Vital record of Rhode Island

1636-1850: first series: births, marriages and deaths.

A family register for the people

(Volume V)

James N. Arnold

Alpha Editions

This edition published in 2019

ISBN : 9789353864804

Design and Setting By
Alpha Editions
email - alphaedis@gmail.com

Vital Record of Rhode Island.

1636=1850.

FIRST SERIES.

BIRTHS, MARRIAGES AND DEATHS.

A Family Register for the People.

BY JAMES N. ARNOLD,

EDITOR OF THE NARRAGANSETT HISTORICAL REGISTER.

"Is My Name Written in the Book of Life?"

Vol 5.   WASHINGTON COUNTY.

Published under the Auspices of the General Assembly.

PROVIDENCE, R. I:
NARRAGANSETT HISTORICAL PUBLISHING COMPANY.
1894.

INTRODUCTION.

KINGS COUNTY, now known as Washington, is a delightful field for the geneologist and historian to labor in. While the compiler of this volume regrets the sad loss of the old Kings Towne Records, he is happy in thinking that the people kept a very good record up to the period of the Revolution. Here, as in all other portions of the State, the recording from 1776 to 1850 is remarkably poor, and the compiler believes, that had this latter period been kept as faithfully as the former, that this work would have been double its present size. The perplexities, difficulties and annoyances the compiler met in other portions of the State have attended him here, the nature and character of which none save those who have and experience in the field can form a just idea.

It is a source of pride with the compiler to realize and know that his labor of years has been a success and is appreciated by the scholar interested in family matters. He is grateful for their words of encouragement, both printed and written. No Rhode Island work has been better received or has received more or better endorsment than his.

THE NAMES OF THE TOWNS.

North Kingstown, incorporated Oct. 28, 1674, as Kings Towne. First settlement 1636. Name was changed to Rochester, June 23, 1786, but restored in 1689. Town divided into North and South Kingstown, Feb. 26, 1722-3, which provided that North Kingstown should be the eldest town.

Under authority of Connecticut the town in 1663 was incorporated as Wickford, called Kings Towne because it was the town given the colony through the pleasure of the King. Original name Aquidnessett.

Westerly, incorporated May 14, 1669. Original name Misquamicutt. Called Haversham, June 23, 1686. Name restored as Westerly in 1689. Called Westerly because it was the most western town in the colony.

South Kingstown, incorporated Feb. 26, 1722-3. Called by the proprietors Pettequomscutt.

Charlestown named from King Charles II. Town incorporated Aug. 22, 1728. Taken from Westerly. Original name Shannock.

Exeter, incorporated March 8, 1742-3. Taken from North Kingstown. Called by the proprietors, Newbury, in honor of Walter Newbury, Treasurer of the company. Original name Yawgoo. Called Exeter after the English town of that name.

Richmond, incorporated Aug. 18, 1747. Taken from Charlestown. Named in honor of William Richmond, a name which served the longest term as Assistant of any yet placed on our records.

Hopkinton, incorporated March 19, 1757. Taken from Westerly. Named in honor of Gov. Stephen Hopkins.

CONDITION OF THE RECORDS.

North Kingstown has several books, but which have been so badly damaged by fire and smoke as to render a pagination impossible. Our copy printed in this volume, with all its imperfections, is a far better one than can be made to-day from the same sources.

South Kingstown has two hooks, hoth in good order. They have also in the old Kings Towne Transcripts a list of hirths, marriages and deaths. These are included in this volume under the North Kingstown records.

Exeter has two books, in good order.

Westerly has five books; two first need hinding; the others in fine condition.

Charlestown's first book needs binding; writing good. The second book is in fine order. Is known as First Council.

Richmond has two books. No. 1 needs hinding. Is known as Land Evidence, No. 1. No. 2 has a good hinding. Is known as Town Meeting, No. 1. Writing in both good.

Hopkinton has five books. Nos. 1, 2 and 3 are known also as Town Meeting 1-2-3. No. 4 is known also as School Committee, No. 1. No. 5 is known also as Militia, No. 1. Writing in all good. The two first need hinding.

ACKNOWLEDGMENTS.

We still have to thank our dear friends again for their continued interest in our work, for their confidence in us personally and for their many kindnesses.

The General Assemhly of the State has again heen liberal, and has hestowed on the work a liheral subscription, for which we thank them, and also the Honorable Committee who favorably reported upon so desirahle a matter to us and so vital to the success of this enterprise.

PLEASE OBSERVE.

We also thank the puhlic for the favor in which they received our previous volumes, and for their good wishes towards us in the future.

I. That the marriages are given in duplicate, hnt that nothing beyond the book and page of the original town record, the names and date are given where the bride is placed first. That under the groom the notes are so extended as to include all the items of the record from whence it was taken. The reader will consider the hride heing placed first, therefore, as merely an index for him to consult the other entry in its proper place. Should they disagree, give the groom the preference, if possihle. That the hirths and deaths are grouped so as to better enable the reader to see at a glance the names and dates in their natural order of the members of the family.

II. That the figures at the left of the name is the hook and page of the original town record, the hyphen separating the two apart.

III. That the indexes for all the towns treated in this work are placed in the fore part of the hook. No one need look farther than the index to discover whether the matter he is in search of is to he found within the covers. These indexes are so constructed as to show:

(a) The names occurring in their natural order.

(b) The names occurring promiscuously, and

(c) The places mentioned in the text.

IV. That each town is separate and distinct in itself, and the indexes are confined strictly to each town, but all are placed in the fore part of the work for the more handy reference of the reader. Should the reader want his copy rebound, he can do so, and the indexes can be differently placed with no injury to the others.

V. The spelling of the given names are as they stand on the Record in many instances, and when they are not far wrong. This accounts for the variety of spelling in this work.

VI. The acts incorporating the several towns of the county are placed hefore the matter itself in that particular town.

VII. Every convenience that would aid the reader, and everything that would naturally perplex him, has been carefully studied. While not claiming perfection for our work, we would say that we have spared no pains in order to make it as simple as possible, and yet be comprehensive. How well we have succeeded in this must be left, however, to the reader himself to say.

VIII. We have not changed dates here given, but we give it just as it stands on the Record itself. We have observed, however, that the Scotch year is more general in this county than in any other that has come to our notice

A REQUEST.

It would be a great favor to the compiler of this work if every reader who consults these pages would copy out and send to him at Providence, R. I., copies from his family record in the Bible, or where else the same may be recorded, or any other information he may be possessed of, in order to make these records in the future as complete as possible. It makes no difference whether the party resides in the State of Rhode Island or not. If they can connect with Rhode Island ancestry it is sufficient. While these matters may seem trifling, yet they may become of incalculable value in the future, and therefore we urgently desire that the Vital Records of Rhode Island may be made complete and that errors, wherever found, may be pointed out and corrected as soon as possible.

ANNOUNCEMENT.

We have substantial encouragement so far that we feel able to here announce that we shall commence the new year (1894) with a new serial, entitled "RHODE ISLAND COLONIAL GLEANINGS." These volumes will be faithful transcripts of the first record books of the oldest towns in the State, and papers illustrating some important State question of history. They will afford much interest to the scholar and will be published so that every poor man can have a copy if he wishes one, as they will be published at popular prices.

The compiler's long experience in reading old manuscript, and his long and close study of our State history, places him in a position to do an able work. When it is taken into account the many perplexities and difficulties that have on every side beset his path, and of such nature that no other man in the State would have had the courage to face it, and then to see the noble work he has already done. The Vital Record alone is a monument to his industry. The grand work the city of Providence is now doing was put into successful operation by him, seconded by several thoughtful and intelligent gentlemen.

If the good people of our State will stand by us and our lamp of life holds out, we pledge ourself Rhode Island will have no need to blush for one of her sons.

The compiler of these Vital Records means business, and he proposes to be as persistent and as untiring in the future as he has been in the past, and he does not propose and will not be put down, but means to be heard. "Hew to the line" is the motto on his banner, and the preservation in print of our historical treasures shall be his object, and he asks the endorsement and good feelings of every intelligent citizen of Rhode Island in his behalf, and he asks them to see to it that he has a fair and square show.

All he asks for himself he is willing to concede to others, and stands ready to record every courtesy to others that he expects others to grant him. The field is broad enough for all, and he only demands that those who enter it shall enter as scholars should enter and conduct themselves as gentlemen should towards each other, and be willing to learn of each other and assist when occasion demands. All that enter the field with these sentiments will find every day in the week and Sundays in the compiler a friend, adviser, sympathizer and man.

INDEX.

TOWN OF NORTH KINGSTOWN.

I.

Names Occurring in Their Natural Order.

Marriages commence with page 5; births and deaths with page 53.

A

Airs, 53.
Aborn, 5.
Albro, 5 53.
Aldrich, 5 53.
Allen, 5 53.
Alverson, 6.
Anthony, 6.
Armstrong, 6 54.
Arnold, 6 55.
Atherby, 6.
Austin, 6 55.
Aylesworth, 7 55.
Ayrault, 56.
Ayres, 8.

B

Babcock, 8 56.
Bailey, 8 56.
Baker, 8 56.
Barber, 8 57.
Barker, 8.
Barnes, 8.
Barney, 9 57.
Bates, 9 57.
Baton, 9.
Beares, 9.
Beasy, 57.
Bentley, 9 57.
Berry, 9.
Bicknell, 9 58.
Bidelcom, 9.
Bissell, 9 58.
Bly, 59.
Boone, 10 59.
Boss, 10 59.
Boltom, 10.
Bowen, 10.
Braman, 10.
Brenton, 10.
Briggs, 10 59.
Browning, 10 60.
Brown, 11 60.
Bullock, 12 62.

Bull, 12 62.
Bundy, 12.
Burke, 62.
Burkemaster, 62.
Burdick, 12.
Burgeuss, 12.
Burge, 12.
Burlingame, 12 62.
Burnham, 12.

C

Cahoone, 12.
Canuda, 12.
Capron, 12.
Carder, 12.
Card, 12, 62.
Carpenter, 13 62.
Casey, 13.
Case, 13 63.
Carr, 13 63.
Carter, 63.
Ceazer, 14.
Chadsey, 14 64.
Chamberland, 14.
Champlain, 14 64.
Chappell, 14.
Chase, 14 64.
Cheeseborough, 64.
Church, 15 65.
Clarke, 15 65.
Cleaveland, 15 65.
Coatney, 65.
Cobb, 15.
Codner, 15.
Coffin, 15.
Coggeshall, 15 65.
Cole, 16 66.
Collins, 16.
Comfort, 16.
Congdon, 16 66.
Connelly, 17.
Cook, 17.
Cooper, 17 68.
Corey, 17 68.
Corpse, 69.

Cornell, 18.
Cottrell, 18 69.
Cozzens, 18 69.
Crandall, 18 69.
Cranston, 18 69.
Crossman, 69.
Crowder, 18.
Crowell, 18.
Crumb, 18.
Culverwell, 18.
Cutter, 18

D

Dake, 18.
Daley, 18.
Dare, 18.
Davis, 18 69.
Dawley, 18 70.
Dayton, 70.
Dean, 19 70.
Dimond, 19 70.
Dickerson, 19.
Dickinson, 19 70.
Dickson, 19 70.
Dick, 19.
Dixon, 19.
Dollmer, 19.
Donison, 19.
Douglass, 19 70.
Downing, 19 70.
Durfee, 70.
Durgan, 19.
Dyre, 19 70.

E

Earle, 19.
Eastlix, 19.
Eldred, 19 71.
Eley, 20.
Ellis, 21 72.
Enos, 21.
Ensworth, 72.
Essex, 21 72.

II.

Names Occurring Promiscuously.

III.

Names of Places.

INDEX.

TOWN OF SOUTH KINGSTOWN.

I.

Names Occurring in Their Natural Order.

Marriages commence with page 5; births page 37; deaths page 61.

II.

Names Occurring Promiscuously.

III.

Names of Places.

INDEX.

TOWN OF EXETER.

I.

Names Occurring in Their Natural Order.

Marriages commence with page 5; births and deaths with page 38.

A

Adams, 5.
Albro, 5 38.
Aldrich, 5.
Allen, 5.
Andrews, 5.
Angell, 5.
Arnold, 5 38.
Austin, 6 38.
Aylesworth, 6 39.

B

Babcock, 6 39.
Bailey, 6.
Baker, 6 39.
Barber, 6 40.
Barney, 8.
Barrows, 40.
Bates, 8 40.
Baten, 8.
Beardmare, 40.
Benjamin, 8.
Bennett, 8.
Benson, 8.
Bentley, 8 40.
Bill, 8.
Bissell, 8 40.
Bly, 8.
Boone, 8 41.
Boss, 8.
Bowen, 8.
Bowdish, 9.
Brayman, 9 41.
Briggs, 9 41.
Brown, 9 41.
Brownell, 9.
Browning, 9 41.
Burdick, 9.

C

Cahoone, 9.
Cammell, 9.

Capwell, 9.
Carden, 9.
Card, 9.
Carney, 10.
Carpenter, 10.
Carr, 10 41.
Carter, 10.
Casey, 10 41.
Case, 10 41.
Chace, 10.
Chambers, 10.
Chapman, 10 42.
Champlain, 10 41.
Church, 10 42.
Clarke, 10 42.
Clawson, 11.
Cleaveland, 11.
Cobb, 11.
Codner, 11 42.
Coldgrove, 11 43.
Comstock, 11.
Congdon, 11 43.
Coone, 12.
Corey, 12.
Cornell, 12.
Corpse, 12 43.
Cottrell, 12 43.
Crandall, 12 43.

D

Davis, 12 44.
Dawley, 13 44.
Dean, 13.
Douglass, 13.
Dunn, 13.
Dupuy, 13.
Dutemple, 13.
Dyre, 13.

E

Earl, 13.
Eldred, 13 44.
Ellis, 14 44.

Ensworth, 14 44.

F

Fenner, 14.
Fisher, 14.
Fones, 14.
Foredice, 44.
Foster, 14.
Fowler, 14.
Franklin, 14.
Frazier, 14.
Freeborn, 14.
Fry, 14.

G

Gardiner, 14 44.
Gates, 15.
Gill, 15 46.
Gorton, 15.
Gould, 15.
Greene, 15 46.
Griffen, 16.

H

Hall, 16 46.
Hammond, 16.
Handy, 16.
Harrington, 16 47.
Harris, 17.
Hathaway, 17.
Haven, 17.
Hawkins, 48.
Hazard, 17.
Heffernan, 17.
Hendrick, 17.
Hesaline, 17.
Hiames, 17 48.
Hill, 17 48.
Hoar, 48.
Holloway, 17 48.
Hood, 17.

II.

Names Occurring Promiscuously.

A

Albro, 5 6 8 9 10 12 13 14 15 16 17 18 19 22 23 25 26 27 28 30 31 32 34 35 36.
Allen, 5 10 11 13 16 28.
Angell, 22.
Arnold, 9 22.
Aylesworth, 35.

B

Babcock, 48.
Barber, 7 18 20 21 24 32.
Bates, 8 10 11.
Bissell, 33.
Bradford, 30.
Briggs, 26.
Brown, 25 56.
Burdick, 20 24.
Burlingame, 13.

C

Campbell, 8.
Carpenter, 54.
Casey, 14 34.
Champlain, 11.
Chapman, 34.
Clarke, 23 40.
Coone, 36.
Crandall, 16 17 19 20 22 24 25 30 34.
Cross, 8.

D

Dean, 28, 34.

E

Edes, 33.
Ellis, 15 33.

F

Fifield, 25.
Fones, 14.
Frank, 13.

G

Gallup, 16.
Gardiner, 5 9 13 15 16 21 24 29 30 33.
Gorton, 26 27 32.
Greene, 8 9 11 14 15 17 18 20 21 24 26 27 29 30 32 36.

H

Hall, 6 9 10 11 13 14 15 16 17 19 22 23 25 26 27 31 32 33 35.
Hammond, 22 28 36.
Hart, 12.
Hazard, 7.
Hill, 10 17 27 29 34.
Hopkins, 60.
Hubbard, 8 28.
Hull, 30.
Huntington, 26.

I J

Jenkins, 9 24 25 29.
Johnston, 5 6 7 9 13 16 17 18 20 21 22 23 24 26 29 31 32 34 37.
Joslin, 7 8 11 18 26 27 28 32 36.
Justin, 17 27.

K

Kenyon, 8 19 20 21 24 29.

L

Lapham, 34.
Lillibridge, 22 24 29.
Locke, 7 8 9 10 20 24 25 26 32 34.

M

Manchester, 5 6 20 21 23 27 28 30 36.
Matteson, 24.
McReady, 28.
Moon, 8 11.
Morey, 12 16 17 31.
Morse, 30.
Moshier, 7 33.
Murch, 15.

N

Nicholas, 20 26.
Northup, 11 12 15 17 27 33.

O P

Palmer, 6 7 9 10 11 12 13 14 15 16 18 19 20 21 22 23 25 26 28 29 30 31 32.

Peckham, 7 16 28 32.
Pendleton, 20 22.
Perkins, 6 7 8 11 12 13 14 16 17 18 23 24 25 28 30 31 32 34 35.
Pierce, 5 6 8 10 11 12 14 15 16 17 23 27 31 32 33 35 36.
Pitcher, 11.
Post, 8.
Potter, 24.

Q R

Rathbun, 24 26.
Reynolds, 5 6 8 10 12 13 15 17 19 20 22 23 25 26 27 29 30 31 32 33 34 35 36 37.
Richmond, 5 18 19 24 27 31 32 35.

S

Sheffield, 23 36.
Sheldon, 7 16 24.
Sherman, 27.
Slocum, 7 8 9 12 14 17 18 19 21 22 28 30 32 33 35.
Spencer, 30.
Sprague, 5 6 7 9 10 11 12 19 23 24 27 29 30 32 34 36.
Stanton, 6 18 19.
Steele, 12.
Stillman, 7 20 26.
Stone, 15.
Sunderland, 7 10 11 17 25 27 35.
Sweet, 19 24 34.

T

Thomas, 27.
Thurston, 30.
Tillinghast, 7 9 12 13 14 16 17 18 19 23 24 26 28 30 31 32 36.
Tripp, 10 12 14 15 25 26 33 35.

U

Underwood, 11.

V W

Waite, 23.
Wakefield, 17.

III.

Names of Places.

INDEX.

TOWN OF WESTERLY.

I.

Names Occurring in Their Natural Order.

Marriages commence with page 5; births and deaths page 72.

Edwards, 29 100.
Eglestone, 30.
Elderton, 30 101.
Eldredge, 30.
Eldred, 30.
Ellis, 30 101.
Enos, 30 101.

F

Fenner, 30.
Fellows, 30.
Ferguson, 30.
Fielden, 30.
Fish, 30.
Fitch, 30.
Fordis, 30.
Foster, 30 101.
Fowler, 30 102.
Frazier, 30 102.
French, 31 102.
Frink, 31 102.
Fry, 31.
Fuller, 31 102.

G

Gage, 31.
Gardiner, 31 102.
Gavitt, 31 102.
Geer, 32
Gibbs, 32.
Gifford, 32.
Gilbert, 33.
Godando, 33.
Goodrich, 33.
Gorton, 33 104.
Gory, 33.
Grant, 33.
Greenell, 33 104.
Greenman, 33 104.
Greene, 33 104.
Griffin, 34.

H

Hadfall, 34.
Hadsall, 34.
Hakes, 34.
Hallum, 34.
Hall, 34 106.
Hammond, 35.
Handcock, 35.
Hardy, 108.
Harris, 36.
Hasell, 36 108.
Hawkins, 36.
Hawk, 36 108.
Haxston, 36.
Hayden, 36.
Hazelton, 36 108.
Helme, 36.
Hern, 36.
Hewitt, 36.
Hex, 108.
Hilliard, 36.
Hill, 36 108.
Hinckley, 36.
Hiscox, 36 108.
Hobert, 37.
Holly, 37.

Holmes, 37.
Holway, 37 109.
Hopkins, 37.
Horick, 37.
Howard, 109.
Hoxsie, 37 109.
Hubbard, 37 110.
Hull, 37 110.
Huntley, 37.

I

Ingraham, 37.
Irish, 37.

J

Jagers, 38.
James, 38.
Jerome, 38.
Johnson, 38 110.
Jones, 38.
Justus, 38.

K

Kenecome, 38.
Kenyon, 38 110.
Kimber, 38.
King, 39.
Knight, 39 110.
Knowles, 39 110.

L

Ladd, 39.
Lake, 39.
Lamb, 39.
Langford, 39.
Langley, 39.
Langworthy, 39.
Lankford, 39.
Lanphear, 39 111.
Larkin, 41 113.
Lawton, 42 113.
Leeds, 42 113.
Lee, 42 113.
Lester, 42.
Lewis, 42 113.
Lillibridge, 44.
Lippitt, 44.
Lock, 44.
Lombard, 44.
Loomas, 44 116.
Long, 44.
Lothrop, 44.
Loveless, 44.
Lovitt, 44.

M

Maceater, 44.
Maccoon, 44 116.
Mackee, 44.
Mackintosh, 45.
Macomber, 45.
Mallerson, 45.
Maine, 45.
Mash, 45.
Mason, 45.

Maxson, 45 116.
McDowell, 46.
McDonnell, 46.
Meekcome, 46 118.
Merriott, 46.
Milliard, 46 119.
Minor, 46.
Mitchell, 46.
Moon, 46.
Moore, 119.
Morris, 47.
Mott, 47 119.
Mulkins, 47 119.
Mumford, 47.
Munro, 47.
Musgrave, 47.

N

Nash, 47 119.
Nett, 47.
Newberry, 47.
Newbury, 47.
Ney, 47.
Nichols, 119.
Niles, 47.
Noogen, 47 119.
Noyes, 47 119.
Nutter, 48.
Nye, 48 120.

O

Odell, 120.
Otis, 48.
Owen, 48.

P

Page, 48.
Palmer, 48 120.
Palmitter, 48 120.
Parker, 48.
Parkinson, 48.
Park, 48 120.
Partelow, 48.
Pearce, 48.
Peckham, 48 121.
Peirce, 49 121.
Pendleton, 50 122.
Perkins, 51 125.
Perry, 51 125.
Pettis, 51.
Phelden, 51.
Phillips, 51.
Phinney, 125.
Pierce, 52.
Poes, 52.
Pooler, 52 125.
Poole, 52.
Popple, 125.
Porter, 52 125.
Potter, 52 126.
Potts, 52.
Powell, 52.
Pratt, 52.
Prentice, 52.
Prosser, 52.
Pullen, 126.
Pullman, 52.
Purdy, 52.

II.

Names Occurring Promiscuously.

C

Campbell, 15 41 56 60 63.
Carr, 53
Case, 57.
Champlain, 24 27 42 61 122.
Chase, 25.
Cheeseborough, 29.
Chester, 41.
Clarke, 7 8 9 10 11 12 13 15 16 17 18 19 20 21 22 23 25 26 27 29 31 32 33 34 37 40 42 43 44 45 46 47 48 49 50 52 53 56 57 59 60 62 63 64 65 66 68 70.
Coggeshall, 21.
Coon, 5 8 12 13 14 15 17 19 20 22 23 26 29 30 31 37 39 40 41 44 46 47 54 55 59 60 62 63 65.
Crandall, 6 7 8 9 10 12 13 14 15 16 17 18 19 20 21 22 23 24 25 26 28 29 30 33 34 35 36 37 38 39 40 41 43 44 46 48 49 50 51 52 53 54 55 56 57 58 59 60 61 64 65 66 67 68 69 70 71.
Crary, 13 27 40 67.
Cross, 9 10 13 15 30 31 41 44 52 58 70.

D

Daman, 63.
Danforth, 69.
Davis, 24 70.
Dawley, 52.
Dehon, 8.
Denison, 10 17 26 37 46 49 51 63 64 67 68.
Dewry, 130.
Dodge, 10.
Dorrance, 17.

E

Eddy, 62.
Edwards, 58.
Eells, 6 7 23 24 30 36 43 50 61.

F

Fish, 6 7 48 58.

G

Gardiner, 12 21 26 30 31 32 47 51 52 55 57 58 61 71.
Gavitt, 47 53.
Gillett, 40.
Gore, 68.
Gorton, 12 20 25 45.

Gould, 48.
Greenman, 5 6 15 36 39 45.
Greene, 9 10 21 62 80.

H

Hanuah, 24.
Hall, 20 42.
Hart, 48 67.
Helme, 21 30 33 52 69.
Hern, 6 11 12 14 15 16 18 19 21 22 24 27 28 33 34 35 36 37 38 39 42 43 45 47 48 50 51 52 55 56 58 59 60 61 62 66 67 68 69 70.
Hiscox, 17 20 22 28 34 35 41 48 60 70 113.
Honeyman, 50.
Hopkins, 49.
Hotchkiss, 69.
Hoxsie, 30 41 42 54.

I J

Johnson, 106.
Joslin, 8 15 65.

K

Kendall, 68.
Kenney, 10.
Knight, 19 29 49 56 59 60 64 70.

L

Lanphear, 27 38 44 47 56 58 109 129 130.
Larkin, 29 36 41 46.
Lewis, 43 45 68.
Lillibridge, 44.
Lost, 95.
Lyons, 45.

M

Maccoon, 6 18 20 30 34 39 67.
Marther, 6.
Maxson, 5 10 11 13 14 15 16 20 21 23 24 27 28 29 30 34 35 36 37 38 39 42 44 45 46 47 48 50 52 53 54 55 56 58 59 60 61 63 64 67 69 70.
McSparran, 18.
Miner, 9 10 11 32 63 64 78.
Moore, 17 33 41 49 58 64.
Mulkins, 74.

N

Newman, 9 23 32 59 64.
Northup, 40 67.
Noyes, 50.

O

Osborn, 5.

P

Palmer, 9 15 23 28 31 38 40 50 58 60 62 65 67 70.
Park, 7 11 12 14 18 19 20 21 24 28 30 31 36 37 42 43 50 53 54 55 56 57 59 60 61 64 67.
Peckham, 39.
Pendleton, 8 9 10 11 13 14 17 22 26 27 29 31 42 47 48 51 59 60 62 64 65 69.
Perry, 13 23 27 52.
Phelps, 8.
Phillips, 65.
Phinney, 10 33 41 42.
Potter, 15 26 27 37 55 66.
Pratt, 9 15 29.

Q R

Randall, 5 11 14 24 40 43 45 51 53 66 68.
Rathbun, 38 44 51 60.
Rhodes, 6 9 11 13 14 15 16 20 24 31 34 36 37 38 39 41 42 44 46 47 48 50 52 53 54 56 60 69.
Richmond, 5 11 14 15 16 17 21 23 27 30 34 36 39 46 47 48 54 56 61 63 66 67 70.
Robinson, 38.
Rogers, 12 28 52 54 58 62 119.
Rossiter, 18 50 65.
Ross, 7 25 28 35 46 55 64 69.

S

Sands, 12.
Sanford, 70.
Saunders, 5 11 16 18 20 23 29 33 34 36 37 41 42 43 45 55 56 59 61 66 110.
Shaw, 26 32 35.
Sheffield, 33 58.
Sheldon, 13.
Sims, 133.
Sisson, 133.
Slocum, 54.
Smith, 9 16 20 23 24 27 32 34 36 37 38 40 45 47 49 50 56 60 62 66 67.
Stanton, 11 14 48 53 120 121.
Stillman, 9 10 11 17 20 32 33 41 44 47 52 58 60 61 63 65 68 70.
Sturgeon, 17.
Sweet, 121.

T

Tabor, 52.
Taylor, 8 10 12 13 16
  20 25 26 31 32 49 52
  60 65.
Throop, 44.
Thurston, 7 19 65.
Tillinghast, 26 39.
Trumbull, 27.
Tuckerman, 5 22 32 33
  49 60 61 63 65.

U V

Vail, 5 13 18 27 29 32
  33 38 39 52 53 58 59
  61 71.
Vars, 132.
Vinton, 49.
Vose, 48 59.

W

Wakefield, 64.
Weight, 39.

Wells, 41 48 49 65 91.
West, 128.
Whitman, 57.
Wilbur, 9 11 22 29 42
  54 66.
Wilcox, 7 8 10 12 14 19
  25 29 32 35 43 46 47
  51 53 58 60 68 69 70.
Woodruff, 44 55 64.
Worden, 38.

X Y Z

York, 20.

III.

Names of Places.

A

Albany, N. Y., 112.
Alfred, N. Y., 37.
Ashton, England, 44.

B

Baltimore, Md., 35.
Bangor, Mass., 55.
Benson, Vt., 5.
Block Island, 38 53.
Boston, Mass., 37.
Bristol, Conn., 62.
Bristol, England, 52.
Bristol, R. I., 89.
Brookfield, N. Y., 26 58
  69.
Brookhaven, L. I., 65.

C

Charlestown, R. I., 5 6
  7 8 9 12 13 16 17 18
  19 20 21 22 24 25 26
  27 29 30 31 32 33 34
  35 36 37 38 39 40 41
  42 43 45 46 48 49 50
  52 54 55 56 57 58 59
  61 64 65 68 71 72 76
  77 78 80 81 82 84 85
  88 95 96 97 103 104
  105 106 107 110 113
  127 130 131 145 1...
Charlotte Precinct, N.
  Y., 86.
Chenango County, N.
  Y., 51.
Clinton, Conn., 15.
Cohoes, N. Y., 52.
Colchester, Conn., 70.
Connecticut, 5 52 58 70.
Coosocky, N. Y., 105.
Cortland County, N. Y.,
  63.
Cranston, R. I., 15.

D

De Kalb, N. Y., 5.
Demarara, W. I., 82.
Dighton, Mass., 83 86.

E

East Greenwich, R. I.,
  11 66.
Exeter, R. I., 10 23 33
  39 46 78 106 132.

F

Falmouth, Mass., 47.
Feversham, R. I., 88.
Freetown, Mass., 89.

G

Glocester, 33.
Groton, Conn., 5 14 32
  33 44 45 47 50 70 77
  104 133 144.

H

Hancock County, Mass.,
  13.
Hanover, Mass., 135.
Hopewell, N. J., 14.
Hopkinton, R. I., 7 8 9
  10 11 14 16 17 19 21
  22 23 24 25 31 33 34
  35 37 38 40 41 43 44
  46 47 48 52 53 54 55
  58 59 60 62 63 64 65
  66 68 70 71 77 78 82
  88 91 93 94 95 96 105
  106 108 109 112 120
  128 131 137 141 142.

I

Ireland, 38.
Isle of Jersey, 68.

J K

Kingsbury, N. Y., 82.
Kings Towne, R. I., 52
  64.

L

Lancashire, England, 44.
Lebanon, Conn., 10 67.
Ledyard, Conn., 45 68.
Little Compton, R. I.,
  54.
Lyme, Conn., 37 52 100
  113.

M

Madison County, N. Y.,
  26.
Mason's Island, Conn.,
  124.
Massachusetts, 29.
Mendon, Mass., 31 52.
Middletown, Conn., 113.
Middletown, R. I., 7 67
  76.
Montville, Conn., 62.

N

Nantucket, Mass., 56.
New Concord, Conn., 44.
New Haven, Conn., 38.
New London, Conn., 5
  12 25 26 36 37 45 50
  54 59 62 87 95.
Newport, R. I., 7 19
  20 21 29 30 36 39 43
  44 45 47 48 50 53 54

INDEX.

TOWN OF CHARLESTOWN.

I.

Names Occurring in Their Natural Order.

Marriages commence with page 5; births and deaths page 17.

O

Olney, 12.

P

Park, 12 24.
Peckham, 13 24.
Peirce, 13.
Perkins, 13.
Perry, 13 25.
Pettis, 13.
Pettey, 25.
Phebe, 13.
Pierce, 13 25.
Pike, 13.
Potter, 13 25.
Pullman. 13.

Q R

Rathbone, 13 25.
Reynolds, 13.
Rhodes, 14 25.
Rodman, 14.
Ross, 14 25.

S

Sands, 14.
Sash, 14.
Saulsbury, 25.
Saunders, 14.
Scribens, 14 25.
Seager, 14.
Shaw, 14.
Sheffield, 14 25.
Sheldon, 14.
Sherman, 14 26.
Simon, 14.
Smith, 14.
Spencer, 14.
Stanton, 14 26.
Stiles, 15.
Stillman, 15.
Sunderland, 15.
Swan, 15.

T

Tanner, 27.
Taylor, 15 27.
Tefft, 15.
Thomas, 15.

Thompson, 15
Tiger, 15.
Trim, 15.
Tucker, 15 27.

U V

Vars, 16.

W

Ward, 16.
Watson, 27.
Webb, 16.
Webster, 16.
Welch, 16 27.
Wells, 16 28.
Wescott, 16.
West, 28.
Wilcox, 16 28.
Williams, 16.
Woodmansee, 16 28.
Worden, 16.

X Y Z

York, 16 28.

II.

Names Occurring Promiscuously.

A

Allen 9 16.
Avery, 14.

B

Babcock, 5 6 7 9 14 15
 16.
Baker, 7 11 15.
Barber, 10 11 13 15.
Billings, 16.
Bliven, 6 8.
Boss, 10.
Brown, 15.
Burdick, 9 14.

C

Card, 6.
Champlain, 8 13.
Church, 9.
Clarke, 6 7 8 9 13 14 16.
Coggswell, 9.
Collins, 13.
Colwell, 5 11.
Congdon, 11.
Coon, 9 10.
Crandall, 5 6 7 8 9 10
 12 13 14 16.
Cross, 5 6 7 8 9 10 11
 12 13 14 15 16.

D

Davis, 26.
Dodge, 10.

E

Evritt, 7.

F G

Gardiner, 8 15.
Gorton, 15.
Griffin, 11 12 15.
Grosvenor, 10.

H

Helme, 7.
Hern, 16.
Hicks, 7 10 12 14 16.
Hill, 8 10.
Hiscox, 8.
Hoxsie, 5 6 7 9 10 11
 12 13 14 15 16 19.

I J

Joslin, 11.

K

King, 12 15.
Knight, 18.

L

Lewis, 7 9 12 14.
Lillibridge, 11.

M

Maxson, 14.
Miner, 14.

N O P

Parks, 5 7 11 12 15.
Perry, 5 6 8 9.
Potter, 8 9.

Q R

Rhodes, 11 12.
Robinson, 7 10 13.
Rosseter, 16.
Ross, 7 9 10.

S

Saunders, 6.
Sekoter, 8.
Sheffield, 9.
Sprague, 6.
Stillman, 5.

T

Taylor, 7.
Tefft, 5.
Tillinghast, 15.

U V

Vail, 10.

Vose, 8.

W

Watson, 5.
Wilbur, 8.
Witter, 8.

X Y Z

III.

Names of Places.

A B

Blanford, Mass., 19.

C D

Dartmouth, Mass., 8.

E

East Greenwich, R. I., 13 14.
Exeter, R. I., 12 13.

F G

Groton, Conn., 21.

H

Hopkinton, R. I., 7 8 9 10 16.

I

Ireland, 28.

J

Jamestown, R. I., 6 8.

K L

Lebanon, Conn., 10.

M

Manville, Conn., 15.

N

Narragansett Tribe, 10 15.
New London, Conn., 6 8.
Newport, R. I., 7.
New Shoreham, R. I., 15 16.
North Kingstown, R. I., 12 28.
North Stonington, Conn., 24.

O P

Providence, R. I., 9.

Q R

Richmond, R. I., 5 11 13

S

South Kingstown, R. I., 5 6 7 9 10 11 12 13 14 15 16 28.
Stonington, Conn., 12 14 15 16 24.

T U V W

Westerly, R. I., 5 6 7 8 9 10 11 12 13 14 15 16.

X Y Z

INDEX.

TOWN OF RICHMOND.

I.

Names Occurring in Their Natural Order.

Marriages commence with page 5; births and deaths page 23.

Moore, 15.
Morey, 15.
Moshier, 15.
Mumford, 15.

N

Ney, 15 31.
Newton, 15.
Nichols, 15 31.
Niles, 16.
Noyes, 16.
Nye, 16.

O

Olney, 16 31.

P

Palmer, 16.
Parker, 16.
Patterson, 16.
Pearce, 16.
Peckham, 16.
Pendleton, 16.
Perrin, 16.
Perry, 16 32.
Peterson, 16.
Pettis, 16 32.
Petty, 16 32.
Phillips, 16 32.
Pierce, 16.
Pollard, 16.
Potter, 16 32.
Powell, 17.
Pullman, 17 33.

Q R

Rathbun, 17.
Record, 17 33.
Reynolds, 17 33.
Rice, 17.
Richmond, 18 33.
Robbins, 18.
Rogers, 18 33.
Ross, 18.
Russell, 18.

S

Sabin, 18.
Sanford, 18.
Saunders, 18.
Serel, 18.
Sheldon, 18 33.
Sherman, 18.
Sisson, 33.
Slocum, 33.
Smith, 18.
Stafford, 33.
Stanton, 18 33.
Star, 18.
Steadman, 18.
Stewart, 18.
Sunderland, 18.
Swan, 19.
Sweet, 19.

T

Tabor, 19.

Tanner, 19.
Tefft, 19 34.
Tennant, 20.
Thomas, 20.
Tillinghast, 20.
Torrey, 20.
Tourgee, 20.
Tripp, 20.
Tucker, 20 35.
Tuck, 20.
Turner, 20.

U V

Vallett, 20.

W

Watson, 20 35.
Weaver, 20.
Webb, 20 35.
Webster, 20 35.
Weeks, 21.
Wells, 21.
West, 21.
Wilbour, 21 36.
Wilcox, 21 36.
Witter, 21.
Woodmansee, 21 36.
Worden, 22.

X Y Z

Yoeman, 22.
Young, 22.

II.

Names Occurring Promiscuously.

A

Albro, 18.
Austin, 19.
Avery, 6 18.

B

Babcock, 5 7 8 9 18 19.
Bailey, 19.
Barber, 7 8 9 11 30.
Beezeley, 17.
Boss, 6 11 17 19.
Burbank, 7 9 10 22.
Burdick, 10 14.

C

Carpenter, 22.
Champlain, 8.
Clarke, 6 8 12 13 16.

Coon, 11 17.
Crandall, 13 20 21.
Cross, 8.
Culver, 10 16.

D

Durfee, 8.

E F G

Gardiner, 11 16.
Greene, 12.

H

Hazard, 13.
Helme, 11.
Hill, 5 11.
Holloway, 11.
Hubbard, 13 15 20.

I J

Johnson, 12 15.
Joslin, 7 9 10 12 14
   15 16 17 19 20 21.

K

Kenyon, 6 7 8 9 10 12
   13 14 16 19 20 21 22.

L

Lewis, 5 7 10 16 18.
Lillibridge, 5 7 11 14 16
   18 21.
Locke, 6 8 18 20 22.

M

Manchester, 11.

Meech, 14.
Moshier, 12.

N

Northup, 17.

O P

Palmer, 6 9 10 11 12 13
    15 17 21.
Peckham, 6.
Pendleton, 6 14 16.
Perry, 5 6 7 8 9 10 11
    12 13 14 15 17 18 19
    20 21 22.
Petty, 10 18.
Phelps, 11.
Potter, 16 18.

Q R

Randall, 11.
Richmond, 5 6 8 10 11
    13 14 16 18 19 20 21.
Rogers, 17.
Rouse, 18.

S

Saunders, 14.
Sheffield, 17.
Slocum, 6.
Sprague, 7 19.
Stanton, 11 13 14 15 19.
Stillman, 6 8 13 18 24.

T

Tefft, 5 6 7 8 9 10 11
    12 13 16 17 19 20 21.

Thomas, 9.
Tillinghast, 7 9 10 12 13
    14 15 16 21 22 27.
Torrey, 9 13 14.
Tripp, 16.

U V W

Watson, 8.
Webb, 10 11 12 15.
Webster, 9 10 11 12 14
    16 18 20 21.
Weightman, 19.
West, 21.
Wilbur, 14 17 18.
Willey, 8.
Williams, 7 20.
Woodmansee, 7 8 11 13
    16 21.

X Y Z

III.

Names of Places.

A B

Barton, Conn., 19.
Brookfield, N. Y., 18.

C

Charlestown, R. I., 6 7
    8 9 10 11 12 13 14 15
    16 17 18 20 21 22 27
    30 31.
Coventry, R. I., 17 18
    21.

D

Dartmouth, Mass., 17
    32.

E

East Greenwich, R. I.,
    10 15 16 20 21 22.
Exeter, R. I., 6 7 8 10
    11 14 15 16 17 18 19
    20 21 22 33.

F

Fall River, Mass., 10.
Foster, R. I., 10.

G

Groton, Conn., 19.

H

Hopkinton, R. I., 6 7 8
    9 10 11 13 14 15 16
    17 18 19 21 22.

I J K

Kingston, R. I., 6.

L

Lonsdale, R. I., 18 22.

M N

North Kingstown, R. I.,
    ·7 9 11 18 21 33.
North Providence, R. I.,
    31.
Norwich, Conn., 17.

O P

Plainfield, Conn., 18.
Preston, Conn., 14.

Q R

Rome, Me., 10.

S

South Kingstown, R. I.,
    6 8 9 11 12 15 16 18
    20 21 33.
Stonington, Conn., 7 10
    11 21.

T U V

Voluntown, Conn., 8 9.

W

Warwick, R. I., 11 21.
Westerly, R. I., 5 6 7
    8 10 11 13 14 16 18
    19 20 21 24.
West Greenwich, R. I.,
    ·7 9 16 17.
Wickford, R. I., 18.

X Y Z

INDEX.

TOWN OF HOPKINTON.

I.

Names Occurring in Their Natural Order.

Marriages commence with page 5; births and deaths page 30.

K

Keeney, 17.
Kenyon, 17 41.
Kezeir, 17.
Kingsley, 17.
King, 17.
Kinney, 42.
Knowles, 17.

L

Lake, 18.
Lamb, 18 42.
Langworthy, 18 42.
Lanphere, 18 43.
Larkin, 18 43.
Latham, 43.
Lawton, 19.
Leonard, 19.
Lewis, 19 43.

M

Maccoon, 20 44.
Maine, 20.
Manchester, 20 44.
Marrian, 20.
Marriott, 20.
Matteson, 20.
Maxson, 20 44.
Maynard, 21.
Millard, 21 46.
Miner, 21.
Morgan, 21.
Morey, 21.
Mott, 21 46.

N

Neff, 21.
Ney, 21 46.
Nichols, 21 46.
Niles, 21.
Northup, 21.
Noyes, 21.

O

Olney, 22.

P

Palmer, 22 47.

Palmitter, 22 47.
Partelow, 22.
Patterson, 22 47.
Pearce, 22.
Peckham, 22 47.
Pendleton, 22.
Perkins, 22.
Perry, 22 47.
Pettey, 22.
Pierce, 2.
Plumber, 22.
Popple, 22 47.
Porter, 22 47.
Potter, 22 47.
Powers, 23.
Prosser, 23.

Q R

Randall, 48.
Rathbun, 23.
Remington, 23.
Reynolds, 23 48.
Rhodes, 23 49.
Richmond, 23.
Rider, 23.
Robinson, 23 49.
Rogers, 24 49.
Ross, 24 49.

S

Salisbury, 24.
Sampson, 24.
Satterlee, 24.
Saunders, 24 49.
Scriven, 24.
Sheffield, 24.
Sheldon, 24 49.
Sherman, 24.
Sissel, 24.
Sisson, 24.
Slack, 24.
Slocum, 24.
Smith, 24.
Snow, 24.
Spencer, 24.
Spicer, 24 49.
Stanton, 25.
Stearns, 25.
Stewart, 25.
Stiles, 49.
Stillman, 25 49.
Stetson, 50.
Stutson, 25.

Sutcliff, 25.
Sweet, 25.

T

Taber, 25.
Tanner, 25 50.
Taylor, 26.
Tefft, 26 51.
Thayer, 26.
Thomas, 26.
Thompson, 26.
Thorp, 26.
Thurston, 26 51.
Tripp, 51.

U

Utter, 26 51.

V

Vars, 26.
Vincent, 51.
Vinson, 26.

W

Waite, 26 51.
Watson, 26.
Ward, 26.
Warren, 52.
Webster, 26.
Wells, 27 52.
West, 27 52.
Wheeler, 27.
Whipple, 27.
White, 27 53.
Whitford, 28.
Wilbur, 28 53.
Wilcox, 28 53.
Wilkinson, 28 53.
Williams, 28.
Will, 28.
Witter, 28 53.
Woodmansee, 29 54.
Wood, 29.
Worden, 29 54.
Wright, 29 54.

X Y Z

York, 29.

II.

Names Occurring Promiscuously.

A

Allen, 31.
Avery, 6 9 14 17 23 24 26 28.

B

Babcock, 7 11 14 15 19 26
Barber, 6 7 9 10 11 13 16 17 19 25 26.

Brown, 12 21 24.
Burdick, 6 7 8 9 10 11 12 13 14 15 16 17 18 19 20 21 22 23 24 25 26 27 28 37 44 49.

C

Campbell, 8 10.
Carr, 19.
Chester, 9 22.
Ohnrch, 27.
Clarke, 5 6 7 8 9 10
   11 12 13 14 16 18 19
   20 21 22 23 24 25 26
   27 28.
Collins, 7 10.
Coon, 6 7 10 11 12 13
   15 17 18 19 20 21 22
   23 24 25 26 27 28.
Crandall, 5 8 11 12 13
   15 17 22 24 26 44.
Cross, 19.

D

Darron, 15.
Davis, 7 10 12 18 19
   24 25 27 29.

E F

Fish, 20.
Foster, 36.

G

Gardiner, 6 7 11 14 15
   17 18 19 22 24 26 27
   28 50.
Greene, 11 14 20 25 48.

H

Hall, 47.
Hazard, 7.
Helme, 7.
Hull, 21 36.

I

Irish, 32

J

Joslin, 6 7 11 12.

K L

Langworthy, 35 43.
Lanphere, 41.
Larkin, 6 8 9 12 16 18
   20 22 25.
Latham, 21 23.
Lewis, 6 7 12 13 14
   15 16 17 18 22 23 24
   26.
Lillibridge, 12.
Locke, 13.

M

Maccoon, 23 25.
Manchester, 9 16.
Maxson, 5 8 10 11 14
   16 17 18 19 20 21 22
   23 24 27 28.
Miner, 11.
Morgan, 15.

N

Nichols, 7 8 21 28.
Northup, 7 11 18 19 43.

O P

Palmer, 8 9 11 12 14
   19 25 26 27.
Patterson, 40.
Pendleton, 7 9 26.
Perry, 5 6 8 28.
Post, 17.
Potter, 17 27 34.

Q R

Randall, 9 14 15 19.

Reynolds, 53.
Richmond, 27.
Rogers, 21.

S

Saunders, 24 25 28 29.
Sheffield. 52.
Sheldon, 18.
Smith, 13.
Stillman, 5 6 9 11 13
   14 15 17 18 20 21 23
   24 25 26 28 29.

T

Tanner, 11 14 19.
Taylor, 35.
Tefft, 9.
Thomas, 32.
Thompson, 16.
Thurston, 35.
Tillinghast, 6 22.

U V W

Wakefield, 27.
Wells. 5 8 10 17 21
   26 28.
West, 6 8 10 11 12 14
   15 16 17 19 21 22 23
   25 26 27 28 29.
Whitman. 16.
Wilbur, 12.
Wilcox, 17 20 39.
Williams, 11.
Witter, 9 17 18 28.
Woodmansee, 14.
Woodruff, 18.
Wright, 35.

X Y Z

III.

Names of Places.

A B

Brookfield, N. Y., 12.

C

Cayuga County, N. Y.,
   39.
Charlestown, R. I., 7
   10 11 14 15 16 17 18
   19 21 22 24 25 26 33
   37 38 44.
Chester, N. Y., 6.
Colchester, Conn., 14.

Connecticntt, 11-
Coventry, R. I., 8 9 16
   24 27.

D E

Eastham, Mass., 10.
East Lyme, Conn., 13.
Exeter, R. I., 6 8 11 12
   15 21 22 26 28.

F G

Genesee, N. Y., 21.

Great Britain, 16.
Griswold, Conn., 24.
Groton, Conn., 15.

H

Hartford, Conn., 21.

I J K L

Lebanon, Conn., 7.
Ledyard, Conn., 34.
Leyden, Conn., 10.
Little Hoosick, N. Y.,
   28.

M

Marthas Vineyard, Mass., 34.
Middletown, R. I., 16.
Milton, N. Y., 39.
Montville, Conn., 21 27.

N

New London, Conn., 11 15 18 24.
Newport, R. I., 6 7 9 11 13 23 35.
New Shoreham, R. I., 7 15 25.
North Kingstown, R. I., 7 15 19.
North Stonington, Conn., 6 9 11 12 15 16 20 28 43.
Norwich, Conn., 9 24 26.

O P

Plainfield, Conn., 16 28.
Preston, Conn., 6 9 20 25 28 33.
Providence, R. I., 21.

Q R

Rhode Island, 11.
Richmond, R. I., 5 6 7 8 9 11 14 15 16 17 18 19 22 25 26 28 36 41 47 48.

S

Shrewsbury, Mass., 38.
South Kingstown, R. I., 7 9 13 18 19 24 25 26 28.
Stonington Conn., 5 6 7 8 10 11 14 15 16 18 19 20 21 22 23 24 27 28 29 36 47.

T

Tiverton, R. I., 26.

U V

Voluntown, Conn., 8 14 20 21 27 36.

W

Warwick, R. I., 14.
Waterford, Conn., 24.
Westerly, R. I., 5 6 7 8 9 10 12 13 14 15 16 17 18 19 20 21 23 24 25 27 28 29 31 33 38 44.
West Greenwich, R. I., 7 10 15 25 28.
Windham, Conn., 21.

X Y Z

Vital Record of Rhode Island.

1636=1850.

FIRST SERIES.

BIRTHS, MARRIAGES AND DEATHS.

A Family Register for the People.

BY JAMES N. ARNOLD,

EDITOR OF THE NARRAGANSETT HISTORICAL REGISTER.

"Is My Name Written in the Book of Life?"

Vol. 5.　　　　NORTH KINGSTOWN.　　　　Part I.

Published under the Auspices of the General Assembly.

PROVIDENCE, R. I:
NARRAGANSETT HISTORICAL PUBLISHING COMPANY.
1894.

ACT INCORPORATING THE TOWNS OF WICKFORD AND KINGS TOWNE.

The Secretary allso is ordered to seud a letter to the Inhabitants of Narraganset in the name of the Councill, and to signify to them, that Mr. Richard Smith, Senr., Capt. Edw'd Hutchiuson, and Lut. Jas. Hews are appointed se lect men at Mr. Smith's trading house, and Mr. Rich Smith, Junr., is appointed Constable for the said Town, and Mr. Rich Smith, Senr., is to adminster an oath to him for a faithful dicharge of his office.

It is ordered that the Plantation aforesaid shall for the future he called by the name of Wickford. The Coppy of the letter to Wickford hangs upon the file.

Colonial Records of Connecticut, Vol. I., page 407.

Voted, by the King's Authority in this Assembly, it is approved the Generall Councill's Acts in ohstrctinge Conecticut Collony from useinge jurisdiction in the Narragansett country, and the Conncill's establishing a towne shipp there, and callinge it Kingstown, with liberty as hath heen granted to New Shoreham, and that the charges of our Councill repairinge thither not exceedinge fifty shillings, for every time, shall he paid out of the Geuerall Treasury; and that futurely, it shall he lawful to summons as many of our inhabitants as they see cause to attend at Narragansett to oppose Connecticut from useinge jurisdiction there; hut not in any hostile manner, or to kill or hurt any person. And further hee it enacted, that the Governor, or Deputy Governor, and the mayor, part of the Magistrates on Rhode Island; as they see cause, may send letters or messengers to the New York Governor, concerning such husiness; and the charge not exceedinge tenu pound, to he paid out of the Generall Treasnry.

Rhode Island Colonial Records, Vol. II., page 525.

In General Assemhly at Newport May 1679.

Voted, The Recorder shall draw forth the copy of the Act of the Generall Assemhly in Octoher, 1674, concerninge the confirming of the act of the Generall Councill in estahlishing a Towneshipp in Narragansett, and calllng it King's Towne, which shall he sent to the inhahitants there under the sale of the Colony.

Rhode Island Colonial Records, Vol. III., page 55.

NORTH KINGSTOWN.

MARRIAGES.

NOTE.—North Kingstown had at one time as fine a Town Record as any town in the State, and full as important and historic. In December, 1869, the records were badly damaged by fire. The books, or rather what remains of them, were so badly burnt and pages become so disarranged that it has become impossible to give original book and page, as in the other towns, and hence are omitted here. No doubt errors in names and dates are here made, but this can be relied on far safer than the present condition of the records. This is an honest attempt, therefore, to save what remained of them in September, 1881.

A

ABORN ———ah, and Joseph Atherby, Dec. 9, 1724.

ALBRO Benoni, and Mary Browning; m. by Benjamin Weight, Justice of Peace, Jan., 1744.
    "   Samuel, Jr., and Jane Cole, Dec. 3, 1758.
    "   Dorcas, and Thomas Phillips, April 23, 1761.
    "   Mrs. Martha, and William Phillips, March 14, 1782.
    "   Ann, and Sewall Kingsley, March, 1784.
    "   Elizabeth, and David Gardiner, Jan. 26, 1794.

ALDRICH Sarah, and Samuel Bissell, —— 19, 1753.
    "   Isaac, of Providence, and Mercy Browning, of North Kingstown; m. by Rev. John H. Rouse, Dec. 22, 1846.

ALLEN Christopher, of Rhode Island, and Elizabeth Segouche, of Little Compton, at Boston, according to the forms of the Church of England, by Rev. Robert Ratcliff, ——, 1687.
    "   Elizabeth, and Thomas Hill, Sept. 16, 1716.
    "   Rebecca Cole, and Thomas Hill, March, 1731.
    "   William, of Prudence Island, and Mary Dyre; m. by George Tibbetts, Justice, Feb. 19, 1737-8.
    "   Abigail and —— Bicknell, Oct., 1738.
    "   Jonathan, and Elizabeth Huling; m. by Thomas Hill, Justice, Nov. 2, 1740.
    "   Thomas, and Patience Greene; m. by Thomas Hill, Justice, —— 20, 1742.
    "   John, of Prudence Island, and Hannah Wall; m. by Thomas Hill, Justice, 1743.
    "   Hannah, and Nicholas Northup Jun., March 29, 1750.
    "   Joshua, and Hannah Watson, Sept. 13, 1750.
    "   Thomas, of John, and Ann Corey, of John, dec.; m. by Jeremiah Gould, Justice, Sept. 4, 1756.
    "   John, of Thomas, jun., and Mary Gould, of Daniel, dec.; both of N. Kingstown, Jan. 1760.
    "   Anna, and John Corey, Dec. 7, 1772.
    "   Jeffrey, and Elizabeth Richardson; m. by Elder Simeon Brown, March 3, 1776.
    "   Phebe, and Oliver Carr, April, 1776.
    "   Benjamin, of N. Kingstown, and Sarah Morey, widow of Robert, of Exeter; m. by George Thomas, Justice, April 23, 1776.
    "   Mary, and Alexander Huling, March 31, 1777.
    "   Marcy, and William Spencer, Oct. 22, 1781.
    "   Sarah, and Samuel Bissell, March 18, 1782.
    "   Lydia, and Immanuel Case, May 12, 1782.

ALLEN Elizabeth, and George Bissell, Dec. 2, 1787.
" ——, and William Gardiner, Dec. 20, 1790.
" Mrs. Dorcus, and —— Congdon, Feb. 23, 1795.
" ——, and Mary Greene.
" John, of Jonathan, and Mary Havens, of Thomas, May 17, 1767.
" Thomas G., and Phebe B. Congdon.
" Caleb, of Joshua, and Ruth Underwood, of Benjamin.
" Freelove, and —— Dawley, 28
" Anne, and —— Warner, Dec. 13, ——.
" Rose, and Thomas, —— —, ——.
" Phebe, of Jonathan, and Jeremiah Aylesworth, of Arthur, July 24, 1768.
" Mary, and William Corey, Dec. 4, 1812.
" Phebe W., (of Thomas G.), and Nathan A(llen) Arnold, Sept. 3, 1820.
" Lucy Ann, and Thomas Hill, Jan. 14, 1821.
" Caroline, and Ishmeal Eldred, May 12, 1830.
" Harriet, and Samuel S. Baker, Sept. 17, 1838.
" Lydia, and Benjamin B. Munroe, March 17, 1840.
" Daniel, and Mrs. Ruth Ann Finey; m. by Elder John Slocum, July 27, 1845.
" (Julie), E(lma), and Thomas W. Noyes, Sept. 28, 1845.
" ——, and —— Gardiner, Nov. 11, 1847.
ALVERSON David, and Martha Card; m. by George Tibbetts, Justice, — 30, 1735.
" Deliverance, and —— Moon, Dec. 27, 1759.
" David, and Phebe Jones, both of N. Kingstown; m. by William Hall, Justice, Jan. 24, 1765.
" ——, and Jenckes Reynolds, May 4, 1767.
ANTHONY Adelaide, and Royal Vaughn, Aug. 17, 1792.
" James B., son of Gideon Thomas Anthony, and Anna Johnson of Lawton, of Coventry, R. I.; m. by Elder Pardon Tillinghast, March 15, 1832.
" Benjamin, and Ann Weeden, both of N. Kingstown; m. by Elder David Avery, May 18, 1845.
ARMSTRONG Mrs. Nancy, and John Northup, Oct. 19, 1845.
ARNOLD Joseph, and Patience Gifford; m. by William Hall, Justice, Nov. 23, 1732.
" Joseph, and Hannah Gifford, both of N. Kingstown; m. by Benjamin Weight, Justice, Aug. —, 1737.
" Hannah, and George Thomas, April 15, 1764.
" Patience, and Abraham Greene, Sept. 5, 1765.
" Ann, and Micah Whitmarsh, June 12, 1774.
" Josiah, of N. Kingstown, and Freelove Case, of W. Greenwich; m. by Elder James Weightman, July 9, 1775.
" Edmund, of Joseph, deceased, and Abigail Hylames, of George, both of N. Kingstown; m. by George Thomas, Justice, April 20, 1777.
" George, and Margaret Slocum; m. by Elder James Weightman, April 26, 1778.
" Elizabeth, and Samuel Spink, Feb. 26, 1798.
" Joseph, of N. Kingstown, and Mercy Browning, of Samuel, Jr., of do.; m. by Francis Willett, Justice, April 24, 17—.
" Oliver, of Josiah, of Exeter, and Anstis Thomas, of George and Hannah of N. Kingstown; m. by Elder William Northup, Aug. 4, 1811.
" Nathan A(llen), of Edmund, and Phebe W. Allen, of Thomas G., of N. Kingstown; m. by Elder John Gardiner, Sept. 3, 1820.
" Abbie, and Benjamin W. Champlain, Nov. 19, 1837.
" Joshua, and Lucy A. Lovell; m. by Elder Benedict Johnson, Jan. 3, 1841.
" Horatio N., of William and Abigail, and Martha G. Card, of Joshua P. and Harriet; m. by Elder Edwin Stillman, March 29, 1842.
" Pardon M., and Mercy A. Taylor, both of N. Kingstown; m. by Elder Edwin Stillman, Dec. 23, 1845.
" Mary Ann, and Lewis D. Lawton, April 8, 1849.
" Perry, and Abigail Sophronia Greene; m. by Elder Preserved S. Greene, Jan. 13, 1850.
ATHERBY Joseph, and ——ah Aborn; m. by William Spencer, Justice, Dec. 9, 1724.
AUSTIN ——, and Margaret Sunderland, Oct. 25, 1725.

AUSTIN Stephen, of North Kingstown, and Mary, of Portsmouth; m. by William
    Sanford, Justice of Peace, April 23, 1729.
"   Benoni, of John, of E. Greenwich, and Mercy Austin, of Jeremiah, of
    N. Kingstown; m. by William Spencer, Justice of Peace, Aug., 1729.
"   Mercy, and Benoni Austin, Aug., 1729.
"   Ann, and Obediah Rathbun, Sept. 16, 1731.
"   Elizabeth, and —— Nichols, Oct. 18, 1736.
"   Robert, and Elizabeth ——; m. by Benjamin Weight, Justice of Peace,
    July 22, 1739.
"   Hannah, and Thomas Cobb, —— 1, 1753.
"   Sarah, of James, and ——, May 4, 1755.
"   James, and Catherine Hunt; m. by William Hall, Justice of Peace, March
    4, 1759.
"   ——, and Jeremiah Macomber, Aug. 3, 1761.
"   ——, and Adam Hunt, —— 3, 1761.
"   Lettice, of John, and ——; m. by George Northup, Justice of Peace, July
    27, 1766.
"   Mary, and Thomas Spencer, Oct. 15, 1767.
"   Patience, and Nathan Tanner, Feb. 28, 1768.
"   Pearces, of John, and Eleanor Smith, of Jeremiah, both of N. Kingstown;
    m. by George Thomas, Justice of Peace, Oct. 21, 1779.
"   Paulipus, of John, and Abigail Northup, of Elizabeth both of N. Kings-
    town; m. at N. K. by George Thomas, Justice of Peace, Dec. 14,
    1779.
"   Prisimus, of John and Elizabeth, and Presilia Smith, of Jeremiah and
    Mary; m. by Elder William Northup, Dec. 11, 1783.
"   Mary, and Benjamin Smith, June 8, 1788.
"   Margaret and Palmer Tanner, Dec. 17, 1789.
"   Catherine, and Daniel Fones, Jan. 9, 1791.
"   Mary, and Jonathan Vaughn, Jan. 11, 1796.
"   ——, and Ann Baker; m. by William Spencer, Justice of Peace, April 9,
    17—.
"   Anne, and Stephen Sweet, Dec. 16, 17—.
"   Mary, and James Northup, March 17, ——.
"   John, and ——
" Russell, of James, and Catherine Essex, of Benajah, of Warwick, R. I.;
    m. by Daniel Eldred, Justice of Peace, Nov. —, 1802.
"   Wanton, of Peace and Eleanor and Elizabeth Havens, of William and
    Lucy; m. by Elder William Northup, rec. Feb. 28, 1817.
"   Mary, and —— Perry, Oct. 22, 1847.
AYLESWORTH Robert, and Ann Davis; m. by William Hall, Justice of Peace, May
    20, 1708.
"   James, of Arthur, of E. Greenwich, and Mary Wood, of William; m. by
    William Spencer, Justice of Peace, Feb. 8, 1733.
"   Robert, Jr., and Susannah Reynolds; m. by Elder Benjamin Harrington,
    —— —, 1737.
"   James, of E. Greenwich, and Mary Wood, of William; m. by William Spen-
    cer, Justice of Peace, Feb. 8, 1739.
"   Mary, and Nathaniel Potter, Sept. 20, 1739.
"   Dorcas, and —— Wanton, Feb. 27, 1758.
"   Elizabeth, and Samuel Ralph, Feb. 16, 1762.
"   Sarah, and Benjamin Tanner, —— —, 1765.
"   Mary, and Richard Essex, July 24, 1768.
"   William, of Arthur, and Catherine Havens, of Rhodes; m. by George
    Thomas, Justice of Peace, June, 1774.
"   Arthur, Jr., and Abigail Dyre, both of N. Kingstown; m. by Elder Nathan
    Hill, Sept. 14, 1783.
"   Martha, and George Thomas, Aug. 19, 1787.
"   Jeremiah, of Arthur, and Anna Spencer, of Henry; m. by Elder Philip
    Jenkins, —— —, 1793.
"   Elizabeth, and John Diamond, April 26, 1798.
"   Jeremiah, of Arthur, and Phebe Allen, of Jonathan, July 24, 1768.
"   John, of Warwick, and Ann Reynolds, of Samuel, of North Kingstown;
    m. by Benoni Hall, Justice of Peace, April 19, ——.
"   Polly, and John Reynolds, Sept. 20, 1801.

AYLESWORTH ——, and —— Chadsey, March 17, 1803.
"   Isaac, of Jeremiah, and Sally Corey, of William and Sarah; m. by Elder William Northup, April 18, 1808.
"   Samuel Rhodes, of Jeremiah, and Alice Chadsey, of John and Alice; m. by Isaac Hall, Justice of Peace, Aug. 17, 1808.
"   Edward D., of Arthur, and Anna Havens, of Coventry, now of Warwick, R. I.; m. by Rev. Thomas Manchester, —— —, 1811.
"   Penelope D., and Merchant Weeden, rec. Feb. 14, 1829.
"   ——, of Samuel Rhodes Aylesworth, and ——; m. by Rev. James R. Stone, May 15, 1843.
"   ——, and Peleg A. Coggeshall, rec. Dec. 19, 1849.
AYRES Mary, and James Reynolds, Jan. 28, 1721-2.
"   Bethiah, and Nahum Chase, March 8, 1727-8.
"   Sarah, of Thomas, dec., of N. Kingstown, and Robert ——, of Robert, of Warwick; m. by Peter Boss, Justice of Peace, Nov. 13, 1736.

B

BABCOCK George, and Elizabeth Hall, Nov. 28, 1694.
"   Job, Jr., and Elizabeth Hull; m. by Rouse Helme, Asst., Oct. 10, 1717.
"   George, Jr., and Susannah Potter; m. by Christopher Allen, Justice, Dec. 20, 1721.
"   Thomas H., and Eunice A. Northup, of Stukeley; m. by Rev. J. H. Rouse, Jan. 21, 1847.
BAILEY Prudence, and Jeremiah Carpenter, March 25, 1806.
BAKER Benjamin, and Mary Ha——; m. by William Hall, Justice, —— 18, 1704-5.
"   ——, and Elizabeth Haxton; m. by Samuel Fones, Justice, March 6, 1715.
"   John, and Susannah Reynolds; m. by Benjamin Nichols, Justice, Feb. 28, 1722-3.
"   ——, daughter of Benjamin and —— Fones, ——. 1725.
"   Sarah, and —— West, Nov. 7, 1731.
"   Joseph, and Sarah Browne; m. by George Thomas, Justice, Feb. —. 1733.
"   Joseph, and —— Clarke; m. by Elisha Clarke, Justice, —— 13, 1754.
"   Susannah, and Richard Briggs, March 3, 1755.
"   Sarah, and William Dyre, Sept. 23, 1770.
"   George, and Elizabeth B——; m. by Christopher Spencer, Justice, Jan. 21, ——.
"   Jeremiah, and Deborah Reynolds; m. by William Spencer, Justice, Jan. 9, ——.
"   ——, of Benjamin, and Ruth ——; m. by Elder William Northup.
"   Ann, and —— Austin, April 9, 17—.
"   William, of Benjamin, and —— Carpenter, of Joshua, Dec. 5, 1803.
"   Thomas S., of Benjamin, and Elizabeth Chadsey, of John, deceased; m. by Elder Joseph W. Allen, Jan. 18, 1838.
"   Capt. Samuel S., and Harriet Allen; m. by Rev. B. C. Grafton, Sept. 17, 1838.
"   Abel S., and Eliza A. Thomas; m. by Rev. J. R. Stone, Dec. 30, 1839.
"   Sally S., and James J. Reynolds, March 2, 1841.
"   Mary W., and Henry Fowler, Jan. 20, 1842.
"   David S., of Capt. Benjamin and Mary C. Waite, of Col. Joseph; m. by Rev. James R. Stone, June 14, 1842.
"   Abigail F. and Nathaniel S. Lewis, Dec. 30, 1849.
"   Abigail F. and William McCotter, Jan. 27, 1850.
BARBER Moses and Susannah Wait, March 24, 1691-2. (Another date reads "20.")
"   Moses and Elizabeth Eldred; m. by John Eldred Assistant, May 23, 1765.
"   William and Mercy Smith; m. by John Eldred, Assistant, March 22, 1710.
"   William and Sarah Mumford; m. by William Spencer, Justice, May 5, 1720.
"   Edward and Mary Northup; m. by John Northup, Justice, May 1, 1773.
"   Elizabeth A. and Charles A. Slocum
BARKER Benajah, of Middletown, and Mary A. Lawton of N. Kingstown; m. by Elder John Slocum, Dec. 31, 1844.
BARNES Thomas, of Glocester, R. I., and Ruth Greene, of Kingstowne; m. by George Tibbetts, Justice, ——. ——, 18—.

BARNEY Richard, of Isaac, of Swanzey, and Frances Northup, of George, of N. Kingstown; m. by Elder William Northup, Aug. 10, 1794.

BATES Francis, and Margaret Nichols; m. by William Spencer, Justice, July 9, 1721, (prob.).

" Samuel, and Elizabeth Nichols; m. by William Spencer, Justice, July 12, 1721.

" James, and Eliza ——; m. by William Hall, Justice, April 25, 1723.

" Hezekiah, and ——, Dec. 24, 1737.

" Mary, and Samuel Codner, Dec. 28, 1740.

" Jonathan, and Mary Himes; m. by Thomas Phillips, Justice, March 26, 1747.

" Amie, and John East'ix, Oct. 24, 1762.

" Ruth, and Samuel Gavitt, Nov. 29, 1766.

" Daniel, of Daniel and Lois, and Ruth Hazard, of John and Abigail; m. by Elder William Northup, June 15, 1799.

" David, and Lowry Sherman, of Benoni.

BATON Mary E., and Alfred Thurston, May 12, 1849.

BEARES Susannah, and Jonathan Greene, March, 1733.

BENTLEY Jane, and John Weightman, Jan. 6, 1700.

" Sarah, and ——man; m. by Elisha Cole, Assistant, March 16, 1721.

" Jane, and Clement Reynolds, — 3, 1726.

" Caleb, and Dorcas Gould; m. by Job Tripp, Justice, Jan. 21, 1738.

" Lewhannah, and James James, May 28, 1738.

" Bethsheba, and John Bissell, March 29, 1761.

" Thomas, and Elizabeth Chamberland; m. by John Eldred, Assistant, June 6, (1706).

" Thomas, and Mary Reynolds; m. by William Spencer, Justice, May 20.

BERRY Charles, and Eleanor Berry; m. by Benjamin Nichols, Justice, Aug. 18, 1728.

" Eleaner, and Charles Berry, Aug. 18, 1728.

" Mary, and William Godfrey, Aug. 7, 1729.

" Dinah (col.), and William Wright, Feb. 13, 1734.

" Mary and Thomas Hill, — 8, 1743.

" Charles, of Nathaniel and Rebecca, and Sarah Mitchell, of Ephraim and Deborah; m. by Christopher Spencer, Justice, Dec. 1, 1757.

" Frances, and William Fowler, Nov. 7, 1765.

" John, and Phebe Nichols; m. by Job Tripp, Justice, Feb. 6, 17—.

" Nathaniel, and Rebecca Nichols; m. by Benjamin Weight, Justice, Jan. 5.

BICKNELL ——, and Abigail Allen, of —— town of Bristol Co., Mass.; m. by George Tibbetts, Justice, Oct., 1738.

" Arnold, and Emeline Himes; m. by J. A. Tillinghast, Justice, Dec. 23, 1849.

" Nehemiah, of Jesse, and Susan A. Gardiner, of James, dec.; m. by J. A. Tillinghast, Justice, Sept. 3, 1850.

BIDELCOM Daniel, and Ruth Tarbox, both of E. Greenwich; m. at N. Kingstown, by William Hall, Justice, April 27, 1760.

BISSELL Anne, and Jeremiah Vallett, Dec. 27, 1753.

" Samuel, (blacksmith), and Sarah Aldrich; m. by Immanuel Northup, Justice, ——, 19, 1753.

" John, of N. Kingstown, and Bathsheba Bentley, of Richmond; m. by Jeremiah Crandall, Justice, March 29, 1761,

" Thomas, and Phebe Congdon, both of N. Kingstown; m. by Elder James Weightman, March 17, 1776.

" Daniel, of Thomas, of N. Kingstown, and Waite Congdon, of Benjamin, dec.; m. by Eber Sherman, Justice, June 4, 1776.

" Samuel, of Thomas, and Sarah Allen, of Jonathan; m. by Elder James Weightman, March 18, 1782.

" George, of Thomas, and Elizabeth Allen, of Capt. Jonathan, both of N. Kingstown; m. by Elder James Weightman, Dec. 2, 1787.

" Samuel, of Thomas, and Ann Spink, of Josiah; m. by Elder Philip Jenkins, Dec. 13, 1798.

" ——, and Izitt Burgess; m. at Jamestown by Tiddeman Hull, Justice, Jan. 16, ——.

" John, of Thomas and Ruth Congdon, of Benjamin, 3d., dec.; m. by George Thomas, Justice, Dec. 15, 17—.

" Thomas, and Hannah Pinder; m. by Thomas Phillips, Justice.

BOONE Sarah, and Capt. Samuel Rhodes, March 6, 1724.
"   Ann, and ——— Jackson, Aug. 15, 1725.
"   Samuel, Jr., and Mer——. Dec. 6, 1736.
"   ———, and Ephraim Smith, Feb. 4, 1741.
"   William, and Ruth Hill; m. by Eld. Samuel Albro, May 21, 1761.
"   Richard, and Harty Carey, both of N. Kingstown; m. by Samuel Albro, Feb. 28, 1765.
"   Samuel, of Samuel, and Margar.t Smith, of Ephraim, of N. Kingstown; m. by George Thomas, Justice, Jan. 7, 1767.
"   Hannah, and Joseph Clarke, Dec. 13, 176—.
"   James, of James, and Mary Weightman, of George; m. by Elder Philip Jenkins, April 19, 1778.
"   Martha, and Peleg Clarke, March 11, 1784.
"   Sarah, and Robert Eldred, Jan. 1, 1789.
"   Thomas, of North Kingstown, son of —— and Mary, and Susannah Gardiner, of Christopher and Mary, Sept. 21, 1794.
"   Thomas G., of Thomas and Luceanna, and Hannah Reynolds, of Benjamin and ——: m by Elder William Northup.
"   ———, and Nicholas Spink.
BOSS Peter, and Anne Gardiner; m. by William Spencer, Justice, Jan. 28, 1719-20. Another record reads "23."
"   Hannah Martin, and Thomas Smith, June 13, 1711.
BOTTOM Sarah, and William Learnard, Feb. —, 1708-9.
BOWEN Stephen, of Aaron and Elnathan, of Coventry, R. I., and Rebecca Hill, of Caleb and Mercy, of N. Kingstown; m. by Elder William Northup, April 22, 1802.
BRAMAN James, of James and Elizabeth Carpenter; m. by Rouse Helme, Justice, Dec. 3, 1721.
"   Hannah, and William Himes. March 28, 1845.
BRENTON Elizabeth McLoughling, and William G. Shaw, M. D., Oct. 16, 1796.
BRIGGS Sarah, and Philip Smith, —, 1720-1.
"   Rose, and Nathaniel Havens, Feb. —, 1733-4.
"   Mary, and —— Fowler, Nov. —, 1737.
"   William, of N. Kingstown, and Deliverance Shippee, of East Greenwich; m. by Benjamin Weight, Justice, May 18, 1740.
"   John, Jr., and Mary Parmelent; m. by Thomas Hill, Justice, Dec. —, 1740.
"   James, and Elizabeth ——; m. by Thomas Hill, Justice, July —, 1741.
"   Richard, of Frances, and Susannah Baker, of Jeremiah; m. by Nicholas Northup, Justice, March 3, 1755.
"   Susannah, and Nathaniel Spencer, March 16, 1758.
"   Hannah, and Samuel Fones, April 26, 1760.
"   Hannah, and —— Congdon, ——. 18, 1760.
"   John, Jr., and Mary Tanner, of Palmer, dec.; m. by William Hall, Justice, Dec. 25, 1763.
"   Eunice, and John Pierce, March 24, 1771.
"   George, of Richard, and Frances Dyre, of Edward; m. by Elder Philip Jenkins, Feb. 10, 1777.
"   Wealthian, and Charles Brown, Jan. 15, 1778.
"   Silas, and Elizabeth Spencer, both of N. Kingstown; m. by Elder James Weightman, March 26, 1780.
"   William, Jr., of William, and Hannah Dixon, of Robert, of N. Kingstown; m. by Elder Nathan Hill, Dec. 23, 1788.
"   Paul, and ——y Carr, of Gideon, of N. Kingstown; m. by Elder Nathan Hill, ——. 1, 1798.
"   ———, and Mary Joslin, —— 4, ——.
"   Henry, of William, and Mary Dickson, of Robert, both of N. Kingstown; m. by George Thomas, Justice, Feb. 7, 1802.
BROWNING John, and Ann Hazard (of Jeremiah); m. by Stephen Hazard, Asst., April 21, 1721.
"   Sarah, and Eleazer Kelley, Oct. 6, 1721.
"   Rebecca, and Isaac Bull, April 8, 1731.
"   Mary, and Benoni Albro, Jun. —, 1744.
"   Isaac, and Elizabeth ——; m. by Samuel Thomas, Justice, Dec. 2, 1754.
"   Samuel, of Isaac, and Lucy Kingsley, of Samuel, both of North Kingstown; m. by Elder Philip Jenkins, Dec. 31, 1778.

BROWNING Gardiner, of Samuel, and Izett Cole, of John, both of North Kingstown; m. by Elder James Wightman, March 27, 1784.

" William, of Samuel, dec., and Sorah Cole, of Capt. John, both of North Kingstown; m. by Eld. James Whitman, Dec. 13, 1787.

" Mercy, and Joseph Arnold, April 24, 17 .

" Samuel, Jr., and Phebe Wo—; m. by Benjamin Weight, Justice.

" Abbie C., and Jeremiah Gardiner, March 16, 1826.

" Mercy, and Isaac Aldrich, Dec. 22, 1846.

BROWN Samuel, and Mary ——; m. by George Hazard, Justice, Oct. 22, 1702.

" (Samuel), and Anna Warner; m. by William Hall, Justice, April 24, 1707.

" William, and Elizabeth Robinson; m. by Christopher Allen, Justice, Nov. 2, 1707.

" Deborah, and Thomas Peckham, Oct. 4, 1722.

" Sarah, and Joseph Baker, Feb. ---, 1733.

" Abigail and (Samuel), Phillips —— 4, 1733.

" Alexander and Honor (Huling), —— --, 1739.   Date wrong, probably 1709.

" —— and Alice Joslin, March 10, 1744.

" Daniel, of Warwick, R. I., and Deliverance Medbury, of North Kingstown; m. by Robert Hall, Justice, Oct. 25, 1747.

" Martha and Nathaniel Gardiner, Aug. 1, 1762.

" Charles, Jr., of Charles, and Mary Congdon, of William; m. by George Thomas, Justice, Dec. 6, 1767.

" William, of Samuel, and Anne Tanner; m. by George Northop, Justice, Sept. 2, 1768.

" Benjamin, and Waite Reynolds, both of N. Kingstown; m. by Elder Samuel Albro, Oct. 17, 1771.

" Elizabeth, and Anthony Rathbun, Nov. 7, 1771.

" Phenix, of Charles, and Dorcas Congdon, of William, dec.; m. by George Thomas, Justice, Jan. 16, 1772.

" Elizabeth, and Nathan Brown, Sept. 27, 1772.

" Nathan, of Ebenezer, and Elizabeth Brown, of John; m. by George Thomas, Justice, Sept. 27, 1772.

" Stukeley, and Sarah Congdon, both of N. Kingstown; m. by Elder James Weightman, July 30, 1775.

" Samuel, Jun., of N. Kingstown, and Anna Ha—, of E. Greenwich; m. by Elder James Weightman, Aug. 27, 1775.

" Elizabeth (widow), and Thomas Phillips, Oct. 27, 1776.

" Charles, of Samuel, of N. Kingstown, and Weathian Briggs, of E. Greenwich; m. by Elder James Weightman, Jan. 15, 1778.

" Mary, and James Eldred, Jan. 28, 1779.

" Mrs Abigail, and Benedict Brown, M— 23, 1780.

" Benedict, of John, and Mrs. Abigail Brown, of Ebenezer, both of N. Kingstown; m. by George Thomas, Justice, May 23, 1780.

" Benjamin, of Benjamin, and Elizabeth Cooper, of James; m. by Elder Phillip Jenkins, Nov. 2, 1780.

" Margaret, and William Weeden, March 29, 1781.

" Penelope, and Anthony Rathbun, Feb. 18, 1787.

" Alexander, of Beriah, of Exeter, and Mary Thurber, of N. Kingstown; m. by Elder Phillip Jenkins, Jan. 2, 1790.

" Abigail, and Elisha Gardiner, ——, —, ——.

" Charles, of Charles, and —— Sherman, of Samual, ——, —, ——.

" Beriah, and Elizabeth Smith; m. by Benjamin Weight, Justice, —— 30, ——.

" ——, and James Eldred, —— —, ——.

" Honor, and Samuel Hopkins, April 23, (1729-30).

" James Eldred, of ——, and Abigail and Thomas, of George and Hannah; m. by Elder William Northup, July 2, 1802.

" Ann, and Henry Spencer, July 10, 1806.

" Mary, and John Eldred, June 8, 1820.

" Sarah, and John Pierce, Nov. 6, 1825.

" Elmathan C., of Samuel and Annie, of Westerly, and Frances G. Hazard, of John, of N. Kingstown, May 11, 1827.

" Joseph, and Desire C. Pierce, both of N. Kingstown; m. by Elder John Gardiner, Feb. 24, 1828.

BROWN Elizabeth, and Samuel A. Toothacker, July 26, 1838.
"   Jane C., and Jeremiah Wills, March 18, 1847.
"   Nathan, of Newport, and Mar— Gardiner, of N. Kingstown; m. by Elder
        John Slocum, July 4, 1847.
"   Harriet, and Daniel Spink, Jun., Oct. 25, 1847.
"   Ann F., and Willett Himes, Oct. 23, 1848.
"   Edmund A., of Daniel, and Margaret C. Tanner, of Abel; m. by Elder
        Joseph W. Allen, March 25, 1849.
"   Amie A., and Samuel Greene, Oct. 15, 1849.
"   William, and Avis Ann Spink; m. by Rev. Alfred H. Taylor, Feb. 11,
        1850.
"   Ebenezer, of (William), and Mrs. Sarah Reynolds, (widow of Daniel,
        dau. Allen Tillinghast), both of N. Kingstown; m. by Elder William
        R. Slocum, April 23, 1850.
"   Elizabeth, and George Baker, Jan. 21, ——.
BULLOCK Celinda, and John P. Case, March 17, 1799.
"   Jabez, of N. Kingstown, and Lydia A. Hammond, of William, dec.; m. by
        Rev. John H. Rouse, Nov. 15, 1841.
BULL William, and Mary Coggeshall, Oct. 27, 1692.   (Another record reads
        " Ephraim.")
"   Ephraim, and Hannah Holway, June 20, 1700. (Another record reads
        " William.")
"   Isaac, and Rebecca Browning; m. by Daniel Coggeshall, Justice, April
        8, 1731.
"   Hannah, and Eber Harrington, ——.
"   John, and Lydia ——; m. by Daniel Coggeshall, Justice, ——.
BUNDY Rebecca, and Edward Rogers, July 16, 1739.
BURDICK Joseph, and Abigail Eldred, of Joseph, of N. Kingstown; m. by George
        Thomas, Justice, Jan. 10, 1776
BURGEUSS Izitt, and —— Bissell, Jan. 16, ——.
BURGE Anne Shaw, and —— Thomas, Aug. 9, 1844.
BURLINGAME Audrey, and Arnold Thomas, ——. 22, 1801.
"   James, and Abbie A. Sweet; m. by Rev. John Slocum, Dec. 13, 1847.
"   Alice, and John Sherman, Nov. 7, 1848.
"   Hazard, and Hannah Gardiner, May 20, 1850.
BURNHAM Alva, and Hannah Holloway Oct. 7, 1839.
BU——— Harriet, and Caleb Carr, Aug. 4, 183—.

C

CAHOONE William and Sarah Carpenter; m. by Benjamin Nichols, Justice,
        March 10, 1730.
CANUDA Jenne, and John Hull, July 11, 1709.
CAPRON Jonathan, of E. Greenwich, and —— Greene, of N. Kingstown; m. by Wil-
        liam Hall, Justice, —— 30, 1756.
"   John, of Greene, and Ruhuma, of E Greenwich, and Mary Eldred, of James
        and Mary ; Dec. 4, 1803.
CARDER Thomas R., and Mary E. Hoxsie, both of E. Greenwich; m. by Rev.
        C. C. Lewis, Sept. 6, 1849.
CARD James, of James, and Martha Wait or West, March 4, 1702-3.
"   Mary, and Joseph Straight, May 15, 1735.
"   Martha, and David Alverson, —— 30, 1735.
"   Stephen and ——; m. by Thomas Northup, Justice, —— 8, 1740.
"   Phillip, of N. Kingstown, and Catherine Davis; m. by Thomas Hill, Jus-
        tice, Dec. 3, 1741.
"   Elizabeth, and ——; m. by Elisha Clarke, Justice, April 12, 1752.
"   ——, and Hannah Dyer; m. by Elisha Clarke, Justice, April 2, 1752.
"   Job, and Martha Eldred; m. by Samuel Albro, Justice, Nov. 1, 1756.
"   Sarah, and John Olin Jun, Oct. 13, 1765.
"   Elizabeth, and Daniel Dawley, Nov. 20, 1774.
"   Job, of N. Kingstown, son of Jo—, dec., and Barbara Smith, widow of
        Samuel, and dau. of Benjamin Northup; m. by Eber Sherman, Justice,
        June 5, 1782.
"   Mary, and ——; m. by William Spencer, Justice, Oct. 15, ——.

CARD ——, and Martha West; m. by William Hall, Justice, March 24, ——.
"   Phillip, of Peleg and Alice, and Anstris Helme, of William, and Margaret; m. by Elder William Northup, Aug. 20, 1807.
"   Robert, of N. Kingstown, and Mary Gardiner, of Exeter; m. by Elder Gershem Palmer, Sept. 5, 1813.
"   Martha G., and Horatio N. Arnold, March 29, 1842.
"   Phillip, and Mrs. Jemima Congdon; m. by Rev. John Slocum, Aug. 11, 1844.
CARPENTER Elizabeth, and James Braman, Dec. 3, 1721.
"   Sarah, and William Cahoone, March 10, 1730.
"   Tabitha, and —— ——; m. by George Thomas, Justice, Feb. 22, 1732.
"   Daniel, and Renewed ——; m. by Daniel Coggeshall, Justice, April 29. 1733.
"   Jeremiah, of East Greenwich, and Elizabeth Reynolds, of N. Kingstown; m. by Samuel Casey, Justice, Dec. 25, 1737.
"   Dinah, of John, and Joshua Greene, Feb. 12, 1746.
"   Sarah, and John Reynolds, Jan. 17, 1762.
"   Elisha, of ——, Kent Co., R. I., and Lydia Greene of N. Kingstown; m. by William Hall, Justice, Sept. 20, 1767.
"   Christopher G., and ——.
"   Hannah, and ——, Oct. 30, 17—
"   —— and Joshua Greene, Feb. 12, ——.
"   Hannah, and Benjn. Rathbun, Oct. 31, ——.
"   Francis, and Elizabeth Case, of Joseph. Oct. 4, 1801.
"   ——, of Joshua, and William Baker, of Benjamin; Dec. 5, 1803.
"   Jeremiah, of Ephraim and Mary, of S. Kingstown, and Prudence Bailey, of Eli and Hannah, of N. Kingstown; m. by Elder Thomas Manchester, March 25, 1806.
"   Jeremiah, of William and Elizabeth Vaughn, of John, of E. Greenwich; m. by Elder Gershem Palmer, Feb. 5, 1809.
"   Sarah, and Pardon Vaughn, March 4, 1809.
"   John J. Jr., of John J. of Providence, and Hannah G. Hall, of Slocum; m. by Rev. James R. Stone, Oct. 22, 1843.
"   Charles S., of E. Greenwich, and Susie R. Carpenter, of N. Kingstown; m. by Rev. John H. Rouse, Oct. 8, 1846.
"   Susie R., and Charles S. Carpenter, Oct. 8, 1846.
CASEY Sarah, and Ebenezer Slocum, Oct. 11, 1772.
"   Joseph, of William and Sarah, and Anna Reynolds, of George and Sarah, of Exeter; m. by Elder William Northup, March 31, 1799.
"   Sally,* and Isaac Aylesworth, April 18, 1808.   *This should be Carey.
CASE Margaret, and Abraham Perkins, June 29, 1718.
"   Sanford, and —— Godfrey, of East Greenwich; m. by William Hall, Justice, Sept. 1, 1761.
"   Immanuel, Jr., and —— A. Rathbun; m. by Elder Samuel Albro, Oct. 4, 1761.
"   Ann, and Benjn. Fowler, Jan. 2, 1763.
"   Sarah, and Thomas Clarke, Dec. 20, 1770.
"   Freelove, and Josiah Arnold, July 9, 1775.
"   Immanuel, of South Kingstown, and Lydia Allen, of North Kingstown; m. by Elder James Weightman, May 12, 1782.
"   ——, dau of Immanuel; m. at N. Kingstown to —— ——, by Eld. Nathan Hill; rec. Sept. 18, 1784.
"   John P., of Immanuel, and Celinda Bullock, of John; m. by Eld. William Northup, March 17, 1799.
"   Elizabeth, and Francis Carpenter, Oct. 4, 1801.
"   Elisha, of Joseph and Abigail, and Anne Clarke, of Thomas and Sarah; m. by Elder William Northup, April 18, 1805.
"   ——, and Harriet Holloway; m. by B. L. Peckham, Justice of Peace, April 21, 1814.
"   Ann P., and William A. Shaw; rec. Feb. 1, 1848.
CARR Anne, and —— Northup, ——, 1745-6,
"   Mercy, and James Wightman, Feb. 1, 1776.
"   Oliver, of Jamestown, and Phebe Allen, of Joshua, April —, 1776.
"   Samuel, of John and Frances Eldred, of Joseph; m. by George Thomas, Justice of Peace, Jan. 17, 1779.

CARR William, of Daniel and Elizabeth Pierce, of Silas, both of N. Kingstown; m. by Elder Phillip Jenkins, —— 13, 1794.

"   ——, and Paul Briggs, —— 1, 1798.

"   Robert Robinson, of ——, and Abbie, of Newport, and Mary Davis, of Benjn. and Phebe, of N. Kingstown; m. by Elder William Northup, Feb. —, 1802.

"   Phebe, and Joseph Eldred, Jan. 15, 1802.

"   Mary, and William Thomas, Jan. 1, 1808.

"   Caleb, of Warwick, and Harriet Bu—, of N. Kingstown; m. by Rev. James R. Stone, Aug. 4, 183—.

"   Mary M., and Ebenezer Rose, June 11, 1843.

"   Phebe Ann, and William Rose, Nov. 22, 1843.

CEASER Solomon, (negro), and —— Sweet; m. by Elder Benjn. Harrington, Dec. 12, 1735.

"   William, and Sarah Wolmesley (col.); m. by George Thomas, Justice of Peace, March 25, 1768.

"   Joseph, of N. Kingstown, and Freelove King, of E. Greenwich; m. by Benjamin Barton, Justice of Peace, Aug. 10, 1789.

CHADSEY Jabez, and Honor Huling (Alexander); m. by Edward Dyre, Justice of Peace, March —, 1751.

"   Jabez, of N. Kingstown, and Mary Corey, of W. Greenwich; m. at N. K. by George Thomas, Justice of Peace, Sept. 1, 1774.

"   William, and Barbara Eldred, both of N. Kingstown; m. by Eber Sherman, Justice of Peace, —— 21, 1776.

"   Jabez, of Jabez and (Hannah) Greene, of Jeremiah, dec., both of N. Kingstown; m. by Eld Phillip Jenkins, Sept. 30, 1779.

"   Honor, and Benjamin Jenkins, April 13, 1780.

"   John, of Jabez, of N. Kingstown, and Alice Pierce, of John, of E. Greenwich; m. at E. G. by George Spencer, Justice of Peace, May 9, 1791.

"   Jabez (of William, dec.), of N. Kingstown, and Martha Greene, widow of Archibald, of E. Greenwich; m. by George Spencer, Justice of Peace, March 21, 1792.

"   Elizabeth, and Jonathan Slocum; m. by Elder Philip Jenkins; rec. Jan. 30, 1794.

"   Circuit, of Jabez and Honor, and Rachel Aylesworth, of Jeremiah and Ann; m. by Elder William Northup, March 17, 1803.

"   Rowland, of Jabez and Honor, and Patty Pearce, of John and Eunice; m. by Elder William Northup, June 22, 1803.

"   George, and Elizabeth Spencer, both of N. Kingstown; m. by Elder William Northup, Oct. 16, 1803; rec. April 21, 1804.

"   Alce, and Samuel R. Aylesworth, Aug. 17, 1808.

"   Henry T., of Jeremiah G. and Almira W Wightman, both of N. Kingstown; m. by Elder J. W. Allen, June 13, 1830.

"   Elizabeth, and Thomas S. Baker, Jan. 18, 1838.

"   Mariah W., and Charles F. Woodworth, Nov. 30, 1846.

CHAMBERLAND Elizabeth, and Thomas Bentley, June 6, ——.

CHAMPLAIN William, and Lucy Lewis; m. by Isaiah Wilcox, Justice, June 18, 1786.

"   Emblem, and ——; m. by Elisha Cole, Assistant, Dec. 25, 1721.

"   Jeffrey, and Mary Northup, of Henry; m. by William Hall, Justice, Sept. 26, 1725.

"   Benjamin, of Daniel G., of Exeter, and Amie Ann Pierce, of Elisha, of N. Kingstown; m. by Elder J. W. Allen, Sept. 28, 1837.

"   Benjamin W. and Abbie Arnold; m. by Elder William Northup, Nov. 19, 1837.

"   George Leroy, of Isaac and Ann, and Clara H. Thomas, of Samuel and Ann, ——, —, 1847.

CHAPPELL James, of S. Kingstown, and Virtue Scranton, of N. Kingstown; m. by Samuel Thomas, Justice, April 4, 1751.

"   Rhoda Ann, and James Eldred, Oct. 3, 1842.

"   Esther C., and Esbon Sanford, Aug. 12, 1850.

CHASE Nahum, (mariner), and Bethiah Ayres; m. by William Spencer, Justice, March 8, 1727-8.

"   Phebe, and Jeremiah Harrington, Feb. —, 1753.

"   Sarah, and Benjn. Congdon, Nov. —, 1748.

"   Annie, and Cato Greene, ——. —, 1779.

CHASE William E. (schoolmaster), of Josiah S., and Charity, of Uxbridge, Mass.,
  aged 25 years, and Hannah B. Reynolds, of Henry and Ruth, aged
  26 years; m. by Rev. Joseph A. Tillinghast, Oct. 3, 1848.
" ——, and James Congdon, ——. —, ——.
" Jonathan, and (Mary Huling, widow of James). Sept. 3, ——.
CHURCH George H., of George H., and Sarah Greene Eldred, of Ishmeal; m.
  by Rev. John Enock Cheshire, June 13, 1853.
" Sarah E., and Henry M. Coffin, Dec. 1, 1868.
CLARKE William, and Ann Greene; m. by William Hall, Assistant, Nov. 3, 1730.
" Margaret, and ——, of E. Greenwich; m. by George Tibbetts, May —,
  1736.
" ——, and Joseph Baker, ——. 13, 1754.
" Cary, of Caleb, and —— Dyre, dau. of Geo. Thomas; m. by Samuel
  Thomas, Justice, April 6, 1755.
" Elisha, and Desire Gardiner; m. by Rev. Samuel Albro, April 10, 1763.
" Sarah, and Carr Northup, March 9, 1766.
" Susannah, and John Nichols, March 19, 1769.
" Joseph, and Hannah Boone, Dec. 13, 176—.
" Thomas, of Elisha, of N. Kingstown, and Sarah Case, of Joseph, of N.
  K.; m. by Elder Solomon Sprague, Dec. 20, 1770.
" Peleg, of Cornelius, of E. Greenwich, and Martha Boone, of James,
  dec., of N. Kingstown; m. at N. K. by George Thomas, Justice, March
  11, 1784.
" Hannah, and Henry Gardiner, Oct. 26, 1796.
" William, of Thomas, of N. Kingstown, and Sarah Hamilton, of Frederic,
  June 18, 1797.
" Patience, and Augustus Morey, May 4, 17—.
" Elizabeth, and James Huling, May 15, ——.
" Margaret, and Peter, —— —, ——.
" May, and ——; m. by Jeremiah Gould, Assistant, June 11, 17—.
" Mary, and Benjamin Wart, Jan. 24, 1805.
" Anna, and Elisha Case, April 18, 1805.
" Elisha, of Thomas and Sarah, and Phebe Reynolds, of Henry and Mary; m.
  by Elder William Northup, Aug. 5, 1810.
" Benjamin T., of Thomas and Sarah, and Mary Ann Reynolds, of Henry
  and Mary; m. by Elder William Northup, Jan. 14, 1811.
" Esther, and —— Dickinson; rec. April 19, 1822.
CLEAVELAND Palmer, and Esther Northup, widow of David; m. by John Cong-
  don, Justice of Peace, July 1, 1751.
" Deborah, and —— Tripp, March 8, 1743.
" Deliverance, of Exeter, and Hannah ——, of N. Kingstown; m. by Thomas
  Hill, Justice of Peace, —— 7, 1743.
" John, Esq., and Elizabeth Enos, widow; m. by George Thomas (of
  Samuel), Justice of Peace, Jan. 28, 1773.
" John, and Mercy Sweet; m. by George Thomas, Justice of Peace, ——
  4, ——.
COBB Thomas, and Hannah Austin; m. by Elisha Clarke, Justice of Peace, ——. 1,
  1753.
" Mercy, and Jeremiah Niles, Dec. 29, 1778.
CODNER Samuel, and Mary Bates; m. by Jeffrey Watson, Justice of Peace, Dec.
  28, 1740.
COFFIN Henry Martin, and Sarah Eldred Church; m. by Rev. Justus Aldrich, Dec.
  1, 1868.
COGGESHALL Mary, and Ephraim Bull, Oct. 27, 1692.
" Mary, and William Bull, Oct. 27, 1692.
" Joshua, and —— Reynolds; m. by Jeremiah Gould, Justice of Peace,
  —— —, 1725-6.
" Waite, and James Gardiner, March 15, 1749.
" Ann, and Ephraim Gardiner, March 12, 1758.
" Elizabeth, and William Hall, Aug. —, 1773.
" Christopher, of Benjamin, of E. Greenwich, and Anna Hall, of Daniel,
  of N. Kingstown; m. by George Thomas, Justice of Peace, Oct. 13,
  1780.
" Mrs. Hannah, and John Magnin, Dec. 13, 1798
" ——, and Samuel Fry, ——. 20, ——.

COGGESHALL ——, and John Sheffield, —— —, ——.
" Peleg A., of Peleg, of Portsmouth, and —— Aylesworth, of Samuel D., of N. Kingstown; m. by Rev. C. C. Lewis, Rec. Dec. 19, 1849.

COLE Rebecca, and —— Hill, March 25, 173—.
" Jane, and Samuel Albro, Dec. 3, 1758.
" Martha, and Stephen Northup, ——. —, 1780.
" Benjamin, Jr., of N. Kingstown, and Patty Wightman; m. by Elder Nathan Hill, Nov. 2, 1783.
" Izitt, and Gardiner Browning, May 27, 1784.
" Sarah, and William Browning, Dec. 13, 1787.
" Benjamin, and ——. widow of Samuel Place; m. by Benjamin Allen, Justice, ——. 19, ——.
" Hutchinson A., and Sally B. ——; m. by Elder William Northup, Oct. 1, 1817.
" George H. T., of Hutchinson A. and Sally B., and Eliza Melissa Crumb, of ——, and Susan; m. by Rev. John H. Rouse, Sept. 19, 1848.

COLLINS William, of the Continental Army, and Catherine Smith of N. Kingstown; m. by Elder Phillip Jenkins, June 3. 1779.

COMFORT Abigail, and ——, Feb. 14, 170—.

CONGDON Benjamin, and Elizabeth Sweet, of Benoni; m. by Elisha Cole, assistant, Nov. 22, 1722.
" ——, and Patience Northup; m. by William Hall, Justice of Peace, Nov. 16, 1727.
" James, and Mary Vaughn; m. by William Spencer, Justice of Peace, March 30, 1732.
" William, and Ann Gifford; m. by Daniel Coggeshall, Justice of Peace, March 30, 1732.
" Benjamin, of Benjamin, Jr., and Sarah Chase, of Jonathan; m. by Immanuel Northup, Justice of Peace, Nov. —, 1748.
" Joseph, of Benjamin, and —— Wall, of John; m. by Samuel Thomas, Justice of Peace, Jan. 10, 1754.
" ——, of Joseph, and Hannah Briggs, of John; m. by George Northup, Justice of Peace, ——. 18, 1760,
" John, Jr., of N. Kingstown, and Abigail Rose, of S. Kingstown; m. by Rev. Joseph Torrey, July 9, 17—; rec. June 29, 1761.
" Patience, and Ephraim Gardiner, Oct. 19, 1761.
" George, of Joseph, and Ann ——. both of N. Kingstown; m. by George Northup, Justice of Peace, April 3, 1764.
" Susannah, and Ezekiel Gardiner, May —, 1764.
" Mary, and Charles Brown, Dec. 6, 1767.
" Dorcas, and Phenix Brown, Jan. 16, 1772.
" Sarah, and Stukeley Brown, July 30, 1775.
" Mary, and Stephen Sweet, Jan. 28, 1776.
" Phebe, and Thomas Bissell, March 17, 1776.
" Waite, and Daniel Bissell, June 4, 1776.
" George, and Deborah Himes; m. by George Thomas, Justice of Peace, Oct. 25, 1781.
" Sarah, and Benjamin Davis, Dec. 6, 1781.
" Henry, of John (of Exeter), dec., and Sarah Vaughn, widow of Jeremiah, late of N. Kingstown, dec.; m. by George Thomas, Justice of Peace, Feb. 8, 1787.
" Abigail, and Esbon Sanford, March 25, 1787.
" Thomas R., of N. Kingstown, and Betsey Stewart, of Preston, Conn.; m. by Elder Levi Hart, —— 19, 1789.
" ——ah, and Benjamin Shaw, Oct. 13, 1793.
" ——. and Mrs. Dorcas, dau. of Capt. Joshua Allen, of N. Kingstown, at do.; m. by George Thomas, Justice of Peace, Feb. 23, 1795.
" Stephen, of N. Kingstown, and Thankful Stewart, of Preston, Conn.; m. by Elder Samuel Tyler, June 24, 1795.
" Henry, of James, of N. Kingstown, and —— Sweet, widow, of N. Kingstown; m. by Elder Nathan Hill, —— 29. 1795.
" Capt. Daniel, and Mrs. Hannah Thurston, of S. Kingstown; m. by Elder Benjamin Weight, Jan. 24, 1797.
" Ruth and John Bissell, Dec. 15, 17—.
" Elizabeth, and Silas Gardiner, Dec. 20, ——.

CONGDON Frances, and George Northup, Dec. 20, ——.
" Phebe B. and Thomas G. Allen.
" Hannah and John J. Reynolds, April 9, 18—.
" Anna and —— Sherman.
" James, of William (dec.) and —— Chase.
" James, of N. Kingstown, and Lydia Hedley, of Portsmouth, dau of ——, and Rachel.
" Frances, of —— and John, m. by Elder David Sprague, June 19, ——.
" George, Jr., of George and ——, of Zubanon; m. by George Thomas, Justice of Peace, Oct. 8, 1807.
" Stephen, of William and Ann, and Mercy Spencer, dau. of Jonathan and Elizabeth Allen, m. at Exeter, Jan. 17, 1814.
" Henry, of James and Lydia, and Waltey Weaver, dau. of David and Mary Cottrell; m. by Elder William Northup, Feb. 5, 1816.
" Joseph, of John and Mary, and Phebe Congdon, dau. of William and Phebe Bailey, m. by Elder William Northup, Feb. 23, 1817.
" Phebe and Joseph Congdon, Feb. 23, 1817.
" ——, of Daniel and Hannah, and Spink, of Samuel and Elizabeth; m. by Elder William Northup, recorded June —, 1821.
" Benjamin H., of Benjamin S., and Abbie Ann Spink, of Job; m. by Elder Edwin Stillman, Feb. 12, 1844.
" Mrs. Jemima, and Philip Card, Aug. 11, 1844.
" Thomas, of Benjamin, and Eliza Ann Spink, of Boone; m. by Rev. Elbridge Gale, Dec. 15, 1845.
" —— W., and Mercy Rathbun, Nov. 8, 1846.
" Gideon G., of Gideon G. and Elizabeth, of Warwick, R. I., and Mary Nichols Reynolds, of William B. and Susan, of N. Kingstown; m. by Rev. A. Judson Chaplin, Dec. 14, 1846.
" Hannah S., and Daniel S. Hazard, rec. July 15, 1847.
" Elizabeth, and Henry S. Tourgee, Nov. 13, 1848.
CONNELLY Bridget R., and George S. A. Patterson.
COOK Sarah (widow), and Daniel McCoone, June 19, 1705.
" Sarah, and John Ney, Oct. 26, 1710.
" Philip, of Charles and Annie, and Hannah Thomas, of Benjamin and Austin; m. by Elder William Northup, Feb. 15, 1799.
COOPER Abigail, and Matthew Cooper, Oct. 15, 1721.
" Matthew, and Abigail Cooper, Oct. 15, 1721.
" Gilbert, of Matthew, and Elizabeth Davis, of John, dec.; m. by Samuel Thomas, Justice of Peace, April 7, 1755.
" ——, and Jemima Hart; m. by Ephraim Gardiner, Justice of Peace, Feb. 28, 1760.
" Matthew, and Rebecca Spink, of Capt. Benjamin; m. by William Smith, Justice of Peace, April 1, 1763.
" Margaret, and John Bawly, Sept. 17, 1772.
" Mary, and John Slocum, Dec. 5, 1779.
" Elizabeth, and Benjamin Brown, Nov. 2, 1780.
" ——, of Thomas, dec., and —— ——, of Capt. Benjamin; m. by Elder Nathan Hill, May —, 1782.
" James, Jr., and Ruth Warner, —— 28, ——.
" Mary, and John P. Whitford, Aug. 5, 1803.
" Edmund, of N. Kingstown, son of Gilbert, and Eleanora Miner, of Snow; m. by Joshua B. Rathbun, Justice of Peace, June 10, 1829.
" Elizabeth, and Daniel Northup, March 30, 1841.
" John, and Mrs. Lydia Smith; m. by Rev. J. R. Stone, Jan. 19, 1842.
COREY Ann, and Thomas Allen, Sept. 4, 1756.
" Harty, and Richard Boone, Feb. 28, 1765.
" John, Jr., and Mary Greene; m. by Elder Samuel Albro, Nov. 13, 1766.
" Job, of John, Jr., and Elizabeth Pearce, of N. Kingstown; m. by George Thomas, Justice of Peace, July 30, 1767.
" William, of Caleb, of N. Kingstown, and Martha Pierce, of Benjamin, of Warwick; m. by Robert Hall, Justice of Peace, 1771; rec. Sept. 14, 1771.
" John, of Thomas, dec., and Anna Allen, of Christopher; m. by Elder Philip Jenkins, Dec. 7, 1772.
" John, of Samuel, of Richmond, R. I., and Abigail Smith, of Thomas, of N. Kingstown; m. by George Thomas, Justice of Peace, Nov. 7, 1773.
(Vit. Rec., Vol. 5.) 2

COREY Mary, and Jabez Chadsey, Sept. 1, 1774.
" 　　Sarah, and Nicholas Hart, March 19, 1779.
" 　　Esther, and Eldred Reynolds, April 26, 1792.
" 　　Mary, and William Hall, June 8, 1803.
" 　　William, of William and Elizabeth, and Mary Allen, of Christopher and
　　　　Margaret; m. by Elder William Northup, Dec. 4, 1812.
" 　　Mary, and Benjamin Gardiner, Jan. 28, 1822.
" 　　William, and ——, Nov. 26, ——.
CORNELL Abigail, and Caleb Sisson, Aug. 27, 1769.
COTTRELL Rachel, and ——; m. by William Spencer, Justice of Peace, March 2,
　　　　1737.
" 　　John, son of Rachel Osborne, and —— Rogers; m. by James Eldred,
　　　　Justice of Peace, Nov. 16, 1752.
" 　　Abigail, and Stephen Reynolds, —— 3, ——.
" 　　Phebe, and ——.
" 　　——, and Elizabeth Gardiner; m. by William Hall, Assistant, Dec. —,
　　　　——.
COZZENS William E., and Elizabeth A. Hunt, Dec. —, ——.
CO—— Sarah, and Simon Smith, Nov. —, 1739.
CRANDALL Jonathan, and ——, July 26, 1739.
" 　　Samuel, and Hannah Reynolds, of Joseph, Dec. 12, ——.
" 　　Anstis, and David Northup, March 9, 1739.
CRANSTON Ann, and Samuel Spink, Nov. 9, 1837.
" 　　Sarah F., and Benj. P. Tucker.
CROWDER Mary, and —— Wilkes, Jan. 14, 1732-3.
CROWELL Sarah, and John Straight, Nov. 19, 1721.
CRO—— Esther, and Silas Helme, May 5, 1800.
CRUMB Eliza Melissa, and George H. T. Cole, Sept. 19, 1848.
CULVERWELL Thomas, and Abigail ——; m. by George Hazard, Justice of Peace,
　　　　Feb. 22, 1719-20.
CUTTER Thomas, and —— Talman; m. by Nicholas Northup, Justice of Peace; rec.
　　　　July 8, 1763.
" 　　John, of W. Greenwich, late of N. Kingstown, and Rosanna Straight of
　　　　W. Greenwich, Oct. 23, ——.

D

DAKE Elizabeth, and Ebenezer Moon, Jr., June 12, 1735.
DALEY Sarah, and James Sweet, — 4, 1736.
DARE Mary, and —— Wescott, Aug. 17, 1718.
DAVIS Ann, and Robert Aylesworth, May 20, 1708.
" 　　Isabelle, and Thomas Loveless, Nov. —, 1734.
" 　　Catherine, and Phillip Card, Dec. 3, 1741.
" 　　Elizabeth, and Gilbert Cooper, Apr. 7, 1755.
" 　　Joshua, and (Hannah) Spink, (dau. of John); m. by Elder Samuel Albro,
　　　　May 18, 1766.
" 　　Mary, and Jonathan Dean, Jan. 4, 1775.
" 　　Abigail, and Christopher Greene, May 19, 177—.
" 　　Benjamin, and Sarah Congdon; m. by George Thomas, Justice of Peace,
　　　　Dec. 6, 1781.
" 　　Elizabeth, and Gardiner Reynolds, Apr. 23, 1786.
" 　　Phebe, and George Thomas, Nov. 15, 1787.
" 　　Rebecca, and Samuel E. Gardiner, March 27, 1799.
" 　　Ephraim, of John, and Mary Fones, of Jeremiah, —— 30, —.
" 　　Stephen, and Anne Hill.
" 　　——, and Daniel Thomas; recorded March 29, ——.
" 　　Mary, and Zarobabel Wescott, Aug. 17, ——.
" 　　Elizabeth, and Smith ——, ——. —, ——.
" 　　Mary, and Robert R. Carr, Feb. —, 1802.
DAWLEY John, and Mary Tripp; m. by William Hall, Justice of Peace, ——. 1,
　　　　1729-30.
" 　　Lydia, and —— Gardiner, ——. —, 1736.
" 　　John, of John, and Margaret Cooper, of Mancer; m. by Elder Phillip
　　　　Jenkins, Sept. 17, 1772.

DAWLEY Daniel, of Nathan, of Exeter, and Elizabeth Card, of N. Kingstown, dau.
of Phillip; m. by George Thomas, Justice, ——. 28, ——.
" ——, and Freelove Allen; m. by George Tibbeth. Justice, ——. 28, ——.
" Mary Abbie, and David Northup, Feb. 18, 1844.
DEAN Jonathan, of W. Greenwich. and —— Nichols, of Thomas, of W. Kings-
town; m. by George Thomas, Justice of Peace, Nov. 14, 1773.
" Jonathan, of W. Greenwich, and Mary Davis, of N. Kingstown; m. by
Elder James Wightman, Jan. 4, 1775.
" William, of N. Y., of Newport, R. I., and Rebecca Williams, of Benja-
min, of N. Kingstown; m. by Elder John Slocum, Oct. 11, 1847.
DIMOND Benjamin, and Abigail Tourgee; m. by Elisha Clarke, Justice, Sept.
27, 1753.
" ——, and Elizabeth Huling; m. by William Hall Justice, April 17, 1760.
" John, of Benjamin, and Elizabeth Aylesworth, of Jeremiah; m. by
Elder Philip Jenkins, April 26, 1798.
" Elizabeth, and John Fowler, March 15, 1804.
" Eunice, and Samuel Munroe, Sept. 9, 1832.
DICKERSON Mary, and Elisha Reynolds, Feb. 19. 1758.
DICKINSON Mary, and Elisha Reynolds, Feb. 9, 1758.
" Charles, and Mary Slocum; m. by George Thomas, Justice, Dec. 20, 1762.
" William A., and Phebe Greene; m. by J. A. Tillinghast, Justice, Jan.
17, 18—.
" ——, of Charles, and Esther Clarke, of Gardiner; m. by Elder William
Northup; recorded April 19, 1822.
DICKSON Mary, and Henry Briggs, Feb. 7, 1802.
DICK Jemima, and John Onyon, Jr., June 15, 1755.
DIXON Hannah, and William Briggs, Dec. 23, 1788.
DOLLINER Rebecca, and ——, Sept. —, 1706.
DONISON Jonathan, of Providence, son of Capt. William, dec., and Avis Huling,
of Alexander, of N. Kingstown; m. by George Thomas, Justice of
Peace, Aug. 8, 1773.
DOUGLASS Mary, and —— Lewiston, May —, 1767.
" Thomas, of N. Kingstown, son of James and Elizabeth Hazard, of James-
town; m. at E. Greenwich by John Briggs, Justice of Peace, Feb. 24,
1776.
" David, and Susan C. Sherman, Jan. 7, 1850.
DOWNING Rebecca, and Thomas Eldred, March 26, 1730.
DURGAN James, and Elizabeth Reynolds, of Thomas; m. by Rev. J. R. Stone,
April 29, 1841.
DYRE Mary, and William Allen, Feb. 19, 1737-8.
" Freelove, and ——; m. by Thomas Hill, Justice of Peace, April 9, 1741.
" Edward, and Elizabeth Fish, Nov. 29, 1750.
" Hannah, and —— Card, April 21, 1752.
" ——, and Cary Clarke, April 6, 1755.
" William, and Sarah Baker; m. by Elder James Wightman, Sept. 23, 1770.
" Frances, and George Briggs, Feb. 10, 1777.
" Abigail, and Arthur Aylesworth, Jr., Sept. 14, 1783.
" Samuel, of John, and Waite Eldred, of Thomas, deceased; m. by Elder
Phillip Jenkins, July 13, 1786.
" Freelove, and John Pierce.
" Ruth, and Ishmeal Spink, March 19, 1804.
" Charles F., and Mrs. Harriet Tourgee; m. by Elder John Slocum, July 21,
1845.

E

EARLE Mary, and Joseph Sheffield, Jan. 27, 1708.
" John, and Sarah Potter; m. by Christopher Allen, Justice of Peace, March
19, 1711-12.
EASTLIX John, of Prudence Island, and Amie Bates, Oct. 24, 1762.
ELDRED Elizabeth, and Mapes Barber, May 23, 1705.
" Mary and Nicholas Gardiner, Oct. 13, 1709.
" Penelope, and Ephraim Gardiner, April 28, 1713.
" Margaret, and William Gardiner, June 12, 1718.

ELDRED Freelove, and Nicholas Northup, June 23, 1720.
   "   Freelove, and Charles Northup. June 23, 1720.
   "   Thomas of N. Kingstown, and Abigail Tucker, of Groton; m. by John Plumb, Justice of Peace, Oct. 12, 1727.
   "   Thomas and Rebecca Downing; m. by William Spencer, Justice of Peace, March 26, 1730.
   "   Capt. John, and Mary Greene, of John; m. by William Hall, Justice of Peace, Aug. 9, 1733.
   "   ——, and Waite Gould; m. by George Thomas, Justice of Peace, Sept. 1, 1734.
   "   Margaret, and Eber Sherman, Feb. —, 1738.
   "   Thankful, and Daniel Scranton, Sept. 22, 1744.
   "   Martha, and Job Card, Nov. 1, 1756.
   "   ——, and Martha Weeden; m. by Elder David Sprague, April —, 1759.
   "   Benedict, and Patience Smith; m. by Thomas Phillips, Justice of Peace, —— —, 1764.
   "   Martha, widow of Thomas, of N. Kingstown, and Nicholas ——, of E. Greenwich; m. by George Thomas, Justice of Peace, July 5, 1769.
   "   Gardiner, and Mrs. Martha ——; m. by Georg eThomas (of Samuel) Justice of Peace, Jan. —, 1773.
   "   Elizabeth, and Havens Sherman, Oct. 10, 1773.
   "   Abigail, and Joseph Burdick, Jan. 10, 1776.
   "   Barbary and William Chadsey, —— 21, 1776.
   "   Rhoda (col.) and Prince Greene, June 21, 1778.
   "   Lydia, and John Spink, Dec 27, 1778.
   "   Frances, and Samuel Carr, Jan. 17, 1779.
   "   James, of Seth, and Mary Brown; m. by George Thomas, Justice of Peace, Jan. 28, 1779.
   "   Waite, and Samuel Dyre, July 13, 1786.
   "   Robert, of James, and Sarah Boone, of James; m. by Elder Nathan Hill, Jan. 1, 1789.
   "   Thomas, of Thomas, and Sarah Spink, of Ishmeal; m. by Elder Philip Jenkins, —— 24, 1790.
   "   Elizabeth, and Vernon Hiames, Aug. 26, 1795.
   "   Daniel, and Mary Phillips; m. by William Smith, pastor Trinity Church, Jan. 10, 1799.
   "   Elizabeth, and Benedict Peckham, Sept. 6, 17—.
   "   Abigail, and John Watson, March 14, ——.
   "   James, and —— Brown, of Samuel; m. by George Thomas, Justice of Peace, —— —, ——.
   "   Elizabeth, and —— ——; m. by George Thomas, Justice of Peace, May —, ——.
   "   Elisha, and Elizabeth, —— —, ——.
   "   Beriah, of James and Lucy, and Elizabeth Peckham, of Benedict and Elizabeth; m. by Elder William Northup, Sept. 7, 1800.
   "   Joseph, of William and Lydia, and Phebe Carr, widow, dau. of James and Ruth Cooper; m. by Elder William Northup, Jan. 15, 1802.
   "   James, of Robert and Hannah, and Joanna Wilson (widow), dau. of George and Joanna Reynolds, of Exeter, though said Joanna is of Richmondtown; m. by Elder William Northup, June 8, 1803.
   "   Mary, and John Capron, Dec. 4, 1804.
   "   Susan, and George Tillinghast, Sept. 4, 1806.
   "   Beriah, and Elizabeth Reynolds, of Hezekiah; m. by George Thomas, Town Clerk, April 27, 1807.
   "   Hannah, and Samuel Spink; rec. Jan. 8, 1814.
   "   John, of Thomas and Mary Brown, of Phenix; m. by Elder Gershum Palmer, June 8, 1820.
   "   Ishmael, of Thomas and Caroline Allen, of Thomas G.; m. by Elder Joseph W. Allen, May 12, 1830.
   "   James, of —— and Phebe, and Rhoda Ann Chappell, of Francis and Bethsheba; m. by Rev. Lemuel N. Burge, Oct. 3, 1842.
   "   Sarah, and Richard Smith, March 9, 1846.
   "   John C., and Abbie F. Rathbun; m. by Elder John Slocum, June 13, 1847.
   "   Sarah G., and George H. Church, June 13, 1853.
ELEY Elizabeth, and George Mariner, Sept. —, 1722.

ELLIS Darius, and ——; m. by Samuel Fones, Justice of Peace, Sept. 23, 1715.
   " ——, and Mary Hall, Feb. 6, 1731-2.
   " Ruth, and William Havens, Jan. 2, 1766.
ENOS Elizabeth, and John Cleaveland, Jan. 28, 1773.
ESSEX Richard, of Hugh, of Warwick, R. I., and Mary Aylesworth, of Arthur, of
     N. Kingstown; m. by John Gorton, Justice of Peace, July 24, 1768.
   " Catherine, and Russell Austin, Nov. —, 1802.
   " Phebe, and Arnold Spink, Nov. 3, 1812.

F

FINEY Mrs. Ruth Ann, and Daniel Allen, July 27, 1845.
FISH Hannah, and ——; m. by Elder Benjamin Harrington, May 7, 1738.
   " Elizabeth, and Edward Dyre, Nov. 29, 1750.
FOSTER Ann, and Bartholomew Hunt, Nov. 30, 1785.
FONES Mary, and Joseph Smith, Dec. 18, 1724.
   " ——, and —— Baker, daughter of Benjamin, ——, 1725.
   " Sarah, and Thomas Scranton, March —, 1725-6.
   " Mary, and Ebenezer Hill, Jan. 1, 1729-30.
   " Mary, widow of Samuel, and ——; m. by Thomas Northup, Justice of
     Peace, Nov. 13, 1738.
   " Elizabeth and John Gardiner, Jan. 4, ——.
   " Mary, and Ephraim Davis, ——.
   " Lydia, and ——.
   " James, and Elizabeth Havens, Feb. ——.
   " Margaret, and Robert Whitford, May 10, ——.
   " Mary, and Edward York, Jan. —, 1755.
   " Mary, and Ebenezer Hill; rec. Nov. 12, 1756.
   " Samuel, and Hannah Briggs; m. by William Hall, Justice of Peace, April
     26, 1760.
FONES ——, and John Spencer; recorded Aug. 3, 1767.
   " Martha, and Daniel ——; m. by George Thomas, Justice of Peace;
     recorded ——. —, 1768.
   " Elizabeth, and Christopher Gardiner, Feb. 18, 1775.
   " Mary, and Henry Reynolds, May 15, 1785.
   " Daniel, and Catherine Austin, of James; m. by Elder Nathan Hill, Jan.
     9, 1791.
   " Rebecca, and Benjamin Tanner, Sept. 25, 1799.
   " ——, of James, and —— Reynolds, of Peter; m. by William Hall, Jus-
     tice of Peace, Dec. 23, ——.
FOWLER Isaac, and Mary Hopkins; m. by Rouse Helme, Justice of Peace, Jan. 15,
     1720-21.
   " Thomas, and Mary Hopkins; m. by Rouse Helme, Justice of Peace, Jan.
     15, 172-.
   " Deborah, and Paske Whitford, July 5, 1723.
   " ——, of E. Greenwich, and Mary Briggs; m. by George Tibbetts, Justice
     of Peace, Nov. —, 1737.
   " Mary, and —— ——; m. by James Eldred, Justice of Peace, Feb. 17,
     1754.
   " ——, and William Weeden, Nov. —, 1755.
   " Benjamin, and Ann Case; m. by Elder Samuel Albro, Jan. 2, 1763.
   " Delewey, and Sarah Hunt; m. by William Hall, Justice of Peace, March
     11, 1764.
   " William, of E. Greenwich, and Frances Berry, of Nathaniel; m. by
     George Thomas (of Samuel), Justice of Peace, Nov. 7, 1765.
   " Benjamin, of N. Kingstown, son of George, and Freelove Nichols, of W.
     Greenwich; m. by Elder Solomon Sprague, Dec. 15, 1771.
   " George, Jun., and Elizabeth Wightman; m. by Elder James Wightman,
     Dec. 10, 1781.
   " Benjamin, of N. Kingstown, and Huldah Randall, of Warwick; m. by Elder
     John Pitman, Oct. 23, 1791.
   " Mary, and Peleg Weeden, —— 5, 1803.
   " John, of Deleway, of E. Greenwich, and Elizabeth Dimond, widow of John,
     dau. of Jeremiah Aylesworth; m. by Judge John Allen, March 15, 1804.

FOWLER Samuel Carr, and Elizabeth Fones Havens; m. by Richard Thomas, Justice of Peace, Aug. 19, 1819.
"   Henry, and Mary W. Baker; m. by Rev. J. R. Stone, Jan. 20, 1842.
FRANKLIN Sylvester R., and Abbie Ann Thomas.
FRARERS Ruth, and Benjamin Smith, Dec. 16, 1761.
FREEBOURNE Thomas, of Portsmouth, and ——, Jan. 30, 1734.
"   Sarah F., and Joseph Sealey, Feb. —, ——.
"   Capt. Gideon, son of Capt. Gideon, dec., and Freelove W. Weeden, of Peleg; m. by Elder Elbridge Gale, Nov. 13, 1825.
"   Huldah S., and Albert Sanford, Dec. 24, 1849.
FRY Thomas G., of E. Greenwich, and Hannah A. U. Reynolds, of N. Kingstown; m. by Rev. J. R. Stone, Feb. 13, 1841.
"   Anne, and Job Gardiner, Dec. —, ——.
"   Samuel, of Thomas, of E. Greenwich, and —— Coggeshall, of Daniel; m. by Jeffrey Watson, Justice, —— 20, ——.

G

GADDIE Robert, of E. Greenwich, son of Joseph and Alice Allen Spencer, of Essex; m. by Rev. Samuel C. Brown, May 4, 1845.
GARDINER Nicholas, of Nicholas, and Mary Eldred, of Thomas; m. by John Eldred, Assistant, Oct. 13, 1709.
"   Henry, and Desire Havens, Aug. 4, 1710.
"   Dorcas, and Abial Sherman, Nov. 20, 1712.
"   Ephraim, and Penelope Eldred, April 28, 1713.
"   William, of Henry, and Margaret Eldred, of Capt. John; m. by Rouse Helme, Justice of Peace, June 12, 1718.
"   Sarah, and Edward Sheffield, April 5, 1719.
"   Amie, and Peter Boss, Jan. 23, 1719-20.
            Another record reads "28."
"   Hannah, and James McSparran, May 22, 1722.
"   Mary, of Kingstown, and ——, of E. Greenwich; m. by Francis Wellett, Justice of Peace, ——, —, 1723.
"   Mary, and Peleg Tripp, J—, 28, 1728.
"   Nicholas, and Martha Havens, of William; m. by William Spencer, Justice of Peace, —— 12, 1729-30.
"   Hannah, and John Sweet, March —, 1733-34.
"   Elizabeth, and Benoni Hall, March —, 1734-5.
"   Nathaniel, Jun., and —— Pierce; m. by Elder Benjamin Harrington, —— 23, 1734.
"   ——, and Lydia Dawley; m. by Peter Boss, Justice of Peace, —— —, 1736.
"   Margaret, and Isaac ——; m. by Peter Boss, Justice of Peace, Dec. 26, 1736
"   Sarah, and ——; m. by Job Tripp, Justice of Peace, April —, 1737.
"   Mary, and John Spencer, March, —, 1739.
"   Mary, and Jarah Mumford, Nov. 29, 1739.
"   James, and Waite Coggeshall, March 15, 1749.
"   Annah, and Robert Reynolds, July —, 1742.
"   Henry, of William, and Mary Helme, of Christopher; m. by Samuel Thomas, Justice of Peace, —— 6, 1750.
"   Nicholas, of Exeter, and Honor Brown, of N. Kingstown; m. by Elder Samuel Albro, —— —, 1757.
"   Ephraim, and Ann Coggeshall; m. by Thomas Hazard, Justice of Peace, March 12, 1758.
"   Ephraim, and Patience Congdon; m. by Frances Willett, Asst., Oct. 19, 1761.
"   Nathaniel, of Exeter, and Martha Brown, of N. Kingstown; m. by Elder Samuel Albro, Aug. 1, 1762.
"   Samuel of E. Greenwich, and Catherine Greene, of N. Kingstown; m. by Elder Samuel Albro, Dec. 18, 1762.
"   Joshua, of Benjamin, of S. Kingstown, and Mercy Tanner, of Palmer, of N. Kingstown; m. by Caleb Hill, Justice of Peace, Feb. 22, 1763.
"   Desire, and Elisha Clarke, April 10, 1763.

GARDINER Ezekiel, and Susannah Congdon; m. by Elder Samuel Albro, May —, 1764.

" Huling, of Nicholas, Esq., of Exeter, and Elizabeth Northup, of Col. Immanuel, of N. Kingstown; m. by George Thomas, Justice of Peace, Feb. 1, 1767.

" Christopher, of South Kingstown, and Elizabeth Fones, of N. Kingstown, dau. of James; m. by George Thomas, Justice of Peace, Feb. 18, 1775.

" Gideon, of Ephraim, and Mrs. Mary Thomas, of George, of N. Kingstown; m. by George Thomas, Justice of Peace, Jan. 3, 1782.

" Josiah, of Ephraim, and Patience Gardiner, of Silas; m. by George Thomas, Justice of Peace, Sept. 3, 1780.

" Patience, and Josiah Gardiner, Sept. 3, 1780.

" Nancy, and Arnold Weeden, Nov. 16, 1783.

" Samuel, of Samuel, dec., and Elizabeth Slocum, of William; m. by Elder Philip Jenkins, March 24, 1789.

" William, of S. Kingstown, and —— Allen, of Capt. Joshua, of N. Kingstown; m. by George Thomas, Justice of Peace, Dec. 20, 1790.

" Amos, of Jo——, of N. Kingstown, and Sarah Watson, dau. of Stephen Champlain, of S. Kingstown; m. by Elder Philip Jenkins, Jan. 7, 1794.

" Susannah, and Thomas Boone, Sept. 21, 1794.

" David, of Benjamin, and Elizabeth Albro, of Robert; m. by George Thomas, Justice of Peace, Jan. 26, 1794.

" Henry, of S. Kingstown, and Hannah Clarke, of Latham; m. by Ezekiel Gardiner, Jr., Justice of Peace, Oct. 26, 1796.

" Samuel E., of James and Waitey, and Rebecca Davis, of Stephen and Anne; m. by Elder William Northup, March 27, 1799.

" Edward C., of James and Sarah, and Mary Slocum, of John and Mary; m. by Elder William Northup, Dec. 9, 1799.

" Penelope, and William Hiscox.

" John, of William, deceased, and Elizabeth Fones; m. by William Spencer, Justice of Peace, Jan. 4, ——.

" ——, and Elizabeth Hall.

" Elizabeth, and —— Cottrell, Dec. —, ——.

" Mary, and —— Place.

" Lydia, and John Northup, June 8, ——.

" Benjamin, of ——, deceased, and Luccanna Northup, of Huling.

" Job, and Anne Fry; m. by Edward Dyre, Justice of Peace, Dec. 6, ——.

" Silas, of E. Greeuwich, son of Isaac, of Exeter, and Elizabeth Congdon, of John, of N. Kingstown; m. by James Gardiner, Justice of Peace, Dec. 20, ——.

" Elisha and Abigail Brown.

" Rebecca and Nathaniel Smith.

" Alexander, and Mrs. Patience Watson; m. by Elder Benjamin Weight, Nov. 25, 1802.

" Isabel, and Benjamin Sherman, July 14, 1805.

" Isabel, and Brudah Thomas, June 16, 1808.

" Mary, and Robert Card, Sept. 5, 1813.

" Benjamin, and Mary Carey; m. by Elder Francis Dane, Jan. 28, 1822.

" Sarah Ann, and Edmund Sheffield, June 8, 1823.

" Amos, of N. Kingstown, and Matilda Perry, of S. Kingstown; m. by Elder William Northup, Dec. 5, 1824.

" Jeremiah, of Jeremiah, and Abbie C. Browning, of Gardiner. March 16, 1826.

GARDINER ——, and —— Allen, of James; m. by Elder Joseph W. Allen, Nov. 11, 1847.
" Mary E., and Henry S. Sherman, April 19, 1849.
" Dulcina, and William Gardiner, Oct. 23, 1849.
" William, of Exeter, and Dulcinna Gardiner, of N. Kingstown; m. by Elder Joseph A. Tillinghast, Oct. 23, 1849.
" Caroline E., and Joseph R. Hood, April 9, 1850.
" Hannah, and Hazard Burlingame, May 20, 1850.
" Susan A., and Nehemiah Bicknell, Sept. 1, 1850.
" Mary R., and Isaac H. Jecoy, Nov. 21, 1850.
" Harriet C., and Stephen B. Reynolds, ——.
GARFIELD ——, and Penelope Rods; m. by William Hall, Assistant, May 4, 1729.
GAVITT Samuel, of Westerly, and Ruth Bates; m. by George Northup, Justice of Peace, Nov. 29, 1766.
GIFFORD Ann, and William Congdon, March 30, 1732.
" Patience, and Joseph Arnold, Nov. 23, 1732.
" Hannah, and Joseph Arnold, Aug. —, 1737.
GILL Sarah, and Samuel Place, Jan 29, 1760.
GODFREY William, and Mary Berry; m. by Benj. Nichols, Justice of Peace, Aug. 7, 1729.
" Weltha, and Edward Kettle, Aug. —, 1756.
" ——, and Sanford Case, Sept. 1, 1761.
" Caleb, and Mary Maxfield; m. by William Hall, Justice of Peace, —— 2, 1762.
" Rebecca, and James Reynolds, Nov. 10, 1762.
GODWORD Nicholas, of E. Greenwich, and Freelove Havens, of N. Kingstown.
GORTON Jane, and Cyrus H. Stuart.
" Louisa, and Stephen N. Himes, Oct. 25, 1847.
GOULDING Sarah, and ——, Jr.; m. by Francis Willett, Justice of Peace, July —, 1723.
GOULD Isaac, and Elizabeth Jackwise; m. by Elisha Cole, Assistant, July 8, 1722.
" Sarah, and Immanuel Northup, —— 24, 1727-8.
" Ann, and Samuel Slocum, —— 4, 1733.
" Waite, and —— Eldred, Sept. 1, 1734.
" Dorcas, and Caleb Bentley, Jan. 21, 1738.
" Ruth, and Samuel Adams, Feb. —, 1739.
" Hannah, and Henry Wall, —— 13, 1742.
" Elizabeth, and Jonathan Vaughn, Jan. 1. 1756.
" Mary, and Benjamin Greene, Sept. 21, ——.
" Mary, and John Allen.
" Thomas J., and Susan Knowles; m. by Elder James Hammond, Sept. 20, 1848.
GREENE Ann, and William Clarke, Nov. 8, 1730.
" Jonathan, of N. Kingstown, and Susannah Beare, of E. Greenwich; m. by Daniel Pearce, Justice of Peace, March —, 1733.
" Mary, and John Eldred, Aug. 9, 1733.
" Daniel, Jr., and Mary Relph, Jan. 9, 1737-8.
" Edward, and —————— Tanner, of William, April 28, 1739.
" Patience, and Thomas Allen, —— 20, 1742.
" Alexander G., of Exeter, and Abbie N. Streeter, of Richmond, ——. —, ——.
" Benjamin, of N. Kingstown, and Ann Utter, of William, of Warwick, R. I.; m. by James Rhodes, Justice of Peace, Jan. —, 1743-4.
" Carpenter, of John, Feb. 12, 1746.

GREENE John, of Daniel, and Sarah Spink, of John; m. by William Hall, Justice of Peace, Dec. 24, 1758.

"   Daniel, of N. Kingstown, son of Robert, and Mary Greene, of Benjamin, dec., of Coventry; m. by Stephen Potter, Justice, Feb. 12, 1761.

"   Mary, and Daniel Greene, Feb. 12, 1761.

"   Peleg, of N. Kingstown, and —— Ralph, of Warwick, R. I., M— 10, 1762.

"   Catherine, and Samuel Gardiner, Dec. 18, 1762.

"   Abraham, of James, of Warwick, R. I., and Patience Arnold, of Joseph, of N. Kingstown; m. by George Northup, Justice of Peace, Sept. 5, 1765.

"   Mary, and John Corey, Nov. 13, 1766.

"   Lydia, and Elisha Carpenter, Sept. 20, 1767.

"   Joshua, of N. Kingstown, and Alice Potter, of S. Kingstown; m. by Elder Phillip Jenkins, Jan. 1, 1771.

"   Abraham, of E. Greenwich, and Mary Reynolds, of N. Kingstown; m. by John Northup, Justice of Peace, Jan. 9, 1774.

"   Prince (negro), and Rhoda Eldred; m. by Elder Phillip Jenkins, June 21, 1778.

"   Christopher, and Abigail Davis; m. by Rev. Charles Holden, May 19, 177–.

"   John, and Mrs. Susannah Pratt, both of Providence; m. by George Thomas, Justice, June 3, 1779.

"   Hannah, and Jabez Chadsey, Sept. 30, 1779.

"   Cato, late belonging to Richard Greene, of Warwick, R. I. (col.), and Anna Chase of N. Kingstown; m. by Elder Phillip Jenkins, —— —, 1779.

"   Hannah, of John and Sarah, and Peleg Spencer, —— 14, 1783.

"   Sally, and Caleb Hill, Jan. 4, 1784.

"   Ann, and Joseph Pearce, Nov. 16, 1784.

"   David, and Lydia Matteson; m. by Elder William Northup, July 3, 1788.

"   Martha, and Jabez Chadsey, March 21, 1792. Should be Grieves or Grieve, widow of Archibald.

"   Mrs. Sarah, and Angustus Huling, April 22, 1792.

"   William, of Abraham and Patience, of N. Kingstown, and Sarah Shaw, of Anthony and Weighty, of Exeter; m. by Elder William Northup, May 29, 1796.

"   William, of N. Kingstown, son of Abraham, and Mary Wilcox, of Robert, dec., of Exeter; m. by Elder Thomas Manchester, March 30, 1809.

"   Samuel, of N. Kingstown, and Amie Ann Brown, of Exeter; m. by Elder J. A. Tillinghast, Oct. 15, 1849.

"   Abigail S., and Perry Arnold, Jan. 13, 1850.

"   Phebe, and William A. Dickerson, Jan. 17, 18—.

GWILLIAM Mary, and Ebenezer Slocum, Jan. 1, 1788.

H

HAGAN David, of N. Kingstown, son of Anthony, of Philadelphia, and Sarah Updike, of Lodowick and Abigail; m. by Isaac Hall, Justice of Peace, Feb. 10, 1807.

"   David U., of David, of N. Kingstown, and Lucinda Harris, of Daniel, dec., of Warwick, R. I.; m. by Rev. Moses Fifield, Sept. 8, ——.

HALEY John, and Mary Saunders, of Westers; m. by Christopher Allen, Justice of Peace, May 18, 1719.

"   Samuel, Jr., of N. Kingstown, late of Thompson, Conn., and Audrey Spencer, of Henry, late of N. Kingstown, dec.; m. by Elder Nathan Hill, Aug. 25, 1791.

HALL Elizabeth, and George Babcock, Nov. 28, 1694.

"   ——, and John Seager, Jr., March 1, 1707.

"   Sarah, and John Spencer, Oct. —, 1725.

"   Mary, and John Lee, March 1726-7.

"   Mary, and —— Ellis, Feb. 6, 1731-32.

"   Benoni, and Elizabeth Gardiner; m. by William Spencer, Justice of Peace, March —, 1732-3.

"   Rebecca, and Thomas Stafford, Feb. —, 1762.

"   Abigail, and Nicholas Spencer, —— —, 1763.

HALL Caleb, of W. Greenwich, and Merabah Havens, of N. Kingstown; m. by
          Elder Solomon Sprague, Oct. 15, 1769.
  "   William, of N. Kingstown, and Elizabeth Coggeshall, of E. Greenwich;
          m. by John Northup, Justice of Peace, Aug. —, 1773.
  "   Lucy, and Ebenezer Spencer, July 9, 1775.
  "   Elizabeth, and —— Hunt, Jan. —, 1777.
  "   Anna, and Christopher Coggeshall, Oct. 13, 1780.
  "   Mary, and John Reynolds, March 17, 1792.
  "   Penelope, and Christopher Northup, Dec. 12, 1795.
  "   Susannah, of N. Kingstown, and ——, of Exeter; m. by Elder Phillip Jen-
          kins, March 7, 1799.
  "   Abigail, and —— Weight, ——.
  "   Elizabeth, and —— Gardiner, ——.
  "   Thurza P., of N. Kingstown, and ——, of E. Greenwich; m. by Elder
          Joseph W. Allen.
  "   Abigail, and Sylvester Watson, June —, 1802.
  "   William, of Robert, and Mary, of E. Greenwich, and Mary Corey, of
          William and Sarah, of N. Kingstown; m. by Elder William Northup,
          June 8, 1803.
  "   John, of Slocum, dec., and Patience Peckham, of Capt. Benedict; m. by
          George Thomas, Jr., Town Clerk, Aug. 23, 1807.
  "   Harriet, and John B. Hartwell, March 21, 1842.
  "   Hannah G., and John J. Carpenter, Oct. 22, 1843.
HAMILTON Sarah, and William Clarke, June 18, 1797.
HAMMOND Lydia A., and Jabez Bullock, Nov. 15, 1841.
  "   Benjamin W., and Sarah R. Johnson; m. by Rev. J. H. Rouse, Dec. 11,
          1848.
HANDLEY Matthew, of James, and Lydia Pierce, of Benjamin, of Richmond, R. I.;
          m. by Elder William Northup, Sept. 22, 1794.
HANNAH Mary, and Nathaniel Niles, Jr., Jan. 26, 1699.
  "   Mary, and George Webb; m. by Christopher Allen, Justice of Peace,
          April 21, 1708.
HARMON Mary, and Oliver White, Jan. 21, 1747.
HARRINGTON Job, and Alice Weightman, of John and Jane; m. by William Spen-
          cer, Justice of Peace, June 8, 1722.
  "   ——, and Elizabeth Spencer; m. by Benj. Nichols, Justice of Peace,
          July 4, 1731.
  "   Jeremiah, and Phebe Chase, of Jonathan; m. by Samuel Thomas, Justice
          of Peace, Feb. —, 1753.
  "   Ebenezer, of Liverpool, England, and Mary Mercy, of Exeter; m. by
          Elder Solomon Sprague, May 20, 1778.
  "   Eber, and Hannah Bull, ——.
  "   Timothy, and ——.
HARRIS Mary, and Job Rathbun, —— 1, 1737.
  "   Lucinda, and David U. Hagan, Sept. 8, ——.
HARTWELL John B., of Providence, and Harriet Hull, of John; m. by Rev. James
          R. Stone, March 21, 1842.
HART Jemima, and —— Cooper, Feb. 28, 1760.
  "   Nicholas, of N. Kingstown, son of Nicholas, and Sarah Carey, of Caleb;
          m. by Elder Phillip Jenkins, March 19, 1779.
HARVEY Lucy C., and Adam M. Thurston, April 2, 1848.
  "   Mrs. Mary F., and Edwin A. Sweet, May 28, 1848.
HATHAWAY Anthony, of E. Greenwich, son of Martha and Lydia Stretson, of Si-
          las, of N. Kingstown; m. by Rev. Elisha Sweet, Aug. 7, 1808.
  "   Edward H., of W. Bridgewater, Mass., son of Nathan and Susan, of New
          Bedford, Mass., and Ruth Pierce, of N. Kingstown; m. by Rev. A. J.
          Chaplain, Feb. —, 1848.
HAVENS Desire, and Henry Gardiner, Aug. 4, 1710.
  "   Phebe, of Thomas, of Kingstowne, and (John Wightman) of George, of
          Warwick, R. I.; m. by William Hall, Justice of Peace, June 14, 1722.
  "   William, of Thomas, and Sarah Pierce, widow of Benoni; m. by Jeremiah
          Gould, Justice of Peace, Nov. 21, 1725.
  "   Martha, and Nicholas Gardiner, —— 12, 1729-30.
  "   Nathaniel, of Joseph, and Rose Briggs, of Robert; m. by Robert Hall, Jus-
          tice of Peace, Feb. —, 1733-4.

HAVENS George, and Mary ——; m. by Thomas Spencer, Justice of Peace, Aug. 25, 1748.
" Sarah, and 'John Vaughn, April 9, 1761.
" William, of Thomas, and Ruth Ellis, of Samuel; m. by George Thomas, Justice of Peace, Jan. 2, 1766.
" Merabah, and Caleb Hall, Oct. 15, 1769.
" ————, of William, and —— Spencer, of Christopher; m. by Robert Hall, Justice of Peace, April 5, 1770.
" Susannah, and Edward Hazard, April 5, 1770.
" Catherine, and William Aylesworth, June —, 1774.
" Robert, of N. Kingstown, son of Thomas, and Elizabeth Wightman, of George, of Warwick, R. I., ——. —, ——.
" ————, and Samson Haxton; m. by William Spencer, Justice of Peace, Jan. 9, ——.
" Rhodes, and Catherine Nichols, of David, ——.
" John, and Jemima Havens; m. by George Thomas, Justice of Peace, Dec. 1, ——.
" Jemima, and John Havens, Dec. 1, ——.
" Freelove, and Nicholas Godward, ——. —. ——.
" Sarah, and —— Smith, Dec. 19, ——.
" Phebe, and Thomas Hill, ——. —. ——.
" Mary, and John Allen, ——. 17, ——.
" James, of N. Kingstown, and Penelope Scott, of Coventry, R. I.; m. by Elder Charles Stone, April 10, 1800.
" Anna, and Edward D. Aylesworth, —— —, 1811.
" Elizabeth, and Wanton Austin, recorded Feb. 28, 1817.
" Elizabeth Fones, and Samuel Carr Fowler, Aug. 19, 1819.
" Sarah D., and Jeremiah Mitchell, —— 5, 1844.
HAXSON Tamson, and —— Havens, Jan. 9, ——.
" Martha, and —— Jess, June 25, 1744.
HAXTON Elizabeth, and —— Baker, March 6, 1715.
HAZARD Mary, and John Robinson, Oct. 19, 1704.
" George, of Thomas, and Mary ——; m. by Stephen Hazard, Assistant, Nov. 17, 1721.
" Thomas, and —— Slocum; m. by Francis Willett, Justice of Peace, Feb. 22, 1727.
" Robert, and Martha ——; m. by Francis Willett, Justice of Peace, March 22, 1727-8.
" Margaret, and Joseph Holmes, ——, 20, 1727.
" Sarah, and Robert Marcy, Oct. 24, 1728.
" Thomas, and Hannah Updike; m. by George Thomas, Justice of Peace, May —, 1738.
" Edward, of Jamestown, and Susannah Havens, of N. Kingstown; m. by George Thomas, Justice of Peace, April 13, 1773.
" Elizabeth, and Thomas Douglass, Feb. 24, 1776.
" Ruth, and Daniel Bates, June 15, 1799.
" Caleb, and Abigail ——; m. by Stephen Hazard, assistant, Nov. 19, ——.
" Frances G., and Elnathan C. Brown, May 11, 1827.
" Hannah M., and Samuel R. Phillips, Jan. 9, 1843.
" Wilbur, of Wilbur, and Lydia Pierce, of William; m. by Rev. Edwin Stillman, Dec. 25, 1843.
" Eliza, and Samuel Weeden, March 13, 1844.
" Daniel S., of Wilbur and Mary, and Hannah S. Congdon, of Benjamin and Mary; m. by Rev. A. J. Chaplain; rec. July 15, 1847.
" Mary, and Samuel Pierce, ——.
HAZELTON William, and Mary Paine; m. by Nathan Niles, Justice of Peace, Sept. 27, 1710.
" Mary, and James Nichols, Nov. 7, ——.
HA—— Mary, and Benjn. Baker, —— 18, 1704-5.
HA(ZZARD) Elizabeth, and (John) Tibbetts, —— 7, 1705.
HA—— Anna, and Samuel Browne, Jr., Aug. 27, 1775.
HEDLEY Lydia, and James Congdon, —— 3, ——.
HELME Rouse, Jr., and Sarah Niles; m. by John Eldred, Assistant, July 21, 1709.
" Mary, and Ebenezer Terry, Nov. 30, 1721.
" Mary, and Henry Gardiner, —— 6, 1750.

HELME Silas, and Esther Cro—, of N. Kingstown; m. by Samuel Northup, Justice of Peace, May 5, 1800.
"   Anstis, and Phillip Card, Aug. 20, 1807.
HENRY James, of Voluntown, Conn., and Mrs. Anna Northup, of N. Kingstown, daughter of James, dec.; m. by George Thomas, Justice of Peace, Jan. 5, 1786.
HILL Thomas, and Elizabeth Allen, Sept. 16, 1716.
"   Ebenezer, of Prudence Island, and Mary Fones, of N. Kingstown; m. by William Spencer, Justice of Peace, Jan. 1, 1729-30.
"   Thomas, and Rebecca Cole Allen, March —, 1731.
"   —, and Rebecca Cole; m. by William Spencer, Justice of Peace, March 25, 173—.
"   Mary, and Paymen Tanner, Jan. —, 1737-8.
"   Thomas, and Mary Berry; m. by Thomas Hill, Justice of Peace, —— 8, 1743.
"   Thomas, and Anna Oatley (proh.), Oct. 24, 1749.
"   Elizabeth, and Benjamin Richardson, Dec. 1, ——.
"   Anne, and Stephen Davis, ——.
"   Thomas, Esq., and Elizabeth Tibbetts; m. by Thomas Hill, Justice of Peace, ——.
"   Thomas, of E. Greenwich, son of Thomas and Phebe Havens, of Rhodes, Jan. —, ——.
"   Caleb, and Mercy Stafford, March 23, 1755.
"   Ebenezer, and Mary Fones, rec. Nov. 12, 1756.
"   Mary, and Thomas Tillinghast, Aug. 27, 1762.
"   Ruth, and William Boone, May 21, 1771.
"   Bridget, and Peter Tourgee, Dec. 6, 1775.
"   Caleb, and Sally Greene, Jan. 4, 1784.
"   Rebecca, and Stephen Bowen, April 22, 1802.
"   Thomas, of Caleb, and Lucy Anna Allen, of John, dec.; m. by Rev. John Gardiner, Jan. 14, 1821.
HIMES Benjamin, of N. Kingstown, and Mary James, of Westerly; m. by Benjamin Nichols, Justice of Peace, June —, 1723.
"   Ann, and —— ——, —. —, 1727.
"   Sarah, and Jeffrey Wilcox, April 24, 1726.
"   John, and Hannah Himes; m. by George Thomas, Justice of Peace, Dec. —, 1734.
"   Hannah, and John Himes, Dec. —, 1734.
"   Mary, and Jonathan Bates, March 26, 1747.
"   Elizabeth, and John Moro——, June —, ——.
"   Abbie A., and John W. Phillips, —. —, ——.
"   Martha, and Albert C. G. Rathbun, ——.
"   Abigail, and Edmund Arnold, April 20, 1777.
"   Martha, and —— ——; m. by Elder James Wightman, Dec. 18, 1777.
"   Deborah, and George Congdon, Oct. 25, 1781.
"   Vernon, of Sylvester and Lois, and Elizabeth Eldred, of Joseph and Sarah; m. by Elder William Northup, Aug. 26, 1795.
"   Stukeley, of George and Martha, and Elizabeth Vaughn, of Joshua and Mary; m. by Elder William Northup, Jan. 13, 1803.
"   George, of George, of N. Kingstown, and Mary Tew, of John, of Jamestown; m. at J. by Daniel Weeden, Warden, Feb. 15, 1815.
"   William, and Hannah Braman; m. by Rev. Edwin Stillman, March 28, 1845.
"   Stephen N., and Louisa Gorton; m. by Elder Joseph W. Allen, Oct. 25, 1847.
"   Willett, and Ann F. Brown; m. by Rev. Joseph A. Tillinghast, Oct. 23, 1848.
"   Sylvester R. J., and Sarah C. Place; m. by Rev. Joseph A. Tillinghast, Nov. 18, 1849.
"   Emeline, and Arnold Bicknell, Dec. 23, 1840.
HISCOX William, Jr., of Westerly, and Penelope Gardiner, of Jeremiah, of N. Kingstown.
"   Eliza C., and Daniel Wall, Feb. 3, 1849.
HOLLAND Sylvester, of Henry, of S. Kingstown, and —— A. Sherman, of Eber, of N. Kingstown; m. by Rev. Edwin Stillman, June 1, 1845.

HOLLOWAY Harriet, and —— Case, April 21, 1814.
  "   Hannah, and Alva Burnham, Oct. 7, 1839.
HOLMES Susannah, and —— Wightman, Feb. —, 1702-3.
  "   Joseph, of Newport, and Margaret Hazard, of N. Kingstown; m. by William Spencer, Justice of Peace, —— 20, 1727.
HOLWAY Hannah, and Ephraim Bull, Jan. 20, 1700.
HOOD Joseph R., and Caroline E. Gardiner, both of Providence; m. by Rev. Joseph A. Taylor, April 9, 1850.
HOOKEY William, of Stephen, of Newport, and Mary Whitman, of George, of N. Kingstown; m. by Elder John Gorton, April 17, 1760.
HOPKINS Samuel, and Honor Brown; m. by William Spencer, Justice of Peace, April 23, 1729-30.
  "   Mary, and Isaac Fowler, Jan. 15, 1720-1.
  "   Mary, and Thomas Fowler, Jan. 15, 1720.
HORTON Ariel B., of Rehoboth, Mass., and Eliza W. Huling, of N. Kingstown; m. by Rev. J. R. Stone, Dec. 21, 1840.
HOXSIE Mary E., and Thomas R. Carder, Sept. 6, 1849.
HULING Elizabeth, and Jonathan Allen, Nov. (2), 1740.
  "   (Alexander), of James, dec., and (Mary) Smith, of William; m. by Robert Hall, Justice of Peace, Feb. 3, 1745.
  "   Virtue, and Peleg Sherman, of Eber (of Ex.), Dec. 25, 17—.
  "   Elizabeth, and —— Dimond, April 17, 1760.
  "   (Avis) Frances, and Jonathan Donison. (Aug. 8), 1773.
  "   Alexander, of Alexander, and Mary Allen; m. by Elder Phillip Jenkins, March 31, 1777.
  "   Abigail, and —— (Hendley); m. by George Thomas Justice of Peace, March 29 (April 12), 1794.
  "   Andrew, of N. Kingstown, and Desire Ann (Deliverance) Spink, of Samuel and Abigail, of W. Greenwich; m. by Elder Nathan Hill, Oct. 28, 1784.
  "   Angustus, of Alexander, and Mrs. Sarah Greene, of John; m. by George Thomas. Justice, April 22, 1792.
  "   (John G., of Andrew), and (Lydia B. Lillibridge, of John); m. by Elder Peleg Peckham, Justice of Peace, May (25), 1823.
  "   Eliza W., of James, and Ansel (Ariel) B. Horton, Dec. 21, 1840.
  "   Virtue (of Alexander), and Peleg Sherman (of Eber), Dec. 25, (175—).
  "   James (of Andrew), and Elizabeth Clarke (of Gardiner), May 15, (1808).
HULL Alice, and John Seager, Jr., March 1, 1707-8.
  "   John, and Jenne Conadn; m. by Nathaniel Niles, Justice of Peace, July 11, 1709.
  "   Elizabeth, and Job Babcock, Jr., Oct. 10, 1717.
  "   John, and Waitey Ann ——, Dec. 8, 1828.
HUNT Roseanna, and Francis Tanner, Feb. 1, 1761.
  "   Adam, and —— Austin; m. by William Hall, Justice of Peace, —— 3, 1761.
  "   Samuel, and Mary Weaver; m. by John Reynolds, Justice of Peace, May 2, 1762.
  "   Sarah, and Delaway Fowler, March 11, 1764.
  "   ——, and Elizabeth Hall; m. by Daniel Hall, Justice of Peace, Jan. —, 1777.
  "   Catherine, and James Austin, March 4, 1759.
  "   William, and Prudence Tourgee; m. by Elder Nathan Hill, Feb. 4, 1783.
  "   Bartholomew, of North Kingstown, and Ann Foster, of Newport; m. by Rev. Gardiner Thurston, Nov. 30, 1785.
  "   George, of Samuel, and Elizabeth Whitford, of Benjamin; m. by Elder Nathan Hill, Dec. 6, 1788.
  "   Daniel, of Samuel, and Susannah Northnp, of Lebbens, of Exeter; m. by Elder Nathan Hill, Dec. 18, 1794.
  "   Elizabeth, and Thomas Letson, March 12, 1797.
  "   ——, and Benjamin Tanner, April 16, 1815.
  "   Elizabeth A., and William E. Cozzens, Dec. —, ——.
  "   Sukey, and David Terry, Feb. 4, 1858.
HUTCHINS Mary, and James Justin, Dec. —, 1728.

I

INMAN Elisha, of Scituate, and Sarah Nichols, of Robert, of N. Kingstown; m. by Henry Spencer, Justice, Jan. 13, 1761.

J

JACKSON ———, and Ann Boone, Aug. 15, 1725.

JACQUES Elizabeth, and Richard Sweet; March 8, 1704.

JACKWISE Nathan, and Hannah Norris; m. by Jeffrey Champlain, Assistant, Apr. 1, 1709.

"   Elizabeth, and Isaac Gould, July 8, 1722.

"   Thomas, and Hannah Spink; m. by William Spencer, Justice of Peace, Oct 24, 1725.

JAMES Mary, and Benjamin Himes, June —, 1723.

"   James, of Westerly, and Lewhannah Bentley; m. by George Thomas, Justice of Peace, May 28, 1738.

JECOY Isaac H., of N. Bridgewater, Mass., and Mary R. Gardiner, of N. Kingstown; m. by Rev. Alfred H. Taylor, Nov. 21, 1850.

JENKINS Rebecca, and Thomas Sherman; recorded July 16, 1761.

"   Christopher, and Ruth Tanner; m. by Elder James Wightman, Sept. 26, 1770.

"   Benjamin, of Phillip and Honor Chadsey, of Jabez; m. by George Thomas, Justice of Peace, April 13, 1780.

"   Phineus, of Phillip and Elizabeth, and Susan Warren; m. by Elder William Northup, July 19, 1787.

"   ———biah, and John Kinsey, ———.

JESS ———, and Martha Haxson; m. by Robert Hall, Justice of Peace, June 25, 1744.

JOHNSON ———, Jr., of Warwick, R. I., and Elizabeth Moon; m. by Benjamin Weight, Justice of Peace, July 10, 1737.

"   Anna, and James B. Anthony, March 15, 1832.

"   Sarah R., and Benjamin W. Hammond, Dec. 11, 1848.

JONES Phebe, and David Alverson, Jan. 24, 1765.

JOSLIN Alice, and —— Brown, March 10, 1744.

"   Mary, and —— Briggs, — 4, ——.

JURDON Mary, and Benjamin Wells, Jan. 21, 1730.

JUSTICE ———, and Alice Trowbridge; m. by Samuel Fones, Justice of Peace, April —, 1709.

JUSTIN Mary, and James ———; m. by William Spencer, Justice of Peace, March 17, 1728.

"   James, and Mary Hutchins; m. by William Spencer, Justice of Peace, Dec. —, 1728.

K

KEIAS Sybel, and Jabez Reynolds, March 14, 1779.

KELLEY George, and Rachel Ladd; m. by Christopher Allen, Justice, Feb. 15, 1719-20.

"   Eleazer, of Yarmouth, son of —— of Boston, and Sarah Browning of Kingstowne; m. by George Hazard, Justice, Oct. 6, 1721.

KENYON John, Jr., and Elizabeth Remington; m. by Thomas Mumford, Justice, July, 1704.

"   James, and Abigail Ladd; m. by Rouse Helme, Justice, Sept. 25, 1720.

"   John, of James and Abigail Ladd; m. by Rouse Helme, Justice, Sept. 25, 1720.

"   Remington, of N. Kingstown, and Elizabeth Spencer, of E. Greenwich, m. by William Hall, Justice, Feb. 27, 1757.

"   Nancy, and William Potter, Aug. —, 1849.

KETTLE Edward, of Mansur, and Weltha Godfrey, of Joshua; m. by William Hall, Justice of Peace, Aug. —, 1756.

KING Thomas, and Robey Scranton, of Thomas; m. by Samuel Thomas, Justice of Peace, —— 19, 1754.

"   Freelove, and Joseph Ceaser, Aug 10, 1789.

KINGSLEY Sarah, and Job Sweet, ——, 18, 1753.
" Lucy, and Samuel Browning, Dec. 31, 1778.
" Sewall, of Coggeshall, of N. Kingstown, and Ann Albro, of James; m. by Eber Sherman, Justice of Peace, March —, 1784.
" Samuel C., and Lydia S. Taylor; m. by Elder Eleazer Bellows, Jan. 7, 1855.
KINSEY John, and ——biah Jenkins; m. by Elisha Cole, Asistant, ——.
KNOWLES Daniel, and Hannah ——; m. by Stephen Hazard, Assistant, May 5, 1721.
" Mary, and Clarke Northup, March 13, 1791.
" Susan, and Thomas J. Gould, Sept. 20, 1848.

L

LADD Rachel, and George Kelley, Feb. 15, 1719-20.
" Abigail, and John Kenyon, Sept. 25, 1720.
" Abigail, and James Kenyon, Sept. 25, 1720.
LATHAM, Hannah, and William Mumford, Mar. 1, 1720-1.
LAWTON Samuel, of Edward, and —— Smith, of Benjamin; m. by George Thomas, Justice, May 8, 1781.
" Anna, and Samuel Thomas, —— —. 1806.
" Mary A., and Benajah Barker, Dec. 31, 1844.
" Beriah H., of Exeter, son of Caleb, and Sarah B. Wightman, of Josiah B., of N. Kingstown; m. by Eld. Joseph W. Allen, 4, 1847.
" Lewis D., and Mary Ann Arnold, April 8, 1849.
" Abbie C., and Michael Peckham, Dec. —, 1849.
LEACH Charles, of Maine, son of Martin, and Sally Sweet, of Constant; m. by Rev. Edwin Stillman, Mar. 16, 1843.
LEARNARD William, and Sarah Bottom; m. by Thomas Mumford, Justice, Feb. (10), 1708-9.
LEE Charles, and Abbie ——; m. by Jeremiah Gould, Justice, March —, 1725-6.
" John, and Mary Hall; m. by Francis Willett, Justice, March —, 1726-7.
LETSON Thomas, of W. Greenwich, son of Ephraim, and Elizabeth Hunt, of Jeremiah, of N. Kingstown; m. by Slocum Hall, Justice, March 12, 1797.
LEWISTON —— (schoolmaster), and Mary Douglass, of George; m. by George Northup, Justice, May ——, 1767.
LEWIS Jonathan, Jun, of Exeter, and Patience Tourgie (widow), of N. Kingstown; m. by George Thomas, Justice, Feb. 7, 1776.
" Tacy, and William Champlain, June 18, 1786.
" Nathaniel S., and Abigail F. Baker; m. by Rev. Alfred H. Taylor, Dec. 30, 1849.
LILLIBRIDGE Samuel, of Elisha, of Richmond, and Mary Peckham, of Benjamin, of N. Kingstown; m. by George Thomas, Justice, Aug. 18, 1808.
" Lydia B., of John, and John G. Huling, of Andrew, May 25, 1823.
LIPPITT George, of N. Kingstown, son of Aaron, and Elizabeth Rodman, of Timothy; m. by Eld. John Slocum, July 22, 1855.
LOCKWOOD Phebe, and George Thomas, Sept. 25, 1763.
" Phebe, and George Thomas, July 10, 1784.
LONG Ezekiel, of E. Greenwich, and Ruth Nichols, of N. Kingstown; m. by William Spencer, Justice, ——. 22, 1724.
LOVELL Nathaniel, of Scituate, and Ruth Vaughn of Isaac; m. by George Thomas (of Samuel), Justice, Nov. 1, 1772.
" Lucy A., and Joshua Arnold, Jan. 3, 1841.
LOVELASS Thomas, of Westerly, and Isabel Davis; m. by George Thomas, Justice, Nov. ——, 1734.
LUTHER Phebe J., and Silas Spink, Jan. 1, 1862

M

MACUMBER Jeremiah, of Middletown, and —— Austin; m. by Joseph Coggeshall, Aug. 3, 1761.

MAGNIN John, and Mrs. Hannah Coggeshall, of Joseph; m. by George Thomas, Justice, Dec. 13, 1798.

MANCHESTER Hannah, and John Spencer, Feb. 17, ——.

"   John, of Matthew and ——, of George, ——.

MARKESFIELD Con——, and Margaret Nichols; m. by William Spencer, Justice, March 4, 1739.

MARINER George, and Elizabeth Eley; m. by Rev. Dr. James McSparrun, Sept. —, 1722.

MARSH John, and Mary Masey, April —, 1732.

"   ——, and Samuel Thomas, ——.

MATTESON ——, and Josiah ——; m. by Elder James Wightman, Jan. 6, 1771.

"   Job, of W. Greenwich, and Margaret Spink, of N. Kingstown; m. by Robert Hall, Justice, Dec. 15, 1772.

"   Lydia, and David Greene, July 3, 1788.

"   Simeon, and Mercy Ann Taylor, ——.

"   ——, of Verbatus, and Mrs. Hannah Rose, age 18 years; born S. Kingstown, dau. of Miner; m. at Hamilton Mills by Elder John Slocum, Oct. 22, 1854.

MAYFIELD Mary, and Caleb Godfrey, —— 2, 1762.

McCOONE Daniel, and Sarah Cook, widow of George; m. by John Eldred, Assistant, June 19, 1705.

McCOTTER William, and Abigail F. Baker; m. by Rev. Alfred H. Taylor, Jan. 27, 1850.

McLOUGHLING John S., of John and Joanna M. Nichols, of Samuel; m. by Elder William Northup, Dec. 8, 1816.

McSPARRAN James, and Hannah Gardiner, of William, May 22, 1722.

MEDBURY Thomas, and ——; m. by Thomas Hill, Justice, March 27, 1744.

"   Deliverance, and Daniel Brown, Oct. 25, 1747.

MERRETT Samuel, of Samuel, of N. Stonington, Conn., and Sally G. Thomas, of Samuel; m. by Elder Joseph W. Allen, Jan. 24, 1830.

MERRILL William H., of Warwick, R. I., and Amanda F. Northup; m. by Rev. John H. Rouse, Jan. 21, 1847.

MINER Abigail, and Samuel Rose, Dec. 28, 1763.

"   Eleanora, and Edmund Cooper, June 10, 1829.

MITCHELL Sarah, and Charles Berry, Dec. 1, 1757.

"   Thomas, and Sarah Reynolds; m. by Robert Hall, Justice of Peace, Aug. 1, 1769.

"   ——, and Sarah Whitford, ——.

"   Samuel, and Margaret ——.

"   George A., and Mary R. Willis; m. by Rev. David Avery, Oct. 13, 1844.

"   Jeremiah, and Sarah D. Havens; m. by Elder John Slocum, ——. 5, 1844.

"   R——, and —— Reily, July 7, 1850.

MONTGOMERY Edwin, of Providence, and Susan W. Wightman, of N. Kingstown, April —, 1850.

MOORE Robert, and Ann Tripp; m. by William Spencer, Justice of Peace, June —, 1729.

"   Ebenezer, Jr., and Elizabeth Dake; m. by Job Tripp, Justice of Peace, June 12, 1735.

"   Elizabeth, and —— Johnson, Jr., July 10, 1737.

"   ——, of Exeter, and Deliverance Alverson, of N. Kingstown; m. by William Hall, Justice of Peace, Dec. 27, 1759.

"   William, and Sarah Pinder, both of Newport; m. by Rev. Gardiner Thurston, Aug. 16, 1775.

MOOT James, of E. Greenwich, and —— ——; m. by William Spencer, Justice of Peace, ——. —, 1738.

MOREY Robert, of Westerly, and Sarah Hazard, of N. Kingstown; m. by Francis Willett, Justice of Peace, Oct. 24, 1728.

"   Hannah, and —— ——; m. by George Thomas, Justice of Peace, ——. 13, 1732.

"   Mary, and John Marsh, April —, 1732.

"   Sarah (widow), and Benjamin Allen, April 28, 1776.

"   Mary, and Ebenezer Harrington, May 20, 1778.

"   Augustus, of Benjamin, and Patience Clarke; m. by George Thomas, Justice of Peace, May 4, 17—.

MORLEY Joseph, of Exeter, and Freelove Slocum, of N. Kingstown, Oct. 21, ——.

MORO John, Jr., and Elizabeth Himes; m. by William Hall Justice of Peace.

MOSS John, and Mary Relph; m. by William Hall, Justice of Peace, July 8, 1725-6.

MOTT Jacob, and Sarah Mott; m. by Elisha Cole, Assistant, March 7, 1720-1.
" Sarah, and Jacob Mott, March 7, 1720-1.
" Rebecca, and John Ray, May 19, 1728.
" Rebecca, of Newport, and ——ing, of Kings Towne; m. by Samuel Fones, Justice of Peace, Nov. —, ——.
" Gilbert, of N. Y., and Mar—— Anstis Slocum, of N. Kingstown; m. at Wickford by Elder David Avery, June 30, 1844.

MUMFORD Thomas, Jr., and Hannah Robinson; m. by John Eldred, Justice of Peace, May 3, 1704-5.
" Thomas, Jr., and Hannah Remington; m. by John Eldred, Assistant, Jan. 3, 1705-6.
" Thomas, Sen., and Esther Tefft; m. by Stephen Hazard, Assistant, Nov. 25, 1708.
" George, and Mary Robinson; m. by Joseph Jenckes, Assistant, Aug. 7, 1709.
" Sarah, and William Barber, May 5, 1720.
" William, and Hannah Latham, of Groton, Conn.; m. by Rev. Ephraim Woodbridge, March 1, 1720-1.
" Jerah, of S. Kingstown, and Mary Gardiner, of N. Kingstown; m. by Benjamin Weight, Justice of Peace, Nov. 29, 1739.
" ——, of Kings Towne, and Mrs. Hannah ——, of Groton, Mass.; m. by Rev. Ephraim Woodbridge, Sept. 7, 1821.

MUNROE Samuel, and Eunice Dimond, of John; m. by Elder Joseph W. Allen, Sept. 9, 1832.
" Benjamin P., of E. Greenwich, and Lydia Allen, of N. Kingstown; m. by Rev. S. Nash, March 17, 1840.

N

NASON Elizabeth, and James Tanner, Oct. 14, 1816.
" Phebe G., and Benoni S. Rose, Sept. 10, 1848.

NEY John, of Sandwich, and Sarah Cook, of Kings Towne; m. by Samuel Fones, Justice of Peace, Oct. 26, 1710.

NICHOLS Margaret, and Francis Bates; (pub.) July 9, 1721.
" Elizabeth, and Samuel Bates, July 12, 1721.
" Jonathan, and Sarah Thomas; m. by William Spencer, Justice of Peace, June 9, 1723.
" Ruth, and Ezekiel Long, ——, 22, 1724.
" ——, of John, (dec.), and Elizabeth Austin, of Joseph, Jun., (dec.); m. by Peter Boss, Justice of Peace, Oct. 18, 1736.
" Margeret, and —— Markesfield, May 4, 1739.
" Sarah, and Elisha Inman, Jan. 13, 1761.
" Thomas, of E. Greenwich, and Elizabeth Reynolds, of N. Kingstown; m. by Caleb Hill, Justice of Peace, Sept. 8, 1765.
" Christopher, of E. Greenwich, and Elizabeth Nichols, of Thomas, of N. Kingstown; m. by George Thomas, Justice of Peace, March 5, 1767.
" Elizabeth, and Christopher Nichols, March 5, 1767.
" John, of E. Greenwich, and Susannah Clarke, of Caleb, of N. Kingstown; m. by George Northup, Justice of Peace, March 19, 1769.
" Freelove, and Benjamin Fowler, Dec. 15, 1771.
" ——, and Jonathan Dean, Nov. 14, 1773.
" Mrs. Susannah, of George, of N. Kingstown, and ——, of John; m. by George Thomas, Justice of Peace, Dec. 5, 1773.
" ——, of George, and —— ; m. by George Thomas, Justice of Peace, Jan. 12, 1779.
" Samuel, of Samuel, of Newport, and Mary Wall, of Henry, of N. Kingstown; m. by Elder Phillip Jenkins, March 16, 1783.
" Brownen, of Jo—, of E. Greenwich, and Dorcas Reynolds, of Francis, of N. Kingstown; m. by Elder Phillip Jenkins, March 6, 1794.

NICHOLS Alexander, of E. Greenwich, and Mercy Spencer, of William, of N. Kings-
        town: m. by Thomas Hill, Justice of Peace, July 13; ——.
"   James, and Mary Hazelton; m. by William Hall, Justice of Peace, Nov.
        7, ——.
"   Phebe, and John Berry, Feb. 6, 17—.
"   Catherine, and Rhodes Havens, ——.
"   Rebecca, and Nathaniel Berry, Jan. 8, ——.
"   Hannah, and Ichabod Smith, ——.
"   Susan, and William Reynolds, Oct. 25, 1808.
"   Joanna M., and John S. McLoughling, Dec. 8. 1816.
NILES Nathaniel, Jr., and Mary Hannah, Jan. 26, 1699.
"   Tabitha, and Abraham Perkins, May 23, 1708.
"   Sarah, and Rouse Helme, Jr., July 21, 1709.
"   Nathaniel, and Ruth Sweet; m. by William Spencer, Justice of Peace,
        —— 3, 1731.
"   Jeremiah, of W. Greenwich, now of N. Kingstown, and Mercy Cobb, of
        N. Kingstown; m. by Daniel Hall, Justice of Peace, Dec. 29, 1778.
NORRIS Hannah, and Nathan Jackwise, April 14, 1709.
NORTHUP Benjamin, and ——, July 3, 1718.
"   Charles, and Freelove Eldred, June 23, 1720.
"   Nicholas, and Freelove Eldred; m. by Rouse Helme, Justice of Peace,
        June 23, 1720.
"   Immanuel, and Ann Tibbetts, of George; m. by William Hall, Justice of
        Peace, May 4, 1721.
"   Hannah, and Thomas Sandford, May 25, 1724.
"   Mary, and Jeffrey Champlain, Sept. 26, 1725.
"   Patience, and —— Congdon, Nov. 16, 1727.
"   Immanuel, and Sarah (Gould); m. by Francis Willett, Justice of Peace, ——
        24, 1727-8.
"   ——, and Anne Carr, ——, 1745-6.
"   Nicholas, Jr., and Hannah Allen; m. by Jeffrey Watson, Assistant, March
        29, 1750.
"   Esther, and Palmer Cleaveland, July 1, 1751.
"   Rufus, and Mary Talman; m. by Nicholas Northup, Justice of Peace,
        March 30, 1760.
"   Carr, of Immanuel, of N. Kingstown, and Sarah Clarke, of Hopkinton; m.
        by George Northup, Justice. March 9, 1766.
"   Elizabeth, and Huling Gardiner, Feb. 1, 1767.
"   Anne, of Immanuel, of N. Kingstown, and ——, of E. Greenwich; m. by
        George Thomas, Justice, Dec. 4, 1768.
"   John, of N. Kingstown, and Margery Talford, of Newport; m. by Rev.
        Gardiner Thurston, Dec. 25, 1771.
"   Mary, and Edmund Barber, May 1, 1773.
"   Samuel, of Stephen, and Waite Thomas, of George; m. by Eber Sherman,
        Justice of Peace, Feb. 25, 1779.
"   Abigail, and Paulipus Austin, Dec. 14, 1779.
"   Hannah, and ——; m. by George Thomas, Justice of Peace, July 10,
        1780.
"   Stephen, of Stephen, and Martha Cole, of Benjamin; m. by George
        Thomas, Justice of Peace, —— —, 1780.
"   Stephen, and Mary Reynolds; m. by Elder Nathan Hill, Nov. 18, 1782.
"   John, of John, dec., and Lucy Spink, of Ishmeal; m. by Nathan Brown,
        Justice of Peace, —— 1, 1783.
"   (Anne), and Nicholas Carr Northup, Dec. 1, 1785.
"   Nicholas Carr, and (Anne) Northup; m. by Elder James Wightman, Dec.
        1, 1785.
"   Mrs. Anna, and James Henry, Jan. 5, 1786.
"   David, of Robert, of N. Kingstown, dec., and Antis Crandall, dau. of
        John Austin, of said town; m. by Eber Sherman, Justice of Peace, March
        9, 1789.
"   Clarke, of Carr, dec., and Mary Knowles, of Reynolds; m. by Elder Phillip
        Jenkins, March 13, 1791.
"   Stephen, of Rufus and Mary, and Mary Slocum, widow of John, dau. of
        James and Almy Cooper; m. by Elder William Northup, Jan. 10, 1793.
"   Frances, and Richard Barney, Aug. 10, 1794.

NORTHUP Susannah, and Daniel Hunt, Dec 18, 1794.
" 	Christopher, of Carr and Sarah, and Penelope Hall, of William and Penelope; m. by Elder William Northup, Dec. 12, 1795.
" 	James, of N. Kingstown, and Mary Austin, of Richmond; m. by George Thomas, Justice, March 17, ——.
" 	Lucy Anna, and Benjamin Gardiner, ——.
" 	John, and Lydia Gardiner, of Jeremiah, Jr.; m. by William Hall, Justice of Peace, June 8, ——.
" 	George, and Frances Congdon, of John; m. by James Gardiner, Justice of Peace, Dec. 20, ——.
" 	William, of Nicholas, and Freelove, and Ann Slocum, of Samuel and Ann, of Jamestown, —— 17, ——.
" 	Mary Ann, and ——; m. by Rev. C. C. Lewis, ——.
" 	Elizabeth, and Samuel Northup, March 1, 1802.
" 	Samuel, of Zebulon and Mary, and Elizabeth Northup, of Stephen and Martha; m. by Elder William Northup, March 1, 1802.
" 	Hannah, and Christopher Spencer; rec. Nov. 22, 1809.
" 	Sarah, and —— Sweet; rec. Oct. 1, 1816.
" 	Thomas, of Warwick, R. I., and Mary Frances Sherman, of N. Kingstown; m. by Rev. Thomas Tew, Aug. 24, 1840.
" 	Daniel, and Elizabeth Cooper; m. by Rev. J. R. Stone, March 30, 1841.
" 	David, of Samuel, of N. Kingstown, and Mary Abbie Dewey, of Champlain, of S. Kingstown; m. by Rev. Edwin Stillman, Feb. 18, 1844.
" 	Stephen, and Mary C. Gardiner; m. by Elder John Slocum, June 28, 1844.
" 	James M., and Penelope Northup, of Stukeley; m. by Rev. John H. Rouse, Nov. 9, 1844.
" 	Penelope, and James M. Northup, Nov. 9, 1844.
" 	John, and Mrs. Nancy Armstrong, Oct. 19, 1845.
" 	Amanda F., and William H. Merrill, Jan. 21, 1847.
" 	Eunice A., and Thomas H. Babcock, Jan. 21, 1847.
" 	Mary F., and Nicholas S. Spink, Jan. 24, 1850.
" 	Stephen, and Elizabeth A. Willis, Feb. 14, 1850.
" 	Mary, and Daniel Sunderland, June 7, 1850.
" 	Abbie O., and George S. Thomas, Sept. 15, 1861.
NOYES Thomas W., of Robert F., of S. Kingstown, and Julia Elmer Allen, of Elder Joseph W.; m. by Rev. Jonathan Brayton, Sept. 28, 1845.

O

OATLEY Anna, (prob.) and Thomas Hill, Oct. 20, 1749.
" 	William, and Harriet Turgee; m. by Rev. Cyrus Wilson, June 19, 1843.
OLIN John, Jun., and Sarah Card, of Phillip; m. by George Northup, Justice, Oct. 13, 1765.
" 	Giles, and Ann Reynolds; m. by George Thomas, Justice, Dec. 17, 1769.
" 	——, and Valentine Whitman, ——.
ONYON John, Jun., of N. Kingstown, and Jemima Dick, of Jamestown; m. by Samuel Thomas, Justice, June 15, 1755.
OSBORNE Rachel, and John Cottrell, Nov. 16, 1752.

P

PAINE Elizabeth, and Jonathan Turner, June 9, 1709.
" 	Mary, and William Hazelton, Sept. 27, 1710.
PARMELENT Mary, and John Briggs, Jun., Dec. —, 1740.
PATTERSON George S. A., of James, and Bridget R. Connelly, of N. Kingstown, age 17 years, late of Ireland.
PECKHAM Thomas, and Deborah Browne; m. by Rev. James McSparran, Oct. 4, 1722.
" 	Benedict, of Newport, and Elizabeth Eldred, of N. Kingstown; m. by Elder James Wightman, Sept. 6, 17—.
" 	Elizabeth, and Beriah Eldred, Sept. 7, 1800.

PECKHAM Patience, and John Hall, Aug. 23, 1807.
"   Mary, and Abraham R. Rathbun, June 17, 1807.
"   Mary, and Samuel Lillibridge, Aug. 18, 1808.
"   Michael, of Middletown, and Abbie C. Lawton, of N. Kingstown; m. by
      Rev. J. A. Tillinghast, Dec. —, 1849.
PERKINS Abraham, and Tabitha Niles; m. by Thomas Mumford, Justice, May 23,
      1708.
"   Abraham, and Margaret Case; m. by Rouse Helme, Justice of Peace, Ju
      ne 29, 1718.
PERRY Mathilda, and Amos Gardiner, Dec. 5, 1824.
"   ——, and Mary Austin; m. by Rev. A. J. Chaplain, Oct. 22, 1847.
PHILLIPS (Samuel, of Samuel, and Elizabeth, and Abigail Brown; m. by William
      Spencer, Justice of Peace, —. 4, 1733.
"   Mary, and Joseph ——; m. by William Spencer, Justice of Peace, Sept. 19,
      1734.
"   John, and —— Wilson; m. by Job Tripp, Justice of Peace, ——. —. 1735.
"   Elizabeth (widow), and George Thomas, Feb. 9, 1738.
"   Charles, and Dorcas Scranton; m. by William Hall, Justice of Peace, Apr.
      12, 1761.
"   Thomas, of Samuel, and Dorcas Albro, of Major Samuel; m. by Samuel Br
      owning, Justice of Peace, Apr. 23, 1761.
"   Sarah, and Jeremiah Wall, Sept. 25, 1768.
"   Thomas, of Samuel, and Elizabeth Brown (widow), dau. of Samuel Brown;
      m. by Daniel Hall, Justice of Peace, Oct. 27, 1776.
"   William, of William, and Mrs. Martha Albro, widow of Capt. James;
      m. by George Thomas, Jr., Justice of Peace, March 14, 1782.
"   Mary, and Daniel Eldred, Jan. 10, 1799.
"   John W., and Abbie A. Himes; m. by Elder John Slocum.
"   Samuel R., of Richmond, son of Nicholas H., and Hannah M. Hazard, of
      N. Kingstown, dau. of Stephen, Jan. 9, 1843.
"   Ezekiel B., of Nicholas H., of Richmond, and Maria Pierce, of Samuel, of
      N. Kingstown; m. by Elder Joseph W. Allen, May 29, 1853.
"   Henry A., and Eliza Spink, Oct. 29, 1860.
"   Eliza, and Edward C. Schoonmaker, Oct. 1, 1865.
PIERCE Mary, and —— ——, —— —, 1715.
"   Benoni, and Sarah Rhodes; m. by Jeremiah Gould, Assistant, Nov. 10,
      1723.
"   Sarah (widow), and William Havens, Nov. 21, 1725.
"   ——, and Nathaniel Gardiner, Jr., ——. 23, 1734.
"   Joseph, of Scituate, and —— Reynolds, of N. Kingstown; m. by George
      Thomas, Justice of Peace, Nov. 3, 1734.
"   Joshua, and —— Smith; m. by Elder David Sprague, April 16, 1747.
"   Elizabeth, and Job Corey, July 30, 1767.
"   John, and Eunice Briggs; m. by Caleb Hill, Justice of Peace, March 24,
      1771.
"   Martha, and William Corey, Sept. 14, 1771.
"   Sylvester, of Joshua, and Martha Warner, of Samuel; m. by Elder Phillip
      Jenkins, Jan. 26, 1775.
"   ——, and —— Spencer, of Henry; m. by Elder Phillip Jenkins, ——.
      —, 1777.
"   Joseph, of Sylvester, dec., and Ann Greene, of John, late of N. Kings-
      town; m. by Elder Phillip Jenkins, Nov. 16, 1784.
"   Alice, and John Chadsey, May 9, 1791.
"   Elizabeth, and William Carr, ——. 13, 1794.
"   Lydia, and Matthew Handley, Sept. 22, 1794.
"   Martha, and Daniel Weeden, Jan. 14, 1796.
"   Samuel, and Mary Hazard, of Ephraim, and Mary; m. by Elder Wil-
      liam Northup, ——, —, ——.
"   John, of E. Greenwich, and Freelove Dyer, of John, of N. Kingstown,
      ——.
"   Deliverance, and Elisha Tillinghast, ——.
"   William, of N. Kingstown and —— of Jamestown, Jan. 27, ——.
"   Jonathan, and Margaret ——, Feb. 22. ——.
"   Nathan, and Abigail Spink; m. by Jeremiah Gould, Assistant, ——. —, 8—.

PIERCE John, of E. Greenwich, and Alice Tibbetts, of N. Kingstown, April 13, ——.

" Pattey, and Rowland Chadsey, June 22, 1803.
" William, of John and Betsey Tanner, of Benjamin; m. by John Allen, Justice, July 3, 1803.
" Sarah, and Wanton Spencer, July 4, 1811.
" Mercy, and Joseph S. Reynolds, Feb. 4, 1816.
" John, of Giles and Desire, and Sarah Brown, of Stukeley and Sarah; m. by Elder John Gardiner, Nov. 6, 1825.
" Desire C., and Joseph Brown, Feb. 24, 1828.
" Amie A., and Benjamin Champlain, Sept. 28, 1837.
" Lydia, and Wilbur Hazard, Dec. 25, 1843.
" Ruth, and Edward H. Hathaway, Feb. —, 1848.
" Maria, and Ezekiel B. Phillips, May 29, 1853.

PIERSON James, and Freelove ——, dau. of Freelove; m. by George Thomas, Justice of Peace, Feb. 28, 1784.

PINDER Sarah, and William Moore, Ang. 16, 1775.
" Hannah, and Thomas Bissell. ——.

(PLACE Joseph, and Johannah ——, Nov. 9, 1698.)
" Mary, and —— Wickham, May 23, 1707.
" Samuel, of N. Kingstown, and Sarah Gill, of W. Greenwich; m. by Ephraim Gardiner, Justice of Peace, Jan. 29, 1760.
" ——, of Thomas, of E. Greenwich, and Mary Gardiner; m. by Christopher Spencer, Justice of Peace. ——.
" Enock, and Hannah Wilcox, March —, ——.
" ——, (widow) and Benjamin Cole, —— 19, ——.
" Scuce, and Joseph Smith, ——.
" Sarah C., and Sylvester R. J. Himes, Nov. 18, 1849.
" Arnold James, and —— E. Wescott; m. by Rev. Edward Bell, Sept. 9, 1860.

PORTER Melissa, and Thomas M. Tourgee, July 27, 1845.

POTTER Sarah, and John Earle, March 19, 1711-12.
" John, of John, and Mercy Robinson; m. by Christopher Allen, Justice of Peace, Oct. 28, 1714.
" Thomas, Sr., and Lydia Sherman; m. by Christopher Allen, Justice of Peace, Dec. 8, 1720.
" Susannah, and George Babcock, Jr., Dec. 20, 1721.
" Nathaniel, of Charlestown, and Mary Aylesworth, of N. Kingstown; m. by Job Tripp, Justice of Peace, Sept. 20, 1739.
" Alice, and Joshua Greene, Jan. 1, 1771.
" Hannah, and Nicholas Spink, Aug. 12, 1802.
" Patience, and William Roome (col.), Jan. —, 1849.
" William, of North Kingstown, and Nancy Kenyon, of Richmond; m. by Elder James Hammond, Aug. —, 1849.

POWELL Mrs. Esther, and ——; m. by Rev. Joseph Torrey, Oct. 3, 1738.

POWERS Ichabod, and Miribah ——; m. by Daniel Coggeshall, Justice of Peace, April 8, 1733.

PRATT Mrs. Susan, and John Greene, June 3, 1779.

Q R

RANDALL Huldah, and Benjamin Fowler, Oct. 23, 1791.

RATHBUN Samuel, of New Shoreham, and ——; m. by William Spencer, Justice of Peace, April 13, 1725.
" Obediah, and Ann Austin; m. by William Spencer, Justice of Peace, Sept. 16, 1731.
" Job, and Mary Harris; m. by Samuel Dorrance, Justice of Peace, —— 1, 1737.
" William, and ——el Sweet; m. by Job Tripp, Justice of Peace, Dec. 16, 1739.
" Sarah, and Abner Wilbonr, Feb. 8, 1753.
" Thomas, and Ho—— ——; m. by Elder Samuel Albro, —— —, 1758.
" ——, and Immanuel Case, Jr., Oct. 4, 1761.

RATHBUN Anthony, of Samuel, and Elizabeth Brown, of Charles; m. by George Thomas, Justice of Peace, Nov. 7, 1771.
" Anthony, of Samuel, dec., and Penelope Brown, of Charles; m. by George Thomas, Justice of Peace, Feb. 18, 1787.
" Albert C. G., of Benjamin, and Martha Himes, ——.
" Benjamin, and Hannah Carpenter; m. by William Hall, Assistant, Oct. 31, ——.
" ——, and Abigail ——, ——.
" Abraham Borden, of Joshua, and Mary Peckham, of Benoni; m. by George Thomas, Justice of Peace, June 19, 1808.
" Thomas R., and Lucy Ann Gardiner; m. by Rev. James R. Stone, May 2. 1841.
" Mercy, and —— W. Congdon, Nov. 8, 1846.
" Abbie F., and John C. Eldred. June 13, 1847.
RAY John, and Rebecca Mott; m. by William Spencer, Justice of Peace, May 19, 1728.
" John, and Mary ——; m. by Elder Benjamin Harrington, March 6, 1735.
RALPH Mary, and Daniel Greene, Jr., Jan. 9, 1737-8.
" Samuel, and Elizabeth Aylesworth; m. by John Reynolds, Justice of Peace, Feb. 16, 1762.
" ——, and Peleg Greene, M—— 10, 1762.
" Mary, and John Moss, 8th, 7m. (1725-6).
REMINGTON Elizabeth, and John Kenyon, Jun., July —, 1704.
" Hannah, and Thomas Mumford, Jun., Jan. 3, 1705-6.
REYNOLDS James, and Sarah ——, Oct. 7, 1705.
" John, and Martha Tibbetts; m. by William Spencer, Justice, Nov. 2, 1721.
" James, and Mary Ayres; m. by Benjn. Nichols, Justice, Jan. 28, 1721-2.
" Susannah, and John Baker, Feb. 28, 1722-3.
" ——, and Joshua Coggeshall, ——. —, 1725-6.
" Clement, and Jane Bentley; m. by Benjamin Nichols, Justice, ——. 3, 1726.
" John, and —— ——, April 9, 1728.
" Elizabeth, and William Tanner, March —, 1729.
" George, and Johannah Spencer; m. by William Spencer, Justice, Sept 14, 1729.
" Hannah, and Henry Tibbetts, Nov. 3, 1734.
" ——, and Joseph Pierce, Nov. 3, 1734.
" Elizabeth, and Jeremiah Carpenter, Dec. 25, 1737.
" Susannah, and Robert Aylesworth, Jr., ——. —, 1737.
" Peter, Jr., and Phebe Reynolds; m. by Job Tripp, Justice, March —, 1738.
" Phebe, and Peter Reynolds, Jr., March —, 1738.
" John, and Deborah Wightman; m. by Benjamin Weight, Justice of Peace, —— 22, 1739.
" Susannah, and John Spencer, 3d, —— 8, 1741.
" Robert, and Annah Gardiner; m. by Benoni Hall, Justice of Peace, July —, 1742.
" Joseph, of John, and Dorcas Tibbetts; m. by William Hall, Justice of Peace, May 23, 1756.
" ——, and Martha Slocum; m. by William Hall, Justice of Peace, Nov. 28, 1757.
" Elisha, of John and Hannah, and Mary Dickinson, of John and Mary; m. by Christopher Spencer, Justice of Peace, Feb. 19, 1758.
" John, of John, and Sarah Carpenter; m. by John Reynolds, Justice of Peace, Jan. 17, 1762.
" James, and Rebecca Godfrey; m. by Caleb Clarke, Justice, Nov. 10, 1762.
" Elizabeth, and Thomas Nichols, Sept. 8, 1765.
" James, of John, and —— Alverson, of Daniel, May 4, 1767.
" Ann, and Giles Olin, Dec. 17, 1769.
" Martha, and Robert Tefft, —— 24, 1769.
" Sarah, and Thomas Mitchell, Aug. 1, 1769.
" Waite, and Benjamin Brown, Oct. 17, 1771.
" ——, and William Wall, Nov. 17, 1771.
" Francis, of John, and Mrs. Martha Tibbetts, of George, dec.; m. by Caleb Hill, Justice of Peace, Oct. 25, 1772.

REYNOLDS Mary, and Abraham Greene, Jan, 9, 1774.
" Esther, and William Reynolds, Jan. 23, 1774.
" William, of John, of Peter, and Esther Reynolds, of John, of James; m. by George Thomas, Justice of Peace, Jan. 23, 1774.
" Jabez, of N. Kingstown, and Sybel Kelas, of Warwick; m. by Daniel Hall, Justice of Peace, March 14, 1779.
" Mary, and Stephen Northup, Nov. 18, 1782.
" ——, and Samuel Watson, May 21, 1784.
" Henry, and Mary Fones; m. by Elder Nathan Hill, May 15, 1785.
' Gardiner, of Exeter, and Elizabeth Davis, of Benjamin, of N. Kingstown; m. by George Thomas, Justice of Peace, Apr. 23, 1786.
" Mary, and John Smith, Oct. 16, 1791.
" John, and Mary Hall; m. by George Thomas, Justice of Peace. March. 17, 1792.
" Eldred, of John, of N. Kingstown. and Esther Corey, of Sheffield, of W. Greenwich; m. by Elder Nathan Hill, April 26, 1792.
" Dorcas. and Brownen Nichols. March 6. 1794.
" Anna, and Joseph Casey, March 31, 1799.
" Jonathan, of Peter, and Mary Tanner, of William, Sept. 4, ——.
" Hannah. and Thomas G. Boone, ——.
" ——, of Jonathan, and ——, of Rufus; m. by George Thomas, Justice of Peace, ——.
" Stephen, of John, and Abagail Cottrell, of Samuel; m. by Eber Sherman, Justice of Peace. ——. 3. ——.
" Deborah. and Jeremiah Baker. Jan. 9, ——.
" Hannah, and Samuel Crandall. Dec. 12. ——.
" Mary, and Thomas Bentley, May 20, ——.
" Ann, and John Aylesworth, April 19, ——.
" Stephen B., of William J., and Harriet C. Gardiner, Aug. 7, ——.
" Anne, of Jonathan and Anstis, and ——; m. by Elder Wm. Northup, ——.
" Jonathan, and Mary Spink, of Nicholas, Jan. 20, 180-.
" ——, daughter of Peter, and —— Fones, of James, Dec. 23, ——.
" John, of Benjamin, and Polly Aylesworth, of Arthur; m. by Elder William Northup, Sept. 20, 1801.
" Jonathan, of William, and Mary Spink, of Nicholas; m. by George Thomas, Justice of Peace, Jan. 20, 1803.
" Elizabeth, and Beriah Eldred, April 27, 1807.
" William, of Benjamin and Susannah, and Susan Nichols, of Samuel and Mary; m. by Elder William Northup, Oct. 25, 1808.
" Phebe, and Elisha Clarke, Aug. 5, 1810.
" Mary Ann, and Benj. T. Clarke, Jan 14, 1811.
" Joseph S., of Eldred, and Mary Pierce, of Sylvester; m. by Elder Gersham Palmer, Feb. 4, 1816.
" John J., and Hannah Congdon; m. by Rev. James R. Stone, April 9, 18--.
" Helena M. W., and Abial Sherman. Sept. 11, 1828.
" Mary M., and Vincent Gardiner, Jan. 18, 1829.
" Almira Amanda, and Boone Spink, Jr., Sept. 14, 1840.
" Hannah A. U., and Thomas G. Fry, Feb. 13, 1841.
" Capt. James J., and Sally S. Baker; m. by Rev. James R. Stone, March 2, 1841.
" Sarah, and James Durgan, April 29, 1841.
" Elizabeth Frances, and Harrison G. O. Gardiner, July 18, 1841.
" Mary Nichols, and Gideon G. Congdon, Dec. 14, 1846.
" Hannah B., and William E. Chase, Oct. 3, 1848.
" Mrs. Sarah, and Ebenezer Brown, April 23, 1850.
" Mary A., and —— Tillinghast; rec. —— 27, 1850.
RHODES Sarah, and Benoni Pierce, Nov. 10, 1723.
" Capt. Samuel, and Sarah Boone; m. by William Spencer, Justice of Peace, ——ber 6, 1724.
" ——, and William Utter, Jan. —, 1743.
RICHARDSON Elizabeth, and Jeffrey Allen, March 3, 1776.
" Benjamin, and Elizabeth Hill; m. by George Thomas, Justice of Peace, Dec. 1, ——.

RIELY ——, of J— E—, of Newport, and R— Mitchell, of Caroline M—; m. by Rev.
    C. C. Lewis, July 7, 1850.
ROBINSON Hannah, and Thomas Mumford, Jr. (should be Remington), May 3, 1704.
    "   John, and Mary Hazard, Oct. 19, 1704.
    "   Elizabeth, and William Brown, Nov. 2, 1707.
    "   Mary, and George Mumford, Aug. 7, 1709.
    "   Mercy, and John Potter, Jr., Oct. 28, 1714.
    "   Lewis, of Rehoboth, Mass., and Margeret Swan, of N. Kingstown; m. by Ro
        bert Hall, Justice of Peace, July 29, 1769.
RODMAN Elizabeth, and George Lippitt, July 22, 1855.
RODS Penelope, and —— Garfield, May 4, 1729.
ROYERS Edward, of Westerly, and Rebecca Bundy, of E. Greenwich; m. by Benja
    min Weight, Justice of Peace, July 16, 1739.
ROOKES Benjamin, of England, and Lucy Ann West, of N. Kingstown; m. by Rev.
    John H. Rouse, July 9, 1843.
ROOME William, and Patience Potter, (col.); m. by Rev. John H. Rouse, Jan.
    —, 1849.
ROSE Abigail, and John Congdon, July 9, 17—.
    "   Samuel, of S. Kingstown, and Abigail Miner, of Stonington, Conn.; m.
        by Rev. Nathaniel Eells, Dec. 28, 1763.
    "   Elizabeth, and John Smith, March 17, 1799.
    "   Ebenezer, of Thomas, and Mary M. Carr, of John, of Jamestown; m. by
        Rev. Edwin Stillman, June 11, 1843.
    "   William, of Thomas, and Phebe Ann Carr, of John, of Jamestown; m.
        by Rev. Edwin Stillman, Nov. 22, 1843.
    "   Benoni S., and Phebe G. Nason; m. by Rev. Joseph A. Tillinghast, Sept.
        10, 1848.
    "   Mrs. Hannah, and —— Matteson, Oct. 22, 1854.
ROUSE ——, and Margaret Young of Edward; m. by Elder Phillip Jenkins, Dec.
    28, 1776.

S

SANFORD Thomas, and Hannah Northup, of Joseph; m. by William Hall, Justice
    of Peace, May 25, 1724.
    "   Joshua, and Mary Westcott; m. by William Hall, Justice of Peace, Jan.
        9, 1757.
    "   Esbon, of Newport, and Abigail Congdon, of William, of N. Kingstown; m.
        by Elder Nathan Hill, March 25, 1787.
    "   Albert, and Huldah S. Freeborne, Dec. 24, 1849.
    "   Esbon, and Esther C. Chappell; m. by Rev. Daniel Henshaw, Aug. 12,
        1850.
SAUNDERS Margaret, and John Haley, May 18, 1719.
SCOTT Penelope, and James Havens, April 10, 1800.
SCRANTON Thomas, of Prudence Island, and Sarah Fones, of N. Kingstown; m.
    by William Spencer, Justice of Peace, March —, 1725-6.
    "   Daniel, and Thankful Eldred; m. by Robert Hall, Justice of Peace, Sept.
        22, 1744.
    "   Virtue, and James Chappell, April 4, 1751.
    "   Robey, and Thomas King, ——. 19, 1754.
SCRANTON Dorcas, and Charles Phillips, April 12, 1761.
SEAGER John, Jr., and Alice Hull; m. by Christopher Allen, Justice, March 1,
    1707-8.
SEALEY Joseph, of New Jersey, and Sarah F. Freeborne.
SEGOUCHE Elizabeth and Christopher Alen, —— —, 1687.
SHAW Benjamin, of Anthony, late of Exeter, dec., and ——ah Congdon, of James,
    of N. Kingstown; m. by George Thomas, Justice, Oct. 13, 1793.
    "   Sarah, and William Greene, May 29, 1796.
    "   William Gardiner, of John and Elizabeth, of Newport, and Elizabeth Mc-
        Laughling Brenton, of Samuel and Susanna; m. by Elder William Nor-
        thup, Oct. 16, 1796.
    "   John A., of Willett, N. Y., and Mrs. Ann S. Slocum, of N. Kingstown.
    "   Joseph, of Warwick, R. I., and Harriet Underwood, of Samuel, of S. Kings-
        town; m. by Rev. Cyrus Wilson, May 1, 1843.

SHAW William A., M. D., and Ann P. Case; m. by Rev. William F. Morgan; recorded, Feb. 1, 1848.

SHEFFIELD Joseph, of Portsmouth, and Mary Earle, of Freetown, dan. of Ralph: m. by William Arnold, Justice, Jan. 27, 1708.

" Elizabeth, and —— Weight, Oct. 17, 1717.

" Edward, and Sarah Gardiner; m. by Samuel Fones, Justice, April 5, 1719.

" Edmund, of Westerly, son of Samuel, and Sarah Ann Gardiner, of Jeremiah, of N. Kingstown; m. by Rev. Joseph W. Allen, June 8, 1823.

" John, of Capt. Benjamin, and —— Cogeshall, of Daniel, ——.

SHERMAN Abial, and Dorcas Gardiner; m. by Christopher Allen, Justice, Nov. 20, 1712.

" Lydia, and Thomas Potter, Sr., Dec. 8, 1720.

" Hannah, and Robert ——; m. by William Spencer, Justice, Dec. 26, 1727.

" Eber, of William, and Margaret Eldred, of Robert; m. by Thomas Northup, Justice, Feb. —, 1738.

" Benoni, and Margaret ——; m. by Benjamin Weight, Justice, Dec. 24, 1741.

" Sylvester, and Mary Sweet; m. by Elder Samuel Albro, July 16, 1758.

" William, of N. Kingstown, and —am Sweet, m. by Jeffrey Watson, Assistant, Jan. 28, 1759.

" Thomas, and Rebecca Jenkins; m. by Frances Willett, Assistant, July 16, 1761.

" Robert, and —— Tabor, (widow); m. by George Thomas, Justice, March 25, 1768.

" Havens, of Benoni, and Elizabeth Eldred, of Sylvester; m. by Eber Sherman, Justice, Oct. 10, 1773.

" Andrew, of Stephen, dec., and Phebe Sherman, of Eber; m. by George Thomas, Justice, Feb. 10, 1774.

" Phebe, and Andrew Sherman, Feb. 10, 1774.

" Moses, of Moses, of Exeter, and Sarah Sherman, of Samuel, Sept. 22, 1774.

" Sarah, and Moses Sherman, Sept. 22, 1774.

" Henry, of Eber, dec., and Mary Sherman, widow of Sylvester; m. by Eber Sherman, Justice of Peace, April 16, 1778.

" Mary and Henry Sherman, April 16, 1778.

" Giffe, and James Sherman, March —, 1798.

" James, of Sylvester and Giffe Sherman; m. by Slocum Hall, Justice of Peace, March —, 1798.

" Peleg, of Eber, of Exeter, and Virtue Huling, of N. Kingstown; m. by James Fones, Justice of Peace, Dec. 25, 175—.

" John, of Henry, and Lydia Whitford; m. by George Northup, Justice of Peace, April 24, ——.

" ——, and Anna Congdon, —, ——.

" Ichabod, and Mary Young; m. by Job Tripp, Justice of Peace, —, ——.

" ——, and Charles Brown, —, ——.

" Lowry, and David Bates, —— ——.

" Jemima, and Job Sweet, —— ——.

" Benjamin, of Remington, and Isabell Gardiner, of Gideon, of S. Kingstown; m. by Oliver Gardiner, Justice of Peace, July 14, 1805.

" Abial, of Nathaniel and Elizabeth, and Helena M. W. Reynolds, of Jonathan and Mary; m. by Elder William Northup, Sept. 11, 1828.

" Mary Frances, and Thomas Northup, Aug. 24, 1840.

" —— A., and Sylvester Holland, June 1, 1845.

" John, and Alice Burlingame, Nov. 7, 1848.

" Henry S., of John Reed and Mary S., and Mary E. Gardiner, of Benjamin and Elizabeth, of S. Kingstown; m. by Rev. J. H. Rouse, April 19, 1849.

" Susan C., and David Douglass, Jan. 7, 1850.

SHIPPEE Deliverance, and William Briggs, May 18, 1740.

" Horace J., of William and Eliza, of E. Greenwich, and Mary G. Wightman, of Daniel G.; m. by Rev. A. Judson, Chaplain, March 8, 1847.

" Martha F., and John F. Tourgee, Aug. —, 1860.

SHOONMAKER Edward C., and Eliza Phillips, Oct. 1, 1865.

SIGWORTH Jemima, and Scipeo Wilbur, Nov. 11, 1743.

SISSON Caleb, of Portsmouth, and Abigail Cornell, of N. Kingstown; m. by George
　　　　Northup, Justice, Aug. 27, 1769.
SLOCUM ——, and Thomas Hazard, Feb. 22, 1727.
　"　　Samuel, and Ann Gould.; m. by George Thomas, Justice, —— 4, 1733.
　"　　Edward, of Samuel, and Mary Watson, of Samuel; m. by Robert Hall,
　　　　Justice, Aug. 20, 1741.
　"　　Moses, and Frances Watson; m. by Jeffrey Watson, Assistant, Aug. 21,
　　　　1746.
　"　　John, of John, and Eleanor Spink, of Joseph; m. by William Hall, Jus-
　　　　tice, Sept. 30, 1756.
　"　　Martha, and —— Reynolds, Nov. 28, 1757.
　"　　Ebenezer, of Ebenezer, and Sarah Casey, of Gideon; m. by George
　　　　Thomas (of Samuel), Justice, Oct. 11, 1772.
　"　　Margaret, and George Arnold, April 26, 1778.
　"　　John, of Ebenezer, and Mary Cooper, of James; m. by Elder Phillip
　　　　Jenkins, Dec. 5, 1779.
　"　　Mary, and Charles Dickinson, Dec. 20, 1782.
　"　　Ebenezer, of William, of N. Kingstown, and Mary Gwilliam, late of Europe;
　　　　m. by Elder Phillip Jenkins, Jan. 1, 1788.
　"　　Elizabeth, and Samuel Gardiner, March 24, 1789.
　"　　Mary (widow), and Stephen Northup, Jan. 10, 1793.
　"　　Jonathan, and Elizabeth Chadsey; m. by Elder Philip Jenkins, rec. Jan.
　　　　30, 1794.
　"　　Mary, and Edward C. Gardiner, Dec. 9, 1799.
　"　　Freelove, and Joseph Morey, Oct. 21, ——.
　"　　Mrs. Ann S., and John A. Shaw ——.
　"　　Ann, and William Northup ——. —, 17—.
　·　　George Washington, of John and Mary, and Anstis Thomas, of Benjamin
　　　　and Anstis; m. by Elder William Northup, Jan. 9, 1800.
　"　　Mar— Anstis, and Gilbert Mott, June 30, 1844.
　"　　Charles A., of William R., and Elizabeth A. Barber, ——.
SMITH John, Jr., and Mercy Wescott; m. by John Eldred, assistant, Jan. 8, 1708.
　"　　Mercy, and William Barber, March 22, 1710.
　"　　Abigail (widow), and Peter Tourgee, April 5, 1722.
　"　　Joseph, and Mary Fones; m. by William Spencer, Justice, Dec. 18, 1724.
　"　　Sarah, and John Weight, Feb. 27, 1728.
　"　　Phillip, and Sarah Briggs; m. by William Spencer, Justice, —— —, 1730-1.
　"　　Simon, and Sarah Co—; m. by Benjamin Weight, Justice, Nov. —, 1739.
　"　　Ephraim, of S. Kingstown, and —— Boone, of N. Kingstown, Feb. 4,
　　　　1741.
　"　　(Mary), and James Huling, Feb. 3, 1745.
　"　　——, and Joshua Pierce April 16, 1747.
　"　　Ichabod, of Jamestown, and Hannah Nichols, of N. Kingstown; m. by
　　　　Elder Samuel Albro, Nov. 25, 1759.
　"　　Precilla, and John Tourgee, Nov. 5, 1761.
　"　　Benjamin, of N. Kingstown, and Ruth Frarers, of S. Kingstown; m. by
　　　　Henry Gardiner, Justice, Dec. 16, 1761.
　"　　Patience, and Benedict Eldred, —— —, 1764.
　"　　Elizabeth, and Thomas Smith, Sept. 14, 1766.
　"　　Thomas, and Elizabeth Smith; m. by George Thomas, Justice, Sept. 14,
　　　　1766.
　"　　Margaret, and Samuel Boone, Jan. 7, 1767.
　"　　Abigail, and John Corey, Nov. 7, 1773.
　"　　Catherine, and William Collins, June 3, 1779.
　"　　Eleanor, and Pearces Austin, Oct. 21, 1779.
　"　　Stephen, and Patience Spooner; m. by George Thomas, Justice, July
　　　　—, 1780.
　"　　——, and Samuel Lawton, May 8, 1781.
　"　　Barbary (widow), and Job Card, June 5, 1782.
　"　　Precilla, and John Austin, Dec. 11, 1783.
　"　　Benjamin, and Mary Austin, June 8, 1788.
　"　　John, of William, dec., of N. Kingstown, and Mary Reynolds, of Ben-
　　　　jamin, of Exeter; m. by Elder Phillip Jenkins, Oct. 16, 1791.
　"　　John, of Benajah and Ruth, and Elizabeth Rose, of James and Thank-
　　　　ful; m. by Elder William Northup, March 17, 1799.

SMITH Elizabeth, and Beriah Brown, —— 30, ——.
" 　John, of S Kingstown, and Abigail ——; m. by George Tibbetts, Justice, May 31, ——.
" 　Joseph, of N. Kingstown, and Scuce Place, of Exeter, ——.
" 　——, and Sarah Havens; m. by William Spencer, Justice, Dec. 19, ——.
" 　——, of Joseph, and Elizabeth Davis, ——.
" 　Nathaniel, and Rebecca Gardiner, ——
" 　Thomas, of Benjamin, and Hannah Martin Boss, of Phillip Martin Boss, of Newport; m. by George Thomas, Justice, Jan. 13, 1811.
" 　Avis Ann, and Oliver Spink, Jan. 28, 1827.
" 　Rachel, and —— Thomas, Sept. 28, 1840.
" 　Mrs. Lydia, and John Cooper, Jan. 19, 1842.
" 　Richard, and Sarah Eldred; m. by Elder Edwin Stillman, March 9, 1846.
SPENCER John, and Sarah Hall; m. by Benjamin Nichols, Justice, Oct. —, 1725,
" 　Johannah, and George Reynolds, Sept. 14, 1729.
" 　Elizabeth, and —— Harrington, July 4, 1731.
" 　John, of E. Greenwich, and Mary Gardiner, of N. Kingstown; m. by William Spencer, Justice, March —, 1739.
" 　John 3d, of E. Greenwich, and Susannah Reynolds, of N. Kingstown; m. by Thomas Hill, Justice, —— 8, 1741.
' 　Elizabeth, and Remington Spencer, Feb. 27, 1757.
" 　Remington, and Elizabeth Spencer, Feb. 27, 1757.
" 　Nathaniel, of William, and Eliza, of E. Greenwich, and Susannah Briggs, of ——, and Mary; m. by Christopher Spencer, Justice, March 16, 1758.
" 　Nicholas, of E. Greenwich, and Abigail Hall, of N. Kingstown; m. by William Hall, Justice, —— —, 1763.
" 　Elizabeth, and John Tibbetts; recorded Aug. 3, 1767.
" 　John, of E. Greenwich, and —— Fones, of Daniel, of N. Kingstown; m. by George Thomas, Justice; recorded Aug. 3, 1767.
" 　Thomas, of E. Greenwich, and Mary Austin, of N. Kingstown; m. by William Hall, Justice, Oct. 15, 1767.
" 　——, and —— Havens, April 5, 1770.
" 　Christopher, and Patience ——; m. by John Northup, Justice, June 24, 1773.
" 　Ebenezer, of John, and Lucy Hall, of William; m. by George Thomas, Justice, July 9, 1775.
" 　——, and —— Pierce, —— —, 1777.
" 　Elizabeth, and Silas Briggs, March 26, 1780.
" 　(William), and Mary Allen; m. by Elder James Wightman, Oct. 22, 1781.
" 　Peleg, of E. Greenwich, and Hannah Greene, of John, of N. Kingstown; m. by George Thomas, Justice, —— 14, 1783.
" 　Audrey, and Samuel Haley, Aug. 25, 1791.
" 　Anna, and Jeremiah Aylesworth, —— —, 1793.
" 　Lydia, and Nathaniel Spink, June 1, 1798.
" 　Ruth, and John Spencer, May 28, ——.
" 　John, and Ruth Spencer; m. by Benjamin Nichols, Justice, May 28, ——.
" 　John, of Christopher, and Hannah Manchester; m. by William Hall, Justice, Feb. 17, ——.
" 　Mercy, and Alexander Nichols, July 13, ——.
" 　Elizabeth, and Benjamin Weight, —— —, 1801.
" 　Elizabeth, and George Chadsey; recorded April 21, 1804.
" 　Henry, of William and Mary, and Ann Brown, of William and Ann; m. by Elder William Northup, July 10, 1806.
" 　Christopher, and Hannah Northup; m. by Elder William Northup; recorded Nov. 22, 1809.
" 　Wanton, of William and Mary, and Sarah Pierce, of Sylvester and Martha; m. by Elder John Gardiner, July 4, 1811.
" 　Mary, and Stephen Congdon, Jan. 17, 1814.
" 　Alice Allen, and Robert Gaddie, May 4, 1845.
SPINK Hannah, and Thomas Jackwise, Oct. 24, 1725.
" 　Eleanor, and John Slocum, Sept. 30, 1756.
" 　Sarah, and John Greene, Dec. 24, 1758.
" 　Rebecca, and Matthew Cooper, April 1, 1763.
" 　Mary, and Stukeley Westcott, Jan. 22, 1764.
" 　(Hannah), and Joshua Davis, May 18, 1766.

SPINK Abigail, and Joshua ——; m. by Robert Hall, Justice, Oct. —, 1769.
"   Margaret, and Job Matteson, Dec. 15, 1772.
"   John, of John, and —ary Weeden, of Daniel; m. by Elder Phillip Jenkins, May 29, 1774.
"   John, of Samuel, dec., and Lydia Eldred, of Joseph; m. by George Thomas, Justice, Dec. 27, 1778.
"   Lucy, and John Northup, —— 1, 1783.
"   Desire (Deliverance) Ann, and Andrew Huling, Oct. 28, 1784.
"   Sarah, and Thomas Eldred, —— 24, 1790.
"   Samuel, of Ishmeal, and Elizabeth Arnold, of Samuel; m. by Elder Phillip Jenkins, Feb. 26, 1798.
"   Nathaniel, of Ishmeal, of N. Kingstown, and Lydia Spencer, of George, of E. Greenwich; m. by Nathaniel Spink, Justice, June 1, 1798.
"   Ann, and Samuel Bissell, Dec. 15, 1798.
"   Abigail, and Nathan Pierce, ——.
"   Benjamin, of E. Greenwich, and Jean ——; m. by George Thomas, Justice, April 7, ——.
"   John, and Sarah Tibbetts; m. by Jeremiah Gould, Justice, (Aug.) 22, (1723).
"   Nicholas, of John, and (Ann) Boone, of Samuel (and Mary), (July 20, 1769).
"   Mary, and Jonathan Reynolds, Jan. 20, 1803.
"   Nicholas, Jr., of Nicholas and Anna, and Hannah Potter, of Robert and Hannah; m. by Elder William Northup, Aug. 12, 1802.
"   Boone, of Nicholas and Anna, and Nancy Tennant, of George and Tabitha; m. by Elder William Northup, April 15, 1803.
"   Ishmeal, of Ishmeal and Waity, and Ruth Dyer, of Samuel and Waity; m. by Elder William Northup, March 19, 1804.
"   Arnold, of Warwick, R. I., and Phebe Essex, of do.; m. by George Tillinghast, Justice, Nov. 3, 1812.
"   Samuel, of —— and Waity, and Hannah Eldred, of Weeden and Mercy; m. by Elder William Northup; recorded Jan. 8, 1814.
"   Oliver, and Avis Ann Smith, of Benjamin; m. by Elder Gershom Palmer, Jan. 28, 1827.
"   ——, and Congdon; recorded June —, 1821.
"   Nicholas N., and Huldah A. Weeden; m. by Rev. B. C. Grafton, July 12, 1837.
"   Samuel, and Ann Cranston, Nov. 9, 1837.
"   Boone, Jr., and Almira Amanda Reynolds; m. by Rev. James R. Stone, Sept. 14, 1840.
"   Margery, and Hazard C. Watson, Oct. 10, 1842.
"   Abbie Ann, and Benjamin H. Congdon, Feb. 12, 1844.
"   Eliza Ann, and Thomas Congdon, Dec. 15, 1845.
"   Daniel, Jr., of Daniel, and Harriet Brown, of Daniel; m. by Elder Joseph W. Allen, Oct. 25, 1847.
"   Frances, and Jonathan C. Waite, Jan. 1, 1849.
"   Nicholas S., and Mary F. Northup; m. by Elder J. A. Tillinghast, Jan. 24, 1850.
"   Avis Ann, and William Brown, Feb. 11, 1850.
"   Eliza, and Henry A. Phillips, Oct. 29, 1860.
"   Silas, and Phebe J. Luther, Jan. 1, 1862.
"   Hannah C., and Charles L. Wightman, Feb. 5, 1866.
SPOONER Patience, and Stephen Smith, July —, 1780.
"   George, of Charles, and Nancy Tillinghast, of Charles; m. by George Thomas, Justice, Sept. 3, 1780.
STAFFORD Mercy, and Caleb Hill, March 23, 1755.
"   Thomas, and Rebecca Hill, of Thomas; m. by Elder John Gorton, Feb. —, 1762.
STONE Rachel, and ——; m. by William Spencer, Justice, —, 1731.
STRAIGHT John, and Sarah Crowell; m. by William Hall, Justice, Nov. 19, 1721.
"   Henry, and ——, July 5, 1733.
"   Joseph, and Mary Card; m. by Elder Benjamin Harrington, May 15, 1735.
"   Roseanna, and John Cutter, Oct. 23, ——.
"   John, of E. Greenwich, and Elizabeth Sunderland, of N. Kingstown; m. by Elder Benjamin Weight, June 17, ——.

STREETER Abbie N., and Alexander G. Greene, ——.
STRETSON Lydia, and Anthony Hathaway, Aug. 7, 1808.
ST—— Hannah, and Robert Westcott, ——.
STUART Betsey, and Thomas R. Congdon, —— 19, 1789.
   "   Thankful, and Stephen Congdon, June 24, 1795.
   "   Cyrus H., and Jane Gorton, ——.
SUNDERLAND Margaret, and —— Anstin. Oct. 25. 1725.
   "   Elizabeth, and John Straight, June 17, ——.
   "   Amle, and —— Gardiner, Jan 22, 1844.
   "   Daniel, and Mary Northup, June 7, 1850.
SWAN Margaret, and Lewis Robinson. July 29, 1769.
SWEET Richard, and Elizabeth Jacques: m. by William Hall, Justice. March 8,
     1704.
   "   Ann. and —— Wightman, Feb. 12, 1729.
   "   Elizabeth, and Benjamin Congdon. Nov. 22, 1722.
   "   Sarah, and Isaac Tripp, June ——, 1729.
   '   Alice, and John West. March ——, 1730-31.
   "   Ruth, and Nathaniel Niles, ——. 3, 1731.
   "   John, and Hannah Gardiner; m. by George Thomas, Justice, March
     ——, 1733-4.
   "   James, of Kingstowne. and Ann Weeden. of Newport; m. by Job Tripp,
     Justice, July 6, 1734.
   "   Bridget, and James Wightman, Sept. 5, 1734.
   "   ——, and Solomon Ceaser (col.), Dec. 12, 1735.
   "   James, and Sarah Daley; m. by Peter Boss, Justice, —— 4, 1736.
   ·   ——, and Mercy Sweet; m. by Samuel Corey, Justice, June ——, 1737.
   "   Mercy, and —— Sweet, June ——, 1737.
   "   —el, and William Rathbun, Dec. 16, 1739.
   ·   Catherine, and Nicholas Whitford, —— 1, 1739.
   "   Benoni, Jr., and Isabel, —— 16, 173—.
   "   Job, of James, and Sarah Kingsley, of John; m. by Samuel Thomas, Jus-
     tice, —— 18, 1753.
   "   Mary, and Sylvester Sherman, July 16, 1758.
   "   —am, and William Sherman, Jan. 28, 1759.
   "   Stephen, and Mary Congdon; m. by Elder James Wightman, Jan. 28, 1776.
   "   Walte, and George Wightman, June 16, 1776.
   "   Lucy, and Job Tibbetts, Oct. 4, 1781.
   "   Godfrey, of Capt. Samuel, of Newport, and Mrs. Henretta Wilrey, of
     John, of N. Kingstown; m. by George Thomas, Justice, Oct 16, 1794.
   "   —— (widow), and Henry Congdon, —— 29, 1795.
   "   Job, and Jemima Sherman; m. by James Gardiner. Justice, ——.
   "   Stephen, late of Charlestown, and Anne Anstin; m. by Nicholas Gardi-
     ner, Justice, Dec. 16, 17—.
   "   Mercy, and John Cleveland, ——. 4, ——.
   "   ——, of —— and Ann, and Sarah Northup of —— and Mary; m. by
     Elder William Northup; recorded Oct. 1, 1816.
   "   Sally, and Charles Leach, March 16, 1843.
   "   Abbie A., and James Burlingame, Dec. 13, 1847.
   "   Edwin A. ot Johnson, R. I., and Mrs. Mercy F. Harvey, of N. Kings-
     town; m. by Elder John Slocum, May 28, 1848.

T

TABOR —— (widow), and Robert Sherman, March 25, 1768.
TALFORD Margery, and John Northup, Dec. 25, 1771.
TANNER John, and Susannah West, of Frances; m. by William Hall, Justice,
     May 9, 1723.
   "   William, and Elizabeth Reynolds; m. by William Spencer, Justice, March
     ——, 1729.
   "   Benjamin, and Abigail Tripp; m. by Job Tripp, Justice, July 20, 1734.
   "   Paymen, and Mary Hill; m. by George Tibbetts, Justice, Jan. —, 1737-8.
   "   ——, and Edward Greene, April 28, 1739.
   "   Anis, and Charles ——; m. by William Hall, Justice. Jan. —, 1760.

TANNER Frances, and Roseanna Hunt; m. by William Hall, Justice, Feb. 1, 1761.
"   Mercy, and Joshua Gardiner, Feb. 22, 1763.
"   Mary, and John Briggs, Dec. 25, 1763.
"   Benjamin, and Sarah Aylesworth, of Arthur; m. by Caleb Hill, Justice, —— —, 1765.
"   Nathan, and Patience Austin; m. by William Hall, Justice, Feb. 28, 1768.
"   Anne, and William Brown, Sept. 2, 1768.
"   Ruth, and Christopher Jenkins, Sept. 26, 1770.
"   Palmer, of Benjamin, and Margeret Austin, of James; m. by Elder Nathan Hill, Dec. 17, 1789.
"   Benjamin, of Benjamin and Sarah, and Rebecca Fones, of John and Ruth; m. by Elder William Northup, Sept. 25, 1799.
"   Mary, and Jonathan Reynolds, Sept. 4, ——.
"   Betsey, and William Pierce, July 3, 1803.
"   Benjamin, of Palmer, and —— Hunt, of William; m. by Rev. Thomas Manchester, April 16, 1815.
"   James, of N. Kingstown, son of Palmer, and Elizabeth Nason, of David, of Newport; m. by Samuel Hunt, Justice, Oct. 14, 1816.
"   Margeret C., and Edmund A. Brown, March 25, 1849.
TARBOX Ruth, and Daniel Bidelcome, April 27, 1760.
TAYLOR Ruth, and George Waite, Jan. 9, 1820.
"   Mercy A., and Pardon M. Arnold, Dec. 23, 1845.
"   Lydia S., and Samuel C. Kingsley, Jan. 7, 1835.
"   Phebe, and Zarobabel Westcott, Jan. 1, 17—.
"   Mercy Ann, and Simeon Matteson, ——.
"   Mercy, and ——.
TEFFT Esther, and Thomas Mumford, Sr., Nov. 25, 1708.
"   Joanna, and John Webb, April 23, 1721.
"   Robert, of Exeter, and Martha Reynolds, of N. Kingstown; m. by Robert Hall, Justice, —— 24, 1769.
TENNANT Nancy, and Boone Spink, of Nicholas, April 15, 1803.
TERRY Ebenezer, and Mary Helme; m. by Rouse Helme, Justice, Nov. 30, 1721.
"   David, and Sukey Hunt; m. by Rev. S. G. Smith, Feb. 4, 1838.
TEW Mary, and George Himes, Feb. 15, 1815.
THOMAS Sarah, and Jonathan Nichols, June 9, 1723.
"   George, and Elizabeth Phillips (widow); m. by William Spencer, Justice, Feb. 9, 1738.
"   Samuel, and Ruth Gould, Feb. —, 1739.
"   ——, and John Tillinghast, Sept. 21, 1742.
"   George, of Samuel, of N. Kingstown, and Phebe Lockwood, of Warwick, R. I.; m. by Elder Charles Holden, Sept. 25, 1763.
"   George, and Hannah Arnold; m. by George Northup, Justice, April 15, 1764.
"   Waite, and Samuel Northup, Feb. 25, 1779.
"   Mary, and Gideon Gardiner, Jan. 3, 1782.
"   George, of Samuel, and Phebe Lockwood, of Amos, of Warwick, R. I.; m. by Rev. Charles Holden, (prob. recorded) July 10, 1784.
"   George, of N. Kingstown, son of Samuel, dec., and Martha Aylesworth, of Phillip, dec., of E. Greenwich; m. by Elder John Gorton, Aug. 19, 1787.
"   George, Jr., and Phebe Davis, of Benjamin; m. by Elder Nathan Hill, Nov. 15, 1787.
"   Hannah, and Phillip Cooke, Feb. 15, 1799.
"   ——, and Rose Allen, ——.
"   Samuel, and —— Marsh, of Plainfield, ——.
"   Daniel, of —— and Phebe, and —— Davis, of Benjamin, and Phebe; m. by Elder William Northup, rec., March 29, ——.
"   Alice, and —— Tillinghast, ——.
"   Abbie Ann, and Sylvester R. Franklin, ——.
"   Anstis, and George Washington Slocum, Jan. 9, 1800.
"   Benjamin, of George and Phebe, and Elizabeth Thomas, of George and Hannah; m. by Elder William Northup, March 27, 1800.
"   Elizabeth, and Benjamin Thomas, March 27, 1800.

THOMAS Arnold, of George, and Audrey Burlingame, of Deacon Elisha, of W.
    Greenwich; m. by Elder Thomas Manchester, —— 22, 1801.
" ——, and James Eldred Brown, July 2, 1802.
" Samuel, of Samuel and Penelope, and Anna Lawton, of Edward and An-
    na; m. by Elder William Northup, —— —, 1806.
" William, of George, Jr., and Mary Carr, of Samuel: m. by George Thomas,
    Justice, Jan. 1, 1808.
" Brudah, of Chloe, and Isabel Gardiner, of Betsey; m. by George Thomas,
    Justice, June 16, 1808.
" Anstis, and Oliver Arnold, Aug. 4, 1811.
" George W., of Daniel, of N. Kingstown, and Sarah Ann Williams, of
    Ebenezer, of E. Greenwich; m. by Elder Pardon Tillinghast; rec. May
    31, 1826.
" Sally G., and Samuel Merrett, Jan. 24, 1830.
" Eliza A., and Abel S. Baker, Dec. 30, 1839.
" ——, and Rachel Smith; m. by Rev. John H. Rouse, Sept. 28, 1840.
" Isaac K., and Elizabeth R. Vaughn; m. by Rev. J. R. Stone, Aug. 31,
    1841.
" ——, and Anne Shaw, dau. of Rev. Lemuel Burge; m. by Rev. John H.
    Rouse, Aug. 9, 1844.
" Clara H., and George Leroy Champlain, —— —, 1847.
" John, and Leucy Ann Watson; m. by Elder Preserved Greene, July 15,
    1849.
" George S., and Abbie O. Northnp; m. by Rev. A. B. Flanders, Sept. 15,
    1861.
THURBER Mary, and Alexander Brown, Jan. 2, 1790.
THURSTON Mrs. Hannah, and Capt. Daniel Congdon, Jan. 24, 1797.
" Adam M., of Westport, Mass., and Lucy C. Harvey, of N. Kingstown;
    m. by Elder John Slocum, April 2, 1848.
" Alfred, of George, of Rhode Island, and Mary E. Baten, of Warwick, R.
    I.; m. by Rev. C. C. Lewis, May 12, 1849.
TIBBETTS (John), of Henry, and Elizabeth Hazzard; m. at E. Greenwich, ——.
    7, 1705.
" Ann, and Immanuel Northup, May 4, 1721.
" Martha, and John Reynolds, Nov. 2, 1721.
" Henry, of George, and Hannah Reynolds, of John; m. by Robert Hall,
    Justice, Nov. 3, 1734.
" Dorcus, and Joseph Reynolds, May 23, 1756.
" George, and Susannah Wall; m. by Robert Hall, Justice, Dec. 11, 1760.
" Nathaniel, of George, dec., and Waite Wall, of Henry; m. by George
    Northup, Justice, Feb. 15, 1766.
" John, of Henry, of E. Greenwich, and Elizabeth Spencer, of John, of
    Warwick; m. by Caleb Hill, Justice; recorded Aug. 3, 1767.
" Mrs. Martha, and Francis Reynolds, Oct. 25, 1772.
' Job, of ——, and Lucy Sweet, of James; m. by George Thomas, Justice,
    Oct. 4, 1781.
" Alice, and John Pierce, April 13, ——.
" Elizabeth, and Thomas Hill, ——.
" Sarah, and John Spink, Aug. 22, 1725.
" Mary, and Caleb Greene, Jan. 24, ——.
TILLINGHAST John, of E. Greenwich, and —— Thomas, of N. Kingstown; m. by
    Thomas Hill, Justice, Sept. 21, 1742.
" John, and Mercy Greene, of David; m. by Jeffrey Watson, Justice, Feb.
    14, 1754.
" Thomas, of Phillip, of E. Greenwich, and Mary Hill, of Thomas, of N. Kings-
    town; m. by Elder John Gorton, Aug. 27, 1762.
" Nancy, and George Spencer, Sept. 3, 1780.
" Elisha, and Deliverance Pierce, of E. Greenwich, ——.
" ——, and Alice Thomas, ——.
" Joseph R., of Phillip, and Anne Tillinghast, of John and Ruth, July 31,
    180—.
" Anne, and Joseph R. Tillinghast, July 31, 180—.
" George, of George and Mary, and Susan Fldred, of Robert and Sarah; m.
    by Elder William Northup, Sept. 4, 1806.
" Anne, and —— Tillinghast, rec. Nov. 27, 1815.

TILLINGHAST ——, of Benjamin and Ann, of E. Greenwich, and Anne Tillinghast,
    of Phillip and Frances, of N. Kingstown; m. by Elder William Northup,
    rec. Nov. 27, 1815.
    "   Harriet E., and Pardon A. Tillinghast, March 3, 1850.
    "   Pardon, and Harriet E. Tillinghast, both of E. Greenwich; m. by Rev.
    Alfred H. Taylor, March 3, 1850.
    "   ——, of Sterling, Conn., son of George, and Mary A. Reynolds, of Rich-
    mond, dau. of Robert; m. by Rev. C. C. Lewis, recorded —— 27, 1850.
TOLMAN Mary, and Rufus Northup, March 30, 1768.
    "   ——, and Thomas Cutter, rec. July 8, 1763.
TOOTHACKER Samuel Allen, of Charles, of Clemsford. Mass., and Elizabeth Brown,
    of Daniel, of N. Kingstown; m. by Elder Joseph W. Allen, July 26, 1838.
TOURGEE Peter, of Prudence Island, and Mary Smith, of Abigail, widow of Wil-
    liam, dec., April 5, 1722.
    "   Abigail, and Benjamin Dimond, Sept. 27, 1753.
    "   John, and Priscilla Smith; m. by Joseph Coggeshall, Justice, Nov. 5, 1761.
    "   Peter, Jr., and Bridget Hill; m. by Elder James Wightman, Dec. 6, 1775.
    "   Patience, and Jonathan Lewis, Feb. 7, 1776.
    "   Prudence, and William Hunt, Feb. 4, 1783.
    "   Harriet, and William Oatley, June 19, 1843.
    ·   Mrs. Harriet, and Charles F. Dyre, July 21, 1845.
    "   Thomas M., of N. Kingstown, and Melissa Porter, of New York; m. by
    Rev. Daniel Avery, July 27, 1845.
    "   Henry S., of Phillip and Peggy, and Elizabeth Congdon, of George and
    Patience; m. by Rev. A. J. Chaplain, Nov. 13, 1848.
    ·   John F., and Martha F. Shippee; m. by Elder John Slocum, Aug. —, 1860.
TRIPP Peleg, of S. Kingstown, and Mary Gardiner, of N. Kingstown; m. by Wil-
    liam Spencer, Justice, J—— 28, 1728.
    "   Mary, and John Dawley, ——. 1, 1729-30.
    "   Ann, and Robert Moon, Jan. —, 1729.
    "   Isaac, and Sarah Sweet; m. by William Spencer, Justice, June —, 1729.
    '   Abigail, and Benjamin Tanner, July 29, 1734.
    "   ——, and Deborah Cleaveland, of Exeter, March 8, 1743.
    "   William, and Mary ——leaches; m. by Job Tripp, Justice, —— —, ——.
TROWBRIDGE Alice, and ——, Justice, April —, 1709.
TUCKER Abigail, and Thomas Eldred, Oct. 12, 1727.
    "   ——, and Sally B. Waite, of Joseph and Mary; m. by Rev. A. J Chap-
    lain, rec., April 5, 1847.
    "   Benjamin P., and Sarah F. Cranston, ——.
TURNER Jonathan, and Elizabeth Paine, June 9, 1709.

U

UNDERWOOD Ruth, and Caleb Allen, ——.
    " Harriet, and Joseph Shaw, May 1, 1843.
UPDIKE Hannah, and Thomas Hazard, May —, 1738.
    "   Daniel E., and Elizabeth Wall; m. by Elder Phillip Jenkins, Feb. 3, 1788.
    ·   Sarah, and David Hagan, Feb. 10, 1807.
UTTER (Ann), of William, of Warwick, R I., and (Benjamin) Greene, of N. Kings-
    town, Jan. or June —, 1743-4.

V

VALLETT Jeremiah, of N. Kingstown, and Anne Bissell, of John, of do.; m. by
    Immanuel Northup, Justice, Dec. 27, 1753.
VAUGHN Isaac, and ——; m. by Daniel Coggeshall, Justice, Feb. 14, 1730.
    "   Mary, and James Congdon, March 30, 1732.
    "   Merabah, and ——; m. by William Spencer, Justice, Jan. —, 1736.
    "   Jonathan, of Isaac, and Elizabeth Gould; m. at E. Greenwich by Thomas
    Aldrich, Justice, Jan. 1, 1736.
    "   John, and Sarah Havens; m. by William Hall, Justice, April 9, 1761.
    "   Mary, and John Whitford, Jr., March 22, 1767.
    "   Ruth, and Nathaniel Lovell, Nov. 1, 1772.

VAUGHN Sarah (widow), and Henry Congdon, Feb. 8, 1787.
" Royal, of N. Kingstown, son of Robert, of E. Greenwich, and Adelaide Anthony, of N. Kingstown; m. by Elder Nathan Hill, Aug. 17, 1792
" Jonathan, and Mary Austin; m. by Nicholas Gardiner, Justice, Jan. 11, 1796.
" ——, of Warwick, R. I., and Abial S., of William, of N. Kingstown.
" Elizabeth, and Stukeley Himes, Jan. 13, 1803.
" Elizabeth, and Jeremiah Carpenter, Feb. 5, 1809.
" Pardon, of Robert, of W. Greenwich, and Sarah Carpenter, of Ephraim, of S. Kingstown; m. by Elder Thomas Manchester, March 4, 1809.
" Elizabeth R., and Isaac K. Thomas, Aug. 31, 1841.

W

WAIT Susannah, and Moses Barber, March 22, 1691-2.
WALL Henry, and Hannah Gould; m. by Thomas Hill, Justice, —— 13, 1742.
" Hannah, and John Allen, —— —, 1743.
" ——, and Joseph Congdon, Jan. 10, 1754.
" Susannah, and George Tibbetts, Dec. 11, 1760.
" Waite, and Nathaniel Tibbetts, Feb. 15, 1766.
" Jeremiah, of Henry, and Sarah Phillips, of Capt. Christopher; m. by George Thomas, Justice, Sept. 25, 1768.
" William, of Henry and —— Reynolds, of John; m. by Elder Phillip Jenkins, Nov. 17, 1771.
" Mary, and Samuel Nichols, March 16, 1783.
" Elizabeth, and Daniel E. Updike,, Feb. 3,, 1788.
" Samuel, and ——; m. by Francis Chappell, Justice, Nov. 29, 1818.
" Daniel,, of Jeremiah, and Elizabeth C. Hiscox, of Thomas J.; m. by Rev. John H. Rouse, Feb. 3, 1849.
WALMESLEY Sarah, and William Ceaser (colored), March 25, 1768.
WANTON ——, and Dorcas Aylesworth; m. by Christopher Spencer, Justice, Feb. 27, 1758.
WARNER Anna, and (Samuel) Brown, April 24, 1707.
" Martha, and Sylvester Pierce, Jan. 26, 1775.
" Susannah, and Phineus Jenkins, July 19, 1787.
" ——, and Anne Allen, Dec. 13, ——.
" Ruth, and James Cooper, —— 28, ——.
WART Benjamin, of Benjamin, of E. Greenwich, and Mary Clarke, of Thomas and Sarah, of N. Kingstown; m. by Elder William Northup, Jan. 24, 1805.
WATSON Mary, and Edward Slocum, Aug. 20, 1741.
" Dorcas, and ——; m. by George Thomas, Justice, Aug. 10, 1736.
" Frances, and Moses Slocum, Aug. 21, 1746.
" Hannah, and Joshua Allen, Sept. 13, 1750.
" Samuel, and —— Reynolds, of Jo——, dec.; m. by George Thomas, Justice, May 21, 1784.
" Sarah, and Amos Gardiner, Jan. 7, 1794.
" Samuel, and Hannah ——; m. by Benjamin Weight, Justice, March 14, ——.
" John, and Abigail Eldred; m. by Elisha Cole, Assistant, March 14, ——.
" Sylvester, of Benjamin, dec., and Abigail Hall, of Slocum, dec.; m. by George Thomas, Justice, June —, 1802.
" Mrs. Patience, and Alexander Gardiner, Nov. 25, 1802.
" John, of Wheeler, of Windham, Greene Co., N. Y., and —— L. Watson, of John and Mary, of S. Kingstown; m. by Elder William Northup; rec. May 23, 1831.
" —— L., and John Watson; rec. May 23, 1831.
" Hazard C., and Margery Spink; m. by Eld. John Slocum, Oct. 10, 1842.
" Lucy Ann, and John Thomas, July 15, 1849.
WEAVER William, of East Greenwich, and —— ——; m. by George Tibbetts, Justice, —— 27, 1735.
" Mary, and Samuel Hunt, May 2, 1762.
" Waitey, and Henry Congdon, Feb. 5, 1816.
WEBB George, and Mary Hannah; m. by Christopher Allen, Justice, April 21, 1708.
" John, and Joanna Tefft; m. by Rouse Helme, Justice, April 28, 1721.
(Vit. Rec., Vol. 5.) 4

WEEDEN Ann, and James Sweet, July 6, 1734.
"   William, and ——— Fowler; m. by William Hall, Justice, Nov. —, 1755.
"   Martha and ——— Eldred, April —. 1759.
"   —ay, and John Spink, May 29, 1774.
"   William, of Daniel, of Jamestown, and Margeret Brown, of John, of N
            Kingstown; m. by George Thomas, Justice, March 29, 1781.
"   Arnold, of Jamestown, and Nancy Gardiner of N. Kingstown; m. by
            Elder Nathan Hill, Nov. 16, 1783.
"   Daniel, of John, of S. Kingstown, and Martha Pierce, of Mercy, of N.
            Kingstown; m. by Elder Phillip Jenkins, Jan. 14, 1796.
"   Peleg, of Benjamin and Susannah, and Mary Fowler, of Benjamin and
            Freelove; m. by Elder William Northup, ——, 5, 1803.
"   Freelove N., and Gideon Freeborne, Nov. 13, 1825.
"   Merchant, of Daniel and Penelope D. Aylesworth; m. by Elder Pardon
            Tillinghast; rec. Feb. 14, 1829.
"   Hudlah A., and Nicholas N. Spink, July 12, 1837.
"   Samuel, and Eliza Hazard; m. by Elder David Avery ———. March 13,
            1844.
"   Ann, and Benjamin Anthony, May 18, 1845.
WEIGHTMAN John, and Jane Bentley, Jan. 6, 1700.
"   (Valentine), and Susannah Holmes; m. by William Hall, Justice, Feb. 17,
            1702-3.
"   Sarah, and ——— Whitford, —— —, 1722-3.
"   ———. and Ann Sweet; m. by William Hall, Assistant, Feb. 12, 1729.
"   John, and ——— ———, of Newport; m. by Job Lawton, Justice, June 4,
            1729.
"   James, of John, and Bridget Sweet, of Samuel; m. by Robert Hall, Jus-
            tice, Sept. 5, 1734.
"   Deborah, and John Reynolds, —— 22, 1759.
"   Paul, and Hannah Whitman; m. by George Thomas, Justice, June 23, 1772.
"   James, of Valentine, and Mercy Carr, of Caleb; m. by George Thomas,
            Justice, Feb. 1, 1776.
"   George, of N. Kingstown, and Waite Sweet, of E. Greenwich; m. by Elder
            James Wightman, June 16, 1776.
"   Frederic, of George, Jr., and Sarah Br———, of Samuel; m. by Elder Phil-
            lip Jenkins, April 19, 1778.
"   Mary, and James Boone, April 19, 1778.
"   Elizabeth, and George Fowler, Dec. 10, 1781.
"   Patty, and Benjamin Cole, Nov. 2, 1783.
"   Elizabeth, and Robert Havens, —— —, ———.
"   Alice, and Job Harrington, June 8, 1722.
"   Almira W., and Henry T. Chadsey, June 13, 1830.
"   ———, and ——— ———; m. by Elder Joseph W. Allen, Sept. 4, 1833.
"   Mary G., and Horace J. Shippee, March 8, 1847.
"   Sarah B., and Beriah H. Lawton, Nov. 4, 1847.
"   Susan W., and Edwin Montgomery, April —, 1850.
"   Charles L., and Hannah C. Spink, Feb. 5, 1866.
WEIGHT ———, and Elizabeth Sheffield; m. by William Spencer, Justice, Oct. 17,
            1717.
"   John, and Sarah Smith; m. by William Spencer, Justice, Feb. 27, 1728.
"   ———, and Abigail Hull; m. by William Spencer, Justice, ———.
"   Joseph, Jun., and Elizabeth, Dec. 29, ———.
"   Benjamin, of Benjamin, and Suah, of Exeter, and Elizabeth Spencer, of
            William and Mercy; m. by Elder William Northup, ——, 1801.
"   George, and Ruth Taylor, Jan. 9, 1820.
"   Mary C., and David S. Baker, June 14, 1842.
"   Sally B., and ——— Tucker; rec. April 5, 1847.
"   Jonathan C., of George, and Frances Spink, of Thomas; m. by Rev. A. J.
            Judson, Jan. 1, 1849.
WELLS Mary, and David Whitford, April 5, 1722.
"   Benjamin, and Mary Jurdon; m. by William Spencer, Justice, Jan. 21,
            1730.
"   John, and ———; m. at Colchester, Conn., by John Bulkeley, Justice, Nov.
            12, 1732.
"   Peter, and ———, Nov. 4, ———.

WELLS ——ab, late of Greenwich, now of N. Kingstown, and ——, late of New Shoreham; m. by George Thomas, Justice, Nov. 16, 17—.

WESCOTT Mercy, and John Smith, Jr., Jan. 8, 1708.
" ——, and Mary Dare, Aug. 17, 1718.
" Mary, and Joshua Sanford, Jan. 9, 1757.
" Stukeley, and Mary Spink; m. by Elder Samuel Albro, Jan. 22, 1764.
" Zorobabel, and Mary Davis, Aug. 17, ——.
" Robert, of N. Kingstown, and Hannah St——, of E. Greenwich; m. at E. Greenwich, ——.
" Zorobabel, and Phebe Taylor; m. by John Spencer, Justice, Jan. 1, 17—.
" —— E., and Arnold Place, Sept. 9, 1800.

WEST Susannah, and Moses Barber, March 20 or 24, 1691-2.
" Susannah, and John Tanner, May 9, 1723.
" John, and Alice Sweet; m. by William Spencer, Justice, March —, 1730-1.
" ——, and Edmund ——; m. by William Spencer, Justice, Aug. 22, 1731.
" ——, and Sarah Baker; m. by William Spencer, Justice, Nov. 7, 1731.
" Martha, and —— Card, March 4, ——.
" Lucy Ann, and Benjamin Rookes, July 9, 1843.

WHITEMAN George, of Thomas, of Warwick, R. I., and Abbie E. Gardiner, of David, dec., of N. Kingstown; m. by Elder Edwin Stillman, March 9, 1845.

WHITE Oliver, and Mary Harmon; m. by Jeffrey Champlain, Justice, Jan. 21, 1747.

WHITFORD David, and Mary Wells; m. by Elisha Cole, Assistant, April 5, 1722.
" ——, and Sarah Weightman; m. by Elisha Cole, Assistant, —— —, 1722-3.
" Paske, Jr., and Deborah Fowler; m. by Frances Willett, Justice, July 5, 1723.
" Nicholas, of E. Greenwich, and Catherine Sweet, of N. Kingston; m. by Benjamin Weight, Justice, —— 1, 1739.
" John, Jr., of John, of Exeter, and Mary Vaughn, of Isaac, of N. Kingstown; m. by George Thomas, Justice, March 22, 1767.
" Elizabeth, and George Hunt, Dec. 6, 1788.
" John P., of Thomas, and Patience, and Mary Cooper, of Gilbert, and Elizabeth; m. by Elder William Northup, Aug. 5, 1803.
" Ezekiel, and —— ——, Dec. 17. ——.
" Lydia, and John Sherman, April 24, ——.
" Robert, of E. Greenwich, and Margaret Fones, of N. Kingstown; m. by William Spencer, Justice, May 10, ——.
" Sarah, and —— Mitchell, ——.

WHITMAN Mary, and William Hookey, April 17, 1760.
" Hannah, and Paul Weightman, June 23, 1772.
" Valentine, and —— Olin, ——.

WHITMARSH Micab, of E. Greenwich, and Ann Arnold, of N. Kingstown; m. by Elder James Wightman, June 12, 1774.

WICKHAM ——, and Mary Place; m. by John Eldred, Assistant, May 23, 1707.

WILCOX Jeffrey, and Sarah Himes; m. by William Hall, Justice, April 24, 1726.
" Mary, and William Greene, March, 30, 1809.
" Hannah, and Enock Place, March, —, ——.
" Thomas, and —— ——, ——.

WILKES ——, and Mary Crowder; m. by William Hall, Assistant, Jan. 14, 1732 3.

WILKEY Mrs. Henrietta, and Godfrey Sweet, Oct. 16, 1794.

WILBOR Scipeo, and Jemima Sigworth, (c.l.), Nov. 11, 1743.
" Abner, and Sarah Rathbone, Feb. 8, 1753.

WILLIAMS Sarah Ann, and George W. Thomas; recorded May 31, 1826.
" Rebecca, and William Dean, Oct. 11, 1847.

WILLIS James, and —— ——, Oct. 18, 1732.
" Mary R., and George A. Mitchell, Oct. 13, 1844.
" Jeremiah, of Abel, and Penelope, of New Shoreham, and Jane C. Brown, of Samuel, and Susanna, of Goshen, N. Y.; m. by Rev. A. J. Chaplain, March 18, 1847.
" Elizabeth A., and Stephen Northup, Feb. 14, 1850.

WILLETT Ann, and —— ——; m. by John Eldred, Justice, ——.

WILSON ——, and John Phillips, —— —, 1735.

WILSON Joanna (widow), and James Eldred, June 8, 1803.
WOODWORTH Charles F., of Monson, Mass., and Mariah W. Chadsey, of Jeremiah G., of N. Kingstown; m. by Rev. A. J. Chaplain, Nov. 30, 1846.
WOOD Mary, and James Aylesworth, Feb. 8, 1733 or 9.
WO—— Phebe, and Samuel Browning, ——.
WRIGHT William (mulatto), and Dinah Berry, (Indian); m. by Daniel Coggeshall, Justice, Feb. 13, 1734.

X Y Z

YORK Edward, and Mary Fones; m. by Samuel Thomas, Justice, Jan. —, 1755.
YOUNG Margaret, and —— Rouse, Dec. 28, 1776.
  "   Mary, and Ichabod Sherman, ——.

NO NAME.

——, of E. Greenwich, and Susannah ——, of N. Kingstown; m. by William Spencer, Justice, April 7, ——.
Caleb, of Westerly, and Elizabeth, ——, of N. Kingstown; m. by William Spencer, Justice, March 16, 1735.

NORTH KINGSTOWN.

BIRTHS AND DEATHS.

(A list of the Births and Deaths of North Kingstown, including Old Kings
Towne, from the Clerk's Records and other sources.)

A

AIRS ——, (dau.) of Thomas and Sarah,		Nov. 23, 1696.
" Sarah,		May 8, 1698.
ALBRO Elizabeth, of John and Barbary,		April 17, 1731.
" ——ston.		Aug. 10, 1735.
" Barbary,		Oct. 27, 1737.
" William,		Feb. 25, ——.
" ——,		Sept. 2, ——.
" Jeremiah, of John and Freeborn,		June —, ——,
" Eunice,		March —, ——.
" Margaret,		Aug. 5, ——.
" ——,		June 27, ——.
" ——, (son)		June 27, ——.
" Mary, born		—— —, ——.
ALDRICH ——, (dau.) of David and Sarah,		April 5, 1734.
" ——,		July 3, 1736.
" ——,		March 29, 1750.
ALLEN James, of Christopher and Elizabeth,		June 15, 1688.
" Rouse, of Matthew and Elizabeth,		Sept. 24, 1701.
" Caleb,		Feb. 27, 1704.
" Benjamin,		April 21, 1707.
" Joshua,		Aug. 19, 1710.
" Elizabeth,		June 20, 1713.
" ——ret, of Thomas, and Ann, Aug. 3, 1714.		
" ——,		Oct. 10, 1716.
" Samuel,		Oct. 21, 1718.
" Elizabeth,		May 13, 1722.
" ——,		April 23, 1724.
" ——,		Aug. 30, 1729.
" Christopher,		Oct. 26, 1731,
" ——tha,		Jan. 28, 1734-5.
" Bathsheba,		Aug. 1, 1738.
" Elizabeth, of Caleb, and Mercy, July 23, 1725.		
" ——,		June 10, ——.
" ——,		Aug. 21, ——.
" ——, (dau.),		June 10, ——.
" ——,		—— —, ——.
" ——,		—— —, ——.
" ——, (dau.), of Thomas, Jr., and Patience, Oct. 20, 1742.		
" ——, (son),		March 26, 1745.
" ——, (son),		March 20, 1748.
" Sarah, of Daniel and Sarah,		Dec. 8, 17—.
" David Sprague,		April 25, 175—.
" Stephen Olney,		Sept. 17, 17—.
" Thomas, of Joshua and Hannah,		Dec. 14, ——.
" Elizabeth,		Dec. 14, ——.

ALLEN Sophia, of Joshua and Hannah,	May 13, 1753.
" Phebe,	—9, 175–.
" Mary,	Dec. 18, 175–.
" Caleb,	Nov. 5, 17–.
" Hannah,	July 7, 17–.
" Anna,	Feb. 17, 17–.
" —— (dau.)	Jan. 27, 17–.
" ——, (dau.)	June 5, 17–.
" ——, (dau.)	July 3, 17–.
" ——mwell, of Nathan and Mary (Reynolds),	May 23, 1779.
" Susanna (dau.)	(May 12,) 1780.
" Elizabeth, (dau.)	Dec. 22, 1782.
" ——, (dau.) of Samuel and Prudence,	Nov. —, 1772.
" ——,	Dec. 25, 1775.
" ——,	June 29, 1776.
" ——, (son)	Feb. 1, 1780.
" Lucretia, of ——, and Mary,	June 2, ——.
" Patience,	May 31, 17–.
" Catherine,	July 3, 177–.
" Thomas Gould, (E. G.)	Sept. 1, 177–.
" Lydia, of —— and Martha,	July 28, 178–.
" John,	May 29, 1788.
" Christopher,	Oct. 31, 1789.
" Ray Greene,	Nov. 22, 1793.
" Mary Gould,	June 25, 1795.
" Samuel,	Sept. 21, 1797.
" Samuel, 2d,	Oct. 21, 1799.
" Lucy Ann,	March 16, 1801.
" ——, of Jeffrey and Sarah,	Aug. 24, 1798.
" ——,	May 13, 1800.
" ——,	March 3, ——.
" ——, —— of Thomas,	March 22, 1803.
" ——,	May 14, 1804.
" Samuel Greene,	Aug. 15, 1805.
" Susan Tillinghast,	Feb. 28, 1807.
" George W. Tillinghast,	July 18, 1809.
" Alice Ann, of Thomas,	Feb. 7, 1813.
" Thomas, Jr.,	June 23, 1814.
" Nicholas Tillinghast,	Dec. 28, 1815.
" Julia Ann,	Aug. 16, 1818.
" Thomas, of Christopher and Margaret,	Aug. 24, ——.
" ——(son) of John and Anna,	March 17, ——.
" ——,	Aug. 29, ——.
" ——,	Nov. 23, ——.
" ——,	April 24, ——.
" ——,	May —, ——.
" Samuel, born ——, died	—— —, ——.
" Hannah, —— —— 26, ——	—— —, ——.
" Matthew, —— —— 14,	—— —, ——.
" Christopher, —— —— —, ——	—— —, ——.
" Thomas, of Jeffrey and Elizabeth,	Dec. 15, ——.
" Samuel, of Benjamin and Elizabeth,	April —, ——.
" ——,	Aug. 24, ——.
" —— and	April 19, ——.
" Mary,	May 21, ——.
" Martha,	April 18, ——.
" Freelove,	May 26, ——.
" Silas,	Aug. 15, ——.
" Christopher,	Feb. 3, ——.
" Benjamin,	Oct. 8, ——.
" Elizabeth,	Oct. 8, ——.
ARMSTRONG Jane, of Michael and Lydia,	Jan. 2, ——.
" Susannah,	July 3, ——.
" Thomas,	Jan. 10, ——.
" George,	Aug. 2, ——.

ARMSTRONG ——, of Michael and Lydia,	—— —, ——.
" ——,	—— —, ——.
" ——,	—— —, ——.
ARNOLD Elizabeth, of Samuel and Mary,	Nov. 6, ——.
" Alice,	April 13, ——.
" Susannah,	Jan. 3, ——.
" Joseph,	Sept. 16, ——.
" Jonathan Nichols,	Aug. 6, ——.
Above recorded March 17, 1779.	
" Edmund, of Joseph and Hannah,	Dec. 8, 17—.
" Dorcas,	Aug. 1, 17—.
" Hannah, (b. Exeter),	July 31, 17—.
" Joseph, (b. Exeter), of Peleg and Margaret,	Sept. 19, 1779.
" ——, (son),	Sept. 6, 1781.
" ——, (son), (N. K.),	June 18, 1783.
" ——, (son), (N. K.),	May 23, 1785.
" Mary,	Aug. 9, 1787.
" —nna,	Nov. 3, 1791.
AUSTIN James, of Edmund and Mary,	June 14, 173—.
" ——,	—ber —, ——.
" ——, (dau.),	—, 10, ——.
" ——, (dau.),	Nov. 10, ——.
" ——, (dau.),	Sept. 22, 176—.
" ——, (son),	Aug. 30, 1767.
" ——, (dau.),	Aug. 18, 1769.
" Margaret,	Sept. 30, 1771.
" ——, (son),	Oct. 24, 1773.
" —ll, (son),	July 7, 1775.
" ——, (dau.),	March 31, 1777.
" ——, of John,	June 20, 1784.
" ——, (dau.),	April 5, 1786.
" William,	Sept. 22, 1788.
" Elizabeth,	July 1, 1790.
" Nichols,	Nov. 13, 1792.
" Stephen Sweet,	March 29, 1794.
" John,	June 1, 1797.
" Patience Ann, of Russell and Katey,	Aug. 4, 1805.
" George W.,	Oct. 20, 1807.
" Penelope,	March 27, 1810.
" Henry, Jun.,	Jan. 13, ——.
" Sarah, of Paske and Mary,	July 26, ——.
" Margaret,	June 9, ——.
" Gideon,	July 16, ——.
" Daniel,	July —, ——.
" Pasque,	March 30, ——
" Isaac,	March 10, ——.
" Hannah,	April 1, ——.
AYLESWORTH Arthur, of Arthur,	Nov. 15, 176—.
" Wm. Pearce, of Sam'l R., and Alce (Chadsey),	Sept. 9, 18—.
" Benjamin,	April 12, 18—.
(They had six others.)	
" Eunice, of Dyre and Mary,	Dec. —, ——.
" Ezra,	Feb. 5, ——.
" Mary,	March —, ——.
" Hannah Savage, of Isaac and Sarah, (Cory; m. April 18, 1808), Oct. 29, ——.
" Isaac,	Feb. —, ——.
" Anne, of Christopher and Phebe,	March 18, ——.
" Russell, (of Jeremiah and Phoebe (Allen),	—. —, ——.
" Elizabeth,	—. —, ——.
" George,	Sept. 15, ——.
" Rachel,	March 29, ——.
" Phillip,	March 29, ——.
" Phillip,	d. following December.
" William,	Dec. 22, ——.
" Dyre,	Jan. 11, ——.

AYLESWORTH Dyre, of Jeremiah and Phoebe (Allen), d. following Sept. 15, ——.
"   Caleb,   Nov. 11, ——.
"   Allen,   June 11, ——.
"   Isaac,   Jan. 6, ——.
"   Samuel Rhodes,   Feb. —, ——.
"   Phebe Ann,   May 7, ——.
"   Charles,   March 18, ——.
"   Mary, of Arthur and Abigail,   June 2, ——.
"   Hazard Dyre,   March —, ——.
"   William,   Nov. —, ——.
"   Samuel Dyer,   May 13, ——.
"   Tamer,   ——. —, ——.
"   Penelope,   ——. —, ——.
"   Josiah Fowler,   May —, ——.
"   ——,   ——. —, ——.
AYRAULT ——, of Daniel,   Oct, —, 1705.

B

BABCOCK Mary, of George and Elizabeth,   Sept. 20, 1695.
"   George,   April 9, 1699.
"   David,   Dec. 22, 1700.
"   Jonathan,   March 22, 1702-3.
"   Elizabeth,   March 16, 1704-5.
"   Abigail,   Feb. 6, 1706-7.
"   Ruth,   March 1, 1709.
"   Eunice,   Jan. 13, 1712-13.
"   Hezekiah,   March 26, 1715.
"   Elisha,   May 18, 1718.
"   Chancey, (born Stafford, Tolland Co., Conn.), of Horace and Elizabeth,
                                                       Oct. —, ——.
BAILEY —— Warren,   Nov. 27, 1795.
"   —— Angustus,   Aug. 19, 1798.
"   Samuel, of George and Sarah,   Nov. 23, ——.
BAKER Thomas, of Thomas and Mary,   Jan. 7, 169—.
"   John,   Sept. 20, 1699.
"   Jeremiah,   July 26, 170—.
"   ——nn,   March 6, 170—.
"   ——ah,   Dec. 15, 170—.
"   ——iah,   Oct. 11, 170—.
"   Joshua,   Feb. 11, 17—.
"   Joseph,   Feb. 2, 17—.
"   Elizabeth,   Jan. 29, ——.
"   Ann,   Oct. 15, ——.
"   Phillip,   Nov. 11, ——.
"   Ruth,   July 12, ——.
"   Ichabod,   March 1, ——.
"   Mary, of Comfort and Elizabeth,   Feb. 3, 1716.
"   Benjamin,   —— —, ——.
"   Lodowick,   Oct. 16, ——.
"   —— (son),   Jan. 13, ——.
"   ——,   —— —, ——.
"   Benjamin, of William, of Benjamin,   Sept. 15, ——.
"   Joshua C.,   Sept. 15, ——.
"   William, Jr.,   March —, ——.
"   Lodowick,   Nov. —, ——.
"   Abel,   Sept. —, ——.
"   Hannah,   March —, ——.
"   Hannah, 2d,   —— —, ——.
"   Rhoda Ann,   —— —, ——.
"   —— (dau.), of James and Penelope,   Oct. 8, ——.
"   Daniel,   —— —, ——.
"   Abel,   —— —, ——.
"   George,   —— —, ——.
"   Alice,   —— —, ——.

BARBER Dinah, of Moses and Susannah,		Jan. 5, 1692-3.
"	Lydia,	Feb. 24, 1694-5.
"	Samuel,	Nov. 8, 1695.
"	Susannah,	Oct. 23, 1697.
"	Thomas,	Oct. 19, 1699.
"	Joseph,	Oct. 16, 1701.
"	Martha,	Nov. 30, 1703.
"	Ruth,	June 23, —705.
"	Benjamin,	March 10, 1706-7.
"	Mercy,	March 13, 1708-9.
"	Ezekiel,	March 6, 1710.
"	Abigail,	Jan 6, 1712-13.
"	Henry, of John and Dorcas, 2d wife,	Jan. 22, 17—.
"	William,	July 6, 17—.
"	Edmund,	May 30, 17—.
"	Mary,	June 3, 17—.
"	Phebe,	— 22, 17—.
"	Robert, died, aged 24y. 1m.,	May 29, 1766.
BARNEY Richard,		— —, —.
"	George Wheaton,	June 25, —.
BATES —, of James and Elizabeth,		Dec. 9, 1723.
"	—,	Dec. 15, 1725.
"	—.	Aug. 30, 1727.
"	—.	Oct. 6, 1729.
"	—.	Dec. 16, 1731.
"	—.	Oct. 13, 1733.
"	—,	Jan. 11, 1735-6.
"	—,	July 17, 1739.
"	Penelope, of Hezekiah and Elizabeth,	July 9, 1738.
"	—,	April 17, 1742.
"	Jonathan, of Daniel,	March 26, —.
"	Daniel,	Sept. 22, —.
"	Francis,	Jan. 8, —.
"	Ruth,	Dec. 7, —.
"	John,	Aug. 24, —.
"	David,	June 23, —.
"	Ebenezer, of Francis and Mary,	March 25, 1696.
"	Samuel,	Dec. 1, 1698.
"	John,	Feb. 25, 1700.
"	Mary,	— —, —.
"	Elizabeth,	— 31, —.
"	Freeborn,	— 2, —.
"	Benjamin,	— 13, —.
"	Amey,	Aug. 24, —.
"	Samuel,	April 29, —.
"	Joseph,	May 2, —.
"	Lydia,	Oct. 20, —.
BEARY Charles, of Nathaniel,		Jan. —, —.
"	Francis,	Jan. —, —.
"	Elisha,	June 11, —.
"	—,	March 30, —.
"	—,	Nov. 14, —.
"	—,	Feb. —, —.
BENTLEY Hannah, of James and Dorothy,		March 25, 1702-3.
"	— (dau.), of James and Hannah,	Dec. 15, 1718.
"	Tillinghast, of William and Eliza,	June 2, 1735.
"	John,	— 22, —.
"	— (son),	— —, —.
"	— (son), of William and Elizabeth,	Dec. —, 1736.
"	— (son), of Benjamin and Sarah,	Aug. 22, 1739.
"	Christopher Coggeshall,	June 15, —.
"	Martha,	April —, —.
"	Mary.	March 2, —.
"	Elizabeth.	June 2, 1797.
"	Elizabeth, 2d,	Oct. 18, —.

BENTLEY Lucy, of Benjamin and Sarah,	June 12, 180—,
"	Thomas.	March 26, 180—.
"	James, had children, names and dates all burnt off.	
"	William, of Samuel and Susannah,	Jan. 20, ——.
"	James,	Dec. 31, ——.
"	Emeline,	Jan. —, ——.
"	Robert,	Oct. —, ——.
"	Sarah, of Benjamin and ——,	May 24, ——.
"	Mary,	Aug. 28, ——.
"	Jeremiah.	Feb. 16, ——.
"	Elizabeth.	Dec. 29, ——.
"	——.	April 10, ——.
BICKNELL Japeth.	— —, ——.
"	——.	Oct. 24, 1787.
"	——.	March 27, 1790.
BISSELL Thomas, of Samuel,	Feb. 28, 1724.
"	Thomas,	d. Oct. 4, 1725.
"	Hannah,	Jan. 5, 1729.
"	—— (son),	Jan. 7, 1732.
"	Susannah, of George and Elizabeth,	July 21, 17—.
"	Thomas,	June 21, 17—.
"	Arter Levy,	Nov. 17, 17—.
"	—— (son), of John and Ann,	July 21, 1728.
"	—— (dau.),	May 4, 1730.
"	—— (son),	April 4, 1732.
"	—— (dau.),	March 26, 1737.
"	—— (dau.),	March 4, 1734.
"	Jonathan, of Samuel and Sarah,	Nov. 10, ——.
"	William,	Jan. 27, ——.
"	William,	d. May 7, ——.
"	William, 2d,	Jan. 14, ——.
"	Betsey,	Dec. 17, ——.
"	Izitt,	Jan. 23, ——.
"	Caleb Allen,	Feb. 15, ——.
"	Sarah,	Nov. 21, ——.
"	Sarah, wife of Samuel,	d. Dec. 11, 17—.
"	Sarah,	Sept. 6, 1754.
"	Samuel,	March 19, 1755.
"	Mary,	Dec. 2, 1757.
"	David,	Feb. 4, 1763.
"	Daniel, of Thomas,	Sept. —, ——.
"	John,	May 25, ——.
"	Thomas,	April 13, ——.
"	Samuel,	Nov. 23, ——.
"	Susannah,	Dec. 17, 1759.
"	William,	Feb. 16, 17—.
"	Mary,	July 16, ——.
"	George,	March 12, 1770.
"	Nathaniel, of Thomas and Phebe,	April —, 1777.
"	—— (son),	March 14, 1779.
"	Abigail,	April 24, 1781.
"	William, of Samuel and Sarah; died off Cape Florida and buried at sea,	
		Sept. 23, 1806.
"	Thomas, of Samuel,	Feb. —, ——.
"	Mary,	Oct. —, ——.
"	Hannah,	— —, ——.
"	Samuel,	June —, ——.
"	Elizabeth,	— —, ——.
"	John P.,	— —, ——.
"	Hannah,	April —, ——.
"	Thomas,	July 23, ——.
"	Thomas, died following	Dec. 23, ——.
"	Randall Mumford,	Aug. —, ——
"	Thomas,	March 30, ——.
"	George,	— —, ——.

BLY Charles, of Jonathan and Eunice,   Aug. 7, 17—.
"   Amie,   June 22, 17—.
"   Lydia,   Jan. 27, 17—.
'   Anna,   Sept. 1, 17—.
"   Daniel,   July 24, 17—.
"   James,   Jan. 13, 17—.
"   Eunice,   June 21, 17—.
"   Hannah,   — —, —.
"   Abigail,   — —, —.
"   Jonathan,   — —, —.
"   Waite,   April —, —.
"   Daniel,   May —, —.
"   Benjamin,   May —, —.
BOONE Hannah, of Samuel (woolcomber) and Mary,   Oct. (13), 1707.
"   Ann,   Sept. (18), 1709.
"   Mary,   Jan. 10, 1711.
"   Freelove,   July 10, 1713.
"   Susannah,   May 7, 1715.
"   Samuel,   April 9, 1717.
"   Sarah,   Feb. 7, 1718.
"   James,   Nov. 28, 1720.
"   Abigail,   April 13, 1723.
"   Elizabeth,   March 19, 1727.
"   ——, of Richard and Harty,   Dec. 24, 17—.
"   ——pha,   Feb. 27, 176—.
"   ——hn,   Jan. 17, 176—.
"   Richard,   Oct. 9, 177—.
"   Penelope, of —— and Susannah,   June 14, —.
"   Thomas G.,   Dec. 8, —.
"   Christopher C.,   Dec. 23, —.
"   Benjamin Reynolds, of Thomas G. and Hannah,   Sept. 19, —.
"   Elizabeth Leroy, of Samuel and Mary, of No. Kingstown, and mother of
        Benedict Peckham, of do., died aged 72 years, 4 months, 7 days,
        July 24, 1799.
BOSS ——, (dau.) of Peter and Amie,   April 20, —.
"   ——,   Jan. 7, —.
"   ——,   Aug. 16, —.
BRIGGS John, of John and Frances,   11m. 25, 1667.
"   James,   (12) m. 12th d., 16(69).
"   Frances,   1m. 23, 1672.
"   Frances,   d. 7m. 2, 1693.
"   Richard (Newport),   12m. 1, 1674.
"   Robert,   9m. 13, 1678.
"   Mary,   7m. 27, 1681.
"   Ann,   7m. 2, (1683).
"   Ann, (d. same m.)   7m. 9, (1683).
"   Sarah,   2m. 12, (1685).
"   Joshua, of Richard and Susannah,   Sept. 30, —.
"   George,   April 5, —.
"   Silas,   March 24, 1758.
"   Abigail,   Feb. 7, 1760.
"   Mary B., of Willett and Frances,   April 10, 1814.
"   Sarah C.,   Nov. 14, 1815.
"   Stukeley B.,   Sept. 21, 1817.
"   Vallett Reynolds,   Dec. 11, 1819.
"   Joseph Vincent,   Nov. 4, 1821.
"   Stephen C.,   May 13, 1825.
"   Hannah, of John, and ——,   April 26, —.
"   John, of John, and Mary, 2d wife,   Sept. 10, —.
"   Pasalment,   Sept. 16, —.
"   Sylvanus,   April 14, —.
"   Mary,   Dec. 13, —.
"   Thomas, of Francis,   Jan. 29, —.
"   ——,   — —, —.
"   ——,   — —, —.

BRIGGS Sarah, of Francis,	—— —, ——.
" Mary,	—— 31, ——.
" John,	—— 14, ——.
" William,	—— 16, ——.
" Deliverance,	—— 3, ——.
" Ebenezer,	July 26, ——.
" Elizabeth, of Paul,	Oct. 13, ——.
" Beriah,	June 5, ——.
" Patience,	May 7, ——.
" Gideon Carr,	March 2, ——.
" Ruth,	Aug. 3, ——.
" Edward Carr,	Feb. 10, ——.
" Hannah,	Oct. 8, ——.
BROWNING——, of Samuel, and Phebe,	June 3, 1743.
" ——,	Nov. 6, 1745.
" ——,	Dec. 5, 1748.
" ——,	Dec. 19, 1751.
" ——,	July 21, 1754.
" Anna, of Samuel, and Lucy,	Sept. 15, 1782.
" Gardiner, (of Samuel),	May 31, 1761.
" Gardiner, (of Samuel), died,	July 23, 1817.
" Izitt (Cole, of John), his wife,	March 31, 1763.
" Izitt (Cole, of John), died,	June 18, 1843.
" Samuel, of Gardiner, and Izitt,	April 12, 1785.
" Mary,	Oct. 24, 1787.
" Gardiner,	March 5, 1791.
" Gardiner, 2d.,	April 12, 1792.
" Hannah,	March 28, 1795.
" William,	May 12, 1798.
" Sarah C.,	Nov. 22, 1800.
" Izitt Cole,	Aug. 13, 1804.
" Abbie Ann Congdon,	Dec. 22, 1807.
" Wm. (of Samuel) and Sarah (Cole, of John) ch	
" Phebe,	
" William,	
" John Arnold,	
" Lois, of Samuel and Mary,	March 16, ——.
" Samuel,	Nov. 11, ——.
" Sarah,	Sept. 11, ——.
" Mercy,	Nov. 18, ——.
" Isaac,	June 17, ——.
BROWN Sarah, of Samuel and Mary,	Dec. 12, 1703.
" Mary,	July 17, 1705.
" Jeremiah,	Oct. 29, 1707.
" Penelope,	Oct. 27, 1709.
" Samuel,	Nov. 5, 1711.
" Elizabeth,	Oct. 28, 1713.
" John,	Nov. 14, 1715.
" Freelove,	Jan. 29, 1717-8.
" Zepheniah,	Dec. 23, 1721.
" John, of William and Elizabeth,	Aug. 6, 1708.
" Mary,	June 4, 1710.
" Thomas,	Aug. 23, 1711.
" Elizabeth,	Feb. 28, 1712-3.
" Ruth,	Sept. 25, 1715.
" Robert,	July 26, 1718.
" George,	Sept. 30, 1721.
" ——nes (son)	May 8, 177—.
" Alexander, of Ebenezer and Martha,	Feb. 17, 1765.
" Alexander,	d. March 1, 1773.
" Mary, of Kingsley and Mary,	May 12, 1773.
" Ruth,	March 14, 1779.
" Allen,	Dec. 24, 1782.
" Elizabeth,	Jan. 14, 1784.
" John,	Sept. 29, 1788.

BROWN ——, of Kingsley and Mary,	March —, 1773.
" ——,	March 31, 1775.
" ——,	April —, 1777.
" ——,	April 16, 1779.
" ——,	Feb. 1, 1781.
" ——,	March 22, 1783.
" ——,	Sept. 14, 1787.
" ——,	April 7, 1785.
" ——,	April 21, 1789.
" ——,	June 19, 1795.
" ——,	June 15, 1798.
" ——,	March 19, 1800.
" Susannah, of (Stukeley) and Sarah (Congdon),	March 2, 1776.
" Mary,	March 9, 177(8).
" Ebenezer,	July 7, 17(80).
" (Susannah), died,	Oct. 7, 177(8).
" (Stukely), (son),	April 14, 178(3).
" (Anna), (dau.),	March 15, 178(5).
" (Anna), (dau.), died,	Dec. 1, 1787.
" (Sarah), (dau.),	May 21, 178(8).
" (Mary), (dau.), died,	April 17, 1789
" (Frances), (dau.),	July 22, 17(90).
" William,	March 4, 179(3).
" Dorcas,	Dec. 9, 179(6).
" Joseph,	May 23, 180?.
" Elizabeth, of Joshua and Elizabeth,	May 30, 1785.
" Daniel,	Aug. 7, 1787.
" Charles,	Oct. 13, 1789.
" Mercy,	Feb. 8, 1793.
" Isaac N.,	Aug. 11, 1796.
" Mary,	May 24, 1798.
" Martha,	March 25, 1803.
" Benjamin, of Reynolds and Nancy,	Jan. 5, 1793.
" William,	Jan. 17, 1795.
" Isaac Guilford,	April 25, 1797.
" Reilley,	June 27, 1799.
" Honeel,	Feb. 20, 1802.
" John, of do., (above b. in N. Carolina)	Aug. —, 1804.
" Harrison,	May 27, 1807.
" Waity Ann, (b. in N. Kingstown)	Feb. 22, 1811.
" ——,	Aug. 9, 1797.
" ——,	May 2, 1800.
" William, of Simeon and Waite,	March 2, ——.
" Honor,	—— —, ——.
" Sarah,	—— —, ——.
" Alexander, of Ebenezer (and Mary Congdon),	June 3, ——.
" Benjamin,	April 26, ——.
" Susannah,	—— 12, ——.
" Mary,	March 30, ——.
" Ebenezer,	April 10, ——.
" Frances,	Feb. —, ——.
" Stukeley, of Ebenezer,	Sept. 28, (1752.)
" Nathan,	Feb. 2, ——.
" Beriab,	March 31, ——.
" Beriah, died	Dec. 12, 1756.
" Honor,	July —, ——.
" Abigail,	Aug. —, ——.
" Sarah,	—— —, ——.
" Sarah, died	—— —, ——.
" ——,	—— —, ——.
" ——,	—— —, ——.
" Honor, of Alexander and Honor,	April 16, ——.
" Abigail,	Nov. 5, (1713.)
" Beriab,	Jan. 16, (1714-15.)
" Sarah,	July 7, ——.

BROWN Ebenezer, of Alexander and Honor,		Sept. 20, ——.
"	Ann,	March 13, ——.
"	Mary,	July 8, ——.
"	—— (son) of —— and Waite,	May 17, ——.
"	Waite,	Jan. —, ——.
"	Arnold,	Jan. 18, ——.
BULLOCK John (Prov), of John and Sarah,		June 14, 178-.
BULL William, of Henry and Ann,		Jan. 23, 1690-1.
"	Mary, of Ephraim and Mary,	July 30, 1693
"	Rebecca,	July 27, 1697.
"	Content,	Nov. 24, 1699.
"	Ephraim, of Ephraim and Hannah,	April 18, 1702.
"	Hannah,	April 18, 1702.
"	Mary, of William and Mary,	July 3(0), 1693.
"	Hezekiah,	July 27, 1697.
"	——,	Nov. 24, 1698-9.
"	Mary, (wife of William), died	Dec. 2, 1699.
"	Ephraim, of William and Hannah (2d wife),	April 18, 1702.
"	Hannah,	April 18, 1702.
BURKE Emeline, died, aged 21y.,		June 13, 1849.
BURKMASTER ——, of John and Margaret,		May 11, 1719.
"	——,	Oct. 6, 1720.
"	——,	Aug. 9, 1722.
"	——,	March 5, 1725.
"	——,	June 26, 1729.
BURLINGAME Nehemiah, of Henry and Nancy B.,		April 18, 1807.

C

CARD James, of James and Martha,		Sept. —, 1703.
"	Martha,	Aug. 24, 1706.
"	—— (son), of James and Barbary,	May —, 1734.
"	—— (dau.), of Jonathan and Renewed,	March 11, 17—.
"	Rebecca,	Nov. 19, 175-.
"	William,	Jan. 1, 1753.
"	Elizabeth,	April 25, 1756.
"	Jonathan,	Feb. 1, 1758.
"	Jeffrey (S. K.), of Jonathan and Phebe,	July 16, 1781.
"	——, of Job and Martha,	Nov. 19, ——.
"	——,	Feb. 2, ——.
"	Job,	recorded Feb. —, 1777.
"	Robert,	recorded, Feb. —, 1777.
"	Martha,	recorded, Feb. —, 1777.
"	Stephen Eldred,	recorded, Feb. —, 1777.
"	Elizabeth, of James and Barbary,	Aug. 18, ——.
"	Jonathan,	Aug. 3, ——.
"	James,	May 12, ——.
CARPENTER Joseph, of Joseph and Mary,		Jan. 7 or 9, 1704.
"	Abigail,	—— —, ——.
"	Ann,	— —. ——
"	Joshua, of Oliver and Sarah,	Jan. —, 1724.
"	Oliver,	July 24, 1727.
"	——, of Nathaniel and Sarah,	March 11, 1730-1.
"	——,	April 4, 1733.
"	Daniel,	— —, ——
"	Abigail,	April 2, 1778.
"	Samuel,	Dec. 5, 17—.
"	Francis, of Francis and Ann,	Oct. 9, 17—.
"	Francis,	d. Jan. 29, 1775.
"	Esther,	April 9, 17—.
"	Willett,	June 17, 17—.
"	James,	April 5, 17—.
"	Mary,	Dec. 31, 17—.
"	Abigail,	Jan. 7, 17—.

CARPENTER Sarah, of Francis and Ann,		April 24, 17—.
"	Francis,	Jan. 21, 17—.
"	Frances Willett, af Francis and Elizabeth,	Sept. 7, 1803.
"	Joseph Case,	Feb. 20. 1806.
"	Benjamin Waite,	Jan. 17, 1808.
"	James Helme,	Feb. 14, 1810.
"	Powell Helme,	Feb. 12 1812.
CARR ——. of William and Elizabeth,		June 9. 1745.
"	——,	Sept. 6, 1746.
"	——,	June 9, 1751.
"	Harty, of Gideon and Elizabeth,	Nov. 2, 1771.
"	Hannah.	July 8, 1773.
CARTER Benjamin, of Samuel and Nancy,		Sept. 8, 1792.
"	Nancy,	Dec. 30, 1793.
"	Samuel.	April 18, 1796.
"	——,	Oct. 18, 1798.
"	William,	March 5, 1801.
"	——,	Sept. 20, 1802.
"	——,	March 17, 1804.
"	——,	Nov. 11, 1805.
CASE Elizabeth, of Joseph and Elizabeth,		Nov. 10, 1686.
"	Ann.	Jan. 18, 1704.
"	Joseph,	Dec. 17, 1706.
"	Mary.	Aug. 29, 1710.
"	Elisha.	June 28, 1712.
"	Joseph, of Joseph and Hannah,	July 16, 1678.
"	William.	May 27, 1681.
"	Mary,	Dec. 2. 1682.
"	Hannah,	July 6, 1687.
"	Margaret,	Aug. 20, 1690.
"	John,	Nov. 20, 1692.
"	Immanuel,	Nov. 2, 1699.
"	William, of William and Elizabeth,	Sept. 8, 1705.
"	Elizabeth,	Dec. 7, 1706.
"	Edward,	Feb. 17, 1708.
"	Hannah,	Nov. 6, 1713.
"	Sarah,	May 3, 1715.
"	Mary,	Jan. 5, 1717-8.
"	Margaret,	Dec. 19, 1720-1.
"	Daniel, of John and Elizabeth,	May 18, 1721.
"	—— (dau.), of Joseph and Sarah,	Sept. 15, 1733.
"	—— (son.),	Aug. 18, 1735.
"	—— (dau.),	Aug. 29, 1739.
"	Joseph,	Dec. 27, 1741.
"	Thomas,	Sept. 30, 1746.
"	William, of Immanuel and Ann,	Aug. 17, 1752.
"	William, died in 22d y.; of do.,	Oct. —, ——.
"	—— Maynard, (dau.) of do.,	June 23, 1766.
"	—— Peck, (son) of do.,	Dec. 18, 1774.
"	Ann, wife of Immanuel, died,	Nov. 9, 1778.
"	Abigail, of ——, and Abigail,	July 27, 17—.
"	Sarah,	April 26, 17—.
"	Joseph,	May 22, 17—.
"	Elisha,	June 9, 17—.
"	Benj. Weight,	June 7, 177—.
"	——, (N), of Samuel, and Dorcas,	—— 16, ——.
"	——, (K.),	—— 26, ——.
"	Freelove,	May 27, ——.
"	Freelove 2d.,	—— 16, ——.
"	Hannah, wife of Joseph, died	May 27, 1712.
"	——, (son), of John and Elizabeth	—— —, ——.
"	——,	May 6, 1805.
"	Waite.	July 1, 1807.
"	—— C.,	March 8, 1810.
"	Caroline Eliza, of John P., and Celinda,	Feb. 21, 1808.

CASE Wm. Henry, of Francis and Elizabeth,		Sept. 3, 1810.
"	Celinda,	Jan. 29, 1813.
*CHADSEY John, of Jabez and Honor,		Dec. 16, 1751.
"	Jabez,	Jan. 31, 1754.
"	Tabitha,	June 20, 1756.
"	Joseph,	Aug. 20, 1758.
"	Elizabeth,	Jan. 16, 1761.
"	Honor,	Sept. 2, 176(3).
"	Rowland,	Feb. 3, 17(66).
"	Sirket (or Circuit), (son),	Aug. 23, 17(68).
"	—,	— —, 1755.
"	—,	June 7, 1757.
"	—,	Sept. 30, 1759.
"	—,	Dec. 1, 1767.
"	—,	Jan. 27, 1769.
"	—,	May 24, 1773.
"	Jeremiah, of Jabez and Hannah (Greene),	Nov. 2, 1780.
"	(George),	Oct. 16, 1782.
"	Henry T.,	Oct. 25, 1806.
"	Almira (Wightman), his wife,	April 4, 1811.
"	John Wightman, of Henry and Almira,	April 2, 1831.
"	Henry Theodore,	June 21, 1833.
"	George Holmes Wightman,	June 18, 1836.
"	Hester Ann,	July 29, 183(8).
"	Mary Catharine,	April 12, 184(0).
"	Anna, of Circuit and Rachel,	April 13, 18—.
"	Caleb A.,	April 11, 18—.
"	Harriet,	July 8, 18—.
"	Robert S., (of George, Jabez and Betsey Spencer),	June 17, (1804).
"	Harriet, (Probably a repetition of above Harriet),	July 8, ——.
"	Robert S., 2d, (of George, Jabez and Betsey),	Aug. 22, (1806).
"	Patty Grieve,	May 16, (1808).
"	Albert Edward,	May 22, (1810).
"	Marbon (Marion) Jones,	June 14, (1812).
"	Euclid, (of Jeremiah, Jabez and Avis Wightman)	(April 19, 1805).
"	John,	—. —, —.
"	Alice, (of John, Jabez and Alice Pearce),	Jan. 22, —.
"	John,	April 15, —.
CHAMPLAIN Emblem, of Jeffrey, Jr., and Susannah,		Jan. 30, 1701-2.
"	Jeffrey,	Feb. 2, 1702-3.
"	Thomas, of Jeffrey, Jr., and Hannah, 2d, w.,	Sept. 3, 1708.
"	Stephen,	Feb. 16, 1709-10.
"	William,	March 3, 1712-13.
"	Hannah, of Jeffrey, Jr., and Susannah 3d, w.,	Jan. 11, 1714.
"	John,	Feb. 12, 1716-17.
"	—, of Jeffrey and Mary,	— 4, 1726.
"	—, (son),	Sept. 17, 1728.
"	—, (dau.),	Jan. —, 1730-1.
"	—, (dau.),	Jan. 12, 1732-3.
"	—, (dau.),	Jan. 1, 1734-5.
"	—, (dau.),	June —, 1737.
"	—,	Oct. 13, 1730.
CHACE —, of Jonathan and Mary,		May 20, 1733.
"	—,	May 23, 1735.
"	Joseph, of Joseph and Mary,	Feb. 16, ——.
"	William,	Nov. 21, ——.
"	—, (son),	Feb. 24, ——.
CHEESEBOROUGH Freelove, of Sylvester and Hannah,		Sept. 14, ——.
"	Esther,	Nov. 24, 176--.
"	Sylvester,	March 9, 1764.
"	Oliver,	March 9, 1764.
"	Elisha,	Feb. 16, 1766.

*See Albert Chadsey MSS. at Wickford.

CHEESEBOROUGH Elisha, 2d, of Sylvester and Hannah,	July 17, 1767.
" Hannah,	May 29, 1769.
" Nathaniel,	Aug. 15, 1771.
" Sarah,	May 20, 1774.
" Mary,	Aug. 15, 1776.
CHURCH Abigail, of Nathaniel and Sarah,	—— 29, ——.
CLARKE —— (dau.), of Caleb and Dinah,	May 31, 1726.
" ——,	Oct. 1, 1727.
" ——,	Jan. 27, 1729-30.
" ——,	Nov. 25, 1732.
" ——,	Jan. 5, 1734.
" ——,	March 28, 173–.
" —— (dau.),	May 11, 174–.
" —— (dau.),	Jan. 10, 174–.
" —— (dau.),	Nov. 23, 174–.
" —— (son),	Jan. 1, ——.
" —— (dau.), of William and Ann,	Sept. 3, 1731.
" —— (dau.),	Jan. 13, 1737.
" —— (dau.),	Nov. 17, 1739.
" —— (dau.),	Oct. 15, 1746.
" —— (son), of Carey and Desire,	April 23, 1757.
" Mary,	Dec. 5, 1758.
" Gardner, of Elisha and Desire (Gardiner of Jeremiah of N. K.),	June 7, 176–.
" Abigail,	April 9, 176–.
" Jabez,	March 19, 1769.
" Benjamin,	Nov. 12, 177–.
" —— (son) of Thomas and Rhobey, (pub.),	July 1, 177–.
" Esther.	Jan. 29, 177–.
" Thomas.	July 23, 177–.
" William.	Jan. 23, 17–.
" Anna.	July 6, 17–.
" Sarah.	Nov. 25, 1782.
" Mary.	May 25, 178–.
" Elisha.	Sept. 16, 178–.
" Benjamin Tillinghast.	—— 20, 1789.
" Hannah.	April 2, 1790.
" John,	Oct. —, 1790.
" ——,	—— —, ——.
" Harriet S., of Elisha, (of Thomas), and Mary,	Jan. 3, 1811.
" William,	Sept. 20, 1812.
" James M., of Benjamin T. and Mary Ann,	March 12, 1813.
" William,	—— —, ——.
" Frederic,	July 21, ——.
" Joseph,	—— —, ——.
" Elisha,	—— —, ——.
" Mary,	July —, ——.
" Thomas,	Aug. 7, ——.
" Sarah,	Jan. 8, ——.
" Benjamin,	Oct. 27, ——.
" Abigail,	—— 22, ——.
CLEAVELAND John, of Palmer and Deborah,	July 12, ——.
" Deborah,	Aug. 9, ——.
" Deliverance,	May —, ——.
" Mercy,	June —, ——.
" Palmer,	Feb. 2, ——.
" John,	Dec. 11, ——.
COATNEY Susannah, dau. of John,	Feb. 3, 1753.
COGGESHALL —— (dau.), of Daniel and Mary,	Nov. —, 1706.
" —— (son),	(Jan.) —, 1708.
" Luranna, of Daniel,	July 2, 1727.
" Mary,	—— 19, ——.
" Weight,	—— 20, ——.
" Joseph,	—— 13, ——.

COGGESHALL Hannah, of Daniel,	— —, —
" — (dau.),	— —, —.
" Christopher, of Joseph and Elizabeth,	Oct. 5, 1758.
" —hod (son),	Sept. 24, 1760.
" —h (dau.),	March 7, 1763.
" — (dau.), of Joseph and Elizabeth,	March 14, 1765.
" — (son),	July 11, 1766.
" Phillip,	March 7, 1770.
" —h (dau.),	Oct. 6, 1773.
" Anbray, of Christopher and Anna.	Dec. 18, 1780.
COLE — (dau.), of John and Ann,	June 10, 1735.
" — (son),	March 13, 1736.
" — (dan.),	April 22, 1739.
" —,	Aug. 21, 1741.
" — (son),	April 4, 1744.
" — (dau.), of John and Mary, 2d.	March 31, 1763.
" — (son),	May 13, 1747.
" — (son),	July 6, 1749.
" — (son),	May 13, 1752.
" — (dan.),	Dec 4, 1754.
" — (son),	Jan. 16, 1760.
" Bradfield, of Capt. Thomas and Nancy,	Sept. 27, 1797.
" George Washington,	Dec. 13, 1781.
" — (son),	Nov. 9, 1784.
" Elizabeth.	— —, 1787.
" —ace.	Feb. 4, 1800.
" Edward.	April 18, 1786.
" Peggy, his wife.	Oct. 3, 1784.
" Sarah, of Edward and Peggy,	March 1, 181—.
" Maria.	July 31, 18—.
" Sybil P..	June 28, —.
" Joseph E..	Nov. 18, —.
" Susan Tillinghast, of Hutchinson A. and Sally B.,	May 9, 1818.
" George Hutchinson Tillinghast, of do.,	April 3, 18—.
" Whitman, of — and Patty,	June 28, —.
" Susannah, of Benjn and Igap,	April —, —.
" Joseph,	July 25, —.
" Benjamin,	Nov. 18, —.
" Mary,	Dec. 4, —.
" Martha,	March 26, —.
" Jeremiah,	May 6, —.
CONGDON William, of William and Mary,	Jan. 25, 1698.
" Elizabeth, wife of Benjn, Jun,	Feb. 20, 1701.
" Elizabeth, of Benjamin, Jr., and Elizabeth,	May 28, 172—.
" Margeret,	Nov. 6, 172—.
" Benjamin,	Nov. 28, 173—.
" — (son),	April 11, 173—.
" —,	July 17, —.
" —,	Oct. 3, —.
" — of John and Patience,	Dec. 12, 1729.
" —,	Sept. 1, 1730.
" —,	July 28, 1733.
" —,	Feb. 21, 1735-6.
" — (dau.),	Sept. 25, 1738.
" — (dau.),	Aug. 15, 1741.
" —,	May 21, 1749.
" — of William and Ann.	Feb. 29, 1732.
" —,	March 25, 1735.
" —,	Dec. 29, 1736.
" —,	Jan. 11, 1739.
" —,	March 28, 1741.
" —,	Feb. 24, 1743.
" —,	Aug. 24, 1744.
" —,	April 30, —.
" —,	May 17, —.

CONGDON —, of William and Ann,		Jan. 20, —.
"	Elizabeth, of James and Mary,	Aug. 26, 1732.
"	— (son),	May 5, 1734.
"	Hannah, of Benjamin and Frances, died	Nov. 3, 1740.
"	— (son),	Dec. 21, 1740.
"	— (dau.),	Dec. —, 1741.
"	— (son),	Feb. 3, 1743.
"	— (son),	April 17, 1746.
"	Rebecca, of William and Abigail,	July 22, 1757.
"	—arey,	Oct. 22, 1758.
"	Phebe, of John and — (Rose, of John, of S. K.)	Aug. 25, —.
"	Abigail,	April 26, —.
"	John,	March 4, —.
"	Susannah,	Feb. 3, —.
"	Thomas Rose,	May 10, —.
"	Ira,	Feb. 11, 176—.
"	Darius,	Sept. 30, —.
"	Stephen,	June 4, 17—.
"	Charles,	Aug. 10, 177—.
"	Elizabeth,	May 9, 177—.
"	— (dau.), of Daniel and Hannah,	Jan. 29, 1798.
"	Rebecca, of William,	July 22, —.
"	Mary,	Oct. 22, 17—.
"	William,	March 24, 17—.
"	William,	died Sept. 6, 17—.
"	Gideon,	Feb 12, 176—.
"	Gideon,	died same year, May 8, 176—.
"	Abigail,	Feb. 5, 176—.
"	Abigail,	died same year, July 8, 176—.
"	Abigail, 2d,	June 17, 1770.
"	Daniel,	Nov. 1, 1772.
"	Frances (dau.),	Sept 27, 1775.
"	Frances,	died Sept. 8, 17—.
"	—,	Sept. 1, 1768.
"	—,	Jan. 1, 1770.
"	—,	April 3, 1772.
"	—,	April 5, 1774
"	—,	Dec. 14, 1775.
"	—,	Oct. 17, 1777.
"	—,	July 20, 1779.
"	—,	March 10, 1782.
"	—,	April 14, 1784.
"	—,	Aug. 27, 1787.
"	William Taylor,	Aug. 10, 1768.
"	William Taylor,	d. Sept. 14, 1768.
"	William Taylor, of Stephen and Mary,	July 19, —.
"	Anna,	April —, —.
"	Dorcas,	July 9, —.
"	Experience,	June —, —.
"	Sarah,	Oct. 7, —.
"	Mary, wife of Stephen,	d. Jan. 15, —.
"	— (dau.), of Thomas R. and Betsey,	Dec. 4, 1789.
"	— (dau.),	Sept. 22, 1791.
"	— (dau.),	Jan. 24, 1793.
"	— (dau.),	July 19, 1796.
"	—, widow of William, Sr.,	d. Feb. 3, 1795.
"	Caleb, of John and Dorcas,	Feb. 18, 17—.
"	Dorcas,	March 8, 17—.
"	Freelove,	June 20, 17—.
"	John,	Jan. 30, 17—.
"	Martha,	Dec. 14, 17—.
"	Abigail,	March 28, 17—.
"	— (son), of Henry, (of —), and Mary,	Feb. —, —.
"	—,	Feb. 3, —.
"	Henry Boone, of Thomas and Eliza Ann,	Sept. 26, 1826.

CONGDON	Mary E., of Thomas and Eliza Ann,	Sept. 27, 1828.
"	Martha S.,	Nov. 9, 1837.
"	Ann Eliza,	Aug. 15, 1841.
"	Mary,	— —, —.
"	Ruth.	— —, —.
"	Waltey,	— —, —.
"	George W., of George (of J——) and Sarah,	Oct. 24, —.
"	Freelove,	— —, —.
"	Benjamin,	— —, —.
"	Joseph,	— —, —.
"	James,	— —, —.
"	Sarah, of Stukeley,	— 22, —.
"	Stukeley,	— 15, —.
"	Jeremiah, of John and Mary,	Nov. 8, —.
"	John,	May 7, —.
"	Mary,	Jan. 30, —.
"	James,	Aug. 28, —.
COOPER	——, of Stephen and Mary.	April —, 1717.
"	Sarah,	June 5, 1721.
"	Thomas, of Matthew and Abigail,	Feb. 25, 1721-2.
"	Thomas, 2d.	April 9, 1723.
"	William, of James (of Stephen) and Ruth,	July 2, 1738.
"	——,	Oct. 20, 1739.
"	——,	Dec. 19, 1741.
"	——,	Dec. 17, 1743.
"	——,	Nov. 20, 1745.
"	Samuel,	Aug. 13, 1748.
"	Lodowick, of Thomas and Mary,	July 26, 175—.
"	Lodowick,	Nov. 20, 1797.
"	Samuel, of Samuel and Margaret,	May 19, —.
"	—— (son),	June 17, —.
"	—— (dau.),	Feb. 25, —.
"	—— (dau.),	June 3, —.
"	Samuel Mitchell, of Abigail,	April 10, —.
COREY	William, of William and Elizabeth,	May 6, 174—.
"	Francis,	April 7, 174—.
"	Esther, of Thomas and Elizabeth (widow of William Corey),	May 30, 17—.
"	John,	April 5, 17—.
"	Daniel,	June 8, 175—.
"	Gideon,	March 21, 1757.
"	Job, of John and Orpha,	Dec. 13, 17—.
"	Harty,	Jan. 29, 174—.
"	Sheffield.	July 30, 174—.
"	Benedict,	Jan. 1, 175—.
"	Peleg,	July 12, 1754.
"	Paris.	April 7, 1757.
"	Abel John,	July 10, 1765.
"	Orpha, of Job and Elizabeth,	Nov. 24, 176—.
"	Harty,	Sept. 25, 1769.
"	Anstis,	Dec. 5, 1771.
"	Peace,	April 20, 1775.
"	Sylvester,	July 10, 1780.
"	Job,	May 11, 1782.
"	Freelove,	Aug. 13, 1784.
"	Joseph, of William and Sarah,	Dec. 13, 1771.
"	Eastla,	Oct. 15, 177—.
"	Frances,	Aug. 6, 177—.
"	Hannah,	Sept. 3, 17—.
"	Mary,	Nov. 10, 17—.
"	John,	Dec. 22, 17—.
"	Daniel,	July 7, 17—.
"	Sarah, of William and Sarah,	May 29, —.
"	William,	Sept. 30, —.
"	Benjamin,	July 10, —.
"	Isaac, of Benjamin C. and Mehitable,	Sept. 28, 1817.

COREY Francis, of Benjamin C. and Mehitable, Sept. 4, 1819.
" Sarah, Oct. 10, 1821.
" William Henry Reynolds, Nov. 10, 182—.
" Albert, Sept. 23, 182—.
" Mary Elizabeth, June 5, —.
" — Mervin, Aug. —, —.
" John, of John and Elizabeth, June 30, —.
CORPES John, —. 24, —.
COTTRELL Hannah, of John, —. 25, 1679.
" —, March 22, —.
" —, Sept. 14, —.
" Samuel, —. —, 1687.
" Elizabeth, of Thomas and Hannah, Oct. 18, 1769.
" Thomas, Sept. 1, 1772.
" Abigail Remington, Nov. 11, 1774.
" Jeremiah, of John and Esther, Sept. 13, 180—.
" Lucy, April 9, 180—.
" Mary Ann, Oct. 19, 180—.
" —, of Samuel and Dorothy, May 10, —.
" —, Aug. 13, —.
" —, April 9, —.
" —, July 9, —.
COZZENS Ruth, — —, —.
" Elizabeth, — —, —.
" Peter, — —, —.
" Phebe, — —, —.
" Mary, — —, —.
" Elizabeth, — —, —.
" Learnard, — —, —.
CRANDALL Samuel, of Peter and Susannah, Feb. 1, 1706-7.
CRANSTON Thomas, of Caleb and Sarah, — —, —.
" Esther, —. 30, —.
" Elizabeth, Nov. 2, —.
" Samuel Northup, March 18, —.
" Sally, April 28, —.
" Penelope, Feb. 9, —.
" William Northup, May 19, —.
" Susannah, Oct. 21, —.
" Avis, April 30, —.
" Jeremiah, June 4, —.
" —, of Caleb, June 8, —.
CROSSMAN Sarah, of Jonathan, May 4, —.
" Mary, Jan. 8, —.
CUTTER Thomas, of Thomas and Freelove, March 29, —.

D

DAVIS Henry, of Henry and Deliverance, March 11, 1729.
" —ut (son), Jan. 26, 1731.
" — (dau.), March 15, 1733.
" Deliverance, June 15, 1735.
" — (son), June 25, 1737.
" William, of Benjamin and Pheaby, Oct. 29, 175—.
" Ruth, July 26, 175—.
" Mary, March 2, 176—.
" Jeffrey, Dec. 17, 176—.
" Benjamin, March 10, —.
" Phebe, May 1, —.
" Elizabeth, Jan. 16, 177—.
" Mary, July 14, 177—.
" Hannah, July 14, 177—.
" Waite, Oct. 27, 177—.
" John Warner, April 22, 1780.
" William, of William and Hester, Nov. 16, —.

DAVIS	Mary, of William and Hester,	— —, —.
"	Dorothy,	— —, —.
"	Phebe,	July 11, —.
"	Benjamin, of Jeffrey,	— —, —.
"	Elizabeth,	— 22, —.
"	Stephen	May —, —.
"	Mary,	— —, —.
"	Joshua,	Nov. 10, —.
DAWLEY	—, of —, and Freelove,	Sept. 2, 1737.
"	—,	May 20, 1740.
DAYTON	John (N.), of Benjamin and Debro.	— 3, 1773.
"	Benedict, (N. K.),	Feb. —, 1777.
"	—, (dau.), (E.),	May 17, 1779.
"	—, (dau.), (E.),	Ang. 28, 1780.
"	—, (N. K.),	— —, 1783.
"	—, (N. K.),	Aug. 17, 1785.
"	—, (N. K.),	Jan. 13, 178—.
"	—, (N. K.),	Jan. 13, 178—.
DEAN	—siah, of Timothy, and Sarah,	Nov. 24, 1773.
DICKINSON	Wm. Allen, of Wm. N., and Mary,	May 21, 1835.
DICKSON	James (son of Anthony, of N. K.,), by wife Ann (dan. of Benj. Mumford, of do.) had son.	
"	Anthony,	horn Aug. 16, 17—.
"	Hannah, of Anthony, and Hannah,	— —, —.
"	John,	Sept. 22, —.
"	Thomas,	Feb. 27, —.
"	Robert,	Oct. 3, —.
"	William,	Sept. —, —.
"	— (dau.), of Robert and Martha,	— —, 1769.
"	— (son),	Sept. 25, 1770.
"	—,	Nov. 15, 1772.
"	— (son),	Oct. 12, 1774.
"	— (son),	Jan. 17, 1777.
"	—,	July 5, 1780.
DIMOND	Benjamin,	— —, —.
"	Mary, of John and Ennice,	Sept. —, —.
"	Benjamin, of Benjamin and Elizaheth, 2d w.,	April 19, —.
"	Abigail,	Dec. 6, —.
"	John,	Sept. 24, 17—.
DOUGLASS	Mary, of George and Susannah,	Nov. 19, 1759.
"	Patience,	Jan. 31, 1764.
"	Mary, of George,	— —, —.
"	— (son),	Jan. —, 1791.
DOWNING	—, of John and R—,	
DURFEE	— (son), of Richard and Susannah,	June 25, 1744.
"	—,	March 25, 1746.
DYRE	— (son), of Edward and Mary,	Jan. —, 1701-2.
"	—, of Samuel,	Dec. 27, 1726.
"	—,	Dec. 3, 1728.
"	—,	March 26, 1731.
"	—,	Oct. 20, 1735.
"	—,	died Nov. 9, 1735.
"	—,	Dec. 26, 1736.
"	—,	Dec. 22, 1739.
"	—,	July 14, 1742.
"	Christopher, of Charles and Penelope,	Feh. 3, 1745.
"	Samuel,	Sept. 16, 1750.
"	Freelove,	March 4, —.
"	Samuel,	March 28, —.
"	—ne (dau.),	June 12, —.
"	Abigail,	July 4, —.
"	Elizabeth,	May 12, 176—.
"	Hannah,	June 24, 176—.
"	Esther,	March 28, 176—.
"	Elizaheth,	March 4, 177—.

DYRE Lydia, of Charles and Penelope,   May 11, 1772.
   "   Abigail, dau. of Col. Charles,   July 14, 176—.
   "   William, of Edward and Elizabeth,   May 2, 175—.
   "   Charles,   July 4, 175—.
   "   Francis,   March 4, 17—.
   "   Benjamin,   Feb. 22, 17—.
   "   Amherst,   July 10, 17—.
   "   Henry,   July 10, 17—.
   "   Susannah,   Feb. 15, 17—.
   "   Anne,   May 26, 17—.
   "   Mary, of Charles, Jr., and Susannah,   Jan. 5, 1789.
   "   Samuel,   May 29, 1790.
   "   Abigail,   Dec. 29, 1792.

E

ELDRED —, of James,   Sept. 1, 1716.
   "   —.   (Doubtful) Nov. 27, 1716.
   "   —, .   Sept. 16, 1720.
   "   —,   April 26, 1724.
   "   —,   Feb. 7, 17—.
   "   Elizabeth.   — —, —.
   "   —bery, (dau.), of Thomas and Rebecca,   April 20, 1730.
   "   Bathsheba,   Dec. —, 173—.
   "   —, (son),   Feb. 26, —.
   "   Robert,   Oct. 23, 1761.
   "   Sarah (Boone of James), wife of Robert,   June 3, 1763.
   "   Susanna Boone, of Robert and Sarah,   Oct. 5, 1789.
   "   James Boone,   May 18, 1792.
   "   James Boone, died   Oct. 3, 1793.
   "   Sarah Boone,   May 28, 1794.
   "   William,   April 21, 1796.
   "   Charles,   Sept. 2, 1798.
   "   Robert,   Dec. 17, 1800.
   "   Richard Boone,   Jan. 2, 1803.
   "   Mary Updike,   Jan. 24, 1806.
   "   Abigail Goddard,   Dec. 25, 1808.
   "   Ezra, of Thomas and Martha (Potter, of Robert of S. K.), April 21, 1760.
   "   Waite,   May 4, 1762.
   "   Lucy.   Feb. 1, 1773.
   "   Weeden,   July 27, 17—.
   "   —,   — —, —.
   "   Samuel, of Joseph and Sarah,   May 30, 1768.
   "   Sarah,   Feb. 7, 1770.
   "   Mary,   Jan. 20, 1772.
   "   Elizabeth,   July 16, 1773.
   "   Martha,   July 25, 1775.
   "   —, of Joseph and Alice, 2d wife,   July 2, —.
   "   —,   — —, —.
   "   Elizabeth, of Daniel and Mary,   Oct. 25, 1790.
   "   Margaret,   Oct. 19, 1792.
   "   Lucy.   Jan. 7, 1795.
   "   Mary,   May 30, 1797.
   "   Sarah Ann Peck,   Jan. 27, 1800.
   "   Lydia Gardiner,   Nov. 9, 1802.
   "   Robert, of James and Lucy,   Oct. 23, 17—.
   "   George,   March 18, 17—.
   "   Christian,   Nov. 16, 17—.
   "   Charles,   May 5, 17—.
   "   Daniel,   Jan. 5, —.
   "   Ann or Nancy (sic.)   Sept. 9, 17—.
   "   Joanna,   July 10, 17—.
   "   Hannah,   July 10, 17—.
   "   Lucy.   Aug. 28, 17—.

ELDRED Beriah Brown, of James and Lucy,		March 21, 17—.
"	Clarke,	Dec. 2, 17—.
"	Phebe,	Nov. 17, 17—.
"	Rowland,	Oct. 4, 1781.
"	Mary,	Nov. 25, 178—.
"	John, of Robert and Hannah.	Nov. 1, ——.
"	Simeon,	March 9, ——.
"	William,	March 15, ——.
"	Hannah,	March 9, ——.
"	Mary,	Sept. 9, ——.
"	James,	Aug. 29, ——.
"	Barberry,	July 21, ——.
"	Joseph Eldred,	—— —, ——.
"	Deborah,	March 8, ——.
"	Phebe,	June 6, ——.
"	Waite S., of Thomas and Sarah,	Sept. 30, ——.
"	John,	Oct. 12, ——.
"	Beriah,	Feb. 25, ——.
"	Mary,	Oct. 11, ——.
"	Ezra,	Jan. 9, ——.
"	Ishmeal S.,	Aug. 19, ——.
"	Thomas,	Jan. 20, ——.
"	Isaac,	June 13, ——.
"	Dorcas, of Henry and Mary,	May 24, ——.
"	William, of Thomas and Hannah,	Feb. 15, ——.
"	Samuel,	May 8, ——.
"	Jeremiah, of William,	Dec. 13, ——.
"	William,	Dec. 26, ——.
"	Ann,	—— —, ——.
"	Mary,	—— —, ——.
"	Abigail,	—— 30, ——.
"	Thomas,	—— 7, ——.
"	Sarah,	—— —, ——.
"	Sarah, of John and Mary,	March 18, ——.
"	Abbie Emeline,	Nov. 29, ——.
"	Mary Ann,	Feb. 7, ——.
"	Mercy Eleanor,	July 14, 1838.
ELLIS ——,		Nov. —, 1732.
"	—— (dau.),	May 16, 1734.
"	—— (dau.),	Nov. 26, 1736.
"	Abigail,	Aug. 5, 1738.
"	George, of John, Jr., and Martha,	Aug. 2, 1760.
"	Silas, of Silas and Hannah,	July 18, 1798.
"	Robert, of Alice, dau. of Samuel,	March 12, ——.
ENSWORTH Nathaniel, of Learnord and Esther,		Oct. 10, ——.
"	Elizabeth Stuart, of Libbeus and Thankful,	Dec. 11, 1803.
ESSEX Corpse,		—— —, ——.
"	Martha,	—— —, ——.

F

FISH Daniel, of Jeremiah and Mary,		June 6, 1722.
"	Samuel,	June 6, ——.
FONES ——, (Jamestown), of Jeremiah and Elizabeth,		June —, 1695.
"	——, (son, Rochester),	Aug, —, 1697.
"	——, (Jamestown),	May —, 1699.
"	——, (dau.), (Jamestown),	May 22, 1701.
	James Fones made oath Nov. 20, 1755, that the above was correct.	
"	Ann, of Samuel, and Anne,	Oct. 28, 16—.
"	Samuel, of Samuel and Meribah, 2d wife,	July 4, 1702.
"	Sarah,	July 3, 1703.
"	Margaret,	July 23, 1704.
"	Mary,	July 1, 1705.
"	—— (dau.), died,	Nov. —, 1705.

FONES —— (son), of Samuel and Meribah, 2d wife,		Dec. 17, 1706.
"	—— (son), of James and Mary,	April 21, 1738.
"	Jane, of John and Hopestill,	April —, 1748.
"	Margaret,	—ber 29, 1750.
"	—— (son),	Oct. 3, ——.
"	Samuel, died aged 90y. 10m. 15d.,	—— 14, 1757.
"	Anne, of Joseph and Sarah,	Sept. 25, 1762.
"	Sarah,	July 28, 176—.
"	Mary, of Capt. Daniel,	——. 4, ——.
"	Martha,	Jan. 11, ——.
"	Elizabeth,	Oct. 26, ——.
"	Daniel,	Dec. 9, ——.
"	—— (dau.), of Joseph,	Nov. 12. ——.
"	Samuel of James and Elizabeth,	Dec. 19, ——.
"	William,	Oct. 17, ——.
"	Joseph,	Oct. 27, ——.
"	Margaret,	Oct. 2, ——.
"	John,	Dec. 21, ——.
"	Meribah,	Nov. 20, ——.
"	Martha,	Jan. 11, ——.
"	Elizabeth,	Ap— —, ——.
"	—— (son),	——.
FOWLER Ann, of Benjn. and Ann (Case, dau. of Joseph),		May 1, 1760.
"	Ann, wife of Benjn, died	—— —, ——.
"	Benjamin, of Benjamin and Freelove,	April 14, 1774.
FREEBORNE Mary Esther, of Gideon and Freelove N.,		Feb. 5, ——.

G

GALLUP ——, (son), of Richard and Lydia,		Dec. 6, 1727.
"	——, (dau.),	Jan. 9, 1738.
GARDINER Henry, of Henry and Abigail, (Remington),		Feb. 25, 1691.
"	Epharaim,	Jan. 7, 1693.
"	William,	Oct. 27, 1697.
"	Henry, of Henry and Desire,	June 16, 1714.
"	John, of William and Abigail,	July 8, 1696.
"	William,	May 21, 1698.
"	Abigail,	Sept. 24, 1700.
"	Thomas,	Oct. 30, 1702.
"	Hannah,	Dec. 7, 1704.
"	Lydia,	June 27, 1706.
"	Sylvester,	June 29, 1708.
"	Job, of William and Margeret,	Dec. 5, 1719-20.
"	——, (dau.), of Henry,	Aug. 4, 1703.
"	Benjamin, of Nathaniel and Mary,	Feb. 26, 1705.
"	Mary,	Nov. 30, 1707.
"	Penelope,	Oct. 11, 1709.
"	Dorcas,	June 10, 1712.
"	Nathaniel,	June 16, 1714.
"	Elizabeth, of Elizabeth ——,	May 17, 1708.
"	Nicholas, of Nicholas and Mary,	Dec. 6, 1710.
"	Ezekiel,	Sept. 29, 1712.
"	Sylvester,	Aug. 3, 1714.
"	Hannah,	Sept. 2, 1717.
"	Amey,	June 17, 1723.
"	Susannah,	—— 9, ——.
"	Thomas,	Oct. 1, 1729.
"	Dorcas,	March 27, ——.
"	Dorcas, of Ephraim and Penelope,	Jan. 31, 1713-14.
"	Penelope,	Oct. 15, 1716.
"	Samuel,	Jan. 16, 1719-20.
"	James,	July 10, 1721.
"	Elizabeth, of Jeremiah,	Nov. 26, 1714.
"	Freelove,	Feb. 28, 1716.

GARDINER Jeremiah, of Jeremiah,   Jan. 28, 1719.
"   Phebe.   Oct. 26, 1722.
"   Sarah.   April 6, 1725.
"   ——.   Dec. 28, 1727.
"   Abigail.   June 23, 1731.
"   ——,   Nov. 6, 1734.
"   ——,   Nov. 11, 1737.
"   ——,   June 9, 174—.
"   John, of William and Margaret,   Dec. 5, 1719-20.
"   Margaret, of John and Mary,   May 7, 1720.
"   ——,   Dec. 24, 1723.
"   ——,   Aug. 2, 1725.
"   ——,   July 27, 1727
"   ——,   Aug. 17, 173—.
"   ——,   Jan. 25, 173—.
"   ——, (dau.) of Jeremiah, Jr., and Tabitha,   Jan. 15, 1741.
"   ——, (dau.),   May 27, 1743.
"   ——, (son),   Nov. 9, 1746.
"   ——, (dau.),   July 30, 1750.
"   ——, (son),   Dec. 7, 1758.
"   Daniel, of James and Waite, who was daughter of Joseph Coggeshall,
                                                Dec. 19, 1751.
"   Daniel,   died Feb. 10, 1755.
"   Mary,   Nov. 3, 1752.
"   Waite,   Sept. 2, 175—.
"   Ann,   March 29, 1759.
"   James,   Sept. 14, 1762.
"   Susannah,   Dec. 6, 1763.
"   Abigail,   Sept. 7, 1766.
"   Samuel,   Jan. 22, 1769.
"   Wanton,   June 7, 177—.
"   David, of Ezekiel, Jun., and Susannah,   Aug. 6. 1764.
"   Mary,   March 3, 1766.
"   Ezekiel,   Jan. 19, 1768.
"   Hannah,   March 6, 1770.
"   Dorcas,   Feb. 3, 1772.
"   Susannah,   April 28, 1774.
"   Ann,   March 15, 1776.
"   Elisha,   Jan. 28, 1778.
"   William,   Oct. 15, 1780.
"   Palmer,   April 29, 1783.
"   Oliver,   May 20, 1785.
"   Jesse,   March 7, 1789.
"   Almy,   March 7, 1789.
"   Jeffrey,   Oct. 21, 1791.
"   Col. Ephraim, died age 80 years,   April 11, 1774.
"   John, (of N. K.), son of Flora, (col.),   Aug. 5, 1799.
"   Clarke,   June 29, ——.
"   Wilbour,   Dec. 16, ——.
"   Jeremiah,   Jan. 3, ——.
"   Dorcas,   Feb. 13, ——.
"   Lawton,   May 18, ——.
"   Mary,   Sept. —, ——.
"   Lydia,   April 7, 1782.
"   Benjm. Waite,   July 7, ——.
"   ——, of Samuel,   Dec. 25, 1796.
"   ——,   Feb. 16, 1799.
"   —— Carpenter,   Jan. 22, 1801.
"   Francis Carpenter,   May 19, 1803.
"   Marinus Willett,   April 9, 1805.
"   —ey Easton,   March 14, 1807.
"   Octavus Fedinand,   June 30, 1809.
"   William Henry,   July 20, 1811.
"   Thomas Rodman,   Sept. 11, 1813.
"   Sally Carpenter,   Dec. 27, 1815.

GARDINER Walter Easton		Nov. 3, 1817.
"	Joseph, of David, and Elizabeth,	March 25, 18—.
"	Stephen Davis, of Samuel and Rebecca,	March 11, 1800.
"	John Reynolds,	April 24, 1827.
"	Nicholas J.,	Oct. 15, 183—.
"	David, of B—— and Elizabeth,	— —, —.
"	Rodman,	April 28, 1826.
"	—,	d. at N. Y. Sept. —, 1834.
"	—.	— —, —.
"	Samuel C.,	May —, —.
"	Sarah Jane,	Feb. 15, —.
"	Lucy Ann, .	April 13, —.
"	Benjamin, of Samuel and Elizabeth,	— —, —.
"	Nicholas Easton, of Christopher,	July 23, —.
"	Henry,	— —, —.
"	Edward.	— —, —.
"	John.	— —, —.
"	Waite,	April 10, —.
"	Idea,	— —, —.
"	Daniel,	— 25, —.
"	Mary, of Job and An——,	Aug. 21, —.
"	Nathaniel,	April 7, —.
"	Mary, of Isaac and Elizabeth,	March 30, —.
"	Elizabeth,	March 24, —.
"	Sarah,	May 5, —.
"	Isaac,	May 5, —.
"	Benoni,	May 31, —.
"	Samuel,	Sept. 27, —.
"	Penelope,	July 19, —.
"	Silas,	Oct. 29, —.
"	Gideon.	— 8, —.
"	John, of Ezekiel and Dorcas,	Oct. 21, —.
"	Hannah,	Feb. 4, —.
"	Ezekiel.	Aug. 25, —.
"	Mary,	Feb. 20, —.
"	Elisha,	June 4, —.
"	George,	July 2, —.
"	David.	Feb. 15, —.
"	Nicholas,	May 29, —.
"	—— (son),	Nov. 24, —.
"	—— (son),	April 20, —.
"	—— (son),	April —, —.
"	Henry,	— —, —.
"	Lydia,	— —, —.
"	Mary,	— 31, —.
"	Caleb,	— 1, —.
"	Nathan,	— 3, —.
"	Tabitha,	— 3, —.
"	—— (dau.), of Henry,	April 14, —.
"	Mary Eleanor, of Vincent, Jr., and Mary,	Feb. 22, —.
"	Jonathan Vincent,	May 23, —.
"	Susan Elizabeth,	Oct. 17. —.
"	Zebulon, of Benjamin R. and Elizabeth,	March —, —.
"	Daniel C., of —— and Lucy,	Sept. —, —.
"	Peleg C..	Sept. 13, —.
"	John H.,	June 26, —.
"	Lucy,	Jan. 10, —.
"	Samuel E.,	March 26, —.
"	Mary,	July 3, —.
"	Peggy,	July 9, —.
"	Rowland,	May 1, —.
"	James S.,	June 4, —.
"	Thomas, of Jeremiah,	d. Feb. 28, —.
"	Wickes, of Benjn. and Elizabeth,	Sept. 12, —.
"	Larry,	May 15, —.

GARDINER Abigail, of Benjn. and Elizabeth,   April 14, ——.
    "   Elizabeth,   Feb. 14, ——.
    "   Patience,   Dec. 12, ——.
    "   Isaac,   July 28, ——.
    "   John,   July 27, ——.
    "   ——miah, of Thomas and Abigail,   Feb. 4, 17—.
    "   —— (son),   April 16, ——.
    "   Clarke, of Benjamin,   Junne —, ——.
    "   Samuel, of Samuel and Catherine   July 25, ——.
    "   Josiah, of Ephraim and Patience,   Jan. 4, ——.
    "   Gideon,   Oct. 4, ——.
    "   Abigail,   Jan. 8, ——.
    "   Sarah,   Jan. 6, ——.
    "   Ephraim Eldred,   May 4, ——.
GIFFORD Elizabeth, of Yelverton.   — 25, ——.
    "   ——nah,   — 30, ——.
    "   ——,   — 20, ——.
GODFREY William, of Caleb,   Jan. 10, ——.
    "   Josiah,   July —, ——.
GOULD Isaac, of Isaac and Elizabeth,   April 11, 1724.
    "   ——. of Daniel,   — —. 1743.
    "   ——,   May 13, 1745.
    "   ——, died   Oct. 8, 1745.
    "   Jeremiah, died   Oct. 8, 1745.
    "   —— Cammell, of Samuel and Sarah,   Aug. 15, 1792.
    "   —— Carney,   July 2, 1795.
    "   —— Brown,   Dec. 6, 1797.
    "   ——,   Jan. 24, 1800.
    "   Joseph (b. at Hrendale),   Feb. 26, 17—.
    "   Joshua (b. at Rehoboth),   March 12, 17—.
    "   George (Providence), of Joseph and Jerusha, April 1, 17—.
    "   William (Providence),   March 17, 179—.
    "   Sarah (N. K.),   June 2, 180—.
    "   Eliza (N. K.),   May 6, 180—.
    "   ——.   — —, ——.
    "   Mary,   — —, ——.
    "   Permilla Bentley.   — —, ——.
    "   Elizabeth, wife of —— ——.   — —, ——.
    "   Sarah.   — —, ——.
    "   Elizabeth.   — —, ——.
    "   Sarah.   — —, ——.
    "   Ann.   — —, ——.
    "   Sarah, of Jeremiah and Elizabeth,   Feb. 23, ——.
    "   Mary,   Aug 27, ——.
    "   Catherine,   Feb. 28, ——.
    "   Elizabeth,   Feb. 14, ——.
    "   Waite,   April 14, ——.
    "   Daniel,   May 2, ——.
    "   Ruth,   Sept. 18, ——.
    "   Hannah,   March 16, ——.
GREENE, Peleg, of Daniel and Rebecca;   Aug. 9, 1690.
    "   Daniel,   Oct. 8, 1692.
    "   Jonathan,   Dec. 1, 1694.
    "   Rebecca,   April 12, 1696.
    "   Rachel,   May 6, 1698.
    "   Sarah,   April 5, 1700.
    "   Jonathan,   June 9, 1705.
    "   Hope, of Peleg and Dinah,   May 22, 1725.
    "   Rachel,   June 27, 1726.
    "   Ann,   Sept. 30, 1728.
    "   ——. (son), of Daniel and Catherine,   ——. 12, 1722.
    "   —— (son), of Peleg and Catherine,   ——. 18, 1727.
    "   Mary, of Joshua and Dinah,   Dec. 30, 174—.
    "   Catherine,   Aug. 1, 174—.
    "   Abigail,   Sept. 10, 175—.

GREENE Daniel, of Joshua and Dinah,	Aug. 30, 175—.
" Elizabeth,	Ang. 5, 175—.
" Fones,	March 4, 1761.
" Susannah,	Dec. 20, 1763.
" Joshua, of Joshua and Alice, 2d w.,	Dec. 23, 1772.
" Capt. Fones, of Warwick, died in his 27th year,	Sept. 12, 1753.
" Hannah, of John (of Daniel) and Sarah,	Nov. —, 1760.
" Timothy, of Paul and Sarah,	June 13, 176—.
" Hannah,	March 15, 176—.
" (David), of David, and Sarah (Allen),	June 4, 1786.
" (Elizabeth),	May 17, 1787.
" (Joshua Allen),	Dec. 13, 1788.
" (Joseph),	April 24, 1790.
" (Caleb),	March 15, 1792.
" James, of Wm. (of Abraham) and Sarah,	March 26, 1797.
" Waity,	Aug. 17, 1798.
" Perry,	Dec. 24, 1799.
" Eliza	May 5, 1802.
" Sally, of Wm. (of Abraham) and Mary,	Feb. 21, 1804.
" Robert Wilcox,	Nov. 4, 1809.
" Thomas, born Nov. 11, 1719,	died Aug. 18, 1813.
" Sally, wife, of Christopher W.,	died June 2, 1836.
" Mary, of David, Jun.,	(June 2, 1727.)
" David,	Aug. (28, 1728.)
" Margeret (Mercy),	(March 8, 1730.)
" Ebenezer,	Jan. —, ——.
" Patience,	Nov. (7, 1733.)
" Alice,	June (16, 1735.)
" Wait,	(June 1, 1739.)
" Phebe,	——. 3, ——.
" Margeret,	——. —, ——.
" Rebecca,	——. —, ——.
" Benjamin, of Benjamin,	April 13, ——.
" Benjamin,	died Jan. 4, ——.
" David, of (David), and Elizabeth,	Nov. 4, (1760.)
" Mary,	June 14, (1765.)
" Jonathan,	July 25, (1767.)
" Elisha, of Peleg,	——. —, ——.
" Lidge,	——. —, ——.
" Peleg,	——. —, ——.
" Mary,	——. —, ——.
" Phebe,	——. —, ——.
" Ann,	——. —, ——.
" John Turner, of John and Sukey,	Jan. 31, Wed'y.
" ——, of Peleg and Catherine,	June 11, ——.
" ——,	Sept. 12, ——.
" ——,	Sept. 26, ——.
" ——,	Sept. 8, ——.
" ——,	March 17, ——.
" Martha, of Ebenezer and Ma——,	May 2, ——.
" John,	Dec. 29, ——.
" Sarah,	April 26, ——.
" Ebenezer,	Sept. 26, ——.
" William,	Aug. 26, ——.

H

HALEY John, of John and Mary,	March 8, 1719-20.
" Mary,	—— —, ——.
" Thomas	—— —, ——.
" Elizabeth, died; aged 4 weeks, 2 days.	
HALL (Alice), of William and Sarah,	June 20, (1698?).
" William,	Jan. 7, 1699-00.
" (Abigail)	Aug. 7, 1702.

HALL (Hannah), of William and Sarah,		Feb. 7, 1704.
"	Alice,	Aug. 16, 1707.
"	William, of John and Mary,	Aug. 3, 1723.
"	—— (son), of Benoni and Elizabeth,	Aug. —, 1734.
"	——. (son),	Nov. 16, 1736
"	—— (son),	—— 30, 1739.
"	——, wife of Robert; died	Oct. —. 1736.
"	——,	June 4, 1741.
"	Elizabeth,	Jan. —, 1726.
"	Izabel,	Feb. 28, 1739.
"	Sarah, of Robert and Isabel.	Jan. 22, 1739.
"	Daniel.	Jan. 22, 1739.
"	——, of John and Ruth,	Dec. 16, 1740.
"	Abigail, of William, (of John), and Mary;	Oct. 29, 1744.
"	Ephraim,	March 20, 1748.
"	Mary,	May 14, 1762.
"	——, of William and Penelope;	Nov. 26, 1745.
"	Elizabeth,	Sept. 19, 1748.
"	——, (dau.),	Jan. 29, 1750.
"	——, (dau.),	Feb. 1, 1753.
"	——. (dau.),	Dec. 13, 1754.
"	——,	Jan. 5, 1757.
"	——,	Oct. 18, 1758.
"	Sarah, of Daniel and Mary;	Feb. 22, ——.
"	Anne,	Oct. 3, ——.
"	Isabel,	March 15, ——.
"	Ruth,	July 22, 1766.
"	Patience,	Aug. 22, 176—.
"	Robert,	March 28, 17—.
"	Dorcas,	Oct. —, ——.
"	Martha,	Oct. —, ——.
"	Benjamin Greene,	May 30, ——.
"	Ruth ——, of Daniel and Mary,	Aug. 22, ——.
"	Daniel Washington,	May 22, ——.
"	Robert, of N. K., died at midnight in 76th y.,	March 2, 1765.
"	Spencer, of William and Mary,	Feb. 16, 1766.
"	——,	——, ——.
"	Frances, of Slocum, and Frances,	March 2, ——.
"	Frances, wife of Slocum,	died March —, 1771.
"	Susannah, of Slocum and Susannah,	Feb. 21, ——.
"	John ——, of Slocum and Almy, 3d w.,	Jan. 3, ——.
"	Abigail,	Jan. 15, ——.
"	Almy,	Feb. —, ——.
"	Christopher,	May 20, ——.
"	Sarah ——, of Henry and Mary,	March 17, 177—.
"	Elizabeth,	June 16, 177—.
"	Anna,	Aug. 14, 177—.
"	Robert ——, of William,	—— 21, ——.
"	William,	Nov. 26, ——.
"	Elizabeth,	—— 9, ——.
"	——.	Jan. —, ——.
"	——,	—— —, ——.
HAMMOND Pardon Tillinghast, of William, Jr., and Alice,		Jan. 31, 1792.
"	Maria,	Oct. 26, 1794.
"	Esther,	March 23, 1797.
"	Ruth F.,	June 20, 1799.
"	William G.	Jan. 21, 1802.
"	George,	Nov. 1, 1804.
"	Lydia Alice,	Jan. 29, 1807.
"	Samuel, of Calvin and Sarah,	—— —, ——.
"	Benjamin,	Oct. 31, 1798.
"	William,	Aug. 24, 1806.
"	James,	Sept. 7, 1808.
HARRINGTON —— (son), of Richard and Sarah,		June 19, 1718.
"	—— (dau.),	Jan. 4, 1719.

HARRINGTON ——, (dau.), of Richard and Sarah,		May 6, 1721.
"	Richard,	April 16, 1724.
"	William,	Oct. 19, 1726.
"	Dorcas ——, of Eleazer and Mary,	Aug. 17, 1779.
"	Susannah,	Nov. 20, 1781.
"	Sarah,	Dec. 17, 1783.
"	Daniel (K.), of Benjamin,	—— ——, ——.
"	Clarke (Prov.),	Aug. —, ——.
"	Sarah (War.),	March 20, ——.
"	Ezekiel (N. K.),	—— ——, ——.
"	Mercy (N. K.),	July 20, ——.
"	Benjamin (N. K.),	Feb. —, ——.
"	Hannah (N. K.),	Dec. —, ——.
"	Sarah. of Job and Alice.	Aug. 13, ——.
"	Lydia.	—— 12, ——.
"	Job,	—— 25, ——.
"	Ebenezer.	—— 2, ——.
"	William.	Dec. 15, ——.
"	Alice,	Oct. 8, ——.
"	Elizabeth.	March 25, ——.
HARVEY Frederic. of William and Waite		March 27, 1765.
"	William.	Dec. 14, 1766.
"	Simeon.	Feb. 13, 1769.
HAVENS ——, dau. (s. b.), of Thomas (of Robert), and Mary,		—— ——, ——.
"	——, dau. of do., born April 23, 1771,	d. May 3, 1771.
"	Joseph, of do.,	Feb. 9, 1773.
"	Susannah,	Nov. 22, 1774.
"	Rhodes, of William and Ruth,	Aug. 12, 1771.
"	Daniel, of —— and Bridget,	March 20, 17—.
"	Darius,	May 23, 176—.
"	Sarah,	May 30, 1767.
"	William,	March 20, 1769.
"	Amie,	July 25, 1771.
"	Elizabeth,	April 16, 1773.
"	Wightman,	Jan. 9, 1775.
"	John Campbell, of Sylvester and Mary,	July 22, 179—.
"	Absalom, of —— and Elizabeth,	Sept. —, ——.
"	Phebe,	Oct. 9, 17—.
"	Elizabeth,	Sept. 30, 17—.
"	Thomas,	Dec. 17, 17—.
"	Mary,	Dec. 4, 17—.
"	Daniel (b. N. K.),	—— ——, ——.
"	Sarah, of Robert,	July 8, ——.
"	Jeremiah,	Oct. 10, ——.
"	Mary,	Feb. 9, ——.
"	Merabah,	Aug. 18, ——.
"	Frances,	Aug. 22, ——.
"	William, of Alexander (Wm.), and Mercy (Stafford),	Oct. 14, 1743.
"	Susannah,	(Nov. 16, 1745.)
HAZARD Mary, of Thomas and Susannah,		Oct. 3, 1683.
"	Hannah,	April 14, 1685.
"	Sarah,	July 15, 1687.
"	Robert,	May 23, 1689.
"	Thomas,	May 11, 1691.
"	Stephen,	June 13, 1693.
"	Jeremiah,	June 5, 1697.
"	George,	Jan. 18, 1698.
"	Benjamin,	Nov. 2, 1702.
"	Jonathan,	Oct. 1, 1704.
"	Abigail, of George and Penelope,	March 19, 1690.
"	Robert,	Nov. 3, 1694.
"	Caleb,	Nov. 24, 1697.
"	George,	Oct. 9, 1700.
"	Thomas,	March 30, 1704.
"	Oliver,	Sept. 30, 1710.

HAZARD Mary, of Stephen and Elizabeth,	July 20, 1695.
" Hannah,	April 20, 1697.
" Susannah, of Stephen and Elizabeth,	April 20, 1699.
" Stephen,	Nov. 29, 1700.
" Robert,	Sept. 12, 1702.
" Samuel,	June 29, 1705.
" Thomas,	July 28, 1707.
" Susannah, of Stephen and Margaret,	May 9, 1715.
" Fones,	Sept. 22, 1717.
" Jeffrey, of Robert and Amie,	Sept. 29, 1698.
" Hannah,	Jan. 16, 1701.
" Hannah, 2d,	Feb. 26, 1703.
" Robert,	Jan. 19, 1709.
" Thomas,	June 18, 1713.
" Amy,	Sept. 20, 1715.
" Mary,	May 14, 1718.
" Mary, of Jeremiah and Sarah,	March 16, 1699.
" Ann,	Feb. 28, 1701.
" Robert,	April 11, 1703.
" Sarah,	Jan. 11, 1706.
" Martha,	Oct. 8, 1708.
" Hannah,	April —, 1714.
" Susanna, of Jeremiah and Sarah,	May 21, 1716.
" Mary, of Robert, (of Thomas), and ——,	Feb. 23, ——.
" Thomas,	May 9, ——.
" Thomas,	d. Dec. 2, 1719.
" Thomas, 2d,	— 15, ——.
" William, of Caleb and Abigail,	April 12, 1721.
" Enock, of George and Mary,	Sept. 1, 1721.
" Oliver, of Oliver and Elizabeth,	March 30, 1739.
" Mercy,	Jan. 21, 1740.
" Elizaebth,	Sept. 13, 1737.
" Easton, of Ephraim and Mary,	Sept. 13, 1783.
" Willett, of Easton and Charlotte,	Nov. 23, 1803.
" Varnum,	Oct. 9, 1805.
" William Robinson, of Nathan G. and Frances,	Jan. 11, 1810.
" Sarah Gardiner,	July 15, 1811.
" Catherine,	June 2, 1818.
" John,	April 30, 1821.
" ——, of Jeremiah, Jr.,	Aug. 3, ——.
" ——,	Sept. 4, ——.
" ——,	June 2, ——.
" ——,	Oct. 28, ——.
" ——, wife of Thomas, died	Jan. 24, 17—.
" Mary,	——. 20, ——.
" Jeremiah,	——. 25, ——.
" Ephraim,	——. 15, ——.
" Gideon,	——. 16, ——.
" ——, (son), of George and Mary,	Sept. —, ——.
HAZELTON, Jarvis, of William and Mercy,	Oct. 28, 1711.
HEFFERNAN, Sukey, of Stephen and Abigail,	July —. ——.
" Sukey, died,	Feb. 28, ——.
" John,	July 6, ——.
" Eunice,	Aug. 20, ——.
" Jeremiah, Cranston,	April 5, ——.
HELME Mary (dau.), of Samuel and Dorcas,	June 14, 1700,
" Christopher,	Mar. 30, 1702-3.
" John,	Feb. 11, 1703-4.
" Samuel,	Oct. 21, 1706.
" Dorcas,	Jan. 14, 1710.
" William,	Mar. 12, 1713-14.
" Thomas,	Jan. 3, 1717-18.
" Mary,	——. —, ——.
" Mary, wife of Rouse, died,	May 9, 1712.
" Rouse, died	May 17, 1712.

HELME Benedict, of Rouse and Sarah, died	Oct. 18, 1718.
" —,	Dec. —, 1721.
" James, of Rouse and Sarah,	May 7, 1710.
" Sands,	Aug. 21, 1711.
" Rouse,	Feb. 11, 1712-3.
" Nathaniel,	Dec. 17, 1714.
" Benedict,	Feb. 17, 1716-7.
" Simeon,	Dec. 15, 1718.
" Benedict,	Oct. 3, 1720.
" —, of James and Esther,	July 20, 1740.
" Keziah, of Rouse, Jr. and Lydia; b. Dec. 15, 1735, d. Feb. 5, 1735-6.	
" Catherine,	March 7, 1736.
" —,	April 14, 1739.
" —,	April 22, 1741.
" —,	Feb. 6, 1742.
" —, (dau.), of —. Jr. and Mercy,	Feb. 19, 1745.
" —,	Feb. 3, 1747.
" —, (dau.),	Aug. 15, 1749.
" —— (dau.),	May 7, 1751.
" —— (dau.), died	Feb. 27, 1754.
" —— (son),	July 7, 1753.
" —,	July 20, 1755.
" —,	Jan. 16, 1757.
" Elizabeth,	March 31, 1760.
" Mercy,	July 11, 1764.
" —— (son),	May 7, 1756.
" Greene Capron, of Esther (col.),	May 19, 181—
" Mary, of William and Margaret,	Feb. 8, ——.
HIAMES Mary, of Sylvester,	
" Sarah,	Jan. 16, 1761.
" ——as (son),	April 16, 1763.
" Cleveland,	Oct. 23, 1765.
" Catherine,	Oct. 10, 1767.
" Sylvester,	Jan. 11, 1770.
" ——rnon (son),	July 22, 1773.
" " ——ais (dau.),	June 22, 1777.
" Elizabeth,	June 20, 1781.
" Joshua Vaughn, of Stukeley and Elizabeth,	May 19, 18—.
" John C.,	Oct. 8, 18—.
" John E.,	— —, ——.
" George, of George and An——,	Oct. 20, ——.
" —, of Benjamin and Mary,	Oct. 27, 1727.
" —,	May 10, 1726.
" —,	Nov. 6, 1728.
HILLARD —— (dau), of Ambrose and Mary,	Nov. 1, ——.
" —— (dau.),	July —, ——.
HILL Stukeley, of Caleb and Mercy,	Dec. 28, 1755.
" Caleb,	Sept. 5, 1758.
" Annie,	Jan. 29, 1761.
" Elizabeth,	Nov. 5, 1764.
" Sarah,	March 2, 1769.
" Rebecca,	Nov. 19, 1772.
" Polly, of Caleb and Sally,	Sept. 30, 1784.
" Fones Greene,	July 27, 1786.
" Wickes,	Sept. 14, 1788.
" Thomas,	Jan. 6, 1793.
" Sally,	Dec. 6, 1800.
" Sally, died	Dec. 26, 1800.
" Sally, 2d,	July 18, 1802.
" Caleb, of Thomas and Elizabeth,	March 29, ——.
" Matthew, of Thomas and Rebecca,	Jan. 21, ——.
" ——nial,	——. —, ——.
" ——d,	——. —, ——.
" Jonathan, of Ebenezer and Mary,	Oct. 30, —.

(Vit. Rec., Vol. 5.) 6

HILL Caleb, died		May 6, 1837.
" Sarah, wife of Caleb, died		Oct. 18, 1839.
HOLLOWAY William (S. K.), of William and Mary,		Nov. 9, ——.
" David Sherman,		March 28, ——.
" Eldred,		May 9, ——.
" Anna,		Feb. 23, ——.
" Mary,		June 7, ——.
" Hannah,		Feb. 15, ——.
HOXSIE Zebulon, of Joseph and Mary,		Aug. 11, 1697.
" Mary,		Sept. 15, 1699.
" Joseph,		Nov. 25, 1701.
" Ann,		Aug. 1, 1704.
" Gideon,		July 31, 1706.
" Lodowick,		Sept. 27, 1708.
" Ann,		Dec. 10, 1716.
" Zebulon,		Sept. 21, 1718.
HULING (Honour, of Alexander, Jr., and Elizabeth),		Sept. (28), 1729.
" (John),		(May 14), 1731.
" (Margaret),		(May) 13, 1733.
" Elizabeth,		Sept. (24), 1735.
" Alexander, of Alexander, of Alexander and Elizabeth,		Jan. 29, 1737-8.
" Virtue,		—— —, 1740-1.
" Catherine,		May 28, 1743.
" Walton,		—— —, 1745.
" Abigail,		—— —, ——.
" Martha,		Nov. 23, 1749.
" Lydia, of Alexander, of James and Mary (Smith),		(April) 5, (1745.)
" William,		March 1, (1748.)
" Avis,		Feb. 24, 17(43).
" Augustus,		March 2, 176(2).
" (James),		—— —, ——.
" Andrew,		March 7, 176(7).
Hannah (another record reads Henrietta), of Catherine,		Dec. 14, 1769.
" James, of Andrew (of Alexander) and Deliverance (Spink),		Nov. 17, 1784.
" William, of Andrew and Ruth,		May 18, 1791.
" Alexander,		March 4, 1793.
" Ray Greene,		Dec. 1, 1794.
" Toleration Harris,		April 18, 1797.
" Jonathan Donnison,		Aug. 25, 1799.
" *John Greene,		March 26, 180(1).
" Christopher,		April 17, 180(3).
" Mary Ann,		(July 6, 1805.)
" John, of Alexander and Susannah (Brown),		Oct. —, (1764.)
(*This was my grandfather. The town record was not correct as to the year of his birth, which was 1801. R. G. H.)		
" James,		Nov. 17, 1784.
" Elizabeth (Clarke), his wife,		Sept. 27, 1790.
" Gardiner C., of James and Elizabeth,		Dec. 19, 1809.
" Samuel S.,		May 3, 1812.
" Abigail S.,		March 7, 1814.
" Eleazer Slocum,		Feb. 29, 1818.
" Elizabeth W.,		Feb. 22, 1819.
" Oliver H. Perry,		Jan. 14, 1821.
" Emeline,		Oct. 27, 1822.
" Burrill James,		March 20, 1825.
" Juliette C.,		June 7, 1827.
" Ruth Esther,	b. Sept. 18, 1832;	d. July 30, 1836.
HULL Mary Ann G., of John and Watty Ann,		Nov. 22, ——.
" John B.,		Nov. 22, ——.
" George, E.,		Dec. 15, ——.
" William B.,		Feb. —, ——.
" Adelia,		—— —, ——.
HUNT Samuel, of Samuel,		Oct. 26, 1769.
" Susan (——), his wife,		Sept. 15, 1773.
" Susan, of Samuel and Susan,		June 1, 1795.
" Sally N.,		Nov. 4, 1796.

HUNT Charlotte, of Samuel and Susan,		Nov. 11, 1798.
"	Ruth Ann,	May 14, 1801.
"	Lucy,	Nov. 10, 1803.
"	Abbie,	March 17, 1807.
"	Mary S. H.,	March 21, 1812.
"	Esther, of George and Heart,	Oct. 23, 1788.
"	Gideon,	Dec. 29, 1790.
"	George,	April 25, 1793.
"	Jeremiah,	Feb. 21, 1796.
"	David, Whitford,	Oct. 4, 1798.
"	Mary Ann,	April 25, 1801.
"	David,	Feb. 20, 1804.
"	Eliza,	Sept. 17, 1806.
"	Charles,	Feb. 9, 1735.
"	Avis (——), his wife,	—— —, 1736.
"	Mary, of Charles and Avis,	—— —, ——.
"	William,	Oct. —, 17—.
"	Charles,	Feb. 17, 17—.
"	Rufus,	Nov. 13, 17—.
"	Elizabeth,	April 20, 17—.
"	Oliver, of Charles and Avis,	Dec. 15, 17—.
"	Jonathan,	July 15, 17—.
"	Ruth,	Oct. 15, 17—.
"	Avis,	April 30, 17—.
"	Sukey, of Samuel and Mary,	May 16, 17—.
"	Allen,	March 8, 179—.
"	Lawton Hazelton,	Feb. 7, 179—.
"	Job, of Rufus and Phebe,	Dec. —, ——.
"	—— (son), of Samuel, Jr.,	April 6, ——.
"	—— (son),	Aug. 18, ——.
"	—— (son),	Aug. 28, ——.
"	——.	Oct. 30, ——.
"	—— (son),	Sept. 9, ——
"	—— (son),	Sept. 21, ——

I

IRISH Jedediah, of Jedediah and Mary,		Nov. 16, 1711.
"	Mary,	Jan. 22, 1713-4.
"	Elizabeth,	Nov. 4, 1715.
"	Lydia,	Nov. 6, 1718.
"	John,	June 9, 1720.

J

JACKSON George, of Stephen,		—— 12, ——.
JACKWISE Ebenezer,		—— —, ——.
"	Lydia,	—— —, ——.
"	Hannah,	—— —, ——.
"	Elizabeth,	Aug. 25, ——.
"	Hannah, of Aaron and Elizabeth,	Jan. 10, ——.
"	Elisha,	Aug. 11, ——.
"	Mary,	Feb. 22, ——.
"	Lydia,	Aug. 2, ——.
JENCKES Waite Ann, of Brown,		Aug. 5, ——.
JENKINS Mary, of Job,		March 11, ——.
"	Elizabeth, of Phineas,	Jan. 31, ——.
"	Mary,	March 7, ——.
"	Amie,	Feb. 5, ——.
"	Azabah,	July 13, ——.
"	Sarah,	May 17, ——.
"	Benjamin Rush,	April 11, ——.
"	William,	April 19, ——.

JENKINS Silas, of Phineas,   Sept. 28, ——.
      Note—Born from 1780 to 1800.
JERKET John B., of Elisha and Mary,   Aug 4, 1806.
   "   James C.,   Aug 4, 1806.
JESS Elizabeth,   —— —, ——.
   "   Mary,   —— —, ——.
JOHNSON Ann, of Ezekiel and Ann,   July 24, 1718.
   "   Elizabeth,   March 5, 1719.
   "   Benjamin,   May 5, 1722.
   "   William, of Sylvester and Elizabeth,   Jan. 10, ——.
JUSTICE Margaret,   —— —, ——.
   "   Ann,   —— —, ——.
JUSTIN Freelove, of Thomas and Mary,   July 4, 1718.
   "   Jonathan, of Melicent,   Sept. 23, 1772.

K

KEAIS William, of William and M——.   Oct. 17, ——.
   "   Mary,   Jan. 30, ——.
   "   Hannah,   March 27, ——.
   "   Sybel,   Jan. 16, ——.
   "   Ebenezer,   June 17, ——.
   "   Alice,   July 23, ——.
   "   Nathan,   Oct. 11, ——.
   "   Hannah,   March 27, ——.
   "   Sybel (above died),   Sept. 26, ——.
   "   Sybel, 2d,   Oct. 15, ——.
KENYON John, of John and Elizabeth,   Nov. 21, 1706.
   "   Thomas,   Dec. 28, 1708.
   "   Sylvester,   April 7, 1710.
   "   George,   Sept. 28, 1712.
   "   Sarah,   Sept. 21, 1715.
KINGSLEY Samuel, of Samuel and Barthonia.   Jan. 4, 175—.
   "   Jonathan,   May 6, 175—.
   "   Lucy,   May 19, 175—.
   "   Samuel,   Jan. 21, 17—.
   "   Elizabeth,   Aug. 8, ——.
   "   Mary,   April 18, ——.
   "   Jedediah,   Nov. 8, ——.
   "   Deliverance,   May 5, ——.
   "   Jonathan, of John and Abiah,   Oct. 8, ——.
   "   Samuel,   March 20, ——.
   "   Mehitable,   Jan. 30, ——.
   "   Jedediah,   April 10, ——.
   "   Sarah,   Feb. 27, ——.
   "   Elizabeth,   Dec. 19, ——.
   "   Abiah,   July 14, ——.

L

LAWTON —— (son), of Thomas and Elizabeth,   Nov. 24, 1742.
   "   George Nichols, of —— and Susannah,   March 14, ——.
   "   Waitey Nichols,   —— —, ——.
   "   Benjamin C.,   —— —, ——.
   "   ——,   —— —, 1802.
   "   Susannah Hall, of ——, Jr., and Susannah,   Jan. —, ——.
   "   Benjamin Clarke,   May 4, ——.
LLUFIO John, of Constantine and Eliza,   Aug. 24, 18)9.
LOVELESS ——, of Thomas and Isabel,   April 11, 1736.

M

MARSHALL Jeremiah, of Jacob and Parmelly,		Jan. —, ——.
"	John,	Nov. —, ——.
"	Joseph,	March —, ——.
"	Abigail,	—— —, ——.
"	Benjamin,	Oct. 16, ——.
MATHERSON Obediah, of Joseph and Martha,		April 13, ——.
"	Jonathan,	—— —, ——.
"	William,	Feb. 2, ——.
"	Alice,	June —, ——.
"	Elizabeth,	Nov. —, ——.
"	Thomas,	May 2, ——.
"	—— (son),	May —, ——.
M'COONE Hannah, of Daniel and Sarah,		May 18, 1706.
"	Abigail,	Dec. 14, 1707.
"	Thankful,	Dec. 17, 1710.
M'KENSIE James, of John and Catherine,		March 22, 17—.
MITCHELL Silas, (N. S.), of Alexander and Dorcas,		May 3, 1805.
"	Ephraim, of Ephraim and Deborah,	March 10, ——.
"	Mary,	Oct. 16, ——.
"	Richard,	April 22, ——.
"	Sarah,	Feb. 22, ——.
"	Elisha,	March 14, ——.
"	James, of William and Sarah,	Jan. 11, ——.
"	Samuel, of Samuel and Margaret,	May 18, ——.
"	Elizabeth,	Oct. 23, ——.
"	Abigail	May 21, ——.
"	Mary,	Dec. 22, ——.
"	Sarah,	Sept. 21, ——.
"	Daniel,	Jan. 20, ——.
MOONE —— (son), of Ebenezer and Elizabeth,		Oct. 18, 1706.
"	—— (dau.),	Aug. 31, 1708.
"	—— (dau.),	Sept. 22, 1711.
"	—— (son),	June 25, 1713.
"	—— (son),	Feb. 3, 1716.
"	Elizabeth,	June 6, 1718.
"	—— (dau.),	Dec. 2, 1720.
"	——, (dau.),	Dec. 4, 1722.
"	——, (dau.),	Nov. 10, 17—.
"	——, (son),	Sept. 21, 17—.
"	——, (dau.),	——. —, ——.
"	——, (dau.),	——. —, ——.
"	Robert, of Robert and Ann,	Oct. —, ——.
"	Mehitable,	Dec. —, ——.
"	Jonathan,	Aug. 13, ——.
"	Deliverance,	——. —, ——.
"	Elizabeth,	——. —, ——.
"	John,	——. —, ——.
MOORE John Pinder, of William and Deborah,		June —, ——.
MOREY Dorcas, of Augustus and Patience,		July 31, 1783.
"	Richard, of John and Lo——,	June 12, ——.
"	John,	May 26, ——.
"	Joseph, of Robert and Sarah,	March 20, ——.
"	Sarah,	——. 13, ——.
"	Jeremiah,	Dec. 20, ——.
"	Mary,	——. 18, ——.
MOTT Sweet, of John,		March 30, ——.
"	John, of John and Elizabeth,	Aug. 9, 1694.
"	Mary,	Sept. 15, 1696.
"	Elizabeth,	April 7, 1700.
"	Jonathan,	Nov. 12, 1703.
"	Hannah,	Aug. —, 1705.
"	Samuel,	March —, 1708.
"	Sarah,	Oct. 16, 1713.

MUMFORD Thomas, of Thomas and Hannah,   Sept. 14, 1706.
  "   John,   May 29, 1714.
  "   Abigail,   Sept. 3, 1710.
  "   Mary, of George and Mary,   Nov. 15, 1710.
  "   Abigail,   April 7, 1713.
  "   William, of William and Hannah,   Dec. 2, 1721.
  "   Henry, of Thomas and Abigail,   May 28, 1753
  "   Henry,   died Oct. 21, 1753.
  "   Thomas,   June 26, 17—.
  "   Stephen, of —— and Judith,   —— —, ——.
  "   Judith,   June 25, ——.
  "   Sarah,   —— —, ——.
  "   Pearce,   —— —, ——.
  "   Perry,   —— 25, ——.
MUNDAY George, of Nathaniel and Elizabeth Ann,   March 18, 1799.

N

NANNIE Robinson, son of (negro) Cotterly, deceased in this town, born Aug. 14,
        1764.
NASON Benjn. Jefferson, of James and Sarah,   Feb. 17, ——.
  "   Elisha,   July 27, ——.
  "   Betsey,   Nov. 2, ——.
  "   John,   Jan. 20, ——.
NEWTON ——, (dau.) of James and Mary,   March —, 1703-4.
        These were not taken from N. K. Records, but from an old paper
        in possession of Mrs. Joseph Brown.
NICHOLS Hannah (wife of Thomas),   b. Dec. 17, 1642.
  "   Thomas, of (Thomas and) Hannah,   Aug. 6, 1660.
  "   Susannah,   Oct. 15, 1662.
  "   John,   April 16, 1666.
  "   Robert,   Nov. 22, 1671.
  "   Hannah,   Aug. 7, 1674.
  "   Benjamin,   Jan. 28, 1676.
  "   Jonathan,   June 10, 1681.
  "   Joseph,   April 18, 1684.
  "   Elizabeth,   June 14, 1688.
            (Place of births uncertain; probably Newport.)
  "   Benjamin, of Benjamin and Mary,   Aug. 22, 1698.
  "   Jonathan,   Nov. 27, 1700.
  "   Ruth,   March 13, 1703.
  "   Joseph,   June 8, 1707.
  "   John,   Dec. 20, 1709.
  "   William,   March 25, 1712.
  "   Thomas,   Feb. 28, 1714.
  "   George,   Aug. 25, 1715.
  "   Ann,   Oct. 16, 1717.
  "   Mary, of Thomas and Rebecca,   April —, 1738.
  "   Benjamin,   Oct. 11, 1739.
  "   ——,   March 20, 1743-4.
  "   Elizabeth,   Dec. 13, 1745.
  "   ——,   March 7, 1747.
  "   ——,   May 30, 1750.
  "   ——, (dau.),   July 30, 17—.
  "   ——,   July 20, 17—.
  "   George, of Benjamin and Mary,   b. Aug. 25, 1715.
  "   Waite Vaughn (of David), his wife,   b. May 2, 1722.
  "   Mary, of George and Weight (Waite) (Vaughn), (Sept. 12, 1744.)
  "   Susannah,   Aug. (26, 1748).
  "   Jonathan,   Aug. 27, 1752.
  "   Sarah,   Sept. (5, 1757).
  "   George, above, d.   Dec. 8, 1794.
  "   Waite, his wife, d.   March 2, 1800.
  "   Lydia, of —— (of Thomas) and Anstrus,   Feb. 17, ——.

NICHOLS Sisson, of —— and Anstrus,	Feb. 24, ——.
"	Hannah,	Nov. 28, ——.
"	Elizabeth,	Jan. 14, 1767.
"	Benjamin,	Nov. 24, 176—.
"	Mary,	Sep. 9, 1770.
"	Russell,	July 7, 1772.
"	George,	Feb. 17, 1773.
"	Sarah, of Col. Thomas, died at Newport,	Sept. —, 1787.
·	John Mendall, of Samuel and Mary.	April 8, ——.
"	Samuel.	Oct. 7, ——.
"	Henry Hall,	Sept. 9, ——.
"	Susannah,	April 20, ——
"	Joseph,	Jan. 5, ——.
"	Joseph, d.	Feb. 7, 1792.
"	Thomas Wall,	April 21, ——.
"	Jeanna Mendall,	July 2, ——.
"	Mary Phillips,	July 25, ——.
"	George Burdict, of George T. and Amie Ann,	April 9, 182—.
"	Annie Frances,	Oct. 5, 182—.
"	Walter S.,	Feb. 6, 183—.
"	Lucinda Caroline,	Nov. 16, 183—.
"	Josephine,	Sept. 27, 183—.
"	Thomas Wilson Dorr,	July 25, 184—.
"	Joseph, of John and Elizabeth,	July 16, ——.
"	John,	—— 30, ——.
NILES Nathan, of Nathaniel and Mary,	Sept. 12, 1700.
"	Robert,	Nov. 9, 1702.
"	Mary,	Aug. 14, 1704.
"	Jeremiah,	April 7, 1707.
"	Sarah,	June 17, 1711.
"	Tabitha,	Nov. 14, 1714.
"	Silas,	May 26, 1718.
"	Paul,	May 16, 1721.
"	Sylvanus,	May 16, 1721.
"	Sylvanus, d.	June —, 1721.
"	James Hazard, of Patience (colored), born in South Kingstown. Dec. 13, ——.
NORTHUP ——, of Joseph and Elizabeth,	Dec. 5, 1727.
"	——,	Aug. 12, 1729.
"	——.	Sept. 15, 1731.
"	——.	June 21, 1734.
"	——,	Sept. 17, 1736.
"	——.	July 17, 1740.
"	——.	Nov. 4, 1745.
"	David, of Robert and Susannah,	May 9, 1746.
"	Dorcus,	Nov. 30, 1748.
"	Nicholas,	Oct. 26, 1751.
"	Hannah,	Aug. 12, 1755.
"	Benjamin,	Dec. 18, 1757.
"	William.	June 4, 1760.
"	David, of Rufus and Mary,	Sept. 29, 175—.
"	Abigail,	April 9, 175—.
"	Stephen,	May 29, 176—.
"	Catherine, of Joseph (of Henry) and Mary,	——. —, ——.
"	Patience,	——. —, ——.
"	Patience,	d. Nov. 15, 175—.
"	Samuel, of Gideon,	Oct. 16, 17—.
"	Ann,	Nov. 4, 175—.
"	William,	July 22, 176—.
"	Sarah,	Nov. 28, 176—.
"	Dorcas,	Jan. 29, 176—.
"	Frederick,	May 30, 176—.
"	Mary, of Joseph and Mary,	Aug. 22, 17—.
"	Henry,	May 4, 175—.
"	John,	April 4, 175—.
"	John, died,	Nov. 15, 175—.

NORTHUP John, 2d, of Joseph and Mary,	Jan. 14, 175--.
" Joseph,	Sept. 1, 175--.
" Patience,	April 8, 175--.
" John, of George and Francis,	Sept. 9, 1754.
" John, died,	Oct. 5, 1754.
" Anne,	June 28, 17--.
" Henry,	April 14, ----.
" Sarah,	June 4, ----.
" Mary,	Feb. 13, ----.
" Tibbith,	Feb. 4, ----.
" Frances,	Oct. 28, ----.
" Frances, died,	April 3, fol'g.
" Frances, 2d,	Jan. 14, ----.
" George,	Feb. --, 1769.
" ----, (son), of John,	July 30, ----.
" Lydia, of John and Phebe, 2d w.,	July 23, 176--.
" Sarah,	April 5, 1767.
" Jeremiah G.,	July 20, 1771.
" Phebe, wife of John, died	July 27, 1771.
" Nichols, son of Nicholas and Ann Slocum, of ----, of Jamestown, their children.	
" Harris,	Jan. 4, ----.
" Remington,	Feb. 1, 1764.
" Gideon,	Jan. 4, 1766.
" Peleg,	Aug. 4, 1769.
" John,	Sept. 9, 1770.
" William,	Nov. 20, 1772.
" Ebenezer,	Dec. 25, 1774.
" Benjamin,	April 10, 1777.
" Benoni,	Nov. 17, 1779.
" Stephen,	Jan. 26, 1782.
" Mary,	July 13, 1784.
" Daniel Gould, of ----, (of Immanuel) and Mary,	Sept. 13, ----.
" --ay,	July 17, 17--.
" ----, died	Oct. 7, 1777.
" Mary,	Dec. 19, 1779.
" Sarah,	Jan, 19, 1781.
" Elizabeth,	Sept. 1, 1782.
" Elizabeth,	d. Nov. 28, 1782.
" Joseph,	Oct. 6, 1783.
" John Gardiner,	Sept. 25, 1785.
" Elizabeth,	Jan. 9, 1788.
" Henry W.,	Aug. 14, 1790.
" ----anin (dau.),	Nov. 30, 1792.
" ---- (dau.), of Stephen (of Stephen) and Martha,	---- 10, 1780.
" ---- (dau.),	April 1, 1783.
" ---- (son),	Aug. 10, 1785.
" ----,	Feb. 20, 178--.
" ----,	Nov. 23, 178--.
" ----,	Feb. 8, 17--.
" Daniel, of Stephen (of Rufus) and Mary,	July 30, 1783.
" ----,	Oct. 4, 1786.
" Mary,	Oct. 19, 1788.
" ---- (dau.), of Stephen (of Rufus) and ----, 2d wife,	Oct. 25, 1793.
" Christopher,	Aug. 27, 179--.
" ----,	April 16, 1794.
" Thomas G., of Cyrus and Sarah,	June 16, 1797.
" Amelia,	March 22, 1800.
" Cyrus,	Sept. 1, 1801.
" ----,	Jan. 8, 180--.
" Sally Smith, of Abial P. and Thurza,	June 5, 1831.
" Elizabeth,	Oct. 10, ----.
" Sarah Clarke,	Sept. 10, ----.
" William Hall,	Oct. 25, ----.
" Christopher Carr,	April 14, ----.

NORTHUP Isaac, of Abial P. and Thurza,		Jan. 14, ——.
" Thomas,		—— —, ——.
" Abigail,		—— —, ——.
" Nicholas,		April —, ——.
" Gideon,		Jan. —, ——.
" Rouse.		March —, ——.
" Daniel,	b. April —, ——;	d. Nov. —, ——.
" Eunice,		Nov. —, ——.
" William,		Dec. 8, ——.
" Immanuel, of Henry and Mary,		June 17, 1699.
" Henry, of Immanuel and Ann Tibbetts, of George		Aug. 7, 1722.
" Mary,		Feb. 9, 1724.
" George,		Aug. 7, 1727.
Note.—Immanuel had three wives. See below.		
" Ann, of Nicholas,		—— 5, ——.
" Benjamin,		—— —, ——.
" Freelove,		—— —, ——.
" Hannah,		—— —, ——.
" ——,		April 5, ——.
" Rufus, of David.		Feb. 19, ——.
" Susannah,		April 11, ——.
" Mary,		March 1, ——.
" Benjamin,		Feb. 25, ——.
" Henry, of Immanuel and Sarah (Gould) (2d wife),		June 26, 1729.
" Henry,		d. Oct. 8, 1736.
" Mary,		March 10, 1732.
" Jeremiah,		April 6, 1734.
" John,		Jan. 16, 1735.
" Daniel,		June 10, 1738.
" Henry, 2d, (3d)		April 23-(2), 1740.
" Sarah, wife of Immanuel		d March 15, 1745.
" David, of David and Susannah,		Dec. 11, ——.
" Stephen,		Oct. 9, ——.
" Benjamin,		June 1, ——.
" Robert,		Aug. 20, ——.
" Gould, of Jeremiah and Sophia,		—— 17, ——.
This is given above on p. 113, also exc. death of 1st wife, Ann. See below at bottom of page.		
" Henry, of Immanuel and Ann,		(Aug. 7, 1722.)
" Mary,		Feb. 9, (1724.)
" George,		Aug. 7, 1727.
" Ann, wife of Immanuel.		died Aug. 28, (1728.)
" Sarah Ann, of Nicholas (Carr) and Anne,		July 14, (1786.)
" Hannah,		Oct. 31, (1787.)
" Elizabeth Bliss,		(June 11, 1789.)
" Carr,		Sept. (25, 1791.)
" Waitey,		Jan. 14, (1793.)
" John Holmes,		Aug. (9, 1796.)
" Immanuel,		July 18, (1798.)
" Mary,		Dec. 31, (1800.)
" Carr, of Immanuel and Ann, 3d wife,		April 1, 1747.
" Ann,		Aug. 20, 1749.
NORTH (Jere)miah, of Thomas and Abigail,		Jan. 24, ——.
" (Susan),		July 23, ——.
" ——, (dan.),		Feb. 15, ——.
" —— (son),		Feb. —, ——.
" —— (son),		—— —, ——.
" Thomas, of John,		—— 2, ——.

O

ONION Nathaniel, of Margaret,	May 9, 1804.
" Joseph,	Feb. 28, 1809.
" Nathaniel, of Sarah,	March 28, ——.

OLIN Harris, of — and Sarah,	Nov. 14, 1765.
" Hannah,	Feb. 8, 176—.
" Isabel,	Aug. 21, 176—.
" Sarah,	April 7, 1770.
" Ezra,	March 23, 1772.
" Phebe,	July 7, 1774.
" Daniel, of Barbara, dau. of John,	March 21, 1768.
" John, of Giles and Ann,	Sept. 24, 1770.
" John,	d. Sept. 26, 1770.
" William,	Nov. 6, 1771.
" —nis,	Nov. 7, 1773.
" —ny,	Aug. 10, 1776.
" —, (son),	Oct. 2, 1775.
" —, (son),	died Nov. 10, 1775.
" Peace,	May 12, 1778.

P

PECKHAM Nathaniel, of Abraham and Tabitha,	Jan. 22, 1710-11.
" Elizabeth,	March 21, 1712-13.
" Sarah,	June 17, 1715.
" Tabitha,	June 17, 1715.
" Benjamin, of Benjamin and Mary,	March 22, 1715.
" Sarah,	May 11, 1717.
" —,	June 23, 1778.
" —,	April 17, 1780.
" —,	Dec. 23, 1782.
" —,	Sept. 17, 1784.
" —,	April 9, 1786.
" Thomas Boone, of Benedict and Mary,	June 18, —.
" Mary, wife of Benedict,	died Dec. 15, —.
" Mary, of Benedict and Elizabeth,	June 6, —.
" Elizabeth,	Dec. 24, —.
" Patience,	Dec. 24, —.
" Benedict Eldred,	Oct. 10, —.
" Benedict Eldred,	d. Oct. 16, 1784.
" Lydia,	April 19, —.
" Clement, of Benedict and Elizabeth,	Feb. 21, —.
" Clement,	d. July 27, —.
" Benedict,	Nov. 15, —.
" Sarah,	Oct. 21, —.
" Sarah,	d. Dec. 23, —.
" Ann,	July 12, —.
PECK Amie, of Aaron and Alsie,	Aug. 6, 1772.
" Nancy,	April 12, 1775.
PERKINS Tabitha, wife of Abraham,	d. Dec. 28, —; b. — 30, 1717.
PHILLIPS —, (dau.) of Samuel and Abigail,	Nov. 1, 1733.
" —, (son),	Jan. 13, 1735.
" —, (dau.),	April 27, 1737.
" —, (son),	Sept. 11, 1739.
" Samuel, of Christopher and Peggy, dau. of Nathaniel Rathbun, late of New Shoreham. Children—	
" —, (dau.),	Jan. 30, 1772.
" —, (son),	April 17, 1774.
" —, (dau.),	April 17, 1774
" Peggy, wife of Samuel,	d. — 7, 1774.
" —,	— 16, —.
" Samuel, of Thomas and —archas,	Feb. 7, 17—.
" Peter,	— —, —.
" Frederic,	— —, —.
" Elizabeth,	July —, —.
" Henry A.,	d. Feb. 26, 1863.
PIERCE James, of Jonathan,	Oct. 9, —.
" Caleb, of — and Freelove,	Nov. 16, —.

PIERCE	Elizabeth, of —— and Freelove,	March 28, ——.
"	Silas,	Dec. 4, 17—.
"	Mary,	Oct. 10, 175—.
"	Abigail,	May 16, 1764.
"	Freelove,	Aug. 28, 1766.
"	Smith,	April 16, 1770.
"	——, of Nathan and Abigail	Aug. 19, 1725.
"	——,	Feb. 10, 172—.
"	Christopher, of Christ., (of Christr) and ——,	—— 18, ——.
"	John, of Benjamin,	Feb. 20, 1750.
"	——, of John,	Oct. 18, 1773.
"	Samuel,	Nov. 10, 1775.
"	Elizabeth,	Nov. 10, 1777.
"	William,	Nov. 4, 1780.
"	John,	Aug. 3, 1783.
PINDER	——, (son), of John and Susannah,	April, —, 1716.
"	——, (son),	March 11, 1720.
"	——, (son),	Dec. 3, 1723.
"	——, (dau.),	Dec. 11, 1725.
"	——, (dau.),	Oct. 1, 1728.
"	Mary,	—— —, ——.
"	John,	—— —, ——.
PLACE	Mary, of Enock and Mary,	Oct. 16, 1697.
"	Mary, of Thomas and Hannah,	Jan. 5, 169—.
"	Marbery,	May 5, 169—.
"	Thomas,	Nov. 2, 169—.
"	John,	April 24, 170—.
"	Sarah,	May 10, 170—
"	Joseph,	Dec. 22, 170—.
"	Samuel,	Sept. —, 170—.
"	——, (son), of Joseph and Johannah,	Jan. 9, 1699.
"	Enoch,	April 12, 1701.
"	——, (dau.),	—— —, 1706.
"	Hannah,	Sept. —, 1709.
"	Peter,	July —, 1714.
"	——, (son), of Samuel and Synee,	Dec. 30, 17—.
"	——, (son),	Nov. 23, 17—.
"	——, (dau.),	Oct. 3, ——.
"	——, (dau.),	Jan. 26, ——.
"	Samuel, of Samuel and Sarah,	Sept. 26, 17—,
"	John,	Sept. 14, 17—
"	Anne,	July 8, 17—.
"	James,	Aug. 20, 17—.
"	Mary,	May 17, 17—.
"	Margaret,	Aug. 3, 17—.
"	Sarah,	April 29, 17—.
"	Sarah,	d. Sept. 19, 1782.
"	Patience, of John and Elizabeth,	June 20, 1756.
"	Thomas, of Enoch and Hannah,	April 24, ——.
"	Stephen,	March —, ——.
"	Benajah,	Dec. 28 ——.
"	George,	June 28, ——.
"	Mary,	July 12, ——.
"	Peter,	June 25, ——.
"	George, of Joseph,	——, 7, ——.
POTTER	Martha, of John and Sarah,	Dec. 20, 1692.
"	John,	May 20, 1695.
"	Samuel,	Sept. 2, 1699.
"	Sarah,	April 15, 1702.
"	Susannah,	Sept. 17, 1704.
"	Mary,	March 2, 1706-7.
"	Samuel,	July 28, 1715.
"	Thomas, of Thomas and Susannah,	Feb. 8, 1695.
"	John,	Oct. 2, 1697.
"	Nathaniel,	April 15, 1700.

POTTER Benjamin, of Thomas and Susannah,   Jan. 19, 1703.
"   Joseph,   Jan. 30, 1706.
"   Mary,   Aug. 16, 1708.
"   Thomas, of Thomas and Mary,   Sept. 14, 1720.
"   (*Barberry), Marbary, of Robert and Elizabeth,   Feb. 2, 1697-8.
"   Martha,   Aug. 10, 1699.
"   Robert,   July 26, 1702.
"   Icbabod,   Nov. 30, 1703.
"   Susan,   Feb. 14, 1705.
"   John, of John and Mercy,   Jan. 3, 1715-16.
"   Christopher,   Nov. 5, 1717.
"   Christopher, 2d,   Nov. 8, 1719.
"   Mary,   May 24, 1721.
"   Lydia, of Robert and Meriam,   March —, ——.
"   John,   May 1, ——.
"   Sarah, of Robert and Meriani,   Aug. 5, ——.
"   Hannah,   Jan. 31, ——.
"   Joseph, of John,   Sept. 24, ——.
"   Benjamin,   Sept. 24, ——.
"   Mary,   Feb. 4, ——.
"   Hannah,   — 28, ——.
"   John,   — 27, ——.
"   Sarah,   — 27, ——.
"   Mattbew,   July 5, ——.

Q R

RATHBUN Mary, of Roger and Mary,   Jan. 25, 1764.
"   Josbua, of A. B. and Waitey,   Dec. 5, 1797.
"   Deborah C.,   Nov. 24, 1799.
"   Elizabeth Thomas,   Oct. 30, 1801.
"   Waite,   Nov. 4, 1803.
"   — P., of A. B. and Mary,   June 26, 18—.
"   Joseph,   July —, ——.
"   Rebecca,   Dec. —, ——.
"   Mary,   Nov. —, ——.
"   Ann,   July 3, ——.
RAY ——, of John and Rebecca,   Nov. 6, 1730.
"   ——, of John and Mary,   May 29, 1736.
"   ——,   Dec. 14, 1737.
"   ——,   Aug. 3, 1739.
"   ——,   April 11, 1741.
REMINGTON Matilda, died aged 27 years,   Dec. 10, 1852.
REYNOLDS John, of James (of William), and Deborah, Oct. 12, 1648, and shot by
        tbe Indians, —— —, 1675.
"   James, of James (of William), and Deborah,   Oct. 28, 1650.
"   Joseph,   Nov. 27, 1652.
"   Henry,   Jan. 1, 1656.
"   Deborah,   —— —, 1658.
"   Francis,   Oct. 12, 1662.
"   Mary,   —— —, 1664.
"   James, of James and Sarah,   Feb. 12, 1705-6.
"   ——, (son), of John and Hannah.   Aug. 23, 1722.
"   Benjamin,   Jan. 31, 1726.
"   ——, (son),   Oct. 9, 172-.
"   ——, (dau.),   Nov. 14, 17—.
"   ——, (dau.),   March 11, 17—.
"   ——,   —, 5, 17—.
"   John,   born —— —. 1723, died about —— —, 1775.
"   ——, of John,   Oct. 5, 1729.
"   ——,   Feb. 17, 1731.
"   ——,   July 18, 1733.
"   Pbebe, of John and Sarah,   Jan. 2, 1747.
"   Wealthian,   April 20, 1749.

REYNOLDS Anna, of John and ——, 2d wife,   Aug. 9, 1751.
"   William,   July 19, 1753.
"   Benjamin,   April 19, 1756.
"   Daniel,   June 3, 1760.
"   Hannah,   May 5, 1743.
"   James,   Nov. 24, 1744.
"   Jonathan, of John and Mehitable,   Jan. 2, 1749.
"   Francis,   Aug. 4, 1750.
"   Sarah,   Aug. 8, 1752.
"   Mehitable,   Feb. 14, 1754.
"   Esther,   Sept. 11, 1755.
"   Henry,   Dec. 21, 1757.
"   Waity,   Dec. 25, 1759.
"   Elizabeth,   Nov. 30, 1761.
"   Colonel,   Jan. 24, 1765.
"   ——, (son), of Jonathan,   March 16, 1747.
"   ——, (dau.),   March 13, 1749.
"   ——, (son),   Feb. 3, 175..
"   ——,   March 16, 1753.
"   ——,   March 12, 1755.
"   ——,   Feb. 3, 1757.
"   ——,   March 31, 1759.
"   ——, (dau.),   Feb. 7, 1761.
"   ——, (son),   Feb. 4, 1763.
"   ——, (son),   May 7, 1765.
"   Abel,   Dec. 10, ——.
"   Anna,   April —, ——.
"   Sarah,   April 21, ——.
"   ——, (dau.) of John (of John) and ——.   July 11, 175--.
"   Dorcas,   March 15, 176--.
"   Eldred,   April 2, 1765.
"   Ruth,   July 23, 1766.
"   Sarah,   May 19, 1768.
"   Joseph, of Jabez and Susannah,   Feb. 1, 1758.
"   Henry,   March 11, 1759.
"   Mary,   March 14, 176--.
"   Phebe,   Jan. 1, 1765.
"   Lucy,   Dec. 1, 1771.
"   Joseph (died)   May 8, 1758.
"   William, of Jabez and Sybel, 2d, wife,   April 20, 1779.
"   Peter, of James and Rebecca,   May 24, 1761.
"   James,   July 5, 1763.
"   Elizabeth,   Nov. 14, 1767.
"   Dorcas, of Francis (of John) and Anna,   Jan. 11, 1773.
"   Mary,   Sept. 26, 1775.
"   Anna,   Dec. 28, 1778.
"   Martha,   April 20, 1781.
"   ——anis,   Aug. 17, 1783.
"   Colonel,   Oct. 17, 1786.
"   Tibbette,   Oct. 15, 1788.
"   ——ah, (dau.), of Jonathan and Anstis,   Dec. 3, 1777.
"   George,   July —, 1780.
"   Anstis,   June 5, 1784.
"   Elizabeth, of Benjn (of John), and Elizabeth   July 19, 1779.
"   John,   Dec. 21, 1780.
"   ——as,   Nov. 8, 1782.
"   Mehitable,   Aug. 18, 1784.
"   Anna,   May 17, 1786.
"   Sarah,   Oct. 15, 1787.
"   Elizabeth,   Aug. 12, 1789.
"   Waite,   Oct. 10, 1791.
"   William W.,   April 26, 1793.
"   George W.,   Sept. 5, 1796.
"   James,   Aug. 11, 1798.
"   Hannah,   June 5, 1802.

REYNOLDS ——, (dau.), of George, (of Joseph), and Sarah,   —— —., 1778.
"   ——, (son),   May 16, 1780.
"   ——,   July 25, 1782.
"   ——,   June 8, 1784.
"   ——,   June 25, 1787.
"   ——,   May 11, 1790.
"   ——,   Oct. 15, 1792.
"   ——,   —— 3, 1795.
"   ——. of Henry (of John) and Mary,   Oct. 24, 1785.
"   ——,   Jan. 4, 1788.
"   Ann,   Oct. 7, 1790.
"   Elizabeth Fones,   June 11, 1793.
"   ——,   June 11, 1793.
"   ——,   Sept. 26, 1796.
"   ——than, of —— and Esther,   March ——, 17—.
"   Nicholas,   Dec. 22, 17—.
"   ——is,   April 7, 17—.
"   ——, (son)   Oct. 17, 17—.
"   ——olon Utter,   Nov. 15, 17—.
"   Esther,   Aug. 19, 178-.
"   William,   March 12, 179--.
"   Saml Watson, .   April 13, 179--.
"   Daniel,   May 13, 1797.
"   ——. of —— and Elizabeth,   Feb. 28, 1795.
"   ——,   Sept. 23, 1798.
"   William M.,   May 3, 1800.
"   ——,   April 3, 1795.
"   ——,   Oct. 26, 179—.
"   ——,   Sept. 27, ——.
"   Susannah Wall, of William, (of Benjamin) and Susannah, Aug. 12, 180—.
"   Esther Chapone, of Jonathan and Mary,   Sept. 1, 180—.
"   Helena Maria Williams,   Jan. 29, 180—.
"   Mary Mehitable,   Aug. 16, 1807.
"   Hannah Anne Utter,   May 15, 1810.
"   John Jonathan,   Dec. 7, 181—.
"   William Peter,   May 21, 181—.
"   William Peter, died,   Oct. 1, 1817.
"   James J., of Geo. W. and Ruth,   Jan. 13, 1818.
"   George W.,   Dec. 30, 1822.
"   Charles E., of George W. and Mary Ann,   May 30, 1830.
"   David G., of Gardiner and Elizabeth,   Nov. 27, ——.
"   Mary,   Oct. ——, ——.
"   Phebe,   ——. 11, ——
"   Benjamin, of John B., (of Benjamin), and Mary,   July 11, ——.
"   Mary,   Oct. 17, ——.
"   John D.,   Jan 5, ——.
"   Hazard D.,   April 6, ——.
"   Abbie,   April 22, ——.
"   William W. A.,   Aug. 31, ——.
"   Elizabeth,   Aug. 9, ——.
"   Ann G.,   Feb. 20, ——.
"   Emma,   April 18, ——.
"   Almira,   April 23, ——.
"   Allen,   Dec. 19, ——.
"   Sarah Leontha,   Dec. ——, ——.
"   Sarah,   —— ——, ——.
"   Stephen,   —— ——, ——.
"   Henry,   —— ——, ——.
"   Mary,   —— ——, ——.
"   Hannah,   —— ——, ——.
"   John,   —— ——, ——.
"   Martha,   —— ——, ——.
"   Peter,   —— ——, ——.
"   Mary,   Aug. 3, ——.
"   Stephen,   Sept. 25, ——.

REYNOLDS —, of Joseph and Susannah, April 27, —.
  " —, March 22, —.
  " —, Dec. 21, —.
  " —, Oct. 18, —.
  " —, Aug. 14, —.
  " —, Dec. 13, —.
  " —, — 7, —.
  " William, July 19, —.
  " Esther, wife of William, Aug. 11, —.
  " Esther, wife of William, d. Sept. 7, —.
  " Jonathan, of William and Esther, March —. —.
  " Nicholas, Dec. —, —.
  " James, April —, —.
  " Nicholas, d. Jan. 19, —.
  " Silas, Oct. —, —.
  " Silas, died (Troy, N. Y.), Oct. 22, —.
  " Zebulon U., Nov. —, —.
  " Esther, Aug. —, —.
  " William J., March —, —.
  " Samuel Watson, April —, —.
  " Daniel, of William and Esther, March —, —.
  " Daniel, died, at Cherrybourne Hospital, near Batavia, N. Y.,
                                                         March 21, 1821.
  " Jabez, of Wm., (of Jabez) and Elizabeth, Jan. 31, 1803.
  " James, Nov. 27, 1804.
  " Lydia. Oct. 9, 1807.
  " William K., Sept. 9, 1812.
  " Bowen, Nov. 11, 1814.
  " Thomas A., Nov. 1, 1817.
  " Richard, June 25, 1820.
  " Obediah B., Feb 13, 1823.
  " Mary Northup, of — and Rebecca, April 22, —.
  " Eliza, Feb. 22, —.
  " Abigail Burrough, Nov. 28, —.
  " Frances, Jan. 24, —.
  " Wm. Hookey, Aug. 29, —.
  " Benjn. Burrough, Jan. 2, —.
  " Sarah Jane, Nov. 21, —.
  " Edwin Nelson, Sept. 20, —.
  " Edwin Nelson, died, April —, —.
  " Christian, of George and Hannah, — —, —.
  " Susannah, — 17, —.
  " Isabel, April 5, —.
  " Ann, Nov. 29, —.
  " Robert, Feb. 21, —.
  " Martha, Feb. 6, —.
  " Mary, Feb. 6, —.
  " Sarah, Aug. 11, —.
  " Thomas, of Samuel, March 16, —.
  " Freelove, Oct. 31, —.
  " Abigail, M— 11, —.
  " Susannah, of Jabez and Mary, Oct. 1, —.
  " James, July 21, —.
  " Jabez, Oct. 22, —.
  " John, — —, —.
  " Mary, — 11, —.
  " Mary, 2d, — 21, —.
  " James, — 15, —.
  " Elizabeth, — 14, —.
  " Ruth, Dec. 28, —.
  " Deborah, — 7, —.
  " Amey, Nov. 18, —.
RICHARDSON Benjamin, of — and Elizabeth, — —, —.
  " Elizabeth, — 20, —.
      By above wife when she bore the name of Hill.

RICHARDSON Mary, of —— and Elizabeth,	Dec. —, ——.
ROBINSON Mary, of John and Mary,	Sept. 30, 1705.
"　　Sarah,	Jan. 22, 1706-7.
"　　Ruth,	March 12, 1708-9.
ROOME William, of Cato and Dorcas,	April 4, ——.
ROSE Charles Henry, of Charles and Lydia,	Nov. —, ——.
ROUSE Mary Grant, of John H. and Sophoronia,	May 31, 1838.
"　　Alexander Billings,	Jan. 20, 1842.
"　　John Frederic Hill,	Sept. 28, 1844.

S

SAMBO Christopher, of Samuel and Eunice,	Dec. 20, ——.
"　　Barbara,	—— —, ——.
"　　James,	—— —, ——.
"　　Job,	—— 30, ——.
"　　Patience,	—— —, ——.
"　　Mercy,	May 20, ——.
"　　George,	Dec. 13, ——.
"　　Samuel,	Nov. 20, ——.
"　　Nancy,	Oct. 13, ——.
"　　Sarah,	Dec. 22, ——.
"　　Thomas,	May 14, ——.
SANDS ——, Maynard, wife of Robert G., died,	July 7, 1795.
SANFORD Joseph C., of Esbon and Abigail,	Jan. 17, 1788.
"　　Mary,	Jan. 28, 1790.
"　　Dorcas,	May 3, 1792.
"　　William C.,	March 13, 1794.
"　　Abigail,	June 3, 1796.
"　　Esbon,	June 21, 1798.
"　　Rebecca,	Aug. 14, 1800.
"　　Lydia,	June 30, 1802.
"　　Esther,	March 21, 1804.
"　　Eliza,	July 10, 1806.
"　　Harriet,	March 6, 1809.
"　　Hannah Hall,	June 12, 1810.
"　　Peleg Clarke,	June 20, 1812.
SCRANTON ——, (son), of Thomas and Sarah,	Nov. 24, 1726.
"　　Desire,	Sept. 7, 1725.
"　　Abigail, of John,	—— —, ——.
"　　Hannah,	May 15, ——.
SHAW ——, of Benjamin and Hannah,	Oct. 14, 1794.
"　　Elizabeth, of William G. and Elizabeth,	June 23, ——.
"　　Samuel,	Nov. 18, ——.
"　　Samuel, died	Sept. 20, 1799.
"　　Brenton,	Dec. 29, ——.
"　　Susannah,	Jan. 29, ——.
"　　Horatio Nelson,	March —, 1800.
"　　——,	—— —, ——.
"　　——,	—— —, ——.
SHEFFIELD Joseph, of Joseph and Mary,	April 1, 1711.
"　　Mary,	Sept. 9, 1712.
"　　Nathaniel,	May 11, 1714.
"　　Elizabeth, of Joseph and Mary,	—— —, ——.
"　　——.	—— —, ——.
"　　—— (dau.), of William and Hannah,	—— —, ——.
SHELDON —— (dau.), of John and Sarah,	May 21, 1728.
"　　Thomas, of Isaac,	—— —, ——.
"　　Susannah,	—— —, ——.
"　　Gideon,	—— —, ——.
SHERMAN —— (son), of Jonathan and Mary,	May 18, 1705.
"　　Martha, of Eber and Martha,	July 25, 1707.
"　　——,	May 15, 1709.
"　　——,	Oct. 30, 1711.

SHERMAN Abigail, of Eben and Martha,		March 22, 1714.
"	William,	Dec. 30, 1716.
"	Mary,	April 13, 1719.
"	Henry,	Jan. 14, 1724.
"	Hannah, of Abial and Dorcas,	Oct. 28, 1713.
"	Ezekiel,	April 13, 1717.
"	Job, of Elisha and Mary,	June 20, 1716.
"	Elisha,	Nov. 17, 1717.
"	Benoni,	July 7, 1719.
"	Elizabeth,	March 24, 1722.
"	Stephen,	March 26, 1724.
"	—,	Aug. 11, 1726.
"	—,	March 20, 173—.
"	—,	Oct. 2, —.
"	—,	Sept. 19, —.
"	Martha, of Stephen and Sarah,	April —, 1722.
"	Samuel,	Aug. 2, 1723.
"	Mary,	Aug. 10, 1725.
"	Isabel,	Sept. 16, 1727.
"	— (son), of Stephen and Margaret,	July 13, 1731.
"	— (son),	May 7, —.
"	—(dau.),	May 20, —.
"	—,	Dec. 29, —.
"	—,	March 30, —.
"	Sarah, of Samuel and Annab,	May 4, 1750.
"	Christopher,	June 5, 1752.
"	Anne,	May 18, 1755.
"	Elizabeth,	Oct. 29, 1758.
"	Susannah,	June 15, 1762.
"	Mercy, .	Oct. 9, 1764.
"	Gideon,	July 8, 1766.
"	Stephen,	Sept. 26, 1768.
"	Samuel,	March 4, 1770.
"	Giffe, of — and Mary,	— 27, 1758.
"	Stephen,	May 4, 17—.
"	Freeborn,	June 30, 176—.
"	James,	May 6, 176—.
"	Mary,	March 31, 1770.
"	Susannah,	Feb. 20, 1772.
"	Jenkins, of Thomas and Bathsheba,	June 11, 1762.
"	Caleb,	March 16, 1764.
"	Martha,	Oct. 5, 1766.
"	Sarah (b. and d.), of —, (of Henry. and Lydia,	— —, —.
"	Sarah, 2d,	Aug. 12, —.
"	Lorey,	Sept. 4, —.
"	Nathaniel,	July 1, —.
"	Anne,	March 26, —.
"	Anne,	d. May 16, 1783.
"	Mary Madelia, of Wm. N. and Mary Madella,	Dec. 29, 18—.
"	James, of Stephen,	Feb. 2, —.
"	George,	May 26, —.
"	Andrew,	June 7, —.
"	Lucy,	Jan. 19, —.
"	Abial,	July 23, —.
"	William Northup,	Feb. 19, —.
"	Cyrus Northup,	May 14, —.
"	Potter, of — and Abbie,	Nov. 8, —.
"	Albert,	July 7, —.
"	George,	Jan. 17, —.
"	Easton,	July 31, —.
"	Edwin,	Feb. 1, —.
"	Galen Wickham,	June 17, —.
"	—, of James and Giffie,	Dec. 30, —.
"	John, of John and Freelove,	Nov. 22, —.
"	Remington,	April 22, —.

(Vit. Rec., Vol. 5.)   7

SHERMAN	Sarah, of John and Freelove,	July 10, ——.
"	Freelove,	Feb. ——, ——.
"	Henry, and his wife, child, who was widow of Sylvester Sherman,	
"	Beriah, born,	——. ——, ——.
"	Innocent, of William, Jr., and Amie,	Feb. ——, ——.
"	Martha,	March 11, ——.
"	Godfrey,	Jan. 28, ——.
"	Abigail,	Feb. 5, ——.
"	Mary,	Aug. 15, ——.
"	Giffie,	July 8, ——.
"	Amie,	June 10, ——.
"	Ichabod, of Peleg,	Dec. 3, ——.
"	Lydia,	April 2, ——.
"	Elizabeth,	—— 11, ——.
"	Mary,	—— 27, ——.
"	Moses,	July 8, ——.
"	Deliverance, of William,	April 10, ——.
"	Eber,	Aug. 7, ——.
"	Phebe,	Jan. 4, ——.
"	Abigail,	Oct. 26, ——.
"	Mary,	June 29, ——.
"	Edward,	March 4, ——.
"	Jemima,	Dec. 14, ——.
"	William,	March 10, ——.
"	Parthenia,	Feb. 16, ——.
"	Jacob,	Nov. 20, ——.
"	Palmer,	May 3, ——.
"	Peleg, of Eber and Margaret,	Nov. 9, ——.
"	Silas,	March 23, ——.
SHIPPEE	William Francis, of Horace J. and Mary G.,	. Jan. 12, 1848.
SHORT	Charles, of Lucy,	Jan. 2, 1771.
SISSON	Abigail, of Caleb and Abigail,	Nov. 23, 1769.
"	——any,	Jan. 1, 1774.
SLOCUM	Mary, of Moses,	Oct. 29, ——.
"	Moses,	March 7, 1748.
"	—— of Ebenezer and Mary,	March 25, 1746.
"	——,	April 5, 1747.
"	—— (dau.),	April 1, 1743.
"	——,	Feb. 21, 1748.
"	—— (dau.),	Jau. 25, 1756.
"	——,	June 26, 1758.
"	Joseph, of William and Sarah,	July 26, 1767.
"	Sarah, of Abel,	June 25, ——.
"	——, (son),	Oct. 7, ——.
"	Elizabeth,	March 25, 178–.
"	Mary, of Ebenezer,	d. Feb. 12, ——.
"	John, of George W. and Anstis,	Nov. 16, Sunday.
"	—— (dau.),	Aug. 13, 1789.
"	—— (dau.),	July 21, 1793.
"	Arnold, of —— and Sally,	Jan. 1, 1804.
"	——,	June 9, 1805.
"	——,	May 28, 1807.
"	——,	June 2, 1809.
"	——— (dau.),	June 18, ——.
"	——— (son),	Dec. 7, ——.
"	—— (dau.),	Oct. 19, ——.
"	—— (son), of Ebenezer and Sarah,	Oct. 19, ——.
"	Abigail,	Dec. 17, ——.
"	Ebenezer,	Nov. 2, ——.
"	—— (dau.), of Samuel,	Feb. 23, ——.
"	—— (dau.),	April 7, ——.
SMITH	Margaret, of John and Mercy;	Oct. 2, (30), 1708.
"	Bathsheba,	April 7, 1710.
"	Freelove, of Ephraim and Margaret,	July 24, 1711.
"	Sarah,	Oct. 4, 1714.

SMITH	Renewed, of Ephraim and Margaret,	May 8, 1717.
"	Margaret,	May 4, 1719.
"	Ephraim,	April 13, 1722.
"	—— (dau.), of William and Avis,	March 1, 1746.
"	——,	d. Dec. 11, 1747.
"	(Edward),	Sept. 20, 1748.
"	William,	July 30, 1750.
"	(Edward),	d. Aug. 20, 1750.
"	——, of William and Elizabeth, 2d w.,	Aug. 12, 1755.
"	——,	Nov. 2, 1756.
"	William, died in 82d year,	Dec. 18, 1745.
"	——, wife of William,	d. Nov. 20, 1759.
"	Christopher, of Thomas and Jerusha,	Oct. 4, 1753.
"	Abigail,	Sept. 8, 1755.
"	Patience,	July 22, 17—.
"	Jeremiah, of Ebenezer and Elizabeth,	Nov. 22, 1755.
"	Jeremiah, of Jeremiah,	Dec. 6, ——.
"	Ebenezer,	Nov. —, ——.
"	Freelove,	June —, ——.
"	Parsallah,	April —, ——.
"	Benajah,	April 6, ——.
"	Lucretia, of Joseph,	— —, ——.
"	Fones,	— —, ——.
"	Joseph,	— —, ——.
"	—— (son), of Benjamin and Mary,	Feb. 17, 1789.
"	—— (son),	April 5, 1790.
"	Elizabeth,	— 28, 1791.
"	——,	— 28, 1791.
"	——,	May 18, 1793.
"	——,	Feb. 5, 1795.
"	——,	Jan. —, 179—.
"	——,	July 3, 179—.
"	——,	Sept. 7, 1800.
"	——,	Sept. 15, 180—.
"	——,	July 8, 180—.

Children's names and dates of birth of John and Presilla Smith entirely burnt off.

"	Catherine, of John and Christiana,	Oct. 1, ——.
"	Thomas, of William and ——,	Dec. 15, ——.
"	Patience,	— 15, ——.
"	Patience,	d. Sept. 30, ——.
"	—— (dau.)	May 18, ——.
"	—— (dau.)	d. Dec. 11, ——.
"	——,	Sept. 27, ——.
"	——,	Aug. 25, ——.
"	Daniel, of Daniel and Ro——	— 16, ——.
SPENCER	—— (son), of William and Elizabeth,	April 16, 1698.
"	Mary,	March 29, 1700.
"	Elizabeth,	May 11, 1702.
"	Jonathan,	Jan. 21, 1704.
"	William,	June 30, 1706.
"	Daniel,	June 20, 1708.
"	William, of John and Sarah,	Feb. 21, 1725-6.
"	Lydia, of Henry and Lydia,	April 29, 17—.
"	Anne,	June 13, 17—.
"	Elizabeth,	June 14, 17—.
"	Sarah,	Oct. 11, 17—.
"	John,	Feb. 12, 17—.
"	Esther,	April 12, 17—.
"	Edna,	Dec. 26, 17—.
"	Henry, father of above children,	d. July 13, 17—.
"	Nicholas, of Christopher and Frances,	April 17, 174—.
"	Frances,	March 27, 17—.
"	Phebe,	Sept. 10, 17—.
"	Mary,	June 12, 175—.

SPENCER —— (son), of Christopher and Abigail,		Aug. 14, 1737.
"	Abigail, wife of Christopher,	d. Aug. 24, 1737.
"	Thomas,	Dec. 23, 1740.
"	——man (dau.),	May 20, 1737.
"	——,	Feb. 20, 1736.
"	——,	Aug. 2, 1734.
"	Palmer, of Nicholas and Abigail,	March 15, 1779.
"	Isabel,	May 28, 178—.
"	Elizabeth,	May 28, 178—.
"	Mary,	— 5, 178—.
"	——,	Nov. 16, 1782.
"	——,	Sept. 22, 1784.
"	——,	Sept. 14, 1786.
"	——,	June 17, 1788.
"	——,	June 16, 1790.
"	——,	May 9, 1795.
"	Henry, of Wanton and Sarah,	March —, 1812.
"	Mercy Allen,	Dec. 21, 1813.
"	——,	March 11, 1822.
"	Elizabeth,	d. ——, ——.
"	—— (son), of William,	June 20, ——.
"	—— (dau.),	Sept. —, ——.
"	Names of rest burnt off.	
"	Elizabeth, of Thomas and ——,	Aug. 4, ——.
"	Amie,	— 4, ——.
"	William,	— 18, ——.
"	Margaret,	Dec. 4, ——.
"	Abigail, of —— and Abigail,	March 5, ——.
"	Lydia,	April 5, ——.
"	William, of Henry,	July 22, ——.
"	Mehitable,	Nov. 3, ——.
"	Benjamin,	Sept. 16, ——.
"	Thomas,	July 13, ——.
"	Amie,	Jan. 22, ——.
"	Mercy,	Feb. 18, ——.
"	Mary,	Feb. 18, ——.
SPINK Samuel, of John and Hannah (Carpenter),		Dec. 31, 1729.
"	Samuel (Ishmael),	Feb. 12, 1731.
"	Oliver,	Dec. 23, 1733.
"	John,	March 21, 1736.
"	Sarah,	Sept. 22, 1741.
"	Silas,	Jan. 24, 1743.
"	Nicholas,	March 3, 1745.
"	Hannah,	July 23, 1746.
"	Abigail, of (above) John and Sarah (Tibbetts),	Sept. 11, 1725.
"	—— (son), of Ishmael and Deliverance),	Jan. 21, 1702.
"	—— (dau.),	Nov. 7, 1704.
"	Capt. John, b. ——, 1753; d. in 84th year,	—— —, 1837.
"	Anne, of Josiah and Anne,	Oct. 6, 175—.
"	Penelope, of —— and Mary	May 20, ——.
"	Oliver,	June 26, 1765.
"	Daniel, of John and Judeth,	Feb. —, 1776.
"	John, of —— and Waite,	July 26, 17—.
"	Silas,	Aug. 23, 17—.
"	Waite,	Jan. 19, 17—.
"	Isaac,	March 3, 17—.
"	Lucia,	May 22, 17—.
"	Samuel,	Oct. 30, 176—.
"	Hannah,	Feb. 23, 176—.
"	Nathaniel,	Nov. 16, 1769.
"	Nicholas, born Jan. 24, 1743,	d. March 3, 1745.
"	Hannah (Boone, of Samuel), his wife,	Aug. 19, 1749.
"	Hannah, of Nicholas and Hannah,	Jan. 30, 1770.
"	John,	June 22, 1771.
"	Mary,	March 25, 1773.

SPINK Samuel, of Nicholas and Hannah,		Feb. 17, 1775.
"	Christopher,	March 17, 1777.
"	Boone,	April 15, 1779.
"	Nicholas,	Feb. 11, 1781.
"	Anna,	Jan. 10, 1783.
"	Lucy,	Jan. 5, 1785.
"	William,	July 12, 1786.
"	Franklin,	March 27, 1788.
"	Martha,	July 24, 1790.
"	Martha, of John and Judeth,	Nov. 21, 1774.
"	——ah (E. G.), of Nathaniel and Lydia,	March —, 1800.
"	——,	Feb. 14, 1802.
"	——, of Thomas,	Feb. 27, 1811.
"	——,	Feb. 18, 1814.
"	Frances Ann,	Jan. 17, 1827.
"	Albert E. N.,	Aug. 30, 1829.
"	Eliza, of —— and ——,	March 14, 1813.
"	Samuel,	Nov. 29, 1815.
"	Arnold,	Sept. 29, 1817.
"	Lucy,	Oct. 27, 1819.
"	Judeth,	Nov. 24, 1821.
"	Mary,	Feb. 12, 1822.
"	Matilda,	Feb. 9, 1825.
"	Emeline,	Sept. 26, 1827.
"	Almira,	April 15, 1830.
"	William,	April 12, 1833.
"	Ruth A.,	Feb. 11, 1836.
"	Samuel,	Nov. 29, 1815.
"	Ann, his wife,	Sept. 21, 1817.
"	Eliza, of Samuel and Ann,	Dec. 22, 1838.
"	Hannah C.,	Jan. 23, 1840.
"	Silas,	Sept. 12, 1841.
"	Eliza, died aged 23 years,	Oct. 10, 1836.
"	Nicholas N.,	Aug. 26, 181—.
"	Huldah A., his wife,	May 11, 1813.
"	Benjn. Weeden, of Nicholas N. and Huldah A.,	April 2, 18—.
"	Frances Ann,	Sept. 26, 18—.
"	Frances Ann,	d. Feb. 17, 1843.
"	Mary Fowler,	Oct. 2, 18—.
"	Mary Fowler,	d. April 25, 1842.
"	Frances Ann,	Feb. 6, 18—.
"	Christopher,	Dec. 23, 18—.
"	Christopher,	d. April 19, 18—.
"	Mary Fowler,	May 14, 18—.
"	Arnold, died aged 47 years,	May 24, 1865.
"	Mahalie,	d. March 12, 1865.
"	Hannah C., died aged 36 years,	June 9, 1876.
"	Ann, died aged 60 yrs. 5mos. 9 days,	April 30, 1878.
"	Walter E., of Silas and Phebe,	June 29, 1862.
"	Hattie A.,	March 28, 1865.
"	Minnie Mabel,	May 9, 1875.
"	George Tennant, of Boone and Anne,	Feb. 14, —.
"	Eliza Ann Sweet,	Feb. 10, —.
"	Mary Eleanor,	Aug. 27, —.
"	Emeline Fry,	Dec. 16, —.
"	Boone,	March 4, —.
"	Charlotte,	July 2, —.
"	Susannah,	Aug. 15, —.
"	Richard Eldred, of Nicholas and Lidge,	Feb. 20, —.
"	Penelope, of Oliver,	May 20, —.
"	Oliver,	June 26, —.
"	Arnold, of Samuel and Elizabeth,	June —, —.
"	Betsey,	Nov. 16, —.
"	Joseph,	Sept. —, —.
"	Mary,	Aug. —, —.

SPRAGUE Mary, of David,   June —, —.
    "   Deborah,   Aug. 10, —.
STANTON ——, of David and Martha,   Nov. 25, 1742.
STEADMAN Henry, of Asa and Sarah, born in Peterboro, Renssalear Co., N. Y.,
        Aug. 6, 1800.
STRAIGHT Henry, of Joseph and Mary,   ·   Feb. —, —.
    "   Ruth,   — 22, —.
SWEET James, of Benoni and Elizabeth,   May 28, 168(7).
    "   Margaret,   Sept. 22, (1689).
    "   Benoni,   March 28, 1692.
    "   Mary,   Dec. 8, 1696.
    "   Elizabeth,   Feb. 22, 1700.
    "   Thomas,   Aug. —, 1703.
    "   ——,   Oct. —, 1715.
    "   ——,   Jan. 5, 1716.
    "   ——,   Aug. 17, 1720.
    "   ——,   Dec. 29, 1721.
    "   ——,   Nov. 2, 1723.
    "   ——,   Jan. 31, 1725.
    "   ——,   Nov. 21, 1727.
    "   ——,   March 30, 1730.
    "   ——,   April 26, 1733.
    "   ——, of John of Catherine,   July 23, 1719.
    "   Catherine,   Feb. 27, 1725-6.
    "   ——,   Feb. 14, 172-.
    "   ——, of Thomas and Tabitha,   Sept. 1, 1728.
    "   ——,   Dec. 2, 1730.
    "   ——,   Oct. 12, 1732.
    "   ——,   Oct. 8, 1742.
    "   ——,   May 26, 1746.
    "   ——, of Benoni, Jun., and Isabel,   June 10, 1740.
    "   Elizabeth,   Oct. 10, 1742.
    "   ——,   April 20, 1745.
    "   Benoni,   Oct. 7, 1748.
    "   ——,   Oct. 3, 1752.
    "   Thankful, of Daniel,   Dec. 30, 1736.
    "   Alice,   Jan. 19, 1744.
    "   Elizabeth,   Sept. 5, 1741.
    "   ——,   Feb. 23, 1743.
    "   —— (dau.),   Feb. 8, 174-.
    "   ——,   Jan. 2, 174-.
    "   —— (son),   April 26, —.
    "   —— (son),   May 31, —.
    "   —— (dau.), of James, Jun.,   Oct. 29, 1740.
    "   —— (dau.), of Job and Jemima, died   Sept. 8, 175-.
    "   Margeret, dau. of James, on oath that the father of her son was James
            Austin, her son Ezra born   April 13, 1767.
    "   ——, of —— and ——,   Feb. 9, 1779.
    "   ——,   Nov. 21, 1780.
    "   Polly,   March 18, 1782.
    "   Christopher A.,   July 29, 1785.
    "   Dorcas,   April 13, 1787.
    "   Samuel,   June 25, 1790.
    "   John A.,   July 15, 1793.
    "   William,   March 20, 1795.
    "   Potter,   Nov. 20, 1796.
    "   Sally,   Nov. 20, 1798.
    "   Jeremiah,   — —, —.
    "   Stephen, of Sylvester and Patience,   Nov. 9, 17-.
    "   Mary,   Nov. 7, 17-.
    "   —— C.,   Nov. 14, 1806.
    "   ——, and ——,   April 24, 1808.
    "   Stephen S., of Scranton E. and Mary,   July 17, 1814.
    "   Betsey C.,   June 19, 1813.
    "   Green A.,   Oct. 28, 1814.

SWEET	William Henry, of Scranton E. and Mary,	April 13, 1816.
"	Mary Ann,	Jan. 13, 1819.
"	George, of Potter and Alceba,	Dec. 19, 1831.
"	William Harris,	July 18, 1833.
"	Washington,	June 22, 1635.
"	Mary R.,	Sept. 26, 1837.
"	Daniel H.,	July 17, 1840.
"	Lucinda,	Dec. 31, 1843.
"	Esther,	Dec. 31, 1843.
"	Parker Hall,	Oct. 24, 1845.
"	Isaac Henry,	May 7, 1848.
"	Sarah Eliza,	May 23, 1851.
"	Amie, of Elnathan,	Nov. —, —.
"	Mary,	July 4, —.
"	Elnathan,	June 24, —.
"	Elizabeth, of John,	May 30, —.
"	Sarah,	June 24, —.
"	John,	Nov. 7, —.
"	Benoni,	May 3, —.
"	Theophilus,	April 30, —.
"	James,	Aug. 24, —.
"	—— (dau.), of James and Mary,	April 30, —.
"	—— (son),	May 28, —.
"	—— (dau.),	May 7, —.
"	—— (son),	Nov. 9, —.
"	Gideon, of Job and Sarah,	April 11, —.
"	James,	April 11, —.
"	Benoni,	Oct. 17, —.
"	Jonathan,	Sept. 6, —.
"	Margaret,	Dec. 4, —.
"	Lydia,	Dec. 4, —.
"	Hannah,	Aug. 3, —.
"	Rufus,	Dec. 6, 174—.
"	Sarah,	April 4, 17—.
"	Ruth, of Samuel and Sarah,	April 24, —.
"	Sarah,	March 14, —.
"	Samuel, of —— and Henrietta,	Aug. 7, —.
"	Thomas,	—— —, —.
"	Mary,	—— —, —.
"	Frances,	—— —, —.
"	Robert,	—— —, —.
"	Abigail,	—— —, —.
"	Benoni, of James and ——,	April 2, —.
"	Eber,	June 5, —.
"	Mary,	Nov. 25, —.
"	James,	—— 4, —.
"	Elisha,	Oct. 18, —.
"	Freelove,	April 12, —.
"	Job,	Dec. 1, —.
"	Elizabeth,	May 13, —.
"	Margaret,	April 4, —.
"	Silas, of Elizabeth,	—— —, —.
"	Elizabeth,	—— —, —.
"	Isabel,	—— —, —.
"	Joshua,	—— 24, —.
"	Patience,	March 21, —.
"	Thankful,	July —, —.
"	Phebe,	March 27, —.
"	Tolding,	Oct. —, —.

T

TANNER	William, of William and Hannah,	Sept. 22, 1712.
"	Benjamin,	June 16, 1714.

TANNER Honor, of William and Hannah,		Dec. 15, 1716.
"	——ah,	Oct. 16, 1723.
"	——,	Jan 19, 172—.
"	Elizabeth, of Francis and Rosanna,	March 30, 176—.
"	Phebe,	Nov. 10, 1763.
"	——, of Benjamin,	Feb. 28, 1766.
"	——,	July 3, 1767.
"	——,	April 9, 1769.
"	——,	May 21, 1771.
"	——,	March 27, 1773.
"	——,	Dec. 25, 1774.
"	——,	June 18, 1776.
"	——,	Nov. 21, 1778.
"	——,	June 13, 1780.
"	——,	March 10, 1782.
"	——,	April 15, 1784.
"	——,	Dec. 5, 1787.
"	Catherine, of Palmer and Margaret,	May 11, 179—.
"	Job,	Dec. 3, 179—.
"	Benjamin,	June 19, 179—.
"	Mary,	Dec. 3, 179—.
"	Palmer,	March 9, 179—.
"	James,	May 8, 179—.
"	Henry,	Jan. 25, 179—.
"	Abel,	Aug. 8, 1800.
"	——, of William and Elizabeth,	Dec. 6, ——.
"	——,	Oct. 11, ——.
"	——,	Sept. 5, ——.
"	——,	Sept. 6, ——.
TAYLOR William Davis, of Sylvia (col.)		July 10, ——.
TENNANT George, (Jamestown)		—— 21, ——.
"	Hannah, wife of George,	—— —, ——.
"	Benajah, (J.) of George and Hannah,	—— —, ——.
"	Mary, (N.)	—— —, ——.
"	Sarah, (N.),	Sept. 22, ——.
"	Luke,	April 23, ——.
"	John, of George and Tabitha,	July 13, ——.
"	Hannah, (Plainfield),	Aug. —, ——.
"	George (Plainfield), of George and Tabitha,	June 13, ——.
"	Daniel (Plainfield),	Jan. —, ——.
"	Nancy, (Plainfield),	Jan. —, ——.
"	Betsey, (Plainfield),	Jan. —, ——.
"	Honor, (Plainfield),	Feb. 28, 17—.
"	——, of George and Anstis,	Feb. 9, 1788.
"	Abigail,	June 1, ——.
"	Abigail,	d. June 21, s. m.
"	Lydia,	Feb. 22, ——.
"	James, of John and Mary,	Dec. —, 1789.
"	John,	—, —, —.
"	Merabah,	—, —, —.
"	——,	—, —, —.
THOMAS ——, (son), of Abraham and Rose,		Dec. —, 1723.
"	Phebe, wife of George, (son of Samuel); d. age1 43 years,	Nov. 19, 1744.
"	Juriah, of Samuel and Ruth,	May 15, 1757.
"	George,	June 7, ——.
"	Gould,	April 7, 174—.
"	Alice,	March 24, 174—.
"	Samuel,	Aug. 1, 17—.
"	Elizabeth,	Feb. 11, ——.
"	Ruth, wife of Samuel, died	Jan. 4, ——.
"	George, of Samuel, and his wife, Phebe Lockwood, dau. of Capt. Amos, of Warwick, R. I., children.	
"	Ruth,	July 1, 1764.
"	George,	March 23, 1766.
"	Gould,	Aug. 17, 1769.

THOMAS	Daniel, of Samuel and Phebe,	Nov. 27, 1771.
"	Sarah,	March 17, 1774.
"	Sarah, died,	Feb. 5, 1775.
"	——, (son),	May 3, 1776.
"	——, (son), died,	May 19, 1776.
"	Amos,	Oct. 23, ——.
"	Amos, died,	Feb. —, ——.
"	Sarah Ann,	Oct. 23, ——.
"	Sarah Ann, died,	—— —, 1778.
"	——, son of George, Jr.,	Nov. 6, 1785.
"	——,	Feb. —, 1788.
"	——,	March 23, 1790.
"	——,	Oct. 11, 1792.
"	——,	Jan. 4, 1795.
"	——, died,	Nov. 7, 1795.
"	——,	July 30, 1796.
"	——,	—— —, 1798.
"	——,	May 7, 1798.
"	——, (dau.),	Oct. 11, 1794.
"	——, (son),	March 3, 1797.
"	Elizabeth,	Feb. 4, 1799.
"	Martha Augusta,	Jan. 5, 1801.
"	Phebe Ann, (Newport),	Jan. 9, 1804.
"	George W., (Newport),	Jan. 9, 1804.
"	Sally,	Nov. 19, 1807.
"	Jane,	—— 2, 1810.
"	Catherine Gould,	June 23, 1813.
"	——ah, (dau.) of —— and Hope,	—— 5, ——.
"	Richard,	Jan. 22, 17—.
"	——ty, (dau.),	Oct. 11, 177—.
"	——, (son), of Benjamin and Elizabeth,	June 10, 1801.
"	Elsie Ann,	Nov. 17, 1803.
"	Mariah,	Feb. 6, 1806.
"	Susannah,	Oct. 12, 1808.
"	Arnold,	July 16, 1811.
"	Nichols Allen,	Sept. 15, ——.
"	Nichols Allen, died, age 9 months,	—— —, ——.
"	Allen Mason,	July 25, ——.
"	Mary of Arnold and Audria,	Aug. 7, 180—.
"	Asel,	Sept. 8, 180—.
"	Rose,	June 3, 180—.
"	——,	April 12, 1807.
"	——,	June 17, 1809.
"	Samuel, Esq., died,	Nov. 22, ——.
"	Dyre, (dau.), of George, Jr., and Abigail,	Aug. —, ——.
"	Waitey, of George, (of John) and ——,	—— —, ——.
"	Mary,	Sept. 22, ——.
"	Alcey,	Dec. 6, ——.
"	Abigail,	April —, ——.
"	Anstress,	Dec. —, ——.
"	Arnold, of George, (of John) and Hannah,	March —, ——.
"	Elizabeth,	Aug. 19, ——.
"	Hannah,	Aug. 19, ——.
"	Coggeshall,	—— —, ——.
"	Elizabeth, of George P.,	April 6, ——.
"	James M.,	Feb. 15, ——.
"	Hannah, of George P.,	March 20, ——.
"	George, of Benj. and Mary,	March 1, ——.
"	Anstis,	Ap—— —, ——.
"	Abigail,	May —, ——.
"	Benjamin,	Feb. —, ——.
"	Mary, of Col. George,	April 20, ——.
"	Sarah,	Nov. 2, ——.
"	George,	Feb. —, ——.
"	John,	April 6, ——.

THOMAS Alice, of Col. George,		June —, ——.
"	Benjn,	July —, ——.
'	Elizabeth,	Oct. —, ——.
"	—— (son),	Dec. —, ——.
TEBBETTS —— (dau.), of George and Dorcas,		Jan. —, 1731-2.
"	—— (dau.),	Jan. 17, 1733-4.
"	— (dau.),	March 14, 1736.
"	—— (dau.),	May 18, 173—.
"	——	Aug. 26, 174—.
"	—— (dau.),	——. —, ——.
"	—— (dau.),	——. —, ——.
"	—— (dau.),	——. —, ——.
" George, of George and —— (Wall, of Wm.),		Sept. —, ——.
'	William,	Feb. 24, ——.
"	Benjamin,	March 2, ——.
"	John,	June 18, ——.
"	John, died	Feb. 3, 1772.
"	Dorcas,	Jan. 23, ——.
"	Hannah, of Nathaniel and Waite,	Feb. 27, 17—.
"	George,	Jan. 6, 17—.
TILLINGHAST Mercy, of —— and Abigail,		June 5, ——.
"	John,	Dec. —, 176—.
"	Pardon,	Jan. 15, 176—.
"	Joseph,	Feb. 10, 1767.
"	Phebe,	Sept. 26, 1768.
"	Charles,	Oct. 25, 17—.
"	Allen,	Oct. 13, 177—.
"	Amie,	Feb. 7, 1774.
"	Anne, of Phillip and Frances,	Jan. 16, 1792.
"	Frances Spencer,	April 25, 1809.
"	Almy R. (N. K.), of Job,	Aug. 24, 18—.
"	Sidney S.,	Dec. 7, 18—.
"	Ann, wife of Benjamin, died,	Jan. 14, ——.
'	Alice, wife of Phillip, dau. of Col. George,	——. —, ——.
"	Thomas,	d. Jan. 19, ——.
"	Phillip, of Capt. Joseph R. and Phebe,	June 9, 1808.
"	William,	Oct. 25, 1810.
"	Joseph Henry,	April 19, 1813.
"	Anne Elizabeth,	March 2, 1815.
"	Harriet Moore,	June 22, 1820.
TOURGEE ——, of Peter and Mary,		Dec. 13, 1722.
"	—— (son),	Oct. 20, 1724.
"	—— (dau.),	Nov. 18, 1728.
"	—— (dau.),	Dec. 1, 1730.
"	—— (son),	Feb. 5, 1733-4.
"	—— (son),	Dec. 23, 1735.
"	——,	May 8, 1739.
"	Desire, of Hollis and Patience,	Dec. 19, 17—.
"	William,	Oct. 3, 175—.
"	Elizabeth,	Jan. 12, 175—.
"	Abigail,	March 12, 1758.
"	Sarah,	Feb. 19, 1761.
"	Charlotte,	Feb. 5, 1763.
"	Prudence, of John and ——,	June 15, 176—.
"	Mary,	Jan. 30, 17—.
"	Peter,	May 12, 17—.
"	Grizell, (dau.), of Thomas,	May —, ——.
"	Phillip,	Nov. 28, ——.
"	Margaret,	May 15, ——.
"	Mary,	June 15, ——.
TRIPP Mary, of Othniel and Mary,		May 22. ——.
"	Othniel,	Aug. 18, ——.
"	Penelope,	Jan. 18, ——.
"	Othniel, 2d,	March 22, ——.
"	Susannah,	Feb. 12, ——.

TRIPP Bridget, of Othniel and Mary,	Oct. 25, ——.
TURNER Mary, of Jonathan and Elizabeth,	Aug. 20, 1711.
" Paine,	May 15, 1713.
" Hannah,	Aug. 7, 1715.

U

UPDIKE —— (son),	April —, 1789.
" ——,	Oct. 1, 1792.
" ——,	April 11, 1795.
" Deblois, (dau.),	April —, 1802.
" —— (dau.),	Feb. 7, 1807.
" Joseph, of James and Freelove,	July —, ——.
" Abbie,	June 26, ——.
" Sally,	Dec. 20, ——.
" John,	March 2. ——.
" James,	Oct. 20, ——.
" Nathaniel,	Oct. 16, ——.
" Susannah,	May 9, ——.
" Celia,	Jan. 10, ——.
" Levina,	Aug. 6, ——.
" ——,	——. —, ——.
" Ceaser,	Oct. 3, ——.
" Christopher,	Aug. 20, ——.

V

VALLETT Mary, of Jeremiah and Anne,	May 16, 175–.
" John,	Feb. 10, 175–.
" Abia,	April 6, 1758.
" Anne,	Feb. 13, 1760.
VAUGHN Nathan, of Aaron and Sarah,	June 29, 1765.
" Elizabeth,	Oct. 6, 1768.
" Joseph Martin,	Dec. 15, 1772.
' Elizabeth, of Capt. Jonathan,	—— 1, 17–.
" Gideon,	Aug. 19, 177–.
" Maria, of Isaac D. and Cynthia,	Oct. 15, 1799.
" Harriet Gardiner,	July 13, 1802.
" Edward Augustus,	July 16, 1805.
" Charles Manuel,	—— —, ——.
" Charlotte,	Sept. 8, ——.
" Nabby,	Sept. 18, ——.
" Christopher,	Ma—— —, ——.
" Isaac,	—— —, ——.
" Jonathan,	—— —, ——.
" Nathan,	—— —, ——.
" John,	—— —, ——.
" Henry, of Daniel,	Oct. 13, ——.
" Elizabeth (Reynolds), his wife,	April 2, ——.
" Abigail, of Henry and Elizabeth,	March —, ——.
" Dorcus,	March —, ——.
" Daniel,	Feb. —, ——.
" Henry,	June —, ——.
" Mary,	April —, ——.
" John G.,	April —, ——.
" Hannah S.,	March —, ——.
VERNER Henry, of John,	Nov. 27, 17—.
" William,	Nov. 29, 17—.
VERRY Elijah, b. (Otter Creek, Vt.,) of John and Sarah,	July 20, ——.

W

WALL Susannah, of Henry and Hannah,	July 2, ——.
" Jeremiah,	March 23, ——.
" Weight,	March 6, ——.
" William,	April 28, ——.
" Henry,	May 22, ——.
" Hannah,	Jan. —, ——.
" Daniel,	Sept. 11, ——.
" Thomas, of Henry and Mary,	Jan. 18, ——.
" Mary,	Feb. 7, ——.
" Hannah, wife of Henry, died June 4, 1759.	
" Coggeshall, of Samuel and Elizabeth,	Feb. 8, 176--.
WARD Wait, of Joseph and Mary,	July 11, 1754.
" Sarah,	Feb. 8, 1756.
" Mary,	June 4, 1758.
" Susannah,	March 10, 1761.
" Thomas,	April 3, 1764.
" Henry,	July 20, 1774.
WATSON Hannah, of John and Hannah,	March 1, 1703-4.
" Ann,	March 27, 1708-9.
" John,	March 13, 1709-10.
" Jeffrey,	Aug. 3, 1712.
" Elisha,	Sept. 14, 1714.
" Dorcas,	Oct. 25, 1716.
" Amie,	Oct. 18, 1719.
" —— (son), of Samuel, Jr.,	——. 23, 1737.
" —— (son),	March 28, 1739.
WEATHERN Thomas, of John and Deborah,	Sept. 5, ——.
WEEDEN Ceaser, of Peter and Lucy,	Feb. 14, 1811.
" Caleb, of Caleb and F——,	Feb. 8, ——.
" Mary Jane, of Marchant and Penelope,	April 10, ——.
" Chas. Williams,	Jan. 2, ——.
" Martha Ann,	Nov. 27, ——.
WEIGHTMAN Catherine, of George and Mary,	Feb. 28, 1725.
" (George),	Nov. 7, 1726.
" (David),	Aug. 24, 1728.
" (John),	Oct. 7, 1730.
" (Valentine),	March 13, 1733.
" —— (dau.),	May 13, 1736.
" Samuel,	——. —, 1739.
" William, of —— and Barbara,	April 27, 1770.
" John,	March 17, 1772.
" John,	d. Sept. 21, 1777.
" Gideon,	Feb. 27, 1774.
" Gideon,	d. Sept. 3, 1777.
" Phebe,	Oct. 24, 1775.
" Phebe,	d. Jan. 19, 177—.
" Giles,	Nov. 26, 1776.
" Giles,	d. Feb. 8, 177—.
" Gideon,	Feb. 22, 177—.
" John,	April 14, 178—.
" Phebe,	June 27, 178—.
" —— B.,	March 19, 1800.
" Charles L., died, aged 35 years,	April 18, 1875.
" Alice, of John and Jane,	Oct. 26, (1702.)
" Sarah,	Jan. 23, (1704.)
" John,	March 11, ——.
" James,	Feb. 17, ——.
" Jean,	M— 20, ——.
" ——,	— 31, ——.
" ——,	—— —, ——.
" Harry H., of John (of Thomas) and Mary,	——. —, ——.
" Mary,	Jan. 13, 1807.
" Isaiah,	Sept. 8, ——.

WEIGHTMAN Sarah, of John and Mary,		Aug. 1, ——.
"	Almidy,	April 4, ——.
"	Fannie,	Sept. 4, ——.
"	Horace,	Oct. 20, ——.
"	Esther Ann,	April 16, ——.
"	John Horace,	Sept. 21, ——.
"	Bridget, of James,	June 22, ——.
"	John,	July 17, ——.
"	Daniel,	July 26, ——.
"	William, of Elizabeth,	Dec. 10, ——.
"	George,	——. ——, ——.
"	Silas,	——. ——, ——.
"	Mary,	April ——, ——.
"	John,	——. ——, ——.
"	Elizabeth,	——. ——, ——.
"	Frederic,	——. ——, ——.
"	Elizabeth, of Valentine,	July 2, ——.
"	Elizabeth, of Holmes and Comfort,	Feb. ——, ——.
"	John,	Oct. 24, ——.
WEIGHT Joseph, of Samuel and Alice,		April 27, 1697.
"	George,	Aug. 14, 1699.
"	Samuel,	Oct. 13, 1701.
"	Benjamin,	——. 17, 1703.
"	Martha,	——. 1, ——.
"	John,	Feb. 22, 1708-9.
"	——,	——. 11, 1725.
"	——,	Sept. 11, 1727.
"	—— (dau.),	Dec ——, 1729.
"	—— (dau.),	May ——, 1732.
"	—— (dau.),	Jan. 22, 1734.
"	—— (dau.),	Jan. 9, 1736.
"	—— (son),	Jan. 5, 1738.
"	Alice, of John and Sarah,	——. 23, 1729.
"	Lydia,	July ——, ——.
"	Eunice,	——. ——, ——.
"	Sion,	——. ——, ——.
"	——,	——. ——, ——.
"	——,	——. ——, ——.
"	——, of Benjamin and Abigail,	July 4, 1742.
"	William Beriah, of George and Ruth,	Oct. 12, 1822.
"	Ann Matilda,	May 20, 1824.
"	Jonathan Card,	April 29, 1826.
"	Martha, of Joseph,	March 10, ——.
"	Reuben,	July 24, ——.
"	Oliver,	——. 13, ——.
"	Henry of Benjamin,	May 27, 1725.
"	Benjamin,	Oct.13, ——.
"	William,	June 9, ——.
"	Sarah,	Jan. 9, ——.
"	Virtue,	May 12, ——.
"	Jonathan,	Aug. 11, ——.
"	—— (son), of Joseph and Elizabeth,	J—— 26, ——.
"	—— (dau.),	Aug. 15, ——.
"	—— (son),	Oct. 16, ——.
"	Elizabeth,	—— 21, ——.
"	Samuel,	—— 28, ——.
"	Alice,	—— 28, ——.
"	Benjamin,	—— 16, ——.
"	Damaries,	—— 14, ——.
"	Phebe,	—— 16, ——.
"	Mary,	—— ——, ——.
WEIR ——, of Daniel and Phebe,		Feb. 27, 1744.
"	Benjamin,	April 14, 1746.
"	William,	Oct. 7, 1747.
"	——,	Jan. 17, 1754.

WEIR ——, of Daniel and Phebe,		Jan. 5, 1756.
WESTCOTT Sarah, of Zerababel and Phebe,		May 15, 1759.
"	Stukeley,	May 13, 1761.
"	Samuel,	Dec. 30, 1764.
"	Lewis,	Nov. 17, 1767.
"	John, of Stukeley and Mary,	Aug. 26, 17–.
"	Hannah,	Oct. 19, ——.
"	Mercy,	Oct. 21, ——.
"	Robert, of Zerobabel and Jane,	Dec. 5, 1700.
"	Margaret,	——. 8, ——.
"	Zerobabel,	Nov. 8, ——.
"	Catherine,	April 17, ——.
"	Robert, of Robert and Hannah,	July 8, (17–).
"	Samuel, ·	June 28, ——.
"	Zerobabel,	Dec. 15, ——.
"	Stukeley,	July 11, ——.
"	Mary,	Nov. 27, ——.
"	Ann,	March 23, ——.
WEST (William, of Francis and Susannah,		May 31, 1681).
(*I have Clement, instead of Thomas, at same date. R. G. H.)		
"	Thomas, of Francis and Susannah,	Sept. 18, 1684.
"	Mary, of Francis,	June 29, 1711.
WHALEY ——, (son) of Jane,		——. 25, 1693.
"	——th, of Thomas and ——nah,	March 5, 1756.
"	Theophilus,	April 19, 1758.
"	Thomas,	March 10, 1760.
"	Lydia, of Lawrence,	May 13, ——.
"	Susannah,	Jan. 21, ——.
"	Theophilus,	Feb. 14, ——.
"	Thomas,	April 10, ——.
WHITFORD Lydia, of Joseph and Sarah,		March 7, 1724.
"	——,	Feb. 7, 1726.
"	——,	Jan. 5, 1728.
"	——,	Oct. 9, 1730.
"	——,	March 6, 1735-6.
"	——,	Jan. 16, 1740.
"	Alice, of Thomas and Patience,	Aug. 10, ——.
"	John Place,	Feb. 23, ——.
"	Caleb,	April 11, ——.
"	Joshua,	Nov. 22, ——.
"	Sarah,	——. ——, ——.
"	Benjamin,	——. ——, ——.
"	Lydia,	——. 22, ——.
"	Elizabeth,	—— ——, ——3.
"	Mary,	Dec. 22, ——.
"	John,	—— —. ——.
"	Mercy,	March —, ——.
"	Martha,	Jan. 21, ——.
"	——, of David and Mary,	June 11, ——.
"	——,	Sept. 6, ——.
"	——,	March 6, ——.
"	——,	March 29, ——.
"	——,	June 23, ——.
"	——,	June 7, ——.
"	——,	Dec. —, ——.
"	——,	Feb. —, ——.
WHITMAN, John,		April 16, ——.
"	——, dau. of above John,	Oct. 26, 1702.
"	Thomas, of —— and Elizabeth,	Jan. —, ——.
"	John,	March —, ——.
"	Elizabeth,	Oct. 23, ——.
"	Frederic,	Sept. 23, ——.
"	Weight,	March 7, ——.
"	George,	Jan. 19, ——.
WHITMAN Mary, of —— and Elizabeth,		April 17, 175–.

WHITMAN Asa, of —— and Elizabeth,	March 28, 176—.
" Valentine,	March 1, 176—.
" Daniel,	Feb. 20, 176—.
" Avis, of George,	Oct. 7, 1780.
" George.	Dec. 11, 1784.
" Sam'l Wart,	Oct. 5, 1789.
" Mary,	Sept. 29, 1791.
" Daniel,	March 6, 1797.
" Thomas Sweet,	Oct. 2, 1799.
WILCOX ——, (son), of Robert and Sarah,	June 26, 1724.
" ——, (son),	Oct. 16, 1725.
WILKEY ——, (son), of John and Jane,	Nov. 17, 1702.
" ——, (dau.),	Dec. 21, 1706.
" ——,	Dec. 27, 1708.
" ——,	April 30, 1710.
" ——,	Nov. 4, 1712.
" ——,	Feb. 4, 1714.
" ——,	March 23, 1716.
" ——,	May 15, 1718.
" ——, (dau.), of Jeremiah and Mary,	July 4, 1735.
" ——, (dau.),	June 16, 173—.
" ——, (son),	Dec. 27, 17—.
" Thomas, of Thomas,	Nov. 12, 1735.
WILLETT ——, of Andrew and Ann,	Sept. 26, 1689.
" ——,	Sept. 21, 1690.
" ——,	June 25, 1693.
" Francis.	May 13, 1696.
" ——,	March 6, 1697-8.
WILSON —— (dau.), of Robert and Catherine,	Aug. 10, 1720.
" —— (dau.),	Sept. 4, 1722.
" —— (dau.),	April 24, ——.
" —— (dau.),	June 28, ——.
" —— (dau.),	Nov. 7, ——.
" —— (dau.),	—— —, ——.
" —— (dau.),	—— —, ——.
WEEDEN Josiah, of Peter and Mary, b. in Harwidge, in county of Barnstable,	May 16, ——.
" Charlotte,	b. in Kingstowne, Feb. 24, 1697.
WOODEN —— (son), of Potter and Mary,	Feb. 24, 1697.
WRIGHT, Susannah, of Capt. Peter,	April 25, ——.
" John,	June 6, ——.
" Hannah,	Nov. 7, ——.
" Samuel,	April 11, ——.
" Mary,	May 29, ——.
" Daniel,	Nov. 11, ——.
" Deborah,	April 4, ——.
" Sarah,	April 16, ——.
" Elizabeth.	April 13, ——.
Recorded Sept. 29, 1779.	

X Y Z

YORK Margaret,	—— —, ——
" James,	—— —, ——.
YOUNG Nicholas, of Thomas and Mary,	Nov. 17, 1691.

NAMES LOST.

Sybil,	Dec. 14, 178—.
Elisha,	Feb. 19, 1789.
Joseph,	July 19, 1791.
Sarah,	Oct. 19, 1793.
Rhodes,	May 29, 1796.
Samuel,	Aug. 27, 1798.
Sarah.	April 14, 1807.

NAMES LOST.

—.	Oct. 16, 1776.
—.	Jan. 13, 1780.
—.	Sept. 8, 1781.
—.	Aug. 13, 1783.
—,	Feb. 22, 1787.
—,	Aug. 22, 1789.
—,	Feb. 11, 1782.
—, and Abigail,	— —, —.
James,	July —, 1727.
—,	April 15, 1729.
—,	Jan. 22, 1731.
—,	Feb. 3, 1733.
—,	March 24, 1734.
William,	May 31, 1681.
—, and Frances,	March 27, 1748.
—,	Sept. 10, 1749.
—.	Jan. 12, 1751.
—, and Mary,	Jan. 27, 1742.
Mary, wife of —, died,	—. 3, 1744.
—, died,	April 26, 1743.
Abigail, his wife, died aged 86 years,	Oct. 3, 1743.
—, (dau.),, of Francis and Mary,	—. —, —.
Ebenezer,	March 25, —.
—, (son),	Dec. 1, —.
—, (son),	Feb. 25, —.
—, (son);	Dec. 9, —.
Francis, father of above, died	—. 15, —.

Vital Record of Rhode Island.

1636=1850.

FIRST SERIES.

BIRTHS, MARRIAGES AND DEATHS.

A Family Register for the People.

By James N. Arnold,

EDITOR OF THE NARRAGANSETT HISTORICAL REGISTER.

"Is My Name Written in the Book of Life?"

Vol. 5.   SOUTH KINGSTOWN.   Part II.

Published under the Auspices of the General Assembly.

PROVIDENCE, R. I:
NARRAGANSETT HISTORICAL PUBLISHING COMPANY.
1894.

ACT DIVIDING THE TOWNE OF KINGS TOWNE.

Voted, that the Act for dividing of Kingstown, be not repealed.

We, whose names are present Subscribed, being appointed and authorized by virtue of an Act of the General Assembly of His Majesty's Colony of Rhode Island, etc., held at Newport, by adjournment, the third Tuesday of June, 1722, to divide the Town of Kingstown into two towns (with all the equality that could be, and to be called by the name of NORTH and SOUTH KINGSTOWN), have proceedeth as followeth, viz.:

Beginning at the Narragansett Bay, at the dividing line between Mr. Francis Willett and Mr. William Robinson, and so continuing said line to the river commonly called Pettaquomscut river, and from thence, a westerly course sixteen degrees southerly into a certtain bound mark in the country road, at a corner of a hedge between Watson and Watson's, and from thence, west four degrees north, until it comes into a highway between Mrs. Mary Haszard and Eber Sherman's and from thence, keeping the highway, which runs west twenty-one degrees north, to a marked tree, near the end of said highway; and from thence, taking a westerly course twenty-seven degrees northerly to a marked tree, something to the southward of Job Babcock, Jr's, house, and so continuing the same course as near as we could, for the badness of the way, taking a marked tree marked on four sides, on the other side of the swamps, continuing the same course into a stake and heap of stones at, or near Misquamocock line, and the line continued in the aforesaid Kingstown, to the southward of said dividing line, to be called SOUTH KINGSTOWN; and all to the northward to be called NORTH KINGSTOWN.

And it is the opinion and intent of the aforesaid subscribers, that if, and in case it should so happen, that the aforesaid line shall run through any man's land, or property, on that side where his house or major part of the land thereunto belonging fall, he shall be one of that Town, and he shall pay rates and taxes into, and do all other duties in the same, for all his said estate as afore mentioned.

As witness our hands this 23d of September, one thousand, seven hundred and twenty-two.

JONATHAN NICHOLS,
WM. WANTON,
T. HULL.

Voted, that this foregoing return be accepted, and that North Kingstown be the eldest Town.

It is voted and enacted by this Assembly, that the Town Meeting to be held at the house of Thomas Joslin, (for the late Town of Kingstown, now North and South Kingstown) on Monday next, to choose jury men to serve in the next General Court of Trials, to be held for this Colony, on the last Tuesday of March next; and that the freemen of each of the respective Towns of North Kingstown and South Kingstown, meet on the third Wednesday of March next, in each of their respective Towns, and some convenient place in each respective Town, as the Assistant or Justices dwelling in each respective Town, shall appoint, and shall then choose deputies, and give in their proxies for the General Election, and appoint their quarter meetings, and that the inhabitants of each Town at their Town Meeting on Monday next, be advised thereof by the Assistants of said Town; and that the Towns of North Kingstown and South Kingstown govern themselves accordingly.

And that the Recorder draw up for each Town their Charter, in order to deliver them to the magistrates at the Election, such as shall be chosen for each respective Town.

And that all former Charters shall cease, upon their receiving their Charters for each Town. And at their respective Town Meetings to be held on the third Wednesday of March next, each Town shall choose two men, to join in a Committee to audit the Treasurer's accounts, that each Town of North and South Kingstown may have their proportion of said money, when they have chosen their respective Treasurer's, in proportion according to their taxes for each Town.

And that the Records of the late Town of Kingstown be put into the hands of the clerk of North Kingstown, to be and remain in said North Kingstown; and that a copy of all Records belonging to South Kingstown, to be drawn out of the Records of the late Kingstown, and to be delivered to the clerk of said South Kingstown, when chosen, and to be paid for out of North and South Kingstown treasuries.

And that Mr. Rouse Helme and Mr. Francis Willet, be, and they hereby are appointed to draw a copy of said Records; and that each Town of North and South Kingstown, shall, after they receive their Charters, choose two petty jurymen, and one grand juryman, to serve at each General Court of Trials, to be held for this Colony.

And it is further ordered, that the day of choice of Town Officers for each Town be mentioned in their Charters.

Voted, that the Act for regulating of North and South Kingstown, be immediately proclaimed.

Rhode Island Colonial Records, Vol. IV., pages 322, 323, 324.

SOUTH KINGSTOWN.

MARRIAGES.

A

1-86 ABB Abigail, residing in South Kingstown, and John Lee, of North Kingstown, Aug. 19, 1743.

1-80 ADAMS Joseph, of Westerly, and Mary Crandall, of South Kingstown; by Isaac Sheldon, Justice, Sept. 4, 1737.

2-2 " Martha, of Ebenezer, and Sarah; and Samuel Bentley, of Caleb and Anne, Nov. 15, 1798.

2-1 " John F., and Ann E. Oatley; by Rev. Pardon Tillinghast, Dec. 31, 1848.

1-105 ALBRO Eunice, and James Whithorne, Oct. 12, 1758.

1-105 " Jeremiah, and Mary Tefft; by Jeremiah Crandall, Justice, Oct. 15, 1758.

1-106 " Hannah, of Richmond, R. I., and Michael Letson, of North Kingstown, Sept. 28, 1760.

2-54 " Edmund B., and Lucy Ann Smith; by Rev. Wilson Cogswell, Feb. 24, 1848.

2-38 " Phebe A., of Exeter, R. I., and Samuel Rose, of South Kingstown, Aug. 4, 1850.

1-68 ALLEN Christopher, of Rhode Island, and Elizabeth Seyonche, of Little Compton, at Boston; by Rev. Robert Hatch, 1687.

1-68 " Caleb, and Marcy Northrup; by Rouse Helme, Assistant, July 15, 1724.

1-70 " Abigail, and Joseph Braman, June 27, 1725.

1-85 " Passaval, and Mary Sherman; by Rouse Helme, Assistant, Dec. 21, 1732.

1-94 " Samuel, and Margaret Congdon; by Samuel Tefft, Justice, June 25, 1784.

1-96 " Joshua, of Caleb, of North Kingstown, and Hannah Watson, of Jeffrey; by Daniel Coggeshall, Assistant, Sept.13, 1750.

1-157 " Mary, of North Kingstown, and Robert Browning, of South Kingstown, March 9, 1777.

1— " Ray, of Charlestown, and Susannah Gould, of South Kingstown; by Samuel Helme, Justice, Dec. 11, 1798.

2-35 " George, and Mercy Perry, of John R. and Sally (Gould), Feb. 26, 1836.

2-17 " Ann, and Nicholas N. Holland; by Rev. Silas Leonard, Feb. 1, 1841.

2-55 " Louisa, and Phineas P. Barber, March 18, 1841.

2-1 " Christopher R., and Elizabeth Jackwurys; by Rev. Wilson Cogswell, Dec. 11, 1842.

2-1 " Jonathan, of Horatio and Alice Hazard; by Rev. Henry C. Coombs, Oct. 6, 1850.

1-01 ANTHONY Mary, and Henry Reynolds, Nov. 9, 1746.

2-1 " Edwin, of Richmond, R. I., and Mary Perkins, of So. Kingstown; by Rev. Wilson Cogswell, July —, 1843.

1-103 ARNOLD Ann, of North Kingstown, and Joseph Babcock, of South Kingstown, Jan. 1, 1758.

2-54 " Stephen, of Warwick, and Rhuhamah Gould, of South Kingstown; by Rev. Nathan Reed, July 15, 1839.

2-1	ARNOLD George, and Eliza Justin; by Rev. Thomas Vernon, Nov. 8, 1839.
2-39	" Sally, and Isaac P. Rodman, July 15, 1847.
1-85	AUSTIN James, and Margaret Gardiner; by Rouse Helme, Assistant, Dec. 29, 1734.
1-104	" Elizabeth, and William Enis, May 27, 1757.
1-156	" Hannah, of Exeter, R. I., and Samuel Whaley, Jr., of South Kingstown, June 11, 1769.
1-84	" Thomas, and Harriet Sweet, of Job; by F. Perry, Justice, Oct. 27, 1791.
2-16	" Eunice, and Robert Hazard, Oct. 25, 1807.
2-54	" George, and Patience Gardiner; by Benjamin Hull, Justice, June 16, 1814.
2-26	" Belinda, of South Kingstown, and Liberty N. May, of Spencer, Mass., July 5, 1840.
2-1	" Charles, and Clarissa Tucker; by Rev. Cyrus Miner. Nov. 29, 1841.
2-44	" Abbie, of George, and William N. Steadman, of Henry, July 2, 1848.
1-98	AYLESWORTH Sarah, and Edward Gardiner, Feb. 25, 1754.

B

1-73	BABCOCK Deborah, and Joseph Hoxsie, Oct. 17, 1728.
1-85	" Ann, and Silas Greenman, March 23, 1730.
1-73	" Ruth, of South Kingstown, and Caleb Hill, of Prudence Island, Feb. 21, 1730.
1-73	" Abigail, of South Kingstown, and Benjamin Hall, of Portsmouth, April 29, 1731.
1-79	" Mrs. Eunice, of South Kingstown, and Capt. Silas Greenman, of Stonington, Conn., May 10, 1737.
1-83	" Hezekiah, of South Kingstown, and Mary Peckham, of Newport, at Newport; by Daniel Gould, Justice, Jan. 3, 1739-40.
1-90	" Mary, of South Kingstown, and Richard Boss, of Charlestown, Aug. 8, 1745.
1-93	" John, and Jemima Reynolds; by John Case, Justice, March 17, 1747.
1-95	" Samuel, and Elizabeth Cottrell; by Benjamin Potter, Justice, Jan. 18, 1748.
1-94	" Job, 3d, and Susannah Hopkins; by Samuel Tifft, Justice, Nov. 20, 1748.
1-95	" Jonathan, and Lydia Lee; by Benjamin Potter, Justice, Nov. 26, 1749.
1-95	" Simeon, of South Kingstown, and Elizabeth Cahoone, of Warwick, R. I.; by Benjamin Potter, Justice, April 19, 1750.
1-99	" James, of Samuel, and Sarah Sheldon, of Isaac, lately deceased; by Jeffrey Watson, Assistant, Jan. 31, 1754.
1-108	" Jonathan, of John and Amey Clarke, of Simeon, of Richmond, R. I.; by Jeffrey Watson, Assistant, March 5, 1755.
1-103	" Joseph, of South Kingstown, and Ann Arnold, of North Kingstown; by Silas Albro, Justice, Jan. 1, 1758.
1-107	" Isabel, and James Stedman, Nov. 11, 1762.
1-108	" John, and Mehitable Sheldon; by Jeremiah Crandall, Justice, Feb. 14, 1765.
1-157	" Mary, of Hezekiah, and Josephus Peckham, May 25, 1774.
1-156	" Augustus, of Hezekiah, and Mary Browning, of Joseph; by Edward Perry, Justice, April 1, 1781.
1-62	" Bridget, of Abijah, and Stephen Browning; by F. Perry, Justice, March 16, 1786.
2-2	" Cudjo, of Charlestown, and Deborah Card, widow of Abram, of South Kingstown; by F. Perry, Justice, Dec. 22, 1791.
1——	" Mehitable, and Caleb Cory, Nov. 11, 1798.
2-32	" Susannah, of Peleg, and John B. Perry, of Samuel, April 11, 1805.
2-23	" Susan S., of South Kingstown, and Jonathan C. Kenyon, of North Providence, Oct. 23, 1839.
2-33	" Hannah E., and Robert C. Peckham, Nov. 14, 1842.

2-43   BABCOCK Rebecca, of Joseph, and William Slocum, of John, of Richmond, R. I., March 30, 1845.

2-28   "   Eliza C., of George, and Arnold W. Nye, of William, July 24, 1845.

2-60   "   Maria S., of Jesse and Sally S., and George N. Crandall. of George W. and Thankful G., Oct. 1, 1845.

2-57   "   Isaac P., and Abbie P. Brown; by Rev. A. Durfee, Dec. 11, 1845.

1-87   BAKER Benjamin, and Mary Sherman; by Isaac Sheldon, Justice, Sept. 16, 1742.

1-108   "   Hannah, and Thomas Hopkins, Jr., Aug. 20, 1765.

1-86   "   Munroe, and Marvel Barber; by Rev. Benjamin Waite, Sept. 8, 1793.

1-63   "   Stafford, of Exeter, and Mary Croncher, of Newport; by Rev. Benjamin Waite, Oct. 27, 1793.

1-68   BARBER Ruth, and George Bentley, March 4, 1723-4.

1-69   "   Joseph, and Rebecca Potter; by Rouse Helme, Assistant, Feb. 4, 1724.

1——   "   Martha, and Thomas Barber, Oct. 3, 1727.

1-——   "   Thomas, and Martha Barber; by Rouse Helme, Assistant, Oct. 3, 1727.

1-70   "   Martha, and Thomas Parker, Oct. 5, 1727.

1-70   "   Mary, and Samuel Tefft, of John, Oct. 1, 1727.

1-70   "   Susannah, and Benjamin Perry, June 11, 1727.

1-75   "   Benjamin, and Mary Tefft; by Rouse Helme, Assistant, Jan. 11, 1729.

1-76   "   Mary, and James Wells, April 22, 1731.

1-85   "   Mercy, and Joseph Carpenter, —— —, 1733.

1-79   "   Ezekiel, of South Kingstown, and Hannah Webster, of John, of Westerly, at Westerly; by Samuel Wilbur, Justice, Nov. 28, 1736.

1-88   "   Samuel, and Abigail Mumford; by Isaac Sheldon, Justice, July 26, 1744.

1-91   "   Lydia, of South Kingstown, and Samuel Hoxsie, of Charlestown, Nov. 27, 1746.

1-93   "   Ann, and James Barber, May 19, 1748.

1-86   "   James, and Ann Barber; by John Case, Justice, May 19, 1748.

1-86   "   George Reynolds, and Amie Popple; by Rev. Benjamin Waite, Aug. 4, 1793.

1-86   "   Marvel, and Munroe Baker, Sept. 8, 1793.

2-2   "   Rowland Robinson, of Allenton, Vermont, and Susannah Whaley, of South Kingstown; by Rev. Benjamin Waite, Oct. 19, 1794.

2-2   "   Moses, and Anne Chapman, of Stonington, Conn.; by Joshua Babcock, Justice, March 30, 1806.

2-2   "   Elizabeth, of Jonathan, and James Barber, of James, April 6, 1809.

2-2   "   James, of James, and Elizabeth Barber, of Jonathan, of Exeter, at Richmond; by Rev. Phineas Palmer, April 6, 1809.

2-3   "   Jesse, of James, of South Kingstown, and Anna Sherman, of Godfrey, of North Kingstown, at Exeter; by John Hopkins, Justice, Nov. 4, 1813.

2-26   "   Susan, of Richmond, R. I., and Silas Ellery Moore, of Cranston, R. I., March 28, 1839.

2-5   "   Elizabeth, and Pitman V. Clarke, both of Richmond, R. I., July 11, 1839.

2-55   "   Henry, and Eliza Ennis, at East Greenwich; by Rev. Thomas Tillinghast, Jan. 20, 1840.

2-55   "   Phineas P., and Louisa Allen; by Rev. Silas Learnard, March 18, 1841.

2-55   "   Albert S., of James, and Waity Peckham, of Reuben S.; by Rev. Ezekiel J. Locke, July 21, 1845.

2-55   "   Davis G., son of Rhoddy, and Susan O. H. Clarke, of Joseph; by Rev. Ezekiel J. Locke, Feb. 1, 1846.

2-50   "   Susannah S., of James, of South Kingstown, and John G. Vaughn, of James T., of West Greenwich, Dec. 24, 1849.

2-56   "   Albert S., of James, of South Kingstown, and Eliza Peckham, of Richmond, R. I., daughter of Reuben S.; by Rev. Ezekiel J. Locke, April 21, 1850.

2-18   BARBER Joanna, of South Kingstown, and Gideon R. Hoxsie, of Richmond, R. I.

2-21   "   Charity, and William H. Johnson, Dec. 24, 1854.

1-—   BARDIN Susannah, and Capt. Abial Brown, Oct. 20, 1795.

2-42, 165 BARNES Sarah, and Benjamin Stanton, Nov. 28, 1839.

1-104   BAUDISH Nathaniel, and Mary Druce; by Thomas Hazard, Justice, Jan. 12, 1738.

1-106   BEARD Hannah, and James Sheldon, Oct. 24, 1762.

1-84   BEARY Richard, and Susannah Saunders; by Joseph Mumford, Justice, Jan. 14, 1726.

1-68   BENTLEY George, and Ruth Barber; by Rouse Helme, Assistant, March 4, 1723-4.

1-70   "   Elizabeth, and Nathaniel Potter, May 30, 1727.

1-70   "   John, and Elizabeth Gardiner; by Rouse Helme, Assistant, May 30, 1727.

1-71, 73   "   Tabitha, and Thomas Sweet, April 11, 1728.

1-106   "   Bathsheba, of Richmond, R. I., and John Bissell, of North Kingstown, March 29, 1761.

1-108   "   Elizabeth, and Reward Tabor, Nov. 6, 1763.

1-108   "   Dorcas, and Josiah Sherman, Dec. 15, 1763.

2-2   "   Samuel, of Caleb and Anne, and Martha Adams, of Ebenezer; by Rev. William Northup, Nov. 15, 1798.

2-6   "   Susan Ann, of South Kingstown, and Daniel Champlain, of Providence, Dec. 11, 1842.

1-81   BENT John, and Sarah Smith; by Rev. Joseph Torrey, Nov. 13, 1737.

2-12   BICKNELL Almira, of North Kingstown, and Robert Gardiner, of South Kingstown, Nov. 4, 1849.

2-16   BILLINGTON Patience Bentley, of South Kingstown, and John Baker Haskell, of Philadelphia, Pa., Dec. 15, 1808.

1-95   BILL Sarah, and William Powers, of Warwick, R. I., April 12, 1750.

1-106   BISSELL John, of North Kingstown, and Bathsheba Bentley, of Richmond, R. I.; by Jeremiah Crandall, Justice, March 29, 1761.

1-157   BOONE Mary, of North Kingstown, and William Gardiner, of South Kingstown, Jan. 26, 1775.

1-84   BOSS Sarah, and George Gardiner, April 22, 1742.

1-90   "   Richard, of Charlestown, and Mary Babcock, of South Kingstown; by Samuel Babcock, Justice, Aug. 8, 1745.

1-90   "   Susannah, and Abiel Sherman, Jan. 30, 1745.

1-108   "   Peter, of South Kingstown, and Susannah Stanton, of Richmond, R. I.; by Jeremiah Crandall, Justice, Dec. 14, 1763.

2-55   BOWEN Ansel, of Thomas, of Providence, R. I., and Sarah A. Woodmansee, of Richmond, R. I., daughter of Job; by Rev. Ezekiel J. Locke, Oct. 14, 1844.

1-70   BRAMAN Joseph, and Abagail Allen; by Rouse Helme, Assistant, June 27, 1725.

1-100   "   Thomas, and Elizabeth Grinnell; by Samuel Tefft, Justice, Jan. 26, 1775.

2-61   "   Austress, and Alfred Cooke, Sept. 15, 1836.

2-10   "   Harty Ann G., of Silas, and William S. Fry, Oct. 27, 1842.

2-60   "   Elizabeth, and Richard Carpenter, Jan. 6, 1850.

2-56   "   Henry, and Mary Elizabeth Harvey; by Rev. Elisha F. Watson, July 15, 1855.

1-77   BRAND Benjamin, of Westerly, and Rebecca Tanner, of South Kingstown; by Isaac Sheldon, Justice, March 16, 1734.

2-42   BRAYTON Abigail, of Portsmouth, and John Segar, of South Kingstown, Nov. 9, 1786.

2-3   BRENTON Frances, of Newport, and Silas Brown, of South Kingstown, Sept. 11, 1796.

2-55   BRIGGS Charles, and Martha Larkin; by Rev. Thomas Vernon, Dec. 25, 1839.

2-34   "   Basheba W., of William, of South Kingstown, and Ezekiel Phillips, of Joseph, Oct. 17, 1847.

2-55   BRIGHTMAN Joseph, of Hopkinton, and Mary P. Segar, of South Kingstown; by Rev. Silas Leonard, Oct. 19, 1740.

1-102   BRISKOW Ann, and Amos Button, June 8, 1755.

1-76   BROOKES John, and Hannah Osborne; by Robert Hannah, Justice, April
            12, 1732.
1-69   BROWNELL Elizabeth, and John Nichols, May 24, 1726.
1-75   "   Esther, and Joseph Tefft, Feb. 22, 1729.
1-90   "   Joseph, of Little Compton, and Elizabeth Congdon, of South
            Kingstown; by Thomas Brown, Justice, Sept. 20, 1746.
1-96   BROWNING Mrs. Hannah, of South Kingstown, and Jedediah Frink, of
            Preston, Conn., Sept. 7, 1748.
1-97   "   Wilkinson, of William, and Susannah Hazard, of Jeffrey; by Jeffrey
            Watson, Assistant, Feb. 4, 1753.
1-98   "   Ann, and John Browning, of William, Jan. 31, 1754.
1-98   "   John, of William, and Ann Browning; by Samuel Tefft, Justice,
            Jan. 31, 1754.
1-106   "   Joseph, of William, and Mary Champlain, of Stephen; by Samuel
            Tefft, Justice, Feb. 12, 1761.
1-157   "   Robert, of South Kingstown, and Mary Allen, of North Kings-
            town; by F. Perry, Justice, March 9, 1777.
1-156   "   Mary, of Joseph, and Angustus Babcock, of Hezekiah, April 1,
            1781.
1-107   "   Rebecca, of William, and Thomas Segar, Feb. 17, 1785.
1-62   "   Stephen, and Bridget Babcock, of Abijah; by F. Perry, Justice,
            March 16, 1786.
1-156   "   Amie, of William, and Henry Knowles, April 28, 1791.
2-3   "   Potter, and Martha Clarke, of Norwich, Conn.; by Rev. John
            Sterry, Dec. 25, 1820.
2-6   "   Martha C., and Peter B. Clarke, Feb. 1, 1843.
2-44   "   Mary Ann, and William F. Segar, Aug. 20, 1848.
2-47   "   Susan, of Samuel and Dorcas, and Palmer Tucker, of Simeon and
            Sally, Feb. 17, 1850.
1-75   BROWN Elizabeth, and Robert Hannah, May 31, 1730.
1-87   "   Ann, of North Kingstown, and Mitihel Case, of South Kings-
            town, March 1, 1743.
1-89   "   Hezekiah, of Providence, R. I., and Sarah Tefft, of South
            Kingstown; by Samuel Tefft, Justice, March 1, 1744.
1-97   "   Robert, Esq., and Sarah Sherman; by Jeffrey Watson, Assistant,
            May 16, 1753.
1-62   "   Jeremiah, Jr., and Eleanor Lillibridge; by Rev. Joseph Torrey,
            Sept. 29, 1776.
1-63   "   Honor, of North Kingstown, and Robert Sherman, of South Kings-
            town, Feb. 26, 1777.
2-23   "   Robert, Jr., of South Kingstown, and Susannah Wells, of Hop-
            kinton; by Rev. Joshua Clarke, Feb. 27, 1791.
1-156   "   William, of Hopkinton, and Thankful Davis, of South Kingstown;
            by Samuel Helme, Justice, Oct. 19, 1791.
1- —   "   Capt. Abiel, and Susannah Bardin; by Samuel Helme, Justice,
            Oct. 20, 1795.
2-3   "   Silas, of South Kingstown, and Frances Brenton, of Newport;
            by Rev. Mr. Smith, of Trinity Church, Newport, Sept. 11, 1796.
1-51   "   Sarah, of South Kingstown, and John Watson, of Jamestown,
            Jan. 24, 1799.
2-3   "   Silas, of South Kingstown, and Mary Potter, of Exeter; by Rev.
            Gresham Palmer, March 9, 1823.
2-55   "   Benjamin B., and Abbie Sherman; by Rev. Oliver Brown, Aug.
            17, 1831.
2-33   "   Sarah, and William Potter, of Alexander (colored), Oct. 23, 1839.
2-17   "   Elizabeth P., of South Kingstown, and Thomas S. Howard, of
            Newport, May 31, 1840.
2-28   "   Elizabeth R., and Isaac Nichols, Dec. 11, 1840.
2-55   "   John K., and Mercy Congdon; by Rev. Silas Leonard, Jan. 28, 1841.
2-24   "   Abbie, of South Kingstown, and Joshua Locke, Jr., April 10, 1842.
2-55, 35 " Palmer A., and Sarah Perry, of John R. and Sally (Gould); by
            Rev. Thomas V. Wells, May 1, 1842.
2-57   "   Abbie P., and Issac P. Babcock, Dec. 11, 1845.
2-38   "   Eliza, of Robert and Hannah, of Warwick, R. I., and Peleg C.
            Rodman, of Christopher G. and Nancy, of South Kingstown,
            March 22, 1846.

2-56   BROWN Joseph S., of Joshua C. and Sally H., and Susan A. Nichols, of Benjamin; by Rev. Thomas Vernon, Nov. 30, 1846.
2-44   "   Sarah E., and Capt. Elias Saunders, of John A., March 3, 1850.
2-56   "   Joseph A., of Palmer, and Mary Adaline Card, of Joshua B.; by Rev. H. C. Coombes, March 17, 1850.
2-49   "   Mary E., and Perry G. Underwood, Dec. 25, 1854.
1-68   BULL Hannah, and Job Card, Aug. 27, 1724.
1-69   "   Amey, and Joseph Coggeshall, Jan. 24, 1724-5.
1-89   "   Nathan, and Abigail Inman; by Samuel Tefft, Justice, Jan. 27, 1740.
1-90   "   Jeremiah, and Ruth Closon; by Samuel Tefft, Justice, June 26, 1745.
2-56   BURDICK Henry B., of Newport, and Margaret R. Patterson; by Rev. Ezekiel J. Locke, Oct. 11, 1846.
1-85   BURNSIDE Joseph, and Abigail Lee; by Rouse Helme, Assistant, 1735.
1-102   BUTTON Amos, and Ann Briskow; by Samuel Segar, Justice, June 8, 1755.

C

1-95   CAHOONE Elizabeth, of Warwick, R. I., and Simeon Babcock, of South Kingstown, April 19, 1750.
1-85   CAMPBELL Charles, and Martha Price; by Rouse Helme, Assistant, Sept. 17, 1732.
1-80   "   John, and Elizabeth ——; m. by Isaac Sheldon, Justice, Dec. 15, 1727.
1-68   CARD Margory, and John Foster, June 11, 1724.
1-68   "   Job, and Hannah Bull; by Rouse Helme, Assistant, Aug. 27, 1724.
1-91   "   Joshua, and Alice Clark; by Thomas Brown, Justice, Feb. 26, 1746.
1-96   "   Phebe, of South Kingstown, and Elijah Champlin, of Charlestown, Nov. 27, 1751.
1-62   "   Ann, of Job, and Jeffrey Champlin, of Elijah, Oct. 23, 1783.
2-2   "   Deborah, widow of Abram, and Cudjo Babcock, of Charlestown, Dec. 22, 1791.
2-21   "   Elizabeth, of Charlestown, and John James, of South Kingstown, Dec. 31, 1849.
2-56   "   Mary Adeline, of Joshua B., and Joseph A. Brown, of Palmer, March 17, 1850.
2-39   "   Harriet P., of Jamestown, and George P. Rose, of South Kingstown, Dec. 5, 1852.
1-108   CARLILE William, and Lois Sunderland; by Jeremiah Crandall, Justice, Jan. 27, 1760.
1-85   CARPENTER Joseph, and Mercy Barber; by Rouse Helme, Assistant, —— —, 1733.
1-88   "   Deborah, and Daniel Knowles, March 24, 1744.
1-98   "   Jeremiah, and Abigail Sheldon; by Samuel Tefft, Justice, June 24, 1752.
1-90   "   Sarah, and Nathaniel Gardiner, Sept. 21, 1752.
1-98   "   Samuel, and Deborah Greenman; by Samuel Tefft, Justice, Nov. 15, 1753.
1-105   "   Elizabeth, of South Kingstown, and Peter Wells, of Westerly, R. I., March 1, 1759.
1-63   "   Mrs. Mary, and Joseph Knowles, March 16, 1783.
1-—   "   Mary Hannah, and Nicholas Bryant Potter, Jan. 28, 1794.
1-—   "   Mary, of Stephen, and John Cooke, Sept. 27, 1798.
2-60   "   Richard, and Elizabeth Braman; by Rev. Henry C. Coombes, Jan. 6, 1850.
2-6, 35   "   Isaac H., and Abbie Perry, of John R., and Sally (Gould); by Rev. Wilson Cogswell, Oct. 30, 1842.
2-45   "   Lavina, and Henry Spear, July 28, 1850.
2-30   "   Susan A., and Adolphus Manuel Open, Nov. 7, 1858.
1-102   CASEY Elizabeth, of Exeter, and Jeremiah Crandall, of South Kingstown, Feb. 2, 1746.

1-71 CASE Elizabeth, and James York, Jan. 11, 1727.
1-70 " Sarah, and Isaac Sheffild, April 20, 1727.
1-71 " Ann, and Aaron Milleman, May 23, 1728.
1-73 " Ann, and Aaron Williams, May 23, 1728.
1-72 " William, and Mercy Crandall; by Rouse Helme, Assistant, Sept. 11, 1729.
1-73 ' Joseph, of Joseph, Jr., and Sarah Mumford; by Christopher Allen, Justice, Dec. 18, 1729.
1-87 " Mitihel, of South Kingstown, and Ann Brown, of North Kingstown; by Rev. David Sprague, March 1, 1743.
1-96 " Hannah, and Samuel Wilson, Dec. 30, 1744.
1-92 " Amie, and Samuel Curtis, March 19, 1746.
1-107 " Mercy, of William, of South Kingstown, and John Clarke, Jr., of Newport, July 16, 1755.
2-240 " Sarah, of South Kingstown, and Robert R. Knowles, of North Providence. R. I., Sept. 20, 1841.
2-6 CASWELL Reuben, and Susannah A. Nichols; by Rev. Elisha F. Watson, Sept. 2, 1844.
2-13 " Mary S., of Gardiner T. and Mary S., and Wm. Gould, of William (marriage not given), recorded May 17, 1780.
1-93 CHAMPLAIN Anne, and Henry Gardiner, June 27, 1736.
1-81 " Mary, and John Craddock (Indians), Feb. 5, 1737.
1-96 " Elijah, of Charlestown, and Phebe Card, of South Kingstown; by Samuel Tefft, Justice, Nov. 27, 1751.
1-106 " Mary, of Stephen, and Joseph Browning, of Wm., Feb. 12, 1761.
1-63 " Stephen, son of Dinah, widow, and Elizabeth Perry, of Freeman; by Rev. Benj. Waite, Dec. 20, 1782.
1-62 " Jeffrey, of Elijah, and Ann Card, of Job; by F. Perry, Justice, Oct. 23, 1783.
1-84 " Gardiner, of William, and Lydia West, of James, of Westerly, R. I.; by Rev. Isaiah Wilcox, Aug. 31, 1791.
2-4 " Thomas Hazard, of Jeffrey, of South Kingstown, and Amie Tripp Perry, of Newport, dau. of Joseph; by Oliver Gardiner, Senator, Oct. 2, 1803.
2-4 " Jeffrey Washington, and Rebecca Perry; by James Congdon, Justice, Jan. 30, 1806.
2-46 " Amie, and Thurston Tucker, Jan. 4, 1841.
2-5 " William, of Richmond, R. I., and Jane Champlain, of South Kingstown; by Rev. Silas Leonard, March 14, 1841.
2-5 " Jane, and William Champlain, March 14, 1841.
2-5 " William, and Adeline B. Tucker; by Rev. Silas Leonard, April 4, 1841.
2-5 " Joseph, 3d., and Mary Whitford; by Rev. Cyrus Miner, Dec. 22, 1841.
2-28 " Elizabeth P., of South Kingstown, and Benjamin Nye, of Charlestown, Oct. 11, 1841.
2 6 " Daniel, of Providence, and Susan Ann Bentley, of South Kingstown, by Rev. Wilson Cogswell, Dec. 11, 1842.
2-46 " Ann, of Robert H. and Esther, and Lyndon G. Tefft, of Elijah and Frances, Aug. 18, 1845.
2-60 " John P., of Samuel, and Mary Whaley, of Ezekiel, by Rev. John Slocum, Dec. 29, 1850.
2-2 CHAPMAN Anne, and Moses Barber, March 30, 1806.
1-107 CHAPPELL Mirabah, and William Osborne, Nov. 13, 1762.
2-4 " Fones and Penelope Hale, by James Helme, Justice, March 12, 1805.
2-60 ". Frederic, of Frederic, and Prudence S. Holley, of John, by Rev. Ezekiel J. Locke, Oct. 12, 1846.
2-60 " William J., of Richard, and Deborah Moore, of Nathan, both of Richmond, by E. J. Locke.
1-68 CLARKE Emmanuel, and Margaret Smith, at North Kingstown, by William Spencer, Justice, Jan. 4, 1725.
1-72 " Sarah, and John Page, Sept. 21, 1729.
1-85 " William, and Rebecca Wells, by Rouse Helme, Assistant, Sept. 4, 1731.

1-85	CLARKE	Judith, and Robert Potter, Jr., Sept. 5, 1731.
1-85	"	Caleb, and Mary Sheffield, by Rouse Helme, Assistant, Dec. 1, 1737.
1-89	"	Latham, of Samuel of Jamestown, and Martha Robinson, of William of South Kingstown, by David Coggeshall, Assistant, April 18, 1745.
1-91	"	Alice, and Joshua Card, Feb. 26, 1746.
1-94	"	Michel, and Martha West, by Samuel Tefft, Justice, Nov. 12, 1748.
1-108	"	Amie, of Simeon of Richmond, and Jonathan Babcock, of John of South Kingstown, March 3, 1755.
1-107	"	John, Jr., of Newport, and Mercy Case, of William, of South Kingstown, July 16, 1755.
1-105	"	James, of Stonington, Conn., and Dorcas Gardiner, of South Kingstown; by Henry Gardiner, Assistant, Nov. 19, 1760.
1-107	"	Lucy, of South Kingstown, and Edward Sand, of Newport, Sept. 15, 1763.
1-63	"	Samuel, and Sarah Niles; by Rev. Joseph Torry, April 13, 1775.
1-62	"	Sarah, and James Helme, Nov. 9, 1777.
2-7	"	William Case, and Sarah Cross; by Nathaniel Gardiner, Justice, July 21, 1781.
2-7	"	Mary Ann, of William C., and George Douglass, of David, Dec. 18, 1805.
2-16	"	Teresa, of South Kingstown, and Bowdoin Hazard, Dec. 6, 1810.
2-3	"	Martha, and Potter Browning, Dec. 25, 1720.
2-5	"	Pittman V., and Elizabeth Barber, both of Richmond; by Rev. John H. Baker, July 11, 1839.
2-6	"	Peter W., and Martha C. Browning; by Rev. Nelson Cogswell, Feb. 1, 1843.
-2-6	"	Simeon P., of Richmond, and Catherine C. Perry, of South Kingstown; by Rev. Leander Witherill, Nov. 8, 1843.
2-6	"	Henry, and Mary T. Tucker; by Rev. Silas Learnard, Dec. 2, 1843.
2-55	"	Susan O. H., of Joseph, and David G. Barber, of Rhoda, Feb. 1, 1846.
2-53	"	Julia F., of Joshua, and John P. Whaley, of Jeremiah W., May 14, 1848.
2-60	"	Rouse R., and Sarah P. Wells, of Thomas R., Jan. 16, 1849.
2-19	"	Cordelia, and John Holland, July 7, 1850.
2-45	"	Jane, of Christopher, and Wm. Steadman, of Oliver, Aug. 5, 1850.
2-31	"	Emeline, and Samuel G. Northup, Sept. 27, 1855.
1-90	CLOSON	Ruth, and Jeremiah Bull, June 26, 1745.
1-09	COGGESHALL	Joseph, and Amey Bull; by Rouse Helme, Assistant, Jan. 24, 1724-5.
1-69	COLE	Catherine, and George Parker, Oct. 18, 1724.
1-78	COLLINS	Jedediah, of Westerly, and Hannah Worden, of South Kingstown, by Isaac Sheldon, Justice, Aug. 13, 1736.
2-4	"	John, of Amos, of North Stonington, Conn., and Eliza Perkins, of James, of South Kingstown; by Rev. Gershom Palmer, Oct. 25, 1809.
1-107	COMSTOCK	Job, of East Greenwich, and Hannah Hookins, of South Kingstown, dau. of Christopher; by John Lillibridge, Justice, Dec. 18, 1763.
2-5	"	Joseph, and Sarah R. Comstock; by Rev. Joel Mann, May 31, 1802.
2-5	"	Sarah R., and Joseph Comstock, May 31, 1802.
1-—	CONGDON	Sarah, of Samuel, and Capt. Robert Robinson, of Christopher, March 15, 1795.
1-90	"	Elizabeth, of South Kingstown, and Joseph Brownell, of Little Compton, Sept. 20, 1746.
1-94	"	Margaret, and Samuel Allen, June 25, 1748.
2-7	"	Mary, of William and Freelove, and John B. Dockray, of John and Mary, Sept. 6, 1779.
1-—	"	Deborah, of William, of South Kingstown, and John Fry, of East Greenwich, June 4, 1795.
2-4	"	John K., of James, of Charlestown, and Sarah Knowles, of South Kingstown, dau. of Major Wm.; by Samuel Perry, Justice, Jan. 12, 1806.

2-5   CONGDON James, of James and Rebecca, of Charlestown, and Renewed Knowles, of William and Sarah; by Rev. William Northup, Oct. 11, 1810.

2-55   "   Mercy, and John K. Brown, Jan. 28, 1841.

2-23   "   Rebecca R., of Charlestown, and Thomas A. Kenyon, of South Kingstown, Oct. 3, 1843.

2-60   CONNOR Daniel, and Susan J. Steadman, of Asa; by Rev. Henry O. Coombes, July 28, 1850.

1-—   COOKE John, and Mary C. Carpenter, of Stephen, by Samuel Helme, Justice, Sept. 27, 1798.

2-61   "   Alfred, and Anstress Braman; m. by William Nichols, Justice, Sept. 15, 1836.

2-12   "   Abbie, of Elisha, and Hazard Gavitt, of Reuben, Oct. 28, 1849.

1-—   COON Lodowick, of Hopkinton, and Thankful Williams, of So. Kingstown; by Samuel Helme, Justice, June 4, 1795.

1-—   CORY Benjamin, and Catherine James; by Samuel Helme, Justice, June, 1798.

1-—   "   Caleb, and Mehitable Babcock; by Samuel Helme, Justice, Nov. 11, 1798.

2-5   "   Benjamin S., and Meriah Perry; by Joseph P. Babcock, Justice, Dec. 15, 1839.

2-24   "   Mrs. Hannah, widow of Gardiner, and Nathan Lillibridge, of Gideon, April 23, 1848.

2-61   "   Angustus, and Clarissa Streeter; m. by Rev. Daniel Carr, Nov. 22, 1875.

1-71, 73   COTTRELL Mary, and Peter Stephens, Sept. 1, 1728.

1-76   "   Mary, and Nathan Tanner, May 28, 1734.

1-80   "   Patience, of South Kingstown, and Benjamin James, of Westerly, Aug. 27, 1737.

1-83   "   George, and Abigail White; by James Sheldon, Justice, Feb. 10, 1739.

1-95   "   Elizabeth, and Samuel Babcock, Jan. 18, 1748.

1-62   "   William (silversmith), and Mary Tefft, of George; by G. Peckham, Justice, Dec. 7, 1786.

2-6   "   Jesse, and Hannah Steadman; by Rev. Silas Learnard, June 21, 1843.

1-—   COYHES William, of Charlestown, and Mary Nocake, of South Kingstown (Indians); by Samuel Helme, Justice, March 19, 1795.

1-76   COX Elizabeth, and Thomas Read, Nov. 3, 1733.

1-81   "   Jacob, of Newport, and Mrs. Mary Heydon, of South Kingstown; by Rev. Joseph Torrey, Sept. 3, 1737.

1-81   CRADDOCK John, and Mary Champlain (Indians), by Rev. Joseph Torrey, Feb. 5, 1737.

1-72   CRANDALL Mercy, and William Case, Sept. 11, 1729.

1-80   "   Mary, of South Kingstown, and Joseph Adams, of Westerly, Sept. 4, 1737.

1-106   "   Elizabeth, and Nathaniel Perkins, March 1, 1739.

1-82   "   Martha, and John Frazer, July 31, 1739.

1-102   "   Jeremiah, of South Kingstown, and Elizabeth Casey, of Exeter; by Rev. David Sprague, Feb. 2, 1746.

2-60   "   George N., of Westerly, R. I., son of George W. and Thankful G., and Maria S. Babcock, of Jesse and Sally S., by Rev. Thomas Vernon, Oct. 1, 1845.

2-21   "   Jane M. H., of William and Randall C. James, of Ezekiel, July 1, 1847.

2-9   "   Benjamin F., and Patience A. Tourjee, by Rev. Elisha F. Watson, Aug. 30, 1852.

2-9   "   Clarke, and Ruth A. Foster, by Rev. Eldredge Crandall, Sept. 17, 1865.

1-109   CROSSMAN Mary, of South Kingstown, and James Pierce, of East Greenwich, Nov. 7, 1773.

1-—   CROSSWELL Mingrel, of Sterling, Conn., and Mary Sias, of South Kingstown, by Samuel Helme, Justice, Nov. 22, 1794.

1-62   CROSS Sarah, and William Case Clarke, July 21, 1781.

2-6   CROSS Charles, of Joseph, of Charlestown, and Martha B. Hazard, of
          Brenton, by Joseph P. Babcock, Justice, Sept. 25, 1842.
1-63   CROUCHER Mary, of Newport, and Stafford Baker, of Exeter, Oct. 27,
          1793.
1-81   CRAWFORD William, of Warwick, and Mary Wells, of South Kingstown; by
          Isaac Sheldon, Justice, Sept. 7, 1738.
2-17   CRUMB Almira P., of Westerly, and Benjamin Holland, of South Kingstown,
          Aug. 2, 1840.
2-17,62,113 "   Mary Ann, and Edward Hazard Holland, Jr., July 4, 1841.
1-92   CURTIS Samuel, and Amie Case, by Jeffrey Hazard, Assistant, March 19,
          1746.

D

1-157 DAKE Benjamin, and Elizabeth Reynolds, by Emmanuel Case, Assistant,
          March 23, 1779.
1-104 DAVIS Martha and Edward Read, Oct. 15, 1758.
1-156   "   Thankful, of South Kingstown, and William Brown, of Hopkinton,
          Oct. 19, 1791.
2-62   "   William A., of Fall River, Mass., and Susan C. Tefft, of South
          Kingstown, by Rev. Thos. Vernon, Dec. 9, 1840.
2-62   DAWLEY John C., and Mary A. Reynolds, both of Exeter, by Rev. Silas
          Learnard, Aug. 28, 1842.
1-70   DENNISON John, and Alice Perry, by Rouse Helme, Assistant, July 21,
          1725.
1-—   Dewy Susannah, of South Kingstown, and Ebenezer Vaughn, of East Green-
          wich, Feb. 7, 1796.
1-81   DICKINSON Mrs. Ann, and Jeremiah Niles, April 21, 1737.
2-62   DIXON George, and Sarah Ann Rodman, by Rev. Silas Learnard, May 3,
          1840.
2-7   DOCKRAY John Bigelow, of John and Mary, and Mary Congdon, of Wil-
          liam and Freelove, by Samuel Tefft, Justice, Sept. 6, 1779.
2-52   "   Mary and Elisha F. Watson, by Rev. James H. Eames, June 6,
          1843.
2-7   DOUGLASS George, of David, and Mary Ann Clarke, of William C., by Rev.
          Thomas Kendall, Dec. 18, 1805.
1-82   DRUCE Ebenezer, and Mary Hazard; by Isaac Sheldon, Justice, June 6,
          1739.
1-104   "   Mary, and Nathaniel Baudish, Jan. 12, 1758.
2-34   DYE Mary W., of Asa and Mary, and Edwin A. Peckham, of Judge William
          Peckham, May 13, 1849.

E

1-77   EARL Susannah, and Daniel Sherman, May 22, 1735.
1-99   "   Abigail, of John, and Isaac Sheldon, of Isaac. Dec. 20, 1746.
2-8   EATON Edgar R., and Mary Ann Smith, by Rev. Wilson Cogswell, Dec. 4,
          1842.
1-70   ELDRED Abigail and Henry Gardiner, June 30, 1726.
1-78   "   Elizabeth, of South Kingstown, and John Rose, of Preston, Conn.,
          June 12, 1734.
1-80   "   William, of North Kingstown, and Abigail Fish, of South Kings-
          town, by Isaac Sheldon, Justice, March 16, 1737.
1-108   "   Esther, and Arnold Proser, July 14, 1764, July 15, 1765 (both
          dates given).
1-104 ENIS Wm., and Elizabeth Austin; by Thomas Hazard, Assistant, May
          27, 1757.
2-55   "   Eliza, and Henry Barber, Jan. 20, 1840.
1-81   ENOS William, and Sarah Ladd, by Rev. Joseph Torrey, Oct. 17, 1736.
1-85   EVERITT Daniel, and Mary Sheffield, by Rouse Helme, Assistant, July
          12, 1739.
1-98   "   Deborah, and Jonathan Holway, May 24, 1753.

F

2-10 FAIRWEATHER Solomon, of George, and Louisa Weeden, of London (col.), by Rev. James Hammond, Oct. 15, 1848.

1-76 FISH Abigail, and Joseph Fox, April 6, 1733.

1-80   "   Abigail, and William Eldred, March 16, 1737.

1-68 FOSTER John, and Margery Card, both of Westerly, by Rouse Helme, Assistant, June 11, 1724.

1-69   "   Jonathan, and Elizabeth Mumford, by Rouse Helme, Assistant, Feb. 4, 1724-5.

2-28   "   Lydia M., of Othniel of South Kingstown, and Thomas P. Nichols, of Newport, July 17, 1844.

2-9   "   Ruth A., and Clarke Crandall, Sept. 17, 1865.

1-72 FOWLER Thomas, and Sybil Knowles, by Robert Hannah, Justice, April 26, 1730.

1-90   "   Simeon, and Mercy Jones, by Samuel Babcock, Justice, March 20, 1745.

1-76 FOX Joseph, and Abigail Fish, by Christopher Allen, Justice, April 6, 1733.

1-94 FRANKLIN Penelope, of Jamestown, and James Sherman, of North Kingstown, Sept. 8, 1748.

1-78 FRAZER Thomas, residing in North Kingstown, and Ann Wells, of South Kingstown, by Isaac Sheldon, Justice, Nov. 26, 1735.

1-82   "   John, and Martha Crandall, by Isaac Sheldon, Justice, July 31, 1739.

1-92   "   Martha, and Edmund Littlefield, Nov. 30, 1746.

1-106   "   Anne, of South Kingstown, and Christopher Potter, of Richmond, Nov. 23, 1760.

1-96 FRINK Jedediah, of Preston, Conn., and Mrs. Hannah Browning, of South Kingstown, by Rev. Joseph Park, Sept. 7, 1748.

1-100 FRY Hannah, of East Greenwich, dau. of Thomas, and James Sherman, of South Kingstown, Feb. 6, 1755.

1-—   "   John, of East Greenwich, and Deborah Congdon, of So. Kingstown, dau. of William, by Samuel Helme, Justice, June 4, 1795.

2-10   "   William S., and Harty Ann G. Braman, of Silas, by Matthew Waite, Justice, Oct. 27, 1842.

G

1-106 GALEN Mercy, and John Young, both of Exeter, Oct. 11, 1760.

1-70 GARDINER Henry, and Abigail Eldred, by Rouse Helme, Assistant, June 30, 1726.

1-71   "   Benjamin, and Mary Howland, by Christopher Allen, Justice, March 22, 1726-7.

1-69   "   Mary, of Nathaniel, and John Kenyon, Jr., March 23, 1726-7.

1-70   "   Elizabeth, and John Bentley, March 30, 1727.

1-73   "   Dorcas, of South Kingstown, and George Tibbitts, Jr., of North Kingstown, March 11, 1730-1.

1-96   "   Ezekiel, of Nicholas, of North Kingstown, and Dorcas Watson, of John, of South Kingstown, by Ephraim Gardiner, Justice, Aug. 29, 1734.

1-85   "   Margaret, and James Anstin, by Rouse Helme, Assistant, Dec. 29, 1734.

1-77   "   Caleb, and Isabel Sherman, by Christopher Allen, Justice, Feb. 20, 1734.

1-93   "   Henry, and Anne Champlain, of Westerly, by Rev. Samuel Scribe, June 27, 1736.

1-80   "   Abigail, and Jeremiah Worden, Nov. 30, 1738.

1-82   "   Hannah, and Caleb Westcott, May 27, 1739.

1-97   "   Mary, of Exeter, R. I., of John, and Jirah Mumford, of South Kingstown, Nov. 29, 1739.

1-84   "   Amie, and Stephen Tefft, Dec. 10, 1741.

1-86, 87   "   George, and Sarah Potter; by Isaac Sheldon, Justice, Feb. 10, 1742.

(Vit. Rec., Vol. 5.) 9

1-84   GARDINER George, and Sarah Boss; by Isaac Sheldon, Justice, April 22, 1742.

1-104   "   John, and Ann Verner; by Robert Hannah, (both came from Ireland) about 1743.

1-95   "   Thomas, and Mary Higinbottom; by Ephraim Gardiner, Justice, April 12, 1744.

1-95   "   William, Jr., and Freelove Joslin; by Ephraim Gardiner, Justice, May 10, 1744.

1-88   "   Edward, of Henry, and Elizabeth Tabor, of William; by William Robinson, Deputy Governor, May 23, 1745.

1-92   "   Mary, and Jonathan Hazard, April 16, 1747.

1-99   "   Nathaniel, Jr., and Sarah Carpenter; by Samuel Tefft, Justice, Sept. 21, 1752.

1-98   "   Edward, and Sarah Aylesworth; by Samuel Albro, Justice, Feb. 25, 1754.

1-104   "   Hannah, of North Kingstown, and Jeffrey Watson, Jr., of South Kingstown, March 24, 1757.

1-105   "   Clarke, and Amie Lillibridge; by William Waite, Justice, Nov. 1, 1759.

1-105   "   Christopher, of South Kingstown, and Mrs. Mercy Wheeler, of Stonington, Conn.; by Rev. Joseph Fish, Jan. 23, 1760.

, 1-105   "   Dorcas, of South Kingstown, and James Clarke, of Stonington, Conn., Nov. 19, 1760.

1-108   "   Thomas, and Abigail Parker; by Jeremiah Crandall, Justice, June 21, 1764.

1-108   "   John, of John (weaver), and Bathsheba Watson, of Jeffrey; by William Potter, Justice, April 30, 1767.

1-109   "   James, and Abigail Tefft, of Ebenezer, by F. Ferry, Justice, June 27, 1771.

1-157   "   William, of South Kingstown, and Mary Boone, of North Kingstown, by Rev. James Whitman, Jan. 26, 1775.

1-157   "   Tabitha, of Caleb, of South Kingstown, and Christopher Nichols, of John, of East Greenwich, March 10, 1779.

2-54   "   Patience, and George Austin, June 16, 1814.

2-52   "   Mary C., and Moses Wilcox, Jr., Nov. 1, 1840.

2-12   "   Robert C., of Exeter, R. I., and Julia Ann Larkin, of Richmond, R. I., by Rev. Dan'l Slocum, Jan. 1, 1844.

2-12   "   Sylvester R., of North Kingstown, and Ruth Northup, of South Kingstown, by Rev. John Slocum, Jan. 21, 1847.

2-12   "   Marvin, of Amos, and Sarah Hathaway, of Nathan, both of Exeter, R. I., by Rev. Ezekiel J. Locke, Oct. 17, 1847.

2-12   "   Elizabeth, and Wanton Gardiner, Aug. 12, 1849.

2-12   "   Wanton, and Elizabeth Gardiner, by Rev. James Hammond, Aug. 12, 1849.

2-12   "   Robert, of South Kingstown, and Almira Bicknell, of North Kingstown, by Rev. Henry C. Coombes, Nov. 4, 1849.

1-——   GAVITT Samuel, and Ruth ——, Nov. 29, 1766.

2-12   "   Hazard, of Reuben, and Abbie Cooke, of Elisha, by Rev. Ezekiel J. Locke, Oct. 28, 1849.

2-33   GINNODO Peggy D., of South Kingstown, and George B. Pitman, of Richmond, R. I., Jan. 27, 1814.

1-108   GOODBODY John, of North Kingstown, and Anna Rose, of South Kingstown, by John Sheldon, Justice, April 4, 1765.

2-12   GOODCHILD Isaac, of Newport, and Ann Whaley, of South Kingstown, by Rev. Silas Learnard, Aug. 29, 1841.

1-——   GOULD Susannah, of South Kingstown, and Ray Allen, of Charlestown, Dec. 11, 1796.

1-——   "   Martha, and Wm. Tourgee, Jr., Nov. 16, 2797.

1-——   "   Hannah, of John, and John Tourjee, Aug. 16, 1798.

2-35   "   Sally, and John Robinson Perry, Oct. 3, 1809.

2-54   "   Ruhannah, and Stephen Arnold, of Warwick, July 15, 1839.

2-17   "   Rhoda Ann, and Raymond H. Holland, May 2, 1841.

2-52   "   Henrietta, and Thomas Webster, March 12, 1846.

2-44   "   Sarah C., of Jonathan P., of South Kingstown, and Henry Sanford, of Joseph, now of Norwich, Conn., Sept. 16, 1849.

2-13 GOULD William, of William, and Mary S. Caswell, of Gardiner T. and Mary S., by Rev. H. C. Coombes, recorded May 17, 1850.

1-91 GRAY Bethany, of Shrewsbury, N. J., and John Steadman, of South Kingstown, Jan. 29, 1746.

1-85 GREENMAN Silas, and Ann Babcock, by Rouse Helme, Assistant, March 28, 1730.

1-79 " Capt. Silas, of Stonington, Conn., and Miss Eunice Babcock, of George, of South Kingstown, by Rev. Daniel Everett, May 10, 1737.

1-98 " Deborah, and Samuel Carpenter, Nov. 15, 1753.

1-100 " Benjamin, and Ruth Sheffield, by Samuel Tefft, Justice, Jan. 23, 1755.

2-33 " Mary H., and Caleb S. Perrigo, of Wrentham, Mass., May 26, 1841.

1-— GREENE Hawkins, and Sarah Tennant, by Samuel Helme, Justice, Feb. 12, 1799.

2-12 " James C., and Susan Hull, by Rev. Silas Learned, March 4, 1841.

2-12 GRINNELL Daniel, Jr., and Susannah Hopkins, by Rouse Helme, Assistant, June 14, 1724.

1-70 " Daniel, Jr., and Jane Lewis, by Rouse Helme, Assistant, May 21, 1727.

1-85 " Mary, and Benjamin Ladd, Oct. 10, 1736.

1-100 " Elizabeth, and Thomas Braman, Jan. 26, 1755.

2-13 " John G., and Rachel A. Perry, by Rev. Augustus Durfee, Oct. 24, 1858.

1-81 GUTRIDGE Mrs. Sarah, and Palne Woodbridge, July 5, 1737,

H

2-17, 42 HADWIN Benjamin, of Barney, of South Kingstown, and Mercy D. Peckham, of Perry, of East Greenwich; by Rev. Nathan Pierce, March 29, 1838.

2-4 HALE Penelope, and Fones Chappell. March 12, 1805.

1-100 HALL Sarah, and Joseph Harvey, Aug. 6, 1754.

1-73 " Benjamin, of Portsmouth, and Abigail Babcock, of South Kingstown; by Christopher Allen, Justice, April 29, 1731.

1-97 " Elisha, and Elizabeth Joslin; by Jeffrey Watson, Assistant, May 17, 1753.

1-100 " Sarah, and Joseph Harvey, Aug. 6, 1754.

2-39 " Benjamin F., and Hannah N. Rodman, Aug. 19, 1854.

1-75 HANNAH Robert, and Elizabeth Brown; by Rouse Helme, Assistant, May 31, 1730.

1-93 " Catherine, and Joseph Holway, March 1, 1740-1.

1-109 HARRINGTON Sarah, of North Kingstown, and Jonathan Sherman, Jr., of South Kingstown, May 17, 1768.

1-100 HARVEY Joseph, and Sarah Hall; by Samuel Tefft, Justice, Aug. 6, 1754.

2-18 " Mary Ann, of Charlestown, and Peter Hazard, May 22, 1842.

2-18 " Hannah S., and Samuel S. E. Harvey, July 13, 1845.

2-18 " Samuel S. E., of Thomas B., and Hannah S., of Benjamin, of Newport; by Rev. Ezekiel J. Locke; July 13, 1845.

2-38 " Lydia Ann, of South Kingstown, and John M. Robbins, of Brooklyn, Conn., June 3, 1849.

2-44 " Alice, and Edward H. Smith, Oct. 7, 1849.

2-56 " Mary Elizabeth, and Henry Braman, July 15, 1855.

2-16 HASKELL John Baker, of Philadelphia, Penn., and Patience Bentley Billington, of South Kingstown, by Syl'r Robinson, Justice, Dec. 15, 1808.

2-12 HATHAWAY Sarah, of Nathan, and Marvan Gardiner, of Amos, both of Exeter, Oct. 17, 1847.

1-— HAWKINS Thomas, and Hannah Mumford; by Rouse Helme, Assistant, March 20, 1728.

1-68 HAZARD Stephen, and Mary Robinson; by Rouse Helme, Assistant, Jan. 9, 1723-4.

1-71 " Abigail, and William Robinson, March 2, 1726-7.

1-72,74 " Elizabeth, and Benjamin Perry, Jr., July 10, 1729.

1-85   HAZARD Amie, and Eber Sherman, Jr., May 30, 1734.
1-78   "   Oliver, of South Kingstown, and Elizabeth Raymond, of the
            North Parish of New London; by Rev. Joseph Torrey, Dec. 9,
            1736.
1-85   "   Mary, and Benjamin Peckham, Jr., March 2, 1739.
1-82   "   Mary, and Ebenezer Druce, June 6, 1739.
1-90   "   Simeon, and Abigail Mumford; by Thomas Brown, Justice, Feb. 6,
            1745.
1-92   "   Jonathan, and Mary Gardiner; by Jeffrey Watson, Assistant, April
            16, 1747.
1-93   "   Jeremiah, Jr., of North Kingstown, and Ruth Potter, of South
            Kingstown; by John Case, Justice, April 24, 1748.
1-108   "   Penelope, of Col. Thomas, and William Potter, of Col. Potter,
            Nov. 18, 1750.
1-108   "   Elizabeth, of Robert, of Pt. Judith, and Col. Robert Hazard, April
            19, 1752.
1-108   "   Col. Robert, and Elizabeth Hazard, of Robert, of Pt. Judith; by
            Rev. Dr. McSparran, April 19, 1752.
1-97   "   Mary, of Stephen, and John Potter, of Ichabod, Aug. 30, 1752.
1-97   "   Susannah, of Jeffrey, and Wilkinson Browning, of William. Feb.
            4, 1753.
1-108   "   Mrs. Hannah, of Col. Thomas, and Col. John Wilson, Nov. 21,
            1762.
1-63   "   Sarah, of Robert, and Job Watson, Feb. 12, 1766.
1-156   "   Alice, and Godfrey Hazard, Feb. 22, 1778.
1-156   "   Godfrey, of Simeon and Abigail, and Alice Hazard, of George
            and Sarah; by Nathaniel Gardiner, Justice, Feb. 22, 1778.
1-62   "   Jonathan, of Stephen, and Mary Robinson, of Sylvester; by N.
            Helme, Justice, May 12, 1785.
1-84   "   Thomas H., and Abigail Robinson, of Sylvester; by Nathaniel
            Gardiner, Justice, Feb. 23, 1790.
1-109   "   Robert R., and Anne Underwood, by Samuel Curtis, Justice, Sept.
            4, 1791.
1- —   "   Sally, and Jeremiah N. Potter, March 23, 1794.
1- —   "   Mumford, of Newport, and Elizabeth Robinson, of Christopher, of
            South Kingstown; by Samuel Helme, Justice, Feb. 18, 1796.
2-16   "   Robert, and Eunice Austin; by Rev. Asher Miner, Oct. 25, 1807.
2-16   "   Bowdoin, and Teresa Clarke, at Stonington, Conn.; by Rev. Wil-
            liam Randall, Dec. 6, 1810.
2-38   "   Eliza, and William H. Robinson, Dec. 13, 1840.
2-6   "   Martha B., of Brenton, and Charles Cross, of Joseph, of Charles-
            town, Sept. 25, 1842.
2-18   "   Peter, and Mary Ann Harvey, of Charlestown; by Rev. Thomas V.
            Wells, May 22, 1842.
2-18   "   Abram, and Susan H. Taylor; by Rev. Wilson Cogswell, Sept. 18,
            1842.
2-33, 35 " Harriet T., and John G. Perry, March 12, 1843.
2-19   "   Carder C., and Susan C. Knowles; by Rev. C. T. Chapman, Dec.
            10, 1848.
2-38   "   Mary A., of Thomas, of South Kingstown, and John A. Rathbun,
            of North Kingstown, Nov. 11, 1849.
2-1   "   Alice, and Jonathan, son of Horatio Allen, Oct. 6, 1850.
2-38   "   Susan T., and George W. Rose, Nov. 20, 1850.
2-24   "   Thomas E., and Elsa Larkin; by Rev. A. Durfee, Sept. 10, 1854.
1-69   HAZLETON Mary, and Joseph Kenyon, Dec. 27, 1724.
2-17   HEALEY Jonathan, of Charlestown, and Sally Reynolds, of South Kings-
            town; by Rev. John H. Baker, Nov. 24, 1839.
1-85   HELME Dorcas, and Nathan Sheffield, Aug. 18, 1734.
1-81   "   James, of South Kingstown, and Esther Powell, of North Kings-
            town; by Rev. Joseph Torrey, Oct. 19, 1738.
1-63   "   James, and Sarah Clarke; by Rev. Joseph Torrey, Nov. 9, 1777.
2-26   "   Mary, and Nathaniel Mumford, Jr., May 3, 1801.
2-16   "   James, of James, and Alice Perry, of Jonathan; by Rev. Thomas
            Kendall, Oct. 7, 1802.

2-19   HELME Powell, of South Kingstown, son of Samuel and Abbie, and Annie E. Kenyon, of Elijah and Mary E.; by Rev. Thomas Vernon, May 24, 1847.

1-81   HEYDON Mrs. Mary, of South Kingstown, and Jacob Cox, of Newport, Sept. 3, 1737.

1-95   • HIGGINBOTTOM Mary, and Thomas Gardiner, April 12, 1744.

1-73   HILL Caleb, of Prudence Island, and Ruth Babcock, of South Kingstown; by Christopher Allen, Justice, Feb. 21, 1730-1.

2-39   HOLBURTON Drusilla, of George, and Hazard Peckham, of Reuben, both of Richmond, Nov. 11, 1849.

2-17   HOLLAND Benjamin, of South Kingstown, and Almira P. Crumb, of Westerly; by Rev. Silas Learned, Aug. 2, 1840.

2-17   HOLLAND Nicholas N., and Ann Allen, by Rev. Silas Learned, Feb. 1, 1841.

2-17   "   Raymond H., and Rhoda Ann Gould, by Rev. Silas Learned, May 2, 1841.

2-17,62,113 "   Edward Hazard, Jr., and Mary Ann Crumb, by Matthew Waite, Justice, July 4, 1841.

2-17   "   Abbie, of John, and Stephen Holland, of Henry, Aug. 21, 1845.

2-17   "   Stephen, of Henry and Abbie Holland, of John, by Ezekiel J. Locke, Aug. 21, 1845.

2-19   "   Courtland B., and Silena E. Sims, by Rev. Milo Frary, recorded April 2, 1849.

2-19   "   John, and Cordelia Clarke, by Ezekiel J. Locke, July 7, 1850.

1-103   HOLLEY Sarah, and Caleb Sheffield, Dec. 3, 1746.

2-60   "   Prudence T., of John and Frdderic Chappell, of Frederic, Oct. 12, 1846.

1-70   HOLWAY Nicholas, and Patience Mott, by Rouse Helme, Assistant, May 8, 1726.

1-93   "   Joseph, and Catherine Hannah, by Rev. Joseph Torrey, March 1, 1740-1.

1-89   "   Penelope, and Samuel Redman, March 10, 1744.

1-93   "   Joseph, and Abigail Niles, by Rev. Joseph Torrey, Nov. 30, 1746.

1-98   "   Jonathan, and Deborah Everett, by Jeffrey Watson, Assistant, May 24, 1753.

2-42   HOLLOWAY Rebecca C., of Charlestown, and George J. Sherman, of Exeter, July 4, 1841.

1-107   HOOKINS Hannah, of Christopher, of South Kingstown, and Job Comstock, of East Greenwich, Dec. 18, 1763.

1-108   HOPKINS Thomas, Jr., and Hannah Baker, by Francis Tanner, Justice, Aug. 20, 1765.

1-68   "   Susannah, and Daniel Grinnell, Jr., June 14, 1724.

1-72-73   "   Thomas, and Hannah Mumford, by Rouse Helme, Assistant, March 20, 1728.

1-94   "   Susannah, and Job Babcock, 3d, Nov. 20, 1748.

2-17   HOWARD Thomas S., of Newport, and Elizabeth P. Brown, of South Kingstown, by Rev. Wm. H. Newman, May 31, 1840.

1-71   HOWLAND Mary, and Benjamin Gardiner, March 22, 1726-7.

1-72   HOXSIE William, and Margaret Knowles, by Rouse Helme, Assistant, April 14, 1728.

1-73   "   Joseph, and Deborah Babcock, by Rouse Helme, Assistant, Oct. 17, 1728.

1-85   "   Stephen, and Elizabeth Kenyon, by Rouse Helme, Assistant, 1735.

1-91   "   Samuel, of Charlestown, and Lydia Barber, of South Kingstown, by Isaac Sheldon, Justice, Nov. 27, 1746.

1-99   "   Mrs. Ann, of Charlestown, and Abial Sherman, of South Kingstown, May 10, 1772.

1-62   "   Samuel, of Stephen, of Richmond, R. I., and Amie Reynolds, of James, of West Greenwich, R. I., by Rev. John Pendleton, June 8, 1783.

2-17   "   Stephen, and Mary Stanton, by Rev. Lewis Jansen, Nov. 1, 1838.

2-26   "   Sally, of Enoch, of Richmond, and Gardiner Moore, of Henry, of South Kingstown, April 1, 1844.

2-18   "   Gideon R., of Rouse, of Richmond, R. I., and Joanna Barber, of South Kingstown, by Rev. Ezekiel J. Locke.

2-18   HOYT Betsey, of Litchfield, Conn., and Wm. Henry Hoyt, of Ezra, of
        Providence, Nov. 25, 1845.
2-18   "   Wm, Henry, of Ezra, of Providence, R. I., and Betsy Hoyt, of Litch-
        field, Conn., by Rev. Thomas Vernon, Nov. 25, 1845.
1-97   HULL Charles, and Abigail Slack, of Samuel, of Westerly, by John Rich-
        mond, Justice, Dec. 30, 1736.
1-82   "   Stephen, and Martha Morey, by Isaac Sheldon, Justice, April 27,
        1738.
1-102   "   Hannah, of Charles and Samuel Segar, of John, Nov. 27, 1755.
2-12   "   Susan, and James C. Greene, March 4, 1841.

I

1-89   INNMAN Abigail, and Nathan Bull, Jan. 27, 1740.
1-85   IRISH Jedediah, and Thankful Lamphere, by Rouse Helme, Assistant. Dec.
        10, 1732.

J

1-85   JACKQUAWS Nathan, and Margaret Littlejohn; by Rouse Helme, Assist-
        ant, May 15, 1737.
1-90   "   Samuel, and Abigail Sabin; by Thomas Brown, Justice, Aug. 26,
        1746.
2-21   "   Taylor, and Mary Mitchell, May 22, 1808.
2-29   "   Mary, and Henry Northup, May 8, 1826.
2-29   "   Hannah, of South Kingstown, and Jonathan R. Nye, of Charles-
        town, Jan. 8, 1831.
2-45   "   Merebah S., and Reuben Wright, Nov. 14, 1841.
2-1   "   Elizabeth, and Christopher R. Allen, Dec. 11, 1842.
2-21   "   Nathan, and Mary Ann M. Thurston; by Rev. A. G. Palmer, July
        25, 1868.
1-80   JAMES Benjamin, of Westerly, and Patience Cottrell, of South Kings-
        town; by Isaac Sheldon, Justice, Aug. 27, 1737.
1-98   "   Sarah, of Charlestown, and Isaac Sheldon, of South Kingstown,
        Jan. 23, 1741.
1- —   "   Catherine, and Benjamin Cory. June, —, 1798.
2-16,21 "   George, of Richmond, R. I., and Sarah Wilcox, of South Kings-
        town; by Rev. Henry O. Hubbard, April 24, 1826.
2-21   "   Randall C., of Ezekiel and Jane, M. H. Crandall, of William; by
        Rev. E. J. Locke, July 1, 1847.
2-21   "   John, of South Kingstown, and Elizabeth Card, of Charlestown;
        by Rev. Ezekiel J. Locke, Dec. 31, 1849.
1-70   JOHNSON Stephen, and Susannah Long; by Rouse Helme, Assistant, Feb.
        2, 1727.
2-21   "   William H., and Charity Barber; by Rev. Pardon Tillinghast,
        Dec. 24, 1854
1-90   JONES Mercy, and Simeon Fowler, March 20, 1745.
1-85   JOSHUA and Sarah (Indians), by Rouse Helme. Assistant, Sept. 28, 1732.
1-72   JOSLIN Mary, and John Lillibridge, March 29, 1730.
1-95   "   Freelove, and William Gardiner, Jr., May 19, 1744.
1-97   "   Elizabeth, and Elisha Hall, May 17, 1753.
1-156   "   Henry, and Mary Tefft, by Jeremiah Crandall, Justice, May 21,
        1769.
1-91   JUSTIN Ruth, of North Kingstown, and Ebenezer Lewis, of South Kings-
        town. Oct. 17, 1746.
2-1   "   Eliza, and George Arnold, Nov. 24, 1839.

K

1-71,73 KEAIS William, and Margaret Knowles, by Rouse Helme, Assistant,
        April 14, 1728.

1-69   KENYON Joseph, and Marcy G. Hazelton; by Rouse Helme, Assistant, Dec. 27, 1724.
1-69   "   John. Jr., and Mary Gardiner, of Nathaniel; by Christopher Allen, Justice, March 23, 1726-7.
1-85   "   Sarah, and Ebenezer Niles, March 25, 1730.
1-85   "   Elizabeth, and Stephen Hoxsie, —— —, 1735.
2-23   "   Susannah, of Gardiner, and Hazard Knowles, of William, Jan. 31, 1813.
2-23   "   Jonathan C., of North Providence, and Susan S. Babcock, of South Kingstown; by Rev. Thomas Vernon, Sept. 2, 1839.
2-23   "   Thomas A., of South Kingstown, and Rebecca R. Congdon, of Charlestown; by Rev. Wilson Cogswell, Oct. 3, 1843.
2-19   "   Anna E., of Elijah and Mary E., and Powell Helme, of Samuel and Abbie, May 24, 1847.
2-35   "   Ellen F., and William Wanton Perry, April 3, 1848.
2-64   "   Martha A., of Amos, and Allen Kingsley, of William, both of Richmond, R. I., Sept. 4, 1848.
2-23   KETTLE Samuel, of West Greenwich, son of Simon and Hannah Wells, of John, of South Kingstown; by Rev. E. J. Locke, June 11, 1843.
2-43   KINGSLEY Dianna, of William, and Alfred Slocum, of John, both of Richmond, R. I., Nov. 20, 1846.
2-64   "   Allen, of William, and Martha A. Kenyon, of Amos, both of Richmond; by Rev. Ezekiel J. Locke, Sept. 4, 1848.
1-72   KNOWLES Margaret, and William Hoxsie, April 14, 1728.
1-71,72   "   Margaret, and William Keais, April 14, 1728.
1-72   "   Sybil, and Thomas Fowler, April 26, 1730.
1-85   "   Stephen, and Francis Roberts, by Rouse Helme, Assistant, Aug. 27, 1732.
1-88   "   Daniel, and Deborah Carpenter; by Isaac Sheldon, Justice, March 24, 1744.
1-100   "   William, and Abigail Segar; by Benedict Helme, Justice, April 29, 1753.
2-23   "   William, and Abigail Segar; by Benedict Helme, Justice, Feb. 19, 1755.
1-63   "   Joseph, Jr., and Mrs. Mary Carpenter, by S. Babcock, Justice, March 16, 1783.
1-156   "   Henry, and Amie Browning, of William, by F. Perry, Justice, April 28, 1791.
2-4   "   Sarah, of Major Wm. of South Kingstown, and John K. Congdon, of James, of Charlestown, Jan. 12, 1806.
2-5   "   Renewed, of Wm. and Sarah, and James Congdon, of James and Rebecca, Oct. 11, 1810.
2-23   "   Hazard, of William, and Susannah Kenyon, of Gardiner; by Daniel Stanton, Justice, Jan. 31, 1813.
2-29   "   Sally F., and Matthew Nichols, Jr., March 18, 1832.
2-23   "   William N., of Jeremiah, and Emeline Lewis; by Matthew Waite, Justice, Dec. 1, 1839.
2-24   "   Robert R., of North Providence, and Sarah Case, of South Kingstown, by Rev. Cyrus Miner, Sept. 20, 1841.
2-64   "   Robert E., of Jeremiah N., and Susan P. Tucker, of Simeon, by Rev. Ezekiel J. Locke, Sept. 25, 1845.
2-46   "   Mary Ann, of Hazard, and Daniel Sherman, of Joseph, June 19, 1848.
2-19   "   Sarah C., and Carder C. Hazard, Dec. 10, 1848.
2-44   "   Mary Ann, and Daniel Sherman, June 19, 1849.

L

1-85   LADD Benjamin, and Mary Grinnell; by Rouse Helme, Assistant, Oct. 10, 1736.
1-81   "   Sarah, and William Enos, Oct. 17, 1736.
1-85   LANPHERE Thankful, and Jedediah Irish, Dec. 10, 1732.

1-72   LARKIN Abigail, and Joseph Potter, Jan. 14, 1730.

2-55   "   Martha, and Charles Briggs, Dec. 25, 1839.

2-12   "   Julia Ann, of Richmond, R. I., and Robert C. Gardiner, of Exeter, Jan. 1, 1844.

2-46   "   Delilla, of John W., and John A. Tucker, of Joshua, Jr., March 6, 1845.

2-24   "   Elsa, and Thomas E. Hazard, Sept. 10, 1854.

1-85   "   Abigail, and Joseph Burnside, 1735.

1-87   "   Nickolas, and Cortent Noyes; by Isaac Sheldon, Justice, June 17, 1743.

1-86   "   John, of North Kingstown, and Abigail Abb, residing in South Kingstown; by Isaac Sheldon, Justice, Aug. 19, 1743.

1-95   "   Lydia, and Jonathan Babcock, Nov. 26, 1749.

1-106   LETSON Michael, of North Kingstown, and Hannah Albro, of Richmond, R. I.; by Jeremiah Crandall, Justice, Sept. 28, 1760.

1- —   "   Thomas Mitchell, of North Kingstown, and Hannah Osborne, of Richmond, R. I.; by Jeremiah Crandall, Justice, Sept. 28, 1760.

1-7   LEWIS Jane, and Daniel Grinnell, May 21, 1727.

1-75   "   Elizabeth, of Westerly, and William Reynolds, July 17, 1732.

1-91   "   Ebenezer, of South Kingstown, and Ruth Justin, of North Kingstown; by Isaac Sheldon, Justice, Oct. 17, 1746.

2-35   "   Phebe Ann, and Robinson Perry, March 11, 1832.

2-23   "   Emeline, and William N. Knowles, of Jeremiah, Dec. 1, 1839.

2-47   "   Eunice A., of Arnold, of Exeter, and Stephen A. Tefft, of Benjamin, of Richmond, R. I., June 20, 1850.

1-72   LILLIBRIDGE John, and Mary Joslin; by Christopher Allen, Justice, March 29, 1730.

1-105   "   Amie, and Clarke Gardiner, Nov. 1, 1759.

1-102   "   John, and Susannah Segar; by Samuel Segar, Justice, July 6, 1755.

1-62   "   Eleanor, and Jeremiah Brown, Jr., Sept. 29, 1776.

2-24   "   Nathan, of Gideon, and Mrs. Hannah Corey, widow of Gardiner; by Rev. E. J. Locke, April 23, 1848.

1-92   LITTLEFIELD Edmund, and Martha Fraser; by Jeffrey Watson, Assistant, Nov. 30, 1746.

1- —   "   Amie, and Abraham Potter, Aug. 11, 1794.

1-85   LITTLEJOHN Margaret, and Nathan Jackways, May 15, 1737.

2-24   LOCKE Joshua, Jr., of Richmond, R. I., and Abbie Brown, of South Kingstown; by Rev. Weeden Barber, April 10, 1842.

2-24   "   William J. S., of Joshua R., of Richmond, R. I., and Catherine Steadman, of Henry, of South Kingstown; by Rev. Ezekiel J. Locke, Sept. 24, 1843.

1-70   LONG Susannah, and Stephen Johnson, Feb. 2, 1727.

2-32   LUNT Sarah, of William, and Samuel H. Pollock, Nov. 27, 1808.

M

1-88   MAJOR Sarah, of South Kingstown, and Robert Money, of Exeter, March 31, 1745.

2-144   MAWNEY Mary, and Elisha R. Potter, July 9, 1810.

2-26   MAY Liberty N., of Spencer, Mass., and Belinda Austin, of South Kingstown; by Rev. Silas Learnard, July 5, 1840.

1-77   McCOON Thankful, and Thomas Williams, Jan. 6, 1734.

1-103   MILLER Thomas, of Dighton, Mass., and Mercy Tefft, of South Kingstown; by Jeremiah Crandall, Justice, Dec. 16, 1756.

1-71,73   MILLEMAN Aaron, and Ann Case; by Rouse Helme, Assistant, May 23, 1728.

2-21   MITCHELL Mary, and Taylor Jackways, May 22, 1808.

1-88   MONEY Robert, of Exeter, R. I., and Sarah Major, of South Kingstown; by Isaac Sheldon, Justice, March 31, 1745.

2-26   MOORE Silas Ellery, of Cranston, R. I., and Susan Barber, of Richmond, R. I., by Rev. Thomas Vernon, March 28, 1839.

2-26   "   Gardiner, of Henry, of South Kingstown, and Sally Hoxsie, of Enock, of Richmond, R. I., by Rev. Ezekiel J. Locke, April 1, 1844.

2-26   MOORE Isaac S., of Nathan, of Richmond, R. I., and Catherine J. C. M. Patterson, of James, of South Kingstown, by Rev. Ezekiel J. Locke, Nov. 24, 1844.

2-60   "   Deborah, of Nathan, and William J. O. Chappell, of Richard, both of Richmond, — —, —.

1-82   MOREY Martha, and Stephen Hull, April 27, 1738.

1-81   "   Sarah, and John Watson, Sept. 28, 1738.

1-70   MOTT Patience, and Nicholas Holway, May 5, 1726.

1-69   MUMFORD Elizabeth, and Jonathan Foster, Feb. 4, 1724-5.

1-72,73   "   Hannah, and Thomas Hopkins, March 20, 1728.

1-73   "   Sarah, and Joseph Case, of Joseph, Jr., Dec. 18, 1729.

1-75   "   William, and Ann Ray (widow), by Rev. Dr. McSparran, April 3, 1729.

1-85   "   John, and Elizabeth Perkins, by Rouse Helme, Assistant, 1735.

1-97   "   Jirah, of South Kingstown, and Mary Gardiner, of John, of Exeter, R. I., at Exeter, by Rev. Benjamin Waite, Nov. 29, 1739.

1-88   "   Abigail, and Samuel Barber, July 26, 1744.

1-90   "   Abigail, and Simeon Hazard, Feb. 6, 1745.

2-26   ·   "   Nathaniel, Jr., and Mary Helme, by Rev. Benjamin Waite, May 31, 1801.

2-249   "   Mary E., of South Kingstown, and Joseph B. Potter, of Richmond, R. I., Oct. 18, 1841.

2-43   "   Abbie, and Clarke B. Sherman, Nov. 5, 1843.

1-156   MURPHY Martin, and Mary Steadman, of Thomas, by F. Perry, Justice, Jan. 7, 1778.

N

1-38   NASH Isaac, Jr., and Elizabeth Tucker, by John Potter, Justice, May 13, 1723.

1-89   "   Elizabeth, and Ebenezer Wells, Oct. 24, 1726.

1-69   NICKOLS John, and Elizabeth Brownell, by Christopher Allen, Justice, May 24, 1726.

1-157   "   Christopher, of East Greenwich, son of John, and Tabitha Gardiner, of Caleb, of South Kingstown, by Stephen Potter, Justice, March 10, 1779.

2-29   "   Matthew, Jr., and Sally F. Knowles, March 18, 1832.

2-28   "   Isaac, and Elizabeth R. Brown, by Rev. Wm. H. Newman, Dec. 11, 1840.

2-28   "   John, Jr., and Ann H. Stanton, by Rev. Cyrus Miner, Jan. 20, 1842.

2-28   "   Thomas P., of Newport, son of William S., and Lydia M. Foster, of Otbneil, of South Kingstown, by Matthew Waite, Justice, July 17, 1844.

2-6   "   Susannah A., and Reuben Caswell, Sept. 2, 1844.

2-56   "   Susan A., of Benjamin, and Joseph S. Brown, of Joshua C. and Sally H., Nov. 30, 1846.

2-29   "   James A., and Mary A. Tefft, by Rev. Pardon Tillinghast, March 11, 1849.

1-71,73   NILES Nathan, and Mary Northup, by Rouse Helme, Assistant, Sept. 12, 1728.

1-85   "   Ebenezer, and Sarah Kenyon, by Rouse Helme, Assistant, March 25, 1730.

1-81   "   Jeremiah, and Mrs. Ann Dickinson, by Rev. Joseph Torrey, April 21, 1737.

1-93   "   Abigail, and Joseph Holway, Nov. 30, 1746.

1-63   "   Sarah, and Samuel Clarke, April 13, 1775.

2-28   "   Edward T., of Simon and Nancy, and Mary Potter, of Aaron and Abbie, by Rev. Thomas Vernon, Dec. 19, 1844.

1-—   NOCAKE Mary, of South Kingstown, and William Coyhes, of Charlestown, (Indians), March 19, 1795.

1-68   NORTHUP Mary, and Caleb Allen, July 15, 1724.

1-71,73   "   Mary, and Nathan Niles, Sept. 12, 1728.

1-89   "   Stephen, and Sarah Roberts, by Samuel Tefft, Justice, Oct. 17, 1744.

2-29 NORTHUP Sarah, and Daniel Tefft, Feb. 9, 1795.
2-28 "   Henry, and Mary Jackways, by Daniel Steadman, Justice, May 8,
              1826.
2-28 "   John V., and Mrs. Hannah B. Sweet, by Rev. Thomas Vernon, Oct.
              27, 1844.
2-12 "   Ruth, of South Kingstown, and Sylvester R. Gardiner, of North
              Kingstown, Jan. 21, 1847.
2-29 "   Gideon S., of James R., and Mary Ann Thomas, of George, by
              Rev. Henry C. Coombes, Oct. 6, 1850.
2-31 "   Samuel G., and Emeline Clarke, Sept. 27, 1855.
1-87 NOYES Content and Nicholas Lee, June 17, 1743.
2-29 "   Azel, and Sarah Jane Sherman, of Exeter, R. I., by Rev. Ezekiel
              J. Locke, March 22, 1849.
1-88 NUTTER Samuel, and Elizabeth Rowler, by Isaac Sheldon, Justice, Oct.
              28, 1744.
2-29 NYE Jonathan R., of Charlestown, and Hannah Jackways, of South Kings-
              town, by Rev. Jonathan Oatley, Jan. 8, 1831.
2-28 "   Benjamin, of Charlestown, and Elizabeth P. Champlain, of South
              Kingstown, by Rev. Wilson Coggswell, Oct. 11, 1841.
2-28 "   Arnold W., of William, and Eliza C. Babcock, of George, by Rev.
              Ezekiel J. Locke, July 24, 1845.

O

1- — OATLEY John, of Samuel, and Susannah Sherman, of Daniel; by Samuel
              Helme, Justice, Sept. —, 1796.
2-1   "   Ann E., and John F. Adams, Dec. 31, 1848.
2-30 OPEN Adolphus Manuel, and Susan A. Carpenter; by Rev. Isaac M.
              Church, Nov 7, 1858.
1-76 OSBORNE Hannah, and John Brooks, April 12, 1732.
1- — "   Hannah, of Richmond, R. I., and Thomas Mitchell Letson, of North
              Kingstown, Sept. 28, 1760.
1-107 "   William, and Mirabah Chappell; by Francis Tanner, Justice, Nov.
              13, 1762.
1-102 OVERING Henry John, of Newport, and Mary Whitehorne, of South Kings-
              town; by Jeremiah Crandall, Justice, Nov. 15, 1755.

P

1-72 PAGE John, and Sarah Clarke; by Robert Hannah, Justice, Sept. 21, 1729.
2-52 PALMER Emma, of Stonington, Conn., (his second wife), and Thomas R.
              Wells, Oct. 10, 1833.
1-69 PARKER George, and Catherine Cole; by Rouse Helme, Justice, Oct. 18,
              1724.
1-70 "   Thomas, and Martha Barber; m. by Rouse Helme, Assistant, Oct.
              5, 1727.
1-92 "   Frances, and Rebecca Veal; by Jeffrey Watson, Assistant, March
              22, 1746.
1-108 "   Abigail, and Thomas Gardiner, Feb. 4, 1765.
1- — PARR Jonathan, and Polly Steadman, of James; by Samuel Helme, Jus-
              tice, Oct. 29, 1795.
2-26 PATTERSON Catherine J. C. M., of James, and Isaac S. Moore, of Nathan,
              Nov. 24, 1844.
2-56 "   Margaret R., and Henry B. Burdick, of Newport, Oct. 11, 1846.
1-109 PEARCE James, of East Greenwich, and Mary Crossman, of South Kings-
              town; by Joseph Torrey, Clerg., Nov. 7, 1773.
2-34 "   George G., of Newport, of George, and Mary N. Robinson, of
              George C., by Rev. Henry C. Coombes, Oct. 15, 1849.
1-85 PECKHAM Benjamin, Jr., and Mary Hazard; by Rouse Helme, Assistant,
              March 2, 1739.
1-83 "   Mary, of Newport, and Hezekiah Babcock, of South Kingstown, at
              Newport, Jan. 3, 1739-40.
1- — "   Sarah, of Benjamin, and John Robinson, of William, April 9, 1761.

1-157 PECKHAM Josephus, of Benjamin, and Mary Babcock, of Hezekiah; by Sylvester Robinson, Justice, May 25, 1774.

1-63 " Mary, of Benjamin, and Joshua Perry, of Freeman, Oct. 17, 1780.

1-62 " Peleg, Jr., and Desire Watson, of John, Jr.; by G. Peckham, Justice, Aug. 25, 1785.

1-— " Phebe, and Benjamin Segar, April 2, 1795.

2-32 " Benjamin T., and Mrs. Mary Waud; by Rev. Benjamin Waite, Dec. 5, 1799.

2 32 " William, Jr., and Susannah Stanton, of Joseph; by Thomas Hoxsie, Senator, Feb. 13, 1803.

2-38 " Mary, of Benjamin, and Samuel Rodman, July 15, 1821.

2-17, 42 " Mercy D., of East Greenwich, dau. of Perry and Benjamin Hadwin, of Barney, March 29, 1838.

2-46 " Sarah, and Samuel Tucker, Sept. 16, 1840.

2-33 " Robert C., and Hannah E. Babcock; by Rev. Wilson Cogswell, Nov. 14, 1842.

2-55 " Waity, of Reuben S., and Albert S. Barber, of James, July 21, 1845.

2-34 " Nathaniel, of Middletown, and Jane P. Tucker, of South Kingstown; by Rev. C. T. Chapman, Jan. 16, 1849.

2-34 " Edwin A., of Judge William, and Mary W. Dye, of Asa and Mary; by Rev. H. C. Coombes, May 13, 1849.

2-34 " Hazard, of Reuben, and Drusilla Holburton, of George, both of Richmond; by Rev. E. J. Locke, Nov. 11, 1849.

2-56 " Eliza, of Richmond, and Albert S. Barber, of James, of South Kingstown, April 21, 1850.

1-85 PERKINS Elizabeth, and John Mumford, —— —, 1735.

1-106 " Nathaniel, and Elizabeth Crandall; by Rev. Daniel Everett, March 1, 1739.

2-144 " Mrs. Mary, and Elisha R. Potter, Nov. 7, 1790.

2-4 " Eliza, of James, of South Kingstown, and John Collins, of Amos, of North Stonington, Conn., Oct. 25, 1809.

2-1 " Mary, of South Kingstown, and Edwin Anthony, of Richmond, R. I., July —, 1843.

2-33 PERRIGO Caleb S., of Wrentham, Mass., and Mary H. Greenman, of South Kingstown; by Rev. Silas Learnard, May 26, 1841.

1-70 PERRY Alice, and John Dennison, July 21, 1725.

1-70 " Benjamin, and Susannah Barber; by Rouse Helme, Assistant, June 11, 1727.

1-72, 74 " Benjamin, Jr., and Elizabeth Hazard; by Rouse Helme, Assistant, July 10, 1729.

1-79 " Mary, and John Potter, Oct. 20, 1736.

1-63 " Jonathan, of James, and Mary Potter, of William; by Emmanuel Case, Justice, May 13, 1777.

1-63 " Joshua, of Freeman, and Mary Peckham, of Benjamin; by Edward Perry, Justice, Oct. 17, 1780.

1-63 " Elizabeth, of Freeman, and Stephen Champlain, of Dinah, Dec. 20, 1782.

1-— " William, and Elizabeth Segar, March 25, 1792.

2-16 " Alice, of Jonathan, and James Helme, of James, Oct. 7, 1802.

2-4 " Amie Tripp, of Joseph, of Newport, and Thomas Hazard Champlain, of Jeffrey, of So. Kingstown, Oct. 2, 1803.

2-32 " John B., of Samuel, and Susannah Babcock, of Peleg, by James Congdon, Justice, April 11, 1805.

2-4 " Rebecca, and Jeffrey Washington Champlain, Jan. 30, 1806.

2-32 " Abigail, and Abram Potter, March 5, 1809.

2-35 " John Robinson, of John and Hannah, and Sally Gould, of John and Mary, Oct. 3, 1809.

2-33 " John B., of John and Mary, and Emeline S. Sunderland, of North Kingstown, of Warham and Mercy, by Rev. Benj. Hazelton, April 27, 1826.

2-35 " Robinson, of John R. and Sally (Gould), and Phebe Ann Lewis, of Westerly, March 11, 1832.

2-35 " Mary, and Esbon S. Taylor, March 6, 1834.

2-35 " Mercy, and George Allen, Feb. 26, 1836.

2-5	PERRY	Mariah, and Benjamin S. Cory, Dec. 15, 1839.
6-55,35	"	Sarah, and Palmer A. Brown, May 1, 1842.
2-6,35	"	Abbie, and Isaac H. Carpenter, Oct. 30, 1842.
2-33,35	"	John G., and Harriet T. Hazard, by Rev. Wilson Cogswell, March 12, 1843.
2-6	"	Catherine C., of South Kingstown, and Simeon P. Clarke, of Richmond, R. I., Nov. 8, 1843.
2-33	"	George G., of George and Dianna, and Louisa Ann Weeden, of London (colored), by Rev. Thomas Vernon, March 5, 1846.
2-35	"	William Wanton, of John R. and Sally (Gould), and Ellen F. Kenyon, April 3, 1848.
2-13	"	Rachel A., and John G. Grinnell, Oct. 24, 1858.
1-70	PHILLIPS	Mary, and Wm. Sunderland, May 26, 1726-7.
1-75	"	Joseph, and Jerusha Thayer, by Rouse Helme, Assistant, Feb. 2, 1729.
2-43	"	Lucinda, of Mehitable, of Richmond, R. I., and Enoch C. Steadman, of Enoch, of So. Kingstown, Oct. 29, 1843.
2-34	"	Ezekiel B., of Joseph, of Richmond, R. I., and Basha W. Briggs, of William, of So. Kingstown, by Rev. E. J. Locke, Oct. 17, 1847.
1-81	PINDAR	Jacob, of North Kingstown, and Mrs. Mary Smith, of Boston, at South Kingstown, by Rev. Joseph Torrey, April 2, 1738.
2-33	PITMAN	George B., of Richmond, R. I., and Peggy D. Ginnodo, of South Kingstown, by John Hopkins, Justice, Jan. 27, 1814.
2-32	POLLOCK	Samuel H., and Sarah Lunt, of Wm., Nov. 27, 1808.
1-84	POPPLESTONE	William, and Sarah Wilcox, by Isaac Sheldon, Justice, Oct. 5, 1740.
1-86	POPPLE	Amie, and George Reynolds Barber, Aug. 4, 1793.
1-68	POTTER	Ichabod, Jr., and Sarah Robinson, by Rouse Helme, Assistant, Jan. 16, 1723-4.
1-69	"	Mary, and Stephen Tallman, Nov. 11, 1724.
1-69	"	Rebecca, and Joseph Barber, Feb. 4, 1724.
1-70	"	Ichabod, and Deborah Reynolds, by Rouse Helme, Assistant, March 20, 1725-6.
1-70	"	Nathaniel, and Elizabeth Bentley, by Rouse Helme, Assistant, May 30, 1727.
1-70	"	Mary, and Joseph Sherman, June 4, 1727.
1-71,73	"	Benjamin, and Ruth Sherman, by Rouse Helme, Assistant, Feb. 1, 1727-8.
1-71,73	"	Susannah, and Elisha Reynolds, June 30, 1728.
1-72	"	Joseph, and Abigail Larkin, by Rouse Helme, Assistant, Jan. 14, 1730.
1-85	"	Robert, Jr., and Judith Clarke, by Rouse Helme, Assistant, Sept. 5, 1731.
1-85	"	Capt. Ichabod, and Margaret Potter, by Rouse Helme, Assistant, Nov. —, 1735.
1-85	"	Margaret, and Capt. Ichabod Potter, Nov. —, 1735.
1-79	"	John, and Mary Perry, by Friends ceremony, Oct. 20, 1736.
1-86,87	"	Sarah, and George Gardiner, Feb. 10, 1742.
1-94	"	Jonathan, and Mary West, by Samuel Tefft, Justice, Jan. 18, 1748.
1-93	"	Ruth, of South Kingstown, and Jeremiah Hazard, Jr., of North Kingstown, April 24, 1748.
1-108	"	William, youngest son of Col. Potter, and Penelope Hazard, eldest dau. of Col. Thomas, by Rev. Dr. McSparran, Nov. 18, 1750.
1-97	"	John, of Ichabod, and Mary Hazard, of Stephen, by Jeffrey Watson, Assistant, Aug. 30, 1752.
1-100	"	Martha, and Daniel Weeden, Jan. 7, 1753.
1-108	"	Thomas, of Ichabod, and Mrs. Elizabeth Reynolds, by Rev. Joseph Torrey, Oct. 29, 1758.
1-106	"	Christopher, of Richmond, R. I., and Anne Frazer, by Jeremiah Crandall, Justice, Nov. 23, 1760.
1-109	"	Lydia, of Capt. Benjamin, and William Potter Taylor, Dec. 11, 1760.
2-32	"	William, of Robert, and Mary Rathbun, by Rev. Joseph Torrey, Jan. 24, 1765.

1-63 POTTER Mary, of South Kingstown, and Jonathan Perry, of James, March 31, 1777.
2-144 " Elisha R., and Mrs. Mary Perkins, by Rev. Benjamin Waite, Nov. 7, 1790.
1- — " Nicholas Bryant, and Mary Hannah Carpenter, by Samuel Helme, Justice, Jan. 28, 1794.
1- — " Jeremiah N., and Sally Hazard, by Samuel Helme, Justice, March 23, 1794.
1- — " Abraham, and Amie Littlefield, by Samuel Helme, Justice, Aug. 11, 1794.
2-52 " Maria, and Thomas Robinson Wells, March 15, 1803.
2-32 " Abram, and Abigail Perry, by Matthew Robinson, Justice, March 5, 1809.
2-144 " Elisha R., and Mary Mawney, by Rev. William Northup, July 9, 1810.
2-3 " Mary, of Exeter, and Silas Brown, of South Kingstown, March 9, 1823.
2-33 " William, of Alexander, and Sarah Brown (colored), by Matthew Waite, Justice, Oct. 23, 1839.
2-249 " Joseph B., of Richmond, R. I., and Mary E. Mumford, of South Kingstown, by Rev. John H. Baker, Oct. 18, 1841.
2-43 " Susan, of South Kingstown, and David Sherman, Jr., of Coventry, R. I., March 21, 1842.
2-47 " Harriet, and Benjamin H. Taylor, Oct. 30, 1842.
2-28 " Mary, of Aaron and Abbie, and Edward T. Niles, of Simon and Nancy, Dec. 19, 1844.
2-34 " Rouse, and Dorcas G. Watson; by Rev. Wilson Coggswell, May 25, 1846.
2-34 " Samuel, of Nicholas E., and Alice Smith, of James W.; by Rev. Ezekiel J. Locke, May 14, 1848.
2-36 " George, and Elizabeth Sherman, Aug. 16, 1838.
1-81 POWELL Mrs. Esther, of North Kingstown, and James Helme, of South Kingstown, Oct. 19, 1738.
1-95 POWERS William, of Warwick, and Sarah Bill, now residing in South Kingstown; by Benjamin Potter, Justice, April 12, 1750.
1-85 PRICE Martha, and Charles Campbell, Sept. 17, 1731.
1-108 PROSSER Arnold, and Esther Eldred, by Jeremiah Crandall, Justice, (both dates given), July 14, 1764—July 15, 1765.

Q R

2-32 RATHBUN Mary, and William Potter, Jan. 24, 1765.
2-38 " John A., of North Kingstown, and Mary A. Hazard, of Thomas, of South Kingstown, by Rev. Henry C. Coombes, Nov. 11, 1849.
1-78 RAYMOND ——, of New London, and Oliver Hazard, of South Kingstown, Dec. 9, 1736.
1-75 RAY ANN (widow), and William Mumford, April 3, 1729.
1-70 REYNOLDS Deborah, and Ichabod Potter, March 20, 1725-6.
1-71,73 " Elisha, and Susannah Potter, by Rouse Helme, Assistant, Jan. 30, 1728.
1-75 " William, and Elizabeth Lewis, residing in Westerly, R. I., at South Kingstown, by Christopher Allen, Justice, July 17, 1732.
1-91 " Henry, and Mary Anthony, by Thomas Brown, Justice, Nov. 9, 1746.
1-93 " Jemima, and John Babcock, March 17, 1747.
1-94 " John, and Abigail Sherman, by Samuel Tefft, Justice, Oct. 24, 1748.
1-106 " Elizabeth, of Exeter, and James Sherman, of South Kingstown, Nov. 19, 1761.
1-108 " Mrs. Elizabeth, and Thomas Potter, of Ichabod, Oct. 29, 1738.
1-157 " Elizabeth, of South Kingstown, and Benjamin Dake, of North Kingstown, March 23, 1779.
1-62 " Amie, of James, of West Greenwich, and Samuel Hoxsie, of Stephen, of South Kingstown, June 8, 1783.

2-17 REYNOLDS Sally, of South Kingstown, and Jonathan Healy, of Charlestown, Nov. 24, 1839.

2-62 " Mary Ann, and John C. Dawley, both of Exeter, Aug. 28, 1842.

1-76 READ Thomas, and Elizabeth Cox, by Rouse Helme, Assistant, Nov. 3, 1733.

1-104 " Edward, and Martha Davis, by Samuel Casey, Justice, Oct. 15, 1758.

2-52 RHODES Elizabeth, of Stonington, Conn., and Thomas R. Wells, of South Kingstown, Sept. 28, 1844.

1-75 RICE William, and Phebe Tripp, by Rouse Helme, Assistant, Dec. 10, 1730.

2-38 ROBBINS John M., of Brooklyn, Conn., and Lydia Ann Harvey, of South Kingstown, by Rev. James Hammond, June 3, 1849.

1-85 ROBERTS Frances, and Stephen Knowles, Aug. 27, 1732.

1-89 " Sarah, and Stephen Northrup, Oct. 17, 1744.

1-90 " Mary, and Stephen Rose, June 10, 1745.

1-68 ROBINSON Mary, and Stephen Hazard, by Rouse Helme, Assistant, Jan. 9, 1723-4.

1-68 " Sarah, and Ichabod Potter, Jr., Jan. 16, 1723-4.

1-71 " William, and Abigail Hazard, by Christopher Allen, Justice, March 2, 1726-7.

1-76 " Ruth, and Joseph Underwood, April 27, 1732.

1-89 " Martha, of William, of South Kingstown, and Latham Clarke, of Samuel, of Jamestown, April 18, 1745.

1- — " John, of William, of South Kingstown, and Sarah Peckham, of Benjamin, April 9, 1761.

1-62 " Mary, of Sylvester, and Jonathan Hazard, of Stephen, May 12, 1755.

1-84 ROBINSON Abigail, of Sylvester, and Thomas H. Hazard, Feb. 23, 1790.

1- — " Capt. Robert, of Christopher and Sarah Congdon, of Samuel, by Samuel Helme, Justice, March 15, 1795.

1- — " Elizabeth, of Christopher, of South Kingstown, and Mumford Hazard, of Newport, Feb. 18, 1796.

2-38 " William H., and Eliza Hazard, by Rev. Silas Learnard, Dec. 13, 1840.

2-34 " Mary N., of South Kingstown, daughter of George C. and George G. Pearce, of George, of Newport, Oct. 15, 1849.

1-89 RODMAN Samuel, and Penelope Holway, by Samuel Tefft, March 10, 1744.

1- — " Penelope, and Nathaniel Tripp, Dec. 15, 1791.

2-38 " Samuel, and Mary Peckham, of Benjamin, by Matthew Robinson, Justice, July 15, 1821.

2-62 " Sarah Ann, and George Dixon, May 3, 1840.

2-38 " Peleg C., of Christopher, and Nancy, of South Kingstown, and Eliza Brown, of Robert and Hannah, of Warwick, R. I., by Rev. Thomas Vernon, March 22, 1846.

2-39 " Isaac P., and Sally Arnold, by Rev. C. T. Brooks, June 15, 1847.

2-39 " Hannah N., and Benjamin F. Hall, Aug. 19, 1854.

1-108 ROGERS Amie, o Samuel and John Rogers, Jr., Jan. 7, 1764.

1-108 " John, Jr., and Amie Rogers, of Samuel, by Jeremiah Crandall, Justice, Jan. 7, 1764.

1-78 ROSE John, of Preston, Conn., and Elizabeth Eldred, of South Kingstown, by Ephraim Gardiner, Justice, June 12, 1734.

1-90 " Stephen, and Mary Roberts; m. by Samuel Tefft, Justice, June 10, 1745.

1-108 " Anna, of South Kingstown, and John Goodbody, of North Kingstown, April 4, 1765.

2-53 " Elizabeth S., of George and James E. B. Walker, Oct. 25, 1849.

2-38 " Samuel, of South Kingstown, and Phebe A. Albro, of Exeter, by Rev. John Slocum, Aug. 4, 1850.

2-38 " George W., and Susan T. Hazard, by Rev. John Slocum, Nov. 20, 1850.

2-39 " George P., of South Kingstown, and Hannah P. Card, of Jamestown, by Rev. James Hammond, Dec. 5, 1852.

1-88 ROWLER Elizabeth, and Samuel Nutter, Oct. 28, 1744.

S

1-90   SABIN Abigail, and Samuel Jackways, Aug. 26, 1746.

1-107 SAND Edward, of Newport, and Lucy Clarke, of South Kingstown, by Silas
       Niles, Justice, Sept. 15, 1763.

2-41   SANFORD Henry, and Joseph, of North Kingstown, now of Norwich, Conn.,
       and Sarah C. Gould, of Jonathan P., of South Kingstown, by
       Rev. Ezekiel J. Locke, Sept. 16, 1849.

1-85   SARAH, and Joshua (Indians), Sept. 28, 1732.

1-84   SAUNDERS Susannah, and Richard Beary, Jan. 14, 1726.

2-44   " Capt. Elias, of John A., and Sarah E. Brown, by Rev. Henry C.
       Coombes, March 3, 1850.

1-85   SCOTAWAY Hannah, and John Swain, Nov. 6, 1731.

1-83   SEAGER Experience, and Ichabod S. Sheffield, April 17, 1740.

1-100 " Abigail, and William Knowles, April 29, 1753.

2-23   " Abigail, and William Knowles, Feb. 19, 1755.

1-102 " Susannah, and John Lillibridge, July 6, 1753.

1-102 " Samuel, of John, and Hannah Hull, of Charles, by Thomas Hazard,
       Assistant, Nov. 27, 1755.

1-108 " Elizabeth, of South Kingstown, and Ichabod Sheffield, of Charles-
       town, Nov. 4, 1764.

1-107 " Thomas, and Rebecca Browning, of William, by F. Perry, Justice,
       Feb. 17, 1785.

2-42   " John, of South Kingstown, and Abigail Brayton, of Portsmouth,
       by Benjamin Foster, Justice, Nov. 9, 1786.

1- —   " Elizabeth, and William Perry, March 25, 1792.

1- —   " Benjamin, and Phebe Peckham, by Samuel Helme, Justice, April
       2, 1795.

2-55   SEAGER Mary P., of South Kingstown, and Joseph Brightman, of Hopkin-
       ton, Oct. 19, 1840.

2-44   " William F., and Mary Ann Browning, by Rev. C. T. Chapman, Aug.
       20, 1848.

1-68   SEGOUCHE Elizabeth, of Little Compton, and Christopher Allen, of R. I.,
       — —, 1687.

1-75   SHAW Richard, and Alice Wilson, by Rouse Helme, Assistant, Aug. 7, 1729.

2-44   SHED George E., and Eliza Ann Tucker, by Rev. C. T. Chapman, Dec. 25,
       1848.

1-70   SHEFFIELD Isaac, and Sarah Case, by Rouse Helme, Assistant, April 20,
       1727.

1-85   " Nathan, and Dorcas Helme, by Rouse Helme, Assistant, April 18,
       1734.

1-85   " Mary, and Caleb Clarke, Dec. 1, 1737.

1-85   " Mary, and Daniel Everett, July 12, 1739.

1-83   " Ichabod, and Experience Seager, by John Potter, Justice, April 17,
       1740.

1-103 " Caleb, and Sarah Holley; m. by Thomas Hazard, Assistant,
       Dec. 5, 1746.

1-100 " Ruth, and Benjamin Greenman, Jan. 23, 1755.

1-108 " Ichabod, of Charlestown (weaver), and Elizabeth Seager, of South
       Kingstown (spinster), by Jeremiah Crandall, Justice, Nov. 4,
       1764.

1- —   " Martha, of Nathan, of South Kingstown, and Samuel Smith, of
       Stonington, Conn., Nov. 8, 1795.

1-68   SHELDON John, and Horred Watson, April 11, 1706.

1-70   " John, Jr., and Sarah Sherman, by Rouse Helme, Assistant, Feb. 2,
       1727-8.

1-70   " Dorcas, and Jonathan Sherman, Jr., Feb. 7, 1726-7.

1-82   " Samuel, and Susannah Sherman, by Isaac Sheldon, Justice,
       Sept. 23, 1739.

1-98   " Isaac, Jr., of South Kingstown, and Sarah James, of Charlestown,
       at C., by Joseph Church, Justice, Jan. 23, 1741.

1-109 " John, of South Kingstown, and Elizabeth Webb, of Charlestown,
       by Nathaniel Lewis, Justice, May 29, 1743.

1-99   SHELDON Isaac, of Isaac, and Abigail Earl, of John, by Rev. Daniel Everett,
            who died before the marriage was asserted; asserted by Jeffrey
            Watson, Assistant, Dec. 20, 1746.
1-98   "   Abigail, and Jeremiah Carpenter, June 24, 1752.
1-99   "   Sarah, of Isaac, and James Babcock, of Samuel, Jan. 31, 1754.
1-106   "   James, and Hannah Beard, by Frances Tanner, Justice, Oct. 24,
            1762.
1-108   "   Mehitable, and John Babcock, Feb. 14, 1765.
2-45   "   Alice, of Rouse, and Daniel Steadman, of Daniel, Sept. 8, 1850.
1-71,73 SHERMAN Ruth, and Benjamin Potter, Feb. 1, 1726-7.
1-70   "   Sarah, and John Sheldon, Jr., Feb. 2, 1726-7.
1-70   "   Jonathan, Jr., and Dorcas Sheldon, by Rouse Helme, Assistant,
            Feb. 1, 1727-8.
1-70   "   Josiah, and Mary Potter, by Rouse Helme, Assistant, June 4, 1727.
1-85   "   Mary, and Passaval Allen, Dec. 21, 1732.
1-77   "   Isabel, and Caleb Gardiner, Feb. 20, 1734.
1-85   "   Eber, Jr., and Amie Hazard, by Rouse Helme, Assistant, May 30,
            1734.
1-77   "   Daniel, and Susannah Earl, by Isaac Sheldon, Justice, May 22,
            1735.
1-82   "   Susannah, and Samuel Sheldon, by Isaac Sheldon, Justice, Sept.
            23, 1739.
1-87   "   Mary, and Benjamin Baker, Sept. 16, 1742.
1-89   "   Alice, and Phillip Sherman, Feb. 14, 1744.
1-89   "   Phillip, of Portsmouth, and Alice Sherman, of South Kingstown,
            by Samuel Tefft, Justice, Feb. 14, 1744.
1-90   "   Abiel, and Susannah Boss, by Samuel Tefft, Justice, Jan. 30, 1745.
1-94   "   James, of South Kingstown, and Penelope Franklin, of Jamestown,
            at Jamestown, by Joseph Clarke, Justice, Sept. 8, 1748.
1-95   "   Experience, and Joseph Taylor, April 6, 1749.
1-97   "   Sarah, and Robert Brown, Esq., May 16, 1753.
1-100   "   James, of South Kingstown, and Hannah Fry, of East Greenwich,
            daughter of Thomas, by Giles Pierce, Justice, Feb. 6, 1755.
1-94   "   Abigail, and John Reynolds, Oct. 24, 1748.
1-102   "   Samuel, of Newport, and Phebe Smith, of South Kingstown, by
            Rev. David Sprague, Sept. 25, 1756.
1-105   "   Lydia, of Benjamin, and Isaac Tanner, Dec. 8, 1759.
1-106   "   James, of South Kingstown, and Elizabeth Reynolds, of Exeter,
            by John Lillibridge, Justice, Nov. 19, 1761.
1-108   "   Josiah, and Dorcas Bentley, by Jeremiah Crandall, Justice, Dec.
            15, 1763.
1-109   "   Jonathan, Jr., of South Kingstown, and Sarah Harrington, of
            North Kingstown, by Rev. Samuel Albro, May 16, 1768.
1-99   "   Abiel, of South Kingstown, and Mrs. Ann Hoxsie, of Charles-
            town, at C., by Rev. Joseph Parks, May 10, 1772.
2-42   "   David, and Hannah Sherman, by James Parker, Justice, Nov. 26,
            1775.
2-42   "   Hannah, and David Sherman, Nov. 26, 1775.
1-63   "   Robert, of South Kingstown, and Honor Brown, of North Kings-
            town, by Rev. James Wightman, Feb. 26, 1777.
1- —   "   Susannah, of Daniel, and John Oatley, of Samuel, Sept. —, 1796.
1- —   "   Sarah, and Benjamin Stanton, Dec. 4, 1796.
2-3   "   Anna, of Godfrey, and Jesse Barber, of James, Nov. 4, 1813.
2-55   "   Abbie, and Benjamin B. Brown, Aug. 17, 1831.
2-42   "   George J., of Exeter, and Rebecca C. Holloway, of Charlestown, by
            Rev. John H. Baker, July 4, 1841.
2-43   "   David, Jr., of Coventry, R. I., and Susan Potter, of South Kings-
            town, by Rev. John H. Baker, March 21, 1842.
2-43   "   Clarke B., of South Kingstown, son of Robert and Abbie Mumford,
            of Oliver, of Richmond, by Rev. E. J. Locke, Nov. 5, 1843.
2-44, 46 "   Daniel, of Joseph, and Mary Ann Knowles, of Hazard; m. by
            Rev. E. J. Locke, June 19, 1848.
2-29   "   Sarah Jane, of Exeter, and Azel Noyes, of South Kingstown,
            March 29, 1848.
2-36   "   Elizabeth, and George Potter, Aug. 16, 1868.

1- — SIAS Mary, of South Kingstown, and Mingull Crosswell, of Sterling, Conn., Nov. 23, 1794.

2-19 SIMS Silence E., and Courtland B. Holland, April 2, 1849.

1-17 SLACK Abigail, of Samuel, and Charles Hull, both of Westerly, Dec. 30, 1736.

2-43 SLOCUM John, Jr., of Richmond, R. I., and Sarah M. Steadman, of Henry of South Kingstown, by Rev. E. J. Locke, Sept. 24, 1843.

2-43 " William, of John of Richmond, R. I., and Rebecca Babcock, of Joseph of South Kingstown, by Rev. E. J. Locke, March 30, 1845.

2-43 " Alfred, of John, and Diana Kingsley, of William, both of Richmond, by Rev. E. J. Locke, November 20, 1846.

1-68 SMITH Margaret, and Emmanuel Clarke, at North Kingstown, Jan. 4, 1725.

1-77 " Bathsheba and Jeffrey Watson, Nov. 30, 1732.

1-85 " Mary, and Benjamin Thomas, Sept. 1, 1737.

1-81 " Sarah, and John Bent, Nov. 13, 1737.

1-81 " Mrs. Mary, of Boston, and Jacob Pindar, of North Kingstown, April 2, 1738.

1-102 " Phebe, of South Kingstown, and Samuel Sherman, of Newport, Sept. 25, 1756.

1- — " Samuel, of Stonington, Conn., and Martha Sheffield, of Nathan of South Kingstown; by Samuel Helme, Justice, Nov. 8, 1795.

2-8 " Mary Ann, and Edgar R. Eaton, Dec. 4, 1842.

2-54 " Lucy Ann, and Edmund B. Albro, Feb. 24, 1848.

2-34 " Alice, of James W., and Samuel Potter, of Nicholas E., May 14, 1848.

2-44 " Edward H., and Alice Harvey; by Rev. James Hammond, Oct. 7, 1849.

2-45 " Esek B., aged 18, son of James W., and Lucy A. Webster, aged 16, dau. of Nathan, by Rev. Ezekiel J. Locke, Nov. 9, 1851.

2-54 " John A., and Ann A. Whaley, by Rev. A. Durfee, Oct. 29, 1854.

2-45 SPEAR Henry, and Levina Carpenter, by Rev. E. J. Locke, July 28, 1850.

2-43 SPRAGUE William, and Adeline Whitford, by Rev Silas Learned, Aug. 28, 1842.

1-95 STANTON Isabel, and Nathan Tefft, Sept. 16, 1742.

1-103 " Robert, of Richmond, R. I., and Elizabeth Whitehorne, of South Kingstown, by Jeremiah Crandall, Justice, Jan. 16, 1757.

1-108 " Susannah, of Richmond, R. I., and Peter Boss, Dec. 14, 1763.

1- — " Benjamin, and Sarah Sherman, Dec. 4, 1796.

2-32 " Susannah, of Joseph, and William Peckham, Jr., Feb. 13, 1803.

2-42,165 ' Benjamin, and Sarah Barnes, by Rev. John H. Baker, Nov. 18, 1839.

2-17 " Mary, and Stephen Hoxsie, Nov. 1, 1838.

2-28 " Ann H., and John Nichols, Jr., by Rev. Cyrus Miner, Jan. 19, 1842.

1-91 STEADMAN, John, of South Kingstown, and Bethany Gray, of Shrewsbury, Monmouth Co., N. J., by Thomas Brown, Justice, Jan. 29, 1746.

1-107 " James, and Isabel Babcock, by Francis Tanner, Justice, Nov. 11, 1762.

1-156 " Mary, and Martin Murphy, Jan. 7, 1778.

1- — " Polly, and Jonathan Parr, Oct. 29, 1795.

2-42 " William, of Oliver, and Elizabeth Tucker, of Joshua, by Joseph P. Babcock, Justice, Jan. 23, 1842.

2-6 " Hannah, and Jesse Cottrell, June 21, 1843.

2-24 " Catherine, of South Kingstown, and William J. S. Locke, of Richmond, R. I., Sept. 24, 1843.

2-43 " Sarah M., and John Slocum, Jr., of Richmond, R. I., Sept 24, 1843.

2-43 " Enoch C., of Enoch, of South Kingstown, and Lucinda Phillips, of Mehitable, of Richmond, R. I., by Rev. E. J. Locke, Oct. 29, 1843.

2-44 " William N., of Henry, and Abbie Austin, of George, by Rev. E. J. Locke, July 2, 1848.

2-60 STEADMAN Susan T., of Asa, and Daniel Connor, July 28, 1850.
2-45 "   William, of Oliver, and Jane Clarke, of Christopher, by Rev. H. C. Coombes, Aug. 5, 1850.
2-45 "   Daniel, of Daniel, and Alice Sheldon, of Rouse, by Rev. H. C. Coombes, Sept. 8, 1850.
1-71,73 STEPHENS Peter, and Mary Cottrell, by Rouse Helme, Assistant, Sept. 1, 1728.
2-61 STREETER Clarrissa, and Augustus Cory, Nov. 25, 1875.
1-70 SUNDERLAND William, and Mary Phillips, by Rouse Helme, Assistant, May 26, 1726-7.
1-108 "   Lois, and William Carlile, Jan. 27, 1760.
2-33 "   Emeline S., of Warham and Mercy, and John B. Perry, of John and Mary, April 27, 1826.
1-85 SWAIN John, and Hannah Scotaway, by Rouse Holme, Assistant, Nov. 6, 1731.
1-71,73 SWEET Thomas, and Tabitha Bentley, by Rouse Helme, Assistant, April 11, 1728.
1-91 "   Lydia, and Ebenezer Tefft, Nov. 6, 1746.
1-84 "   Harriet, of Job and Thomas Austin, Oct. 27, 1791.
1- — "   Gideon, and Silence Williams, by Samuel Helme, Justice, Nov. 30, 1794.
2-28 "   Mrs. Hannah B., and John V. Northrup, Oct. 27, 1844.
1-77 "   Rebecca, of S. K., and Benjamin Brand, of Westerly, March 16,

T

1-88 TABOR Elizabeth, of William, and Edward Gardiner, of Henry, May 23, 1745.
1-108 "   Reward, and Elizabeth Bentley, by Jeremiah Crandall, Justice, Nov. 6, 1763.
1-69 TALLMAN Stephen, and Mary Potter, by Rouse Helme, Assistant, Nov. 11, 1724.
1-72,73 TANNER Francis, and Mary Tosk, by Rouse Helme, Assistant, Feb. 26, 1728.
1-77 "   Rebecca, and Benjamin Brand, March 16, 1734.
1-76 "   Nathan, and Mary Cottrell, by Isaac Sheldon, Justice, May 28, 1734.
1-105 "   Isaac, and Lydia Sherman, of Benjamin, by Wm. Waite, Justice, Dec. 8, 1759.
1-95 TAYLOR Joseph, and Experience Sherman, by Jeffrey Watson, Assistant, April 6, 1749.
2-35 "   Esbon S., of William, of North Kingstown, and Mary Perry, of John R., and Sally (Gould), March 6, 1834.
1-109 "   Wm. Potter, and Lydia Potter, of Capt. Benjamin, by Rev. James Rogers, Dec. 11, 1760.
2-18 "   Susan H., and Abram Hazard, Sept. 18, 1842.
2-47 "   Benjamin H., and Harriet Potter, Oct. 30, 1842.
1-75 TEFFT Joanna, and John Webb, April 28, 1721.
1-70 "   Samuel, of John, and Mary Barber, by Rouse Helme, Assistant, Oct. 1, 1727.
1-75 "   Mary, and Benjamin Barber, Jan. 11, 1729.
1-75 "   Joseph, and Esther Brownell, by Rouse Helme, Assistant, Feb. 22, 1729.
1-84 "   Stephen, and Amie Gardiner, by Isaac Sheldon, Justice, Dec. 10, 1741.
1-95 "   Nathan, and Isabel Stanton, by Rev. Daniel Everett, Sept. 16, 1742.
1-89 "   Sarah, and Hezekiah Brown, of Providence, March 1, 1744.
1-91 "   Ebenezer, and Lydia Sweet, by Isaac Sheldon, Justice, Nov. 6, 1746.
1-103 "   Mercy, and Thomas Miller, of Dighton, Mass., Dec. 16, 1756.
1-103 "   John, and Virtue Wightman, by Jeremiah Crandall, Justice, Dec. 25, 1757.
1-105 "   Mary, and Jeremiah Albro, Oct. 15, 1758.

1-156 TEFFT Mary, and Henry Joslin, May 21, 1769.
1-109   "   Abigail, of Ebenezer and James Gardiner, June 27, 1771.
1-109   "   James, Jr., and Mary Westcott, by F. Perry, Justice, Feb. 6, 1772.
1-62   "   Mary, of George, and William Cottrell, Dec. 7, 1786.
1-62   "   Martha, and Levi Totten, Julg 8, 1789.
1-—   "   Daniel, and Sarah Northrup, by Samuel Helme, Justice, Feb. 9, 1795.
2-62   "   Susan C., of South Kingstown, and William A. Davis, of Fall River, Mass., Dec. 9, 1840.
2-46   "   Lyndon G., of Elijah and Frances, and Ann Champlain, of Robert H. and Esther, by Rev. Thomas Vernon, Aug. 18, 1845.
2-46   "   Amie and Benjamin G. Tefft, Nov. 28, 1844.
2-46   "   Benjamin G., of Augustus and Abbie, and Amie Tefft, of Elijah and Frances, by Rev. Thomas Vernon, Nov. 28, 1844.
2-29   "   Mary Ann, and James A. Nichols, March 11, 1849.
2-46   "   Stephen Hazard, of Stephen and Mary B., of North Kingstown, and Phebe Weeden Watson, of Freeman P., and Phebe, of South Kingstown, at Lonsdale, R. I., by Rev. E. F. Watson, Jan. 23, 1849.
2-47   "   Stephen A., of Benjamin, of Richmond, R. I., and Eunice A. Lewis, of Arnold, of Exeter, by Rev. George K. Clarke, Jan. 20, 1850.
1-— TENNANT Sarah, and Hawkins Greene, Feb. 12, 1799.
1-75 THAYER Jerusha, and Joseph Phillips, Feb. 2, 1729.
1-85 THOMAS Benjamin, and Mary Smith, by Rouse Helme, Assistant, Sept. 1, 1737.
2-29   "   Mary Ann, of George, and Gideon S. Northrup, of James R., Oct. 6, 1850.
2-52 THOMPSON Phebe M., of Richmmond, R. I., and Joseph C. Woodmansee, of Richmond, July 18, 1841.
2-21 THURSTON Mary Ann M., and Nathan Jackways, July 25, 1868.
1-73 TIBBETTS George, Jr., of North Kingstown, and Dorcas Gardiner, of South Kingstown, by Christopher Allen, Justice, March 11, 1730-1.
2-46 TIZZARD William, and Abbie A. Woodmansee, both of Exeter, by Rev. E. J. Locke, Sept. 29, 1847.
1-62 TOTTEN Levi, and Martha Tefft, of George, by Nicholas Gardiner, Justice, July 8, 1789.
1-72,73 TOSH Mary, and Francis Tanner, Feb. 26, 1728.
1-— TOURJEE William, Jr., and Martha Gould, by Samuel Helme, Justice, Nov. 16, 1797.
1-—   "   John, and Hannah Gould, of John, by Samuel Helme, Justice, Aug. 16, 1798.
2-9   "   Patience A., and Benjamin F. Crandall, Aug. 30, 1852.
1-75 TRIPP Phebe, and William Rice, Dec. 10, 1730.
1-—   "   Nathaniel, and Penelope Rodman, by Samuel Helme, Justice, Dec. 15, 1791.
1-68 TUCKER Elizabeth, and Isaac Nash, Jr., May 13, 1723.
2-46   "   Samuel, and Sarah Peckham, by Rev. Silas Learnard, Sept. 16, 1840.
2-46   "   Thurston, and Amie Champlain, by Rev. Silas Learnard, Jan. 4, 1841.
2-5   "   Adeline B., and William Champlain, April 4, 1841.
2-1   "   Clarissa, and Charles Austin, Nov. 29, 1841.
2-42   "   Elizabeth, of Joshua, and William Steadman, of Oliver, Jan. 23, 1842.
2-6   "   Mary T., and Henry Clarke, Dec. 2, 1843.
2-46   "   John A., of Joshua, Jr., and Delilla Larkin, of John W., by Rev. E. J. Locke, March 6, 1845.
2-64   "   Susan P., of Simeon, and Robert E. Knowles, of Jeremiah N., Sept. 25, 1845.
2-46   "   Eunice C., and Samuel P. Tucker, Nov. 7, 1848.
2-46   "   Samuel P., and Eunice C. Tucker, by Rev. C. T. Chapman, Nov. 7, 1849.

2-44   TUCKER Eliza Ann, and George E. Shed, Dec. 25, 1848.
2-34   "   Jane P., of South Kingstown, and Nathaniel Peckham, of Middle-
            town, Jan. 16, 1849.
2-47   "   Palmer, of Simeon and Sally, and Susan Browning, of Samuel and
            Dorcus, by Rev. H. C. Coombes, Feb. 17, 1850.

U

1-76   UNDERWOOD Joseph and Ruth Robinson, by Christopher Allen, Justice,
            April 27, 1732.
1-109 "   Anne and Robert R. Hazard, Sept. 4, 1791.
2-49   "   Perry G., and Mary E. Brown; m. by Rev. A. Durfee, Dec. 25,
            1854.

V

2-50   VALLETT Gilbert, of John, of Richmond, R. I., and Catherine Wilcox, of
            Othniel, of Exeter, by Rev. E. J. Locke, Jan. 1, 1846.
1-—   VAUGHN Ebenezer, of East Greenwich, and Susan Dewy, of South Kings-
            town, by Samuel Helme, Justice, Feb. 7, 1796.
2-50   "   John G., of James, of West Greenwich, and Susannah S. Barber,
            of James, of South Kingstown, by Rev. E. J. Locke, Dec. 24,
            1849.
1-92   VEAL Rebecca, and Francis Parker, March 22, 1746.
1-104 VERNER Ann, and John Gardiner, (both came from Ireland); m. by Robert
            Hannah, Justice, about 1743.

W

2-53   WALKER James E. B., and Elizabeth S. Rose, of George, by Rev. H. C.
            Coombes, Oct. 25, 1849.
1-68   WATSON Horred, and John Sheldon, April 11, 1706.
1-77   "   Jeffrey, and Bathsheba Smith, by Christopher Allen, Justice, Nov.
            40, 1732.
1-96   "   Dorcas, of John, and Ezekiel Gardiner, of Nicholas, Aug. 29,
            1730.
1-81   "   John, and Sarah Morey, by Isaac Sheldon, Justice, Sept. 28, 1738.
1-96   "   Hannah, of Jeffrey, and Joshua Allen, of Caleb, Sept. 13, 1750.
1-104 "   Jeffrey, Jr., of South Kingstown, and Hannah Gardiner, of North
            Kingstown, by Rev. Samuel Albro, March 24, 1757.
1-63   "   Job, and Sarah Hazard, of Robert, by Rev. Joseph Torrey, Feb. 12,
            1766.
1-108 "   Bathsheba, of Jeffrey, and John Gardiner, of John, April 30,
            1767.
1-62   "   Desire, of John, Jr., and Peleg Peckham, Jr., Aug. 25, 1785.
1-—   "   Capt. John, Jr., and Mary Watson, by Samuel Helme, Justice,
            Dec. 18, 1794.
1-—   "   Mary, and Capt. John Watson, Jr., Dec. 18, 1794.
2-51   "   John, of Jamestown, and Sarah Brown, of South Kingstown, by
            Rev. Theodore Dehon, Jan. 24, 1799.
2-51   "   Isabel, and John Watson, Aug. 4, 1805.
2-51   "   John, and Isabel Watson, at Suffield, Conn., by Rev. Daniel
            Waldo, Aug. 4, 1805.
2-51   "   Freeman P., of South Kingstown, and Phebe Watson, of James-
            town, at Stonington, Conn., by Rev. Nathaniel Miner, Dec. 13,
            1811.
2-51   "   Phebe, and Freeman P. Watson, Dec. 13, 1811.
2-52   "   Elisha F., and Mary Dockray, by Rev. James H. Eames, June 6.
            1843.
2-52   "   Henry, of Cyrus and Experience, and Harriet Weeden, of Lon-
            don and Eliza (colored), by Rev. Thomas Vernon, March 19,
            1846.

2-34   WATSON Dorcas G., and Rouse Potter, May 25, 1846.
2-46   "   Phebe Weeden, and Stephen H. Tefft, Jan. 23, 1849.
2-53   "   William W., of South Kingstown, and Susan C. Woodmansee, of Exeter, by Rev. E. J. Locke. Jan. 30, 1850.
2-32   WAUD Mrs. Mary, and Benjamin T. Peckham, Dec. 5, 1799.
1-75   WEBB John, and Joanna Tefft, by Rouse Helme, Assistant April 28, 1721.
1-109   "   Elizabeth, of Charlestown, and John Sheldon, of South Kingstown, May 29, 1743.
1-79   WEBSTER Hannah, of John, and Ezekiel Barber, Nov. 28, 1736.
2-52   "   Thomas, and Henrietta Gould, by Rev. Eldridge Crandall, March 12, 1846.
2-45   "   Lucy Ann, of Nathan, and Esek B. Smith, of James W., Nov. 9, 1851.
1-100   WEEDEN Daniel, and Martha Potter, by Rev. Joseph Torrey, Jan. 7, 1753.
2-33   "   Louisa Ann, and George G. Perry (colored), March 5, 1846.
2-52   "   Harriet, and Henry Watson (colored), March 19, 1846.
2-10   "   Louisa, and Solomon Fairweather (colored), Oct. 15, 1848.
1-89   WELLS Ebenezer, and Elizabeth Nash, by Christopher Allen, Justice, Oct. 24, 1726.
1-76   "   James, and Mary Barber, by Robert Hannah, Justice, April 22, 1731.
1-85   "   Rebecca, and William Clarke, Sept. 4, 1731.
1-78   "   Ann, and Thomas Frazer, Nov. 26, 1735.
1-81   "   Mary, of South Kingstown, and William Crawford, of Warwick, Sept. 7, 1738.
1-105   "   Peter, of Westerly, and Elizabeth Carpenter, of South Kingstown, by Joseph Crandall, Justice, March 1, 1759.
2-23   "   Susannah, of Hopkinton, and Robert Brown, Jr., of South Kingstown, Feb. 27, 1791.
2-51   "   Palmer, of Westerly, son of Thompson, of Hopkinton, R. I., and Susannah Wells, of Jonathan, of South Kingstown, by Rev. Thomas Kendall, Sept. 20, 1802.
2-51   "   Susannah, and Palmer Wells, Sept. 20, 1802.
2-52   "   Thomas Robinson, born in Hopkinton, Oct. 20, 1874, and Maria Potter, born in Rhinebeck, N. Y., May 24, 1790, by Rev. Thomas Kendall, March 15, 1808.
2-52   "   Thomas R., and Emma Palmer, of Stonington, Conn. (his 2d wife), by Rev. John C. Nichols, Oct. 10, 1833.
2-23   "   Hannah, of John, and Samuel Kettle, of Simon, June 11, 1843.
2-52   "   Thomas R., of South Kingstown, and Elizabeth Rhodes, of Stonington, Conn., by Rev. James D. Moore, Sept. 28, 1844.
2-60   "   Sarah P., of Thomas R., and Rouse R. Clarke, Jan. 16, 1849.
1-82   WESCOTT Caleb, and Hannah Gardiner, by Isaac Sheldon, Justice, May 27, 1739.
1-109   "   Mary, and James Tefft, Jr., Feb. 6, 1772.
1-94   WEST Martha, and Mitihel Clarke, Nov. 12, 1748.
1-103   "   James, of Exeter, and Mary ——, of South Kingstown, by Jeremiah Crandall, Justice, Aug. 26, 1756.
1-84   "   Lydia, of James, of Westerly, and Gardiner Champlain, of William, Aug. 31, 1791.
1-94   "   Mary, and Jonathan Potter, Jan. 18, 1848.
1-156   WHALEY Samuel, Jr., of South Kingstown, and Hannah Anstin,, of Exeter, by Jeremiah Crandall, Justice, June 11, 1769.
2-2   "   Susannah, of South Kingstown, and R. R. Barber of Allenton, Vt., Oct. 19, 1794.
2-12   "   Ann, of South Kingstown, and Isaac Goodchild, of Newport, Aug. 29, 1841.
2-53   "   John P., of Jeremiah W., and Julia F. Clarke, of Joshua, by Rev. Ezekiel J. Locke, May 14, 1848.
2-60   "   Mary H., of Ezekiel, and Joseph P. Champlain, of Samuel, Dec. 29, 1850.
2-54   "   Ann A., and John A. Smith, Oct. 29, 1854.
1-105   WHEELER Mrs. Mercy, of Stonington, Conn., and Christopher Gardiner, of South Kingstown, Jan. 23, 1760.

1-102 WHITHORNE Mary, of South Kingstown, and Henry John Overring, of Newport, Nov. 15, 1755.

1-103 " Elizabeth, of South Kingstown, and Robert Stanton, of Richmond, R. I., Jan. 16, 1757.

1-105 " James, and Eunice Albro, by Jeremiah Crandall, Justice, Oct. 12, 1758.

1-83 WHITE Abigail, and George Cottrell, Feb. 10, 1739.

2-5 WHITFORD Mary, and Joseph Champlain, Dec. 22, 1841.

2-43 " Adeline, and William Sprague, Aug. 28, 1842.

1-103 WHITMAN Virtue, and John Tefft, Dec. 25, 1757.

1-84 WILCOX Sarah, and William Popplestone, Oct. 5, 1740.

2-16,21 " Sarah, and George James, April 24, 1826.

2-52 " Moses, Jr., and Mary C. Gardiner, by Rev. Silas Learnard, Nov. 1, 1840.

2-50 " Catherine, and Gilbert Vallett, Jan. 1, 1846.

1-73 WILLIAMS Aaron, and Ann Case, by Rouse Helme, Assistant, May 23, 1728.

1-77 " Thomas, and Thankful McCoon, by Christopher Allen, Justice, Jan. 6, 1734.

1— " Silence, and Gideon Sweet, Nov. 30, 1794.

1— " Thankful, of South Kingstown, and Lodowick Coon of Hopkinton, Aug. 9, 1795.

1-75 WILSON Alice, and Richard Shaw, Aug. 7, 1729.

1-96 " Samuel, and Hannah Case, by Rev. Joseph Torrey, Dec. 30, 1744.

1-108 " Col. John, and Mrs. Hannah Hazard, of Col. Thomas, by Rev. Joseph Torrey, Nov. 21, 1762.

1-81 WOODBRIDGE Paine, and Mrs. Sarah Gutridge, by Rev. Joseph Torrey, July 5, 1737.

2-52 WOODMANSEE Joseph C., of Richmond, R. I., and Phebe M. Thompson, of Columbia, now of Richmond, R. I., by Rev. John H. Baker, July 18, 1841.

2-55 " Sarah Ann, of Job, of Richmond, R. I., and Ansel Bowen, of Thomas, of Providence, Oct. 14, 1844.

2-46 " Abbie A., and William Tizzard, both of Exeter, R. I., Sept. 29, 1847.

2-53 " Susan C., of Exeter, and William W. Watson, of South Kingstown, Jan. 30, 1850.

1-78 WORDEN Hannah, of South Kingstown, and Jedediah Collins, of Westerly, Aug. 13, 1736.

1-80 " Jeremiah, and Abigail Gardiner, by Henry Gardiner, Justice, Nov. 30, 1738.

2-45 WRIGHT Reuben, and Merebah S. Jacques, Nov. 14, 1841.

X Y Z

1-71 YORK James, and Elizabeth Case, by Rouse Helme, Assistant, Jan. 11, 1727-8.

1-106 YOUNG John, Jr., and Mercy Galen, both of Exeter, by Jeremiah Crandall, Justice, Oct. 11, 1760.

SOUTH KINGSTOWN.

BIRTHS.

A

1-119	ALMY, Mrs. Abigail, servants.		
1-119	"	Bristol, son of negro woman Phillis,	Jan. 4, 1733.
1-119	"	Temera, daughter of negro woman Phillis,	Feb. 2, 1748.
1-131	ALLEN	Christopher, of Samuel and Margaret,	Feb. 8, 1748.
1-131	"	Deliverance,	March 17, 1751.
1-131	"	Mary,	Feb. 3, 1754.
1-126	"	Deborah, of Benjamin and Waitstill,	March 10, 1753.
1-126	"	Waitstill,	Sept. 26, 1754.

B

1-7	BABCOCK	Mary, of Samuel and Bethiah,	Dec. 18, 1721.
1-7	"	Jonathan,	Nov. 26, 1723.
1-10	"	Samuel,	Nov. 5, 1725.
1-10	"	John,	June 27, 1727-8.
1-11	"	Job,	Jan. 20, 1729-30.
1-16	"	Simon,	Jan. 6, 1731-2.
1-113	"	James,	June 14, 1734.
1-113	"	Joseph,	Oct. 4, 1737.
1-6	"	Mary, of Jonathan and Elizabeth,	Sept. 1, 1724.
1-31	"	Caleb, of Hezekiah and Mary,	Dec. 7, 1740.
1-31	"	Peleg,	April 18, 1742.
1-31	"	Caleb, of Hezekiah and Mary,	July 10, 1741.
1-122	"	Stephen, of Simeon and Elizabeth,	July 19, 1751.
1-122	"	Bethiah,	Dec. 1, 1752.
1-128	"	Champlain, of Job (of Samuel) and Susannah,	Oct. 10, 1752.
1-125	"	Elizabeth,	Feb. 27, 1775.
1-125	"	George, of George and Mehitable,	Sept. 22, 1753.
1-125	"	Lucy,	Dec. 15, 1754.
1-125	"	Cyrus,	Dec. 11, 1756.
1-125	"	Mary,	Jan. 17, 1767.
1-125	"	Frederick,	Sept. 10, 1771.
1-128	"	James, of James and Sarah,	Jan. 22, 1755.
1-137	"	Sarah, of Jonathan and Amie,	Oct. 30, 1755.
1-137	"	John,	Aug. 18, 1757.
1-137	"	Elizabeth,	Nov. 28, 1760.
1-137	"	Amie,	July 2, 1763.
1-137	"	Thankful,	Feb. 15, 1766.
1-137	"	Seager,	May 8, 1769.
1-143	"	Gideon, of John and Jemima,	April 28, 1757.
1-143	"	Joseph,	Aug. 19, 1759.
1-143	"	Mary,	Feb. 4, 1762.
1-151	"	Ephraim, of George and Mehitable,	May 19, 1758.
1-151	"	Susannah,	May 2, 1760.
1-151	"	Thomas Wheeler, of George and Mehitable,	Aug. 13, 1773.
2-74	"	Mehitable of Peleg and Lucy,	Sept. 23, 1770.
2-74	"	Esther,	May 24, 1772.
2-74	"	Peleg,	July 14, 1774.

2-74	BABCOCK	George P., of Peleg and Lucy,	Oct. 19, 1776.
2-74	"	Lucy,	Dec. 2, 1778.
2-74	"	Mary,	March 22, 1781.
2-74	"	Joseph P.,	Jan. 17, 1783.
2-74	"	Watty,	Jan. 22, 1787.
2-74	"	Susannah,	Jan. 22, 1787.
2-74	"	Ethan,	Aug. 7, 1789.
2-74	"	Charles,	March 14, 1792.
2-74	"	Abigail,	Oct. 26, 1795.
2-74	"	Frances Hazard, of Peleg and Lucy,	Sept. 5, 1798.
2-74	"	Amie, of Gideon J. and Hannah,	Dec. 27, 1777.
2-74	"	John,	Feb. 1, 1730.
2-74	"	Samuel,	March 22, 1782.
2-74	"	Henry,	Aug. 3, 1784.
2-74	"	Hannah,	July 1, 1786.
2-74	"	Charles,	July 24, 1791.
2-74	"	Lydia,	Aug. 12, 1795.
2-76	"	Joseph Browning, of Wm. Browning and Mary,	March 6, 1810.
2-76	"	Frederic, of Frederic and Nancy,	May 31, 1820.
1-2	BARBER	Moses, of Moses, Jr., and Elizabeth,	Feb. 15, 1705-6.
1-2	"	William,	Sept. 4, 1707.
1-2	"	John,	April 19, 1709.
1-3	"	Elizabeth,	March 18, 1711.
1-3	"	Nicholas,	Dec. 23, 1713.
1-3	"	Bridget,	Jan. 23, 1715-16.
1-3	"	Daniel, of Moses and Susannah,	April 22, 1714.
1-3	"	Anna,	Oct. 8, 1717.
1-4	"	Sarah, of Samuel and Ann,	Nov. 28, 1719.
1-4	"	Mary,	June 12, 1721.
1-4	"	Benjamin,	May 30, 1723.
1-24	"	Martha, of Thomas and Avis,	Oct. 9, 1726.
1-24	"	Dinah,	May 3, 1729.
1-24	"	Thomas,	June 5, 1731.
1-24	"	Mary,	Aug. 18, 1733.
1-24	"	Zebulon,	Jan. 22, 1736.
1-13	"	Lydia, of Benjamin and Mary,	April 16, 1730.
2-77	"	Israel A., 2d son of Willett A. and Lucy Ann (Austin)	Feb. 25, 1843.
2-75	"	Henry, of James, Jr., and Eliza,	March 20, 1810.
1-123	BATES	Ruth, of Hezekiah, and Elizabeth,	July 4, 1746.
1-123	"	Nathan,	Sept. 18, 1750.
2-77	BELCHER	Louis H., of Gideon and Eunice,	Dec. 21, 1839.
1-131	BENTLEY	John, of William and Rachel,	Sept. 24, 1755.
1-131	"	Sarah,	Oct. 11, 1757.
1-145	"	Aggrippa,	Oct. 14, 1759.
1-145	"	Samuel,	July 24, 1761.
1-145	"	Charlotte,	April 21, 1765.
1-9	BERRY	Elizabeth, of Richard and Susannah,	Aug. 18, 1727.
1-141,149	BILLINGTON	Jane, of Joseph and Abigail,	Nov. 13, 1762.
1-141,149	"	Elisha,	June 24, 1768.
1-141,149	"	Abigail,	June 24, 1768.
1-144	BILL	Mary, of Joshua and Sarah,	June 15, 1766.
1-1	BRAYMAN	Jane,	Oct. 28, 1695.
1-1	"	James,	Nov. 17, 1697.
1-1	"	Mary,	May 4, 1700.
1-1	"	Joseph,	March 24, 1703.
1-1	"	Benjamin,	April 3, 1705.
1-1	"	John,	March 15, 1707.
1-1	"	Freelove,	Jan. 11, 1708.
1-27	"	Abigail, wife of Joseph, Jr.,	Nov. 29, 1700.
1-27	"	Sarah, of Joseph and Abigail,	Feb. 19, 1725.
1-27	"	Abigail,	Dec. 23, 1727.
1-27	"	Joseph,	Feb. 23, 1729.
1-27	"	Ann,	Aug. 12, 1731.
1-27	"	Thomas,	April 23, 1734.

1-27	BRAYMAN John, of Joseph and Abigail,	May 2, 1737.
1-27	" Paul,	July 21, 1743.
2-75	BRIGGS Charles W., of Palmer and Amie,	July 21, 1813.
1-10	BROWNING William, of William and Mary,	Nov. 28, 1724.
1-23	" Wilkinson,	July 14, 1731.
1-23	" John,	July 26, 1733.
1-23	" Mary,	June 10, 1735.
1-23	" Dinah,	Sept. 6, 1736.
1-131	" William, of William, Jr., and Elizabeth,	April 21, 1756.
1-132	" Christopher, of William, Jr., and Elizabeth,	Sept. 25, 1758.
1-137	" Rebecca, of William, Jr., and Elizabeth,	March 13, 1762.
1-137	" Mary, of Joseph and Mary,	March 14, 1762.
1-137	" Susannah,	Aug. 26, 1764.
1-132	" Stephen,	Sept. 5, 1767.
2-75	" Thomas K., of Thomas and Anne,	Jan. 20, 1811.
1-22	BROWN Mary, of Samuel, Jr., and Sarah,	April 25, 1735.
1-22	" Anstis, of John and Ruth,	Oct. 15, 1742.
1-135	" John,	Jan. 14, 1744.
1-135	" Susannah,	July 10, 1747.
1-135	" Penelope,	Aug. 10, 1749.
1-135	" Ruth,	July 5, 1751.
1-135	" Lucy,	Feb. 24, 1755.
1-135	" Hannah,	April 6, 1757.
1-135	" Lydia,	July 16, 1759.
1-135	" George,	Sept. 27, 1761.
1-135	" Elisha,	Nov. 24, 1763.
1-118	" George, of Robert and Sarah,	Jan. 10, 1745.
1-118	" William,	Sept. 13, 1747.
1-118	" John,	Dec. 15, 1748.
1-118	" Franklin,	May 25, 1750.
1-118	" Abigail, wife of Joseph,	Nov. 29, 1700.
1-118	" Abiel, of Jeremiah and Hannah,	June 17, 1746.
1-118	" Jeremiah,	Jan. 7, 1747.
1-118	" Joseph,	Sept. 29, 1749.
1-118	" Benjamin,	Nov. 4, 1753.
1-128	" Joanna, of Hezekiah and Sarah (1. of Prov.),	Oct. 13, 1746.
1-128	" Sarah,	Jan. 16, 1748.
1-146	" Christopher, of Zephaniah and Alice,	Feb. 16, 1756.
1-146	" Mary,	Dec. 28, 1757.
1-146	" Alice,	Feb. 17, 1761.
1-146	" Freelove,	March 4, 1763.
1-146	" Darius,	March 3, 1766.
1-146	" Sarah,	Aug. 13, 1768.
2-75	" Robert, of Robert and Elizabeth,	Nov. 19, 1763.
2-75	" Susannah, wife of Robert (Hopkinton),	Dec. 14, 1770.
2-75	" Peter C., of Robert and Susannah,	March 15, 1792.
2-75	" Barker W.,	Dec. 8, 1793.
2-75	" Robert,	Dec. 16, 1795.
2-75	" Phillip,	Sept. 26, 1797.
2-75	" George Wells,	Oct. 21, 1799.
2-75	" Henry,	Jan. 17, 1803.
2-75	" Edmund,	Feb. 10, 1805.
2-75	" David,	Sept. 13, 1807.
1-153	" Benjamin, of Jeremiah, Jr., and Eleanor,	June 6, 1777.
1-153	" Amie,	Feb. 14, 1779.
1-153	" Hannah,	Nov. 19, 1780.
1-153	" Jeremiah,	Nov. 16, 1782.
1-153	" John,	Nov. 19, 1784.
2-76	" Benjamin Brenton, of Silas and Frances,	July 11, 1797
2-76	" Silas,	Jan. 2, 1800.
2-76	" Fannie,	Feb. 18, 1803.
2-76	" Susannah,	June 22, 1807.
2-76	" Elizabeth,	Oct. 4, 1808.
2-76	" Sarah Ann,	April 2, 1810.

2-76	BROWN Benj. Brenton, of Silas and Frances,		June, 28, 1811.
2-77	"	Lucy, of Palmer and Mary,	Aug. 5, 1814.
2-77	"	Robert Champlain,	March 24, 1816.
2-77	"	Peleg,	Oct. 29, 1817.
2-77	"	Laura,	Aug. 5, 1819.
2-77	"	Palmer Armstrong,	April 17, 1821.
2-77	"	Mary,	Feb. 6, 1823.
2-77	"	Sally Stanton, of James H. and Hannah S.,	March 20, 1822.
2-77	"	James Dennis,	March 10, 1824.
2-77	"	Hannah Maria,	March 2, 1826.
2-77	"	Mary Ann,	April 22, 1828.
1-10, 35	BULL Hannah, of Ephraim and Patience,		Sept. 26, 1727.
1-35	"	Ephraim,	Sept. 6, 1729.
1-35	"	Jireh,	Jan. 15, 1731-2.
1-35	"	Joseph,	Feb. 18, 1733-4.
1-35	"	Catherine,	May 9, 1736.
1-35	"	Hannah, 2d,	Aug. 4, 1738.
1-35	"	Thomas,	Nov. 7, 1740.
1-35	"	John,	Feb. 19, 1742-3.
1-35	"	Patience,	Aug. 13, 1745.
1-15	"	John, of Isaac and Rebecca,	May 15, 1732.
1-34	"	Elizabeth, of Timothy and Patience,	Jan. 8, 1744.
1-36	"	Aaron, of Nathan and Abijah,	Aug. 27, 1746.
1-36	"	Mary, of Joshua and Sarah.	Jan. 15, 1766.
2-77	BURDICK George S., of Stephen and Mary,		Dec. 28, 1861.
2-27	"	Mary E.,	Dec. 28, 1861.

C

1-127	CASEY Edmund, of Gideon and Jane.		Aug. 16, 1747.
1-127	"	Gideon,	June 17, 1751.
1-127	"	Sarah,	Jan. 14, 1754.
1-141	"	Mary, of Samuel and Martha,	Feb. 7, 1754.
1-141	"	Samuel,	Feb. 4, 1758.
1-141	"	William,	July 25, 1760.
1-141	"	Willett,	Feb. 14, 1764.
1-29	CASE Mitchell, of Joseph and Elizabeth,		May 29, 1722.
1-7	"	Amie, of Emanuel and Hannah,	Dec. 4, 1725.
1-9	"	Hannah,	Nov. 12, 1727.
1-11	"	Mary,	Aug. 19, 1730.
1-16	"	Joseph,	Jan. 27, 1732.
1-23	"	Penelope,	July 27, 1736.
1-12	"	Emmanuel,	Nov. 8, 1739.
1-12	"	Susannah, of William and Mercy,	July 30, 1733.
1-20	"	William,	June 22, 1735.
1-20	"	Mercy,	Oct. 11, 1737.
1-21	"	Abigail, of Sanford and Mary,	May 24, 1745.
1-21	"	Hannah,	Aug. 29, 1746.
1-21	"	Alexander,	Nov. 19, 1747.
1-136, 137	"	William, of Emmanuel, Jr., and Ann,	Aug. 18, 1762.
1-136, 137	"	Ann Maynard,	June 23, 1766.
1-136, 137	"	John Peck,	Dec. 18, 1774.
1-151	"	Thomas Allen, of Emmanuel and Lydia,	March 30, 1783.
1-1	CARPENTER Elizabeth, of Solomon and Elizabeth.		Jan. 4, 1703.
1-1	"	Solomon,	Feb. 16, 170--.
1-1	"	Daniel,	Dec. 28, 1712.
1-1	"	Sarah,	Aug. 24, 1716.
1-33	"	Samuel, of Solomon and Deborah,	April 4, 1733.
1-33	"	Joseph,	June 22, 1736.
1-33	"	Elizabeth,	May 10, 1741.
1-33	"	Jeremiah, of Daniel and Renewed,	April 13, 1734.
1-33	"	Sarah,	Oct. 10, 1736.
1-33	"	Jonathan,	Aug. 2, 1739.
1-33	"	Elizabeth,	Oct. 2, 1741.

1-113	CARPENTER	Daniel, of Daniel and Renewed,	Sept. 8, 1744.
1-113	"	Renewed,	Aug. 4, 1746.
1-134	"	Margaret,	Sept. 1, 1749.
1-134	"	Mercy,	Dec. 8, 1752.
1-134	"	Hannah,	June 29, 1754.
1-134	"	James,	Feb. 26, 1756.
1-134	"	Mary,	Dec. 11, 1759.
1-134	"	Stephen,	May 31, 1763.
1-129	"	Solomon, of Samuel and Deborah,	April 21, 1754.
1-143	"	Ephraim, of Jeremiah and Abigail,	May 25, 1753.
1-143	"	Dorcas,	June 5, 1755.
1-143	"	Sarah,	Aug. 30, 1757.
1-143	"	Esther,	Jan. 1, 1760.
1-143	"	Susannah,	April 9, 1762.
1-143	"	Jeremiah,	June 23, 1764.
1-33	CHAMPBELL	Charles, of Charles and Martha,	July 7, 1733.
1-33	"	Mary,	May 31, 1735.
1-33	"	George,	June 26, 1739.
1-114	CHAMPLIN	Stephen, of Stephen and Mary,	Sept. 29, 1734.
1-114	"	Hannah,	Jan. 20, 1735.
1-114	"	Sarah,	Aug. 18, 1737.
1-114	"	Mary,	April 14, 1739.
1-114	"	Susannah,	March 26, 1742.
1-114	"	Jeffrey,	March 21, 1744-5.
1-114	"	Robert,	April 12, 1747.
1-128	"	Hazard, of Thomas and Hannah,	Sept. 13, 1754.
1-137	"	Mary, of Stephen and Dinah,	June 26, 1760.
1-137	"	Stephen,	Aug. 3, 176.
1-137	"	Hannah,	June 5, 1765.
1-137	"	Susannah,	Dec. 9, 1772.
1-144	"	Thomas H., of Thomas and Hannah	Oct. 9, 1768.
1-147	"	Mary, of Jeffrey (of Stephen) and Mary,	April 7, 1769.
1-147	"	Stephen Gardiner,	Jan. 31, 1771.
1-147	"	Robert, of Robert and Mary,	Nov. 1, 1769.
1-147	"	Sarah,	June 1, 1771.
1-147	"	John,	April 7, 1773.
2-85	"	Robert H., of Stephen and Mary,	Oct. 18, 1796
2-85	"	Ann,	Feb. 26, 1798.
2-85	"	Mary,	Oct. 7, 1799.
2-85	"	Stephen,	March 12, 1801.
2-85	"	Sarah,	March 4, 1803.
2-85	"	George,	March 11, 1805.
2-85	"	John B.,	Dec. 28, 1807.
2-85	"	Abigail,	Jan 3, 1810.
1-131,136	CHAPPELL,	William, of Caleb and Sarah,	Nov. 25, 1757.
1-131,136	"	Holley,	May 15, 1759.
1-131,136	"	Frederic,	July 1, 1761.
1-131,136	"	William,	July 5, 1764.
1-131,136	"	Susannah,	Sept. 19, 1766.
1-1	CLARKE	Sarah, of Benjamin and Mary,	Feb. 26, 1693.
1-1	"	Benjamin,	April —, 1694.
1-1	"	Ebenezer Lion,	Sept. 2, 1717.
1-2	"	Emmanuel, of Benjamin,	April 4, 1697.
1-7	"	Latham, of William and Hannah,	Nov. 19, 1724.
1-7	"	John,	July 13, 1726.
1-18	"	Benjamin, of Emmanuel and Margaret,	July 12, 1728.
1-113	"	Mary, of Latham (of Samuel of Jamestown) and Mary,	Sept. 2, 1748.
1-131	"	Wm. Case, of John, Jr. and Mercy,	July 21, 1756.
1-152	"	Sarah, of John, Jr., and Mercy,	Sept. 23, 1758.
1-152	"	Hannah Niles, of Samuel and Sarah,	Jan. 17, 1777.
1-152	"	Latham,	March 31, 1778.
1-152	"	Silas Niles,	Feb. 10, 1780.
1-152	"	Samuel,	May 19, 1783.
1-154	"	Mercy, of Wm. Case and Sarah,	May 19, 1783.
1-154	"	Mary Ann,	July 18, 1785.

1-154	CLARKE John, of Wm. Case and Sarah,	Dec. 6, 1787.
1-154	" Nathaniel Helme, of Wm. Case and Sarah,	Dec. 10, 1789.
2-87	CLEARY Hugh George, of Stephen and Ann (Grinnell),	July 4, 1857.
2-87	" Maggie,	April 6, 1861.
2-87	" Ann Stanton,	July 17, 1866.
2-87	" Stephen Henry,	Jan. 28, 1868.
2-87	" Theresa, (b. Moosup, Conn.),	Dec. 29, 1869.
1-16	COGGESHALL Hannah, of Joseph and Amey,	Oct. 20, 1725.
1-27	COLLINS Mary, of Hezekiah and Katherine,	Sept. 6, 1736.
1-27	" Joseph,	April 18, 1738.
2-85	COMSTOCK Sarah, of Charles and Anne,	April 13, 1802.
2-86	" Joshua Perry, of Joseph and Sarah R.,	March 31, 1803.
2-86	" Mary,	July 29, 1804.
2-86	" Esther,	Feb. 12, 1806.
2-86	" Elizabeth,	March 16, 1809.
2-86	" Joseph Erasmus Darwin, of Joseph and Sarah R.,	July 20, 1812.
1-21	CONGDON William, of Joseph and Mary,	June 1, 1724.
1-21	" Barberry,	May 18, 1726.
1-21	" Mary,	July 28, 1730.
1-21	" Samuel,	Feb. 18, 1733.
1-23	" Mary, of William and Mary,	June 5, 1729.
1-23	" Robert,	Jan. 27, 1733.
1-23	" Sarah,	May 9, 1735.
1-22	" Ann, of William (of Benj.) and Ann,	Feb. 28, 1733.
1-22	" Hannah,	March 25, 1735.
1-138	" Joseph, of Samuel and Sarah,	March 1, 1758.
1-138	" Hannah,	July 15, 1759.
1-138	" George,	Dec. 9, 1760.
1-138	" Margaret, of Wm. (of James) and Rebecca,	Oct. 24, 1759.
1-138	" Anne, of William and Rebecca,	March 3, 1762.
1-138	" Thomas Taylor,	March 6, 1764.
1-138	" Sarah,	March 31, 1766.
2-84	" Stephen Champlain, of Sam'l and Susannah.	Dec. 9, 1805.
1-110	COOKE, Alice, of John and Elizabeth,	May 15, 1740.
1-110	" Sarah,	June 14, 1742.
1-110	" George,	Jan. 12, 1744.
2-87	" Daniel,	May 10, 1854.
2-87	" Mary S.,	July 15, 1853.
2-87	" Samuel, of Alfred and Austrers (Broman),	Feb. 12, 1945.
2-87	" Jesse F.,	Oct. 1, 1855.
1-5	CRANDALL, James, of Peter and Susannah.	April 17, 1709.
1-5	" Mary,	Feb. 17, 1711.
1-5	" Peter,	July 4, 1713.
1-5	" John,	June 18, 1716.
1-5	" Elizabeth,	Feb. 1, 1718-19.
1-125	" Samuel, of Jeremiah and Elizabeth,	Sept. 18, 1750.
1-125	" Esther	March 13, 1753.
1-125	" Jeremiah,	Sept. 19, 1755.
1-125	" Dorcas,	May 24, 1758.
1-134	CROSS, Hannah, of Samuel and Ann,	March 27, 1760.
1-121	COTTRELL, Elizabeth, of Stephen, Jr., and Lydia,	Dec. 4, 1747.
1-121	" David,	April 7, 1752.
1-135	" Abel, of Thomas and Mary,	Oct. 22, 1747.
1-144	" Lydia, of Stephen and Lydia,	April 6, 1755.
1-144	" Stephen,	Aug. 20, 1758.
1-144	" Elizabeth,	Sept. 3, 1761.
1-151	" William, of Thomas and Sarah,	Jan. 14, 1762.
1-150	" Thomas Paine, of John and Margaret,	June 28, 1768.
1-150	" Susannah,	Oct. 29, 1770.
1-150	" Sarah,	June 27, 1775.
1-150	" Susannah,	April 29, 1780.
1-150	" Abel, of Abel and Mary,	Feb. 9, 1771.
1-150	" Mary,	Jan. 8, 1773.
1-150	" Silence,	April 1, 1775.
1-150	" James Arnold, of Abel and Mary,	June 22, 1777.

1-150	COTTRELL Thomas, of Abel and Mary,	May 7, 1781.
2-84	" Margaret,	Dec. 26, 1784.
2-84	" Benjamin Potter,	May 30, 1788.
2-89	CRUMB Mary Jane, of Levi Lewis, and Susan, of ——,	March 25, 1854.
2-89	" Amanda,	Dec. 7, 1855.
2-89	" Ella F.,	Feb. 22, 1860.
2-89	" George L.,	May 12, 1868.
1-137	CURTIS Samuel, of Samuel and Amie,	Aug. 14, 1747.
1-137	" Sarah,	Feb. 25, 1752.

D

1-6	DICKINSON Charles, of Charles and Mary,	Feb. 27, 1716-7.
1-6	" Philip,	March 17, 1718-19.
1-6	" Sarah,	Jan. 18, 1722-3.
2-92	DOCKRAY Ann, of John Bigelow and Mary,	Oct. 18, 1779.
2-92	" John Bigelow,	Oct. 25, 1780.
1-6	" Mary,	May 7, 1784.
2-92	DOUGLASS Maria, of George and Mary Ann,	July 21, 1808.
2-92	" Eliza,	June 30, 1811.
2-92	" William,	May 10, 1813.
2-92	" Susan,	May 12, 1816.
2-92	" Horace,	Oct. 31, 1820.
2-92	" George Horace,	March 18, 1823.
1-28	DYRE Hannah, of Charles and Penelope,	Feb. 13, 1736-7.
1-115	" William, of William and Mercy,	Oct. 11, 1749.

E

1-12	EARL Benjamin, of John and Sarah,	Dec. 18, 1712.
1-12	" Susannah,	June 25, 1715.
1-12	" Abigail,	Aug. 7, 1724.
1-12	" Lydia,	Dec. 30, 1726.
1-34	EASTON Sarah, of James and Waite,	Jan. 30, 1735.
1-34	" Mary,	July 17, 1737.
1-34	" Mercy,	Aug. 24, 1740.

F

1-130	FRANKLIN Sarah, of John and Elizabeth,	May 5, 1756.
1-130	" Mary,	Oct. 29, 1758.
1-130	" Frances,	Jan. 11, 1761.
1-130	" William,	March 14, 1763.
1-130	" Robert,	Sept. 26, 1765.
1-6	FISH Jeremiah, of Jeremiah and Mary,	July 4, 1724.
1-8	" Thomas,	Sept. 14, 1726.
1-10	" Patience,	Jan. 28, 1728.
1-12	" Mary,	Aug. 30, 1730.
1-16	" Isabel,	Feb. 2, 1732.
1-5	FOREDICE James, of James and Mary,	June 2, 1714.
1-5	" Abigail,	March 14, 1717-8.

G

1-28	GARDINER Samuel, of Ephraim and Penelope,	Jan. 16, 1719.
1-8	" Christopher,	June 3, 1726.
1-7	" George, of George and Susannah,	July 25, 1720.
1-7	" Hannah,	May 27, 1723.
1-7	" Amie,	Aug. 15, 1725.
1-32	" Austis, of John and Mary,	March 23, 1721.
1-32	" Hannah,	April 22, 1723.

1-32	GARDINER	Thomas, of John and Mary,	March 11, 1725.
1-32	"	Amos,	March 27, 1729.
1-32	"	Abigail,	Sept. 26, 1740.
1-32	"	William,	March 18, 1741-2.
1-32	"	Mary, 2d wife of above John, mother of two last children.	
1-19	"	Job, of Nathaniel and Mary,	July 23, 1723.
1-20	"	Edward, of Henry, Jr., and Catherine,	Sept. 8, 1723.
1-20	"	Mary,	July 25, 1728.
1-20	"	Abigail,	March 9, 1732.
1-9	"	Henry, of William and Margaret,	Jan. 9, 1726-7.
1-17	"	Abiel, of Benjamin and Mary,	Jan. 20, 1727-8.
1-20	"	Nathaniel, of Nathaniel and Sarah,	May 18, 1735.
1-111	"	Paris,	July 28, 1743.
1-111	"	James,	May 30, 1746.
1-127	"	Sarah, of Caleb and Isabel,	April 29, 1736.
1-127	"	Dorcus,	March 16, 1739.
1-127	"	Nicholas,	Dec. 8, 1744.
1-127	"	Tabitha,	April 8, 1748.
1-127	"	Experience,	Nov. 1, 1751.
1-110	"	Christopher, of Henry and Anne,	Feb. 7, 1737.
1-110	"	George,	Jan. 3, 1739.
1-110	"	Jonathan,	Oct. 14, 1741.
1-110	"	Henry,	June 10, 1748.
1-110	"	James,	Sept. 30, 1749.
1-110	"	Desire,	March 31, 1751.
1-117	"	Clarke, of William and Freelove,	Aug. 3, 1737.
1-117	"	Thomas,	March 7, 1738.
1-117	"	Stephen,	June 7, 1740.
1-117	"	Mary,	Feb. 13, 1744.
1-117	"	Desire,	Nov. 26, 1749.
1-117	"	Gideon,	Nov. 15, 1751.
1-31	"	William, of John and Mercy,	Aug. 1, 1743.
1-31	"	Mary,	Aug. 1, 1743.
1-31	"	John,	June 17, 1745.
1-29	"	John, son of Margaret Rustin, of North Kingstown, b. ——. —, ——.	
1-31	"	Alan, of John and Mercy,	June 3, 1748.
1-124	"	Mary, of Nathan and Catherine,	March 5, 1743.
1-124	"	Nathan,	May 15, 1747.
1-124	"	Sarah,	Dec. 29, 1751.
1-124	"	Susannah, of George, Jr., and Sarah,	June 16, 1743.
1-124	"	George,	March 18, 1745.
1-124	"	Rufus,	March 9, 1747.
1-124	"	William,	Sept. 8, 1749.
1-124	"	Levi,	Sept. 29, 1751.
1-117	"	Mary, of Thomas and Mary,	Nov. 23, 1744.
1-117	"	Richard,	Feb. 3, 1745.
1-117	"	Thomas,	March 23, 1746.
1-117	"	Tabitha,	May 24, 1752.
1-123	"	Frederic, of Thomas (of John) and Martha,.	Aug. 24, 1751.
1-35	"	Rowland, of George and Sarah,	Dec. 1, 1743.
1-35	"	Thankful,	Feb. 22, 1744-5.
1-129	"	Benoni, of Nathan and Sarah,	Nov. 5, 1753.
1-129	"	Cynthia,	Dec. 27, 1756.
1-129	"	Susannah,	Oct. 7, 1758.
1-147	"	Stephen Champlain, of Nicholas and Hannah,	Dec. 3, 1755.
1-147	"	George,	June 9, 1757.
1-147	"	Rowland,	March 18, 1759.
1-147	"	Hannah,	Oct. 7, 1763.
1-147	"	Jeffrey,	Nov. 12, 1765.
2-102	"	George Perry, of George and Elizabeth,	June 14, 1793.
1-154	GAVITT	Oliver, of Samuel and Ruth,	Dec. 23, 1766.
1-154	"	Daniel,	Oct. 20, 1768.
1-154	"	Mary,	Aug. 2, 1770.
1-154	"	Esther,	Feb. 26, 1772.
1-154	"	Elizabeth,	Nov. 12, 1773.

1-154	GAVITT Samuel, of Samuel and Ruth,		Nov. 10, 1775.
1-154	"	Hannah,	April 4, 1779.
1-154	"	John,	March 9, 1781.
1-154	"	Ruth.	Nov. 9, 1784.
1-154	"	Arnold,	Jan. 9, 1787.
1-154	"	Perry,	May 19, 1789.
1-27	GOULD Mary, of William and Penelope,		March 11, 1731.
1-27	"	Elizabeth,	Dec. 23, 1733.
1-27	"	Waite,	June 10, 1736.
1-27	"	Tabitha,	July 12, 1738.

H

1-20	HALEY Joshua, of John and Mary,		Dec. 27, 1721.
1-20	"	Martha,	April 7, 1723.
1-20	"	Elizabeth,	Aug. 17, 1726.
1-153	HAMMOND Nathaniel, of Thomas and Rebecca,		March 11, 1746.
1-153	"	Mercy,	Jan. 18, 1747.
1-6	HANDSOM Anne, of John and Mary,		Feb. 4, 1720-1.
1-6	"	Sarah,	Nov. 6, 1722.
1-6	"	John,	Dec. 10, 1724.
1-9	"	Abigail,	Sept. 14, 1726.
1-2	HANNAH Mary, of Robert and Catherine,		Feb. 1, 1713-14.
1-2	"	Sarah,	Dec. 10, 1716.
1-2	"	Tabitha,	Feb. 21, 1717 18.
1-2	"	George,	March 26, 1719.
1-2	"	Catherine,	June 2, 1721.
1-2	"	Hannah,	Oct. 13, 1723.
1-2	"	Elizabeth,	March 17, 1725.
1-12	"	Ruth, of Robert and Elizabeth,	April 18, 1731.
1-16	"	Desire,	Feb. 11, 1732.
1-21	"	Ann,	Feb. 28, 1734.
1-29	HATCH Ezekiel, of Ezekiel (of Newport), and Mary		July 2, 1746.
1-151	HAYES Stove, (a dau.) of Moses M. and Rachel,		June 29, 1779.
1-21	HAZARD Oliver, of George and Penelope,		Sept. 13, 1710.
1-36	"	Mary, of Robert, of Thomas and Sarah, of Richard Borden of Tiverton, Feb. 23, 1716.	
1-36	"	Thomas, of Robert, of Thomas and Sarah, of Richard Borden of Tiverton, May, 9, 1718.	
1-36	"	Thomas, 2d, of Robert, of Thomas and Sarah, of Richard Borden, of Tiverton, Sept. 15, 1720.	
1-36	"	Jonathan, of Robert, of Thomas and Sarah, of Richard Borden, of Tiverton, Aug. 17, 1726.	
1-36	"	Richard, of Robert, of Thomas and Sarah, of Richard Borden, of Tiverton, Dec. 31, 1730.	
1-36	"	Sarah, of Robert, of Thomas and Sarah, of Richard Borden, of Tiverton, June 27, 1734.	
1-26	"	Mary, of Hon. George, Esq., and Sarah,	July 16, 1722.
1-26	"	George,	June 15, 1724.
1-26	"	Abigail,	March 12, 1726.
1-26	"	Sarah,	Sept. 15, 1729.
1-26	"	Penelope,	May 7, 1732.
1-26	"	Carder,	Aug. 11, 1734.
1-26	"	Arnold,	May 15, 1738.
1-3	"	Robert, of Caleb and Abigail,	May 1, 1723.
1-6	"	Caleb,	Jan. 21, 1724-5.
1-9	"	Caleb, 2d,	Sept. 22, 1726.
1-32	"	Benjamin, of George (of Thomas) and Mary,	May 22, 1723.
1-32	"	Simon, of George (of Thomas) and Mary,	Aug. 9, 1725.
1-32	"	Mary, of George (of Thomas) and Mary,	Nov. 23, 1727.
1-32	"	George, of George (of Thomas) and Mary,	April 16, 1730.
1-32	"	Susannah, of George (of Thomas) and Mary,	Dec. 18, 1732.
1-32	"	Enoch, of George (of Thomas) and Mary,	Dec. 6, 1735.
1-32	"	Thomas, of George (of Thomas) and Mary,	Oct. 11, 1738.

1-8, 25	HAZARD	Stephen, of Stephen H. and Mary,	July 10, 1723.
1-8, 25	"	Mary,	Sept. 18, 1725.
1-25	"	Elizabeth,	July 17, 1729.
1-25	"	John,	June 26, 1731.
1-7	"	Jeremiah, of Jeffrey and Mary,	Aug. 13, 1726.
1-18	"	Thomas, of Jonathan and Abigail,	Feb. 22, 1727.
1-18	"	Susannah,	March 24, 1729.
1-18	"	Mary,	March 22, 1737-8.
1-10	"	George,	May 22, 1742.
1-16, 24	"	Joseph, of Robert and Esther,	May 21, 1728.
1-16, 24	"	Elizabeth,	May 31, 1730.
1-16, 24	"	Esther,	Dec. 7, 1732.
1-24	"	Stephen,	June 13, 1736.
1-24	"	Robert,	June 13, 1736.
1-23	"	Penelope, of Capt. Thomas and Alice,	Feb. 11, 1730.
1-22	"	Hannah,	Aug. 5, 1732.
1-22	"	Sarah,	Jan. 23, 1734.
1-22	"	Alice,	Aug. 30, 1737.
1-80	"	Elizabeth, of Oliver and Elizabeth,	Sept. 13, 1737.
1-29	"	Sarah, of Samuel and Abigail,	Nov. 26, 1738.
1-33	"	Thomas, of Thomas (of Stephen) and Hannah,	Nov. 30, 1741.
1-32	"	Hannah, of Thomas (of Stephen) and Hannah,	Dec. 22, 1745.
1-113	"	Stanton, of Robert, Esq., and Esther,	June 8, 1743.
1-34	"	Martha, of Thomas and Elizabeth,	June 14, 1745.
1-112	"	Sarah,	Jan. 10, 1745.
1-113	"	Joseph, of William and Phebe,	Dec. 20, 1748.
1-142	"	Hannah, of Richard and Susannah,	April 14, 1753.
1-142	"	Robert,	April 11, 1755.
1-142	"	George,	Sept. 22, 1756.
1-142	"	Benjamin,	Dec. 26, 1757.
1-142	"	Susannah,	April 11, 1760.
1-142	"	Richard,	Nov. 14, 1761.
1-145	"	Abigail, of Dr. Robert and Elizabeth,	Aug. 29, 1753.
1-145	"	Esther,	July 26, 1755.
1-145	"	Elizabeth,	Nov. 28, 1757.
1-145	"	Sylvester Gardiner, of Dr. Robert and Elizabeth,	July 27, 1760.
1-145	"	Nancy, of Dr. Robert and Elizabeth,	April 29, 1764.
1-145	"	Charles, of Dr. Robert and Elizabeth,	July 14, 1766.
1-142	"	Alice, of George and Sarah,	Nov. 15, 1754.
1-142	"	Thomas,	Oct. 3, 1757.
1-142	"	George,	April 8, 1762.
1-142	"	Thomas, 2d, (also 1-145),	March 3, 1765.
1-134	"	Robert Hull, of Carder and Alice,	April 10, 1758.
1-134	"	Peter Bowers (Bours),	Dec. 5, 1759.
1-129	"	Robert, of Joseph and Hannah,	Jan. 31, 1762.
1-129	"	Mary,	May 29, 1764.
1-153	"	Mary, of Enock and Mary,	Sept. 6, 1763.
1-153	"	Sarah,	Aug. 13, 1768.
1-153	"	Enock,	Dec. 28, 1775.
1-153	"	Alice,	Jan. 11, 1778.
1-152	"	Benjamin, of Thomas (of Benj.) and Hannah,	Nov. 4, 1784.
1-152	"	Thomas, of Thomas (of Benj.) and Hannah,	May 8, 1787.
1-154	"	James Robinson, of Jonathan N. and Mary,	Feb. 10, 1789.
1-154	"	Alice Robinson, of Jonathan and Mary,	Dec. 12, 1790.
1-154	"	Stephen, of Jonathan and Mary,	Sept. 20, 1792.
1-154	"	Jonathan Nickols, of Jonathan and Mary,	Jan. 16, 1795.
1-154	"	Sylvester Robinson, of Thomas H. and Abigail,	March 3, 1791.
2-110	"	Eliza Clarke, of Borden and Teresa,	Sept. 1, 1813.
2-110	"	Arnold W.,	Oct. 4, 1815.
2-110	"	Alfred,	Jan. 15, 1818.
2-110	"	Harriet Teresa,	Jan. 15 1820.
2-110	"	William Rhodes,	April 21, 1821.
2-110	"	Marietta,	Feb. 18, 1823.
2-110	"	John Lafayette,	Feb. 4, 1825.
2-110	"	Nathaniel,	Feb. 4, 1827.

2-110	HAZARD Isaac Peace, of Borden and Terese,		Feb. 4, 1829.
2-110	"	Edwin Clarke,	April 4, 1831.
2-112	HEALEY Horace Dighton, of Jonathan and Sally,		Oct. 1, 1841.
1-35	HELME Benedict, of Christopher and Mary,		March 22, 1723-4.
1-35	"	Christopher,	Jan. 31, 1725-6.
1-35	"	Samuel,	Sept. 7, 1728.
1-35	"	Mary,	March 9, 1732.
1-10	"	Silas, of Rouse and Sarah,	May 20, 1724.
1-11	"	Sarah,	May 16, 1727.
1-11	"	Jonathan,	Oct. 14, 1729.
1-30	"	Oliver,	June 17, 1731.
1-30	"	Samuel,	June 3, 1734.
1-29	"	Robert, of Nathaniel and Mary,	Aug. 12, 1739.
1-112	"	Esther, of James and Esther,	July 20, 1740.
1-112	"	Powell,	June 17, 1742.
1-112	"	Rouse,	April 10, 1744.
1-112	"	Sarah,	Jan. 30, 1745.
1-112	"	Elizabeth,	Feb. 15, 1747.
1-112	"	James,	March 12, 1749.
1-112	"	Adam,	Nov. 29, 1752.
1-136	"	Samuel,	Feb. 7, 1755.
1-136	"	Sarah,	July 6, 1757.
1-136	"	Gabriel,	Oct. 26, 1759.
1-136	"	Nathaniel,	Dec. 24, 1761.
1-144	'	Catherine, of Robert and Elizabeth,	April 25, 1764.
1-144	"	Nathaniel,	Sept. 15, 1765.
1-153	"	Mary Hannah, of Robert and Elizabeth,	April 2, 1768.
1-153	"	Ann Harris,	June 3, 1773.
1-153	"	Martha Perry,	Jan. 25, 1781.
1-153	"	Robert Hanibal,	Sept. 11, 1785.
1-153	"	Cyril Ray,	March 18, 1788.
1-152	"	James, of James and Sarah,	Aug. 14, 1778.
1-152	"	Adam Powell, of James and Sarah,	April 5, 1780.
1-152	"	Mary,	Jan. 6, 1782.
1-152	"	John Clarke,	Sept. 30, 1783.
1-152	"	Esther,	June 28, 1785.
1-152	"	Bernon,	March 16, 1787.
1-152	"	Elizabeth,	May 11, 1789.
1-152	"	Sarah,	May 8, 1791.
1-152	"	Mary,	May 20, 1794.
1-152	"	Nathaniel,	Sept. 16, 1796.
2-110	"	Sarah Clarke, of James, Jr., and Alice,	April 8, 1804.
2-110	"	Mercy,	Aug. 28, 1805.
2-110	"	James,	May 11, 1807.
2-110	"	Jonathan Perry	Jan. 13, 1809.
2-110	"	Adam,	May 25, 1811.
2-111	"	Esther, of John Clarke and Susannah,	May 28, 1805.
2-111	"	Mary,	Sept. 24, 1807.
2-111	"	Anne,	June 14, 1809.
1-3	HIGINBOTTOM Mary, of Charles and Mary,		March 30, 1724.
1-25	"	Charles,	March 27, 1726.
1-25	"	Mary,	Oct. 19, 1727.
1-25	"	Ann,	Sept. 15, 1730.
1-151	HOLLAND Henry Hooper, of Henry Hooper and Susannah,		July 24, 1767.
1-151	"	John,	Nov. 24, 1769.
2-113	"	Edward Hazard,	Feb. 4, 1822.
2-113	"	Mary Ann (Crumb), his wife, b. Westerly,	Aug. 1, 1824.
2-113	"	Julia Ann, of Edward H. and Mary A.,	May 26, 1844.
2-113	"	John Burrell,	Aug. 6, 1848.
2-113	"	Jesse Babcock,	July 3, 1854.
2-113	"	Nellie Knowles,	June 7, 1858.
2-113	"	Lizzie,	Aug. 1, 1863.
2-112	"	Louisa, of Stephen and Abbie,	April 20, 1852.
2-112	"	Stephen,	May 14, 1855.

1-130	HOLLEY Daniel, of Jonathan and Deborah,		Feb. 11, 1754.
1-130	"	Henry,	Dec. 10, 1755.
1-130	"	George,	Oct. 24, 1757.
1-148	"	William, of William and Sarah,	Dec. 28, 1767.
1-148	"	Benjamin,	Oct. 10, 1769.
1-148	"	Penelope,	May 21, 1771.
1-8	HOLWAY Silence, of Benjamin and Penelope,		Aug. 11, 1722.
1-8	"	Daniel,	July 14, 1726.
1-111	"	Robert Hannah, of Joseph and Catherine,	April 12, 1742.
1-111	"	Joseph,	May 31, 1744.
1-111	"	Joseph, of Joseph and Abigail	Nov. 2, 1747.
1-36	HOPKINS Thomas, of Thomas,		March 24, 1742.
1-36	"	Mary,	Aug. 6, 1745.
1-138	HULL Joseph, of Tristam,		Oct. 1, 1706.
1-138	"	Elizabeth (Hull), wife of Joseph,	Aug. 23, 1715.
1-138	"	Martha, 2d, wife of Joseph,	April 5, 1722.
1-133	"	Sarah, of Joseph and Elizabeth,	Sept. 8, 1732.
1-133	"	Tristam,	May 28, 1734.
1-133	"	Hannah,	May 13, 1736.
1-133	"	Elizabeth,	April 7, 1738.
1-31	"	Elizabeth, of Joseph and Martha,	June 20, 1741.
1-31	"	Joseph,	Feb 23, 1742.
1-132	"	Thomas,	Jan. 30, 1744.
1-132	"	Benjamin,	Jan. 22, 1748.
1-132	"	Thomas,	Jan. 23, 1750.
1-132	"	Charles,	Sept. 20, 1752.
1-132	"	Martha,	Oct. 26, 1755.
1-133	"	Lydia,	Sept. 23, 1759.
1-115	"	William, of William and Mary,	Oct. 7, 1737.
1-115	"	James,	Aug. 31, 1744.
1-115	"	Mary,	Oct. 8, 1746.
1-115	"	Sylvester,	Oct. 18, 1757.
1-122	"	Bathsheba, of Charles and Abigail,	June 13, 1738.
1-122	"	Hannah,	June 23, 1740.
1-122	"	Samuel,	May 20, 1742.
1-122	"	Gideon,	March 6, 1744.
1-122	"	Charles,	Jan. 26, 1755.
1-146	"	Joseph, of Stephen and Martha,	March 22, 1739.
1-146	"	Elizabeth,	May 15, 1741.
1-146	"	Stephen,	Sept. 17, 1743.
1-146	"	Latham,	Feb. 17, 1749.
1-146	"	Samuel Dyre,	Jan. 20, 1745.
1-146	"	Elias,	April 13, 1748.
1-146	"	Sarah,	July 1, 1752.
1-146	"	Hannah,	Aug. 22, 1754.

I

1-5	IRISH Thankful, of Jedediah and Mary,		Aug. 24, 1722.
1-5	"	Joseph,	April 20, 1724.

J K

1-10	KEAIS Samuel, of William and Margeret,		Aug. 19, 1728.
1-11	"	Sybil,	Jan. 10, 1729.
1-1	KENYON James, of James and Ruth,		April 17, 1693.
1-9	"	Elisha, of Thomas and Mary,	Oct. 26, 1716.
1-9	"	Daniel,	June 24, 1721.
1-9	"	Desire,	Nov. 24, 1723.
2-121	"	Ellen L., of Thomas G. and Susan,	Feb. 12, 1859.

L

1-138	LEWIS Nathaniel, of Nathaniel and Elizabeth,	April 3, 1763.
1-29	LILLIBRIDGE Champlain, of John and Amie,	Sept. 15, 1739.
1-3	" Dorcas,	Aug. 27, 1747.
1-131	LITTLEFIELD Samuel, of Edmund and Martha,	Sept. 28, 1747.
1-131	" Sarah,	June 24, 1749.
1-131	" Penelope,	Jan. 1, 1753.
1-149	LUNT Mary, of William and Bethany,	Oct. 10, 1781.
1-149	" Joshua,	Aug. 29, 1783.

M

1-23	MASH John, of John and Mary,	July 6, 1734.
1-23	" Rowland,	Aug. 16, 1736.
1-113	" Mary,	Oct. 19, 1741.
2-128	MAWNEY Mary, wife of Elisha R. Potter, April 25, 1779.	
2-128	MAY Elisha G., of Liberty N. and Belinda,	Nov. 30, 1844.
2-128	" Horace A.,	Jan. 15, 1852.
2-128	" George L.,	April 29, 1853.
1-17	MOREY Mary, of Joseph and Sarah,	Oct. 18, 1704.
1-17	" Robert,	Aug. 31, 1706.
1-17	" Joseph,	Aug. 24, 1708.
1-17	" Benjamin,	May 2, 1710.
1-17	" Roger,	July 2, 1712.
1-17	" Martha,	Dec. 5, 1714.
1-17	" Sarah,	Aug. 31, 1717.
2-128	MITCHELL Mary A., of John R. and Mercy E.,	Aug. 4, 1858.
2-128	" Martha S.,	April 8, 1860.
1-13	MUMFORD James, of George and Mary,	Feb. 7, 1715.
1-13	" Robinson,	May 1, 1718.
1-13	" Mary,	Nov. 27, 1721.
1-13	" Rebecca,	May 2, 1724.
1-26	" Jirah, of Peleg (of Peleg) and Mary,	Aug. 5, 1717.
1-26	" Peleg,	July 25, 1719.
1-26	" Abigail,	Nov. 28, 1721.
1-26	" Samuel,	Feb. 2, 1723.
1-26	" Content,	March 23, 1725.
1-26	" Sarah,	Sept. —, 1728.
1-26	" Peleg,	Nov. —, 1729.
1-26	" Thomas,	May 30, 1733.
1-28	" Stephen, of Joseph and Hannah,	March 2, 1718.
1-7	" Phebe, of Benjamin and Anne,	Nov. 25, 1721.
1-7	" Samuel,	Jan. 20, 1723.
1-7	" Thomas,	March 7, 1724-5.
1-9	" Peter,	March 9, 1727-8.
1-7	" Lucy, of William and Hannah,	Jan. 29, 1725.
1-17	" William, of William and Hannah,	Sept. 14, 1728.
1-17	" Nathaniel, of William and Ann, 2d wife,	Dec. 29, 1729.
1-17	" Abigail, of William and Ann, 2d wife,	Dec. 27, 1731.
1-25	" Paul,	March 5, 1734.
1-25	" Sarah,	March 26, 1737.
1-27,34	" Simon Ray,	April 25, 1739.
1-34	" Gideon,	Dec. 17, 1741.
1-34	" Augustus,	July 7, 1744.
1-123	" Walte, of Jirah and Mary,	June 27, 1742.
1-123	" Gardiner William, of Jirah and Mary,	Nov. 26, 1744.
1-123	" Jirah,	May 30, 1747.
1-123	" Mary,	Aug. 24, 1749.
1-123	" Mary, 2d,	June 17, 1751.
1-123	" Sarah,	May 1, 1753.
1-123	" Hannah,	Jan. 18, 1755.
2-128	" Paul, of Gardiner William and Elizabeth,	Jan. 8, 1770.

2-128	MUMFORD Dorcas, of Gardiner William and Elizabeth,	April 8, 1772.
2-128	"	Amie,	May 20, 1774.
2-128	"	Silas G.,	March 4, 1776.
2-128	"	Oliver,	Jan. 12, 1778.
2-128	"	Augustus,	Jan. 29, 1780.
2-128	"	Elizabeth,	Feb. 4, 1782.
2-128	"	Davis,	May 8, 1786.

N

1-15	NASH Ann Engley, of Ruth Nash,	Nov. 25, 1714.
1-12	NICKOLS Esther, of John and Elizabeth,	Oct. 27, 1726.
1-12	"	Thomas, of John and Elizabeth,	Oct. 24, 1728.
1-12	"	Jean,	Oct. 2, 1730.
2-132	NICHOLS William H. H., of Matthew and Sally,	Nov. 5, 1840.
1-111	"	Martha, of Andrew and Rachel,	Oct. 24, 1741.
1-111	"	Eunice,	July 6, 1745.
1-12	NILES Ebenezer, of Ebenezer and Abigail,	March 4, 1709-10.
1-124	"	Catherine, of Nathaniel and Mary,	March 5, 1724-5.
1-10,16	"	Catherine, of Nathan and Mary,	July 18, 1729.
1-16	"	Mary,	May 19, 1731.
1-16	"	Sarah,	Oct. 22, 1732.
1-120	"	Silas, of Silas and Hannah,	Oct. 19, 1745.
1-120	"	Nathaniel, of Silas and Hannah,	Feb. 17, 1747.
1-120	"	Mary,	Aug. 16, 1750.
1-137	"	Sarah, of Jeremiah and Ann,	March 31, 1743.
1-137	"	Ann,	Sept. 12, 1744.
1-137	"	Martha,	April 21, 1746.
1-33	"	Simon, of Mingo and Dinah,	Nov. 23, 1776.

O

1-30	OATLEY Samuel, of Jonathan,	Oct. 23, 1726.
1-30	"	Rebecca,	Sept. 10, 1728.
1-30	"	Rhoda,	Dec. 29, 1730.
1-30	"	Benedict,	Dec. 25, 1732.
1-30	"	Joseph,	March 14, 1739.
2-136	O'NEIL Abbie Randall, of James and Mary,	Jan. 18, 1851.
2-136	"	Mary Ann,	April 8, 1853.
2-136	"	Susan	Dec. 19, 1858.
2-136	"	James Daniel,	Sept. 2, 1861.
1-2	OSBORNE Hannah, of Nathaniel and Hannah,	Aug. 23, 1703.
1-2	"	Nathaniel,	Nov. 20, 1708.
1-2	"	William,	Sept. 30, 1711.
1-2	"	Ann,	Sept. 13, 1714.
1-2	"	John,	Dec. 30, 1715.
1-2	"	Abigail,	Feb. 25, 1718-9.
1-6	"	Joseph,	May 31, 1724.

P

2-143	PITMAN Sarah Ann, of George B. and Peggy D.,	Dec. 10, 1815.
1-34	PECKHAM Peleg, of Benjamin and Mary,	June 28, 1723.
1-13	"	Joseph,	Jan. 14, 1725-6.
1-13	"	Isaac,	Dec. 23, 1728.
1-13	"	Mary,	May 28, 1730.
1-24	"	Timothy,	July 19, 1737.
1-27	"	George Hazard, Jr.,	April 14, 1739.
1-32	"	Josephus,	Feb. 21, 1742.
1-112	"	Peleg,	June 11, 1762.
1-151	"	Sarah, of William and Mercy,	Nov. 28, 1777.
1-151	"	Alice,	Jan. 19, 1780.

1-151	PECKHAM	William, of William anl Mercy,	Nov. 11, 1781.
1-151	"	Mercy,	July 11, 1783.
1-151	"	Dorcas,	Feb. 7, 1787.
1-151	"	Perry,	June 30, 1789.
1-151	"	Elizabeth,	Nov. 9, 1792.
1-150	"	Elizabeth, of Peleg, Jr., and Desire (N. K.)	July 25, 1786.
1-150	"	Rufus Wheeler, of Peleg, Jr., and Desire (N. K.)	Sept. 27, 1789.
1-150	"	Peleg Brown, of Peleg, Jr., and Desire (N. K.)	July 17, 1792.
1-150	"	George, of Peleg, Jr., and Desire (N. K.)	Feb. 24, 1796.
2-140	"	Mary, of William and Mercy,	Aug. 27, 1795.
2-143	"	Josephus, of Josephus and Mary,	May 26, 1788.
2-143	"	George,	Feb. 15, 1785.
2-143	"	William Robinson,	July 4, 1791.
2-143	"	Hannah,	May 17, 1795.
2-141	"	Susannah Stanton, of William and Susannah,	Jan. 3, 1804.
2-141	"	Sarah, of William and Susannah,	June 23, 1805.
2-141	"	Benjamin,	Nov. 18, 1806.
2-141	"	William Stanton,	Sept. 22, 1808.
2-141	"	Mercy Perry,	April 29, 1810.
2-141	"	Dorcas, of William and Susannah,	June 5, 1812.
2-141	"	Jane Hazard,	June 8, 1814.
2-141	"	George Hazard,	Feb. 18, 1816.
2-141	"	James Perry,	March 25, 1819.
2-141	"	Edwin Alexander,	Dec. 10, 1820.
2-141	"	John Cross,	Nov. 30, 1822.
2-141	"	Alice Rathbone,	March 8, 1826.
2-141	"	Carder, of Benjamin and Mary,	Jan. 22, 1800.
2-141	"	Henry Wand,	July 22, 1804.
2-141	"	Renewed,	Jan. 19, 1805.
2-140	"	Edward Hazard, of George and Elizabeth,	Jan. 2, 1809.
1-10	PERRY,	Benjamin, of Benjamin and Susannah,	Nov. 7, 1729.
1-115	"	Edward,	March 28, 1731.
1-115	"	Freeman,	Jan. 23, 1733.
1-115	"	Mary,	Nov. 19, 1735.
1-115	"	Susannah,	Nov. 19, 1735.
1-135	"	Mercy, of James and Mary,	Feb. 24, 1754.
1-135	"	Anna,	March 16, 1756.
1-135	"	James,	May 26, 1758.
1-135	"	William,	June 19, 1759.
1-135	"	John,	July 28, 1760.
1-151	"	John, of John and Hannah,	Aug. 7, 1784.
1-142	"	Robert N., of John B. and Susan,	Dec. 27, 1805.
1-142	"	Susan,	March 16, 1810.
1-31	"	John B.,	Feb. 14, 1814.
1-31	PERKINS	Nathaniel, of Nathaniel and Elizabeth,	Jan. 1, 1739.
1-31	"	Susannah,	Jan. 13, 1742.
1-110	"	Elizabeth,	Dec. 25, 1745.
1-136	"	Abraham,	March 9, 1747-8.
1-136	"	William,	Nov. 20, 1754.
1-136	"	Sands,	May 12, 1757.
1-136	"	James,	March 13, 1760.
1-136	"	Jenckes,	—— —, ——.
1-134	"	Ebenezer, of Edward and Elizabeth,	April 4, 1741.
1-134	"	Ann,	May 19, 1743.
1-134	"	Brenton,	March 23, 1745.
2-145	PERRY	John Robinson, of John, and Hannah,	Aug. 7, 1784.
2-145	"	Sarah (Gould, of John and Mary), his wife,	Feb. 19, 1789.
2-145	"	Mercy, of John R., and Sarah,	Aug. 27, 1810.
2-145	"	Robinson,	Oct. 10, 1811.
2-145	"	Abigail,	Jan. 12, 1813.
2-145	"	Mary,	July 1, 1814.
2-145	"	John Gould,	June 2, 1817.
2-145	"	Sarah,	Aug. 21, 1819.
2-145	"	George Thomas,	Jan. 30, 1822.
2-145	"	Oliver Hazard,	May 12, 1824.

2-145	PERRY Rowland, of John R., and Sarah,	Jan. 26, 1826.
2-145	" Rowland, 2d,	May 1, 1827.
2-145	" William Wanton,	Sept. 9, 1829.
2-145	" James,	June 2, 1834.
2-145	" Amos R.,	March 22, 1832.
1-134	PERKINS Edward, of Edward and Elizabeth,	May 20, 1747.
1-134	" Joseph,	Sept. 24, 1749.
1-134	" Abram,	Jan. 19, 1752.
1-134	" Hannah,	Nov. 19, 1753.
1-134	" Benjamin,	Feb. 7, 1756.
1-5	PHILLIPS Joseph, of Bartholomew and Mary,	Aug. 11, 1703.
1-5	" Elizabeth,	Sept. 10, 1705.
1-5	" Mary,	Feb. 7, 1710.
1-24	" Abigail, of Joseph and ——.	Jan. 26, 1729.
1-24	" Dorcas,	Dec. 15, 1731.
1-24	" Bartholomew,	Nov. 10, 1734.
1-24	" Joseph,	May 8, 1737.
2-143	PITMAN Sarah Ann, of George B. and Peggy D.,	Nov. 6, 1817.
2-140	POLLOCK John W., of Wm. Wilson and Mary,	March 28, 1785.
2-143	" Samuel Holden, of William and Lydia,	Sept. 28, 1787.
2-143	" Sally S., of Sam'l Holden and Sarah,	Oct. 27, 1809.
2-143	" Abbie C.,	April 14, 1811.
2-143	" Simon S.,	April 11, 1813.
1-5	POTTER Rouse, of Ichabod and Margaret,	Feb. 13, 1702-3.
1-5	" William,	March 4, 1709.
1-5	" Margaret,	Oct. 11, 1714.
1-4	" Samuel, of John and Sarah,	July 28, 1715.
1-18	" William, of John and Mercy,	Jan. 21, 1722-3.
1-18	" Samuel,	Jan. 20, 1724-5.
1-18	" Mercy,	Aug. 15, 1727.
1-18	" Sarah,	Aug. 11, 1730.
1-11	" John, of Ichabod and Sarah,	July 29, 1724.
1-11	" Simeon,	Sept. 25, 1726.
1-11	" Ruth,	Jan. 19, 1727-8.
1-11	" Rouse,	Dec. 10, 1729.
1-8	" Joseph, of John, son of Thomas,	Sept. 24, 1724.
1-8	" Benjamin,	Sept. 24, 1724.
1-8	" Mary,	Feb. 4, 1726.
1-9	" Robert, of Ichabod and Deborah,	Nov. 26, 1726-7.
1-10	" Elizabeth,	Dec. 18, 1728.
1-18,19	" Deborah,	Feb. 15, 1732.
1-19	" Ichabod,	Sept. 13, 1734.
1-15	" Ruth, of Benjamin and Ruth,	Nov. 8, 1728.
1-19	" Thomas Benjamin,	March 8, 1732.
1-16	" Lydia,	Sept. 13, 1734.
1-16	" Joshua, of Joseph and Abigail,	March 7, 1730-1.
1-16	" Abigail	Jan. 7, 1732.
1-26	" Robert, of Robert and Judith,	March 6, 1732.
1-26	" Martha,	May 15, 1736.
1-36	" Hannah,	Aug. 24, 1738.
1-36	" William,	Jan. 5, 1742.
1-135	" Judith,	July 16, 1745.
1-135	" Rouse,	Jan. 3, 1748.
1-135	" Elizabeth,	Oct. 3, 1750.
1-135	" Marberry,	June 17, 1753.
1-135	" Samuel,	March 6, 1757.
1-20	" Christopher, of Ichabod (of Ichabod), and Sarah,	Nov. 15, 1732.
1-35	" Nicholas,	Aug. 31, 1735.
1-35	" Mary,	Sept. 26, 1737.
1-128	" Thomas, of Ichabod (of Robert), and Margaret,	July 2, 1738.
1-128	" William,	Nov. 14, 1739.
1-128	" Margaret,	June 11, 1743.
1-136	" Mercy, of William and Penelope,	Nov. 26, 1751.
1-126	" Thomas Hazard,	Dec. 8, 1753.
1-126	" Alice,	April 20, 1756.

1-126	POTTER Susannah, of William and Penelope,	April 25, 1758.
1-126	" William Robinson,	July 13, 1760.
1-126	" Benedict Arnold,	Sept. 12, 1761.
1-126	" Penelope,	March 7, 1764.
1-126	" William Pitt,	April 10, 1766.
1-126	" Edward,	Feb. 15, 1768.
1-147	" Simeon,	April 25, 1770.
1-137	" Sarah,	Dec. 13, 1771.
1-147	" John,	May 24, 1774.
1-147	" Pelham,	Dec. 7, 1776.
1-135	" Mary, of Benjamin and Margaret,	Jan. 2, 1747-8.
1-136	" Susannah, of Thomas, Jr., and Elizabeth,	Aug. 21, 1759.
1-136	" Margaret,	May 23, 1761.
1-136	" Thomas,	Dec. 2, 1762.
1-136	" Elisha Reynolds,	Nov. 5, 1764.
1-136	" Asa,	Sept. 4, 1766.
1-136	" Elizabeth,	June 21, 1770.
1-136	" Peggy,	May 7, 1778.
1-123	" Paul Munford, of Deborah,	Dec. 7, 1764.
1-146	" Benjamin, of William and Lydia,	Aug. 20, 1763.
1-142	" James, of Ichabod and Deborah,	July 26, 1764.
1-150	" Robert, of William (of Robert) and Mary,	Dec. 28, 1766
1-149	" Stephen, of Stephen and Abigail,	May 31, 1775.
2-140	" John, of George and Sarah,	March 25, 1789.
2-140	" Alice, of John and Mary,	April 8, 1792.
2-140	" William,	March 4, 1794.
2-140	" Mary,	Aug. 30, 1795.
2-144	" Mary (Perkins), 1st wife of Elisha R.,	——. —, ——.
2-144	" Mary (Mawney), 2d wife of Elisha R.,	April 25, 1779.
2-144	" Elisha Reynolds, of Elisha R. and Mary,	June 20, 1811.
2-144	" Thomas,	May 4, 1813.
2-144	" Thomas Mawney,	Aug. 12, 1814.
2-144	" William Henry,	Nov. 2, 1816.
2-144	" James B. Mason,	Oct. 1, 1818.
2-144	" Mary Elizabeth,	Aug. 11, 1820.
2-145	" James H., of Frederic A. and Esther,	Oct. 28, 1850.
2-145	" Sarah A., of Frederic A. and Anna A.,	Aug. 31, 1853.
1-151	POWERS, Samuel Hoxie, of Samuel and Anne,	June 2, 1785.
1-151	" Mary,	April 20, 1787.
1-151	" Martha,	June 4, 1789.
1-151	" Annie,	June 29, 1791.
1-127	PROSSEY, of Arnold and Esther,	Oct. 9, 1764.

Q R

1-133	READ Thomas, of Joseph (alias Robinson) and Bettey,	—— —, ——.
1-36	RECORDS Virtue, of John and Deborah,	May 19, 1746.
1-10	REYNOLDS, Elisha, of Elisha and Susannah,	June 30, 1729.
1-19	" Mary,	April 11, 1731.
1-19	" Ichabod, of Elisha and Susannah,	Sept. 5, 1732.
1-19	" Susannah,	May 16, 1734.
1-119	" Elizabeth,	Sept. 11, 1737.
1-119	" Henry,	Oct. 13, 1741.
1-119	" Sarah,	Nov. 9, 1743.
1-121	" Benjamin, of Job and Abigail,	Sept. 5, 1746.
1-121	" Abigail,	Nov. 27, 1749.
1-121	" Phebe,	March 20, 1731.
1-121	" George,	Oct. 7, 1753.
1-121	" Mary,	Aug. 31, 1760.
1-120	" Alice, of Henry and Mary,	April 17, 1749.
1-120	" Sarah,	March 28, 1751.
1-126	" Stephen, of John and Abigail,	Dec. 5, 1749.
1-126	" Henry,	July 23, 1751.
1-126	" Mary,	April 20, 1753.

1-150	REYNOLDS Elisha, of Henry and Mary,		April 19, 1762.
1-150	"	Sarah,	June 29, 1764.
1-150	"	Mary,	Oct. 18, 1766.
1-150	"	James,	Jan. 7, 1769.
1-150	"	Thomas,	Jan. 13, 1771.
1-150	"	Henry,	Jan. 13, 1774.
1-150	"	Jessie,	April 1, 1780.
1-143	"	Lydia, of Lydia Seerant, of Col. Elisha,	Aug. 24, 1773.
1-143	"	Jennie.	April 14, 1775.
1-143	"	Nancy.	March 21, 1777.
1-132	RHODES Annie, of James and Annie,		Oct. 20, 1755.
1-132	"	Joseph,	Sept. 10, 1758.
2-152	ROBBINS Thomas, of Thomas and Elizabeth (also 2-255)		Oct. 6, 1771.
1-6, 8	ROBINSON Rowland, of William and Martha,		Oct. 8, 1719.
1-6, 8	"	John,	July 23, 1721.
1-6, 8	"	Marah, or Mary,	Jan. 27, 1722-3.
1-6, 8	"	Elizabeth,	June 16, 1724.
1-8	"	Martha,	Nov. 11, 1725.
1-9	"	Christopher, of William and Abigail,	Dec. 31, 1727.
1-11	"	William,	Aug. 1, 1729.
1-23	"	Mary,	Oct. 8, 1736.
1-27	"	James, of William and Abigail,	Dec. 31, 1738.
1-110	"	John,	Jan. 13, 1742-3.
1-110	"	Christopher,	Dec. 31, 1747.
1-121	"	Hannah, of Rowland and Anstis,	May 10, 1740.
1-111	"	Mary,	Aug. 15, 1751.
1-111	"	William,	Sept. 13, 1758.
1-121	"	Hannah, of William and Sarah,	Feb. 21, 1751.
1-121	"	Abigail,	Aug. 24, 1753.
1-121	"	Philip,	Oct. 6, 1755.
1-132	"	James, of Sylvester and Alice,	Oct. 3, 1756.
1-132	"	William,	Dec. 20, 1760.
1-132	"	Abigail, of Christopher and Ruhamah,	Jan. 20, 1755.
1-132	"	Christopher,	Nov. 26, 1756.
1-132	"	George,	Aug. 3, 1758.
1-132	"	Elizabeth,	June 14, 1760.
1-148	"	Benjamin, of John and Sarah,	Aug. 5, 1763.
1-148	"	Sarah,	Dec. 10, 1764.
1-148	"	William,	April 25, 1766.
1-148	"	John,	Dec. 16, 1767.
1-148	"	Sylvester,	July 12, 1769.
1-148	"	Thomas,	May 5, 1771.
1-4	RODMAN Thomas, of Thomas and Catherine,		March 9, 1707.
1-4	"	Patience,	March 22, 1709-10.
1-4	"	John,	Dec. 26, 1711.
1-4	"	Joseph,	Oct. 1, 1713.
1-4	"	Samuel,	March 22, 1716.
1-4	"	Ann,	April 20, 1718.
1-4	"	Robert,	June 11, 1720.
1-4	"	William,	May 3, 1723.
1-28	"	Joseph, of Joseph and Tabitha,	March 23, 1733.
1-28	"	Mary,	Feb. 7, 1736.
1-28	"	John,	March 24, 1737.
1-30	"	Thomas,	July 1, 1740.
1-4	"	Benjamin,	July 22, 1726.
1-144	"	Hannah, wife of Benjamin,	Oct. 26, 1723.
1-144	"	Catherine, of Benjamin and Hannah,	Dec. 29, 1753.
1-144	"	Mary, of Benjamin and Hannah,	Dec. 16, 1755.
1-144	"	Anne,	Dec. 11, 1757.
1-144	"	Luceanna,	April 28, 1760.
1-144	"	Ruth,	Aug. 12, 1763.
1-144	"	Deborah,	Aug. 5, 1766.
2-152	"	Isaac P., eldest son of Samuel and Mary, Aug. 18, 1822.	
2-152	"	Sally, his wife, daughter of Lemuel H. Arnold, Feb. 25, 1826.	
2-152	"	Isaac P., of Isaac P. and Sally,	April 21, 1848.

2-152	RODMAN Sally Lyman, of Isaac P. and Sally,	Feb. 10, 1850.
2-152	" Mary Peckham,	March 25, 1852.
2-152	" Samuel,	Feb. 6, 1854.
2-152	" Thomas,	March 23, 1856.
2-152	" Samuel,	April 11, 1858.
1-153	" Elizabeth Arnold.	July 24, 1860.
1-119	ROSE Samuel. of John and Elizabeth,	Oct. 21, 1734.
1-119	" Abigail,	July 1, 1736.
1-119	" Thomas,	Jan. 30, 1739.
1-119	" John,	June 13, 1742.
1-119	" James,	Dec. 19, 1744.
1-119	" Phebe,	Dec. 4, 1746.
1-119	" Phillip,	Dec. 11, 1748.
1-119	" Stephen,	March 1, 1750.
2-153	" Mary E., of George P. and Harriet P.,	Sept. 3, 1853.
2-153	" George A.,	July 25, 1856.
2-153	" Thomas,	Dec. 3, 1858.
1-116	ROGERS Mary, of James and Mary,	Jan. 20, 1743.

S

2-162	SANDS Wm. Case, of Robert G. and Anne,	June 27, 1785.
2-162	" Anne Maynard,	April 15, 1787.
2-164	SEAGER Abigail, of John and Abigail,	March 7, 1787.
2-164	" John,	Nov. 5, 1788.
2-164	" Elizabeth,	April 3, 1790.
2-164	" Sarah,	Jan. 18, 1792.
2-164	" Francis Brayton,	Feb. 24, 1794.
2-164	" Joseph Taylor,	April 11, 1796.
2-164	" David Anthony,	March 12, 1798.
2-164	" Alice,	June 17, 1802.
2-164	" Hannah,	Dec. 27, 1805.
1-30	SHEFFIELD George. of Joseph and Mary,	July 12, 1718.
1-30	" Martha Tefft,	Sept. 29, 1719.
1-1	" Ezekiel, of Edmund and Sarah,	Jan. 31, 1720-1.
1-1	" Elizabeth,	March 16, 1722-3.
1-7	" Edmund,	May 17, 1725.
1-12	" Jeremiah, of Deborah,	May 8, 1729.
1-25	" William, of Nathan and Dorcas,	Jan. 23, 1730.
1-25	" Christopher,	Nov. 18, 1732.
1-25	" Elizabeth,	Aug. 8, 1734.
1-25	" Susannah,	Feb. 29, 1736.
1-25	" Nathan,	Oct. 23, 1737.
1-32	" Sarah, of Isaac and Sarah,	Jan. 3, 1735.
1-130	" Dorcas, of William and Lois,	May 12, 1753.
1-130	" Sarah,	May 7, 1755.
1-145	" Edmund, of Joseph and Mary,	June 21, 1749.
1-145	" Prudence,	June 12, 1751.
1-145	" Joseph,	Jan. 19, 1754.
1-145	" John,	Jan. 24, 1757.
1-3	SHELDON John, of John and Horred,	Feb. 10, 1706-7.
1-3	" Dorcas,	Jan. 4, 1707-8.
1-3	" George,	May 25, 1709.
1-3	" Samuel,	Jan. 15, 1713-14.
1-3	" William,	March 27, 1714.
1-3	" Elizabeth,	March 31, 1720.
1-3	" Sarah,	Feb. 26, 1721-2.
1-8	" Thomas, of Isaac and Susannah,	Feb. 18, 1708-9.
1-8	" Roger,	Dec. 15, 1710.
1-8	" Elizabeth,	Nov. 8, 1713.
1-8	" Isaac,	March 4, 1715-16.
1-8	" John,	Aug. 21, 1718.
1-8	" Susannah,	Oct. 23, 1720.
1-8	" Joseph,	March 17, 1721-2.

1-8	SHELDON	Palmer, of Isaac and Susannah,	May 16, 1724.
1-8	"	Benjamin,	March 4, 1727.
1-31	"	Sarah, of Isaac and Sarah,	Jan. 3, 1735.
1-31	"	Herodias, of John and Sarah,	May 21, 1729.
1-31	"	John,	May 21, 1729.
1-31	"	Dorcas,	Feb. 12, 1732.
1-31	"	Abigail,	March 3, 1734.
1-31	"	Sarah,	May 22, 1736.
1-31	"	George,	Dec. 17, 1738.
1-1, 127	"	James, of Isaac and Sarah,	April 11, 1743.
1-1, 127	"	Samuel, of Isaac and Abigail,	June 30, 1747.
1-1, 127	"	Lydia,	Aug. 23, 1749.
1-1, 127	"	Sarah,	Aug 17, 1751.
1-1, 127	"	Isaac,	July 22, 1755.
1-1, 127	"	Benjamin,	July 28, 1758.
1-149	"	Palmer, of John and Elizabeth,	Jan. 28, 1745.
1-149	"	Mehitable,	July 20, 1746.
1-149	"	John,	April 29, 1748.
1-149	"	Isaac,	May 11, 1750.
1-149	"	Nathan,	March 29, 1752.
1-149	"	Jonathan,	May 4, 1755.
1-149	"	George,	Oct. 11, 1757.
1-149	"	Joanna,	April 10, 1760.
2-162	"	Augustus, of James and Hannah,	Feb. 23, 1763.
2-162	"	Henry,	March 30, 1765.
2-162	"	Sarah,	May 7, 1767.
2-162	"	Hannah,	July 17, 1770.
2-162	"	Dorcas,	Sept. 17, 1773.
2-162	"	William J.,	July 15, 1776.
2-162	"	Waite, of James and Elizabeth (2d wife),	Oct. 13, 1782.
2-162	"	Elizabeth,	Sept. 20, 1784.
2-162	"	William, of Jonathan and Dorcas,	March 27, 1785.
2-162	"	Susannah,	Aug. 24, 1786.
2-162	"	Hannah,	Aug. 12, 1788.
2-162	"	Samuel,	May 2, 1790.
2-162	"	Elizabeth,	April 29, 1792.
1-21	SHERMAN	Daniel, of Daniel and Susannah,	Aug. 28, 1735.
1-22	"	Mary, of Josiah and Mary,	Aug. 1, 1727.
1-125	"	Abigail, of Jonathan and Mary,	Oct. 25, 1737.
1-125	"	Jonathan,	Oct. 14, 1731.
1-125	"	Gideon,	Oct. 25, 1741.
1-125	"	Mary,	Nov. 5, 1745.
1-125	"	Robert,	Sept. 14, 1752.
1-36	"	Amie, of Abiel and Susannah,	June 1, 1746.
1-129	"	Nathaniel, of Henry and Ann,	Aug. 15, 1748.
1-129	"	John,	Oct. 24, 1750.
1-129	"	Mary,	March 11, 1753.
1-129	"	Charles,	Feb. 1, 1756.
1-129	"	Henry,	March 31, 1759.
1-129	"	Martha,	March 9, 1762.
1-129	"	Sarah,	March 29, 1765.
1-143	"	Josias, of Benjamin and Mary,	Sept. 21, 1745.
1-143	"	Waite, of Jonathan, Jr., and Sarah,	Jan. 11, 1755.
1-143	"	Elizabeth,	Aug. 12, 1757.
1-143	"	Gideon,	Feb. 22, 1763.
1-150	"	Jonathan, of Robert and Honor,	July 20, 1779.
2-163	"	Catherine Greene, of John R, and Margaret,	March 5, 1801.
2-166	"	David, son of David,	April 18, 1786.
2-166	"	Hannah, wife of David,	Feb. 3, 1785.
2-166	"	David, of David and Hannah,	Sept. 2, 1805.
2-166	"	Lydia B.,	April 24, 1808.
2-166	"	Ruth B.,	Jan. 7, 1811.
2-166	"	George Washington, of David and Hannah,	Jan. 9, 1815.
2-166	"	Susannah E.,	Aug. 16, 1817.
2-166	"	Nehemiah K.,	May 14, 1820.

2-166	SHERMAN Arnold S., of David and Hannah,	April 28, 1823.
2-166	" Horace Dunn,	Sept. 5, 1826.
2-163	" Abner O., of David and Salome (2d wife),	Jan. 3, 1839.
2-163	" Jane E.,	Dec. 28, 1841.
2-163	" Clarissa A.,	Feb. 12, 1843.
2-163	" Joseph,	March 5, 1846.
2-163	" Mary C.,	March 5, 1846.
1-25	SMITH John, of John and Mary,	July 26, 1712.
1-25	" Mary,	July 17, 1715.
1-25	" Mary 2d,	Aug. 5, 1717.
1-25	" William,	Oct. 9, 1719.
1-27	" Phillis,	Sept. 29, 1723.
1-30	" Arnold, of Ephraim and Mercy,	June 30, 1739.
1-33	" Stafford,	March 11, 1740.
1-33	" Abigail,	Dec. 19, 1743.
1-137	" James Alexander Seabury, son of Wm. and Magdalen, baptized by Bishop Seabury, born Moy 29, 1788.	
1-34	STANTON Latham, of David and Martha,	Jan. 13, 1744-5.
2-165	" Benjamin, of Benjamin and Sarah,	June 21, 1800.
2-165	" Daniel,	April 3, 1802.
2-165	" Abigail,	April 24, 1804.
2-165	" Wm. Knowles,	Nov. 6, 1806.
2-165	" Ann Hoxsie,	Jan. 8, 1809.
2-165	" Sarah Sheffield,	July 9, 1811.
2-165	" Hannan Sherman,	July 10, 1811.
2-165	" James Sherman of Benjamin and Sarah,	Jan. 20, 1814.
2-165	" Mary,	Oct. 6, 1816.
2-165	" John Sherman,	March 23, 1820.
1-8	STEADMAN John, of Thomas and Hannah,	Sept. 21, 1725.
1-8	" Samuel,	Dec. 4, 1726.
1-114	" Daniel,	Oct. 10, 1728.
1-114	" Thomas,	Oct. 10, 1730.
1-114	" Enoch,	Nov. 5, 1734.
1-114	" Hannah,	Feb. 6, 1736.
1-114	" James,	March 3, 1738.
1-114	" Sarah,	Aug. 30, 1742.
1-114	" William,	May 4, 1745.
1-114	" Matthew Gracy, of John and Bethany,	July 4, 1748.
1-114	" Martha,	Nov. 19, 1750.
2-166	" William Henry, of William and Abbie N.,	May 6, 1855.
2-166	" Hattie Ann,	May 6, 1855.
2-166	" Herbert,	April 26, 1862.
2-166	" Abbie N., (mother of above)	born Nov.20, 1833.
1-142	SUNDERLAND George, of William and Penelope,	Dec. 29, 1754.
1-142	" Augustus,	Dec. 19, 1758.
1-22	SWAIN Elizabeth, of John and Hannah,	Sept. 28, 1731.

T

1-8	TANNER Nathan, of William and Elizabeth,	Feb. 20, 1709.
1-116	TAYLOR Mary, of Joseph and Experience,	Nov. 21, 1749.
1-148	" Ann, of William and Ann,	April 26, 1741.
1-148	" Sarah,	June 2, 1744.
1-4	TEFFT Samuel, of Samuel and Abigail,	Jan. 19, 1711-12.
1-4	" Daniel,	June 14, 1714.
1-4	" Stephen,	Oct. 5, 1758.
1-4	" Tennant,	Sept. 29, 1720.
1-4	" Ebenezer,	Feb. 14, 1723-4.
1-30	" James, of John and Joanna,	April 21, 1715.
1-29	" Abigail, of Samuel and Mary,	Dec. 24, 1731.
1-29	" Mary,	Jan. 28, 1732.
1-29	" Mercy,	April 24, 1735.
1-142	" Hannah, of Tennant and Tabitha,	June 28, 1741.
1-142	" Caleb,	Oct. 11, 1743.

1-118	TEFFT	Sophia, of Samuel, Jr., and Mary,	—— -, ——.
1-118	"	Samuel,	June 20, 1742.
1-118	"	Oliver,	March 22, 1743.
1-118	"	Alexander,	July 30, 1746.
1-115	"	Stanton, of Nathan and Isabel,	July 9, 1744.
1-115	"	Isabel,	March 14, 1745.
1-115	"	Mercy,	Dec. 14, 1749.
1-115	"	Nathan,	Aug. 28, 1752.
1-115	"	John,	March 24, 1756.
1-115	"	Mary,	May 2, 1758.
1-115	"	Sarah,	Aug. 14, 1762.
1-21	TORREY	Elizabeth, of Joseph and Elizabeth,	July 19, 1731.
1-21	"	Joseph,	Feb. 4, 1732-3.
1-21	"	Oliver,	Feb. 14, 1734-5.
1-21	"	Ann,	May 13, 1737.
2-170	TOTTEN	John Levi, of Levi and Martha,	July 30, 1790.
2-170	"	Eliza,	March 26, 1792.
2-170	"	Henry Morris,	March 9, 1794.

U

1-18	UNDERWOOD	John, of Joseph and Ruth,	Dec. 24, 1732.
1-19	"	Joseph,	April 12, 1734.
1-116	"	Anne, of William and Susannah,	June 26, 1748.
1-116	"	Joseph,	Oct. 21, 1744.
1-128	"	Henry,	Jan. 25, 1752.
1-128	"	Alice,	Aug. 24, 1753.
1-116	"	Samuel,	Jan. 29, 1756.
2-170	"	Anne E., of Perry G. and Mary E.,	Sept. 20, 1855.

V W

2-181	WAITE	Dorcas, of Matthew and Mercy,	Sept. 25, 1816.
2-181	"	Benjamin Case,	April 10, 1819.
2-181	"	John,	April 10, 1821.
2-181	"	Samuel,	June 16, 1823.
2-181	"	William,	Sept. 12, 1826.
2-181	"	William,	Sept. 27, 1837.
1-13	WALMESLEY	Thomas, of Thomas and ——,	Jan. 3, 1706.
1-13	"	Mary,	Nov. 16, 1708.
1-13	"	Patience,	Jan. 5, 1710.
1-13	"	James,	July 17, 1713.
1-13	"	Sarah,	Nov. 6, 1715.
1-13	"	Joseph,	Dec. 27, 1717.
1-14	"	Samuel,	Dec. 29, 1720.
1-14	"	Benjamin,	Dec. 27, 1723.
1-20	WATSON	Hannah, of Jeffrey and Bathsheba,	June 2, 1733.
1-116	"	Jeffrey,	Oct. 16, 1734.
1-116	"	Elisha,	July 10, 1736.
1-116	"	Mercy,	July 10, 1740.
1-116	"	Dorcas,	June 5, 1742.
1-116	"	Sarah,	Jan. 11, 1743.
1-116	"	William,	April 25, 1745.
1-116	"	Bathsheba,	Sept. 16, 1748.
1-130	"	John, of John, Jr., and Isabel,	May 23, 1737.
1-130	"	Hannah,	Sept. 28, 1738.
1-130	"	Bridget,	Dec. 24, 1741.
1-130	"	Job,	Aug. 7, 1744.
1-130	"	Mary,	Sept. 3, 1746.
1-130	"	Elisha,	Aug. 5, 1748.
1-130	"	Isabel,	May 7, 1753.
1-131	"	Walter,	May 7, 1753.

1-122	WATSON Robert, of Benjamin and Sarah,	March 27, 1750.
1-122	" Avis,	July 10, 1752.
1-152	" Isabel, of Job and Sarah,	Sept. 22, 1766.
1-152	" Job,	Oct. 25, 1767.
1-152	" Robert Hazard,	Feb. 28, 1769.
1-152	" Walter,	June 10, 1770.
1-152	" Borden,	Feb. 9, 1772.
2-180	" John,	Nov. 1, 1774.
1-149	" George, of John and Desire,	Dec. 16, 1783.
2-180	" Mary, of Elisha, Jr., and Miriam,	April 6, 1775.
2-180	" Elisha,	Oct. 1, 1776.
2-180	" Joseph Dennison, of Elisha, Jr., and Miriam,	Aug. 30, 1778.
2-180	" Asa,	May 24, 1780.
2-180	" George,	March 24, 1782.
2-180	" William,	Dec. 26, 1783.
2-180	" Freeman, of Elisha, Jr., and Susannah,	May 16, 1787.
2-180	" Susannah,	March 13, 1789.
2-180	" Elizabeth,	June 24, 1790.
2-180	" Miriam,	Oct. 30, 1793.
1-3	WEBB Margaret, of John and Joanna,	Aug. 21, 1721.
1-3	" Elizabeth,	March 27, 1724.
1-122	WEEDEN Mercy, of Caleb and Lydia,	Sept. 24, 1750.
1-128	" John, of Daniel and Martha,	April 16, 1754.
1-128	" Judah (a dau.),	Jan. 18, 1756.
1-120	WEIR James, of Daniel and Phebe,	Nov. 9, 1749.
1-20	WELCH Henry, of William and Catherine,	Oct. 1, 1735.
1-18	WELLS James, of Peter, Jr., and Ann,	Sept. 30, 1706.
1-18	" Ann,	Oct. 20, 1708.
1-18	" Rebecca,	Dec. 30, 1710.
1-18	" Peter,	May 4, 1713.
1-18	" John,	April 14, 1716.
1-18	" Samuel,	Feb. 2, 1725.
1-131	" James, of James (of Westerly) and Mary,	Nov. 1, 1732.
1-131	" Barbara,	Aug. 1, 1734.
1-131	" Peter,	Aug. 29, 1737.
1-131	" Barker,	May 16, 1750.
1-131	" Joshua,	Aug. 24, 1753.
2-52	" Thomas Robinson, b. Hopkinton,	Oct. 20, 1785.
2-52	" Maria (Potter, b. Rhinebeck, N. Y.), his wife,	Aug 24, 1790.
2-181	" Thomas Potter, of Thomas R. and Maria,	April 28, 1809.
2-181	" Mary Robinson,	March 20, 1811.
2-181	" Hannah Hagadon,	May 8, 1813.
2-181	" John Hagadon,	Jan. 28, 1817.
2-181	" Elizabeth Maria,	Dec. 15, 1819.
2-181	" Sarah Palmer,	Oct. 12, 1823.
2-181	" Amos Palmer, of —— and Emma, 2d wife,	Sept. 12, 1834.
1-10	WILCOX Mary, of Robert and Sarah,	June 4, 1727-8.
1-10	" Robert,	Sept. 9, 1729.
1-12	" Arnold,	June 7, 1731.
1-22	WILLIAMS McCoon, of Thomas and Thankful,	Aug. 15, 1735.
1-24	" Henry,	Feb. 11, 1736.
1-120	" Thomas,	June 10, 1742.
1-120	" Daniel,	April 2, 1744.
1-120	" Mary,	Feb. 2, 1745.
1-120	" Martha,	April 5, 1747.
1-19	WILSON Mary, of Jeremiah and Mary,	Nov. 13, 1721.
1-19	" Samuel,	March 23, 1723.
1-19	" Jeremiah,	May 11, 1726.
1-19	" John,	May 11, 1726.
1-19	" James,	Sept. 2, 1728.
1-19	" George,	Feb. 7, 1730.
1-19	" Alice,	June 15, 1733.
1-117	" Samuel, of Samuel and Hannah,	Jan. 16, 1746.
1-117	" Samuel, 2d,	Jan. 21, 1747.
1-117	" John, of Samuel and Hannah,	Jan. 25, 1849.

1-138	WILSON John, 2d, of Samuel and Hannah,		March 29, 1752.
1-138	"	James,	May 20, 1754.
1-138	"	Hannah,	Oct. 5, 1756.
1-138	"	George,	Dec. 20, 1758.
1-138	"	William,	Oct. 2, 1761.
1-129	"	George, of Jeremiah and Abigail,	Nov. 26, 1754.
1-129	"	William,	Feb. 24, 1756.
1-129	"	Mary,	Dec. 6, 1759.
1-141	"	John, of John and Hannah,	July 24, 1763.
1-141	"	Hazard,	Not given.
1-141	"	Arnold,	Not given.
1-11	WORDEN Phebe, of Samuel and Abigail,		June 30, 1724.
1-11	"	Benjamin,	June 7, 1726.
1-11	"	Penelope,	March 24, 1728-9.
2-181	WRIGHT Reuben,		June 6, 1807.

X Y Z

2-189	YOST Caroline, of Charles and Margaret,		May 30, 1854.
2-189	"	Charles,	Sept. 10, 1856.
2-189	"	Albert J.,	Feb. 15, 1861.
2-189	"	Louisa,	July 27, 1868.

SOUTH KINGSTOWN.

DEATHS.

A

2-210	ALLEN Ray, aged 60y.,	Feb. 6, 1831.

B

1-139	BABCOCK Caleb, of Hezekiah and Mary,	July 10, 1741.
2-212	" Amie, of Gideon and Hannah, in 19th year,	July 31, 1796.
1-141	BROWNING Mary, of Joseph and Mary,	March 14, 1762.
1-141	" Susannah,	Aug. 26, 1764.
1-141	" William,	Sept. 5, 1767.
1-139	BROWN Sarah, wife of Robert,	May 31, 1750.
2-76	" Benjamin Brenton, of Silas and Frances, aged 6y. 3m. 6d.,	Oct. 17, 1803.
2-112	" Sally, wife of Palmer A., dau. of John R. and Sally Perry; also 2-250, Dec. 9, 1854.	

C

1-155	CASE Anne, wife of Immenuel, Esq., in 37y.,	Nov. 9, 1773.
1-155	" William, of Immenuel and Anne, in 22y.	Oct. 2, 1783.
1-131	CHAPPELL William, of Caleb and Sarah,	April 15, 1758.
1-141	CLARKE Sarah, of John and Mary,	Sept. 23, 1758.

D E F G

1-32	GARDINER Hannah, of John and Mary,	Dec. 31, 1727.
1-140	" Mary, wife of Thomas,	June 9, 1752.
2-231	GOULD John; also 2-250,	Sept. 23, 1828.

H

1-36	HAZARD Thomas, of Robert and Sarah (Berden),	Dec. 2, 1719.
1-139	" Hon. George, Deputy Governor,	June 24, 1738.
1-139	" Jonathan, of Thomas,	Oct. 15, 1746.
1-139	" Benjamin, of George,	Jan. 24, 1748.
1-140	" Sarah, wife of George,	March 17, 1765.
1-140	" Thomas, of George and Sarah,	Nov. 14, 1761.
1-11	HELME Jonathan, of Rouse and Sarah,	May —, 1730.
1-139	" Sands, in Surinam,	May 20, 1738.
1-139	" Simeon, in S. Kingstown,	March 11, 1737.
1-139	" Rouse, Esq.,	Aug. 28, 1751.
1-140	" Esther, wife of James,	March 22, 1764.
2-232	" James, Esq., 67y., 0m., 1 d.,	May 19, 1777.
2-232	" Powell, in 38y.,	April 27, 1780.

2-232	HELME Rouse, Jr., in 46y., of Rouse and Sarah,	Oct. 13, 1789.
2-232	" Nathaniel, Jr., in 28y.,	Nov. 19, 1789.
2-232	" Adam, in 43y.,	Jan. 3, 1794.
2-232	" Alice, wife of James, Jr., in 28y.,	Aug. 16, 1811.
1-152	" Esther, of James and Sarah, 11 1-2m.,	June 14, 1786.
1-152	" Sarah,	Dec. 27, 1792.
1-152	" Mary,	May 13, 1797.
2-113	HOLLAND Edward Hazard,	March 8, 1868.
2-113	" Julia Ann, of Edward H. and Mary Ann,	May 23, 1866.
1-111	HOLWAY .Joseph, of Joseph and Catharine,	Oct. 4, 1744.
1-111	" Catharine, wife of Joseph,	Sept. 15, 1745.
1-111	" Abigail, wife of Joseph,	Nov. 5, 1747.
1-20	HULL Peter Ball, of William (of William) and Mary,	Feb. 13, 1734.
1-140	" Elizabeth, wife of Joseph, 24y. 1m. 16d.,	Oct. 9, 1739.
1-140	" Elizabeth, of Joseph, and Elizabeth,	June 20, 1738.
1-140	" Tristam, of Joseph and Elizabeth, 16y. 4m. 11d.,	Oct. 8, 1750.
1-140	" Thomas, of Joseph and Martha, 2d wife, 4y. 4m. 23d., June 21, 1749.	
1-144	" Charles, of Joseph and Martha, 2d wife, 11w. 7d. 10min., Aug. 23, 1753.	
2-232	" Hannah, wife of Christopher, dan. of John and Hannah (Robinson) Perry; also 2-249, July 1, 1832.	

I J K L

1-138	LEWIS Nathaniel, of Nathaniel and Elizabeth,	—. —, —.

M

1-123	MUMFORD Waite, of Jirah and Mary,	Oct. 7, 1743.
1-123	" Mary,	Dec. 30, 1749.
1-123	" Mary 2d,	Feb. 26, 1752.
2-224	" Mrs. Frances, in 85y.,	Dec. 15, 1814.

N

2-246	NICHOLS William H. H., 20y., 8m., 15d.,	July 21, 1861.
2-246	" Sally T., in 60y.,	Oct. 5, 1872.

O P

1-40	PERKINS Ebenezer, of Edward and Elizabeth,	—. —, —.
2-249	PERRY John B., of Samuel Esq.,	Nov. 19, 1816.
2-249	" Sally, wife of John Robinson, 58y. 11m. 12d., dan. of John and Mary (Gould), March 22, 1847.	
2-249	" William Wanton, of John R. and Sally (Gould), at Hartford Conn., May 21, 1886.	
2-249	" James, of above, 2y. 2m. 8d.,	Aug. 10, 1836.
2-249	" Rowland, of above,	Aug. 22, 1826.
2-249	" John,	Sept. 14, 1834.
2-249	" Hannah, widow of John,	Aug. 29, 1849.
2-249	" John Robinson, 73y. 3m. 24d.	Nov. 24, 1857.
2-249	" John, of James, in New York State,	Sept. 14, 1834.
2-249	" Hannah, his widow,	Aug. 29, 1849.
2 249	PITMAN, Peggy D., wife of George B.,	April 29, 1817.
2-249	" Sarah Ann, of George B. and Peggy D.,	Nov. 6, 1817.
2-249	POLLOCK Lydia, wife of William W., Jr.,	Sept. 21, 1811.
1-140	POTTER Col. John, of John and Sarah,	April 11, 1739.
1-140	" Mary, wife of Col. John,	Oct. 23, 1762.
1-155	" Mary, wife of William (of Robert), in 25th year,	Oct. 14, 1768.

1-136 POTTER Margaret, of Thomas and Elizabeth,   Nov. 24, 1769.
2-144   "   Mary, wife of Elisha R.,   March 7, 1809.
2-144   "   Thomas, of Elisha and Mary,   June 15, 1814.
2-249   "   Mary, wife of Elisha R., dau. of Pardon Mawney, at brother-in-law, Jeffrey Davis, in North Kingstown, July 26, 1835.
2-249   "   Elisha R.,   Sept. 26, 1835.

Q R

1-150 REYNOLDS James, of Henry and Mary,   Aug. 28, 1769.
1-150   "   Thomas, of Henry and Mary,   Sept. 16, 1773.
1-155   "   Susannah, wife of Elisha, 84y., 14d.,   March 10, 1790.
1-155   "   Col. Elisha,   Nov. —, 1791.
1-9 ROBINSON Mary, of William and Martha,   April 16, 1723.
1-139   "   Hon William,   Sept. 19, 1731.
1-148   "   Sarah, wife of John, in 31y.; also 1-156,   Jan. 11, 1775.
2-256 RODMAN Second son of Isaac P. and Sally,   March 3, 1856.

S

2-164 SEAGER Sarah, of John and Abigail,   Dec. 20, 1792.
1-149 SHELDON Elizabeth, wife of John, in 40y.,   Nov. 23, 1763.

T

1-156 TAYLOR William, late of Barnstable, Eng.,   Sept. 21, 1770.

U V W

1-139 WATSON Elisha,   Sept. 11, 1737.
1-140   "   Isabel, wife of John, Jr.,   May 22, 1753.
1-82 WORDEN Samuel,   Sept. 17, 1727.
2-268 WRIGHT, Reuben, 76y. 6m.,   Nov. 18, 1883.

X Y Z

1-140 YORK Elizabeth, widow of James, of Charlestown, in South Kingstown, in 78y., March 27, 1784.

Vital Record of Rhode Island.

1636=1850.

FIRST SERIES.

BIRTHS, MARRIAGES AND DEATHS.

A Family Register for the People.

BY JAMES N. ARNOLD,

EDITOR OF THE NARRAGANSETT HISTORICAL REGISTER.

"Is My Name Written in the Book of Life?"

Vol. 5.   EXETER.   Part III.

Published under the Auspices of the General Assembly.

PROVIDENCE, R. I:
NARRAGANSETT HISTORICAL PUBLISHING COMPANY.
1894.

ACT INCORPORATING THE TOWN OF EXETER.

AN ACT for incorporating the west end of the Town of North Kingstown into a Township, and the same to be distinguished and known by the name of Exeter.

Be it enacted by the General Assembly of this Colony, and by the authoriety thereof it is enacted that the Town of North Kingstown, in the County of King's County, be divided into two Towns, by a line beginning at the south side of said Town, at the middle of the highway that runs between the farm, now or late of Jeoffry Haszard. and the farm of Eber Sherman, to extend from thence northerly to the extent of said highway, as the same runs northwardly; and from the middle of said way, where it meets the cross highway, to extend northwardly in a straight line, to meet the highway that runs between the land of William Hall and Christopher Spencer; and from thence to extend northwardly, as said highway runs to East Greenwich, south lines and that the eastward part of said Town retain the Charter, and name of NORTH KINGSTOWN, and the western part to be called by the name of EXETER, and be incorporated into a Township; and to have and enjoy the like privileges with other Towns in this Colony.

And be it further enacted by the authority aforesaid, that each Town receive, and have a proportion of the money in, and belonging to, the Treasury of said North Kingstown, acording to the money for which the lands in each Town is mortgaged to the Colony; and that all Justices living within the bounds of said new Town, retain their authoriety, and act as such therein, until the next General Election.

Colonial Records of Rhode Island, Vol. V., pages 57, 58.

EXETER.

MARRIAGES.

A

3-220   ADAMS Esther, and Sheffield Rathbun, Jan. 1, 1833.

3-42   ALBRO Thomas, of Exeter, and Sarah Hopkins, of West Greenwich; m. by the Rev. James Weightman, Jan. 27, 1772.

3-29   "   Ruth, and Waite Albro, Jan. 25, 1776.

3-29   "   Waite, son of Elder Samuel, of Exeter, and Ruth Albro, dau. of John, of Exeter; m. by Rev. James Weightman, Jan. 25, 1776.

3-138   "   Oliver, and Olive Crandall; m. by Thomas Allen, Justice, Feb. 18, 1793.

3-273   "   Amie, and Jeremiah Franklin, May 30, 1819.

3-175   "   Jebus (sic), of Waite, both of Exeter, and Edith Lewis, of Exeter, dau. of Capt. Stephen; m. by Elder Thomas Manchester, ——.

2-166   ALDRICH Martha, and John Angell, Feb. 4, 1765.

3-191   "   Sarah, and John Shippee, ——.

1-191   ALLEN Margeret, and Benjamin Nichols, Nov. 27, 1757.

1-154   "   William, and Mercy Mumford; m. by Stephen Richmond, Justice, Dec. 17, 1761.

3-15   "   Chloe, and David Hill, Feb. 11, 1770.

3-55   "   Patience, and David Davis, Feb. 9, 1715.

3-115   "   Penelope, and Daniel Champlin, Dec. 22, 1778.

3-13   "   George W., and Lucy Ann Dupuy; m. by Elder Benedic Johnson, Aug. 30, 1841.

3-104   "   Mrs. Louisee, and Joseph C. Reynolds, April 25, 1853.

3-111   ANDREWS Peleg, of Exeter, son of Samuel, and Jemima Hunt, of North Kingstown dau. of George; m. at North Kingstown, by Elder John Gardiner, Nov. 10, 1816.

3-14   "   Martha R., and Russell J. Barber, Sept. 13, 1841.

3-279   "   Mary, and Charles Lewis, June 23, ——.

2-166   ANGELL John, of Johnston, R. I., and Martha Aldrich, of Exeter; m. by Elder Samuel Albr , Feb. 4, 1765.

1-188   ARNOLD Abigail, and Stephen Watson, Sept. 4, 1757.

1-157   "   Stephen, of North Kingstown, and Martha Gardiner, of Exeter, dau. of Nicholas; m. by Benjamin Reynolds, Justice, March 3, 1760.

3-4   "   Mary, and Joseph Reynolds, Oct. 29, 1769.

3-5   "   Sarah, and Amos Whitford, March 28, 1770.

3-66   "   Oliver, of North Kingstown, son of Joseph, and Hannah Reynolds, of Exeter, dau. of Joseph; m. by George Pierce, Justice, Nov. 24, 1782.

3-128   "   Oliver, and Phebe Lawton; m. by Elder Solomon Sprague, May 8, 1785.

3-79   "   Gideon, and Rebecca Rathbun; m. by Elder Solomon Sprague, Aug. 18, 1785.

3-83   "   Peleg, and Lucy Hopkins; m. by Elder Solomon Sprague, Oct. 20, 1785.

3-93   "   Hannah, and Silas Pierce, Nov. 24, 1785.

3-114   "   Russell, of Caleb, and Merabah Terry, dau. of William Booth, of Exeter; m. by Stephen Reynolds, Justice, Oct. 24, 1790.

3-160   "   Deborah, and Jeremiah Northup, May 25, 1794.

3-271   ARNOLD Mary, and Avery Browning, July 17, 1808.
3-276   "   Lucy, and Daniel G. Champlain, Dec. 22, 1814.
3-83   "   Rowland, of Exeter, and Elizabeth Ellis, dau. of Arnold, of West
             Greenwich; m. by Elder Gershom Palmer, Feb. 18, 1816.
3-46   "   Freelove B., and Samuel Hopkins, Nov. 7, 1824.
3-184   "   Abbie, and Nicholas Gardiner, May 16, 1826.
3-184   "   Elizabeth, and Phillip Tillinghast, May 4, 1826.
3-277   "   Esther, and Samuel Arnold, April 16, 1839.
3-277   "   Samuel, and Esther Arnold, both of North Kingstown; m. by
             Elder Benedick Johnson, April 16, 1839.
1-243   AUSTIN Jemima, and Gideon Ellis, Feb. 14, 1744.
1-238   "   Freelove, and Benjn. Sherman, March 16, 1744.
1-191   "   Sarah, and Moses Sherman, March 31, 1745.
1-180   "   Margaret, and Thomas Hill, Feb. 15, 1753.
1-186   "   Jeremiah, and Hannah Harrington, both of Exeter, by Benoni
             Hall, Justice, April 13, 1756.
1-187   "   Paskow, and Mary Northup, by Elder Samuel Albro, Sept. 5, 1756.
1-156   "   Jeremiah, of Exeter, and Isabel Little, by Elder Samuel Albro,
             Sept. 28, 1760.
3-5   "   William, of R., son of Joseph, and Martha Rogers, by Newman
             Perkins, Justice, Feb. 4, 1770.
3-89   "   Mary, and John Carr, May 12, 1786.
3-275   "   Abigail, and Richard Corey, Jr., May 11, 1816.
3-19   "   Abbie, and Barber Kenyon, Jan. 5, 1845.
1-182   AYLESWORTH Phillip, Jr., of North Kingstown, and Deborah Dyre, of
             Exeter, widow of William, of said North Kingstown; m. at
             Exeter by Benoni Hall, Justice, July 1, 1753.
1-190   "   Amie, and Joshua Rathbun, Jan. 2, 1755.
1-194   "   Mary, and Jeremiah Niles, Dec. 8, 1755.
3-29   "   John, of East Greenwich, son of Anthony, dec., and Bethana Fry,
             of Exeter, dau. of James; at Exeter, by George Pierce, Jus-
             tice, March 4, 1771.
3-52   "   Anna, and William Petty, Sept. 2, 1772.

B

1-189   BABCOCK Joseph, of Samuel, and Sarah Waite, of John; by Benjamin
             Reynolds, Justice, Feb. 9, 1758.
1-199   "   Deborah, and Asa Moon, Aug. 13, 1758.
1-155   "   Lydia, and Joseph Holloway, Oct. 11, 1761.
3-27   "   George Waite of Exeter, son of John, and Susannah Fowler, dau.
             of Simeon, of Exeter; by Elder Solomon Sprague, Feb. 21, 1771.
3-220   "   Penelope, and Sheffield Rathbun, Dec. 20, 1829.
1-188   BAILEY Robert, of East Greenwich, and Phebe Waite, of Exeter; by Elder
             Samuel Albro, Jan. 28, 1738.
3-223   "   Ely S., son of Col. Silas, of West Greenwich, and Mercy Clarke,
             dau. of James, of Exeter; by Elder Thomas Manchester, Jan.
             26, 1806.
3-281   "   Sarah, dau. of Job, and Seth Lewis, Sept. 22, 1849.
1-244   BAKER Mary, and Phillip Greene, Dec. 31, 1750.
1-177   "   Elisha, of Exeter, and Sarah Harrington, of Job; by Benoni
             Hall, Justice, Feb. 6, 1752.
1-177   "   Susannah, and Joseph Sunderland, Feb. 7, 1752.
1-190   "   Abel, of North Kingstown, and Anne Reynolds, dau. of George;
             by Benoni Hall, Justice, Oct. 7, 1758.
1-160   "   Asa, and William Cahoone, May 20, 1759.
1-193   "   Mary, and Giles Brownell, June 3, 1759.
2-165   "   William, Jr., of Exeter, and Anne Gardiner, of West Greenwich;
             m. by David Stanton, Justice, June 22, 1764.
2-171   "   Sarah, and Pheneas Solomon Lemoine, Feb. 19, 1768.
3-46   "   Sarah, and William Harrington, Oct. 10, 1771.
1-194   BARBER Mary, and Jonathan Barney, Dec. 1, 1754.
1-194   "   Zebulon, and Elizabeth Nichols; m. by Newman Perkins,
             Justice, March 21, 1755.

1-187	BARBER	Eleanor, and Josias Barber, Nov. 20, 1756.
1-187	"	Josias, and Eleanor Barber; m. by Rev. Daniel Barber, Nov. 20, 1756.
1-195	"	Susannah, and Jonathan Rathbun, March 3, 1757.
1-158	"	Susannah, and Jeremiah Coldgrove, Oct. 18, 1759.
1-153	"	Mary, and John Wilcox, Jan. 31, 1762.
3-13	"	Daniel, of Daniel, of Exeter, and Charity Rathbun, of John, of do.; by Daniel Sunderland, Justice, Aug. 11, 1769.
3-16	"	Deliverance, and Joseph Barber, Jan. 6, 1770.
3-16	"	Joseph, of Hopkinton, son of William, and Deliverance Barber, of Daniel, of Exeter; by Daniel Sunderland, Justice, Jan. 8, 1770.
3-7	"	Lydia, and Daniel Lewis, March 21, 1770.
3-132	"	Rebecca, and Isaac Wilcox, Jan. 7, 1773.
3-26	"	Levi, son of Nicholas, and Elizabeth Ney, of John; m. by Gideon Moshier, Justice, April 29, 1773.
3-26	"	Lillibridge, of Susannah, of Exeter, and Alice Wilcox, of Abraham, of Exeter; by Newman Perkins, Justice, Dec. 30, 1773.
3-58	"	Thankful, and James Lewis, Jan. 15, 1775.
3-198	"	Asa, of Hopkinton, son of Josiah, and Meriam Barber, of Daniel, of Exeter; m. by Elder Solomon Sprague, May 13, 1780.
3-198	"	Meriam, and Asa Barber, May 13, 1780.
3-150	"	Henry, of Exeter, son of Capt. Jonathan, and Anne Rathbun, of Simeon, of Exeter; by Jeffrey Hazard, Justice, Nov. 1, 1792.
3-156	"	Mary, and Daniel James, Feb. 5, 1793.
3-155	"	Moses, Jr., of Exeter, son of Moses, and Mary Clarke, of Richmond, dau. of Moses; m. by Elder Henry Joslin, March 20, 1794.
3-173	"	Wilcox, of Lillibridge, of Exeter, and Mrs. Patience Tefft, of Hezekiah, of Richmond; by J. W. Sheldon, Justice, June 1, 1797.
3-208	"	Ruth, and Samuel Lewis, Jr., March 2, 1797.
3-193	"	Susannah, and John Browning, March 2, 1797.
3-182	"	Alce, and Thomas Tillinghast, Feb. 7, 1799.
3-210	"	Alce, and Isaac Wilcox, Feb. 10, 1803.
3-226	"	Polly, and John Wilcox,, Sept. 1, 1805.
3-239	"	Rhoda, and Caleb Hall, March 16, 1808.
3-240	"	Gardiner, and Eleanor Lewis; by Elder Matthew Stillman, April 17, 1808.
3-253	"	Reuben, and Mary Terry; by Elder Phineas Palmer, Feb. 18, 1810.
3-274	"	Joanna, and Job Reynolds, Feb. 17, 1811.
3-281	"	Hannah, and Daniel Lillibridge, Aug. 18, 1811.
3-299	"	Learnard E., of Lillibridge, and Phebe B. Rathbun, of Rowland; by Elder Gersham Palmer, Nov. 21, 1816.
3-307	"	Thomas C., and Susan Congdon; by Elder Gershom Palmer, Feb. 2, 1824.
3-124	"	Silas B., of Samuel, and Lydia Lewis of Simon; by Elder Peleg Peckham, June 6, 1824.
3-300	"	Mrs. Nellie, and Roswell Palmer, Oct. 29, 1829.
3-280	"	Rowland R., of Norwich, Conn., and Mary Browning of Exeter; by Elder Benedick Johnson, Jan. 12, 1840.
3-13	"	Rachel, and Joseph W. Lillibridge, Sept. 6, 1841.
3-14	"	Russell J., of Exeter, and Martha R. Andrews of Richmond; by Elder Benedick Johnson, Sept. 13, 1841.
3-241	"	Edward, of Samuel, and Sally B. Rathbun of Rowland; by Elder John Tillinghast, April 9, 1844.
3-71	"	Mary, and Beriah Ney, Dec. 2, 1844.
3-16	"	Benjamin T., of Robert, of Exeter, and Maria Champlain, of Ethan, of Hopkinton, by Elder Daniel Slocum, April 14, 1845.
3-10	"	Hiram, of South Kingstown, son of Moses, and Susan E. Sherman, of Samuel, of Exeter, by Elder Ezekiel J. Locke, Dec. 28, 1845.
3-269	"	Thomas D., of Hopkinton, and Olive Lewis, of Exeter, by Elder Thomas Tillinghast, March 9, 1846.
3-228	"	Mary, and Thomas Woodmansee, Dec. 12, 1848.
3-228	"	Samuel K., of Hopkinton, and Hannah Tillinghast, of Exeter, by Elder Thomas Tillinghast, Dec. 12, 1848.
3-205	"	Delia, and John Sarle, June 10, 1849.

3-237 BARBER Jesse W., of Hopkinton, and Mary A. Lewis of Voluntown, by
          Rev. J. G. Post, July 3, 1853.
1-194 BARNEY Jonathan, of Newport, and Mary Barber of Exeter, by Newman
          Perkins, Justice, Dec. 1, 1754.
1-159 BATES John, of Exeter, and Still Morey, of Exeter, dau. of Joseph, by
          Benjamin Reynolds, Justice, Aug. 10, 1759.
1-156   "   Hannah, and Benjamin Bentley, Aug. 23, 1761.
2-170   "   Mary, and William Heffernan (also 3-96), Feb. 8, 1767.
3-15   "   George, of Jonathan, and Joanna Briggs, of Peleg, by Jonathan
               Bates, Justice, Dec. 14, 1779.
3-136   "   Elizabeth, and Lebbeus Wilcox, June 27, 1793.
3-9   "   Benjamin, of John, and Rebecca Wilcox, dau. of Abraham Booth, of
               Exeter, by Elder Elisha Greene, Jan. 28, 1793.
3-10   "   Mary W., and John Davis Mius, July 28, 1811.
3-15   "   Morcy, of Exeter, and Hannah Potter, of Richmond, at Rich-
               mond, by Elder Henry C. Hubbard, June 18, 1826.
3-298   "   Olive, and Thomas T. Wilcox, Oct. 21, 1829.
3-169   "   Perry, of Mowry, of Exeter, and Eliza Clarke, of Ann, of Rich-
               mond, by Elder Daniel Slocum, July 2, 1846.
3-185   "   James W., of Philip, and Harriet N. Palmer, of Gershom, by
               Elder Ezekiel J. Locke, Nov. 8, 1847.
3-95   "   Lewis, of Morey, of Exeter, and Nancy Matteson, widow of
               Joseph, late of Coventry, dec., by Elder Isaac Greene, Oct.
               1, 1854.
3-217 BATEN Benjamin, of East Greenwich, and Caroline F. Knight, of Warwick,
          R. I., by Elder Daniel Slocum, Nov. 27, 1843.
3-178   "   Francis E., of East Greenwich, and Massena Sunderland, of
               Warwick, by Elder Daniel Slocum, Aug. 19, 1844.
3-230 BENJAMIN Betsey, and Job Kenyon, Feb. 15, 1807.
3-182 BENNETT Harriet, and Ezekiel W. Matteson, Sept. 25, 1843.
2-177 BENSON John, and Mercy Casey, by Hopson Wilcox, Justice, April 28,
          1768.
1-132 BENTLEY Hannah, and Robert Reynolds, July 15, 1753.
1-185   "   Tillinghast, of Exeter, and Sarah Thomas, now of South
               Kingstown; by Elder Samuel Albro, May 29, 1755.
1-155   "   Benjamin, and Hannah Bates, by Elder Samuel Albro, Aug. 23,
               1761.
3-11   "   Anna, and James Coldgrove, Jan. 12, 1766.
3-60   "   Benjamin, Jr., and Ruth Fowler, by Elder James Weightman, Aug.
               24, 1780.
3-34   "   Gideon, of Exeter, and Elizabeth Neagers, of North Kingstown, by
               Elder James Weightman, April 5, 1781.
3-77   "   Lucy, and Benjamin Reynolds, Dec. 22, 1785.
3-110   "   Nathaniel, of Exeter, and Sarah Card, of Richmond, by Elder Henry
               Joslin, Dec. 24, 1789.
1-156 BILL Hannah, and John Hoxsie, May 21, 1761.
1-189 BISSELL Anna, and Thomas Wells, June 9, 1758.
2-167   "   Samuel, and Mary Frazier, both of North Kingstown, by Elder
               Samuel Albro, March 2, 1766.
3-92   "   David, son of Samuel, and Elizabeth West, dau. of Capt. Benjamin,
               by George Pierce, Justice of Peace, March 10, 1785.
3-110 BLY Job, of Job, of Voluntown, Conn., and Freelove Watson, of Stephen,
          of Exeter, by Job Kenyon, Justice of Peace, July 14, 1811.
3-104 BOONE Orpha, and John Gorton, June 18, 1789.
3-176   "   Richard, Jr., of Exeter, and Betsey Sheffield, of Voluntown,
               Conn., by Allen Campbell, Justice, April 23, 1795.
3-170   "   James, of Richard, of Exeter, and Patience Terry, of Silas, of
               Charlestown, by Peleg Cross, Justice, Jan. 8, 1797.
3-192   "   Elizabeth, and Stephen Vaughn, Dec. 16, 1799.
3-237   "   Sarah, and James Clarke, Feb. 28, 1805.
1-243 BOSS Edward, of Richmond, and Mary Nichols, of Exeter, dau. of James,
          by Robert Moon, Justice, Oct. 22, 1748.
3-68   "   Mary (widow), and Abraham Wilcox, Dec. 13, 1791.
3-75   "   Elizabeth, and John Browning, Jan. 12, 1817.
3-286 BOWEN Desire M., and Benoni Wells, April 3, 1836.

1-188	BOWDISH Mary, and Jeremiah Gardiner, June 23, 1757.	
3-55	" Martha, and Jonathan Lewis, Aug. 12, 1779.	
1-237	BRAGMAN Solomon, of Exeter, and Content Mumford, of South Kingstown, by Elder David Sprague, April 9, 1744.	
3-235	" Lucy, and Joshua Vaughn, Dec. 31, 1798.	
3-18	" Ann, and William C. Potter, April 20, 1843.	
3-15	BRIGGS Joanna, and George Bates, Dec. 14, 1779.	
3-97	" Peleg, Jr., of Exeter, and Elizabeth Chambers, of Newport, by Nicholas Gardiner, of East Greenwich, Justice, Oct. 15, 1786.	
3-181	" Mercy, and Samuel Holloway, March 17, 1794.	
3-292	" Mary Ann, and George Ray Palmer, May 18, 1823.	
3-196	" Cynthia, and William R. Kenyon, Oct. 3, 1842.	
3-185	" Charles H., of South Kingstown, son of Gorton, and Elizabeth H. Woodmansee, of Richmond, by Elder E. J. Locke, Nov. 10, 1847.	
1-241	BROWN Ann, and Mitchell Case, March 1, 1743.	
1-180	" James, and Damarius Tombs, by Nicholas Gardiner, Justice, Dec. 7, 1752.	
1-196	" Jeremiah, of South Kingstown, and Amie Tanner, of Exeter, by Caleb Arnold, Justice, Jan. 19, 1758.	
2-181	" Sarah, and Caleb Greene, April 16, 1769.	
3-26	" Sarah, and Jenckes Wright, Feb. 11, 1779.	
3-57	" Penelope, and Daniel Tillinghast, Oct. 17, 1779.	
3-130	" Eleanor, and Timothy Money, Dec. 9, 1792.	
3-202	" Freelove, and Rowland Rathbun, May 11, 1794.	
3-297	" Dinah, and Fortune Congdon, Aug. 16, 1829.	
3-277	" Ebenezer, and Almy Franklin, by Elder Benedict Johnson, April 21, 1839.	
3-15	" Hannah, and Albert Himes, Dec. 5, 1841.	
3-15	" Stukeley, of Exeter, and Susan Ann Sanford, of West Kingstown, by Elder Benedict Johnson, Jan. 24, 1842.	
3-230	" Elisha, and Louisa Capwell, both of West Greenwich, by Elder Daniel Slocum, Sept. 24, 1843.	
3-155	" Martha, and Samuel A. Lawton, Oct. 9, 1843.	
3-177	" Dianna, and Burrell Hopkins, Feb. 22, 1844.	
3-314	" Ambrose, of Seth, and Lydia Lewis, of Thomas, at Exeter, by Elder John Tillinghast, Sept. 17, 1848.	
1-193	BROWNELL Giles, and Mary Baker, of John, late of Exeter, deceased, by Benoni Hall, Justice, June 3, 1759.	
3-6	" Mary, and Abel Fowler, June 3, 1770.	
3-74	BROWNING John, and May Davis, Feb. 28, 1765.	
3-74	" John, and Eunice Williams, Aug. 3, 1777.	
3-193	" John, of John, and Susannah Barber, of Lillibridge, by Elder Elisha Greene, March 2, 1797.	
3-217	" Eunice, and Preserved Hall, April 12, 1804.	
3-271	" Avery, of John and Mary, and Mary Arnold, of Peleg, by Elder Gershom Palmer, July 17, 1808.	
3-75	" John, of Exeter, and Elizabeth Boss, of West Greenwich, by Elder Stafford Greene, Jan. 12, 1817.	
3-280	" Mary, and Rowland R. Barber, Jan. 12, 1840.	
3-229	BURDICK Rawson P., of Hopkinton, and Lydia N. Palmer, of Exeter, by Elder Charles A. Weaver, April 3, 1843.	

C

1-160	CAHOONE William, of Exeter, and Asa Baker, of West Greenwich, by Elder Samuel Albro, May 20, 1759.	
1-154	" Reynolds, and Rebecca Rathbun, by Elder Samuel Albro, Nov. 5, 1761.	
2-179	" Reynolds, and Mercy Rathbun, by Elder Philip Jenkins, Feb. 12, 1769.	
2-167	CAMMELL Deborah, and Jeremiah Greene, July 20, 1765.	
3-230	CAPWELL Louisa, and Elisha Brown, Sept. 24, 1843.	
3-227	CARDEN Mary Ann, and Charles Phillips, Feb. 29, 1852.	
3-68	CARD Mary, and Abraham Wilcox, Feb. 14, 1770.	
3-110	" Sarah, and Nathaniel Bentley, Dec. 24, 1789.	

2-177   CARNEY Rachel, and George Codner, Feb. 20, 1769.
1-241   CARPENTER Hannah, and Benjamin Rathbun, Oct. 31, 1732.
3-11   "   Thankful Knowles, and Wm. Waite Potter, Sept. 7, 1816.
3-23   CARR Abigail, and John Congdon, March 8, 1778.
3-12   "   Freelove, and Elder Nathan Hill, June 6, 1782.
3-89   "   John, of Jamestown, and Mary Austin of Exeter, by Daniel
              Sunderland, Justice, May 12. 1786.
3-244   "   Hannah, and Michael Dawley, Jan. 19, 1809.
3-5   "   Mary, and Giles S. Jenkins, Feb. 13, 1825.
3-286   CARTER Sally, and John Mycock, Jan. 25, 1846.
1-243   CASEY Gideon, and Jane Roberts, by Peleg Tripp, Justice, July 31, 1747.
2-177   "   Mercy, and John Benson, April 28, 1768.
3-273   "   Sarah, and John Rathbun, Oct. 10, 1776.
1-241   CASE Mitchell, of South Kingstown, and Ann Brown, of North Kingstown,
              by Elder David Sprague, March 1, 1743.
2-165   "   Joseph, of North Kingstown, and Abigail Waite of Exeter, by
              Elder Samuel Albro, Dec. 29, 1763.
3-65   "   Elijah, of Alexander, and Silence Potter, of Joseph, by Elder
              Solomon Sprague, —— —, 1774.
3-63   "   Samuel, of West Greenwich, and Cate Wheeler Crandall, of Exeter,
              by Elder Ellet Locke, Nov. 26, 1780.
3-127   CHACE Hannah Huling Abbie, and George Whitman, Oct. 3, 1790.
3-97   CHAMBERS Elizabeth, and Peleg Briggs, Oct. 15, 1786.
2-166   CHAPMAN John, of Exeter, and Elizabeth Clarke, of Joseph, of North
              Kingstown, by Caleb Allen, Justice, Jan. 8, 1765.
3-15   "   Rufus, of Warwick, R. I., and Dorcas Sewall, of Exeter, by Elder
              Solomon Sprague, May 19, 1770.
3-131   "   Mary, and Jeremiah Peckham, Sept. 27, 1792.
1-186   CHAMPLAIN Elizabeth, and John Gardiner, June 3, 1756.
2-163   "   Benjamin, and Elizabeth Gardiner, by Elder Samuel Albro, Feb.
              8, 1763.
2-166   "   Christopher, and Mary Cottrell, (also 3-1), by Elder Samuel Albro,
              Feb. 27, 1763.
3-16   "   Susannah, and Arnold Wilcox. Jan. 22, 1767.
3-64   "   Jeffrey, of Jeffrey, of Exeter, and Hannah Hazard, of South Kings-
              town, dau. of Robert. dec., by Elder Solomon Sprague, April
              1, 1777.
3-75   "   Samuel, of Exeter, and Alice Reynolds, of Benjamin, by Elder
              Nathan Hill, Dec. 10, 1782.
3-73   "   Thomas, of John, of Exeter, and Thankful Coone, of Joseph, of
              Voluntown, Conn., by Jonathan Dutes, Justice, Dec. 17, 1783.
3-115   "   Daniel, of Benjamin, of Exeter, and Penelope Allen, of Matthew,
              of North Kingstown, by Elder Nathan Hill, Dec. 22, 1788.
3-120   "   William, of John, dec., and Abigail Sherman, of Eber, by Stephen
              Reynolds, Justice, April 5, 1790.
3-141   "   Stephen, and Dorcas Dawley, by Elder Ellet Locke, Feb. 9, 1796.
3-284   "   George G., of Exeter, and Mary Wilcox, of South Kingstown, by
              Elder Phenens Palmer, Dec. 1, 1811.
3-276   "   Daniel G., of Daniel, and Lucy Arnold, of Oliver, by Elder Gersham
              Palmer, Dec. 22, 1814.
3-299   "   Waity, and Samuel C Potter, Jan. 2, 1831.
3-17   "   Dorcas, and Nelson B. Hazard, Dec. 19, 1841.
3-16   "   Maria, and Benj. T. Barber, April 14, 1845.
2-171   CHURCH Benedict of Jamestown, and Martha Wilkey, of Jeremiah, of
              Exeter; by William Hall, Justice. March 14, 1768.
3-241   "   Phebe Ann, and James Tew, March 22, 1836.
3-308   "   Susan E., and Palmer G. Perkins, Jan. 4, 1852.
1-181   CLARKE Mary, and Thomas Rathbun, June 3, 1753.
1-187   "   Mary, and Caleb Gardiner, March 7, 1754.
1-156   "   Joshua, of Richmond, and Dorcas Smith, of Simon, of Exeter; by
              Benjamin Reynolds, Justice, April 23, 1760.
2-166   "   Anne, and Robert Gardiner, Sept. 28, 1764.
2-166   "   Elizabeth, and John Chapman, Jan. 8, 1765.
2-171   "   William, of Jonathan, of Newport, and Catharine Stanton, of Exe-
              ter, dau. of David; by George Pierce, Justice, May 10, 1767.

3-28	CLARKE	Benjamin, of N. Kingstown, son of Joseph, of Warwick, R. I., and Patience Rathbun, of John, of Exeter, by Jonathan Bates, Justice, Jan. 2, 1780.
3-71	"	Abigail, and Joseph Walte, Feb. 23, 1783.
3-166	"	John, of James and Barberry, and Mary Waite, of Benj. and Sarah, by Elder William Northnp, Jan. 17, 1786.
3-155	"	Mary, and Moses Barber, March 20, 1794.
3-172	"	Phebe, and Job Dawley, March 16, 1797.
3-179	"	Moses, Jr., of Moses, of Richmond, and Abigail Reynolds, of Stephen, by Elder Henry Joslin, Feb. 22, 1798.
3-237	"	James, Jr., of James, and Sarah Boone, of Richard, by Elder Stephen Allen, Feb. 28, 1805.
3-223	"	Mercy, and Ely S. Bailey, Jan. 26, 1806.
3-255	"	James, and Hannah Sepson, by Elder Gershom Palmer, Oct. 27, 1811.
3-289	"	Susannah, and Daniel Slocum, Oct. 24, 1822
3-110	"	Lydia (widow), and Robert Richmond, Dec. 21, 1826.
3-283	"	Deborah P., and Nicholas Marsh, Feb. 21, 1840.
3-169	"	Eliza, and Perry Bates, July 2, 1846.
3-8	CLAWSON	Bethany, and John Wilkey, June 24, 1770.
1-237	CLEAVELAND	Mercy, and Thomas Stafford, Nov. 25, 1743.
3-2	"	Margaret, and Peter Wells, Nov. 19, 1769.
3-145	"	Deliverance, and Benjamin Lewis, Feb. 10, 1780.
3-94	COBB	Hannah, and Jonathan Rogers, Feb. 18, 1781.
3-99	"	Lucy, and Benjamin Rogers, Dec. 27, 1787.
1-243	CODNER	Ephariam, of Exeter, and Mary Morey, of South Kingstown, by Robert Moon, Justice of Peace, Nov. 20, 1748.
2-166	"	David, and Martha Wilbur, by Newman Perkins, Justice, Jan. 16, 1763.
2-177	"	George, of Ephariam, and Rachel Carney, by Newman Perkins, Justice, Feb. 20, 1769.
3-247	"	John C., of Exeter, son of Elizabeth, and Fannie Tillinghast, of John, late of Exeter, dec., by Stephen Champlain, Justice, July 22, 1810.
1-190	COLDGROVE	Mary, and David Pittey, April 23, 1758.
1-158	"	Jeremiah, and Snsannah Barber, of Thomas, by Newman Perkins, Justice, Oct. 18, 1759.
1-158	"	Mary, and Samuel Coldgrove, Oct. 18, 1759.
1-158	"	Samuel, and Mary Coldgrove, both of Coventry, R. I., by Newman Perkins, Justice, Oct. 18, 1759.
1-158	"	Benjamin, of Coventry, R. I., son of Stephen and Sarah Coldgrove, of Exeter, dau. of Ebenezer, by Newman Perkins, Justice, Oct. 21, 1759.
1-158	"	Sarah, and Benjamin Coldgrove, Oct. 21, 1759.
3-11	"	James, of Exeter, and Anna Bentley, of South Kingstown, by Daniel Sunderland, Justice, Jan. 12, 1766.
3-197	COMSTOCK	Joel, of Jonathan, of West Greenwich, and Hannah Lawton, of James, of Exeter, by Elder Henry Joslin, Aug. 19, 1798.
1-182	CONGDON	Elizabeth, and Samuel Gardiner, May 3, 1750.
1-181	"	John, son of James, dec., and Mary Reynolds, of John, by Benoni Hall, Justice, March 25, 1753.
3-23	"	John, of Exeter, and Mrs. Naomi Tew, of Jamestown, at Jamestown, by Benjamin Underwood, Justice, Oct. 22, 1770.
3-23	"	John, of Exeter, and Abigail Carr, of Jamestown, by Elder Solomon Sprague, March 8, 1778.
3-9	"	John, Jr., of Exeter, son of John, and Sarah Morris, of Newport, dau. of William, by Jonathan Bates, Jr., Justice, March 1, 1781.
3-76	"	Benjamin, of Exeter, son of John, and Sarah Sweet, of Warwick, at Exeter, by George Pierce, Justice, Sept. 11, 1785.
3-245	"	Jonathan, of John, late of Exeter, dec., and Abigail Whitman, of James, by Jonathan Pitcher, Justice, April 13, 1809.
3-307	"	Susan, and Thomas C. Barber, Feb. 2, 1824.
3-297	"	Fortune, and Dinah Brown, now residing in Exeter, by Isaac Greene, Justice, Aug. 16, 1829.

3-289   CONGDON Sally M., and William W. Tillinghast, July 3, 1843.
8-309   "   Emeline, and Joseph H. Congdon, Sept. 6, 1846.
3-309   "   Joseph J. H., son of Nancy, of North Kingstown, and Emeline
                Congdon, of Matilda, of Charlestown, at Exeter, by Elder
                Daniel Slocum, Sept. 6, 1846.
3-103   "   Susan A., and William A. Morriss, Aug. 27, 1849.
3-73   COONE Thankful, and Thomas Champlain, Dec. 17, 1783.
3-122   "   Nancy, and Newman Perkins, July 9, 1791.
3-284   "   Almira, and Arnold Ellis, March 30, 1845.
2-177   CAREY Prudence, and Uriah Perkins, July 1, 1768.
3-275   "   Richard, Jr., and Abigail Austin, of Solomon, by Elder Gershom
                Palmer, May 11, 1816.
3-312   CORNELL Benjamin, of Warren, Bradford Co., Penn., now residing in
                Exeter, and Mrs. Susan A. Wilbur, of Richmond, now re-
                siding in Coventry, by Elder Thomas Tillinghast, Jan. 21, 1841.
1-185   CORPSE Mary, and James Whitford, Dec. 1, 1754.
1-177   COTTRELL Samuel, and Susannah Reynolds, by Elder David Sprague, Feb.
                6, 1752.
1-192   "   Nathaniel, Jr., and Martha Reynolds, of George, by Benjamin Rey-
                nolds, Justice, Dec. 21, 1758.
2-163   "   Nathaniel, and Sarah Smith, by Elder Samuel Albro, June 10,
                1762.
2-166   "   Mary, and Christopher Champlain, (also 3-1), Feb. 27, 1763.
3-14   "   Sarah, and Benjamin Reynolds, Aug. 27, 1769.
3-70   "   Abigail, and Stephen Reynolds, March 3, 1774.
3-7   "   David, of Nathaniel, of Exeter, and Sarah Sherman, of Benoni, of
                North Kingstown, by Elder William Northup, Jan. 28, 1817.
2-163   CRANDALL Sarah, and Christopher Harrington, Nov. 16, 1762.
2-181   "   John, Jr., of Exeter, son of John, and Kezia Shaw, of Voluntown,
                Conn., dau. of Thomas, by Newman Perkins, Justice, May 18,
                1768.
2-177   "   Hannah, and Thomas James, July 3, 1768.
3-2   "   John, of Exeter, and Phillia Freeborn, of Portsmouth, R. I., by
                Elder Solomon Sprague, Sept. 26, 1780.
3-63   "   Cate Wheeler, and Samuel Case, Nov. 26, 1780.
3-33   "   Joseph, of Exeter, and Olive Wheeler, of Norwich, Conn., by
                Rev. Levi Hart, May 24, 1781.
3-118   "   Charity, and Zebulon Kenyon, Jan. 12, 1792.
3-144   "   Robert, and Margaret Gardiner, by Elder Solomon Sprague, July
                1, 1792.
3-133   "   Olive, and Oliver Albro, Feb. 18, 1793.
3-184   "   Elizabeth, and Waite Reynolds, April 28, 1798.
3-3   "   Robert, of Exeter, and Mrs. Lettice Hubbard, of Providence, R. I.;
                m. at Tunbridge, Orange Co., N. Y., by Jason Steele, Justice,
                Oct. 21, 1824.
3-295   "   Mary A., and Moses B. Lewis, Jan. 14, 1827.
3-275   "   James, of Joseph, of Hopkinton, and Tacy Greene, of Peleg, of
                Westerly, by Elder Daniel Slocum, Nov. 30, 1844.
3-226   "   Catharine, and John Turner, May 25, 1845.

D

1-196   DAVIS Elizabeth, and Isaac Gardiner, March 24, 1709.
1-180   "   John, and Mary Sherman, of Peleg, by Benjamin Morey, Justice,
                Dec. 21, 1752.
1-158   "   Barney, and Catherine Wilcox, of Robert, by Job Tripp, Justice,
                Sept. 26, 1759.
3-74   "   Mary, and John Browning, Feb. 28, 1765.
3-106   "   Experience, and Joseph Reynolds, Oct. 31, 1771.
3-52   "   William, now of Exeter, and Mary Greene, of Philip, of West
                Greenwich, by George Pierce, Justice of Peace, Sept. 7, 1772.
3-55   "   David, and Patience Allen, by Hopson Wilcox, Justice, Feb. 9,
                1775.

2-287 DAWLEY John, of Exeter, and Sally Rice, of Warwick, by Elder Pardon Tillinghast, April 26, 1841.

1-240 " Daniel, and Hannah Sweet, by Nicholas Gardiner, Justice, April 26, 1744.

1-184 " Nathan, and Alice Whitford, at North Kingstown, by Benjamin Allen, Justice, Jan. 4, 1746.

1-179 " Elizabeth, and John Rathbun, Dec. 13, 1752.

3-12 " Margaret, and Joseph Rathbun, Aug. 17, 1766.

2-175 " Benjamin, and Millie Sherman, by Hopson Wilcox, Justice, March 4, 1768.

2-175 " Oliver, and Mercy Sherman, by Hopson Wilcox, Justice, March 31, 1768.

2-177 " Peleg, of John, of West Greenwich, late dec., and Margeret Rathbun, of Obediah, of Exeter, by Newman Parkins, Justice, Nov. 27, 1768.

3-158 " Molly, and Samuel Littlefield, Feb. 19, 1795.

3-141 " Dorcas, and Stephen Champlain, Feb. 9, 1796.

3-172 " Job, and Phebe Clarke, both of Litchfield, Herkimer Co., N. Y., according to the rites of the Dutch Reformed Church at Plattsburg, N. Y., by John Frank, Justice, March 16, 1797.

3-228 " David, of David, of Exeter, and Mary Reynolds, of Benjn., by Elder Gershom Palmer, Dec. 11, 1806.

3-241 " Vincent, and Sarah Harrington, by Elder Gershom Palmer, Oct. 13, 1808.

3-244 " Michael, of Oliver, and Hannah Carr, of John, by Elder Gershom Palmer, Jan 19, 1809.

3-30 " William, of Nathan, and Phebe Lawton, of Edward, by Elder Gershom Palmer March 23, 1809.

3-264 " Sally, and James Sheldon, Dec. 6, 1811.

3-272 " Susannah, and Solomon Sprague, July 9, 1815.

3-2 ' Beriah, of Job, of Coventry, and Charlotte Rouse, of Sterling, Conn., by Elder James Burlingame, Jan. 8, 1824.

3-34 " Peleg A., of Shibney, and Abbie P. Northnp, of Benjamin, by Elder Gershom Palmer, Jan. 19, 1826.

3-195 DEAN Abigail, and George Gardiner, Feb. 20, 1800.

3-172 DOUGLASS Allen C., of Joseph, of Exeter, and Catherine Stanton, of Daniel P., of Preston, Conn., by Elder Gershom Palmer, Dec. 23, 1824.

1-184 DUNN Bathsheba, and John Dyre, March 17, 1754.

3-13 DUPUY Lucy Ann, and George W. Allen, Aug. 30, 1841.

3-9 DUTEMPLE Nathan, and Annis T. Joslin, by Elder Benedict Johnson, April 17, 1841.

1-182 DYRE Deborah, and Phillip Aylesworth, July 1, 1753.

1-184 " John, and Bathsheba Dunn, both of North Kingstown, by Elder Samuel Albro, March 17, 1754.

3-137 • Anna, and Anthony Shaw, April 25, 1793.

3-152 " Isabel, and John Watson, April 1, 1800.

3-248 " Permerle, and Reynolds Kenyon, March 8, 1810.

E

1-179 EARL Wilbur, and Sarah Rathbun, of Thomas, of Exeter, by Benoni Hall, Justice, Dec. 10, 1752.

1-237 ELDRED Abigail, and John Sweet, Feb. 5, 1743-4.

1-159 " Mary, and Benjamin West, Oct. 7, 1759.

1-155 " Jeremiah, and Ordery Harrington, dau. of Job, by Benjamin Reynolds, Justice, Oct. 29, 1761.

2-163 " John, and Sarah West, by Elder Samuel Albro, March 29, 1762.

2-165 " Abigail, and John Eldred, Jan. 31, 1764.

2-165 " John, of Scituate, and Abigail Eldred, of Exeter, by Elder Samuel Albro, Jan. 31, 1764.

2-175 " Joseph, of North Kingstown, and Sarah Spink, of East Greenwich, by William Hall, Justice Peace, Aug. 29, 1767.

2-38   ELDRED Jane, and Jeremiah Sweet, July 12, 1771.
3-63   "   Mary, and Isaac Rathbun, Jan. 14, 1776.
1-243   ELLIS Gideon, of West Greenwich, and Jemima Austin, of Exeter, by Samuel
        Casey, Justice, Feb. 14, 1744.
1-160   "   Jeremiah, and Priscilla Greene, both of West Greenwich, by Elder
        Samuel Albro, Oct. 21, 1759.
3-154   "   Oliver, of Gideon, of West Greenwich, and Hannah Reynolds, of
        Henry, of Exeter, by Elder Elisha Greene, March 1, 1792.
3-260   "   Sarah, and Reynolds Lillibridge, Oct. 5, 1806.
3-83   "   Elizabeth, and Rowland Arnold, Feb. 18, 1813.
3-284   "   Arnold, of Jeremiah, of West Greenwich, and Almira Coone,
        of Elisha, of Hopkinton, by Elder Daniel Slocum, March 30,
        1848.
3-148   ENSWORTH Leonard, of Joseph, of Canterbury, Conn., and Esther Wilcox,
        of Capt. Job, of Exeter, by Elder Elisha Greene, Jan. 17,
        1793.

F

3-204   FENNER Mary, and Isaac Morey, March 22, 1802.
3-17   FISHER Lucy Ann, and Dutee J. Hall, Jan. 23, 1842.
1-191   FONES Eunice, and Francis West, Oct. 1, 1758.
1-195   FOSTER Mary, and Daniel Rathbun, May 28, 1758.
3-6   FOWLER Abel, of Simeon, and Mary Brownell, dau. of Mary (widow), by
        George Pierce, Justice, June 3, 1770.
3-9   "   Job J., of Simeon, and Ruth Gardiner, of Benoni, by George
        Pierce, Justice, June 28, 1770.
3-27   "   Susannah, and George Waite Babcock, Feb. 21, 1771.
3-60   "   Ruth, and Benjamin Bentley, Aug. 24, 1780.
3-283   "   Elizabeth, and John Slocum, May 23, 1819.
3-116   FRANKLIN, Mary, and Abraham Terry, April 4, 1791.
3-273   "   Jeremiah, of West Greenwich, son of Joshua and Amie Albro, of
        Exeter, dau. of Silas, by Elder Gershom Palmer, May 30,
        1819.
3-277   "   Almy, and Ebenezer Brown, April 21, 1839.
3-229   "   Joseph P., of Exeter, and Mary S. Vaughn, of West Greenwich, by
        Elder Thomas Tillinghast, Nov. 25, 1844.
3-229   "   Albert G., of Exeter, and Clancey G. Vaughn, of West Greenwich;
        by Elder Thomas Tillinghast, Dec. 18, 1848.
2-167   FRAZIER Mary, and Samuel Bissell; March 2, 1766.
3-2   FREEBORN Philla, and John Crandall, Sept. 26, 1780.
3-29   FRY Bethany, and John Aylesworth, March 4, 1771.

G

1-196   GARDINER Isaac, and Elizabeth Davis, both of Kings Towne, by Samuel
        Fones, Justice, March 24, 1709.
1-240   "   Mary, and John Spencer, March 23, 1732.
1-182   "   Samuel, and Elizabeth Congdon, by Job Tripp, Justice, May 3,
        1750.
1-244   "   Gideon, and Tabitha Gardiner, dau. of John, by Benoni Hall, Jus-
        tice, Sept. 9, 1750.
1-244   "   Tabitha, and Gideon Gardiner, Sept. 9, 1750.
1-244   "   Joshua, and Deliverance Reynolds, by Benoni Hall, Justice, April
        28, 1751.
1-178   "   Dorcas, and Henry Tanner, April 13, 1752.
1-182   "   Benjamin, of Benjamin, deceased, and Elizabeth Olin, of Joseph, by
        Benoni Hall, Justice, Nov. 11, 1753.
1-187   "   Caleb, of Thomas, and Mary Clarke, by Newman Perkins, Justice,
        March 7, 1754.
1-183   "   Bridget, and Thomas Newcomb, Jr., June 2, 1754.
1-185   "   Mary, and William Hall, Aug. 25, 1754.

1-186 GARDINER John, of North Kingstown, and Elizabeth Champlain, of Exeter, by Elder Samuel Albro, June 3, 1756.

1-188 " Jeremiah, of Thomas, of Exeter, and Mary Bowdish, of West Greenwich, dau. of Joseph, by Joseph Ellis, Justice, June 23, 1757.

1-192 " Mary, and Oliver Reynolds, Feb. 8, 1759.

1-157 " William, and Martha Reynolds, dau. of Capt. John, by Benjamin Reynolds, Justice, March 2, 1760.

1-157 " Martha and Stephen Arnold, March 3, 1760.

1-154 " Ann, and Samuel Morey, Feb. 28, 1762.

2-163 " Nicholas, Jr., and Deborah Vincent (also 3-53), by Elder Samuel Albro, Oct. 19, 1762.

2-163 " Elizabeth, and Benjamin Champlain, Feb. 8, 1763.

2-165 " Anne, and William Baker, June 22, 1764.

2-165 " Jonathan, of Newport, and Mary Morey, of Exeter, by Elder Samuel Albro, July 22, 1764.

2-170 " Othniel, and Lydia Reynolds, by William Hall, Justice, Aug. 16, 1764.

2-166 " Robert, and Anne Clarke, by Elder Samuel Albro, Sept. 28, 1764.

2-166 " Elizabeth, and Joseph Reynolds, April 12, 1765.

3-51 " Benjamin, of Jeremiah, and Tabitha ——, May 22, 1766.

2-170 " Amie, and Joseph Nicholas, Jan. 25, 1767.

2-170 " Margaret, and John Reynolds, Jr., April 6, 1767.

3-48 " Elizabeth, and Joseph Holloway, April 9, 1769.

3-9 " Ruth, and Job J. Fowler, June 28, 1770.

3-50 " Sylvester, son of Nicholas, and Hannah Reynolds, of Jonathan, by George Pierce, Justice, June 6, 1773.

3-60 " Mary, and Joshua Vaughn, Feb. 4, 1779.

3-144 " Margaret, and Robert Crandall, July 1, 1792.

3-169 " Elizabeth, and Clarke Sisson, Nov. 3, 1796.

3-195 " George, of Abel, and Abigail Dean, of Jonathan, of West Greenwich, by Elder Charles Stone, Feb. 20, 1800.

3-216 " Amie, and James Tillinghast, Feb. 5, 1801.

3-215 " Ruth, and James Reynolds, March 27, 1803.

3-246 " John, of Exeter, and Francis Hall, of West Greenwich, by Elder Gershom Palmer, July 16, 1809.

3-285 " William H., of Exeter, son of Gould, and Patience A. Hendrick, of James, of North Kingstown, by Elder Gershom Palmer, Dec. 7, 1817.

3-220 " Elizabeth, and Benjamin Griffin, Jr., Nov. 18, 1821.

3-188 " Susannah, and Benjamin Lillibridge, Sept. 29, 1825.

3-184 " Nicholas, of Benjamin C., and Abbie Arnold, of Benjamin, by Elder Gershom Palmer, March 16, 1826.

3-296 " Mercy, and Stephen A. Gardiner, Feb. 1, 1829.

3-296 " Stephen A., and Mary Gardiner; m. by Elder John Gardiner, Feb. 1, 1829.

3-297 " Joseph W., of Gould, and Sally, of Exeter, and Mary W. Hendrick, of James and Hannah, of North Kingstown; m. by Elder William Northnp, Feb. 19, 1829.

3-301 " Zebulon, and Miss Sarah G. Sweet; m. by Elder Levi Murch, Sept. 4, 1831.

3-10 " Mary, and George A. Wells, Nov. 30, 1845.

3-314 " Sarah, and George B. Sunderland, Jan. 22, 1870.

3-205 GATES Mary, and Job Wilcox, Feb. 7, 1771.

3-287 GA——, and Mrs. Caroline, and Joseph Robinson, March 4, 1830.

1-160 GILL Daniel, Jr., of West Greenwich, and Mercy Whitford, of John, of Exeter; m. by Benjamin Reynolds, J. P., Jan. 1, 1760.

3-104 GORTON John, of Samuel, and Orpha Boone, dau. of Richard Booth; m. by Elder Elisha Greene, June 18, 1789.

3-281 " Elizabeth, and Thomas A. James, June 1, 1817.

3-249 " Mary, and Willard W. Perkins, June 15, 1834.

1-237 GOULD Sarah, and Alexander Nichols, Jan. 29, 1743-4.

1-244 GREENE Philip, and Mary Baker; m. by Peleg Tripp, Justice, Dec. 31, 1750.

1-178   GREENE Benjamin, of West Greenwich, son of Henry, dec., and Mehitable Tripp, of Job; m. by Benoni Hall, Justice, Sept. 22, 1752.
3-10   "   Mary, and George Pierce, Dec. 2, 1753.
1-160   "   Precilla and Jeremiah Ellis, Oct. 21, 1759.
2-163   "   David, and Penelope Northrup, by Elder Samuel Albro, Aug. 15, 1762.
2-167   "   Jeremiah, and Deborah Cammell, by Elder Samuel Albro, July 20, 1765.
2-181   "   Caleb, of West Greenwich, son of Benjamin, and Sarah Brown of Exeter, dau. of Benjamin, by Newman Perkins, Justice, April 16, 1769.
3-52   "   Mary, and William Davis, Sept. 7, 1772.
3-100   "   Mrs. Sarah, and William Rathbun, July 9, 1786.
3-246   "   Job R., of East Greenwich, and Mary Johnson, of West Greenwich, by Elder Gershom Palmer, Feb. 28, 1813.
3-282   "   Lucy, and Thomas Lewis, Mar. 7, 1813.
3-50   "   Isaac, of Benjamin, and Eliza Kenyon, of John, late of Exeter, by Elder Peleg Peckham, Nov. 24, 1825.
3-275   "   Tacy, and James Crandall, Nov. 30, 1844.
3-309   "   Clarke S., and Mary T. Whitford, by Elder Pardon Tillinghast, Oct. 15, 1848.
3-220   GRIFFEN Benjamin, Jr., of Exeter, and Elizabeth Gardiner, of North Kingstown, dau. of David, by Elder Gershom Palmer, Nov. 18, 1821.

H

1-185   HALL William, son of Benoni, and Mary Gardiner, of Robert, by Benjamin Morey, Justice, Aug. 25, 1754.
2-167   "   George, of Coventry, R. I., and Ruth Nichols, of Exeter, by William Hall, Justice, Feb. 10, 1766.
3-25   "   William, of William, of North Kingstown, and Lydia Reynolds, of Robert, of Exeter, by George Pierce, Justice, Dec. 20, 1771.
3-67   "   Frances, and Phillip Tillinghast, April 13, 1791.
3-9   "   James, and Mrs. Lucy Hoxsie, dau. of Capt. John Hoxsie, by J. W. Sheldon, Justice, Nov. 4, 1792.
3-214   "   Abigail, and Christopher, Joslin, Feb. 20, 1803.
3-217   "   Preserved H, of Caleb, late of West Greenwich, and Eunice Browning, of John, of Exeter, by Elder Stephen Allen, April 12, 1804.
3-239   "   Caleb, of Caleb, of West Greenwich, and Rhoda Barber, of Lillibridge, of Exeter, by Robert Crandall, Justice, March 6, 1808.
3-246   "   Francis, and John Gardiner, July 16, 1809.
3-166   "   Mary, and Samuel B. Reynolds, June 30, 1825.
3-280   "   Phebe, and Palmer Lewis, Sept. 22, 1841.
3-17   "   Dutee J., of Exeter, and Lucy Ann Fisher, of Warwick, by Elder Benedict, Johnson, Jan. 23, 1842.
3-7   HAMMOND William, of Exeter, son of Joseph, of Newport, and Lucy Waite, dau. of Samuel, of Exeter, by George Pierce, Justice, Aug. 15, 1779.
3-125   "   Jounna, and Smith Tanner, March 4, 1792.
3-310   HANDY William J., of Andrew, of West Greenwich, and Mary Ann Lanphere, of Oliver, late of Exeter, dec, by Elder Nathan N. Gallup, Sept. 28, 1846.
1-237   HARRINGTON Lydia, and Abraham Wilcox, June 5, 1739.
1-237   "   Ebenezer, and Rebecca Spencer, by Nicholas Gardiner, Justice, Dec. 18, 1743.
1-177   "   Alce, and Daniel Sunderland, Feb. 6, 1752.
1-177   "   Sarah, and Elisha Baker, Feb. 6, 1752.
1-186   "   Hannah, and Jeremiah Austin, April 13, 1756.
1-100   "   Amie, and James Reynolds, Jan. 10, 1760.
1-156   "   Anna, and Benjamin Reynolds, Nov. 16, 1760.
1-155   "   Ordery, and Jeremiah Eldred, Oct. 29, 1761.
2-163   "   Christopher, and Sarah Crandall, by Elder Samuel Albro, Nov. 16, 1762.
2-167   "   Freelove, and Henry Harrington, May 30, 1765.

2-167 HARRINGTON Henry, and Freelove Harrington, by Elder Samuel Albro, May 30, 1765.

3-3   "   David, and Walte Tripp, by William Hall, Justice, March 27, 1768.

3-46   "   William, of Exeter, and Sarah Baker, of Richmond, at Richmond, by George Webb, Justice, Oct. 10, 1771.

3-128   "   Christopher, of Christopher, and Amie Lillibridge, of Benjamin, by Stephen Reynolds, Justice, Oct. 21, 1792.

3-241   "   Sarah, and Vincent Dawley, Oct. 13, 1808.

2-171 HARRIS Elijah, of Plainfield, Conn., and Hannah Wilkey, of Preston, Conn., by Robert Crandall, Justice, Feb. 25, 1768.

3-233 HATHAWAY Nancy, and John Sunderland, May 17, 1807.

1-184 HAVEN Samuel, and Margaret Rathbun, both of North Kingstown, by Elder Samuel Albro, Jan. 3, 1754.

3-64 HAZARD Hannah, and Jeffrey Champlain, April 1, 1777.

3-17   "   Nelson B., and Dorcas Champlain, both of Exeter, at South Kings-'town, by Elder Elbridge Crandall, Dec. 19, 1841.

3-240   "   Jason P., of Thomas T., of West Greenwich, and Betsey M. Lewis, dau. of Moses, late of Exeter, by Elder John Tillinghast, March 15, 1847.

2-170 HEFFERNAN William, of South Kingstown, and Mary Bates, of Exeter, (also 3-96); m. by Thomas Justin, Justice, Feb. 8, 1767.

3-285 HENDRICK Patience A., and William H. Gardiner, Dec. 7, 1817.

3-297   "   Mary W., and Joseph W. Gardiner, Feb. 19, 1829.

3-127   "   William A., and Mrs. Sarah Money, m. at Cumberland, by Rev. Samuel Wakefield, April 14, 1838.

3-170 HESALINE William, and Mary Tefft, by Elder Elisha Greene, Jan. 4, 1787.

1-195 HIAMES Spink, and Elizabeth Richmond, by Newman Perkins, Justice, Oct. 6, 1757.

3-15   "   Albert, of North Kingstown, and Hannah Brown, of Exeter, by El-der Benedict Johnson, Dec. 5, 1841.

1-180 HILL Thomas, of George, of East Greenwich, and Margaret Austin, dau. of Paskow, of Exeter, by Benjamin Morey, Justice, Feb. 15, 1753.

2-163   "   Samuel, and Meriam Rathbun, by Elder Samuel Albro, Feb. 29, 1762.

2-165   "   Mercy, and Benjamin Sweet, Dec. 13, 1764.

3-15   "   Davis, of William, and Chloe Allen, of Jeremiah, by Daniel Sunderland, Justice, Feb. 11, 1770.

3-12   "   Elder Nathan, of Exeter, and Freelove Carr, of North Kingstown, widow of Slocum Carr, by Elder James Weightman, June 6, 1782.

3-190   "   Sarah, and John Rhodes, March 14, 1799.

3-155 HOLLOWAY Joseph, and Lydia Babcock, by Elder Samuel Albro, Oct. 11, 1761.

3-48   "   Joseph, and Elizabeth Gardiner, by George Northup, Justice, April 9, 1769.

2-179   "   Joseph, Jun., son of Joseph, and Sarah Tripp, dau. of Peleg, by George Pierce, Justice, May 23, 1769.

3-63   "   Catherine, and Robert Wheaton, March 3, 1776.

3-140   "   Abigail, and Dr. Simon Sprague, Jan. 13, 1782.

3-181   "   Samuel, of Joseph, of Exeter, and Mercy Briggs, of Gardiner, of East Greenwich, by Elder Nathan Hill, March 17, 1794.

3-8   "   Julia A. and Jeremiah A. Kenyon, June 30, 1844.

3-257 HOOD James C., of West Greenwich, and Desire C. Richmond, of Volun-town, Conn., by Elder Williad R. Slocum, Sept. 4, 1850.

3-126 HOPKINS Honor, and Stukeley Tillinghast, Nov. 22, 1762.

3-42   "   Sarah, and Thomas Albro, Jan. 27, 1772.

3-44   "   Phebe (widow), and John Morey, Jan. 26, 1781.

3-83   "   Lucy, and Peleg Arnold, Oct. 20, 1785.

3-46   "   Samuel, of Exeter, son of Rufus and Amie, and Freelove B. Ar-nold, dau. of Elijah and Sally Ann, of Warwick, R. I., by Rev. Jonathan Wilson, Nov. 7, 1824.

3-177   "   Burrell, and Dianna Brown, both of West Greenwich, by Elder Daniel Slocum, Feb. 22, 1844.

3-64   "   Rufus, of Exeter, and Sally Kettle, of West Greenwich, by Elder Daniel Slocum, March 2, 1844.

1-241   "   Phebe, and Simeon Toms, March 13, 1745.

1-156   HOXSIE John, of Richmond, and Hannah Bill of Exeter, by Elder Samuel Albro, May 21, 1761.

3-36   "   Samuel, of Richmond, son of Stephen, and Anna Wilcox, of Thomas, of Exeter, at Exeter, by Robert Stanton, Justice, Sept. 30, 1772.

3-68   "   Anna (widow), and Abraham Wilcox, Aug. 20, 1781.

3-133   "   Mary, and Freeman Phillips, April 16, 1786.

3-9   "   Mrs. Lucy, and James Hall, Nov. 4, 1792.

3-291   "   Collins, of John, dec., and Sarah James, of Joseph, by Elder Gershom Palmer, Sept. 9, 1824.

3-276   "   Mercy, and Thomas Phillips, Jr., Feb. 26, 1828.

3-302   "   Sarah S., and James Sheldon, March 24, 1839.

3-224   "   Thankful, and Stephen James, ——.

3-3   HUBBARD Mrs. Lettice, and Robert Crandall, Oct. 21, 1824.

3-239   HULING George W., of North Kingstown, and Joanna E. Lillibridge, of Exeter, by Elder Samuel West, Dec. 16, 1824.

3-193   HULL Sarah, and John Spencer, Feb. 25, 1759.

3-111   HUNT Jemima, and Peleg Andrews, Nov. 10, 1816.

I J

2-177   JAMES Thomas, of Richmond, and Hannah Crandall, of Exeter, by Newman Perkins, Justice, July 3, 1768.

3-156   "   Daniel, of Joseph, and Mary Barber, of Caleb, by Elder Benjamin Barber, Feb. 5, 1793.

3-268   "   Elizabeth, and Newman Perkins, April 9, 1815.

3-281   "   Thomas A., of Exeter, and Elizabeth Gorton, of West Greenwich, by Elder Stafford Greene, June 1, 1817.

3-291   "   Sarah, and Collins Hoxsie, Sept. 9, 1824.

3-15   "   Alce, and George Tefft, April 1, 1827.

3-306   "   Ruth E., and Horace Johnson, July 6, 1837.

3-8   "   Susan, and Henry D. Rathbun, March 14, 1841.

3-227   "   Reynolds, and Alice Potter, both of Richmond, by Elder Daniel Slocum, March 31, 1844.

3-8   "   Phebe A., and Benjamin H. Reynolds, June 30, 1844.

3-224   "   Stephen, of Deacon Joseph, and Thankful Hoxsie, by Elder Henry Joslin, not given.

1-178   JENCKES Ancillis, and Samuel Waite, June 26, 1752.

3-5   JENKINS Giles S., son of Lydia Miers, of Exeter, and Mary Carr of Newport, dau. of Samuel Greene, by Elder Gershom Palmer, Feb. 13, 1825.

3-246   JOHNSON Mary, and Job R. Greene, Feb. 28, 1813.

3-306   "   Horace, of Exeter, and Ruth E. James, of Richmond, by Elder Thomas Tillinghast, July 6, 1837.

3-201   "   Clara, and George W. Wilcox, Sept. 16, 1849.

1-183   JOHNS Benjamin, and Prudence Thompson, both of Canterbury, Conn.; m. at Exeter, by Newman Perkins, Justice, March 20, 1754.

2-179   JONES Martha, and Thomas Phillips, Feb. 9, 1769.

3-141   JOSLIN Joanna, and John Rathbun, March 3, 1793.

3-214   "   Christopher, of John of Exeter, and Abigail Hall, of Caleb, by Elder Thomas Tillinghast, Feb. 20, 1803.

3-8   "   Betsey, and Joseph W. Lewis, March 16, 1841.

3-9   "   Annis T., and Nathan Dutemple, April 17, 1841.

3-7   "   John H., of Exeter, and Julia Ann Vaughan, of East Greenwich; m. by Elder Benedict Johnson, Aug. 30, 1841.

K

1-186   KENYON John, and Freelove Reynolds, by Daniel Barber, Justice, June 8, 1755.

1-158   "   Dorcas, and Gideon Rathbun, Feb. 18, 1759.

1-159   "   Christopher, and Mary Rathbun, by Stephen Richmond, Justice, Dec. 27, 1759.

1-188   KENYON Mercy, and Stephen Watson, March 2, 1780.
3-118   "   Zebulon, of John, and Charity Crandall, of Joseph, by Stephen
                Reynolds, Justice, Jan. 12, 1792.
8-230   "   Job, of John, and Betsey Benjamin, of David, by Elder Gershom
                Palmer, Feb. 15, 1807.
3-248   "   Reynolds, of Exeter, and Permerle Dyre, of Ashford, Conn., by
                Robert Crandall, Justice, March 8, 1810.
3-125   "   Charity, and David Terry, June 6, 1824.
3-50   "   Eliza, and Isaac Greene, Nov. 24, 1825.
3-302   "   Mary, and William B. Wilcox, Nov. 8, 1830.
3-303   "   Sarah, and Ezra Reynolds, Oct. 20, 1836.
3-196   "   William R., of Exeter, and Cynthia Briggs, of West Greenwich, by
                Elder Thomas Tillinghast, Oct. 3, 1842.
3-8   "   Jeremiah A., of Richmond, and Julia A. Holloway, of Charles-
                town; m. at Exeter, by Elder Daniel Slocum, June 30, 1844.
3-19   "   Barber, of Exeter, son of Benedict, and Abbie Austin, dau. of Let-
                tice, by Daniel Slocum, Jan. 5, 1845.
3-129   KEPPARD John, and Hannah Sherman, by Elder Solomon Sprague, March
                7, 1797.
3-64   KETTLE Sally, and Rufus Hopkins, March 2, 1844.
3-42   "   Nancy, and William H. Reynolds, July 3, 1848.
3-202   KEZER Anna, and Samuel Perkins, March 12, 1820.
3-14   KINGSLEY Dorcas, and David D. Northup, Oct. 12, 1841.
2-175   KING Earle, of South Kingstown, and Content Richmond, of Stephen, of
                Exeter, by David Stanton, Justice, Jan. 24, 1768.
3-105   "   Stephen, and Dorcas Watson, by Pheneus Kenyon, Justice, Feb.
                24, 1789.
3-217   KNIGHT Caroline F., and Benjamin Baton, Nov. 27, 1843.
1-221   KNOWLES Margaret, and Ezekiel Sherman, Feb. 26, 1747.
2-175   "   Samuel, and Abigail Wilcox, by Hopson Wilcox, Justice, March
                31, 1768.

L

3-119   LADD Mrs. Elizabeth, and Solomon Lewis, July 18, 1790.
3-221   "   Eleanor, and Moses Lewis, Nov. 18, 1804.
3-251   "   Esther, and Jesse Lewis, Nov. 4, 1810.
3-310   LANPHERE Mary Ann, and Wm J. Handy, Sept. 28, 1846.
3-291   "   Mrs. Eliza, and Jonathan Robbins, Dec. 19, 1847.
1-117   LAWTON Benjamin, of Exeter, and Anna Phillips, of North Kingstown, by
                Benoni Hall, Justice, May 3, 1752.
2-163   "   Oliver, and Ann Rathbun, by Elder Samuel Albro, Oct. 21, 1762.
2-170   "   Mary, and Ezekiel Tripp, April 29, 1765.
2-176   "   Timothy, and Deborah Reynolds, by Elder Samuel Albro, Nov. 21,
                1765.
3-128   "   Phebe, and Oliver Arno'd, May 8, 1785.
3-117   "   Eleanor, and Asa Wilcox, Oct. 16, 1791.
3-197   "   Hannah, and Joel Comstock, Aug. 19, 1798.
8-30   "   Phebe, and William Dawley, March 23, 1809.
3-155   "   Samuel A., of Caleb, late of Exeter, dec., and Martha Brown, of
                Joshua, of Exeter, at East Greenwich, by Elder Pardon Tilling-
                hast, Oct. 9, 1843.
2-171   LEMOINE Phenens Solomon, and Sarah Baker; m. at Exeter by William
                Hall, Justice, Feb. 19, 1768.
3-95   LEWIS Sylvester, of Exeter, and Sarah Reynolds, of West Greenwich, by
                Elder David Sprague, June 3, 1748.
3-88   "   George, of George, and Elizabeth Pendleton, Jan. 12, 1757.
3-88   "   Caleb, and Sybel ——, at Preston, Conn., April 7, 1757.
2-167   "   Randall, of Hopkinton, and Alce Rathbun, of Exeter, by Stephen
                Richmond, Justice, Nov. 21, 1765.
3-47   "   Stephen, son of John, and Alice Sheldon, of Roger, by William
                Sweet, Justice, Jan. 26, 1770.
3-7   "   Daniel, of Jonathan, and Lydia Barber, by Robert Crandall, Justice,
                March 21, 1770.

3-207	LEWIS	Joseph, and Mary Stanton, Jan. 6, 1774.
3-58	"	James, and Thankful Barber, Jan. 15, 1775.
3-108	"	John, of Jonathan, and Amie Sheldon, of Roger, by Elder Caleb Nicholas, Sept. 28, 1777.
3-55	"	Jonathan, 3d, of Exeter, son of Jonathan, 2d, and Martha Bowdish, of Nathaniel, of Preston, Conn., by Elder John Pendleton, Aug. 12, 1779.
3-145	"	Benjamin, and Deliverance Cleaveland, dau. of Deliverance, both of West Greenwich, by Elder Elisha Greene, Feb. 10, 1780.
3-146	"	Elizabeth, and Roger Sheldon, Feb. 14, 1783.
3-171	"	William, of Thomas, of Exeter, and Eleanor Straight, of John, of West Greenwich, by Elder Elisha Greene, Nov. 29, 1786.
3-119	"	Solomon, of Exeter, and Mrs. Elizabeth Ladd, of Coventry, R. I., by Elder John Burdick, July 18, 1790.
3-163	"	Lucy, and Stephen Rathbun, Dec. 17, 1795.
3-208	"	Samuel, Jr., of Samuel, and Ruth Barber, of Reynolds, by Elder Elisha Greene, March 2, 1797.
3-189	"	Stephen, son of Capt. Stephen, and Hannah Lewis, of Samuel, by Elder Thomas Manchester, Nov. 7, 1799.
3-189	"	Hannah, and Stephen Lewis, Nov. 7, 1799.
3-183	"	James, and Olive Rathbun, by Robert Crandall, Justice, Oct. 18, 1798.
3-186	"	Ruth, and Allen Tillinghast, July 11, 1799.
3-211	"	Lucy, and Nathaniel Wilcox, Dec. 23, 1802.
3-213	"	John, of Elisha, of Exeter, and Lydia Tanner, of Benjamin, of South Kingstown, by Stephen Reynolds, Justice, May 29, 1803.
3-222	"	Lydia, and Silas Lewis, Oct. 28, 1804.
3-222	"	Silas, of Jonathan, Jr., of Exeter, and Lydia Lewis, of James M., of Exeter, by Elder Ellet Locke, Oct. 28, 1804.
3-221	"	Moses, of Jonathan, Jr., of Exeter, and Eleanor Ladd, of John, of West Greenwich, by Elder Ellet Locke, Nov. 18, 1804.
3-232	"	Dorcas, and Abel Rathbun, Nov. 30, 1806.
3-2, 238	"	Nathan B., of James, and Sally Richmond, of Stephen, by Elder Gershom Palmer, Feb. 4, 1808.
3-240	"	Eleanor, and Gardiner Barber, April 17, 1808.
3-242	"	Annis, and Caleb Strange, April 16, 1809.
3-250	"	Jonathan, Jr., and Mariah Lewis, by Robert Crandall, Justice, March 8, 1810.
3-250	"	Mariah, and Jonathan Lewis, Jr., March 8, 1810.
3-251	"	Jesse, of Jonathan, and Esther Ladd, of John, of Coventry, R. I., by Elder Gershom Palmer, Nov. 4, 1810.
3-263	"	Prudence, and Roger Sheldon, April 11, 1811.
3-254	"	Daniel, of Elisha, of Exeter, and Elizabeth Lewis, of Daniel, of West Greenwich, by Elder Ellet Locke, Oct. 17, 1811.
3-254	"	Elizabeth, and Daniel Lewis, Oct. 17, 1811.
3-262	"	Sanford, and Aseneth Palmer, by Job Kenyon, Justice, Jan. 24, 1813.
3-282	"	Thomas, of Exeter, son of Stephen, and Lucy Greene, of West Greenwich, dau. of Stafford, by Elder Gershom Palmer, March 7, 1813.
5-133	"	Reynolds, of Caleb, of Voluntown, Conn., and Bridget Young, of Benjamin, of Exeter, by Job Kenyon, Justice, June 26, 1814.
3-281	"	Eliza, and Benjamin Richmond, April 14, 1815.
3-279	"	Geriah, and Stephen Richmond, Dec. 3, 1815.
3-124	"	Lydia, and Silas B. Barber, June 6, 1824.
3-295	"	Moses B., of James, of Exeter, and Mary A. Crandall, of Samuel of Hopkinton, at Hopkinton, by Elder Matthew Stillman, Jan. 14, 1827.
3-281	"	James, of Exeter, and Mary Sisson, of Hopkinton, by Elder Weeden Barber, Sept. 2, 1838.
3-8	"	Joseph W., of Richmond, and Betsey Joslin, of West Greenwich, by Elder Benedict Johnson, March 16, 1841.
3-9	"	Caleb S., of Hopkinton, and Catharine S. Matteson, of West Greenwich, by Elder Benedict Johnson, May 9, 1841.

3-280   LEWIS Palmer, of Exeter, and Phebe Hall of West Greenwich, by Elder Benedict Johnson, Sept. 22, 1841.

3-269   "   Olive, and Thomas D. Barber, March 9, 1846.

3-240   "   Betsey M., and Jason P. Hazard, March 15, 1847.

3-214   "   Lydia, and Ambrose Brown, Sept. 17, 1848.

3-281   "   Seth, of Exeter, and Miss Sarah Bailey, of West Greenwich, by Elder Benedict Johnson, Sept. 22, 1849.

3-237   "   Mary A., and Jesse W. Barber, July 3, 1853.

3-279   "   Charles, of Hopkinton, and Mary Andrew of Coventry, R. I., by Elder Benedict Johnson, June 23, ——.

3-175   "   Edith, and Jeous Albro, not given.

1-237   LILLIBRIDGE Benjamin, and Amie Sherman, by Nicholas Gardiner, Justice, Dec. 15, 1743.

3-277   "   Alice, and Christopher Morey, April 6, 1772.

3-128   "   Amie, and Christopher Harrington, Oct. 21, 1792.

3-260   "   Reynolds, of Jonathan, of Exeter, and Sarah Ellis, of Capt. Augustus, of West Greenwich, by Elder Thomas Manchester, Oct. 5, 1806.

3-266   "   Deborah, and Samuel Reynolds, July 31, 1808.

3-281   "   Daniel, of Gardiner, and Hannah Barber, of Lillibridge, by Elder Gershom Palmer, Aug. 18, 1811.

3-267   "   Elizabeth, and John Sheldon, Dec. 25, 1814.

3-286   "   John, Jr., of Exeter, son of John, and Mrs. Phebe Swan, of Griswold, Conn., at Griswold, by Elder Levi Walker, June 4, 1820.

3-290   "   Whitman W., of John; Mercy Whitman, of James, by Elder Gershom Palmer, March 7, 1823.

3-239   "   Johannah E., and George W. Huling, Dec. 16, 1824.

3-188   "   Benjamin, of Clarke, and Susannah Gardiner of Jeffrey, by Elder Gershom Palmer, Sept. 29, 1825.

3-13   "   Joseph W., and Rachel Barber, by Elder Benedict Johnson, Sept. 6, 1841.

3-158   LITTLEFIELD Samuel, son of Sarah Rathbun, of Stephenstown, N. Y., and Molly Dawley, of Margaret, of Exeter, by Elder Benjamin Barber, Feb. 19, 1795.

1-156   LITTLE Isabel, and Jeremiah Austin, Sept. 28, 1760.

3-236   LOCKWOOD Oliver, and Amie H. Thurston, now residing in Exeter, by Elder Steadman Kenyon, Nov. 5, 1849.

M

3-302   MAKER Mrs. Ruth, and Asia E. Wood, —— 29, 1833.

1-153   MANTON Abigail, and Libbeus Northup, Jan. 19, 1764.

3-283   MARSH Nicholas, of Newport, and Deborah P. Clarke, now residing in Exeter, by Elder Benedict Johnson, Feb. 21, 1840.

1-189   MATTESON Elizabeth, and Theophilus Spencer, Nov. 11, 1757.

3-304   "   Hannah, and Willett Rathbun, Sept. 9, 1832.

3-9   "   Catherine S., and Caleb S. Lewis, May 9, 1841.

3-72   "   Uriah, and Betsey Moone, both of West Greenwich, by Elder Caleb Greene, June 5, 1842.

3-182   "   Ezekiel P., of Coventry, R. I., and Harriet Bennett, of West Greenwich, by Elder Daniel Slocum, Sept. 25, 1843.

3-308   "   Samuel K., of West Greenwich, son of Levi, and Almira Spencer, of Edmund, of East Greenwich, by Elder Daniel Slocum, Sept. 6, 1846.

3-95   "   Nancy, and Lewis Bates, Oct. 1, 1854.

3-10   MIAS John David, and Mary W. Bates, of James; m. by Elder Gershom Palmer, July 28, 1811.

2-167   MAXSON Polly, and John Richmond, March 2, 1801.

1-183   M'QUEEN Mary, and John Skellion, May 28, 1754.

3-9   MERISS Sarah, and John Congdon, Jun., March 1, 1781.

3-103   "   William A., of William, and Susan A. Congdon, of Clarke, all of Exeter, by Isaac Greene, Justice, Aug. 27, 1849.

3-130 MONEY Timothy, of Samuel, of Exeter, and Eleanor Brown, of West Greenwich, at Exeter, by Stephen Reynolds, Justice, Dec. 9, 1792.

3-188 " Sarah, and James Young, Sept. 26, 1799.

3-252 " Allen, of Exeter, and Penelope Westcott, of North Kingstown, by Elder Gershom Palmer, pub. Dec. 10, 1818.

3-127 " Mrs. Sarah, and William A. Hendrick, April 14, 1838.

1-179 MOON Robert, Jun., and Eleanor Waite, of Samuel, by Benoni Hall, Justice, Nov. 23, 1752.

1-199 " Asa, of Exeter, and Deborah Babcock, of South Kingstown, by Jeremiah Crandall Justice, Aug. 13, 1758.

2-167 " John, and Ruth Moon, by Elder Samuel Albro, April 28, 1765.

2-167 " Ruth, and John Moon, April 28, 1765.

3-59 " Mary, and Harris Weaver, Dec. 20, 1772.

3-170 " Lyman, and Sarah Thurston, by Simon Lillibridge, Justice, Sept. 7, 1839.

3-72 " Betsey, and Uriah Matteson, June 5, 1842.

3-278 MOORE Alce, and Daniel Reynolds, Feb. 18, 1813.

3-231 " John, of Isaac, of West Greenwich, and Betsey Potter, of George, of Richmond, by Elder Daniel Slocum, Dec. 28, 1845.

1-243 MOREY Mary, and Ephraim Codner, Nov. 20, 1748.

1-183 " Mary, and John Wilbur, April 28, 1754.

1-194 " Mary, and Jeremiah Wilcox, Nov. 9, 1755.

1-159 " Still, and John Bates, Aug. 10, 1759.

1-154 " Samuel, and Ann Gardiner, of Nicholas; m. by Benjamin Reynolds, Justice, Feb. 28, 1762.

2-165 " Mary, and Jonathan Gardiner, July 22, 1764.

2-167 " Sarah, and John Richmond, Oct. 20, 1765.

3-5 " Lucy, and Stephen Richmond, Jan. 18, 1770.

3-277 " Christopher, of Benjamin, late of Exeter, and Alice Lillibridge, of John, of South Kingstown, late deceased, by William Hammond, Justice, April 6, 1772.

3-57 " Benjamin, of Joseph, and Ruth Sweet, of John, by Elder John Pendleton, Jan. 18, 1775.

3-44 " John, and Phebe Hopkins (widow), by Matthew Wells, Justice, Jan. 26, 1781.

3-204 " Isaac, and Mary Fenner by Benjamin Angell, Justice, March 22, 1802.

3-234 " Tillinghast, of Exeter, and Elizabeth Vaughn, of Sterling, Conn., Dec. 26, 1805.

3-291 " Esther, and Thomas Wilcox, Nov. 1, 1841.

3-282 MORGAN Elisha, of Madison, Conn., and Mary Ann Newton, of Exeter, by Elder Benedict Johnson, Feb. 21, 1840.

1-196 MOSHIER Ichabod, and Anna Tripp, by Caleb Arnold, Justice, July 13, 1760.

2-179 " Anna, and Benjamin Tripp, March 29, 1769.

1-181 MOTT Lydia, and William Sweet, March 18, 1753.

1-239 MUMFORD John, Jr., of North Kingstown, son of John, and Mercy Reynolds, of James, of West Greenwich, at East Greenwich, Oct. 14, 1742

1-237 " Content, and Solomon Brayman, April 9, 1744.

1-154 " Mercy, and William Allen, Dec. 17, 1761.

3-286 MYCOCK John, of Coventry, R. I., and Sally Carter, of Exeter, by Elder Daniel Slocum, Jan. 25, 1846.

N

2-167 NASH Mary, and Benjamin Reynolds, Nov. 11, 1765.

3-34 NEAGERS Elizabeth, and Gideon Bentley, April 5, 1781.

1-183 NEWCOMB Thomas, Jr., of Poughkeepsie, N. Y., and Bridget Gardiner, of Isaac, of Exeter, by Benoni Hall, Justice, June 2, 1754.

3-282 NEWTON Mary Ann, and Elisha Morgan, Feb. 21, 1840.

3-26 " Elizabeth, and Levi Barber, April 29, 1773.

3-10 NEY Abbie A., and Gershom P. Sherman, July 24, 1843.

3-71   NEY Beriah, of Isaac, and Mary Barber, of Samuel, m. at Exeter, by
         Elder John Tillinghast, Dec. 2, 1844.

2-170   NICHOLAS Joseph, of West Greenwich, and Amie Gardiner, of Exeter, by
         William Hall. Justice, Jan. 25, 1767.

3-293   "   David, of Coventry, R. I., and Lydia R. Sherman, of Exeter, by
         Elder Thomas Tillinghast, Jan. 8, 1837.

1-237   NICHOLS Alexander, of East Greenwich, and Sarah Gould of Exeter, by
         Benoni Hall, Justice. Jan. 29, 1743-4.

1,242   "   Martha, and Richard Sweet, May 3, 1747.

1-243   "   Mary, and Edward Boss, Oct. 22, 1748.

1-194   "   Elizabeth, and Zebulon Barber, March 21, 1755.

1-194   "   Joseph, of Plainfield, Con., and Anna Rathbun, of Exeter, dau. of
         John, dec., by Newman Perkins, Justice, Jan. 13, 1757.

1-195   "   Benjamin, of Exeter, son of James, and Margaret Allen, of East
         Greenwich, by Newman Perkins, Justice, Nov. 27, 1757.

2-167   "   Ruth, and George Hall, Feb. 10, 1766.

3-55   "   John, of Andrew, of South Kingstown, and Phebe Reynolds, of
         John, of Exeter, by George Pierce, Justice, July 23, 1775.

1-194   NILES Jeremiah, of West Greenwich, and Mary Aylesworth, of Exeter, dau.
         of Robert, Jr., by Newman Perkins, Justice, Dec. 8, 1755.

3-26   "   Elizabeth, and Levi Barber, April 29, 1773.

3-13   "   Deborah, and Stephen Weightman, April 12, 1781.

3-176   "   Mary, and Samuel Sherman, Jan. 18, 1794.

1-187   NORTHUP Mary, and Paskow Austin, Sept. 5, 1756.

2-163   "   Penelope, and David Greene, Aug. 15, 1762.

1-153   "   Lebbeus, and Abigail Manton, by W. Waite, Justice, Jan. 19, 1764.

3-157   "   Francis, and Solomon Reynolds, Dec. 24, 1793.

3-160   "   Jeremiah, son of Judge John, late of North Kingstown, dec., and
         Deborah Arnold. of Job, late of Coventry, R. I.; m. at Coven-
         try, by Elder Thomas Manchester, May 25, 1794.

3-162   "   Stukeley, son of Mary, of North Kingstown, and Phebe Rathbun,
         of Isaac, by Stephen Reynolds, Justice, Oct. 4, 1795.

3-34   "   Abbie P., and Peleg A. Dawley, Jan. 19, 1826.

3-14   "   David D., of Richmond, and Dorcas Kingsley, of North Kings-
         town, by Elder Benedict Johnson, Oct. 12, 1841.

O

1-182   OLIN Elizabeth, and Benjamin Gardiner, Nov. 11, 1753.

1-185   "   Henry, of Warwick, R. I., and Charity Vaughn, of North Kings-
         town, by Elder Samuel Albro, Sept. 1, 1754.

1-238   OSBORNE Abigail, and Thomas Wilcox, March 3, 1744.

P

3-177   PALMER Mary, and Joseph Pettey, March 5, 1801.

3-262   "   Aseneth, and Sanford Lewis, Jan. 24, 1813.

3-292   "   Amie, and Samuel Sherman, Jr., June 9, 1822.

3-292   "   George Ray, of Gershom, of Exeter, and Mary Ann Briggs, of
         North Kingstown, dau. of Henry, by Elder Gershom Palmer,
         May 18, 1823.

3-293   '   Gershom, Jr., and Sarah Reynolds, of Benjamin, by Elder Gershom
         Palmer, Aug. 18, 1824.

3-300   "   Roswell, and Mrs. Nellie Barber, by Elder Nathaniel Sheffield, Oct.
         29, 1829.

3-12   "   Almira, and Willett Peckham, June 10, 1841.

3-229   "   Lydia N., and Ranson P. Burdick, April 3, 1843.

3-185   "   Harriet N., and James W. Bates, Nov. 8, 1847.

3-66   "   James A., of Westerly, R. I., and Susan Elvira Perkins, of Exeter,
         by Elder Henry Clarke, Oct. 3, 1867.

3-131   PECKHAM Jeremiah, of Newport, R. I., and Mary Chapman, of Exeter,
         by Elder Solomon Sprague, Sept. 27, 1792.

3-131   PECKHAM Jeremiah, of Benoni, of Newport, R. I., and Elizabeth Whitman, of Daniel, of Exeter, by Elder Ellet Lockee, March 18, 1802.

3-12   "   Willett, of South Kingstown, and Almira Palmer, of Exeter, by Elder Benedict Johnson, June 10, 1841.

3-7   "   James H., of Warwick, R. I., and Mary W. Tripp, of Exeter, by Elder Benedict Johnson, Dec. 12, 1841.

3-88   PENDLETON Elizabeth, and George Lewis, Jan. 12, 1757.

1-186   PERKINS Charity, and Thomas Rathbun, Dec. 21, 1732.

2-177   "   Uriah, of Exeter, son of Newman, and Prudence Corey, of James, of Stonington, Conn., by Stephen Richmond, Justice, July 1, 1768.

3-121   "   Silas, of Ebenezer, of Exeter, and Huldah Saunders, of James, of Westerly, R. I., by Robert Burdick, Justice, Aug. 26, 1789.

3-122   "   Newman, and Nancy Coon, at Hopkinton, by Thomas J. Gardiner, Justice, July 9, 1791.

3-124   "   John, of Exeter, and Mary Wilcox, of Foster, R. I., by Caleb Potter, Justice, Feb. 16, 1792.

3-268   "   Newman, Jr., of Exeter, son of Newman, and Elizabeth James, of West Greenwich, dau. of Joseph, by David Matteson, Justice, April 9, 1815.

3-202   "   Samuel, of Exeter, and Anna Kezer, of Lisbon, Conn., by Rev. Horatio Waldo, March 12, 1820.

3-4   "   Rhodes, of John, of Exeter, and Mary Tourgee, of Smith, of North Kingstown, by Simon Lillibridge, Justice, March 28, 1823.

3-249   "   Williard W., of Exeter, and Mary Gorton, of West Greenwich, by Elder Stafford Greene, June 15, 1834.

3-308   "   Palmer G., of John P., and Susan E. Church, dau. of Norris H., by Elder Steadman Kenyon, Jan. 4, 1852.

3-184   "   Mrs. Hannah M., and Almond S. Reynolds, Jan. 1, 1864.

3-66   "   Susan Elvira, and James A. Palmer, Oct. 3, 1867.

1-190   PETTY David, of Richmond, and Mary Coldgrave, of Exeter, by Daniel Barber, Justice, April 23, 1758.

3-52   "   William, and Anna Aylesworth, by William Sweet, Justice, Sept. 2, 1772.

3-177   "   Joseph, of Nathaniel, and Mary Palmer of Amos, by Nathan Rathbun, Justice, March 5, 1801.

1-177   PHILLIPS Anna, and Benjn. Lawton, May 3, 1752.

1-195   "   Mary, and Samuel Thomas, June 12, 1757.

1-195   "   Samuel, of Exeter, and Phebe Thomas, of Richmond, by Newman Perkins, Justice, Oct. 27, 1757.

1-153   "   Mary, and Jeremiah Rathbun, Aug. 8, 1763.

2-179   "   Thomas, of Exeter, son of Samuel, and Martha Jones, of Silas, of East Greenwich, by Elder Phillip Jenkins, Feb. 9, 1769.

3-133   "   Freeman, and Mary Hoxsie, by J. W. Sheldon, Justice, April 16, 1786.

3-276   "   Thomas, Jun., of Exeter, and Mercy Hoxsie, of West Greenwich, at Warwick, R. I., by Rev. Jonathan Wilson, Feb. 26, 1828.

3-18   "   Sabra, and Benjamin Richmond, Feb. 20, 1842.

3-311   "   Elisha P., of Plainfield, Conn., and Lucy Reynolds, of Exeter, at Exeter, by Elder Alfred B. Burdick, April 23, 1848.

3-267   "   Royal L., and Susan A. Straight, by Elder Pardon Tillinghast, March 15, 1849.

3-227   "   Charles, of Sarah, of Hopkinton, and Mary Ann Carden, dau. of Peter, of Ireland, by Elder Isaac Greene, Feb. 29, 1852.

3-10   PIERCE George, of East Greenwich, and Mary Greene of West Greenwich, at West Greenwich, by Phillip Greene, Justice, Dec. 2, 1753.

3-62   "   Amie, and Oliver Spink, Dec. 16, 1774.

3-93   "   Giles, of Exeter, son of George, and Hannah Arnold, of North Kingstown, dau. of Joseph, at North Kingstown, by Elder Solomon Sprague, Nov. 24, 1785.

1-242   PLACE Thomas, Jr., and Jemima Spencer, both of Exeter, by Elder David Sprague, Dec. 13, 1747.

1-153   "   Peace, and Joseph Smith, Jan. 3, 1763.

2-171   POPPLE Stephen, and Susannah Itullman, by Robert Crandall, Justice, Jan. 24, 1768.

1-242   POTTER Joseph, of Exeter, and Catherine Spencer, of East Greenwich, by Elder David Sprague, Feb. 14, 1747.

1-242   "   Benjamin, and Susannah Sweet, by Peleg Tripp, Justice, Sept. 15, 1748.

1-195   "   Gideon, of Hopkinton, and Hannah Rathbun, by Newman Perkins, Justice, Oct. 30, 1757.

3-19   "   Mary, and Nathan Wilcox, June 15, 1764.

3-31   "   Abel, of Exeter, son of Joseph, and Abigail Staffard, of Coventry, R. I., dau. of Thomas, by Elder Phillip Jenkins, Dec. 16, 1770.

3-65   "   Silence, and Elijah Case, ——,——, 1774.

3-178   "   Joshua, of Smitheon, of Richmond, and Deborah Young, of Caleb, of Exeter, by Stephen Reynolds, Justice, March 18. 1798.

3-11   "   William Waite, of Exeter, son of William, and Thankful Knowles Carpenter, of Jeremiah, of South Kingstown, by Elder Gershom Palmer. Sept. 7, 1816.

3-12   "   Jesse. of Clarke, and Betsey Sherman, of Eber, by Elder Gershom Palmer, March 17, 1825.

3-192   "   Clarke, son of William, dec., and Sarah Sherman, of Wanton, by Elder Gershom Palmer. Sept. 1, 1825.

3-299   "   Samuel C., of Clarke, and Watty Champlain, of Nathaniel, by Elder Moses Fifield, Jan. 2, 1831.

3-15   "   Hannah, and Mary Bates, June 18, 1826.

3-18   "   William C., of Benjamin, and Ann Brayman, of Solomon, by Elder E. J. Locke, April 20, 1843.

3-227   "   Alice, and Reynolds James, March 31, 1844.

3-231   "   Betsey, and John Moore, Dec. 28, 1845.

3-17   "   Lourania B., and Prince A. Taylor, Aug. 10, 1861.

2-171   PULLMAN Susannah, and Stephen Popple, Jan. 24, 1768.

3-164   "   Mercy, and Joseph Wilcox, Jan. 7, 1796.

Q R

1-241   RATHBUN Benjamin, and Hannah Carpenter, by William Tripp, Justice, Oct. 31, 1732.

1-186   "   Thomas, of North Kingstown, and Charity Perkins, of Ebenezer, of Valentine, by John Brown, Justice, Dec. 31, 1732.

1-179   "   Sarah, and Wilbur Earl, Dec. 10, 1752.

1-179   "   Capt. John, and Elizabeth Dawley, of John, Jr., by Benoni Hall, Justice, Dec. 13, 1752.

1-181   "   Thomas, of Exeter, and Mary Clarke, widow of John, late of Newport, by Benoni Hall, Justice, June 3, 1753.

1-184   "   Margaret, and Samuel Havens, Jan. 3, 1754.

1-190   "   Joshua, and Amie Aylesworth, by Newman Perkins, Justice, Jan. 2, 1755.

1-186   "   John, and Mary Ross, by Elder Samuel Albro, July 31, 1755.

1-194   "   Anna, and Joseph Nichols, Jan. 13, 1757.

1-195   "   Jonathan, of John. dec., and Susannah Barber, of Joseph, by Newman Perkins, Justice, March 3, 1757.

1-195   "   Hannah, and Gideon Potter, Oct. 30, 1757.

1-195   "   Daniel, and Mary Foster, by Newman Perkins, Justice, May 28, 1756.

1-158   "   Gideon, and Dorcas Kenyon, by Newman Perkins, Justice, Feb. 18, 1759.

1-159   "   Sarah, and John Wilcox, Sept. 30, 1759.

1-159   "   Mary, and Christopher Kenyon, Dec. 27, 1759.

1-154   "   Rebecca, and Reynolds Cahoone, Nov. 5, 1761.

2-163   "   Marian, and Samuel Hill, Feb. 29, 1762.

2-163   "   Ann, and Oliver Lawton, Oct. 21, 1762.

1-153   "   Jeremiah, and Mary Phillips, by Elder Samuel Albro, Aug. 8, 1763.

2-167   "   Alce, and Randall Lewis, Nov. 21, 1765.

3-19   "   Joseph, of Obedinh, and Margeret Dawley, of John, by Daniel Sunderland, Justice, Aug. 17, 1766.

3-13   "   Charity, and Daniel Barber, Aug. 11, 1769.

2-177	RATHBUN Margaret, and Peleg Dawley, Nov. 27, 1768.	
2-179	" Mercy, and Reynolds Cahoone, Feb. 12, 1769.	
3-63	" Isaac, of John, and Mary Eldred, of Samuel, by Samuel Gorton, Justice, Jan. 14, 1776.	
3-273	" John, of John, of Exeter, and Sarah Casey, of John of West Greenwich, by Elder Caleb Nicholas, Oct. 10, 1776.	
3-28	" Patience, and Benjamin Clarke, Jan. 2, 1780.	
3-79	" Rebecca, and Gideon Arnold, Aug. 18, 1785.	
3-100	" William, and Mrs. Sarah Greene, at Norwich, by Jonathan Huntington, Hon. Justice, July 9, 1786.	
3-118	' Phebe, and Jonathan Wilcox, Jan. 1, 1792.	
3-150	" Anna, and Henry Barber, Nov. 1, 1792.	
3-141	" John, and Joanna Joslin, by Thomas Albro. Justice, March 3, 1793.	
3-202	" Rowland, of John, of Exeter, and Freelove Brown, of Zephaniah, of Hopkinton, by Elder Henry Joslin, May 11, 1794.	
3-158	" Sarah and Samuel Littlefield, Feb. 19, 1795.	
3-162	" Phebe, and Stukeley Northup, Oct. 4, 1795.	
3-163	" Stephen, of Gideon, and Lucy Lewis, of Elisha, by Stephen Reynolds, Justice, Dec. 17, 1795.	
3-174	" Paul, son of Joshua, and Patience Wilcox, widow of Thurston, dau. of Nathaniel Kenyon, by Nathan Rathbun, Justice, Sept. 4, 1796.	
3-183	" Olive, and James Lewis, Oct. 18, 1798.	
3-249	" Anna, and John Rathbun, April 25, 1802.	
3-249	" John, 3d, son of John, Jr., of Exeter, and Anna Rathbun, of Joshua, of Tyringham, Conn., by Elder Elliot Locke, April 25, 1802.	
3-209	" Charity, and Harrington Wilcox, Aug. 1, 1802.	
3-220	" Olive, and Sheffield Rathbun, Feb. 10, 1803.	
3-220	" Sheffield, of Joshua, and Olive Rathbun, of John, by Nathan Rathbun, Justice, Feb. 10, 1803.	
3-232	" Abel, of John, Jr., of Exeter, and Dorcas Lewis, of Jacob, of West Greenwich, by Elder Ellet Locke, Nov. 30, 1806.	
3-299	" Phebe B., and Samuel E. Barber, Nov. 21, 1816.	
3-280	" Joshua, 2d, and Susannah Richmond, of John, by Elder Gershom Palmer, May 22, 1817.	
3-220	" Sheffield, of Exeter, and Dorcas Babcock, of Richmond, by Elder Matthew Stillman, Dec. 20, 1829.	
3-220	" Sheffield, of Exeter, and Esther Adams, of Killingly, Conn., by Elder Stafford Greene, Jan. 1, 1833.	
3-304	" Willett, of Exeter, son of Sheffield, and Hannah Matteson, of West Greenwich, dau. of Reuben, by Elder Stafford Greene, Sept. 9, 1832.	
3-257	" Beriah L., of Exeter, and Hannah Rathbun, of West Greenwich, by Elder Thomas Tillinghast, Oct. 31, 1839.	
3-257	" Hannah, and Bertha L. Rathbun, Oct. 31, 1839.	
3-8	" Henry D., and Susan James, by Elder Benedict Johnson, March 14, 1841.	
3-241	" Sally B., and Edward Barber, April 9, 1844.	
3-247	" Sally, and Ira A. Wilcox, Sept. 18, 1842.	
3-214	" Sheffield, of Joshua, of Exeter, and Betsey Wood of Joab, of Coventry, R. I., dau. of Caleb Briggs, by Isaac Greene, Justice, June 9, 1850.	
1-239	REYNOLDS Mercy, and John Mumford, Oct. 14, 1742.	
1-241	" William, and Hannah Wilcox, by William Tripp, Justice, Nov. 12, 1745.	
1-242	" Benjamin, of John, of Exeter, and Alice Waite, of John, by Benoni Hall, Justice, March 19, 1746.	
3-95	" Sarah, and Sylvester Lewis, June 3, 1748.	
3-139	" Isabel, and Solomon Sprague, June 3, 1750.	
1-244	" Deliverance, and Joshua Gardiner, April 28, 1751.	
1-177	" Susannah, and Samuel Cottrell, Feb. 6, 1752.	
1-181	" Mary, and John Congdon, March 25, 1753.	

1-182 REYNOLDS Robert, of Joseph, of West Greenwich, and Hannah Bentley, of Exeter, dau. of James, at Exeter, by Benoni Hall, Justice, July 15, 1753.

1-186 " Freelove, and John Kenyon, June 8, 1755.

1-187 " Robert, of George, and Eunice Waite, of John, by Elder David Sprague, Jan. 20, 1757.

1-189 " Mary, and Reuben Waite, July 13, 1758.

1-190 " Anne, and Abel Baker, Oct. 7, 1758.

1-192 " Martha, and Nathaniel Cottrell, Dec. 21, 1758.

1-192 " Oliver, of Capt. John, and Mary Gardiner, of Nicholas, by Benoni Hall, Justice, Feb. 8, 1759.

1-160 " James, of James, and Amie Harrington, by Stephen Richmond, Justice, Jan. 10, 1760.

1-157 " Martha, and William Gardiner, March 2, 1760.

1-156 " Benjamin, of South Kingstown, and Anna Harrington, of John, late of Exeter, by Benjamin Reynolds, Justice, Nov. 16, 1760.

1-154 " Elizabeth, and James Sherman, Nov. 19, 1761.

2-170 " Lydia, and Othniel Gardiner, Aug. 16, 1764.

2-166 " Joseph, and Elizabeth Gardiner, by Elder Samuel Albro, April 12, 1765.

2-167 " Benjamin, and Mary Nash, both of South Kingstown, by Elder Samuel Albro, Nov. 11, 1765.

2-176 " Deborah, and Timothy Lawton, Nov. 21, 1765.

2-170 " John, Jr., and Margaret Gardiner, by Thomas Justin, Justice, April 6, 1767.

3-14 " Benjamin, of Job, and Sarah Cottrell, of Nathaniel, by Daniel Sunderland, Justice, Aug. 27, 1769.

3-4 " Joseph, of Benjamin, of Exeter, and Mary Arnold, of Joseph, of North Kingstown, at North Kingstown, by George Thomas, Justice, Oct. 29, 1769.

3-106 " Joseph, of George, of Exeter, and Experience Davis, of William, of West Greenwich, by Elder Solomon Sprague, Oct. 31, 1771.

3-25 " Lydia, and William Hall, Dec. 20, 1771.

3-38 " Henry, of Henry, of West Greenwich, and Mrs. Jemima Weightman, of George, of Warwick, R. I., by Elder John Gorton, Sept. 27, 1772.

3-50 " Hannah, and Sylvester Gardiner, June 6, 1773.

3-70 " Stephen, of North Kingstown, and Abigail Cottrell, of Exeter, by Eber Sherman, Justice, March 3, 1774.

3-55 " Phebe, and John Nichols, July 23, 1775.

3-59 " George, of Job, and Nancy Reynolds, of Jonathan, by George Pierce, Justice, May 30, 1779.

3-59 " Nanney, and George Reynolds, May 30, 1779.

3-267 " Anna, and Phillip Tillinghast, April 14, 1782.

3-66 " Hannah, and Oliver Arnold, Nov. 24, 1782.

3-75 " Alice, and Samuel Champlain, Dec. 10, 1782.

3-77 " Benjamin, of Clement, and Lucy Bentley, by George Pierce, Justice, Dec. 22, 1785.

3-112 " Benjamin, Jr., of Exeter, and Elizabeth Whitford, of David, by Elder Nathan Hill, May 6, 1790.

3-154 " Hannah, and Oliver Ellis, March 1, 1792.

3-129 " Margaret, and William Weaver, Nov. 11, 1792.

3-157 " Solomon, of Robert and Eunice, of Exeter, and Frances Northup, of Rouse and Sarah, of North Kingstown, by Elder William Northup, Dec. 24, 1793.

3-184 " Waite, of Thomas, of West Greenwich, and Elizabeth Crandall, of Joseph, (dec.), of Exeter, by Elder Elisha Greene, April 28, 1796.

3-179 " Abigail, and Moses Clarke, Jr., Feb. 22, 1798.

3-187 " Lucy, and Benjamin T. Tefft, Sept. 8, 1799.

3-215 " James, of Amos, and Ruth Gardiner, of John, late of Exeter, by Elder Thomas Manchester, March 27, 1803.

3-218 " John, of Stephen, of Exeter, and Mercy Tefft, of Benjamin, of Richmond, by Elder Henry Joslin, June 4, 1804.

3-228 " Mary, and David Dawley, Dec. 11, 1806.

3-243	REYNOLDS Stephen, Jr., and Abigail Terry, of Seth, by Elder Stephen Allen, Aug. 30, 1807.
3-266	" Samuel, of Stephen, of Exeter, and Deborah Lillibridge, of Champlain, of Richmond, by Elder Gershom Palmer, July 31, 1808.
3-274	" Job, of Exeter, son of Stephen, and Joanna Barber, of Richmond, dan. of Caleb, by Elder Gershom Palmer, Feb. 17, 1811.
3-256	" Sarah, and Moses Terry, Jan. 23, 1812.
3-278	" Daniel, of Exeter, son of Stephen, and Alice Moore, of Richmond, dan. of George, by Elder Gershom Palmer, Feb. 18, 1813.
3-293	" Sarah, and Gershom Palmer, Jr., Aug. 15, 1824.
3-166	" Samuel B., and Mary Hall, by Elder Peleg Peckham, June 30, 1825.
3-301	" Margeret, and Stephon Terry, June 20, 1835.
3-303	" Ezra, of Exeter, and Sarah Kenyon, of Richmond, by Elder Thomas Manchester, Oct. 20, 1836.
3-8	" Benjamin H., of Richmond, and Phebe A. James, of Exeter, by Elder Daniel Slocum, June 30, 1844.
3-311	" Lucy, and Elisha P. Phillips, April 23, 1848.
3-42	" William H., now residing in Coventry, R. I., and Nancy Kettle, of West Greenwich, now residing in Warwick, R. I., by Elder Thomas Manchester, July 3, 1848.
3-104	" Joseph C., of Exeter, and Mrs. Louisa Allen of Providence, by Elder Joseph McReady, April 25, 1853.
3-184	" Almond F., of Daniel, and Hannah M. Perkins, of John P., by Elder Wm. R. Slocum, Jan. 1, 1864.
3-190	RHODES John, of John, dec., and Sarah Hill, of Barnett, by Elder Thomas Manchester, March 14, 1799.
2-287	RICE Sally, and John Dawley, April 26, 1841.
1-195	RICHMOND Elizabeth, and Spink Hiames, Oct. 6, 1757.
1-158	" Rebecca, and Robert Watson, Aug. 3, 1758.
2-167	" John, and Sarah Morey, by Newman Perkins, Justice, Oct. 20, 1765.
2-175	" Content, and Earl King, Jan. 24, 1768.
3-5	" Stephen, Jr., of Stephen, and Lucy Morey, of Sarah, Jr., by Newman Perkins, Justice, Jan. 18, 1776.
3-225	" John, of Stephen, late of Exeter, dec., and Polly Maxson, of George, late of Hopkinton, dec., by Elder Henry Joslin, March 2, 1801.
3-238	" Sally, and Nathan B. Lewis, Feb. 4, 1808.
3-265	" Stephen, of Exeter, and Margaret Wilcox, of Jeremiah, of Foster, R. I., by Elder John Hammond, Sept. 29, 1808.
3-281	" Benjamin, and Eliza Lewis, by Elder Gershom Palmer, April 14, 1815.
3-279	" Stephen, of Exeter, son of Edward, and Geriah Lewis, of Rowswell, by Rowswell Palmer, Justice, Dec. 3, 1815.
3-280	" Susannah, and Joshua Rathbun, 2d, May 22, 1817.
3-110	" Robert, of Exeter, son of Stephen, dec., and Lydia Clarke (widow), of Charlestown, by Elder Gershom Palmer, Dec. 21, 1826.
3-18	" Benjamin, of Exeter, and Sabra Phillips, of Voluntown, Conn., now of Exeter, by Elder John Tillinghast, Feb. 20, 1842.
3-257	" Desire C., and James C. Hood, Sept. 4, 1850.
1-243	ROBERTS Jane, and Gideon Casey, July 31, 1847.
3-287	ROBINSON Joseph, and Mrs. Caroline Ga——ana, by Elder Henry C. Hubbard, March 4, 1830.
3-291	ROBINS Jonathan, and Mrs. Eliza Lanphere, by Elder John Tillinghast, Dec. 19, 1847.
3-5	ROGERS Martha, and William Austin, Feb. 4, 1770.
3-94	" Jonathan, of Exeter, and Hannah Cobb, of North Kingstown, now residing in Western New York, by Jonathan Dean, Justice, Feb. 18, 1781.
3-99	" Benjamin, of Thomas, of Exeter, and Lucy Cobb, of West Greenwich, by Jonathan Dean, Justice, Dec. 27, 1787.
3-2	ROUSE Charlotte, and Beriah Dawley, Jan. 8, 1824.
2-165	ROSS Jonathan, of Richmond, and Phebe Tripp, of Exeter; m. by Elder Samuel Albro, April 8, 1764.
1-186	" Mary, and John Rathbun, July 31, 1755.

S

3-15, 111 SANFORD Susan Ann, and Stukeley Brown, Jan. 24, 1842.

3-205 SAILE John, and Delia Barber, widow of John, by Isaac Greene, Justice, June 10, 1849.

3-121 SAUNDERS Huldah, and Silas Perkins, Aug. 26, 1789.

3-255 SEPSON Hannah, and James Clarke, Oct. 27, 1811.

3-15 SEWALL Dorcas, and Rufus Chapman, May 19, 1770.

2-181 SHAW Kezia, and John Crandall, May 18, 1768.

3-137 " Anthony, of Exeter, and Anna Dyre, of North Kingstown, at East Greenwich, by Elder Nathan Hill, April 25, 1793.

1-238 SHEFFIELD Mary, and Stephen Wilcox, Oct. 17, 1744.

3-176 " Betsey, and Richard Boone, Jr., April 23, 1795.

3-47 SHELDON Alice, and Stephen Lewis, Jan. 26, 1770.

3-108 " Amie, and John Lewis, Sept. 28, 1777.

3-146 " Roger, and Elizabeth Lewis, by Phineas Kenyon, Justice, Feb. 14, 1783.

3-237 " Lucy, and John H. Sherman, Sept. 5, 1810.

3-111 " Roger, Jr., of Exeter, and Prudence Lewis, of West Greenwich, dau. of Jacob, by Elder Gershom Palmer, April 11, 1811.

3-264 " James, of Roger, and Sally Dawley, of James, by Elder Gershom Palmer, Dec. 6, 1811.

3-267 " John, of Roger, and Elizabeth Lillibridge, of Gardiner, by Elder Gershom Palmer, Dec. 25, 1814.

3-302 " James, of Exeter, and Sarah T. Hoxsie, of Richmond, by Elder Benedict Johnson, March 24, 1839.

1-237 SHERMAN Amie, and Benjamin Lillibridge, Dec. 15, 1743.

1-238 " Benjamin, of Exeter, and Freelove Anstin, of North Kingstown, by Elder David Sprague, March 16, 1744.

1-240 " Moses, and Sarah Austin, by Nicholas Gardiner, Justice, March 31, 1745.

1-221 " Ezekiel, of Jonathan, and Mary, and Margeret Knowles, of John, Feb. 26, 1747.

1-244 " Susannah, and Peregrine Tripp, Jan. 22, 1749.

1-179 " Stephen, of North Kingstown, and Giffe Sweet, of Exeter, by Nicholas Gardiner, Justice, July 15, 1749.

1-180 " Mary, and John Davis, Dec. 21, 1752.

1-191 " Moses, and Mary Tarbox, by Benjamin Reynolds, Justice, July 13, 1758.

1-154 " James, of South Kingstown, and Elizabeth Reynolds, of Exeter, by John Lillibridge, Justice, Nov. 19, 1761.

1-154 " Silas, and Lydia Sweet, by Benjamin Reynolds, Justice, March 7, 1762.

2-175 " Millie, and Benjamin Dawley, March 4, 1768.

2-175 " Mercy, and Oliver Dawley, March 31, 1768.

3-120 " Abigail, and William Champlain, April 5, 1790.

3-176 " Samuel, of Moses, of Exeter, and Mary Niles, of Jeremiah, of West Greenwich, by Elder Phillip Jenkins, Jan. 18, 1794.

3-129 " Hannah, and John Keppard, March 7, 1797.

3-201 " Elizabeth, and William Underwood, Nov. 12, 1801.

3-237 " John H., of North Kingstown, and Lucy Sheldon, of Exeter, by Elder Gershom Palmer, Sept. 5, 1810.

3-246 " Freelove, and Reynolds Sherman, March 22, 1811.

3-246 " Reynolds, of Exeter, and Freelove Sherman, of North Kingstown, by Stephen Reynolds, Justice, March 22, 1811.

3-7 " Sarah, and David Cottrell, Jan. 28, 1817.

3-292 " Samuel, Jr., and Amie Palmer, of Gershom, by Elder Gershom Palmer, June 9, 1822.

3-12 " Betsey, and Jesse Potter, March 17, 1825.

3-192 " Sarah, and Clarke Potter, Sept. 1, 1825.

3-3 " Othniel, Jr., and Mary Whitman, of James, dec., by Elder Gershom Palmer, Oct. 2, 1826.

3-293 " Lydia R., and David Nicholas, Jan. 8, 1837.

3-10   SHERMAN Gershom, of Exeter, and Abbie A. Ney, of North Providence, at Pawtucket, by Rev. S. S. Bradford, July 24, 1843.

3-10   "   Susan E., and Hiram Barber, Dec. 28, 1845.

3-285 SHIPPEE Albert G., of John, of East Greenwich, and Mary Sunderland, of Nathaniel, of Exeter, by Elder Daniel Slocum, Dec. 15, 1844.

3-288 "   Pardon V., of Allen, of East Greenwich, and Hannah M. Stone, of Wanton, of Coventry, R. I., at Exeter, by Elder Daniel Slocum, March 15, 1846.

3-191 "   John, of Thomas, and Sarah Aldrich, of Philip, both of Glocester, R. I., by Stephen Reynolds, Justice, not given.

3-169 SISSON Clarke, of Rodman, of Richmond, and Elizabeth Gardiner, of Exeter, dau. of Nicholas, Jr., by Elder Elisha Greene, Nov. 3, 1796.

3-281 "   Mary, and James Lewis, Sept. 2, 1838.

3-174 "   John S., and —— ——, by Elder Thomas Tillinghast, March 19, 1844.

1-183 SKILLION John, of Coventry, R. I., and Mary McQueen, transient woman, at Exeter, by Newman Perkins, Justice, May 28, 1754.

3-283 SLOCUM John, of Capt. Eleazer, of Exeter, and Elizabeth Fowler, of John, of North Kingstown, by Elder Thomas Manchester, May 23, 1819.

3-289 "   Daniel, son of Eleazer, of Exeter, and Susannah Clarke, of Richmond, dau. of Moses, Jr., by Elder Gershom Palmer, Oct. 24, 1822.

1-192 SMITH Hannah, and John Smith, March 19, 1759.

1-192 "   John, of South Kingstown, and Hannah Smith, widow of Benjamin, late of Newport, by Benjamin Reynolds, Justice, March 19, 1759.

1-193 "   Patience, and William Thorn, April 12, 1759.

1-156 "   Dorcas, and Joshua Clarke, April 23, 1760.

2-163 "   Sarah, and Nathaniel Cottrell, June 10, 1762.

1-153 "   Joseph, of North Kingstown, and Peace Place, of Exeter, by Elder Samuel Albro, Jan. 3, 1763.

3-69   SNOW Samuel, Jr., of Taunton, Mass., and Ann M. Walker, of Exeter, at Exeter, by Elder Pardon Tillinghast, Feb. 3, 1851.

1-240 SPENCER John, of Peleg, of East Greenwich, and Mary Gardiner, of Isaac, of North Kingstown, at North Kingstown, by William Spencer, March 23, 1732.

1-237 "   Rebecca, and Ebenezer Harrington, Dec. 18, 1743.

1-242 "   Catherine, and Joseph Potter, Feb. 14, 1747.

1-242 "   Jemima, and Thomas Place, Dec. 13, 1747.

1-189 "   Theophilus, of Exeter, and Elizabeth Matteson, of West Greenwich, by Elder Samuel Albro, Nov. 11, 1757.

1-193 "   John, of East Greenwich, and Sarah Hull, now residing in Exeter, widow of Teddeman Hull, of Jamestown, by Benjamin Reynolds, Justice, Feb. 25, 1759.

3-308 "   Almira, and Samuel K. Matteson, Sept. 6, 1846.

2-175 SPINK Sarah, and Joseph Eldred, Aug. 29, 1767.

3-62   "   Olive, of North Kingstown, son of Oliver (dec.), and Amie Pierce, of Exeter, dau. of George; m. at Exeter by Elder Solomon Sprague, Dec. 16, 1774.

3-139 SPRAGUE Solomon, and Isabel Reynolds, by Joshua Morse, Justice, June 3, 1750.

3-140 "   Dr. Simon, of Exeter, and Abigail Holloway, of Newport; m. at Newport by Rev. Gardiner Thurston, Jan. 13, 1782.

3-272 "   Solomon, of Jeremiah, and Susannah Dawley, of Daniel, by Elder Gershom Palmer, July 9, 1815.

1-237 STAFFORD Thomas, and Mercy Cleveland, by Nicholas Gardiner, Justice, Nov. 25, 1743.

3-31   "   Abigail, and Abel Potter, Dec. 16, 1770.

2-171 STANTON Catherine, and William Clarke, May 10, 1767.

2-171 "   Latham, and Martha Watson, by Robert Crandall, Justice, Jan. 3, 1768.

3-207 "   Mary, and Joseph Lewis, Jan. 6, 1774.

3-172 STANTON Catherine, and Allen C. Douglass, Dec. 23, 1824.

3-288 STONE Hannah M., and Pardon V. Shippee, March 15, 1846.

3-242 STRANGE Caleb, of William, and Annie Lewis, of Elisha, by Joshua Pierce, Justice, April 16, 1809.

3-171 STRAIGHT Eleanor, and William Lewis, Nov. 29, 1786.

3-267 " Susan A., and Royal L. Phillips, March 15, 1849.

1-237 SUNDERLAND Mercy, and Thomas Thurston, Oct. 18, 1743.

1-177 " Daniel, of William, and Alce Harrington, of Job, by Benoni Hall, Justice, Feb. 6, 1752.

1-177 " Joseph, of Exeter, and Susannah Baker, of John, by Benoni Hall, Justice, Feb. 7, 1752.

1-157 " Mary, and John Sweet, March 23, 1760.

3-143 " George, of William (dec.), and Deborah Wilcox, of Jeffery, by Hapson Wilcox, Justice, Sept. 25, 1774.

3-314 " George B., and Mrs. Sarah Gardiner; m. by Rev. Pardon Tillinghast, Jan. 22, 1870.

3-233 " John, of George, and Nancy Hathaway, of Nathan, by Elder Gershom Palmer, May 17, 1807.

3-178 " Massena, and Francis E. Briton, Aug. 19, 1844.

3-285 " Mary, and Albert G. Shippee, Dec. 15, 1844.

3 286 SWAN, Mrs. Phebe, and John Lillibridge, June 4, 1820.

1-237 SWEET, John, and Abigail Eldred, by Benoni Hall, Justice, Feb. 5, 1743-4.

1-240 " Hannah, and Daniel Dawley, April 26, 1744.

1-242 " Richard, of North Kingstown, son of John, (dec.) and Martha Nichols, of Exeter, by Benoni Hall, Justice, May 3, 1747.

1-242 " Susannah, and Benjamin Potter, Sept. 15, 1748.

1-179 " Giffe, and Stephen Sherman, July 15, 1749.

1-178 " William, and Elizabeth Whitford, of John, by Benjamin Morey, Justice, March 8, 1752.

1-181 " William, and Lydia Mott, both of North Kingstown, by Benoni Hall, Justice, March 18, 1753.

1-157 " John, and Mary Sunderland, dau. of William, by Benjamin Reynolds, Justice, March 23, 1760.

1-156 " Jonathan, and Ede Wilcox, by Stephen Richmond, Justice, Nov. 13, 1760.

1-155 " Samuel, and Sarah Wilcox, by Elder Samuel Albro, May 10, 1761.

1-154 " Lydia, and Silas Sherman, March 7, 1762.

1-165 " Benjamin, and Mercy Hill, by Elder Samuel Albro, Dec. 13, 1764.

3-38 " Jeremiah, of Exeter, and Jane Eldred, of West Greenwich, by Elder James Whitman, July 12, 1771.

3-57 " Ruth, and Benjamin Morey, Jan. 16, 1775.

3-76 " Sarah, and Benjamin Congdon, Sept. 11, 1785.

3-205 " Thomas, and Elizabeth Tingley, by Elder Thomas Tillinghast, Sept. 2, 1802.

3-301 " Miss Sarah G., and Zebulon Gardiner, Sept. 4, 1831.

3-11 " Albert, of Exeter, and Clarissa D. Vaughn, of East Greenwich, by Elder Benedict Johnson, Aug. 23, 1841.

T

1-178 TANNER, Henry, and Dorcas Gardiner, of Nicholas, late of Exeter (dec.), by Benjamin Morey, Justice, Aug. 13, 1752.

1-184 " James, of West Greenwich, and Mercy Wilcox, of George, of Stonington, Conn., by Newman Perkins, Justice, Dec. 24, 1753.

1-196 " Amie, and Jeremiah Brown, Jan. 19, 1758.

1-153 " Thomas, and Mary Whitford, of John, by Benjamin Reynolds, Justice, April 15, 1762.

3-125 " Smith, of Thomas, and Joanna Hammond, by Stephen Reynolds, Justice, March 4, 1792.

3-213 " Lydia, and John Lewis, May 29, 1803.

3-226 " John, of Reuben, of Exeter, and Catherine Crandall, of Joseph, of Richmond, at West Greenwich, by Elder John Tillinghast, May 25, 1845.

3-178   TARBOX Mary, and Moses Sherman, July 13, 1758.
3-178   "   Robert W., of Fones W., of West Greenwich, and Harriet M.
                Wells, of John, of East Greenwich, by Elder Daniel Slocum, Dec.
                8, 1845.
3-17   TAYLOR Prince A., and Laurania B. Potter, by Elder Pardon Tillinghast,
                Aug. 10, 1861.
3-170   TEFFT Mary, and William Hesaline, Jan. 4, 1787.
3-173   "   Mrs. Patience, and Wilcox Barber, June 1, 1797.
3-187   "   Benjamin T., of Thomas, of Richmond, and Lucy Reynolds, of
                Stephen, of Exeter, by Moses Barber, Justice, Sept. 8, 1799.
3-213   "   Mercy, and John Reynolds, June 4. 1804.
3-15   "   George, of John, of Exeter, and Alce James, of Richmond, dau. of
                Stephen, by Elder Gershom Palmer, April 1, 1827.
3-236   "   Alice, and Amos Tefft, Dec. 29, 1839.
3-236   "   Amos, and Alice Tefft, by Elder Benedict Johnson, Dec. 29, 1839.
3-114   TERRY Merebah, and Russell Arnold, Oct. 24, 1790.
3-170   "   Patience, and James Boone, Jan. 8, 1797.
3-116   "   Abraham, of Exeter, and Mary Franklin, of Hannon, by John Rich-
                mond, Justice, April 4, 1791.
3-243   "   Abigail, and Stephen Reynolds, Aug. 30, 1807.
3-253   "   Mary, and Reuben Barber, Feb. 18, 1810.
3-256   "   Moses, of Seth, and Sarah Reynolds, of Stephen, by Elder Gershom
                Palmer, Jan. 23, 1812.
3-125   "   David, of Seth, and Charity Kenyon, of John, by Elder Peleg
                Peckham, June 6, 1824.
3-301   "   Stephen, and Margaret Reynolds, by Isaac Greene, Justice, June
                20, 1835.
3-216   "   Sarah, and William Young, Nov. 1, 1846.
3-23   TEW Mrs. Naomi, and John Congdon, Oct. 22, 1770.
3-241   "   James, of Warwick, R. I., and Phebe Ann Church, of Exeter,
                by Elder John Gorton, March 22, 1836.
1-185   THOMAS Sarah, and Tillinghast Bentley, May 25, 1755.
1-195   "   Samuel, of Richmond, and Mary Phillips, of Exeter, by Newman
                Perkins, Justice, June 12, 1757.
1-195   "   Phebe, and Samuel Phillips, Oct. 27, 1757.
3-305   "   Hannah, and Gardiner Tillinghast, Oct. 30, 1834.
1-183   THOMPSON Prudence, and Benjamin Johns, March 20, 1754.
1-193   THORNE William, of West Greenwich, and Patience Smith, of East Green-
                wich; m. at Exeter by Elder Samuel Albro, April 12, 1759.
1-153   "   Edward, of West Greenwich, and Hannah Tripp, of Exeter, by
                Thomas Joslin, Justice, May 20, 1762.
1-237   THURSTON Thomas, of West Greenwich, and Mercy Sunderland, by Be-
                noni Hall, Justice, Oct. 18, 1743.
3-170   "   Sarah, and Lyman Moon, Sept. 7, 1839.
3-236   "   Amie H., and Oliver Lockwood, Nov. 5, 1849.
3-266   TILLINGHAST Stukeley, of Exeter, son of Pardon, of West Greenwich,
                and Honor Hopkins, of Samuel, of West Greenwich, Nov. 22,
                1762.
3-57   "   Daniel, of Pardon, and Penelope Brown, widow of Christopher, by
                Geo. Pierce, Justice, Oct. 17, 1779.
3-2,67   "   Phillip, son of Phillip, and Anna Reynolds, of Joseph, by George
                Pierce, Justice, April 14, 1782.
3-67   "   Phillip, of Exeter, and Frances Hall, of North Kingstown, at
                North Kingstown, by Elder Solomon Sprague, April 13, 1791.
3-182   "   Thomas, of Thomas, of West Greenwich, and Alice Barber, of
                Lillibridge, of Exeter, by Stephen Reynolds, Justice, Feb. 7,
                1799.
3-186   "   Allen, of West Greenwich, son of Charles (dec.), and Ruth Lewis,
                of Sylvester, of Exeter, by Stephen Reynolds, Justice, July 11,
                1799.
3-216   "   James, and Annie Gardiner, by Elder Ellet Locke, Feb. 5, 1801.
3-236   "   Anna, and Thomas Tillinghast, Dec. 13, 1807.
3-236   "   Thomas, of West Greenwich, son of Pardon, and Anna Tilling-
                hast, of Exeter, widow of John, by Elder Gershom Palmer,
                Dec. 13, 1807.

3-247   TILLINGHAST Fannie, and John C. Codner, July 22, 1810.
3-184   "   Phillip, of Samuel and Martha, and Elizabeth Arnold, of Benjn.
            and Elizabeth; m. at North Kingstown by Elder William
            Northup, May 4, 1826.
3-305   "   Gardiner, of Samuel and Martha, and Hannah Thomas, of Cogswell
            and Sally, by Elder William Northup, Oct. 30, 1834.
3-289   "   William W., of East Greenwich, son of Thomas, and Sally M.
            Congdon, of West Greenwich, dau. of John; m. at Exeter by
            Elder Daniel Slocum, July 3, 1843.
3-228   "   Hannah, and Samuel K. Barber, Dec. 12, 1848.
3-203   TINGLEY Elizabeth, and Thomas Sweet, Sept. 2, 1802.
1-180   TOMBS Damarius, and James Brown, Dec. 7, 1732.
1-241   TOMS Simeon, of Exeter, and Phebe Hopkins, of West Greenwich, by Nicho-
            las Gardiner, Justice, March 13, 1745.
3-4   TOURGEE Mary, and Rhodes Perkins, March 28, 1823.
1-238   TRIPP Capt. William, of Exeter, and Mary Waite, of West Greenwich, by
            Jeremiah Ellis, Justice, Nov. 13, 1743.
1-244   "   Peregrine, of Exeter, and Susannah Sherman, of South Kingstown,
            by Peleg Tripp, Justice, Jan. 22, 1749.
1-178   "   Mehitable, and Benjamin Greene, Sept. 22, 1752.
1-187   "   Job, Jr., of Exeter, and Virtue Waite, dau. of Benjamin, of West
            Greenwich, by Preserved Hall, Justice, March 24, 1755.
1-160   "   Virtue, and John Vaughn, Sept. 9, 1759.
1-155   "   Mary, and Thomas Weeden, May 11, 1760.
1-196   "   Anna, and Ichabod Moshier, July 13, 1760.
1-153   "   Hannah, and Edward Thorne, May 20, 1762.
2-165   "   Phebe, and Jonathan Ross, April 8, 1764.
2-170   "   Ezekiel, and Mary Lawton, by William Hall, Justice, April 29,
            1765..
3-3   "   Waite, and David Harrington, March 27, 1768.
2-177   "   Catherine, and Robert Wilcox, April 14, 1768.
2-179   "   Benjamin, of Job, of Exeter, and Anna Moshier, of James, of
            Richmond, by Gideon Moshier, Justice, March 29, 1769.
2-179   "   Sarah, and Joseph Holloway, May 23, 1769.
3-16   "   Sarah, and Jeremiah Vaughn, June 23, 1776.
3-268   "   Charles, of Exeter, and Margaret Weeden, of Providence, by Rev.
            Henry Edes, Dec. 9, 1816.
3-7   "   Mary W., and James H. Peckham, Dec. 12, 1841.

U

3-201   UNDERWOOD William, of Samuel, of South Kingstown, and Elizabeth
            Sherman, of Eber, Jr., of Exeter, by Stephen Reynolds, Jus-
            tice, Nov. 12, 1801.

V

1-185   VAUGHN Elizabeth, and Joseph Wood, May 12, 1754.
1-185   "   Charity, and Henry Olin, Sept. 1, 1754.
1-160   "   John, of North Kingstown, and Virtue Tripp, widow of Job, at
            Exeter, by Benoni Hall, Justice, Sept. 9, 1759.
3-16   "   Jeremiah, of North Kingstown, son of Isaac, and Sarah Tripp, of
            Exeter, dau. of Peregrine, by George Pierce, Justice, June 23,
            1776.
3-60   "   Joshua, of North Kingstown, son of Isaac, and Lucy Brayman,
            of New London, dau. of James, of Exeter, by Samuel Bissell,
            Justice, Dec. 31, 1793.
3-192   "   Stephen, of West Greenwich, son of George, and Elizabeth Boone,
            of Exeter, dau. of Richard, by Stephen Reynolds, Justice,
            Dec. 13, 1799.
3-234   "   Elizabeth, and Tillinghast Morey, Dec. 26, 1805.
3-11   "   Clarissa D., and Albert Sweet, Aug. 23, 1841.
3-7   "   Julia Ann, and John H. Joslin, Aug. 30, 1841.

3-229   VAUGHN Mary S., and Joseph P. Franklin, Nov. 25, 1844.
3-229   "   Clancey G., and Albert G. Franklin, Dec. 18, 1848.
2-163   VINCENT Deborah, and Nicholas Gardiner, (also 3-53), Oct. 19, 1762.

W

1-238   WAITE Mary, and William Tripp, Nov. 13, 1743.
1-242   "   Alce, and Benjamin Reynolds, March 19, 1746.
1-243   "   Elizabeth, and George Weightman, Dec. 21, 1746.
1-178   "   Samuel, and Ancillis Jenckes, at Smithfield, R. I., by Thomas Lapham, Justice, July 26, 1752.
1-179   "   Eleanor, and Robert Moon, Nov. 23, 1752.
1-187   "   Virtue, and Job Tripp, Jr., March 24, 1705.
1-188   "   Phebe, and Robert Bailey, Jan. 28, 1757.
1-187   "   Eunice. and Robert Reynolds, June 2, 1757.
1-190   "   Domarius, and Daniel Whitman, June 5, 1757.
1-180   "   Sarah and Joseph Babcock, Feb 9, 1758.
1-189   "   Reuben, and Mary Reynolds, of George, by Benjamin Reynolds, Justice, July 13, 1758.
2-165   "   Abigail, and Joseph Case, Dec. 29, 1763.
3-26   "   Jenckes, of Exeter, and Sarah Brown, of North Kingstown, by Elder Solomon Sprague, Feb. 11, 1779.
3-7   "   Lucy, and William Hammond, Aug. 15, 1779.
3-71   WAITE Joseph, of North Kingstown, son of Benjn., and Abigail Clarke, of Exeter, by Elder Natham Hill, Feb. 23, 1783.
3-166   "   Mary, and John Clarke, Jan. 17, 1786.
3-69   WALKER Ann M., and Samuel Snow, Jr., Feb. 3, 1851.
3-227   WALTON Sybel, and Isaiah Wilcox, Sept 21, 1806.
1-188   WATSON Stephen, of North Kingstown, and Abigail Arnold, of Exeter, by Elder Samuel Albro, Sept. 4, 1757.
1-158   "   Robert, and Rebecca Richmond, by Newman Perkins, Justice, Aug. 3, 1758.
2-171   "   Martha, and Latham Stanton, Jan. 3, 1768.
3-28   "   Stephen, of Robert, and Mercy Kenyon, of John, by Newman Perkins, Justice, March 2, 1780.
3-105   "   Dorcas, and Stephn King, Feb. 24, 1789.
3-152   "   John, of E., son of Stephen, and Isabel Dyre, dau. of James, of Ashford, Conn., by Robert Crandall, Justice, April 1, 1800.
3-110   "   Freelove, and Job Bly, July 14, 1811.
3-59   WEAVER Harris, and Mary Moon, by William Sweet, Justice, Dec. 20, 1772.
3-129   "   William, and Margaret Reynolds, of Benjamin, by Elder Nathan Hill, Nov. 11, 1792.
1-155   WEEDEN Thomas, and Mary Tripp, by Elder Samuel Albro, May 11, 1760.
3-268   "   Margaret, and Charles Tripp, Dec. 9, 1816.
1-243   WEIGHTMAN George, of North Kingstown, and Elizabeth Waite, of Exeter, by Thomas Casey, Justice, Dec. 21, 1746.
3-38   "   Mrs. Jemima, and Henry Reynolds, Sept. 27, 1772.
3-13   "   Stephen, of Exeter, and Deborah Niles, of West Greenwich, by Jonathan Dean, Justice, April 12, 1781.
1-189   WELLS Thomas, of Peter, of East Greenwich, and Anna Bissell, of Exeter, by Benjamin Reynolds, Justice, June 9, 1758.
3-2   "   Peter, of Peter, of East Greenwich, and Margaret Cleveland, of Palmer, of Exeter (dec.), by John Chapman, Justice, Nov. 19, 1769.
3-286   "   Benoni, of Exeter, and Desire M. Bowen, of Coventry, R. I., by Elder W. E. Johnson, April 3, 1836.
3-10   "   George A., of Silas, of Exeter, and Mary Gardiner, of Jeffrey, of Exeter, by Elder Ezekiel J. Locke, Nov. 30, 1845.
3-178   "   Harriet M., and Robert W. Tarbox, Dec. 8, 1845.
3-252   WESTCOTT Penelope, and Allen Money (prob.), Dec. 10, 1818.
1-191   WEST Frances, and Eunice Fones, by Benjamin Reynolds, Justice, Oct. 1, 1758.

1-159	WEST Benjamin, and Mary Eldred, by Benjamin Reynolds, Justice, Oct. 7, 1759.
2-163	"	Sarah, and John Eldred, March 29, 1762.
3-92	"	Elizabeth, and David Bissell, March 10, 1785.
3-63	WHEATON Robert, and Catherine Holloway, dau. of Joseph, by George Pierce, Justice, March 3, 1776.
3-83	WHEELER Olive, and Joseph Crandall, May 24, 1781.
1-184	WHITFORD Alce, and Nathan Dawley, Jan. 4, 1746.
1-178	"	Elizabeth, and William Sweet, March 8, 1752.
1-185	"	James, and Mary Corpse, of John, of North Kingstown, by Benoni Hall, Justice, Dec. 1, 1754.
1-160	"	Mercy, and Daniel Gill, Jr., Jan. 1, 1760.
1-153	"	Mary, and Thomas Tanner, April 15, 1762.
3-5	"	Amos, son of John, and Sarah Arnold, of Caleb, by George Pierce, Justice, March 28, 1770.
3-112	"	Elizabeth, and Benjamin Reynolds, May 6, 1790.
3-177	"	Caleb, of Solomon, of West Greenwich, and Roxsey Ann Young, dau. of Benjamin, of Exeter, by Elder Daniel Slocum, Oct. 9, 1843.
3-306	"	Mary T., and Clarke S. Greene (also 3-111), Oct. 15, 1848.
1-190	WHITMAN Daniel, of North Kingstown, and Damarius Waite, of Exeter, by Elder Samuel Albro, June 5, 1757.
3-127	"	George, and Hannah Huling Abbie Chace, both of Exeter, by Daniel Sunderland, Justice, Oct. 3, 1790.
3-131	"	Elizabeth, and Jeremiah Peckham, March 18, 1802.
3-245	"	Abigail, and Jonathan Congdon, April 13, 1809.
3-290	"	Mercy, and Whitman A. Lillibridge, March 7, 1823.
3-3	"	Mary, and Othniel Sherman, Oct. 2, 1826.
1-183	WILBUR John, of Exeter, and Mary Morey, dau. of Robert, late of Exeter (dec.), by Newman Perkins, Justice, April 28, 1754.
2-166	"	Martha, and David Codner, Jan. 16, 1763.
3-312	"	Mrs. Susan A., and Benjamin Cornell, Jan. 21, 1841.
1-237	WILCOX Abraham, and Lydia Harrington, June 5, 1739.
1-238	"	Thomas, and Abigail Osborne, of Rachel, by William Tripp, Justice, March 3, 1744.
1-238	"	Stephen, Jr., of Charlestown, and Mary Sheffield, of Exeter, by William Tripp, Justice, Oct. 17, 1744.
1-241	"	Hannah, and William Reynolds, Nov. 12, 1745.
1-184	"	Mary, and James Tanner, Dec. 24, 1753.
1-194	"	Jeremiah, of Richmond, and Mary Morey, of Exeter, dau. of Joseph, by Newman Perkins, Justice, Nov. 9, 1755.
1-158	"	Catherine, and Barney Davis, Sept. 26, 1759.
1-159	"	John, of South Kingstown, and Sarah Rathbun, of Exeter, by Stephen Richmond, Justice, Sept. 30, 1759.
1-156	"	Ede, and Jonathan Sweet, Nov. 13, 1760.
1-155	"	Sarah, and Samuel Sweet, May 10, 1761.
1-153	"	John, of Abraham, and Mary Barber, of Daniel, by Newman Perkins, Justice, Jan. 31, 1762.
3-19	"	Nathan, of Exeter, son of Thomas, and Mary Potter, of Joseph, of South Kingstown, by Daniel Sunderland, Justice, June 15, 1764.
3-16	"	Arnold, of Jeremiah, of South Kingstown, and Susannah Champlin, of Stephen, of Exeter, by Daniel Sunderland, Justice, Jan. 22, 1767.
2-175	"	Abigail, and Samuel Knowles, March 31, 1768.
2-177	"	Robert, and Catherine Tripp, by Hopson Wilcox, Justice, April 14, 1768.
3-5	"	Ishmeal, and Mary Wilcox, by Newman Perkins, Justice, Jan. 15, 1770.
3-5	"	Mary, and Ishmeal Wilcox, Jan. 15, 1770.
3-68	"	Abraham, Jr., of Exeter, and Mary Card, of West Greenwich, at West Greenwich, by Judeth Aylesworth, Justice, Feb. 14, 1770.
3-203	"	Job, and Mary Gates, Feb. 7, 1771.
3-36	"	Anna, and Samuel Hoxsie, Sept. 30, 1772.

3-132	WILCOX	Isaac, and Rebecca Barber, by Elder Solomon Sprague, Jan. 7, 1773
3-26	"	Alice, and Lillibridge Barber, Dec. 30, 1773.
3-143	"	Deborah, and George Sunderland, Sept. 25, 1774.
3-68	"	Abraham, son of Abraham, of Exeter, and Anna Hoxsie, widow of Thomas (dec.), of West Greenwich, by Elder Elisha Greene, Aug. 20, 1781.
3-117	"	Asa, of Job, and Eleanor Lawton, of Josiah, by Stephen Reynolds, Justice, Oct. 16, 1791.
3-68	"	Abraham, Jr., son of Abraham, of Exeter, and Mary Boss, widow of Elder Charles, late of Richmond, by Stephen Reynolds, Justice, Dec. 13, 1791.
3-118	"	Jonathan, son of Abraham, Jr., and Phebe Rathbun, of Nathan, by Stephen Reynolds, Justice, Jan. 1, 1792.
3-124	"	Mary, and John Perkins, Feb. 16, 1792.
3-148	"	Esther, and Leonard Ensworth, Jan. 17, 1793.
3-136	"	Lebbens, of Abraham, and Elizabeth Bates, of John, by Elder Elisha Greene, Jan. 27, 1793.
3-9	"	Rebecca, and Benjn. Bates, Jan. 28, 1793.
3-164	"	Joseph, of Exeter, son of Isaac, and Mary Pullman, of Nathaniel, of West Greenwich, by Elder Elisha Greene, Jan. 7, 1796.
3-174	"	Patience, and Paul Rathbun, Sept. 4, 1796.
3-200	"	Rebecca, and Job Wood, Jan. 25, 1798.
3-209	"	Harrington, of Capt. Job, of Exeter, and Charity Rathbun, of Parish, formerly of Exeter, by Elder Henry Joslin, Aug. 1, 1802.
3-211	"	Nathaniel, and Lucy Lewis, both of Exeter, by Elder Abraham Coone, Dec. 23, 1802.
3-210	"	Isaac, and Alce Barber, by Elder Abram Coone, Feb. 10, 1803.
3-226	"	John, of Major Abraham, and Polly Barber, of Reynolds, by Elder Henry Joslin, Sept. 1, 1805.
3-227	"	Isaiah, of Isaac, late of Exeter (dec.), and Sybel Walton, of Oliver, of Preston, Conn., by Stephen Reynolds, Justice, Sept. 21, 1806.
3-265	"	Margaret, and Stephen Richmond, Sept. 29, 1808.
3-284	"	Mary, and George G. Champlain, Dec. 1, 1811.
3-298	"	Thomas T., and Olive Bates, at Coventry, R. I., by William Hammond, Justice, Oct. 21, 1829.
3-302	"	William B., of Griswold, Conn., and Mary Kenyon, of Exeter, at Voluntown, Conn., by Elder Nathaniel Sheffield, Nov. 8, 1830.
3-291	"	Thomas, of Jonathan, of Exeter, now of East Greenwich, and Esther Morey, of Amos, of Exeter, by Elder Pardon Tillinghast, Nov. 1, 1841.
3-247	"	Ira A., of Nathan, of West Greenwich, and Sally Rathbun, of Sheffield, of Exeter, by Elder John Tillinghast, Sept. 18, 1842.
3-201	"	George W., of Exeter, and Clara Johnson, of Coventry, R. I., by Elder John Tillinghast, Sept. 16, 1849.
2-171	WILKEY	Hannah, and Elijah Harris, Feb. 25, 1768.
2-171	"	Martha, and Benedict Church, March 14, 1768.
3-8	"	John, of Jeremiah, and Betheny Clawson, by George Peirce, Justice, June 24, 1770.
3-74	WILLIAMS	Eunice, and John Browning, Aug. 3, 1777.
3-185	WOODMANSEE	Elizabeth H., and Charles H. Briggs, Nov. 10, 1847.
3-228	"	Thomas, of Hopkinton, and Mary Barber, of Exeter, by Elder Thomas Tillinghast, Dec. 12, 1848.
1-185	WOOD	Joseph, of Scituate, R. I., and Elizabeth Vaughn, of North Kingstown, by Elder Samuel Albro, May 12, 1754.
3-200	"	Job, of Silas, of Stephentown, N. Y., and Rebecca Wilcox, of Isaac, by Elder Thomas Manchester, Jan. 25, 1798.
3-202	"	Asia E., of East Greenwich, and Mrs. Ruth Maker, of Providence*, by Elder Thomas Tillinghast, —— 29, 1833.
3-214	"	Betsey, and Sheffield Rathbun, June 9, 1830.

X Y Z

3-178   YOUNG Deborah, and Joshua Potter, March 18, 1798.

3-188   "   James, of Caleb, and Sarah Money, of Samuel, by Stephen Reynolds, Justice, Sept. 26, 1799.

3-133   "   Bridget, and Reynolds Lewis, June 26, 1814.

3-177   "   Roxey Ann, and Caleb Whitford, Oct. 9, 1843.

3-216   "   William, and Sarah Terry, by Elder Benedict Johnson, Nov. 1, 1846.

EXETER.

BIRTHS AND DEATHS.

A

1-218	ARNOLD Abigail, of Joseph and Patience (1st wife),	Jan. 24, 1733.
1-218	" Joseph, of Joseph and Hannah (2d wife),	Feb. 3, 1738.
1-218	" Stephen,	April 20, 1739.
1-218	" Samuel,	Jan. 16, 1741.
1-218	" Josias,	Dec. 31, 1743.
1-218	" Patience,	July 16, 1745.
1-218	" Mary,	Oct. 9, 1747.
1-218	" Peleg,	Feb. 15, 1749.
1-218	" Oliver,	Oct. 15, 1750.
1-219	" Elizabeth, of Caleb and Hannah,	Jan. 1, 1749.
1-219	" Sarah,	Jan. 11, 1752.
1-219	" Hannah,	Oct. 11, 1753.
1-219	" Caleb,	Nov. 11, 1755.
1-219	" Samuel,	Dec. 24, 1757.
1-219	" Oliver,	Dec. 12, 1759.
1-219	" Peleg,	March 21, 1762.
1-219	" Gideon,	Dec. 18, 1763.
1-219	" Samuel,	died Aug. 7, 1821.
3-128	" Amie, of Oliver and Phebe,	June 15, 1785.
3-128	" Mercy,	July 16, 1787.
3-128	" Dorcas,	March 17, 1790.
3-128	" James, of Oliver and Phebe,	Aug. 4, 1796.
3-83	" Beriah, of Peleg and Lucy,	Dec. 30, 1787.
3-83	" Mary,	June 8, 1791.
3-83	" Rowland,	May 10, 1794.
3-114	" Wm. Terry, of Russell and Meribah,	Feb. 9, 1791.
3-114	" Caleb,	Aug. 21, 1798.
3-114	" Lydia,	Sept. 28, 1804.
3-114	" Sarah,	March 8, 1807.
3-114	" Sheffield,	Aug. 10, 1808.
3-83	" Peleg, of Rowland and Elizabeth,	Aug. 22, 1817.
3-83	" Lucetta,	March 9, 1820.
3-83	" Gideon E.,	Dec. 22, 1821.
3-83	" Mary,	Nov. 5, 1823.
3-83	" Stephen,	June 12, 1826.
3-83	" Hannah,	May 5, 1829.
3-83	" Robert C.,	Oct. 22, 1830.
3-83	" Clarke,	Jan. 27, 1834.
1-242	ALBRO John, of Samuel and Alice,	April 16, 1739.
1-202	" Alce,	Feb. 19, 1743.
1-202	" Thomas,	July 28, 1745.
1-202	" Samuel,	Oct. 12, 1749.
1-202	" Martin,	Feb. 2, 1752.
1-165	" Mary, of Stephen and Alce,	July 31, 1752.
1-165	" Benjamin,	Oct. 24, 1754.
2-172	AUSTIN Sarah, of Paskow,	July 26, 1727.
2-172	" Margaret,	June 9, 1729.
2-172	" ——,	—— —, ——.
2-172	" Gideon,	July 16, 1731.

2-172	AUSTIN Daniel, of Paskow,	July 6, 1733.
2-172	" Paskow,	March 30, 1735.
2-172	" Isaac,	March 10, 1737.
2-172	" Hannah,	April 1, 1739.
2-172	" Jeremiah,	March 16, 1741.
2-172	" Betsey,	Oct. 27, 1744.
2-172	" David,	May 12, 1745.
2-172	" Jonathan,	June 29, 1747.
2-172	" Stephen,	May 30, 1751.
1-202	" Jeremiah, of Jeremiah and Sarah,	Sept. 9, 1730.
1-202	" Elizabeth,	June 29, 1733.
1-202	" Sarah,	Aug. 15, 1738.
1-202	" Thomas,	Aug. 8, 1741.
1-202	" Daniel,	March 17, 1743.
1-202	" Catherine,	June 14, 1746.
1-202	" John,	July 4, 1750.
1-202	" Abigail, of Stephen and Mary,	Aug. 21, 1733
1-202	" Kezia,	Aug. 19, 1739.
1-202	" Rufus,	April 11, 1742.
1-202	" Eunice,	March 31, 1745.
1-202	" Lucy,	July 8, 1747.
3-5	" Joseph, of William and Martha,	Nov. 12, 1770.
3-211	" Palmer, of Simeon and Dorcas,	July 7, 1807.
1-220	AYLESWORTH Mary, of Robert, Jr., and Susannah,	June 12, 1739.
1-220	" Sarah,	March 5, 1740.
1-220	" Robert,	Feb. 1, 1742.
1-220	" Susannah,	Sept. 16, 1745.
1-220	" Elizabeth,	Aug. 16, 1747.
1-220	" Joseph,	April 1, 1750.
1-220	" Amie, 1st,	May 18, 1752.
1-220	" Amie, 2d,	Sept. 4, 1754.
1-220	" Amie, 1st,	d. Aug. 28, 1754.
1-222	" William, of Ephraim and Alce,	Oct. 3, 1744.
1-222	" Anne,	Aug. 3, 1746.
1-222	" Mary,	Feb. 13, 1748.
1-222	" Ephraim,	Dec. 2, 1750.

B

1-220	BABCOCK Mercy, of Jonathan and Lydia,	Oct. 14, 1750.
1-220	" Mary, born Oct. 15, 1751; d. Nov. 17, 1751.	
1-227	" John, died March 30, 1760, aged 32y. 2m. 3d.	
1-226	" George Waite, of John and Lydia,	June 25, 1751.
1-220	" Samuel, of do, b. Jan. 1, 1754; d. Feb. 24, 1757.	
1-226	" Sarah, of John and Lydia,	July 17, 1756.
1-226	" John,	Nov. 28, 1758.
1-227	" Samuel,	Oct. 19, 1760.
1-164	" James, of James and Sarah,	June 22, 1755.
1-164	" Sarah,	Aug. 10, 1756.
1-164	" Mary,	Aug. 4, 1758.
1-164	" Elizabeth, of Joseph and Sarah,	Nov. 29, 1758.
1-164	" Joseph,	March 29, 1768.
3-27	" George Waite, of George Waite and Susannah,	May 11, 1778.
1-169	BAKER Benjamin, of Samuel and Abigail,	Jan. 21, 1749.
1-169	" Amos,	Feb. 2, 1750.
1-169	" Thomas,	Oct. 29, 1751.
1-169	" Ruth,	Feb. 24, 1753.
1-169	" Mary,	Nov. 24, 1756.
1-169	" John,	July 16, 1759.
1-169	" Peleg,	May 23, 1761.
1-169	" Mehitable,	March 10, 1764.
1-165	" Dorcas, of Elisha and Sarah,	May 18, 1754.
1-165	" David,	Dec. 6, 1755.
1-165	" Harrington,	Oct. 8, 1756.
1-165	" Christian,	May 18, 1758.

1-215	BARBER	Rebecca, of Nathaniel and Charity,	June 16, 1755.
3-43	"	Mary, of Moses and Barberry,	May 16, 1764.
3-43	"	Moses,	Nov. 13, 1768.
3-294	"	Moses, Jr., b. Nov. 13, 1768.	
3-294	"	Mary (Clarke), wife of Moses, Jr.,	Feb. 1, 1774.
3-294	"	Moses, 3d, of Moses and Mary,	June 23, 1794.
3-294	"	Robert,	Aug. 21, 1796.
3-294	"	Thomas C.,	Dec. 29, 1798.
3-294	"	Aaron,	Nov. 8, 1800.
3-294	"	Samuel A.,	Feb. 19, 1803.
3-294	"	Washington,	Jan. 11, 1807.
3-294	"	Jefferson,	Jan. 11, 1807.
3-294	"	Naratien,	April 6, 1809.
3-294	"	Benjamin,	Aug. 10, 1814.
3-294	"	Edward,	Feb. 14, 1816.
3-123	"	Wilcox, of Lillibridge and Alice,	March 2, 1774.
3-123	"	Alice,	Aug. 28, 1777.
3-123	"	Edward,	July 17, 1779.
3-123	"	Susannah,	July 17, 1779.
3-123	"	Learnard,	Nov. 30, 1787.
3-123	"	Rhoda,	July 6, 1791.
3-198	"	West, of Asa and Marian,	July 21, 1781.
3-198	"	Asa,	Aug. 28, 1787.
3-198	"	Smith,	Nov. —, 1789.
3-253	"	Mary, of Reuben and Mary,	April 29, 1811.
3-299	"	Rowland Rathbun, of Sam'l C. and Phebe B.,	Sept. 23, 1817.
3-299	"	Sally Rathbun,	April 1, 1824.
3-307	"	Henry, of Thomas C. and Susan,	May 23, 1825.
3-307	"	Clarke,	Dec. 5, 1826.
3-307	"	Mary Ann,	March 5, 1838.
3-238	BARROWS	Catherine 2d, dau. of Joseph and Deborah,	March 25, 1780.
3-6	BATES	Joseph, of Jonathan, Jr., and Anna,	Sept. 25, 1778.
1-201	BEARDMARE	John, of Thomas and Eleanor,	May 17, 1740.
1-201	"	Gideon,	May 11, 1743.
1-201	"	Mary,	Sept. 26, 1745.
1-201	"	Anna,	Aug. 2, 1749.
1-201	"	Nicholas,	May 15, 1752.
1-201	"	Damarius,	May 19, 1754.
1-201	"	Nickolas,	May 13, 1756.
1-201	"	Thomas,	July 6, 1758.
1-201	BENTLEY	Caleb, of Benjamin, Jr., and Sarah,	Aug. 25, 1739.
1-201	"	Joseph,	March 25, 1740-1.
1-201	"	Thomas,	Jan. 4, 1743.
1-201	"	Samuel,	Jan. 4, 1746.
1-201	"	Benjamin,	May 5, 1749.
1-224	"	Patience, of Thomas, Jr., and Margaret,	July 22, 1752.
1-224	"	Sarah,	Sept. 14, 1754.
1-224	"	Benjamin,	March 15, 1757.
1-224	"	John,	Aug. 23, 1760.
1-224	"	Zerviah,	April 4, 1763.
2-169	"	Sarah, of Caleb and Leah,	May 12, 1764.
2-169	"	Hannah,	Feb. 12, 1766.
2-169	"	William,	Jan. 17, 1768.
		Note—Eldest born East Greenwich; the others Exeter.	
1-170	"	Niobe, of Caleb and Martha,	Nov. 2, 1761.
3-34	"	Isaac, of Gideon and Elizabeth,	Aug. 12, 1781.
3-34	"	Christopher,	July 6, 1783.
3-34	"	Thomas,	Jan. 13, 1785.
3-87	BISSELL	Mary, of Samuel and Sarah,	Oct. 16, 1779.
3-87	"	John,	Sept. 15, 1781.
3-87	"	Stephen,	Sept. 29, 1783.
3-87	"	Sarah,	Aug. —, 1785.
3-288	"	Thomas, of Caleb A. and Mary,	July 22, 1823.
3-288	"	Thomas,	died Dec. 19, 1824.
3-288	"	Mary Ann,	Oct. 30, 1824.

3-176	BOONE Lydia Sheffield, of Richard and Betsey,	Feb. 4, 1796.
3-176	" Thomas,	Sept. 13, 1797.
1-202	BRAYMAN Solomon, of James and Elizabeth,	July 2, 1723.
1-202	" Sarah,	Sept. 18, 1731.
3-97	BRIGGS James, of Peleg and Elizabeth,	May 3, 1787.
3-74, 75	BROWNING John, b. Nov. 15, 1742,	died Feb. 24, 1832.
3-74, 75	" Mary, wife of John,	died July 5, 1776.
3-74, 75	" Eunice,	died April 15, 1816.
3-74, 75	" Jedediah, of John and Mary,	Sept. 4, 1767.
3-74, 75	" John,	Oct. 20, 1770.
3-74, 75,	" George Hazard, of John and Eunice,	July 7, 1779.
3-74, 75	" George Hazard,	died April 26, 1795.
3-74, 75	" Mary,	June 1, 1781.
3-74, 75	" Eunice,	June 4, 1783.
3-74, 75	" Avery,	Feb. 8, 1786.
3-74, 75	" Annie,	March 16, 1788.
3-74, 75	" Jesse,	Aug. 31, 1792.
3-74, 75	" George Williams,	Aug. 10, 1796.
3-193	" Thurston, of John and Susannah,	May 3, 1778.
3-271	" Arnold, of Avery and Mary,	May 27, 1810.
3-271	" Hiram,	Oct. 6, 1813.
3-271	" Beriah H.,	Sept. 13, 1819.
3-271	" Eunice Williams,	Dec. 27, 1824.
3-271	" Eunice Williams,	died Feb. 6, 1831.
3-271	" Clarke,	March 10, 1829.
3-15	BROWN James E. (also 3-165),	died March 26, 1846.

C

3-89	CARR Hannah, of John and Mary,	Oct. 9, 1786.
3-89	" John Chapman,	April 10, 1787.
3-89	" Mercy,	March 4, 1789.
3-89	" James Casey,	March 13, 1791.
3-89	" Stephen,	Jan. 30, 1794.
1-214	CASEY Sarah, of John and Mercy,	May 18, 1745.
1-214	" Sarah,	died June 2, 1752.
1-214	" Mary,	April 24, 1747.
1-214	" Mary,	died June 26, 1752.
1-214	" Samuel,	April 14, 1750.
1-214	" Mercy,	April 28, 1752.
1-214	" John,	Feb. 28, 1754.
1-214	" Sarah,	Nov. 7, 1755.
1-214	" Mary,	Feb. 7, 1758.
1-214	" Abel, of John and Mercy,	May 21, 1760.
1-214	" Dorcas,	May 11, 1769.
1-223	" Edmund, of Gideon and Jean,	Aug. 20, 1747.
1-223	" Dorcas, of Thomas and Alce,	June 16, 1749.
1-223	" Mary,	April 6, 1751.
3-17	CASE Elijah, of Alexander and Mary,	April 3, 1753.
3-17	" Lydia,	Feb. 25, 1757.
3-17	" Joseph, 4th son,	Aug. 6, 1759.
3-17	" Hannah,	Aug. 7, 1763.
3-17	" Susannah,	Jan. 12, 1767.
	Note—3 eldest born South Kingstown, 2 youngest Exeter.	
1-208	" Elisha, of Mitchell and Ann,	June 23, 1745.
3-65	" Mary, of Elijah and Silence,	Dec. 12, 1774.
3-65	" Elijah,	Sept. 11, 1776.
1-205	CHAMPLAIN Jeffrey, of Jeffrey and Mary,	Oct. 4, 1726.
1-205	" Thomas,	Sept. 17, 1728.
1-205	" Susannah,	Jan. 1, 1730-1.
1-205	" Mary,	Jan. 12, 1732-3.
1-205	" Emblem,	Jan. 31, 1734-5.
1-205	" Elizabeth,	June 20, 1737.
1-205	" Christopher,	Oct. 13, 1739.

1-205	CHAMPLAIN Benjamin, of Jeffrey and Mary,		Oct. 13, 1741.
1-205	"	Daniel,	June 11, 1744.
1-220	"	John, of John and Freelove,	July 30, 1744.
1-220	"	Samuel,	July 17, 1746.
1-220	"	William,	Aug. 15, 1749.
1-220	"	Stephen,	Aug. 27, 1751.
1-220	"	Thomas.	Jan. 23, 1754.
1-220	"	Abigail,	June 23, 1756.
1-220	"	Elisha,	Nov. 11, 1758.
1-220	"	Susannah,	Oct. 31, 1761.
1-220	"	Freelove,	June 15, 1767.
1-217	"	Jeffrey, of Jeffrey, Jr., and Mary,	Oct. 6, 1749.
1-217	"	George Gardiner,	July 19, 1754.
1-217	"	William,	May 19, 1756.
1-217	"	Stephen,	Feb. 19, 1761.
1-217	"	Mary,	Nov. 1, 1762.
1-217	"	Susannah,	Aug. 19, 1764.
1-217	"	Hannah,	Aug. 19, 1764.
1-217	"	Ezekiel,	April 24, 1767.
1-217	"	Rowland Gardiner,	March 29, 1770.
3-1	"	Christopher, of Christopher and Mary,	March 11, 1764.
3-1	"	Nathaniel,	Nov. 30, 1765.
3-1	"	—— (dau.),	Oct. 17, 1767; died May 26, 1769.
3-1	"	Mary,	d. May, 26, 1769.
3-5	"	Nicholas, of Benjamin and Elizabeth,	Jan. 18, 1764.
3-5	"	Daniel,	Oct. 3, 1769.
3-73	"	Watson, of Thomas and Thankful,	July 11, 1784.
3-98	"	Jordan Sprague, of Elisha and Phebe,	Dec. 15, 1784.
3-98	"	Elizabeth,	Dec. 16, 1787.
3-75	"	John, of Samuel and Alice,	March 26, 1785.
3-75	"	Benjamin,	May 9, 1786.
3-75	"	Hannah,	Dec. 30, 1788.
3-75	"	Waite,	March 20, 1791.
3-75	"	Russell,	July 23, 1793.
3-75	"	Samuel,	Aug. 24, 1796.
3-151	"	Jesse, of Christopher, Jun., and Dorcas,	June 23, 1787.
3-151	"	Hannah,	Dec. 4, 1789.
3-151	"	Mary,	Jan. 6, 1792.
3-151	"	Martha Cottrell,	Jan. 13, 1794.
3-141	"	Hannah, of Stephen and Dorcas,	Aug. 20, 1799.
3-141	"	Hannah, of Stephen and Dorcas,	died, Sept. 6, 1822.
3-141	"	Stephen,	March 9, 1801.
3-1	"	Christopher, died May 26, 1801, in 62d year.	
3-1	"	Mary, widow of do., died Jan. 12, 1813, in 76th year.	
3-1	"	William, of Watson,	Aug. 17, 1808.
3-284	"	Sylvester W., of George G., and Mary,	Aug. 11, 1813.
2-173	CHAPMAN Isaac, of John and Elizabeth,		Feb. 14, 1766.
2-173	"	Mary,	Aug. 8, 1767.
3-167	CHURCH Martha, of Nathaniel and Lucy,		Jan. 27, 1796.
3-167	"	Benedick,	Oct. 19, 1797.
3-167	"	Benedick,	March 16, 1798.
3-167	"	Susannah,	Aug. 7, 1799.
3-28	CLARKE John, of Benjamin and Patience,		Sept. 22, 1780.
3-28	"	Lydia,	March 7, 1783.
3-179	"	Alce, of Moses, Jr., and Abigail,	Sept. 30, 1798.
3-179	"	Stephen,	Dec. 20, 1799.
3-179	"	Susannah,	April 16, 1801.
3-179	"	Abigail,	Sept. 20, 1803.
1-224	CODNER George, of Ephariam, Jr., and Mary,		Feb. 13, 1749.
1-224	"	Nathan.	March 4, 1752.
1-224	"	Ephariam,	Feb. 3, 1753.
3-146	"	Elizabeth, of Ephariam and Peace,	Dec. 29, 1778.
3-146	"	Anna,	Aug. 29, 1780.
3-146	"	Patience,	Oct. 29, 1782.
3-146	"	Barber,	March 27, 1785.
3-146	"	Kenyon,	May 1, 1787.

3-146	CODNER Stephen, of Ephraim and Peace,	April 1, 1789.
3-146	" David,	June 10, 1791.
3-146	" Merabah,	Oct. 18, 1794.
3-146	" Charlotte,	July 15, 1798.
3-146	" Phebe,	March 29, 1800.
1-204	COLDGROVE Sarah, of John and Susannah,	Oct. 18, 1738.
1-204	" Susannah,	May 21, 1740.
1-204	" John,	Jan. 21, 1743.
1-204	" James,	June 29, 1746.
3-11	" Susannah, of James and Ann,	Sept. 4, 1766.
3-11	" Dorcas,	March 27, 1768.
3-11	" Sarah,	Jan. 28, 1770.
3-11	" Russell,	April 2, 1772.
	Note—Youngest bor'n Richmond.	
1-228	CONGDON James, of John and Mary,	Nov. 23, 1753.
1-228	" Hannah,	March 4, 1755.
1-228	" John,	March 23, 1757.
1-228	" Henry,	July 24, 1759.
1-228	" Jonathan,	July 9, 1761.
1-228	" Benjamin,	May 8, 1763.
1-228	" Joseph,	April 18, 1765.
1-228	" Mary,	July 31, 1766.
1-228	" Elizabeth,	Aug. 17, 1768.
3-23	" Azariah, of John and Naomi,	June 18, 1771.
3-23	" J. Naomi,	June 18, 1771.
3-23	" William,	Jan. 1, 1773.
3-23	" Oliver,	April 15, 1775.
3-23	" Mary,	March 15, 1777.
3-23	" Abigail, of John and Abigail (2d m.)	Dec. 2, 1778.
3-23	" Carey	Oct. 21, 1780.
3-23	" Gideon,	Feb. 9, 1783.
3-23	" Peleg,	Oct. 9, 1784.
2-178	CORPSE Anna, of David and Susannah,	Dec. 30, 1763.
1-214	COTTRELL Abigail, of Nathaniel and Deborah,	Feb. 16, 1727.
1-214	" Samuel,	Nov. 27, 1729.
1-214	" Deborah,	Nov. 19, 1731.
1-214	" Joshua,	Sept. 2, 1733.
1-214	" John,	Aug. 15, 1735.
1-214	" John,	died April 11, 1737.
1-214	" Mary,	May 17, 1737.
1-214	" Nathaniel,	Jan. 18, 1739.
1-214	" David,	March 15, 1742.
1-214	" Sarah,	June 10, 1745.
1-214	" Hannah,	Feb. 23, 1748.
3-153	" Abigail, of Samuel and Susannah,	Dec. 11, 1752.
3-153	" John,	Sept. 29, 1755.
3-153	" Lucy,	Feb. 23, 1758.
3-153	" Nathaniel,	Oct. —, 1760.
3-153	" Nathaniel,	died Dec. —, 1762.
3-153	" Martha,	July 22, 1762.
3-153	" Samuel,	April 25, 1765.
3-153	" Freelove,	March 30, 1768.
3-153	" Susannah,	March 30, 1768.
3-194	" Benjamin B., of Samuel, Jr., and Susannah,	March 25, 1792.
3-194	" Mary,	Feb. 11, 1794.
3-194	" Peckham,	March 6, 1796.
3-194	" Jesse,	June 3, 1798.
3-35	CRANDALL Robert,	Feb. 21, 1735.
3-35	" Elizabeth, of Robert and Mary,	July 6, 1766.
3-35	" Annie,	June 5, 1768.
3-35	" Robert,	Dec. 31, 1769.
3-35	" Joseph, of John,	April 22, 1738.
3-33	" Hannah, of Joseph and Olive,	June 14, 1767.
3-33	" Charity,	March 4, 1770.
3-33	" Joseph,	July 13, 1771.

3-33	CRANDALL Olive, of Joseph and Olive,	Oct. 27, 1773.
3-33	" Cate Wheeler,	Nov. 23, 1782.
3-33	" Waite,	Dec. 21, 1784.
3-33	" Edward Wheeler,	May 14, 1788.
3-144	" John G., of Robert and Margaret,	April 21, 1793.
3-144	" Mary,	March 12, 1795.
3-144	" Amie,	April 4, 1797.
3-144	" Robert H.,	April 12, 1798.
3-144	" Joseph,	April 16, 1800.
3-144	" Waite G.,	July 9, 1802.
3-144	" Sarah,	Sept. 29, 1804.
3-144	" Margaret,	Feb. 14, 1807.
3-144	" Hannah,	July 8, 1809.
3-290	" Silas C., of Joseph and Hannah C.,	March 29, 1832.
3-290	" Mary C.,	July 19, 1834.

D

3-52	DAVIS Benjamin, of William and Mary,	Jan. 9, 1774.
3-62	" James, (2d son) of David and Patience,	June 10, 1782.
3-62	" Samuel, (3d son)	Aug. 1, 1785.
3-180	DAWLEY Daniel, Jr., of Daniel,	April 9, 1789.
3-241	" Matilda, of Vincent and Sarah,	July 17, 1809.
3-241	" Christopher Harrington,	Aug. 3, 1811.
3-30	" Alcey Ann, of William and Phebe,	Nov. 27, 1814.
3-30	" William,	Sept. 13, 1817.
3-30	" Roxanna,	Aug. 11, 1822.
3-30	" Elizabeth,	June 22, 1811.

E

1-162	ELDRED Jeremiah, of William and Abigail,	Dec. 13, 1738.
1-162	" William,	Dec. 26, 1744.
1-162	" John,	March 5, 1742.
1-162	" Ruth,	Aug. 5, 1744.
1-162	" Daniel,	Oct. 29, 1746.
1-162	" James,	May 12, 1749.
1-162	" Thomas,	Feb. 26, 1752.
3-154	ELLIS Ann, of Oliver and Hannah,	Nov. 25, 1792.
3-154	" Gideon,	March 11, 1794.
3-168	ENSWORTH Betty, of Learnard and Esther,	Oct. 4, 1795.
3-168	" Esther,	Feb. 25, 1798.
3-168	" Joseph.	June 24, 1803.
3-168	" Job Wilcox,	Aug. 29, 1805.

F

1-208	FOREDICE James, of John and Lucianna,	Jan. 30, 1734.
1-208	" Sarah,	Nov. 18, 1737.
1-208	" John,	May 24, 1740.
1-208	" Lucianna.	Dec. 12, 1744.

G

1-196	GARDINER Isaac, of Benoni and Mary,	Jan. 7, 1687-8.
1-196	" Mary, of Isaac and Elizabeth,	Mar. 30, 1711.
1-196	" Elizabeth,	Mar. 24, 1714-5.
1-196	" Sarah,	May 5, 1716.
1-196	" Isaac,	May 5, 1718.
1-196	" Benoni,	May 31, 1720.
1-1,197	" Samuel,	Sept. 27, 1722.

1-1, 197	GARDINER	Penelope, of Isaac and Elizabeth,	July 19, 1725.
1-1,197	"	Silas,	Oct. 29, 1727.
1-1,197	"	Gideon,	Jan. 8, 1729.
1-1,197	"	Bridget,	Aug. 21, 1734.
1-200	"	Mary, of Nicholas and Martha,	Sept. 22, 1732.
1-200	"	William,	Sept. 9, 1734.
1-200	"	Margaret,	June 13, 1736.
1-200	"	Nicholas,	Mar. 2, 1738.
1-200	"	Martha,	Aug. 31, 1739.
1-200	"	Ann,	May, 28, 1741.
1-200	"	Elizabeth,	Sept. 22, 1743.
1-200	"	Huling,	Aug. 18, 1745.
1-217	"	Peleg. of Isaac, Jr., and Margaret,	June 2, 1740.
1-217	"	Oliver,	June 24, 1742.
1-217	"	Isaac,	Aug. 16, 1744.
1-217	"	Nickolas,	May 30, 1748.
1-217	"	Waite,	Oct. 3, 1751.
1-217	"	Mary,	Sept. 24. 1754.
1-217	"	John,	Nov. 29, 1756.
1-213	"	Lydia, of Jeremiah and Tabitha,	June 15, 1741.
1-213	"	Phebe,	May 27, 1745.
1-213	"	Benjamin,	Nov. 9, 1747.
1-213	"	Othniel, of Benoni and Elizabeth,	June 24, 1742.
1-213	"	Elizabeth,	Dec. 21, 1743.
1-213	"	Latham,	Jan. 11, 1745.
1-168	"	Latham,	died, Feb. 27, 1747.
1-168	"	Benoni,	Aug. 18, 1747.
1-168	"	Benoni,	died Feb. 27, 1749.
1-168	"	Ruth,	Jan. 12, 1750.
1-168	"	Benoni,	Jan. 7, 1752.
1-168	"	Lucy,	May 15, 1755.
1-168	"	Lucy,	died Oct. 27, 1756.
1-163	"	Abel, of John and Amie,	Sept. 2, 1747.
1-163	"	Waite,	May 4, 1750.
1-163	"	Zilpha,	Jan. 14, 1752.
1-163	"	Zilpha,	died Feb. 9, 1752.
1-163	"	John,	April 7, 1753.
1-163	"	Henry Greene,	April 5, 1755.
1-163	"	Samuel,	May 13, 1757.
3-51	"	Benjamin, of Jeremiah, Jun.,	Nov. 9, 1747.
3-51	"	Tabitha, wife of Benjamin,	Sept. 4, 1748.
3-51	"	Clarke, of Benjamin and Tabitha,	June 29, 1767.
3-51	"	Wilbur,	Dec. 16, 1769.
3-51	"	Jeremiah,	Jan. 3, 1772.
3-51	"	Dorcas,	Feb. 13, 1774.
3-61	"	James, of Nicholas and Dorcas,	Oct. 26, 1750.
3-61	"	Sylvester,	Aug. 30, 1752.
3-61	"	Francis,	April 4, 1755.
3-61	"	Dorcas,	March 12, 1760.
3-61	"	Martha, wife of Nicholas,	died Sept. 25, 1746.
3-61	"	Dorcas,	died March 23, 1775.
1-161	"	Benoni, of Samuel and Elizabeth,	March 30, 1751.
1-161	"	Mary,	Jan. 16, 1753.
1-161	"	James,	Oct. 1, 1754.
1-163	"	Sarah, of Caleb and Mary,	May 3, 1754.
1-163	"	Clarke,	Sept. 13, 1755.
1-163	"	Ann,	March 5, 1757.
1-163	"	Heart,	July 15, 1759.
1-176	"	Simeon, of Benj. and Elizabeth,	Oct. 22, 1754.
1-176	"	Alice,	May 6, 1756.
1-176	"	Mary,	Jan. 31, 1757.
1-176	"	Benjamin,	Sept. 13, 1759.
1-176	"	Elizabeth,	Sept. 12, 1761.
1-176	"	Howland,	Sept. 1, 1763.

1-176	GARDINER Nathaniel, of Benj. and Elizabeth,		Oct. 11, 1765.
1-176	"	Caleb,	Feb. 14, 1768.
3-101	"	Samuel, of John and Annie,	May 5, 1757.
3-101	"	Mary,	April 7, 1759.
3-101	"	Amie,	July 1, 1761.
3-101	"	Margaret,	Aug. 27, 1767.
1-166	"	Patience, of Jeremiah and Mary,	Dec. 31, 1757.
1-166	"	Thomas,	May 23, 1760.
1-170	"	Elizabeth, wife of Isaac,	died May 20, 1759.
3-53	"	Honor, of Nicholas and Deborah,	Jan. 3, 1763.
3-53	"	Vincent,	Dec. 9, 1764.
3-53	"	Elizabeth,	April 10, 1767.
3-53	"	Nicholas,	Aug. 11, 1769.
3-53	"	Beriah,	Nov. 16, 1771.
3-53	"	Willett,	Feb. 13, 1774.
3-53	"	Elizabeth,	Oct. 6, 1776.
3-53	"	Benjamin Champlin,	April 27, 1779.
3-56	"	Sarah, of Huling and Elizabeth,	Oct. 7, 1768.
3-56	"	Gould,	Oct. 17, 1772.
3-56	"	Wanton,	Dec. 5, 1775.
3-56	"	Mary,	March 22, 1778.
	Note—Eldest born North Kingstown, the others Exeter.		
3-80	"	Sweet, of Abel and Dorothy,	June 1, 1773.
3-80	"	George,	Aug. 19, 1775.
3-80	"	Mary,	Aug. 14, 1777.
3-80	"	Amie,	Aug. 16, 1780.
3-252	"	Nicholas, of George and Dorcas,	Nov. 7, 1803.
3-229	"	Nathan Allen, of John (of James) and Elizabeth,	Nov. 17, 1805.
3-297	"	Harrison, of Joseph Warren and Mary,	May 18, 1830.
3-297	"	Greene,	Nov. 24, 1831.
3-297	"	Mary Fields,	Sept. 10, 1834.
3-297	"	Joseph Warren,	March —, 1836.
3-297	"	Owen G.,	Jan. 8, 1845.
3-297	"	Massena T.,	Nov. 9, 1846.
3-297	"	Ansel B.,	Jan. 29, 1849.
3-297	"	Calvin P.,	April 24, 1851.
1-211	GILL John, of Daniel and Hannah,		June 29, 1732.
1-211	"	Sarah,	Sept. 30, 1733.
1-211	"	Daniel,	Sept. 25, 1734.
1-211	"	Hannah,	April 2, 1740.
1-211	"	Susannah,	June 30, 1746.
1-211	"	Samuel,	May 1, 1752.
1-213	GREENE Prudence, of Philip and Hannah,		March 7, 1746.
1-213	"	Mary,	Aug. 7, 1748.
1-175	"	Eunice, of Benjamin and Mehitable,	Feb. 6, 1754.
1-175	"	Waite,	June 1, 1755.
1-175	"	Son (b. and d.),	Sept. 27, 1756.
1-175	"	Henry,	Aug. 16, 1757.
1-175	"	Margaret,	Feb. 24, 1759.
1-175	"	Joseph,	Dec. 1, 1760.
1-175	"	Sarah,	Dec. 10, 1762.
1-175	"	Benjamin,	Aug. 13, 1764.
1-175	"	Mary,	May 24, 1766.
1-175	"	Duty,	May 27, 1768.
1-175	"	William,	May 20, 1770.

H

1-170	HALL Sarah, wife of William,		died July 12, 1733.
1-170	"	Mary,	May —, 1741.
1-170	"	Mercy,	Sept. 27, 1757.
1-170	"	William, in his 87th year,	July 9, 1759.
1-198	"	William, of Benoni and Elizabeth,	Aug. 3, 1734.
1-198	"	Henry,	Nov. 16, 1736.

1-198	HALL Isaac, of Benoni and Elizabeth,		Sept. 30, 1739.
1-198	"	Olive,	June 3, 1741.
1-198	"	Rowland,	March 6, 1744.
1-198	"	Sarah,	Sept. 19, 1749.
1-198	"	Elizabeth,	Nov. 25, 1755.
1-212	"	Rufus, of Samuel and Dinah,	June 8, 1744.
1-212	"	Alice,	May 24, 1746.
1-212	"	Rachel,	July 15, 1750.
1-219	"	Timothy, of Benjamin and Temperance,	Jan. 12, 1750.
1-166	"	Benoni, of William, Jr., and Mary,	June 20, 1755.
1-166	"	Waite,	Feb. 4, 1757.
1-166	"	Waite,	died July 2, 1758.
1-166	"	Isaac,	April 6, 1761.
3-69	"	Sybel, of Caleb,	Dec. 27, 1794.
3-69	"	Meriam,	July 24, 1796.
3-69	"	Sarah,	March 15, 1800.
3-69	"	Daniel,	April 5, 1804.
1-208	HARRINGTON Alce, of Job and Elizabeth,		Oct. 8, 1733.
1-208	"	Elizabeth,	March 25, 1734-5.
1-208	"	Sarah,	Aug. 13, 1736.
1-208	"	Henry,	Sept. 28, 1738.
1-208	"	Andra,	Sept. 2, 1740.
1-208	"	Christopher,	Aug. 12, 1742.
1-208	"	Mercy,	June 8, 1744.
1-208	"	Ruth,	June 11, 1747.
1-198	"	Mary, of John and Anna,	Sept. 15, 1737.
1-198	"	Anna,	Feb. 24, 1738.
1-198	"	Amie,	Nov. 12, 1740.
1-198	"	Freelove,	Oct. 13, 1742.
1-198	"	Desire,	June 14, 1744.
1-198	"	Desire,	died Jan. 26, 1744.
1-198	"	Elizabeth,	Dec. 2, 1745.
1-198	"	William,	Jan. 11, 1746.
1-198	"	Abigail,	May 23, 1748.
1-198	"	John,	Aug. 31, 1750.
1-198	"	Benjamin,	Sept. 14, 1752.
1-198	"	Benjamin,	died April 4, 1753.
1-198	"	John (Senior),	died Jan. 27, 1753.
1-203	"	Esther, of Eber and Hannah,	June 28, 1738.
1-203	"	Richard,	July 2, 1739.
1-203	"	Hannah,	Oct. 8, 1742.
3-113	"	Henry,	Sept. 27, 1738.
3-113	"	Freelove, wife of Henry,	Oct. 13, 1742.
3-113	"	John, of Henry and Freelove,	March 27, 1766.
3-113	"	Job,	March 19, 1768.
3-113	"	Henry,	Feb. 16, 1770.
3-113	"	Gideon,	Jan. 11, 1772.
3-113	"	Gideon,	died April 22, 1774.
3-113	"	Annie,	April 20, 1774.
3-113	"	Abigail,	Jan. 27, 1776.
3-113	"	Elizabeth,	Oct. 13, 1777.
3-113	"	Freelove,	Aug. 3, 1779.
3-113	"	Daniel,	April 6, 1781.
3-113	"	Alice,	May 12, 1783.
3-113	"	Mary,	May 24, 1785.
1-161	"	Thomas, of Ebenezer and Rebecca,	April 4, 1744.
1-161	"	Benjamin,	Oct. 22, 1745.
1-161	"	Alce,	Oct. 22, 1747.
1-161	"	Lydia,	Oct. 2, 1749.
1-161	"	Ebenezer,	April 11, 1752.
1-161	"	Elizabeth,	April 19, 1754.
1-161	"	Ebenezer Weightman,	May 1, 1756.
3-37	"	Alice, of Christopher and Sarah,	Dec. 12, 1762.
3-37	"	Christopher,	Nov. 17, 1764.
3-37	"	William,	Oct. 16, 1766.

3-37	HARRINGTON Sarah, of Christopher and Sarah,	June 20, 1769.
3-37	" Crandall,	Sept. 5, 1771.
3-37	" Hannah.	Aug. 31, 1774.
3-3	" Christian, of David and Weight,	Sept. 5, 1768.
3-3	" Nicholas,	Dec. 11, 1771.
3-3	" Warder,	Jan. 2, 1773.
3-3	" Sarah,	March 25, 1774.
3-3	" Martha,	Feb. 25, 1776.
3-3	" Mary,	April 28, 1778.
3-3	" Hannah,	April 18, 1781.
3-3	" Waite,	June 9, 1783.
3-4	" Lucy,	March 22. 1785.
3-4	" David,	June 24, 1787.
3-4	" Elizabeth,	June 13, 1789.
3-4	" Phebe,	April 6, 1792.
3-206	" William, of William and Sarah,	March 15, 1772.
3-206	" Benjamin,	Oct. 4, 1773.
3-206	" Sarah, dau. of Waite,	July 8, 1799.
2-287	HAWKINS Thomas Hazard,	born Sept. 20, 1795.
1-222	HILL Mary, of Robert and Freelove,	April 23, 1750.
1-222	" Daniel,	Jan. 7, 1752.
3-49	HIMES Stephen, of James and Abigail,	Jan. 6, 1750.
3-49	" Walter,	Jan. 28, 1753.
3-49	" Mary,	Oct. 6, 1755.
3-49	" Lydia,	June 2, 1758.
3-49	" Meriam,	June 23, 1762.
3-49	" Potter,	Dec. 21, 1764.
3- —	HOAR Hezekiel, and Deborah, his wife; no children recorded.	
3-48	HOLLOWAY Catherine, of Joseph and Lydia,	July 19, 1756.
3-48	" Elizabeth,	Dec. 10, 1758.
3-48	" Lydia,	May 7, 1763.
3-48	" Lydia,	died Nov. 23, 1766.
3-48	" John Weight,	June 18, 1765.
3-48	" John Weight,	died Sept. 7, 1779.

Note—J. W. H. was killed Sept. 7, 1779, at 11 o'clock a. m., lat. 48 deg. 00m. N., long. 40 deg. 00m. W., on board the private ship-of-war Gen. Mifflin, Capt. Geo. Waite Babcock, being shot by a cannon ball by the enemy while he was contending for the rights of his country.

3-48	" Lydia, wife of Joseph; age 36y. 0m. 26d.;	Aug. 18, 1768.
3-48	" Christopher, of Joseph and Elizabeth,	Dec. 19, 1769.
3-48	" Samuel,	March 25, 1772.
3-48	" Elizabeth, wife of Joseph,	died Nov. 23, 1773
3-181	" Penelope, of S. K., widow of Benjamin, died Nov. 20, 1773.	
3-181	" John, of Samuel and Mercy,	Oct. 22. 1794.
3-181	" Elizabeth,	Oct. 25, 1796.
3-46	HOPKINS Rufus, of Samuel and Freelove B.,	May 6, 1825.
3-46	" Arnold,	March 30, 1827.
3-46	" Sarah Ann,	Feb. 14, 1829.
3-46	" Alexander S.,	Feb. 15, 1831.
3-46	" Bradford,	March 25, 1833.
3-46	" Bradford,	d. Feb. 27, 1835.
3-46	" Emeline,	Feb. 6, 1835.
3-46	" Crawford,	March 12, 1837.
3-46	" Crawford,	d. July 16, 1838.
3-46	" Hiram,	Nov. 27, 1840.
3-46	" Samuel,	April 1, 1845.
3-78	HOXSIE Sarah, of John and Hannah,	Aug. 7, 1761.
3-78	" James,	March 8, 1763.
3-78	" Deborah,	April 22, 1764.
3-78	" John,	April 20, 1765.
3-78	" Bill,	Nov. 1, 1766.
3-78	" Mary,	April 22, 1768.
3-78	" Phebe,	June 7, 1769.
3-78	" Lucy,	July 7, 1771.

3-78	HOXSIE Joshua, of John and Hannah,	Oct. 22, 1772.
3-78	" Abigail,	May 22, 1774.
3-78	" Thomas,	Dec. 5, 1776.
3-78	" Calvin,	June 4, 1778.
3-78	" Wanton,	March 10, 1780.
3-78	" Hannah, of John and Phebe, 2d wife,	Nov. 20, 1786.
3-78	" Thankful.	May 3, 1788.
3-78	" Catherine,	Nov. 21, 1789.
3-78	" Olive,	Aug. 3, 1791.
3-78	" Eason,	Oct. 6, 1793.
3-36	" Susannah, of Samuel and Anna,	Feb. 3, 1773.

I J

3-156	JAMES Sarah, of Daniel and Mary,	Dec. 4, 1795.
3-156	" Elizabeth,	Dec. 4, 1795.
3-156	" Caleb B.,	Oct. 10, 1797.
3-156	" Phebe,	June 27, 1801.
3-156	" Rodman,	Feb. 23, 1804.
3-156	" Ruth.	Feb. 23, 1804.
1-163	JENKINS Christian, of Philip and Mary,	Jan. 4, 1751.
1-163	" Christopher,	Jan. 26, 1753.
1-163	" Gideon,	Oct. 6, 1754.
1-163	" Philip,	Oct. 6, 1756.
1-225	JOSLIN Henry, of Thomas and Sarah,	April 24, 1748.
1-225	" Thomas,	Sept. 26, 1750.
1-225	" Potter,	Aug. 3, 1753.
1-225	" Freeborn,	July 24, 1756.
1-225	" John,	Dec. 12, 1758.
1-172	" Henry, of John and Joanna.	June 2, 1755.
1-172	" Andrew,	April 16, 1757.
1-172	" Rufus.	April 8, 1759.

K

3-199	KENYON Gardiner, of John,	Sept. 24, 1755.
3-199	" Mercy,	Nov. 18, 1757.
3-199	" John,	July 3, 1760.
3-199	" Zebulon,	Aug. 25, 1764.
3-199	" Freelove,	July 3, 1766.
3-199	" Freeman,	Jan. 28, 1769.
3-199	" Remington,	July 27, 1771.
3-199	" Lewis,	July 20, 1774.
3-199	" Amos,	July 18, 1781.
3-199	" Job,	June 24, 1783.
3-199	" Reynolds,	Aug. 21, 1786.
3-199	" Lydia,	March 18, 1789.
3-199	" Joseph Greene,	May 19, 1792.

L

2-176	LAWTON Phebe, of Timothy and Deborah,	May 6, 1768.
2-176	" Elizabeth,	(sic) Aug. 9, 1768.
1-211	LEWIS Hannah, of James and Elizabeth,	Nov. 29, 1743.
1-211	" James,	Nov. 20, 1745.
2-164	" Daniel, of Jonathan and Sarah,	July 12, 1745.
2-164	" John,	Nov. 10, 1746.
2-164	" Jean,	Aug. 29, 1748.
2-164	" Jonathan,	Aug. 15, 1752.
2-164	" Benjamin,	April 9, 1755.

Note—Two eldest born Richmond, the others Exeter.

2-164	" Joseph,	b. April 7, 1750.

3-207	LEWIS	Susannah, of Joseph and Mary,	Nov. 22, 1775.
3-207	"	Job,	Sept. 10, 1776.
3-207	"	Hannah,	Nov. 18, 1779.
3-207	"	R. Kenyon,	Feb. 18, 1782.
3-207	"	Joseph,	July 26, 1784.
3-207	"	Mary,	Oct. 25, 1786.
3-207	"	B. Stanton,	Aug. 26, 1789.
3-207	"	Charity,	Oct. 27, 1792.
3-207	"	John R.,	Jan. 17, 1795.
3-45	"	Caleb, of Caleb and Sybel,	Aug. 15, 1755.
3-45	"	Hannah,	June 14, 1761.
3-45	"	Elijah,	March 28, 1764.
3-45	"	Joel,	Nov. 7, 1768.
3-45	"	Edmund,	Feb. 28, 1772.

Note—Also recorded 2-164.

3-88	"	Abigail, of George and Elizabeth,	Oct. 28, 1757.
3-88	"	George,	June 15, 1760.
3-88	"	Obediah,	Dec. 10, 1764.
3-88	"	Mary,	Aug. 17, 1766.
3-88	"	Asa,	May 22, 1769.
3-88	"	Betsey,	March 3, 1772.
3-88	"	Rawland,	Dec. 5, 1775.
3-4	"	Mary, of James and Elizabeth,	Nov. 16, 1763.
3-58	"	Abigail, of James and Thankful,	Sept. 19, 1775.
3-58	"	James,	Feb. 28, 1778.
3-58	"	Elizabeth,	April 27, 1780.
3-58	"	Hannah,	April 1, 1782.
3-58	"	Thankful,	July 22, 1784.
3-58	"	Lydia,	June 12, 1786.
3-58	"	Esther,	Feb. 12, 1788.
3-58	"	Nathan Barber,	March 30, 1790.
3-58	"	Moses B.,	April 19, 1797.
3-58	"	David Maxon,	June 24, 1799.
3-58	"	Sarah Gates,	— —, —.
3-108	"	John, of John and Amie,	April 3, 1780.
3-108	"	Sabra,	Aug. 11, 1782.
3-108	"	Susannah,	Feb. 7, 1785.
3-108	"	Amie,	May 1, 1787.
3-108	"	Benjamin,	Oct. 14, 1778.
3-55	"	Moses, of Jonathan, 3d, and Martha,	Sept. 20, 1779.
3-55	"	Sarah,	Feb. 24, 1781.
3-55	"	Anna,	Oct. 19, 1782.
3-55	"	Silas,	July 21, 1784.
3-55	"	Hannah,	Jan. 9, 1786.
3-55	"	Jonathan,	June 7, 1788.
3-56	"	Jesse,	May 5, 1790.
3-56	"	Joseph Bowdish,	May 31, 1792.
3-56	"	Martha,	June 28, 1794.
3-56	"	Peleg,	Oct. 19, 1796.
3-145	"	Amos, of Benjamin and Deliverance,	July 8, 1780.
3-145	"	Sinthean,	Dec. 12, 1781.
3-145	"	Jason,	March 13, 1783.
3-145	"	Jareb,	Oct. 2, 1786.
3-145	"	Annis,	June 22, 1788.
3-145	"	Benjamin,	June 13, 1790.
3-145	"	Hannah,	Oct. 6, 1793.
3-171	"	Mary, of William and Eleanor,	March 29, 1787.
3-171	"	Sarah,	Jan. 29, 1789.
3-171	"	Sarah,	d. Dec. 6, 1790.
3-171	"	Thomas,	Oct. 9, 1790.
3-171	"	Olive,	Feb. 27, 1792.
3-171	"	Andrew,	Oct. 5, 1793.
3-171	"	Rowland,	Jan. 25, 1795.
3-171	"	John,	Dec. 4, 1796.
3-93	"	Prosper, George Dyre, of Abigail (single),	June 1, 1788.

3-20	LEWIS Betsey, of Asa,		Aug. 20, 1789.
3-20	" Arabella,		Dec. 13, 1791.
3-20	" George,		Feb. 17, 1794.
3-20	" Desire,		April 14, 1796.
3-20	" Cynthia,		April 17, 1798.
3-20	" Asa,		May 22, 1800.
3-183	" James, of James and Olive,		Jan. 17, 1799.
3-183	" Simeon Rathbun,		March 24, 1801.
3-183	" Henry Barber,		March 28, 1803.
3-208	" Abraham, of Samuel, Jr., and Ruth,		July 18, 1799.
3-208	" Daniel,		Aug. 12, 1802.
3-213	" Francis Tanner, of John and Lydia,		July 11, 1803.
3-213	" Ira Lane, (prob.)		Nov. 14, 1804.
3-213	" Sally Celinda,		Feb. 10, 1807.
3-221	" Isaac, of Moses and Eleanor,		Sept. 23, 1805.
3-221	" Beede,		Aug. 13, 1808.
3-221	" John Ladd,		May 1, 1811.
3-221	" Sarah,		Oct. 16, 1812.
3-221	" Sarah,		d. Oct. 16, 1813.
3-221	" Jonathan,		Aug. 25, 1814.
3-221	" Moses,		June 21, 1817.
3-222	" Rodman, of Silas and Lydia,		Nov. 8, 1805.
3-2	" James, of Nathan B. and Sally,		Oct. 11, 1810.
3-2	" Lucy,		July 2, 1813.
3-2	" Thankful,		Feb. 26, 1816.
3-2	" Esther,		Aug. 29, 1818.
3-250	" Prony, of Jonathan, Jr., and Mariah,		Oct. 23, 1811.
3-250	" Hannah,		Sept. 10, 1813.
3-251	" Anna, of Jesse and Esther,		Dec. 19, 1811.
3-251	" Benjamin,		April 30, 1815.
3-270	" Phebe, of Moses and Wealthen,		Sept. 27, 1813.
3-270	" Lydia,		May 4, 1815.
3-270	" Lydia,		d. May 7, 1817.
3-270	" Mary Ann,		Oct. 23, 1817.
3-270	" Mary Ann,		died March 3, 1821.
3-270	" John T.,		Oct. 23, 1817.
3-270	" Betsey M.,		June 27, 1822.
3-270	" Moses A.,		May 7, 1824.
3-270	" Daniel J.,		Aug. 18, 1826.
3-282	" Stafford G., of Thomas and Lucy,		May 3, 1814.
3-282	" Palmer,		May 21, 1816.
3-282	" Seth,		July 17, 1818.
3-295	" Mary Elizabeth, of Moses B. and Mary,		Jan. 21, 1828.
3-295	" Nathan Barber, of James and Mary,		Feb. 26, 1842.
3-295	" Mary Francis,		Oct. 10, 1845.
3-295	" John Nelson,		April 23, 1847.
3-295	" Saunders,		May 3, 1849.
3-295	" Saunders,		died Aug. —, 1872.
3-295	" Peleg,		May 3, 1849.
3-295	" Peleg,		died ——, 1869.
1-213	LILLIBRIDGE, David, of Benjn and Amie,		Sept. 18, 1744.
1-213	" Mary,		May 29, 1746.
1-213	" Josias,		Aug. 18, 1749.
1-213	" Jonathan,		Aug. 23, 1751.
1-213	" Gideon,		June 16, 1754.
1-213	" Benjamin,		Aug. 14, 1756.
1-213	" Gardiner,		Sept. 19, 1758.
1-213	" Amie,		May 16, 1765.
	Note—Also recorded 1-221.		
3-281	" Gardiner, of Daniel and Hannah,		Feb. 1, 1812.
3-281	" Daniel,		July 27, 1814.
3-281	" David,		Aug. 17, 1818.
3-281	" Joseph W.,		Dec. 20, 1821.
3-204	" Wauton, of Warren and Mary,		May 16, 1825.
3-238	" Gardiner, a Rev. soldier,		died July 22, 1824.
3-205	LOCKE, Charles B., of Elliot and Mary,		May 15, 1787.

M

3-109	MAGUIRE Ruth, of John and Susan,	Oct. 6, 1784.
3-109	" Constantine,	July 4, 1786.
3-109	" Phebe,	July 13, 1790.
3-109	" Sophia,	Sept. 7, 1799.
1-206	MARSHALL Thomas, of Jacob and Penelope,	April 23, 1742.
3-10	MIAS Philip Bates, of John and Mary W.,	April 5, 1813.
1-209	MONEY Joseph, of Robert and Sarah,	Dec. 20, 1745.
1-209	" Samuel,	March 14, 1747.
1-209	" Elizabeth,	March 31, 1750.
3-252	" John Allen, born	Jan. 15, 1793.
3-252	" John Wescott, of John A. and Penelope,	Sept. 22, 1821.
3-252	" Mary Eleanor,	Oct. 27, 1822.
3-252	" George Brown,	Dec. 12, 1825.
3-252	" Timothy Allen,	Aug. 23, 1829.
3-252	" Amie Ann,	March 24, 1831.
3-252	" Sarah Eanos,	July 28, 1833.
3-252	" James Burrell,	May 29, 1835.
3-252	" Mercy Ann,	Jan. 26, 1838.
3-280	" Daniel Lyman, of Hannah,	Feb. 6, 1813.
2-164	MOON Mary, of Jonathan and Lydia,	Dec. 1, 1758.
2-164	" Ann,	July 6, 1760.
2-164	" Darius,	Sept. 28, 1763.
3-39	" Amie, of John and Elizabeth,	Dec. 25, 1771.
3-39	" Daniel, of Sanford and Elizabeth,	April 12, 1772.
3-39	" Rebecca, of Elizabeth (dec.),	Oct. 3, 1803.
3-39	" Robert, of Ebenezer and Sarah,	June 23, 1782.
3-39	" Elizabeth,	June 3, 1784.
3-39	" William W.,	July 29, 1787.
3-39	" Sylvester,	Jan. 1, 1791.
3-258	MOORE Thompson (4th son), of John and Sarah,	Aug. 9, 1792.
3-212	" Joshua Vaughn, of Thomas and Elizabeth,	Nov. 8, 1798.
3-212	" Thomas Paine,	June 3, 1800.
3-212	" Daniel,	Dec. 2, 1801.
3-212	" Alexander Pope,	April 22, 1804.
3-212	" Lydia Jenkins,	July 14, 1806.
1-200	MOREY Hazard, of Benjamin and Dorcas,	May 6, 1739.
1-200	" Samuel,	Jan. 30, 1740.
1-200	" Benjamin,	March 13, 1742.
1-200	" Mary,	May 6, 1745.
1-200	" Christopher,	Dec. 23, 1746.
1-200	" Joseph,	June 28, 1749.
1-200	" Stephen,	March 13, 1751.
1-200	" Augustus,	Jan. 31, 1753.
1-198	" Joshua, of Robert and Sarah,	July 1, 1740.
1-198	" Anna,	Dec. 22, 1742.
1-173	" Asa, of Joseph and Sarah,	April 8, 1747.
1-173	" Jesse,	Nov. 26, 1750.
1-173	" Benjamin,	Jan. 10, 1752.
1-173	" Robert,	Feb. 13, 1754.
1-173	" John,	Sept. 4, 1757.
1-173	" Elizabeth,	July 10, 1760.
3-54	" Martha, of Samuel and Ann,	July 5, 1762.
3-54	" Dorcas,	Jan. 13, 1765.
3-54	" Hazard,	April 18, 1766.
3-54	" Sarah,	April 18, 1766.
3-54	" Elizabeth,	Feb. 14, 1768.
3-54	" Gardiner,	Feb. 4, 1770.
3-54	" George,	March 28, 1772.
3-54	" Enock,	March 28, 1772.
3-54	" Ann,	Aug. 21, 1773.
3-54	" George,	d. Aug. 7, 1772.
3-54	" Enock,	d. Aug. 4, 1772.

Note—Gardiner (above) born West Greenwich.

3-27	MOREY Christopher, of Christopher and Alice,		June 21, 1773.
3-27	"	Mary,	Jan. 2, 1776.
		Note—⸺ born South Kingstown, ⸺ Exeter.	
1-173	"	Hazard (N. K.), of Joseph and Freelove,	Dec. 24, 1780.
1-173	"	Joseph,	May 22, 1782.
3-82	"	Lydia, of John and Margaret,	Oct. 11, 1778.
3-82	"	Isaac,	Sept. 28, 1781.
3-39	MOSHEIR Mehitable, of Ichabod and Anna,		March 3, 1761.
3-39	"	Joseph,	Feb. 5, 1765.
3-39	"	Jonathan,	Feb. 20, 1770.
		Note—Joseph (above) born Richmond; the others Exeter.	
1-204	MUMFORD John, of John, Jr., and Mary,		Aug. 5, 1743.
1-204	"	Freeman,	May 14, 1746.
1-204	"	Judeth, 1st wife of John, Jr.,	d. Oct. 21, 1739.
2-180	"	Ruth, of Thomas,	Oct. 12, 1756.
2-180	"	Robinson,	Jan. 13, 1758.
2-180	"	Sarah,	Jan 17, 1760.
2-180	"	Mary,	Dec. 10, 1761.
2-180	"	George,	Aug. 6, 1764.
2-180	"	Hannah,	Nov. 20, 1766.
2-180	"	Abigail	Sept. 23, 1768.
1-174	"	Mary, of Perry and Hannah,	Dec. 15, 1758.
1-174	"	Judeth,	May 3, 1760.

N

1-167	NEWCOMB Elizabeth, of Thomas and Bridget,		July 14, 1755.
1-167	"	James,	Dec. 13, 1756.
1-167	"	Frederick,	May 4, 1758.
1-219	NILES William, of Nathaniel and Martha,		Dec. 14, 1753.
1-219	"	Freelove,	May 25, 1755.
1-219	"	Abigail,	Jan. 14, 1757.
1-219	"	Elizabeth,	May 24, 1759.
1-219	"	Henry,	April 20, 1761.

O

1-213	OLIN Rahanna, of Joseph and Mary,		March 8, 1733.
1-213	"	Elizabeth,	(sic) June 2, 1735.
1-213	"	Mary,	Jan. 10, 1738.
1-213	"	Joseph,	Feb. 27, 1740.
1-213	"	Phillip,	Dec. 5, 1742.
1-213	"	Wealthiam,	Jan. 27, 1744.
1-213	"	William,	Nov. 13, 1747.
1-213	"	Ruth,	Aug. 5, 1750.
1-213	"	Anne,	July 30, 1752.
1-213	"	Sarah,	March 31, 1756.

P

3-292	PALMER Elijah, of Gershom and Betsey,		June 2, 1806.
3-292	"	Mary Ann,	July 1, 1810.
3-292	"	Susan Sherman,	Feb. 25, 1815.
3-292	"	Betsey, wife of Gershom, died in her 85th year,	July 3, 1826.
3-292	"	Elvira, of George Ray and Mary Ann,	July 16, 1824.
3-292	"	Amanda,	June 9, 1826.
3-292	"	Angeline,	Sept. 26, 1828.
3-130	PECKHAM Elizabeth Clarke Chapman, of Jeremiah and Mary,		May 23, 1796.
3-67	"	Mary C., died	Nov. 12, 1797.
1-227	PERKINS John, of Newman and Mehitable,		May 30, 1733.
1-227	"	Oliver,	June 14, 1735.
1-227	"	Ebenezer,	Aug. 20, 1736.

1-227	PERKINS Uriah, of Newman and Mehitable,		May 12, 1738.
1-227	"	David,	Aug. 1, 1741.
1-227	"	Samuel,	July 15, 1745.
1-227	"	Martha,	Aug. 21, 1747.
3-134	"	Thomas, of Uriah,	Oct. 8, 1770.
3-134	"	Pardon,	Dec. 2, 1779.
3 134	"	Uriah,	Sept. 10, 1780.
3-134	"	James,	July 29, 1784.
3-165	"	Newman, Jr., of Newman and Anna,	Oct. 5, 1792.
3-165	"	Nancy,	Jan. 13, 1794.
3-261	"	Marvel,	Dec. 31, 1796.
3-261	"	Samuel,	Feb. 15, 1799.
3-261	"	Abigail,	April 5, 1801.
3-261	"	Hannah,	June 26, 1803.
3-261	"	Polly Spooner,	Oct. 27, 1805.
3-261	"	Rhoda,	Dec. 14, 1807.
3-261	"	Paul,	March 13, 1810.
3-261	"	Andrew Allen,	Aug. 13, 1814.
3-310	"	Susan H., of Palmer G. and Susan E.,	Jan. 7, 1853.
3-310	"	Byron F.,	July 9, 1858.
3-310	"	George H.,	Oct. 13, 1860
3-122	PHILLIPS Thomas, April 20, 1770,		died Feb. 11, 1840.
3-122	"	Lydia (Whitford), his wife,	—— —, ——.
3-122	"	Dorcas, of Thomas and Lydia,	Jan. 17, 1794.
3-122	"	Elizabeth,	Oct. 14, 1796.
3-122	"	Thomas,	Jan. 23, 1798.
3-122	"	Mary,	March 21, 1801.
3-122	"	John,	March 13, 1803.
3-122	"	Lydia,	March 2, 1805.
3-122	"	James,	July 23, 1807.
3-122	"	Samuel,	Jan. 21, 1810.
3-122	"	Abbie Ann,	March 22, 1812.
3-177	"	Samuel (3d son) Jr., of Samuel and Susannah,	April 18, 1799.
3-177	"	Annie Eliza, of Thomas, Jr., and Mercy,	Jan. 14, 1830.
3-177	"	Thomas H.,	Jan. 1, 1835.
3-177	"	Abbie M.,	Aug. 2, 1838.
1-164	PIERCE, Amie, of George and Mary,		Sept. 19, 1754.
1-164	"	Christopher,	Oct. 3, 1759.
1-164	"	Giles,	April 22, 1765.
	Note.—Also recorded 3-10, eldest born at East Greenwich, the others Exeter.		
3-93	"	George, (N. K.) of Giles and Hannah,	March 3, 1786.
3-93	"	Amie (E.),	Dec. 12, 1787.
3-93	'	Sarah, (E.),	May 23, 1789.
3-93	"	Oliver Spink,	Feb. 11, 1791.
3-185	PILLSBURY, Elizabeth, of Tobias, and Susannah,		Jan. 24, 1785.
3-185	"	Ruth, of do, Sept. 23, 1786,	died, Feb. 9, 1787.
3-185	"	Mehitable, of do,	Feb. 20, 1790.
1-169	POTTER Abel, of Joseph and Catherine,		Nov. 13, 1748.
1-169	"	Hannah,	April 10, 1750.
1-169	"	Silence,	Jan. 22, 1753.
1-169	"	Mary,	Jan. 24, 1755.
1-169	"	Martha,	Feb. 26, 1757.
1-169	"	Sarah,	May 3, 1759.
1-228	"	Eunice, of John and Ruth,	Nov. 3, 1753.
1-228	"	John,	March 6, 1755.
1-228	"	Hannah,	June 16, 1758.
1-228	"	Deliverance,	Sept. 7, 1760.
3-31	"	John, of Abel and Abigail,	Sept. 23, 1771.
3-31	"	Joseph,	March 29, 1773.
3-31	"	Barberry,	March 6, 1775.
3-11	"	William Waite,	Aug. 8, 1789.
3-11	'	Thankful Knowles (Carpenter), his wife, Nov. 28, 1795.	
3-11	"	Samuel Carey, of William and Thankful,	Dec. 8, 1817.
3-11	"	William Robert,	May 19, 1821.

3-11	POTTER Jeremiah Carpenter, of William and Thankful,	May 24, 1823.
3-11	" Isaiah Knowles,	Feb. 7, 1826.
3-11	" Nathan L.,	April 18, 1828.
3-11	" Willett F.,	Sept. 13, 1830.
3-11	" George W.,	March 4, 1833.
3-11	" John S.,	Oct. 28, 1835.
3-11	" Daniel B.,	March 4, 1838.

Q R

3-41	RATHBUN Sarah, of Obediah and Anna,	June 15, 1732.
3-41	" Mary,	May 25, 1734.
3-41	" Dorcas,	May 5, 1737.
3-41	" William,	Jan. 28, 1744.
3-41	" Joseph,	Sept. 22, 1745.
3-41	" Margeret,	Feb. 20, 1748.
3-41	" Susannah,	April 21, 1750.
1-228	" Oliver, of Thomas and Charity,	Feb. 15, 1734.
1-228	" Charity,	April 12, 1735.
1-228	" Thomas,	Dec. 5, 1736.
1-228	" Hannah,	July 3, 1741.
1-228	" Simeon,	May 10, 1745.
1-228	" Oliver,	Feb. 2, 1747.
1 228	" Mary,	March 25, 1750.
1-228	" Nathan,	May 25, 1753.
1-211	" Joseph, of Joseph Jr., and Abigail,	July 16, 1735.
1-211	" Rebecca,	Dec. 27, 1736.
1-211	" Mary,	Nov. 22, 1738.
1-211	" Ann,	July 30, 1740.
1-211	" Jeremiah,	March 27, 1742.
1-211	" George,	March 7, 1743.
3-90	" John Peck, of Nathaniel and Ann,	March 23, 1746.
3-90	" Margeret (3d dau.),	July 16, 1749.
3-91	" Capt. Nathaniel,	d. June or July —, 1750.
3-91	" Thankful, of Joshua and Amie,	Nov. 29, 1735.
1-167	" Mercy,	Feb. 25, 1758.
3-82	" Margaret, of John and Elizabeth,	Feb. 7, 1758.
3-82	" John,	June 8, 1770.
3-202	" Rowland,	born, Sept. 10, 1765.
3-202	" Phebe Brown, of Rowland and Freelove,	March 16, 1795.
3-202	" Sally Brown,	March 21, 1797.
3-202	" Thomas, of Simeon and Anna,	Oct. 19, 1771.
3-202	" Anna,	Sept. 26, 1774.
3-202	" Charity,	Sept. 26, 1774.
3-202	" Mary,	Jan. 7, 1778.
3-202	" Olive,	Feb. 10, 1780.
3-202	" Russell,	Jan. 20, 1782.
3-202	" Simeon,	Sept. 14, 1784.
3-202	" Nathan,	May 17, 1788.
3-202	" Eunice,	Feb. 5, 1790.
3-84	" Joseph, of George and Mercy,	June 25, 1779.
3-269	" Nathan D., of Nathan and Sarah,	Feb. 6, 1807.
3-269	" Charity D.,	May 28, 1809.
3-269	" Mary A.,	Sept. 29, 1811.
3-269	" John H.,	Oct. 14, 1814.
3-100	" Jerome B., of Nathan and Mary,	Dec. 8, 1859.
1-197	REYNOLDS George, of John and Martha,	March 1, 1728.
1-197	" Ann,	June 7, 1732.
1-197	" Ann,	d. Aug. —, 1734.
1-197	" Mary,	April 3, 1736.
1-197	" Mary,	d. Jan. 7, 1737.
1-197	" Oliver,	June 21, 1739.
1-197	" Martha,	May 8, 1741.
1-197	" Martha 2d,	Sept. 19, 1744.

1-197	REYNOLDS George, of John and Martha,	Sept. 18, 1751.
1-197	" John,	Dec. 9, 1753.
1-197	" Lueza, of George and Joanna,	July 8, 1743.
1-197	" George,	April 27, 1745.
1-197	" Lydia,	April 4, 1747.
1-197	" Joseph,	July 9, 1749.
1-197	" Elizabeth,	July 9, 1749.
1-197	" George,	Dec. 30, 1751.
1-197	" George,	d. July 1, 1753.
1-197	" Joanna,	March 12, 1755.
1-210	" Henry, of John, (carpenter),	Sept. 22, 1724.
1-210	" Thomas, of Henry and Mehitable,	March 18, 1746.
1-210	" Hannah,	Feb. 1, 1748.
1-210	" Henry,	April 17, 1751.
1-215	" Joseph, of Benjamin and Alce,	July 26, 1747.
1-215	" Jonathan,	Aug. 6, 1749.
1-215	" Hannah,	Oct. 14, 1752.
1-215	" Hannah,	Jan. 26, 1754.
1-215	" Alce.	July 21, 1755.
1-215	" Benjamin,	Oct. 6, 1757.
1-215	" John,	Aug. 20, 1759.
1-215	" Mary,	(July) Aug. 10, 1763.
1-215	" Margaret,	Dec. 14, 1766.
1-215	" Stephen,	Aug. 10, 1772.
1-215	" Stephen,	d. March 27, 1773.
	Note.—Also recorded 3-135.	
1-212	" Christopher, of Christian, dau. of George,	Aug. 16, 1747.
1-212	" Christopher,	d. Aug. 26, 1747.
1-175	" Hannah, of Jonathan and Ann,	July 20, 1756.
1-175	" Ann,	May 6, 1758.
1-175	" Jonathan,	Oct. 7, 1760.
1-171	" Sarah, of Robert and Eunice,	Oct. 17, 1757.
1-171	" Ann,	Dec. 15, 1759.
1-171	" Ann,	d. March 10, 1760.
1-171	" George,	Feb. 19, 1761.
1-171	" Waite,	Dec. 26, 1763.
1-171	" Waite,	d. March 13, 1769.
1-171	" Eunice,	Dec. 29, 1765.
1-171	" Phenews,	Feb. 23, 1768.
1-171	" Anna,	Dec. 11, 1769.
3-25	" John, of Elisha,	March 31, 1758.
3-25	" Mary,	May 28, 1760.
3-25	" Elisha,	Oct. 29, 1763.
3-25	" Thomas,	July 19, 1765.
3-25	" Sellah,	Feb. 12, 1768.
3-25	" Phillipa,	Sept. 18, 1770.
3-25	" Waite,	Oct. 24, 1773.
3-159	" Henry,	born Aug. 31, 1759.
3-159	" Mercy (Brown), his wife,	Aug. 8, 1761.
3-159	" Margaret, of Henry and Mercy,	Dec. 31, 1784.
3-159	" Martha,	May 8, 1786.
3-159	" Charles,	May 8, 1787.
3-159	" Job,	May 20, 1790.
3-159	" Elizabeth,	Dec. 3, 1791.
3-159	" Benjamin,	Feb. 28, 1796.
3-159	" Abel,	May 25, 1798.
3-159	" Phebe,	March 1, 1801.
3-159	" Mercy,	April 18, 1804.
3-159	" Henry,	April 22, 1811.
3-5	" Anna, of Joseph, (of Robert) and Elizabeth,	June 28, 1765.
3-14	" Amon, of Benjamin and Sarah,	June 17, 1770.
3-14	" Benjamin,	Dec. 12, 1772.
3-4	" Mary, of Joseph and Mary,	Nov. 2, 1771.
3-38	" Hannah, of Henry, Jr., and Jemima,	March 16, 1773.
3-38	" Elizabeth,	July 4, 1774.

3-38	REYNOLDS Mehitable, of Henry, Jr., and Jemima,	Nov. 18, 1778.
3-38	"	Sarah,	May 13, 1781.
3-38	"	Weightman,	Jan. 26, 1783.
	Note—Two eldest born West Greenwich, the others Exeter.
3-142	"	George, of Joseph and Elizabeth,	Jan. 24, 1774.
3-142	"	William,	Feb. 23, 1773.
3-142	"	Stephen,	Aug. 7, 1778.
3-142	"	Abigail,	Dec. 17, 1781.
3-142	"	David,	July 17, 1784.
3-142	"	Sarah,	Jan. 20, 1787.
3-70	"	Susannah, of Stephen and Abigail,	Feb. 11, 1775.
3-70	"	Abigail,	Oct. 11, 1776.
3-70	"	Lucy,	April 5, 1778.
3-70	"	John,	Aug. 29, 1780.
3-70	"	Stephen,	May 19, 1782.
3-70	"	Samuel,	June 7, 1784.
3-70	"	Daniel,	July 21, 1786.
3-70	"	Job,	Dec. 7, 1788.
3-70	"	Martha,	Feb. 11, 1791.
3-70	"	Sarah,	Sept. 1, 1793.
3-59	"	Anna, of George and Amie,	Aug. 22, 1784.
3-59	"	George,	July 14, 1786.
3-59	"	John Gardiner,	Dec. 2, 1790.
3-59	"	Abel,	May 8, 1793.
3-59	"	Dutee,	Nov. 24, 1795.
3-59	"	Samuel,	Oct. 6, 1800.
3-180	"	Joseph, of Henry and Anna,	April 25, 1785.
3-180	"	Harris,	Nov. 15, 1786.
3-180	"	Susannah,	Sept. 3, 1788.
3-180	"	Lucy,	March 7, 1791.
3-180	"	Patience,	April 9, 1794.
3-180	"	Jabez,	Jan. 14, 1797.
3-161	"	John, d., aged 83y. 11m. 8d., Aug. 18, 1794.
3-161	"	Abigail, widow of John, died, aged 83y. 3m. 8d., July 30, 1798.
3-218	"	Gardiner C., of John and Mercy,	Oct. 10, 1804.
3-218	"	Asa T.,	Aug. 17, 1806.
3-218	"	Susannah,	Oct. 23, 1808.
3-218	"	Deborah,	May 18, 1811.
3-218	"	Abigail,	May 18, 1811.
3-218	"	Mercy,	Jan. 14, 1814.
3-218	"	John,	Feb. 2, 1816.
3-218	"	Jesse Burdick,	March 18, 1818.
3-218	"	Benjamin Hoxsie,	March 23, 1820.
3-218	"	Stephen,	July 11, 1822.
3-243	"	Ezra, of Stephen, Jr., and Abigail,	Jan. 5, 1808.
3-243	"	Joanna,	Feb. 5, 1811.
3-243	"	Clarke,	Jan. 12, 1816.
3-43	"	Lucinda Nud,	Dec. 17, 1824.
3-259	"	William, of Samuel and Deborah,	Jan. 12-13, 1809.
3-259	"	Stephen,	April 26, 1812.
3-266	"	Amie,	Sept. 8, 1819.
3-274	"	Barber, of Job and Joanna,	June 14, 1811.
3-274	"	Lucy,	June 14, 1813.
3-274	"	Nathaniel,	June 14, 1815.
3-274	"	Nathaniel,	d. Dec. 6, 1815.
3-274	"	Job,	d. Feb. 7, 1850.
3-278	"	Greene, of Daniel and Alce,	June 4, 1813.
3-278	"	Ruth,	March 24, 1815.
3-278	"	Waite,	Sept. 3, 1818.
3-278	"	Abigail,	April 17, 1821.
3-278	"	Aley Ann,	June 15, 1825.
3-298	"	Whitman G., of Almond S. and Hannah M.,	Aug. 25, 1853.
3-298	"	Climer A.,	May 4, 1858.
2-169	RICHMOND William, of Adam and Mary,	Nov. 21, 1762.
2-169	"	Preserved,	June 25, 1764.

2-169	RICHMOND Dorcas, of Adam and Mary,	April 27, 1766.
3-5	" John, of Stephen and Lucy,	Dec. 25, 1777.
3-225	" Susannah, of John and Polly,	March 22, 1802.
3-225	" Sarah,	Feb. 10, 1804.
3-225	" Stephen Hazard,	Dec. 7, 1805.
3-225	" John Maxson,	Dec. 25, 1808.
3-225	" Mary,	Jan. 3, 1811.
3-225	" George W.,	April 8, 1813.
3-225	" Robert H.,	March 9, 1815.
3-225	" Nancy,	June 15, 1817.
3-225	" Lucy,	Nov. 21, 1819.
3-225	" Almira,	Aug. 21, 1821.
3-35	" Eliza, of Stephen and Margaret,	Nov. 13, 1819.
3-35	" Ephraim,	Dec. 12, 1811.
3-35	" Benjamin,	Aug. 12, 1815.
1-215	ROGERS Thankful, of Joseph and Margaret,	Oct. 8, 1742.
1-215	" Joanna,	March 20, 1744.
1-215	" Elizabeth,	March 10, 1746.
1-215	" Margaret,	Dec. 28, 1748.

S

3-44	SANFORD Jeremiah, of William C.,	Jan. 16, 1856.
3-44	" Lydia,	Jan. 22, 1858.
3-44	" Edwin A.,	Sept. 1, 1861.
3-111	SHELDON Roger, of Roger and Elizabeth,	Jan. 1, 1785.
3-111	" James,	Feb. 15, 1787.
3-111	" John,	June —, 1789.
3-264	" James Seager, of James and Sally,	April 23, 1812.
3-264	" Palmer,	Sept. 24, 1814.
3-264	" Joseph,	Aug. 15, 1817.
3-264	" Elizabeth,	July 2, 1820.
3-264	" Cazanda,	Feb. 13, 1825.
3-264	" Gardiner Dawley,	April 19, 1827.
3-267	" Hannah, of Roger, Jun., and Prudence,	Nov. 26, 1812.
3-267	" Sarah, of John and Elizabeth,	July 1, 1816.
3-267	" Daniel,	March 2, 1818.
3-202	" Benjn., of James and Sarah T.,	Nov. 18, 1841.
1-221	SHERMAN Ezekiel, of Jonathan and Mary,	June 23, 1721.
1-221	" Elizabeth, of Ezekiel and Margaret,	Aug. 18, 1748.
1-221	" William,	May 18, 1750.
1-221	" Mary,	Dec. 4, 1751.
1-221	" John,	Aug. 31, 1753.
1-222	" Joseph, of Benjamin and Freelove,	Jan. 4, 1746.
1-222	" Sarah,	Feb. 20, 1747.
1-222	" Freelove,	Dec. 4, 1753.
1-224	" Mellicent, of Moses and Sarah,	July 20, 1747.
1-224	" Elizabeth,	Oct. 4, 1749.
1-224	" Hannah,	Feb. 26, 1752.
1-224	" Moses,	March 7, 1756.
2-174	" Rufus, of Moses and Mary,	Jan. 28, 1759.
2-174	" Sarah,	Jan. 15, 1761.
2-174	" Abiel,	Feb. 5, 1767.
3-85	" Gideon, of Robert and Hannah,	Nov. 22, 1781.
3-85	" Ebenezer B.,	April 20, 1783.
3-85	" Arnold C.,	Feb. 15, 1785.
3-85	" Daniel C.,	March 4, 1787.
3-85	" Robert N.,	Sept 10, 1790.
3-85	" Willett H.,	Jan. 31, 1792.
3-85	" William Pitt,	March 2, 1794.
3-85	" Stukeley B.,	Feb. 14, 1796.
3-277	" David,	Sept. 26, 1798.
3-277	" Sarah,	April 21, 1801.
3-292	" Gersham Palmer, of Sam'l, Jr., and Amie,	Sept. 26, 1823

3-292	SHERMAN Peleg Arnold, of Sam'l, Jr., and Amie,		Aug. 23, 1826.
1-206	SLOCUM Hannah, of Benjn. and Elizabeth,		July 5, 1737.
1-206	"	Mary,	Dec. 12, 1738.
1-206	"	Peleg,	July 29, 1740.
1-206	"	Elizabeth,	Sept. 3, 1742.
1-206	"	Sarah,	Feb. 14, 1743.
3-259	"	Sarah F., of Charles A. and Elizabeth A.,	June 23, 1855.
3-259	"	Georgianna,	March 8, 1858.
1-206	SMITH Christopher, of Simon and Sarah,		June 18, 1740.
1-206	"	Dorcas,	Jan. 31, 1741-2.
1-206	"	Sarah,	Aug. 11, 1744.
3-149	"	Samuel, of Samuel and Sarah,	April 27, 1791.
3-149	"	Reuben,	March 22, 1793.
3-149	"	Sarah,	April 22, 1795.
3-69	SNOW Paulina E., of Samuel and Ann M.,		March 31, 1854.
3-69	"	Willard R.,	June 13, 1856.
3-69	"	James B.,	Sept. 9, 1862.
1-207	SPENCER Robert, of Mitchell and Abigail,		Feb. 20, 1740.
1-207	"	Nathaniel,	July 30, 1742.
1-207	"	Michell,	April 18, 1744.
1-207	"	Nathan,	April 23, 1746.
1-207	"	Joanna,	Jan. 15, 1747.
1-207	"	Caleb, of Michell and Abigail,	Dec. 27, 1750.
1-207	"	Samuel,	Aug. 15, 1752.
1-207	"	James,	Feb. 26, 1753.
1-207	"	Theodosia,	March 2, 1755.
1-207	"	Lydia,	Aug. 8, 1756.
1-206	"	Sarah,	July 17, 1758.
1-206	"	Mary,	July 17, 1758.
2-168	"	William, of John and Hannah,	Dec. 12, 1760.
2-168	"	Nicholas,	Sept. 1, 1762.
2-168	"	Abigail,	March 26, 1764.
2-168	"	Elizabeth,	July 3, 1766.
2-168	"	George,	July 8, 1768.
1-201	SPRAGUE Solomon, of David and Experience,		April 2, 1730.
1-201	"	David,	March 14, 1731-2.
1-201	"	Sarah,	March 16, 1733-4.
1-201	"	Esther,	May 4, 1736.
1-201	"	Experience,	Oct. 20, 1738.
1-201	"	Lydia,	March 13, 1740-1.
1-201	"	Jeremy,	July 4, 1743.
1-201	"	Abigail,	(sic.) Jan. 12, 1744.
1-201	"	Joseph,	March 12, 1746.
1-201	"	Joseph,	d. March 19, 1746.
1-201	"	Benjamin,	March 12, 1746.
1-201	"	Benjamin,	d. March 16, 1746.
3-139	"	George, of Solomon and Isabel,	April 16, 1752.
3-139	"	Simon,	Jan. 17, 1754.
3-139	"	Jeremiah,	June 30, 1761.
3-139	"	Phebe,	Oct. 7, 1764.
3-139	"	David,	Nov. 28, 1765.
3-139	"	Isabel,	Aug. 26, 1768.
3-139	"	Sarah,	July 14, 1771.
3-140	"	Elizabeth, of Dr. Simon and Abigail,	June 24, 1782.
3-140	"	Mary,	April 5, 1784.
3-140	"	Isabel,	Feb. 6, 1786.
3-140	"	Sarah,	Dec. 6, 1788.
3-140	"	Jordan,	Aug. 26, 1790.
3-140	"	Abigail,	June 3, 1792.
3-140	"	Abigail,	d. Oct. 13, 1795.
3-140	"	Penelope Holloway,	Feb. 10, 1797.
2-1	STANTON Daniel, of John and Sarah,		Oct. 30, 1765.
2-168	STRANGE Sarah, of William and Hannah,		April 12, 1779.
3-147	"	Mary,	April 12, 1779.
3-147	"	Caleb,	April 14, 1781.
3-5	"	Sarah (2d dau.), of Caleb and Annis,	Feb. 10, 1811.

3-143	SUNDERLAND William, of George and Deborah,	April 13, 1775.
3-143	"	Warham,	July 2, 1777.
3-143	"	Mary,	Feb. 9, 1781.
3-143	"	George,	March 1, 1783.
3-143	"	John,	May 27, 1788.
3-143	"	Augustus,	Dec. 8, 1792.
3-247	"	Joseph Wilcox, of Gideon G. and Mary (Wilcox),	July 17, 1845.
1-207	SWEET Freelove, of Samuel and Sarah,	Nov. 1, 1734.
1-207	"	Samuel,	Feb. 1, 1736.
1-207	"	Jonathan,	Aug. 9, 1739.
1-207	"	Albro,	March 14, 1743.
1-207	"	Elizabeth,	March 11, 1744.
1-199	"	Dorothy, of George and Ruth,	Nov. 12, 1742.
1-199	"	Susannah,	May 17, 1745.
1-199	"	Mary,	June 20, 1747.
1-199	"	George,	Sept. 28, 1749.
1-199	"	Jabez,	Oct. 9, 1751.
1-199	"	Hannah,	April 12, 1754.
1-199	"	Ruth,	May 31, 1757.
1-199	"	Elizabeth,	Aug. 10, 1759.
1-199	"	Almy,	Jan. 7, 1762.
1-199	"	Orpha, of Robert and Elizabeth,	Aug. 11, 1743.
1-199	"	Benjamin,	Jan. 30, 1744.
1-199	"	Zilpha,	May 1, 1746.
1-199	"	Elizabeth,	Oct. 7, 1747.
1-199	"	Robert,	April 20, 1749.
1-199	"	Nathan,	April 18, 1751.
1-199	"	Ann,	Sept. 14, 1752.
1-199	"	Dinah,	June 13, 1754.
1-199	"	Patience,	April 2, 1756.
1-245	"	Jeremiah, of John and Abigail,	Nov. 14, 1744.
1-245	"	Jsesuball,	Sept. 21, 1746.
1-205	"	George,	Nov. 28, 1748.
1-205	"	Elizabeth,	Jan. 28, 1750.
1-205	"	Ruth,	June 12, 1753.
1-223	"	Naomi, of Henry and Freelove,	Dec. 21, 1754.
3-21	"	John, of John and Mary,	Jan. 13, 1762.
3-21	"	William,	Jan. 13, 1764.
3-21	"	George,	April 30, 1766.
3-21	"	Hannah,	March 27, 1768.
3-69	"	William, of Elisha and Martha,	April 5, 1784.
3-258	"	Palmer, of Hannah, grandson of John,	May 4, 1797.

T

1-223	TANNER Gideon, of Joseph and Joanna,	Jan. 26, 1749.
1-223	"	Joanna,	May 3, 1742.
1-223	"	John,	July 22, 1745.
1-223	"	Joshua,	March 23, 1748.
1-223	"	Joseph,	Aug. 27, 1750.
1-162	"	William, of William and Susannah,	Aug. 15, 1752.
3-126	TILLINGHAST Stukeley (of Exeter), son of Pardon (of West Greenwich), born in Warwick, R. I.,	Nov. 24, 1741.
3-126	"	Honor (Hopkins), (West Greenwich), his wife,	Jan. 6, 1745.
3-126	"	Anna, (West Greenwich), of Stukeley and Honor,	May 26, 1763.
3-126	"	Amos, (Exeter),	Oct. 23, 1764.
3-126	"	Stephen,	June 13, 1766.
3-127	"	Amie, of Stukeley and Honor,	Oct. 29, 1767.
3-126	"	Honor,	May 24, 1769.
3-126	"	Pardon,	Feb. 3, 1771.
3-126	"	Hannah,	Dec. 26, 1772.
3-126	"	Stukeley,	June 29, 1774.
3-126	"	Mary,	Jan. 21, 1776.
3-126	"	Sarah,	Oct. 10, 1777.

3-126	TILLINGHAST Ruth, of Stukeley and Honor,		Jan. 29, 1780.
3-126	" Anstis,		Jan. 18, 1782.
3-126	" Clarke,		April 17, 1784.
3-126	" James,		Aug. 21, 1786.
3-22	" Alice, (3d dau.) of Pardon and Ruth,		May 21, 1767.
3-22	" Ruth, (4th dau.),		April 22, 1773
3-22	" Ruth, wife of Pardon,	d. Aug. 21, 1776.
3-57	" —, of Penelope, (Jamestown),		Sept. 28, 1780.
3-57	" Daniel Holloway, of Daniel and —,		—. —, —.
3-57	" Pardon (Exeter),		March 23, 1782.
3-67	" Joseph R., of Phillip and Anna,		Dec. 29, 1782.
3-186	" Amie, of Allen and Ruth,		Oct. 11, 1799.
3-186	" Abigail,		Sept. 11, 1801.
3-186	" Charles,		Nov. 18, 1803.
3-186	" John,		Dec. 30, 1805.
3-209	" John, of Pardon S.,		Feb. 1, 1808.
2-180	TEFFT Abigail, of Robert and Abigail,		Oct. 6, 1755.
2-180	" John,		Feb. 19, 1758.
2-180	" Robert,		Feb. 4, 1761.
2-180	" Joseph,		Oct. 13, 1763.
2-180	" Patience,		Dec. 10. 1766.
3-22	" Martha, of Robert and Martha,		May 7, 1771.
3-107	" Robert, of John and Anna,		March 1, 1779.
3-107	" Abigail,		Oct. 6, 1781.
3-107	" Jeremiah,		July 23, 1782.
3-107	" Simon,		April 27, 1784.
3-107	" Mary,		June 23, 1786.
3-107	" David,		July 3, 1788.
3-187	" Lydia, of Benjamin T. and Lucy,		Feb. 3, 1800.
3-187	" Abigail,		Feb. 20, 1802.
3-187	" Lucy,		April 25, 1804.
3-187	" Rebecca,		Feb. 15, 1806.
3-187	" Hannah,		March 25, 1808.
3-187	" Benjamin B.,		May 6, 1810.
3-161	" Lucy, wife of Benjamin T., dau. of Stephen and Abigail Reynolds, aged 33y., 5m., 6d,		Sept. 11, 1811.
3-102	TERRY Seth,		Jan. 22, 1764.
3-102	" Abigail, of Seth and Mary,		Jan. 11, 1786.
3-102	" Joanna,		March 28, 1787.
3-102	" Moses,		Dec. 2, 1788.
3-256	" Charles, of Othniel and Nancy,		Sept. 14, 1811.
3-256	" William R., of Moses and Sarah,		June 2, 1812.
3-256	" Stephen,		Nov. 3, 1814.
3-256	" Seth W.,		Jan. 31, 1816.
3-256	" Burgness P.,		Aug. 1, 1817.
3-256	" Whitman Barber,		May 23, 1818.
3-256	" Whitman Barber,	d. April 8, 1823.
3-256	" Ellet,		April 3, 1820.
3-256	" Silas Whitman,		April 3, 1822.
1-203	TRIPP Job,	b. April 20, 1701.
1-203	" Sarah, his wife,	b. May 20, 1704.
1-203	" Peleg, of Job and Sarah,		June 13, 1723.
1-203	" Peregrine,		Aug. 19, 1725.
1-203	" Charles,		Oct. 1, 1727.
1-203	" Charles,	d. in Surinam, April —, 1748.
1-203	" Mehitable,		Dec. 1, 1729.
1-203	" Sarah,		Dec. 20, 1731.
1-203	" Job,		June 28, 1734.
1-203	" Amos,		Sept. 8, 1736.
1-203	" Mary,		March 28, 1739.
1-203	" Phebe,		Aug. 13, 1741.
1-203	" Ezekiel,		March 9, 1743-4.
1-203	" Charles,		Sept. 30, 1749.
1-203	" Thomas, of William and Mary,		May 12, 1740.

1-216	TRIPP Hannah, of Peleg and Sarah,	Jan. 19, 1743.
1-216	" Sarah,	Nov. 11, 1745.
1-216	" Louis,	Aug. 16, 1747.
1-216	" Waite,	April 1, 1749.
1-216	" Sarah, of Peregrine and Susannah,	Oct. 1, 1749.
1-216	" Ruth,	April 15, 1751.
1-216	" Susannah,	Jan. 1, 1753.
3-169	" Lucy Ann, of John S.,	April 15, 1818.
3-169	" Samuel Burrell,	Feb. 23, 1820.
3-169	" Huldah Eliza	Oct. 12, 1821.
3-169	" Perry Greene,	Oct. 12, 1823.

U V

3-235	VAUGHN Joshua, born	Nov. 1, 1773.
3-235	" Lucy, his wife, born	March 21, 1772.
3-235	" Pitt, of Joshua and Lucy,	Sept. 24, 1799.
3-235	" Ray Greene,	Aug. 3, 1801.
3-235	" Maria Flagg,	April 18, 1803.
3-235	" Catherine Isabel,	Nov. 18, 1804.
3-197	" Isaac Watton, of Richard and Esther,	March 4, 1798.
3-197	" Lucy,	Jan. 5, 1800.
3-197	" Mary,	Jan. 10, 1802.
3-197	" Sybel,	April 21, 1803.
3-197	" Abigail,	Dec. 4, 1806.
3-197	" Betsey,	Feb. 17, 1815.
3-197	" Daniel,	Oct. 31, 1813.

W

1-226	WAINMAN Sarah, of Richard and Avis,	June 10, 1753.
1-226	" Penelope,	Jan. 9, 1755.
1-226	" Charles,	Oct. 22, 1757.
1-209	WAITE Deborah, of Samuel, Jr., and Sarah,	July 11, 1725.
1-209	" Caleb,	Sept. 11, 1727.
1-209	" Martha,	Dec. 4, 1729.
1-209	" Ruth,	May 12, 1732.
1-209	" Lucretta,	Jan. 22, 1734.
1-209	" Eleanor,	Jan. 9, 1736.
1-209	" Samuel,	Jan. 1, 1738.
1-209	" Catherine,	June 19, 1740.
1-209	" Henry,	Jan. 7, 1742-3.
1-209	" Jonathan,	Jan. 7, 1742-3.
1-209	" Benjamin,	Jan. 5, 1745-6.
1-209	" Alce,	June —, 1747.
1-209	" George,	March 22, 1749.
1-174	" Martha, of Joseph and Elizabeth,	March 10, 1738.
1-174	" Reuben,	July 24, 1740.
1-174	" Oliver,	June 15, 1741.
1-174	" Elverton,	Sept. 14, 1743.
1-227	" Mary, of William and Mary,	Feb. 18, 1751-2.
1-227	" Benjamin,	Sept. 3, 1753.
1-227	" Isaiah,	Jan. 30, 1756.
1-227	" John,	Dec. 29, 1757.
1-227	" William,	Jan. 10, 1760.
1-227	" Stephen,	Oct. 11, 1761.
1-227	" Nicholas,	April 17, 1763.
1-226	" Jenckes, of Samuel, Jun., and Ansilles,	Feb. 6, 1753.
1-226	" Lucia,	June 6, 1756.
1-226	" Jenckes,	March 3, 1759.
1-172	" Beriah, of Benjamin and Sarah,	Nov. 28, 1757.
1-172	" Joseph,	Jan. 27, 1759.
1-172	" Stephen,	Jan. 26, 1761.

1-172	WAITE Honor, of Benjamin and Sarah,	Aug. 18, 1762.
1-172	" Elizabeth,	Feb. 18, 1765.
1-172	" Edmund,	Feb. 26, 1767.
1-172	" Lydia,	Dec. 25, 1769.
1-172	" Mary,	Jan. 14, 1772.
3-81	" Benjamin,	Jan. 8, 1776.
3-81	" Sarah,	Oct. 8, 1780.
3-81	" John,	Aug. 22, 1785.
1-173	" Elizabeth, of Reuben and Mary,	July 19, 1759.
3-26	" Jenckes, of Jenckes and Sarah,	May 24, 1781.
3-71	" George, of Joseph and Abigail,	Aug. 10, 1784.
1-176	WATSON Stephen, of Robert,	Dec. 7, 1760.
3-152	" Samuel (2d son), of Robert and Rebecca,	May 10, 1778.
3-152	" John (3d son),	June 22, 1782.
3-177	" John, of Stephen and Mercy,	Nov. 24, 1782.
3-177	" Gardiner,	Jan. 17, 1785.
3-177	" Freelove,	April 6, 1790.
	Note.—Also recorded 3-28.	
3-152	" Patience, of John and Isabel,	Sept. 7, 1801.
3-152	" John Kenyon,	March 15, 1804.
3-152	" Stephen Dyer,	Oct. 25, 1806.
3-152	" John Mumford,	June 20, 1809.
1-171	WEEDEN Peleg, of Caleb and Lydia,	Sept. 15, 1759.
1-171	" John,	Dec. 22, 1761.
1-225	WEIGHTMAN Thankful, of Titus and Hannah,	Sept. 19, 1752.
3-13	" Mary, (b. in Warwick), of Stephen and Abigail,	Oct. 12, 1773.
3-13	" Abigail, wife of Stephen, died	Feb. 22, 1780.
1-210	WHITFORD Sarah, of John and Martha,	Sept. 17, 1727.
1-210	" Benjamin,	May 1, 1729.
1-210	" Lydia,	Nov. 22, 1730.
1-210	" Elizabeth,	April 3, 1733.
1-210	" Mary,	Dec. 22, 1735.
1-210	" John,	Dec. 1, 1737.
1-210	" Mercy,	March 25, 1739.
1-210	" Martha,	Jan. 21, 1740.
1-210	" Amos,	July 25, 1743.
1-225	WHITMAN Elizabeth, of George and Bridget,	Sept. 23, 1752.
3-103	WILBUR Abigail, of John and Abigail,	May 1, 1752.
3-206	" John, died	Nov 5, 1798.
1-199	WILCOX John, of Abraham and Lydia,	July 9, 1741.
1-199	" Job,	Feb. 4, 1743
3-24	" Thurston, of John and Mary,	June 4, 1762.
3-24	" Lydia,	March 11, 1764.
3-24	" Daniel,	May 1, 1767.
3-24	" Mary,	June 4, 1771.
3-24	" Deliverance,	March 17, 1774
3-68	" Libbeus, of Abraham and Mary,	Aug. 22, 1763.
3-203	" Asa, of Job and Mary,	April 7, 1772.
3-203	" Nathan,	Aug. 16, 1774.
3-203	" Esther,	Aug. 20, 1776.
3-203	" Simon,	Sept. 3, 1778.
3-203	" Eunice,	Aug. 17, 1780.
3-203	" Job,	March 12, 1782.
3-203	" Harrington,	Sept. 22, 1783.
3-203	" Mary,	Aug. 22, 1785.
3-203	" Prudence,	April 2, 1787.
3-203	" Gates,	Sept. 21, 1790.
3-203	" Hannah,	Oct. 7, 1794.
3-203	" Thurston,	Nov. 2, 1796.
3-132	" Joseph, of Isaac and Rebecca,	Sept. 1, 1774.
3-132	" Charity,	July 20, 1776.
3-132	" Rebecca,	Dec. 23, 1779.
3-132	" Isaac,	Feb. 22, 1781.
3-132	" Nathaniel,	March 20, 1783.
3-132	" Josiah,	June 5, 1785.

3-132	WILCOX	Arehaba, of Isaac and Rebecca,	Dec. 26, 1787.
3-132	"	Jacob,	Jan. 10, 1790.
3-132	"	Isaac, died	March 16, 1801.
3-231	"	Jeffrey H., (3d son) of Jeffrey and Sarah,	Oct. 11, 1783.
3-106	"	Gardiner, of Stephen,	June 15, 1797.
3-227	"	Rebecca Walton, of Isaiah and Sybel,	May 23, 1807.
3-257	"	Charles T., of Othniel and Nancy,	Sept. 14, 1811.
3-207	WILKEY	Mary, of Jeremiah and Mary,	July 4, 1735.
3-207	"	Martha,	June 16, 1737.
3-207	"	Thomas,	March 27, 1739.
3-207	"	Peter,	Oct. 27, 1740.
3-207	"	John,	Jan. 19, 1742.
3-207	"	Lydia,	April 13, 1745.
3-207	"	Abignil,	May 23, 1747.
3-207	"	Jeremiah,	Dec. 17, 1750.
3-207	"	Elizabeth,	Aug. 17, 1759.
3-207	"	Peter, died	Jan. 11, 1741.
3-8	"	Sarah, of Martha,	April 1, 1761.
3-8	"	John, of John and Bethany,	Aug. 2, 1771.
3-8	"	Jenerate,	Nov. 5, 1774.
3-8	"	Joseph Spencer,	Sept. 16, 1779.

X Y Z

Vital Record of Rhode Island.

1636=1850.

FIRST SERIES.

BIRTHS, MARRIAGES AND DEATHS.

A Family Register for the People.

BY JAMES N. ARNOLD,

EDITOR OF THE NARRAGANSETT HISTORICAL REGISTER.

"Is My Name Written in the Book of Life?"

Vol. 5. **WESTERLY.** **Part IV.**

Published under the Auspices of the General Assembly.

PROVIDENCE, R. I:
NARRAGANSETT HISTORICAL PUBLISHING COMPANY.
1894.

ACT INCORPORATING THE TOWN OF WESTERLY.

This Court taking notice of the returne of the Committee, to witt, Mr. John Easton, Mr. Benjamin Smith, James Greene, Edward Smith, Caleb Carr and William Weeden, in reference to the petition or desire of the people inhabiting at Mosquanocott and Pawcatucke in the Kings Province to be made a towneshipp, it being and lying within this jurisdiction, as by his Majesty's Letters Pattents it may appear and considering the power by his Majestye given to this Assembly to order and settle townes, cities and corporations within this said jurisdiction, as shall seem meet and seeing there doth alsoe appeare good evidence of the trust and good affection of the said people unto his Mejestyes government, established in this Collony, and being also sensibell that the said inhabitants have suffered much in vindicating the same and are a competent number to carry on the affairs there, as in condition of a towneship.

Bee it therefore enacted by this Assembly, and by the authority thereof, that the said inhabitants of Musquamacott being seated adjoining to Pawcatucke, alias Narragansett or Narragansett River on the west part and boundary of this Collony, and within that part thereof known by the name of the King's Province aforesaid, to wit, Mr. John Crandall, Mr. Tobias Sanders and all such others as now are, or hereafter shall be legally admitted as freemen and inhabitants in the said place called Musquamacott, etc., shall be knowne and called by the name of WESTERLY, and shall be reputed and deemed the fifth Towne of this Collony, and shall have use and enjoy all such privilidges and exercise all such methods and forms for the well ordering their towne affaires, as any other towne in this Collony may now use and exercise, and they shall have liberty to elect and send two Deputies to sitt and act in the Generall Assemblys of this Collony from time to time, and are enjoyned to choose and send to the General Court of Trialls one grand jury man, and one for the jury of trials from time to time, and further this Assembly for their the said peoples better governing themselves, and such as come amongst them, and untill his Majestyes pleasure be father knowne doe recommend the care and speciall regard or ordering and appeynting Conservators of the Peace among them unto the Governor, Deputye Governor and Assistants of this Collony, as was by the Governor and Councill began in the year 1665, and hath been since continued disiringe it may still be ordered, and by the said justices, renewed and as occasion requires compleated and established, as they shall see meett, even to erecting Courts for Triall of such small matters as other particular Courts in this Collony may doe in that respect.

Rhode Island Colonial Records Vol. II., pages 250, 251.

WESTERLY.

MARRIAGES.

A

2-84   ADAMS Thomas, and Mary Hall (of Edward, dec.); m. by John Richmond, Justice, Nov. 23, 1732.

3-80   "   James, and Mary Randall, both of Groton, Conn.; m. by Silas Greenman, Justice, Aug. 3, 1756.

5-89   AKINS Andrew J., of Volney, Oswego Co., N. Y., and Hannah Vars, of Westerly; m. by Rev. Thomas G. Osborn, Dec. 2, 1846.

5-101 ALEXANDER Dixon, of Benson, Vt., M. D., son of Alexander, of De Kalb, N. Y., and Mary Elizabeth Wentworth, of Erastus, of Conn.; m. by Rev. Thomas H. Vail, Oct. 2, 1849.

2-119 ALLEN Gideon, and Lydia ——, Nov. 6, 1705.

2-119 "   Samuel, and Catherine Morris, Aug. 20, 1707.

2-87   "   Patience, and William Meekcome, April 2, 1738.

2-94   "   Sarah, and Thomas Burdick, Dec. 6, 1742.

2-73   "   John, and Lydia Richmond; m. by Elder Joseph Maxson, March 30, 1744.

3-93   "   Thankful, and Isaiah Lanphear, Oct. 16, 1763.

3-155 "   Rachel, and Paul Edwards, April 13, 1782.

4-64   "   Polly, and William Noyes, April 21, 1792.

4-120 "   Joshua, of James, of Charlestown, and Rachel Bliven, of Daniel, of Westerly; m. by Samuel Bliven, Justice, March 1, 1798.

4-212 "   Greene, of Charlestown, and Amey Bliven, of Westerly; m. by Elder Abram Coon, Feb. 12, 1804.

4-257 "   Amelia, and Benjamin Gavitt, May 17, 1914.

5-97   "   Frederic Lee, of New London, Conn., and Waite Harris Lippitt, of Christopher, of Westerly; m. by Rev. Thomas H. Vail, June 4, 1849.

2-72   ALLOBY Sarah, and William Davis, Feb. 7, 1739-40.

5-67   AMOS Rufus, and Betsey White; m. by Rev. Oliver P. Tuckerman, Jan. 25, 1846.

3-66   AUSTIN Cornellus, of Scltnate, and Thankful Saunders, of Westerly; m. by John Richmond, Justice, Oct. 25, 1733.

3-17   "   Barbara, and Daniel Button, Oct. 7, 1752.

4-103 "   Champlain, of Stephen, of Charlestown, and Dolly Hall, of Abigail, of Westerly; m. by Samuel Bliven, Justice, (also 4-109), Nov. 20, 1796.

5-52   "   Charles W., and Emma Ann Bliven; m. by Rev. Oliver P. Tuckerman, April 25, 1844.

5-25   "   Rhoda N., and William R. Burdick, July 4, 1846.

3-32   AVERY Charles, of Groton, and Mary Thurston, of Stonington; m. by Benjamin Randall, Justice, Aug. 28, 1753.

3-17   "   Elizabeth, and Benajah Williams, Sept. 1, 1754.

B

2-115 BABCOCK Mary, and Thomas Potter, March 19, 1717-8.

2-58   "   Lydia, and Roger Elderton, Sept. 20, 1722.

2-112 "   Samuel, and Ann Pendleton; m. by John Saunders, Justice, May 15, 1723.

2-95   BABCOCK Stephen, and Anna Thompson, Oct. 12, 1726.
2-95   "   Mercy, and Tobias Brand. April 30, 1730.
2-92   "   William, of Westerly, and Sarah Denison, of Seabrook; m. by Rev. Hezekiah Marther, Aug. 11, 1730.
2-88   "   Joseph, and Susannah Thompson; m. by Theodoty Rhodes, Justice, Dec. 9, 1730.
2-94   "   David, of South Kingstown, and Dorcas Brown, of Westerly; m. by George Babcock, Justice, Feb. 24, 1730-1.
2-88   "   Anne, and Silas Greenman, March 23, 1730-1.
2-87   "   James, and Content Maxson; m. by Theodoty Rhodes, Justice, July 7, 1731.
2-94   "   Ichabod, and Jemima Babcock; m. by Theodoty Rhodes, Justice, Dec. 1, 1731.
2-94   "   Jemima, and Ichabod Babcock, Dec. 1, 1731.
2-84   "   Amey, and Ezekiel Gavitt, Aug. 9, 1732.
2-76   "   Joshua, and Hannah Stanton; m. by Rev. John Maxson, Aug. 11, 1735.
2-73   "   Mary, and Benjamin Randall, Oct. 22, 1735.
2-72   "   Amos, and Elizabeth Brand; m. by William Hern, Justice, Dec. 20, 1738.
2-14   "   Ezekiel, and Eunice Billings; m. by Elder John Maxson, Oct. 26, 1740.
2-14   "   Abigail, and Henry Mulkins, Nov. 4, 1740.
2-94   "   Content, and William Hiscox (also 3-39), Dec. 22, 1742.
3-11   "   Mary, and William Wilbur, April 17, 1745.
3-6   "   Isaac, of Westerly, and Mary, Worden, of Stonington; m. by Rev. Nathaniel Eells, April 17, 1746.
3-12   "   Nathan, of Samuel, of Westerly, and Deborah Stafford, of Warwick; m. by Elder Joseph Maxson, May 19, 1748.
3-28   "   Susannah, and Benjamin Clarke, Nov. 3, 1748.
3-61   "   William, of Daniel, and Patience Cottrell; m. by William Babcock, Justice, Jan. 28, 1749.
3-20   "   Anne, and Joseph Davis, Jan. 18, 1749-50.
3-9   "   George, Jr., of Westerly, and Mehitable Wheeler, of Stonington; m. by Rev. Joseph Fish, June 26, 1751.
3-25   "   Lucy, and Nathan Breed, June —, 1751.
3-3   "   Elizabeth, and John Burdick, Dec. 1, 1751.
3-25   "   Hannah, and Joseph Reynolds, Sept. —, 1752.
3-29   "   Mary, and Joseph Davis, Jan. 10, 1753.
3-35   "   Caleb, of Westerly, and Susanna Hall, of Richmond; m. by Daniel Maccoon, Justice, Jan. 14, 1753.
3-30   "   James, and Mary Satterly, Feb. 21, 1753.
3-31   "   John, of Westerly, and Abigail Pearce, of Richmond; m. by Daniel Maccoon, Justice, March 8, 1753.
3-9   "   Sarah, and Stephen Chalken, Nov. 5, 1753.
3-33   "   Joshua, of Daniel, and Sarah Berry; m. by William Hern, Justice, Jan. 10, 1754.
3-41   "   Elizabeth, and Nathan Smith, Sept. 19, 1754.
3-42   "   James, and Sarah Stanton; m. by Silas Greenman, Justice, Dec. 2, 1754.
3-43   "   Prudence, and William Saunders, Jr., Jan. 9, 1755.
3-43   "   Samuel, Jr., and Mary Smith; m. by Joseph Crandall, Justice, Jan. 23, 1755.
3-9   "   Ichabod, Jr., of Westerly, and Esther Stanton, of Charlestown; m. by Joseph Crandall, Justice, March 17, 1756.
3-51   "   Anne, and Capt. Simon Rhodes, Dec. 15, 1756.
3-44   "   Job, and Sarah Porter; m. by Daniel Maccoon, Justice, Feb. 10, 1757.
3-55   "   James, Jr., of Stonington, and Lucretia Babcock, of Westerly; m. by Silas Greenman, Justice, July 21, 1757.
3-55   "   Lucretia, and James Babcock, Jr., July 21, 1757.
3-22   "   Ceazar, and Reensy Greenman; m. by William Hern, Justice, April 7, 1758.
3-72   "   Sarah, and John Gorton, Nov. 9, 1760.

3-77   BABCOCK Oliver, and Silvestre Belcher; m. by Joseph Crandall, Justice, July 2, 1761.

3-81   "   Elkanah, and Esther Crandall; m. by James Bliven, Justice, (also 4-66), March 28, 1762.

3-86   "   Thankful, and Joseph Stanton, Jr., July 14, 1762.

3-94   "   Benedict, of South Kingstown, and Mary Thompson, of Capt. Joshua, of Westerly; m. by Rev. Joseph Park, March 2, 1763.

4-19   "   Jesse, of Joseph, and Abigail Mulkin, of Henry; m. by Ichabod Babcock, Justice, March 8, 1763.

3-94   "   Mary, and Pheneas Clarke, Nov. 23, 1763.

3-12   "   Nathan, of Westerly, and Elizabeth Brown, of Stonington; m. by Rev. Joseph Fish, May 20, 1764.

3-09   "   Joseph, Jr., and Hannah Champlain; m. by Rev. Joseph Park, March 31, 1765.

3-104   "   Prudence, and Elijah Lewis, Nov. 10, 1765.

3-105   "   Ephraim, of Westerly, and Ann Peckham, of Charlestown; m. by Rev. Joseph Park, Aug. 10, 1766.

3-109   "   Phebe, and Ezekiel Gavitt, Jr., March 22, 1767.

3-115   "   Major James, of Westerly, and Joanna McDowell, of Stonington, at Stonington, by Rev. Nathaniel Eells, Aug. 27, 1769.

3-114   "   Elizabeth, and John Worden, Nov. 12, 1769.

3-123   "   Desire, and Zaccheus Reynolds, Dec. 11, 1771.

3-126   "   Rebecca, and Champlain Lanphear, March 9, 1772.

3-126   "   Anne, and William West, Nov. 1, 1772.

3-130   "   Anna and Robert Thompson, March 18, 1773.

3-141   "   Amelia, and Nathan Pendleton, Jan. 22, 1775.

3-149   "   James, 3d, of James, and Sarah Ross, of John; m. by Elder Isaiah Wilcox, Jan. 26, 1777.

4-61   "   Deborah, and Nathaniel Stillman, Feb. 26, 1777.

3-160   "   Lucy, and Christopher Crandall, April 17, 1777.

3-173   "   Anne, and Rowland Champlain, May 10, 1777.

3-153   "   Prentice, of Isaac, and Anna Gavitt, of William, dec.; m. by Joseph Crandall, Justice, March 15, 1778.

3-154   "   Henry, of James, and Prudence Gavitt, of Hezekiah; m. by Elder Isaiah Wilcox, Aug. 4, 1778.

3-163   "   Samuel, of Nathan, 2d, and Lucy Wilcox, of David, dec.; m. by Elder Isaiah Wilcox, May 22, 1779.

3-164   "   Nathan, of Samuel, dec., of Westerly, and Nancy Lewis, of Nathaniel, dec., of Hopkinton; m. by Elder Isaiah Wilcox, Aug. 26, 1779.

3-177   "   Simon, and Mrs. Hannah Champlain; m. by Elder Oliver Babcock, April 6, 1780.

3-170   "   Hon. Joshua, of Westerly, and Mrs. Anna Maxson, late of Newport; m. by Joseph Clarke, Justice, May 28, 1780.

3-127   "   Isaac, and Amey Gavitt, of Deacon Ezekiel; m. by Joseph Crandall, Justice, Nov. 12, 1780.

3-171   "   Paul, of Samuel, of Westerly, and Charlotte Crandall, of James, of Richmond; m. by Joseph Crandall, Justice, (also 4-76), Nov. 30, 1780.

4-43   "   Sarah, and Sylvester Gavitt, Sept. 30, 1781.

3-176   "   Elizabeth, and William Blackington, Nov. 27, 1781.

3-176   "   Amos, of Isaac, and Mary Babcock, of Joseph; m. by Elder Thomas Ross, (also 4-84), Dec. 2, 1781.

3-176   "   Mary, and Amos Babcock, (also 4-84), Dec. 2, 1781.

3-176   "   Mary, and Peleg Ross, Jr., Dec. 2, 1781.

3-175   "   Dorcas, and Nathan Babcock, Feb. 6, 1782.

3-175   "   Nathan, of Samuel, dec., of Westerly, and Dorcas Babcock, of David, of South Kingstown; m. by Elder Isaiah Wilcox, Feb. 6, 1782.

4-113   "   Christopher, Jr., of Charlestown, and Polly Potter, of Middletown; m. by Rev. Gardiner Thurston, June 16, 1782.

3-118   "   Joseph, Jr., son of Ichabod, Jr., and Sarah Babcock, of Christopher; m. by Elder Isaiah Wilcox, Aug. 4, 1782.

3-118   "   Sarah, and Joseph Babcock, Jr., Aug. 4, 1782.

4-7   "   Mary, and William Babcock, Sept. 8, 1782.

4-7	BABCOCK	William, of Christopher, and Mary Babcock, of Ichabod; m. by Elder Isaiah Wilcox, Sept. 8, 1782.
4-68	"	Mary, and Henry Davis, Aug. 21, 1783.
4-13	"	Christopher, of Christopher, and Polly Burdick, of Oliver, dec.; m. by Elder Isaiah Wilcox, Nov. 30, 1783.
4-100	"	Anna, and Walter Brand, Jan. 28, 1784.
4-4	"	Daniel, of James, dec., of Westerly, and Hannah Burdick, of Peter, of Stonington; m. by Joseph Crandall, Justice, March 1, 1784.
4-20	"	Silas, of Westerly, and Mercy Kenyon, of John, of Richmond, at Richmond; m. by Elder John Burdick, Jan. 18, 1787.
4-27	"	Rhoda, and George Gavitt, March 31, 1788.
4-68	"	Jared, of Samuel, of Westerly, and Martha Lewis, of Daniel, of Hopkinton; m. by Elder Joshua Clarke, Oct. 25, 1789.
4-55	"	Jesse, of Isaac, and Hannah Thompson, of Isaac; m. by Elder Isaiah Wilcox, Jan. 23, 1789.
4-97	"	Joanna, and Joseph Wilbur, Jr., Jan. 6, 1790.
4-49	"	John, of John, dec., of Westerly, and Anna Maxson, of Jonathan, of Richmond; m. by Eld. Henry Joslin, Jan. 10, 1790.
4-60	"	Arnold, of Oliver, dec., and Lucy Davis, of Joseph; m. by Elder Isaiah Wilcox, Jan. 17, 1790.
4-100	"	Lydia, and Walter Brand, May 16, 1791.
4-74	"	Charles, and Lucy Langworthy; m. by Daniel Babcock, Justice, Jan. 1, 1792.
4-77	"	Joshua, and Ruth Greene; m. by Elder Isaiah Wilcox, March 11, 1792.
4-75	"	Deborah, and George Pendleton, Oct. 25, 1792.
4-86	"	Delight, and Lemuel Vose, March 13, 1794.
4-105	"	John, of Joseph, and Damarius Crandall; m. by Joseph Clarke, Justice, Dec. 4, 1794.
4-108	"	Hannah, and Arnold West (also 4-112), Nov. 17, 1796.
4-149	"	James, of James, and Sarah Ross, of John; m. by Elder Isaiah Wilcox, Jan. 26, 1797.
4-106	"	Jesse, of Westerly, and Mary Barnes, widow, of Hopkinton; m. at Hopkinton by Elder Asa Coon, Aug. 19, 1798.
4-124	"	Lois, and William Hebert, Nov. 20, 1798.
4-209	"	Capt. Dudley, and Ann Wright, both of Stonington; m. by Charles Phelps, Justice, Jan. 7, 1799.
4-139	"	Elizabeth and Joseph Noyes, Jr., Jan. 13, 1799.
4-140	"	Hannah, and Richard Berry, March 4, 1799.
4-151	"	Asa, of Christopher, and Molly Babcock, of Joseph; m. by Samuel Bliven, Justice, Jan. 16, 1800.
4-151	"	Molly, and Asa Babcock, Jan. 16, 1800.
4-154	"	Martha, and Sanford Noyes, Feb. 2, 1800.
4-165	"	Rouse, of Rouse, of Westerly, and Hannah Brown, of George, of South Kingstown; m. at South Kingstown, by Rev. Theodore Dehon, Jan. 13, 1801.
4-168	"	Stephen, of Christopher, and Phebe Burch; m. by Samuel Bliven, Justice, March 22, 1801.
4-180	"	Joseph, of Joseph, of Westerly, and Keturah Gavitt, of John, of Charlestown; m. by Nathan Taylor, Justice, April 12, 1801.
4-174	"	Elizabeth, and John Wilbur, Sept. 21, 1801.
4-164	"	Ruth, and Sylvester Crumb, Jr., Oct. 11, 1801.
4-173	"	Daniel, of Joseph, and Nancy Babcock, of James; m. by Joseph Pendleton, Justice, Oct. 29, 1801.
4-173	"	Nancy, and Daniel Babcock, Oct. 29, 1801.
4-171	"	Phineas, of Christopher, and Thankful Babcock, of Joseph; m. by Samuel Bliven, Justice, Nov. 29, 1801
4-171	"	Thankful, and Phineas Babcock, Nov. 29, 1801.
4-172	"	Joshua, of Elder Elkanah, and Nancy Crandall, of John; m. by Samuel Bliven, Justice, Dec. 13, 1801.
4-175	"	James, of Joseph and Hannah Rhodes, of Capt. Joseph; m. by Samuel Bliven, Justice, May 6, 1802.
4-54	"	Nancy, and William Bliven, 2d, Jan. 16, 1803.
4-147	"	Charlotte, and Augustus Crandell, Sept. 17, 1803.
4-205	"	Damarius, and Nathan Burch, Dec. 22, 1803.

4-208	BABCOCK	Nathan, of Nathan, dec., and Patty Barber, of Peleg; m. by Joseph Pendleton, Justice, March 18, 1805.
4-214	"	Nancy, and William Thompson, March 31, 1805.
4-151	"	Asa, of Christopher, of Westerly, and Elizabeth Barber, of Thomas, de ., of Hopkinton; m. by Charles Greene, Justice, Dec. 19, 1805.
4-211	"	Dorcas, and Nathan Barber, 3d, Jan. 12, 1806.
4-227	"	Benjamin, of Westerly, and Ann Wilcox, of Col. Edward, of Charlestown; m. at Charlestown, by Peleg Cross, Justice, Jan. 26, 1806.
4-250	"	Esther, and Stephen Smith, Sept. 6, 1807.
4-241	"	David, of Nathan, dec., and Fanny Tefft, of John; m. by Joseph Pendleton, Justice, April 7, 1808.
4-255	"	Eunice, and Thomas Barber, May 25, 1809.
4-247	"	Paul, Jr., and Amey Clarke, of Job B.; m. by Elder Matthew Stillman, Sept. 5, 1811.
4-253	"	Asa 2d, and Mary Gavitt; m. by Elder Jesse Babcock, Sept. 12, 1813.
4-256	"	Mary, and Joseph Potter, Jr., Oct. 28, 1813.
4-256	"	Elisha, and Celia Wilbur; m. at Stonington, by Nathaniel Miner, Justice, Jan. 17, 1814.
4-263	"	Hannah, and Robert F. Ferguson, Jan. 23, 1814.
5-15	"	Nancy, and John P. Hall, Sept. 3, 1826.
5-48	"	Edward W., and Martha B. Cross; m. by Eller Matthew Stillman, Nov. 27, 1833.
5-32	"	Henry, of Stonington, and Mary Caroline Ross, of Westerly; m. by Rev. James Pratt, Feb. 4, 1839.
5-35	"	Charlotte, and James R. Irish, Aug. 26, 1839.
5-60	"	Sarah A., and Dr. John G. Peirce, June 1, 1840.
5-40	"	Perry G., and Eliza Sheffield; m. by Rev. A. G. Palmer, April 11, 1841.
5-25	"	Ezekiel, and Mary W. Lee; m. by George D. Cross, Justice, Feb. 13, 1842.
5-43	"	Mary Ann, and Benjamin R. Champlin, Sept. 22, 1842.
5-33	"	Susan, and George W. Barber, Dec. 7, 1842.
5-49	"	Rhoda, and Matthew S. Barber, Jan. 8, 1843.
5-47	"	Horace, and Abby Jane Cross; m. by Rev. William H. Newman, Sept. 11, 1843.
5-46	"	Lydia A., and William P. Taylor, Oct. 5, 1843.
5-74	"	Harriet, and Horatio Nelson Campbell, Sept. 8, 1846.
5-75	"	Esther, and Charles A. Stillman, Oct. 4, 1946.
5-76	"	Mary Ann, and George G. Crandall, Oct. 4, 1846.
5-87	"	Matilda, and Perry Hoxsie, July 3, 1848.
3-37	BACON	Ephraim, of Pomfret, and Mary Vincent, of Westerly; m. by Benoni Smith, Justice, Feb. 20, 1754.
2-110	BAILEY	Hannah, and Francis Coldgrove, (also 2-115), March 5, 1718-9.
2-96	"	Mary, and Edward Rogers, July 22, 1728.
2-72	"	Samuel, and Charity Clossen; m. by Samuel Wilbur, Justice, Feb. 12, 1735.
2-72	"	Judeth, and Thomas Brand, May 17, 1739.
2-10	"	Mary, and Jonathan Tefft, Jan. 29, 1740.
3-68	"	Samuel, Jr., and Hannah York; m. by Joseph Crandall, Justice, Jan. 8, 1761.
3-162	"	Silas, of Caleb, and Amey Stillman, of Joseph, dec.; m. by Joseph Clarke, Justice, May 22, 1777.
2-88	BARBER	Dinah, and Edward Wilcox, June 14, 1716.
2-92	"	Moses, and Mary Larkin; m. by Theodoty Rhodes, Justice, April 9, 1729.
2-82	"	Ezekiel, of South Kingstown, and Hannah Webster, of Westerly; m. by Samuel Wilbur, Justice, Nov. 28, 1736.
3-41	"	Mary, and Timothy Peckham, Sept. 19, 1754.
3-56	"	Mary, and Darius Waterman, Sept. 23, 1757.
4-21	"	Mary, and John Wilbur (also 4-10) Dec. 30 or 31, 1780.
4-15	"	Eunice, and Thomas Dunbar, Aug. 29, 1784.

4-9   BARBER Benjamin, of Capt. Nathan, and Fanny Bliven, of Major Edward, dec.; m. by Joseph Crandall, Justice, Dec. 1, 1784.
4-41   "   John, of Nathan, and Sally Wilcox, of Isaiah; m. by Elder Isaiah Wilcox, Jan. 9, 1790.
4-190   "   Perry, of John and Molly, of Exeter, and Hannah Miner, of Charles, and Eunice, of Stonington; m. by Elder Eleazer Brown, March 30, 1794.
4-42   "   Hosea, and Cattern Lanphere; m. by Joseph Clarke, Justice, Dec. 18, 1794.
4-125   "   Lucy, and Rogers Crandall, Feb. 12, 1797.
4-122   "   Ruth, and Daniel Bliven, Jan. 28, 1802.
4-197   "   Sprague, of Joseph, and Leney Stillman, of Col. George; m. by Joseph Pendleton, Justice, April 7, 1804.
4-208   "   Patty, and Nathan Babcock, March 18, 1805.
4-151   "   Elizabeth, and Asa Babcock, Dec. 19, 1805.
4-211   "   Nathan, 3d, of Nathan, Jr., and Dorcas Babcock, of Nathan, dec.; m. by Joseph Pendleton, Justice, Jan. 12, 1806.
4-260   "   Benjamin P., of Westerly, and Hannah Merriott, of Hopkinton; m. at Hopkinton, by Elder Matthew Stillman, March 13, 1806.
4-255   "   Thomas, of Peleg, and Eunice Babcock, of Joseph, dec.; m. by Joseph Pendleton, Justice, May 25, 1809.
4-245   "   Peleg Sherman, and Louisa Gavitt; m. by Elder Jesse Babcock, March 15, 1810.
4-41   "   John, of Westerly, and Barbara Maxson, of Lebanon, Conn.; m. by Nathaniel Dodge, Justice, Dec. 9, 1810.
4-254   "   Thankful, and Capt. Thomas Dunbar, Jan. 30, 1814.
4-268   "   Amos, Jr., of Amos, of Westerly, and Lucinda Champlain, of Paris, of Hopkinton; m. by Daniel Babcock, Justice, Dec. 7, 1815.
4-267   "   Jered, Jr., of Westerly, and Lois Lewis, of Elias, of Hopkinton; m. at Hopkinton, by Elder Matthew Stillman, March 6, 1817.
4-273   "   Hosea, of Westerly, and Fanny Pendleton, of Stonington; m. at Stonington, by Elder Asher Miner, Oct. 4, 1821.
4-248   "   Keturah, and Capt. Clarke Lanphere, March 31, 1823.
4-273   "   Jared, of Westerly, an Eliza Stanton, of Stonington; m. by Elder Asher Miner, Feb. 12, 1825.
5-5   "   Paul M., of Westerly, and Almira Dewry, of North Stonington; m. by Elder Asher Miner, Dec. 30, 1827.
5-61   "   George S., of Westerly, and Mary A. Boss, of Hopkinton; m. at Hopkinton, by Elder John Greene, March 13, 1842.
5-33   "   George W., and Susan Babcock; m. by George D. Cross, Justice, Dec. 7, 1842.
5-49   "   Matthew S., and Rhoda Babcock; m. by George D. Cross, Justice, Jan. 8, 1843.
5-47   "   Dorcas, and Thomas W. Sisson, Dec. 3, 1843.
5-56   "   Nancy M., and Davis Lanphere, Sept. 9, 1844.
5-84   "   George S., and Julia A. Otis; m. by Rev. P. F. Kenney, Jan. 28, 1848.
5-100   "   Mary E., and Clarke D. Crandall, Aug. 27, 1849.
5-105   "   George H. S., of Nathan, and Frances M. Hall, of John; m. by Rev. John Taylor, Feb. 4, 1850.
2-72   BARKER Barberry, and Jarvis Hazleton, Jan. 21, 1735-6.
4-142   BARNES Bessy, and Amos Cross, Dec. 9, 1798.
4-214   "   Sally, and George Brown, Dec. 9, 1804.
5-90   "   Matthew, of Amos, and Martha G. Burdick, of Ichabod; m. by Rev. Fred Denison, Sept. 4, 1848.
3-65   BARRONS Mrs. Lydia, and William Pendleton, March 10, 1725-6.
5-53   BATES Lewis, Jr., of Exeter, and Sarah Sims, of Westerly; m. by Rev. Ralph Phinney, July 29, 1844.
1-102   BEBEE Mary, and John Clarke, Nov. 1, 1705.
2-73   "   Gideon, and Ruth Clarke; by Elder John Maxson, Nov. 25, 1735.
3-49   "   Mrs. Patience, and Thomas Hiscox, March 2, 1756.
4-63   BEERS Elizabeth, and John Burdick, Jr., Sept. 23, 1779.
3-99   BELCHER Elizabeth, and Job Stanton, Nov. 11, 1764.
3-77   "   Silvestre, and Oliver Babcock, July 2, 1761.

3-46   BELL Anna, and Samuel Hern, July 28, 1754.

2-76   BENNETT Richard, of Stonington, and Mary Loveless, of Westerly; m. by John Richmond, Justice, Jan. 12, 1726.

2-79   BENTLEY William, and Bathsheba Lewis; m. by Samuel Wilbur, Justice, Aug. 1, 1734.

3-94   "   Ruth, and Gideon Satterly, Jan. 3, 1764.

3-121   BENT John, Jr., of John, of Hopkinton, and Hannah Saunders, of widow Elizabeth, of Westerly; m. by Rev. Joseph Park, Oct. 10, 1770.

4-139   "   Hannah, and William Chapman, Jr., Jan. 24, 1799.

3-33   BERRY Sarah, and Joshua Babcock, Jan. 10, 1754.

3-47   "   Elisha, of Westerly, and Dinah Spencer, of East Greenwich; m. by William Hern, Justice, Jan. 8, 1756.

3-99   "   Elijah, and Dinah Saunders; m. by Rev. Joseph Parks, Oct. 24, 1764.

4-18   "   Peleg, and Mary Kenyon; m. by Elder Stephen Babcock, April 17, 1774.

4-65   "   Mrs. Hannah and Sanford Gavitt, Feb. 23, 1787.

4-89   "   Elizabeth, and Paul Lanphere, Feb. 18, 1789.

4-89   "   Polly, and Pardon Lanphere, Feb. 25, 1790.

4-149   "   Lydia, and Oliver Thurston, March 21, 1793.

4-134   "   Peleg, and Hannah Chapman; m. by Elder Elkanah Babcock, Jan. 21, 1798.

4-129   "   Foxton, and Grace Pendleton; m. by Elder Elkanah Babcock, Feb. 25, 1798.

4-140   "   Richard, and Hannah Babcock; m. by Elder Elkanah Babcock, March 4, 1799.

4-160   "   Nancy, and James Larkin, Nov. 23, 1800.

4-165   "   Nancy, and Pardon Crandall, Feb. 25, 1802.

4-193   "   Lyman, of Elijah, of Westerly, and Sally Stillman, of Nathaniel; m. by Joseph Pendleton, Justice, Nov. 22, 1802.

4-216   "   Bridget, and John Thompson, 3d, Feb. 27, 1805.

4-228   "   Betsey, and Marshall Frink, May 1, 1805.

4-227   "   Wain, of Westerly, and Rosanna Frink, of Stonington; m. by Elder Asher Miner, Dec. 7, 1806.

4-232   "   Susannah, and Enock Lanphere, Jan. 29, 1807.

4-253   "   Samuel F., and Lucy Stanton; m. at North Stonington by Elder Jedediah Randall, April 13, 1813.

5-13   "   Horatio S., and Welthia Stillman; m. by Elder Matthew Stillman, Aug. 23, 1832.

3-121   BESSY, Sarah, and Ebenezer Rathbun, July 23, 1721.

2-85   "   Mary, and John Burch, June 20, 1737.

2-72   BILLINGS Benajah, and Bethia Holmes, both of Stonington; m. by William Hern, Justice, Mar. 24, 1739-40.

2-17   "   Trustum, and Elizabeth Lester; m. by Elder Joseph Maxson, Sept. 10, 1740.

2-14   "   Eunice, and Ezekiel Babcock, Oct. 26, 1740.

3-57   "   Jesse, and Grace Breed, both of Stonington; m. by Richard Berry, Justice, Mar. 5, 1761.

3-176   BLACKINGTON, William, and Elizabeth Babcock, of Elder Oliver; m. by Joseph Clarke, Justice, Nov. 27, 1781.

2-84   BLEASON, Rachel, and Stephen Saunders, Nov. 19, 1721.

4-243   BLISS Sally Thurston, and Paul, Stillman, Nov. 19, 1807.

2-121   BLIVEN Edward, and Isabel Maccoon; m. by Tobias Saunders, Justice, Oct. 2, 1691.

2-220   "   Edward, Jr., and Ann Ross; m. by Joseph Stanton, Justice, May 30, 1743.

2-119   "   Joan, and William Clarke, Sept. 9, 1703.

2-110   "   Edward, and Freelove Swaros; m. by Joseph Stanton, Justice, May 12, 1719.

2-98   "   John, and Mercy Rathbone; m. by Theodoty Rhodes, Justice, Nov. 8, 1727.

2-69   "   James, and Anna Rhodes; m. by John Richmond, Justice, Jan. 22, 1734.

2-118   "   Freelove, and Joshua Saunders, Oct. 25, 1739.

3-19   "   Mary, and Joseph Lewis, Sept. 20, 1752.

3-29	BLIVEN	John, and Elizabeth Hern; m. by Joseph Crandall, Justice, Jan. 3, 1753.
3-38	"	Sarah, and Wait Lewis, Oct. 2, 1754.
3-45	"	Nathan, and Elizabeth Lewis; m. by William Hern, Justice, March 15, 1755.
3-52	"	James, and Sarah Stetson; m. by Joseph Crandall, Justice, Dec. 16, 1756.
3-86	"	Daniel, of Westerly, and Hannah Greene, of Charlestown; m. by Joseph Crandall, Justice, Nov. 21, 1762.
4-52	"	Daniel, of Westerly, and Hannah Greene, of Charlestown; m. by Joseph Crandall, Justice, Nov. 21, 1762.
3-94	"	Mary, and Lieut. Hezekiah Saunders, Nov. 20, 1763.
4-194	"	Samuel, of James and Ann, of Westerly, and Ruth Greene, of Josiah, and Hannah, of Charlestown; m. by Joseph Crandall, Justice, (also 3-104), March 17, 1766.
3-123	"	William, of Edward, Jr., and Eleanor Maxson, of John; m. by Elder Joshua Clarke, Oct. 31, 1771.
3-156	"	Patience, and Thompson Burdick, March 17, 1773.
3-132	"	Edward, 3d, of Edward, and Mary Champlain, of Capt. Samuel; m. by Joseph Crandall, Justice, Jan. 6, 1774.
3-136	"	Anne, and Pardon Clarke, April 6, 1774.
3-145	"	Elizabeth, and Jonathan Sisson, May 12, 1776.
3-151	"	Isaac Ross, of Major Edward, and Nancy Champlain, of William; m. by Joseph Clarke, Justice, Aug. 17, 1777.
3-157	"	Thankful, and Peleg Ross, Jan. 15, 1778.
3-160	"	James, Jr., of James, and Mary Hall, widow, dau. of Peleg Ross; m. by Joseph Crandall, Justice, Feb. 22, 1780.
4-19	"	George, of Edward, and Vashti Gavitt, of Capt. Samuel, dec.; m. by Elder Isaiah Wilcox, Aug. 12, 1784.
4-9	"	Fanny, and Benjamin Barber, Dec. 1, 1784.
4-9	"	Nancy, and Peter Crandall, Feb. 9, 1785.
4-121	"	Arnold, of Edward, dec., of Westerly, and Nancy Wilcox, of Joseph, of Charlestown; m. by Elder Isaiah Wilcox, Feb. —, 1788.
4-33	"	John, of Westerly, and Lucretia Dodge, of New Shoreham; m. at New Shoreham, by John Sands Warden, Feb. 8, 1789.
4-28	"	Fanny, and Pardon Greene, April 9, 1789.
4-29	"	Hannah, and Jesse Rogers, Dec. 23, 1789.
4-121	"	Arnold, of Edward, of Westerly, and Mary Wilcox, of Joseph, of Charlestown; m. by Elder Isaiah Wilcox, Dec. 31, 1789.
4-34	"	Theodoty, of Daniel, of Westerly, and Bathana Rogers, of Nathan, of New London; m. by Elder Davis Rogers, March 18, 1790.
4-37	"	Samuel, Jr., and Elizabeth Hull, of Isaac; m. by Samuel Bliven, Justice, Jan. 24, 1790.
4-44	"	John, of Daniel, of Westerly, and Barbara Davis, of Joseph, of Charlestown; m. by Samuel Bliven, Justice, at Charlestown, Jan. 16, 1791.
4-54	"	William, of William, 2d, of Westerly, and Rozina Dodge, of New Shoreham; m. at New Shoreham, by John Gorton Worden, April 6, 1791.
4-71	"	Elizabeth, and Anthony Bennett Ross, Aug. 26, 1792.
4-72	"	Luther, of Westerly, and Rebecca Cook, of Preston, Conn.; m. by Elder Paul Park, Nov. 28, 1792.
4-96	"	Joshua, of Westerly, and Rhoda Brown, of Stonington; m. by Elder Simeon Brown, July 30, 1795.
4-101	"	Lucy, and George Gavitt, Sept. 6, 1795.
4-48	"	Henry, of Nathan, and Nancy Bliven, of Edward; m. by Nathan Taylor, Justice, Dec. 31, 1797.
4-48	"	Nancy, and Henry Bliven, Dec. 31, 1797.
4-181	"	Capt. Nathan, Jr., and Mrs. Polly Taylor; m. by Elder William Gardiner, Feb. 1, 1798.
4-120	"	Rachel, and Joshua Allen, March 1, 1798.
4-122	"	Ethan, of Samuel, and Mary Hiscox, of Ephraim; m. by Elder Asa Coon, May 12, 1798.
4-145	"	Ruth, and Nathaniel Frazier, Oct. 6, 1799.
4-154	"	Desire, and George Clarke, Jan. 19, 1800.

4-167 BLIVEN William P., of Major William, of Westerly, and Amey Taylor, of Nathan, of Charlestown; m. at Charlestown by Lemuel Bliven, Justice, April 5, 1801.

4-122 " Daniel, of Samuel, and Ruth Barber, of Joseph; m. by Joseph Pendleton, Justice, Jan. 28, 1802.

4-54 " William, 2d, and Nancy Babcock; m. by Elder Jesse Babcock, Jan. 16, 1803.

4-199 " Fanny, and Samuel Saunders, Jan. 1, 1804.

4-212 " Amey, and Greene Allen, Feb. 12, 1804.

4-244 " Thankful, and Joseph Gavitt, Nov. 29, 1809.

5-56 " Betsey, and Silas W. Edwards, Nov. 22, 1827.

5-7 " Erastus, and Phebe C. States; m. by George D. Cross, Justice, Nov. 5, 1829.

5-52 " Emma Ann, and Charles W. Austin, April 25, 1844.

5-37 " Nancy, and Willard B. Tefft, June 26, 1846.

5-108 " Abby Jane, and Evan C. Burdick, July 15, 1850.

4-16 BLY Abigail, and Clarke Stillman, March 17, 1779.

5-61 BOSS Mary A., and George S. Barber, March 13, 1842.

5-93 BRACKETT Lucy E., and John A. Taylor, March 21, 1849.

4-13 BRADFORD Alexander, of Alexander (dec.), of Stonington, and Lois Pendleton, of Capt. Benjamin, of Westerly; m. by Joseph Crandall, Justice, July 14, 1785.

5-28 " Alexander, of Stonington, and Eunice Crandall, of Westerly; m. by Elder Daniel Coon, Dec. 20, 1840.

5-31 " Col. Charles, and Fanny Fowler; m. by Rev. Thomas H. Vail, Sept. 30, 1846.

5-100 " Charles H., of Lewis, of Worcester, Mass., and Martha Taylor, of Isaac R., of Stonington; m. by Rev. John Taylor, Aug. 27, 1849.

4-104 BRAGDON Joseph, of Sullivan, Hancock, Co., Mass., and Content Davis, of James, of Westerly; m. by Joseph Clarke, Justice, Nov. 10, 1793.

3-55 BRAMAN Freelove, and Thomas Brand, Oct. 28, 1734.

4-223 BRAMBLEY Perry, and Dorcas Pendleton; m. by Samuel Bliven, Justice, March 4, 1807.

2-105 BRAND Isabel, and Peleg Rogers, Aug. 25, 1726.

2-95 " Tobias, and Mercy Babcock; m. by Theodoty Rhodes, Justice, April 30, 1730.

2-85 " Rebecca, and Caleb Church, Sept. 16, 1731.

2-95 " Benjamin, of Westerly, and Rebecca Tanner, of South Kingstown; m. at South Kingstown, by Isaac Sheldon, Justice, March 16, 1734.

2-71 " James, and Rachel Hall; m. by Elder John Maxson, March 11, 1735-6.

2-72 " Elizabeth, and Amos Babcock, Dec. 20, 1738.

2-72 " James, and Rachel Hall; m. by Elder John Maxson, Aug. 10, 1737.

2-72 " Thomas, and Judeth Bailey; m. by Elder John Maxson, May 17, 1739.

2-118 " Mercy and Henry Wells, July 30, 1739.

2-72 " Benjamin, and Lucy Cottrell; m. by Elder John Maxson, June 25, 1740.

2-42 " James, and Grace Viley; m. by Elder John Maxson, Feb. 22, 1741.

2-37 " Mary, and Benjamin Broomer, May 8, 1743.

3-55 " Thomas, and Freelove Braman; m. by Samuel Perry, Justice, Oct. 28, 1734.

3-5 " Robert, and Prudence Lanphere; m. by Joseph Crandall, Justice, Nov. 14, 1751.

3-34 " Judeth, and Moses Warren, Dec. 27, 1753.

3-37 " Isabel, and Nelson Millard, March 31, 1754.

3-99 " Hannah, and Joseph Crumb, March 17, 1765.

3-132 " Thomas, of Samuel and Nancy Brown, of George, dec.; m. by Oliver Crary, Justice, Nov. 28, 1773.

3-147 BRAND David, of Stonington, son of Benjamin, and Lovice Chase, of Capt. Oliver, of Westerly; m. by Elder Isaiah Wilcox, July 18, 1776.

5-170 " Samuel, of Samuel, of Westerly, and Anne Sheffield, of Nicholas, of Richmond; m. by Robert Stanton, Justice, March 9, 1777.

4-136 " Capt. Nathan, of Samuel, and Susannah Vincent, of Dr. William; m. by Elder Oliver Babcock, Oct. 24, 1779.

4-100 " Walter, and Anna Babcock, Jan. 28, 1784.

4-100 " Walter, and Lydia Babcock, May 16, 1791.

4-241 " Russell, of Thomas, and Hannah Thompson, of Elias; m. by Joseph Pendleton, Justice, Jan. 1, 1803.

4-210 " Susan, and Thomas C. Slattery, Oct. 13, 1805.

3-111 BRAUGHTON Eunice, and Elijah Crandall, May 20, 1768.

3-25 BREED Nathan, of Stonington, and Nancy Babcock, of Westerly; m. by Benjamin Randall, Justice, June 16, 1751.

3-57 " Grace, and Jesse Billings, March 5, 1761.

3-94 BRIAN Mary, and Deacon Ezekiel Gavitt, May 8, 1763.

3-91 BRIGGS Jacob, and Freegift Saunders; m. by Joseph Crandall, Justice, March 14, 1767.

5-35 BRIGHT John, of Hopewell, N. J., and Martha Stillman, of Westerly; m. by Elder Daniel Coon, Aug. 25, 1839.

2-37 BROOMER Benjamin, and Mary Brand, of Thomas; m. by Elder Joseph Maxson, May 8, 1743.

2-79 BROWNING William, of South Kingstown, and Mary Wilkinson, of Westerly; m. by George Babcock, Justice, Aug. 5, 1728.

3-139 " Sarah, and George Sheffield, Jr., Jan. 22, 1775.

2-155 " Anna, and Samuel Sheffield, Dec. 3, 1778.

2-72 BROWN Elizabeth, of Thomas, of Stonington, and James Pendleton, Jan. 6, 1717-8.

2-106 " Peter, and Elizabeth Saunders; m. by Theodoty Rhodes, Justice, Dec. 15, 1726.

2-96, 97 " Mary, and Matthew Button, Dec. 20, 1727.

2-96 " George, and Elizabeth Tosh; m. by Theodoty Rhodes, Justice, Sept. 25, 1729.

2-92 " John, of Westerly, and Abigail Randall, of Stonington; m. by Rev. Ebenezer Bussell, Oct. 16, 1729.

2-95 " Benjamin, and Abigail Maccoon; m. by Theodoty Rhodes, Justice, April 6, 1730.

2-88 " William, and Dorothy Crandall; m. by Theodoty Rhodes, Justice, Sept. 10, 1730.

2-94 " Dorcas, and David Babcock, Feb. 24, 1730-1.

2-94 " Abigail, and James Pendleton, March 22, 1731.

2-78 " George, Jr., and Jerusha Lewis, of Joseph; m. by John Richmond, Justice, April 4, 1734.

2-37 " Simeon, of Stonington, and Dorothy Hern, of Westerly; m. by William Babcock, Justice, March 1, 1742-3.

3-8 " Rebecca, and Gideon Worden, May 1, 1748.

3-20 " Samuel, of Westerly, and Eleanor Haxston, of North Kingstown; m. by William Hern, Justice, July 9, 1749.

3-25 " Jesse, of Stonington, and Hannah Leeds, of Groton, Conn; m. by Benjamin Randall, Justice, Jan. —, 1752.

3-23 " John, of John, and Ruth Saunders; m. by Joseph Crandall, Justice, June 25, 1752.

3-28 " Hannah, and Jonathan Hakes, Nov. 23, 1752.

3-27 " Elizabeth, and James Hall, Jr., Feb. 11, 1753.

3-48 " Ebenezer, of Westerly, and Anna Wells, of Stonington; m. by William Hern, Justice. Feb. 5, 1756.

3-54 " Jonathan, and Elizabeth Burdick; m. by William Hern, Justice, March 1, 1757.

3-62 " James, and Lois Willis; m. by Rev. Joseph Parks, May 25, 1757.

3-59 " Benajah, and Mary Tefft; m. by William Hern, Justice, Jan. 25, 1758.

3-61 " Capt. Joshua, of Hopkinton, and Abigail Saunders, of Westerly; m. by Joseph Crandall, Justice, June 19, 1758.

3-82 " Sarah, and Elias Lanphere, April 22, 1762.

3-86	BROWN Elisha, and Ruth Pendieton; m. by Joseph Crandall, Justice, Dec. 30, 1762.	
3-12	" Elizabeth, and Nathan ·Babcock, May 20, 1764.	
3-102	" Elizabeth, and John Moon, Oct. 17, 1768.	
3-125	" Mary, and John Ruggles Searl, June 24, 1772.	
3-132	" Nancy, and Thomas Brand, Nov. 28, 1773.	
4-27	" Samuel, of Westerly, and Amie J. Clarke, of Stonington; m. by Elder Joshua Clarke, March 1, 1778.	
3-172	" Olive, and Oliver Burdick, Jr., Dec. 14, 1780.	
3-160	" Jeptha, of Elder Simeon, and Lydia Gardiner, of Abial, both of Stonington; m. by Joseph Crandall, Justice, Oct. 13, 1782.	
4-8	" Jeptha, of Simeon, and Dorcas Gardiner, of Abial, both of Stonington; m. by Joseph Crandall, Justice, at Westerly, Oct. 31, 1784.	
4-77	" Robert, of Reuben, of Stonington, and Hannah Burdick, of John, of Westerly; m. by Elder Elkanah Babcock, March 4, 1792.	
4-96	" Rhoda, and Joshua Bliven, July 30, 1795.	
4-166	" Mary, and Jesse Babcock, Aug. 19, 1798.	
4-165	" Hannah, and Rouse Babcock, Jan. 13, 1801.	
4-214	" George, and Sally Barnes; m. by Elijah Palmer, Justice, Dec. 9. 1804.	
5-22	" Sarah, and Francis S. West, Sept. 24, 1836.	
5-34	" Avery Nelson, and Maria Louisa Peckham; m. by Rev. James Pratt, July 14, 1839.	
5-23	" Randall T., of North Stonington, and Emma Chapman, of Westerly; m. by Elder Daniel Coon, Jan. 3, 1841.	
5-65	" Emily, and Aaron Peirce, April 14, 1845.	
5-75	" Elizabeth, and Joseph F. Langley, Oct. 4, 1847.	
5-102	" Elizabeth S., and Charles H. James, Nov. 6, 1849.	
4-126	BUDINGTON Luke, of Eliphal, and Charlotte Crandall, of Lewis; m. by Joseph Potter, Justice, Oct. 12, 1797.	
5-49	BUEL Samuel J., of Clinton, Conn., and Elizabeth N. Chapman, of Westerly; m. by Rev. Alexander Campbell, Jan. 21, 1844.	
5-69	BUFFINTON William, of Cranston, R. I., and Mary A. Stillman, of Westerly; m. by Rev. Alexander Campbell, Sept. 9. 1845.	
2-123	BUNDY Nathaniel, of Westerly, and Mary Palmister, April 26, 1724.	
3-61	" Joseph, of Preston, Conn., and Mary Tefft, of Westerly; m. by Silas Greenman, Justice, Oct. 31, 1758.	
2-47	BURCH Mary, and John Palmister, Nov. 22, 1712.	
2-85	" John, and Mary Bessy; m. by Elder John Maxson, June 20, 1737.	
2-1	" Zeriah, and John Newbury, Nov. 26, 1739.	
2-7	" Thomas, of Stonintgon, and Martha Davis; m. by William Hern, Justice, Oct. 10, 1740.	
2-119	" Isaiah, and Sarah Dixon, both of Stonington; m. at Westerly, by Elder Joseph Maxson, Jan. 20, 1742-3.	
3-167	" Hannah, and Seth White, Sept. 3, 1760.	
4-168	" Phebe, and Stephen Babcock, March 22, 1801.	
4-180	" Thomas, of Henry, and Susannah Pendleton, of Benjamin; m. by Elder Henry Joslin, Jan. 31, 1802.	
4-205	" Nathan, and Damarias Babcock; m. by John Cross, Justice, Dec. 22, 1803.	
4-229	" Thomas, and Mary Burdick; m. by Elder Jesse Babcock, Nov. 27, 1806.	
2-115	BURDICK Mary, and Peter Crandall, Feb. 27, 1717-8.	
2-118	" Mary, and John Lewis, Jr., March 12, 1718.	
2-97	" Abigail, and William Griffin, Feb. 9, 1726-7.	
2-77	" Peter, of Benjamin, and Desire Reynolds, of Sarah; m. by John Richmond, Justice, April 17. 1726.	
2-109	" Susannah, and William Wilcox, Jan. 11, 1727-8.	
3-9	" Susannah, and William Hiscox, Jan. 11, 1727-8.	
2-90	" John, and Rebecca Thompson; m. by Theodoty Rhodes, Justice, Oct. 21, 1730.	
2-86	" Edward, and Sarah Clarke; m. by Theodoty Rhodes, Justice, Nov. 26, 1730.	

2-88	BURDICK	Robert, and Susannah Clarke; m. by Theodoty Rhodes, Justice, Dec. 31, 1730.
2-88	"	Ebenzer, and Elizabeth Stewart; m. by John Richmond, Justice, Jan. 21, 1730-1.
2-87	"	Samuel Herbert, and Avis Maxson; m. by Theodoty Rhodes, Justice, Nov. 5, 1731.
2-83	"	David, and Mary Thompson; m. by John Richmond, Justice, July 25, 1733.
2-76	"	Joshua, and Abigail Lanphere; m. by John Babcock, Justice, Dec. 26, 1734.
2-76	"	Joseph, and Pase Clarke; m. by Elder John Maxson, Aug. 13, 1735.
2-84	"	Mary, and George Stillman, Nov. 3, 1737.
2-69	"	Benjamin, and Elizabeth Tanner; m. by Elder John Maxson, Dec. 28, 1737.
2-25	"	Thomas, of Stonington, and Penelope Rhodes, of Westerly; m. by John Richmond, Justice, Feb. 9, 1737-38.
2-26	"	Elisha, and Mary Slack; m. by Elder John Maxson, Feb. 25, 1739.
2-4	"	Margaret, and John Lewis, May 3, 1739.
2-38	"	Martha, and John Corey, Jan. 25, 1741-2.
2-94	"	Thomas, and Sarah Allen, both of Stonington; m. by Elder Joseph Maxson, Dec. 6, 1742.
2-79	"	Nathan, and Goodeth Maxson; m. by Elder John Maxson, Oct. 14, 1743.
2-77	"	Hubbard, and Avis Lewis; m. by Elder John Maxson, Nov. 1, 1743.
3-39	"	Simeon, and Isabel Saunders; m. by Edward Saunders, Justice, Sept. 20, 1747.
3-2	"	Edmund, and Thankful Enos; m. by Joseph Crandall, Justice, April 23, 1749.
3-11	"	Ezekiel, and Amey Downing; m. by William Hern, Justice, July 14, 1750.
3-2	"	Abigail, and Isaac Hall, Nov. 5, 1750.
3-3	"	John, and Elizabeth Babcock; m. by William Hern, Justice, Dec. 1, 1751.
3-33	"	Elias, and Hannah Cottrell; m. by Joseph Crandall, Justice, Jan. 17, 1754.
3-33	"	Peter, Jr., of Charlestown, and Esther Gavitt, of Westerly; m. by William Hern, Justice, Jan. 24, 1754.
3-34	"	Rebecca, and Abel Peckham, Feb. 24, 1754.
3-40	"	Parker, and Thankful Burdick; m. by Joseph Crandall, Justice, June 13, 1754.
3-40	"	Thankful, and Parker Burdick, June 13, 1754.
3-42	"	Carey, and Dorcas Cottrell; m. by Benoni Smith, Justice, Dec. 27, 1754.
3-54	"	Elizabeth, and Jonathan Brown, March 1, 1757.
3-63	"	Oliver, and Lydia Eldertou; m. by Joseph Crandall, Justice, Oct. 19, 1758.
3-61	"	Zacharius, of Hopkinton, and Elizabeth Smith, of Westerly; m. by William Hern, Justice, Feb. 19, 1759.
3-75	"	Ruth, and Joseph Sheldon, May 3, 1761.
3-75	"	Judith, and Joseph Johnson, Jr., Feb. 28, 1762.
3-89	"	Christopher, and Chloe Greenman; m. by Joseph Clarke, Jr., Justice, March 24, 1762.
3-82	"	Susannah, and Joseph Hiscox, Jr., April 15, 1762.
3-88	"	Eunice, and Peleg Coon, Jan. 26, 1763.
3-94	"	Lois, and Benjamin Pendleton, Feb. 9, 1763.
3-112	"	Ichabod, of Robert, and Bathsheba Mackee, of John and Bathsheba; m. by John Taylor, Justice, Feb. 6, 1764.
3-114	"	Edith, and Joshua Ross, April 27, 1769.
3-120	"	Clarke, and Amy Sisson; m. by Elder Joshua Clarke, Dec. 12, 1770.
3-156	"	Thompson, of David, and Patience Bliven, of John; m. by Joseph Clarke, Justice, May 17, 1773.

4-110	BURDICK	Simeon, and Mary Davis; m. by Samuel Bliven, Justice, Nov. 29, 1776.
3-153	"	Anne, and Joseph Peckham, Jan. 21, 1778.
3-152	"	Asa, of Jonathan, and Isabel Davis, of Samuel; m. by Joseph Crandall, Justice, Jan. 28, 1778.
3-153	"	Esther, and James Ross, April 9, 1778.
3-159	"	Hannah, and Clarke Crandall, Nov. 21, 1778.
4-63	"	John, Jr., and Elizabeth Beers; m. by Elder Joshua Clarke, Sept. 23, 1779.
3-172	"	Oliver, Jr., and Olive Brown; m. by Elder John Burdick, Dec. 14, 1780.
4-13	"	Polly, and Christopher Babcock, Nov. 30, 1783.
4-4	"	Hannah, and Daniel Babcock, March 1, 1784.
4-14	"	Ichabod, of Robert, and Mary Chapman, of William; m. by Joseph Clarke, Jr., Justice, Oct. 21, 1784.
4-81	"	Simeon, of Simeon, of Westerly, and Susannah Gardiner, of Deacon Samuel, of Hopkinton; m. by Joseph Crandall, Justice, Feb. 4, 1786.
4-29	"	James, of Ephraim, of Charlestown, and Prudence Ross, of Joshua, dec., of Westerly; m. by Simeon Burdick, Justice, Dec. 10, 1788.
4-54	"	Kenyon, of Phineas, and Nancy Hiscox, of Thomas; m. by Joseph Clarke, Justice, Jan. 18, 1790.
4-111	"	Rowland, of Oliver, and Hester Crandall, of Joseph; m. by Samuel Bliven, Justice, Oct. 22, 1790.
4-47	"	Mary, and Russell Saunders, March 31, 1791.
4-56	"	Amey, and Capt. Charles Greene, Nov. 19, 1791.
4-77	"	Hannah, and Robert Brown, March 4, 1792.
4-65	"	Ethan, late of Stephentown, N. Y., and Esther Stillman, of Westerly; m. by Joseph Clarke, Justice, Dec. 26, 1792.
4-105	"	Thompson, and Amey Sisson; m. by Elder Asa Coon, May 28, 1796.
4-159	"	Clarke, and Abigail Hiscox; m. by Elder Elkanah Babcock, June 20, 1799.
4-198	"	Thankful, and Peleg Wilcox, April 25, 1804.
4-199	"	Nancy, and Lemuel Chester, Sept. 20, 1804.
4-217	"	Rowland, and Martha Chester; m. by Elder Matthew Stillman, March 30, 1806.
4-218	"	Christopher, of John, of Westerly, and Polly Fellows, of Ambrose, of Stonington; m. by Joseph Pendleton, Justice, Nov. 27, 1806.
4-229	"	Mary, and Thomas Burch, Nov. 27, 1806.
4-244	"	Ruth, and Oliver Stillman, March 1, 1810.
4-163	"	Hannah, and Ephraim Hiscox, Nov. 29, 1810.
4-252	"	Susan, and William Lanphere, Jan. 24, 1835.
5-36	"	Maria A., and William S. Sisson, Dec. 17, 1839.
5-58	"	Clarke, of Hopkinton, and Clarissa C. Crandall, of Westerly; m. by Elder Weeden Barber, Jr., March 31, 1844.
5-25	"	William R., and Rhoda N. Austin; m. by Rev. E. T. Hiscox, July 4, 1846.
5-81	"	Joseph, of Charlestown, son of Joseph, and Susan M Clarke, of Westbrook, Conn., dau. of Clewson; m. by Rev. Isaac Moore, Nov. 4, 1847.
5-90	"	Martha G., and Matthew Barnes, Sept. 4, 1848.
5-88	"	Frances, and John M. Gage, June 18, 1849.
5-106	"	Lucinda, and David C. Larkin, May 4, 1850.
5-108	"	Evan C., of Joseph G., and Abby Jane Bliven, of Luther; m. by Rev. Fred. Denison, July 15, 1850.
5-86	BURLINGAME	Mary D., and George D. Cross, Jr., May 8, 1848.
5-104	"	Maria, and William Sturgeon, Jan. 2, 1850.
2-109	BURROUGH	Lydia, and William Pendleton, March 10, 1725-6.
2-96, 97	BUTTON	Matthew, of Westerly, and Mary Brown, of John, of Stonington; m. by John Richmond, Justice, Dec. 20, 1727.
3-13	"	Joseph, and Abigail Rood; m. at Voluntown, by Samuel Dorrance, Justice, Dec. 22, 1737.

3-1   BUTTON Daniel, of Stonington, and Elizabeth Palmeter, of Westerly; m. by
       William Hern, Justice, Sept. 24, 1744.
3-25   "   Abigail, and George Thurston, Aug. —, 1752.
3-17   "   Daniel, Jr., and Barbara Austin; m. by Daniel Moccoon, Justice,
              Oct. 7, 1752.
3-32   "   Deborah, and John Palmeter, Nov. 9, 1752.
3-37   BYRNS Mary, and Benajah Sack, Feb. 7, 1754.
3-96   BYRNS Mary, and William Warden, Oct. 4, 1764.

C

5-74   CAMPBELL Horatio Nelson, of Winthrop, of Voluntown, Conn., and Har-
              riet Babcock, of Rouse, dec.; m. by Rev. Thomas H. Vail,
              Sept. 8, 1846.
2-112 CARD Martha, and Joshua Rathbone, Nov. 30, 1721.
2-82   "   Margary, and John Foster, June 11, 1724.
5-9   CARPENTER Nancy A., and Orman Taft, Feb. 16, 1845.
5-50   "   Susan, and William H. Sherman, June 21, 1846.
5-73   "   Sarah P., and Joseph D. Rathbone, Aug. 9, 1846.
4-224 CARTRIGHT Rebecca, and Frederic Chace, Feb. 1, 1807.
4-246   "   Nancy, and John C. Chester, April 4, 1808.
4-185 CARR Resolved, of Westerly, and Betsey Hincidey, of Stonington; m. at
              Stonington by Elder Simeon Brown, Dec. 6, 1792.
5-5   "   Phebe, and Jonathan P. Stillman, Oct. 28, 1827.
5-14   "   Hannah, and Amos Stillman, Oct. 28, 1832.
2-96   CASE Immanuel, of South Kingstown, and Hannah Gavitt, of Westerly; m.
              by John Saunders, Justice, Dec. 3, 1714.
4-266   "   Hannah, and John Noyes, Dec. 24, 1809.
3-9   CHALKEN Stephen, of Seabrook, Conn., and Sarah Babcock, widow of Wil-
              liam; m. by William Hern, Justice, Nov. 5, 1753.
2-122 CHAMPLAIN Ann, and Samuel Clarke, Jan. 19, 1698-9.
1-102   "   William, Jr., of William, and Mary Clarke, of Joseph, Jr.; m. by
              Joseph Clarke, Justice, Jan. 18, 1699-1700.
2-125   "   Christopher, Jr., and Elizabeth Denison; m. by Peter Crandall,
              Justice, Dec. 5, 1705.
2-112   "   Susannah, and Samuel Clarke, May 26, 1720.
2-45   "   Christopher, and Hannah Hill; m. by Rev. James McSparran, April
              22, 1730.
2-90   "   Mary, and Joseph Stanton, Aug. 9, 1738.
3-68   "   James, of Westerly, and Mrs. Prudence Hallam, of Stonington; m.
              by Rev. Ebenezer Rossiter, Jan. 15, 1734-5.
3-3   "   Andrew, and Eunice Greenman; m. by William Hern, Justice, Jan.
              15, 1745-6.
3-20   "   Joseph, of Stonington, and Sarah Saunders, of Westerly; m. by
              William Hern, Justice, May 24, 1748.
3-23   "   Mary, and Stephen Lanphere, Oct. 26, 1749.
3-5   "   Sarah, and Sylvester Pendleton, June 16, 1751.
3-9   "   William, Jr., and Sarah Pendleton; m. by William Hern, Justice,
              Dec. 4, 1751.
3-45   "   Susannah, and Benjamin Lanphere, March 27, 1755.
3-47   "   Esther, and Jonathan Langford, Dec. 25, 1755.
3-49   "   Capt. John, of Charlestown, and Thankful Thompson, of Westerly;
              m. by Joseph Crandall, Justice, Feb. 26, 1756.
3-51   "   Col. Christopher, of Charlestown, and Mrs. Lucy Stanton, of Wes-
              terly; m. by William Hern, Justice, Aug. 19, 1756.
4-127   "   William, Jr., and Sarah Pendleton; m. by William Hern, Justice,
              Dec. 8, 175—.
3-83   "   Mary, and Samuel Thompson, July 18, 1762.
3-84   "   Susannah, and John Stanton, June 8, 1763.
3-94   "   Rowland, and Hannah Stetson; m. by Rev. Joseph Park, Dec. 21,
              1763.
3-96   "   Eunice, and Daniel Larkin, Aug. 29, 1764.
3-98   "   Asa, of Charlestown, and Mary Thompson, of Westerly; m. by
              Joseph Crandall, Justice, March 21, 1765.

3-99   CHAMPLAIN Hannah, and Joseph Babcock, Jr., March 31, 1765.

3-101   "   William, 3d, and Mary Gardiner; m. by Joseph Crandall, Justice, Dec. 19, 1765.

3-132   "   Mary, and Edward Bliven, 3d, Jan. 6, 1774.

3-135   "   Sarah, and William Greene, (also 4-40), March 18, 1774.

3-173   "   Rowland, of William, dec., and Anne Babcock, of Nathan; m. by Elder Isaiah Wilcox, May 10, 1777.

3-151   "   Nancy, and Isaac Ross Bliven, Aug. 17, 1777.

3-174   "   Oliver, of Capt. Samuel, and Thankful Gavitt, of Stephen; m. by Elder Isaiah Wilcox, Jan. 25, 1779.

3-160   "   Sarah, and William Rhodes, Jan. 31, 1779.

3-167   "   Samuel, of Capt. Samuel, and Freelove Ross, of Isaac; m. by Joseph Clarke, Justice, Jan. 12, 1780.

3-167   "   Abigail, and Thomas Slattery, Jan. 16, 1780.

3-177   "   Mrs. Hannah, and Simeon Babcock, April 6, 1780.

4-21   "   George, and Patience Lamphere, Oct. 5, 1780.

4-155   "   Adam B., of Westerly, and Henrietta Coggesnall, of Newport; m. by Rev. Gardiner Thurston, March 27, 1793.

4-93   "   Sally, and Stephen Wilcox, May 17, 1795.

4-187   "   George, of South Kingstown, and Lydia Thurston, of Westerly; m. by Elder Elkanah Babcock, March 20, 1800.

4-226   "   Hannah, and Isaac Ross, May 11, 1807.

4-228   "   Eliza, and Jedediah Knight, Aug. 21, 1807.

4-245   "   Margaret, and Barker Noyes, March 18, 1810.

4-268   "   Lucinda, and Amos Barber, Dec. 7, 1815.

5-1   "   Charlotte, and William Stillman, Jr., April 30, 1818.

5-2   "   Sally, and George H. Sheffield, Jan. 2, 1825.

5-57   "   Sarah Ann, and Wanton Lillibridge, Nov. 7, 1841.

5-43   "   Benjamin R., and Mary Ann Babcock; m. by Elder Daniel Coon, Sept. 22, 1842.

5-53   "   James, of Paris, dec., and Phebe A. Gavitt, widow of Isaac P., dau. of Silas Edwards; m. by Jedediah W. Knight, Justice, July 4, 1844.

3-19   CHAPMAN, Andrew, of Stonington, and Hannah Smith, of Westerly; m. by William Hern, Justice, Oct. 15, 1745.

3-48   "   Sumner, and Elizabeth Herick; m. by William Hern, Justice, Feb. 23, 1756.

3-109   "   John, and Mary Crandall; m. by Elder Joseph Park, Mar. 8, 1767.

4-51   "   William, Jr., of William, of Westerly, and Bridget Johnson, of Daniel, of Charlestown; m. by Elder Stephen Babcock, March 14, 1773.

3-139   "   Elizabeth, and James Davis, Jan. 5, 1775.

3-138   "   Mary, and Abram Perkins, Jan. 17, 1775.

3-181   "   Timothy, of Sumner, and Nancy Pendleton, of Major Joseph; m. by Elder Oliver Babcock, March 14, 1782.

4-14   "   Mary, and Ichabod Burdick, Oct. 21, 1784.

4-182   "   Plumb, of William, dec., and Lois White, of Seth; m. by Joseph Clarke, Justice, Nov. 14, 1784.

4-18   "   Sumner, of Sumner, and Nancy Greenman, of Silas; m. by Joseph Crandall, Justice, Aug. 27, 1786.

4-28   "   Prudence, and Paul Crandall, March, 26, 1789.

4-87   "   Joseph, of Westerly, and Elizabeth Kenyon, of Hopkinton; m. at Hopkinton, by Daniel Babcock, Justice, Dec. 21, 1791.

4-119   "   Israel, and Polly Kenyon; m. by Samuel Brown, Justice, Oct. 20, 1796.

4-131   "   Hannah, and Peleg Berry, Jan. 21, 1798.

4-117   "   Lucy, and Joseph Sisson, Feb. 4, 1798.

4-139   "   William, Jr., and Hannah Bent; m. by Elder Abram Conn, Jan. 24, 1799.

4-206   "   Elizabeth, and Sanford Sisson, March 3, 1799.

4-51   "   William, of William, and Mary Johnson, of Reuben; m. by Elder Elkanah Babcock, June 14, 1799.

4-163   "   Case, and Polly Pendleton; m. by Elder Abram Coon, Feb. 15, 1801.

4-189 CHAPMAN Nancy. and William Clarke, Feb. 6, 1803.
4-237   "   Samuel, of William, of Westerly, and Abigail Johnson, of John, of
               Charlestown; m. by Samuel Bliven, Justice, May 13, 1810.
4-255   "   Phebe, and Jeremy Crandall, Dec. 20, 1812.
4-265   "   John, and Abigail Sisson; m. by Daniel Babcock, Justice, March
               28, 1816.
4-272   "   Thomas, of Plumb, of Westerly, and Anna Peckham, of James, of
               Charlestown; m. at Charlestown, by Elder Matthew Stillman,
               Dec. 26, 1819.
5-3   "   Joseph, and Eunice Clarke; m. by Elder Matthew Stillman, Jan.
               7, 1826.
5-23   "   Emma, and Randall T. Brown, Jan. 3, 1841.
5-58   "   Abby, and Elias R. Maine, May 31, 1843.
5-49   "   Elizabeth N., and Samuel J. Bull, Jan. 21, 1844.
5-76   "   Julia, and Charles W. Thompson, Dec. 8, 1847.
5-96   "   Albert, of Case, of Westerly, and Martha Greene, of Sheffield,
               of Charlestown; m. by Rev. John Taylor, May 7, 1849.
2-222 CHASE Joshua, and Mary Maxson; m. by Elder Joseph Maxson, May 12,
               1748.
3-62   "   Elizabeth, and Elisha Saunders, May 17, 1758.
3-116   "   Mary, and Angus McDonnell, Nov. 22, 1769.
3-128   "   Eunice, and Nathan Dye, Nov. 26, 1772.
3-147   "   Lavice, and David Brund, July 18, 1776.
3-152   "   Rebecca, and William Sims, Nov. 20, 1777.
4-12   "   Martha, and Christopher Chester, Jan. 3, 1779.
4-5   "   Frederic, of Capt. Oliver and Ruth Fry; m. by Elder Oliver Bab-
               cock, Feb. 2, 1783.
4-166   "   Maxson, and Polly Merriatt; m. by Elder Jesse Babcock, Dec.
               10, 1803.
4-224   "   Frederic, Jr., of Frederic, of Westerly, and Rebecca Cartright, of
               Edward, of New Shoreham; m. at New Shoreham, by John
               Gorton Worden, Feb. 1, 1807.
5-21   "   Eliza, and Samuel Russel, May 1, 1836.
5-72   "   Nathaniel J. L.,and Martha A. Wilcox; m. by Rev. E. T. His-
               cox, Jan. 1, 1846.
3-65   CHEESEBOROUGH Mrs. Mary, and Col. William Pendleton, April 25, 1751.
3-58   "   James, of Stonington, and Lucy Pendleton, of Westerly; m. by
               Benoni Smith, Justice, Feb. 10, 1758.
3-85   "   Zebulon, and Lydia Pendleton; m. by Rev. Joseph Park, Dec. 10,
               1761.
3-104   "   Molly, and Thomas Randall, Dec. 1, 1765.
3-164   "   Amos, of Stonington, son of Amos, dec., and Anna Gavitt, of
               Westerly, (widow,) dau. of Stanton York, of Charlestown; m.
               by Joseph Crandall, Justice, Nov. 10, 1779.
4-12   CHESTER Christopher, and Martha Chase; m. by Joseph Clarke, Justice,
               Jan. 3, 1779.
4-199   "   Samuel, and Nancy Burdick; m. by Elder Abram Coon, Sept.
               20, 1804.
4-217   "   Martha, and Rowland Burdick, March 30, 1806.
4-246   "   John C., and Nancy Cartright; m. at Shelter Island, N. Y., by
               Elder Daniel Hall, April 4, 1808.
2-85   CHURCH Caleb, and Rebecca Brand; m. by Theodoty Rhodes, Justice,
               Sept. 16, 1731.
3-49   "   Joshua, and Katherine Kenyon; m. by Daniel Maccoon, Justice,
               March 29, 1756.
1-57   CLARKE Joseph, of Westerly, and Bethia Hubbard, dau. of Samuel, of
               Newport; m. by James Barker, Assistant, Nov. 16, 1664.
1-57   "   Joseph, Jr., and Dorothy Maxson, of John, of Westerly; m. by
               Tobias Saunders, Justice, Jan. 5, 1692.
1-95   "   Sarah, of Joseph, and Thomas Reynolds, Oct. 11, 1683.
2-78   "   Judith, and John Maxson, Jan. 19, 1687-8.
2-122   "   Samuel, and Ann Champlain, Jan. 19, 1698-9.
1-102   "   Mary, and William Champlain, Jan. 18, 1699-1700.
2-73   "   Bethiah, and Thomas Hiscox, Oct. 31, 1703.
1-102   "   John, of Joseph, Jr., and Mary Beebe, of Samuel, Nov. 1, 1705.

2-119 CLARKE William, and Joan Bliven; m. by Peter Crandall, Justice, Sept. 9, 1709.

2-112 " Samuel, of Westerly, and Susannah Champlain, of South Kingstown; m. by William Greene, Justice, May 26, 1720.

2-110 " Anna, and John Lewis, Nov. 24, 1720.

2-88 " Sarah, and Edward Burdick, Nov. 26, 1730.

2-88 " Susannah, and Robert Burdick, Dec. 31, 1730.

2-85 " William, Jr., of Westerly, and Rebecca Wells, of South Kingstown; m. by Rouse Helme, Assistant, Sept. 1, 1731.

2-76 " Pose, and Robert Burdick, Aug. 13, 1735.

2-73 " Ruth, and Gideon Beebe, Nov. 25, 1735.

2-88 " Abigail, and William Clarke, Oct. 20, 1736.

2-88 " William, of Westerly, and Abigail Clarke, of Newport, of Capt. Lawrence; m. at Newport by Thomas Coggeshall, Justice, Oct. 20, 1736.

2-88 " Simeon, and Elizabeth Sanford; m. by Elder John Maxson, Dec. 20, 1736.

2-90 " Thomas, and Thankful Violet; m. by Elder John Maxson, May 27, 1740.

2-113 " Ephraim, and Elizabeth Dake; m. by Rev. Joseph Parks, Dec. 12, 1745.

3-10 " Joseph, and Deborah Crandall; m. by John Richmond, Justice, April 25, 1729.

3-177 " Sarah, and Joseph Lewis, June 16, 1743.

3-24 " Elisha, and Mary Potter, Feb. 15, 1743-44.

3-1 " Walter, of Charlestown, and Rachel Sisson, of Westerly; m. by William Hern, Justice, March 19, 1743-4.

3-15 " Ichabod, and Marcy ——; m. by William Babcock, Justice, March —, 1744.

3-1 " Ephraim, and Hannah Lanphere; m. by William Hern, Justice, Dec. 15, 1744.

3-19 " Mary, and John Stillman, Dec. 12, 1745.

3-14 " Stephen, and Sarah Mitchell; m. by William Hern, Justice, Dec. 29, 1745.

3-15 " Thankful, and Ebenezer Crandall, April 22, 1746.

3-28 " Benjamin, of Charlestown, and Susannah Babcock, of Westerly; m. by William Babcock, Justice, Nov. 3, 1748.

3-21 " William, and Jemima Vincent; m. by William Hern, Justice, Nov. 13, 1749.

3-2 " Katharine, and John Millard, Oct. 1, 1752.

3-54 " Joan, and Daniel Edwards, Sept. 9, 1756.

3-56 " Joseph, 4th, and Thankful Davis; m. by Joseph Crandall, Justice, Sept. 15, 1757.

3-67 " Eunice, and William Satterly, Sept. 13, 1759.

4-144 " Mary, and Peleg Saunders, (also 3-73), Jan. 1 or 21, 1761.

3-177 " Mary, and Joseph Lewis, May 14, 1761.

3-83 " John, and Mary Saunders; m. by Joseph Crandall, Justice, Nov. 18, 1762.

3-94 " Phineas, of Hopkinton, and Mary Babcock, of Capt. Nathan, of Westerly; m. by Rev. Joseph Park, Nov. 23, 1763.

3-82 " William, of Newport, and Ruth Peckham, of Westerly; m. by Joseph Crandall, Justice, Nov. 24, 1765.

3-109 " Nancy, and Joshua Pendleton, Jan. 6, 1768.

3-122 " Sarah, and Silas Maxson, March 20, 1771.

3-135 " David, of Ephraim, and Jane Peckham, of Isaac; m. by Elder John Gardiner, June 8, 1772.

3-129 " Hannah, and William Sweet Peckham, (also 4-102), Jan. 6, 1773.

3-120 " Mary, and Samuel Crandall, Feb. 4, 1773.

3-136 " Pardon, of Benjamin, of Stonington, and Anne Bliven, of Major Edward, of Westerly; m. by Elder Joshua Clarke, April 6, 1774.

3-143 " Lydia, and Nicholas Young, Feb. 1, 1776.

3-143 " Ethan, of Joshua and Hannah of Hopkinton, and Anna Ward, of Samuel, of Westerly; m. by Elder Joshua Clarke, Feb. 4, 1776.

3-151 " Anne, and Isaac Peckham, Jr., Sept. 28, 1777.

3-151 " Anne, and Job Johnson, Oct. 30, 1777.

4-99	CLARKE	George, of Elisha, and Keturah Maxson, of Joseph; m. by Elder Joshua Clarke, Jan. 29, 1778.
4-27	"	Amey, and Samuel Brown, March 1, 1778.
3-154	"	Susannah, and James Rathbone, (also 4-53), Sept. 27, 1778.
4-134	"	Nicholas, of William (dec.) and Jemima, of Westerly, and Barbara Wells, of Peter and Elizabeth, of Hopkinton; m. at Hopkinton, by Elder Joshua Clarke, Jan. 20, 1779.
4-2	"	Jemima, and John Clarke, May 26, 1781.
4-2	"	John, and Jemima Clarke, of Daniel; m. by Elder John Burdick, May 26, 1781.
3-172	"	Lucy, and Benedicte Crandall, Dec. 7, 1780.
3-180	"	Martha, and Edward Saunders, (also 4-56), March 14, 1782.
3-181	"	Perry, and Patience York Peckham; m. by Joseph Clarke, Justice, Dec. 1, 1782.
3-131	"	Hannah, and James Crandall, Dec. 21, 1782.
4-259	"	Hannah, and James Crandall, Nov. 20, 1783.
4-17	"	Isabel, and Joseph Varin, Jan. 26, 1786.
4-58	"	Joshua, and Wealthy Stillman; m. by Joseph Clarke, Justice, Feb. 16, 1786.
4-23	"	Ichabod, Jr., of Ichabod, and Mary, or Polly Rock, of Robert, dec.; m. by Joseph Crandall, Justice, Nov. 22, 1787.
4-46	"	Hannah, and Arnold Saunders, Oct. 21, 1790.
4-174	"	Abel, and Eunice Lanphere; m. by Elder Elkanah Babcock, Oct. 13, 1791.
4-153	"	Wait, of William, and Abigail Lanphere, of Nathan; m. by Elder John Burdick, Nov. 14, 1799.
4-154	"	George, of George, and Desire Bliven, of William; m. by Elder Asa Coon, Jan. 19, 1800.
4-153	"	Sally, and Joseph Tefft, Jan. 24, 1800.
4-189	"	William, of South Kingstown, son of Nicholas, and Nancy Chapman, of Timothy; m. by Joseph Pendleton, Justice, Feb. 6, 1803.
4-185	"	Sophia, and Jessie Maxson, Jr., (also 5-24,) March 20, 1803.
4-212	"	John, and Mercy Lanphere; m. by Elder Jesse Babcock, Nov. 29, 1804.
4-237	"	Sally, and Cornelius Stetson, Jr., Dec. 13, 1807.
4-247	"	Deborah, and Hezekiah Lanphere, Feb. 17, 1811.
4-247	"	Amey, and Paul Babcock, Jr., Sept. 5, 1811.
4-248	"	Wealthy, and Clarke Lanphere, March 1, 1812.
5-3	"	Eunice, and Joseph Chapman, Jan. 7, 1826.
5-67	"	Frances M., and Edward Peirce, Jan. 26, 1846.
5-81	"	Susan M., and Joseph Burdick, Nov. 4, 1847.
2-94	CLOSSON	Bathsheba, and Edward Pierce, Dec. 3, 1731.
2-72	"	Charity, and Samuel Bailey, Feb. 12, 1735.
4-5	"	John, of Ichabod, of Charlestown, and Marcy Kenyon, of James, dec., of said Town; m. by Joseph Crandall, Justice, March 11, 1784.
4-230	"	Polly, and Parker Wilcox, April 26, 1807.
4-231	CLAWSON	Eunice, and Isaac Wilcox, Jan. 17, 1808.
3-20	COATS	Christopher, of Stonington, and Thankful Pendleton, of Westerly; m. by William Hern, Justice, May 2, 1748.
2-51	"	Victorias, and Isaac Hilliard, April 5, 1751.
4-175	COAZEN	Betsy, and Jabez Lewis, Nov. 24, 1801.
2-108	COBB	Benjamin, and Mary Enos; m. by George Babcock, Justice, Jan. 30, 1728-9.
5-68	CODNER	Thomas J., and Elizabeth L. Edwards; m. by Rev. Oliver P. Tuckerman, June 2, 1846.
4-155	COGGESHALL	Henrietta, and Adam B. Champlain, March 27, 1793.
4-158	"	Abigail, and Samuel Thompson, Dec. 25, 1794.
2-110	COLDGROVE	Francis, and Hannah Bailey; m. by Thomas Hiscox, Justice, (also 2-115), March 5, 1718-9.
4-75	"	Susannah, and John Pendleton, Dec. 11, 1791.
2-74	COLLINS	Hezekiah, and Catherine Gifford; m. by Samuel Wilbur, Justice, Nov. 6, 1735.
3-146	COMSTOCK	Sarah, and Eliphalet Harris, July 10, 1776.

2-86   CONGDON James, of Westerly, son of James, of Providence, R. I., and Celinda Holway, of Benjamin; m. by Samuel Perry, Justice, May 2, 1732.

5-103   "   Prudence G., and Peter Stevenson, Nov. 19, 1849.

4-72   COOK Rebecca, and Luther Bliven, Nov. 28, 1792.

3-88   COON William, of Hopkinton, and Freegift Stetson, of Westerly; m. by Stephen Saunders, Justice, Jan. 6, 1763.

3-88   "   Peleg, of Hopkinton, and Eunice Burdick, of Westerly; m. by Stephen Saunders, Justice, Jan. 26, 1763.

3-91   "   Thomas, of Hopkinton, and Anne Crandall, of Westerly; m. by Lawton Palmer, Justice, June 16, 1763.

3-68   "   Jemima, and David Crandall, June 14, 1764.

3-98   "   Samuel, of Hopkinton, and Esther Saunders, of Westerly; m. by Joseph Crandall, Justice, March 25, 1765.

3-112   "   John, Jr., of John, of Hopkinton, and Amie Hiscox, of Ephraim, of Westerly; m. by Elder Joshua Clarke, May 15, 1771.

2-41   COREY Rachel, and Theodosius Lanphere, June 22, 1707-8.

2-4   "   James, and Sarah Lanphere; m. by Peter Crandall, Justice, March 21, 1708.

2-76   "   Mary, and Thomas Nett, Dec. 25, 1734.

2-43   "   Isaac, of Westerly, and Lydia Davis of Stonington, Conn.; m. by John Richmond, Justice, March 23, 1736-7.

2-118   "   Hosea, and Lydia Davis; m. by John Richmond, Justice, March 23, 1736-7.

2-58   "   James, and Mary Lanphere; m. by Elder John Maxson, Jan. 21, 1738-9.

2-38   "   John, and Martha Burdick, both of Stonington; m. by Elder John Maxson, Jan. 25, 1741-2.

5-50   "   Alfred B., of North Kingstown, and Eliza Ann Lock, of Richmond; m. by Rev. William H. Newman, April 9, 1843.

2-105   COTTRELL Dorothy, and John Randall, Dec. 22, 1726.

2-76   "   Amey, and Joseph Crumb, June —, 1734.

2-75   "   Nicholas, and Rebecca Randall; m. by Elder John Maxson, Oct. 3, 1735.

2-70   "   Eleanor, and Nathan Randall, July 22, 1736.

2-72   "   Lucy, and Benjamin Brand, June 23, 1740.

2-73   "   Prudence, and Nathaniel Lanphere, July 7, 1743.

3-1   "   Dorcas, and Elisha Lewis, Oct. 25, 1744.

3-10   "   Nathaniel, of Westerly, and Mary Niles, of Stonington; m. by Rev. Nathaniel Eells, March 3, 1744-5.

3-1   "   Elizabeth, and Sands Niles, Sept. 4, 1745.

3-61   "   Patience, and William Babcock, Jan. 28, 1749.

3-33   "   Hannah, and Elias Burdick, Jan. 17, 1754.

3-42   "   Dorcas, and Carey Burdick, Dec. 27, 1754.

3-66   "   Joshua, of Exeter, and Desire Crandall, of Westerly; m. by Benoni Smith, Justice, March 15, 1759.

3-89   "   Mary, and Robert Owen, June 3, 1762.

3-147   "   Elias, of Major John, and Phalley Gavitt, of Joseph; m. by Joseph Crandall, Justice, Nov. 7, 1776.

4-1   "   Abigail, and Thomas Sisson, Jan. 19, 1783.

4-1   "   Lois, and Angustus Saunders, Jan. 19, 1783.

4-86   "   Daniel, and Merebah Saunders; m. by Elder Joshua Clarke, May 21, 1789.

4-45   "   Lebbeus, and Mary Saunders; m. by Joshua Clarke, Justice, May 17, 1793.

4-249   "   John, and Lydia Stillman; m. by Elder Abram Coon, Nov. 13, 1808.

4-242   "   Lois, and Daniel Stillman, Nov. 17, 1808.

4-254   "   Russell, and Betsey Pendleton; m. by Elder Abram Coon, Jan. 31, 1810.

2-121   CRANDALL Deborah, and George Stillman (also 2-123), April 13, 1706.

2-82   "   Joseph, and Ann Langworthy; m. by Peter Crandall, Justice, Feb. 15, 1715-6.

2-115   "   Peter, and Mary Burdick, Feb. 27, 1717-8.

2-78   "   Lucy, and John Lewis, of James, March 3, 1717.

2-78	CRANDALL	Jane, and Cyrus Richmond, Jan. 29, 1718-9.
3-10	"	Deborah, and Joseph Clarke, April 25, 1729.
2-88	"	Dorothy, and William Brown, Sept. 10, 1730.
2-90	"	John, and Mary Crandall; m. by Theodoty Rhodes, Justice, Nov. 19, 1730.
2-90	"	Mary, and John Crandall, Nov. 19, 1730.
3-26	"	Eber, and Mary Long; m. at South Kingstown by Robert Hannah, Justice, Feb. 10, 1732.
2-75	"	Elizabeth, and Samuel Larkin, Jan. 21, 1734-5.
2-71	"	Joseph, and Edith Hiscox; m. by Elder John Maxson, May 2, 1736.
2-72	"	Mary, and Samuel Langworthy, Aug. 7, 1736.
2-119	"	Lucy, and Thomas William Davis, Dec. 8, 1737.
2-88	"	John, and Elizabeth Lewis; m. by Elder John Maxson, June 28, 1738.
2-45	"	Elizabeth, and Joseph Crandall, Dec. 13, 1738.
2-45	"	Joseph, and Elizabeth Crandall; m. by William Hern, Justice, Dec. 13, 1738.
2-72	"	John, and Esther Lewis; m. by William Hern, Justice, April 19, 1740.
2-42	"	Peter, and Esther Frink; m. by William Babcock, Justice, Dec. 22, 1740.
2-90	"	James, of Westerly, and Damarias Kenyon, of Charlestown; m. by William Champlain, Justice, Feb. 27, 1742.
2-119	"	Ann, and Henry Hull, Sept. 6, 1742.
3-7	"	James, of Westerly, and Damarias Kenyon, of Charlestown; m. by William Champlain, Justice, Feb. 27, 1743-4.
3-108	"	Simeon, and Mary Sweet; m. by Elder Joseph Park, June 23, 1745.
3-15	"	Ebenezer, and Thankful Clarke; m. by William Hern, Justice, April 22, 1746.
3-7	"	Deborah, and William Crandall, March 12, 1746-7.
3-7	"	William, and Deborah Crandall; m. by William Babcock, Justice, March 12, 1746-7.
3-1	"	Jonathan, and Hannah Downing; m. by William Hern, Justice, April 12, 1747.
3-29	"	Anna, and James Rhodes, Dec. 14, 1752.
3-29	"	Edward, of Westerly, and Sarah Kenyon, of Charlestown; m. by Joseph Crandall, Justice, Jan. 18, 1753.
3-30	"	Eber, of John, Jr., and Elizabeth Crandall, of Eber; m. by John Larkin, Justice, Feb. 22, 1753.
3-30	"	Elizabeth, and Eber Crandall, Feb. 22, 1753.
3-98	"	Benajah, of John, late of Hopkinton, dec., and Elizabeth Slack, of Samuel, dec.; m. by Benjamin Randall, Justice, March 18, 1754.
3-46	"	Abijah, of Westerly, and Sarah Yeoman, of Stonington; m. at Stonington by Rev. Nathaniel Eells, Aug. 29, 1754.
3-56	"	Mrs. Hannah, and Nathan Rogers, Sept. 17, 1757.
3-66	"	Edey, and Isaac Thorn, Feb. 27, 1759.
3-66	"	Desire, and Joshua Cottrell, March 15, 1759.
3-70	"	Jonathan, and Elizabeth Wells; m. by William Hern, Justice, April 3, 1760.
3-69	"	Bridget, and Thomas Curtis, April 30, 1760.
3-78	"	Joseph, and Esther Hull; m. by Renoni Smith, Justice, Aug. 24, 1761.
3-81	"	Esther, and Elkanah Babcock (also 4-66), March 28, 1762.
3-87	"	Abigail, and Joshua Crandall, Oct. 20, 1762.
3-87	"	Joshua, and Abigail Crandall; m. by Elder Joseph Davis, Oct. 20, 1762.
3-91	"	Anne, and Thomas Coon, June 16, 1763.
3-95	"	Susannah, and Comfort Shaw, April 5, 1764.
3-68	"	David, and Jemima Coon; m. by Joseph Crandall, Justice, June 14, 1764.
3-97	"	Amey, and Nathan Lanphere, Oct. 28, 1764.
3-99	"	Anna, and John Tefft, Dec. 16, 1764.

3-99	CRANDALL	Eunice, and Augustus Stanton, Feb. 6, 1765.
3-101	"	Damarias, and Joseph Pendleton, Jan. 19, 1766.
3-102	"	Ezekiel, and Mary Pendleton; m. by Joseph Crandall, Justice, May 22, 1766.
3-109	"	Mary, and John Chapman, March 8, 1767.
3-111	"	Thomas, of Westerly, and Ruth Rogers, of New London; m. by Elder Stephen Gorton, May 19, 1767.
3-111	"	Elijah, of Joseph, and Eunice Braughton, of John; m. by Elder Thomas Ross, May 20, 1768.
3-111	"	James, of Charlestown, and Elizabeth Saunders, of Westerly (widow), dau. of Oliver Chase; m. by Joseph Crandall, Justice, June 26, 1768.
3-134	"	Elias, of Peter, and Sarah Stillman, of Capt. George; m. by Joseph Clarke, Justice, April 30, 1769.
3-127	"	Joseph, of Joseph, dec., of Westerly, and Martha Crandall, of John, of Hopkinton, dec.; m. by Job Taylor, Justice, Sept. 17, 1772.
3-127	"	Martha, and Joseph Crandall, Sept. 17, 1772.
3-129	"	Samuel, of Samuel, of Charlestown, and Mary Clarke, of Daniel, of Westerly; m. by Joseph Crandall, Justice, Feb. 4, 1773.
3-128	"	Enoch, of James, and Hannah Crandall, of Col. John, dec.; m. by Joseph Crandall, Justice, March 24, 1773.
3-128	"	Hannah, and Enoch Crandall, March 24, 1773.
4-91	"	Elizabeth, and James Saunders, Oct. 3, 1774.
3-140	"	Joseph, 4th, of Joseph of Westerly, and Mary Ladd, of John, of Charlestown; m. by Nathan Burdick, Justice, Feb. 16, 1775.
3-146	"	Lydia, and Joseph Saunders, June 30, 1776.
4-70	"	Nancy, and Joseph Pendleton, March 23, 1777.
3-160	"	Christopher, of James and Lucy Babcock; m. by Elder Isaiah Wilcox, April 17, 1777.
3-150	"	Elizabeth, and Henry Crandall, July 17, 1777.
• 3-150	"	Henry, of Capt. William, of Westerly, and Elizabeth Crandall, of Abijah, of Hopkinton now of Charlestown; m. by Joseph Crandall, Justice, July 17, 1777.
4-95	"	John, and Anna Gardiner; m. by Elder Simeon Brown, at Stonington, Nov. 9, 1777.
3-159	"	Clarke, of James, and Hannah Burdick, of Jonathan; m. by Joseph Crandall, Justice, Nov. 21, 1778.
3-161	"	Sally, and Nicholas Davis, June 6, 1779.
3-162	"	Elijah, of Joseph, of Westerly, and Mercy Kenyon, of James, dec., of Charlestown; m. by Joseph Crandall, Justice, July 18, 1779.
3-169	"	Anna, and Jonathan Greene, Aug. 27, 1780.
3-171	"	Charlotte, and Paul Babcock (also 4-76), Nov. 30, 1780.
3-172	"	Benedict, of James, of Westerly, and Tacy Clarke, of Ephraim, of Charlestown; m. by Joseph Crandall, Justice, Dec. 7, 1780.
5-150	"	Henry, of Capt. William, and Mary Greenman, of Silas; m. by Joshua Clarke, Justice, Feb. 24, 1782.
3-180	"	Ruth, and Theodoty Johnson, March 31, 1782.
3-131	"	James, of James, of Westerly, and Hannah Clarke, of Ephraim, of Charlestown; m. by Joseph Crandall, Justice, Dec. 21, 1782.
3-174	"	Rebecca, and Samuel Taylor (also 4-202), Jan. 6, 1783.
4-2	"	Rhoda, and Lebbeus Ross, March 23, 1783.
4-3	"	Elizabeth, and Benjamin Watson, July 9, 1783.
4-259	"	James, of James and Sarah, and Hannah Clarke, of Ephraim, Nov. 20, 1783.
4-14	"	Elbridge, of Joshua, of Westerly, and Mary Crandall, of Abijah, of Charlestown; m. by Elder Isaiah Wilcox, March 4, 1784.
4-14	"	Mary, and Elbridge Crandall, March 4, 1784.
4-9	"	Peter, of Joshua, and Nancy Bliven, of Daniel; m. by Joseph Crandall, Justice, Feb. 9, 1785.
4-22	"	Enock, of James, and Mary Pendleton, of Simeon; m. by Joseph Clarke, Justice, Sept. 18, 1787.
4-19	"	Arnold, of Capt. William, dec., and Dinah Gavitt, of Hezekiah; m. by Joseph Crandall, Justice, Dec. 6, 1787.

4-25	CRANDALL	Barney, of Capt. William, dec., and Hannah Davis, of William, dec.; m. by Joseph Crandall, Justice, March 12, **1788**.
4-26	"	Joseph, of Joshua, of Westerly, and Molly Greene, of Joshua, of Charlestown, Nov. 25, 1788.
4-28	"	Paul, of James, and Prudence Chapman, of William; m. by Joseph Crandall, Justice, March 26, 1789.
4-41	"	Mary, and Ebenezer Rathbone, Sept. 23, 1790.
4-111	"	Hester, and Rowland Burdick, Oct. 22, 1790.
4-44	"	Clement, of Joshua, of Westerly, and Susannah Davis, of Joseph, of Charlestown; m. by Samuel Bliven, Justice, at Charlestown, Jan. 16, 1791.
4-71	"	Stannett, of Capt. William, dec., and Caty Greenman. of Silas; m. by Samuel Bliven, Justice, Aug. 26, 1792.
4-176	"	Grace, and David Stillman, Feb. 20, 1794.
4-105	"	Damarius, and John Babcock, Dec. 4, 1794.
4-166	"	Nancy, and Nathan Lanphere, Dec. 23, 1794.
4-118	"	Joseph, of Westerly, and Nancy Lanphere, of Stonington; m. by Samuel Brown, Justice, April 3, 1796.
4-110	"	Rebecca, and Joseph Saunders, Dec. 27, 1796.
4-125	"	Rogers, of Phineas, of New London, and Lucy Barber, of widow Content Potter; m. by Joseph Potter, Justice, Feb. 12, 1797.
4-172	"	Joel, of William, and Ruth Peckham, of Sweet; m. by Elder John Gardiner, May 14, 1797.
4-126	"	Charlotte, and Luke Budington, Oct. 12, 1797.
4-143	"	Esther, and Maxson Stillman, Dec. 8, 1798.
4-150	"	Caty, and Theodoty Hall, Jr., May 5, 1799.
4-150	"	James Kenyon, of Elijah, and Lydia Ross, of John; m. by Elder William Gardiner, Dec. 15, 1799.
4-172	"	Nancy, and Joshua Babcock, Dec. 13, 1801.
4-105	"	Pardon, of Major Ethan, of Charlestown, and Nancy Berry, of Capt. Peleg, dec., of Westerly; m. by Samuel Bliven, Justice, Feb. 25 , 1802.
4-147	"	Augustus, Jr., of Brookfield, N. Y., son of Augustus, and Charlotte Babcock, of Paul, of Westerly; m. by Joseph Pendleton, Justice, Sept. 17, 1803.
4-238	"	James, Jr., of James, and Dorcas Hall, of Mrs. Anna; m. by Samuel Bliven, Justice, Dec. 4, 1808.
4-249	"	Joseph, and Sarah Gavitt, widow of Stephen; m. by Samuel Bliven, Justice, May 3, 1812.
4-255	"	Jeremy, and Phebe Chapman; m. by Elder Jesse Babcock, Dec. 20, 1812.
4-269	"	Elijah, and Esther Gavitt; m. by Elder Jesse Babcock, May 17, 1813.
5-8	"	Charles, and Lydia Saunders; m. by Elder Benjamin Shaw, March 18, 1827.
5-7	"	Lovina, and John A. Saunders, Dec. 6, 1829.
5-9	"	John, of Brookfield, Madison Co., N. Y., and Sally Saunders, of Westerly; m. by Elder Thomas Tillinghast, Feb. 20, 1830.
5-110	"	Barbara, and James Crandall, Jan. 26, 1840.
5-110	"	James, and Barbara Crandall; m. by Elder Daniel Coon, Jan. 26, 1840.
5-28	"	Eunice, and Alexander Bradford, Dec. 20, 1840.
5-43	"	Hannah, G., and William L. Dennis, June 5, 1842.
5-57	"	Warren, G., and Sophia W. Saunders; m. by Elder Weeden Barber, Jr., Oct. 1, 1842.
5-58	"	Clarissa C. and Clarke Burdick, March 31, 1844.
5-76	"	George G., of Their I. and Mary Ann Babcock, of Charles; m. by Elder Henry Clarke, Oct. 4, 1846.
5-85	"	Francis F. and Henry Crandall, May 7, 1848.
5-85	"	Henry, of Westerly, and Frances F. Crandall, of Troy, N. Y.; m. by Rev. Fred. Denison, May 7, 1848.
5-94	"	Emeline E., and John S. Peckham, Feb. 11, 1849.
5-100	"	Clarke D., of Abel, of Stonington, and Mary E. Barber, of Henry M., of Westerly; m. by Rev. John Taylor, Aug. 27, 1849.

3-55 CROCKER Asa, of Norwich, Conn., and Elizabeth Vose, of Westerly; m. by William Hern, Justice, July 4, 1757.

4-251   "   George. of Waterford, Conn., son of Stephen and Nancy Lanphere, of Daniel, of Westerly; m. by Joseph Pendleton, Justice, Dec. 6, 1812.

3-1 CROSS Phebe, and Jonathan Palmeter, Sept. 24, 1744.

4-183   "   Mary, and Joshua Kenyon, May 5, 1774.

3-165   "   Anne, and Simeon Lewis, Jan. 13, 1780.

4-119   "   John, Jr., of South Kingstown, and Mary Hoxsie, of Gideon, of Charlestown; m. by Freeman Perry, Justice, at Charlestown, Jan. 23, 1791.

4-142   "   Amos, and Bessy Barnes; m. by Joseph Potter, Justice, Dec. 9, 1793.

5-26   "   George D., of Westerly, and Abby Hinckley, of Stonington; m. at Stonington by Gershom Trumbull, Justice, Oct. 25, 1829.

5-48   "   Martha B., and Edward W. Babcock, Nov. 27, 1833.

5-17   "   Abby Jane. and Horace Babcock, Sept. 11, 1843.

5-86   "   George D., Jr., of Hon. George D. and Mary D. Burlingame, of Gen. Ray G.; m. by Rev. Thomas H. Vail, May 8, 1848.

2-110 CRUMB Rachel, and Joseph Hazell, Nov. 10, 1715.

2-84   "   Elizabeth, and Samuel Saunders, Nov. 30, 1732.

2-76   "   Joseph, and Amey Cottrell; m. by John Babcock, Justice, June —, 1734.

2-70   "   William, and Hannah Lewis; m. by Elder John Maxson, April 25, 1736.

3-20   "   Hannah, and Stephen Hall, March 27, 1747-8.

3-59   "   Elizabeth, and Nathan Saunders, Feb. 23, 1758.

3-67   "   Joseph, and Rebecca Hall; m. by Benoni Smith, Justice, July 26, 1759.

3-95   "   William, and Mrs. Edith Thorn; m. by Stephen Lanphere, Justice, April 13, 1764.

3-99   "   Joseph, Jr., and Hannah Brand; m. by Stephen Lanphere, Justice, March 17, 1765.

3-124   "   David, of Joseph, of Westerly, and Hannah Denison, of Joseph, of Stonington; m. by Oliver Crary, Justice, Dec. 12, 1771.

4-59   "   Simeon, of William, and Harriet Pendleton, of Samuel; m. by Joseph Clarke, Justice, May 25, 1783.

4-26   "   Sylvester, and Grace Culver; m. by Joseph Clarke, Justice, Jan. 23, 1799.

4-164   "   Sylvester, Jr., of Sylvester, and Ruth Babcock, of Samuel; m. by Joseph Pendleton, Justice, Oct. 11, 1801.

4-176   "   Lucy, and Matthew Lanphere, Oct. 22, 1801.

4-269   "   Alice, and Joshua Sisson, May 20, 1811.

4-274   "   Charles, and Susannah Hiscox; m. by Elder Jesse Babcock, April 25, 1822.

5-63   "   Charlotte L., and Allen Gory, May 12, 1845.

2-52 CULVER Thankful, and Ebenezer Hill, Sept. 10, 1744.

4-26   "   Grace, and Sylvester Crumb, Jan. 23, 1799.

5-107   "   Cynthia A., and Benjamin F. Sisson, June 2, 1850.

3-1 CURTIS John, of Westerly, and Margaret Curtis, of Stonington; m. by William Hern, Justice, March 11, 1744-5.

3-1   "   Margaret, and John Curtis, March 11, 1744-5.

3-69   "   Thomas, of Stonington, and Bridget Crandall, of Westerly; m. by William Hern, Justice, April 30, 1760.

D

2-97 DAERISET Andrew, and Rebecca Enos, of John; m. by John Richmond, Justice, March 1, 1727-8.

2-98 DAKE George, and Susannah ——; m. by Christopher Champlain, Justice, June 15, 1721.

2-119   "   Richard, and Content Maxson; m. by Elder John Maxson, Dec. 4, 1739.

2-113   "   Elizabeth, and Ephraim Clarke, Dec. 12, 1745.

4-135   DANIELS Susannah, and Samuel Sheffield, Feb. 14, 1799.
2-118   DARBY Elias, of William, and Lydia Darby, April 23, 1739.
2-118   "   Lydia, and Elias Darby, April 23, 1739.
2-60   "   William, and Experience Prentice; m. by Elder Joseph Parks,
                Feb. 9, 1743-4.
2-92   DAVISON Rebecca, and Samuel Turner, March 4, 1727-8.
2-106   DAVIS John, and Elizabeth Maxon; m. by Thomas Hiscox, Justice, Aug.
                25, 1715.
2-43   "   Lydia, and Isaac Corey, March 23, 1736-7.
2-118   "   Lydia, and Hosea Corey, March 23, 1736-7.
2-119   "   Thomas William, and Lucy Crandall; m. by Elder John Maxson,
                Dec. 8, 1737.
2-69   "   Thomas, and Bethiah Maxson; m. by Elder John Maxson, Jan. 5,
                1737.
2-72   "   William, and Sarah Allaby; m. by William Hern, Justice, Feb. 7,
                1739-40.
2-69   "   Amey, and John Witter, Jr., Sept. 7, 1740.
2-7   "   Martha, and Thomas Burch, Oct. 10, 1740.
2-10   "   James, and Judeth Maxson; m. by Elder John Maxson, Jan. 10,
                1740.
2-35   "   Jedediah, and Annie Dodge, m. by Elder John Maxson, June 5,
                1741.
2-83   "   William, and Mary Lewis; m. by William Hern, Justice, April
                24, 1745.
3-18   "   Joseph, and Comfort Langworthy, both of Stonington; m. at
                Stonington by Elder Wait Palmer. — — —, 1745.
3-20   "   Joseph, and Anne Babcock; m. by William Hern, Justice, Jan.
                18, 1749-50.
3-29   "   Joseph, of William, and Mary Babcock, of Stephen; m. at South
                Kingstown by Elder James Rogers, Jan. 10, 1753.
3-54   "   Nathan, of Westerly, and Tabitha Niles, of Stonington; m. by Wil-
                liam Hern, Justice, March 3, 1757.
3-56   "   Thankful, and Joseph Clarke, 4th, Sept. 15, 1757.
3-60   "   Mary, and Elisha Stillman, Jan. 23, 1759.
3-63   "   Mary, and Elisha Stillman, Dec. 23, 1759.
3-103   "   Elder Joseph, and Penelope Lewis; m. by Elder Thomas Ross,
                May 14, 1763.
3-139   "   James, of William, and Elizabeth Chapman, of William; m. by
                Elder Joseph Park, Jan. 5, 1775.
3-141   "   Marvel, and James Schrivens, March 2, 1775.
3-152   "   Isabel, and Asa Burdick, Jan. 28, 1778.
4-110   "   Mary, and Simeon Burdick, Nov. 29, 1776.
3-161   "   Nicholas, of William, and Sally Crandall (so called), dau. of
                Zerdiah West, dec.; m. by Joseph Crandall, Justice, June 6,
                1779.
4-68   "   Henry, of Westerly, and Mary Babcock, of Stonington; m. at
                Stonington by Elder Simeon Brown, Aug. 21, 1783.
4-25   "   Hannah, and Barney Crandall, March 12, 1788.
4-60   "   Lucy, and Arnold Babcock, Jan. 17, 1790.
4-44   "   Barbara, and John Bliven, Jan. 16, 1791.
4-44   "   Susannah, and Clement Crandall, Jan. 16, 1791.
4-69   "   Clarke, of Westerly, and Polly Miner, of Stonington; m. by Eld.
                Eleazer Brown, Oct. 21, 1792.
4-104   "   Content, and Joseph Bragdon, Nov. 10, 1793.
4-96   "   Nancy, and Thomas Duran, Sept. 6, 1795.
4-242   "   James, Jr., and Lydia Saunders; m. by Elder Jesse Babcock,
                Sept. 10, 1815.
3-36   DEAK John, and Hannah Foster; m. by Elder Joseph Maxson, Feb. 26,
                1746-7.
3-52   "   Content, and Timothy Peckham, June 24, 1756.
5-39   "   Denly, and John Ryan, Jan. 18, 1841.
2-125   DENISON Elizabeth, and William Babcock, Dec. 5, 1705.
2-92   "   Sarah, and William Babcock, Aug. 14, 1730.
5-41   "   Mary Ann, and Whitman T. Lewis, July 18, 1841.
3-124   "   Hannah, and David Crumb, Dec. 12, 1771.

5-43 DENNIS William L., of Newport, and Hannah G. Crandall, of Westerly; m. by Elder Daniel Coon, June 5, 1842.

5-34 DERBY Levi Lothrop, and Esther Saunders; m. by Rev. James Pratt, June 24, 1839.

3-68 DETTEOCK Hannah, and Rufus Perkins, March 2, 1760.

4-42 DEWRY Sarah, and Luke Saunders, Oct. 29, 1781.

4-191 " Amey, and Ebenezer Shelley, Nov. 15, 1799.

5-5 " Almira, and Paul M. Barber, Dec. 30, 1827.

3-157 DICKINS Trustam, of Amos, of New Shoreham, and Martha Wilcox, of Hezekiah; m. by Joseph Crandall, Justice, Oct. 27, 1782.

2-119 DIXON Sarah, and Isaiah Burch, Jan. 20, 1742-3.

2-107 DODGE John, and Elizabeth ——, Oct. 19, 1710.

2-84 " Mary, and Theodoty Vars. Dec. 21, 1732.

2-82 " Elizabeth, and Samuel Rathbone, March 15, 1732-3.

2-35 " Annie, and Jedediah Davis, June 5, 1741.

3-51 " Trustam, of New Shoreham, and Hannah Larkin, of Westerly; m. by Joseph Crandall, Justice, Oct. 28, 1764.

4-33 " Lucretia, and John Bliven, Feb. 8, 1789.

4-31 " Lydia, and George Wells, Oct. 15, 1789.

4-54 " Rozina, and William Bliven, April 6, 1791.

4-158 " Dea Oliver, and Dorothy Lanphere; m. by Joseph Pendleton, Justice, March 26, 1800.

2-87 DOWNING Sarah, and Gideon Johnson, Oct. 23, 1743.

3-1 " Hannah, and Jonathan Crandall, April 12, 1747.

3-11 " Amey, and Ezekiel Burdick, July 14, 1750.

3-1 " Mercy, and Joshua Vose, March 3, 1752.

3-157 DRISCOL William, of William, and Elizabeth Ross, of John; m. by Joseph Crandall, Justice, July 27, 1778.

4-15 DUNBAR Thomas, of John, dec., and Eunice Barber, of Nathan; m. by Elder Isaiah Wilcox, Aug. 29, 1784.

4-254 " Capt. Thomas, and Thankful Barber; m. by Elder Elisha Cheeseborough, at Stonington, Jan. 30, 1814.

5-54 DUNHAM William R. F., of Freeman, dec., and Eunice Sisson, of Sanford; m. by Jedediah W. Knight, Justice, Aug. 18, 1844.

5-77 DUNN Mary Ann, and Henry R. Gavitt, Aug. 2, 1847.

5-103 " Edward M., of John E. and Desire A. Gavitt, of Benajah; m. by Thomas H. Vail, Dec. 24, 1849.

4-96 DURAN Thomas, of Massachusetts, and Nancy Davis, of Westerly; m. by Samuel Bliven, Justice, Sept. 6, 1795.

4-198 DURFEE John, of James, of Stonington, and Rebecca Saunders, of Joshua, of Westerly; m. by Joseph Pendleton, Justice, Sept. 15, 1804.

3-81 DYE Esther, and Remington Sears, Feb. 1, 1761.

3-128 " Nathan, of Jonathan, of Stonington, and Eunice Chase, of Oliver, of Westerly; m. by Joseph Crandall, Justice, Nov. 26, 1772.

2-105 DYRE Deborah, and Daniel Lombard, Sept. 24, 1747.

E

2-71 EAGLESTONE, Ichabod and Thankful Hadfall; m. by Samuel Wilbur, Justice, June 27, 1736.

2-74 EDWARDS, Christopher and Phebe Wells; m. by Elder John Maxson, Oct. 24, 1735.

2-119 " Thomas and Garthrat Greenman; m. by Elder John Maxson (also 3-38), Nov. 1, 1742.

3-54 " Daniel, of Charlestown, and Joan Clarke, of Westerly; m. by Stephen Saunders, Justice, Sept. 9, 1756.

4-133 " Clarke, of Daniel, dec., of Charlestown, and Catharine Maxson, of Tory, of Westerly; m. by Joseph Clarke, Justice, April 6, 1780.

3-171 " Sarah, and Joseph Gavitt, Oct. 1, 1780.

3-155 " Paul, of Westerly, and Rachel Allen, of Stonington, m. at Stonington by Elder Eleazer Brown, April 13, 1782.

4-191 " Mary, and Samuel Ellis, Nov. 7, 1801.

4-243 " Nancy, and Arnold Hiscox, Feb. 7, 1810.

5-29   EDWARDS Hannah, and Albert Stillman, May 5, 1818.
5-28   "   Phebe Ann, and Isaac Gavitt, Oct. 7, 1827.
5-56   "   Silas W., and Betsey Bliven; m. by George D. Cross, Justice, Nov. 22, 1827.
5-68   "   Elizabeth L., and Thomas J. Codner, June 2, 1846.
3-19   EGLESTONE Dorcas, and William Hadsall Dec. 4, 1745.
8-96   "   Deliverance, and Benjamin Jones, Sept. 24, 1764.
2-58   ELDERTON Roger, and Lydia Babcock; m. by John Babcock, Justice, Sept. 20, 1722.
3-30   "   Anna, and John Hawk, Sept. 9, 1751.
3-63   "   Lydia, and Oliver Burdick, Oct. 19, 1758.
3-79   "   Patience, and Wait Saunders, Dec. 16, 1761.
3-137 ELDREDGE Peter, of Newport, and Esther Pendleton, of Samuel, of Westerly; m. by Joseph Crandall, Justice, Nov. 20, 1774.
4-160 ELDRED Esther, and Stephen Gavitt, Sept. 29, 1800.
2-77   ELLIS Zerniah, and Joshua Lanphere, Oct. 17, 1734.
3-31   "   Mary, and Samuel Tefft, May 5, 1753.
4-83   "   Phebe, and Thompson Wells, Sept. 27, 1792.
4-191 "   Samuel, and Mary Edwards; m. by Elder Abram Coon, Nov. 7, 1801.
2-84   ENOS Joseph, and Margaret Webster, Sept. 20, 1716.
2-97   "   Rebecca, and Andrew Daleriset, March 1, 1727-8.
2-108 "   Mary, and Benjamin Cobb, Jan. 30, 1728-9.
2-77   "   John, and Mercy Hall; m. at Stonington by Rev. Nathaniel Eells, Dec. 26, 1743.
3-2   "   Thankful, and Edmund Burdick, April 23, 1749.
3-2   "   Sarah, and John Millard, April 21, 1751.
3-54   "   Elizabeth, and Joshua Lewis, Feb. 23, 1757.
3-57   "   Lydia, and Zebulon Lewis, Feb. 12, 1758.

F

5-51   FENNER Eliza, and Charles Gear, Dec. 17, 1843.
4-218 FELLOWS Polly, and Christopher Burdick, Nov. 27, 1806.
4-263 FERGUSON Robert F., of Philadelphia, Penn., and Hannah Babcock, of Westerly; m. by Elder Jesse Babcock, Jan. 23, 1814.
——   FIELDEN see Phelden.
3-92   FISH Abigail, and Andrew Lothrop, Sept. 14, 1763.
5-71   FITCH Waitey, and Jesse W. Hall, Jan. 8, 1846.
2-79   FORDIS John, and Susannah Pettes; m. by John Hoxsie, Justice, Dec. 27, 1733.
2-82   FOSTER John, and Margarey Card; m. by Rouse Helme, Assistant, June 11, 1724.
2-97   "   Elizabeth, and John Lanphere, March 3, 1727-8.
2-72   "   Caleb, and Elizabeth Irish; m. by John Richmond, Justice, Sept. 24, 1735.
2-70   "   Thomas, and Mary Stewart; m. by Elder John Maxson, April 5, 1736.
3-36   "   Hannah, and John Deak, Feb. 26, 1746-7.
3-34   "   Jonathan, Jr., of Richmond, and Anna Lawton, of Westerly; m. Daniel Maccoon, Justice, Nov. 29, 1753.
3-142 "   Sarah, and Abel Larkin, April 1, 1770.
4-120 "   Thomas, of Westerly, and Nabby York, of Stonington; m. by Elder Simeon Brown, Sept. 4, 1791.
4-92   FOWLER John, of Westerly, and Hannah Helmes, of Stonington; m. at Stonington by Elder Simeon Brown, Aug. 5, 1792.
5-31   "   Fanny, and Col. Charles Bradford, Sept. 30, 1846.
3-100 FRAZIER Gideon, and Mercy Gibbs; m. by Elder Joseph Park, Oct. 22, 1767.
4-12   "   Gideon, and Elizabeth Greene, of William; m. by Joseph Crandall, Justice, March 1, 1785.
4-145 "   Nathaniel, of Gideon and Ruth Bliven, of Samuel; m. by Elder John Gardiner, Oct. 6, 1799.
4-221 "   Judith, and Lyman Ross, Jan. 8, 1807.

5-115 FRAZIER Frances, and Arnold Saunders, Jr., Jan. 29, 1826.
2-74 FRENCH William, and Prudence Gavitt; m. by Joseph Pendleton, Justice, March 1, 1738-9.
2-42 FRINK Esther, and Peter Crandall, Dec. 22, 1740.
4-228 " Marshall, of Stonington, and Betsey Berry, of Westerly; m. by Elijah Palmer, Justice, May 1, 1805.
4-227 " Rosannah, and Wain Berry Dec. 7, 1866.
4-5 FRY Ruth, and Frederic Chase, Feb. 2, 1783.
4-229 FULLER Lindall A., of Pomfret, Conn., and Sarah Wells of Hopkinton; m. at Hopkinton, by Elder Abram Coon, March 1, 1806.

G

5-98 GAGE John M., of Moses, of Mendon, Mass., and Frances Burdick, of Welcome, of Charlestown; m. by Rev. John Taylor, June 18, 1849.
3-88 GARDINER Lydia, and Joseph Sheffield, Jan. 13, 1763.
3-101 " Mary, and William Champlain, Dec. 19, 1765.
3-131 " Lydia, and Sanford Taylor (also 4-98), June 17, 1773.
4-95 " Anna, and John Crandall, Nov. 9, 1777.
3-169 " Waitey, and Isaac Vars, Oct. 15, 1780.
4-8 " Dorcas, and Jeptha Brown, Oct. 31, 1784.
4-81 " Susannah, and Simeon Burdick, Feb. 4, 1786.
4-184 " Caty, and Russell Saunders, March 1, 1801.
3-160 " Lydia, and Jeptha Brown, Oct. 13, 1782.
4-195 " Lydia, and John Thompson, March 8, 1804.
2-96 GAVITT Hannah, and Immanuel Case, Dec. 3, 1714.
2-84 " Ezekiel, and Amey Babcock; m. by Theodoty Rhodes, Justice, Aug. 9, 1732.
2-42 " Mary, and William Lewis, Oct. 10, 1733.
2-74 " Prudence, and William French, March 1, 1738-9.
2-113 " Benajah, and Lois Pendleton; m. by Rev. Joseph Parks, Sept. 7, 1746.
3-33 " Esther, and Peter Burdick, Jan. 24, 1754.
3-62 " John, of Westerly, and Anna York, of Charlestown; m. by Rev. Joseph Park, April 19, 1758.
3-84 " Anna, and William Gavitt, May 19, 1760.
3-84 " William, and Anna Gavitt; m. by Peleg Cross, Justice, May 19, 1760.
3-94 " Deacon Ezekiel, of Westerly, and Mary Brian of Stonington; m. by Rev. Joseph Park, May 8, 1763.
3-109 " Ezekiel, Jr., and Phebe Babcock; m. by Rev. Joseph Park, March 22, 1767.
2-118 " Margary, and Oliver Gavitt, Oct. 1, 1770.
3-118 " Oliver, of Samuel, dec., and Margary Gavitt, of Joseph, both of Charlestown; m. at Charlestown, by Peleg Cross, Justice, Oct. 1, 1770.
4-11 " George, and Abigail Hiscox; m. by Elder Joshua Clark, Nov. 4, 1772.
4-186 " John, of Joseph, of Westerly, and Desire Wilcox, of Joseph, of Charlestown; m. by Peleg Cross, Justice, Dec. 28, 1773.
3-138 " Stephen, and Mercy West, both of Westerly; m. at Stonington, by Elder Ebenezer Brown, May 11, 1775.
3-147 " Phalley, and Elias Cottrell, Nov. 7, 1776.
3-153 " Anna, and Prentice Babcock, March 15, 1778.
3-154 " Prudence, and Henry Babcock, Aug. 4, 1778.
3-174 " Thankful and Oliver Champlain, Jan. 25, 1779.
3-164 " Anna, and Amos Cheeseborough, Nov. 10, 1779.
3-171 " Joseph, of Westerly, and Sarah Edwards, of Charlestown; m. by Elder John Gardiner, Oct. 1, 1780.
3-127 " Amey, and Isaac Babcock, Nov. 12, 1780.
4-43 " Sylvester, of Benajah, dec., and Sarah Babcock, of Col. James, dec.; m. by Elder Oliver Babcock, Sept. 30, 1781.
4-19 " Vashti, and George Bliven, Aug. 12, 1784.

4-231	GAVITT	Stephen, Jr., of Stephen, and Mary Lewis, of Joseph; m. by Elder Isaiah Wilcox, Oct. —, 1785.
4-65	"	Sanford, of Deacon Joseph, and Mrs. Hannah Berry, of Elijah; m. by Joseph Clarke, Justice, Feb. 23, 1787.
4-19	"	Dinah, and Arnold Crandall, Dec. 6, 1787.
4-43	"	Sylvester of Benajah, dec., and Keturah Pendleton, of William, dec.; m. by Elder Isaiah Wilcox, March 16, 1788.
4-27	"	George, of Deacon Ezekiel, and Rhoda Babcock, of Isaac; m. by Elder Isaiah Wilcox, March 31, 1788.
4-101	"	George, of George, and Lucy Bliven, of John; m. by Elder John Gardiner, Sept. 6, 1795.
4-108	"	Thomas, of George, of Westerly, and Melinda Kennicome, of Groton, Conn.; m. by Samuel Bliven, Justice, Nov. 17, 1796.
4-120	"	Eunice, and William Thompson, April 9, 1798.
4-160	"	Stephen, of Stephen, and Esther Eldred, widow, dan. of Samuel Pendleton, dec.; m. by Samuel Bliven, Justice, Sept. 29, 1800.
4-204	"	Ephraim, and Sally Larkin; m. by Elder Jesse Babcock, Feb. 17, 1805.
4-211	"	Ezekiel, of Oliver of Westerly, and Hannah Wilcox, of Joseph, dec., of Charlestown; m. at Charlestown, by Samuel Bliven, Justice, Nov. 21, 1805.
4-221	"	Samuel and Rebecca Taylor; m. by Elder Jesse Babcock, July 24, 1806.
4-230	"	Abigail, and Merchant Haff, Dec. 17, 1807.
4-244	"	Joseph, of Col. John, and Thankful Bliven, of Major William; m. by Elder Jesse Babcock, Nov. 29, 1809.
4-245	"	Louisa, and Peleg Sherman Barber, March 15, 1810.
4-249	"	Sarah, and Joseph Crandall, May 3, 1812.
4-253	"	Mary, and Asa Babcock, 2d, Sept. 12, 1813.
4-257	"	Benjamin, of Oliver, dec., and Amelia Allen, of Samuel, dec.; m. by Samuel Bliven, Justice, May 17, 1814.
4-265	"	Rhoda, and Capt. Nathan Pendleton, Oct. 20, 1816.
4-267	"	Lucy, and James Wells, April 20, 1817.
4-269	"	Esther, and Elijah Crandall, May 17, 1818.
5-111	"	David, of Stephen, dec., and Martha Hall, of Benjamin; m. by Elder Matthew Stillman, Dec. 21, 1823.
4-203	"	Benajah, and Rhoda Gavitt; m. at Stonington, by Elder Asher Miner, Feb. 29, 1824.
4-203	"	Rhoda, and Benajah Gavitt, Feb. 29, 1824.
4-266	"	Wells, of Stephen, dec., and Eunice Lanphere, of Matthew, dec., by Elder Matthew Stillman, Dec. 30, 1826.
5-28	"	Isaac, and Phebe Ann Edwards; m. by Rev. Benjamin Shaw, Oct. 7, 1827.
5-18	"	Thankful, and Job W. Rathbone, March 28, 1831.
5-53	"	Phebe A., and James Champlain, July 4, 1844.
5-77	"	Henry K. of Henry C. and Mary Ann Dunn, of John K.; m. by Rev. Thomas H. Vail, Aug. 2, 1847.
5-78	"	Keturah V., and Peleg Saunders, Sept. 22, 1847.
5-88	"	Timothy P., and Freelove V. Thompson; m. by Rev. John Taylor, June 5, 1848.
5-103	"	Desire A., and Edward M. Dunn, Dec. 24, 1849.
5-106	"	Abbie C., and Avery P. Peckham, March 2, 1850.
5-109	"	Abbie, and Maxson White, Aug. 5, 1850.
3-37	GEER	William, and Lydia Hall, both of Preston, Conn.; m. by Benoni Smith, Justice, March 20, 1754.
3-42	"	Jonathan, of Groton, and Lois Lanphere, of Westerly; m. by Benoni Smith, Justice, Jan. 2, 1755.
5-50	"	Ebenezer, and Ruth M. Perkins; m. by Rev. William H. Newman, April 23, 1843.
5-51	"	Charles H., of Westerly, and Eliza Fenner, of Warwick; m. by Rev. Oliver P. Tuckerman, Dec. 17, 1843.
3-109	GIBBS	Mercy and Gideon Frazier, Oct. 22, 1767.
2-74	GIFFORD	Catharine and Hezekiah Collins, Nov. 6, 1735.

5-67 GILBERT John, of Groton, Conn., and Lydia Perry, of Westerly; m. by Rev. Oliver P. Tuckerman, May 31, 1845.

3-80 GODANDO (mustie), and Mary Mitchell; m. by Joseph Crandall, Justice, Jan. 28, 1762.

5-68 GOODRICH, Samuel W., and Sarah E. Hayden, both of New York; m. by Rev. Thomas H. Vail, March 15, 1847.

3-72 GORTON John, and Sarah Babcock; m. by William Hern, Justice, Nov. 9, 1764.

4-41 " Hannah E., and Pardon S. Peckham, May 25, 1841.

5-63 GORY Allen, of Westerly, son of Peter and Martha, of Glocester, R. I., and Charlotte L. Crumb, of Arnold and Lucinda, of Westerly; m. by Rev. Ralph Phinney, May 12, 1845.

4-218 GRANT Prudence, and Samuel Wilcox, ——, 1798.

2-94 GREENELL Daniel, Jr., and Jane Lewis, of Israel; m. at South Kingstown by Rouse Helme, Assistant, May 21, 1727.

2-88 GREENMAN Silas, of Stonington, and Anne Babcock, of Westerly; m. by Rouse Helme, Assistant, March 23, 1730-1.

3-21 " Margaret, and Joseph Greene, Sept. 20, 1747.

2-119 " Garthrot, and Thomas Edwards (also 3-38), Nov. 1, 1742.

3-3 " Eunice, and Andrew Champlain, Jan. 15, 1745-6.

3-22 " Reeasey, and Ceazer Babcock. April 7, 1758.

3-89 " Chloe. and Christopher Burdick, March 24, 1762.

3-94 " Elizabeth, and Robert Helme, Feb. 10, 1763.

3-94 " Catharine, and Oliver Helme, Dec. 25, 1763.

3-41 " Nathan, of Exeter, and Eunice Saunders, of Westerly; m. by Joseph Crandall, Justice, March 19, 1766.

3-119 " Abigail, and James Rhodes, Feb. 21, 1768.

3-120 " Catherine, and Nathan Lanphere, Jr., Aug. 16, 1770.

3-150 " Mary, and Henry Crandall, Feb. 24, 1782.

4-18 " Nancy, and Sumner Chapman, Aug. 27, 1786.

4-71 " Caty, and Stennett Crandall, Aug. 26, 1792.

4-94 " Silas and Polly Stillman; m. by Daniel Babcock, Justice, Oct. 17, 1793.

4-274 " Silas, Jr., of Westerly, and Thankful Wells, of Samuel, dec., of Hopkinton; m. by Elder Matthew Stillman, Dec. 20, 1821.

5-79 " William, of Silas, and Frances Hall, of Stanton; m. by Rev. Isaac Moore, Sept. 29, 1847.

2-85 GREENE Benjamin, and Eleanor Randall. March 19, 1714.

2-69 " Phebe, and Thomas Wells, Sept. 22, 1717.

2-94 ' Sarah, and Joseph Hiscox, March 28, 1739.

3-27 " Sarah, and Joseph Hiscox, March 28, 1739.

3-21 " Joseph, of Westerly, and Margaret Greenman, of Charlestown; m. by William Hern, Justice, Sept. 20, 1747.

3-22 " Matthew, and Judith Maxson, Dec. 1, 1748-9.

3-26 " Amey, and Elisha Lewis, Jan. 10, 1751.

3-59 " William, of Charlestown, and Judith Rathbone, of Westerly; m. at Charlestown by Nathaniel Sheffield, Justice, Jan. 25, 1756.

3-86 " Hannah, and Daniel Bliven (also 4-52), Nov. 21, 1782.

3-104 " Ruth, and Samuel Bliven (also 4-194), March 17, 1766.

3-136 " Christopher, of Nathaniel, of Warwick, dec., and Catharine Ward, of Samuel, of Westerly; m. by Elder Joshua Clarke, Dec. 23, 1773.

3-135 " William, and Sarah Champlain, of Joseph. dec.; m. by Stephen Saunders, Justice, (also 4-40), March 18, 1774.

3-141 " John, of Exeter, son of Josias, dec., and Prudence Saunders, of Joseph, of Westerly; m. by Joseph Crandall, Justice (also 4-200), March 2, 1775.

3-158 " Samuel, of Joshua, of Westerly, and Desire Ross, of Elder Thomas, of Charlestown; m. by Joseph Crandall, Justice, Nov. 19, 1778.

3-169 " Jonathan, of Josias, dec., of Charlestown, and Anna Crandall, of James, of Westerly; m. by Joseph Crandall, Justice, Aug. 27, 1780.

3-180 " William Rathbone, of Capt. William, of Westerly, and Esther Johnson, of Nathaniel, of Hopkinton; m. by Elder Joshua Clarke, (also 4-178), March 21, 1781.

4-169 GREENE Keziah, and Dennis Taylor, Feb. 17, 1782.
4-12   "   Elizabeth, and Gideon Frazier, March 1, 1785.
4-21   "   Benjamin, of Capt. William, of Westerly, and Mary Johnson, of
                   Nathaniel, of Hopkinton; m) by Joseph Crandall, Justice,
                   Jan. 28, 1787.
4-26   "   Molly, and Joseph Crandall, Nov. 25, 1788.
4-28   "   Pardon, of Capt. William and Fanny Bliven, of Capt. William;
                   m. by Joseph Crandall, Justice, April 9, 1789.
4-56   "   Capt. Charles of Petersborough, N. Y., and Amey Burdick, widow
                   of Robert, of Charlestown; m. by Joseph Clark, Justice, Nov.
                   19, 1791.
4-55   "   Dorcas, and Thomas Thompson, Jr., Dec. 21, 1791.
4-77   "   Ruth, and Joshua Babcock, March 11, 1792.
4-204   "   William, of Jonathan, and Sally Hall of Isaac; m. by Samuel
                   Bliven, Justice, Jan. 17, 1805.
4-234   "   Betsey and Benjamin Potter, March 6, 1808.
5-30   "   Amey K., and Samuel Saunders, Jr., Nov. 6, 1834.
5-25   "   Millen S., of Stonington, and Thankful Stillman, of Westerly; m.
                   by E. T. Hiscox, Sept. 1, 1846.
5-96   "   Martha, and Albert Chapman, May 7, 1849.
2-97   GRIFFIN William, and Abigail Burdick; m. by John Richmond, Justice,
                   Feb. 9, 1726-7.

H

2-71   HADFALL Rachel and Obadiah Pendleton, June 4, 1736.
2-71   "   Thankful, and Ichabod Eagleston, June 27, 1736.
2-86   "   Sarah, and Samuel Hill, Dec. 3, 1738.
3-19   HADSALL and Dorcas Eglestone; m. by William Hern, Justice, Dec. 4,
                   1745.
3-28   HAKES Jonathan and Hannah Brown, of Jonathan; m. by Benoni
                   Smith, Justice, Nov. 23, 1752.
3-68   HALLAM Mrs. Patience, and James Champlain, Jan. 15, 1734-5.
2-83   HALL James, Jr., and Rachel Meckcome; m. by Peter Crandall, Justice,
                   April 17, 1721.
2-106   "   Benjamin, and Lydia Hall; m. by Theodoty Rhodes, Justice, Jan.
                   6, 1726-7.
2-106   "   Lydia, and Benjamin Hall, Jan. 6, 1726-7.
2-84   "   Mary, and Thomas Adams, Nov. 23, 1732.
2-75   "   Hannah, and Israel Styles, April 10, 1735.
2-71   "   Rachel, and James Brand, March 11, 1735-6.
2-81   "   Sarah, and Simeon Tucker, May 1, 1737.
2-72   "   Rachel, and James Brand, Aug. 10, 1737.
2-119   "   Henry, and Ann Crandall; m. by Elder John Maxson, Sept. 6, 1742.
2-57   "   Anna, and Nathan Meekame, Dec. 23, 1743.
2-77   "   Mercy, and John Enos, Dec. 26, 1743.
3-1   "   Sarah, and Benjamin Ross, April 26, 1741.
2-77   "   Anna, and Nathan Maxson, Dec. 23, 1843.
3-51   "   Anna, and Nathan Maccoon, Dec. 23, 1743.
3-1   "   Phebe, and Samuel Pendleton, Feb. 13, 1744-5.
3-1   "   Gideon, and Rebecca Hern; m. by William Hern, Justice, March
                   11, 1744-5.
3-20   "   Stephen, and Hannah Crumb; m. by William Hern, Justice, March
                   27, 1747-8.
3-20   "   David, and Judeth Wilbur; m. by William Hern, Justice, May —,
                   1748.
3-2   "   Isaac, and Abigail Burdick; m. by Joseph Crandall, Justice, Nov.
                   5, 1750.
3-25   "   Susanna, and Caleb Babcock, Jan. 14, 1753.
3-27   "   James, Jr., of Westerly, and Elizabeth Brown, of Norwalk; m. by
                   Daniel Maccoon, Justice, Feb. 11, 1753.
3-34   "   Henry, of Henry, and Sarah Hall, of James; m. by John Saun-
                   ders, Justice, before 1754.
3-34   "   Sarah, and Henry Hall, before 1754.

3-37	HALL	Lydia, and William Geer, March 20, 1754.
3-40	"	Benjamin, and Penelope Palmeter; m. by William Hern, Justice, Sept. 14, 1754.
3-63	"	Joseph, of Hopkinton, and Teresia Wilcock, of Westerly; m. by Joseph Crandall, Justice. Dec. 18, 1758.
3-67	"	Rebecca, and Joseph Crumb, July 26, 1759.
3-65	"	Hezekiah, of Hopkinton, and Dorcas Peckham, of Westerly; m. by Joseph Crandall, Justice, Oct. 11, 1759.
3-78	"	Esther, and Joseph Crandall, Aug. 24, 1761.
3-117	"	Sarah, and Benjamin Ross, March 4, 1770.
4-82	"	Martha, and Charles Saunders, Nov. 25, 1773.
3-140	"	Esther, and Stephen Peckham, Feb. 26, 1775.
3-142	"	Theodoty, Jr., of Theodoty, and Mary Peckham, of Isaac; m. by Joseph Crandall, Justice, Jan. 3, 1776.
4-135	"	Thomas, of Isaac, of Westerly, and Eunice Johnson, of Reuben, dec., of Charlestown; m. by Elder Thomas Ross, at Charlestown, May 1, 1777.
3-166	"	Mary, and James Bliven, Jr., Feb. 22, 1780.
3-166	"	William, of William, dec., of Hopkinton, and Rachel Saunders, of James, of Westerly; m. by Joseph Crandall, Justice, March 16, 1780.
4-14	"	Mary, and Benjamin Peckham, June 11, 1785.
4-20	"	Rachel, and Joseph Lewis, Dec. 27, 1786.
4-85	"	Capt. Lyman, of Joseph, dec., and Eunice Pendleton, of John; m. by Elder Isaiah Wilcox (also 4-30), Jan. 27, 1787.
4-24	"	James, of Ephraim, of Charlestown, and Sarah Larkin, of Moses, of Westerly; m. by Joseph Crandall, Justice, Dec. 31, 1787.
4-29	"	Freegift, and Phelia Millard, Dec. 17, 1789.
4-37	"	Elizabeth and Samuel Bliven, Jr., June 24, 1790.
4-115	"	Braddock, and Susannah Wilcox; m. by Elder Isaiah Wilcox, July 30, 1790.
4-95	"	David, and Hannah Young; m. by Elder Elkanah Babcock Nov. 20, 1791.
4-103	"	Dolly, and Champlain Austin (also 4-109), Nov. 20, 1796.
4-115	"	Lyman, of Westerly, and Phebe Palmer, of Stonington; m. by Joshua Babcock, Justice, Nov. 27, 1796.
4-206	"	Benjamin, and Huldah Wilbur; m. by Elder Elkanah Babcock, June 8, 1797.
4-150	"	Theodoty, Jr., and Caty Crandall, of Elijah; m. by Paul Maxson, Justice, May 5, 1799.
4-151	"	Amey, and Isaac Nash, Jan. 30, 1800.
5-37	"	Stanton, of Westerly, and Mercy Perkins, of Charlestown; m. by Elder Oliver Bright, July 8, 1800.
4-161	"	Wilbur, of David, and Polly Saunders, of Joshua; m. by Paul Maxson, Justice, Nov. 16, 1800.
5-171	"	Barbara, and Nathan Nash, Oct. 11, 1801.
4-204	"	Sally, and William Greene, Jan. 17, 1805.
4-223	"	Varnum, of Theodoty and Caty Saunders, of Joseph; m. by Samuel Bliven, Justice, Feb. 25, 1807.
4-230	"	Merchant, and Abigail Gavitt; m. by Elder Jesse Babcock, Dec. 17, 1807.
4-238	"	Dorcas, and James Crandall, Jr., Dec. 4, 1808.
5-12	"	Hezekiah, of Westerly, and Jane Smith, of Baltimore, Md.; m. at Baltimore, by Rev. John E. Barstow, Nov. 12, 1822.
5-111	"	Martha, and David Gavitt, Dec. 21, 1823.
5-15	"	John P., and Nancy Babcock; m. by Rev. Benjamin Shaw, Sept. 3, 1826.
5-50	"	Kesiah, and Alvey Taylor, April 18, 1843.
5-45	"	Susan, and George Sisson, May 28, 1843.
5-71	"	Jesse W., and Waitey Fitch; m. by Rev. E. T. Hiscox, Jan. 8, 1846.
5-79	"	Francis, and William Greenman, Sept. 29, 1847.
5-105	"	Frances M., and George H. S. Barber, Feb. 4, 1850.
4-162	HAMMOND	Ann, and Christopher Rhodes, Dec. 28, 1800.
4-207	HANDCOX	Hannah, and Joshua Saunders, April 18, 1805.

3-166   HARRIS Eliphalet, of Henry, dec., of Westerly, and Sarah Comstock, of
           Caleb, of New London; m. by Joseph Crandall, Justice, July 10,
           1776.
2-110   HASELL Joseph, and Rachel Crumb; m, by Peter Crandall, Justice, Nov. 10,
           1715.
3-73   HAWKINS Mary, and John Pois, Jan. 8, 1765.
3-30   HAWK John, of Charlestown, and Anna Elderton, of Westerly; m. by John
           Larkin, Justice, Sept. 9, 1751.
3-20   HUXSTON Ellinor, and Samuel Brown, July 9, 1749.
5-68   HAYDEN Sarah E., and Samuel W. Goodrich. March 15, 1847.
2-72   HAZELTON Jarvis, and Barberry Barker; m. by Elder John Maxson, Jan.
           21, 1735-6.
3-94   HELME Robert, of South Kingstown, and Elizabeth Greenman, of Wes-
           terly; m. by Rev. Joseph Park, Feb. 10, 1763.
3-94   "   Oliver, of South Kingstown, and Catharine Greenman, of Wes-
           terly; m. by Rev. Joseph Park, Dec. 25, 1763.
4-92   "   Hannah, and John Fowler, Aug. 5, 1792.
4-183   "   Mary, and Christopher Leeds. May 23, 1800.
2-119   HERN William, and Mary Lewis; m. by Elder John Maxson, Oct. 26, 1742.
2-37   "   Dorothy, and Simeon Brown, March 1, 1842-3.
3-1   "   Rebecca, and Gideon Hall, March 11, 1744-5.
3-23   "   William, Jr., and Eunice Wilcox; m. by Joseph Crandall, Justice,
           June 25, 1752.
3-29   "   Elizabeth, and John Bliven, Jan. 3, 1753.
3-46   "   Samuel, of Westerly, and Anna Bell, of Stonington; m. by Rev.
           Nathaniel Eells, July 28, 1754.
5-160   HEWITT Edmund, of Edmund, dec., of Stonington, and Hannah Peckham,
           of Isaac, of Westerly; m. by Joseph Crandall, Justice, March
           7, 1779.
2-51   HILLIARD Isaac, and Victorias Coats, both of Stonington; m. at Westerly
           by John Larkin, Justice, April 5, 1751.
2-45   HILL Hannah, and Christopher Champlain, April 22, 1730.
2-83   "   Mary, of Josias, and Ebenezer Lamb, July 26, 1732.
2-86   "   Samuel, and Sarah Hadfall; m. by William Hern, Justice, Dec. 3,
           1738.
2-7   "   Samuel (negro), and Anna (mulatto); m. by William Hern, Justice,
           Oct. 21, 1740.
2-52   "   Ebenezer, and Thankful Culver, Sept. 10, 1744.
4-185   HINCKLEY Betsey, and Resolved Carr, Dec. 6, 1792.
5-26   "   Abby, and George D. Cross, Oct. 25, 1820.
2-73   HISCOX Thomas, of Newport, and Bethiah Clarke, of Westerly; m. at
           Westerly by Elder Joseph Parks, Oct. 31, 1703.
2-81   "   Ephraim, and Abigail Saunders; m. by John Richmond, Justice,
           Oct. 29, 1733.
2-71   "   Edith, and Joseph Crandall, May 2, 1736.
2-54   "   Hannah, and Jonathan Rogers, Oct. 26. 1737.
2-94   "   Joseph, and Sarah Greene; m. by Elder John Maxson, March 24,
           1739.
2-98   "   William, and Content Babcock; m. by Elder Joseph Maxson, Dec.
           22, 1742.
3-39   "   William, and Susannah Burdick; m. by Theodoty Rhodes, Justice,
           Jan. 11, 1727-8.
3-27   "   Joseph, and Sarah Greene; m. by Elder John Maxson, March 28,
           1739.
3-39   "   William, and Content Babcock; m. by Elder Joseph Maxson, Dec.
           —, 1742.
3-24   "   Sarah, and Edward Saunders (also 4-57), Aug. 13, 1752.
3-41   "   Thomas, Jr., and Elizabeth Saunders; m. by Benoni Smith, Justice,
           Nov. 14, 1754.
3-42   "   Joseph, and Bathsheba Mackee; m. by Benoni Smith, Justice, Dec.
           30, 1754.
3-49   "   Thomas, of Westerly, and Mrs. Patience Bebee, of Southold, L. I.;
           m. by Silas Greenman, Justice, March 2, 1756.
3-82   "   Joseph, Jr., and Susannah Burdick; m. by Stephen Saunders, Jus-
           tice, April 15, 1762.

3-99   HISCOX Nathan, and Ruth Saunders; m. by Rev. Joseph Park, May 7, 1764.

3-112   "   Amey, and John Coon, Jr., May 15, 1771.

4-11   "   Abigail, and George Gavitt, Nov. 4, 1772.

4-142   "   Ephraim, of Ephraim, and Mary Sisson, of Thomas; m. by Joseph Clarke, Justice, Oct. 21, 1773.

4-3   "   Clarke of Joseph and Bathsheba, and Sarah Saunders, of Edward; m. by Elder Joshua Clarke, Dec. 12, 1782.

4-14   "   Bethiah, and David Thayer, March 7, 1786.

4-54   "   Nancy, and Kenyon Burdick, Jan. 18, 1790.

4-122   "   Mary and Ethan Bliven, May 12, 1798.

4-159   "   Abigail, and Clarke Burdick, Jan. 20, 1799.

4-130   "   Thomas, of Westerly, and Susanna Wood, of Westport, Mass.; m. at Westport by William Almy, Justice, Nov. 13, 1797.

4-163   "   Ephraim, and Susannah Lanphere; m. by Elder Abram Coon, Dec. 25, 1800.

4-239   "   Clarke, Jr., of Hopkinton, and Mary White, of Westerly; m. by Elder Abram Coon, Jan. 11, 1809.

4-243   "   Arnold, of Hopkinton, and Nancy Edwards, of Charlestown; m. at Charlestown by Elder Abram Coon, Feb. 7, 1810.

4-163   "   Ephraim, Jr., and Hannah Burdick; m. by Elder Jesse Babcock, Nov. 29, 1810.

4-274   "   Susannah, and Charles Crumb, April 25, 1822.

4-124   HOBERT William, of Westerly, and Lois Babcock, of Hopkinton; m. by Joseph Potter, Justice, Nov. 20, 1798.

4-126   HOLLY Sally, and Stephen Lanphere, Aug. 12, 1798.

2-72   HOLMES Bethiah, and Benajah Billings, March 24, 1739-40.

3-45   "   Thomas, and Zerviah Mason, both of Stonington; m. by Benoni Smith, Justice, Feb. 5, 1755.

2-86   HOLWAY Celinda, and James Congdon, May 2, 1732.

3-20   HOPKINS Sarah, and Mark Williams, July 2, 1749.

3-48   HORICK Elizabeth, and Sumner Chapman, Feb. 23, 1756.

3-133   HOXSIE Sarah, and James Sheffield, Dec. 26, 1773.

4-119   "   Mary, and John Cross, Jr., Jan. 23, 1791.

5-87   "   Perry, of New London, and Matilda Babcock, of Westerly; m. by Rev. Fred Denison, July 3, 1848.

1-57   HUBBARD Bethiah, and Joseph Clarke, Nov. 16, 1664.

2-103   "   Thomas, of Boston, and Lydia Ray, of Westerly; m. by Rev. Joseph Park, May 7, 1747.

4-69   "   Tacy, and Edward Sheffield Wells, Jan. 6, 1791.

4-136   "   James, and Amey Stillman; m. by Elder John Burdick, Jan. 26, 1799.

2-86   HULL Joseph, and Elizabeth Richmond; m. by Theodoty Rhodes, Justice, Nov. 11, 1731.

2-77   "   Joan, and Thomas Kimber, Nov. 7, 1743.

3-123   "   Benjamin, of Joseph and Lydia Saunders, of Stephen; m. by Elder Joshua Clarke, Nov. 7, 1771.

3-136   "   Martha, and Charles Saunders, Nov. 25, 1773.

3-140   "   Benjamin, of Joseph, and Mary Ross, of Peleg; m. by Joseph Crandall, Justice, Feb. 9, 1775.

4-72   "   Thomas, of Thomas, dec., of Westerly, and Amey Peckham, of Abel, of Charlestown; m. by Robert Burdick, Justice, Aug. 27, 1791.

4-156   HUNTLEY Joseph, of Lyme, Conn., and Susanna Peckham, of Westerly; m. by Elder Asa Coon, June 15, 1800.

I

3-20   INGRAHAM Jeremiah, and Elizabeth Lanphere, both of Stonington; m. by William Hern, Justice, Nov. 11, 1748.

2-81   IRISH Johanna, and Edward Robinson, Oct. 11, 1708.

2-81   "   Mary, and John Robinson, Aug. 23, 1733.

2-72   "   Elizabeth, and Caleb Foster, Sept. 24, 1735.

3-26   "   Lydia, and Elisha Lewis, Oct. 30, 1740.

5-35   "   James R., of Alfred N. Y., and Charlotte Babcock, of Westerly; m. by Elder Daniel Coon Aug. 26, 1830.

J

2-83   JAGERS Sarah, and Joseph Stewart, Sept. 6, 1732.
5-102   JAMES Charles H., of William, and Elizabeth S. Brown, of Arnold; m. by
         Rev. Fred Denison, Nov. 6, 1849.
4-271   JEROME Sally, and James Stillman, Dec. 2, 1819.
2-13   JOHNSON Joseph, and Mary Lanphere; m. by Elder John Maxson, June
         18, 1739.
2-87   "   Gideon, of Westerly, and Sarah Downing, of Block Island; m. at
              Block Island, by Samuel Rathbone, Deputy Warden, Oct. 23,
              1743.
3-75   "   Joseph, Jr., of Charlestown, and Judith Burdick, of Westerly; m.
              by Joseph Crandall, Justice, Feb. 28, 1762.
3-97   "   Stephen, of Hopkinton, son of Stephen, and Lois Ross, of Westerly,
              dau. of Thomas; m. by Simeon Burdick, Justice, Dec. 10, 1767.
4-51   "   Bridget, and William Chapman, Jr., March 14, 1773.
4-135   "   Eunice, and Thomas Hall, May 1, 1777.
3-151   "   Job, of Joseph, of Charlestown, and Anne Clarke, of Daniel, of
              Westerly; m. by Joseph Crandall, Justice, Oct. 30, 1777.
3-166   "   Hannah, and Thomas Taylor, Feb. 6, 1780.
2-178   "   Esther, and William Rathbone Greene (also 3-180), March 21,
              1781.
3-180   "   Theodoty, of Daniel, of Charlestown, and Ruth Crandall, of James
              of Westerly; m. by Joseph Crandall, Justice, March 31, 1782.
4-21   "   Mary, and Benjamin Greene, Jan. 28, 1787.
4-51   "   Mary, and William Chapman, June 14, 1799.
4-237   "   Abigail, and Samuel Chapman, March 13, 1810.
5-28   "   George M., of Scotland, and Elizabeth Quall, of Ireland; m. by
              Rev. Thomas H. Vail, Sept. 14, 1847.
3-96   JONES Benjamin, and Deliverance Eaglestone, both of Stonington, published
         by Sylvester Warden, Justice, sometime ago, published also by
         Elder Wait Palmer, at Stonington, Sept. 18, 1764; m. at Wes-
         terly, by Stephen Lanphere, Justice, Sept. 24, 1764.
2-14   JUSTUS Lydia, and Elisha Lewis, Nov. 30, 1740.

K

3-56   KENECOME Abigail, and Valentine Wilcox, Aug. 10, 1757.
4-108   "   Malinda, and Thomas Gavitt, Nov. 17, 1796.
2-106   KENYON Peter, and Naomi Wells; m. by Theodoty Rhodes, Justice, Sept.
         15, 1726.
2-35   "   George and Anna Lewis; m. by Elder John Maxson, June 16,
              1741.
2-90   "   Damarias, and James Crandall (also 3-7), Feb. 27, 1742-3.
3-29   "   Sarah, and Edward Crandall, Jan. 18, 1753.
3-37   "   Nathaniel, and Elliner Utter; m. by Benoni Smith, Justice, March
              21, 1754.
3-49   "   Katherine, and Joshua Church, March 29, 1756.
4-18   "   Mary, and Peleg Berry, April 17, 1774.
4-183   "   Joshua, and Mary Cross, both of Charlestown; m. by Sylvester
              Robinson, Justice, C. C. Pleas, May 5, 1774.
3-162   "   Mercy, and Elijah Crandall, July 18, 1779.
4-5   "   Mercy, and John Closson, March 11, 1784.
4-20   "   Mercy, and Silas Babcock, Jan. 18, 1787.
4-87   "   Elizabeth, and Joseph Chapman, Dec. 21, 1791.
4-119   "   Polly, and Israel Chapman, Oct. 20, 1796.
4-154   "   Sally, and Luther Palmer, Dec. 12, 1799.
4-205   "   Betsey, and Oates Pendleton, Dec. 6, 1801.
5-11   "   Hannah, and Horace Wilcox, March 11, 1831.
5-30   "   Bridget, and Ichabod Sisson, Dec. 27, 1846.
5-95   "   Harriet M., and John A. Weller, April 2, 1849.
2-77   KIMBER Thomas, of New Haven, (sailor), and Joan Hull, of Westerly; m.
         by William Hern, Justice, Nov. 7, 1743.

3-32 KING Susannah, and Edmund Pendleton, April 9, 1738.
2-77 "   Mary, and John Pullman, March 17, 1750-1. ·
4-228 KNIGHT Jedediah, and Eliza Champlain; m. by Elder Abram Coon. Aug. 21, 1807.
5-32 "   J. Whitney, of Westerly, and Mary Ann Perkins, of Sterling, Conn.; m. by Elder Peleg Peckham, Nov. 26, 1838.
4-192 KNOWLES Joseph M., of South Kingstown, and Mrs. Dorcas Tillinghast, of Exeter; m. at Exeter, by Elder Benjamin Weight, Jan. 7, 1802.
5-19 "   John T., of Westerly, and Elizabeth R. Stanton, of Charlestown; m. by Elder Thomas Tillinghast, Oct. 23, 1833.

L

3-140 LADD Mary, and Joseph Crandall, 4th, Feb. 16, 1775.
2-70 LAKE Jeremiah, and Thankful Palmister; m. by Elder John Maxson, April 1, 1737.
2-83 LAMB Ebenezer, and Mary Hill, of Jarvis; m. by John Richmond, Justice, July 26, 1732.
3-31 "   ——, and Sarah Larkin; m. by Daniel Maccoon, Justice, April 27, 1753.
3-47 LANGFORD Jonathan, and Esther Champlain; m. by Silas Greenman, Justice, Dec. 25, 1755.
5-75 LANGLEY Joseph F., of Newport, and Elizabeth Brown, of Westerly; m. by Rev. Thomas H. Vail, Oct. 4, 1847.
2-82 LANGWORTHY Ann, and Joseph Crandall, Feb. 15, 1715-6.
2-72 "   Samuel, and Mary Crandall; m. by Elder John Maxson, Aug. 7, 1736.
2-119 "   Mary, and Nathan Lanphere (also 3-15), June 22, 1739.
3-12 "   John, Jr., and Abigail Munro; m. by Stephen Richmond, Justice, May 27, 1742.
3-18 "   Comfort, and Joseph Davis. ——. —. 1745.
4-74 "   Lucy, and Charles Babcock, Jan. 1. 1792.
4-156 "   Betsey, and Sylvanus Maxson, Sept. 24. 1797.
5-29 "   Lucy P., and Alfred Lewis, Sept. 28 1840.
2-42 LANKFORD Ann, and John Lewis (Fuller), June 3, 1741.
2-41 LANPHERE Theodosius, and Rachel Carey; m. by Peter Crandall, Justice, Jan. 22. 1707-8.
2-4   "   Sarah, and James Corey, March 21, 1708.
2-124 "   Elizabeth, of George, and James Pendleton, Jan. 12, 1709-10.
2-105 "   Experience, and John Satterly. Jan. 5, 1726-7.
2-97 "   John, and Elizabeth Foster; m. by John Richmond, Justice, March 3, 1727-8.
2-95 "   Anna, and John Lanphere, July 24, 1730.
2-95 "   John, and Anna Lanphere; m. by Theodoty Rhodes, Justice, July 24, 1730.
2-88 "   Daniel. and Cattron Prosser; m. by John Richmond, Justice, Jan. 24. 1730-1.
2-77 "   Joshua, of Westerly, and Zerniah Ellis, of Stonington; m. by John Richmond, Justice, Oct. 17, 1734.
2-76 "   Abigail, and Joshua Burdick, Dec. 25, 1734.
2-73 "   Patience, and Ichabod Prosser, Nov. 26, 1735.
2-58 "   Mary, and James Casey, Jan. 21, 1738-9.
2-119 "   Mary, and Joseph Johnson, June 18, 1739.
2-119 "   Nathan. and Mary Langworthy; m. by Elder John Maxson (also 3-15). June 22, 1739.
2-73 "   Nathaniel, and Prudence Cottrell; m. by William Hern, Justice, July 7, 1743.
3-1   "   Mercy, and Joseph Saunders (also 3-168), April 5, 1744.
3-1   "   Hannah, and Ephraim Clarke, Dec. 15, 1744.
3-19 "   Jerusha, and William Sims. March 24. 1747-8.
3-20 "   Jerusha, and William Lewis, March 22, 1747-8.
3-20 "   Elizabeth, and Jeremiah Ingraham, Nov. 11, 1748.
3-18 "   Amey, and Joba Satterly, Dec. 4, 1748.

3-23	LANPHERE	Stephen, and Mary Champlain; m. by Benjamin Randall, Justice, Oct. 26, 1749.
3-5	"	Prudence, and Robert Brand, Nov. 14, 1751.
3-32	"	Martha, and Tony Maxson. Oct. 18, 1753.
3-42	"	Lois, and Jonathan Geer, Jan. 2, 1755.
3-45	"	Benjamin, and Susannah Champlain; m. by Benoni Smith, Justice, March 27, 1755.
3-47	"	Content, and Timothy West, Dec. 3, 1755.
3-52	"	Mary, and Joshua Vosc, Jr., May 3, 1757.
3-63	"	Mary, and William Steward, Nov. 30, 1758.
3-67	"	Nahor, and Anne Lewis; m. by Joseph Crandall, Justice. Jan. 24, 1760.
3-89	"	Barbara, and Samuel Lewis, Oct. 15, 1761.
3-87	"	David. and Sarah Smith; m. by Joseph Clarke, Jr., Justice, March 4, 1762.
3-82	"	Elias, and Sarah Brown; m. by Benoni Smith, Justice, April 22, 1762.
3-93	"	Isaiah, of Westerly, and Thankful Allen, of Stonington; m. by Joseph Crandall, Justice, Oct. 16, 1763.
3-97	"	Nathan, Jr., of Westerly, and Amey Crandall, of Charlestown; m. by Joseph Crandall, Justice, Oct. 28, 1764.
4-76	"	Daniel, of Westerly, and Weltha Worden, of Stonington; m. at Stonington by Elder Simeon Brown, Nov. 13, 1765.
3-120	"	Nathan, Jr., and Catharine Greenman; m. by Elder Joshua Clarke, Aug. 16, 1770.
3-123	"	Nathan, Jr., of Nathan, and Sarah Landers, of John; m. by Elder Joshua Clarke (also 4-100), Oct. 31, 1771.
3-124	"	Abram, of John, of Westerly, and Sarah Lanphere, of Ebenezer, of Hopkinton; m. by Elder Joshua Clarke, Dec. 29, 1771.
3-124	"	Sarah, and Abram Lanphere, Dec. 29, 1771.
3-126	"	Champlain, of Stephen, and Rebecca Babcock, of Joseph; m. by Oliver Crary, Justice. March 9, 1772.
3-126	"	Amey, and William Weaver, March 10, 1772.
4-4	"	Wealtha, and Christopher Seager, March 17, 1777.
4-21	"	Patience, and George Champlain, Oct. 5, 1780.
4-22	"	Hannah, and Nathan Stillman, Nov. 10, 1785.
4-89	"	Paul, and Elizabeth Berry; m. by Joseph C'arke, Justice, Feb. 18, 1789.
4-89	"	Pardon, and Polly Berry; m. by Joseph Clarke, Justice, Feb. 25, 1790.
4-201	"	Cynthia, and Barney Sisson, March 7, 1790.
4-174	"	Eunice, and Abel Clarke, Oct. 13, 1791.
4-42	"	Cattern, and Hosea Barber, Dec. 18, 1794.
4-101	"	Lydia, and Elisha West, Nov. 23, 1794.
4-166	"	Nathan, of David, and Nancy Crandall; m. by Joseph Clarke, Justice, Dec. 23, 1794.
4-137	"	Maxson, of Nathan, dec., of Westerly, and Susannah Freeman, of Southold, L. I.; m. at Southold, by Elder Elisha Gillett, Nov. 19, 1795.
4-114	"	Elisha, of Nathan. and Betsey Potter, of George, dec.; m. by Elder John Burdick, Dec. 17, 1795.
4-118	"	Nancy, and Joseph Crandall, April 3, 1796.
4-111	"	Joshua, of Champlain, and Ruth Thompson, of William; m. by Elder Samuel Northup. Nov. 4, 1797.
4-123	"	Joseph C., of Westerly, and Lucretia Yeomans, of Daniel, of Stonington; m. by Elijah Palmer, Justice, June 6, 1798.
4-126	"	Stephen, of Champlain, of Westerly, and Sally Holly, of South Kingstown; m. by Samuel Bliven, Justice, Aug. 12, 1798.
4-140	"	Pally W., and Isaac Peckham, June 30, 1799.
4-153	"	Abigail, and Walt Clarke, Nov. 14, 1799.
4-158	"	Dorothy, and Dea. Oliver Dodge, March 26, 1800.
4-163	"	Susannah, and Ephraim Hiscox, Dec. 25, 1800.
4-176	"	Matthew, of Westerly, and Lucy Crumb, of Stonington; m. by Elijah Palmer, Justice, Oct. 22, 1801.
4-215	"	Simeon, and Susannah Stillman; m. by Elder Abram Coon, Jan. 26, 1804.

4-212 LANPHERE Mercy. and John Clarke, Nov. 29, 1804.
4-227 " Asa, and Susanna Saunders, of Stephen; m. by Elder Jesse Babcock, Jan. 15, 1807.
4-232 " Enock, and Susannah Berry; m. by John Cross, Justice, Jan. 29, 1807.
4-225 " Prentice, of Westerly, and Anna Merriott, of Hopkinton; m. at Hopkinton by Elder Matthew Stillman, March 13, 1807.
4-247 " Hezekiah, and Deborah Clarke; m. by Elder Abram Coon, Feb. 17, 1811.
4-248 " Clarke, and Wealthy Clarke; m. by Elder Jesse Babcock, March 1, 1812.
4-251 " Nancy, and George Crocker, Dec. 6, 1812.
4-252 " William, 2d, and Eliza Miner; m. by Elder Jesse Babcock, Dec. 23, 1812.
4-264 " Acors, of Westerly, and Wealthy Stillman, of Hopkinton; m. by Daniel Babcock, Justice C. C. Pleas, Nov. 30, 1815.
4-264 " Amelia, and Daniel Rathbone, March 7, 1816.
4-248 " Capt. Clarke, of David, and Keturah Barber, of Amos, of Hopkinton; m. by Elder Matthew Stillman, March 31, 1823.
5-4 " Abby, and Thomas Lewis, Nov. 20, 1825.
4-266 " Eunice, and Wells Gavitt, Dec. 30, 1826.
5-6 " Frank, of Westerly, and Waitey Lewis, of Hopkinton; m. at Hopkinton by Elder Amos P. Wells, Oct. 5, 1828.
4-252 " William, and Susan Burdick; m. at Hopkinton by Elder Christopher Chester, Jan. 24, 1835.
5-62 " Perry, and Sophia A. Slocum; m. by Rev. E. T. Hiscox, Sept. 1, 1844.
5-56 " Davis, and Nancy M. Barber; m. by Rev. Ralph P. Phinney, Sept. 9, 1844.
5-80 " Horace V., of Stonington. son of Daniel and Sybel G. Sharp, of Charles, of Westerly; m. by Rev. Isaac Moore, Oct. 9, 1847.
5-91 " Juliet, and Frank Maxson, Nov. 27, 1848.
2-106 LARKIN John, and Sarah Tucker; m. by Theodoty Rhodes, Justice, June 15, 1726.
2-92 " Mary, and Moses Barber. April 9, 1729.
2-95 " Roger, and Rebecca Tucker; m. by Theodoty Rhodes, Justice, March 19, 1730.
2-95 " John, and Mary Maccoon; m. by Theodoty Rhodes, Justice. July 24. 1730.
2-95 " Joseph, and Johannah York; m. by Theodoty Rhodes, Justice, July 24. 1730.
2-75 " Samuel, and Elizabeth Crandall; m. by John Hoxsie, Justice, Jan. 21. 1734-5.
2-75 " Rebecca, and David Lewis. Aug. 28, 1734.
3-31 " Sarah, and Ebenezer Lamb, April 27, 1753.
3-62 " Daniel, of John, and Susannah Rathbone; m. by Stephen Saunders, Justice, Feb. 27, 1758.
3-96 " Daniel, and Eunice Champlain; m. by Joseph Crandall, Justice, Aug. 29, 1764.
3-51 " Hannah, and Trustam Dodge, Oct. 28, 1764.
3-142 " Abel, of John, and Sarah Foster; m. by John Larkin, Justice, April 1, 1770.
4-24 " Sarah, and James Hall, Dec. 31, 1787.
4-39 " Lydia, and William Loomas, Aug. 22, 1790.
4-129 " Abel, Jr., of Westerly, and Hannah Larkin, of Hopkinton; m. by Elder Asa Coon, Jan. 25, 1797.
4-129 " Hannah, and Abel Larkin, Jr., Jan. 25, 1797.
4-160 " James, of Kenyon, of Charlestown, and Nancy Berry, of Samuel, of Westerly; m. by Samuel Bliven, Justice, Nov. 23, 1800.
4-217 " Jonathan, and Ann Rhodes, of James; m. by John Cross, Justice, Nov. 22, 1804.
4-204 " Sally, and Ephraim Gavitt, Feb. 17, 1805.
5-55 " Samuel S., of Westerly, and Mary A. Potter, of Richmond; m. by Rev. Alexander Campbell, Sept. 2, 1844.
5-71 " Susan E., and Joseph Ross, Sept. 22, 1845.

5-106 LARKIN David C., of Richmond, and Lucinda Burdick, of Charlestown; m. by Elder Henry Clarke, May 4, 1850.
2-1 LAWTON Mary, and Sanford Noyes, Nov. 24, 1738.
3-34 " Anna, and Jonathan Foster, Jr., Nov. 29, 1753.
3-44 " Jane, and David Lewis, June 11, 1755.
3-105 " Thomas, of Portsmonth and Amey Poole, of Westerly; m. by Rev. Joseph Park, May 20, 1766.
3-25 LEEDS Hannah, and Jesse Brown, Jan. —, 1752.
4-183 " Christopher, of Thomas, of Stonington, and Mary Helme, of Simeon, of Westerly; m. by Joseph Pendleton, Justice, March 23, 1800.
5-25 LEE Mary W., and Ezekeil Babcock, Feb. 13, 1842.
5-50 " Mary Esther, and Stiles Sherley, May 1, 1843.
5-54 " Henry, and Nancy Tefft; m. by Rev. Ralph Phinney, Sept. 1, 1844.
2-17 LESTER Elizabeth, and Trustum Billings, Sept. 10, 1740.
2-86 LEWIS Ann, and William Ross, April 18, 1711.
2-78 " John, of James, and Lucy Crandall; m. by Joseph Hall, Justice, March 3, 1717.
2-118 " John, Jr., and Mary Burdick, March 12, 1718.
2-113 " Israel, and Mary Mash; m. by Joseph Hall, Justice, March 27, 1718.
2-112 " Israel, and Bathsheba ——; m. by Christopher Champlain, Justice, June 30, 1720.
2-110 " John, and Anna Clarke, Nov. 24, 1720.
2-94 " Jane, of Israel, and Daniel Greenell, Jr., May 21, 1727.
2-96 " Mary, and Nathaniel Lewis, Nov. 13, 1729.
2-96 " Nathaniel, and Mary Lewis; m. by Theodoty Rhodes, Justice, Nov. 13, 1729.
2-87 " Joseph, and Mary Lewis; m. by Theodoty Rhodes, Justice, April 1, 1731.
2-87 " Mary, and Joseph Lewis, April 1, 1731.
2-42 " William, and Mary Gavitt; m. by John Saunders, Justice, Oct. 10, 1733.
2-80 " George, and Sarah Lewis; m. by John Hoxsie, Justice, Nov. 22, 1733.
2-80 " Sarah, and George Lewis, Nov. 22, 1733.
2-78 " Jerusha, and George Brown, Jr., April 4, 1734.
2-79 " Bathsheba, and William Bentley, Ang. 1, 1734.
2-75 " David, and Rebecca Larkin; m. by Samuel Wilbur, Justice, Ang. 28, 1735.
2-70 " Hannah, and William Crumb, April 25, 1736.
2-88 " Elizabeth, and John Crandall, June 28, 1738.
2-4 " Thankful, and John Lewis, Jan. 21, 1738-9.
2-4 " John, and Thankful Lewis; m. by Elder John Maxson, Jan. 21, 1738-9.
2-4 " John, and Margaret Burdick; m. by Elder John Maxson, May 3, 1739.
2-72 " Esther, and John Crandal, April 19, 1740.
2-14 " Elisha, and Lydia Justus; m. by Elder Joseph Maxson, Nov. 30, 1740.
2-42 " John (Fuller), and Ann Lankford; m. by Elder Joseph Maxson, June 8, 1741.
2-35 " Anna, and George Kenyon, June 16, 1741.
2-119 " Mary, and William Hern, Oct. 26, 1742.
2-77 " Avis, and Hubbard Burdick, Nov. 1, 1743.
2-58 " Martha, and John Maxson, Sept. 13, 1744.
2-83, 97 " Mary, and William Davis, April 24, 1745.
3-26 " Elisha, and Lydia Irish; m. by Elder Joseph Maxson, Oct. 30, 1740.
3-177 " Joseph, and Sarah Clarke; m. by Elder Joseph Maxson, June 16, 1743.
3-1 " Elisha, and Dorcas Cottrell; m. by William Hern, Justice, Oct. 25, 1744.
3-5 " John, Jr., and Prudence Mitchell; m. by Joshua Clarke, Justice, Sept. 20, 1746.

3-28 LEWIS Jonathan, and Tacy Maxson; m. by Joshua Clarke, Justice, Jan. 22, 1746-7.

3-16 " Stephen, and Martha Witter; m. by Nathaniel Lewis, Justice, Oct. 18, 1747.

3-20 " William, of North Kingstown, and Jerusha Lanphere, of Westerly; m. by William Hern, Justice, March 22, 1747-8.

3-22 " Elias, and Susannah Reynolds; m. by Benjamin Randall, Justice, Sept. 15, 1749.

3-25 " Keziah, and Charles Phillips, Nov. 3, 1749.

3-26 " Elisha, and Amey Greene, Jan. 10, 1751.

3-26 " Abel, and Thankful Maccoon; m. by Benjamin Randall, Justice, Aug. 2, 1751.

3-19 " Joseph, and Mary Bliven; m. by William Hern, Justice, Sept. 20, 1752.

3-38 " Wait, and Sarah Bliven; m. by William Hern, Justice, Oct. 2, 1754.

3-45 " Elizabeth, and Nathan Bliven, March 15, 1755.

3-44 " David, of Westerly, and Jane Lawton, of Newport; m. by William Hern, Justice, June 11, 1755.

3-47 " Hannah, and Peleg Ross, Dec. 10, 1755.

3-54 " Joshua, and Elizabeth Enos; m. by Stephen Saunders, Justice, Feb. 23, 1757.

3-57 " Zebulon, and Lydia Enos; m. by Joseph Crandall, Justice, Feb. 12, 1758.

3-63 " Esther, and Ezekiel Saunders, Dec. 14, 1758.

3-67 " Anna, and Nahor Lanphere, Jan. 24, 1760.

3-177 " Joseph, of Westerly, and Mary Clarke, of Stonington; m. by Elder Nathaniel Eells, May 14, 1761.

3-89 " Samuel, and Barbara Lanphere; m. by Joseph Clarke, Jr., Justice, Oct. 15, 1761.

3-79 " Sarah, and Isaiah Wilcox, Oct. 15, 1761.

3-103 " Penelope, and Elder Joseph Davis, May 14, 1763.

3-104 " Elijah, of Hopkinton, and Prudence Babcock, of Westerly; m. by Rev. Joseph Park, Nov. 10, 1765.

3-105 " Maxson, of Hopkinton, and Dorcas Rathbone, of Westerly; m. by Rev. Joseph Park, Dec. 22, 1765.

4-157 " Capt. Oliver, of Joseph, dec., and Ruhamah Lewis, of Capt. John; m. by Elder Stephen Babcock, Feb. 10, 1766.

4-157 " Ruhamah, and Capt. Oliver Lewis, Feb. 10, 1766.

3-135 " Hezekiah, of Westerly, and Anna Maine, of Stonington; m. at Stonington, by Elder Simeon Brown, March 16, 1766.

4-92 " Mrs. Mary, and John Tefft, Nov. 24, 1773.

3-169 " John, of John, dec., and Amey Wilcox, of David, dec.; m. by Elder Isaiah Wilcox, March 16, 1775.

3-143 " Elizabeth, and Elias Millard, April 16, 1777.

3-164 " Nancy, and Nathan Babcock, Aug. 26, 1779.

3-170 " Content, and David Wilcox, Jan. 1, 1780.

3-165 " Simeon, of Capt. John, of Westerly, and Anne Cross, of Peleg, of Charlestown; m. by Joseph Crandall, Justice, Jan. 13, 1780.

4-157 " Capt. Oliver, of Joseph, dec., and Elizabeth Vincent, of Nicholas, dec.; m. by Elder Oliver Babcock, Aug. 2, 1781.

4-38 " William, of John, and Hannah Thompson, of Samuel, dec.; m. by Elder Isaiah Wilcox, Dec. 22, 1781.

4-6 " Betsey, and Thomas Ross, March 28, 1784.

4-231 " Mary, and Stephen Gavitt, Jr., Oct. —, 1785.

4-20 " Joseph, of Joseph, dec., and Rachel Hall, of Theodoty, dec.; m. by Simeon Burdick, Justice, Dec. 27, 1786.

4-68 " Martha, and Jared Babcock, Oct. 25, 1789.

4-32 " Nancy, and Nathan Wilcox, Feb. 17, 1790.

4-80 " Matthew, of Eleazor, of Voluntown, Conn., and Hannah Saunders, of Hezekiah, of Westerly; m. by Elder Isaiah Wilcox, Feb. 12, 1792.

4-81 " Dorcas, and Lyman Ross, Aug. 29, 1793.

4-94   LEWIS Prentice, and Polly Thompson; m. by Joseph Clarke, Justice, Dec. 7. 1794.

4-106   "   Simeon, and Lydia Sheffield; m. by Samuel Brown, Justice, Dec. 20, 1795.

4-216   "   Elias, of Westerly, and Priscilla Lewis, of Stonington; m. at Stonington by Valentine W. Rathbone, V. D. M., Dec. 22, 1796.

4-216   "   Priscilla, and Elias Lewis, Dec. 22, 1796.

4-102   "   Dorcas, and William Sweet, Peckham, Apr'l 30, 1797.

4-196   "   Jabez, 3d, of Hezekiah, of Westerly, and Lois Lewis, of William, of Stonington; m. by Rev. Hezekiah Woodruff about 1797.

4-196   "   Lois, and Jabez Lewis, about 1797.

4-175   "   Jabez, of Westerly, and Betsey Couzen, of Groton, Conn.; m. by Joseph Allen, Justice, Nov. 24, 1801.

4-179   "   Abigail, and Benjamin Ross, Jan. 7, 1802.

4-187   "   Frances, and Simeon Lewis, March 27, 1803.

4-187   "   Simeon, of Westerly, and Frances Lewis, of Hopkinton; m. by Elder Abram Coon, March 27, 1803.

4-225   "   Maxson, of Westerly, and Polly Maine, of Stonington; m. by Elder David Lillibridge, Oct. 21, 1805.

4-267   "   Lois, and Jared Barber, Jr., March 6, 1817.

5-4   "   Thomas, of Henry, and Abby Lanphere, of Perry; m. by Elder Matthew Stillman, Nov. 20, 1825.

5-6   "   Waitey, and Frank Lanphere, Oct. 5, 1828.

5-29   "   Alfred, and Lucy P. Langworthy; m. by Elder Daniel Coon, Sept. 28, 1840.

5-41   "   Whitman T., and Mary Ann Denison: m. by George D. Cross, Justice. July 18, 1841.

2-105   LILLIBRIDGE Thomas, and Mary Woodmansee; m. by Theodoty Rhodes, Justice, June 12, 1726.

5-57   "   Wanton, of Richmond, and Sarah Ann Champlain, of Westerly; m. by Rev. Weeden Barber, Jr., Nov. 7, 1841.

5-97   LIPPITT Waite Harris, and Frederic Lee Allen, June 4, 1849.

5-50   LOCK Eliza Ann, and Alfred B. Corey, April 9, 1843.

2-105   LOMBARD Daniel. of Newport, and Deborah Dyre, of Westerly; m. by Elder Joseph Clarke, Sept. 24, 1747.

4-39   LOOMAS William, of William, of Ashton, Lancashire, Great Britain, and Lydia Larkin, of Daniel (dec.); m. by Joseph Crandall, Justice, Aug. 22, 1790.

3-26   LONG Mary, and Eber Crandall, Feb. 10, 1732.

3-92   LOTHROP Andrew, of Norwich, Conn., and Abigail Fish, of Groton; published Sept. 6, 1763, by Rev. Benjamin Throop, at New Concord, Norwich; m. at Westerly, by Stephen Lanphere, Justice, Sept. 14, 1763.

2-76   LOVELESS Mary, and Richard Bennett, Jan. 12, 1726.

2-4   "   Joseph, and Elizabeth Tems; m. by Elder John Maxson, Jan. 20, 1728.

2-81   "   Ann, and Solomon Partelon, April 21, 1731.

4-180   LOVITT Keturah, and Joseph Babcock, April 12, 1801.

M

3-52   MACEATER Anne, and Elder John Maxson. Oct. 31, 1756.

2-121   MACCOON Isabel, and Edward Bliven, Oct. 2, 1691.

2-95   "   Abigail, and Benjamin Brown, April 6, 1730.

2-95   "   Mary, and John Larkin, July 24, 1730.

3-51   "   Nathan, and Anna Hall; m. by Elder Joseph Maxson, Dec. 23, 1743.

3-22   "   Lois, and Caleb Wells, Jan. 18, 1748-9.

3-26   "   Thankful, and Abel Lewis, Aug. —, 1751.

3-54   "   Anna, and Samuel West, March 17, 1757.

3-42   MACKEE Bathsheba, and Joseph Hiscox. Dec. 30, 1754.

3-112   "   Bathsheba. and Ichabod Burdick, Feb. 6, 1764.

3-38	MACKINTOSK Andrew, of Stonington, and Bridget Perry, of Westerly; m. by Silas Greenman, Justice, May 29, 1754.
3-88	MACOMBER Jonathan, of Charlestown, and Sarah Varse, of Westerly; m. by Stephen Saunders, Justice, Sept. 8, 1765.
3-77	MALLERSON Joseph, Jr., of Groton, and Sarah Stewart, of Stonington; m. by Joseph Clarke, Justice, Aug. 18, 1761.
3-43	MAINE Jonas, and Patience Peckham, both of Stonington; m. by Benoni Smith, Justice, June 3, 1756.
3-59	" Jeremiah, of Stonington, and Bathsheba Vose; m. by William Hern, Justice, Feb. 22, 1758.
3-135	" Anna, and Hezekiah Lewis, March 16, 1766.
3-131	" Elizabeth, and Isaac Peckham, July 18, 1773.
4-225	" Polly, and Maxson Lewis, Oct. 21, 1805.
5-58	" Elias R., of Ledyard, Conn., and Abby Chapman, of Westerly; m. by Elder Weeden Barber, Jr., May 31, 1843.
2-113	MASH Mary, and Israel Lewis, March 27, 1718.
3-45.	MASON Zerviah, and Thomas Holmes, Feb. 5, 1755.
2-78	MAXSON John, and Judeth Clarke, Jan. 19, 1687.
1-57	" Dorothy, and Joseph Clarke, Jr., Jan. 5, 1692.
2-116	" Jonathan, and Content Rogers, May 1, 1707.
2-106	" Elizabeth, and John Davis, Aug. 25, 1715.
2-125	" John, Jr., and Thankful Randall, Sept. 26, 1724.
2-87	" Content, and James Babcock, July 7, 1731.
2-87	" Avis, and Samuel Hubbard Burdick, Nov. 5, 1731.
2-77	" Elizabeth, and Jonathan Wells, Nov. 29, 1734.
2-73	" Jonathan, and Jemima Mumford; m. by Elder John Maxson, Jan. 6, 1735.
2-47	" John, of Westerly, and Lucy Rogers, of New London; m. by Elder Stephen Gorton, Oct. 27, 1736.
2-69	" Bethiah, and Thomas Davis, Jan. 5, 1737.
2-119	" Content, and Richard Dake, Dec. 4, 1739.
2-10	" Judeth, and James Davis, Jan. 10, 1740.
2-111	" Joshua, and Anna Slack; m. by Elder Joseph Maxson, Sept. 20, 1742.
3-3	" Samuel, of Westerly, and Ruth Rogers, of New London; m. by Rev. Eliphalet Adams, Oct. 13, 1742.
2-79	" Goodeth, and Nathan Burdick. Oct. 14, 1743.
2-79	" William, and Hannah Reynolds; m. by Elder John Maxson, Oct. 14, 1743.
2-77	" Nathan, and Anna Hall; m. by Elder Joseph Maxson, Dec. 23, 1743.
2-58	" John, and Martha Lewis; m. by John Lewis, Justice, Sept. 13, 1744.
3-28	" Lucy, and Jonathan Lewis, Jan. 22, 1746-7.
3-20	" Matthew, and Lucy Wilbur; m. by William Hern, Justice, May 2, 1748.
2-222	" Mary, and Joshua Chase, May 12, 1748.
3-22	" Judeth, and Matthew Greene, Dec. 1, 1748-9.
3-21	" Matthew, and Martha Potter; m. by Benjamin Randall, Justice, Dec. 21, 1748-9.
3-22	" Isaiah, and Judith Reynolds; m. by Benjamin Randall, Justice, Oct. 19, 1749.
3-102	" Jesse, and Keturah Randall; m. by Rev. John Lyons, Sept. 11, 1753.
3-32	" Tory, and Martha Lanphere; m. by Benjamin Randall, Justice, Oct. 18, 1753.
3-41	" Content, and George Potter, Sept. 18, 1754.
3-52	" Elder John, of Newport, and Anne Maccarter, widow, of Westerly; m. by Elder Thomas Clarke, Oct. 31, 1756.
3-80	" Daniel, and Barredel Ross; m. by Joseph Clarke, Jr., Justice, March 31, 1762.
3-122	" Silas, of David, and Sarah Clarke, of Joseph; m. by Elder Joshua Clarke, March 20, 1771.
3-123	" Eleanor, and William Bliven, Oct. 31, 1771.
3-148	" Thomas, and Hannah Sisson; m. by Elder Joseph Clarke, Dec. 17, 1772.

3-156 MAXSON Elizabeth, and Joseph Stillman, Jan. 27, 1773.
3-181   "   Asa, of David, and Lois Stillman, of Joseph; m. by Joseph Clarke, Justice, Dec. 6, 1775.
4-99   "   Keturah, and George Clarke, Jan. 29, 1778.
4-90   "   Paul, and Susannah Stillman; m. by Joseph Clarke, Justice, Dec. 22, 1779.
4-133   "   Catherine, and Clarke Edwards, April 6, 1780.
3-170   "   Mrs. Anna, and Hon. Joshua Babcock, May 28, 1780.
4-4   "   Augustus, of Joseph and Thankful Ross, of John; m. by Elder Isaiah Wilcox, June 5, 1783.
4-7   "   Hannah, and Joseph Varse, July 18, 1784.
4-31   "   Amos, and Hannah Potter; m. by Joseph Clarke, Justice, Jan 3, 1789.
4-49   "   Anna, and John Babcock, Jan. 10, 1790.
4-32   "   Prudence, and Benjamin Stillman, Feb. 11, 1790.
4-31   "   Joshua, and Mrs. Thankful Stillman; m. by Elder John Burdick, March 4, 1790.
4-156   "   Sylvanus, of Hopkinton, and Betsey Langworthy, of Stonington; m. at Stonington by Elder Joshua Babcock, Justice, Sept. 24, 1797.
4-208   "   Elizabeth Ward, and Joseph Stillman, Dec. 23, 1804.
5-24   "   Jesse, Jr., and Sophia Clarke; m. by Elder Abram Coon (also 4-85), March 20, 1803.
4-239   "   Silas, and Betsey Stillman; m. by Elder Abram Coon, Oct. 13, 1808.
4-91   "   Barbara, and John Barber, Dec. 9, 1810.
5-36   "   William E., and Elizabeth M. Smith; m. by Elder Daniel Coon, Dec. 2, 1839.
5-91   "   Frank, of Asa, and Juliet Lanphere, of William; m. by Rev. Fred Denison, Nov. 27, 1848.
3-115 McDOWELL Joanna, and Major James Babcock, Aug. 27, 1769.
3-116 McDONNELL Angus, and Mary Chase, of Capt. Oliver; m. by Joseph Crandall, Justice, Nov. 22, 1769.
2-83 MEEKCOME Rachel, and James Hall, Jr., April 17, 1721.
2-75   "   Joseph, and Jemima Ross; m. by John Richmond, Justice, Jan. 9, 1734.
2-87   "   William, and Patience Allen; m. by Theodoty Rhodes, Justice, April 2, 1738.
2-57   "   Nathan, and Anna Hall; m. by Elder Joseph Maxson, Dec. 23, 1743.
4-166 MERRIOTT Polly, and Maxson Chase, Dec. 10, 1803.
4-260   "   Hannah, and Benjamin P. Barber, March 13, 1806.
4-225   "   Anna, and Prentice Lanphere, March 13, 1807.
4-268   "   Lucy, and Pardon Thompson, Dec. 10, 1816.
3-2 MILLARD John, of Charlestown, and Sarah Enos, of Westerly; m. by Joseph Crandall, Justice, April 21, 1751.
3-2   "   John, of Charlestown, and Katharine Clarke, of Westerly; m. by John Larkin, Justice, Oct. 1, 1752.
3-37   "   Nelson, of Charlestown, and Isabel Brand, of Westerly; m. by Joseph Crandall, Justice, March 31, 1754.
3-143   "   Elias, of Holmes, and Elizabeth Lewis, of Joshua; m. by Elder Thomas Ross, April 16, 1777.
4-29   "   Phelia, of Stephentown, N. Y., and Freegift Hall, of Westerly; m. by Joseph Crandall, Justice, Dec. 17, 1789.
1-58 MINOR Deborah, and Joseph Pendleton, July 8, 1696.
4-69   "   Polly, and Caleb Davis, Oct. 21, 1792.
4-190   "   Hannah, and Perry Barber, March 30, 1794.
4-252   "   Eliza, and William Lanphere, 2d, Dec. 23, 1812.
3-14 MITCHELL Sarah, and Stephen Clarke, Dec. 29, 1745.
3-5   "   Prudence, and John Lewis, Jr., Sept. 20, 1746.
3-80   "   Mary, and Godando, Jan. 28, 1762.
3-59   "   Elizabeth, and Samuel Tefft, July 26, 1767.
4-176   "   Betsey, and Jonathan Nash, Jr., Jan. 7, 1793.
3-102 MOON John, of Exeter, son of Robert, and Elizabeth Brown, of Jonathan. dec., of Westerly; m. by Simeon Burdick, Justice, Oct. 17. 1768.

2-119 MORRIS Catharine, and Samuel Allen, Aug. 20, 1707.
2-111 MOTT Phebe, and Cyrus Richmond, March 27, 1734.
2-86 " Sarah, and William Thorn, July 16, 1738.
2-77 " Jonathan, and Johannah Page; m. by Stephen Richmond, Justice, Oct. 11, 1740.
2-14 MULKINS Henry, and Abigail Babcock; m. by Elder John Maxson, Nov. 4, 1740.
4-19 " Abigail, and Jesse Babcock, March 8, 1763.
2-73 MUMFORD Jemima, and Jonathan Maxson, Jan 6, 1735.
3-12 MUNRO Abigail, and John Langworthy, May 27, 1742.
2-166 " Sarah, and Job Taylor, Nov. 18, 1742.
5-69 MUSGRAVE Eleanor, and Allen Stevenson, July 18, 1847.

N

4-176 NASH Jonathan, Jr., of Jonathan, of Westerly, and Betsey Mitchell, of George, of Groton, Conn.; m. by Elder Isaiah Wilcox, Jan. 7, 1793.
4-132 " Asa, of Jonathan, and Anna Ross, Feb. 4, 1799.
4-151 " Isaac, of Jonathan, and Amey Hall, of Thomas; m. by Samuel Bliven, Justice, Jan. 30, 1800.
5-171 " Nathan, of Jonathan, and Barbara Hall, of Joshua; m. by Joseph Pendleton, Justice, Oct. 11, 1801.
2-76 NETT Thomas, and Mary Corey; m. by John Babcock, Justice, Dec. 25, 1734.
5-94 NEWBERRY Jeremy, and Prudence Satterly; m. by Stephen Lanphere, Justice, Jan. 4, 1764.
2-1 NEWBURY John, and Zeriah Burch; m. by Elder John Maxson, Nov. 26, 1739.
5-63 " Adeline, and Jonathan Tubbs, July 4, 1844.
5-102 " Maria, and Elisha Kenyon Rathbone, Nov. 19, 1849.
5-21 NEY Samuel Russell, of Samuel, dec., and Eliza Chase, of Westerly, dau. of Maxson; m. by Benajah Gavitt, Justice, May 1, 1836.
3-10 NILES Mary, and Nathaniel Cottrell, March 3, 1744-5.
3-1 " Sands, of Stonington, and Elizabeth Cottrell, of Westerly; m. by William Hern, Justice, Sept. 4, 1745.
3-43 " Stephen, of Stonington, and Desire Pendleton, of Westerly; m. by Benoni Smith, Justice, Jan. 9, 1755.
3-54 " Tabitha, and Nathan Davis, March 3, 1757.
4-124 NOOGEN Elisha, and Prudence Thompson, of William; m. by Samuel Bliven, Justice, June 6, 1798.
2-87 NOYES Thomas, and Mary Thompson; m. by Theodoty Rhodes, Justice, May 1, 1731.
2-1 " Sanford, and Mary Lawton; m. by John Maxson, Nov. 24, 1738.
3-144 " Joseph, and Barbara Wells; m. by William Hern, Justice, (also 3-10), July 31, 1754.
3-174 " Thomas, of Col. Joseph, of Westerly, and Lydia Rogers, late of Newport; m. by Elder Joshua Clarke, (also 4-141), Jan. 31, 1781.
4-64 " William, and Polly Allen, of Samuel; m. by Samuel Bliven, Justice, April 21, 1792.
4-139 " Joseph, Jr., and Elizabeth Babcock; m. by Elder William Gardiner, Jan. 13, 1799.
4-138 " Polly, and Thomas Noyes, April 14, 1799.
4-138 " Thomas, of Stonington, and Polly Noyes, of Westerly; m. by Elder William Gardiner, April 14, 1799.
4-155 " Sanford, of Westerly, and Martha Babcock, of Hopkinton; m. by Elder Abram Coon, Feb. 2, 1800.
4-266 " John, of Westerly, and Hannah Case, of Falmouth; m. by Elder Jesse Babcock, Dec. 24, 1809.
4-245 " Barker, of Col. Joseph, dec., and Margaret Champlain, of William, dec.; m. by Elder Matthew Stillman, March 18, 1810.

4-270   NOYES Grace, and Joshua Noyes, May 6, 1810.
4-270   "   Joshua, of Westerly, and Grace Noyes, of Stonington; m. by Rev. Ira Hart, May 6, 1810.
5-10   "   Sanford, Jr., and Eunice Witter, both of Hopkinton; m. by Elder Amos P. Wells, Dec. 19, 1845.
3-89   NUTTER Abigail, and Samuel Turner, Nov. 26, 1761.
4-173   NYE Samuel, of Stephen, of Charlestown, and Sally Saunders, of Joseph, of Westerly; m. by Samuel Bliven, Justice, Dec. 27, 1801.

O

5-84   OTIS Julia A., and George S. Barber, Jan. 28, 1848.
3-89   OWEN Robert, and Mary Cottrell, both of Stonington; m. by Joseph Clarke, Jr., Justice, June 3, 1762.

P

2-77   PAGE Johannah, and Jonathan Mott, Oct. 11, 1740.
2-128   PALMER Elihu, and Deborah Reynolds; m. by Theodoty Rhodes, Justice, Jan. 19, 1726-7.
4-128   "   Mary, and Simeon Pendleton, Jan. 15, 1760.
4-115   "   Phebe, and Lyman Hall, Nov. 27, 1796.
4-197   "   Cynthia, and Samuel Taylor, 2d, Aug. 25, 1799.
4-153   "   Luther, of Sanford, of Stonington, and Sally Kenyon, of Joshua, of Westerly; m. by Joseph Pendleton, Justice, Dec. 12, 1799.
2-47   PALMITTER John, and Mary Burch; m. by Peter Crandall, Justice, Nov. 22, 1712.
2-123   "   Mary (widow), and Nathaniel Bundy, April 26, 1724.
2-76   "   Thankful, and Jeremiah Lake, April 1, 1737.
2-84   "   Freelove, and David Tefft, Nov. 26, 1737.
2-45   "   Joshua, and Hannah Tucker; m. by William Hern, Justice, Jan. 19, 1738-9.
2-72   "   Daniel, and Elizabeth Palmitter; m. by Elder John Maxson, July 10, 1739.
2-72   "   Elizabeth, and Daniel Palmitter, July 10, 1739.
3-1   "   Jonathan, and Phebe Cross; m. by William Hern, Justice, Sept. 24, 1744.
3-1   "   Elizabeth, and Daniel Button, Sept. 24, 1744.
3-32   "   John, of Westerly, and Deborah Button, of Stonington; m. by Rev. Joseph Fish, Nov. 9, 1752.
3-40   "   Penelope, and Benjamin Hall, Sept. 14, 1754.
3-59   "   Jonathan, and Sarah Wilcox; m. by William Hern, Justice, Jan. 25, 1758.
3-37   PARKER Hannah, and Hezekiah Wilcox, March 31, 1754.
4-169   "   Sarah, and David Saunders, Dec. 16, 1790.
5-64   PARKINSON William E., and Eliza A. Peckham; m. by Rev. E. T. Hiscox, Jan. 5, 1845.
3-62   PARK Ann, and Peleg Pendleton, (also 3-146), Sept. 7, 1758.
2-81   PARTELOW Solomon, and Ann Loveless; m. by John Richmond, Justice, April 21, 1731.
4-8   "   Thomas, of Stonington, and Elizabeth Tefft, of Westerly; m. by Joshua Vose, Justice, April 29, 1784.
3-31   PEARCE Abigail, and John Babcock, March 18, 1753.
4-166   "   Nancy, and William Lewis Ross, Feb. 24, 1801.
2-112   PECKHAM Daniel, and Mary Ross; m. by Joseph Stanton, Justice, Feb. 11, 1719-20.
3-14   "   John, of Isaac, and Deborah Sweet, both of Newport; m. by Daniel Gould, Justice, Dec. 25, 1735.
3-2   "   Isaac, and Mary York; m. by Joseph Crandall, Justice, April 11, 1750.
3-34   "   Abel, of Charlestown, and Rebecca Burdick, of Westerly; m. by Joseph Crandall, Justice, Feb. 24, 1754.

3-41   PECKHAM Timothy, of Stonington, and Mary Barber, of Westerly; **m. by** Benoni Smith, Justice, Sept. 19, 1754.

3-43   "   Patience, and James Maine, June 3, 1756.

3-52   "   Timothy, and Content Drake; m. by Elder Thomas Clarke, June 24, 1756.

3-60   "   Isaac, Jr., of Westerly, and Dorcas Sweet, of West Greenwich; m. by Samuel Hopkins, Justice, Oct. 25, 1757.

3-65   "   Dorcas, and Hezekiah Hall, Oct. 11, 1759.

3-95   "   Anne, and William York, Nov. 15, 1764.

3-82   "   Ruth, and William Clarke, Nov. 24, 1765.

3-105   "   Ann, and Ephraim Babcock, Aug. 10, 1766.

3-135   "   Jane, and David Clarke, June 8, 1772.

3-129   "   William Sweet, of John, of Westerly, and Hannah Clarke, of Joseph, of Charlestown; m. by Joseph Crandall, Justice (also 4-102), Jan. 6, 1773.

3-131   "   Isaac, of Westerly, and Elizabeth Maine, of Stonington; m. at Stonington, by Elder Eleazer Brown, July 18, 1773.

3-140   "   Stephen, of Isaac, and Esther Hall, of Charles; **m. by Joseph** Crandall, Justice, Feb. 26, 1775.

3-142   "   Mary, and Theodoty' Hall, Jr., Jan. 3, 1776.

3-151   "   Isaac, Jr., of Isaac, and Anne Clarke, of Joseph; m. by Joseph Crandall, Justice, Sept. 28, 1777.

3-153   "   Joseph, and Ann Burdick, of David; m. by Thomas Wells, Justice, Jan. 21, 1778.

3-160   "   Hannah, and Edmund Hewitt, March 7, 1779.

3-171   "   Anna, and James York Peckham, Nov. 23, 1780.

3-171   "   James York, of Isaac, and Anna Peckham, widow; m. by Joseph Crandall, Justice, Nov.' 23, 1780.

3-181   "   Patience York, and Perry Clarke, Dec. 1, 1782.

4-16   "   Rebecca, and Edward Vars, Dec. 22, 1785.

4-14   "   Benjamin, of Isaac, and Mary Hall, of Isaac; **m. by** Joseph Crandall, Justice, June 11, 1785.

4-23   "   Peleg, of Abel, and Betsey Stetson, of Stephen, dec.; m. by Joseph Crandall, Justice, Oct. 25, 1787.

4-72   "   Amey, and Thomas Hull, Aug. 27, 1791.

4-102   "   William Sweet, and Dorcas Lewis; m. by Elder Elkanah Babcock, April 30, 1797.

4-172   "   Ruth, and Joel Crandall, May 14, 1797.

4-140   "   Isaac, of Isaac, dec., of Westerly, and Polly W. Lanphere, of Samuel L., dec., of Stonington; m. by Samuel Bliven, Justice, June 30, 1799.

4-156   "   Susanna, and Joseph Huntley, June 15, 1800.

4-190   "   Deborah, and John Rider, Dec. 21, 1800.

4-272   "   Anna, and Thomas Chapman, Dec. 26, 1819.

5-34   "   Maria Louisa, and Avery Nelson Brown, July 14, 1839.

5-39   "   Abby, and Samuel Sweet, April 4, 1841.

5-41   "   Pardon S., and Hannah E. Gorton; m. by Jedediah W. Knight, Justice, May 25, 1841.

5-64   "   Eliza A., and William E. Parkinson, Jan. 5, 1845.

5-73   "   Hannah Amelia, and Thomas H. Sherman, Feb. 23, 1847.

5-89   "   John D., of John, and Eliza A. Thompson, of William; m. by Rev. John Taylor, Oct. 9, 1848.

5-94   "   John S., of Joseph, of Preston, Conn., and Emeline E. Crandall, of Benjamin, of Westerly; **m. by** Rev. Isaac Moore, Feb. 11, 1849.

5-99   "   Amanda F., and Franklin Purdy, Aug. 16, 1849.

5-106   "   Avery P., of John, and Abby C Gavitt, of Isaac W.; m. by Rev. Fred Denison, March 2, 1850.

5-60   PEIRCE Dr. John G., and Sarah A. Babcock; m. by Rev. Alexander H. Vinton, June 1, 1840.

5-65   "   Aaron, and Emily Brown; m. by' Rev. Oliver P. Tuckerman, April 14, 1845.

5-67   "   Edward, of North Kingstown, and Frances M. Clarke, of Westerly; m. by Rev. Oliver P. Tuckerman, Jan. 26, 1846.

1-58   PENDLETON Joseph, and Deborah Minor, of Ephraim, of Stonington; m. by Rev. James Noyes, July 8, 1696.

1-58   "   Joseph, of Westerly, and Patience Potts, of William, of New London: m. by Nehemiah Smith, Justice, Dec. 11, 1700.

2-124 "   James, of Caleb, and Elizabeth Lanphere, of George, Jan. 12. 1709-10.

2-72   "   James, and Elizabeth Brown, of Thomas, of Stonington, Jan. 6, 1717-8.

2-112 "   Caleb, and Mary Randall, Oct. 25, 1716.

2-112 "   Ann, and Samuel Babcock, May 15, 1723.

2-85   "   Joseph, and Sarah Worden; m. at Newport, by Rev. James Honeyman, Jan. 9, 1723.

2-109 "   William, of Westerly, and Lydia Burrough, of Groton: m. at Stonington, by Rev. Ebenezer Rossiter, March 10, 1725-6.

3-65   "   William, of Westerly, and Mrs. Lydia Barrons, of Groton; m. by Rev. Ebenezer Rossiter, March 10, 1725-6.

2-91   "   Bryant, of Westerly, and Anna Wilcox, of Stonington; m. at Stonington, by Daniel Palmer, Justice, March 11, 1725.

2-105 "   Ruth, and Renoni Smith. Dec. 28, 1726.

2-94   "   James, of James, of Westerly. and Abigail Brown, of Stonington; m. by Theodoty Rhodes. Justice, March 22, 1731-2.

2-71   "   Obadiah, and Rachel Hadfull; m. by Elder John Maxson, June 4, 1736.

2-83   "   Rebecca, and Oliver Stewart, Aug. 21, 1741.

2-113 "   Lois, and Benajah Gavitt. Sept. 7, 1746.

3-50   "   Reed, and John Saunders, Oct. 31, 1728.

3-32   "   Edmund, and Susannah King; m. at Stonington by Rev. Ebenezer Rossiter, April 9, 1738.

3-1   "   Samuel, and Phebe Hall; m. by William Hern, Justice, Feb. 13, 1744-5.

3-20   "   Thankful, and Christopher Coats, May 2, 1748.

3-65   "   Col. William, of Westerly, and Mrs. Mary Cheeseborough, of Stonington; m. by Rev. Nathaniel Eells, April 25, 1751.

3-5   "   Sylvester, and Sarah Champlain; m. by William Hern, Justice, Jan. 16, 1751.

3-6   "   Freelove, and Grace Sheffield, Aug. 1, 1751.

3-9   "   Sarah, and William Champlain, Jr. (also 4-127), Dec. 4 or 8, 1751.

3-43   "   Desire, and Stephen Niles, Jan. 9, 1755.

3-58   "   Lucy, and James Cheesebo ough, Feb. 10, 1758.

3-62   "   Peleg, of Westerly, and Anna Park, af Charlestown; m. by Rev. Joseph Park (also 3-146), Sept. 7, 1758.

4-128 "   Simeon, of Col. Joseph, of Westerly, and Mary Palmer, of Walter, of Stonington; m. at Stonington by Rev. Nathaniel Eells, Jan. 15, 1760.

3-86   "   Ruth, and Elisha Brown, Dec. 30, 1762.

3-87   "   Wealthian, and Thomas Sheffield, Jan. 12, 1763.

3-94   "   Benjamin, and Lois Burdick; m. by Rev. Joseph Park, Feb. 9, 1763.

3-148 "   Hannah, and David Wilbur, April 27, 1765.

3-104 "   John, and Sebra Thompson; m. by Rev. Joseph Park, Sept. 22, 1765.

3-101 "   Joseph, and Damarias Crandall; m. by Joseph Crandall, Justice, Jan. 19, 1766.

3-102 "   Mary, and Ezekiel Crandall, May 22, 1766.

3-109 "   Ephraim, and Sarah Thompson; m. by Eld. Joseph Park (also 4-148), Dec. 17, 1767.

3-109 "   Joshua, and Nancy Clarke; m. by Elder Joseph Park, Jan. 6, 1768.

4-88   "   Deborah, and Samuel Sims, Oct. 20, 1770.

3-137 "   Esther, and Peter Eldredge, Nov. 20, 1774.

3-141 "   Nathan, of Col. William. and Amelia Babcock, of Col. James; m. by Rev. Joseph Park, Jan. 22, 1775.

4-70   "   Joseph, and Nancy Crandall; m. by Joseph Clarke, Justice, March 23, 1777.

4-59   "   Harriet, and Simeon Crumb, May 25, 1783.

3-181 "   Nancy, and Timothy Chapman, March 14, 1782.

4-10 PENDLETON Anne, and Jesse Wilcox, Dec. 9, 1784.
4-13   "   Lois, and Alexander Bradford, July 14, 1785.
4-30   "   Eunice, and Capt. Lyman Hall, (also 4-85), Jan. 27, 1787.
4-22   "   Mary, and Enoch Crandall, Sept. 18, 1787.
4-33   "   Polly, and Isaiah Wilcox, Jan. 22, 1788.
4-43   "   Keturah, and Sylvester Gavitt, March 16, 1788.
4-75   "   John, and Susannah Colegrove; m. by Elder Isaiah Wilcox, Dec. 11, 1791.
4-66   "   David, of Benjamin, and Sally Pendleton, of Simeon; m. by Elder Isaiah Wilcox, Feb. 13, 1792.
4-66   "   Sally, and David Pendleton, Feb. 13, 1792.
4-75   "   George, and Deborah Babcock; m. by Elder Isaiah Wilcox, Oct. 25, 1792.
4-147   "   Joseph, Jr., of Major Joseph, of Westerly, and Hannah Stanton, of Job, of Stonington; m. by Elder Whitman Rathbone, Feb. 28, 1793.
4-88   "   Anna, and Samuel Sims, Feb. 8, 1794.
4-117   "   Paul, and Sabra Pendleton; m. by Elder William Gardiner, Nov. 20, 1796.
4-117   "   Sabra, and Paul Pendleton, Nov. 20, 1796.
4-125   "   Eunice, and Oliver Rhodes, Dec. 14, 1796.
4-118   "   Joshua, of Norwich, Conn., and Milly Pendleton, of Westerly; m. by Samuel Brown, Justice, Jan. 19, 1797.
4-118   "   Milly, and Joshua Pendleton, Jan. 19, 1797.
4-129   "   Grace, and Foxton Berry, Feb. 25, 1798.
4-146   "   Abel, of Major Joseph, of Westerly, and Abigail Stanton, of Job, of Stonington; m. by Elder Whitman Rathbone, Sept. 30, 1799.
4-167   "   Christopher Segar, and Bridget Thompson, of Joshua; m. by Joseph Pendleton, Justice, Feb. 15, 1801.
4-163   "   Polly, and Case Chapman, Feb. 15, 1801.
4-205   "   Oates, of Amos, and Betsey Kenyon, of Joshua; m. by Joseph Pendleton, Justice, Dec. 6, 1801.
4-180   "   Susannah, and Thomas Burch, Jan. 31, 1802.
4-166   "   Fannie, and Joshua Thompson, Feb. 12, 1804.
4-219   "   Lucy, and Abial Sherman, Dec. 1, 1805.
4-220   "   Charles Lee, of John, and Nably Taylor, of Jude; m. by Joseph Pendleton, Justice, July 13, 1806.
4-223   "   Dorcas, and Perry Brambley, March 4, 1807.
4-254   "   Betsey, and Russell Cottrell, Jan. 31, 1810.
4-248   "   William, and Anna Taylor, both of Westerly; m. at North Stonington by Stephen Avery, Justice, Feb. 26, 1812.
4-265   "   Capt. Nathan, of Norwich, Chenango Co., N. Y., and Rhoda Gavitt, of Westerly; m. by Elder Jesse Babcock, Oct. 20, 1816.
4-273   "   Fanny, and Hosea Barber, Oct. 4, 1821.
5-6   "   Taylor, of Stonington, and Clarinda R. Smith, of Westerly; m. by Thomas J. Wilcox, Justice, Feb. 4, 1829.
5-51   "   Mary B., and Joseph L. Thompson, Oct. 23, 1843.
5-101   "   William D., of William, and Frances M. Thurston, of John C.; m. by Rev. Fred Denison, Nov. 5, 1849.
3-68 PERKINS Rufus, and Hannah Dettroch, both of Norwich; m. by William Hern, Justice, March 2, 1760.
3-138   "   Abram, of Nathaniel, dec., of South Kingstown, and Mary Chapman, widow, dan. of Col. John Crandall, dec., of Westerly; m. by Joseph Crandall, Justice, Jan. 17, 1775.
5-37   "   Mercy, and Stanton Hall, July 8, 1800.
5-32   "   Mary Ann, and J. Whitney Knight, Nov. 26, 1838.
5-50   "   Ruth M., and Ebenezer Gear, April 23, 1843.
3-38 PERRY Bridget, and Andrew Mack Intosh, May 29, 1754.
4-188   "   Susannah, and Palmer Wells, Sept. 20, 1802.
5-66   "   Mary Ann, and Charles N. Smith, May 5, 1845.
5-67   "   Lydia, and John Gilbert, May 31, 1845.
2-79 PETTIS Susannah, and John Fordis, Dec. 27, 1733.
3-50 PHELDEN Sarah, and Stephen Potter, Sept. 2, 1756.
3-25 PHILLIPS Charles, and Keziah Lewis; m. by Benjamin Randall, Justice, Nov. 3, 1749.

2-94   PIERCE Edward, and Bathsheba Closson; m. by Theodoty Rhodes, Justice, Dec. 3, 1731.

3-73   POIS John, and Mary Hawkins (both Indians); m. by Elder John Gardiner, Jan. 8, 1765.

2-111   POOLER George, and Amey Vars; m. by Elder Joseph Maxson, Aug. 8, 1742.

2-106   "   Zaccheus, of Westerly, and Jean Tanner, of Charlestown; m. by Joseph Clarke, Justice, Nov. 27, 1746.

3-105. POOLE Amey, and Thomas Lawton, May 20, 1766.

3-44   PORTER Sarah, and Job Babcock, Feb. 10, 1757.

2-115   POTTER Thomas, of Thomas, of Kings Towne, and Mary Babcock, of George, of Westerly; m. by Ronse Helme, Justice, March 19, 1717-8.

3-24   "   Mary, and Elisha Clarke, Feb. 15, 1743-4.

3-21   "   Martha, and Matthew Maxson, Dec. 21, 1748-9.

3-41   "   George, and Content Maxson; m. by Joseph Crandall, Justice, Sept. 18, 1754.

3-50   "   Stephen, of Richmond, and Sarah Phelden, of Charlestown; m by Simeon Perry, Justice, Sept. 2, 1756.

4-48   "   Polly, and John Stillman, April 10, 1776.

4-45   "   George, Jr., and Polly Stillman; m. by Joseph Clark, Justice, April 26, 1780.

4-113   "   Polly, and Christopher Babcock, June 16, 1782.

4-9   "   Joseph, of Westerly, and Phebe Wells, of Hopkinton; m. by Elder John Burdick, April 7, 1784.

4-31   "   Hannah, and Amos Maxson, Jan. 3, 1789.

4-184   "   Martha, and William Stillman, April 28, 1791.

4-114   "   Betsey, and Elisha Lanphere, Dec. 17, 1795.

4-131   "   Nathan, of George, of Westerly, and Lucy Rogers, of Ezekiel, of Connecticut; m. by Elder Davis Rogers, June 14, 1792.

4-220   "   Polly, and James Ross, April 29, 1804.

4-234   "   Benjamin, of George, and Betsey Greene, of Pardon; m. at Newport by Elder Henry Burdick, March 6, 1808.

4-251   "   George, of Westerly, and Betsey Rogers, of Waterford, Conn.; m. at Waterford, by Pardon T. Tabor, Justice, Oct. 11, 1809.

4-256   "   Joseph, Jr., of Westerly, and Mary Babcock, of Peleg, of Stonington; m. at Stonington, by Eld. Matthew Stillman, Oct. 28, 1818.

5-16   "   Matthew, and Nancy Saunders; m. by George D. Cross, Justice, July 2, 1828.

5-55   "   Mary Ann, and Samuel S. Larkin, Sept. 2, 1844.

1-58   POTTS Patience, and Joseph Pendleton, Dec. 11, 1700.

5-108   POWELL John D., of Morris D., of Bristol, Eng., and Mrs. Diantha C. Williamson, dau. of Peleg E. Dawley, of North Kingstown; m. by Rev. John Taylor, July 14, 1850.

5-92   PRATT Benjamin W., of Benjamin W., of Mendon, Mass., and Elizabeth H. Rogers, of Joseph, of Lyme, Conn.; m. by Rev. Thomas H. Vail, March 18, 1849.

1-58   PRENTICE Experience, and William Darby, Feb. 9, 1743-4.

2-88   PROSSER Cattron, and Daniel Lanphere, Jan. 24, 1730-1.

2-73   "   Ichabod, and Patience Lanphere; m. by Elder John Maxson, Nov. 26, 1735.

5-83   "   Abby A., and Milton P. Saunders, Jan. 10, 1848.

5-55   "   Mary S., and Saunders Sisson, Sept. 2, 1844.

2-77   PULLMAN John, and Mary King; m. by William Hern, Justice, March 17, 1750-1.

4-112   "   Susannah, and James West, Dec. 16, 1751.

5-99   PURDY Franklin, of Cohoes, N. Y., and Amanda F. Peckham, of John, of Stonington; m. by Rev. Thomas H. Vail, Aug. 16, 1849.

Q

5-28   QUAIL Elizabeth, and George M. Johnson, Sept. 14, 1847.

R

2-85	RANDALL	Eleanor, and Benjamin Greene, March 19, 1714.
2-71	"	Mercy, and Stephen Wilcox, July 12, 1716.
2-112	"	Mary, and Caleb Pendleton, Oct. 25, 1716.
2-125	"	Thankful, and John Maxson, Jr., Sept. 26, 1724.
2-109	"	Elizabeth, and Edward Wells, Jan. 12, 1725-6.
2-105	"	John, and Dorothy Cottrell; m. by Theodoty Rhodes, Justice, Dec. 22, 1726.
2-95	"	Abigail, and John Brown, Oct. 16, 1729.
2-75	"	Rebecca, and Nicholas Cottrell, Oct. 3, 1735.
2-73	"	Benjamin, and Mary Babcock; m. by Elder John Maxson, Oct. 22, 1735.
2-70	"	Nathan, and Eleanor Cottrell; m. by Stephen Babcock, Justice, July 22, 1736.
3-102	"	Returah, and Jesse Maxson, Sept. 11, 1753.
3-50	"	Mary, and James Adams, Aug. 3, 1756.
3-104	"	Thomas, of Stonington, and Molly Cheeseborough, of Westerly; m. by Rev. Joseph Park, Dec. 1, 1765.
2-112	RATHBONE	Joshua, of Block Island, and Martha Card, of Westerly; m. by Joseph Stanton, Justice, Nov. 30, 1721.
3-121	"	Ebenezer, of Block Island, and Sarah Bessey, of Westerly; m. by Joseph Stanton, Justice, July 23, 1721.
2-98	"	Mercy, and John Bliven, Nov. 8, 1727.
2-82	"	Samuel, and Elizabeth Dodge; m. by Theodoty Rhodes, Justice, March 15, 1732.
3-59	"	Judeth, and William Greene, Jan. 25, 1756.
3-53	"	Anna, and John Thurston, Feb. 20, 1757.
4-107	"	Anna, and John Thompson, April 17, 1757.
3-62	"	Susannah, and Daniel Larkin, Feb. 27, 1758.
3-105	"	Dorcas, and Maxson Lewis, Dec. 22, 1765.
3-154	"	James, of Thomas, and Susannah Clarke, of Joseph; m. by Joseph Crandall, Justice, (also 4-53), Sept. 27, 1778.
3-161	"	Stephen, of Thomas, and Elizabeth Taylor, of David; m. by Elder Isaiah Wilcox, March 25, 1779.
4-41	"	Ebenezer, of Ebenezer, dec., and Mary Crandall, of James; m. by Joseph Crandall, Justice, Sept. 23, 1790.
4-79	"	Mercy, and Asa Wilcox, Nov. 28, 1791.
4-264	"	Daniel, and Amelia Lanphere; m. by Elder Jesse Babcock, March 7, 1816.
5-18	"	Job W., of Stephen, dec., and Thankful Gavitt, of Joseph, dec.; m. by Benajah Gavitt, Justice, March 28, 1831.
5-73	"	Joseph D., of Christopher, and Sarah P. Carpenter; m. by Elder Henry Clarke, Aug. 9, 1846.
5-102	"	Elisha Kenyon, and Maria Newbury (adopted daughter), of Catherine, both of Stonington; m. by Rev. Thomas H. Vail, Nov. 19, 1849.
2-90	"	Anna, and Samuel Ward (also 3-30), Dec. 20, 1745.
2-105	"	Lydia, and Thomas Hubbard, May 7, 1747.
1-95	REYNOLDS	Thomas, of John, of Stonington, and Sarah Clarke, of Joseph, of Newport, aged 20 years, Jan. 29, 1683; m. at Newport by Caleb Carr, Assistant, Oct. 11, 1683.
2-113	"	Mary, and John Tafft, Nov. 11, 1721.
2-77	"	Desire, and Peter Burdick, April 17, 1726.
2-123	"	Deborah, and Elihu Palmer, Jan. 19, 1726-7.
2-91	"	Joseph, and Prescilla Richmond; m. by George Babcock, Justice, July 14, 1729.
2-79	"	Hannah, and William Maxson, Oct. 14, 1743.
3-25	"	Joseph, and Hannah Babcock; m. by Benjamin Randall, Justice, Sept. —, 1752.
3-22	"	Susannah, and Elias Lewis, Sept. 15, 1749.
3-22	"	Judeth, and Isaiah Maxson, Oct. 19, 1749.
3-123	"	Zaccheus, Jr., of Zaccheus, of Hopkinton, and Desire Babcock, of Nathan, of Westerly; m. by Elder Joshua Clarke, Dec. 11, 1771.

2-69	RHODES Anna, and James Bliven, Jan. 22, 1734.
2-25	" Penelope, and Thomas Burdick, Feb. 9, 1737-8.
3-29	" James, and Anna Crandall; m. by Benjamin Hoxsie, Justice, Dec. 14, 1752.
3-51	" Capt. Simon, of Newport, and Anne Babcock, of Westerly; m. by Elder Joseph Park, Dec. 15, 1756.
3-119	" James, of Hopkinton, and Abigail Greenman, of Westerly; m. by Rev. Joseph Park, Feb. 21, 1768.
3-160	" William, of James, of Stonington, and Sarah Champlain, of Col. Christopher, of Charlestown; m. by Joseph Crandall, Justice, Jan. 31, 1779.
4-125	" Oliver, and Eunice Pendleton; m. by Elder Elkanah Babcock, Dec. 14, 1796.
4-159	" James, of Westerly, and Martha Rhodes, of Hopkinton; m. at Hopkinton, by Elder Abram Coon, May 12, 1800.
4-159	" Martha, and James Rhodes, May 12, 1800.
4-162	" Christopher, of William and Ann Hammond; m. by Eld. Asa Coon, Dec. 28, 1800.
4-175	" Hannah, and James Babcock, May 6, 1802.
4-217	" Ann, and Jonathan Larkin, Nov. 22, 1804.
3-53	RICHARDSON Prudence, and Samuel Woodburn, March 4, 1757.
2-78	RICHMOND Cyrus, and Jane Crandall; m. by John Babcock, Justice, Jan. 29, 1718-19.
2-111	" Rebecca, and Peter Worden, May 26, 1720.
2-91	" Prescilla, and Joseph Reynolds, July 14, 1729.
2-86	" Elizabeth, and Joseph Hull, Nov. 11, 1731.
2-111	" Cyrus, and Phebe Mott; m. by John Hoxsie, Justice, March 27, 1734.
2-73	" Lydia, and John Allen, March 30, 1744.
4-190	RIDER John, of Charlestown, and Deborah Peckham, of Westerly; m. by Elder Abram Coon, Dec. 21, 1800.
2-81	ROBINSON Edward, son of Margaret Hull, widow, of Newport, and Johannah Irish, of John, of Little Compton; m. by Giles Slocum, Assistant, Oct. 11, 1708.
2-81	" John, and Mary Irish; m. by John Richmond, Justice, Aug. 23, 1733.
2-119	" Mercy, and Edward Wilcox, Jan. 5, 1738-9.
3-40	ROCK Valentine, of New Shoreham, and Hannah Saunders, of Westerly; m. by Joseph Crandall, Justice, Oct. 29, 1765.
4-23	" Mary, and Ichabod Clarke, Jr., Nov. 22, 1787.
2-81	ROGERS Samuel, and Patience ————; m. by John Babcock, April 28, 1707.
2-116	" Content, and Jonathan Maxson, May 1, 1707.
2-105	" Peleg, and Isabel Brand; m. by Theodoty Rhodes, Justice, Aug. 25, 1726.
2-96	" Edward, and Mary Bailey; m. by George Babcock, Justice, July 22, 1728.
2-87	" Robert, and Mary Williams; m. by George Babcock, Justice, Oct. 7, 1728.
2-45, 77	" Thomas, of James (deceased), and Zerniah Woodmansee, of Joseph; m. by Samuel Wilbur, Justice, Oct. 3, 1734.
2-47	" Lucy, and John Maxson, Oct. 27, 1736.
2-84	" Jonathan, of New London, and Hannah Hiscox, of Westerly; m. by Elder John Maxson, Oct. 26, 1737.
5-3	" Ruth, and Samuel Maxson, Oct. 13, 1742.
3-56	" Nathan, of New London, Conn., and Mrs. Hannah Crandall, of Hopkinton; m. by Elder John Maxson, Sept. 17, 1757.
3-111	" Ruth, and Thomas Crandall, May 17, 1767.
3-174	" Lydia, and Thomas Noyes (also 4-141), Jan. 31, 1721.
4-29	" Jesse, of New London, son of Nathan, and Hannah Bliven, of Westerly, dau. of Daniel; m. by Elder Davis Rogers, Dec. 23, 1789.
4-34	" Bathana, and Theodoty Bliven, March 18, 1790.
4-131	" Lucy, and Nathan Potter, June 14, 1792.
4-251	" Betsey, and George Potter, Oct. 11, 1809.

4-143	ROGERS Sarah, and Clarke Saunders, Feb. 15, 1798.
5-59	"	Emeline, and Albert Stillman, Sept. 23, 1844.
5-92	"	Elizabeth H., and Benjamin W. Pratt, March 18, 1849.
3-13	ROOD Abigail, and Joseph Button, Dec. 22, 1737.
2-86	ROSS William, and Anna Lewis; m. by John Saunders, Justice, April 18, 1711.
2-112	"	Mary, and Daniel Peckham, Feb. 11, 1719-20.
2-75	"	Jemima, and Joseph Meekcome, Jan. 9, 1734.
2-72	"	William, and Abigail Swaros; m. by William Hern, Justice, Oct. 25, 1739.
2-87	"	Thomas, and Lois Wells; m. by Elder Joseph Maxson, March 7, 1739-40.
2-7	"	John, and Hannah Saunders; m. by William Hern, Justice, Feb. 27, 1740-1.
2-220	"	Ann, and Edward Bliven, Jr., May 30, 1743.
3-1	"	Benjamin, and Sarah Hall; m. by William Hern, Justice, April 26, 1741.
3-47	"	Peleg, and Hannah Lewis; m. by Joseph Crandall, Justice, Dec. 10, 1735.
3-89	"	Barredel, and Daniel Maxson, March 31, 1762.
3-97	"	Lois, and Stephen Johnson, Dec. 10, 1767.
3-114	"	Joshua, of Elder Thomas, and Edith Burdick, of Simeon; m. by Joseph Crandall, Justice, April 27, 1769.
3-117	"	Benjamin, of Elder Thomas, and Sarah Hall, of William; m. by Joseph Crandall, Justice, March 4, 1770.
3-125	"	Eunice, and Sheffield W cox, Dec. 11, 1771.
3-138	"	John, Jr., and Lois Tay or; m. by Elder Joseph Park, April 11, 1773.
3-137	"	Abigail, and Jnde Taylor, March 13, 1774.
3-140	"	Mary, and Benjamin Hull, Feb. 9, 1775.
3-149	"	Sarah, and James Babcock, 3d, Jan. 26, 1777.
3-157	"	Peleg, of Peleg, and Thankful Bliven, of James; m. by Elder Daniel Saunders, Jan. 15, 1778.
3-153	"	James, of John, of Westerly, and Esther Burdick, of Peter, of Stonington; m. by Joseph Crandall, Justice, April 9, 1778.
3-157	"	Elizabeth, and William Driscoll, July 27, 1778.
3-158	"	Desire, and Samuel Greene, Nov. 19, 1778.
3-137	"	Freelove, and Samuel Champlain, Jan. 12, 1780.
3-176	"	Peleg. Jr., of Peleg, and Mary Babcock, of Isaac; m. by Elder Thomas Ross, Dec. 2, 1781.
4-2	"	Lebbeas, of Peleg, and Rhoda Crandall, of Capt. William; m. by Joseph Crandall, Justice, March 23, 1783.
4-4	"	Thankful, and Augustus Maxson, June 5, 1783.
4 6	"	Thomas, of Peleg, of Westerly, and Betsey Lewis, of James, of Newport; m. by Joseph Crandall, Justice, March 28, 1784.
4-20	"	Prudence, and James Burdick, Dec. 10, 1788.
4-71	"	Anthony Bennett, of Isaac, dec., and Elizabeth Bliven, of Samuel; m. by Samuel Bliven, Justice, Aug. 26, 1792.
4-81	"	Lyman, of Codaudo, dec., of Westerly, and Dorcas Lewis, of Exchange, of Hopkinton; m. by Samuel Bliven, Justice, Aug. 29, 1793.
4-138	"	Joshua, and Thankful Saunders; m. by Joseph Potter, Justice, March 17. 1796.
4-149	"	Sarah, and James Babcock, Jan. 26, 1797.
4-132	"	Anna, and Asa Nash, Feb. 4, 1799.
4 150	"	Lydia, and James Kenyon Crandall, Dec. 15, 1799.
4-166	"	William Lewis, of Westerly, and Nancy Pearce, of Bangor, Mass. (Me.); m. by Elder Abram Coon, Feb. 24, 1801.
4-179	"	Benjamin, and Abigail Lewis; m. by Rev. Hezckiah N. Woodruff, Jan. 7, 1802.
4-218	"	John, Jr., of John, of Westerly, and Phebe Taylor, of Nathan, of Charlestown; m. by Elder William Gardiner, Dec. 5, 1802.
4-220	"	James, and Polly Potter; m. by Elder Abram Coon, April 29, 1804
4-213	"	David, of John, of Westerly, and Sarah Taylor, of Nathan, of Charlestown; m. at Charlestown by Samuel Bliven, Justice, Feb. 6, 1806.

4-221 ROSS Lyman, of John, and Judeth Frazier, of Gideon; m. at Charles-
             town by Samuel Bliven, Justice, Jan. 8, 1807.
4-226   "   Issac, late of Nantucket, and Hannah Champlain, of Westerly;
             by Samuel Bliven, Justice, May 11, 1807.
5-32   "   Mary, Caroline, and Henry Babcock, Feb. 4, 1839.
5-109   "   Ruth Ann, and James B. Wilbur, July 26, 1840.
5-71   "   Joseph, of Charlestown, and Susan E. Larkin, of Westerly; m.
             by Rev. Alexander Campbell, Sept. 22, 1845.
3-62 RUDD Zerviah, and William Vincent, June 22, 1758.
3-112 RUSSELL Levi, of Preston, and Abigail Sisson, of Westerly: m. by Joseph
             Crandall, Justice, Dec. 1, 1768.
5-39 RYAN John, and Lydia Denby, widow of William; m. by Jedediah W.
             Knight, Justice, Jan. 18, 1841.

S

2-105 SATTERLEE John, and Experience Lanphere; m. by Theodoty Rhodes,
             Justice, Jan. 5, 1726-7.
3-20   "   Dorothy, and John Worden, May 1, 1746.
3-18   "   John, and Amey Lanphere; m. by William Hern, Justice, Dec.
             4, 1748.
3-30   "   Mary, and James Babcock, Feb. 21, 1753.
3-67   "   William, and Eunice Clarke; m. by William Hern, Justice, Sept.
             13, 1759.
3-94   "   Gideon, and Ruth Bentley; m. by Stephen Lanphere, Justice, Jan.
             3, 1764.
3-94   "   Prudence, and Jeremy Newbury, Jan. 4, 1764.
2-70 SAMPSON Sarah, and Joseph Sawcross, April 27, 1737.
2-88 SANFORD Elizabeth, and Simeon Clarke, Dec. 20, 1736.
2-84 SAUNDERS Stephen, and Rachel Bleason; m. by John Saunders, Justice,
             Nov. 19, 1721.
2-406   "   Elizabeth, and Peter Brown, Dec. 15, 1726.
3-50   "   John, and Reed Pendleton; m. by Samuel Clarke, Justice, Oct.
             31, 1728.
2-84   "   Samuel, and Elizabeth Crumb; m. by Theodoty Rhodes, Justice,
             Nov. 30, 1732.
2-80   "   Thankful, and Cornelius Stetson (also 3-66), Oct. 25, 1733.
2-81   "   Abigail, and Ephraim Hiscox, Oct. 29, 1733.
2-80   "   William, and Mary Vars; m. by John Richmond, Justice, Nov. 15,
             1733.
2-118   "   Joshua, and Freelove Bliven; m. by Elder John Maxson, Oct. 25,
             1739.
2-10   "   Mary, and Thomas Sisson, Oct. 10, 1740.
2-7   "   Hannah, and John Ross, Feb. 27, 1740-1.
2-85   "   Stephen, Jr., of Westerly, and Lydia Wilcox, of Charlestown; m.
             by William Babcock, Justice, Aug. 12, 1744.
3-1   "   Joseph, and Mercy Lanphere; m. by William Hern, Justice (also
             3-68), April 5, 1744.
3-39   "   Isabel, and Simeon Burdick, Sept. 20, 1747.
3-20   "   Sarah, and Joseph Champlin, May 24, 1748.
3-4   "   Mary, and Benjamin Stillman, Feb. 28, 1750-1.
3-23   "   Ruth, and John Brown, June 25, 1752.
3-24   "   Edward, and Sarah Hiscox; m. by Joseph Crandall, Justice (also
             4-57), Aug. 13, 1752.
3-33   "   Gideon, and Elizabeth Stetson; m. by Joseph Crandall, Justice,
             Sept. 30, 1753.
3-41   "   Elizabeth, and Thomas Hiscox, Jr., Nov. 14, 1754.
3-43   "   William, Jr., and Prudence Babcock; m. by Benoni Smith, Jus-
             tice, Jan. 9, 1755.
3-59   "   Nathan, and Elizabeth Crumb; m. by William Hern, Justice, Feb.
             23, 1758.
3-62   "   Elisha, and Elizabeth Chase; m. by Rev. Joseph Park, May 17,
             1758.
3-61   "   Abigail, and Capt. Joshua Brown, June 19, 1758.

3-63	SAUNDERS	Ezekiel, and Esther Lewis: m. by William Hern, Justice, Dec. 14, 1758.
3-64	"	Martha, and John Varse, Nov. 19, 1759.
3-69	"	David, and Eleanor Smith; m. by William Hern, Justice, March 17, 1760.
4-144	"	Peleg, of Stephen, dec., and Mary Clarke, of Thomas, dec.; m. by Joseph Crandall, Justice, Jan. 1, 1761.
3-73	"	Peleg, and Mary Clarke; m. by Joseph Crandall, Justice, Jan. 21, 1761.
3-79	"	Wait, and Patience Elderton; m. by Joseph Crandall, Justice, Dec. 16, 1761.
3-83	"	Mary, and John Clarke, Nov. 18, 1762.
3-94	"	Lieut. Hezekiah, and Mary Bliven; m. by Rev. Joseph Park, Oct. 20, 1763.
3-99	"	Ruth, and Nathan Hiscox, May 7, 1764.
3-99	"	Dinah, and Elijah Berry, Oct. 24, 1764.
3-98	"	Esther, and Samuel Coon, March 25, 1765.
3-40	"	Hannah, and Valentine Rock, Oct. 29, 1765.
3-41	"	Eunice, and Nathan Greenman, March 19, 1766.
3-91	"	Freegift, and Jacob Briggs, March 14, 1767.
3-111	"	Elizabeth, and James Crandall, June 26, 1768.
3-121	"	Hannah, and John Bent, Jr., Oct. 10, 1770.
4-17	"	Jonathan, and Elizabeth Woodworth; m. by Elder Timothy Whitman, June 25, 1771.
3-123	"	Sarah, and Nathan Lanphere, Jr. (also 4-100), Oct. 31, 1771.
3-123	"	Lydia, and Benjamin Hull, Nov. 7, 1771.
3-128	"	Joshua, of Daniel, of Charlestown, and Mary Taylor, of Humphrey, of Westerly; m. by Joseph Crandall, Justice, Dec. 27, 1772.
3-136	"	Charles, of Stephen, and Martha Hall, of Joseph, dec.; m. by Elder Joshua Clarke (also 4-82), Nov. 25, 1773.
4-78	"	Stephen, and Tacy Stillman; m. by Joseph Clarke, Justice, Jan. 12, 1774.
4-91	"	James. Jr., and Elizabeth Crandall, Oct. 3, 1774.
3-141	"	Prudence, and John Greene (also 4-200), March 2, 1775.
3-146	"	Joseph, of Joseph, and Lydia Crandall, of James; m. by Joseph Crandall. Justice, June 30, 1776.
3-159	"	Augustus, of Stephen, dec.. and Elizabeth Vars, of Isaac; m. by Joseph Crandall, Justice, Dec. 31, 1778.
3-155	"	Freelove, and John Tanner, April 8, 1779.
3-166	"	Rachel, and William Hall, March 16, 1780.
4-5	"	Dorcas, and Luke Saunders, Feb. 15, 1781.
4-5	"	Luke, of Elisha, dec., of Westerly, and Dorcas Saunders, of Tobias, of Charlestown; m. by Elder John Gardiner, Feb. 15, 1781.
4-42	"	Luke, of Charlestown, and Sarah Dewry, of Stonington; m. by Elder Eleazer Brown, Oct. 29, 1781.
3-180	"	Edward, of Capt. Edward, and Martha Clarke. of Elisha; m. by Elder Joshua Clarke (also 4-56), March 14, 1782.
4-3	"	Sarah, and Charles Hiscox, Dec. 12, 1782.
4-1	"	Augustus, of Daniel, of Charlestown, and Lois Cottrell, of John, of Westerly; m. by Joshua Case, Justice, Jan. 19, 1783.
4-6	"	Peleg, of Stephen, dec., and Sarah Vars, of Isaac; m. by Joseph Crandall, Justice, June 28, 1784.
4-86	"	Mereba, and Daniel Cottrell, May 21, 1789.
4-33	"	George, of Hezekiah, and Lydia Saunders, of Charles; m. by Joseph Crandall, Justice, April 15, 1790.
4-33	"	Lydia, and George Saunders, April 15, 1790.
4-46	"	Arnold, of Capt. Edward. dec., and Hannah Clarke, of Elisha; m. by Elder Joshua Clarke, Oct. 21, 1790.
4-169	"	David, of Westerly, and Sarah Parker, widow of Richmond; m. by Edmund Burdick, Justice, Dec. 16, 1790.
4-47	"	Russell, of Capt. Edward, dec., and Sarah, and Mary Burdick, of Clarke, dec., and Amey; m. by Ichabod Burdick, Justice, March 31, 1791.
4-80	"	Hannah, and Matthew Lewis, Feb. 12, 1792.

4-45	SAUNDERS Mary, and Lebbeus Cottrell, May 17, 1793.
4-138	" Thankful, and Joshua Ross, March 17, 1796.
4-110	" Joseph, of Westerly, and Rebecca Crandall, of Hopkinton; m. by Samuel Bliven, Justice, Dec. 27, 1796.
4-143	" Clarke, of Peleg, of Westerly, and Sarah Rogers, of Ezekiel, of Connecticut; m. by Elder Davis Rogers, Feb. 15, 1798.
4-168	" Dora, and Stephen Saunders, Jr., April 15, 1798.
4-168	" Stephen, Jr., and Dora Saunders; m. by Thomas P. Gardiner, Justice, April 15, 1798.
4-161	" Polly, and Wilbur Hall, Nov. 16, 1800.
4-222	" Desire, and Capt. Benjamin York, Jan. 21, 1801.
4-184	" Russell, of Westerly, and Caty Gardiner, of Hopkinton; m. by Daniel Edwards, Justice, March 1, 1801.
4-173	" Sally, and Samuel Nye, Dec. 27, 1801.
4-199	" Samuel, and Fanny Bliven; m. by Elder Jesse Babcock, Jan. 1, 1804.
4-198	" Rebecca, and John Durfee, Sept. 15, 1804.
4-207	" Joshua, of Westerly, and Hannah Handcox, of Stonington; m. at Stonington, by Elijah Palmer, Justice, April 18, 1805.
4-227	" Susannah, and Asa Lauphere, Jan. 15, 1807.
4-223	" Caty, and Namund Hall, Feb. 25, 1807.
5-20	" Elias, and Fanny Vars; m. by Elder Matthew Stillman, Sept. 24, 1809.
4-252	" Mary, and Lodowick Sisson, March 27, 1813.
4-242	" Lydia, and James Davis, Jr., Sept. 10, 1815.
5-115	" Arnold, Jr., and Frances Frazier, of Nathaniel; m. by Elder Matthew Stillman, Jan. 29, 1826.
5-8	" Lydia, and Charles Crandall, March 18, 1827.
5-16	" Nancy, and Matthew Potter, July 2, 1828.
5-7	" John A., of Westerly, and Lavina Crandall, of Hopkinton; m. at Hopkinton by Elder Matthew Stillman, Dec. 6, 1829.
5-9	" Sally, and John Crandall, Feb. 20, 1830.
5-31	" Samuel, Jr., of Westerly, and Amey K. Greene, of Charlestown; m. by Elder Matthew Stillman, Nov. 6, 1834.
5-34	" Esther, and Levi Lothrop Derby, June 24, 1839.
5-57	" Sophia W., and Warren G. Crandall, Oct. 1, 1842.
5-40	" Rebecca, and Joseph Scott, Oct. 5, 1842.
5-78	" Peleg, of Elias, and Keturah V. Gavitt, of Benajah; m. by Rev. Thomas H. Vail, Sept. 22, 1847.
5-83	" Milton P., of Brookfield, N. Y., son of William B., and Abby A. Prosser, of Welcome, of Westerly; m. by Rev. Isaac Moore, Jan. 10, 1848.
2-70	SAWCROSS Joseph, and Sarah Sampson; m. by Elder John Maxson, April 27, 1737.
3-141	SCHRIVEN James, of William, of Westerly, and Marval Davis, of Elder Joseph, of Hopkinton; m. by Joseph Crandall, Justice, March 2, 1775.
5-40	SCOTT Joseph, and Rebecca Saunders; m. by Rev. John H. Cross, Justice, Oct. 5, 1842.
4-4	SEAGER Christopher, and Wealtha Lanphere, of Ebenezer; m. by Elder Isaiah Wilcox, March 17, 1777.
4-224	" Sally, and William Sims, Jr., April 9, 1807.
2-70	SEALLENGER Martha, and William Wright, March 24, 1745-6.
3-125	SEARL John Ruggles, of Benoni, and Mary Brown, of Humphrey, both of Stonington; m. by Joseph Crandall, Justice, June 24, 1772.
3-81	SEARS Remington, of Westerly, and Esther Dye, of Stonington; m. by Rev. Joseph Fish, Feb. 1, 1761.
5-80	SHARP Sybel G., and Horace V. Lanphere, Oct. 9, 1847.
3-95	SHAW Comfort, and Susannah Crandall; m. by Stephen Lanphere, Justice, April 5, 1764.
3-25	SHEFFIELD Elizabeth, and Edward Wells, Dec. —, 1749.
3-6	" Isaac, and Freelove Pendleton; m. by William Hern, Justice, Aug. 1, 1751.
3-87	" Thomas, of Charlestown, and Wealthian Pendleton, of Westerly; m. by Nathaniel Sheffield, Justice, Jan. 12, 1763.

3-88	SHEFFIELD Joseph, of Charlestown, and Lydia Gardiner, of Westerly; m. by Stephen Saunders, Justice, Jan. 13, 1763.
3-133	"	James, of George, of Westerly, and Sarah Hoxsie, of Benjamin, of Charlestown; m. by Elder Joseph Park, Dec. 26, 1773.
3-139	"	George, of George, of Westerly, and Sarah Browning, of Jeremiah, of Charlestown; m. by Joseph Crandall, Justice, Jan. 22, 1775.
5-170	"	Anne, and Samuel Brand, March 9, 1777.
3-155	"	Samuel, of George, of Westerly, and Anna Browning, of John, of Charlestown; m. by Joseph Crandall, Justice, Dec. 3, 1778.
4-106	"	Lydia, and Simeon Lewis, Dec. 20, 1795.
4-135	"	Samuel, of Charlestown, and Susannah Daniels, of New London; m. by Elder Abram Coon, Feb. 14, 1799.
5-2	"	George H., and Sally Champlain; m. by Jedediah W. Knight, Justice, Jan. 2, 1825.
5-30	"	Martha, and James B. Thompson, Aug. 27, 1837.
5-40	"	Eliza, and Perry G. Babcock, April 11, 1841.
3-75	SHELDON Joseph, and Ruth Burdick; m. by Joseph Crandall, Justice, May 3, 1761.
4-11	"	Abigail, and Thomas Vars, Feb. 10, 1785.
4-191	SHELLEY Ebenezer, and Amey Dewry; m. by Elder Abram Coon, Nov. 15, 1799.
5-50	SHERLEY Stiles, of Stonington, and Mercy Esther Lee, of Westerly; m. by Rev. William H. Newman, May 1, 1843.
4-219	SHERMAN Abial, and Lucy Pendleton, of Simeon; m. by Joseph Pendleton, Justice, Dec. 1, 1805.
5-50	"	William H., of South Kingstown, and Susan Carpenter, of Westerly; m. by Elder Henry Clarke, June 21, 1846.
5-73	"	Thomas H., of George H., of Hopkinton, and Hannah Amelia Peckham, of John; m. by Rev. Thomas H. Vail, Feb. 23, 1847.
4-210	SHORT Eunice, and Stanton Stephens, Jan. 10, 1802.
3-19	SIMS William, of North Kingstown, and Jerusha Lanphere, of Westerly; m. by William Hern, Justice, March 24, 1747-8.
4-88	"	Samuel, of Westerly, and Deborah Pendleton, of Stonington; m. by Elder Simeon Brown, Oct. 20, 1770.
3-152	"	William, of William, dec., and Rebecca Chase, widow, dau. of Samuel Pendleton; m. by Joseph Crandall, Justice, Nov. 20, 1777.
4-88	"	Samuel, and Anna Pendleton; m. by Elder Elkanah Babcock, Feb. 8, 1794.
4-193	"	Deborah, and Lemuel Smith, Nov. 7, 1802.
4-213	"	Phebe, and Gilbert Sisson, Feb. 16, 1806.
4-224	"	William, Jr., and Sally Seager; m. by Elder Jesse Babcock, April 9, 1807.
4-257	"	Samuel P., of William, and Sally Sisson, of Barney; m. by Joseph Pendleton, Justice, March 17, 1814.
5-53	"	Sarah, and Lewis Bates, Jr., July 29, 1844.
2-10	SISSON Thomas, and Mary Saunders; m. by Elder John Maxson, Oct. 10, 1740.
3-1	"	Rachel, and Walter Clarke, March 19, 1743-4.
3-103	"	Peleg, and Content West, widow; m. by Joseph Crandall, Justice, Feb. 26, 1767.
3-112	"	Abigail, and Levi Russell, Dec. 1, 1768.
3-120	"	Amey, and Clarke Burdick, Dec. 12, 1770.
3-148	"	Hannah, and Thomas Maxson, Dec. 17, 1772.
4-142	"	Mary, and Ephraim Hiscox, Oct 21, 1773.
3-145	"	Jonathan, of William, dec., and Elizabeth Bliven, of Nathan; m. by Joseph Crandall, Justice, May 12, 1776.
4-152	"	Peleg, Jr., of Peleg, and Esther West, of Timothy, dec.; m. by Joseph Clarke, Justice, Feb. 10, 1777.
4-1	"	Thomas, of William, dec., and Abigail Cottrell, of Major John; m. by Joshua Vose, Justice, Jan. 19, 1783.

4-201	SISSON	Barney, of Peleg, and Cynthia Lanphere, of Elias; m. by Elder Isaiah Wilcox, March 7, 1790.
4-62	"	Sion, of Westerly, and Betsey Welden, of Stonington; m. at Stonington by Valentine Raihbun, Justice, Dec. 11, 1791.
4-105	"	Amey, and Thompson Burdick, May 28, 1796.
4-117	"	Joseph, of Peleg, and Lucy Chapman, of William; m. by Samuel Bliven, Justice, Feb. 4, 1798.
4-206	"	Sanford, and Elizabeth Chapman; m. by Elder Elkanah Babcock, March 3, 1799.
4-219	"	Hannah, and James Stetson, Dec. 2, 1804.
4-213	"	Gilbert, of Peleg, and Phebe Sims, of William; m. by Samuel Bliven, Justice, Feb. 16, 1806.
4-252	"	Lodowick, of Peleg, of Westerly, and Mary Saunders, of Uriah, of Hopkinton; m. by Elder Matthew Stillman, March 27, 1813.
4-257	"	Sally, and Samuel P. Sims, March 17, 1814.
4-265	"	Abigail, and John Chapman, March 28, 1816.
4-269	"	Joshua, of Peleg, and Alice Crumb, of Simeon; m. by Joseph Pendleton, Justice, May 20, 1811.
5-33	"	Libbeus, and Nancy G. Smith; m. by Rev. Albert G. Palmer, March 24, 1839.
5-36	"	William S., of Stonington. and Maria A. Burdick, of Westerly; m. by Elder Daniel Coon, Dec. 17, 1839.
5-45	"	George, of Ichabod B., and Susan Hall, of Hezekiah; m. by Jedediah W. Knight, Justice, May 28, 1843.
5-47	"	Thomas W., of Ichabod B., and Dorcas Barber, of Benjamin P.; m. by Jedediah W. Knight, Justice, Dec. 3, 1843.
5-54	"	Eunice, and William R. F. Dunham, Aug. 18, 1844.
5-55	"	Saunders, and Mary S. Prosser, both of Hopkinton; m. by Rev. Alexander Campbell, Sept. 2, 1844.
5-30	"	Ichabod, and Bridget Kenyon; m. by Rev. Oliver P. Tuckerman, Dec. 27, 1846.
5-107	"	Benjamin F., of Ichabod, of Westerly, and Cynthia A. Culver, of Abram, of Stonington : m. by Rev. John Taylor, June 2, 1850.
3-99	SKEESUCH	Daniel, and Sarah Skeesuch (both Indians); m. by Rev. Joseph Park, May 10, 1764.
3-99	"	Sarah, and Daniel Skeesuch, May 10, 1764.
2-26	SLACK	Mary, and Elisha Burdick, Feb. 25, 1739.
2-111	"	Anna, and Joshua Maxson, Sept. 20, 1742.
3-37	"	Benajah, and Mary Button; m. by Benoni Smith, Justice, Feb. 7, 1754.
3-98	"	Elizabeth, and Benajah Craudall, March 18, 1754.
3-167	SLATTERY	Thomas, and Abigai' Champlain, of Capt. Samuel; m. by Joseph Clarke, Justice, Jan. 16, 1780.
4-210	"	Thomas C., and Susan Brand: m. at Stonington, by Stephen Avery, 2d, Justice, Oct. 13, 1805.
5-62	SLOCUM	Sophia A., and Perry Lanphere, Sept. 1, 1844.
2-105	SMITH	Benoni, and Ruth Pendleton; m. by Theodoty Rhodes, Justice, Dec. 28, 1726.
2-17	"	Mehitable, and Isaac Worden, Aug. 31, 1740.
3-19	"	Hannah, and Andrew Chapman, Oct. 15, 1745.
3-41	"	Nathan, and Elizabeth Babcock; m. by Joseph Crandall, Justice, Sept. 19, 1754.
3-43	"	Mary, and Samuel Babcock, Jr., Jan. 23, 1755.
3-61	"	Elizabeth, and Zacharias Burdick, Feb. 19, 1759.
3-69	"	Elleanor, and David Saunders, March 17, 1760.
3-75	"	Nathan, and Mary Stillman; m. by William Hern, Justice, Feb. 19, 1761.
3-87	"	Sarah, and David Lanphere, March 4, 1762.
4-193	"	Lemuel, Jr., of Stonington, son of Lemuel, and Deborah Sims, of Samuel, of Westerly; m. by Joseph Pendleton, Justice, Nov. 7, 1802.
4-250	"	Stephen, and Esther Babcock; m. at North Stonington by Stephen Avery, Justice, Sept. 6, 1807.
5-12	"	Jane, and Hezekiah Hall, Nov. 12, 1822.
5-6	"	Clarina R., and Taylor Pendleton, Feb. 4, 1829.

5-33	SMITH Nancy G., and Libbeus Sisson, March 24, 1839.
5-36	" Elizabeth M., and William E. Maxson, Dec. 2, 1839.
5-66	" Charles V., and Mary Ann Perry; m. by Rev. Oliver P. Tuckerman, May 5, 1845.
3-47	SPENCER Dinah, and Elisha Berry, Jan. 8, 1756.
3-12	STAFFORD Deborah, and Nathan Babcock, May 19, 1748.
2-119	STANTON Hannah, and James York, Nov. 13, 1695.
2-76	" Hannah, and Joshua Babcock, Aug. 11, 1735.
2-44	" Thankful, and Elias Thompson, March 24, 1736.
2-90	" Joseph, and Mary Champlain; m. by Elder John Maxson, Aug. 9, 1738.
3-13	" Sarah, and Joshua Thompson, May 27, 1736.
3-42	" Sarah, and James Babcock, Dec. 2, 1754.
3-9	" Esther, and Ichabod Babcock, Jr., March 17, 1756.
3-51	" Mrs. Lucy, and Col. Christopher Champlain, Aug. 19, 1756.
2-86	" Joseph, Jr., of Charlestown, and Thankful Babcock, of Westerly; m. by Rev. Joseph Park, July 14, 1762.
3-10	" Daniel, of Charlestown, and Mercy Wilcox, of Westerly; m. by William Champlain, Justice, July 18, 1762.
3-107	" Mary, and Elias Thompson, Oct. 14, 1762.
3-84	" John, of Stonington, and Susanna Champlain, of Westerly; m. by Thomas Gardiner, Justice, June 8, 1763.
3-99	" Job, and Elizabeth Belcher; m. by Rev. Joseph Park, Nov. 11, 1764.
3-99	" Angustus, of Charlestown, and Eunice Crandall, of Westerly; m. by Rev. Joseph Park, Feb. 6, 1765.
4-147	" Hannah, and Joseph Pendleton, Feb. 28, 1793.
4-146	" Abigail, and Abel Pendleton, Sept. 30, 1799.
4-253	" Lucy, and Samuel F. Berry, April 13, 1813.
4-273	" Eliza, and Jared Barber, Feb. 12, 1825.
5-19	" Elizabeth R., and John T. Knowles, Oct. 23, 1833.
5-38	STATES Mary Ann, and Lemuel Vose, Jr., Dec. 29, 1825.
5-7	" Phebe C., and Erastus Bliven, Nov. 5, 1829.
4-215	STEPHENS Sally, and Joshua P. Thompson, Oct. 25, 1789.
4-210	" Stanton, of Westerly, and Unice Short, of Stonington; m. by Elder William Gardiner, Jan. 10, 1802.
3-33	STETSON Elizabeth, and Gideon Saunders, Sept. 30, 1753.
3-52	" Sarah, and James Bliven, Dec. 16, 1756.
3-88	" Freegift, and William Coon, Jan. 6, 1763.
3-88	" Ruth, and William Thurston, Jan. 17, 1763.
3-94	" Hannah, and Rowland Champlain, Dec. 21, 1783.
3-153	" Cornelius, and Susanna West; m. by Elder Daniel Saunders, July 13, 1777.
4-23	" Betsey, and Peleg Peckham, Oct. 25, 1797.
4-219	" James, and Hannah Sisson; m. by Elder Matthew Stillman, Dec. 2, 1804.
4-237	" Cornelius, Jr, and Sally Clarke; m. by Elder Jesse Babcock, Dec. 13, 1807.
5-69	STEVENSON Allen, of Norwich, Conn., and Eleanor Musgrove, of Thomas, of Westerly; m. by Rev. Thomas H. Vail, July 18, 1847.
5-103	" Peter, of Philadelphia, Pa., and Prudence G. Congdon, of Stonington; m. by Rev. Thomas H. Vail, Nov. 19, 1849.
3-63	STEWARD William, and Mary Lanphere; m. by William Hern, Justice, Nov. 30, 1758.
2-88	STEWART Elizabeth, and Ebenezer Burdick, Jan. 21, 1730-1.
2-83	" Joseph, and Sarah Jagers; m. by John Richmond, Justice, Sept. 6, 1732.
2-70	" Mary, and Thomas Foster, April 5, 1736.
2-75	" Sarah, and Joseph Witter, Dec. 9, 1736.
2-83	" Oliver, and Rebecca Pendleton; m. by Rev. Nathaniel Eells, Aug. 21, 1741.
3-79	" Sarah, and Joseph Malleson, Aug. 18, 1761.
2-121	STILLMAN George, and Deborah Crandall; m. by Peter Crandall, Justice, (also 2-123), April 13, 1706.

2-84	STILLMAN	George, and Mary Burdick; m. by Elder John Maxson, Nov. 3, 1737.
2-35	"	Deborah, and Benjamin Tanner, April 13, 1741.
3-19	"	John, and Mary Clarke; m. by William Hern, Justice, Dec. 12, 1745.
3-4	"	Benjamin, and Mary Saunders; m. by Benoni Smith, Justice, Feb. 28, 1750-1.
3-58	"	Esther, and George Stillman, 3d, (also 4-93), Feb. 11, 1758.
3-58	"	George, 3d, and Esther Stillman; m. by Benoni Smith, Justice, (also 4-93), Feb. 11, 1758.
3-60	"	Elisha, and Mary Davis; m. by Elder Thomas Clarke, Jan. 23, 1759.
		(Another entry in 3-63 says Dec. 23, 1759.)
3-75	"	Mary, and Nathan Smith, Feb. 19, 1761.
3-134	"	Sarah, and Elins Crandall, April 30, 1769.
3-156	"	Joseph, of George and Mary, and Elizabeth Maxson, of David and Abigail; m. by Joseph Clarke, Justice, Jan. 27, 1773.
4-78	"	Tacy, and Stephen Saunders, Jan. 12, 1774.
3-181	"	Lois, and Asa Maxson, Dec. 6, 1775.
4-48	"	John, and Polly Potter; m. by Joseph Clarke, Justice, April 10, 1776.
4-61	"	Nathaniel, and Deborah Babcock; m. by Joseph Clarke, Justice, Feb. 26, 1777.
3-162	"	Amey, and Silas Bailey, May 22, 1777.
4-16	"	Clarke, of Westerly, and Abigail Bly, of West Greenwich; m. by Elder Elisha Greene, March 17, 1779.
4-90	"	Susannah, and Paul Maxson, Dec. 22, 1779.
4-45	"	Polly, and George Potter, Jr., April 26, 1780.
4-22	"	Nathan, of Benjamin, dec., and Hannah Lanphere, of Nathan; m. by Joseph Clarke, Justice, Nov. 10, 1785.
4-58	"	Wealthy, and Joshua Clarke, Feb. 16, 1786.
4-32	"	Benjamin, and Prudence Maxson; m. by Elder John Burdick, Feb. 11, 1790.
4-31	"	Mrs. Thankful, and Joshua Maxson, March 4, 1790.
4-184	"	William, of Bristol, Conn., and Martha Potter, of Jonathan, of Richmond, R. I.; m. at Richmond, by Elder John Babcock, April 28, 1791.
4-65	"	Esther, and Ethan Burdick, Dec. 26, 1792.
4-94	"	Polly, and Silas Greenman, Oct. 17, 1793.
4-176	"	David, and Grace Crandall; m. by Daniel Babcock, Justice, Feb. 20, 1794.
4-162	"	Nancy, and Daniel Truman, Dec. 10, 1795.
4-143	"	Maxson, of Col. George, of Westerly, and Esther Crandall, of New London, dau. of Phenias, of Montville, Conn.; m. by Elder Davis Rogers, Dec. 8, 1798.
4-136	"	Amey, and James Hubbard, Jan. 26, 1799.
4-193	"	Sally, and Lyman Berry, Nov. 22, 1802.
4-215	"	Susannah, and Simeon Lanphere, Jan. 26, 1804.
4-192	"	Desire, and Ichabod Wilbur, Feb. 2, 1804.
4-197	"	Leney, and Sprague Barber, April 7, 1804.
4-208	"	Joseph, of Deacon Joseph, of Westerly, and Elizabeth Ward Maxson, of Caleb, of Newport; m. by Elder William Bliss, Dec. 23, 1804.
4-243	"	Paul, of Joseph, of Westerly, and Sally Thurston Bliss, of Newport, dau., of Thomas; m. by Elder Michael Eddy, Nov. 19, 1807.
4-232	"	Rhene, and Isaac B. Taylor, Feb. 21, 1808.
4-233	"	Nathaniel, and Mrs. Polly Thompson; m. by Elijah Palmer, Justice, March 31, 1808.
4-239	"	Betsey, and Silas Maxson, Oct. 13, 1808.
4-249	"	Lydia, and John Cottrell, Nov. 13, 1808.
4-242	"	Daniel, and Lois Cottrell; m. by Elder Abram Coon, Nov. 17, 1808.
4-244	"	Oliver, of Nathaniel, dec., of Westerly, and Ruth Burdick, of Simeon, of Hopkinton; m. at Hopkinton, by Joseph Pendleton, Justice, March 1, 1810.

4-246 STILLMAN Zebulon, of Westerly, and Ennice Wells, of Hopkinton; m. by Elder Abram Coon, Nov. 17, 1810

4-259 " Phebe, and Rouse Stillman, Dec. 20, 1812.

4-259 " Rouse, and Phebe Stillman; m. by Daniel Babcock, Justice, Dec. 20, 1812.

4-264 " Wealthy, and Acors Lanphere, Nov. 30, 1815.

5-1 " William, Jr., and Charlotte Champlain, of Adam, of Hopkinton; m. by Elder Matthew Stillman, April 30, 1818.

5-29 " Albert, and Hannah Edwards; m. at Stonington, by Elder Asher Miner, May 5, 1818.

4-27 " James, of Westerly, and Sally Jerome, of Waterford, Conn.; m. by Elder Francis Daman, Dec. 2, 1819.

5-1 " Ephraim, of William, of Westerly, and Mary Tanner, of William, of Hopkinton; m. by Elder Matthew Stillman, Feb. 19, 1824.

5-5 " Jonathan P., of William, and Phebe Carr, of Resolved; m. by Elder Matthew Stillman, Oct. 28, 1827.

5-13 " Weithia, and Horatio S. Berry, Aug. 23, 1832.

5-14 " Amos, and Hannah Carr; m. by Elder Matthew Stillman, Oct. 28, 1832.

5-42 " Phebe Ann, and Joshua Thompson, Oct. 30, 1837.

5-35 " Martha, and John Bright, Aug. 25, 1839.

5-59 " Albert, and Emeline Rogers; m. by Rev. Alexander Campbell, Sept. 23, 1844.

5-69 " Franklin W., of New York city, and Lucy E. Wells, of Westerly; m. by Rev. Alexander Campbell, May 28, 1845.

5-70 " Abby E., and Ezra Stillman, Sept. 9, 1845.

5-70 " Ezra, and Abby E. Stillman; m. by Rev. Alexander Campbell, Sept. 9, 1845.

5-69 " Mary A., and William Buffington, Sept. 9, 1845.

5-25 " Thankful, and Millen S. Greene, Sept. 1, 1846.

5-75 " Charles A., of Westerly, and Esther V. Babcock, of Scott, Cortland Co., N. Y.; m. by Rev. Alexander Campbell, Oct. 4, 1846.

5-104 STURGEON William, of William, and Maria Burlingame, of Charles; m. by Rev. Fred Denison, Jan. 2, 1850.

2-80 STUTSON Cornelius, of Scituate, now of Westerly, and Thankful Saunders, of Westerly; m. by John Richmond, Justice, Oct. 25, 1733.

2-75 STYLES Israel, and Hannah Hall; m. by John Richmond, Justice, April 10, 1735.

5-19 SULLIVAN Mary Ann, and Asa Worden, Feb. 28, 1845.

2-110 SWAROS Freelove, and Edward Bliven, May 12, 1719.

2-72 " Abigail, and William Ross, Oct. 25, 1739.

3-14 SWEET Deborah, and John Peckham, Dec. 25, 1735.

3-108 " Mary, and Simeon Crandall, June 23, 1745.

3-60 " Dorcas, and Isaac Peckham, Jr., Oct. 25, 1757.

5-39 " Samuel, of South Kingstown, and Abby Peckham, of New Shoreham; m. by Elder Daniel Coon, April 4, 1841.

T

5-9 TAFT Orman, of Worcester. Mass., and Nancy A. Carpenter, of Westerly; m. by Rev. O. D. Tuckerman, Feb. 16, 1845.

2-95 TANNER Rebecca, and Benjamin Brand, March 16, 1734.

2-69 " Elizabeth, and Benjamin Burdick, Dec. 28, 1737.

2-35 " Benjamin, and Deborah Stillman; m. by Elder John Maxson, April 13, 1741.

2-106 " Jean, and Zaccheas Pooler, Nov. 27, 1746.

3-47 " William, of Richmond, and Susannah Thurston, of Westerly; m. by Stephen Richmond, Justice, Nov. 6, 1755.

3-155 " John, and Freelove Sanuders, both of Newport; m. by Elder Joshua Clarke, April 8, 1779.

5-1 " Mary, and Ephraim Stillman, Feb. 19, 1824.

2-166 TAYLOR Job, and Sarah Munro; m. by Stephen Richmond, Justice, Nov. 18, 1742.

3-128 " Mary, and Joshua Saunders, Dec. 27, 1772.

3-138	TAYLOR	Lois, and John Ross, Jr., April 11, 1773.
3-131	"	Sanford, of John, of Westerly, and Lydia Gardiner, of Samuel, of Hopkinton; m. by Elder Stephen Babcock (also 4-98), June 17, 1773.
3-131	"	Sarah, and Joseph Thurston, Nov. 7, 1773.
3-137	"	Jude, of David, and Abigail Ross, of Isaac; m. by Elder Joseph Park, March 13, 1774.
3-161	"	Elizabeth, and Stephen Rathbun, March 25, 1779.
8-166	"	Thomas, of Humphrey, of Westerly, and Hannah Johnson, of Nathaniel, of Hopkinton; m. by Joseph Crandall, Justice, Feb. 6, 1780.
4-169	"	Dennis, and Kesiah Greene, both of Hopkinton; m. by Elder Joshua Clarke, Feb. 17, 1782.
3-170	"	Samuel, of David, dec., and Rebecca Crandall, of Capt. William; m. by Joseph Crandall, Justice (also 4-202), Jan. 6, 1783.
4-181	"	Mrs. Polly, and Capt. Nathan Bliven, Jr., Feb. 1, 1798.
4-197	"	Samuel, 2d, of Westerly, and Cynthia Palmer, of Stonington; m. at Stonington, by Rev. Hezekiah Woodruff, Aug. 25, 1799.
4-167	"	Amey, and William P. Bliven, April 5, 1801.
4-218	"	Phebe, and John Ross, Jr., Dec. 5, 1802.
4-213	"	Sarah, and David Ross, Feb. 6, 1806.
4-220	"	Nabby, and Charles Lee Pendleton, July 13, 1806.
4-221	"	Rebecca, and Samuel Gavitt, July 24, 1806.
4-232	"	Isaac R., of Jude and Rhene Stillman, of Nathaniel; m. by Joseph Pendleton, Justice, Feb. 21, 1808.
4-248	"	Anna, and William Pendleton, Feb. 26, 1812.
5-50	"	Alvey, of Charlestown, and Kesiah Hall, of Westerly; m. by Rev. W. H. Newman, April 18, 1843.
5-46	"	William P., of Stonington, and Lydia A. Babcock, of Westerly; m. by Rev. Shuball Wakefield, Oct. 5, 1843.
5-93	"	John A., of Stonington, son of Benjamin F., and Lucy E. Brackett, of Preston, Conn., dan. of Samuel; m. by Rev. Fred Denison, March 21, 1849.
5-100	"	Martha, and Charles H. Bradford, Aug. 27, 1849.
2-113	TEFFT	John, of Kings Towne, and Mary Reynolds, of Westerly; m. by John Babcock, Justice, Nov. 11, 1721.
2-84	"	David, and Freelove Palmitter; m. by Elder John Maxson, Nov. 26, 1737.
2-119	"	Sarah, and Thomas Wilcox, July 2, 1739.
2-10	"	Jonathan, and Mary Bailey; m. by Elder John Maxson, Jan. 29, 1740.
3-31	"	Samuel, of Westerly, and Mary Ellis, of Preston, Conn.; m. at Stonington, by Simeon Miner, Justice, May 5, 1753.
3-59	"	Mary, and Benajah Brown, Jan. 25, 1758.
3-61	"	Mary, and Joseph Bundy, Oct. 31, 1758.
3-99	"	John, and Anna Crandall; m. by Joseph Parks, Dec. 16, 1764.
3-59	"	Samuel, of Westerly, and Elizabeth Mitchell, widow, dan. of Joseph Bundy; m. by Rev. Thomas Ross, July 26, 1767.
4-92	"	John, of Samuel, dec., and Mrs. Mary Lewis, of Joseph, dec.; m. by Elder Stephen Babcock, Nov. 24, 1773.
4-8	"	Elizabeth, and Thomas Partelow, April 29, 1784.
4-153	"	Joseph, and Sally Clarke; m. by Elder Elkanah Babcock, Jan. 24, 1800.
4-241	"	Fanny, and David Babcock, April 7, 1808.
5-54	"	Nancy, and Henry Lee, Sept. 1, 1844.
5-37	"	Willard B., and Nancy Bliven; m. by Jedediah W. Knight, Justice, June 26, 1846.
5-82	"	Peleg S., of John, and Sally West, of Simeon; m. by Rev. Isaac Moore, May 12, 1847.
4-103	TENNANT	Sarah, and Peleg Vars, Jan. 5, 1794.
4-14	THAYER	David, of Worcester, Mass., and Bethiah Hiscox, of Ephraim, of Westerly; m. by Joseph Crandall, Justice, March 7, 1786.
2-113	THOMPSON	Samson, and Edward Wilcox, May 1, 1698.
2-45	"	Anna, and Stephen Babcock, Oct. 12, 1726.
2-90	"	Rebecca, and John Burdick, Oct. 21, 1730.

2-88	THOMPSON	Susannah, and Joseph Babcock, Dec. 9, 1730.
2-87	"	Mary, and Thomas Noyes, May 1, 1731.
2-83	"	Mary, and David Burdick, July 25, 1733.
2-94	"	Elias, and Thankful Stanton; m. by Rev. Elias Rossiter, March 24, 1736.
3-4	"	Ruth, and William Thompson, Oct. 19, 1732.
3-4	"	William, and Ruth Thompson, he of Westerly, she of Brookhaven, L. I.; m. by George Phillips, Justice, Oct. 19, 1732.
3-13	"	Joshua, of Westerly, and Sarah Stanton, of Stonington; m. by Daniel Palmer, Justice, March 27, 1736.
3-17	"	Sarah, and Thomas Wells. Jr., April 3, 1745.
3-32	'	Mary. and Charles Avery, Aug. 28, 1753.
3-49	"	Thankful, and John Champlain, Feb. 26, 1756.
3-53	"	John, of Westerly, and Anna Rathbone, of Stonington; m. at Stonington, by Elder Wait Palmer (also 4-107, says April 17, 1757), Feb. 20, 1757.
3-83	"	Samuel, and Mary Champlain; m. by Joseph Crandall, Justice, July 18, 1762.
3-107	"	Elias, Jr., of Elias, of Westerly, and Mary Stanton, of Joseph, of Charlestown; m. at Charlestown, by Abram Barden, Justice, Oct. 14, 1762.
3-94	"	Mary, and Benedick Babcock, March 2, 1763.
3-98	"	Mary, and Asa Champlain, March 21, 1765.
3-104	"	Sebra. and John Pendleton, Sept. 22, 1765.
3-100	"	Hannah, and Jonathan Wilbur, Nov. 7, 1765.
3-109	"	Sarah, and Ephraim Pendleton (also 4-148), Dec. 17, 1767.
3-130	"	Robert, of Col. Elias and Anna Babcock, of William; m. by Joseph Crandall, Justice, March 18, 1773.
4-38	"	Hannah, and William Lewis, Dec. 22, 1781.
4-30	"	Nancy, and Simeon West, Oct. 30, 1784.
4-215	"	Joshua P., and Sally Stephens; m. by Joseph Clarke, Justice, Oct. 25, 1789.
4-55	"	Hannah, and Jesse Babcock, Dec. 23, 1789.
4-55	"	Thomas, Jr., of Thomas, of Westerly, and Dorcas Greene, of Capt. Amos, of Charlestown; m. by Elder Henry Joslin, Dec. 21, 1791.
4-94	"	Colby, and Prentice Lewis, Dec. 7, 1794.
4-158	"	Samuel, of Westerly, and Abigail Coggeshall, of Newport; m. by Elder Gardiner Thurston, Dec. 25, 1794.
4-106	"	Nancy, and Benjamin Wilcox, Sept. 28, 1796.
4-111	"	Ruth, and Joshua Lanphere, Nov. 4, 1797.
4-124	"	Prudence, and Elisha Noogen, June 6, 1798.
4-120	"	William, of William, dec., and Eunice Gavitt, of Capt. Samuel. dec.; m. by Samuel Bliven, Justice, April 9, 1798.
4-167	"	Bridget, and Christopher Seagor Pendleton, Feb. 15, 1801.
4-241	"	Hannah, and Russell Brand, Jan. 1, 1803.
4-166	"	Joshua, of John and Fannie Pendleton, of John; m. by Joseph Pendleton, Justice, Feb. 12, 1804.
4-195	"	John, and Lydia Gardiner; m. by Elder Jesse Babcock, March 8, 1804.
4-216	"	John, 3d, of Joshua, and Bridget Berry, of Samuel; m. by Joseph Pendleton, Justice, Feb. 27, 1805.
4-214	"	William, of John and Nancy Babcock, of Henry; m. by Elder Jesse Babcock, March 31, 1805.
4-233	"	Mrs. Polly, and Nathaniel Stillman, March 31, 1808.
4-268	"	Pardon, of Westerly, and Lucy Merriott, of Henry, of Hopkinton; m. by Elder Matthew Stillman, Dec. 10, 1816.
5-30	"	James B., and Martha Sheffield; m. by Rev. Thomas V. Wells, Aug. 27, 1837.
5-42	"	Joshua, Jr., and Phebe Ann Stillman; m. by Elder Daniel Coon, Oct. 30, 1837.
5-51	"	Joseph L., and Mary B. Pendleton; m. by Rev. Oliver P. Tuckerman, Oct. 23, 1843.
5-72	"	Henrietta M., and Dudley R. Wilcox, Nov. 6, 1845.
5-76	"	Charles W., and Julia Chapman; m. by Rev. John Taylor, Dec. 8, 1847.

5-88   THOMPSON Freelove V., and Timothy P. Gavitt, June 5, 1848.

5-89   "   Eliza A., and John D. Peckham, Oct. 9, 1848.

2-86   THORN William, and Sarah Mott, of Edward; m. by John Richmond, Justice, July 16, 1738.

3-66   "   Isaac, and Edey Crandall; m. by Benoni Smith, Justice, Feb. 27, 1759.

3-95   "   Mrs. Edeth, and William Crumb, April 13, 1764.

3-25   THURSTON George, and Abigail Button; m. by Benjamin Randall, Justice, Aug. —, 1752.

3-47   "   Susannah, and William Tanner, Nov. 6, 1755.

3-88   "   William, of Hopkinton, and Ruth Stetson, of Westerly; m. by Stephen Saunders, Justice, Jan. 17, 1763.

3-131   "   Joseph, of George, of Hopkinton, and Sarah Taylor, of John, of Westerly; m. by Joseph Crandall, Justice, Nov. 7, 1773.

4-149   "   Oliver, of Hopkinton, and Lydia Berry, of Westerly; m. by Daniel Babcock, Justice, March 21, 1793.

4-187   "   Lydia, and George Champlain, March 20, 1800.

5-102   "   Frances M., and William D. Pendleton, Nov. 5, 1849.

2-81   TIKON Sampson, of Westerly, and Bettey Wogg, of Stonington; m. by William Hern, Justice, June 15, 1748.

4-192   TILLINGHAST Mrs. Dorcas, and Joseph M. Knowles, Jan. 7, 1802.

2-4   TOMS Elizabeth, and Joseph Loveless, Jan. 20, 1728.

2-96   TOSH Elizabeth, and George Brown, Sept. 25, 1729.

4-137   TRUMAN Susannah, and Maxson Lanphere, Nov. 19, 1795.

4-162   "   Daniel, of Southold, L. I., and Nancy Stillman, of Westerly; m. by Joseph Potter, Justice, Dec. 10, 1795.

5-63   TUBBS Jonathan, of Norwich, Conn., and Adeline Newbury, of Westerly; m. by Rev. E. S. Hiscox, July 4, 1844.

2-106   TUCKER Sarah, and John Larkin, June 15, 1726.

2-95   "   Rebecca, and Roger Larkin, March 19, 1730.

2-81   "   Simeon, and Sarah Hull; m. by Samuel Wilbur, Justice, May 1, 1737.

2-45   "   Hannah, and Joshua Palmiter, Jan. 19, 1738-9.

2-92   TURNER Samuel, and Rebecca Davison, both of Stonington; m. at Westerly, by John Richmond, Justice, March 4, 1727-8.

3-89   "   Samuel, and Abigail Nutter, both of Stonington; m. by Joseph Clarke, Jr., Justice, Nov. 26, 1761.

U

2-79   UTTER Thankful, and Thomas Weeks, Nov. 8, 1741.

3-37   "   Eleanor, and Nathaniel Kenyon, March 21, 1754.

V

4-17   VARIN Joseph, of James, dec., and Isabel Clarke, of Ichabod; m. by Robert Burdick, Justice, Jan. 26, 1786.

2-84   VARS Theodoty, and Mary Dodge; m. by John Richmond, Justice, Dec. 21, 1732.

2-80   "   Mary, and William Saunders, Nov. 15, 1733.

2-111   "   Amey, and George Pooler, Aug. 8, 1742.

3-88   "   Sarah, and Jonathan Macumber, Sept. 8, 1765.

3-64   "   John, and Martha Saunders; m. by Joseph Crandall, Justice, Nov. 19, 1759.

4-7   "   Joseph, of Isaac, and Hannah Maxson, of Joseph; m. by Joseph Crandall, Justice, July 18, 1784.

3-159   "   Elizabeth, and Augustus Saunders, Dec. 31, 1778.

3-169   "   Isaac, of Westerly, and Waitey Gardiner, of East Greenwich, or Warwick; m. by Joseph Crandall, Justice, Oct. 15, 1780.

4-6   "   Sarah, and Peleg Saunders, June 28, 1784.

4-11   "   Thomas, of Isaac, of Westerly, and Abigail Sheldon, of Capt. Isaac, dec., of South Kingstown; m. by Joseph Crandall, Justice, Feb. 10, 1785.

4-16 VARS Edward, of Isaac and Rebecca Peckham, of Abel; m. by Joseph Crandall, Justice, Dec. 22, 1785.

4-103   "   Peleg, of John and Martha, of Middletown, and Sarah Tennant, of George and Hannah, of North Kingstown; m. by Elder William Northup, Jan. 5, 1794.

5-20   "   Fanny, and Elias Saunders, Sept. 24, 1809.

5-89   "   Hannah, and Andrew J. Akins, Dec. 2, 1846.

2-42 VILEY Grace, and James Brand, Feb. 22, 1741.

3-21 VINCENT Jemima, and William Clarke. Nov. 13, 1749.

3-37   "   Mary, and Ephraim Bacon. Feb. 20, 1754.

3-62   "   William, of Westerly, and Zerriah Rudd, of Norwich, Conn, June 22, 1758.

4-136   "   Susannah, and Capt. Nathan Brand. Oct. 24, 1779.

4-157   "   Elizabeth, and Capt. Oliver Lewis. Ang. 2, 1781.

2-90 VIOLET Thankful, and Thomas Clarke. May 27, 1740.

3-1 VOSE Joshua, and Mercy Downing; m. by Benoni Smith, Justice, March 3, 1752.

3-52   "   Joshua, Jr., and Mary Lanphere; m. by William Hern, Justice. May 3, 1757.

3-54   "   Elizabeth, and Asa Crocker, July 4, 1757.

3-59   "   Bathsheba, and Jeremiah Maine. Feb. 22, 1758.

4-86   "   Lemuel, of Joshua, and Delight Babcock, of Elder Elkanah; m. by Samuel Brown, Justice, March 13, 1794.

4-132   "   Joshua, Jr., and Prudence Wilcox; m. by Elder Elkanah Babcock, Jan. 3, 1799.

5-3   "   Sophia, and Stephen Wilcox, Jr., Oct. 21, 1824.

5-38   "   Lemuel, Jr., of Westerly, and Mary Ann States, of Stonington; m. by Rev. Ira Hart, Dec. 29, 1825.

W

2-90 WARD Samuel, and Anna Ray; m. by Rev. Joseph Park (also 3-30), Dec. 20, 1745.

3-136   "   Catharine, and Christopher Greene, Dec. 23, 1773.

3-143   "   Anna, and Ethan Clarke, Feb. 4, 1776.

3-34 WARREN Moses, and Judeth Brand; m. by Daniel Maccoon, Justice, Dec. 27, 1753.

3-56 WATERMAN Darius, and Mary Barker, both of Lebanon, Conn.; m. at Westerly by Benoni Smith, Justice, Sept. 23, 1757.

4-3 WATSON Benjamin, of Benjamin, of North Kingstown, and Elizabeth Crandall, of Jonathan, of Westerly; m. by Joseph Crandall, Justice, July 9, 1783.

3-126 WEAVER William, of Elisha, of Stonington, and Amey Lanphere, of Stephen, of Westerly; m. by Oliver Crary, Justice, March 10, 1772.

2-84 WEBSTER Margaret, and Joseph Enos, Sept. 20, 1716.

2-82   "   Hannah, and Ezekiel Barber, Nov. 28, 1736.

2-79 WEEKS Thomas, of Warwick, and Thankful Utter, of Westerly; m. by Elder Joseph Maxson, Nov. 8, 1741.

4-62 WELDEN Betsey, and Sion Sisson, Dec. 11, 1791.

5-95 WELLER John A., of Stonington, and Harriet M. Kenyon, of Westerly; m. by Rev. Fred Denison, April 2, 1849.

2-69 WELLS Thomas, of Westerly, and Phebe Greene, of Stonington; m. by Daniel Palmer, Justice, at Stonington, Sept. 22, 1717.

2-109   "   Edward, of Westerly, and Elizabeth Crandall, of Stonington; m. by John Richmond, Justice, Jan. 12, 1725-6.

2-106   "   Naomi, and Peter Kenyon, Sept. 15, 1726.

2-85   "   Rebecca, and William Clarke, Jr., Sept. 1, 1731.

2-77   "   Jonathan, and Elizabeth Maxson; m. by Elder John Maxson, Nov. 29, 1734.

2-74   "   Phebe, and Christopher Edwards, Oct. 24, 1735.

2-118   "   Henry, and Mercy Brand; m. by Elder John Maxson, July 30, 1739.

2-27   "   Lois, and Thomas Ross, March 7, 1739-40.

3-17	WELLS Thomas, Jr., and Sarah Thompson; m. by William Hern, Justice, April 3, 1745.
3-22	"	Caleb, and Lois Maccoon; m. by Benjamin Randall, Justice, Jan. 18, 1748-9.
3-25	"	Edward, and Elizabeth Sheffield; m. by Benjamin Randall, Justice, Dec. —, 1749.
3-10	"	Barbary, and Joseph Noyes (also 3-144), July 31, 1754.
3-48	"	Anna, and Ebenezer Brown, Feb. 5, 1756.
3-70	"	Elizabeth, and Jonathan Crandall, April 3, 1760.
4-134	"	Barbara, and Nicholas Clarke, Jan. 20, 1779.
4-9	"	Phebe, and Joseph Potter, Aug. 7, 1784.
4-24	"	Elisha, of Matthew, of Hopkinton, and Eunice Wilcox, of David, dec., of Westerly; m. by Elder Isaiah Wilcox, June 28, 1787.
4-31	"	George, of Hopkinton, and Lydia Dodge, of Westerly; m. by Elder Joshua Clarke, Oct. 15, 1789.
4-69	"	Edward Sheffield, of Hopkinton, and Lucy Hubbard, of Westerly; m. by Elder Joshua Clarke, Jan. 6, 1791.
4-83	"	Thompson, of Westerly, and Phebe Ellis, of Charlestown; m. by Elder Isaiah Wilcox, Sept. 27, 1792.
4-188	"	Palmer, of Westerly, son of Thompson, of Hopkinton, and Susannah Perry, of Jonathan, dec., of South Kingstown; m. by Rev. Thomas Kendall, Sept. 20, 1802.
4-229	"	Sarah, and Lindall A. Fuller, March 1, 1806.
4-246	"	Eunice, and Zebulon Stillman, Nov. 17, 1810.
4-267	"	James, of Edward S., of Hopkinton, and Lucy Gavitt, of George, of Westerly; m. by Elder Matthew Stillman, April 20, 1817.
4-274	"	Thankful, and Silas Greenman, Jr., Dec. 20, 1821.
5-69	"	Lucy E., and Franklin W. Stillman, May 28, 1845.
5-101	WENTWORTH Mary Elizabeth, and Dixon Alexander, Oct. 2, 1849.
4-112	WEST James, and Susanna Pullman; m. by Nathaniel Lewis, Justice, Dec. 18, 1751.
3-47	"	Timothy, and Content Lanphere; m. by Joseph Crandall, Justice, Dec. 3, 1755.
3-54	"	Samuel, and Anna Maccoon; m. by William Hern, Justice, March 17, 1757.
3-83	"	John, and Amey Wilcox; m. by Joseph Crandall, Justice, Dec. 29, 1765.
3-103	"	Content, and Peleg Sisson, Feb. 26, 1767.
3-126	"	William, of Timothy (as is said), and Anne Babcock, of Joseph; m. by Joseph Crandall, Justice, Nov. 1, 1772.
3-138	"	Mercy, and Stephen Gavitt, May 11, 1775.
4-152	"	Esther, and Peleg Sisson, Jr., Feb. 10, 1777.
3-153	"	Susanna, and Cornelius Stetson, July 10, 1777.
4-30	"	Simeon, and Nancy Thompson; m. by Joseph Clarke, Justice, Oct. 30, 1784.
4-101	"	Elisha, and Lydia Lanphere; m. by Joseph Clarke, Justice, Nov. 23, 1794.
4-108	"	Arnold, of James, dec., and Hannah Babcock, of Joseph; m. by Samuel Bliven, Justice (also 4-112), Nov. 17, 1796.
5-22	"	Francis S., of the Isle of Jersey, and Sarah Brown, of Westerly; m. at Ledyard, Conn., by Asa Gore, Justice, Sept. 24, 1836.
5-82	"	Sally, and Peleg S. Tefft, May 12, 1847.
3-9	WHEELER Mehitable, and George Babcock, Jr., June 26, 1751.
3-167	WHITE Seth, and Hannah Burch; m. by Joseph Clarke, Justice, Sept. 3, 1780.
4-182	"	Lois, and Plumb Chapman, Nov. 14, 1784.
4-239	"	Mary, and Clarke Hiscox, Jr., Jan. 11, 1809.
5-67	"	Betsey, and Rufus Ames, Jan. 25, 1846.
5-109	"	Maxson, of Charles, of North Stonington, and Abby Gavitt, of Perry, of South Kingstown; m. by Rev. Fred. Denison, Aug. 5, 1850.
4-218	WHITTLES Mehitable, and Capt. Peleg Wilcox, Sept. 15, 1790.
3-11	WILBUR William, of Seconnett, and Mary Babcock, of Westerly; m. by William Babcock, Justice, April 17, 1745.
3-20	"	Lucy, and Matthew Maxson, May 2, 1748.

3-20 WILBUR Judith, and David Hall, May —, 1748.

3-148 " David, and Hannah Pendleton; m. by Richard Barry, Justice, April 27, 1765.

3-100 " Jonathan, and Hannah Thompson; m. by Joseph Crandall, Justice, Nov. 7, 1765.

4-21 " John, of Joseph, and Mary Barber, of Capt. Nathan; m. by Elder Oliver Babcock (also 4-10), Dec. 30, 1780.

4-97 " Joseph, Jr., of Joseph, and Joanna Babcock, of Col. James, dec.; m. by Elder Isaiah Wilcox, Jan. 6, 1790.

4-206 " Huldah, and Benjamin Hall, June 8, 1797.

4-174 " John, of Brookfield, N. Y., son of Joseph, and Elizabeth Babcock, of Westerly, daughter of Nathan; m. by Joseph Pendleton, Justice, Sept. 21, 1801.

4-192 " Ichabod, of David, and Desire Stillman, of Thaniel; m. by Joseph Pendleton, Justice, Feb. 21, 1804.

4-256 " Celia, and Elisha Babcock, Jan. 17, 1814.

4-274 " Desire, and Isaiah Wilbur, Aug. 14, 1825.

4-274 " Isaiah, and Desire Wilbur, both of Westerly; m. at North Stonington by Elder William Bendall, Aug. 14, 1825.

5-109 " James B., of Westerly, and Ruth Ann Ross, of Saybrook; m. at Saybrook by Rev. Fred William Hotchkiss, July 26, 1840.

2-113 WILCOX Edward, of Westerly, and Tamson Thompson, of Taunton; m. by Elder Samuel Danforth, May 1, 1698.

2-88 " Edward, of Westerly, and Dinah Barber, of South Kingstown; m. by Rouse Helme, Justice, June 14, 1716.

2-71 " Stephen, and Mercy Randall; m. by John Babcock, Justice, July 12, 1716.

2-91 " Anna, and Bryant Pendleton, March 11, 1725.

2-109 " William, and Susannah Burdick; m. by Theodoty Rhodes, Justice, Jan. 11, 1727-8.

2-119 " Edward, of Stonington, and Mercy Robinson; m. by William Hern, Justice, Jan. 5, 1738-9.

2-119 " Thomas, and Sarah Tefft; m. by Elder Joseph Maxson, July 2,1739.

2-85 " Lydia, and Stephen Saunders, Jr., Aug. 12, 1744.

3-23 " Eunice, and William Hern, June 25, 1752.

3-37 " Hezekiah, and Hannah Parker; m. by William Hern, Justice, March 31, 1754.

3-56 " Valentine, and Abigail Kenecome; m. by Joseph Crandall, Justice, Aug. 10, 1757.

3-59 " Sarah, and Jonathan Palmitter, Jan. 25, 1758.

3-63 " Teresa, and Joseph Hall, Dec. 18, 1758.

3-79 " Isaiah, and Sarah Lewis; m. by Joseph Crandall, Justice, Oct. 15, 1761.

3-10 " Mercy, and Daniel Stanton, July 18, 1762.

3-83 " Amey, and John West, Dec. 29, 1765.

3-125 " Sheffield, of Edward, and Esther, of Richmond, and Eunice Ross, of Thomas, of Westerly; m. by Jeffrey Wilcox, Justice, Dec. 11, 1771

4-186 " Desire, and John Gavitt, Dec. 28, 1773.

3-169 " Amey, and John Lewis, March 16, 1775.

3-163 " Lucy, and Samuel Babcock, May 22, 1779.

3-170 " David, of David, dec., and Content Lewis, of John; m. by Elder Thomas Ross, Jan. 1, 1780.

3-172 " Daniel, of Hezekiah, of Westerly, and Prudence Wilcox, of Edward, of Stonington; m. by Joseph Crandall, Justice, Dec. 28, 1780.

3-172 " Prudence, and Daniel Wilcox, Dec. 28, 1780.

3-157 " Martha, and Trustam Dickins, Oct. 27, 1782.

4-10 " Jesse, of Hezekiah, and Anne Pendleton, of Capt. Peleg; m. by Joseph Crandall, Justice, Dec. 9, 1784.

4-24 " Eunice, and Elisha Wells, June 28, 1787.

4-33 " Isaiah, and Polly Pendleton; m. by Elder Isaiah Wilcox, Jan. 22, 1788.

4-121 " Nancy, and Arnold Bliven, Feb. —, 1788.

4-121 " Mary, and Arnold Bliven, Dec. 31, 1789.

4-41 WILCOX Sally, and John Barber, Jan. 9, 1790.
4-32 "   Nathan, of Elder Isaiah, and Nancy Lewis, of Hezekiah; m. by Elder Isaiah Wilcox, Feb. 17, 1790.
4-115 "   Susannah, and Braddock Hall, July 30, 1790.
4-218 "   Capt. Peleg, and Mehitable Whittles; m. by Joseph Clarke, Justice, Sept. 15, 1790.
4-79 "   Asa, and Mercy Rathbone; m. at Colchester, Conn., by Rev. Abel Palmer, Nov. 28, 1791.
4-93 "   Stephen, of Elder Isaiah, dec., and Sally Champlain, of Capt. William; m. by Samuel Bliven, Justice, May 17, 1795.
4-106 "   Benjamin, of Valentine, and Nancy Thompson, of John; m. by Samuel Bliven, Justice, Sept. 28, 1796.
4-218 "   Samuel, of Hezekiah, of Westerly, and Prudence Grant, of Connecticut, — —, 1798.
4-132 "   Prudence, and Joshua Vose, Jr., Jan. 3, 1799.
4-198 "   Peleg, and Thankful Burdick, of Oliver, Jr.; m. by John Cross, Jr., Justice, April 25, 1804.
4-211 "   Hannah, and Ezekiel Gavitt, Nov. 21, 1805.
4-227 "   Ann, and Benjamin Babcock, Jan. 26, 1806.
4-230 "   Parker, and Polly Closson; m. at Stonington by Elijah Palmer, Justice, April 26, 1807.
4-231 "   Isaac, and Eunice Clawson; m. by Elijah Palmer, Justice, Jan. 17, 1808.
5-3   "   Stephen, Jr., and Sophia Vose, of Samuel; m. by Elder Matthew Stillman, Oct. 21, 1824.
5-11 "   Horace, and Hannah Kenyon; m. by Jedediah W. Knight, Justice, March 11, 1831.
5-72 "   Dudley R., and Henrietta M. Thompson; m. by Rev. E. T. Hiscox, Nov. 6, 1845.
5-72 "   Martha A., and Nathaniel J. L. Chase, Jan. 1, 1846.
2-79 WILKINSON Mary, and William Browning, Aug. 5, 1728.
5-108 WILLIAMSON Mrs. Dianna C., and John D. Powell, July 14, 1850.
2-87 WILLIAMS Mary, and Robert Rogers, Oct. 7, 1728.
3-17 "   Benajah, and Elizabeth Avery, both of Groton; m. by Joseph Crandall, Justice, Sept. 1, 1754.
3-20 "   Mark, and Sarah Hopkins; m. by William Hern, Justice, July 2, 1749.
3-62 WILLIS Lois, and James Brown, May 25, 1757.
2-75 WITTER Joseph, and Sarah Stewart; m. by Elder John Maxson, Dec. 9, 1736.
2-69 "   John, Jr., and Amey Davis; m. by Stephen Richmond, Justice, Sept. 7, 1740.
3-16 "   Martha, and Stephen Lewis, Oct. 18, 1747.
5-10 "   Eunice, and Sanford Noyes, Jr., Dec. 19, 1845.
2-81 WOGG Betty, and Sampson Tikon, June 15, 1748.
3-53 WOODBURN Samuel, and Prudence Richardson, both of Stonington; m. by Elder Stephen Babcock, March 4, 1757.
4-17 WOODWORTH Elizabeth, and Jonathan Saunders, June 25, 1771.
4-130 WOOD Susannah, and Thomas Hiscox, Nov. 13, 1797.
2-105 WOODMANSEE Mary, and Thomas Lillibridge, June 12, 1726.
2-45, 77 " Zerniah, and Thomas Rogers, Oct. 3, 1734.
2-111 WORDEN Peter, Jr., and Rebecca Richmond, May 26, 1720.
2-85 "   Sarah, and Joseph Pendleton, Jan. 9, 1723.
2-17 "   Isaac, and Mehitable Smith; m. by Elder Joseph Maxson, Aug. 31, 1740.
3-6   "   Mary, and Isaac Babcock, April 17, 1746.
3-20 "   John, and Dorothy Satterly; m. by William Hern, Justice, May 1, 1746.
3-8   "   Gideon, of Westerly, and Rebecca Brown, of Portsmouth; m. at Portsmouth, by William Sanford, Justice, May 1, 1748.
3-96 "   William, of Stonington, and Mary Byrns, of Rhode Island; m. by Elder Joseph Davis, Oct. 4, 1764.
4-76 "   Weltha, and Daniel Lanphere, Nov. 13, 1765.
3-114 "   John, of John, dec., of Hopkinton, and Elizabeth Babcock, of Joshua, Jr., dec., of Westerly; m. by Joseph Crandall, Justice, Nov. 12, 1769.

5-19   WORDEN Asa, of Hopkinton, and Mary Ann Sullivan, of Westerly; m. by
        Rev. Thomas H. Vail, Feb. 28, 1845.

2-70   WRIGHT William (mulatto), and Martha Scallenger (Indian); m. by Wil-
        liam Babcock, Justice, March 24, 1745-6.

4-209   "   Ann, and Capt. Dudley Babcock, Jan. 7, 1799.

X Y Z

3-46   YEOMAN Sarah, and Abijah Crandall, Aug. 29, 1754.

4-123   "   Lucretia, and Joseph C. Lanphere, June 6, 1798.

2-119   YORK James, and Hannah Stanton, Nov. 13, 1695.

2-95   "   Johannah, and Joseph Lorkin, July 24, 1730.

3-2   "   Mary, and Isaac Peckham, April 11, 1750.

3-62   "   Anna, and John Gavitt, April 19, 1758.

3-68   "   Hannah, and Samuel Bailey, Jr., Jan. 8, 1761.

3-95   "   William, and Anne Peckham; m. by Joseph Crandall, Justice,
        Nov. 15, 1764.

4-120   "   Nabby, and Thomas Foster, Sept. 4, 1791.

4-222   "   Capt. Benjamin, of William and Desire Saunders, of Joshua, both
        of Charlestown; m. by Elder William Gardiner, Jan. 21, 1801.

3-143   YOUNG Nicholas, of Samuel and Lydia Clarke, of Daniel; m. by Joseph
        Crandall, Justice, Feb. 1, 1776.

4-95   "   Hannah, and David Hall, Nov. 20, 1791.

WESTERLY.

BIRTHS AND DEATHS.

A

1-173	ADAMS	James, of James,	Jan. 20, 1697-8.
1-173	"	John,	May 26, 1700.
1-173	"	Jonathan,	Sept. 28, 1702.
1-173	"	Henry,	Sept. 27, 1704.
2-120	"	Honor, of James and Honor,	July 11, 1706.
2-120	"	Nathaniel,	March 25, 1708-9.
2-120	"	Thomas,	March 24, 1710.
2-120	"	Joseph,	March 4, 1714-5.
2-96	"	David, of Nathaniel and Hannah,	Sept. 20, 1737.
2-96	"	Elijah,	Aug. 8, 1734.
2-118	ALLEN	Mary, of Samuel and Catherine,	Sept. 17, 1709.
2-118	"	Catherine,	Dec. 20, 1711.
2-118	"	Elizabeth,	Sept. 4, 1713.
2-118	"	Joshua,	April 2, 1715.
2-118	"	Samuel,	June 26, 1717.
2-119	"	Lydia, of Gideon and Lydia,	Feb. 16, 1710.
2-119	"	Sarah,	Sept. 19, 1711.
2-122	"	Christopher, of Zachariah and Sarah,	Jan. 28, 1711-2.
3-35	"	Thankful, of Jonathan and Rachel,	Sept. 14. 1744.
3-115	"	Pamola, of Samuel and Isabel,	June 9, 1769.
3-115	"	Anne,	Nov. 11, 1770.
3-115	"	Polly,	Nov. 20, 1772.
3-115	"	Rhode,	July 26, 1790.
4-120	"	Betsey, of Joshua and Rachel,	Jan 8, 1799.
4-120	"	Patty,	June 23, 1800.
4-120	"	Joshua,	March 6, 1802.
4-120	"	Fanny,	Sept. 6, 1803.
4-120	"	Samuel,	Oct. 3, 1805.
		Note.—Patty born at Charlestown.	
4-212	"	Greene, of Greene and Amey,	Dec. 13, 1805.
3-66	AUSTIN	Freegift, of Cornelins, and Thankful,	June 26, 1738.
3-66	"	Sarah,	Oct. 2, 1740.
3-66	"	Hannah,	Nov. 30, 1742.
3-66	"	Ruth,	March 27, 1745.
3-66	"	Stephen,	May 17, 1747.
3-66	"	Cornelins,	Aug. 7, 1749.
3-101	"	Edward, of Thomas, and Martha,	Sept. 23, 1754.
3-101	"	Sarah,	Jan. 29, 1757.
3-101	"	Martha,	March 24, 1759.
3-101	"	Thomas,	April 24, 1761.
3-101	"	David,	Oct. 27, 1763.
		Note—Thomas born Westerly, all others Charlestown.	
3-71	"	Hannah, of Jedediah, and Anne,	Nov. 26, 1756.
3-71	"	Dorcas,	July 7, 1759.
3-71	"	John,	Aug. 24, 1761.
3-71	"	Anne,	Oct. 15, 1763.
3-71	"	Jedediah,	June 22, 1766.

B

-2-124	BABBITT Mary, died Nov. 8, buried 9th, 1711.		
1-172	BABCOCK James, of Capt. James, Jr.,		Dec. 23, 1688.
1-172	"	Elizabeth,	Feb. 8, 1691.
1-172	"	Samuel,	Feb. 15, 1697.
1-172	"	Daniel,	April 23, 1699.
1-172	"	Anna, of Capt. James, Jr., and Elizabeth,	Nov. 29, 1701.
1-172	"	Sarah,	Dec. 13, 1704.
1-172	"	Sarah,	d. Nov. 13, 1705.
2-121	"	Joshua,	May 17, 1707.
1-95	"	John, of John and Mary,	May 4, 1701.
1-95	"	Ichabod,	Nov. 21, 1703.
1-95	"	Stephen,	May 2, 1706.
2-113	"	Mary, of Robert and Lydia,	Aug. 31, 1702.
2-113	"	Lydia,	Nov. 5, 1703.
2-113	"	Robert,	May 8, 1706.
2-113	"	Elisha,	June 5, 1708.
2-113	"	Sarah,	March 28, 1710.
2-113	"	Patience,	Dec. 23, 1711.
2-113	"	Simeon,	Oct. 17, 1714.
2-113	"	Ezekiel,	June 22, 1716.
2-113	"	Joseph,	April 9, 1718.
2-113	"	Remember,	Feb. 11, 1720.
2-109	"	Susannah, of Oliver and Susannah,	Sept. 20, 1705.
2-109	"	Thomas,	March 7, 1710.
2-109	"	Mary,	Feb. 8, 1712-3.
2-109	"	Nathan,	Oct. 12, 1715.
2-109	"	Simeon,	Sept. 27, 1717.
2-109	"	John,	May 12, 1720.
2-109	"	Oliver,	Sept. 16, 1722.
2-109	"	Joseph,	Oct. 18, 1726.
2-120	"	William, of John and Mary,	April 15, 1708.
2-120	"	Amey,	Feb. 8, 1712-3.
2-120	"	Mary,	July 23, 1716.
2-120	"	Ann,	Sept. 14, 1721.
2-124	"	John, Jr., of John and Mary, died July 10, buried	— 11, 1719.
2-109	"	Jonathan, of James, (blacksmith) and Mary,	Feb. 18, 1723.
2-74	"	Isaac, of Daniel and Abigail,	April 24, 1724.
2-74	"	William,	March 11, 1725-6.
2-74	"	Joshua,	Dec. 7, 1728.
2-74	"	Elizabeth,	Jan. 13, 1730-1.
2-74	"	James,	June 2, 1733.
2-74	"	Daniel,	March 14, 1735.
2-74	"	Elkanah,	Aug. 21, 1738.
2-90	"	Elizabeth, of George and Susannah,	Jan. 25, 1725-6.
2-90	"	George,	Dec. 27, 1727.
2-90	"	Martha,	Dec. 8, 1729.
2-90	"	Susannah,	March 10, 1731-2.
2-90	"	Christopher,	Feb. 27, 1736-7.
2-90	"	Samuel,	May 30, 1739.
2-90	"	Hezekiah,	May 30, 1739.
2-90	"	Rouse,	April 29, 1746.
2-112	"	Nathan, of Samuel and Ann,	Nov. 25, 1726.
2-112	"	Elizabeth,	May 6, 1729.
2-112	"	Samuel,	May 16, 173?.
2-95	"	John, of Stephen and Anna,	July 16, 1727.
2-95	"	Anna,	Jan. 30, 1729.
2-88	"	Hosannah, of Joseph and Susannah,	April 1, 1730.
2-88	"	Prudence,	Oct. 22, 1732.
2-88	"	Joseph,	Dec. 9, 1734.
2-88	"	Jesse,	April 3, 1737.
2-88	"	Hannah,	Jan. 27, 1739-40.
2-88	"	Joseph,	Jan. 9, 1741-2.
2-88	"	Rebecca,	April 11, 1744.

2-88	BABCOCK	Joshua, of Joseph, and Susannah,	Oct. 5, 1747.
2-88	"	Anne,	June 18, 1749.
2-88	"	Ichabod,	June —, 1751.
2-92	"	William, of William, and Sarah,	May 19, 1731.
2-92	"	Joshua,	Dec. 2, 1732.
2-92	"	Christopher,	Sept. 12, 1734.
2-92	"	Sarah,	Oct. 17, 1736.
2-92	"	Elijah,	July 19, 1738.
2-124	"	Elijah,	d. Dec. 11, 1738.
2-92	"	Elias,	July 28, 1740.
2-94	"	Ichabod of Ichabod and Jemima,	Dec. 12, 1731.
2-94	"	Mary,	May 9, 1733.
2-94	"	Joseph,	Feb. 3, 1736.
2-94	"	John,	July 27, 1739.
2-87	"	Ann, of Capt. James and Content,	March 30, 1732.
2-87	"	James,	Nov. 1, 1734.
2-87	"	Jonathan,	Oct. 11, 1736.
2-113	"	Andrew, of Samuel, and Ann,	April 12, 1733.
2-113	"	Silas,	Dec. 31, 1734-5.
2-94	"	David, of David and Dorcas,	April 10, 1734.
2-94	"	Jonathan,	Nov. 19, 1735.
2-94	"	Benedick,	Oct. 21, 1737.
2-118	"	Penelope, of Elisha and Sarah,	Oct. 6, 1734.
2-118	"	Eunice,	Jan. 27, 1738-9.
2-76	"	Henry, of Joshua and Hannah,	April 26, 1736.
2-76	"	Luke,	July 6, 1738.
2-76	"	Adam,	Sept. 27, 1740.
2-76	"	Hannah,	Jan. 22, 1742-3.
2-76	"	Frances,	May 11, 1745.
2-76	"	Paul,	Dec. 5, 1748.
2-76	"	Amelia,	April 19, 1751.
2-76	"	Harriet,	May 18, 1756.
2-76	"	Sally,	Oct. 18, 1753.
2-76	"	Elisha, of William and Sarah,	d. Dec. 12, 1738.
2-76	"	William,	d. Feb. 6, 1751.
2-76	"	Pheneus,	Sept. 29, 1742.
2-76	"	Mercy,	July 14, 1745.
2-76	"	Samuel,	Sept. 4, 1747.
3-100	"	Abigail, wife of Jesse, (dau. of Henry Mulkins and Abigail, his wife), born Oct. 15, 1741.	
2-124	"	Capt. John, died March 28, 1746.	
2-95	"	Thankful, of Stephen and Anne,	Nov. 17, 1747.
2-124	"	Rebecca, widow of Joseph, died	July 15, 1747.
3-6	"	Phebe, of Isaac and Mary,	July 24, 1748.
3-6	"	John Prentice,	Oct. 4, 1750.
3-6	"	Isaac,	Jan. 15, 1754.
3-6	"	Mary,	March 11, 1757.
3-6	"	Amos,	Aug. 1, 1759.
3-6	"	Rebecca,	Oct. 21, 1761.
3-6	"	Rhoda,	Aug. 21, 1764.
3-6	"	Judah,	July 13, 1766.
3-6	"	Jesse,	June 16, 1768.
3-6	"	Abigail,	June 16, 1768.
3-6	"	Hannah,	June 23, 1770.
3-6	"	Joshua,	June 23, 1770.
3-12	"	Thomas, of Nathan and Deborah,	July 29, 1749.
3-12	"	Benjamin,	April 7, 1751.
3-12	"	Anne,	Nov. 9, 1752.
3-12	"	Mercy,	Oct. 12, 1754.
3-12	"	Samuel,	March 22, 1757.
3-12	"	Nathan,	June 19, 1759.
3-61	"	William, of William and Patience,	Feb. 23, 1750.
3-61	"	Anna,	March 26, 1753.
3-61	"	Esther,	Jan. 27, 1755.
3-61	"	Eunice,	Feb. 23, 1757.

3-61	BABCOCK	Hannah, of William and Patienre,	May 29, 1763.
2-92	"	William, Esq., died Jan. 15, 1751-2.	
3-120	"	James, of James and Mary,	July 31, 1753.
3-120	"	Daniel,	Feb. 25, 1755.
3-120	"	Henry,	June 23, 1757.
3-120	"	Mary,	Sept. 22, 1761.
3-120	"	Content,	March 19, 1764.
3-120	"	Barredell,	Jan. 19, 1766.
3-120	"	Lois,	May 20, 1768.
3-120	"	Patience,	Dec. 25, 1770.
3-120	"	Gideon,	April 30, 1773.
3-33	"	Susannah, of Joshua and Sarah,	Jan. 11, 1755.
3-33	"	Richard,	Feb. 10, 1756.
3-33	"	Daniel,	Sept. 10, 1757.
4-109	"	William, of Christopher and Mehitable,	Dec. 16, 1755.
4-109	"	Amey,	June 12, 1757.
4-109	"	Joshua,	March 15, 1759.
4-109	"	Joshua,	d. Oct. —, 1786.
4-109	"	Christopher,	July 26, 1761.
4-109	"	Sarah,	March 10, 1763.
4-109	"	Eunice,	Dec. 28, 1764.
4-109	"	Jeremiah,	Nov. 23, 1766.
4-109	"	Asa,	July 6, 1768.
4-109	"	Asa,	died April —, 1777.
4-109	"	Wealthy,	June 12, 1770.
4-109	"	Wealthy,	died June —, 1772.
4-109	"	Stephen,	Feb. 27, 1772.
4-109	"	Elias,	Oct. 26, 1773.
4-109	"	Elias,	died April —, 1794.
4-109	"	Phenias,	Feb. 14, 1776.
4-109	"	Asa,	Oct. 7, 1777.
3-42	"	Amelia, of James and Sarah,	—— — 1755.
3-42	"	Simeon,	Feb. 27, 1758.
3-42	"	Sarah,	March 25, 1764.
3-43	"	William, of Samuel and Mary,	Dec. 22, 1756.
3-43	"	Naham,	March 5, 1758.
3-43	"	Paul,	March 30, 1760.
3-43	"	Fanny,	Jan. 25, 1762.
3-43	"	Silas,	April 10, 1764.
3-43	"	Jared,	Feb. 11, 1766.
3-43	"	Thankful,	Feb. 15, 1768.
3-9	"	Ichabod, of Ichabod, Jr. and Esther,	Jan. 15, 1758.
3-9	"	Lucy,	July 24, 1760.
3-9	"	Joseph,	April 1, 1762.
3-9	"	Mary,	April 8, 1765.
3-9	"	Lodowick,	Feb. 18, 1767.
3-9	"	Angustus,	Jan. 30, 1769.
3-12	"	John Barber, of John and Elizabeth,	Aug. 2, 1759.
4-66	"	Linda, of Elkanah and Esther,	Feb. 25, 1763.
4-66	"	Joshua,	May 8, 1766.
4-66	"	Delight,	Feb. 8, 1768.
4-66	"	Amelia,	March 5, 1770.
4-66	"	Bradley,	May 14, 1772.
4-66	"	Luke,	May 1, 1774.
4-66	"	Hannah,	May 28, 1777.
4-66	"	Chancey,	Nov. 28, 1779.
4-66	"	Lodowick,	Jan. 27, 1781.
4-66	"	Esther,	April 9, 1784.
4-66	"	Elkanah,	June 29, 1786.
		Note—First 5 recorded also 3-81.	
3-12	"	Andrew, of Nathan and Elizabeth,	April 6, 1765.
3-12	"	Jonathan,	Dec. 14, 1766.
3-136	"	Lucy, of John and Lucy,	Aug. 14, 1765.
3-136	"	Jemimah,	Dec. 28, 1767.

3-136	BABCOCK	John, of John and Lucy,	Jan. 13, 1769.
3-99	"	Hannah, of Joseph (of Ichabod) and Hannah, 4-112, 3-122),	1st wife (also Jan. 2, 1767.
3-99	"	Elizabeth, of Nathan and Elizabeth,	Oct. 30, 1768.
3-99	"	Charles,	Aug. 23, 1770.
3-99	"	Deborah,	Aug. 16, 1772.
3-99	"	Mercy, of Nathan and Anna, 2d wife,	July 21, 1780.
3-115	"	Joanna, of Major James and Joanna,	June 10, 1770.
3-115	"	James,	Dec. 10, 1771.
3-115	"	Ezra,	May 13, 1773.
3-115	"	Charlotte,	Nov. 30, 1775.
3-115	"	Anna,	Dec. 19, 1779.
4-83	"	Jason, of Elder Oliver and Silvestre.	March 30, 1774.
4-83	"	Stephen,	July 26, 1777.
4-83	"	Oliver,	March 29, 1780.
4-53	"	Nancy, of William and Penelope,	Jan. 27, 1775.
4-53	"	John,	Oct. 14, 1780.
4-53	"	Sylvester,	July 10, 1783.
4-53	"	Jesse,	Oct. 1, 1785.
4-53	"	Daniel,	July 10, 1788.
4-53	"	Clarke,	Sept. 28, 1790.
4-53	"	Eunice,	Dec. 17, 1793.
4-149	"	Hannah, of James and Sarah,	Sept. 3, 1777.
4-149	"	Jesse,	May 20, 1784.
4-149	"	Abigail,	July 20, 1786.
4-149	"	Martha,	March 30, 1789.
4-149	"	Joshua,	March 20, 1793.

Note—Two last born South Kingstown, in 3-149, name of first is given as Hannah Clarke.

3-153	"	Stauton Prentice, of Prentice and Anna,	Dec. 15, 1778.
4-37	"	Henry, of Henry and Prudence,	July 22, 1779.
4-37	"	James,	Oct. 16, 1781.
4-37	"	Ezekiel,	Oct. 22, 1783.
4-37	"	Asa,	April 26, 1786.
4-37	"	Nancy,	Oct. 17, 1788.
4-37	"	Joshua,	April 18, 1791.
4-37	"	Joshua,	d. Jan. —, 1794.
4-37	"	Hannah,	Sept. 18, 1794.
4-37	"	Sarah,	July 17, 1796.
4-74	"	Benjamin, of Rouse and Ruth,	Sept. 2, 1779.
4-74	"	Sally,	April 6, 1782.
4-74	"	Nancy,	May 13, 1786.
4-74	"	Rouse, died June 13, 1801.	
4-76	"	Charlotte, of Paul and Charlotte,	Sept. 15, 1781.
4-76	"	Damarias,	Oct. 14, 1783.
4-76	"	Mary,	May 2, 1787.
4-76	"	Paul,	June 3, 1791.
4-76	"	Hannah,	Jan. 16, 1800.
4-7	"	Wealthy, of William and Mary,	Nov. 22, 1782.
4-7	"	William,	June 13, 1784.
4-113	"	Mary Ann, of Christopher and Polly,	Jan. 22, 1783.
4-113	"	James,	Nov. 10, 1784.
4-113	"	Martha,	Aug. 21, 1786.
4-113	"	Christopher,	May 23, 1788.
4-113	"	Elizabeth,	Oct. 28, 1790.
4-113	"	Benjamin Perry,	Dec. 8, 1792.
4-113	"	Charles,	Aug. 8, 1794.
4-113	"	Susannah,	Feb. 10, 1799.
4-113	"	Susannah,	died Oct. 27, 1803.
4-113	"	Martha,	died Oct. 27, 1803.
4-113	"	Christopher, Sr.,	died July 28, 1803.

Note—One born Middletown, next three Charlestown, the others Westerly.

4-84	"	Charlotte, of Amos and Mary,	Nov. 4, 1784.
4-84	"	Amos,	March 30, 1790.

4-84	BABCOCK	Anna, of Amos and Mary,	April 1, 1793.
3-127	"	Lucy, of Isaac and Amey,	March 19, 1783.
3-127	"	Sarah,	April 18, 1785.
3-175	"	Nathan, of Nathan and Dorcas,	Oct. 30, 1782.
3-175	"	David,	Aug. 16, 1784.
3-175	"	Dorcas,	April 20, 1786.
4-4	"	Hannah, of Daniel and Hannah,	Feb. 12, 1785.
4-4	"	Daniel,	Nov. 17, 1787.
4-4	"	Hannah,	March 30, 1789.
4-4	"	James,	Jan. 16, 1791.
4-4	"	Daniel Lee,	Jan. 26, 1795.
4-4	"	Desire,	Feb. 21, 1797.

Note—Hannah, 2d, born Stonington.

3-134	"	John Prentice, of Isaac, Jr., and Amey,	Oct. 13, 1787.
3-134	"	Denison Avery, at Groton,	Feb. 28, 1792.
4-20	"	Samuel, of Silas and Mary,	Oct. 19, 1787.
4-20	"	Silas,	Aug. 9, 1789.

Note—1st born Preston, Conn.

3-173	"	Asa, of Nathan and Dorcas, 4th wife,	Feb. 25, 1788.
4-68	"	Martha, of Jared and Martha,	Aug. 8, 1790.
4-68	"	Jared,	Aug. 8, 1792.
4-68	"	Clarke,	May 21, 1796.
4-55	"	Hannah, of Jesse and Hannah,	Sept. 22, 1790.
4-55	"	Beley (dau.),	Oct. 7, 1792.
4-55	"	Polly,	Oct. 8, 1794.
4-55	"	Rhoda,	March 7, 1798.
4-55	"	Lucy Ann,	July 31, 1800.
4-55	"	Phebe,	Sept. 3, 1802.
4-55	"	Jesse,	Aug. 31, 1806.
4-55	"	Lydia Ann,	Feb. 3, 1809.
4-55	"	Abby,	June 21, 1811.
4-55	"	John Champlain,	July 1, 1814.
4-60	"	Lucy, of Arnold and Lucy,	March 25, 1791.
4-60	"	John,	Feb. 4, 1793.
4-60	"	Amey,	Dec. 29, 1794.
4-74	"	Charles, of Charles and Tacy,	Aug. 24, 1792.
4-74	"	Jonathan,	July 26, 1794.
4-74	"	Tacy,	Nov. 14, 1796.

Note—Two eldest born Hopkinton.

4-77	"	Oliver, of Joshua and Ruth,	Dec. 21, 1792.
4-77	"	Silva,	Aug. 19, 1794.
4-77	"	Ephraim,	March 15, 1796.
4-77	"	Lodowick,	Feb. 14, 1798.
4-77	"	Thankful,	Feb. 1, 1800.
4-164	"	Jonathan, of Jonathan and Elizabeth,	Sept. 13, 1795.
4-164	"	Harry,	March 11, 1797.
4-164	"	Betsey,	June 20, 1799.
4-164	"	Nancy,	Jan. 24, 1801.

Note—1st two born Norwich, Conn.; last two Charlestown.

4-105	"	John, of John and Damarias,	Feb. 18, 1796.
4-209	"	Frances Ann, of Capt. Dudley and Ann,	Oct. 20, 1799.
4-209	"	Dudley Right,	Jan. 5, 1802.
4-209	"	Paul,	Feb. 11, 1805.

Note—Eldest born Stonington.

4-151	"	Caroline, of Asa and Molly,	Sept. 18, 1801.
4-151	"	Molly, wife of Asa,	d. Dec. 31, 1802.
4-180	"	Desire, of Joseph and Keturah,	Sept. 25, 1801.
4-180	"	Desire,	d. Nov. 15, 1802.
4-180	"	Hannah,	Sept. 10, 1803.
4-180	"	Hannah,	d. July 21, 1804.
4-180	"	Desire Gavitt,	Dec. 19, 1805.

Note—Two eldest born Charlestown; youngest Westerly.

4-165	"	Rouse, of Rouse and Hannah,	Oct. 27, 1801.
4-165	"	Rouse,	d. May 3, 1802.
4-165	"	Rouse, 2d,	May 4, 1803.

4-165	BABCOCK Hannah, of Rouse and Hannah,	Nov. 4, 1805
4-168	" Phebe, of Stephen and Phebe,	March 5, 1802.
4-168	" Stephen,	May 10, 1804.
4-168	" Elias,	March 19, 1806.
4-168	" Nathan,	July 27, 1808.
4-168	" Nathan,	died Dec. 11, 1814.
4-168	" Amanda,	Nov. 29, 1810.
4-168	" Amanda,	died Sept. 19, 1912.

Note.—Two born Hopkinton; next three Stonington.

4-171	" Avilda, of Phineas and Thankful,	Aug. 1, 1802.
4-171	" Phineas,	Sept. 24, 1804.
4-171	" Christopher Denison,	Jan. 2, 1806.
4-171	" Mary,	Oct. 2, 1807.
4-171	" Hannah,	March 31, 1811.
4-171	" Nancy B.,	Nov. 15, 1912.
4-172	" Nancy, of Joshua and Nancy,	May 26, 1802.
4-172	" Joshua,	died Aug. 2, 1802.
4-173	" Nancy, of Daniel and Nancy,	Nov. 29, 1803.
4-173	" Emory,	Feb. 6, 1806.
4-173	" Oliver,	June 26, 1811.
4-173	" Joseph,	Dec. 24, 1813.
4-173	" Ezra,	Jan. 16, 1816.
4-175	" James Rhodes, of James and Hannah,	Aug. 16, 1803.
4-175	" Joseph,	July 31, 1805.
4-208	" Frank, of Nathan, Jr., and Patty,	Jan. 17, 1806.
4-151	" Thomas, of Asa and Elizabeth,	Sept. 24, 1806.
4-227	" Benjamin, of Benjamin and Ann,	April 25, 1807.
4-241	" David Fenner, of David and Fanny,	Sept. 21, 1809.
5-45	" Stanton, of Chancey W. and Prudence,	Feb. 8, 1812.
4-247	" Merian, of Paul, Jr., and Amey,	May 21, 1812.
2-247	" Charlotte,	May 30, 1816.
4-271	" Hannah Almy, of Daniel, Jr., and Anne,	Oct. 13, 1819.
5-8	" Nathan, of Oliver and Phebe,	Nov. 19, 1825.
5-8	" Phebe Maria,	Feb. 20, 1827.
5-8	" Amanda,	Oct. 20, 1828.
5-8	" Daniel,	Dec. 4, 1829.
5-17	" Paul, died April 21, 1845.	
4-190	BARBER Perry, of John and Molly, born at Exeter,	June 1, 1767.
4-190	" Hannah (Miner, of Charles and Eunice), his wife, born Stonington, Oct. 3, 1767.	
4-190	" Perry, of Perry and Hannah,	Dec. 3, 1794.
4-190	" Charles Miner,	Sept. 13, 1796.
4-190	" Silas Holmes,	July 6, 1799.
4-190	" Ezra Styles,	Oct. 30, 1803.

All born Stonington except youngest in Westerly.

4-263	" Thomas, of Peleg and Isabel,	Oct. 24, 1783.
4-263	" Peleg Sherman,	July 4, 1785.
4-263	" Patty,	May 11, 1787.
4,263	" Abial,	Aug. 14, 1789.
4-263	" Merchant,	Feb. 20, 1791.
4-263	" Experience,	April 6, 1793.
4-263	" Mercy,	May 7, 1794.
4-263	" Hannah,	April 17, 1796.
4-263	" Susannah,	April 18, 1798.
4-263	" Isaac,	Jan. 20, 1800.
4-263	" Wealthy Ann,	May 21, 1802.

Note—First, born Hopkinton; next five Charlestown; sixth, Hopkinton; the others Westerly.

4-42	" Hosea, of Hosea and Cattern,	Sept. 13, 1799.
4-42	" Jared,	Sept. 19, 1801.
4-42	" Caty,	Nov. 12, 1803.
4-42	" Paul Maxson,	Feb. 28, 1806.
4-42	" Eunice,	April 1, 1813.
4-197	" Sprague, of Sprague, and Seney,	July 27, 1804.
4-197	" Sally,	June 11, 1806.

4-260	BARBER	Henry Merriott, of Benjamin P., and Hannah,	May 7, 1807.
4-260	"	Lucinda Merriott,	March 8, 1809.
4-260	"	Joshua,	Dec. 23, 1810.
4-260	"	George Washington,	March 18, 1813.
4-255	"	Thomas, of Thomas and Eunice,	June 4, 1809.
4-255	"	Sarah,	Nov. 17, 1810.
4-255	"	Phebe,	April 27, 1812.
4-255	"	Joseph R.,	Jan. 10, 1814.
4-41	"	Sally, wife of John, died July 5, 1810.	
4-41	"	John Maxson, of John and Barbara,	Oct. 2, 1811.
4-41	"	Wealtha,	June 8, 1813.
4-41	"	Phineas Wheeler,	April 18, 1816.
4-272	"	Mariah, of Susan,	Nov. 9, 1815.
4-272	"	Rhoda Ann, of Mercy,	June 27, 1816.
5-18	"	Charles Albert, of Charles P. and Celestine Lucy Ann,	
			Sept. 27, 1834.
5-61	"	Mary Frances, of George S. and Mary A.,	Feb. 3, 1843.
5-61	"	Harriet Louisa,	June 11, 1844.
5-61	"	Josephine,	Feb. 8, 1846.
3-11	BARTLETT,	Charles Frederick, of John and Lucretia,	Feb. 22, 1766.
2-79	BENTLEY,	William, of William and Bathsheba,	May 29, 1735.
3-121	BENT,	Hannah, of John, Jr., and Hannah,	July 10, 1771.
2-79	BEMES,	Ephraim, of James and Sarah,	Jan. 11, 1712-3.
2-79	"	James,	April 3, 1716.
2-25	BERRY,	Elisha, of Richard and Susannah,	Sept. 7, 1731.
2-25	"	Mariah,	March 11, 1732-3.
2-25	"	Elijah,	Feb. 23, 1734-5.
2-25	"	Susannah,	Sept. 11, 1737.
3-96	"	Bridget,	Sept. 17, 1729.
3-69	"	Elizabeth,	Aug. —, 1726.
3-69	"	John,	Nov. 27, 1738.
3-69	"	Simeon,	May 26, 1741.
3-69	"	Samuel,	Sept. 27, 1744.
3-69	"	Peleg,	May 30, 1746.

Note—3-69 gives Elizabeth, birthplace South Kingstown, and
Elisha, birth, Sept. 6, 1730; Sarah, March 11, 1732, and Susannah, Sept. 7, 1736.

3-47	"	Mary, of Elisha and Dinah,	April 22, 1763.
4-16	"	Hannah,	May 20, 1765.
4-16	"	Sexton Palmer,	May 8, 1767.
4-16	"	Lydia,	March 9, 1769.
4-16	"	Peleg,	July 23, 1772.
4-16	"	Sarah,	June 20, 1776.
4-16	"	Lyman,	May 20, 1779.
4-16	"	Samuel,	Aug. 27, 1781.
4-16	"	Susannah,	May 21, 1784.
3-152	"	Molly, of Samuel, and Molly,	Feb. 9, 1769.
3-152	"	Elizabeth,	Dec. 20, 1770.
3-152	"	Susanna,	Nov. 23, 1772.
3-152	"	Richard,	Jan. 28, 1775.
3-152	"	Anne,	Nov. 23, 1776.
3-152	"	Esther,	April 28, 1779.
3-152	"	Bridget,	June 28, 1781.
3-152	"	Catherine,	Oct. 26, 1783.
3-152	"	Samuel Foster,	Dec. 13, 1785.
4-18	"	Peleg, of Peleg and Mary,	June 10, 1775.
4-18	"	George Washington,	June 11, 1779.
4-18	"	Anna,	April 29, 1780.
4-18	"	Richard Wain,	June 1, 1782.
4-18	"	Elizabeth,	Oct. 17, 1784.
4-18	"	Elijah,	March 14, 1787.
4-18	"	John Simeon,	Aug. 28, 1789.
4-18	"	Elisha,	Dec. 20, 1792.
4-140	"	Henrietta, of Richard and Hannah,	June 3, 1800.
4-131	"	Bridget, of Peleg and Hannah,	June 13, 1800.

4-193	BERRY	Nancy, of Lyman and Sally,	Feb. 28, 1804.
4-227	"	Richard Wane, of Wain and Rosanna; born at Stonington, Sept. 28, 1807.	
4-253	"	Lucy Ann, of Samuel and Lucy,	Jan. 23, 1814.
4-253	"	Catherine,	Nov. 21, 1815.
4-253	"	Eliza Esther,	Feb. 5, 1818.
4-253	"	Samuel Spicer,	Jan. 29, 1820.
4-253	"	Charles Henry,	Sept. 12, 1823.
4-253	"	Eunice Cowline,	May 16, 1826.
2-121	BLIVEN	Joan, of John and Isabel,	May 1, 1692
2-121	"	Edwin,	Aug. 5, 1694.
2-121	"	Rachel,	March 19, 1697.
2-121	"	James,	Oct. 27, 1702.
2-121	"	John,	Jan. 22, 1707.
2-121	"	Freelove, of Edward and Freelove,	Dec. 20, 1719.
2-121	"	Joshua,	March 21, 1720.
2-121	"	Edward,	May 30, 1722.
2-121	"	Isabel,	Oct. 22, 1723.
2-121	"	Patience,	June 3, 1725.
2-121	"	Peter,	Feb. 1, 1727.
2-121	"	John,	Sept. 22, 1730.
2-121	"	Nathan,	Nov. 20, 1732.
2-121	"	Mary,	Feb. 16, 1734.
2-121	"	Sarah,	May 26, 1736.
2-98	"	Mercy, of John and Mercy,	Nov. 25, 1728.
2-98	"	John,	died Aug. 25, 1728.
2-69	"	James, of James and Anna,	March 22, 1735.
2-98	"	John,	March 22, 1735.
2-69	"	Daniel,	March 12, 1737.
2-69	"	Mary,	May 13, 1739.
2-69	"	Theodoty,	May 3, 1741.
2-69	"	Samuel,	March 12, 1744.
2-220	"	Joshua, of Edward, Jr., and Ann,	July 13, 1743.
2-220	"	William,	Dec. 15, 1745.
2-220	"	Edward,	July 12, 1748.
2-220	"	Isaac,	July 13, 1750.
2-220	"	Ann,	March 10, 1755.
2-220	"	Arnold,	Feb. 7, 1757.
2-220	"	George,	Sept. 16, 1759.
2-220	"	Fannie,	July 16, 1761
2-220	"	Jonathan Burdick,	Aug 12, 1764.
2-220	"	Jessie Champlain,	Nov. 14, 1766.
4-194	"	Samuel, of James and Ann, born Westerly,	March 12, 1744.
4-194	"	Ruth (Greene of Josiah and Hannah), his wife, born Charlestown, March 16, 1746.	
4-194	"	Elizabeth, of Samuel and Ruth,	Dec. 27, 1766.
4-194	"	Samuel,	Dec. 15, 1768.
4-194	"	Luther,	Oct. 30, 1770.
4-194	"	Ruth,	Feb. 5, 1773.
4-194	"	Mary,	June 14, 1776.
4-194	"	Ethel,	May 28, 1778.
4-194	"	Daniel,	Aug. 20, 1780.
4-194	"	James,	June 27, 1787.
4-194	"	Ruth, wife of Samuel, d.	Dec. 18, 1803.
3-29	"	Patience, of John and Elizabeth,	Sept. 15, 1753.
3-29	"	Freelove,	Jan. 26, 1756.
3-29	"	John,	Dec. 23, 1758.
3-29	"	William,	May 19, 1762.
3-29	"	Elizabeth,	Dec. 31, 1764.
3-29	"	Lucy,	April 25, 1768.
3-29	"	Joshua,	April 29, 1773.
3-29	"	Ruth Seager,	March 9, 1773.
3-175	"	Elizabeth, of Nathan and Elizabeth,	Aug. 4, 1755.
3-175	"	Nathan,	April 17, 1761.
3-175	"	Mary,	Feb. 15, 1764.

3-175	**BLIVEN**	Henry, of Nathan and Elizabeth,	Nov. 27, 1766.
3-175	"	Freelove,	June 16, 1770.
3-175	"	Abigail,	Nov. 3, 1774.
3-175	"	Joseph Lewis,	May 5, 1778.
3-52	"	Thankful, of James and Sarah,	Sept 16, 1757.
3-52	"	James,	Nov. 20, 1760.
3-52	"	Freeman,	March 26, 1766.
3-52	"	Sarah,	Oct. 25, 1768.
3-52	"	Luke,	June 20, 1771.
4-52	"	Theodoty, of Daniel and Hannah,	Aug. 23, 1763.
4-52	"	Anna,	June 29, 1765.
4-52	"	John,	April 5, 1767.
4-52	"	Hannah,	Feb. 26, 1770.
4-52	"	Rachel,	March 5, 1772.
4-52	"	Daniel,	Feb. 20, 1774.
4-52	"	Greene,	April 30, 1776.
4-52	"	Isaac,	June 10, 1778.
4-52	"	Amey,	Sept. 19, 1780.
4-52	"	Fanny,	April 16, 1783.
4-52	"	Polly,	Oct. 13, 1786.
4-52	"	Daniel, Sr; died	Nov. 15, 1803.
		Note.—First seven recorded also 3-86.	
3-104	"	Elizabeth, of Samuel and Ruth,	Dec. 27, 1766.
3-104	"	Samuel,	Dec. 15, 1768.
3-104	"	Luther,	Oct. 30, 1770.
3-104	"	Ruth,	Feb. 5, 1773.
3-104	"	Mary,	June 14, 1776.
3-104	"	Ethel,	May 28, 1778.
3-150	"	Fanny, of William and Eleanor,	Aug. —, 1772.
3-150	"	Pardon Clarke,	Jan. 4, 1774.
3-150	"	Eleanor,	April 1, 1776.
3-150	"	William Barton,	Nov. 7, 1777.
3-150	"	Desire,	Aug. 11, 1790.
3-150	"	Edward,	May 20, 1783.
3-150	"	John Maxson,	April 21, 1785.
3-150	"	Thankful,	July 27, 1787.
3-150	"	Isaac Ross,	Dec. 20, 1790
3-150	"	Maria,	Feb. 10, 1793
3-132	"	Nancy, of Edward, 3d, and Mary,	May 1, 1774.
3-54	"	Simon Ray, of James and Sarah,	April 28, 1774.
3-54	"	Martha,	May 22, 1776.
4-181	"	Polly (——), wife of Capt. Nathan,	Dec. 11, 1774.
4-181	"	Robert Ellery, of Capt. Nathan and Polly,	Sept. 21, 1798.
4-181	"	Ann Mariah,	Feb. 7, 1800.
4-181	"	Francis,	Jan. 3, 1802.
4-181	"	Francis,	died Sept. 29, 1804.
4-181	"	Elizabeth,	March 24, 1803.
4-181	"	Francis,	Aug. 26, 1805.
		Note—Two eldest born Charlestown.	
3-157	"	Isaac, of Daniel and Hannah,	June 10, 1778.
3-157	"	Amey,	Sept. 19, 1780.
3-157	"	Fanny,	April 16, 1783.
3-28	"	Isaac, of John and Elizabeth,	Sept. 20, 1778.
3-166	"	Hannah, of James and Mary,	April 2, 1781.
3-166	"	Benjamin Hall,	June 17, 1787.
3-166	"	Betsey,	June 30, 1791.
		Note—First born Westerly, 2d Valuntown, 3d Newport.	
4-19	"	Nancy, of George and Vashti,	Dec. 4, 1784.
4-19	"	Edward,	May 7, 1786.
4-19	"	Polly,	May 27, 1788.
4-19	"	Samuel,	Feb. 28, 1792.
4-19	"	Henry,	April 3, 1794.
4-19	"	Noyes,	March 17, 1796.
3-168	"	Daniel, of Samuel and Ruth,	Aug. 20, 1780.
3-168	"	James,	June 27, 1787.

4-121	BLIVEN	Nancy, wife of Arnold,	died July 12, 1788.
4-121	"	Joshua, of Arnold and Mary,	July 25, 1790.
4-121	"	Joseph,	Jan. 31, 1792.
4-121	"	Nancy,	March 6, 1794.
4-121	"	Arnold,	Feb. 24, 1796.
4-121	"	Charles Ross,	Feb. 12, 1799.
4-121	"	Isaac Ross,	Feb. 27, 1801.
4-121	"	Desire,	April 21, 1803.
4-37	"	Samuel, of Samuel and Elizabeth,	Oct. 1, 1790.
4-37	"	Isaac,	May 30, 1793.
4-37	"	Thomas,	March 26, 1794.
4-37	"	Luther,	Sept. 23, 1801.
4-37	"	Benjamin,	Sept. 6, 1803.
4-37	"	Darius,	Dec. 1, 1805.
4-37	"	Elizabeth,	Feb. 2, 1808.
4-37	"	Mary,	May 14, 181).

Note—Benjamin born Hopkinton and Darius at Charlestown.

4-34	"	Daniel, of Theodoty and Bathana,	Feb. 27, 1791.
4-34	"	Esther	May 25, 1795.
4-34	"	Nathan Rogers,	April 19, 1797.

Note—Esther born Hopkinton, and Nathan R. at Charlestown.

4-44	"	Hannah, of John and Barbara,	Oct. 19, 1792.
4-54	"	Rozina, of William and Rozina,	Aug. 7, 1793.
4-54	"	Rozina, wife of William,	died July 4, 1800.
4-72	"	Sally, of Luther and Rebecca,	Jan. 18, 1794.
4-72	"	Polly,	July 13, 1796.
4-72	"	Samuel Greene,	Jan. 1, 1799.

Note—All born at Kingsbury, N. Y.

3-28	"	Elizabeth, wife of John,	died May 14, 1796.
3-28	"	Isaac, of John and Elizabeth, died at Demarara, Jan. 24, 1800.	
4-96	"	Joshua, of Joshua and Rhoda,	Oct. 2, 1796.
4-96	"	Ledyard,	March 8, 1798.
4-96	"	Ira,	Nov. 22, 1799.
4-96	"	Rhoda,	Sept. 20, 1801.
4-96	"	Russell,	April 20, 1803.
4-122	"	Betsey Sisson, of Ethel and Mary,	July 13, 1798.
4-122	"	Pardon,	July 2, 1800.
4-122	"	Alfred,	May 30, 1803.

Note—Two youngest born Newport.

4-48	"	Abigail, of Henry and Nancy,	Aug. 18, 1798.
4-48	"	Henry,	May 8, 1801.
4-48	"	Royal,	March 7, 1803.
4-48	"	Avery,	Jan. 6, 1805.
4-48	"	Albert,	Oct. 28, 1809.
4-48	"	Harriet,	July 25, 1812.
4-48	"	Horace,	Aug. 7, 1815.
4-48	"	Joseph Charles,	March 28, 1818.
4-48	"	Thomas N.,	July 22, 1820.
4-194	"	Ira, of Daniel (of Samuel),	May 14, 1802.
4-167	"	Cranston, of William P. and Amey,	Sept. 10, 1802.
4-167	"	Prudence,	Feb. 14, 1804.
4-122	"	Arestes, of Daniel and Ruth,	July 24, 1803.
4-54	"	Coddington, of William and Nancy,	Oct. 11, 1803.
4-54	"	Asa,	Dec. 1, 1804.
4-54	"	William Dudley,	April 22, 1806.
4-54	"	Bradley,	Jan. 15, 1808.
4-54	"	John Emery,	(Postumous), May 6, 1810.
2-43	BOSS	Richard, of Jeremiah and Martha,	Feb. 26, 1724-5.
2-43	"	Edward,	April 20, 1725.
2-43	"	Susannah,	Feb. 19, 1728-9.
2-43	"	Jeremiah,	May 17, 1729.
2-43	"	Martha,	Feb. 12, 1731-2.
2-43	"	Peter,	Sept. 30, 1732.
2-43	"	Joseph,	Nov. 2, 1734-5.

2-43	BOSS John, of Jeremiah and Martha,		Oct. 14, 1735.
2-42	" Martha,		Oct. 11, 1737.
4-104	BRAGDON, Anna, of Joseph and Content,		March 2, 1794.
2-15	BRAMAN Dorcas, of Benjamin and Martha,		Feb. 24, 1731-2.
3-103	BRAMBLEY Asa, of William and Elizabeth,		Feb. 22, 1746.
3-103	" David,		Oct. 27, 1748.
3-103	" Joshua,		March 20, 1750.
3-103	" Simeon,		Feb. 17, 1752.
3-103	" Paul,		April 17, 1754.
3-103	" Paine,		April 17, 1754.
3-103	" William,		March 27, 1756.
3-103	" Perry,		Nov. 12, 1758.
3-103	" Elizabeth,		March 11, 1761.
3-103	" Lucy,		Oct. 27, 1762.
3-103	" Rhoda,		April 11, 1764.
3-103	" Amelia,		April 11, 1764.
2-51,95	BRAND Amos, of Benjamin and Rebecca,		Feb. 8, 1735-6.
2-51,95	" Rebecca and Lucy,		June 28, 1741.
2-51,95	" Benjamin,		Oct. 2, 1742.
2-51,95	" David,		Jan. 11, 1744-5.
3-55	" Isabel, of Thomas and Freelove,		April 28, 1737.
3-55	" Jane,		Sept. 24, 1742.
3-88	" Susanna, of Samuel and Rachel,		July 6, 1741.
3-88	" Samuel,		Oct. 16, 1743.
3-88	" Hannah,		March 6, 1746.
3-88	" Thomas,		July 26, 1752.
3-88	" Nathan,		Aug. 15, 1754.
3-88	" Anne,		April 9, 1757.
3-88	" Walter,		May 25, 1760.
3-88	" Elizabeth,		July 5, 1762.
3-88	" Royzell,		April 10, 1775.
3-85	" Sarah, of John and Mary,		May 18, 1754.
3-85	" John,		Jan. 18, 1757.
3-85	" Abigail,		—— 17, 1758.
3-85	" Thomas,		Sept. 10, 1761.
3-141	" Fanny, of John and Isabel,		May 6, 1771.
3-141	" Hannah,		March 11, 1775.
5-170	" Lucy, of Samuel and Anne,		Sept. 1, 1777.
4-136	" Nathan, of Capt. Nathan and Susannah,		Feb. 12, 1785.
4-136	" Samuel,		Feb. 16, 1788.
4-136	" William,		Nov. 5, 1790.
4-136	" Betsey,		Dec. 23, 1793.
4-100	" Sally, of Walter and Anna,		July 16, 1785.
4-100	" Alpheus,		June 8, 1787.
4-100	" Samuel,		June 13, 1789.
4-100	" Nancy, of —— and Lydia,		Sept. 13, 1791.
4-241	" Thomas, of Russell and Hannah,		Dec. 13, 1804.
4-241	" Rachel Thompson,		July 9, 1809.
3-91	BRIGGS Anne, of Jacob and Freegift,		May 10, 1768.
3-91	" Abigail,		July 2, 1771.
2-4	BRITON Mary, of James, late of Dighton, Mass.,		died Dec. 23, 1750.
2-114	BROWN Elizabeth, of Daniel,		March 13, 1703.
2-114	" Mary,		Aug. 3, 1706.
2-114	" Benjamin,		March 16, 1708.
2-114	" Daniel,		Nov. 15, 1709.
2-114	" Elisha,		Jan. 26, 1711.
2-114	" Dorcas,		May 23, 1713.
2-114	" John,		Feb. 18, 1714.
2-114	" Desire, and Frances, 2d wife,		Jan. 8, 1723.
2-115	" Mary, of John and Ann,		Feb. 20, 1708.
2-115	" Martha,		Sept. 24, 1709.
2-115	" John,		Oct. 4, 1711.
2-115	" Ann,		Nov. 2, 1714.
2-115	" Thomas,		Oct. 18, 1717.
2-115	" Philip, of —— and Martha, 2d wife,		Sept. 2, 1721.

2-95	BROWN	John, of —— and Abigail,	July 15, 1730.
2-95	"	Joshua,	Jan. 19, 1732-3.
2-95	"	Abigail,	June 8, 1735.
2-95	"	Benjamin, of Benjamin and Abigail,	March 27, 1731.
2-95	"	Desire,	June 18, 1733.
2-95	"	Frances,	March 12, 1735.
2-95	"	James,	March 13, 1737.
2-95	"	John,	April 3, 1739.
2-95	"	Jeremiah,	April 4, 1741.
2-95	"	Desire,	March 23, 1743.
2-95	"	Jesse,	April 11, 1745.
2-95	"	Elijah,	June 10, 1747.
2-95	"	Abijah,	Nov. 3, 1749.
2-96	"	Mary, of George and Elizabeth,	Nov. 20, 1729.
3-48	"	Caleb, of Ebenezer and Anna,	Dec. 3, 1756.
3-48	"	Hannah,	March 17, 1759.
3-48	"	Lydia,	July 9, 1761.
3-48	"	John,	March 12 1764.
3-48	"	Amey,	Sept. 22, 1766.
3-48	"	Sarah,	March 3, 1769.
3-100	"	Dorothy,	Dec. 11, 1771.
3-100	"	Nathan,	——. —, 1774.
4-27	"	Polly, of Samuel and Amey,	Feb. 8, 1779.
4-27	"	Samuel,	March 2, 1782.
4-27	"	Benjamin,	Sept. 23, 1786.
4-27	"	Stanton,	April 16, 1789.
4-27	"	Phebe,	Jan. 14, 1791.
4-27	"	Nancy,	July 26, 1793.
4-27	"	Abigail,	Aug. 3, 1795.
4-27	"	Elnathan Clarke,	April 5, 1797.
4-77	"	Charles, of Robert and Hannah,	Dec. 16, 1792.
4-77	"	Thomas,	Jan. 21, 1798.
4-77	"	Susanna Stillman,	April 8, 1801.
4-77	"	Sebra,	Jan. 2, 1804.
4-214	"	Lorenzo Dow, of George and Sally,	Dec. 27, 1805.
4-126	BUDINGTON	Luke, of Luke and Charlotte,	Sept. 15, 1799.
4-126	"	Ludowick,	March 6, 1801.
4-126	"	Charlotte,	Jan. 21, 1803.
4-126	"	Rhoda Ann,	July 15, 1806.
4-180	BURCH	John Irish, of Thomas and Susanna,	Nov. 4, 1802.
4-229	"	Thomas, of Thomas and Mary,	Aug. 25, 1807.
2-119	BURDICK,	Mary, of Benjamin and Mary,	July 26, 1699.
2-119	"	Rachel,	July 5, 1701.
2-119	"	Peter,	Aug. 5, 1703.
2-119	"	Benjamin,	Nov. 25, 1705.
2-119	"	John,	March 24, 1708.
2-119	"	David,	Feb. 24, 1710.
2-119	"	William,	June 12, 1713.
2-119	"	Elisha,	Sept. 22, 1716.
2-125	"	Hubard, of Hubard,	Nov. 24, 1716.
2-125	"	Nathan,	Feb. 19, 1718-9.
2-125	"	John,	May 19, 1721.
2-77,90	"	Elnathan, of Peter and Desire,	Jan. 14, 1727.
2-77,90	"	Mary,	June 28, 1728.
2-77,90	"	Peter,	May 12, 1730.
2-77,90	"	Content,	April 1, 1735.
2-77,90	"	Oliver,	June 8, 1737.
2-77, 90	"	Ketnrah,	Jan. 30, 1741.
2-77, 90	"	Elnathan,	April 11, 1743.
2-77, 90	"	Elisha,	Aug. 1, 1747.
2-77, 90	"	Samuel Park (b. Charlestown),	Sept. 10, 1750.
2-76	"	Parker, of Joshua and Abigail,	Sept. 11, 1735.
2-79	"	Sylvanus, of Nathan and Goodeth,	Sept. 17, 1747.
3-70	"	Jonathan, of Jonathan and Judeth,	April 1, 1730.
3-70	"	Joseph,	Nov. 10, 1733.

3-70	BURDICK	Oliver, of Jonathan and Judeth,	March 27, 1735.
3-70	"	Ruth,	Dec. 10, 1737.
3-70	"	Judith,	May 21, 1740.
3-70	"	Wealthy,	June 18, 1743.
3-70	"	Ephraim,	May 1, 1746.
3-70	"	Benjamin,	Aug. 27, 1748.
3-70	"	Asa,	Aug. 6, 1751.
3-70	"	Hannah,	Oct. 29, 1755.
3-70	"	Joseph (grandson of the above, said son Joseph supposed to be deceased),	born March 18, 1755.
3-71	"	Lois, of David and Mary,	April 1, 1738.
3-71	"	David,	April 15, 1740.
3-71	"	Thompson,	Dec.15 1744.
3-71	"	Clarke,	Feb. 25, 1748.
3-71	"	Anne,	May 17, 1757.
3-39	"	Stephen, of Simeon and Isabel,	March 16, 1748.
3-39	"	Edith,	July 27, 1750.
3-39	"	Isabel,	Feb. 23, 1753.
3-39	"	Abigail,	Aug. 11, 1760.
3-39	"	Simeon,	Aug. 25, 1762.
3-39	"	Content,	Nov. 17, 1764.
3-39	"	Jonathan,	Sept. 26, 1767.
3-106	"	Maxson, of John and Elizabeth,	Jan. 22, 1751.
3-106	"	Thompson,	Sept. 1, 1753.
3-106	"	Anne,	Feb. 2, 1755.
3-106	"	John,	Sept. 20, 1756.
3-106	"	Paul,	Oct. 24, 1759.
3-106	"	Abigail,	Nov. 22, 1761.
3-106	'	Sarah,	Sept. 7, 1763.
3-106	"	Frances,	March 29, 1765.
3-11	"	Amey, of Ezekiel, and Amey,	June 29, 1751.
3-33	"	Esther, of Peter and Esther,	Nov. 5. 1754.
3-33	"	Cynthia,	Nov .26. 1759.
3-33	"	Henry,	March 1, 1764.
3-33	"	Hannah,	April 20, 1768.
3-33	"	Desire,	April 20, 1768.
3-149	"	Oliver, of Oliver and Lydia,	Feb. 7, 1760.
3-149	"	Sarah,	Aug. 4, 1761.
3-149	"	Hazard,	April 21, 1764.
3-149	"	Roger,	March 13, 1767.
3-149	"	Rowland,	June 26, 1769.

Note—1st and 4th born Charlestown, 2d and 5th Westerly, 3d South Kingstown.

3-22	"	Stanton, of Oliver and Susannah,	April 7, 1760.
3-22	"	Mary,	Nov. 9, 1761.
3-92	"	Ruth, of Zaccheas and Elizabeth,	June 24, 1760.
3-92	"	Smith,	May 3, 1762.
3-89	"	John, of Christopher and Chloe,	Sept. 25, 1762.
3-89	"	Lodowick,	April 5, 1764.
3-112	"	Clarke, of Ichabod and Bathsheba,	March 11, 1765.
3-112	"	Henry,	June 2, 1767.
3-176	"	Mary, of Clarke and Amey,	July 28, 1771.
3-176	"	David,	Oct. 8, 1773.
3-176	"	Amey,	Aug. 23, 1776.
3-176	"	Clarke,	April 5, 1779.

Note—First and 4th born Westerly, 2d Newport, 3d South Kingstown.

3-156	"	Thompson, of Thompson and Patience,	April 15, 1774.
3-156	"	Elizabeth,	July 13, 1776.
3-156	"	Samuel Allen,	Dec. 30, 1779.
3-156	"	Mary,	Jan. 3, 1783.
3-156	"	Freelove Bliven,	Oct. 11, 1785.
3-156	"	Lucy Bliven	(b. Stonington), Nov. 15, 1792.
4-63	'	John, of John and Elizabeth,	Feb. 9, 1781.
4-63	"	Polly,	April 13, 1783.

4-63	BURDICK Sarah, of John and Elizabeth,		June 5, 1786.
4-63	"	Paul,	May 17, 1788.
4-63	"	Hannah,	Dec. 10, 1791.
4-63	"	Rouse Babcock,	March 6, 1794.
4-63	"	Ira Kilburn,	March 14, 1798.
3-152	"	Ruth, of Asa and Isabel, born in the Charlotte Precinct, in the Grant of the Nine Partners, N. Y.,	June 24, 1783.
4-81	"	Simeon, of Simeon and Susannah,	Jan. 29, 1787.
4-81	"	Simeon,	died Sept. 12, 1806.
4-81	"	Susannah,	March 16, 1789.
4-81	"	Ruth,	April 28, 1792.
4-81	"	Lucy,	May 30, 1794.
4-81	"	Sally,	May 18, 1797.
4-81	"	Caty,	June 5, 1800.
4-81	"	Matilda,	March 10, 1803.
4-81	"	Simeon,	July 23, 1807.
4-54	"	Nancy, of Kenyon and Nancy,	Dec. 28, 1790.
4-54	"	Kenyon,	Nov. 19, 1792.
4-54	"	Thomas Hiscox,	July 2, 1794.
4-54	"	Henry,	Feb. 3, 1797.
4-54	"	Beley (dau.),	April 16, 1799.
4-54	"	Esther,	June 10, 1801.
4-54	"	Edward Hiscox,	Nov. 5, 1803.
4-54	"	Phineas,	Oct. 17, 1805.
4-54	"	Lois,	April 17, 1808.
4-54	"	Hannah,	April 17, 1808.
4-65	"	Esther, of Ethan and Esther,	Jan. 9, 1794.
4-65	"	Dorcas,	June 15, 1795.
4-65	"	Ethan,	Oct. 30, 1796.
4-65	"	Cary,	April 12, 1798.
4-105	"	Thomas Thompson, of Thompson and Amey,	Feb. 20, 1797.
4-105	"	Rodman Sisson,	Feb. 11, 1799.
4-105	"	Polly,	Nov. 29, 1800.
4-105	"	Desire,	June 20, 1803.
4-105	"	Sion Sisson,	March 6, 1805.
4-105	"	Eliza,	Oct. 25, 1807.
4-105	"	Content,	Aug. 5, 1809.
4-105	"	Samuel Lee	Feb. 3, 1812.
4-217	"	Rowland Chester, of Rowland and Martha,	Sept. 20, 1807.
4-217	"	William Coon,	March 30, 1809.
4-217	"	Horatio Nelson,	Sept. 20, 1811.
4-217	"	Martha Chase,	June 14, 1813.
4-217	"	John Davis,	April 25, 1815.
4-217	"	Esther Crandall,	April 30, 1817.
4-217	"	Alfred Bailey,	Feb. 1, 1819.
4-217	"	James Palmer,	Nov. 21, 1820.
5-11	"	Amanda, of Jed. and Sally,	May 23, 1823.
5-11	"	Lucanna,	March 23, 1825.
5-11	"	Asahel L.,	April 28, 1827.
5-11	"	Thomas E.,	March 24, 1829.
2-96	BUTTON John, of Matthew and Mary,		Sept. 1, 1728.
2-96	"	Mary,	March 10, 1730.
2-96	"	Matthew,	April 22, 1732.
2-60	"	Charles, of Joseph, and Abigail,	April 17, 1739.
2-60	"	Mary, of James, late of Dighton, Mass., (deceased), and Hannah, his wife,	died Dec. 23, 1750.
3-13	"	Charles, of Joseph, and Abigail,	April 17, 1739.
3-13	"	Elisha,	Jan. 5, 1741-2.
3-13	"	Stanberry,	June 27, 1744.
3-13	"	Joseph,	July 16, 1746.
3-13	"	Mary,	Aug. 25, 1750.
3-13	"	Joseph, Sr.,	died May 20, 1750.

C

4-185	CARR	Daniel, of Resolved and Betsey,	Oct. 14, 1793.
4-185	"	Samuel,	Oct. 29, 1795.
4-185	"	Elizabeth,	Oct. 1, 1797.
4-185	"	Phebe,	March 26. 1800.
4-185	"	Joanna,	Jan. 20, 1802.
4-185	"	Vincent,	Dec. 3, 1804.
4-218	CASSON	Charles, of John and Phebe,	Oct. 3, 1803.
4-218	"	Nancy Taylor,	Aug. —, 1805.
1-102	CHAMPLAIN	William of William and Mary,	May 31, 1702.
1-102	"	Jeffrey,	March 6, 1704.
2-125	"	Christopher, of Christopher, Jr., and Elizabeth,	Nov. 30, 1707.
2-125	"	Joseph.	Aug. 4, 1709.
2-125	"	Ann,	March 29, 1714.
2-125	"	George,	Feb. 15, 1715-6.
2-125	"	Elizabeth,	Jan. 10, 1718-9.
2-125	"	Thankful,	March 27, 1721.
2-125	"	Lydia,	Nov. 19, 1723.
2-125	"	Jabez,	Aug. 31, 1728.
2-125	"	Oliver,	May 12, 1730.
2-125	"	Mary,	June 29, 1731.
2-98	"	Andrew, of Joseph and Sarah,	Feb. 25, 1722-3.
2-98	"	Joseph,	July 20, 1725.
2-45	"	Christopher, of Christopher and Hannah,	Feb. 7, 1730-1.
2-45	"	John,	Dec. 18, 1732.
2-45	"	Rhuhamah,	Jan. 11, 1735-6.
2-45	"	Elizabeth,	May 22, 1737.
2-124	"	Christopher,	died April 2, 1732.
4-127	"	William, May 31, 1702.	died April 14, 1774.
3-97	"	Mary, of William and Sarah,	July 13, 1722.
3-97	"	Samuel,	Oct. 6, 1724.
3-97	"	Jeffrey,	Sept. 30, 1726.
3-97	"	Anna,	Jan. 15, 1729.
3-97	"	William,	Aug. 14, 1731.
3-97	"	John,	Sept. 30, 1733.
3-97	"	Sarah,	March 5, 1735.
3-97	"	Oliver,	Aug. 21, 1737.
3-97	"	Anstis,	Oct. 8, 1739.
3-97	"	Rowland,	Jan. 8, 1741-2.
3-97	"	Eunice,	Feb. 15, 1744.
3-68	"	Phebe, of James and Prudence,	Aug. 18, 1735.
3-68	"	Wealthian,	Jan. 1, 1737.
3-68	"	James,	Sept. 18, 1742.
3-68	"	Paul,	June 20, 1743.
3-68	"	Silas,	Nov. 20, 1747.
3-68	"	Prudence	(b. New London), Oct. 19, 1753.
3-84	"	William, of Samuel and Hannah,	Nov. 6, 1745.
3-84	"	Hannah,	Dec. 9, 1747.
3-84	"	Martha,	Jan. 27, 1750.
3-84	"	Mary,	Aug. 16, 1752.
3-84	"	Henry,	Jan. 18, 1756.
3-84	"	Samuel,	Sept. 18, 1758.
3-84	"	Oliver,	March 17, 1761.

Note—First born New Shoreham, 2d South Kingstown, others Westerly.

3-3	"	John, of Andrew and Eunice,	Nov. —, 1746.
3-3	"	Silas,	Sept. 8, 1748.
3-3	"	Eunice,	Jan. 28, 1762.
3-3	"	Catharine,	Sept. 15, 1764.

Note—Two youngest born Stonington.

4-127	"	William, of William and Sarah,	Aug. 13, 1752.
4-127	"	Anne,	May 19, 1754.
4-127	"	Lucy,	May 17, 1756.
4-127	"	Deborah,	April 12, 1758.

4-127	CHAMPLAIN Parmelia, of William and Sarah,		June 5, 1760.
4-127	"	Adam,	July 24, 1762.
4-127	"	Lois,	July 27, 1764.
4-127	"	Sally,	Aug. 1, 1766.
4-127	"	Eunice,	Sept. 18, 1768.
4-127	"	Elizabeth,	Dec. 24, 1769.
4-127	"	Phebe,	Feb. 1, 1772.
4-127	"	Phebe,	died Aug. 22, 1791.
4-127	"	Joseph,	Oct. 1, 1774.
4-127	"	Polly,	Oct. 23, 1776.
4-127	"	Oliver,	June 6, 1778.
3-9	"	William, of William, Jr., and Sarah,	Aug. 13, 1752.
3-9	"	Anne,	May 19, 1754.
3-9	"	Lucy,	May 17, 1756.
3-9	"	Deborah,	April 12, 1758.
3-9	"	Pamela,	June 5, 1760.
3-9	"	Adam,	July 24, 1762.
3-9	"	Lois,	July 27, 1764.
3-149	"	Hampton, of Rowland and Hannah,	May 20, 1766.
3-149	"	Fanny,	June 7, 1768.
3-149	"	Paul,	March 12, 1774.
3-149	"	Rowland, and Anna, 2d wife,	June 8, 1776.
3-149	"	Jeffrey,	Aug. 27, 1783.
3-127	"	Keturah, of Sila and Wealthy, born at Stonington,	March 23, 1772.
3-173	"	Hannah, of Rowland, and Anne,	Oct. 31, 1779.
3-173	"	Hannah,	d. April 18, 1780.
3-173	"	Nathan,	Sept. 7, 1780.
3-174	"	John, of Oliver, and Thankful,	Aug. 10, 1780.
3-174	"	Abigail,	April 15, 1783.
3-167	"	Polly, of Samuel, and Freelove,	March 12, 1781.
3-167	"	Martha,	May 20, 1783.
3-167	"	Martha,	d. March 25, 1785.
3-167	"	Martha, 2d,	Nov. 19, 1800.
3-167	"	Isaac Ross,	Jan. 6, 1786.
3-167	"	Lemuel,	Sept. 14, 1788.
3-167	"	Nancy or Amey,	March 9, 1791.
3-167	"	Phebe,	Nov. 21, 1794.

Note—Two youngest born Charlestown.

5-170	"	J. B., of William (of William, dec.) and Elizabeth,	Nov. 20, 1781.
5-170	"	James W.,	March 20, 1784.
5-174	"	Elizabeth,	Oct. 4. 1787.
5-174	"	Margaret,	Nov. 2, 1791.
5-174	"	William,	April 15, 1794.
5-174	"	Sally,	June 27, 1796.
5-174	"	William, Sr.,	died Aug. 31, 1803.

Note—Two youngest born South Kingstown, the others Newport.

4-21	"	Sally, of George and Patience,	Jan. 7, 1784.
4-21	"	Susannah,	March 18, 1786.
4-21	"	George,	March 18, 1788.
4-21	"	Joseph,	June 3, 1790.
4-21	"	Edward,	Oct. 6, 1792.
4-21	"	Nancy,	Nov. 30, 1796.
4-21	"	Patience, wife of George, died at South Kingstown,	March 5, 1799.

Note—3d and 5th born Hopkinton, 4th Richmand, 6th South Kingstown.

4-155	"	Charlotte Coggeshall, of Adam B. and Henrietta,	March 7, 1795.
4-155	"	Henrietta,	Dec. 21, 1796.
4-155	"	James Dean,	March 3, 1799.
4-155	"	Oliver,	Aug. 7, 1801.
4-161	"	Lydia, of George and Lydia,	Nov. 18, 1800.
4-161	"	Josiah Bliss,	July 31, 1802.
4-161	"	Mary,	March 24, 1804.

Note—All born South Kingstown, also recorded 4-187.

1-95	CHAPMAN Richard, of Hope, of Westerly, alias Feverham,		Feb. 20, 1687.
4-182	"	Plumb, March 23, 1752.	

4-182	CHAPMAN Lois, of Plumb and Lois,	Sept. 29, 1785.
4-182	" George Greene,	April 11, 1788.
4-182	" Phebe,	Aug. 17, 1790.
4-182	" Nancy,	June 1, 1794.
4-182	" Esther,	Sept. 30, 1796.
4-182	" Thomas,	April 11, 1799.
3-48	" John, of Sumner and Elizabeth,	Jan. 3, 1758.
3-48	" Timothy,	May 28, 1760.
3-48	" Elizabeth,	Dec. 12, 1762.
3-48	" Sumner,	April 23, 1765.
3-48	" Joseph,	July 29, 1767.
3-48	" Israel,	June 27, 1770.
3-48	" Case,	Dec. 28, 1772.
4-51	" Hannah, of William, Jr., and Bridget,	Nov. 6, 1773.
4-51	" William,	April 21, 1775.
4-51	" Lucy,	Sept. 4, 1776.
4-51	" Elizabeth,	Sept. 17, 1778.
4-51	" Sarah,	Dec. 25, 1780.
4-51	" Abigail,	Feb. 6, 1782.
4-51	" John,	March 20, 1784.
4-51	" Samuel,	April 18, 1786.
4-51	" Amey,	June 17, 1788.
4-51	" Polly,	Aug. 26, 1790.
4-51	" Bridget, wife of William, died Nov. 21, 1798.	
3-181	" Nancy Pendleton, of Timothy and Nancy,	Aug. 11, 1783.
3-181	" Rebecca,	Dec. 8, 1785.
3-181	" Joseph,	March 21, 1788.
3-181	" Damarius,	Jan. 31, 1791.
3-181	" Oliver Rhodes,	Feb. 5, 1794.
3-87	" John, of Joseph and Elizabeth,	Sept. 23, 1792.
3-87	" Benjamin Kenyon.	Aug. 9, 1794.
3-87	" Elizabeth,	May 9, 1797.
3-87	" Joseph,	Sept. 13, 1799.
3-87	" Mary Ann.	March 28, 1802.
3-87	" William Robinson,	Aug. 21, 1804.
3-87	" Rouse,	Sept. 21, 1806.
3-181	" Sumner. of Timothy and Nancy,	April 1, 1797.
3-181	" John Case,	Sept. 13, 1799.
3-181	" Enock Crandall,	March 22, 1802.
3-181	" Freeman Clarke,	Oct. 9, 1804.
4-119	" Joshua Kenyon, of Israel and Polly,	Jan. 8, 1798.
4-119	" John,	Sept. 30, 1901.
4-119	" Anne Palmer,	Feb. 4, 1804.
	Note—Two youngest born Stonington.	
4-163	" Case, of Case and Polly,	Aug. 1, 1801.
4-139	" Hannah, of William, Jr., and Hannah,	Jan. 6, 1800.
4-139	" William.	Jan. 28, 1802.
4-139	" Saunders Brown,	July 16, 1804.
3-64	CHASE Oliver, born Bristol, July, 11, 1715.	
3-64	" Elizabeth, his wife, Dec. 5, 1716.	
3-64	" Mary, of Oliver and Elizabeth,	Jan. 5, 1738-9.
3-64	" Seth,	Sept. 2, 1742.
3-64	" Abner,	Oct. 7, 1745.
3-64	" Consider.	Dec. 20, 1747.
3-64	" Lovice,	June 9, 1750.
3-64	" Eunice.	June 9, 1750.
3-64	" Martha,	March 27, 1753.
3-64	" Frederick,	Feb. 2, 1758.
	Note—Eldest born Freetown, Mass., the next two are also recorded 2-84.	
2-222	" Mary, of Joshua and Mary,	March 27, 1749.
2-222	" Joshua,	June 15, 1750.
2-222	" Maxson,	May 9, 1752.
3-145	" Maxson, of Maxson and Rebecca,	Feb. 17, 1776.
4-5	" Frederic, of Frederic and Ruth,	Feb. 5, 1784.

4-166	CHASE	Mary Ann, of Maxson and Polly,	Nov. 16, 1804.
4-166	"	Maxson,	Jan. 16, 1806.
4-166	"	Isaac,	Nov. 2, 1807.
4-166	"	Eliza,	Sept. 6, 1809.
4-166	"	Rebecca,	June 22, 1811.
4-166	"	Nathan Merriott,	May 6, 1813.
4-166	"	Susan,	March 15, 1815.
4-166	"	Harriet Lavina,	Dec. 28, 1819.
4-12	CHESTER	Martha, of Christopher and Martha,	Jan. 16, 1780.
4-12	"	Christopher,	June 4. 1781.
4-12	"	Christopher,	died Oct. 6, 1785.
4-12	"	Lemuel,	Jan. 6, 1783.
4-12	"	John Chase,	July 8, 1785.
4-12	"	Christopher,	Feb. 24, 1792.
4-199	"	Lemuel, of Lemuel and Nancy,	July 1, 1805.
4-199	"	Ann,	Sept. 19, 1806.
4-199	"	Frederic Oliver Chase,	May 12, 1808.
4-199	"	Elizabeth Martha,	March 22, 1810.
4-199	"	Hannah,	March 22, 1812.
4-199	"	Sophronia,	April 18, 1814.
4-199	"	Eunice,	May 26, 1816.
4-199	"	Ursula,	Nov. 30, 1818.
4-246	"	John Edward, of John C. and Nancy,	July 19, 1809.
1-95	CHURCH	Caleb, of Caleb and Rebecca,	March 6, 1732.
1-95	"	Joshua,	June 4, 1734.
1-95	"	Charles,	July 26, 1736.
1-95	"	Samuel,	Oct. 30, 1738.
1-57	CLARKE	Joseph, b. Newport,	Feb. 11, 1642.
1-57	"	Judith, of Joseph and Bethiah,	Oct. 12, 1667.
1-57	"	Joseph,	April 4, 1670.
1-57	"	Samuel,	Sept. 29, 1672.
1-57	"	John.	Aug. 25, 1675.
1-57	"	Bethiah,	April 11, 1678.
1-57	"	Mary,	Dec. 27, 1680.
1-57	"	Susannah,	Aug. 31, 1683.
1-57	"	Thomas,	March 17, 1686.
1-57	"	William,	April 21, 1688.
1-57	"	Freegift, of Joseph, Jr., and Dorothy,	July 4, 1694.
1-57	"	Dorothy,	May 28, 1696.
1-57	"	Experience,	July 6, 1699.
2-122	"	Samuel, of Samuel and Ann,	Jan. 19, 1699-1700.
2-122	"	Mary,	Nov. 27, 1701.
2-122	"	Bethiah,	July 18, 1703.
2-122	"	Joseph,	Aug. 29, 1705.
2-122	"	Ann,	Sept. 3, 1707.
2-122	"	William,	May 21, 1709.
2-122	"	James,	Jan. 20. 1710-1.
2-122	"	Joshua.	Sept. 22, 1712.
2-122	"	Amos.	Nov. 14, 1714.
2-122	"	Simeon.	April 7, 1716.
2-122	"	Christopher,	Oct. 26. 1717.
2-122	"	Samuel, Jr.,	May 6, 1719.
		Note—Samuel, 1st, died about this time.	
2-122	"	Amey, of Samuel and Susannah,	May 3, 1721.
2-122	"	Benjamin,	July 13, 1722.
1-102	"	John, of John and Mary,	Sept. 4, 1706.
2-106	"	Samuel,	Jan. 15, 1707-8.
2-106	"	Mary,	Nov. 15, 1709.
2-106	"	Ebenezer,	July 1, 1711.
2-106	"	Benjamin,	June 21, 1713.
2-106	"	Elizabeth,	June 19, 1715.
2-106	"	Bathsheba,	Oct. 26, 1717.
		Note—Also second 2-121.	
2-119	"	Judeth, of William and Joan,	July 7, 1710.
2-119	"	Susannah,	Feb. 8, 1711.

2-119	CLARKE	Lucy, of William and Jean,	Feb. 21, 1713-4.
2-119	"	William,	Dec. 25, 1715.
2-114	"	Sarah, of Thomas and Elizabeth,	May 11, 1712.
2-114	"	Thomas,	March 4, 1715.
2-114	"	Joshua,	April 26, 1717.
2-114	"	James,	March 3, 1720.
2-114	"	Elisha, of Joseph (dec.), and Anna,	Nov. 17, 1718.
3-10	"	Mary, of Thomas, Jr., and Deborah,	July 5, 1729.
3-10	"	Joseph,	March 30, 1737.
2-79	"	Mary, of Thomas, Jr., and Thankful,	April 15, 1741.
2-79	"	Thomas,	April 23, 1743.
2-119	"	Elisha, of Joseph,	Feb. 25, 1742.
3-71	"	Robert, of Daniel and Mary,	Dec. 11, 1744.
3-71	"	Mary,	Sept. 4, 1748.
3-71	"	Anne,	Nov. 20, 1750.
3-71	"	Daniel,	Dec 26, 1752.
3-71	"	Edward,	June 16, 1755.
3-71	"	Lydia,	May 10, 1758.
3-71	"	Roger,	April 13, 1760.
3-24	"	Mary, of Elisha and Mary,	Jan. 12, 1744-5.
3-24	"	Anna,	Oct. 7, 1747.
3-24	"	Elisha,	Jan. 28, 1750-1.
3-24	"	Thomas,	Feb. 29, 1751-2.
3-24	"	Martha,	Feb. 17, 1757.
3-24	"	Joshua,	June 20, 1759.
3-24	"	Luke,	Oct. 10, 1761.
3-91	"	Jesse, of Ephraim and Hannah,	April 18, 1745.
3-91	"	David,	April 26, 1747.
3-91	"	Susannah,	Sept. 1, 1749.
3-91	"	Ichabod,	May 29, 1750.
3-91	"	Amey,	Oct. 10. 1753.
3-91	"	Tacy,	June 3, 1756.
3-91	"	Jane,	Aug. 13, 1758.
3-91	"	Lucy,	March 13, 1760.
3-91	"	Hannah,	Sept. 28, 1761.
3-91	"	Judeth,	May 1, 1765
3-91	"	Marcy,	Aug. 19, 1767.
3-14	"	Mitchell,	April 9, 1746.
3-14	"	Nathan,	Aug. 7, 1748.
3-14	"	Philena,	Oct. 4, 1750.
4-134	"	Nicholas, of William, dec., and Jemima,	March 21, 1752.
4-134	"	Barbara (Wells, of Peter and Elizabeth), his wife, born Hopkinton, Jan. 17, 1760.	
4-134	"	William, of Nicholas and Barbara,	Dec. 1, 1780.
4-134	"	Peter Wells,	Jan. 10, 1783.
4-134	"	Freeman,	Dec. 17, 1784.
4-134	"	Barbara,	Feb. 6, 1787.
4-134	"	Arnold Wells,	April 5, 1789.
4-134	"	Betsey,	Sept. 19, 1792.
4-134	"	Henry,	Jan. 28, 1795.
4-134	"	Joshua,	April 23, 1797.
3-90	"	Eleanor, of Ichabod and Marcy,	Oct. 8, 1752.
3-90	"	Isabel,	Aug. 25, 1757.
3-90	"	Ichabod,	Feb. 2, 1763.
3-90	"	Sarah, of Joseph, Jr., and Deborah,	June 24, 1753.
3-90	"	Samuel,	Dec. 11, 1754.
3-90	"	Nathan,	May 9, 1756.
3-90	"	Nancy,	May 24, 1758.
3-90	"	Asa,	May 25, 1760.
3-90	"	Simeon,	Feb. 13, 1762.
3-56	"	Thankful, of Joseph and Thankful,	Dec. 1, 1758.
3-56	"	Lucy,	June 9, 1761.
3-56	"	Desire,	July 27, 1763.
3-56	"	Deborah,	Jan. 26, 1766.

3-56	CLARKE	Lucretia, of Joseph and Thankful,	June 14, 1768.
3-56	"	Chally,	Sept. 24, 1770.
3-173	"	Patience, of Daniel and Mary,	Nov. 16, 1762.
3-173	"	Jemima,	Sept. 21, 1764.
3-173	"	Bridget,	April 6, 1766.
3-173	"	Content,	May 22, 1771.
3-83	"	John, of John and Mary,	Feb. 20, 1763.
3-83	"	Sarah,	Oct. 15, 1765.
3-83	"	Martha,	March 22, 1768.
3-83	"	Stephen,	June 26, 1771.
3-83	"	Peleg,	Sept. 11, 1774.
3-83	"	Mary,	Jan. 9, 1776.
3-117	"	Stanton, of Phineas and Mary,	May 17, 1764.
3-117	"	Elnathan,	July 13, 1766.
3-117	"	Joshua,	Oct. 25, 1768.
4-1	"	Sarah, of William and Eunice,	Jan. 14, 1771.
4-1	"	Jemima,	Feb. 17, 1773.
4-1	"	Waite,	April 16, 1775.
4-1	"	Eunice,	May 22, 1777.
4-1	"	Bathsheba,	July 9, 1780.
3-113	"	Jesse, of Jesse and Susannah,	June 20, 1771.
3-135	"	Joshua, of David and Jane,	Feb. 26, 1772.
3-135	"	Ephraim,	April 27, 1773.
3-135	"	Waite,	Dec. 29, 1774.
3-135	"	William,	May 18, 1776.
3-135	"	Joseph,	Oct. 30, 1779.
3-135	"	Jesse,	May 26, 1781.
3-135	"	Amey,	June 18, 1784.
3-143	"	Davis, of Joseph, 3d, and Thankful,	June 6. 1773.
3-143	"	Alpheus,	Aug. 8, 1775.
3-170	"	Catherine, of Lemuel and Cloe,	Aug. 3. 1777.
3-170	"	Maxson,	Sept. 20, 1779.
3-170	"	Samuel,	Dec. 1, 1782.
3-170	"	David,	June 15, 1785.
3-170	"	Joseph,	Oct. 12, 1787.
3-170	"	Truman,	April 9, 1790.
3-170	"	Clarissa,	May 21, 1793.
3-170	"	Hosea Barber,	Nov. 16, 1797.
3-143	"	Samuel Ward, of Ethan and Anna,	Oct. 17, 1778.
3-143	"	Anna,	April 22, 1780.
4-99	"	George, of George and Keturah,	May 29, 1779.
4-99	"	Angustus,	Oct. 9, 1781.
4-99	"	Jude,	Oct. 1, 1784.
4-99	"	Keturah,	Sept. 16, 1789.
4-99	"	Phebe,	July 15, 1792.
4-99	"	Joseph,	Oct. 15, 1794.
4-2	"	William, of Nicholas and Barbara,	Dec. 1, 1780.
4-2	"	Peter Wells,	Jan. 10, 1783.
4-2	"	Freeman,	Dec. 17, 1784.
4-2	"	Barbara,	Feb. 6, 1787.
4-2	"	Arnold,	April 5, 1790.
4-2	"	Lydia, of John, Jr., and Jemima,	Dec. 4, 1781.
4-58	"	Joshua, of Joshua and Wealtha,	Feb. 16, 1787.
4-58	"	Elisha,	Aug. 3, 1788.
4-58	"	Benjamin,	Jan. 20, 1790.
4-58	"	Wealtha,	May 30, 1791.
4-58	"	Polly,	March 29, 1793.
4-58	"	Simon,	Sept. 17, 1794.
4-58	"	Henry,	April 26, 1796.
4-58	"	Ephraim,	May 27, 1798.
4-58	"	Ephraim,	died April 3, 1802.
4-58	"	Nathan,	April 10, 1800.
4-58	"	Clarissa,	Aug. 29, 1802.
4-58	"	Phebe,	July 20, 1804.
4-58	"	Lydia,	May 9, 1806.

4-58	CLARKE Caty, of Joshua and Wealtha,	April 16, 1809.
4-23	" Sarah, of Ichabod, Jr., and Mary,	Sept. 7, 1788.
4-23	" Polly,	April, 4, 1790.
4-23	" William,	June 27, 1792.
4-23	" Esther,	Sept. 12, 1794.
4-23	" Roy Greene,	June 27, 1796.
4-23	" Robert Palmer,	Nov. 3, 1799.
4-23	" Charles Babcock,	Oct. 21, 1803.
4-153	" William, of Waite and Abigail,	July 30, 1801.
4-153	" Ephraim,	Aug. 11, 1803.
4-153	" Susan,	July 2, 1805.
4-212	" Gamilla, of John and Mercy,	April 27, 1807.
4-212	" Nancy,	Feb. 20, 1809.
5-16	" John T.,	died April 12, 1845.
2-110	COLDGROVE Anna, of Francis and Hannah,	Jan. 23, 1721 2.
2-110	" Sarah,	June 20, 1724.
2-110	" Hannah,	June 20, 1724.
	Note—Also recorded 2-115.	
2-121	COLLINS Hezekiah, of John and Susannah,	Aug. 18, 1707.
2-121	" Sarah,	June 18, 1709.
2-121	" Jedediah,	Nov. 5, 1711.
3-74	COON Anna, of John and Patience,	March 10, 1736.
2-58	COREY James,	March 1, 1687.
2-58	" Sarah, of James and Sarah,	Jan. 11, 1707.
2-58	" Mary,	Sept. 3, 1709.
2-58	" Hope,	Sept. 15, 1712.
2-58	" James, Jr.,	June 24, 1715.
2-58	" John,	March 16, 1717.
2-58	" Joseph,	May 16, 1719.
2-58	" Samuel,	Oct. 15, 1721.
2-58	" Elisha,	March 7, 1724.
2-58	" Elisha,	died Dec. 7, 1730.
2-58	" Elizabeth,	March 2, 1726.
2-118	" Elisha, of Hosea and Sarah,	Feb. 3, 1737-8.
2-41	COTTRELL Elizabeth, of John and Elizabeth,	April 6, 1733.
2-41	" Hannah,	May 4, 1735.
2-41	" Dorcas,	May 4, 1737.
2-41	" Thomas,	Sept. 4, 1739.
2-41	" Benjamin,	Sept. 14, 1742.
2-41	" John,	March 12, 1745.
3-10	" Dorothy, of Nathaniel and Mary,	Jan. 22, 1746-7.
4-6	" John, of Major John (dec.) and Lois,	Sept. 22, 1760.
3-147	" Thankful, of Elias and Phalley,	Sept. 23, 1779.
3-147	" John,	May 19, 1781.
3-147	" Elias,	Dec. 2, 1782.
3-147	" Russell,	March 31, 1785.
3-147	" Phalley,	March 3, 1787.
3-147	" Lois,	April 11, 1789.
3-147	" Lebbeus,	Jan. 29, 1792.
3-147	" Joshua Gorton,	Feb. 10, 1794.
4-86	" Daniel, of Daniel and Mereba,	Feb. 13, 1792.
4-86	" Amelia,	Feb. 8, 1795.
4-86	" Polly,	Sept. 21, 1797.
4-86	" Peleg Saunders,	Jan. 29, 1799.
4-86	" John Boardman,	July 3, 1802.
4-86	" Lois Ann,	Sept. 23, 1806.
4-45	" Mary, of Lebbeus and Mary,	Sept. 8, 1793.
4-249	" Silas H., of John and Lydia,	Aug. 25, 1809.
4-254	" Russell, 2d, of Russell and Betsey, born at Hopkinton, Dec. 10, 1813.	
2-82	CRANDALL Joseph, of Joseph and Ann,	Jan. 21, 1716-7.
2-82	" James,	May 12, 1719.
2-82	" William,	Aug. 6, 1721.
2-82	" Simeon,	Jan. 15, 1724-5.
2-82	" Joshua,	Oct. 15, 1727.

2-82	CRANDALL	Ezekiel, of Joseph and Ann,	Nov. 21, 1730.
2-82	"	Ann,	July 2, 1733.
2-82	"	Benjamin,	Nov. 29, 1736.
3-153	"	Nathaniel, of Eber and Mary,	Feb. 28, 1718.
2-115	"	Peter, of Peter and Mary,	May 30, 1719.
2-115	"	Amos,	May 19, 1721.
2-115	"	Samuel,	July 6, 1724.
2-115	"	Edward,	Oct. 11, 1726.
2-115	"	Mary,	April 25, 1729.
3-26	"	Elizabeth, of Eber and Mary,	Jan. 8, 1734.
3-26	"	Amey,	Jan. 14, 1736.
3-26	"	Desire,	June 16, 1738.
3-26	"	Eber,	March 13, 1741.
3-26	"	Thankful,	Feb. 29, 1742.
3-26	"	Benjamin,	April 7, 1748.
3-26	"	Mary,	June 20, 1750.
3-26	"	Apharinah,	May 4, 1752.
3-113	"	Martha, of John and Hannah, born at Hopkinton,	Dec. 18, 1736.
2-49	"	Jonathan, of Joseph, Jr., and Elizabeth,	Feb. 16, 1739-40.
2-49	"	Phendas.	April 7, 1743.
2-49	"	Anna,	Aug. 23, 1745.
2-49	"	Elijah,	Jan. 17, 1747-8.
2-49	"	Joseph,	Feb. 17, 1750.
2-49	"	Sylvester,	Nov. 7, 1752.
2-49	"	Elisha,	April 15, 1756.
2-49	"	Eunice, of James and Damarius,	Jan. 24, 1743-4.
3-98	"	Esther, of John and Esther,	Feb. —, 1742.
3-98	"	Ann,	Aug. —, 1740.
3-98	"	Lewis,	Aug. —, 1738.
3-98	"	Mercy,	Feb. —, 1734.
3-98	"	John,	Jan. —, 1732.
3-98	"	Hannah,	June —, 1730.
3-31	"	Esther, of Peter and Esther,	Nov. 21, 1743.
3-31	"	Peter,	Jan. 4, 1745-6.
3-31	"	Elias,	Oct 17, 1747.
3-31	"	Azariah,	Dec. 22, 1749.
3-31	"	Asher,	Feb. 7, 1751-2.
3-7	"	Eunice, of James and Damarius,	Jan. 24, 1744-5.
3-7	"	Ezekiel,	Oct. 11, 1746.
3-7	"	Damarius,	Sept. 8, 1749.
3-7	"	Enoch,	Nov. 1, 1752.
3-7	"	Christopher,	Sept. 1, 1755.
3-7	"	Augustus,	March 27, 1761.
3-7	"	Cynthia,	Feb. 4, 1763.
3-7	"	Charlotte,	May 10, 1764.
3-7	"	James,	July 16, 1766.
3-108	"	Amey, of Simeon and Mary,	Oct. 24, 1745.
3-108	"	Caleb,	April 7, 1747.
3-1	"	Amos, of Amos and Hannah,	April 3, 1747.
3-1	"	Edward,	Jan. 6, 1750.
3-15	"	Thomas, of Ebenezer and Thankful,	May 8, 1747.
3-15	"	Bethany,	June 17, 1749.
3-15	"	Elizabeth,	Sept. 9, 1751.
3-15	"	Jasper,	Sept. 26, 1754.
3-7	"	Anstress, of William and Deborah,	Feb. 18, 1748-9.
3-7	"	William,	Oct. 8, 1751.
3-7	"	Henry,	Jan. 7, 1754.
3-7	"	Ruhamah,	May 26, 1756.
3-7	"	Rhoda,	July 27, 1758.
3-7	"	Arnold,	Oct. 24, 1760.
3-7	"	Rebecca,	May 1, 1763.
3-7	"	Barney,	Oct. 11, 1765.
3-7	"	Stennet,	Nov. 1, 1767.
3-7	"	Joel,	Jan. 19, 1771.
3-7	"	Beriah, of Joshua and Eunice,	July 5, 1752.

3-7	CRANDALL	Sarah, of Joshua and Eunice,	April 21, 1754.
3-7	"	Lucy,	May 2, 1756.
3-7	"	Luke,	May 29, 1758.
3-7	"	Eldredge,	March 5, 1760.
3-7	"	Joshua,	April 16, 1762.

Note—Three youngest born South Kingstown.

3-29	"	Mary, of Edward and Sarah,	Aug. 28, 1753.
3-29	"	Remember,	Oct. 11, 1755.
3-29	"	Alice,	Jan. 12, 1758.
3-29	"	Gideon,	June 10, 1760.
3-108	"	Lydia, of James, Jr., and Sarah,	Nov. 25, 1754.
3-108	"	Clarke,	Sept. 16, 1756.
3-108	"	Benedick,	Sept. 1, 1758.
3-108	"	Anne,	May 4, 1761.
3-108	"	James,	Sept. 20, 1763.
3-108	"	Ruth,	Jan. 13, 1766.
3-108	"	Peter,	Jan. 26, 1768.
3-108	"	Paul,	Jan. 26, 1768.
3-108	"	Gardner,	March 5, 1770.
3-108	"	Mary,	Dec. 6, 1773.
3-46	"	Moses, of Abijah and Sarah,	Oct. 12, 1755.
3-46	"	Sibbel,	June 9, 1759.
3-46	"	Amariah,	April 3, 1762.
3-80	"	Anne, of Benjamin and Alice,	June 25, 1760.
3-80	"	Luke,	Aug. 15, 1761.
3-80	"	Amelia,	Feb. 4, 1763.
3-80	"	Rowland,	April 21, 1764.
3-80	"	Benjamin,	Dec. 5, 1765.
3-80	"	Sarah,	Jan. 2, 1767.
3-80	"	Rowland, 2d,	June 25, 1769.

Note—Eldest born Charlestown.

3-70	"	Trepbenia, of Jonathan and Elizabeth,	April 29, 1761.
3-70	"	Lyman,	Oct. 15, 1762.
3-70	"	Elizabeth,	May 7, 1764.
3-70	"	Huldah,	Feb. 13, 1766.
3-70	"	Saberry,	April 15, 1768.

Note—Eldest born South Kingstown, third Charlestown.

3-8	"	Peter, of Joshua and Abigail,	Aug. 1, 1763.
3-8	"	Joseph,	Nov. 18, 1765.
3-8	"	Betty,	March 1, 1768.
3-8	"	Clement,	May 7, 1770.
3-8	"	William,	March 4, 1773.
3-8	"	Martin Luther,	March 28, 1776.
4-259	"	James, Sept. 20, 1763.	
4-259	"	Lydia, of James and Hannah,	July 10, 1783.
4-259	"	James,	July 12, 1789.
4-259	"	Fanny,	May 4, 1791.
4-259	"	Theodoty,	March 29, 1795.
4-259	"	William,	Jan. 25, 1797.
4-259	"	Nathaniel C.,	March 31, 1798.
4-259	"	Paul,	Nov. 2, 1802.
3-102	"	Eunice, of Ezekiel and Mary,	Jan. 16, 1767.
3-111	"	Silas, of Thomas and Ruth,	March 3, 1768.
3-111	"	Grace,	Dec. 7, 1769.
3-111	"	Rogers,	March 24, 1772.
3-111	"	Esther,	Aug. 17, 1775.
3-111	"	Ruth,	Feb. 28, 1778.
3-111	"	Lydia,	Sept. 1, 1781.
3-111	"	Ezekiel,	Sept. 7, 1783.
3-111	"	Desire,	Nov. 9, 1786.

Note—First born Westerly, next four Hopkinton; the youngest at New London.

3-115	"	Samuel Clarke, nat. son of Samuel Crandall, Jr., and Isabel Lost, June 8, 1768.	
3-111	"	Elizabeth, of James and Elizabeth,	Aug. 8, 1769.

3-111	CRANDALL Mary, of James and Elizabeth,	Aug. 3, 1771.
3-111	" Oliver,	Sept. 30, 1773.
	Note—Eldest born Charlestown.	
3-134	" Tacy, of Elias and Sarah,	Nov. 30, 1769.
3-134	" Esther,	Nov. 22, 1772
3-134	" Elias,	Sept. 11, 1773.
3-134	" Mary,	March 4, 1777.
3-134	" George,	Dec. 12, 1778.
3-134	" Sarah,	Sept. 18. 1781.
3-111	" Eunice, of Elijah and Eunice,	July 14, 1770.
3-111	" Russell,	July 14, 1772.
3-111	" Mary,	Oct. 29, 1774.
3-130	" Prudence, of Benjamin and Alice,	July 10, 1771.
3-133	" Damarias, of James and Elizabeth,	July 26? 1776.
3-133	" Nancy,	Sept. 4, 1778.
3-133	" Fanny,	Sept. 4, 1778.
	Note—Eldest born Charlestown.	
3-160	" Pardon, of Christopher and Tacy,	Jan. 8, 1778.
3-160	" Prudence,	Oct. 29, 1779.
3-133	" Charlotte, of Lewis and Betbiah,	March 19, 1778.
3-133	" Joshua,	Aug. 8, 1781.
3-133	" Lodowick,	Oct. 23, 1790.
3-133	" Lewis,	Oct. 24, 1769.
3-133	" Rhoda,	Sept. 1, 1771.
3-133	" John Bradley,	Jan. 23, 1773.
3-133	" Russell Smith,	Feb. 15, 1775.
3-133	" Dudley,	April 11, 1776.
4-95	" Anna, of John, and Anna,	April 26, 1778.
4-95	" John,	May 3. 1780.
4-95	" Dorcas,	Aug. 23, 1782.
4-95	" Gardiner,	March, 6 1786.
4-95	" Jeremiah,	June 2, 1788.
4-95	" Hannah,	Sept. 23, 1790.
4-95	" Joshua,	Nov. 31, 1793.
4-95	" Charles,	Feb. 3, 1797.
4-95	" Daniel,	July 16, 1799.
4-95	" John, son of above, named Dorcas,	June 15, 1809.
4-22	" Enock, of Enock and Mary,	July 7, 1778.
4-22	" Hannah,	June 16, 1780.
4-22	" Bathsheba,	May 8, 1782.
3-140	" Elizabeth, of Joseph and Mary, born at Hopkinton,	Oct. 15, 1778.
3-159	" Clarke, of Clarke, and Hannah,	Jan. 15, 1779.
3-159	" James,	Sept. 3, 1780.
3-159	" Ephraim,	Sept. 1, 1782.
3-159	" Joseph,	March 23, 1785.
3-159	" Benjamin,	Oct. 17, 1787.
3-159	" Hannah,	June 27, 1790.
3-159	" Peter,	June 1, 1792.
3-159	" Hoxsie,	Jan. 23, 1796.
5-150	" Lydia, of Henry and Elizabeth,	March 8, 1779.
3-55	" Nathan, of Joshua and Abigail,	July 20, 1779.
3-162	" James Kenyon, of Elijah and Mercy,	April 30, 1780.
3-162	" Catherine,	May 6, 1784.
	Note—1st born Charlestown; 2d Westerly.	
3-172	" Hannah, of Benedick and Lucy,	Sept 22, 1781.
3-172	" John Dodge,	Sept. 13, 1783.
3-172	" Amey,	Sept. 10, 1785.
3-172	" Tacy,	Sept. 8, 1787.
3-150	" William, of Henry and Mary,	Dec. 28, 1782.
3-150	" Betsey	Dec. 24, 1785.
3-150	" Hannah,	Nov. 26, 1787.
3-150	" Henry,	Feb. 18, 1790.
3-150	" Timothy,	Sept. 7, 1795.
	Note—Youngest born Petersbury, N. Y.	
3-124	" Alexander, of Jonathan and Elizabeth,	Jan. 7, 1783.

3-124	CRANDALL	Barton, of Jonathan and Elizabeth,	Jan. 30, 1781.
3-124	"	Jonathan,	April 3, 1770.
3-124	"	Wells,	Feb. 16, 1772.
3-124	"	Daniel Ross,	April 12, 1774.
3-124	"	Falley,	May 2, 1776.
4-8	"	Elizabeth, of Elias and Sarah,	Aug. 7, 1784.
4-8	"	Rhoda,	March 15, 1786.
4-14	"	Eunice, of Eldredge and Mary,	July 8, 1785.
4-14	"	William,	March 6, 1787.

Note—Both born in Charlestown.

4-9	"	Daniel, of Peter and Nancy,	Dec. 23, 1786.
4-9	"	Luke,	Dec. 21, 1788.
4-9	"	Greene,	March 23, 1791.
4-19	"	Susannah, of Arnold and Dinah,	July 21, 1788.
4-19	"	Deborah,	Oct. 1, 1790.
4-19	"	William Gorton,	Oct. 1, 1790.
4-19	"	Erastus,	Oct. 14, 1793.
4-25	"	Rhoda, of Barney and Hannah,	Jan. 25, 1788.
4-25	"	William,	Sept. 25, 1790.
4-25	"	Ellery,	April 7, 1791.
4-25	"	Amos Collins,	Nov. 9, 1793.
4-25	"	Henry,	Dec. 5, 1794.

Note—Second born Richmond.

4-34	"	Molly, of Benedick and Lucy,	May 9, 1789.
4-34	"	Judeth,	July 22, 1791.
4-34	"	Gardner,	Dec. 7, 1793.
4-26	"	Maxson, of Joseph and Molly,	Sept. 17, 1789.
4-26	"	Betsey,	July 3, 1791.
4-28	"	Paul, of Paul and Prudence,	Dec. 26, 1790.
4-28	"	Abigail,	April 13, 1791.
4-28	"	Abigail,	died Dec. 25, 1792.
4-28	"	Thomas Baster,	Aug. 7, 1795.
4-28	"	Acors Rathbone,	Dec. 15, 1797.
4-28	"	Gardner,	Dec. 3, 1799.
4-28	"	Gardner,	died Dec. 11, 1799.
4-28	"	John,	March 10, 1801.
4-28	"	William Clarke,	July 14, 1803.
4-44	"	Joseph Davis, of Clement and Susannah, born at Charlestown, Oct. 13, 1791.	
4-71	"	Silas, of Stennett and Caty,	March 16, 1793.
4-118	"	Sophronia, of Joseph and Nancy,	Jan. 9, 1797.
4-118	"	Hannah,	Jan. 10, 1799.
4-172	"	William Hazard, of Joel and Ruth,	Feb. 21, 1798.
4-172	"	Harry,	Aug. 30, 1800.
4-172	"	John,	Aug. 2, 1803.
4-172	"	Joseph,	March 15, 1806.
4-172	"	Hannah,	May 10, 1809.
4-172	"	Amos,	Feb. 29, 1812.
3-133	"	Dudley, of Rhoda (dau. of Lewis and Bethiah),	July 29, 1798.
4-125	"	Jaros, of Rogers and Lucy,	Jan. 17, 1799.
4-125	"	Susannah,	Sept. 5, 1801.
5-38	"	Charles, of William and Catharine,	May 13, 1816.
5-38	"	Hannah G.,	July 6, 1818.
5-38	"	Mary Ann,	April 11, 1821.
5-38	"	Warren G.,	Dec. 2, 1823.
5-38	"	John N.,	Oct. 3, 1826.
5-38	"	Clarissa Catherine,	Sept. 11, 1828.
5-8	"	Anna, of Charles and Lydia,	Feb. 4, 1828.
5-8	"	Sally Maria,	Feb. 16, 1829.
3-81	CRARY	Lucy, of Oliver and Hopestill,	March 1, 1763.
3-81	"	Oliver,	July 29, 1771.
2-70	CROSS	Samuel, May 7, 1724.	
2-70	"	Joseph, Dec. 2, 1727.	
2-70	"	John, July 31, 1729.	
2-70	"	William, June 3, 1730.	

2-70	CROSS	Mary, March 24, 1732.	
2-70	"	Susannah, Dec. 6, 1734.	
2-70	"	Edward, May 23, 1735.	
4-119	"	Dorcas, of John and Mary,	June 26, 1791.
4-119	"	Elizabeth,	Dec 3, 1795.
4-119	"	George Delwin,	Jan. 24, 1799.
4-119	"	Susannah,	April 26 1801.
4-119	"	Mary,	April 26, 1803.
4-119	"	Sarah Alexander,	Aug. 2, 1805.
4-119	"	James Madison,	March 5, 1809.
5-26	"	John Hobert, of George D. and Abby	Aug. 31, 1821.
5-26	"	George Dillwyn,	Jan. 17, 1823.
5-26	"	Abby Jane,	Nov. 8, 1824.
5-26	"	James,	Oct. 22, 1826.
5-26	"	Sally Babcock,	Sept. 5, 1828.
5-26	"	Sally Babcock,	died, Jan. 29, 1831.
5-26	"	Benjamin Franklin,	March 3, 1831.
5-26	"	William Henry,	April 21, 1833.
5-26	"	Samuel Hazard,	May 22, 1835.
5-26	"	Harriet Babcock,	Jan. 8, 1838.
5-26	"	Anna Hobert,	Nov. 11, 1840.
5-26	"	Calvin Richard,	May 31, 1843.
5-26	"	Clara Hobert,	Dec. 12, 1845.
2-70	CRUMB	Elizabeth, of Joseph and Amey,	Dec. 27, 1734-5.
2-70	"	Joseph,	Sept. 22, 1737.
2-120	"	Samuel, of William and Hannah,	Nov. 9, 1740.
2-70	"	Daniel,	Aug. 19, 1737
3-44	"	Elizabeth, of Joseph and Amey,	Dec. 27, 1734.
3-44	"	Joseph,	Sept. 20, 1738.
3-44	"	Samuel,	Aug. 22, 1740.
3-44	"	Wait,	July 6, 1742.
3-44	"	Amey,	July 6, 1745.
3-44	"	William,	Aug. 31, 1747.
3-44	"	David,	July 18, 1749.
3-44	"	Sylvester,	Feb. 23, 1751.
3-99	"	Amey, of Joseph, Jr., and Hannah,	March 30, 1765.
3-99	"	Joseph.	Feb. 10, 1768.
3-99	"	Samuel,	March 14, 1769.
3-124	"	Denison, of David and Hannah,	March 31, 1772.
3-124	"	Rebecca,	Aug. 27, 1777.
3-147	"	David,	Oct. 19, 1773.
3-147	"	Hannah,	Nov. 21, 1775.
4-26	"	Sylvester, of Sylvester and Grace,	Oct. 18, 1779.
4-26	"	William,	April 21, 1782.
4-26	"	Elizabeth.	July 23, 1784.
4-26	"	Joel,	Oct. 7, 1786.
4-26	"	Culver,	Dec. 8, 1788.
4-26	"	Hannah,	April 14, 1791.
4-26	"	Sands Niles,	July 18, 1793.
4-26	"	John,	May 1, 1795.
4-26	"	Waite,	Oct. 29, 1797.
4-59	"	Nancy, of Simeon and Harriet,	Sept. 15, 1783.
4-59	"	Fanny,	Dec. 25, 1784.
4-59	"	Else,	Aug. 24, 1786.
4-59	"	Simeon,	March 22, 1788.
4-59	"	Rhoda,	April 11, 1790.
4-59	"	Prudence,	Feb. 25, 1792.
4-59	"	Betsey,	April 13, 1795.
4-59	"	Phenias,	Feb. 15, 1797.
4-59	"	Charles,	Nov. 12, 1798.
4-59	"	Rowland,	Oct. 1, 1800.
4-59	"	George Washington,	June 11, 1803.

D

2-98	DAKE	Mary, of George and Su annah,	Jan. 17, 1721.
2-98	"	John,	Feb. 22, 1724.
2-98	"	Elizabeth,	April 15, 1727.
2-85	DARBY	William, of William and Lydia (also 2-114),	March 4, 1736-7.
2-113	DAVIS	John, of John and Elizabeth,	May 5. 1696.
2-100	"	Elizabeth,	April 17. 1717.
2-100	"	William,	May 15. 1719.
2-100	"	Martha,	Aug. 14, 1721.
2-100	"	John,	Sept. 18, 1723.
2-100	"	Joseph,	Sept. 24, 1726.
2-100	"	Anna,	Jan. 23, 1728-9.
2-100	"	Judeth,	April 7, 1731.
2-79	"	Martha, of William and Experience,	May 13, 1721.
2-79	"	William,	Jan. 25, 1722-3.
2-79	"	Joseph,	May 28, 1726.
2-79	"	Mary,	April 29, 1732.
2-79	"	Nathan,	April 24, 1736.
2-79	"	Thankful,	March 6, 1738-9.
2-79	"	Desire,	May 30, 1741.
2-79	"	William, died Sept. 30, 1740.	
3-118	"	Sarah, of William (of Peter) and Sarah,	Feb. 6, 1743.
3-118	"	Mary,	April 14, 1745.
3-118	"	William,	Feb. 20, 1747.
3-118	"	Peter,	Nov. 9, 1749.
3-118	"	James,	May 19, 1752.
3-118	"	Martha,	March 20, 1754.
3-118	"	Nicholas,	Jan. 30, 1756.
3-118	"	Aaron,	March 6, 1759.
3-118	"	Hannah,	July 31, 1762.
3-18	"	Martha, of Joseph and Comfort,	May 25, 1746.
3-19	"	Samuel,	Feb. 28, 1747-8.
3-29	"	Anna, of Joseph and ——,	Aug. 7, 1750.
3-29	"	Henry, of Joseph and Mary, 2d wife,	Oct. 15, 1754.
3-122	"	Henry, of Joseph (of William) and Mary, 2d wife,	Oct. 15, 1754.
3-122	"	Lucretia,	Sept. 20, 1756.
3-122	"	Mary,	Aug. 21, 1758.
3-122	"	Joseph,	Aug. 27, 1760.
3-122	"	Lucy,	Nov. 7, 1763.
3-122	"	Ephraim,	Sept. 12, 1765.
3-122	"	Lydia,	June 7, 1767.
3-122	"	Amey,	March 6, 1769.
3-122	"	Clarke,	Feb. 23, 1771.
3-79	"	Niles, of Nathan and Tabitha,	Nov. 12, 1757.
3-79	"	William,	Dec. 13, 1759.
3-117	"	George, of William (of John) and Anna,	Jan. 20, 1769.
3-117	"	Joshua,	March 6, 1770.
3-117	"	William,	Oct. 21, 1771.
4-50	"	Elizabeth, of James and Elizabeth,	Nov. 8, 1775.
4-50	"	Anne,	Nov. 8, 1775.
4-50	"	Content,	July 18, 1777.
4-50	"	Mary,	May 25, 1781.
4-50	"	Armella,	Oct. 11, 1782.
4-50	"	James,	Aug. 16, 1784.
4-50	"	Sarah,	Jan. 23, 1787.
4-59	"	Lydia,	Sept. 27, 1788.
4-50	"	William,	Aug. 2, 1790.
4-50	"	John Chapman,	May 2, 1793.
4-50	"	Hannah,	July 20, 1795.
4-50	"	Abigail,	Feb. 25, 1802.
3-168	"	Mary, of Martha (also 4-90),	Nov. 19, 1779.
4-90	"	Martha, March 4, 1787.	
4-84	"	Polly Griffith, alias, of Mary,	March 7, 1798.
3-36	"	——, of John and Hannah,	June 18, 1747.

3-36	DAVIS Christopher, of John and Hannah,	Aug. 21, 1749.
3-36	" John,	Aug. 16, 1752.
3-36	" Joseph,	Nov. 27, 1753.
3-36	" Benjamin,	Nov. 27, 1753.
2-119	DENISON Sarah, of Daniel and Mary,	Jan. 18, 1709-10.
2-119	" Samuel,	Oct. 23, 1711.
5-34	DERBY Horace Babcock, of Levi Lothrop and Esther,	Sept. 19, 1840.
5-34	" Harriet Elizabeth,	June 8, 1842.
5-34	" William Blanchard,	May 11, 1844.
4-114	" Jesse, of Tristam and Martha,	Aug. 3, 1783.
4-114	" Amos,	July 14, 1785.
4-114	" Hezekiah,	July 9, 1787.
4-114	" Martha,	March 19, 1789.
4-114	" Nabby,	Jan. 3, 1791.
4-114	" Tristam,	Nov. 14, 1793.
4-114	" Sylvester,	Jan. 7, 1795.
4-114	" Susannah,	Sept. 7, 1796.
4-114	" Margaret,	May 30, 1801.
4-114	" Henry,	March 30, 1804.
	Note—Two youngest born Stonington.	
2-107	DODGE John, of John and Elizabeth,	Aug. 24, 1711.
2-107	" Mary,	March 12, 1713.
2-107	" Elizabeth,	Dec. 18, 1714.
2-107	" Amey,	Feb. 20, 1717.
2-107	" Joseph,	June 29, 1719.
2-107	" Walter,	Aug. 23, 1721.
2-107	" Catherine,	Aug. 16, 1723.
2-107	" Oliver,	April 20, 1726.
3-110	" Lydia, of Oliver and Mary,	Jan. 22, 1768.
3-175	" Susanna, of Joseph, Jr., and Lucretia,	Feb. 14, 1779.
3-175	" John,	Dec. 16, 1780.
	Note—First born Westerly, 2d, Stonington.	
1-173	DOYLE William, of William and Elizabeth,	Aug. 2, 1698.
2-123	" Joseph, of William and Eleanor,	Sept. 19, 1718.
3-74	" William, of Philip and Sarah,	July 2, 1755.
3-74	" Philip,	June 14, 1757.
3-74	" Prudence,	Aug. 1, 1759.
3-74	" Barbara,	March 25, 1762.
3-74	" Ezekiel,	May 2, 1765.
3-157	" William, of William and Elizabeth,	June 9, 1779.
3-157	" Philip,	March 13, 1781.
3-157	" Hannah,	Aug. 21, 1783.
3-157	" James,	Sept. 5, 1785.
3-157	" Lydia,	Dec. 27, 1787.
3-93	" Ezekiel, of Ezekiel (supposed dead) and Desire, both Stonington,	May 17, 1785.
3-31	DUNBAR John, of John and Anstrus,	Aug. 18, 1759.
3-31	" Thomas,	May 20, 1764.
3-31	" Abigail,	Jan. 28, 1766.
	Note—Eldest born Lyme, Conn.	
4-15	" Anstress, of Thomas and Eunice,	Oct. 6, 1786.
4-15	" Thomas,	Nov. 8, 1788.
4-15	" Sally Freebody,	Nov. 9, 1790.
4-15	" Nathan Barber,	Nov. 20, 1796.
4-15	" John,	May 30, 1794.
4-15	" William Champlain,	Sept. 20, 1798.
4-15	" Eunice,	Oct. 3, 1800.
4-15	" Oliver Champlain,	Dec. 27, 1807.

E

2-116	EDWARDS Sarah, of Thomas and Josepha,	Jan. 24, 1720-1.
2-116	" Daniel,	March 15, 1722-3.
2-74	" Phebe, of Christopher and Phebe,	July 18, 1737.

2-74	EDWARDS Peleg, of Christopher and Phebe,	Sept. 3, 1741.
2-74	" Paine,	Feb. 3, 1743-4.
2-74	" Patience,	May 16, 1746.
2-74	" Phineas,	Oct. 17, 1749.
2-74	" Prudence,	April 4, 1752.
2-74	" Perry,	Dec. 3, 1755.
3-38	" Leah, of Thomas and Garthrot,	Feb. 26, 1743.
3-38	" Garthrot,	June 18, 1745.
3-38	" Thomas,	Oct. 12, 1747.
3-38	" Paul,	March 4, 1749.
3-38	" Silas,	July 6, 1752.
3-147	" Mary, of Thomas and Mary,	Sept. 1, 1775.
6-147	" Thomas,	Dec. 29, 1777.
3-147	" Sarah,	June 15, 1780.
3-147	" Anna,	April 1, 1783.
3-147	" Silas,	Feb. 10, 1786.
3-147	" Greenman,	Nov. 15, 1789.
3-147	" Daniel,	Aug. 2?, 1792.
3-155	" Paul, of Paul and Rachel,	Jan. 9, 1781.
3-155	" Thomas,	March 25, 1782.
3-155	" Jonathan,	March 25, 1782.

Note—Eldest born Westerly, others Westerly.

4-133	" Patty, of Clarke and Catherine,	Feb. 11, 1781.
4-133	" Polly,	June 3, 1783.
4-133	" Clarke,	March 29, 1785.
4-133	" Daniel,	March 4, 1787.
4-133	" Daniel,	died April —, 1791.
4-133	" Maxson,	Sept. 7, 1789.
4-133	" Thomas,	Aug. 22, 1791.
4-133	" Benjamin,	Sept. 18, 1793.
4-133	" John,	May 25, 1796.
4-133	" Hannah,	July 25, 1798.
4-133	" Caty,	Sept. 29, 1801.
4-39	" Hannah, of Paul and Rachel,	Nov. 6, 1783.
4-39	" Sarah,	Aug. 26, 1786.
4-39	" Hazard,	Sept. 6, 1788.
4-39	" Patience,	May 30, 1790.
2-58	ELDERTON Joseph, of Roger and Lydia,	Jan. 6, 1723.
2-58	" Robert,	March 12, 1724.
2-58	" Bridget,	March 27, 1726.
2-58	" Mary,	April 10, 1728.
2-58	" Anna,	Nov. 5, 1730.
2-58	" Sarah,	Jan. 8, 1732.
2-58	" Lydia,	Dec. 10, 1736.
2-58	" Joseph, 2d,	Jan. 10, 1744-5.
4-191	ELLIS Mary Ann, of Samuel and Mary,	June 20, 1803.
2-92	ENOS Joseph, of Joseph and Margaret,	June 10, 1718.
2-92	" Mercy,	Nov. 1, 1720.
2-92	" Benjamin,	Oct. 25, 1725.
2-92	" Margaret,	May 27, 1729.
2-92	" Benjamin,	Feb. 26, 1733.
2-92	" Hannah,	April 7, 1736.

F

2-82	FOSTER Card, of John and Marjory,	April 17, 1725.
2-82	" Mary,	April 20, 1726.
2-82	" John,	Sept. 10, 1727.
2-82	" Hannah,	May 19, 1729.
2-82	" Christopher,	July 6, 1731.
3-36	" Gideon,	Sept. 11, 1734.
3-36	" John,	Feb. 25, 1746.
4-120	" Sally, of Thomas and Nabby,	Jan. 30, 1794.
4-120	" Thomas,	Oct. 17, 1797.

4-92	FOWLER Damarias, of John and Hannah,		June 8, 1793.
4-92	"	Sally,	Dec. 27, 1794.
4-92	"	Harriet,	Jan. 10, 1797.
4-92	"	Fanny,	Aug. 28, 1798.
4-92	"	Mary Ann,	Aug. 1, 1801.
4-92	"	Oliver Hull,	April 6, 1803.
4-92	"	Powell Helme,	June 25, 1805.
4-92	"	Emeline,	Nov. 1, 1808.

Note—Eldest born Stonington.

3-109	FRAZIER Nathaniel, of Gideon and Mercy,		Jan. 24, 1768.
3-109	"	Gideon,	Oct. 25, 1773.
3-109	"	Anne,	Dec. 23, 1775.
3-159	"	Elizabeth,	Sept. 7, 1778.
3-159	"	Gideon,	Oct. 20, 1782.
3-159	"	Thomas,	April 30, 1784.
4-12	"	Mercy, of George and Elizabeth,	Dec. 8, 1785.
4-12	"	Mercy,	died Dec. 13, 1785.
4-12	"	Judeth,	June 6, 1787.
4-12	"	William Greene,	Dec. 9, 1788.
4-12	"	Joseph,	July 26, 1790.
4-12	"	John Greene,	April 14, 1792.
4-12	"	Thomas,	March 8, 1794.
4-145	"	Nathaniel Warren Gibbs, of Nathaniel and Ruth,	July 17, 1800.
4-145	"	Fanny Hoxsie,	July 19, 1801.
4-145	"	William Robinson,	Nov. 7, 1803.
4-145	"	Gideon Wells,	March 8, 1806.
4-145	"	Charles Greene,	Feb. 25, 1809.
2-98	FRENCH John, of William and Prudence,		Nov. 15, 1739.
2-98	"	Prudence,	June 7, 1743.
4-228	FRINK Marshall, of Marshall and Betsey,		July 15, 1806.
4-228	"	Mary,	June 29, 1808.
4-228	"	Peleg,	July 4, 1810.
4-229	FULLER Sarah W., of Lindall A. and Sarah,		July 8, 1807.

G

3-67	GARDINER Benaiah, of Thomas and Martha,		March 8, 1754.
3-67	"	Abigail,	April 29, 1756.
3-67	"	Thomas,	Aug. 27, 1758.

Note—Eldest born South Kingstown.

2-84	GAVITT Elijah, of Ezekiel,		May 28, 1734.
2-84	"	John,	July 13, 1736.
2-84	"	William,	Nov. 11, 1737.
2-84	"	Amey,	Dec. 1, 1739.
2-84	"	Ezekiel,	June 15, 1741.
2-84	"	Hannah,	March 8, 1742-3.
2-84	"	Lucy,	Dec. 5, 1744.
2-84	"	Elijah,	Jan. 6, 1746-7.
2-84	"	Ichabod,	Oct. 30, 1750.
3-57	"	Oliver, of Samuel and Mary,	Feb. 11, 1738.
3-57	"	Susannah,	June 14, 1741.
3-57	"	Samuel,	Sept. 8, 1743.
3-57	"	Edward,	May 6, 1747.
3-57	"	Hannah,	Aug. 17, 1751.
3-57	"	Eunice,	Aug. 3, 1753.
3-57	"	Vashti,	Sept. 4, 1755.
3-73	"	John, of Joseph and Thankful,	July 13, 1744.
3-73	"	Marjory,	Sept. 4, 1746.
3-73	"	Joseph,	May 13, 1749.
3-73	"	Phalley,	May 13, 1752.
3-73	"	Sanford,	June 28, 1760.
3-73	"	Samuel,	March 29, 1763.
3-73	"	Mary,	Jan. 1, 1768.
3-61	"	Mary, of Stephen and Mary,	Aug. 14, 1744.

4-11		GAVITT George, of Stephen, Nov. 21, 1745.	
4-11	"	George of George and Abigail,	April 16, 1773.
4-11	"	Thomas,	Feb. 26, 1775.
4-11	"	Ephraim,	Oct. 22, 1777.
4-11	"	Abigail,	July 10, 1780.
4-11	"	Asa,	March 29, 1782.
4-11	"	Arnold Saunders,	Nov. 16, 1784.
4-11	"	Mary,	March 16, 1787.
3-143	"	Thankful, of Stephen and Mary,	Oct. 15, 1754.
3-84	"	Anna, of William and Anna,	Dec. 29, 1761.
3-84	"	John,	Feb. 19, 1764.
3-84	"	William,	April 2, 1766.
3-110	"	Amey, of Ezekiel and Mary,	July 27, 1764.
3-110	"	George,	Oct. 28, 1766.
3-129	"	Oliver, of Samuel and Ruth,	Dec. 23, 1766.
3-129	"	Daniel Pearce,	Oct. 20, 1768.
3-129	"	Mary,	Aug. 2, 1770.
3-129	"	Esther,	Feb. 26, 1772.
3-118	"	Joseph, of Oliver and Marjory,	Jan. 26, 1771.
3-118	"	Benjamin,	July 10, 1772.
3-118	"	Ezekiel,	June 26, 1775.
3-118	"	Thankful,	Feb. 25, 1781.
3-118	"	Mary,	Oct. 18, 1787.
3-138	"	Elizabeth, of Stephen and Mercy,	Aug. 27, 1775.
3-138	"	Martha,	Feb. 13, 1778.
4-186	"	Keturah, of John and Desire,	Dec. 8, 1778.
4-186	"	Joseph,	Jan. 10, 1781.
4-186	"	Samuel,	March 19, 1784.
4-186	"	Thankful,	Jan. 21, 1787.
4-186	"	Benjah,	June 30, 1791.
4-186	"	Polly,	May 7, 1795.
4-186	"	Daniel Lee.	Aug. 4, 1799.
		Note—Three youngest born Charlestown.	
3-171	"	Sarah, of Joseph and Sarah, 2d wife,	Nov. 20, 1781.
3-171	"	Thankful,	July 3, 1785.
4-43	"	Lois, of Sylvester and Sarah,	Nov. 8, 1783.
4-24	"	Mary, of Eunice, June 27, 1787.	
4-65	"	Samuel, of Sanford and Hannah,	Oct. 1, 1787.
4-65	"	Sexton Berry,	Oct. 1, 1789.
4-65	"	John,	Dec. 1, 1791.
4-65	"	Joseph,	March 4, 1794.
4-65	"	Susannah,	June 9, 1797.
4-65	"	Hannah,	Jan. 5, 1800.
4-65	"	Sanford,	Aug. 11, 1802.
4-65	"	Saunders,	Jan. 20, 1804.
4-331	"	Stephen, of Stephen, Jr., and Mary,	Feb. 5, 1790.
4-43	"	Keturah, of Sylvester and Keturah,	Sept. 15, 1791.
4-43	"	Sarah,	Sept. 3, 1793.
4-43	"	Rhoda,	March 28, 1795.
4-43	"	Sylvester,	April 3, 1797.
4-43	"	Charles Pendleton,	Dec. 17, 1799.
4-43	"	William Pendleton,	Feb. 19, 1801.
4-43	"	Isaac Pendleton,	May 9, 1805.
4-101	"	Lucy, of George and Lucy,	July 7, 1796.
4-101	"	Reley,	Dec. 7, 1798.
4-101	"	Isaac Bliven,	April 24, 1801.
4-101	"	Abby,	Feb. 11, 1803.
4-101	"	John Bliven,	Feb. 9, 1806.
4-101	"	George Washington,	Feb. 9, 1806.
4-101	"	Frank,	March 12, 1808.
4-101	"	Arnold,	May 17, 1810.
4-104	"	Mary Hix,	July 18, 1812.
4-204	"	Daniel, of Ephraim and Sally,	March 3, 1804.
4-204	"	Sally,	Dec. 24, 1805.
4-204	"	Edwin,	July 23, 1808.

4-204	GAVITT	Mary Ann, of Ephraim and Sally,	April 9, 1810.
4-204	"	Abby,	June 23, 1812.
4-204	"	Martha Rhodes.	Sept. 21, 1814.
		Note.—Second born Norwich. Conn.	
4-211	"	Lydia, of Ezekiel and Hannah.	June 30, 1806.
4-211	"	Joseph.	Aug. 7, 1808.
4-221	"	Albert, of Samuel and Rebecca.	Feb. 14, 1807.
4-244	"	John Emory, of Joseph and Thankful,	May 11, 1811.
4-244	"	Francis.	May 11, 1811.
4-244	"	William Sidney,	April —, 1813.
		Note.—Youngest born Charlestown.	
5-28	"	Isaac P., of Isaac and Phebe Ann,	Dec. 1, 1827.
5-28	"	Sylvester.	Feb. 27, 1830.
5-28	"	Phebe Ann.	March 1, 1832.
5-28	"	Amos.	Oct. 16, 1837.
3-40	GORTON	Grant, of Samuel and Mercy,	April 5, 1753.
3-40	"	Mary.	Sept. 27, 1755.
		Note.—First born Groton, Conn.; second. Richmond.	
2-94	GREENELL	Susannah, of Daniel and Jane,	July 29, 1728.
2-94	"	Susannah,	died, June 17, 1733.
2-94	"	George,	March 2, 1731-2.
2-94*	"	Susannah,	Dec. 25, 1733.
2-94	"	Jane,	May 30, 1736.
2-96	GREENMAN	Catherine, of Silas and Eunice,	April 22, 1738.
2-96	"	Abigail,	April 15, 1740.
2-96	"	Anna,	Jan. 30, 1741-2.
2-96	"	Elizabeth,	Nov. 5, 1744.
3-41	"	Rhahama, of Nathan and Eunice,	March 23, 1767.
3-41	"	Nathan,	Oct. 12, 1774.
3-41	"	Ethan,	May 22, 1776.
3-155	"	Luke.	Oct. 18, 1779.
4-94	"	Sarah, of Silas and Polly,	Oct. 22, 1794.
4-94	"	Silas,	Nov. 26, 1796.
4-94	"	Polly,	Dec. 1, 1798.
4-94	"	Lucy,	Jan. 25, 1800.
4-94	"	Lucy,	d. March 2, 1803.
4-94	"	Caty,	June 11, 1803.
2-85	GREENE	Sarah, of Benjamin and Eleanor,	Feb. 28, 1714-5.
2-85	"	Humility,	Feb. 6, 1716.
2-85	"	Eleanor,	March 2, 1718.
2-85	"	Benjamin,	March 2, 1720.
2-85	"	Matthew,	March 13, 1722.
2-85	"	Amey,	Jan. 7, 1727.
2-85	"	Caleb,	March 21, 1729.
2-85	"	Joseph,	June 23, 1731.
3-80	"	Margaret, of William and Judeth,	Aug. 14, 1759.
3-80	"	William Rathbone,	Dec. 22, 1761.
3-80	"	Elizabeth,	Feb. 4, 1764.
3-80	"	Benjamin,	Dec. 14, 1765.
3-80	"	Pardon,	April 24, 1769.
3-80	"	Judeth, of William and Sarah, 2d wife,	Nov. 23, 1774.
3-80	"	Margaret,	July 5, 1776.
3-80	"	Sarah,	Oct. 17, 1777.
3-21	"	Charles, of Joseph and Margaret,	June 14, 1749.
3-21	"	Luke,	Sept. 18, 1751.
3-21	"	John,	Jan. 10, 1754.
3-21	"	Rhody,	April 29, 1756.
3-21	"	Edward,	March 20, 1760.
3-21	"	Perry,	Feb. 20, 1762.
3-21	"	Joseph,	Oct. 31, 1764.
3-21	"	Olive,	March 5, 1768.
4-3	"	Lois, of Samuel and Lois,	Jan. 22, 1771.
4-3	"	Betsey,	May 25, 1774.
4-3	"	Bathsheba,	Oct. 10, 1777.
4-3	"	Samuel,	May 21, 1780.

4-3	GREENE	Margaret, of Samuel and Lois,	Oct. 3, 1782.
4-3	"	Stephen,	June 18, 1785.
4-3	"	Hannah,	Sept. 24, 1788.
4-3	"	Ruth,	April 5, 1791.

Note—Three youngest born Voluntown, Conn.

4-40	"	Judeth, of William and Sarah,	Nov. 23, 1774.
4-40	"	Margaret,	July 5, 1776.
4-40	"	Sarah,	Oct. 17, 1777.
4-40	"	Hannah,	April 13, 1779.
4-40	"	Elisha Cheeseborough,	Feb. 13, 1781.
4-40	"	John,	June 11, 1782.
4-40	"	Nathaniel,	March 3, 1784.
4-40	"	Prudence,	Oct. 31, 1785.
4-40	"	Coggeshall,	Aug. 29, 1787.
4-40	"	Thomas,	Sept. 29, 1790.
4-200	"	Saunders, of John and Prudence,	March 15, 1776.
4-200	"	Nathan,	Nov. 9, 1777.
4-200	"	Oliver Davis,'	Jan. 15, 1780.
4-200	"	Abigail,	April 22, 1782.
4-200	"	Hannah,	Oct. 15, 1784.
4-200	"	Rowland Thurston,	Oct. 23, 1786.
4-200	"	George Saunders,	Sept. 15, 1788.
4-200	"	Alpheus Miner,	July 27, 1790.
4-200	"	John,	Oct. 28, 1792.

Note—Hannah born Charlestown, the next two Hopkinton, the two youngest Stonington.

3-135	"	Hannah, of William and Sarah,	April 13, 1779.
3-135	"	Nathaniel,	March 3, 1784.
3-135	"	Prudence,	Oct. 31, 1785.
3-80	"	Elisha Cheeseborough,	Feb. 13, 1781.
3-80	"	John,	June 11, 1782.
3-80	"	Coggeshall,	Aug. 29, 1787.
3-169	"	Josias, of Jonathan and Anna,	Dec. 23, 1780.
3-169	"	Jonathan,	Sept. 18, 1783.
3-169	"	William,	Sept. 18, 1783.
3-169	"	Tacy,	May 15, 1786.
3-169	"	Mary,	Aug. 11, 1789.
3-169	"	Lucinda,	July 8, 1792.
3-169	"	Christopher,	June 1, 1795.
3-169	"	Christopher,	died March 16, 1798.
3-169	"	Gardner,	March 27, 1797.
4-178	"	William Rathbone, of William R. and Esther,	Dec. 15, 1781.
4-178	"	William Rathbone,	died May 13, 1782.
4-178	"	Pegy,	Feb. 4, 1783.
4-178	"	William Rathbone,	April 13, 1785.
4-178	"	Pardon,	June 17, 1787.
4-178	"	Sally,	Feb. 22, 1790.
4-178	"	Polly,	Feb. 18, 1792.
4-178	"	Nancy,	May 9, 1794.
4-178	"	Nancy,	died March 11, 1796.
4-178	"	Lucy,	Jan. 11, 1798.
4-178	"	Fanny,	June 13, 1800.
4-178	"	Charles Keene,	April 12, 1803.

Note—1st also recorded 3-180.

4-21	"	Judeth, of Benjamin and Mary,	June 3, 1787.
4-21	"	Matila, born at Richmond, Dec. 4, 1790, died at Voluntown, Conn., July 18, 1790. (sic.)	
4-28	"	Pardon Clarke, of Pardon and Fanny,	Jan. 1, 1790.
4-28	"	Betsey,	Nov. 8, 1791.
4-28	"	William Bliven,	Feb. 9, 1794.
4-28	"	Luther Bliven,	Aug. 29, 1796.
4-28	"	Pardon died at Cooksocky, N. Y.,	Aug. 12, 1799.

Note—3d born Hopkinton; 4th Cooksocky, N. Y.

4-44	"	Lydia, of Benjamin, and Polly,	April 21, 1791.
4-44	"	Christopher,	Feb. 1, 1794.

4-44	GREENE Olive, of Benjamin and Polly,		Jan. 27, 1795.
4-44	"	Benjamin Barber,	Nov. 5, 1797.
4-44	"	Pardon,	March 1, 1800.
4-44	"	Perry,	Oct. 25, 1802.

Note—Three eldest born Voluntown, next two Richmond, youngest Hopkinton.

3-140	"	Richard, of John, and Abigail, born in Exeter; date not given.	

H

2-111	HALL Sarah, of James and Sarah,		Dec. 25, 1693.
2-111	"	Jane,	Aug. 29, 1695.
2-111	"	Honor,	Aug. 14, 1697.
2-111	"	Eliah,	Aug. 23, 1699.
2-111	"	James,	Sept. 17, 1701.
2-111	"	Joseph,	July 8, 1703.
2-111	"	Mary,	Nov. 10, 1705.
2-111	"	Benjamin,	Nov. 19, 1707.
2-111	"	Amey,	Sept. 26, 1709.
2-111	"	Jonathan,	Nov. 18, 1711.
2-83	"	Benjamin, of James and Rachel,	April 17, 1722.
2-83	"	David,	Dec. 11, 1723.
2-83	"	Anna,	May 1, 1725.
2-83	"	Timothy,	Dec. 20, 1726.
2-83	"	James,	May 11, 1729.
2-83	"	Amos,	July 8, 1731.
4-15	"	Amos, of David and Judeth,	Feb. 14, 1749.
4-15	"	Rachel,	June 8, 1750.
4-15	"	Deborah,	Oct. 27, 1752.
4-15	"	Judeth,	Oct. 20, 1754.
4-15	"	Lydia,	April 20, 1757.
4-15	"	David,	Sept. 20, 1759.
4-15	"	Abigail,	March 11, 1764.
4-15	"	Wilbur,	July 21, 1766.
4-15	"	Daniel,	May 31, 1768.
4-15	"	Nathan,	Aug. 22, 1770.
4-15	"	Benjamin,	June 1, 1772.
4-15	'	John White,	Oct. 4, 17..

Note—Youngest born Hopkinton.

3-107	"	Elizabeth, of Theodoty and Elizabeth,	May 3, 1749.
3-107	"	Margaret,	June 21, 1751.
3-107	"	Theodoty,	Aug. 23, 1754.
3-107	"	Rhodes,	March 23, 1757.
3-107	"	Chloe,	July 1, 1759.
3-107	"	Rachel,	July 26, 1762.
3-107	"	Adam,	April 3, 1766.
3-107	"	Freegift,	May 26, 1768.
4-135	"	Thomas, of Isaac, born Westerly,	Jan. 4, 1754.
4-135	"	Eunice (Johnson, of Reuben), his wife, born Charlestown,	May 20, 1754.
4-135	"	Eunice, of Thomas and Eunice,	Sept. 23, 1779.
4-135	"	Anna,	March 20, 1780.
4-135	"	Barbara,	Feb. 12, 1782.
4-135	"	Olive,	May 20, 1785.
4-135	"	Lydia,	Jan. 17, 1787.
3-2	"	Thomas, of Isaac and Abigail,	Jan. 4, 1754.
3-2	"	Nathan,	March 7, 1776.
3-107	"	Lucy, of Charles and Esther,	March 27, 1755.
3-107	"	Esther,	Aug. 3, 1756.
3-107	"	Charles,	March 9, 1758.
3-107	"	Amey,	April 14, 1760.
3-107	"	Samuel,	May 20, 1762.
3-107	'	Lebbens,	Nov. 9, 1764.
3-107	"	Penelope,	March 12, 1768.

3-107	HALL	Dorcas, of Charles and Esther,	Feb. 11, 1771.
3-107	"	Acars Tosh,	Oct. 23, 1773.
3-175	"	Joseph, of Joseph (dec.), and Tamson,	Nov. 19, 1759.
3-175	"	Lyman,	Aug. 30, 1762.
3-175	"	Braddick,	April 7, 1767.
3-175	"	Dennis,	May 27, 1770.
3-175	"	Warren,	Oct. 23, 1772.
3-175	"	Merchant,	May 6, 1775.
3-65	"	Zilpah, of Hezekiah and Dorcas,	Feb. 18, 1763.
3-65	"	Amey,	Feb. 6, 1767.
3-65	"	Frances,	Feb. 23, 1769.
3-65	"	Deborah,	Oct. 3, 1771.
3-168	"	Susanna,	Dec. 4, 1774.
3-168	"	Anne,	Jan. 24, 1777.
3-168	"	Hezekiah,	April 1, 1779.
3-142	"	Mary, of Theodoty and Mary,	Jan. 24, 1777.
3-142	"	Theodoty,	May 2, 1779.
3-142	"	Stanton,	March 14, 1784.
4-38	"	Eunice, of Thomas and Eunice,	Sept. 23, 1778.
4-38	"	Amey,	March 20, 1780.
4-38	"	Barbara,	Feb. 12, 1783.
4-38	"	Olive,	May 17, 1785.
4-38	"	Lydia,	June 17, 1789.

Note.—2d born Charlestown.

3-166	"	Weeden, of William and Rachel,	April 28, 1782.
3-173	"	Varnum, of Theodoty and Mary,	Sept. 21, 1786.
3-173	"	Freegift,	April 3, 1789.
3-173	"	Peckham,	Aug. 4, 1791.
3-173	"	Margaret,	Sept. 3, 1794.
4-85	"	Eunice, of Capt. Lyman and Eunice,	Dec. 27, 1788.
4-85	"	Joseph,	June 6, 1790.
4-85	"	Joseph,	died July 15, 1790.
4-85	"	Lyman,	Sept. 7, 1791.
4-85	"	Lyman,	died Oct. 8, 1791.
4-85	"	Lyman, 2d,	Sept. 18, 1792.
4-85	"	John Pendleton,	March 30, 1794.
4-85	"	Eunice, wife of Lyman,	died March 31, 1794.

Note—Eldest child also recorded 4-30.

4-115	"	Joseph, of Braddick and Susannah,	Dec. 15, 1791.
4-115	"	Hezekiah,	March 2, 1794.
4-115	"	Elisha,	April 23, 1797.
4-115	"	Thomas,	Feb. 2, 1799.
4-115	"	Polly,	Aug. 29, 1800.
4-115	"	Polly,	died April 9, 1801.
4-115	"	Susanna,	Feb. 26, 1802.
4-115	"	Tamson,	July 13, 1805.
4-115	"	Abigail,	Oct. 5, 1808.
4-115	"	Hannah,	Nov. 7, 1810.
4-115	"	Nancy,	Feb. 4, 1812.
4-206	"	Daniel, of Benjamin and Huldah,	June 21, 1798.
4-206	"	Patty,	Oct. 30, 1799.
4-206	"	David,	Nov. 29, 1801.
4-206	"	Benjamin,	Aug. 20, 1804.
4-206	"	Judah Ann,	Sept. 12, 1806.
4-115	"	Palmer, of Lyman and Phebe,	Jan. 8, 1799.
4-115	"	Palmer,	died July 29, 1807.
4-115	"	Phebe,	Aug. 4, 1801.
4-115	"	Elizabeth,	May 11, 1803.
4-115	"	Palmer,	Nov. 11, 1810.
4-150	"	Caty, of Theodoty and Caty,	Feb. 8, 1800.
4-150	"	Theodoty,	April 13, 1802.
4-223	"	Varnum Sannders, of Varnum and Caty,	Dec. 10, 1807.
4-223	"	Elizabeth,	Nov. 20, 1809.
4-223	"	Prudence,	April 27, 1812.

4-230	HALL	Francina, of Merchant and Abigail,	March 27, 1809.
4-230	"	Gordon,	March 1, 1812,
4-230	"	Mary Ann,	June 9, 1815.
5-12	"	Susannah, of Hezekiah and Jane,	March 24, 1826.
5-12	"	Elisha,	Oct. 2, 1827.
5-12	"	Charles,	May 20, 1829.
5-15	"	Eunice Ann, of John P. and Nancy,	April 23, 1828.
5-15	"	John Franklin,	Oct. 3, 1829.
5-15	"	Frances Maria,	April 14, 1832.
2-110	HASSELL	Thankful, of Joseph and Rachel,	July 22, 1716.
2-110	"	Mercy,	Feb. 4, 1718.
2-110	"	Sarah,	Sept. 17, 1719.
2-110	"	Joseph,	May 17, 1721.
2-110	"	William,	March 19, 1723.
2-110	"	James,	Feb. 4, 1726.
2-110	"	Jemima,	Sept. 8, 1727.
3-116	HARDY	Esther Babcock, of Sarah, Jr.,	March 27, 1790.
3-4	HAWK	Ann, of John and Ann,	April 26, 1754.
2-88	HAZELTON	Barbara, of Jarvis and Barbara,	July 27, 1736.
4-124	HERBERT	Polly, of William and Lois,	Aug. 23, 1797.
4-124	"	John,	Nov. 30, 1798.
2-77	"	Dorothy, of William and Dorothy,	Feb. 14, 1726.
2-77	"	William,	Sept. 22, 1727.
2-77	"	Samuel,	Jan. 14, 1730-1.
2-77	"	Elizabeth,	April 29, 1734.
2-77	"	Joshua,	Sept. 19, 1738.
3-23	"	Matthew, of William, Jr., and Eunice,	Aug. 31, 1752.
3-23	"	Lucy,	May 19, 1754.
3-23	"	Anne,	April 4, 1756.
3-23	"	Marcy,	March 30, 1758.
3-23	"	Eunice,	Sept. 15, 1767.
3-23	"	William,	March 2, 1772.

Note.—Two youngest born Hopkinton.

3-91	HEX	Lydia of John and Anne,	March 29, 1752.
3-91	"	Anne,	April 15, 1754.
3-91	"	John,	May 1, 1756.
3-91	"	Joseph,	March 10, 1758.
1-173	HILL	John, of John,	Oct. 3, 169—.
1-173	"	Mary,	Feb. 27, 1701-2.
2-87, 97	"	Ebenezer and Mercy,	March 25, 1733-4.
2-87, 97	"	Tacy,	Dec. 17, 1727.
2-87, 97	"	Jonathan,	April 25, 1730.
2-87, 97	"	John,	Nov. 21, 1734.
2-87, 97	"	David,	Nov. 18, 1736.
3-35	"	Samuel, of Josiah and Mary,	Dec. 11, 1712.
3-35	"	Josiah,	Oct. 28, 1714.
3-35	"	John,	Nov. 10, 1717.
3-35	"	Ebenezer,	April 8, 1719.
3-35	"	Josiah, Sr.,	died Jan. 27, 1754.
2-52	"	Josiah, of Ebenezer and Thankful.	May 25, 1745.
2-52	"	Josiah,	died Nov. 13, 1745.
2-52	"	Mary,	Feb. 27, 1747.
2-52	"	Timothy,	Jan. 28, 1749.
2-52	"	Josiah,	Sept. 13, 1754.
2-52	"	Ebenezer,	Jan. 15, 1757.
2-73	HISCOX	William, of Thomas and Bethiah,	May 31, 1705.
2-73	"	Ephraim,	June 2, 1707.
2-73	"	Edith,	Sept. 6, 1709.
2-73	"	Mary,	July 12, 1713.
2-73	"	Thomas,	May 17, 1715.
2-73	"	Joseph,	April 22, 1717.
2-73	"	Hannah,	Jan. 22, 1719-20.
3-39	"	William, of William and Susannah,	July 13, 1731.
3-39	"	David, of William and Content,	Feb. 9, 1743.
3-39	"	Susannah,	May 7, 1745.

3-39	HISCOX	Content, of William and Content,	April 21, 1747.
3-39	"	Lucy,	May 19, 1749.
3-27	"	Joseph, of Joseph and Sarah,	Jan. 1, 1739-40.
3-27	"	Simeon,	April 28, 1742.
3-27	"	Thomas,	March 16, 1744.
3-27	"	Eunice,	Nov. 9, 1747.
3-165	"	Joshua, of Thomas and Elizabeth,	Sept. 30, 1755.
3-165	"	Edward,	May 9, 1760.
3-163	"	Hannah,	April 18, 1763.
3-165	"	Nancy,	May 5, 1766.
3-165	"	Thomas,	May 22, 1770.
3-42	"	Clarke, of Joseph and Bathsheba,	Oct. 14, 1760.
4-8	"	Waitey, of William, Jr., and Penlope,	Oct. 25, 1762.
4-8	"	William,	May 12, 1764.
4-8	"	Gardiner,	June 2, 1770.
3-148	"	Ruth, of Nathan and Ruth,	Oct. 12, 1765.
3-148	"	Catherine,	Jan. 8, 1767.
3-148	"	Nathan,	March 23, 1769.
3-148	"	Abigail,	June 15, 1772.
3-148	"	George Saunders,	May 22, 1778.
4-142	"	Amey, of Ephraim, Jr., and Mary,	Feb. 26, 1774.
4-142	"	Amey,	died March 5, 1774.
4-142	"	Abigail,	Nov. 10, 1775.
4-142	"	Mary,	Nov. 10, 1775.
4-142	"	Ephraim,	April 7, 1778.
4-142	"	Amey,	Dec. 19, 1780.
4-142	"	Pardon,	April 15, 1783.
4-142	"	John,	Jan. 31, 1786.
4-142	"	Sumner,	May 11, 1789.
4-3	"	Sarah, of Clarke and Sarah,	Nov. 3, 1783.
4-3	"	Sarah,	died Oct. 30, 1788.
4-3	"	Bathsheba,	Sept. 3, 1785.
4-3	"	Clarke,	May 28, 1787.
4-3	"	Arnold,	April 11, 1789.
4-3	"	Sarah,	April 14, 1792.
4-3	"	Polly,	June 5, 1794.
4-3	"	John,	Aug. 16, 1796.
4-3	"	Joseph,	June 16, 1799.
4-130	"	Susan, of Thomas and Susanna,	Sept. 1, 1798.
4-130	"	Thomas Jefferson,	April 25, 1801.
4-130	"	Daniel Chase,	Oct. 17, 1805.
5-17	"	William B., of Ephraim and Hannah,	Sept. 4, 1811.
5-17	"	Almira,	May 30, 1814.
5-17	"	Ira F.,	Sept. 14, 1816.
5-17	"	Paul E.,	Oct. 17, 1823.
4-243	"	Rowland, of Arnold and Nancy,	Dec. 22, 1810.
4-243	"	John S.,	Oct. 2, 1813.
		Note.—First born Hopkinton.	
4-163	"	Susannah (Lanphere), wife of Ephraim,	died Feb. 4, 1810.
5-46	"	Charles Edward, of Edward T. and Caroline,	March 4, 1846.
2-91	HOLWAY	Benjamin, of Benjamin and Penelope,	Dec. 30, 1714
2-91	"	Experience,	July 4, 1716.
2-91	"	Experience,	died Jan. 21, 1726.
2-91	"	Joseph,	Feb. 10, 1717.
2-91	"	Penelope,	Jan. 12, 1719.
2-91	"	William,	Feb. 18, 1721.
2-91	"	Samuel,	April 3, 1723.
2-91	"	Hannah,	Dec. 7, 1724.
2-91	"	Hannah,	died Dec. 15, 1730.
3-115	HOWARD	Henry, of Henry and Thankful,	Aug. 12, 1755.
3-115	"	Robert,	Feb. 3, 1759.
3-115	"	Thankful,	Oct. 5, 1761.
2-80	HOXSIE	Martha, of Joseph and Mary,	April 13, 1729.
2-80	"	Gideon,	Dec. 14, 1729.
2-80	"	Sarah,	Sept. 14, 1731.

2-80	HOXSIE Joseph, of Joseph and Mary,		May 8, 1733.
4-136	HUBBARD Amey, of James and Amey,		Oct. 6, 1799.
4-136	"	James,	May 31, 1802.
2-86	HULL Sarah, of Joseph and Elizabeth,		Sept. 8, 1732.
2-86	"	Trustam,	May 28, 1734.
2-86	"	Hannah,	May 13, 1736.
2-86	"	Elizabeth,	April 7, 1738.
3-132	"	Thomas, of Thomas and Hannah,	April 22, 1770.
3-132	"	Lydia,	April 15, 1772.
3-132	"	Joseph,	May 9, 1775.
3-132	"	James,	Aug. 7, 1777.
3-132	"	Martha,	June 6, 1780.
3-132	"	Benjamin,	Oct. 19, 1782.
3-158	"	Mary (so called), dau. of Rachel Saunders (single woman),	
			Jan. 31, 1775.
4-72	"	Thomas, of Thomas and Amey,	June 21, 1792.

I J

2-122	JOHNSON John, of Jonah and Mary,		Sept. 8, 1709.
2-74	"	Ezekiel, of Stephen and Susannah,	Oct. 23, 1728.
2-74	"	Stephen,	Sept. 23, 1730.
2-74	"	Elizabeth,	Jan. 24, 1732-3.
2-74	"	Mary,	May 24, 1735.
3-127	"	Nathaniel, of Nathaniel and Sarah,	Aug. 19, 1753.
3-127	"	Christopher,	June 30, 1773.
		Note—Youngest born Charlestown.	
3-150	"	Hannah, of Nathaniel and Sarah,	July 5, 1757.
3-151	"	Polly,	Feb. 17, 1765.

K

2-68	KENYON Martha, of Joseph,		May 8, 1725.
2-68	"	John,	Dec. 4, 1727.
2-68	"	Mary,	July 20, 1729.
2-68	"	Paine,	April 20, 1733.
2-68	"	Joseph,	Feb. 5, 1736.
2-118	"	Mary, of Peter and Naomi,	Aug. 3, 1737.
4-183	"	Sally, of Joshua and Mary,	Feb. 29, 1776.
4-183	"	Polly,	Feb. 5, 1779.
4-183	"	Betsey,	June 23, 1783.
4-183	"	Nancy,	Feb. 25, 1786.
4-183	"	Nabby,	Dec. 11, 1788.
4-183	"	Patty,	June 18, 1791.
4-183	"	Rowland,	Dec. 17, 1797.
		Note—All born Charlestown except youngest, in Westerly.	
4-150	"	Lois Ross, of James and Lydia,	Sept. 26, 1800.
4-228	KNIGHT Margaret C., of Jedediah and Eliza		May 13, 1809.
4-228	"	Elizabeth D.,	Oct. 24, 1812.
4-228	'	Elizabeth D.,	died June 21, 1825.
4-228	"	Jedediah Whitney,	Feb. 21, 1815.
4-228	"	David Crane,	July 24, 1817.
4-192	KNOWLES Samuel, of Joseph M. and Dorcas,		Nov. 12, 1802.
4-192	"	Samuel,	died Oct 5, 1805.
4-192	"	John Tillinghast,	March 10, 1804.
4-192	"	Sally,	Oct. 24, 1805.
4-192	"	Anna,	Jan. 11, 1808.
4-192	"	Joseph,	July 3, 1810.
4-192	"	Celia,	May 29, 1812.
4-192	"	Jerah M.,	Dec. 17, 1814.
4-192	"	William,	Aug. 28, 1816.
4-192	"	Mumford Gardiner,	Sept. 9, 1821.

L

2-41	LANPHERE	Theodorius, of Theodorius and Rachel,	Jan. 31, 1707-8.
2-41	"	James,	Nov. 22, 1710.
2-41	"	Joshua,	Nov. 23, 1712.
2-41	"	Abigail,	March 27, 1715.
2-41	"	Susannah,	Dec. 14, 1716.
2-41	"	Nathaniel,	March 22, 1718.
2-41	"	Mary,	Dec. 14, 1721.
2-41	"	Samuel,	Dec. 23, 1723.
2-41	"	Stephen,	Feb. 5, 1725-6.
2-41	"	Jabez,	March 25, 1731.
2-41	"	Joseph,	Sept. 20, 1736.
2-108	"	Elizabeth, of Seth and Sarah,	Aug. 10, 1715.
2-109	"	Amey, of Richard and Mary,	June 22, 1715.
2-109	"	Lucy,	July 3, 1718.
2-109	"	Esther,	Feb. 21, 1720-1.
2-109	"	Sophia,	Oct. 12, 1724.
2-109	"	Josepha,	Jan. 25, 1725-6.
2-124	"	George, died Oct. 6, buried	Oct. 7, 1731.
3-15	"	Mary, of Nathan and Mary,	April 5, 1740.
3-15	"	Nathan,	Feb. 18, 1742.
3-15	"	Elisha,	Jan. 21, 1744.
3-15	"	Jonathan,	April 19, 1748.
3-15	"	Langworthy,	Feb. 5, 1753.
3-15	"	Amey,	March 20, 1755.
3-23	"	Champlain, of Stephen and Mary,	July 14, 1750.
3-23	"	Amey,	April 20, 1753.
3-23	"	Susannah,	Feb. 25, 1755.
3-23	"	Huldah,	March 14, 1760.
3-23	"	Anson,	Feb. 22, 1764.
3-23	"	Anson,	died March 9, 1764.
3-23	"	Ansin, 2d,	Jan. 28, 1765.
3-23	"	Lua,	Dec. 6, 1768.
3-23	"	Polly,	July 1, 1771.
3-45	"	Ruth, of Benjamin and Susannah,	May 27, 1757.
3-100	"	Prudence, of Daniel, Jr., and Eunice,	Oct. 30, 1759.
3-100	"	George,	March 31, 1761.
3-100	"	Lucretia,	Nov. 12, 1762.
3-100	"	Elizabeth,	June 26, 1764.
3-100	"	Rhoda,	Aug. 18, 1766.
3-100	"	Daniel,	May 16, 1768.
3-100	"	Jesse,	Jan. 20, 1770.
3-100	"	Eunice,	Sept. 21, 1772.
3-15	"	Patience, of Nathan and Anna, 2d wife,	May 26, 1760.
3-15	"	Paul,	Feb. 25, 1762.
3-15	"	Pardon,	Feb. 25, 1762.
3-15	"	Anne,	Feb. 20, 1767.
3-87	"	Benoni Smith, of David and Sarah,	Sept. 28, 1762.
3-121	"	Mary, of Nathan, 2d, and Amey,	Aug. 24, 1765.
3-121	"	Hannah,	Nov. 22, 1767.
3-121	"	Ethan,	Jan. 19, 1770.
4-76	"	Luther, of Daniel and Wealtha,	July 27, 1768.
4-76	"	Tacy,	May 14, 1770.
4-76	"	Eunice,	Feb. 21, 1772.
4-76	"	Oliver,	Aug. 18, 1774.
4-76	"	Lois,	Nov. 16, 1777.
4-76	"	Joshua,	Oct. 1, 1787.
4-76	"	Keturah,	Aug. 9, 1790.
3-119	"	Maxson, of Nathan and Ann, 2d wife,	Dec. 5, 1769.
3-119	"	Catharine,	Nov. 9, 1779.
4-100	"	Amey, of Nathan, Jr., and Sarah,	July 4, 1772.
4-100	"	Elisha,	Nov. 19, 1773.
4-100	"	Simeon,	Nov. 5, 1776.
4-100	"	Abigail,	June 27, 1778.

4-100	LANPHERE	Susannah, of Nathan, Jr., and Sarah,	May 10, 1780.
4-100	"	Enock,	Jan. 14, 1782.
4-100	"	Samuel,	Oct. 14, 1783.
4-100	"	Hezekiah,	Oct. 14, 1783.
4-100	"	Joseph,	Oct. 12, 1785.
4-100	"	William,	May 24, 1787.
4-100	"	Acors,	Feb. 28, 1790.
4-100	"	Silas,	Oct. 3, 1791.
3-126	"	Asa, of Champlain and Rebecca,	Sept. 19, 1772.
3-126	"	Joshua,	March 5, 1774.
3-126	"	Joseph,	Oct. 3, 1775.
3-126	"	Stephen,	Aug. 16, 1778.
3-126	"	Prentice,	July 11, 1781.
3-126	"	Rebecca,	May 5, 1784.
3-126	"	Polly,	Jan. 11, 1786.
4-67	"	Russell, of Daniel and Nancy,	Dec. 2, 1776.
4-67	"	Mercy,	Jan. 3, 1782.
4-67	"	William,	Oct. 13, 1785.
4-67	"	Nancy,	Sept. 16, 1787.
4-67	"	Triphena,	Oct. 7, 1789.
4-67	"	Daniel,	Dec. 22, 1792.
4-39	"	Perry, of David and Eunice,	Oct. 13, 1783.
4-39	"	Clarke,	Aug. 24, 1787.
4-64	"	Wheeler, of Henry and Priscilla,	Oct. 16, 1788.
4-64	"	Susannah,	Oct. 15, 1790.
		Note—1st born Albany, N. Y., 2d Stephentown, N. Y.	
4-89	"	Abel, of Paul and Elizabeth,	Jan. 25, 1790.
4-89	"	Clarke,	April 27, 1792.
4-89	"	Susannah,	March 6, 1795.
4-89	"	Pardon, of Pardon and Polly, b. Hopkinton,	Dec. 27, 1790.
4-166	"	Sally, of Nathan and Nancy,	Jan. 29, 1795.
4-166	"	Fanny,	Dec. 9, 1797.
4-114	"	Elisha, of Elisha and Betsey,	July 20, 1796.
4-114	"	Elisha,	died Aug. 26, 1800.
4-114	"	Betsey,	Feb. 1, 1799.
4-137	"	Polly, of Maxson and Susannah.	Jan. 27, 1797.
4-137	"	Truman,	Oct. 23, 1798.
4-137	"	Nancy,	Dec. 5, 1800.
4-137	"	Clarissa,	Nov. 26, 1803.
4-137	"	Jonathan,	Sept. 16, 1808.
4-137	"	Bathsheba,	Nov. 20, 1811.
4-137	"	Ephraim,	Nov. 9, 1815.
4-123	"	Sally, of Joseph C., and Lucretia,	Aug. 16, 1798.
4-123	"	Asa,	June 16, 1801.
4-123	"	George Washington,	Feb. 19, 1803.
4-111	"	Polly, of Joseph and Ruth,	Dec. 3, 1798.
4-111	"	Sally,	Jan. 27, 1801.
4-111	"	Asel,	April 30, 1803.
4-111	"	Franklin,	June 23, 1805.
4-111	"	Celia Anne,	Dec. 5, 1807.
4-111	"	William Thompson,	March 7, 1810.
4-111	"	Lucinda Bernice,	June 18, 1812.
4-111	"	Lewis Thompson,	May 25, 1815.
		Note—Three youngest born North Stonington.	
4-126	"	Nancy, of Stephen and Sally,	April 4, 1800.
4-248	"	Wealthy, of Clarke and Wealthy,	Jan. 9, 1814.
4-248	"	George C.,	Jan. 28, 1816.
4-248	"	Belinda,	Oct. 2, 1818.
4-248	"	Wealthy, wife of Clarke,	died Nov. 24, 1822.
4-252	"	Joanna C., of William, 2d, and Eliza,	April 21, 1814.
4-252	"	Thomas M.,	June 28, 1816.
4-252	"	Gordon M.,	Aug. 11, 1818.
4-252	"	Silas H.,	Feb. 7, 1821.
4-252	"	Horace,	Jan. 25, 1823.
4-252	"	Sarah P.,	Oct. 6, 1824.

4-252	LANPHERE	Juliet, of William, 2d, and Eliza,	Oct. 5, 1826.
2-124	LARKIN	Rebecca, of John (dec.) and widow Rebecca,	Oct. 14. 1701.
2-97	"	Joseph, of Joseph and Johannah,	Feb. 12, 1730-1.
2-97	"	Joshua,	Aug. 20, 1732,
2-69	"	John, of John and Mary,	May 1, 1731.
2-69	"	Nathan,	June 13, 1732-3.
2-69	"	Daniel,	Dec. 19, 1734-5.
2-69	"	Timothy,	Oct. 10, 1736.
2-69	"	Lebbeus,	June 5, 1738-9.
2-41	"	Benajah, of Samuel and Sarah,	June 18, 1732,
3-72	"	Daniel, of Samuel and Sarah,	April 1, 1739.
3-128	"	Moses, of Simeon and Jane,	Feb. 11, 1747.
3-128	"	Sarah, of Moses and Jane,	Aug. 29, 1769.
3-128	"	Thomas,	Dec. 19, 1771.
3-128	"	Isabel,	Feb. 15, 1774.
3-128	"	Stephen ——. and Barbara, 2d wife,	May 2, 1797.
		Note—Youngest born at Charlestown.	
3-83	"	Simeon, of Simeon, dec.,	Sept. 18, 1748.
3-62	"	Mary, of Daniel and Susannah,	July 31, 1759.
3-62	"	John,	Feb. 4, 1760.
3-142	"	Abel, of Abel and Sarah,	June 14, 1771.
3-142	"	Sarah,	Feb. 7, 1773.
3-142	"	Jonathan,	Jan. 12, 1775.
3-142	"	Anna,	Feb. 24, 1778.
3-142	"	Anna,	died March 6, 1819.
3-142	"	Daniel,	Dec. 26, 1781.
3-142	"	John,	Dec. 1, 1784.
3-161	"	Simeon, of Moses and Barbara, born Charlestown,	Oct. 22, 1778.
3-176	"	Barbara, of Moses and Barbara, born Stonington,	April 5, 1781.
4-129	"	Abel, of Abel and Hannah,	July 4, 1798.
4-129	"	Abel,	died July 14, 1799.
4-129	"	Hannah,	May 2, 1800.
4-129	"	Nathan,	Aug. 17, 1802.
4-129	"	Hirris,	Dec. 30, 1804.
4-129	"	Sally Ann,	Jan. 9, 1807.
4-217	"	Jonathan, of Jonathan and Ann,	June 24, 1805.
5-112	"	Daniel F., of Daniel and Rhoda,	Jan. 10, 1817.
5-112	"	Martha (Hiscox, of Clarke and Mary), his wife,	March 19, 1817.
5-112	"	Franklin, of Daniel F. and Martha,	April 14, 1844.
5-112	"	Martha Jane,	June 14, 1846.
5-112	"	Sarah Elizabeth,	May 17, 1850.
5-112	"	Albert Clarke,	Aug. 6, 1852.
3-1	LAWTON	Thomas, of Josiah and Elizabeth,	May 23, 1751.
4-183	LEEDS	Frank, of Christopher and Mary,	Nov. 30, 1802.
4-183	"	——,	Feb. 22, 1804.
4-179	LEE	William Elliott, of Daniel and Lydia Ann,	Nov. 6, 1784.
4-179	"	Nancy Atwater,	April 30, 1787.
4-179	"	Sophia,	Feb. 20, 1789.
4-179	"	Harriet,	Jan. 10, 1791.
4-179	"	Fanny,	Oct. 20, 1792.
4-179	"	Sophronia,	Aug. 25, 1794.
4-179	"	Benjamin Franklin,	May 9, 1796.
4-179	"	Daniel Mather,	Jan. 15, 1798.
4-179	"	Allen Campbell,	Oct. 25, 1799.
4-179	"	Charlotte,	Aug. 16, 1801.
4-179	"	Sally,	March 10, 1803.
		Note—Eldest born Middletown, Conn., next two Lyme, the others Westerly.	
1-172	LEWIS	Joseph, of John,	Oct. 16, 1683.
1-172	"	Sarah,	Aug. 17, 1687.
1-172	"	Mary,	May 4, 1689.
1-172	"	Anna,	Jan. 6, 1691.
1-172	"	Abigail,	May 20, 1693.
1-172	"	John,	Jan. 30, 1698.
1-172	"	William,	Feb. 1, 1701-2.

1-204	LEWIS	Israel, of Israel and Joanna,	June 22, 1695.
1-204	"	Benjamin,	June 8, 1697.
1-204	"	Joanna,	May 21, 1700.
1-204	"	Anna,	July 13, 1704.
1-204	"	Nathaniel,	March 23, 1706.
2-117	"	Jerusha, of John and Ann,	Jan. 11, 1706-7.
2-116	"	Jerusha, of Joseph and Mary,	July 13, 1707.
2-116	"	Joseph,	Dec. 25, 1709.
2-116	"	Thankful,	June 15, 1720.
2-116	"	Absolam,	Nov. 25, 1724.
2-116	"	Hannah,	Nov. 21, 1726.
2-107	"	Hannah, of George and Elizabeth,	Jan. 15, 1713.
2-107	"	Samuel,	Dec. 21, 1715.
2-107	"	Mary,	Sept. 21, 1716.
2-107	"	James,	Dec. 18, 1719.
2-107	"	Ebenezer,	March 18, 1722.
2-107	"	Othniel,	April 15, 1723.
2-78	"	John, of John, Jr., and Mary,	April 19, 1719.
2-78	"	Elisha,	Dec. 30, 1722.
2-78	"	Mary,	Jan. 22, 1723-4.
2-78	"	Joseph,	March 2, 1728.

Note—Also recorded 2-117.

2-78	"	Stephen, of John (of James and Tacy),	April 9, 1719.
2-78	"	Joseph, of John and Mercy, 2d wife,	April 21, 1721.
2-78	"	Mercy,	July 1, 1726.
2-78	"	Edward,	June 19, 1728.
2-78	"	Joshua,	Nov. 20, 1729.
2-78	"	Nathan,	May 23, 1733.
2-78	"	Zebulon,	Sept. 3, 1734.
2-78	"	Samuel,	Sept. 15, 1736.
2-78	"	Anne,	Jan. 29, 1737-8.
2-78	"	Penelope,	March 29, 1739.
2-78	"	John,	July —, 1751.
2-112	"	Elisha, of Israel and Mary,	Feb. 4, 1718-9.
2-112	"	Enock, of Israel and Bathsheba,	Oct. 13, 1720.
2-110	"	Jonathan, of John and Anna,	Aug. 21, 1721.
2-110	"	John,	April 13, 1723.
2-110	"	Avis,	Aug. 8, 1725.
2-110	"	Anna,	Nov. 13, 1727.
2-110	"	Kezia,	June 12, 1730.
2-110	"	Joshua,	May 13, 1733.
2-42	"	Ezekiel, of William and Mary,	Dec. 16, 1723.
2-42	"	William,	April 8, 1725.
2-42	"	Prudence,	April 2, 1727.
2-42	"	Sarah,	May 15, 1731.
2-42	"	Mary,	Sept. 26, 1733.
2-42	"	Anne,	May 31, 1735.
2-42	"	Hannah,	March 1, 1737-8.
2-42	"	Benjamin, of John and Ann,	Jan. 24, 1748-9.
2-96	"	Amos, of Nathaniel and Mary,	April 29, 1731.
2-96	"	Nathaniel,	Feb. 28, 1732-3.
2-96	"	Mary,	July 31, 1735.
2-96	"	Jean,	June 22, 1737.
2-96	"	Rhabamah,	Oct. 7, 1739.
2-96	"	Elijah,	Oct. 11, 1741.
2-96	"	Mary,	July 10, 1743.
2-96	"	Israel,	Sept. 15, 1745.
2-77	"	Elizabeth, of Joseph, Jr., and Mary,	July 18, 1731.
2-77	"	David,	Nov. 12, 1733.
2-77	"	Joseph,	Nov. 25, 1735.
2-77	"	Oliver,	Sept. 23, 1738.
2-77	"	Esther,	March 2, 1741.
2-77	"	Betsey,	July 28, 1744.
2-77	"	Mary,	July 24, 1747.
2-77	"	Peleg,	June 2, 1749.

2-1	LEWIS	Bethana, of Elisha and Dorcas (or Tabitha),	Jan. 7, 1745.
2-1	"	Mary,	Nov. 3. 1746.
2-1	"	Joseph, died Sept. 23, 1751.	
3-139	"	John, of John and Thankful,	July 17, 1739.
3-139	"	Cloe,	Aug. 26, 1741.
3-139	"	Ruhama,	May 19, 1743.
3-139	"	Hezekiah,	Oct. 24, 1744.
3-139	"	Elias,	Nov. 25, 1746.
3-139	"	Simeon,	Dec. 25, 1753.
3-139	"	Hannah,	Sept. 7, 1755.
3-139	"	Bernice,	Feb. 1, 1758.
3-139	"	William,	June 24, 1760.
3-139	"	Jeptha,	May 17, 1763.
3-139	"	Anne,	Sept. 22, 1765.
2-14	"	Mosh. of Elisha and Lydia (also 3-26),	Jan. 12, 1741 2.
3-177	"	James, of Joseph and Sarah,	Aug. 7, 1745.
3-177	"	Catherine,	May 11, 1746.
3-177	"	Valentine,	Nov. 29, 1749.
3-177	"	Mary,	June 9, 1752.
3-177	"	Joseph, of —— and Mary, 2d wife,	June 18, 1764.
		Note—Born at Stonington.	
3-16	"	Stephen, of Stephen and Martha,	June 18, 1748.
3-16	"	Lydia,	March 21, 1749-50.
3-28	"	Jonathan, of Jonathan and Tacy,	Jan. 28, 1748-9.
3-35	"	Abel, of Abel and Thankful,	Oct. 14, 1751.
3-35	"	Augustus,	April 30, 1753.
3-35	"	Thankful,	March 23, 1755.
3-35	"	Nathaniel,	Jan. 8, 1757.
3-35	"	Phineas,	March 2, 1759.
3-26	"	Lydia, of Elisha and Amey,	Jan. 16, 1752.
3-26	"	Asa,	Jan. 20, 1754.
3-22	"	Eunice, of Elias and Susannah,	Feb. 23, 1753.
3-19	"	Freelove, of Joseph and Mary,	March 15, 1753.
3-19	"	Wealthian,	June 24, 1755.
3-19	"	Mary,	Feb. 20, 1757.
3-19	"	Silva,	Feb. 12, 1759.
3-19	"	Anna,	Feb. 1, 1761.
3-19	"	Joseph,	Oct. 27, 1762.
4-157	"	Rozzell, of Capt. Oliver and Ruhama,	Sept. 6, 1736.
4-157	"	Thankful,	Dec. 22, 1768.
4-157	"	Thankful,	d. Dec. 5, 1770.
4-157	"	Elias,	Nov. 25, 1770.
4-157	"	Oliver,	May 1, 1772.
4-157	"	Simeon,	July 18, 1774.
4-157	"	Ichabod,	July 22, 1776.
4-157	·	Ichabod.	d. Oct. —, 1776.
4-157	"	Jabez,	Oct. 18, 1778.
4-157	"	Molly.	Sept. 18, 1780.
4-157	"	Ruhama, wife of Capt. Oliver,	d. March 27, 1781.
4-157	"	Capt. Oliver,	d. Sept. 27, 1804.
3-135	"	Jared, of Hezekiah and Anna,	March 6, 1767.
3-135	"	Anne,	Sept. 10, 1768.
3-135	"	Prentice,	March 16, 1772.
3-135	"	John,	April 28, 1776.
3-135	"	Maxson,	Dec. 13, 1782.
3-135	"	Amey,	Jan. 18, 1784.
3-135	"	Josiah,	July 31, 1789.
3-135	"	Hezekiah,	July 31, 1789.
		Note—Eldest born Stonington.	
3-174	"	Ichabod, of Nathaniel and Elizabeth,	May 7, 1767.
3-174	"	Lodowick,	April 22, 1771.
3-174	"	Elizabeth,	April 7, 1773.
3-174	"	Horatio Gates,	Jan. 16, 1778.
3-174	"	Martha,	Oct. 21, 1780.
4-79	"	Elizabeth, of David and Mary,	Oct. 1. 1776.

4-79	LEWIS	Ruth, of David and Mary,	Sept. 21, 1778.
4-79	"	Mary,	Oct. 8, 1780.
4-79	"	David,	April 3, 1783.
4-79	"	Soloman,	June 29, 1785.
4-79	"	Patience,	Sept. 3, 1787.
4-79	"	Prudence,	Jan. 14, 1790.
4-79	"	Tacy,	Jan. 14, 1790.
4-79	"	Jacob,	Sept. 3, 1792.
4-79	"	Ichabod Prosser,	May 18, 1796.
4-79	"	Augustus,	Oct. 31, 1798.
3-165	"	Simeon, of Simeon and Anne,	June 10, 1782.
3-165	"	Nathaniel,	March 11, 1784.
3-165	"	Peleg Cross,	Jan. 11, 1791.
3-165	"	Anne,	Jan. 18, 1793.
3-165	"	Jobn,	Ang. 16, 1795.
3-165	"	Jason Lee,	March 31, 1801.
3-165	"	Anne, wife of Simeon,	died Dec. 5, 1802.
4-38	"	William, of William and Hannah,	Oct. 26, 1782.
4-38	"	Hannah,	Sept. 19, 1784.
4-38	"	Chloe,	Dec. 16, 1787.
4-38	"	Samuel,	May 14, 1791.
4-38	"	Jeptha,	Feb. 20, 1794.
4-38	"	Pardon Thompson,	Oct. 17, 1796.
4-38	"	Abel,	Oct. 26, 1799.
4-20	"	Joseph, of Joseph and Rachel,	April 25, 1787.
4-20	"	Molly,	Oct. 14, 1789.
4-78	"	Fanny, of Jeptha and Fanny,	Sept. 14, 1788.
4-78	"	Samuel Gardner,	Jan. 23, 1789.
4-80	"	Saunders, of Matthen and Hannah,	April 1, 1793.
4-08	"	Polly, of Prentice and Polly,	Oct. 23, 1795.
4-94	"	Prentice,	Sept. 27, 1797.
4-94	"	Bridget,	Dec. 21, 1800.
4-94	"	Bridget,	died Nov. 14, 1801.
4-94	"	Rhoda,	Feb. 21, 1802.
4-94	"	Anna,	April 2, 1805.
4-216	"	Phineas, of Elias and Prescilla,	Feb. 4, 1798.
4-216	"	Deney,	Nov. 7, 1799.
4-216	"	Prescilla,	Jan. 16, 1802.
4-216	"	Prescilla,	April 3, 1802.
4-216	"	Rhuhumah,	March 23, 1806.
4-216	"	Elizabeth,	March 23, 1806.
4-196	"	John, of John and Lois,	April 20, 1798.
4-196	"	William,	Aug. 29, 1799.
4-196	"	Margery,	July 28, 1801.
4-196	"	Hezekiah,	March 8, 1804.
4-187	"	Jeptha Malbone, of Simeon and Frances,	March 31, 1804.
4-187	"	Enock,	Dec. 5, 1805.
4-39	LOMAS	Martha, of William and Lydia,	Sept. 4, 1791.
4-39	"	William,	Aug. 26, 1794.
4-39	"	James,	May 26, 1797.

Born at Voluntown, Conn.

M

3-51	MACCOON	Mary, of Nathan and Anna,	Oct. 21, 1744.
3-51	"	Nathan,	May 29, 1746.
3-51	"	Isabel,	July 17, 1748.
3-51	"	Timothy,	Feb. 9, 1750.
3-51	"	Abram,	April 15, 1753.
2-78	MAXSON	Judeth, of John and Judeth,	Sept. 23, 1689.
2-78	"	Mary,	Oct. 26, 1691.
2-78	"	Mary,	d. March 16, 1692.
2-78	"	Betniah,	July 31, 1693.
2-78	"	Elizabeth,	Nov. 7, 1695.

2-78	MAXSON	Hannah, of John and Judeth,	June 13, 1698.
2-78	"	John,	April 21, 1701.
2-78	"	Dorothy,	Oct. 20, 1703.
2-78	"	Susannah,	Oct. 19, 1706.
2-78	"	Joseph,	Dec. —, 1709.
2-78	"	Avis,	Dec. 27, 1712.
2-78	"	Joseph,	d. Dec. —, 1710.
2-60	"	Joseph, Jr.,	March 10, 1692.
2-60	"	Bethiah (——), wife of Joseph, Jr.,	July 31, 1693.
2-60	"	Bethiah, of Joseph, Jr., and Bethiah,	Oct. 19, 1716.
2-60	"	Mary,	Aug. 28, 1718.
2-60	"	Judeth,	Sept. 17, 1720.
2-60	"	Joseph,	Jan. 20, 1722-3.
2-60	"	Zebulon,	April 15, 1725.
2-60	"	Susan,	Aug. 25, 1727.
2-60	"	Mason,	March 6, 1729-30.
2-60	"	Content,	Dec. 31, 1732.
2-60	"	Nathan,	Sept. 30, 1736.
2-116	"	Jonathan, of Jonathan and Content,	Jan. 16, 1707-8.
2-116	"	Content,	Jan. 28, 1708.
2-116	"	Joseph,	Jan. 14, 1711-2.
2-116	"	John,	March 2, 1714.
2-116	"	Naomi,	May 6, 1716.
2-116	"	Samuel,	July 20, 1718.
2-116	"	Caleb,	Nov. 1, 1721.
2-116	"	Mary,	Nov. 20, 1723.
2-58	"	William, of John (of Joseph) and Hannah,	Jan. 20, 1717-8.
2-58	"	Amos,	March 16, 1720.
2-58	"	Joshua,	Feb. 1, 1721-2.
2-58	"	Isaiah,	Jan. 21, 1723-4.
2-58	"	Goodeth,	June 5, 1726.
2-58	"	Tacy,	Dec. 15, 1728.
2-58	"	Judeth,	Jan. 17, 1730-1.
2-58	"	Torrey,	Jan. 22, 1732-3.
2-58	"	Sylvanus,	May 3, 1735.
2-58	"	Hannah,	Dec. 3, 1737.
2-58	"	Mary,	Nov. 23, 1739.
2-58	"	Jesse, and Martha, 2d wife,	June 11, 1745.
2-58	"	Ruth,	Jan. 31, 1746-7.
2-125	"	John, of John, Jr., and Thankful,	Aug. 27, 1725.
2-125	"	Matthew,	April 27, 1727.
2-125	"	David,	July 24, 1729.
2-125	"	Joseph,	March 23, 1731.
2-125	"	Benjamin,	Feb. 21, 1733.
2-125	"	Stephen,	May 3, 1735.
2-125	"	Thankful,	July 16, 1737.
2-125	"	Daniel,	Sept. 25, 1739.
2-125	"	Joel,	May 28, 1742.
2-125	"	Eleanor,	Jan. 24, 1748-9.
2-47	"	Jonathan, of John and Tacy,	Aug. 24, 1737.
2-47	"	Esther,	June 13, 1739.
2-47	"	Anne,	Jan. 24, 1740-1.
2-79	"	William, of William and Hannah,	Nov. 16, 1745.
3-3	"	Samuel, of Samuel and Ruth,	Sept. 5, 1743.
3-3	"	Ruth,	March 5, 1747.
3-3	"	Elisha,	April 20, 1749.
3-21	"	Thomas, of Matthew, and Martha,	Jan. 7, 1750.
3-21	"	Peleg,	Jan. 7, 1752.
3-21	"	Matthew,	Jan. 6, 1754.
3-21	"	George,	Oct. 10, 1756.
3-21	"	Nathan,	Dec. 9, 1758.
3-21	"	Abel,	Jan. 1, 1761.
3-21	"	Luke,	April 18, 1763.
3-49	"	Silas, of David and Abigail,	Dec. 29, 1750.
3-49	"	Asa,	March 6, 1752.

3-49	MAXSON Elizabeth, of David and Abigail,		July 14, 1754.
3-49	"	Paul,	Aug. 2, 1757.
3-49	"	Chloe,	Oct. 15, 1759.
3-49	"	Wealthy,	March 9, 1762.
3-49	"	Sarah,	Dec. 23, 1763.
3-77	"	Amos, of Torrey and Martha,	Feb. 27, 1754.
3-77	"	John,	Nov. 1, 1755.
3-77	"	Catherine,	April 16, 1758.
3-77	"	Tacy,	June 2, 1761.
3-77	"	Joshua,	Jan. 27, 1763.
3-77	"	Prudence,	Aug. 18, 1765.
3-77	"	Martha,	Oct. 20, 1767.
3-77	"	Hannah,	Dec. 18, 1770.
3-77	"	Benjamin,	Feb. 27, 1773.
3-102	"	Jedediah, of Jesse and Keturah,	Aug. 3, 1754.
3-102	"	Hannah,	April 9, 1757.
3-102	"	Keturah.	March 3, 1759.
3-102	"	Augustus,	Nov. 8, 1761.
3-102	"	Joseph,	Nov. 2, 1765.
3-102	"	Samuel Randall,	July 26, 1772.
3-89	"	Joel, of Daniel and Borredell,	Jan. 1, 1763.
3-89	"	Elias,	Sept. 11, 1770
3-122	"	Silas, of Silas and Sarah,	Mar. 25, 1772.
3-122	"	Elizabeth,	Nov. 25, 1773.
3-148	"	Hannah, of Thomas and Hannah,	Oct. 4, 1773.
3-148	"	Thomas,	Aug. 17, 1775.
3-181	"	Asa, of Asa and Lois,	July 1, 1776.
3-181	"	Lois,	Aug. 25, 1778.
3-181	"	Mary,	July 14, 1781.
3-181	"	David,	Sept. 27, 1788.
3-181	"	Wealtha,	Aug. 18, 1790.
4-90	"	Paul, of Paul and Susannah,	Oct. 28, 1780.
4-90	"	Silas,	Sept. 7, 1782.
4-90	"	Jarus,	Jan. 15, 1785.
4-90	"	Susanna,	Dec. 19, 1788.
4-90	"	Jesse,	June 12, 1791.
4-90	"	George Stillman,	Aug. 18, 1793.
4-90	"	Sally,	Jan. 27, 1795.
4-90	"	Abigail,	Jan. 20, 1798.
4-90	"	Esther,	April 11, 1800.
4-90	"	David,	Nov. 20, 1802.
4-4	"	Augustus, of Augustus and Thankful,	March 19, 1784.
4-156	"	Betsey, of Sylvanus and Betsey,	Sept. 6, 1798.
4-156	"	Cynthia,	Aug. 1, 1800.
4-156	"	Altana,	Sept. 19, 1802.
4-156	"	Sanford Langworthy,	Dec. 5, 1806.
4-156	"	Lydia Ann,	Oct. 5, 1809.
4-156	"	Abby,	Sept. 9, 1811.
4-156	"	Sylvanus,	Oct. 29, 1813.
4-185	"	Jesse, of Jesse and Sophia,	Jan. 29, 1804.
4-185	"	Jesse,	died Oct. 18, 1824.
4-185	"	Courtland,	Dec. 26, 1806.
4-185	"	Courtland,	died Dec. 1, 1808.
		Note—Also recorded 5-24.	
4-239	"	Eliza, of Silas and Betsey,	Aug. 20, 1809.
4-239	"	Silas,	Sept. 25, 1811.
4-239	"	Silas,	died March 27, 1813.
4-239	"	Paul,	Dec. 7, 1813.
4-239	"	Paul,	died May 4, 1815.
4-239	"	Silas Franklin,	April 6, 1816.
4-239	"	William Ellery,	Nov. 18, 1818.
4-239	"	Cyrus Henry,	March 17, 1821.
4-239	"	George Franklin,	Feb. 9, 1824.
2-75	MEEKCOME Joseph, of Joseph and Jemima,		Oct. 10, 1735.
2-75	"	Thomas,	Dec. 24, 1737.
2-75	"	Elias,	Oct. 5, 1739.

2-75	MEEKCOME Peleg, of Joseph and Jemima,		Oct. 24, 1741.
2-75	" Jeremiah,		Jan. 10, 1743-4.
2-75	" Anna,		March 15, 1745-6.
2-75	" William,		March 15, 1745-6.
2-75	" Benjamin,		June 27, 1748.
2-75	" Ross,		June 16, 1751.
2-75	" Joseph, Sr.,		died Jan. 22, 1750-1.
3-37	MILLARD Elias, of Nelson and Isabel,		March 6, 1755.
3-37	" Stephen,		Dec. 2, 1759.
2-114	MOORE Stephen, of John,		April 20, 1716.
2-114	" George,		May 28, 1719.
2-114	" David,		Sept. 13, 1721.
2-125	MOTT Hannah, of Samuel and Hannah,		Dec. 30, 1726.
2-125	" Deborah,		Aug. 9, 1729.
2-125	" Thankful,		Aug. 9, 1729.
2-86	" Edward, of Jonathan and Hannah,		Dec. 16, 1731.
2-86	" Abigail,		Sept. 12, 1734.
2-86	" Samuel,		Oct. 31, 1736.
2-114	" Edward, of John,		Dec. 15, 1736.
2-14	MULKINS Abigail, of Henry and Abigail,		March 21, 1741-2.

N

4-176	NASH Betsey, of Jonathan, Jr., and Betsey,		Dec. 28, 1794.
4-176	" Jonathan,		June 20, 1797.
4-176	" Joseph,		Sept. 9, 1799.
4-176	" James Sheffield,		Sept. 16, 1801.
4-132	" Mary Ann, of Asa and Anna,		Nov. 5, 1799.
4-132	" Peggy,		Sept. 20, 1801.
4-132	" William Pendleton,		Dec. 4, 1803.
4-132	" Nancy,		Dec. 12, 1806.
2-97	NICHOLS David, of David and Sarah,		March 27, 1734-5.
2-97	" Elizabeth,		Dec. 17, 1736.
4-124	NOOGEN Elisha, of Elisha and Prudence,		Dec. 27, 1799.
4-124	" William Thompson,		June 24, 1802.
2-120	NOYES James, of James and Ann,		March, 18, 1707-8.
2-120	" Bridget,		May 25, 1710.
2-120	" Dorothy,		Oct. 1, 1712.
2-120	" Sarah,		Nov. 17, 1714.
2-120	" Elizabeth,		April 17, 1717.
3-144	" Thomas, of Joseph and Barbara,		Oct. 3, 1754.
3-144	" Sanford,		Oct. 20, 1756.
3-144	" Sanford,		died Sept. 30, 1759.
3-144	" Joseph, 3d,		May 9, 1758.
3-144	" Sanford,		Jan. 18, 1761.
3-144	" Mary,		Oct. 11, 1763.
3-144	" James,		Feb. 8, 1768.
3-144	" Betsey,		July 31, 1770.
3-144	" Joshua,		Dec. 5, 1772.
3-144	" Barker,		March 13, 1775.
4-141	" Thomas, of Col. Joseph and Barbara (also 3-10),		Oct. 3, 1754.
4-141	" Lydia (Rogers, of William) his wife, born Newport,		May 19, 1760.
4-141	" Sally, of Thomas and Lydia,		Dec. 6, 1781.
4-141	" Sally,		died April 23, 1782.
4-141	" William Rogers,		March 19, 1783.
4-141	" James Wells,		Dec. 22, 1784.
4-141	" Thomas,		Nov. 22, 1786.
4-141	" Joseph,		Nov. 27, 1788.
4-141	" Martha,		April 25, 1791.
4-141	" Daniel Rogers,		Aug. 22, 1793.
4-141	" Abby,		Sept. 29, 1795.
4-141	" Sanford Barker,		Nov. 4, 1797.
4-141	" Lydia, wife of Thomas,		died Nov. 15, 1798.
3-53	" Sanford, of Joseph and Barbara,		Oct. 20, 1756.

8-53	NOYES	Sanford, of Joseph and Barbara,	Oct. 20, 1756.
3-53	"	Joseph,	May 9, 1758.
3-53	"	Sanford,	Jan. 18, 1761.
3-53	"	Mary,	Oct. 11, 1763.
3-53	"	James,	Feb. 8, 1768.
3-70	"	Barker, of Capt. Joseph and Barbara,	March 13, 1775.
4-64	"	Samuel Allen, of William and Polly,	July 7, 1792.
4-64	"	Sally,	Oct. 23, 1793.
4-64	"	Lydia,	April 15, 1795.
4-64	"	Robert Fanning,	March 21, 1798.
4-64	"	William,	Oct. 7, 1799.
4-64	"	John Harvey,	March 18, 1801.
4-64	"	Polly,	Feb. 28, 1803.
4-64	"	Jesse,	July 30, 1804.
4-64	"	Joshua,	Jan. 11, 1809.
4-139	"	Eliza, of Joseph, Jr., and Elizabeth.	July 4, 1800.
4-155	"	Ann Maria, of Sanford and Martha,	Jan. 6, 1801.
4-155	"	Sanford,	Jan. 9, 1802.
4-155	"	Lydia Rogers,	Sept. 1, 1804.
4-155	"	Patty,	March 11, 1806.
		Note—Youngest born Hopkinton.	
4-270	"	Grace, of Joshua and Grace,	Sept. 19, 1811.
4-270	"	Joshua,	June 6, 1814.
4-270	"	Peleg,	July 18, 1816.
4-270	"	Barbara,	Feb. 16, 1819.
4-245	"	William Champlain, of Barker and Mariett,	March 22, 1813.
4-245	"	Joseph Barker,	Nov. 26, 1814.
4-245	"	David Marvin,	Dec. 30, 1825.
4-173	NYE	Lydia Ann, of Samuel and Sally,	Oct. 30, 1802.
5-62	"	Hannah A., of Jonathan R. and Hannah,	Sept. 13, 1852.

O

2-93	ODELL	Joseph, of Joseph and Elizabeth,	Aug. 14, 1718.

P

2-122	PALMER	John, of John and Hannah,	March 27, 1694.
2-122	"	Ephraim,	Feb. 21, 1699.
2-122	"	Joseph,	Sept. 2, 1704.
2-122	"	Hannah,	Sept. 5, 1706.
2-122	"	Mary,	Nov. 1, 1709.
4-154	"	Elias Sanford, of Luther and Sally,	March 27, 1801.
4-154	"	Polly Maria,	March 1, 1803.
2-47	PALMITTER	Benoni, of John and Mary,	Sept. 7, 1713.
2-47	"	Benajah,	Nov. 28, 1714.
2-47	"	Thankful,	April 8, 1716.
2-47	"	Daniel,	April 20, 1718.
	"	Jonathan, of Jonathan and Penelope,	Feb. 21, 1721.
	"	Elizabeth,	Dec. 13, 1725.
	"	John,	April 24, 1729.
	"	Penelope,	May 17, 1734.
3-78	"	Mercy, of Jonathan and Phebe,	Nov. 16, 1745.
3-78	"	Joseph,	March 1, 1748.
3-78	"	Phebe,	Nov. 26, 1756.
3-78	"	Jonathan,	Sept. 18, 1758.
3-78	"	Penlope,	Oct. 1, 1760.
3-32	"	John, of John and Deborah,	July 23, 1753.
3-32	"	Deborah,	June 10, 1755.
2-93	PARK	Joseph, of Joseph and Abigall,	Nov. 1, 1756.
2-93	"	Benjamin,	Nov. 1, 1756.
3-102	"	Benjamin, of Benjamin and Hannah (Stanton),	Sept. 16, 1765.
3-102	"	Thomas,	Sept. 1, 1767.

3-102	PARK John, of Benjamin and Hannah (Stanton),	Aug. 29, 1769.
3-102	" Hannah Stanton,	July 12, 1771.
2-80	PECKHAM Hannah, of Daniel and Mary,	Oct. 23, 1720.
2-80	" Mary,	Feb. 22, 1722.
2-80	" Daniel,	Sept. 25, 1726.
2-80	" Sarah,	Aug. 31, 1729.
2-80	" Abel.	Feb. 17, 1733.
	Note—also recorded 2-112.	
3-14	" John, born Newport, ——, 1712.	
3-14	" Deborah (Sweet), his wife, Sept. 15, 1711.	
3-14	" Isaac, of John and Deborah,	Feb. 21, 1737-8.
	Died in expedition to Ticonderoga, July 8, 1768; born in Newport.	
3-14	" Dorcas, of John and Deborah,	Dec. 26, 1740.
3-14	" Ruth.	March 19, 1743.
8-14	" Clement,	Aug. 1, 1745.
3-14	" Clement,	died Nov. 12, 1768.
3-14	" John,	Nov. 8, 1747.
3-14	" John,	died June 16, 1764.
3-14	" William Sweet,	April 22, 1750.
3-14	" Deborah, wife of John, died in 60th year, June 20, 1780.	
3-48	" Isaac of Isaac, of Newport, born at Newport, Oct. 20, 1713.	
3-48	" Bethiah, his wife, July 1, 1715, died Jan. 19, 1748-9.	
3-48	" Barbara, of Isaac and Bethiah,	Aug. 1, 1738.
3-48	" Benjamin,	June 2, 1740.
3-48	" Joan,	Oct. 26, 1741.
3-48	" Joshua,	March 29, 1743.
3-48	" Ann,	Sept. 4, 1744.
3-48	" Isaac,	May 8, 1747.
3-48	" Bethiah,	Jan. 13, 1748-9.
3-2	" Joseph, of Isaac and Mary,	Feb. 7, 1751.
3-2	" Stephen,	Oct. 23, 1752.
3-2	" Mary,	Oct. 11, 1754.
3-2	" Hannah.	Jan. 14, 1758.
3-2	" James York,	May 21, 1760.
3-2	" Patience,	Sept. 6, 1763.
3-60	" William, of Isaac and Dorcas, March 14, 1758.	
	Born in West Greenwich.	
4-102	" Hannah, of William S. and Hannah,	May 1, 1774.
4-102	" John Hazard,	June 23, 1776.
4-102	" John Hazard,	died May 29, 1783.
4-102	" Ruth,	Dec. 19, 1778.
4-102	" Deborah,	April 2, 1781.
4-102	" Susannah.	June 29, 1783.
4-102	" William Sweet,	Sept. 6, 1785.
4-102	" Joseph Clarke,	Oct. 25, 1792.
4-102	" Nancy,	Nov. 3, 1795.
4-102	" Hannah, wife of William S., died Nov. 5, 1795.	
	Note—The above, except two youngest, recorded 3-129.	
3-140	" Lucy, of Stephen and Esther,	Jan. 6, 1776.
3-140	" Stephen,	May 19, 1777.
3-151	" Isaac, of Isaac, Jr., and Anne,	June 23, 1778.
3-153	" Mary, of Joseph and Anna,	Oct. 19, 1778.
3-153	" Betsey,	March 1, 1780.
3-153	" Joseph,	March 19, 1782.
3-153	" Betsey,	Oct. 2, 1783.
3-171	" Hannah, of James York and Anna,	Sept. 18, 1781.
3-154	" Lois, of Joseph and Anna,	June 8, 1785.
4-23	" Peleg, of Peleg and Betsey,	Feb. 9, 1789.
4-23	" Rowland,	June 20, 1791.
4-140	" Hannah Perry, of Isaac and Polly W.,	Oct. 17, 1800.
4-140	" Hannah,	died Nov. 10, 1801.
4-140	" Mary Ann,	Dec. 7, 1801.
4-140	" Nancy,	Feb. 17, 1804.
5-60	PEIRCE Sarah Augusta, of Dr. John G. and Sarah A., March 24, 1841.

1-58	PENDLETON	Joseph, of James and Hannah, born Sudbury, Mass., Dec. 29, 1664.	
1-58	"	Deborah, of Joseph and Deborah,	Aug. 29, 1697.
1-58	"	Deborah, wife of Joseph,	died Sept. 8, 1797.
1-58	"	Joseph, of Joseph and Patience,	March 3, 1702.
1-58	"	Joseph,	died Feb. 18, 1706.
1-58	"	William,	March 23, 1704.
1-58	"	Joshua,	Feb. 22, 1705-6.
2-124	"	James, of James and Elizabeth,	Nov. 21, 1710.
2-124	"	Obadiah,	Nov. 1, 1712.
2-124	"	Christopher,	April 12, 1715.
2-124	"	Elizabeth,	April 12, 1715.
2-124	"	James, of James and Elizabeth, 2d wife,	Jan. 3, 1718-9
2-124	"	Samuel,	Sept. 21, 1720.
2-124	"	Thankful,	July 14, 1725.
2-124	"	Read,	Feb. 24, 1728-9.
2-124	"	Hannah,	July 3, 1731.
2-124	"	Ruth,	Dec. 19, 1734.
2-112	"	Abigail, of Caleb and Mary,	Dec. 10, 1717.
2-112	"	Sarah,	July 27, 1723.
2-112	"	Mary,	April 2, 1727.
2-112	"	Benajah,	July 24, 1729.
2-85	"	Joseph, of Joseph and Sarah,	Oct. 26, 1724.
2-85	"	Patience,	June 13, 1726.
2-85	"	Lois,	Aug. 22, 1728.
2-85	"	Sylvester,	Aug. 5, 1730.
2-85	"	Eunice,	Sept. —, 1731.
2-91	"	John, of Bryant and Anna,	Sept. 26, 1727.
2-91	"	Nathan,	Dec. 3, 1729.
2-91	"	Anna,	March 26, 1732.
2-98	"	Amos, of William and Lydia,	June 21, 1728.
2-109	"	William,	Feb. 11, 1726-7.
2-109	"	Freelove,	Oct. 30, 1731.
2-109	"	Peleg,	July 9, 1733.
2-109	"	John,	May 20 or 22, 1737.
2-109	"	Benjamin,	Sept. 18, 1738.
2-109	"	Lydia,	March 22, 1740-1.
2-109	"	Joshua,	May 6, 1744.
2-109	"	Ephraim,	July 14, 1746.
		Note.—Also recorded 3-65.	
2-32	"	Anna, of Priam,	March 20, 1731.
2-32	"	Caleb,	Dec. 7, 1734.
2-72	"	Ichabod, of James and Abigail,	May 9, 1732.
3-5	"	Sarah, wife of Sylvester, March 5, 1735.	
3-5	"	Sylvester, of Sylvester and Sarah,	Jan. 14, 1752.
3-5	"	Anne,	Sept. 20, 1754.
3-5	"	Katherine,	March 13, 1757.
3-5	"	Deborah,	Nov. 11, 1758.
3-5	"	Sarah,	May 26, 1760.
3-5	"	Abigail,	March 13, 1762.
3-5	"	Oliver,	Nov. 14, 1763.
3-32	"	Edmund, of Edmund and Susannah,	Jan. 8, 1738.
3-32	"	William,	Feb. 3, 1740.
3-32	"	Daniel,	Feb. 20, 1744.
3-32	"	David,	Feb. 20, 1747.
3-32	"	Solomon,	Feb. 15, 1751.
3-97	"	Joseph, of Joseph Jr., (dec.), and Anne,	Jan. 17, 1747.
3-97	"	William,	July 15, 1740.
		Note—Grandchildren of William Champlain and Sarah, his wife.	
3-65	"	Lucy, of Col. William and Mary,	April 22, 1752.
3-65	"	Nathan,	April 2, 1754.
3-65	"	Isaac,	June 23, 1757.
3-65	"	Keturah,	Jan. 25, 1761.
3-110	"	Amos, of Amos and Susannah,	Nov. 5, 1754.

3-110	PENDLETON Andrew, of Amos and Susannah,		July 7, 1756.
3-110	"	Molly,	Aug. 4, 1758.
3-110	"	Lebulon,	May 27, 1760.
3-110	"	Charles,	April 24, 1762.
3-110	"	Frederic,	June 13, 1766.
3-110	"	Jonathan, —— and 2d wife,	Sept. 19, 1769.
3-110	"	Nancy,	July 22, 1771.
3-110	"	Acors,	July 28, 1773.
3-110	"	William,	July 23, 1775.
3-110	"	Isaac,	Nov. 22, 1777.
3-110	"	Otis,	March 7, 1780.
3-110	"	Gibbert,	Sept. 7, 1782.
3-110	"	Harris,	Nov. 17, 1786.
3-60	"	Rebecca, of Samuel and Phebe,	Sept. 2, 1755.
3-60	"	Stephen,	Feb. 4, 1758.
3-60	"	Gideon,	May 15, 1759.
3-60	"	Anna,	March 18, 1760.
3-60	"	Harriet,	Feb. 4, 1762.
3-60	"	Lucy,	May 27, 1766.
3-68	"	Simeon, of James and Abigail,	June 3, 1756.
4-128	"	Mary, of Simeon and Mary,	May 12, 1760.
4-128	"	Grace,	Jan. 15, 1762.
4-128	"	Grace,	died March 15, 1764.
4-128	"	Bathsheba,	July 13, 1763.
4-128	"	Jabez,	Sept. 15, 1765.
4-128	"	Jabez,	died Sept. 25, 1773.
4-128	"	Hannah,	Oct. 8, 1767.
4-128	"	Hannah,	died Oct. 3, 1773.
4-128	"	Grace,	Jan. 18, 1770.
4-128	"	Sarah,	July 2, 1772.
4-128	"	Lucretia,	March 15, 1775.
4-128	"	Ethan,	April 3, 1777.
4-128	"	William,	Sept. 7, 1781.
4-128	"	William,	died Jan. 20, 1782.
4-128	"	Lucy,	March 3, 1783.
3-146	"	Peleg, of Peleg and Anna,	June 22, 1760.
3-146	"	Anna,	June 4, 1762.
3-146	"	Abigail,	Dec. 2, 1764.
3-146	"	Abigail,	died, Dec. 7, 1769.
3-146	"	Thomas,	July 4, 1767.
3-146	"	William,	June 17, 1769.
3-146	"	Joseph,	June 17, 1769.
3-146	"	Abigail,	Aug. 11, 1771.
3-146	"	Lydia,	Aug. 11, 1771.
3-146	"	Greene,	——. 21, 1774.
3-146	"	Prudence,	Oct. 5, 1777.
3-177	"	Benjamin, of Benjamin and Lois,	Feb. 7, 1764.
3-177	"	Lois,	March 8, 1766.
3-177	"	Lydia,	March 7, 1768.
3-177	"	David,	May 13, 1770.
3-177	"	Paul,	May 4, 1772.
3-177	"	Lebbeus,	Feb. 15, 1774.
3-177	"	Christopher,	Sept. 18, 1776.
3-177	"	Jabez Cheeseborongh,	May 21, 1778.
3-177	"	Susannah,	July 25, 1783.
3-101	"	Anne, of Joseph and Damarias, 1st wife.	June 19, 1766.
3-101	"	Abel,	Sept. 21, 1768.
3-101	"	Joseph,	June 30, 1771.
3-101	"	Alice. Nancy, 3d wife,	March 19, 1781.
3-101	"	Mary Miner,	July 17, 1783.
3-101	"	Martha.	April 28, 1785.
3-104	"	Eunice, of John and Sebra,	Aug. 26, 1766.
3-104	"	George,	July 24, 1768.
3-104	"	John Gardner,	May 7, 1770.

(Vit. Rec., Vol. 5.)   24

3-104	PENDLETON	Sebra, of John and Sebra,	Aug. 19, 1773.
3-104	"	John Lee,	March 4, 1777.
4-13	"	Sarah, of Ephraim and Sarah, born Mason's Island, Conn., Sept. 16, 1768.	
4-13	"	Ephraim, of Ephraim and Sarah,	Oct. 25, 1770.
4-13	"	Lodowick,	May 5, 1772.
4-13	"	Elizabeth,	Dec. 28, 1773.
4-13	"	Mary or Polly,	Sept. 20, 1775.
4-13	"	Nathaniel Miner,	May 5, 1777.
4-13	"	Keturah,	Jan. 19, 1779.

Note—Also recorded 3-161 and 4-148.

4-148	"	Lodowick, died at the West Indies Feb. 2, 1795.	
4-148	"	Edward Denison,	May 5, 1777.
4-148	"	Edward Denison,	d. July 2, 1778.
4-148	"	Ephraim, Sr.,	d. Jan. 2, 1780.
3-137	"	Joshua, of Joshua and Anna,	May 25, 1770.
3-137	"	Anne,	June 3, 1772.
3-137	"	Martha,	March 3, 1774.
3-137	"	Lucy,	March 14, 1776.
3-137	"	Clarrasaharlo,	April 24, 1778.
3-137	"	Polly,	Aug. 16, 1780.
3-137	"	William,	May 27, 1782.
3-137	"	Elisha Clarke,	May 16, 1784.
3-137	"	Adam,	Dec. 4, 1786.
3-101	"	Damarias, of Joseph and Damarias,	Aug. 9, 1773.
3-163	"	Simeon, of Simeon (of James) and Tabitha,	Aug. 12, 1775.
3-163	"	David,	Sept. 9, 1779.
3-163	"	Tabitha,	Dec. 1, 1783.
3-163	"	Elizabeth,	July 30, 1787.
3-163	"	Ely,	July 2, 1789.
3-163	"	Zerriah,	Oct. 11, 1791.
3-163	"	James,	April 7, 1796.
3-141	"	Amelia, of Nathan and Amelia,	Oct. 20, 1775.
3-141	"	Sally,	Aug. 13, 1777.
3-141	"	Nathan,	June 1, 1779.
3-141	"	Isaac,	Jan. 16, 1781.
3-141	"	Keturah,	Dec. 5, 1782.
3-141	"	Charlotte,	Oct. 24, 1784.
3-141	"	Molly,	Dec. 16, 1786.
3-141	"	Catharine,	July 22, 1789.
3-141	"	Simon,	Feb. 7, 1792.
3-141	"	Simon,	died Aug. 31, 1792.
3-141	"	Simon, 2d,	July 30, 1793.
3-141	"	William,	April 29, 1795.

Note—Youngest born at Stonington.

4-70	"	Armelia, of Joseph and Nancy,	July 4, 1779.
4-70	"	Alice,	March 17, 1781.
4-70	"	Mary,	July 7, 1783.
4-70	"	Martha,	April 28, 1785.
4-70	"	Fanny,	Dec. 11, 1787.
4-70	"	Elizabeth,	April 8, 1790.
4-70	"	William,	July 3, 1792.
4-70	"	Benjamin Crandall,	Nov. 11, 1794.
4-70	"	Gurdon,	July 4, 1797.
4-70	"	Lucy Ann,	April 15, 1799.
4-70	"	Ellet,	May 4, 1801.
4-70	"	Rowland,	Oct. 28, 1803.
3-101	"	Amelia, of Joseph and Anna, 2d wife,	July 4, 1779.
4-116	"	Benjamin, of Capt. Benjamin and Lucy,	Feb. 16, 1787.
4-116	"	Joseph,	March 25, 1789.
4-116	"	Frederic,	June 24, 1791.
4-116	"	Lucy,	Dec. 14, 1793.
4-116	"	Lodowick,	Feb. 22, 1796.
4-116	"	Harry,	Oct. 6, 1798.
4-116	"	Lois,	May 24, 1801.

4-116	PENDLETON Oliver, of Capt. Benjamin and Lucy,	Nov. 18, 1803.
3-173	" Fanny, of John and Sib:a,	Dec. 13, 1778.
3-173	" William,	Nov. 24, 1787.
3-101	" Elizabeth, of Joseph and Nancy, 3d wife,	April 8, 1790.
3-101	" Fanny,	Dec. 11, 1787.
4-40	" Rebecca, born Oct. 13, 1789.	
4-75	" Eunice, of John and Susannah,	Sept. 6, 1792.
4-75	" Freelove,	Feb. 20, 1795.
4-75	" John Gardner,	May 16, 1800.
4-66	" David, of David and Sally,	Aug. 19, 1793.
4-66	" Mercy,	Dec. 31, 1795.
4-66	" William Champlain,	Nov. 2, 1798.
4-66	" Polly,	July 14, 1802.
4-66	" Ethan,	Oct. 24, 1804.
4-147	" Hannah, of Joseph and Hannah,	Oct. 5, 1793.
4-147	" Amey,	May 25, 1795.
4-147	" Job Stanton,	Feb. 9, 1797.
4-147	" Samuel Clarke,	Feb. 15, 1799.
4-75	" Deborah, of George and Deborah,	Oct. 23, 1793.
4-75	" George,	June 30, 1795.
4-146	" Nancy, of Abel and Abigail,	Jan. 6, 1796.
4-146	" Charles,	March 1, 1798.
4-146	" Frances,	March 19, 1799.
4-146	" Damarias,	March 5, 1800.
4-146	" Amelia,	March 19, 1801.
4-146	" John S.,	Feb. 5, 1804.

Note—Eldest and two youngest born Stonington.

4-117	" Sabrina, of Paul and Sabra,	Aug. 26, 1797.
4-117	" Paul Washington,	Dec. 1, 1799.
4-117	" Charles Lee,	May 16, 1802.
4-118	" Amelia, of Joshua and Milly,	March 4, 1798.
4-195	" Jabez, of Lebbeus,	Jan. 4, 1800.
4-195	" Frank,	Nov. 16, 1801.
4-195	" Lucretia,	July 22, 1803.
4-195	" Dudley,	Oct. 3, 1806.
4-167	" Almira, of Christopher S. and Bridget,	March 7, 1803.
4-167	" Christopher,	July 23, 1805.
4-167	" Mary,	Oct. 10, 1807.
4-205	" Joshua Kenyon of Oates and Betsey,	Aug. 20, 1803.
4-248	" William Taylor, of William and Anna,	Feb. 8, 1813.
4-248	" Anna Loesa,	July 26, 1815.
4-248	" John,	March 9, 1818.
4-91	PERKINS Huldah, of Silas and Huldah, of West Greenwich,	Dec. 3, 1790.
2-98	PERRY Elizabeth, of Samuel and Susannah,	Nov. 8, 1719.
2-98	" Mary,	June 10, 1721.
2-98	" Samuel,	April 19, 1723.
2-98	" Simeon,	March 31, 1726.
2-98	" Hannah,	April 13, 1728.
5-52	Phinney John Edwin Clapp, of Ralph and Eliza,	Feb. 19, 1845.
2-106	POOLER Sarah, of Zaccheus and Jean,	July 17, 1747.
2-106	" John,	Aug. 25, 1749.
2-106	" Mary,	May 29, 1752.
3-92	POPPLE Stephen, of John and Dorcas,	Feb. 25, 1745.
3-92	" Theodoty,	March 16, 1747.
3-92	" William,	Sept. 23, 1750.
3-92	" Anne,	Feb. 23, 1753.
3-92	" Hannah,	Feb. 23, 1753.
3-92	" George,	Feb. 16, 1756.
3-92	" John,	Sept. 24, 1758.
3-92	" Penelope,	April 5, 1762.
2-40	PORTER Timothy, of John and Desire,	Dec. 15, 1725.
2-40	" Hannah,	Nov. 7, 1728.
2-40	" John,	Nov. 25, 1730.
2-40	" Desire,	Feb. 11, 1732-3.
2-40	" Sarah,	Aug. 19, 1735.

2-40	PORTER Samuel, of John and Desire,		May 9, 1737.
2-40	"	Thankful,	Dec. 7, 1739.
2-40	"	Nathan,	June 26, 1742.
2-115	POTTER Susannah, of Thomas and Mary,		Feb. 20, 1718-9.
2-115	"	Elizabeth,	Jan. 29, 1727-8.
2-115	"	Martha,	Jan. 3, 1729-30.
2-115	"	George,	Jan. 3, 1731-2.
4-45	"	Polly, of George, Jr., and Polly,	March 12, 1781.
4-45	"	George,	April 17, 1783.
4-45	"	Benjamin,	June 18, 1785.
4-45	"	Polly,	June 20, 1787.
4-45	"	Ephraim,	May 30, 1789.
4-45	"	Sally,	Aug. 11, 1792.
4-45	"	John,	May 13, 1795.
4-45	"	Content,	Aug. 9, 1797.
4-45	"	Charles,	Sept. 17, 1799.
4-9	"	Thomas, Wells, of Joseph and Phebe,	Jan. 26, 1785.
4-9	"	Joseph,	Aug. 4, 1787.
4-9	"	Henry,	March 12, 1790.
4-9	"	Robert Thompson,	July 31, 1794.
4-9	"	William,	May 8, 1800.
4-131	"	Hannah, of Nathan and Lucy,	Jan. 29, 1793.
4-131	"	Susannah,	March 5, 1795.
4-131	"	Cynthia,	Feb. 26, 1797.
4-131	"	Amelia,	April 3, 1799.
4-131	"	Nathan,	July 12, 1801.
4-131	"	David Rogers,	Jan. 3, 1804.
4-256	"	Julia, of Joseph and Mary,	Jan. 9, 1815.
2-90	PULLEN Mary, of William and Mercy,		Nov. 18, 1715.

Q R

2-70	RANDALL Nathan, of Nathan and Mary,		Oct. 10, 1735.
2-70	"	Mary, wife of Nathan,	died Dec. 2, 1735.
3-121	RATHBONE Thomas, of Ebenezer and Sarah,		Nov. 23, 1721.
3-121	"	Tamsin,	Oct. 8, 1724.
3-121	"	Sarah,	March 27, 1728.
3-121	"	Eleanor,	Sept. 10, 1732.
3-121	"	Mercy,	Jan. 16, 1737.
3-121	"	Ebenezer,	Jan. 29, 1740.
3-113	"	Thomas, of Ebenezer and Sarah,	Nov. 23, 1721
3-113	"	Stephen, of Thomas and Anna,	Nov. 17, 1750.
3-113	"	Priscilla,	Nov. 12, 1752.
3-113	"	James,	Aug. 6, 1754.
3-113	"	Paul Wilcox,	Dec. 29, 1756.
3-113	"	Mary,	April 29, 1758.
3-113	"	Thomas,	March 8, 1768.
4-53	"	Anne, of James and Susanna,	March 23, 1779.
4-53	"	Hannah Perry,	Oct. 27, 1782.
4-53	"	Hannah Perry,	died Feb. 7, 1788.
4-53	"	James,	May 20, 1786.
4-53	"	Hannah Perry 2d,	Aug. 11, 1791.
	Note.—Also recorded 3-154.		
3-161	"	Anne, of Stephen and Elizabeth,	April 4, 1781.
3-161	"	Job Wilbur,	June 20, 1784.
3-161	"	David Taylor,	Nov. 6, 1792.
4-41	"	Ebenezer, of Ebenezer, Jr., and Mary,	July 30, 1791.
4-41	"	Sarah,	Sept. 1, 1792.
4-41	"	Mary,	May 15, 1794.
4-41	"	Christopher,	Feb. 13, 1796.
4-41	"	Lydia,	April 19, 1798.
4-41	"	Prudence,	Feb. 17, 1800.
4-41	"	James Noyes,	March 4, 1802.
4-41	"	Susannah,	Feb. 12, 1806.

4-112	RATHBONE William, of Acors and Sarah,	18th 2d mo., 1796.
4-112	" Sarah,	11th 11th mo., 1797.
4-112	" Solomon,	1st 6th mo., 1799.
4-99	RECORDS Abigail, of Daniel and Lydia,	Aug. 13, 1784.
1-95	REYNOLDS Joseph, of Thomas,	born Newport, June 21, 1684.
2-91	" Richmond, of Joseph and Priscilla,	Jan. 22, 1729-30.
3-119	RHODES Oliver, of James and Abigail,	June 16, 1769.
3-119	" Abigail,	Jan. 1, 1772.
3-119	" Anne,	May 9, 1765.
3-160	" Christopher, of William and Sarah,	July 23, 1779.
3-160	" William,	Oct. 9, 1784.
3-160	" Thomas Randall,	July 23, 1786.
3-160	" Sally,	Feb. 23, 1788.
3-160	" Joshua,	Oct. 12, 1790.
4-203	" Lodowick Hoxsie, of James and Elizabeth, born Charlestown, Jan. 31, 1784.	
4-125	" Phebe, of Oliver and Eunice,	Sept. 26, 1797.
4-125	" Abigail,	Feb. 4, 1801.
4-125	" Oliver,	Dec. 26, 1803.
4-125	" William Babcock,	Sept. 9, 1805.
4-125	" Joseph Pendleton,	July 12, 1807.
4-125	" Caroline,	March 5, 1811.
4-240	" Martha, widow of Col. James,	died, March 31, 1809.
2-111	RICHMOND Lydia, of Cyrus and Jane,	Nov. 4, 1719.
2-111	" Elizabeth,	July 30, 1722.
2-111	" John,	June 19, 1724.
2-111	" Ann,	Sept. 1, 1726.
2-111	" Cyrus,	Dec. 8, 1730.
2-82	" Mary, of Stephen,	April 4, 1731.
2-82	" John,	Feb. 24, 1733.
2-82	" Elizabeth,	April 21, 1735.
2-82	" Adam,	March 24, 1737.
2-82	" Rebecca,	March 17, 1739.
2-82	" Content,	June 22, 1741.
2-124	" Jane, wife of Cyrus,	died April 26, 1733.
2-78	" Joan, of Cyrus and Phebe,	June 7, 1735.
2-78	" Cyrus,	May 26, 1737.
4-190	" Deborah, of John and Deborah,	Jan. 20, 1802.
4-190	" John,	died at Newport Oct. 9, 1802.
2-120	ROGERS Lucy, of Samuel and Patience,	May 24, 1708.
2-120	" Patience,	Oct. 23, 1709.
2-120	" Samuel	Sept. 15, 1711.
2-120	" Thankful,	Sept. 11, 1713.
2-120	" Mary,	Oct. 12, 1715.
2-120	" Grace,	July 27, 1717.
2-120	" Peleg,	Jan. 3, 1720-1.
2-124	" Patience,	died Nov. 18, 1715.
4-29	" Hannah, of Jesse and Hannah,	Sept. 19, 1792.
1-173	ROSS Anna, of William,	Jan. 3, 1694.
1-173	" Mary,	May 21, 1700.
2-86	" Jemima, of William and Ann,	March 14, 1711-12.
2-86	" William,	Aug. 3, 1715.
2-86	" Thomas,	Sept. 11, 1719.
2-86	" Isaac,	April 5, 1722.
2-86	" Ann,	Jan. 21, 1725-6.
2-86	" Hannah,	Oct. 14, 1727.
2-86	" Peleg,	Sept. 9, 1733.
3-28	" William, of William, Jr., dec., and Abigail,	April 30, 1740.
3-90	" Lois, of Thomas and Lois,	June 9, 1740.
3-90	" Thomas (died young),	Oct. 4, 1742.
3-90	" Joshua,	April 16, 1745.
3-90	" Benjamin,	March 26, 1748.
3-90	" Eunice, Nov. 14, 1750.	
3-90	" Desire, Aug. 19, 1753.	
3-90	" Jemima, Jan. 10, 1757.	

3-90	ROSS	William, Jan. 19, 1760.	
		Note—Children of Thomas and Lois.	
3-72	"	John, of John and Hannah,	Sept. 12, 1741.
3-72	"	James,	Feb. 6, 1744.
3-72	"	Hannah,	Sept. 27, 1746.
3-72	"	Daniel,	April 21, 1749.
3-72	"	Sarah,	Aug. 28, 1751.
3-72	"	Elizabeth,	May 2, 1754.
3-72	"	Edward,	June 21, 1757.
3-72	"	Mary,	April 2, 1760.
3-86	"	Borredell, of Isaac and Isabel,	Feb. 8, 1744.
3-86	"	Isaac,	July 7, 1746.
3-86	"	Anne,	Feb 9, 1749.
3-86	"	Abigail,	Feb. 18, 1754.
3-86	"	Jesse,	Nov. 7, 1756.
3-86	"	Freelove,	May 26, 1759.
3-86	"	Melleta,	Feb. 7, 1762.
3-86	"	Peter,	July 28, 1764.
3-86	"	Anthony Bennett,	July 16, 1768.
3-86	"	Frances,	Aug. 16, 1770.
3-47	"	Mary, of Peleg and Hannah,	Aug. 1, 1756.
3-47	"	Peleg,	Oct. 17, 1758.
3-47	"	Lebbens,	March 29, 1761.
3-47	"	Thomas,	Aug. 29, 1763.
3-47	"	Amey,	Jan. 14, 1766.
3-47	"	Abijah,	July 4, 1768.
3-47	"	Hannah,	Dec. 24, 1770.
3-47	"	Anna,	March 10, 1773.
3-47	"	William Lewis,	Nov. 9, 1775.
3-138	"	John, of John and Lois,	Aug. 20, 1774.
3-138	"	Lawton,	March 4, 1776.
3-138	"	Lydia,	Feb. 10, 1778.
3-138	"	Daniel,	March 5, 1781.
3-154	"	Benjamin, of Peleg and Hannah,	Oct. 15, 1778.
3-154	"	Ezekiel,	June 15, 1781.
3-157	"	Rowland, of Peleg and Thankful,	Jan. 15, 1779.
3-153	"	Esther, of James and Esther,	Aug. 20, 1779.
3-153	"	James,	March 16, 1781.
3-153	"	Hannah,	Aug. 23, 1784.
3-176	"	Prentice Babcock, of Peleg and Mary,	June 22, 1782.
3-176	"	Mary,	June 28, 1784.
3-176	"	Anne,	Oct. 26, 1786.
3-176	"	Peleg Babcock,	May 27, 1789.
3-176	"	Isaac Babcock,	May 12, 1793.
		Note—1st born Westerly, 2d Hopkinton, 3d Voluntown, 4th Westerly, 5th Sheffield, Mass.	
4-108	"	Nancy Babcock, alias, of Hannah West, (now wife of Arnold West), dau. of Edward West,	Feb. 16, 1783.
3-164	"	David, of John and Lois,	April 3, 1783.
3-164	"	Lyman Crandall,	Jan. 28, 1785.
3-164	"	Nathan,	Sept. 16, 1787.
4-2	"	William Crandall, of Lebbeus and Rhoda, born Preston, Conn.,	July 31, 1785.
3-165	"	Cynthia, of James and Esther,	June 12, 1786.
3-165	"	Mary,	March 10, 1788.
3-165	"	Lois,	April 30, 1790.
3-165	"	Desire Hannah,	July 9, 1795.
4-71	"	Anthony, of Anthony B. and Elizabeth,	May 24, 1793.
4-71	"	Betsey,	June 16, 1796.
4-71	"	Dianna,	Feb. 28, 1798.
4-71	"	Luther Bliven,	March 11, 1801.
4-71	"	James Noyes,	Oct. 5, 1804.
4-71	"	Dudley Palmer,	June 6, 1806.
		Note—Youngest born Stonington.	
4-138	"	Joshua, of Joshua and Thankful,	Dec. 17, 1796.

4-138	ROSS	James Saunders, of Joshua and Thankful,	Dec. 3, 1798.
4-226	"	Robinson C., of Isaac and Hannah,	Jan. 6, 1799.
4-220	"	James Potter, of James and Polly,	Aug. 17, 1805.
4-220	"	Huram,	Oct. 22, 1807.
4-220	"	Henry,	Jan. 5, 1810.
4-213	"	Avery, of David and Sarah,	Sept. 13, 1806.
4-179	"	Benjamin, of Benjamin and Abigail,	June 24, 1811.
4-179	"	Peleg,	June 16, 1813.

S

1-94	SATTERLEE	Penelope, of Nicholas and Mary,	Nov. 15, 1698.
1-94	"	John,	Feb. 24, 1701-2.
1-94	"	Mary,	Oct. 21, 1703.
1-174	SAUNDERS	Mary, of John and Silena,	Jan. 6, 1699-1700.
1-174	"	Hannah,	Dec. 17, 1701-2.
1-174	"	Elizabeth,	Oct. 27, 1703.
1-120	"	Edward, of Edward and Sarah,	Jan. 10, 1702-3.
1-120	"	John, of John and Silena,	Oct. 13, 1705.
1-120	"	Susanna,	Dec. 4, 1707.
1-120	"	Samuel,	Feb. 28, 1710.
1-120	"	Prudence,	Jan. 19, 1712.
1-120	"	Joseph,	July 5, 1721.
2-79	"	Mary, of Benjamin and Ann,	Jan. 29, 1714.
2-79	"	Joshua,	March 6, 1716.
2-79	"	Daniel,	Nov. 1, 1717.
2-79	"	Lucy,	Nov. 13, 1719.
2-79	"	Tacy,	Feb. 4, 1722.
2-79	"	Nathan,	March 17, 1724.
2-79	"	Ann,	Dec. 15, 1726.
2-84	"	Stephen, of Stephen and Rachel,	Aug. 3, 1722.
2-84	"	Rachel,	Sept. 18, 1724.
2-84	"	Isabel,	Oct. 14, 1726.
2-84	"	Ruth,	July 1, 1729.
2-84	"	Tobias,	March 28, 1732.
2-84	"	Mary,	July 9, 1734.
2-84	"	Peleg,	March 4, 1737.
2-84	"	Martha,	Nov. 27, 1740.
2-87	"	Mary, of John, Jr., and Reede,	May 13, 1731.
2-87	"	Elisha,	May 29, 1733.
2-87	"	Benjamin,	Jan. 8, 1742-3.
		Note—Youngest also recorded 2-119.	
4-57	"	Edward, Feb. 13, 1726.	
4-57	"	Sarah, his wife, Nov. 20, 1734.	
4-57	"	Edward, of Edward and Sarah,	July 13, 1756.
4-57	"	Sarah,	Aug. 9, 1758.
4-57	"	Abigail,	Sept. 17, 1760.
4-57	"	Arnold,	March 20, 1763.
4-57	"	Elizabeth,	Jan. 27, 1766.
4-57	"	Russell,	March 11, 1768.
4-57	"	Philip,	Oct. 12, 1771.
4-57	"	Esther,	Dec. 10, 1775.
4-57	"	Freelove,	Oct. 9, 1778.
3-50	"	Mary, of John and Reed,	May 13, 1731.
3-50	"	Elisha,	May 29, 1733.
3-50	"	David,	May 10, 1738.
3-50	"	Waite,	June 1, 1740.
3-50	"	Benjamin,	Jan. 8, 1742.
3-50	"	Joshua,	Oct. 28, 1745.
3-50	"	Sarah,	April 26, 1747.
3-168	"	Hannah, of Joseph and Mary (Lanphere),	Sept. 28, 1745.
3-168	"	Freegift,	Oct. 5, 1748.
3-168	"	Prudence,	May 20, 1754.
3-168	"	Joseph,	May 25, 1758.

3-168	SAUNDERS Mercy, of Joseph and Mary (Lamphere),		April 1, 1760.
3-168	"	George,	Feb. 27, 1762.
3-158	"	Eunice, of James and Rachel,	Nov. 3, 1745.
3-158	"	James,	April 16, 1748.
4-158	"	Hannah,	Feb. 27, 1751.
3-158	"	Rachel,	Jan. 9, 1754.
3-158	"	Amey,	Feb. 11, 1758.
3-158	"	Lucy,	May 1, 1765.
3-158	"	Huldah,	April 5, 1768.
3-158	"	Jesse,	May 27, 1771.
4-17	"	Jonathan, June 19, 1746.	
4-17	"	Elizabeth, his wife, July 11, 1749.	
4-17	"	Cyrus, of Jonathan and Elizabeth,	April 8, 1772.
4-17	"	Benjamin Woodworth,	Nov. 29, 1774.
4-17	"	Elisha Smith,	July 14, 1776.
4-17	"	Jonathan,	Jan. 30, 1778.
4-17	"	Elizabeth,	April 16, 1780.
4-17	"	Henry Bliss,	July 6, 1783.
4-17	"	Zebe,	Jan. 16, 1785.
3-58	"	Dinah, of Stephen and Lydia,	Dec. 12, 1746.
3-58	"	Esther,	May 4, 1747.
3-58	"	Stephen,	April 28, 1749.
3-58	"	Lydia,	July 10, 1751.
3-58	"	Charles,	March 4, 1755.
3-58	"	Augustus,	July 5, 1757.
3-58	"	Peleg,	Sept. 5, 1759.
3-24	"	Edward, of Edward and Sarah,	July 12, 1756.
3-24	"	Sarah,	Aug. 9, 1758.
4-42	"	Luke, of Tobias and Martha, born Charlestown, April 12, 1758.	
4-42	"	Sarah (Dewry, of David and Deborah, of Stonington), born Charlestown, Feb. 28, 1758.	
4-42	"	Sarah, of Luke and Sarah,	Feb. 27, 1783
4-42	"	Martha,	Aug. 25, 1785.
4-42	"	Parish,	Jan. 4, 1788
4-42	"	Jabez,	Dec. 5, 1790
3-72	"	Luke, of Elisha and Elizabeth,	Dec. 1, 1758
3-72	"	Silvester (dau.),	Jan. 27, 1761
3-91	"	Elizabeth, of Gideon and Mary,	Dec. 29, 1758
3-79	"	Waite, of Waite and Patience,	Aug. 25, 1762.
4-144	"	Marble, of Peleg and Mary,	Jan. 11, 1763.
4-144	"	Amelia,	March 1, 1765.
4-144	"	Polly,	July 10, 1767.
4-144	"	Patty,	June 1, 1770.
4-144	"	Patty,	died March 24, 1791.
4-144	"	Nancy,	Aug. 24, 1773.
4-144	"	Clarke,	Jan. 24, 1776.
4-144	"	Peleg,	April 5, 1784.
4-144	"	Peleg,	died July 26, 1799.
4-50	"	Anna, of Hezekiah and Mary,	Aug. 12, 1764.
4-50	"	George,	July 25, 1766.
4-50	"	Hezekiah,	Aug. 26, 1768.
4-50	"	Hannah,	Dec. 31, 1770.
4-50	"	Gideon,	June 25, 1773.
4-50	"	Asa,	Oct. 29, 1775.
4-50	"	Phineas,	March 5, 1778.
4-50	"	Freeman,	Aug. 6, 1780.
		Note—Eldest also recorded 3-98.	
3-152	"	Thomas, of Joshua and Martha,	Dec. 1, 1770.
3-152	"	Simeon,	Dec. 8, 1772.
3-152	"	Mary,	March 20, 1776.
3-128	"	Richard, of Joshua and Mary,	July 24, 1773.
4-82	"	Lydia, of Charles and Martha,	May 7, 1774.
4-82	"	Lodowick,	Nov. 5, 1775.
4-82	"	Martha,	March 5, 1777.
4-82	"	Charles,	Nov. 10, 1778.

4-82		SAUNDERS Hall, of Charles and Martha,	July 12, 1780.
4-82	"	Hall,	died Aug. 27, 1781.
4-82	"	Sarah,	July 10, 1782.
4-82	"	Hall,	April 24, 1784.
4-82	"	Nancy,	April 20, 1786.
4-82	"	Celia,	July 24, 1788.
4-82	"	dan., born and died,	Nov. 23, 1790.
4-82	"	Lucretia,	May 19, 1792.
4-82	"	Mereba,	July 30, 1795.
4-78	"	Mary, of Stephen and Lucy,	Oct. 12, 1774.
4-78	"	Stephen,	May 21, 1776.
4-78	"	Esther,	April 26, 1778.
4-78	"	Samuel,	Aug. 20, 1780.
4-78	"	Susannah,	Jan. 1, 1784.
4-78	"	John Aldrich,	March 25, 1787.
4-78	"	Elias,	June 20, 1789.
4-78	"	Lydia,	Feb. 29, 1792.
4-78	"	Caty,	Sept. 20, 1795.

Note.—Also recorded 3-164.

4-91	"	Thankful, of James, Jr., and Elizabeth,	Jan. 19, 1776.
4-91	"	James,	Feb. 24, 1778.
4-91	"	Walter,	April 21, 1780.
4-91	"	Bethana,	April 11, 1782.
4-91	"	Eunice,	July 2, 1784.
4-91	"	Mary,	Jan. 6, 1787.
4-91	"	Jared,	Nov. 23, 1790.
4-91	"	Elizabeth,	March 8, 1792.
4-91	"	Abel,	April 21, 1794.

Note—Two eldest also recorded 3-158.

3-146	"	Sarah, of Joseph and Lydia,	Aug. 8, 1778.
3-146	"	Russell,	July 12, 1782.
3-146	"	Esther,	May 27, 1785.
3-159	"	Elizabeth of Angustus and Elizabeth,	Oct. 5, 1780.
3-159	"	Elizabeth,	died Sept. 13, 1782.
3-159	"	Elizabeth, 2d,	March 5, 1782.
3-159	"	Augustus,	July 12, 1784.
3-159	"	Joel,	March 7, 1787.
3-159	"	Billings,	Dec. 11, 1796.
3-159	"	Lydia,	May 26, 1799.
4-5	"	Elisha, of Luke and Dorcas,	Dec. 4, 1781.
4-5	"	Dorcas,	Feb. 11, 1783.
4-5	"	Luke,	Nov. 29, 1784.
4-5	"	Silva,	Feb. 13, 1787.
4-5	"	Ezekiel,	Nov. 26, 1789.

Note—Eldest born Charlestown, 3d Westerly, the others Hopkinton.

4-176	"	Rebecca, of Joshua and Martha,	June 14, 1782.
4-176	"	Joshua,	Aug. 24, 1784.
4-176	"	Fanny,	Nov. 29, 1787.
4-176	"	Zebulon,	Nov. 29, 1789.
4-176	"	Russell,	June 23, 1792.
4-56	"	Martha, of Edward and Martha,	April 18, 1783.
4-56	"	Edward,	May 19, 1785.
4-56	"	Nancy,	May 9, 1787.
4-56	"	Elisha Clarke,	Feb 25, 1789.
4-56	"	Ethan,	Feb. 15, 1795.
4-56	"	Permilla,	Feb. 15, 1795.
4-56	"	Fanny,	Sept. 12, 1797.

Note—Two eldest recorded 3-180.

4-6	"	Peleg, of Capt. Peleg and Sarah,	Aug. 22, 1785.
4-6	"	Lyman,	May 14, 1787.
4-6	"	Rowland,	Nov. 16, 1789.
4-6	"	Sally,	May 28, 1791.
4-6	"	Stephen,	Aug. 11, 1793.
5-20	"	Elias,	June 20, 1789.

5 20	SAUNDERS Fanny (Vars of Isaac), his wife,	July 11, 1790.
5-20	"	Frances, of Elias and Fanny,	May 14, 1810.
5-20	"	Esther,	May 30, 1812.
5-20	"	Oliver P.,	March 30, 1814.
5-20	"	Mary Ann,	Dec. 4, 1816.
5-20	"	Stephen,	Dec. 12, 1818.
5-20	"	Peleg,	Oct. 16, 1820.
5-20	"	Elias,	Dec. 20, 1822.
5-20	"	Sally,	Jan. 3, 1828.
5-20	"	Tacy,	April 25, 1830.
5-20	"	Harriet,	Oct. 19, 1832.
4-33	"	George, of George and Lydia,	March 4, 1791.
4-169	"	John, of David and Sarah,	June 5, 1791.
4-169	"	John,	died July 6, 1791.
4-169	"	Polly,	Aug. 17, 1792.
4-169	"	Sarah,	July 12, 1794.
4-169	"	Nancy,	Aug. 31, 1796.
4-46	"	Hannah, of Arnold and Hannah,	Oct. 27, 1791.
4-46	"	Arnold,	June 27, 1793.
4-46	"	Charlotte,	Feb. 4, 1795.
4-46	"	Sarah,	March 20, 1797.
4-46	"	Polly,	Feb. 18, 1800.
4-46	"	Betsey,	Feb. 18, 1800.
4-46	"	Elisha,	May 19, 1802.
4-47	"	Russell, of Russell and Mary,	Aug. 11, 1792.
4-143	"	Clarke, of Clarke and Sarah,	Dec. 7, 1798.
4-143	"	Ezekiel,	April 1, 1801.
4-143	"	Mary,	May 30, 1803.
4-143	"	Hannah,	April 23, 1805.
4-184	"	Nathan Gardner, of Russell and Caty,	Nov. 9, 1802.
4-184	"	Rowland Clarke,	April 1, 1803.
4-184	"	Joseph Potter,	Sept. 4, 1804.
4-184	"	John Alancan,	Feb. 19, 1806.
4-184	"	Polly Gardner,	May 1, 1907.
4-142	"	Stephen, of Susannah, dau. of Stephen,	July 8, 1803.
4-199	"	Daniel Bliven, of Samuel and Fanny,	Sept. 30, 1804.
4-199	"	Samuel,	Nov. 28, 1807.
4-199	"	Fanny,	Aug. 18, 1809.
4-199	"	Hannah,	April 15, 1811.
4-199	"	Charles,	Feb. 11, 1819.
5-31	"	Samuel P., of Samuel and Amey K.,	June 28, 1835.
5-31	"	Charles Henry,	Sept. 10, 1838.
3-85	SCRIVEN William, of James,	June 6, 1727.
3-85	"	Mary, wife of William,	July 1, 1726.
3-85	"	Alice, of William and Alice,	Feb. 10, 1750.
3-85	"	James,	Aug. 28, 1751.
3-85	"	John,	Aug. 28, 1751.
3-85	"	Joshua,	May 17, 1754.
3-85	"	Hannah,	May 17, 1754.
3-85	"	William,	Feb. 23, 1756.
3-85	"	Zebulon,	Oct. 23, 1759.
3-85	"	Mercy,	Feb. 8, 1761.
3-85	"	Thomas (born Exeter),	July 26, 1762.
3-85	"	Joseph,	April 10, 1766.
3-85	"	Isaac, and Elipha, 2d wife,	Aug. 15, 1770.
4-4	SEAGER Ruth, of Christopher and Wealtha,	Oct. 11, 1777.
4-4	"	Mary Kingston,	Oct. 11, 1777.
4-4	"	Sarah,	March 13, 1785.
4-4	"	Malicha,	Oct. 13, 1788.
4-4	"	Christopher,	Jan. 26, 1794.
4-130	SHAW Thomas, of Peleg and Lucretia, both of Stonington, born Westerly,	Feb. 3, 1798.
4-130	"	Nancy, of Peleg and Lucretia,	Dec. 16, 1799.
2-112	SHEFFIELD Mary, of Isaac and Jane,	Sept. 29, 1721.
2-112	"	Martha,	Nov. 20, 1723.

3-95	SHEFFIELD Nathaniel, of Joseph and Lydia,		Oct. 19, 1763.
3-110	"	Dorcas, of Nathan and Martha,	April 30, 1768.
3-139	"	Polly, of George, Jr., and Sarah,	Nov. 28, 1775.
4-46	"	William, of William (of George, dec.), and Bridget,	April 27, 1784.
4-46	"	James,	May 2, 1786.
4-46	"	Eunice,	March 5, 1788.
4-46	"	Dudley,	July 2, 1790.
		Note—Two eldest born Groton, Conn., next Southold, L. I., youngest Westerly.	
4-135	"	Rhoda, of Samuel and Susannah,	April 26, 1799.
3-75	SHELDON Phebe, of Joseph and Ruth,		June 15, 1757.
3-75	"	Susanna,	Aug. 19, 1758.
4-191	SHELLEY Charles, of Ebenezer and Amey,		Aug. 20, 1802.
4-191	"	George Washington Chester,	March 25, 1804.
3-19	SIMS Samuel, of William and Jerusha,		Nov. 1, 1748.
3-19	"	Elizabeth,	Oct. 20, 1752.
3-19	"	William,	Aug. 13, 1756.
3-19	"	Esther,	May 11, 1758.
3-152	"	Esther, of William and Rebecca,	May 14, 1778.
3-152	"	Phebe,	April 29, 1782.
3-152	"	William,	Aug. 27, 1784.
3-152	"	Jeremiah Babcock,	Dec. 23, 1787.
3-152	"	Samuel Pendleton,	May 3, 1790.
3-152	"	Elizabeth,	May 25, 1792.
4-88	"	Deborah, of Samuel and Deborah,	Sept. 10, 1780.
4-88	"	Nancy,	Aug. 16, 1783.
4-88	"	Sylvester Pendleton,	Oct. 22, 1785.
4-88	"	Sally,	April 11, 1788.
4-88	"	Samuel,	Dec. 11, 1790.
4-88	"	Oliver,	April 27, 1793.
4-97	"	Joseph Thompson, of William and Rebecca,	Oct. 9, 1794.
4-97	"	James, \	Sept. 10, 1797.
4-273	"	Ichabod Babcock (called Sisson), son of Phebe Sims,	Jan. 3, 1802.
4-224	"	William, of William, Jr., and Sally,	Aug. 26, 1807.
4-224	"	Charles Edway,	Nov. 6, 1808.
3-73	SISSON Oliver, of William and Hannah,		March 30, 1738.
3-73	"	Nathan,	April 14, 1740.
3-73	"	Hannah,	Jan. 17, 1742.
3-73	"	Hannah,	died soon.
3-73	"	William,	July 12, 1744.
3-73	"	Bennaja,	Sept. 2, 1746.
3-73	"	James,	Aug. 25, 1748.
3-73	"	Abigail,	Oct. 24, 1750.
3-73	"	Jonathan,	May 2, 1753.
3-73	"	Hannah,	June 7, 1755.
3-73	"	Thomas,	April 4, 1758.
3-93	"	John, of Thomas, Jr. and Mary,	March 3, 1741.
3-93	"	Amey,	May 10, 1745.
3-93	"	Mary,	June 23, 1747.
3-93	"	George,	Feb. 5, 1750.
3-93	"	Ann,	July 19, 1753.
3-93	"	Elizabeth,	April 9, 1756.
3-82	"	Samuel, of Giles and Elizabeth,	Dec. 4, 1747.
3-82	"	John,	April 10, 1749.
3-82	"	Jane,	April 27, 1751.
3-82	"	Content,	May 20, 1753.
3-82	"	Sarah,	March 28, 1755.
3-82	"	Esther,	Aug. 6, 1757.
3-82	"	Anne,	Sept. 5, 1759.
3-82	"	Ruth,	Dec. 23, 1761.
3-113	"	Sion, of John and Knturah,	April 16, 1768.
3-113	"	Keturah,	Sept. 6, 1769.
3-113	"	Content,	June 23, 1771.
3-145	"	William, of Jonathan, and Elizabeth,	Oct. 5, 1776.
3-145	"	Elizabeth,	March 8, 1778.

3-145	SISSON	Jonathan, of Jonathan and Elizabeth,	March 27, 1780.
3-145	"	Nathan,	March 23, 1782.
3-145	"	Oliver,	March 23, 1784.
3-145	"	Mary,	April 1, 1786.
3-145	"	Sarah,	April 12, 1788.
3-145	"	Nancy,	June 17, 1790.
3-145	"	Fanny,	Oct. 4, 1792.
3-145	"	Desire,	Dec. 9, 1794.
3-145	"	Henry Bliven,	Aug. 12, 1798.
4-152	"	Timothy, of Peleg, Jr., and Esther,	July 22, 1777.
4-152	"	Joshua,	Feb. 14, 1780.
4-152	"	Gilbert,	April 10, 1783.
4-152	"	Rebecca,	March 14, 1785.
4-152	"	Esther,	March 5, 1787.
4-152	"	Lucy,	July 14, 1790.
4-152	"	Lodowick,	July 14, 1790.
4-152	"	Robert,	Sept. 14, 1795.
4-152	"	Caty,	Aug. 17, 1797.
4-152	"	Peleg,	March 10, 1799.
4-1	"	Thomas, of Thomas and Abigail,	Dec. 2, 1783.
4-1	"	Hannah,	Sept. 25, 1785.
4-1	"	Joshua Cottrell,	Sept. 2, 1787.
4-1	"	Lois,	Aug. 7, 1789.
4-1	"	Daniel,	March 29, 1791.
4-1	"	Abigail,	March 9, 1793.
4-201	"	Cynthia, of Barney and Cynthia,	June 14, 1790.
4-201	"	Barney,	July 15, 1792.
4-201	"	Sally,	Oct. 11, 1794.
4-201	"	Charles,	May 20, 1797.
4-201	"	Hannah,	Aug. 16, 1800.
4-201	"	Rhoda,	Aug. 7, 1803.
4-206	"	Elizabeth, of Sanford and Elizabeth,	July 20, 1800.
4-206	"	Sophia,	Jan. 30, 1802.
4-206	"	Damarias,	Aug. 13, 1804.
4-269	"	Maria Catherine, of Joshua and Alice,	Dec. 28, 1812.
4-269	"	Joshua Franklin,	Sept. 28, 1814.
4-269	"	Caroline,	Oct. 1, 1817.
2-27	SLACK	Abigail, of Samuel and Abigail,	Aug. 10, 1715.
2-27	"	William,	March 27, 1717.
2-27	"	Mary,	March 24, 1719.
2-27	"	Anna,	Dec. 17, 1724.
2-27	"	Temperance,	Oct. 13, 1727.
2-27	"	Elizabeth,	April 26, 1731.
2-27	"	Benajah,	April 24, 1733.
		Note—Also recorded 2-118.	
3-37	"	William, of Benajah and Mary,	Dec. 8, 1755.
3-167	SLATTERY	Thomas C., of Thomas and Abigail,	June 13, 1781.
3-167	"	Abigail,	March 31, 1787.
4-210	"	Susan, of Thomas C. and Susan,	Dec. 9, 1805.
4-210	"	Celia,	July 6, 1807.
4-210	"	Abby Ann,	Aug. 6, 1809.
4-210	"	Dudley,	Nov. 1, 1813.
2-105	SMITH	Hannah, of Benoni and Ruth,	Nov. 19, 1727.
2-105	"	William,	Feb. 13, 1729.
2-105	"	William,	died June 19, 1754.
2-105	"	Nathan,	Dec. 22, 1731.
2-105	"	Nathan,	died Jan. 11, 1734-5.
2-105	"	Nathan, 2d,	Feb. 18, 1732-3.
2-105	"	Mary,	Oct. 2, 1737.
2-105	"	Elizabeth,	May 22, 1739.
2-105	"	Eleanor,	June 22, 1741.
2-105	"	Sarah,	July 11, 1745.
2-105	"	Joseph,	April 4, 1749.
2-105	"	Joseph,	died May 5, 1749.
3-41	"	Joseph, of Nathan and Elizabeth,	June 15, 1755.

3-41	SMITH William, of Nathan and Elizabeth,		March 18, 1757.
3-41	" Joshua,		May 6, 1759.
3-12	" Elizabeth, wife of Nathan,	died	Nov. 12, 1760.
3-75	" Joseph, of Nathan and Mary,	died	May. 15, 1774.
4-250	" Levi Hart, of Stephen and Clarina,		June 23, 1799.
4-250	" Clarina,		Jan. 9, 1801.
4-250	" John Wilson,		March 17, 1803.
4-250	" Clarina, wife of Stephen,	died	Feb. 20, 1807.
4-250	" Stephen, of Stephen and Esther, 2d wife,		Aug. 19, 1808.
4-250	" Esther Babcock,		March 7, 1810.
4-250	" David,		Dec. 8, 1811.
4-250	" Mary Fitch,		May 10, 1814.
4-250	" Martha Harvey,		Sept. 27, 1816.
4-250	" Elizabeth Moore,		June 7, 1818.
4-250	" Charles Vose,		Oct. 31, 1819.
4-250	" William Oakes,		Sept. 1, 1821.
4-250	" Harriet Newell,		June 5, 1823.
4-250	" Esther, wife of Stephen,	died	Feb. 17, 1833.
4-193	" Charles Granderson, of Lemuel, Jr., and Deborah,		Jan. 23, 1803.
3-28	STANTON Elizabeth, wife of Jesse, of Stonington, died Aug. 7, 1803.		
4-210	STEPHENS Eunice, of Stanton and Eunice,		July 24, 1803.
4-210	" Stanton,		Oct. 5, 1805.
4-210	" Hannah Clarke,		Nov. 14, 1807.
4-210	" John,		Aug. 7, 1809.
4-210	" John,	died	March 22, 1810.
4-210	" Joshua F.,		July 15, 1811.
3-119	STETSON Brenton, of Stephen and Dorcas,		April 14, 1768.
3-119	" Elizabeth,		Nov. 20, 1769.
3-119	" Sarah,		Oct. 5, 1771.
3-119	" Stephen,		July 23, 1773.
3-153	" Cornelins,		Jan. 27, 1779.
3-153	" James,		March 1, 1781.
3-153	" Isaac,		Jan. 26, 1785.
3-153	" Thankful,		June 19, 1787.
4-10	" Thomas, of Thomas and Mary (of Hanover, Plymouth Co., Mass.), March 9, 1786.		
4-219	" James Robinson, of James and Hannah,		Aug. 7, 1805.
4-219	" Hannah,		Nov. 9, 1807.
4-219	" Abigail S.,		Feb. 29, 1808.
4-219	" Susannah,		Sept. 15, 1810.
3-93	STEWARD Martha, of William and Mary,		June 14, 1759.
3-93	" William,		March 7, 1761.
3-93	" Elisha,		June 15, 1763.
3-93	" Mary,		March 16, 1765.
2-83	STEWART Daniel, of Oliver and Rebecca,		Feb. 23, 1742-3.
2-83	" Sarah,		March 7, 1743-4.
2-83	" Rebecca,		Oct. 31, 1746.
2-75	STILES John, of Israel and Hannah,		March 5, 1736.
2-121	STILLMAN Deborah, of George and Deborah,		Jan. 11, 1706-7.
2-121	" Nathaniel,		May 2, 1709.
2-121	" Mary,		Sept. 27, 1711.
2-121	" George,		Feb. 13, 1713-4.
2-121	" Joseph,		Dec. 5, 1716.
2-121	" John,		June 14, 1719.
2-121	" Elisha,		April 25, 1722.
2-121	" Benjamin,		Jan. 25, 1725-6.
	Note.—Also recorded 2-123 and 2-116.		
2-84	" George, of George and Mary,		May 19, 1739.
2-84	" Sarah,		April 1, 1746.
2-84	" Joseph,		Aug. 30, 1752.
2-84	" Tacy,		April 14, 1755.
3-10	" Elizabeth, of John and Mary,		Feb. 4, 1746-7.
3-19	" John,		March 13, 1752.
3-19	" Clarke,		April 13, 1754.
3-19	" Anna,		Aug. 23, 1756.

3-19	STILLMAN	Deborah, of John and Mary,	April 15, 1760.
3-19	"	Kelorah,	Sept. 28, 1762.
3-109	"	Samuel, of Elisha and Hannah,	Feb. 5, 1747.
3-109	"	Hannah,	Aug. 13, 1753.
3-109	"	Martha,	May 16, 1756.
3-109	"	Judeth, of Elisha and Mary, 2d wife,	Oct. 28, 1759.
3-109	"	Elisha,	Feb. 26, 1761.
3-109	"	Amos,	April 24, 1762.
3-109	"	Elizabeth,	Dec. 6, 1765.
3-109	"	William,	May 4, 1767.
3-4	"	Eunice, of Benjamin and Mary,	Oct. 8, 1751.
3-4	"	Nathaniel,	May 29, 1753.
3-4	"	Nathan,	Feb. 1, 1757.
3-4	"	Waite (son),	Nov. 27, 1758.
3-4	"	Lydia,	May 6, 1760.
3-4	"	Mary,	March 8, 1762.
3-4	"	Benjamin,	Nov. 15, 1763.
3-4	"	Wealthy,	June 24, 1765.
3-4	"	Thankful,	April 17, 1767.
3-4	"	David,	March 27, 1769.
3-4	"	Ephraim,	Dec. 15, 1771.
3-66	"	Anne, of Joseph and Mary,	April 7, 1754.
3-66	"	Lois,	April 18, 1756.
4-93	"	Susannah, of George, 3d, and Esther,	Oct. 8, 1758.
4-93	"	George,	Sept. 3, 1760.
4-93	"	Esther,	Feb. 9, 1763.
4-93	"	Sarah,	Nov. 9, 1766.
4-93	"	Sylvester,	July 26, 1769.
4-93	"	Mary,	Feb. 19, 1772.
4-93	"	Maxson,	June 28, 1774.
4-93	"	Luke.	Oct. 5, 1776.
4-93	"	Lucy,	May 30, 1779.
4-93	"	Elias,	June 13, 1782.
4-93	"	Amey,	March 25, 1785.

Note—First five also recorded 3-58.

4-25	"	Sabra, of Dea. Joseph and Eunice.	Oct. 28, 1771.
4-25	"	Lois,	Sept. 7, 1773.
4-25	"	Amey,	Feb. 20, 1777.
4-25	"	Joseph,	Jan. 14, 1779.
4-25	"	Lydia,	Oct. 16, 1780.
4-25	"	Paul,	Sept. 19, 1782.
4-25	"	Zebulon.	June 21, 1784.
4-25	"	Daniel.	June 3, 1787.
3-156	"	Asa, of Joseph and Elizabeth,	Dec. 7, 1773.
3-156	"	Tacy,	Jan. 8, 1776.
3-156	"	Jesse.	Feb. 27, 1778.
3-156	"	Silas.	Aug. 6, 1780.
4-48	"	Fanny, of John and Mary,	Jan. 14, 1777.
4-48	"	Susannah,	Sept. 12, 1778.
4-48	"	Betsey,	Feb. 17, 1782.
4-48	"	Caty,	Feb. 15, 1784.
4-48	"	Polly,	April 30, 1786.
4-48	"	Phebe,	July 17, 1788.
4-48	"	Content,	Feb. 1, 1791.
4-61	"	Nancy, of Nathaniel and Deborah,	Oct. 31, 1777.
4-61	"	Sarah,	Aug. 27, 1779.
4-61	"	Desire,	Oct. 3, 1781.
4-61	"	Nathaniel,	Sept. 24, 1783.
4-61	"	Oliver Davis,	Aug. 28, 1785.
4-61	"	Benjamin,	July 1, 1789.
4-61	"	Ezra,	July 8, 1789.
4-61	"	Rahamah	July 11, 1791.
4-61	"	Javis,	Aug. 28, 1794.
4-61	"	Nathaniel, Sr., drowned at Mr. Burdick's mill dam, Pawcatuck river, April 7, 1804.	

4-61	STILLMAN Betsey, of Joseph, 2d, and Elizabeth,		Aug. 30, 1782.
4-61	"	Henry,	Nov. 19, 1784.
4-61	"	David,	May 8, 1787.
4-61	"	Abigail,	Nov. 1, 1789.
4-61	"	Jared,	March 29, 1792.
4-61	"	Joseph	June 24, 1795.
		Note—Also recorded 4-98.	
4-16	"	Clarke, of Clarke and Abigail,	April 22, 1785.
4-16	"	Russell,	Sept. 1, 1786.
4-16	"	Rouse,	Feb. 1, 1788.
4-16	"	Nancy,	Nov. 4, 1789.
4-16	"	Naba,	Dec. 18, 1790.
4-22	"	Amey, of Nathan and Hannah.	Nov. 30, 1786.
4-25	"	Abel, of Dea. Joseph and Eunice,	June 14, 1789.
4-25	"	Barton,	March 26, 1791.
4-25	"	Adam,	Nov. 3, 1792.
4-184	"	William, of William and Martha,	Oct. 2, 1792.
4-184	"	Ezra,	—— 13, 1794.
4-184	"	Albert,	April 27, 1796.
4-184	"	Jonathan Potter,	Feb. 10, 1798.
4-184	"	Martha,	Feb. 21, 1800.
4-184	"	Ephraim,	Jan. 31, 1802.
4-176	"	Wealthy, of David and Grace,	Sept. 21, 1794.
4-176	"	Sophia,	Dec. 12, 1797.
4-176	"	David,	Aug. 13, 1800.
4-143	"	Maxson, of Maxson and Esther,	Sept. 29, 1799.
4-143	"	Silas,	Aug. 6, 1801.
4-143	"	Susannah,	Dec. 29, 1803.
4-243	"	Edwin, of Paul and Sally,	Oct. 21, 1808.
4-242	"	Daniel, of Daniel and Lois,	March 10, 1810.
4-244	"	Oliver Davis, of Oliver and Ruth,	Oct. 2, 1810.
4-244	"	Albert,	June 7, 1812.
4-244	"	Weeden,	Dec. 17, 1814.
2-244	"	Lucy Ann,	Jan. 20, 1817.
		Note—Eldest born in Hopkinton.	
4-259	"	Phebe Ann, of Rouse and Phebe,	April 29, 1814.
4-259	"	Phebe, wife of Rouse,	died Aug. 15, 1814.
5-1	"	William Henry, of William and Charlotte,	Jan. 7, 1819.
5-1	"	Abram Coggeshall,	Dec. 8, 1820.
5-1	"	Ezra,	Jan. 10, 1823.
5-1	"	Elizabeth Coggeshall,	Dec. 7, 1824.
		Note—Eldert born Hopkinton.	
5-29	"	Albert, of Albert and Hannah,	June 8, 1821.
5-29	"	Albert,	died Oct. 14, 1821.
5-2	"	Mary Adella, of Ephraim and Mary,	April 22, 1825.
5-2	"	Horace,	April 25, 1827.
5-15	"	Adam, died May 26, 1845.	
1-174	SWAIT Richard, of Richard and Mehitable,		Feb. 23, 1675-6.
1-174	"	——,	Feb. 17, 1677-8.
1-174	"	——,	Feb. 10, 1679-80.
1-174	"	——,	Nov. 4, 1682.
1-174	"	——,	June 13, 1687.

T

3-108	TAYLOR Lucy, of Joseph and Ruth.		March 6, 1768.
4-98	"	Samuel,	May 1, 1774.
4-98	"	Ruth,	Feb. 18, 1776.
4-98	"	Lydia,	Oct. 1, 1778.
4-98	"	Sarah,	Aug. 14, 1780.
4-98	"	Lucretia,	Nov. 6, 1783.
4-98	"	Martha,	March 13, 1786.
4-98	"	Sanford,	Aug. 21, 1789.
4-98	"	Gardner Wilbur,	May 14, 1795.

3-137	TAYLOR	David, of Jude and Abigail,	Sept. 19, 1774.
3-137	"	Martha,	Aug. 5, 1776.
3-137	"	David,	Aug. 14, 1781.
3-137	"	Abigail,	Feb. 6, 1784.
3-137	"	Isaac Ross,	Jan. 6, 1797.
3-137	"	Fanny,	Sept. 21, 1789.
3-137	"	Anna,	Sept. 29, 1792.
3-137	"	Aseneth,	Dec. 30, 1795.
3-166	"	Hannah, of Thomas and Hannah,	Dec. 22, 1780.
3-166	"	Humphrey,	July 24, 1784.
3-166	"	John,	June 21, 1787.
3-166	"	Thomas,	Jan. 26, 1789.
3-166	"	Martha,	Nov. 4, 1791.
3-166	"	Reuben,	Dec. 5, 1793.
3-166	"	Lydia,	July 15, 1798.
4-169	"	Lyndon, of Dennis and Keziah,	Aug. 29, 1782.
4-169	"	Thomas,	Sept. 26, 1784.
4-169	"	Hannah,	Nov. 25, 1787.
4-169	"	Nancy,	July 3, 1792.
4-169	"	Ruth,	Nov. 1, 1795.
4-58	"	Elizabeth, of John and Elizabeth,	Oct. 15, 1782.
4-202	"	William, of Samuel and Rebecca,	Feb. 21, 1784.
4-202	"	Constant,	May 22, 1786.
4-202	"	Rebecca,	March 1, 1788.
4-202	"	Samuel,	March 30, 1791.
4-202	"	Mercy,	Aug. 7, 1793.
4-202	"	Lois,	Nov. 12, 1795.
4-202	"	David,	Sept. 8, 1797.
4-202	"	Anstress,	Dec. 14, 1799.
4-202	"	Benjamin,	May 11, 1802.
4-202	"	Amos,	July 7, 1804.

Note—Portions of this family are recorded 3-170, 172.

4-197	"	Cecelia,	July 25, 1800.
4-197	"	Mary,	Jan. 15, 1802.
4-197	"	Samuel Palmer,	Sept. 21, 1803.
4-197	"	Loisa,	Dec. 12, 1805.
4-232	"	Mary Ann, of Isaac R. and Phene,	Aug. 16, 1808.
4-232	"	Aseneth,	May 17, 1811.
4-232	"	Desire,	March 22, 1813.
1-173	TEFFT	Peter, of Peter,	Dec. 19, 1699.
2-111	"	Samuel, of Peter and Mary,	Feb. 24, 1705.
2-111	"	John,	Dec. 27, 1706.
2-111	"	Joseph,	Jan. 8, 1710.
2-111	"	Daniel,	April 10, 1712.
2-111	"	Sarah,	Feb. 14, 1715.
3-116	"	Mary, of John and Anna,	Aug. 19, 1765.
3-116	"	Nathan,	Feb. 5, 1767.
3-116	"	John,	Sept. 4, 1768.
3-116	"	Samuel,	May 4, 1770.
3-116	"	Lucy,	Feb. 12, 1772.
4-92	"	Joseph, of John and Mary,	Oct. 17, 1774.
4-92	"	Peleg,	May 18, 1777.
4-92	"	David,	March 21, 1779.
4-92	"	Stephen,	April 9, 1781.
4-92	"	Lewis,	Nov. 11, 1783.
4-92	"	Fanny,	March 27, 1788.
4-92	"	Anna,	July 9, 1790.
1-95	THOMPSON	Mary, of Isaac and Mary,	July 1, 1697.
1-95	"	Isaac,	Sept. 26, 1698.
1-95	"	Samuel,	July 29, 1700.
1-95	"	Abigail,	Jan. 1, 1701.
1-95	"	Sarah,	March 3, 1703.
1-95	"	William,	April 10, 1704.
1-95	"	Nathaniel,	Dec. 31, 1705.
2-121	"	Anna,	Sept. 4, 1707.

2-121	THOMPSON Elias, of Isaac and Mary,		Nov. 14, 1708
2-121	"	Mary,	March 18, 1709-10.
2-121	"	Abigail,	Oct. 14, 1711.
2-121	"	Susannah,	Nov. 25, 1713.
2-121	"	Joshua,	Aug. 13, 1714.
2-121	"	Prudence,	March 11, 1716.
2-94	"	Thankful, of Elias and Thankful,	June 4, 1737.
2-94	"	Mary,	June 11, 1739.
2-94	"	Elias,	June 8, 1741.
2-94	"	Mary,	July 12, 1743.
2-94	"	Thomas,	March 17, 1745-6.
2-94	"	Samuel,	Jan. 14, 1746-7.
2-94	"	Samuel,	died, May 14, 1805.
2-94	"	Isaac,	May 7, 1749.
2-94	"	Robert,	May 21, 1752.
3-4	"	John, of William and Ruth,	March 17, 1732.
3-4	"	Samuel,	Aug. 1, 1738.
3-4	"	Hannah,	July 14, 1741.
3-4	"	William.	Sept. 5, 1746.
3-4	"	Nathaniel,	July 29, 1749.
3-13	"	Lois, of Joshua and Sarah,	Nov. 23, 1736.
3-13	"	Iska Gardner,	June 25, 1738.
3-13	"	Mary,	April 17, 1741.
3-13	"	Sabra,	Oct. 31, 1743.
3-13	"	Sarah,	Jan. 31, 1747-8.
3-13	"	Joshua,	June 25, 1749.
3-13	"	Sarah, wife of Joshua, died Sept. 18, 1751.	
3-106	"	William, of William and Ruth,	Sept. —, 1745.
3-13	"	Nathan, of Joshua and Elizabeth, 2d wife,	Sept. 22, 1756.
3-13	"	George,	Jan. 22, 1758.
4-107	"	Anna, of John and Anna,	Feb. 4, 1758.
4-107	"	Anna,	died May 14, 1759.
4-107	"	Ruth,	Sept. 13, 1759.
4-107	"	John,	April 16, 1761.
4-107	"	Asa,	Aug. 10, 1763.
4-107	"	Asa,	died Nov. 5, 1781.
4-107	"	Susannah,	April 3, 1768.
4-107	"	Anna,	Jan. 24, 1772.
4-107	"	Prudence,	Jan. 20, 1774.
4-107	"	Molly,	Feb. 19, 1776.
4-107	"	Nathan.	March 17, 1778.
4-107	"	William,	March 19, 1780.
4-107	"	Asa,	March 30, 1783.
4-107	"	Whitman Rathbone,	June 1, 1787.
	Note—First six also recorded 3-53.		
3-83	"	Samuel, of Samuel and Mary,	Jan. 22, 1763.
3-83	"	Hannah,	Jan. 10, 1765.
3-83	"	Bridget,	Aug. 26, 1767.
3-83	"	Jonathan,	March 15, 1770.
3-83	"	Pardon.	Nov. 2, 1772.
3-83	"	Mary,	March 19, 1776.
3-105	"	Elias, of Elias, Jr., and Mary,	April 23, 1764.
3-105	"	Thankful,	Nov. 25, 1765.
	Note—Elias is also recorded 3-107.		
3-127	"	Thomas, of Thomas and Hannah,	Dec. 8, 1766.
3-127	"	Hannah,	Oct. 25, 1758.
3-127	"	Elizabeth,	July 19, 1770.
3-127	"	Isaac, of Thomas and Hannah,	March 25, 1772.
3-127	"	Jesse,	Nov. 21, 1773.
3-127	"	Samuel,	March 18, 1775.
3-127	"	George,	Oct. 23, 1776.
3-127	"	Christopher,	April 23, 1778.
3-127	"	Robert,	March 27, 1781.
3-127	"	Asa,	May 13, 1783.

3-127	THOMPSON	John, of Thomas and Hannah,	Aug. 30, 1739.
4-73	"	Mary, of William and Hannah,	Feb. 4, 1773.
4-73	"	Thankful,	March 7, 1774.
4-73	"	William,	March 22, 1776.
4-73	"	Ruth,	July 14, 1777.
4-73	"	Prudence,	May 31, 1779.
4-73	"	Rhuhama,	April 11, 1781.
4-73	"	Reuben,	April 11, 1781.
4-73	"	Nancy,	March 18, 1783.
4-73	"	Bernice,	March 10, 1786.
4-73	"	Rebecca,	June 12, 1789.
4-73	"	John Lewis,	(sic) Sept. 3, 1789.
4-73	"	Lucinda,	Aug. 1, 1791.
4-73	"	Harnah,	Sept. 27, 1793.
4-73	"	Abel,	March 1, 1796.
4-73	"	Abel,	died April 1, 1796.
4-73	"	Rhuhamah, dau. of above Rhuhama,	March 16, 1803.
3-131	"	Mary, of William and Hannah,	Feb. 4, 1773.
3-131	"	Thankful,	March 7, 1774.
3-131	"	William,	March 22, 1776.
3-131	"	Ruth,	July 11, 1777.
3-69	"	Prudence, of John and Anna,	Jan. 20, 1774.
3-163	"	Prudence, of William and Hannah,	May 30, 1779.
3-130	"	Robert, of Robert and Anna,	March 28, 1788.
4-215	"	Joshua, of Joshua P. and Sally,	Jan. 15, 1790.
4-215	"	Polly,	Jan. 28, 1791.
4-215	"	Nathan,	Nov. 21, 1792.
4-215	"	Lydia,	Dec. 29, 1794.
4-215	"	Sally,	Nov. 22, 1796.
4-215	"	Esther,	Jan. 28, 1798.
4-215	"	Joseph,	Sept. 26, 1799.
4-215	"	Nancy,	Dec. 8, 1801.
		Note—First five recorded 4-87.	
4-158	"	Martha Champlain, of Samuel and Abigail,	Sept. 2, 1795.
4-158	"	Samuel Coggeshall,	Dec. 2, 1796.
4-195	"	John Gardiner, of John and Lydia,	Jan. 17, 1805.
4-195	"	Lydia,	Aug. 20, 1806.
4-216	"	Burrell, of John, 3d, and Bridget,	Nov. 25, 1805.
4-166	"	Joshua R., of Joshua and Fanny,	Nov. 4, 1806.
4-166	"	Fanny Maria,	Aug. 27, 1808.
4-166	"	Eunice,	Dec. 16, 1810.
4-268	"	Pardon Henry, of Pardon and Lucy,	Jan. 3, 1822.
5-30	"	James Noyes, of James B. and Martha,	Oct. 7, 1838.
5-30	"	Harriet Fitch,	July 16, 1842.
5-30	"	Stanton Sheffield,	Feb. 5, 1846.
5-42	"	Joshua Lorenzo, of Joshua and Phebe Ann,	Dec. 20, 1838.
5-42	"	Phebe Maria,	Sept. 27, 1841.
4-149	THURSTON	Oliver, of Oliver and Lydia,	Oct. 29, 1793.
2-81	TIKON	Sampson, of Sampson and Battey,	May 10, 1749.
2-81	"	Mary,	Aug. 22, 1751.
2-81	"	Elizabeth,	Feb. 22, 1754.
2-81	"	Freelove,	March 4, 1756.
		Note—2d born Westerly, the others Stonington.	

U

1-173	UTTER	John, of Thomas,	Jan. 29, 1703.
2-83	"	Abraham, of John and Elizabeth,	Nov. 18, 1732.
2-83	"	Eleanor,	Feb. 10, 1733.
2-83	"	Isaac,	Jan. 4, 1736-7.
2-83	"	Jemima,	—— 24, 1738.

V

4-17	VARIN Nathan, of Joseph and Isabel,	Sept 9, 1788.
4-17	" Joseph,	March 15, 1790.
3-105	VARSE Thomas, of Isaac and Elizabeth,	Aug. 21, 1756.
3-105	" Elizabeth,	Aug. 20, 1758.
3-105	" Joseph,	Nov. 7, 1760.
3-105	" Edward,	March 13, 1763.
3-105	" Anne,	March 13, 1765.
3-105	" Sarah,	March 25, 1768.
3-105	" Catherine,	Oct. 19, 1770.
3-105	" Lydia,	March 4, 1772.
3-64	" Prudence, of John and Martha,	May 30, 1760.
3-64	" Mary,	Jan. 15, 1763.
3-64	" Fanny,	Oct. 7, 1765.
	Note—Two youngest born Newport.	
4-7	" Jasper, of Joseph and Hannah,	April 22, 1782.
4-7	" Isaac,	May 17, 1785.
4-7	" Samuel,	Nov. 24, 1786.
3-169	" Polly, of Isaac and Waitey,	Sept. 3, 1781.
3-169	" Isaac,	July 6, 1788.
3-169	" Fanny,	July 11, 1790.
4-16	" Theodoty, of Edward and Rebecca,	April 29, 1738.
4-16	" Rebecca,	June 11, 1792.
4-16	" Edward,	April 12, 1794.
	Note—2d born Stonington, 3d Hopkinton.	
4-103	" Sally, of Peleg and Sarah,	Sept. 28, 1794.
4-103	" William Augustus,	March 7, 1797.
3-62	VINCENT Susannah, of William and Zerviah,	Nov. 12, 1760.
3-62	" Joshua,	Sept. 11, 1762.
3-62	" William,	March 31, 1764.
3-62	" Nicholas,	Jan. 22, 1768.
3-124	" Sarah,	March 8, 1770.
3-124	" Joseph,	April 19, 1772.
2-76	VOSE Joshua, of Joshua and Prudence,	March 15, 1737-8.
3-52	" Abigail, of Joshua and Mary,	Aug. 13, 1758.
3-52	" Lemuel,	Dec. 2, 1767.
3-52	" Joshua,	Jan. 23, 1775.
4-86	" Lemuel, of Lemuel and Delight,	Oct. 9, 1796.
4-86	" Sophia,	Oct. 8, 1799.
4-86	" Charles Babcock,	Feb. 6, 1807.
4-132	" Prudence, of Joshua and Prudence,	April 23, 1800.
4-132	" Sally,	Jan. 14, 1804.
5-38	" John Denison, of Lemuel and Mary Ann,	Oct. 2, 1828.
5-38	" Eliza States,	Aug. 7, 1832.

W

3-30	WARD Hannah, of Samuel and Anna,	April 12, 1749.
3-30	" Ann,	Aug. 24, 1750.
3-30	" Catherine,	Oct. 2, 1752.
3-30	" Mary,	Dec. 3, 1754.
3-30	" Samuel,	Nov. 17, 1756.
3-30	" Deborah,	Oct. 12, 1758.
3-30	" Simon Ray,	Oct. 4, 1760.
3-83	" John,	July 25, 1762.
3-83	" Elizabeth,	Aug. 16, 1767.
2-111	WARNER Thankful, of William and Hannah,	March 27, 1718.
2-111	" William,	Sept. 15, 1719.
2-111	" Joshua,	July 1, 1723.
2-111	" Mary,	May 1, 1724.
2-78	WEAVER Alice, of Thomas and Sarah,	May 12, 1737.
2-78	" John,	Feb. 2, 1739.
2-78	" Prudence,	Sept. 2, 1740.
2-78	" Davis,	April 7, 1748.

2-45	WELCH	William, of William and Martha,	Aug. 27, 1737.
2-123	WELLS	Naomi, of Nathaniel and Mary,	May 11, 1707.
2-123	"	Elizabeth,	Jan. 9, 1709-10.
2-123	"	Jonathan,	June 22, 1712.
2-123	"	Tacy,	Jan. 4, 1714-15.
2-123	"	Ruth,	Sept. 6, 1717.
2-69	"	Phebe, of Thomas and Phebe,	Oct. 7, 1718.
2-69	"	Lewis,	Nov. 30, 1720.
2-69	"	Thomas,	April 5, 1722.
2-69	"	Benjamin,	Nov. 23, 1727.
2-69	"	Caleb,	May 15, 1731.
2-69	"	Joshua,	Oct. 29, 1733.
2-69	"	Nathan,	Feb. 12, 1737.
2-60	"	Edward, of Edward and Elizabeth,	Feb. 23, 1726-7.
2-60	"	Joseph,	April 16, 1729.
2-60	"	David,	July 20, 1731.
2-60	"	Elizabeth,	Oct. 13, 1733.
2-60	"	Matthew,	Feb. 17, 1735 0.
2-60	"	Thomas,	Sept. 13, 1738.
2-60	"	Mary,	Oct. 17, 1740.
2-60	"	John,	June 4, 1742.
2-60	"	Thankful,	Dec. 6, 1745.
2-60	"	Randall,	Sept. 30, 1747.
2-60	"	Sarah,	July 26, 1751.
4-24	"	Eunice, of Elisha and Eunice,	March 31, 1788.
4-24	"	Elisha,	Aug. 20, 1789.
4-24	"	Amey,	Jan. 28, 1791
4-83	"	Lucy, of Thompson and Phebe,	Aug. 16, 1793.
4-83	"	Abigail,	Nov. 12, 1795.
4-83	"	Joseph Taylor,	Dec. 14, 1797.
4-83	"	Elnathan Clarke,	May 6, 1800.
		Note—Youngest born Hopkinton.	
4-69	"	Daniel L., of Edward S., and Lucy,	March 26, 1796.
4-69	"	Elizabeth,	April 30, 1797.
4-188	"	Thompson, of Palmer and Charlotte,	Aug. 1, 1796.
4-188	"	Elisha,	Feb. 14, 1798.
		Note—Born Stonington.	
4-31	"	Oliver Dodge, of George and Lydia,	Sept. 2, 1802.
4-188	"	Palmer, of Palmer and Susannah,	Sept. 10, 1803.
4-188	"	Susan Potter,	July 5, 1805.
3-72	WEST	Samuel, of Francis and Mary,	Feb. 2, 1732.
4-112	"	James, of James and Susannah,	Aug. 11, 1752.
4-112	"	Mary,	July 12, 1753.
4-112	"	Susannah,	April 9, 1756.
4-112	"	Robert,	March 25, 1758.
4-112	"	Robert,	died Aug. 2, 1759.
4-112	"	Lydia,	July 6, 1760.
4-112	"	Arnold,	Sept. 11, 1762.
4-112	"	Robert,	May 11, 1765.
4-112	"	James, Sr.,	died Sept. 29, 1764.
3-74	"	Samuel, of Samuel and Anne,	April 14, 1757.
3-74	"	Anne,	April 11, 1759.
3-74	"	Amey,	Dec. 25, 1760.
4-108	"	Arnold, of James and Susannah,	Sept. 11, 1762.
4-108	"	Hannah, (Babcock of Joseph), his wife,	Jan. 2, 1767.
3-130	"	Henry, of John and Amey,	May 24, 1766.
3-130	"	Hannah,	Sept. 12, 1769.
3-130	"	Elisha,	Jan. 6, 1771.
3-130	"	Abigail,	July 30, 1773.
3-130	"	Thomas,	April 13, 1776.
3-130	"	Esther,	Jan. 26, 1780.
3-130	"	Peleg,	Sept. 15, 1782.
3-130	"	Mary,	March 4, 1787.
3-132	"	Frederic, of Timothy and Mary,	May 10, 1767.
3-126	"	Sarah, of William and Anne,	March 11, 1773.

-3-126	WEST	Timothy, of William and Anne,	June 22, 1774.
3-126	"	Prudence,	Aug. 19, 1775.
3-126	"	Jesse Babcock,	May 31, 1779.
4-60	"	Joseph, of William and Anna,	May 8, 1781.
4-60	"	Jesse,	Oct. 9, 1783.
4-60	"	Nancy,	May 4, 1785.
4-60	"	William,	Feb. 24, 1787.
4-60	"	George,	Feb. 18, 1789.
4-60	"	Assa,	Feb. 18, 1789.
4-30	"	Nancy, of Simeon and Nancy,	July 13, 1788.
4-30	"	Simeon,	Sept. 11, 1789.
4-30	"	Sally,	Aug. 16, 1791.
4-30	"	Christopher Champlain,	Jan. 16, 1794.
4-30	"	Margaret,	Dec. 5, 1799.
4-24	"	Zilpha, of Hannah, granddaughter of John,	March 1, 1791.
4-101	"	Lydia, of Elisha and Lydia,	Sept. 12, 1795.
4-101	"	Elisha,	Dec. 11, 1797.
4-101	"	John,	Nov. 9, 1800.
4-101	"	Amey,	April 1, 1803.
4-101	"	Stiles,	Sept. 23, 1805.
5-22	"	Francis Edward, of Francis S. and Sarah,	Sept. 7, 1837.
5-22	"	Francis Edward,	died Oct. 13, 1838.
5-22	"	Francis Stephen,	Feb. 22, 1839.
5-22	"	Charles Henry,	April 10, 1841.
5-22	"	Charles Henry,	died Aug. 10, 1841.
5-22	"	Mary Ann Elizabeth,	June 10, 1842.
5-22	"	Sarah Jane,	Oct. 1, 1844.
2-90	WHEELER	Susannah, of Jeremiah and Susannah,	Feb. 10, 1749-50.
4-15	WHITE	Lucy, of Walter and Sophia,	Dec. 12, 1775.
4-15	"	Abby Soule,	Feb. 20, 1778.
4-15	"	Walter Ellery,	Sept. 1, 1785.
4-15	"	Sophia,	May 11, 1787.
4-15	"	Lydia,	Sept. 25, 1787.
4-15	"	Polly,	Nov. 26, 1791.
4-15	"	Matilda,	Dec. 10, 1795.
4-15	"	Martha,	April 15, 1810.

Note—Two youngest born Hopkinton.

2-97	WILBUR	Samuel, of Stephen,	Nov. 2, 1739.
2-97	"	Stephen,	Oct. 25, 1741.
2-76	"	Anna, of William and Mary,	May 13, 1748.
3-11	"	Mary, of William and Mary,	March 14, 1746.
3-11	"	William,	May 17, 1747.
3-11	"	Anne,	May 13, 1749.
3-11	"	Martha,	May 25, 1751.
-3-114	"	Jeremiah, of Joseph and Sarah,	July 8, 1759.
3-114	"	John,	Aug. 30, 1760.
3-114	"	Sarah,	June 30, 1762.
3-114	"	Ruth,	Dec. 25, 1763.
3-114	"	Lucy,	July 26, 1765.
3-114	"	Joseph,	Jan. 14, 1767.
3-114	"	Benjamin,	Jan. 14, 1767.
3-114	"	Daniel,	June 5, 1769.
3-114	"	Lydia,	March 8, 1771.
3-114	"	Benjamin,	April 14, 1773.
3-114	"	Keturah,	Dec. 13, 1776.
3-114	"	Delight,	May 20, 1778.
3-125	"	Deborah, of John and Elizabeth,	Aug. 16, 1765.
3-125	"	Elizabeth,	Dec. 4, 1767.
3-125	"	Mary,	Feb. 11, 1770.
3-125	"	Esther,	Aug. 12, 1787.
3-148	"	Hannah, of David and Hannah,	March 3, 1766.
3-148	"	David,	Sept. 27, 1767.
3-148	"	Isaiah,	Aug. 29, 1771.
3-148	"	Bathsheba,	July 24, 1773.
3-148	"	Huldah,	Jan. 23, 1776.

3-148	WILBUR	Christopher, of David and Hannah,	March 26, 1778.
3-148	"	Ichabod,	Nov. 18, 1780,
3-148	"	Esther,	Jan. 22, 1786.
3-100	"	Jonathan, of Jonathan and Hannah,	July 14, 1766.
3-165	"	Prudence, of Joseph and Sarah,	March 12, 1790.
3-165	"	Charlotte,	June 12, 1782.
4-10	"	Mary, or Polly, of John and Mary,	Sept. 25, 1781.
4-10	"	Eunice,	April 19, 1783.
4-10	"	John,	March 5, 1785.
4-10	"	Esther,	Aug. 12, 1787.
4-10	"	Thankful,	April 28, 1789.
4-10	"	Nathan,	Feb. 7, 1791,
4-10	"	Susannah,	Jan. 28, 1793.
4-21	"	Mary, of John,	Sept. 25, 1781.
4-21	"	Eunice,	April 19, 1782.
4-21	"	John,	March 5, 1785.
4-97	"	Joanna, of Joseph and Joanna,	Oct. 18, 1790.
4-97	"	Ethan,	Jan. 20, 1792.
4-97	"	Ethan,	died Jan. 31, 1792.
4-97	"	Sally,	Jan. 22, 1793.
4-97	"	Mary Ann,	April 17, 1795.
4-97	"	Celia,	Aug. 17, 1797,
4-97	"	Charlotte,	Nov. 2, 1800.
4-192	"	Clarke, of Ichabod and Desire,	Aug. 14, 1804.
4-192	"	John Cottrell,	May 18, 1807.
4-274	"	Jarvis Stillman, of Isaiah and Desire,	Oct. 6, 1826.
5-109	"	Ruth Ann, of James B. and Ruth Ann,	July 7, 1841.
2-113	WILCOX	Sarah, of Edward and Tamsen,	May 30, 1700.
2-113	"	Thomas,	Feb. 18, 1701-2.
2-113	"	Hezekiah,	April 4, 1704.
2-113	"	Elisha,	July 9, 1706.
2-113	"	Amey,	Oct. 18, 1709.
2-113	"	Susannah,	April 4, 1712.
2-88	"	Mary, of Edward and Dinah,	Oct. 4, 1717.
2-88	"	Hannah,	Oct. 29, 1720.
2-88	"	Lydia,	April 6, 1725.
2-88	"	Susannah,	Oct. 4, 1727.
2-88	"	Joseph,	Aug. 27, 1730.
2-71	"	David, of Stephen and Mercy,	Feb. 13, 1720-1.
2-71	"	Mercy,	Aug. 6, 1724.
2-71	"	Eunice,	May 22, 172 .
2-71	"	Stephen,	April 21, 1728.
2-71	"	Valentine,	Feb. 14, 1733-4.
2-124	"	Edward,	died Nov. 5, 1715.
2-124	"	Thomas, of Edward and Tamson,	died Jan. 15, 1721-2.
3-81	"	David, of David and Tabitha,	Aug. 8, 1746.
3-81	"	Sarah,	Nov. 16, 1749.
3-81	"	Elias,	March 19, 1755.
3-81	"	Amey,	Dec. 25, 1756.
3-81	"	Lucy,	Feb. 25, 1759.
3-81	"	Stephen,	Nov. 19, 1760.
3-81	"	Eunice,	Aug. 3, 1762.
3-81	"	John,	Oct. 30, 1769.
3-37	"	Hezekiah, of Hezekiah and Hannah,	July 30, 1755.
3-37	"	Daniel,	Feb. 9, 1757.
3-37	"	Peleg,	Jan. 4, 1759.
3-37	"	Martha,	Nov. 5, 1760.
3-16	"	Thomas, of Thomas (of Groton, Conn.,) and Jerusha,	Sept. 27, 1755.
3-56	"	Benjamin, of Valentine and Abigail,	May 24, 1758.
3-56	"	John,	Nov. 12, 1760.
3-56	"	Rebecca,	Sept. 13, 1762.
3-56	"	Daniel,	July 3, 1764.
3-56	"	Sarah,	Sept. 13, 1766.
3-56	"	Ezekiel,	Feb. 13, 1772.

3-123	WILCOX Jesse, of Hezekiah and Hannah,		Dec. 29, 1762.
3-123	"	Asa,	Sept. 28, 1764.
3-123	"	Susanna,	Sept. 22, 1767.
3-123	"	Abigail,	Jan. 4, 1770.
3-123	"	Thomas,	Oct. 2, 1772.
3-123	"	Sylvester,	Aug. 11, 1774.
3-123	"	Samuel,	June 10, 1777.
3-79	"	Isaiah, of Isaiah and Sarah,	Jan. 31, 1763.
3-79	"	Asa,	Sept. 1, 1764.
3-79	"	Nathan,	April 10, 1766.
3-79	"	Sarah,	Dec. 19, 1767.
3-79	"	Mercy,	March 23, 1769.
3-79	"	Stephen,	Oct. 10, 1770.
3-79	"	Oliver,	June 26, 1773.
3-79	"	Prudence,	March 10, 1775.
3-79	"	Mary,	Jan. 8, 1777.
3-134	"	David, of David and Content,	Oct. 23, 1770.
3-134	"	Jonathan,	July 7, 1772.
3-134	"	Elias,	Feb. 9, 1774.
3-172	"	Daniel, of Daniel and Prudence,	April 14, 1781.
3-172	"	Nathan,	May 3, 1783.
5-218	"	Peleg, of Capt. Peleg and Lucy,	Aug. 26, 1783.
5-218	"	Parker,	July 5, 1787.
5-218	"	Isaac,	June 9, 1789.
4-33	"	Polly, of Isaiah and Polly,	Jan. 4, 1789.
4-33	"	Isaiah,	Nov. 30, 1791.
		Note—Both born Preston, Conn.	
4-32	"	Nancy, of Nathan and Nancy,	Oct. 3, 1790.
4-32	"	Sally,	Nov. 12, 1792.
4-218	"	Frederic, of Capt. Peleg and Mehitable,	Jan. 13, 1793.
4-218	"	Gilbert,	July 28, 1796.
4-218	"	Greene,	Feb. 21, 1798.
4-218	"	William,	Aug. 6, 1800.
4-93	"	Stephen, of Stephen and Sally,	May 7, 1796.
4-93	"	Phebe,	Sept. 11, 1798.
4-93	"	Thomas Jefferson,	Aug. 15, 1800.
4-106	"	Nancy, of Benjamin and Nancy,	Oct. 1, 1797.
4-106	"	Daniel,	Oct. 9, 1800.
4-106	"	Abigail,	April 29, 1805.
4-106	"	John Thompson,	April 13, 1806.
4-218	"	Freelove, of Samuel and Prudence,	Sept. 11, 1799.
4-218	"	Samuel,	March 28, 1801.
4-218	"	Eunice,	Aug. —, 1803.
4-218	"	Polly,	Dec. 30, 1805.
4-198	"	Peleg, of Peleg and Thankful,	Sept. 18, 1805.
4-230	"	Lucy, of Parker and Polly,	June 5, 1808.
5-27	"	Nancy, of George S. and Ann Maria,	Aug. 13, 1823.
5-27	"	Huldah,	Nov. 17, 1824.
5-27	"	George E.,	Sept. 7, 1826.
5-27	"	Nathan B., —— and Elizabeth, 2d wife,	Oct. 17, 1828.
5-27	"	Thomas C.,	April 17, 1830.
5-27	"	Joseph F.,	July 14, 1834.
		Note—The four eldest born Charlestown.	
5-3	"	Enock Hazard, of Stephen and Sophia,	July 26, 1825.
5-3	"	Enock Hazard,	died June 25, 1828.
5-3	"	Stephen,	Feb. 12, 1830.
2-114	WILLIS William, of Henry and Sarah,		Sept. 10, 1721.
2-118	WINSLOW Benjamin, of James and Elizabeth,		June 19, 1707.
2-114	WORDEN Elizabeth, of Peter, Jr., and Rebecca,		March 29, 1721.
2-114	"	Gideon (also 3-8),	Dec. 22, 1722.
3-8	"	Gideon, of Gideon and Rebecca,	Feb. 17, 1748-9.
3-8	"	Rebecca,	Feb. 20, 1749-50.
3-114	"	Dolly, of John and Elizabeth,	Feb. 28, 1771.
3-114	"	Abigail Babcock,	Oct. 1, 1772.

X Y Z

4-123	YEOMAN Lucretia, of Daniel (of Stonington, Ct., born at Stonington, Jan. 13, 1775.		
2-119	YORK Hannah, of James and Hannah,		March 21, 1697.
2-119	"	Joanna,	Dec. 31, 1699.
2-119	"	James,	Sept. 6, 1702.
2-119	"	Anna,	Jan. 21, 1704.
2-119	"	Hanson,	March 14, 1708.
2-119	"	Thankful,	Feb. 26, 1711.
3-64	"	Edward, of James and Elizabeth,	April 18, 1730.
3-64	"	Elizabeth,	Feb. 11, 1732.
3-64	"	Stephen,	May 24, 1735.
3-64	"	Hannah,	Feb. 28, 1738.
3-64	"	James,	Nov. 20, 1740.
3-64	"	William,	Jan. 20, 1742.
4-222	"	Saunders, of Capt. Benjamin and Desire,	Oct. 30, 1801.
4-222	"	Isaac,	June 24, 1804.
4-222	"	Welcome,	Feb. 6, 1807.
		Note.—Two eldest born Charlestown.	
4-261	"	Wanton, of Stephen and Mary,	Feb. 8, 1808.
4-261	"	Ruth Ann,	Sept. 11, 1810.
4-261	"	Mary,	Sept. 16, 1815.

Vital Record of Rhode Island.
1636=1850.

FIRST SERIES.

BIRTHS, MARRIAGES AND DEATHS.

A Family Register for the People.

By James N. Arnold,

EDITOR OF THE NARRAGANSETT HISTORICAL REGISTER.

"Is My Name Written in the Book of Life?"

Vol. 5.   **CHARLESTOWN.**   Part V.

Published under the Auspices of the General Assembly.

PROVIDENCE, R. I:
NARRAGANSETT HISTORICAL PUBLISHING COMPANY.
1894.

ACT INCORPORATING THE TOWN OF CHARLESTOWN.

AN ACT for dividing and incorporating the Town of Westerly into two Towns and the same to be known and distinguished by the names of Westerly and Charlestown.

Whereas, the present Town of Westerly is very large and its inhabitants are numerous, many of whom live at a very remote distance from the place of meeting appointed for the transacting the public, and prudential affairs of the Town and the rivers there (especially in the middle part thereof) being very large so that the way to said meeting is rendered difficult, as well as dangerous, and many of the inhabitants are thereby often impeded and hindered in attending thereon, which proves a great injury and hurt to them.

And, whereas the said Town is well situated and lies commodious for a division into two Towns which being divided will tend to the general interest and advantage of all its inhabitants.

Be it enacted by the General Assembly of this Colony and by the authority thereof it is enacted that the line for dividing said Town be as follows, viz.:

Beginning northerly where Wood river enters the line between the said Town of Westerly and North Kingstown, and so running by the natural course thereof so far until said river empties itself into a river called Pawcatuck and then to run or extend as said Pawcatuck river runs by the bank thereof westward three miles, and from thence a south or southerly course to the sea, and that for the future of the town of WESTERLY extend no further eastward than the aforesaid line.

And be it further enacted by the authority aforesaid that all the rest of said lands heretofore westerly situate, lying and being to the eastward of the aforesaid line be and they are hereby incorporated and erected a Town and called and distinguished by the name of CHARLESTOWN, and that the inhabitants thereof have all the liberties, privileges and immunities in the same manner as the other Towns in the government enjoy by Charters.

And be it further enacted by the authority aforesaid that Jeremiah Gould, John Rice, and William Gould, Esqs., be appointed a Committee to run a line between the aforesaid Towns and erect and make thereon proper monuments and bounds for distinguishing the same and to perform the same forwith.

And be it further enacted by the authority aforesaid that the Justice of the Peace in the Town of Charlestown as soon as conveniently may be issue forth a warrant to summon in the freemen to elect and make choice of their Town Officers for the management of the prudential affairs of said Town and also for the choice of two deputies for said Town to represent the same at the General Assembly in the October Session next, and so on from time to time as by Charter is appointed and that the Town of Westerly send two deputies to be chosen in manner as usual.

And be it further enacted by the authority aforesaid that each of the said Towns have their proportion of the interest of the bank money appropriated for the Towns in this Colony in the same proportion and according to the sums that the lands in each Town are mortgaged for.

And be it further enacted by the authority aforesaid that the Town of Westerly send three grand jurors to attend on the General Sessions of the Peace for the County of Kings County, and two petit jurors to attend at the Inferior Court for said County, and that the Town of Charlestown send two grand jurors to attend on said Court of General Sessions of the Peace, and two petit jurors to attend on said Inferior Court.

And it is likewise further enacted that the Towns of Westerly and Charlestown shall each send to the Superior Court one grand juror and one petit juror to attend on the same.

Colonial Record of Rhode Island, Vol. V., pages 545, 546, 547.

CHARLESTOWN.

MARRIAGES.

A

2-171 ADAMS Ebenezer, and Martha Taylor, both of Charlestown; m. by Rev. Jos. Parks, Sept. 14, 1763.

1-31, 42 " Mary, and John Johnson, March 4, 1788.

1-66 " Simeon, and Dorcas Burdick; m. by Samuel Perry, Justice, Court of Common Pleas, Nov. 4, 1805.

2-62 ALLEN Sarah, and John Earle, March 11, 1744.

2-171 " Joun, and Tacy Saunders, both of Charlestown; m. by Nathan Tefft, Justice, May 19, 1763.

1-96 AMMONS Gideon, and Caroline Rodman; m. by John Colwell, Minister of the Gospel, Nov. 10, 1846.

1-19 ARES Jos., and Mary Harvey, both of Charlestown; m. by Peleg Cross, Justice, Nov. 16, 1773.

2-61 AUCHMUDY Ann (wid.) and Enock Kenyon, Nov. 24, 1747.

2-226 " Mary, and Abijah Crandall, March 28, 1754.

2-171 " Isabel, and Stephen Crandall, Dec. 16, 1762.

2-103 AUSTIN Mrs. Abigail, and John Ball, May 22, 1750.

2-162 " Jediah, of Westerly, and Ann King, of Richmond, dau. of Ann King, widow; m. by Benj'm Hoxsie, Justice, Feb. 3, 1756.

1-49 " Joshua, of Robert, and Thankful Peirce, of James; m. by Peleg Cross, Justice, April 29, 1801.

B

2-227 BABCOCK Ichabod, of Westerly, and Esther Stanton, of Charlestown; m. by Jos. Crandall, Justice, March 17, 1756.

2-165 " David, of David, of South Kingstown, and Sarah Perry, of Samuel, of Charlestown; m. by Benj'm Hoxsie, Justice, March 30, 1757.

2-167 " Jonathan, of David, of South Kingstown, and Susannah Perry, of Samuel, of Charlestown; m. by Gideon Hoxsie, Justice, Feb. 10, 1759.

1-2 " Thankful, and Jos. Stanton, Jun., July 14, 1762.

1-43 " Lucy, and Peleg Hoxsie, June 1, 1777.

1-48 " Ceazar, and Elce Cook (col.); m. by Peleg Cross, Justice, Dec. 13, 1700.

1-67 " Benjamin, of Westerly, and Ann Wilcox, of Charlestown; m. by Peleg Cross, Justice, Jan. 26, 1806.

1-71 " Elizabeth, and Daniel Miner, Nov. 23, 1807.

1-81 " Jared, and Annie Lewis; m. by Nathan Stillman, Justice, June 25, 1830.

2-61 BAILEY Richard, and Abigail Woodmansee, both of Westerly; m. by George Babcock, Justice, April 25, 1729.

1-76 " Cloe, and Capt. Hazard Hoxsie, Dec. 25, 1806.

2-103 BALL John, of Charlestown, and Mrs. Abigail Austin, of do.; m. by Jeffrey Watson, Assistant, May 22, 1750.

2-62 BARBER Sarah, and Jonathan Lewis, Jun., July 27, 1744.

2-103 BARKER Abigail, and Consider Hall, April 23, 1750.

2-170 BASSETT Mary, and John Davis, July 12, 1762.

1-35   BLIVEN John, of Daniel, of Westerly, and Barbara Davis, of Joseph, of
            Charlestown; m. by Samuel Bliven, Justice, Jan. 16, 1791.
1-69   "   Mary, and Stephen York, March 19, 1807.
1-77   "   Maria, and Joseph Wilcox, 2d, Jan. 30, 1814.
2-61   BRAMAN Benjamin, and Martha Hall, both of Charlestown; m. by George
            Babcock, Justice, April 28, 1729.
2-103   "   Freelove, and John Miliard, Jan. 23, 1751.
2-226   "   Benjamin, and Rebecca Johnston, both of Charlestown; m. by
            Joseph Crandall, Justice, March 17, 1754.
2-165   "   John, Jun., of Westerly, and Mary Willard, of John, of Charles-
            town; m. by Stephen Saunders, Justice, Nov. 5, 1756.
1-20   "   Elizabeth, and Thomas Harvey, Dec. 29, 1782.
1-9   BROWNING Annie, and Gideon Hoxsie, Oct. 20, 1774.
1-36   "   Mary, and Thomas Hoxsie, Dec. 28, 1777.
1-15   "   Annie, and Samuel Sheffield, Dec. 3, 1778.
1-65   "   Sarah, and David Crandal, March 21, 1805.
1-90   "   Dorcas, and William Mumford, Jan. 3, 1843.
1-4   BROWN Bridget, and James Cornell, Sept. 14, 1774.
1-50   BURCH Rhoda, and George Sheffield, Jan. 3, 1802.
2-103   BURDICK Mary, and Jos. Wilcox, July 28, 1748.
2-227   "   Robert, 3d, and Hannah Hall, of John, Jun., of Charlestown;
            m. by Stephen Saunders, Justice, March —, 1759.
1-28   "   Lydia, and John Welch, Aug. 27, 1774.
1-18   "   Tacy, and Jonathan Hazard, Jr., Dec. 20, 1781.
1-25   "   Anna, and Jonathan Burdick, Feb. 2, 1786.
1-25   "   Jonathan, son of Jonathan, of Charlestown, and Anna Burdick,
            of Ephraim, of Charlestown; m. by Joseph Crandall, Justice,
            Feb. 2, 1786.
1-31   "   Annie, and Mathias Enos, March 2, 1788.
1-32   "   Hannah, and Lodowick Thompson, Aug. 29, 1788.
1-66   "   Dorcas, and Simeon Adams, Nov. 4, 1805.
1-72   "   Samuel, of Gideon, and Sally Sheffield, of Stanton; m. by Peleg
            Cross, Justice, Jan. 21, 1808.
1-73   "   Martha, and Joseph Cross, Oct. 16, 1808.

C

2-62   CARD Martha, and Thomas Potter, April 20, 1746.
1-63   "   Dorcas, and Gideon Holloway, Nov. 22, 1787.
1-101   "   Pardon, and Martha Clarke; m. by Joshua Card, Jr., Justice,
            Sept. 4, 1817.
1-67   CARR John, of Jamestown, and Mary Cross, of Charlestown, dau. of Peleg,
            Jr.; m. by Samuel Perry, Justice, Court of Common Pleas, Dec.
            23, 1805.
2-101   CHAMPLAIN Mary, and Joseph Stanton, Jr., Aug. 9, 1738.
2-162   "   John, of William, of New London, and Rebecca Stanton, of Daniel,
            of Charlestown; m. by Benj'n Hoxsie, Justice, Dec. 14, 1756.
2-166   "   Ann, and James Peckham, Aug. 19, 1757.
1-4   "   Jesse, of Charlestown, and Hannah Potter, of South Kingstown; m.
            by David Sprague, Clergyman, April 17, 1774.
1-22   "   Sarah, and William Rhodes, Jan. 31, 1779.
1-16   "   Jonathan, and Mary Moon; m. by Peleg Cross, Justice, April 2,
            1780.
1-20   "   John, of Charlestown, and Hannah Congdon, of Samuel, of South
            Kingstown; m. by Freeman Perry, Justice, June 14, 1781.
1-21   "   Nancy, and Joseph Rhodes, Dec. 9, 1781.
1-38   "   Joshua, of Christopher, of Charlestown, and Mary Congdon, of Sam-
            uel, of South Kingstown; m. at South Kingstown, by Peleg
            Cross, Justice, Sept. 13, 1792.
1-74   "   Amey, and Job Taylor, Nov. 9, 1809.
1-1   CHAPMAN Abigail, and John Park, Nov. 4, 1772.
1-98   CHAPPELL Scranton, and Zilpha Perkins; m. by Rev. George K. Clarke,
            Nov. 18, 1849.
1-102   CHURCH Charles, and Susannah ——, Jan. 12, 1759.

1-41	CHURCH Charles, and Mary Cross, both of Charlestown; m. by Peleg Cross, Justice, Nov. 23, 1794.
1-44	"	Caleh, of Isaac, and Lucy Potter, of William; m. by Peleg Cross, Justice, Dec. 13, 1795.
2-31	CLARKE William, and Hannah Knight; April 15, 1700.
2-169	"	Sarah, and Edward Greenman, Jr., May 11, 1721.
2-60	"	Elisha, of Charlestown, and Judith Seager, of South Kingstown; m. by Rouse Helme, Asst., Dec. 18, 1739.
2-35	"	Jonathan, of Charlestown, and Tahitha Westcott, of South Kingstown; m. by Elder Daniel Evritt, Feb. 8, 1739.
2-226	"	Bertha, and William Clarke; May 26, 1754.
2-226	"	William, and Bertha Clarke, both of Charlestown; m. by Elisha Babcock, Justice, May 26, 1754.
1-2	"	Hannah, and William S. Peckham, Jan. 6, 1773.
1-7	"	Ichabod, of Ephraim, of Westerly, and Mary Crandall, of Edward, of Charlestown; m. by Joseph Crandall, Justice, Jan. 10, 1773.
1-2	"	Edward, of Westerly, and Tamar Crandall, of Charlestown; m. by Elder Thomas C. Ross, May 31, 1773.
1-17	"	Tacy, and Benedict Crandall, Dec. 7, 1780.
1-22	"	Judea, and Gideon Crandall, Dec. 12, 1782.
1-27	"	Simeon, of Joshua, and Silva Hall, of Peter, both of Charlestown; m. by Peleg Cross, Justice, May 10, 1786.
1-33	"	Mary, and Newman Tucker, Nov. 27, 1788.
1-101	"	Martha, and Pardon Card, Sept. 4, 1817.
1-90, 92	"	Sarah, and Thomas Johnson, March 10, 1842.
1-31	COLLINS Hezekiah, of Jas., and Mary Hoxsie, of Stephen, Jr.; m. by Peleg Cross, Justice, Dec. 20, 1787.
1-5	CONGDON John, of South Kingstown, and Sarah Hoxsie, of Charlestown; m. by John Hicks, Justice, Oct. 6, 1745. (Also 2-62.)
2-62	"	James, Jr., and Elizabeth Pike, both of Charlestown; m. by John Hicks, Justice, Jan. 30, 1745.
2-166	"	James, of James and Lehorah Potter, both of Charlestown; m. by Jos. Hoxsie, Justice, Nov. 23, 1757.
2-168	"	Susannah, and Timothy Peckham, March 11, 1759.
2-168	"	Margaret, and Cahoone Williams, March 25, 1759.
1-14	"	James, of John, and Elizabeth Sherman, of Hopkinton; m. by Elder Joshua Clarke, Jan. 23, 1773.
1-20	"	Hannah, and John Champlain, June 14, 1781.
1-19	"	Catey, and Peleg Cross, Jr., June 28, 1781.
1-38	"	Mary, and Joshua Champlain, Sept. 16, 1792.
1-45	"	Ceasar, and Eunice Niles; m. by Peleg Cross, Justice, Dec. 26, 1797.
1-50	"	Bristol, Jr., and Hannah Trim (col.); m. by Peleg Cross, Justice, Jan. 3, 1802.
1-48	COOK Elce, and Ceazer Babcock, Dec. 13, 1800.
1-48	COREY Abigail, and Hazard Perry, Nov. 23, 1800.
1-4	CORNELL James, of Newport, and Bridget Brown, of Charlestown, dau. of William; m. by Sylvester Robinson, Justice, Sept. 14, 1774.
1-83	COGGSWELL Wilson, and Ahhie Kenyon, of James, all of Charlestown; m. by Elder John H. Baker, Feb. 11, 1841.
2-162	CRARY Oliver, of Westerly, and Hopestill York, of Charlestown; m. by Elder Joseph Park, March 16, 1756.
2-224	CRANDALL Joshua, of Westerly, and Eunice Kenyon, of Charlestown; m. by Nathaniel Lewis, Justice, Sept 18, 1750.
2-224	"	Nathan, of Westerly, and Bathsheba Pierce, of Edward, of Charlestown; m. by Benjamin Hoxsie, Justice, April 5, 1753.
2-226	"	Ahijah, and Mary Auchmady; m. by Joseph Crandall, Justice, March 28, 1754.
2-167	"	Benjamin, and Alice Kenyon, both of Charlestown; m. by Joseph Crandall, Justice, June 26, 1758.
2-171	"	Stephen, of Hopkinton, and Isabel Anchmady, of Charlestown; m. by Joseph Crandall, Justice, Dec. 16, 1762.
1-2	"	Joseph, Jr., of Westerly, and Martha Crandall, of John, of Hopkinton; m. by Job Taylor, Justice, Sept. 17, 1772.

1-2 CRANDALL Martha, and Joseph Crandall, Jr., m. Sept. 17, 1772.
1-7   "   Mary, and Ichabod Clarke; m. Jan. 10, 1773.
1-2   "   Tamar, and Edward Clarke; m. May 31, 1773.
1-11   "   Jared, of Simeon, of Charlestown, and Zilpha Potter, of Benj'n, of
             Dartmouth, Mass.; m. by Jos. Crandall, Justice, July 2, 1776.
1-17   "   Benedict, of James, of Westerly, and Tacy Clarke, of Ephriam, of
             Charlestown; m. by Jos. Crandall, Justice, Dec. 7, 1780.
1-18   "   Asa, of Simeon, and Phebe Taylor, of Job, both of Charlestown;
             m. by Jos. Crandall Justice, Dec. 28, 1780.
1-21   "   Simeon, and Katherine Welch. both of Charlestown; m. by Jos.
             Crandall, Justice, Feb. 22, 1781.
1-20   "   Asa, of Simeon, and Sarah Tefft, of Nathan, both of Charlestown;
             m. by Jos. Crandall, Justice, Sept. 12, 1782.
1-22   "   Gideon, of Edward, and Judea Clarke. of Ephriam, both of Charles-
             town; m. by Joshua Vose, Justice, Dec. 12, 1782.
1-35   "   Clement, of Joshua, of Westerly, and Susannah Davis, of Jos., of
             Charlestown; m. by Samuel Bliven, Justice, Jan. 16, 1791.
1-48   "   Hannah, and John B. Stanton, Oct. 12, 1800.
1-65   "   Potter, and Patty Taylor; m. by Peleg Cross, Justice, April 11,
             1803.
1-65   "   Bathsheba, and Lewis Crandall, Feb. 20, 1805.
1-65   "   Lewis, of New London, and Bathsheba Crandall, of Charlestown;
             m. by Peleg Cross, Justice, Feb. 20, 1805.
1-65   "   David, and Sarah Browning; m. by Elder John Sekoter, March 21,
             1805.
2-101 CROSS Jos., and Abigail Gould, both of Charlestown; m. by William Clarke,
             Justice, Nov. 14, 1746.
1-38   "   Peleg, and Mary ——; m. by Capt. John Hill, Justice, Dec. 30,
             1753.
2-226 "   William, and Abigail Darling, both of Charlestown; m. by Robert
             Potter, Justice, Jan. —, 1754.
2-171 "   Edward, and Elizabeth Moon, both of Charlestown; m. by Christo-
             pher Champlain, Justice, Aug. 7, 1763.
1-16   "   Annie, and Simeon Lewis; m. Jan. 13, 1780.
1-19   "   Peleg, Jun., and Catey Congdon, of John, both of Charlestown; m.
             by Edward Perry, Justice, Court Common Pleas, June 28, 1781.
1-27   "   Jos., of Jos., and Abigail Worden, of Christopher; m. by Elder
             John Gardiner, April 25, 1785.
1-41   "   Mary, and Charles Church; m. Nov. 23, 1794.
1-64   "   Susannah, and Hoxsie Perry, Dec. 4, 1803.
1-67   "   Mary, and John Carr, Dec. 23, 1805.
1-73   "   Jos., of Gideon and Martha Burdick, of Isaiah, both of Charles-
             town; m. by Peleg, Jr., Justice, Oct. 16, 1808.

D

2-170 DAVIS, John, of Hopkinton, and Mary Bassett, of Charlestown; m. by John
             Witter, Justice, July 12, 1762.
1-35   "   Barbara, and John Bliven; m. Jan. 16, 1891.
1-35   "   Susannah, and Clement Crandall; m. Jan. 16, 1791.
1-81   "   Sophia, and George Hazard Sherman, Dec. 14, 1814.
2-226 DEARLING Abigail, and William Cross; m. Jan. —, 1754.
2-224 DECK Isaac, of Jomestown, and Hannah Sash, of Charlestown; m. by
             Robert Potter, Justice, Oct. 25, 1753.

E

2-62   EANOS Mary, and John Lillibridge; m. Oct. 12, 1743.
2-77   "   Jos., and Margaret Webster; m. in Westerly by Thomas Hiscox,
             Justice, Sept. 20, 1716.
2-60   "   Jos., Jun., and Keziah Woodmansee, both of Charlestown; m. by
             Samuel Wilbur, Justice, Dec. 21, 1738.

1-31 EANOS Mathias, of Stephen, of South Kingstown, and Anne Burdick, of Samuel, of Charlestown; m. by Peleg Cross, Justice, March 2, 1788.

2-62 EARLE John, son of Freelove Parker, and Sarah Allen, of William, both of Charlestown; m. by Stephen Hoxrie, Justice, March 11, 1744.

1-51 EDWARDS Daniel, of Charlestown, and Lois Stillman, of Westerly; m. by Elder Asa Coon, Sept. 16, 1797.

1-73 " Jos., and Bathsheba Hiscox; m. by Elder Abram Coon, Jan. 12, 1809.

1-15 ELLIS Jonathan, of Providence, and Phebe Taylor, of Charlestown; m. by Elder Thomas Ross, May 17, 1778.

F

2-62 FOSTER Sarah, and Benjamin Pettis, April 2, 1746.

G

2-172 GARDNER Luci, and William Greene; m. Aug. 20, 1767.

1-94 GAVITT Oliver, and Martha Perry; m. by Elder Wilson Coggswell, June 30, 1843.

2-169 GREENMAN Edward, Jun., of Westerly, and Sarah Clarke, of South Kingstown; m. in S. K. by Christopher Allen, Justice, May 11, 1721.

2-35 " Silas, and Sarah Peckham, both of Charlestown; m. by Joseph Crandall, Justice, Oct. 27, 1751.

2-60, 164 GREENE Amos, and Amie Knowles, both of Charlestown; m. by William Clarke, Justce, June 19, 1740.

2-227 " William, and Judith Rathbone; m. by Nathan Sheffield, Justice, Jan. 25, 1756.

2-163 " Mary, and Nathan Kenyon; m. April 18, 1757.

2-172 " Amos, Jun., and Dorcas Hall, both of Charlestown; m. by Edward Perry, Justice, June 9, 1763.

2-172 " William, of Charlestown, and Luci Gardiner, of Hopkinton; m. by Nathan Burdick, Justice, Aug. 20, 1767.

1-41 " Amos, of Charlestown, and Elizabeth Thompson, of Westerly; m. by Eld. E. Babcock, Dec. 25, 1793.

1-51 " Robert, and Abigail Tefft; m. by James Potter, Justice, Dec. 27, 1798.

1-100 " Alvin, and Esther Holburton; m. by Asa Church, Justice, July 18, 1822.

1-88 " Edward L., and Elizabeth ——; m. Jan. 6, 1823.

1-83 " Jason B., and Hannah Sannders; m. March 18, 1839.

1-96 " Nancy C., and Bradford Kenyon; m. July 5, 1846.

2-60 GRIFFIN Phillip, of Charlestown, and Elizabeth Reynolds, of Westerly; m. by William Clarke, Justice, June 17, 1740.

2-62 " John, and Abigail Ladd, both of Charlestown; m. by Nathaniel Lewis, Justice, Oct. 16, 1743.

1-71 " Stephen, and Hannah Hazard, both of Charlestown; m. by Peleg Cross, Justice, Nov. 26, 1807.

1-27 GOULD Abigail, and Jos. Cross; m. Nov. 14, 1746.

H

2-61 HALL Martha, and Benj'm Braman; m. April 28, 1729.

2-62 " William, of Westerly, and Sarah Kenyon, of Charlestown; m. by William Clarke, Justice, July 14, 1744.

2-103 " Consider, of John, Jun., and Abigail Barker, of Thomas, all of Charlestown; m. by Benj'n Hoxsie, Justice, April 23, 1750.

2-103 " Martha, and Tobias Sannders; m. April 9, 1752.

2-224   HALL Potter, and Hannah Lovatt; m. by Benj'n Hoxsie, Justice, Feb.
            5, 1753.
2-162   "   Jonathan, of Westerly, and Jane Harvey, of Charlestown; m. by
                Benj'n Hoxsie, Justice, March 8, 1756.
2-166   "   Ephraim, of Benj'n, and Penelope Hall, widow, both of Hopkin-
                ton; m. by Benj'n Hoxsie, Justice, Dec. 11, 1757.
2-166   "   Penelope, widow, and Ephraim Hall; m. Dec. 11, 1757.
2-227   "   Hannah, and Robert Burdick; m. March —, 1759.
2-172   "   Dorcas, and Amos Greene, Jun.; m. June 9, 1768.
1-27   "   Silvia, and Simeon Clarke; m. May 10, 1786.
1-65   "   Jane, and Henry Figer, March —, 1804.
1-69   HANCOCK Freelove, and Nathaniel Sheffield; m. Jan. 13, 1805.
1-69   "   Zebulon, and Catherine Sheffield, of Thomas; m. by Peleg Cross,
                Justice, Feb. 15, 1807.
2-162   HARVEY Jane, and Jonathan Hall; m. March 8, 1756.
1-19   "   Mary, and Jos. Ares; m. Nov. 16, 1773
1-20   "   Thomas, of Charlestown, and Elizabeth Braman, of South Kings-
                town; m. by Peleg Cross, Justice, Dec. 29, 1782.
1-85   "   Harriet, and Jos. Thompson; m. Feb. 9, 1840.
1-65   HAWKINS Hannah, and Daniel Swan, April 3, 1804.
1-18   HAZARD Jonathan, Jun., and Tacy Burdick, both of Charlestown; m. by
                Elder Thomas Ross, Dec. 29, 1781.
1-71   "   Hannah, and Stephen Griffin; m. Nov. 26, 1807.
1-101   "   Arnold W., of South Kingstown, and Sarah S. Hoxsie of Charles-
                town; m. by Rev. Charles P. Grosvenor, Jan. 8, 1837.
1-93   "   William H., and Sarah M. Thomas, both of the Narragansett Tribe;
                m. by Elder Weeden Barber, Dec. 30, 1844.
1-73   HISCOX Bathsheba, and Jos. Edwards; m. Jan. 12, 1809.
1-89   "   Arnold, Jun., and Martha B. Macomber, both of Charlestown;
                m. by Elder Daniel Coon, April 12, 1842.
1-100   HOLBURTON Esther, and Alvin Greene; m. July 18, 1822.
1-63   HOLLOWAY Gideon, and Dorcas Card; m. by Elder Charles Boss, Nov.
            22, 1787.
2-166   HOXSIE Sarah, and John Congdon; m. Oct. 6, 1745. (also 1-5).
2-165   "   Joseph, of Joseph, of Charlestown, and Mary Peckham, of Benja-
                min, of South Kingstown; m. by John Hill, Justice, Feb. 5,
                1754.
2-166   "   Mary, and Amos Lewis; m. April 20, 1755.
1-9   "   Gideon, Jr., of Charlestown, and Amie Browning, of William, of
                South Kingstown; m. by Sylvester Robinson, Justice, Oct. 20,
                1774.
1-43   "   Peleg, of Gideon, and Lucy Babcock, of Ichabod, of Westerly;
                m. by Peleg Cross, Justice, June 1, 1777.
1-36   "   Thomas, of Benjamin, and Mary Browning, of Wilkerson; m. by
                Peleg Cross, Justice, Dec. 28, 1777.
1-31   "   Mary, and Hezekiah Collins; m. Dec. 20, 1787.
1-40   "   Elizabeth, and Peter Perry; m. June 8, 1794.
1-42   "   Lodowick, and Ruth Taylor, both of Charlestown; m. by Peleg
                Cross, Justice, Jan. 4, 1795.
1-76   "   Capt. Hazard, and Cloe Bailey; m. at Lebanon, Conn., by Rev.
                Nehemiah Dodge, Dec. 25, 1806.
1-101   "   Sarah S., and Arnold W. Hazard; m. Jan. 8, 1837.
1-95   "   Samuel B., of Hazard, and Maria Wilcox, of Joseph, Jr.; m. by
                Rev. Thomas H. Vail, Sept. 10, 1846.

I   J

2-61   JAMES Hannah, and Robert Moore; m. Nov. 30, 1741.
2-62   "   Jonathan, and Mehitable Webb, both of Charlestown; m. by John
                Hicks, Justice, Jan. 17, 1744.
2-62   "   Mary, and David Moore; m. Nov. 24, 1745.
2-226   JOSHUA, son of Negro Will, of Charlestown, and Phebe, a mulatto woman,
                of Westerly; m. by Joseph Crandall, Justice, Nov. 5, 1753.
2-226   JOHNSON Rebecca, and Benjamin Braman; m. March 17, 1754.

2-170 JOHNSON Lucy, and John Stiles; m. Feb. 11, 1760.
1-13   "   Mary, and Benjamin Tucker; m. April 15, 1777.
1-31, 42   "   John, of Reuben, and Mary Adams, of Thomas, both of Charlestown;
           m. by Peleg Cross, Jr., Justice, March 4, 1788.
1-40   "   Sarah, and Pardon Perry; m. March 13, 1803.
1-90, 92   "   Thomas, and Sarah Clarke; m. by Elder Weeden Barber, March 10,
           1842.

K

2-60 KENYON Ebenezer, and Amie ——; m. Nov. 14, 1717.
2-60   "   Mary, and Stephen Larkin; m. March 9, 1740.
2-60   "   Sarah, and Nicholas Larkin; m. Dec. 18, 1740.
2-61   "   Sarah, and Nathaniel Pullman, Jr.; m. Jan. 14, 1741.
2-61   "   Mary, and Enoch Lewis; m. Feb. 27, 1742.
2-61   "   Elizabeth, and James Lewis (also 1-101); m. Feb. 27, 1742.
2-62   "   Sarah, and William Hall, July 14, 1744.
2-60   "   Hannah, and Thomas Kenyon; m. April 13, 1746.
2-60   "   Thomas, of John, and Hannah Kenyon, of David, both of Charles-
           town; m. by Robert Lillibridge, Justice, April 13, 1746.
2-61   "   Enock, and Ann Anchmndy; m. by Elder Joseph Park, Nov. 24,
           1747.
2-224   "   Eunice, and Joshua Crandall, m. Sept. 18, 1750.
2-163   "   Nathan, and Mary Greene, both of Charlestown; m. by Gideon
           Hoxsie, Justice, April 18, 1757.
2-167   "   Alice, and Benjamin Crandall; m. June 26, 1758.
2-62   "   Sarah, and William Potter, Jr.; m. July 24, 1763.
1-36   "   James, of Daniel, and Lydia Sheffield, of Elisha, both of Charles-
           town; m. by Peleg Cross, Justice, April 22, 1786.
1-34   "   Nathan, Jr., of Richmond, and Sarah Tefft, of South Kingstown;
           m. by Elder Henry Joslin, April 12, 1789.
1-45   "   Sarah, and Robert Potter; m. Sept. 30, 1797.
1-84   "   James N., and Mary Stanton, both of Charlestown; m. by Rev.
           John H. Baker, March 23, 1840.
1-86   "   Abbie, and Wilson Cogswell; m. Feb. 11, 1841.
1-96   "   Bradford, of Richmond, and Nancy C. Greene, of Charlestown;
           m. by Rev. John W. Colwell, July 5, 1846.
1-97   "   James A., and Frances Rathbone, both of Charlestown; m. by
           Jos. H. Griffin, Justice, July 27, 1847.
2-162 KING Ann, and Jediah Austin; m. Feb. 3, 1756.
2-31 KNIGHT Hannah, and William Clarke; m. April 15, 1700.
2-60 KNOWLES Amie, and Amos Greene (also 2-164); m. June 19, 1740.
2-103   "   Robert, of Daniel, and Abigail Smith; m. by John Congdon, Jus-
           tice, April 22, 1750.
1-83   "   Celia, and John Stanton; m. May 26, 1833.

L

2-62 LADD Abigail, and John Griffin; m. Oct. 16, 1743.
2-60 LANPHERE Susannah, and John Stanton; m. Oct. 16, 1734.
2-60 LARKIN Stephen, of Edward, of Westerly, and Mary Kenyon, of Ebenezer,
           of Charlestown; m. by Stephen Hoxsie, Justice, March 9,
           1740.
2-60   "   Nicholas, of Edward, of Westerly, and Sarah Kenyon, of John, of
           Charlestown; m. by Stephen Hoxsie, Justice, Dec. 18, 1740.
2-60 LEWIS Mary, and Nathaniel Lewis; m. Nov. 13, 1729.
2-60   "   Nathaniel, and Mary Lewis; m. by Theo. Rhodes, Justice, Nov.
           13, 1729.
2-60   "   Jacob, and Prudence Lewis; m. by Stephen Hoxsie, Justice, Sept.
           9, 1739.
2-60   "   Prudence, and Jacob Lewis; m. Sept. 9, 1739.
2-60   "   Mary, and Jos. Rogers; m. Jan. 17, 1739.

2-61 LEWIS Enoch, and Mary Kenyon, of John, both of Charlestown; m. by John Hicks, Justice, Feb. 27, 1742.

2-61 " James, of North Kingstown, and Elizabeth Kenyon, of Jonathan, of Charlestown (also 2-101); m. by John Hicks, Justice, Feb. 27, 1742.

2-62 " Jonathan, Jr., of Exeter, and Sarah Parber, of Charlestown; m. by John Hicks, Justice, July 27, 1744.

2-224 " A muster man, son of Negro Will, of Charlestown, and Mary Matthews, of same town; m. by Nathaniel Lewis, Justice, Feb. 7, 1753.

2-166 " Amos, and Mary Hoxsie, both of Charlestown; m. by John Hicks, Justice, April 20, 1755.

1-16 " Simeon, of Capt. John, of Westerly, and Annie Cross, of Peleg, of Charlestown; m. by Jos. Crandall, Justice, Jan. 13, 1780.

1-81 " Anne, and Jared Babcock; m. June 25, 1830.

2-60 LILLIBRIDGE Thomas, and Mary Woodmansee; m. by Theo Rhodes, Justice, June 12, 1726.

2-62 " John, and Marcy Enos, both of Charlestown; m. by Nathaniel Lewis, Justice, Oct. 12, 1743.

2-224 LOVATT Hannah, and Potter Hall; m. Feb. 5, 1753.

2-61 LYSTER Hannah, and Jos. Woodmansee, July 7, 1719.

M

1-85 MACOMBER Nancy A., and William Ney; m. Jan. 13, 1840.

1-89 " Martha B., and Arnold Hiscox, Jr.; m. April 12, 1842.

2-224 MATTHEWS Mary, and son of Negro Will Lewis; m. Feb. 7, 1753.

2-103 MILLARD John, and Freelove Braman, both of Charlestown; m. by Joseph Crandall, Justice, Jan. 23, 1751.

2-165 " Mary, and John Braman, Jr., Nov. 9, 1756.

1-71 MINER Daniel, of Stonington, and Eliztbeth Babcock, of Ephraim, of South Kingstown; m. by Peleg Cross, Justice, Nov. 23, 1807.

2-171 MOON Elizabeth, and Edward Cross; m. Aug. 7, 1763.

1-16 " Mary, and Jonathan Champlin; m. April 2, 1780.

2-61 MOORE Robert, of John, of Charlestown, and Hannah James, of William, of Charlestown; m. by Stephen Hoxsie, Justice, Nov. 30, 1741.

2-62 " David, and Mary James, both of Charlestown; m. by John Hicks, Justice, Nov. 24, 1745.

2-167 " Deliverance, and Edward Perry; m. Jan. 7, 1759.

1-66 MOREY Gardiner, and Lydia Sheffield; m. by Peleg Cross, Justice, April 16, 1804.

1-90 MUMFORD William, and Dorcas Browning; m. by Joseph H. Griffin, Justice, Jan. 3, 1843.

N

1-85 NEY William, and Nancy A. Macomber; m. by Daniel King, Justice, Jan. 13, 1840.

1-45 NILES Eunice, and Ceaser Congdon; m. Dec. 26, 1797.

O

1-66 OLNEY Lemuel, and Mary Simon; m. by Peleg Cross, Justice, March 25, 1804.

P

2-467 PARK Benjamin, and Hannah Stanton York; m. by Rev. Jos. Park, Dec. 4 (prob.), 1757.

1-1 " John, of Jos., of Charlestown, and Abigail Chapman, of William, of Westerly; m. by Rev. Jos. Park, Nov. 4, 1772.

2-35	PECKHAM	Sarah, and Silas Greenman; m. Oct. 27, 1751.
2-165	"	Mary, and Jos. Hoxsie; m. Feb. 5, 1754.
2-166	"	James, of Daniel, and Ann Champlin, of Jeffrey, both of Charlestown; m. by Benj'n Hoxsie, Justice, Aug. 19, 1757.
2-168	"	Timothy, of South Kingstown, and Susannah Congdon, of Charlestown; m. by Jos. Crandall, Justice, March 11, 1759.
1-2	"	William S., of John, of Westerly, and Hannah Clark, of Jos., of Charlestown; m. by Jos. Crandall, Justice, Jan. 6, 1773.
1-25	"	Isaac, of Westerly, and Susannah Sunderland, of Charlestown; m. by Jos. Crandall, Justice, July 27, 1786.
1-90	"	Charles, of Charlestown, and Mary Ann Saunders, of Westerly; m. by Eld. Weeden Barber, Jr., Oct. 17, 1841.
1-49	PEIRCE	Thankful, and Joshua Austin, April 29, 1801.
1-98	PERKINS	Zilpha, and Scranton Chappell; m. Nov. 18, 1849.
2-165	PERRY	Sarah, and David Babcock; m. March 30, 1757.
2-167	"	Edward, of Charlestown, and Deliverance Moore, of Exeter; m. by Gideon Hoxsie, Justice. Jan. 7, 1759.
2-167	"	Susannah, and Jonathan Babcock; m. Feb. 10, 1759.
1-1	"	Edward, of Benj'n, of Richmond, and Ruth Perry, of Samuel; m. by Sylvester Robinson, Justice, Oct. 7, 1770.
1-1	"	Ruth, and Edward Perry; m. Oct. 7, 1770.
1-2	"	Merebah, and Jeremiah Pierce; m. Jan. 27, 1773.
1-40	"	Peter, a mustee man, of Charlestown, and Elizabeth Hoxsie, mustee, of same town; m. by John Collins, Justice, June 8, 1794.
1-48	"	Hazard, and Abigail Corey; m. by Peleg Cross, Justice, Nov. 23, 1800.
1-63	"	Pardon, and Sarah Johnson; m. by Peleg Cross, Justice, March 13, 1803.
1-64	"	Hoxsie, and Susannah Cross; m. by Peleg Cross, Justice, Dec. 4, 1803.
1-80	"	Mary, and Samuel Ward; m. Jan. 12, 1826.
1-86	"	Mary, and Jonathan Tucker; m. Sept. 30, 1840.
1-94	"	Martha, and Oliver Gavitt, June 30, 1843.
2-62	PETTIS	Benjamin, and Sarah Foster, m. by William Clarke, Justice, April 20, 1746.
2-226	PHEBE	a mulatto, and Joshua, son of Negro Will; m. Nov. 5, 1753.
2-224	PIERCE	Bathsheba, and Nathan Crandall; m. April 5, 1753.
1-2	"	Jeremiah, of East Greenwich, son of John, and Merebah Perry, of Samuel, of Charlestown; m. by Sylvester Robinson, Justice, Jan. 27, 1773.
2-62	PIKE	Elizabeth, and James Congdon, Jr.; m. Jan. 30, 1745.
2-62	POTTER	Thomas, of Ichabod, and Martha Card, of Charlestown; m. by William Clarke, Justice, April 20, 1746.
2-166	"	Deborah, and James Congdon, Nov. 23, 1757.
2-62, 171	"	William, Jr., of South Kingstown, and Sarah Kenyon, of Charlestown, m. by Christopher Champlin, Justice, July. 24, 1763.
1-4	"	Hannah, and Jesse Champlin; m. April 17, 1774.
1-11	"	Zilpha, and Jesse Chamall; m. July 2, 1776.
1-44	"	Lucy, and Caleb Church; m. Dec. 13, 1795.
1-45	"	Robert, and Sarah Kenyon; m. by Peleg Cross, Justice, Sept. 30, 1797.
2-61	PULLMAN	Nathaniel, Jr., and Sarah Kenyon, of Jonathan, both of Charlestown; m. by William Clarke, Justice, Jan. 14, 1741.

Q R

2-61	RATHBONE	Joshua, and Dorcas Wells, both of Charlestown; m. by William Clarke, Justice, May 4, 1742.
2-227	"	Judeth, and William Greene; m. Jan. 25, 1756.
1-97	"	Frances, and James A. Kenyon; m. July 27, 1847.
2-60	REYNOLDS	Elizabeth, and Phillip Griffin; m. June 17, 1740.
1-47	"	Elizabeth, and Samuel Stanton; m. April 11, 1799.

1-22   RHODES William, of James, of Stonington, and Sarah Champlin, of Christopher, of Charlestown; m. by Joseph Crandall, Justice, Jan. 31, 1779.

1-21   "   Joseph, of Col. James, of Stonington, and Nancy Champlin, of Col. Christopher, of Charlestown; m. by Joseph Crandall, Justice, Dec. 9, 1781.

1-96   RODMAN Caroline, and Gideon Ammons; m. Nov. 10, 1846.

2-60   "   ROGERS Joseph, and Mary Lewis; m. by Stephen Hoxsie, Justice, Jan. 17, 1739.

2-61   "   Joseph, of James, and Margaret Webb, of Charlestown; m. by Joseph Hoxsie, Justice, April 22, 1742.

2-62   "   Isaac, and Sarah Ross, both of Charlestown; m. by John Hicks, Justice, March 31, 1745.

2-62   ROSS Sarah, and Isaac Rogers; m. March 31, 1745.

1-6   "   Anna, and Job Taylor, Jr.; m. Dec. 10, 1772.

1-33   "   Annie, and Samuel Stanton; m. Oct. 1, 1788.

1-93   "   Katherine, and Moses Stanton; m. June 9, 1844.

S

1-66   SANDS Hannah T., and Peleg S. Thompson; m. March 18, 1805.

2-224   SASH Hannah, and Isaac Dick; m. Oct. 25, 1753.

2-103   SAUNDERS Tobias, of Westerly, and Martha Hall, of John, of Charlestown; m. by Joseph Crandall, Justice, April 9, 1752.

2-171   "   Tacy, and John Allen; m. May 19, 1763.

1-21   "   Mary, and William Scribens; m. May 31, 1781.

1-83   "   Hannah, and Jason B. Greene; m. March 18, 1839.

1-90   "   Mary Ann, and Charles Peckham; m. Oct. 17, 1841.

1-21   SCRIBENS William, and Mary Saunders, of Isaac, both of Charlestown; m. by Elder John Burdick, May 31, 1781.

2-60   SEAGER Judeth, and Elisha Clarke; m. Dec. 18, 1739.

2-224   SHAW Mrs. Jemima, and Stanto York, April 30, 1730.

2-101   SHEFFIELD Nathaniel, and Rebecca Stanton, both of Charlestown; m. Feb. 6, 1740.

2-60   "   Martha, and Thomas Spencer, Jr.; m. June 18, 1741.

2-35   "   Abigail, and Jos. Stanton; m. March 6, 1748.

1-35   "   Samuel, of George, of Westerly, and Annie Browning, of John, of Charlestown; m. by Jos. Crandall, Justice, Dec. 3, 1778.

1-36   "   Lydia, and James Kenyon; m. April 22, 1786.

1-50   "   George, and Rhoda Burch; m. by John Cross, Justice, Jan. 3, 1802.

1-66   "   Lydia, and Gardiner Morey, April 16, 1804.

1-69   "   Nathaniel, of Charlestown, and Freelove Hancock, of Stonington, Conn.; m. by Nathaniel Miner, Justice, Jan. 13, 1805.

1-69   "   Catherine, and Zebulon Hancock, Feb. 15, 1807.

1-72   "   Sally, and Samuel Burdick; m. Jan. 21, 1808.

2-62   SHELDON John, of South Kingstown, and Elizabeth Wells, of Charlestown; m. by Nathaniel Lewis, Justice, May 29, 1744.

1-24   "   Abigail, and Thomas Vars; m. Feb. 10, 1785.

1-14   SHERMAN Elizabeth, and James Congdon; m. Jan. 23, 1773.

1-81   "   George Hazard, and Sophia Davis; m. by Elder Christopher Avery, Dec. 14, 1814.

1-66   SIMON Mary, and Lemuel Olney, March 25, 1844.

2-103   SMITH Abigail, and Robert Knowles; m. April 22, 1750.

2-60   SPENCER Thomas, Jr., of East Greenwich, and Martha Sheffield of Charlestown; m. by William Clarke, Justice, June 18, 1741.

2-60   STANTON John, and Susannah Lanphere; m. by John Babcock, Justice, Oct. 16, 1734.

2-101   "   Jos., Jr., and Mary Champlain; m. by Elder John Maxson, Aug. 9, 1738.

2-101   "   Rebecca, and Nathaniel Sheffield; m. Feb. 6, 1740.

2-35   "   Jos., of Daniel, and Abigail Sheffield; m. by Benj'n Hoxsie, Justice, March 6, 1748.

2-227   "   Esther, and Ichabod Babcock; m. March 17, 1756.

2-162	STANTON	Rebecca, and John Champlin; m. Dec. 14, 1756.
1-2	"	Jos., Jun., of Charlestown, and Thankful Babcock, of Westerly; m. by Joseph Park, Clerg., July 14, 1762.
1-33	"	Samuel, of Daniel, and Annie Ross, of Peleg, both of Charlestown; m. by Elder John Gardiner, Oct. 1, 1788.
1-48	"	Samuel, of this town, and Elizabeth Reynolds, of South Kingstown; m. by Thomas Hoxsie, Senator, April 11, 1799.
1-48	"	John B., of Job, and Hannah Crandall, of Enock; m. by Peleg Cross, Justice, Oct. 12, 1800.
1-68	"	Ethan, of Augustus, and Nancy Stanton, of Henry; m. by Peleg Cross, Justice, Feb. 9, 1807.
1-68	"	Nancy, and Ethan Stanton, Feb. 9, 1807.
1-83	"	John, son of Samuel, and Celia Knowles, of Jos.; m. by Eld. Thomas Tillinghast, May 26, 1833.
1-84	"	Mary, and James N. Kenyon; m. March 23, 1840.
1-93	"	Moses, and Katherine Ross, both of the Narragansett Tribe; m. by Eld. Weeden Barber, June 9, 1844.
1-97	"	Mary, and Job Taylor, of ——; m. March 24, 1849.
2-170	STILES	John, and Lucy Johnson; m. by Peleg Cross, Justice, Feb. 11, 1760.
1-51	STILLMAN	Lois, and Daniel Edwards; m. Sept. 16, 1797.
1-25	SUNDERLAND	Susannah, and Isaac Peckham; m. July 27, 1786.
1-05	SWAN	Daniel, of Stonington, and Hannah Hawkins, of Charlestown; m. by Senator Thomas Hoxsie, April 3, 1804.

T

2-171	TAYLOR	Martha, and Ebenezer Adams; m. Sept. 14, 1763.
1-6	"	Job, Jr., of Charlestown, and Anna Ross, of Isaac, of Westerly; m. by Jos. Park, Clerg., Dec. 10, 1772.
1-15	"	Phebe, and Jonathan Ellis; m. May 17, 1778.
1-18	"	Phebe, and Asa Crandall; m. Dec. 28, 1780.
1-42	"	Ruth, and Lodowick Hoxsie; m. Jan. 4, 1795.
1-65	"	Patty, and Potter Crandall, April 11, 1803.
1-74	"	Job, of Nathan, and Amie Champlain, of Samuel, of Westerly; m. by Rev. Jesse Babcock, Nov. 9, 1809.
1-91	"	Joseph W., and Lucinda ——; m. at Manville, Conn., July 4, 1813.
1-97	"	Job, and Mary Stanton, both of Charlestown; m. by Rev. Joseph P. Brown, March 24, 1849.
1-20	TEFFT	Sarah, and Asa Crandall; m. Sept. 12, 1782.
1-34	"	Sarah, and Nathan Kenyon, Jr.; m. April 12, 1789.
1-51	"	Abigail, and Robert Greene; m. Dec. 27, 1798.
1-93	THOMAS	Sarah M., and William H. Hazard; m. Dec. 30, 1844.
1-32	THOMPSON	Lodowick, of Westerly, of Elias, Jr., and Hannah Burdick, of Samuel, of Charlestown; m. by Peleg Cross, Justice, Aug. 29, 1788.
1-41	"	Elizabeth, and Amos Greene; m. Dec. 25, 1793.
1-66	THOMPSON	Peleg S., of Charlestown, and Hannah T. Sands, of New Shoreham; m. by John Gorton, Warden, March 18, 1805.
1-85	"	Joseph, and Harriet Harvey; m. by Dan. King, Justice, Feb. 9, 1840.
1-65	TIGER	Henry, and Jane Hall; m. by Peleg Cross, Justice, March —, 1804.
1-50	TRIM	Hannah, and Bristol Congdon, Jr., (col.) Jan. 3, 1802.
1-13	TUCKER	Benjamin, and Mary Johnson, of Gideon, both of Charlestown; m. April 15, 1777.
1-33	"	Newman, and Mary Clarke, both of Charlestown; m. by Peleg Cross, Justice, Nov. 27, 1788.
1-86	"	Jonathan, of South Kingstown, and Mary Perry, of this town; m. by Rev. John H. Baker, Sept. 30, 1840.
1-92	"	Joseph B., and Dorcas T. Webster; m. by Joseph H. Griffin, Justice, July 19, 1842.
1-99	"	Hannah, and Thomas M. Webster; m. March 3, 1850.

U V

1-24   VARS Thomas, of Isaac, of Westerly, and Abigail Sheldon, of Isaac, of South Kingstown; m. by Joseph Crandall, Justice, Feb. 10, 1785.

W

1-80   WARD Samuel, of New Shoreham, and Mary Perry, of Charlestown; m. at Stonington, Conn., by Coddington Billings, Justice, Jan. 12, 1820.

2-61   WEBB Margaret, and Joseph Rogers; m. April 22, 1742.

2-62   "   Mehitable, and Jonathan James; m. Jan. 17, 1744.

2-77   WEBSTER Margaret, and Joseph Eanos; m. Sept. 20, 1716.

2-61   "   Mary, and Joseph Woodmansee; m. Aug. 17, 1741.

2-61   "   James, and Hannah Woodmansee; m. by John Hicks, Justice, Sept. 12, 1742.

1-92   "   Dorcas T., and Joseph B. Tucker, July 19, 1842.

1-99   "   Thomas M., and Hannah Tucker; m. by Elder Henry Clarke, March 3, 1850.

1-28   WELCH John, of Charlestown, and Lydia Burdick, of Hopkinton; m. by Peleg Cross, Justice, Aug. 27, 1774.

1-21   "   Katherine, and Simeon Crandall; m. Feb. 22, 1781.

2-61   WELLS Dorcas, and Joshua Rathbone; m. May 4, 1742.

2-62   "   Elizabeth, and John Sheldon; m. May 29, 1744.

2-35   WESCOTT Tabitha, and Jonathan Clarke; m. Feb. 8, 1739.

2-103   WILCOX Joseph, and Mary Burdick, both of Charlestown; m. by William Hern, Justice, July 26, 1748.

1-67   "   Ann, and Benjamin Babcock, Jan. 26, 1806.

1-77   "   Joseph, 2d, and Mariah Bliven; m. by Elder Jesse Babcock, Jan. 20, 1814.

1-95   "   Maria, and Samuel B. Hoxsie; m. Sept. 10, 1846.

2-168   WILLIAMS Cahoone, of Thomas, of South Kingstown, and Margaret Congdon, of James, of Charlestown; m. by Gideon Hoxsie, Justice, March 25, 1769.

2-61   WOODMANSEE Joseph, and Hannah Lyster, both of Westerly; m. by Christopher Allen, Justice, July 7, 1719.

2-60   "   Mary, and Thomas Lillibridge; m. June 12, 1726.

2-61   "   Abigail, and Richard Bailey; m. April 25, 1729.

2-60   "   Keziah, and Joseph Eanos, Jr.; m. Dec. 21, 1738.

2-61   "   Joseph, of Joseph, and Mary Webster, of John, both of Charlestown; m. by Stephen Hoxsie, Justice, Aug. 17, 1741.

2-61   "   Hannah, and James Webster; m. Sept. 12, 1742.

1-27   WORDEN Abigail, and Joseph Cross; m. April 25, 1786.

1-49, 51   "   Gardiner, of Christopher, and Nancy Worden, of William; m. by Peleg Cross, Justice, March 18, 1793.

1-49, 51   "   Nancy, and Gardiner Worden; m. March 18, 1793.

X Y Z

2-224   YORK Stanton, of Charlestown, and Mrs. Jemima Shaw, of Stonington, Conn.; m. at Stonington, by Rev. Ebenezer Rosseter, April 30, 1730.

1-162   "   Hopestill, and Oliver Crary; m. March 16, 1756.

2-167   "   Hannah Stanton, and Benjamin Park; m. (Prob.) Dec. 4, 1757.

1-69   "   Stephen, and Mary Bliven; m. by Peleg Cross, Justice, March 19, 1807.

CHARLESTOWN.

BIRTHS AND DEATHS.

A

1-19	ARES Ezra, of Joseph, and Mary,	Feb. 23, 1774.
1-19	" Solomon,	May 17, 1775.
1-19	" Mary,	April 9, 1777.
1-19	" Abigail,	Nov. 18, 1779.
1-19	" Silas,	April 1, 1782.
2-32	AUSTIN Joseph, of David and Dinah,	Feb. 1, 1731.
2-32	" Martha,	Dec. 7, 1733.
2-32	" Mary,	Sept. 5, 1735.
2-32	" Dinah,	Jan. 8, 1738.
2-32	" David,	July 21, 1740.
2-32	" Mercy,	Jan. 16, 1743.

B

1-79	BABCOCK Welcome B., son of Jared,	Nov. 22, 1819.
1-79	" Daniel L.,	June 19, 1822.
1-79	" Elias L.,	Dec. 9, 1829.
1-13	BARTLETT Leander, son of Dr John,	Nov. 26, 1777.
1-13	" Paschal Paoli,	Nov. 2, 1779.
1-13	" Susannah,	Feb. 25, 1777.
2-34	BASSETT William, born	June 2, 1703.
2-34	" Experience, his wife,	Dec. 15, 1702.
2-34	" Mary, of William and Experience,	March 24. 1735.
2-34	" Martha,	Aug. 22, 1737.
2-34	" Lettise,	March 19, 1740.
2-34	" Sarah,	March 18, 1744.
2-34	" James,	March 18, 1744.
2-31	BOSS Richard, of Jeremiah and Martha,	Feb. 26, 1724.
2-31	" Edward,	April 20, 1725.
2-31	" Susannah,	Feb. 9, 1728.
2-31	" Jeremiah,	May 17, 1729.
2-31	" Martha,	Feb. 12, 1731.
2-31	" Peter,	Sept. 30, 1732.
2-31	" Joseph,	March 2, 1734.
2-31	" John,	Oct. 14, 1735.
2-31	" Hannah,	Oct. 11, 1737.
2-31	" Jonathan,	July 14, 1739.
2-33	BRAMAN Freelove, of Benjamin and Martha,	Dec. 9, 1729.
2-173	BROWNING William, of John and Annie (of John),	Dec. 1, 1755.
2-173	" Annie,	May 6, 1757.
2-173	" Ruth,	Feb. 9, 1759.
2-173	" John,	Jan. 1, 1761.
2-173	" Ephraim,	Jan. 16, 1763.
1-10	BURDICK James, of Ephraim and Anna,	Dec. 17, 1766.
1-10	" Anna,	Feb. 20, 1768.
1-10	" Ruth,	Oct. 11, 1769.
1-10	" Benjamin,	June 18, 1772.
1-10	" Sarah,	May 25, 1774.

1-75	BURDICK James, Jr., of James,	March 8, 1790.
1-75	" Edith,	April 11, 1793.
1-75	" Joshua R.,	July 14, 1794.
1-75	" Nancy,	July 10, 1796.
1-75	" Isaiah,	Sept. 28, 1799.
1-75	" Prudence,	April 23, 1802.
1-75	" Wealthy,	May 9, 1805.
1-75	" Sally,	April 3, 1809.
1-75	" Ephraim,	April 6, 1812.

C

2-163	CHAMPLAIN Thankful, of John.	Nov. 10, 1756.
2-163	" John,	July 10, 1759.
2-163	" Hannah,	Nov. 29, 1763.
1-20	" Thankful, of John and Hannah,	July 9, 1782.
1-20	" Sarah,	Sept. 30, 1785.
1-20	" John,	Oct. 11, 1787.
1-20	" Mary,	Nov. 30, 1788.
1-20	" Hannah,	Nov. 5, 1790.
1-102	CHURCH Charles, Aug. 26, 1737, died Dec. 21, 1785.	
1-102	" Susannah, his wife, Sept. 4, 1741, died Aug. 8, 1831.	
1-102	" Lydia, of Charles, and Susannah,	March 21, 1759.
1-102	" Sylvester,	June 28, 1761.
1-102	" Sylvester,	died May 3, 1762.
1-102	" Penelope,	Aug. 8, 1763.
1-102	" Asa,	July 13, 1766.
1-102	" Anna,	Oct. 1, 1768.
1-102	" Elizabeth,	July 21, 1771.
1-102	" Charles, Jr.,	April 17, 1774.
1-102	" Mary,	April 8, 1776.
1-102	" Samuel K.,	May 21, 1778.
1-102	" Rebecca,	Nov. 4, 1780.
1-102	" Rebecca,	died Dec. 16, 1782.
1-102	" Susannah,	July 13, 1782.
1-102	" Rebecca, 2d,	April 17, 1784.
1-102	" Anna, wife of Sylvester 2d,	died March 21, 1795.
1-103	" Asa, of Charles and Susannah, July 13. 1766.	
1-103	" Dorcas, wife of Asa, Sept. 24, 1769.	
1-103	" Charles, of Asa and Dorcas,	Aug. 25, 1794.
1-103	" Dorcas,	Oct. 18, 1796.
1-103	" Mary,	July 20, 1800.
1-103	" Mary,	died Oct. 5, 1801.
1-103	" Mary, 2d,	June 22, 1802.
1-103	" Joseph C.,	April 7. 1805.
1-103	" Anna,	Oct. 23, 1807.
1-103	" Asa, Jr.,	April 13, 1810.
1-103	" Albert,	March 4, 1813.
2-31	CLARKE William, born	May 27, 1673.
2-31	" Hannah (Knight), his wife,	April 3, 1680.
2-31	" William, of William and Hannah,	Aug. 26, 1701.
2-31	" Jonathan,	Oct. 18, 1702.
2-31	" Hannah,	Sept. 8, 1704.
2-31	" Thomas,	March 13, 1706.
2-31	" Ruth,	July 15, 1708.
2-31	" Robert,	Oct. 28, 1710.
2-31	" Judith,	Aug. 8, 1712.
2-32	" Elisha,	July 10, 1714.
2-32	" Caleb,	July 20, 1716.
2-32	" James, of William and Rebecca, Aug. 3, 1732.	
2-32	" Ann,	(prob.) Feb. 15, 1734.
2-32	" Hannah,	Feb. 15, 1734.
2-32	" William,	Feb. 19, 1736.
2-32	" Gideon,	Oct. 15, 1738.

2-33	CLARKE Ruth, of William and Rebecca,		Jan. 22, 1742.
2-33	" Peter,		April 18, 1745.
2-33	" Joshua,		Feb 19, 1749.
2-35	" Jonathan, of Jonathan and Tabitha, Dec. 17, 1739.		
2-35	" Abraham,		March 29, 1731.
2-35	" Josiah,		July 14, 1742.
2-33	" Almy, of Simeon, Aug. 23, 1737.		
2-33	" Thankful, Feb. 23, 1738.		
2-36	" Elisba, of Elisha and Judith, March 5, 1741.		
2-36	" Robert,		April 9, 1742
2-36	" Benjamin, of Ichabod and Mary, Dec. 5, 1773.		
1-47	" John, of Simeon,		Sept. 4, 1786.
1-47	" Stephen,		Sept. 10, 1789.
1-47	" Henry,		May 17, 1792.
1-47	" Simeon,		Sept. 22, 1801.
1-47	" Jabez,		Jan. 8, 1806.
1-47	" Mary, of Stephen (Blanford, Mass.),		Oct. 23, 1816.
1-47	" Sarah,		Oct. 23, 1816.
2-164	COLLINS, John, of John and Mehitable,		April 13, 1745.
2-164	" Susannah,		Feb. 16, 1747.
2-164	" Amos,		July 27, 1749.
2-164	" Benjamin,		Sept. 16, 1751.
2-164	" Samuel,		April 24, 1754.
2-164	" Sarah,		Dec. 6, 1756.
1-74	" James K., of James and Hannah,		Aug. 9, 1802.
1-74	" Clara,		Jan. 17, 1803.
1-74	" Richard B.,		March 26, 1805.
1-75	" Jedediah,		March 25, 1808.
1-75	" Sarah,		Dec. 30, 1809.
1-75	" Esther,		Dec. 4, 1811.
1-75	" Elkanah B.,		Feb. 26, 1814.
1-75	" Lucy A.,		April 25, 1820.
1-75	" Anna S.,		Feb. 3, 1822.
2-76	CONGDON James 3d, of James and Silence,		July 23, 1732.
2-76	" Benjamin,		Oct. 23, 1733.
2-76	" Margaret,		June 7, 1735.
2-76	" Gideon,		March 10, 1737.
2-76	" Joseph,		Jan. 30, 1739.
2-76	" Christopher,		Nov. 9, 1740.
2-76	" Stephen,		June 26, 1743.
1-5	" Margaret, of John and Sarah,		Aug. 6, 1741.
1-5	" James,	March 4, 1742, died July 2, 1746.	
1-5	" John,	Nov. 6, 1739, d. Jan. 19, 1740-1.	
1-5	" Sarah, wife of above John,		died Nov. 8, 1743.
1-5	" Sarah (Hoxsie), of John and Mary, born Sept. 13, 1731.		
1-5	" James, of John and Sarah (2d wife),		Oct. 13, 1747.
1-5	" Joseph,		Oct. 13, 1749.
1-5	" Sarah,		March 12, 1752.
1-5	" Isaac,		Dec. 16, 1754.
1-5	" Isaac,		died June 14, 1758.
1-5	" Mary,		Dec. 4, 1756.
1-5	" Catherine,		March 31, 1759.
1-5	" Martha,		April 5, 1761.
1-5	" Penelope,		April 5, 1761.
1-5	" Mary,		died June 26, 1763.
1-5	" Mary, 2d,		Nov. 30, 1763.
1-5	" Frances,		March 9, 1771.
1-5	" John,		Jan. 29, 1773.
1-5	" Sarah,		died June 3, 1774.
1-39	" Peleg C., of Joseph and Mary,		Oct. 30, 1776.
1-39	" Benjamin,		Nov. 6, 1778.
1-39	" Benjamin,		died May 23, 1789.
2-169	CRARY Joseph, of Oliver and Hopestill,		Jan. 25, 1757.
2-169	" Christopher,		June 24, 1759.
1-34	CRANDALL Zilpha, of Caleb and Patience,		July 15, 1767.
1-34	" Benjamin,		Nov. 10, 1769.

1-34	CRANDALL Mary, of Caleb and Patience,		Nov. 16, 1771.
1-34	"	Amie,	Nov. 16, 1771.
1-34	"	Nathan,	Oct. 20, 1773.
1-11	"	Elizabeth, of James and Elizabeth,	Aug. 8, 1769.
1-11	"	Damarius,	July 26, 1776.
1-11	"	Hannah, of Jesse and Zilpah,	Sept. 17, 1778.
1-11	"	Polly,	April 21, 1780.
1-11	"	Jesse,	Oct. 22, 1781.
1-11	"	Potter,	July 18, 1788.
1-11	"	Asa,	Feb. 17, 1789.
1-22	"	Member, of Gideon and Judea,	April 28, 1783.
1-38	CROSS Peleg, born Dec. 6, 1723; died Dec. 27, 1812.		
1-38	"	Mary, wife of Peleg; born July 30, 1735; died May 27, 1812.	
1-38	"	Mary, of Peleg and Mary,	May 1, 1755.
1-38	"	Thankful,	Sept. 7, 1757.
1-38	"	Peleg,	June 24, 1759.
1-38	"	Mercy,	April 28, 1761.
1-38	"	Anna,	Dec. 8, 1763.
1-38	"	Ruhamah,	July 27, 1767.
2-172	"	Ruth, of Samuel and Annie,	Feb. 20, 1763.
2-172	"	Dorcas,	Feb. 15, 1765.
2-172	"	Martha,	March 17, 1767.
2-139	"	Elizabeth, of Edward and Elizabeth,	Jan. 9, 1764.
1-19	"	Mary, of Peleg, Jr., and Catey,	Nov. 29, 1781.
1-19	"	Sarah,	March 31, 1783.
1-19	"	Peleg,	Dec. 17, 1784.
1-19	"	Catey C.,	Dec. 20, 1786.
1-19	"	Anna,	March 26, 1789.
1-19	"	John C.,	March 21, 1791.
1-46	"	Nathaniel L.,	March 26, 1793.
1-46	"	Benjamin C.,	May 19, 1795.
1-46	"	Joseph H.,	May 28, 1797.
1-46	"	Celia,	May 31, 1800.
1-46	"	George W.,	Oct. 22, 1802.
1-99	"	James F., of Charles and Martha B.,	Dec. 3, 1843.
1-99	"	Carrie E.,	July 22, 1845.
1-99	"	Mary A.,	Dec. 8, 1846.
1-99	"	Millard F.,	Sept. 10, 1850.
1-99	"	Frank P.,	April 10, 1853.
1-99	"	George C.,	June 27, 1855.
		Present Town Clerk.	

D

1-100	DEVOLL William W., of David S. and Mary C.,		July 28, 1841.
2-79	DODGE Elizabeth, of Joseph and Mary,		July 19, 1744.
2-77	EANOS Joseph, Jun., of Joseph and Margaret,		June 10, 1718.
2-77	"	Mercy,	Nov. 1, 1720.
2-77	"	Margaret,	Oct. 25, 1728.
2-77	"	Benjamin,	Feb. 26, 1732.
2-77	"	Hannah,	April 7, 1736.
2-77	"	Amie,	June 30, 1738.
2-24	"	Mercy, of Joseph, Jun., and Keziah,	Sept. 1, 1739.

E

1-51	EDWARDS Joseph, of Daniel and Lois,		Nov. 13, 1782.
1-51	"	William,	May 1, 1787.
1-51	"	Nancy,	Jan. 20, 1789.
1-51	"	Daniel,	Oct. 8, 1798.
1-51	"	John,	Sept. 18, 1801.

F

2-32, 36	FOSTER Mary, of Caleb and Elizabeth,	May 5, 1738.
2-32, 36	" Dorcas,	March 29, 1740.
2-32, 36	" Caleb,	Jan. 18, 1741.
1-30	FRANKLIN Elizabeth, R., of Abel and Anna (Groton, Ct.), on Dec. 28, 1773.	
1-96	FRY Mary E., of James,	April 28, 1839.
1-96	" Martha S.,	Oct. 21, 1842.

G

2-169	GREENMAN Silas, of Edward and Sarah,	June 11, 1724.
2-169	" Margaret,	Oct. 17, 1725.
2-169	" Abigail,	Nov. 21, 1727.
2-169	" Edward,	March 9, 1731.
2-169	" Catherine,	Aug. 18, 1732.
2-169	" Mary,	April 12. 1735.
2-169	" Prudence.	Oct. 28, 1736.
2-169	" Chloe,	April 8, 1739.
2-169	" Nathan,	Feb. 21, 1740.
2-170	" Hannah, of Silas and Sarah (also 2-225),	Aug. 4, 1753.
2-170	" Mary (also 2-225),	June 26, 1755.
2-170	" Timothy (also 2-225),	March 22, 1757.
2-170	" Sarah (also 2-225),	Sept. 1, 1760.
2-164	GREENE Amos, of Amos and Amie,	March 25,1741.
2-164	" William,	Feb. 13, 1743.
2-164	" Hannah,	May 7, 1746.
2-164	" Elizabeth,	Aug. 17, 1748.
2-164	" Ruth,	May 17, 1751.
2-164	" John,	Aug. 13, 1754.
2-164	" Amie,	Sept. 14, 1756.
1-34	" Dorcas, of Braddock,	Dec. 7, 1786.
1-34	" Hazard,	Oct. 22, 1789.
1-167	" William Ellery, of Lucretia,	Jan. 15, 1799.
1-51	" William, of Robert and Abigail,	Nov. 24, 1799.
1-51	" Jeremiah,	March 28, 1801.
1-88	" Edward L.,	Dec. 28, 1794.
1-88	" Elizabeth —, wife of Edward L., Nov. 2, 1796.	
1-88	" Martha E., of Edward L. and Elizabeth,	April 17, 1823.
1-88	" Martha E.,	d. Sept. 28, 1923.
1-88	" Mary A.,	Oct. 15, 1824.
1-88	" Mary A. K.,	Oct. 11, 1826.
1-88	" Ruth E.,	Aug. 9, 1828.
1-88	" Almira F.,	Aug. 2, 1830.
1-88	" Martha J.,	March 12, 1832.
1-88	" Mariah L.,	May 10, 1834.
1-88	" Hannah A.,	Jan. 9, 1837.
1-88	" Dorcas D. B.,	June 7, 1840.
1-88	" Braddock C., of Nathan, April 27, 1827.	
2-35	GRIFFITH George, of Philip and Elizabeth.	Aug. 30, 1743.
2-32	GRINNELL Susannah, of Daniel and Jane,	Dec. 24, 1734.
2-32	" Jane,	May 30, 1736.

H

1-40	HALL Hannah, of Rhodes and Hannah,	Dec. 6, 1779.
1-40	" Elizabeth,	Jan. 9, 1781.
1-40	" Rhodes,	Aug. 16, 1784.
1-40	" Lydia,	March 23, 1786.
1-40	" Thankful,	May 5, 1789.
1-40	" Dorcas,	Aug. 6, 1792.
1-32	" Joseph,	died April 17, 1798.

2-79	HARVEY William, of William,	Dec. 5, 1747.
2-79	" Solomon,	Nov. 5, 1749.
1-73	HAZARD William Wanton, of Brenton and Ann,	March 11, 1810.
2-35	HICKS Ephraim, of Elizabeth,	Jan. 15, 1744.
1-79	HISCOX Arnold, Jr., of Arnold,	July 15, 1818.
1-79	" Anna,	March 29, 1821.
2-33	HOXSIE Sarah, of Joseph and Mary,	Sept. 17, 1731.
2-33	" Joseph, Jr.,	May 8, 1733.
2-33	" Deborah,	May 23, 1735.
2-33	" Mary,	June 26, 1737.
2-30	" Barnabas, of Stephen and Elizabeth,	Nov. 1, 1735.
2-30	" Stephen,	May 8, 1738.
2-30	" Elizabeth,	July 13, 1740.
2-30	" Edward,	Jan. 19, 1742.
2-30	" Hannah,	Jan. 7, 1744.
1-29	" Benjamin, Jr., of Benjamin and Sarah,	March 14, 1742.
1-29	" Bathsheba,	Nov. 13, 1744.
1-29	" Sarah,	Oct. 22, 1746.
1-29	" Ann,	Aug. 3, 1748.
1-29	" Mary,	July 5, 1750.
1-29	" Sarah, mother of above children, May 9, 1722; died July 11, 1750.	
1-29	" Sarah, of Benjamin and Mary (2d wife),	July 25, 1753.
1-29	" Thomas,	Feb. 13, 1755.
2-166	" Gideon, of Gideon and Dorcas,	July 11, 1752.
2-166	" Martha,	Sept. 6, 1754.
2-166	" Peleg,	Sept. 15, 1756.
1-37	" Mary, of Stephen, Jr., and Elizabeth,	Dec. 8, 1767.
1-37	" Lodowick,	Dec. 22, 1769.
1-37	" Luke,	Oct. 14, 1771.
1-37	" John,	Aug. 12, 1773.
1-37	" Solomon,	Aug. 2, 1778.
1-37	" Ruth,	Feb. 18, 1784.
1-43	" Lucy, of Peleg and Lucy,	March 29, 1779.
1-43	" Peleg,	May 17, 1780.
1-43	" Dorcas,	March 30, 1782.
1-43	" John,	March 12, 1784.
1-43	" Esther,	May 15, 1785.
1-43	" Zebulon,	May 22, 1787.
1-43	" Masah,	June 7, 1789.
1-43	" Ichabod,	Aug. 30, 1791.
1-43	" Hannah B.,	April 7, 1793.
1-36	" Hazard, of Thomas and Mary,	June 17, 1782.
1-36	" Mary,	April 28, 1786.
1-76	" Benjamin, of Capt. Hazard and Cloe,	Nov. 2, 1807.
1-76	" Mary,	Jan. 18, 1810.
1-76	" Lydia A.,	Aug. 27, 1811.
1-76	" Gordon H.,	March 24, 1813.
	President of the Town Council, 1882.	
1-76	" Thomas S., of Capt. Hazard and Cloe,	Feb. 27, 1815.
1-76	" Abbie C.,	July 2, 1818.
1-76	" Sarah S.,	Sept. 14, 1820.
1-76	" Samuel B.,	Oct. 9, 1824.

I J

2-30	JOHNSON Stephen, March 25, 1704.	
2-30	" Susannah, wife of Stephen, Oct. 4, 1709.	
2-30	" Ezekiel, of Stephen and Susannah,	Oct. 23, 1728.
2-30	" Stephen,	Sept. 24, 1730.
2-30	" Elizabeth,	Jan. 25, 1732.
2-30	" Mary,	May 24, 1735.
2-30	" Susannah,	Nov. 18, 1737.
2-30	" Sarah,	Nov. 22, 1740.
2-30	" Stephen,	March 17, 1744.

2-30	JOHNSON Hannah, of Stephen and Susannah,		March 29, 1747.
2-35	"	Joseph, of Joseph and Mary,	April 17, 1730.
2-76	"	Joseph, of Joseph,	April 17, 1740.
2-76	"	John,	Jan. 23, 1743.
2-76	"	Mary,	Feb. 13, 1745.
2-76	"	Manuel,	Feb. 3, 1746.
2-76	"	Michael,	April 6, 1752.
2-76	"	Job,	March 2, 1755.
2-76	"	Jared,	July 29, 1757.
2-227	"	Joseph, of Joseph and Judeth,	March 19, 1763.
2-227	"	Benjamin,	Oct. 12, 1764.
2-227	"	Eliphal,	Sept. 10, 1766.
2-135	JONES Robert,		died May 2, 1775.

K

2-6	KENYON Mary, of Ebenezer and Amie,		March 22, 1722.
2-6	"	Sarah,	March 28, 1724.
2-6	"	Ruth,	April 1, 1727.
2-6	"	Amie,	Oct. 12, 1730.
2-6	"	William,	Dec. 5, d. 28, 1732.
2-6	"	Catharine,	Dec. 27, 1733.
2-6	"	Eunice,	Feb. 2, 1736.
2-6	"	Infant,	March 29, d. April 2, 1739.
2-32	"	David, Jr., of David and Mary,	Jan. 7, 1724.
2-32	"	Hannah,	Dec. 21, 1727.
2-32	"	Thomas,	Nov. 7, 1729.
2-32	"	William,	Jan. 30, 1731.
2-32	"	Mary,	Nov. 24, 1733.
2-32	"	Robert,	Jan. 10, 1735.
2-32	"	Peleg,	Feb. 3, 1737.
2-32	"	Elizabeth,	Jan. 25, 1740.
2-32	"	Sarah,	April 24, 1742.
2-33	"	Pheneus,	Oct. 3, 1744.
2-77	"	John, of John and Mary,	Sept. 29, 1730.
2-77	"	Remington,	Feb. 6, 1732.
2-77	"	Mary,	Feb. 4, 1734.
2-77	"	Dorcas,	Aug. 4, 1737.
2-77	"	Hannah,	Nov. 1, 1739.
2-77	"	Nathaniel,	Jan. 4, 1741.
2-77	"	Elizabeth.	June 20, 1743.
2-79	"	George, of Thomas and Catherine,	Feb. 4, 1733.
2-79	"	Elizabeth,	March 5, 1735.
2-79	"	Thomas,	March 14, 1738.
2-79	"	Stephen,	Jan. 25, 1741.
2-79	"	John, .	Feb. 25, 1744.
1-33	KERGROIN John Hazard, of Amo',		March 26, 1787.
1-33	"	Abigail,	Sept. 11, 1789.
1-37	KNOWLES Charles, of Daniel and Antries,		May 5, 1776.

L

2-35, 76	LADD James, of John,		April 22, 1746.
2-35, 76	"	Daniel,	Dec. 7, 1748.
2-76	"	Elizabeth,	Dec. 7, 1750.
2-76	"	Mary,	May 27, 1752.
2-76	"	Dorcas,	May 27, 1754.
2-76	"	John,	May 8, 1756.
2-76	"	Lydia,	July 8, 1759.
2-76	LARKIN Reuben T., of Reuben and Arliville,		July 30, 1844.

2-34	LEWIS Nathaniel, of Nathaniel and Mary,		Feb. 28, 1732.
2-34	"	Amos,	April 29, 1731.
2-34	"	Mary,	July 31, 1735.
2-34	"	Jane,	June 22, 1737.
2-34	"	Ruhama,	Oct. 27, 1739.
2-34	"	Elijah,	Aug. 10, 1741.
2-172	"	Augustus J., of Amos and Mary,	Oct. 10, 1759.
1-80	"	Susannah, of Jos. H. and Margaret, Dec. 17, 1815;	
			d. March 18, 1818.
1-80	"	Mary L.,	May 27, 1818.
1-80	"	Nathaniel,	Jan. 16, 1822.
1-80	"	Augustus,	Jan. 12, 1824.
1-80	"	Oliver F.,	May 20, 1827.
2-34	LILLIBRIDGE Sarah, of Thomas and Mary,		March 20, 1727.
2-34	"	Thomas,	Dec. 4, 1729.
2-34	"	Edward,	March 25, 1732.

M

1-12	MACUMBER Abigail, of Jonathan and Sarah,		June 17, 1767.
1-12	"	Annie,	Dec. 30, 1769.
1-12	"	Benjamin,	May 5, 1772
1-12	"	Sarah,	Nov. 13, 1774.
1-12	"	Joseph,	Aug. 24, 1782.
1-12	"	Dianna,	Oct. 4, 1798.
1-77	"	Francis, of Joseph and Fannie,	Feb. 12, 1809.
1-77	"	Abigail,	Oct. 17, 1812.
1-77	"	John R.,	April 12, 1815.
1-77	"	Martha,	Dec. 23, 1817.
1-77	"	Mary B.,	Dec. 21, 1821.
1-33	MICAEL Tury, of Ruth (Indian),		April 9, 1778.
1-33	"	Sarah,	Sept. 9, 1780
1-33	"	Alice,	June 22, 1788.
2-170	MILLARD Martha, of John, Jun.,		July 13, 1753.
2-170	"	Abigail,	July 4, 1755.
2-170	"	Benjamin,	March 22, 1758.
2-170	"	Elizabeth,	June 14, 1760.

N

1-74	NILES Robert, of Paul and Charity (N. Shoreham),		Dec. 1, 1788.
1-74	"	Sands,	(Stonington), June 6, 1793.
1-74	"	Nathaniel,	June 6, 1793.

O P

2-168	PARK Mary, of Benjamin and Hannah S.,		Sept. 8, 1758.
2-168	"	Jonathan,	March 5, 1760.
2-168	"	Joseph,	Nov. 13, 1763.
1-4	"	John, of John and Abigail,	Sept. 23, 1773.
1-4	"	Abigail,	March 17, 1775.
1-4	"	Annie,	Sept. 28, 1776.
1-4	"	Samuel,	Aug. 15, 1778.
1-4	"	Joseph,	June 20, 1780.
1-4	"	Kate K.,	April 28, 1782.
1-4	"	Benjamin,	April 27, 1784.
1-4	"	Marah,	April 5, 1786.
2-233	PECKHAM Hannah, of Daniel and Mary,		Sept. 23, 1720.
2-233	"	Mary,	Feb. 22, 1722.
2-233	"	Daniel, Jun.,	Sept. 25, 1726.
2-233	"	Sarah,	Aug. 31, 1729.
2-233	"	Abel,	Feb. 17, 1733.

2-233	PECKHAM James, of Daniel and Mary,	Nov. 4, 1736.
2-233	" Annie,	Sept. 20, 1742.
2-225	" Mary, of Daniel, Jr., and Mary,	Dec. 19, 1751.
2-225	" Abigail,	April 26, 1752.
2-225	" Daniel,	Oct. 25, 1754.
2-225	" Mary,	Sept. 19, 1756.
2-225	" John H. G. H., of George H.,	Oct. 24, 1775.
1-39	PERRY Rowland, son of Annie Browning,	May 11, 1789.
1-49	" James, of Capt. James and Deborah,	March 1, 1798.
2-9	PETTEY Nathaniel, of William and Mary,	May 17, 1714.
2-34	" Susannah,	July 6, 1716.
2-34	" Alice,	June 4, 1718.
2-34	" Ephraim,	Dec. 12, 1719.
2-34	" William,	June 24, 1722.
2-34	" Joseph,	Oct. 27, 1724.
2-34	" Charles,	Aug. 10, 1727.
2-34	" John,	Nov. 23, 1729.
2-34	" Mary,	Jan. 3, 1732.
2-34	" David,	March 29, 1735.
2-34	" James,	Nov. 14, 1737.
2-76	PIERCE Stephen, of Isaac,	Nov. 25, 1740.
2-76	" Benjamin,	April 9, 1743.
2-76	" James,	Feb. 25, 1744.
2-76	" Timothy,	March 13, 1747.
2-76	" Isaac,	March 8, 1749.
2-79	POTTER Benjamin, of Nathaniel and Mary,	Aug. 9, 1721.
2-79	" Rouse,	April 28, 1728.
2-79	" Mary,	Oct. 10, 1731.
2-79	" Nathaniel,	Aug. 27, 1739.
2-79	" Thomas,	May 9, 1734.
2-79	" Susannah,	Dec. 20, 1742.
2-79	" Ebenezer,	Sept. 4, 1745.
2-36	" Ruth, of Thomas and Martha,	Sept. 13, 1746.
2-163	" Annie, of Robert,	July 7, 1755.
2-163	" Hannah,	March 20, 1758.
2-163	" Elizabeth,	July 28, 1760.
2-163	" Robert,	May 24, 1762.
2-163	" Thomas,	March 1, 1764.

Q R

2-33	RATHBONE Joshua, of Joshua and Dorcas,	Jan. 8, 1742.
2-225	RHODES William, of James and Anna,	Sept. 13, 1753.
2-225	" William, of Deborah,	Jan. 18, 1789.
2-225	" Charles,	Sept. 16, 1797.
2-165	ROSS, Barberry, of Abigail,	June 15, 1743.
2-165	" Annie,	Aug. 16, 1747.

S

2-173	SAULSBURY, Martin,	born Sept. 16, 1767.
1-21	SCRIBENS, Williams, of William and Mary,	April 6, 1782.
2-101	SHEFFIELD, Thomas, of Nathaniel and Hannah,	Nov. 25, 1741.
2-101	" Joseph,	Aug. 15, 1742.
2-101	" Mary,	Jan. 9, 1745.
1-30	" Joseph, of Thomas and Wealthy,	Oct. 14, 1763.
1-30	" Amos,	Feb. 12, 1766.
1-30	" Samuel,	June 27, 1768.
1-30	" Dorcas,	April 11, 1771.
1-30	" James,	Aug. 27, 1773.
1-30	" Thomas,	Jan. 9, 1776.
1-30	" George,	June 27, 1778.

1-30	SHEFFIELD Anna, of Thomas and Wealthy,		Aug. 30, 1780.
1-30	"	Nathaniel,	Dec. 19, 1783.
1-30	"	Abel,	April 27, 1786.
1-35	"	Lydia, of Joseph and Phebe,	July 8, 1781.
1-35	"	Amos,	Nov. 17, 1783.
1-35	"	Joseph,	Feb. 1, 1787.
1-35	"	Jonathan,	Jan. 30, 1790.
1-35	"	Mary, of Stanton and Anna,	March 18, 1785.
1-35	"	Sarah,	April 11, 1787.
1-35	"	Stanton,	Aug. 23, 1789.
1-35	"	Anna,	Nov. 21, 1792.
1-35	"	Belinda,	April 3, 1797.
1-35	"	Benjamin,	June 8, 1799.
1-35	"	Martha,	April 25, 1802.
1-35	"	Elizabeth,	Nov. 6, 1804.
1-35	"	Robert,	April 12, 1807.
1-35	"	Rebecca,	June 21, 1809.
	SHERMAN George Hazard, June 5, 1788.		
	"	Sophia (Davis), his wife, March 9, 1794.	
	"	Thomas Hazard, of Geo. H. and Sophia,	March 10, 1816.
	"	Thomas Hazard,	d. March 20, 1818.
	"	Lucy A.,	May 2, 1818.
	"	Lorina,	March 18, 1820.
	"	Thomas H.,	March 22, 1822.
	"	James,	Sept. 20, 1824.
	"	Catherine W.,	Aug. 3, 1827.
	"	Martha B.,	Feb. 8, 1830.
	"	John R.,	May 22, 1832.
	"	Hannah E.,	Feb. 23, 1835.
	"	Mary E.,	July 23, 1838.
2-36	STANTON Joseph, Jr.; also 101, born April 23, 1717.		
2-36	"	Mary, his wife; also 101, born July 13, 1722.	
2-36	"	Joseph (also 2-101),	July 19, 1739.*
2-36	"	Esther (also 2-101),	Nov. 23, 1741.
2-36	"	Mary (also 2-101),	June 18, 1743.
2-36	"	Augustus (also 2-101),	March 22, 1745.**
2-36	"	Hannah (also 2-101),	Feb. 24, 1747. ***
	Note—In another list the year is given. *1738; **1744, and ***1746, respectively.		
2-36	"	Lodowick (also 2-101),	May 27, 1749.
2-34	"	Robert, of John and Susannah,	Aug. 18, 1735.
2-34	"	Job,	Feb. 16, 1737.
2-34	"	Susannah,	Aug. 17, 1738.
2-34	"	Benjamin,	July 4, 1740.
2-34	"	Hannah,	March 28, 1742.
2-34	"	Elizabeth,	Jan. 2, 1743.
2-34	"	Samuel,	Dec. 2, 1745.
2-135	"	Col. Joseph (70 years old),	April 23, 1752.
2-135	"	Col. Joseph,	died Aug. 2, 1752.
1-31	"	Abigail, of Daniel, Jun., and Sarah,	May 18, 1785.
1-31	"	Thomas,	Jan. 21, 1787.
1-31	"	Abel,	March 28, 1791.
1-47	"	Samuel, of Samuel and Elizabeth,	Oct. 27, 1803.
1-47	"	Sarah A.,	Nov. 23, 1805.
1-47	"	Elizabeth,	Oct. 23, 1808.
1-47	"	John,	July 21, 1810.
1-47	"	Mary,	March 6, 1814.
1-47	"	Elizabeth, mother of above children,	died May 3, 1826.
1-83	"	Caroline E., of John and Celia,	March 10, 1834.
1-83	"	Dorcas,	May 12, 1836.
1-83	"	William,	May 13, 1839.
1-83	"	John H.,	July 16, 1844.
1-83	"	Caroline E.,	died Dec. 11, 1836.
1-83	"	William,	died Dec. 20, 1846.
1-83	"	John H.,	died Jan. 2, 1847.

T

2-36	TANNER Joseph, of John and Jane,	Feb. 2, 1719.
2-36	" Jane,	Jan. 24, 1721.
2-36	" George, of John and Susannah,	Nov. 9, 1723.
2-36	" Sarah,	Oct. 7, 1720.
2-36	" William,	Feb. 28, 1727.
2-36	" John,	Nov. 11, 1730.
2-36	" Susannah,	Feb. 18, 1732.
2-36	" Mary,	Jan. 9, 1734.
2-36	" Esther,	Aug. 22, 1738.
2-36	" Job,	April 5, 1740.
1-68	TAYLOR Nathan, of Nathan and Prudence,	May 4, 1773.
1-68	" Polly,	Dec. 16, 1774.
1-68	" Kittury,	March 25, 1776.
1-68	" Martha,	Jan. 6, 1778.
1-68	" Amie,	Dec. 6, 1780.
1-68	" Phebe,	Feb. 4, 1782.
1-68	" Sarah,	June 26, 1784.
1-68	" Joseph,	Aug. 4, 1786.
1-68	" Job,	June 9, 1789.
1-68	" Gilbert,	March 16, 1791.
1-1	" Phillip, of Joseph and Ruth,	Dec. 12, 1770.
1-1	" Ichabod,	June 28, 1773.
1-74	" Margaret, of Job and Amie,	Oct. 1, 1773.
1-74	" Julia A.,	Sept. 1, 1810.
1-74	" Gilbert,	Aug. 22, 1813.
1-74	" Alvah,	Sept. 22, 1815.
1-74	" Mary,	May 17, 1818.
1-75	" George W.,	Oct. 2, 1820.
1-75	" Harriet,	Oct. 26, 1823.
1-75	" Eliza,	Aug. 2, 1826.
1-75	" Martha,	June 10, 1833.
1-91	" Charles E., of Joseph W. and Lucinda,	June 17, 1814.
1-91	" Charles E.,	d. March 8, 1818.
1-91	" Ransford S., of Joseph and Lucinda,	Oct. 14, 1815.
1-91	" Caroline B.,	Sept. 1, 1817.
1-91	" Caroline B.,	d. Feb. 8, 1819.
1-91	" Sarah A., of Joseph and Lucinda,	Feb. 2, 1819.
1-91	" Margaret M.,	June 13, 1820.
1-91	" John E.,	March 25, 1822.
1-91	" Joseph E.,	March 4, 1824.
1-91	" Lydia M., of Joseph and Lucinda,	Sept. 15, 1825.
1-91	" Job I.,	April 29, 1827.
1-91	" Hannah M.,	Oct. 31, 1829.
1-91	" George A.,	June 24, 1831.
1-91	" Phebe L.,	Jan. 4, 1833.
1-1	TUCKER Susannah,	born Nov. 24, 1766.
1-1	" Newman,	born Jan. 24, 1767.
1-1	" Mary,	born Oct. 31, 1769.
1-1	" Rebecca,	born Oct. 1, 1749.
1-1	" Hannah,	born Oct. 21, 1755.

U V W

2-35	WATSON Simeon, of William and Mary,	Feb. 21, 1726.
2-35	" Abigail,	June 5, 1729.
2-35	" Elizabeth,	June 5, 1732.
2-35	" John,	Jan. 20, 1735.
2-33	WELCH Charles, of William and Catherine,	March 30, 1739.
2-33	" Mary,	Jan. 29, 1741.
2-33	" John,	May 8, 1746.

1-28	WELCH William, from Ireland, died aged 85 years, 10 months and 15 days,		
	March 10, 1796.		
1-28	"	Patrick, of John and Lydia,	March 18, 1775.
1-28	"	John,	Feb. 9, 1776.
1-28	"	Henry,	Dec. 20, 1779.
1-28	"	Katie,	Aug. 9, 1781.
1-28	"	Gilbert,	Nov. 15, 1783.
1-28	"	Sarah,	Feb. 1, 1786; d. April 28, 1786.
1-28	"	Lois, of John and Lydia,	Feb. 16, 1787; d. March 11, 1787.
2-33	WELLS Dorcas, of Peter and Amie, (S. K.),		Sept. 17, 1720.
2-79	WEST Mary, of Clement and Sarah,		Feb. 28, 1726.
2-79	"	Richard,	Dec. 24, 1728.
2-79	"	Clement (N. K.),	Jan. 1, 1731.
2-79	"	Susannah (N. K.),	July 14, 1733.
2-79	"	John,	Dec. 18, 1736.
2-79	"	Elizabeth,	May 20, 1738.
2-79	"	Thomas,	Aug. 6, 1740.
2-79	"	Eliza,	Feb. 6, 1742.
2-79	"	Sarah,	July 23, 1745.
1-78	WILCOX George S., of Joseph,		Feb. 9, 1799.
1-78	"	Mary.	Aug. 11, 1801.
1-78	"	Rebecca,	July 11, 1804.
1-78	"	Edward,	Aug. 1, 1806.
1-78	"	Hannah,	Feb. 25, 1809.
1-78	"	Rebecca,	Aug. 24, 1811.
1-78	"	Nancy,	Feb. 22, 1814.
1-78	"	Charlie W.,	Dec. 6, 1827.
1-78	"	Joseph D.,	Feb. 12, 1829.
1-78	"	Eliza A.,	March 16, 1830.
1-78	"	Susan F.,	March 26, 1831.
1-78	"	John G.,	May 25, 1832.
	Present Rep.		
1-78	"	Nathan,	Nov. 17, 1833.
1-78	"	Benjamin F.,	July 7, 1835.
1-95	"	Governor Edward, died Sept. 7, 1838.	
2-77	WOODMANSEE Keziah, of Joseph and Hannah,		Aug. 10, 1719.
2-77	"	Joseph,	July 28, 1722.
2-77	"	Hannah,	June 25, 1724.

X Y Z

2-223	YORK Hopestill, of Stanton and Jemima,		May 24, 1734.
2-223	"	Jemima,	Feb. 17, 1739.
2-223	"	Anna,	April 7, 1741.
1-44	"	Hannah, of William and Anna,	Nov. 15, 1770.
1-44	"	James,	Feb. 6, 1772.
1-44	"	Isaac,	April 4, 1776.
1-44	"	Augustus,	July 28, 1778.
1-44	"	William,	Oct. 15, 1780.
1-44	"	Elizabeth,	March 5, 1785.
1-44	"	Anna,	Aug. 24, 1788.

Vital Record of Rhode Island.

1636=1850.

FIRST SERIES.

BIRTHS, MARRIAGES AND DEATHS.

A Family Register for the People.

By James N. Arnold,

EDITOR OF THE NARRAGANSETT HISTORICAL REGISTER.

"Is My Name Written in the Book of Life?"

Vol. 5.   RICHMOND.   Part VI.

Published under the Auspices of the General Assembly.

PROVIDENCE, R. I.:
NARRAGANSETT HISTORICAL PUBLISHING COMPANY.
1894.

ACT INCORPORATING THE TOWN OF RICHMOND.

AN ACT for incorporating the north part of the Town of Charlestown, in King's County, into a Township, the same to be distinguished and known by the name of Richmond.

Be it enacted by the General Assembly of this Colony, and by the authority thereof, it is enacted, that the Town of Charlestown, in the County of Kings County, etc., be divided into two Towns, by a river that runs across said Town, known by the name of Pawcatuck River; all the lands to the southward of said river, shall retain the name of CHARLESTOWN; and that all the lands to the northward of said river, be, and hereby is incorporated into a Township, by the name of RICHMOND; and to have and enjoy the like privileges as other Towns in this Colony

And be it further enacted by the authority aforesaid, that each of said Towns shall have, and receive a proportion of the money in, and belonging to the treasury of said Charlestown, according to the money for which the lands in each Town is mortgaged to the Colony; and that all Justices of the Peace and Military Officers living within the bounds of said new Town called Richmond, retain their authority, and act as such therein until the next General Election; and that the eldest Justice of each of said Towns is hereby empowered to grant forth their warrants to some proper officer, whom they shall appoint, to warn the inhabitants of said Towns to assemble and meet together in some proper place, in said Town, on Friday, the 28t day of this instant August, in order to choose deputies, to represent them at the October Session of this Assembly; and also, to choose Town Officers for said Towns, agreeably to the laws of this Colony; and that each Town shall send one grand juror, and one petit juror, to each of the Inferior and Superior Courts in Kings County.

Rhode Island Colonial Records, Vol. V., pages 220, 221.

RICHMOND.

MARRIAGES.

A

1-285   ADAMS Mary, and Nathan Lewis, Dec. 16, 1756.
1-78   "   Anna, and Andrew Nichols, June 14, 1764.
1-78   "   Thomas, and Abigail Larkin; m. by Edward Perry, Justice, July 10, 1764.
1-80   "   Patience, and Thomas Webster, Nov. 17, 1765.
1-135   "   Sarah, and Jedediah Collins, Nov. 29, 1767.
1-84   ALBRO Alice, and Joseph Tefft, Jr., May 22, 1771.
1-128   "   Martha, and Noah Wilcox, Nov. 15, 1789.
2-51   ALEXANDER Esther Ann, and John Allen, Sept. 11, 1848.
       (N. B.—Another entry says L.)
2-51   ALLEN John, and Esther Ann Alexander. (or L.); m. by Rev. Chris. C. Lewis, Sept. 11, 1848.
1-11   AUSTIN Joseph, and Abigail Rogers; m. by Stephen Richmond, Justice, Aug. 26, 1750.
1-285   "   Dinah, and Thomas Rogers, Sept. 7, 1755.
1-286   "   Daniel, and Anna Barber; m. by Samuel Tefft, Justice, April 22, 1757.
1-123   "   Joseph, and Mary Rogers, (widow); m. by Thomas Petit, Justice, Dec. 8, 1777.
1-123   "   Elizabeth, and James Griffeth, March 25, 1779.
2-50   "   Elizabeth, and Clarke Cahoone, Sept. 20, 1847.
1-92   AYLESWORTH Alce, and Moses Clarke, Nov. 18, 1773.

B

1- —   BABCOCK Jane, and Izrael Lewis, about 1696.
2-273   "   Elisha, and Elizabeth ——; m. by John Hill, Justice, July 4, 1744.
1-255   "   Elizabeth, and Richard Dye, May 4, 1752.
1-147   "   Susannah, and John Worden, Jan. 1, 1769.
1-82   "   Eunice, and Nathaniel Clarke, March 6, 1771.
1-175   "   Thankful, and Caleb Barber, July 19, 1781.
2-40   "   Sarah G., and Sanford W. Foster, April 7, 1839.
2-49   "   Sarah P., and Stephen Bates, April 21, 1845.
2-49   "   Harriet N., and Albert H. Russell, Aug. 25, 1845.
2-53   "   Frances A., and Asa F. Noyes, Dec. 1, 1850.
2-55   "   Ruth, and Richard Chappell, March 12, 1848.
1-281   BAILEY Richard, and Abigail Woodmansee, both of Westerly; m. by George Babcock, Justice, April 25, 1729.
1-11   "   Abigail, and John Sunderland, March 2, 1748-9.
1-10   "   Mary, and Thomas Lewis, Sept. 1, 1748.
1-286   "   Sarah, and Jonathan Irish, Jan. 27, 1757.
1-554   "   Richard, Jr., and Judeth Clarke, both of R.; m. by Thomas Lillibridge, Justice of Peace, April 8, 1762.
1-161   "   Anne, and William Sheldon, June 7, 1767.
1-161   "   Hannah, and Ezekiel James, Jan. 3, 1768.
1-147   "   Major Richard, and Mrs. Judeth Card; m. by Edward Perry, Justice, Jan. 7, 1768.

1-84   BAILEY Clarke, of Richard, of Richmond, and Sarah James, of John, of Exeter; m. by Edward Perry, Justice, March 19, 1772.
1-554 BAKER Susannah, and Thomas Stanton, Dec. 10, 1761.
1-43   " Mercy, and George Holloway, Dec. 5, 1762.
1-135 " Solomon, and Lydia Kenyon, of David, Jr.; m. by Edward Perry, Justice, Feb. 4, 1770.
1-278 BARBER Bridget, and Thomas Clarke, Dec. 17, 1732.
1-11   " Susannah, and David Potter, Jan. 5, 1748-9.
1-256 " Nathaniel, and Charity Rathbun, both of Exeter; m. by Samuel Tefft, Justice, March 8, 1753.
1-286 " Edward, and Charity Briggs; m. by Samuel Tefft, Justice, Nov. 11, 1754.
1-284 " Caleb, and Elizabeth Niles; m. by Stephen Richmond, Justice, Jan. 26, 1755.
1-286 " Anna, and Daniel Austin, April 22, 1757.
1-551 " Dinah, and Joseph Enos, Jan. 11, 1759.
1-551 " Samuel, Jr., and Elizabeth Kenyon; m. by Edward Perry, Justice, April 26, 1759.
1-551 " Moses, and Abigail Niles; m. by Edward Perry, Justice, Dec. 27, 1759.
1-80   " Desire, and David Nichols, Jr., Jan. 23, 1760.
1-552 " Amie, and Benedict Kenyon, May 29, 1760.
1-552 " Mary, and Gideon Dickinson, Dec. 4, 1760.
1-552 " Benjamin, of Kingston, and Desire Moon, of Exeter; m. by Stephen Richmond, Justice, May 28, 1761.
1-78   " Joshua, and Mary Barber; m. by Edward Perry, Justice, May 17, 1764.
1-78   " Mary, and Joshua Barber, May 17, 1764.
1-92   " Lydia, and Thomas Tefft, Dec. 10, 1772.
1-123 " Benjamin, of Ezekiel, and Susannah Boss, of Peter; m. by Thomas Tefft, Justice, Nov. 25, 1778.
1-175 " Caleb, of Samuel, of Richmond, and Thankful Babcock, of Samuel, of Westerly; m. by Elder John Pendleton, July 19, 1781.
1-126 " Sarah, and Taber Tefft, Jan. 25, 1782.
1-428 " Samuel, son of Benjamin, and Thankful Kenyon, of William; m. by Simeon Clarke, Justice, Dec. 27, 1782.
1-128 " Benjamin, of Caleb, and Sarah Tefft, of Joseph; m. by Elder Charles Boss, Oct. 16, 1785.
1-128 " Mary, and Moshier Webster, Feb. 12, 1789.
2-8   " Charity, and John Kenyon, May 1, 1808.
3-153 " Deborah, and Gideon Hoxsie, Jr., Feb. 11, 1810.
2-1   " Joanna, and Job Reynolds, Feb. 17, 1811.
2-31   " Elizabeth, and Wells Reynolds, May 26, 1811.
2-8   " Peter, and Lucy Potter; m. by Elder Phineas Palmer, Feb. 13, 1814.
2-18   " Edward, of Exeter, and Dianna Wilcox, of Richmond; m. by Elder Phineas Palmer, April 24, 1817.
2-23   " Archibald, of Caleb, and Nancy Card, of Enoch; m. by Elder Matthew Stillman, Oct. 18, 1821.
2-28   " Joseph T., of Edward, and Nancy James, of Thomas; m. by Elder Peleg Peckham, Jan. 27, 1825.
2-30   " John, of Samuel, dec., and Sarah Tefft, of Thomas; m. by Elder Gersham Palmer, Feb. 2, 1826.
2-23   " Mrs. Watty, and Corey Kenyon, June 1, 1828.
2-31   " Chloe, and Willett R. Lillibridge, May 13, 1832.
2-46   " Thomas T., of Hopkinton, and Mrs. Angelina P. Richmond, of Richmond; m. by Rev. David Avery, July 10, 1843.
2-49   " John A., of Rhoda, of South Kingstown, and Deborah Tefft, of Richmond; m. by Elder Daniel Slocum, Nov. 5, 1846.
2-51   " Jesse C., of Benjamin, and Sarah Tefft, of Silas; m. by Elder E. J. Locke, Dec. 27, 1847.
2-52   " Peleg, and Mary Boss; m. by Elder Steadman Kenyon, March 18, 1849.
1-255 BASSETT William, and Mary Closson, both of Charlestown; m. by Stephen Richmond, Justice, April 12, 1752.

1-43	BATES Sarah, and Stephen Wilcox, April 24, 1763.
2-49	" Stephen, of Exeter, son of Lewis, and Sarah P. Babcock, of Simeon, of Richmond; m. by Rev. J. P. Burbank, April 21, 1845.
1-10	BENTLEY John, of Richmond, and Mary Cottrell, of Westerly; m. by Samnel Tefft, Justice, Dec. 21, 1749.
1-256	" William, and Abigail Millemam; m. by Elisha Babcock, Justice, April 21, 1754.
1-159	" William, and Elizabeth Enos; m. by Jos. Woodmansee, Justice, April 1, 1778.
1-1	" Ezekiel, and Alice Sabin; m. by Thomas Lillibridge, Justice, Sept. 16, 1765.
2-50	BICKNELL Louisa H., and Elias T. Burdick, Sept. 8, 1846.
1-123	BITGOOD John, Jr., of Stonington, Conn., son of John and Lydia Mitchell, of Richmond, dau. of Elisha, late of North Kingstown; m. by Thomas Tefft, Justice, Dec. 23, 1779.
2-59	BLANCHARD Ephraim A., and Emily Larkin; m. by Rev. A. D. Williams, July 1, 1850.
1-43	BOSS Martha, and Peregrine Fry Tripp (also 1-553), Sept. 14, 1760.
1-550	" Joseph, and Content Peterson; m. by Edward Perry, Justice, Oct. 27, 1757.
1-1	" Hannah, and Isaac Tanner, April 28, 1765.
1-96	" Charles, of Richmond, and Ruth Tripp, of Exeter; m. by Elder Solomon Sprague, Feb. 9, 1775.
1-159	" Charles, and Mary Webster; m. at Exeter by Elder Solomon Sprague, April 16, 1778.
1-123	" Susannah, and Benjamin Barber, Nov. 25, 1778.
2-1	" Martha, and David Gardiner, Nov. 26, 1812.
2-40	" Eliza, and Abner N. Woodmansee, Feb. 14, 1839.
2-52	" Mary, and Peleg Barber, March 18, 1849.
1-165	BRAMAN Mary, and Matthew Potter, Sept. 8, 1796.
2-53	" Harriet L., and Brightman Tucker, Feb. 15, 1845.
1-286	BRIGGS Charity, and Edward Barber, Nov. 11, 1754.
1-552	" Precilla, and Giles Kenyon, Jan. 3, 1760.
2-50	" Sarah, and Thomas Wilbour, Jan. 21, 1847.
2-36	BROWNING Joanna, and Thomas Reynolds, Oct. 5, 1825.
1-175	BROWN Elizabeth, and Jonathan Maxson, Jan. 6, 1791.
1-552	BURDICT Amos, of Stonington, Conn., and Elizabeth Nichols, of Richmond; m. by Edward Perry, Justice, Feb. 4, 1761.
2-46	" Stephen, and Mrs. Elizabeth Eldred; m. by Elder Weeden Barber, Jr., Oct. 17, 1839.
2-45	" George F., of Charlestown, and Mrs. Mary James, of Richmond; m. by Elder Thomas Tillinghast, Aug. 16, 1842.
2-47	" Reuben, of Hopkinton, and Mrs. Hannah E. Cooke, of Richmond; m. by Elder Weeden Barber, Jr., Dec. 4, 1842.
2-50	" Elias T., and Louisa A. Bicknell, both of Hopkinton; m. by Elder Charles C. Lewis, Sept. 8, 1846.
2-51	" Lydia P., and Nelson M. Pearce, Oct. 13, 1847.

C

2-255	CAHOONE Damaries, and Daniel Pierce, Feb. 3, 1752.
2-50	" Clarke, of Hopkinton, and Elizabeth Austin, of West Greenwich; m. by Elder Steadman Kenyon, Sept. 29, 1847.
1-13	CARD Prudence, and Elisha Clarke, Feb. 25, 1746.
1-147	" Mrs. Judeth, and Richard Bailey, Jan. 7, 1768.
1-72	" Joseph, and Elizabeth Lewis; m. by Elder Henry Joslin, Oct. 8, 1789.
2-20	" Mary, and Joseph Griffin, Aug. 24, 1798.
2-11	" Judeth, and Sheffield James, June 28, 1812.
2-23	" Nancy, and Archibald Barber, Oct. 18, 1821.
2-47	" Alzada W., and Clarke H. Reynolds, Dec. 25, 1842.
1-175	CARPENTER Margaret, and Park Enos, March 29, 1790.
1-82	CHAMPLAIN Hannah, and Simeon Clarke, Oct. 22, 1766.
2-45	" Hannah, and Joseph James Woodmansee, Feb. 19, 1843.

2-53	CHAMPLAIN Stephen, of South Kingstown, son of George, and Eliza A. James, of George, of Richmond; m. by Elder Geo. K. Clarke, March 10, 1850.
2-55	CHAPPELL Richard, and Ruth Babcock, at Richmond; m. by Elder A. Durfee, March 12, 1848.
1-256	CHURCH Caleb, of Westerly, and Lydia Larkin, of Richmond; m. by Stephen Richmond, Justice, July 29, 1753.
1-285	" Samuel, of Westerly, and Hannah Rogers, of Richmond; m. by Simeon Perry, Justice, July 18, 1756.
1-286	" Charles, of Hopkinton, and Susannah Kenyon, of Richmond; m. by Thomas Kenyon, Justice, Jan. 12, 1758.
2-54	" Ebenezer K., of Richmond, and Sophia Robbins, of Voluntown, Conn.; m. by John Willey, Justice, at Voluntown, Nov. 27, 1817.
1-12	CLOSSON Alce, and Joseph Woodmansee, Sept. 27, 1750.
1-255	" Mary, and William Bassett, April 12, 1752.
1-12	CLARKE Joseph, and Sarah Reynolds; m. by Christopher Champlain, Justice, Nov. 15, 1727.
2-278	" Thomas, and Bridget Barber, Dec. 17, 1732.
1-13	" Elisha, and Prudence Card, both of Charlestown; m. by Joseph Clarke, Justice, Feb. 25, 1746.
1-13	" Anne, and Samuel Perry, Dec. 26, 1746.
1-13	" Joseph, Jun., and Hannah Perry, of Samuel, Jun., of Charlestown; m. by Joseph Clarke, Justice, Dec. 26, 1746.
1-284	" Hannah, and John Tefft, Jun., March 14, 1750-1.
1-284	" James, and Elizabeth Kenyon; m. by Stephen Richmond, Justice, April 24, 1755.
1-286	" Anne, and Samuel Cross, March 13, 1757.
1-286	" William, 3d, and Mary Tefft; m. by Elisha Babcock, Justice, March 20, 1757.
1-286	" Ruth, and Thomas Rathbun, June 20, 1757.
1-550	" Thomas, Jun., of Richmond, and Hannah Yeomans; m. by Samuel Tefft, Justice, Dec. 8, 1758.
1-553	" Samuel, and Susannah Stanton, both of Richmond; m. by Joshua Clarke, Justice, Sept. 16, 1761.
1-553	" Sarah, and Thomas Wells, Sept. 17, 1761.
1-554	" Judeth, and Richard Bailey, Jun., April 8, 1762.
1-80	" Lois, and Daniel Potter, Dec. 1, 1765.
1-82	" Simeon, of Capt. Simeon, of Richmond, and Hannah Champlain, of Jeffrey, of Exeter; m. by Jeffrey Watson, Justice, Oct. 22, 1766.
1-147	" Elizabeth, and John Phillips, Jan. 18, 1768.
1-68	" Joshua, and Elizabeth Dodge; m. by Peleg Cross, Justice, Feb. 26, 1769.
1-82	" Nathaniel, of Jonathan, of Charlestown, and Eunice Babcock, of Elisha, of Richmond; m. by Edward Perry, Justice, March 6, 1771.
1-92	" Moses, of Richmond, and Alce Aylesworth, of Exeter; m. by Edward Perry, Justice, Nov. 18, 1773.
1-96	" Stephen, of Hopkinton, and Susannah Potter, of Richmond; m. by Edward Perry, Justice, Nov. 24, 1774.
1-159	" Benjamin, now residing in South Kingstown, and Mercy Kenyon, of Richmond, at Richmond; m. by Joseph Woodmansee, Justice, Feb. 26, 1778.
1-202	" Samuel, of Simeon, and Elizabeth Sheldon, of James; m. by Elder Ellet Locke, June 4, 1801.
2-17	" Luke, of Joshua, and Sarah Tefft, of Clarke; m. by Elder Matthew Stillman, Feb. 28, 1806.
1-—	" Susannah, and Joseph W. Watson, Oct. 16, 1806.
1-—	" Joseph, of Joshua, and Joanna Tefft, of Joseph; m. by Elder Matthew Stillman, Dec. 20, 1810.
2-8	" Elizabeth, and Champlain Wilcox, Oct. 14, 1815.
2-30	" Alice, and John R. Congdon, April 7, 1825.
2-38	" Sally, and James T. Webster, Sept. 9, 1832.
2-46	" James W., and Waity M. Taber; m. by Elder Weeden Barber, Jr., Dec. 29, 1839.

2-46   CLARKE William, and Mary A. Jordan; m. by Elder Weeden Barber, Jr.,
       Feb. 27, 1840.
2-42   "   Mrs. Mary, and Edward Lillibridge, Aug. 30, 1840.
2-47   "   John S., son of Bradford, and Pamelia C. Kenyon, dau. of Lewis;
       m. by Elder J. P. Burbank, Oct. 2, 1844.
2-36   "   Reynolds H., and Isabella W. Ney; m. by Elder Thomas Tilling-
       hast, Jan. 20, 1845.
2-51   "   Frances E., and William Perrin, Dec. 4, 1847.
1-128,175   COLDGROVE Eli, of Richmond, of Oliver, and Mary Coon, of David, of
       Hopkinton; m. by Elder Henry Joslin, Dec. 16, 1790.
1-78   "   Oliver, of Charlestown, and Esther Tefft, of Joseph, of Richmond;
       m. by Edward Perry, Justice, April 28, 1765.
1-554   COLLINS Susannah, and Ephraim Larkin, March 24, 1762.
1-135   "   Jedediah, and Sarah Adams; m. by James Kenyon, Justice, Nov.
       29, 1767.
2-6   CONGDON Abigail, and William Reynolds, Nov. 25, 1810.
2-3   "   John R., of West Greenwich, son of Samuel D., and Alice Clarke,
       of Moses; m. by Elder Gershom Palmer, April 7, 1825.
2-47   COOKE Hannah E., and Reuben Burdick, Dec. 4, 1842.
1-128   COON Mary, and Eli Coldgrove, (also 1-175), Dec. 16, 1790.
1-92   COREY Richard, now residing in this town, and Mary Sherman, (widow);
       m. by Elder Joseph Torrey, Oct. 25, 1773.
1-159   "   John, of Samuel, of Richmond, and Abigail Smith, of Thomas, of
       North Kingstown, at North Kingstown; m. by George Thomas,
       Justice, Nov. 7, 1773.
1-10   COTTRELL Mary, and John Bentley, Dec. 21, 1749.
1-43   CRANDALL George, of South Kingstown, and Tacy Tanner, of Richmond,
       at Richmond; (also 1-553), m. by John Webster, Justice, Sept.
       20, 1761.
1-72   "   Mercy, and Jonathan Kenyon, Jan. 21, 1790.
2-45   "   Ruth, and Daniel Larkin, Sept. 5, 1842.
2-51   "   Sarah, and Silas W. Tefft, Dec. 27, 1847.
1-286   CROSS Samuel, of Charlestown, and Anne Clarke, of Richmond; m. by
       Elisha Babcock, Justice, March 13, 1757.

D

1-110   DAKE Mary, and Joseph Lane, April 19, 1781.
2-52   DAVIS Sallie E., and Kenyon Johnson, Sept. 23, 1849.
1-550   DAWLEY Michael, of West Greenwich, and Mary Moore, of Richmond; m.
       by Samuel Tefft, Justice, Dec. 29, 1758.
1-552   DICKINSON Gideon, now residing in Hopkinton, and Mary Baker, now re-
       siding in Richmond; m. by Edward Perry, Justice, Dec. 4, 1760.
1-68   DODGE Elizabeth, and Joshua Clarke, Feb. 26, 1769.
1-552   DOUGLASS William, of Voluntown, Conn., and Mary Petty, of Richmond;
       m. by Edward Perry, Justice, May 1, 1760.
1-255   DYE Richard, and Elizabeth Babcock, both of Richmond; m. by Samuel
       Tefft, Justice, May 4, 1752.
1-550   "   John, and Thankful Potter, of William, Jr., of Richmond; m. by
       Edward Perry, Justice, March 22, 1758.
1-550   "   Thankful, and Jonathan James, Jr., Dec. 7, 1758.
2-42   "   Thomas P., of Hopkinton, and Deborah Kenyon, of Richmond; m.
       by Elder Thomas Tillinghast, Jan. 1, 1840.

E

2-46   ELDRED Mrs. Elizabeth, and Stephen Burdick, Oct. 17, 1839.
1-284   ENOS Hannah, and Samuel Wilbur, March 16, 1755.
1-284   "   Amie, and John Larkin, Jr., March 30, 1755.
1-551   "   Joseph, Jr., and Dinah Barber, both of Richmond; m. by Edward
       Perry, Justice, Jan. 21, 1759.
1-551   "   Catherine, and Joseph Kenyon, June 14, 1759.

(Vit. Rec., Vol. 5.)   28

1-147 ENOS Benjamin, and Jerusha Phillips, both of Richmond; m. by Edward
Perry, Justice, Jan, 14, 1768.
1-159 " Elizabeth, and William Bentley, April 1, 1778.
1-175 " Mary, and Jesse Larkin, Feb. 18, 1790.
1-175 " Park, of Benjamin, of Richmond, (dec.), and Margaret Carpenter,
of Daniel, of Richmond; m. by Elder Henry Joslin, March 29,
1790.
1-175 " Benjamin, of Benjamin, of Richmond (dec.), and Penelope Kenyon, dau. of James (dec.), of Charlestown; m. by Elder
Henry Joslin, Jan. 13, 1791.
2-42 ESSEX Lucy. and Rowland Hiscox, Oct. 4, 1840.

F

2-50 FENNER Nathan, of Richmond, and Harriet B. Olney, of Fall River; m. by
Elder Christopher C. Lewis. Sept. 21, 1846.
2-52 " Gilbert, of Hopkinton, and Martha S. Tuck, of Richmond; m. by
Elder Steadman Kenyon, Oct. 30, 1847.
2-52 " Hildah A., and Rufus J. Johnson, April 10, 1849.
2-40 FORD James, of Foster, R. I., and Anstis T. Hoxsie, of Richmond; m. by
Elder Daniel Webb, May 15, 1838.
1-48 FOREDICE John, of Richmond, and Elizabeth Stanton, of David, of Exeter; m. by William Petty, Justice, Dec. 6, 1764.
1-48 " Sarah, and John Stanton, Dec. 24, 1764.
1-11 FOSTER Abagail, and Joseph Lawton, March 17, 1749.
1-255 " Caleb, and Abigail Watson; m. by Stephen Richmond, Justice,
Feb. 9, 1752.
1-256 " Elizabeth, and Jabez Tucker, Jan. 16, 1754.
1-550 " Gideon, of Hopkinton, and Judeth Mumford, of Richmond; m. by
Samuel Tefft, Justice, Oct. 12, 1758.
1-48 " Eleanor, and William Sheldon, Jr., Jan. 21, 1765.
1-524 " Lawton, of Jonathan, late of Stonington (dec.), and Susannah
Tefft, of Samuel, of Richmond; m. by Edward Burdick, Justice,
Nov. 4, 1792.
2-40 " Sanford W., of Rome, Me., and Sarah G. Babcock, formerly of
Westerly, but now of Richmond, at East Greenwich; m. by
Elder Thomas Tillinghast, April 7, 1839.
2-51 " Albert G., of Richmond, and Levina Foster, of Hopkinton; m. by
Elder Steadman Kenyon, Feb. 5, 1849.
2-51 " Levina, and Albert G. Foster. Feb. 5, 1849.
1-43 FRAZER John, and Sarah Gurgon; m. by John Webster, Justice, Dec. 6,
1762.

G

1-84 GARDINER Amie, and Samuel Tefft, Jr., Dec. 9, 1770.
1-96 " Mary, and Robert Pettis, Feb. 7, 1771.
1-58 " Amie, and Isreal Lewis, Feb. 24, 1780.
2-1 " David, of Exeter, son of Nicholas (dec.), and Martha Boss, widow
of Jonathan, of Richmond; m. by Elder Gershom Palmer,
Nov. 26, 1812.
1-428 GREENE Catherine, and Phillip Kenyon. March 13, 1780.
1-160 " John, of Charlestown, son of Allen, and Elizabeth Hoxsie; m. by
Thomas Tefft, Justice. Oct. 28, 1802.
2-53 " Almira, and Benjamin B. Greene, March 2, 1851.
2-53 " Benjamin B., of Charlestown, and Almira Greene, of Richmond;
m. by Elder David Culver, March 2, 1851.
1-161 GRIFFETH James, and Desire Potter; m. by Edward Perry, Justice, Dec.
29, 1766.
1-134 " Phillip, of John, and Margaret Webster, of James; m. by Edward
Perry, Justice, May 21, 1769.
1-433 " Joshua, and Penelope Minturn, of Jonah; m. by Edward Perry,
Justice, Dec. 19, 1773.

1-123 GRIFFETH James, and Elizabeth Austin; m. by Joseph Woodmansee, Justice, March 25, 1799.

1-433   "   Phillip, of John, and Mary Minturn, of Jonas; m. by Elder Charles Boss, Feb. 23, 1783.

2-20 GRIFFIN Joseph, of Richmond, and Mary Card, of Peleg, at North Kingstown; m. by Elder Nathan Hill, Aug. 24, 1798.

1-43 GURGON Sarah, and John Frazer, Dec. 6, 1762.

H

1-10 HALL John, of Westerly, and Hannah Rogers, of Richmond; m. by Samuel Tefft, Justice, Dec. 28, 1749.

1-285   "   Eunice. and Amos Patterson, Dec. 28, 1756.

1-551   "   Susannah, and John Tanner, Aug. 14, 1759.

1-551   "   Sylvester, and Ruth Larkin; m. by Edward Perry, Justice, May 1, 1760.

1-48   "   Mrs. Anna, and Valentine Hall, Nov. 22, 1764.

1-48   "   Valentine, of Richmond, and Mrs. Anna Hall, of Stonington, Conn., at Stonington; m. by Rev. Charles Phelps, Nov. 22, 1764.

1-285 HARRINGTON Hannah, and John Watson, Oct. 31, 1756.

1-552   "   Paul, and Thankful Webster, both of Exeter; m. by Edward Perry, Justice, Oct. 12, 1764.

2-47 HAZARD Anthony, and Patience Woodmansee; m. by Elder Weeden Barber, Jr., Jan. 6, 1842.

1-26 HIDE John, and Hannah Stewart, both of Westerly; m. by Stephen Richmond, Justice, June 9, 1751.

1-26 HILL John, and Jane West; m. by Benjamin Randall, Justice, ——. —, 1751.

2-42 HISCOX Rowland, of Hopkinton, and Lucy Essex, of Richmond; m. by Elder Daniel Coon, Oct. 4, 1740.

1-43 HOLLOWAY George, of Richmond, and Mercy Baker, of South Kingstown; m. by Thomas Lillibridge, Justice, Dec. 5, 1762.

1-553 HOLWAY Elizabeth, and Hopson Wilcox, Dec. 10, 1761.

1-82 HOXSIE Stephen, of John (dec.), and Elizabeth Kenyon, of John (dec.); m. by Rouse Helme, Justice, Feb. 27, 1734-5.

1-13   "   Job, of Richmond, and Anne Rathburn, of Exeter, at Richmond; m. by John Webster, Justice, March 25, 1749.

1-256   "   Mary, and Thomas Lillibridge, Jun., Dec. 12, 1754.

1-43, 553   "   Joseph, of Richmond, and Alice Weekes, of Warwick, at Richmond; m. by John Webster, Justice, April 23, 1761.

1-286   "   Elizabeth, and Thomas Rogers, Jun., March 20, 1763.

1-48   "   Jeremiah, and Sarah Niles; m. by Samuel Tefft, Justice, June 11, 1764.

1-1   "   Stephen, and Elizabeth Tefft; m. by George Webb, Justice, Oct. 12, 1766.

1-159   "   John, of Stephen, of Richmond, and Bridget Tripp, of Peregrine, of Exeter; m. by Robert Stanton, Justice, Feb. 14, 1779.

1-165   "   Presbury, of Richmond, son of Stephen and Elizabeth, and Alice Perry, of Charlestown, dau. of Edward and Deliverance, Feb. 27, 1791.

1-202   "   Joseph, son of Job, late of Richmond, dec., and Hannah Tillinghast, of Stukely, of Exeter; m. by Elder Thomas Manchester, Nov. 16, 1797.

2-23   "   Joseph, and Susannah ——, Oct. 8, 1801.

1-160   "   Elizabeth, and John Greene, Oct. 28, 1802.

1-353   "   Potter, of Richmond, son of Gideon, and Mary Sunderland, of George, of Exeter; m. by Samuel Holloway, Justice, March 15, 1807.

1-353   "   Gideon, Jun., and Deborah Barber, of Caleb; m. by Elder Gershom Palmer, Feb. 11, 1810.

2-18   "   Martha T., and George Kenyon, Nov. 30, 1817.

2-35   "   Hannah, and Robert Reynolds, Sept. 17, 1820.

2-53   "   Ruth T., and John T. Sheldon, May 10, 1829.

2-46   "   Samuel A., and Malinda James; m. by Elder John Gardiner, Oct. 2, 1830.

2-40   HOXSIE Anstis T., and James Ford, May 15, 1838.
2-45   "   Barber, and Mehitable James; m. by Elder Benedict Johnson,
             Jan. 1, 1843.
2-47   "   Mary T., and Robert E. Moore, Nov. 28, 1844.
1-48   HULL Samuel, of South Kingstown, and Freelove Thomas, of Richmond;
             m. by Samuel Tefft, Justice, Sept. 29, 1763.

I

1-286   IRISH Jonathan, and Sarah Bailey; m. by Samuel Tefft, Justice, Jan. 27,.
             1757.

J

1-256   JAMES Elizabeth, and John Tefft, Dec. 26, 1752.
1-285   "   Patience, and Job Wilcox, Dec. 9, 1756.
1-551   "   Amos, and Nancy Swan; m. by John Webster, Justice, Oct. 1,.
             1758.
1-550   "   Jonathan, Jr., and Thankful Dye; m. by John Tefft, Justice, Dec.
             7, 1758.
1-78   "   Benjamin, Jr., and Rhoda Kenyon; m. by Edward Perry, Justice,
             June 23, 1764.
1-48   "   William, and Elizabeth Sabens; m. by George Webb, Justice, May
             14, 1767.
1-161   "   Ezekiel, of Edward, and Hannah Bailey, of Richard; m. by Gideon
             Moshier, Justice, June 3, 1768.
1-84   "   Sarah, and Clark Bailey, March 19, 1772.
1-110   "   Thomas, Jr., of Col. Thomas, and Dorcas Perry, of George; m. by
             Elder Henry Joslin, May 30, 1805.
2-11   "   Sheffield, and Judith Card; m. by Elder Phineas Palmer, June 28,
             1812.
2-25   "   Caleb B., and Lucy Reynolds; m. by Elder Daniel Greene, May 4,
             1823.
2-28   "   Frances, and Gardiner Kenyon, Nov. 25, 1824.
2-28   "   Nancy, and Joseph T. Barber, Jan. 27, 1825.
2-46   "   Malinda, and Samuel A. Hoxsie, Oct. 2, 1830.
2-43   "   John L., and Mrs. Eliza Kenyon; m. by Elder Thomas Tillinghast,.
             March 22, 1841.
2-43   "   Simeon C., and Mrs. Elizabeth S. Locke; m. by Elder Benedict
             Johnson, Oct. 3, 1841.
2-45   "   Mrs. Mary, and George F. Burdick, Aug. 16, 1842.
2-45   "   Mehitable, and Barber Hoxsie, Jan. 1, 1843.
2-53   "   Eliza A., and Stephen Champlain, March 10, 1850.
1-256   JOHNSON Ezekiel, of Charlestown, and Mercy Kenyon, of Richmond; m. by
             John Webster, Justice, Feb. 3, 1754.
2-55   "   Mercy, and William Kenyon, Sept. 25, 1825.
2-52   "   Rufus J., and Hildah A. Fenner; m. by Elder Steadman Kenyon,
             April 10, 1849.
2-52   "   Kenyon, of Jonathan, and Sally E. Davis, of Preserved; m. by Elder
             George K. Clarke, Sept. 23, 1849.
1-553   JONES Hannah, and Peter Wilbur, Sept. 25, 1761.
2-46   JORDAN Mary A., and William Clarke, Feb. 27, 1840.

K

1-96   KELLEY Charles, and Sarah Moshier; m. by Edward Perry, Justice, Dec.
             28, 1775.
1-82   KENYON Elizabeth, and Stephen Hopkins, Feb. 27, 1734-5.
1-31,2-55 " John, and Elizabeth Webster; m. by Joseph Clarke, Justice, Jan.
             18, 1748.
1-10   "   Hannah, and Simeon Watson, Oct. 24, 1748.
1-10   "   Penelope, and Simeon Perry, April 13, 1749.

1-26	KENYON David Jr., and Mary Potter; m. by Stephen Richmond, Justice, April 21, 1751.
1-256	"	Mercy, and Ezekiel Johnson, Feb. 3, 1754.
1-256	"	Mary, and William Tefft, March 21, 1754.
1-284	"	William, and Hannah Niles; m. by Stephen Richmond, Justice, March 9, 1755.
1-284	"	Elizabeth, and James Clarke, April 24, 1755.
1-285	"	Thomas, of David, and Ruth Tefft; m. by Stephen Richmond, Justice, April 15, 1756.
1-286	"	Susannah, and Charles Church, Jan. 12, 1758.
1-551	"	Elizabeth, and Samuel Barber, April 26, 1759.
1-551	"	Joseph, Jr., and Catherine Enos; m. by Edward Perry, Justice, June 14, 1759.
1-552	"	Giles, and Presilla Briggs; m. by Samuel Tefft, Justice, Jan. 3, 1760.
1-552	"	Sarah, and Sylvester Kenyon, Jr., Feb. 14, 1760.
1-552	"	Sylvester, Jr., and Sarah Kenyon; m. by Samuel Tefft, Justice, Feb. 14, 1760.
1-552	"	Benedict, and Amie Barber; m. by Thomas Kenyon, Justice, May 29, 1760.
1-78	"	Rhoda, and Benjamin James, Jr., June 23, 1764.
1-84	"	Thomas, Jr., and Sarah Steadman; m. by Rev. Joseph Torrey, Nov. 15, 1764.
1-101	"	Peleg, and Elizabeth Stanton; m. by Edward Perry, Justice, Oct. 1, 1766.
1-161	"	Mercy, and George Ney, Sept. 6, 1767.
1-135	"	Lydia, and Solomon Baker, Feb. 4, 1770.
1-12	"	Abigail, and James Woodmansee, Jan. 7, 1773.
1-43	"	Esther, and Joshua Webb, Feb. 16, 1777.
1-159	"	Mercy, and Benjamin Clarke, Feb. 26, 1778.
1-428	"	Philip, of Richmond, and Catharine Greene, of Charlestown; m. by Joseph Woodmansee, Justice, March 13, 1780.
1-58	"	Jonathan, of Samuel, of Charlestown, and Martha Kenyon, of George, of Richmond; m. by Robert Stanton, Justice, May 30, 1780.
1-58	"	Martha, and Jonathan Kenyon, May 30, 1780.
1-53	"	Thomas, of John, of Richmond, and Silvia Saunders, of Elisha, late of Westerly (dec.); m. by Joseph Crandall, Justice, Nov. 30, 1780.
1-428	"	Thankful, and Samuel Barber, Dec. 27, 1782.
1-370	"	Mary, and John Lillibridge, Nov. 2, 1789.
1-72	"	Anna, and Joseph Webster, Nov. 29, 1789.
1-72	"	Jonathan, of Richmond, and Mercy Crandall, of Hopkinton; m. by Elder Joshua Clarke, Jan. 21, 1790.
1-175	"	Penelope, and Benjamin Enos, Jan. 18, 1791.
1-255	"	John, and Elizabeth Webster, Jan. 18, 1748.
2-8	"	John, of Richmond, and Charity Barber, of Hopkinton; m. by Elder Phineas Palmer, May 1, 1808.
2-18	"	George, of John, and Martha T. Hoxsie, of Joseph; m. by Elder Gershom Palmer, Nov. 30, 1817.
2-25	"	Barber, of Benedict, and Honor Reynolds, of Jesse; m. by Elder Gershom Palmer, June 8, 1823.
2-28	"	Gardiner, of Silas, and Frances James, of Thomas; m. by Elder Matthew Stillman, Nov. 25, 1824.
2-33	"	Corey, and Mrs. Waitey Barber; m. by Elder Henry C. Hubbard, June 1, 1828.
2-55	"	William, and Mercy Johnson, of Stephen; m. by Thomas A. Hazard, Justice, Sept. 25, 1825.
2-35	"	Ruth Ann, and William W. Kenyon, March 19, 1838.
2-35	"	William W., of Richmond, and Ruth Ann Kenyon, of Hopkinton; m. by Elder Thomas Tillinghast, March 19, 1838.
2-42	"	Deborah, and Thomas P. Dye, Jan. 1, 1840.
2-42	"	Hannah E. C., and George S. Peckham, Jan. 13, 1840.
2-43	"	Mrs. Eliza, and John L. James, March 22, 1841.
2-49	"	Amie A., and Silas Moore, Jan. 1, 1843.

2-47   KENYON Pamelia C., and John S. Clarke, Oct. 2, 1844.
2-50   "   Lavina, and Nathan L. Richmond, Sept. 21, 1846.
2-50   "   Clarissa, and George C. Sanford, Oct. 29, 1847.
1-10   "   Abigail, and John Weaver, Dec. 20, 1747.
2-52   "   Benjamin F., of Hopkinton, and Mary J. Kenyon, of Richmond;
              m. by Elder Steadman Kenyon, Jan. 28, 1850.
2-52   "   Mary J., and Benjamin F. Kenyon, Jan. 28, 1850.

L

1-110 LANE Joseph, of Preston, Conn., and Mary Dake, of Richmond; m. by
              Edward Perry, Justice, April 19, 1781.
1-256 LARKIN Lydia, and Caleb Church, July 29, 1753.
1-284 "   John, Jr., and Amie Enos, of Richmond; m. by Sylvester Ken-
              yon, Justice, March 30, 1755.
1-551 "   Ruth, and Sylvester Hall, May 1, 1760.
1-554 "   Ephraim, of Hopkinton, and Susannah Collins, of Richmond; m.
              by Elder Thomas Tillinghast, March 24, 1762.
1-78   "   Abigail, and Thomas Adams, July 10, 1764.
1-48   "   Samuel, Jr., of Hopkinton, and Sarah Larkin, of Captain Nicholas,
              of Richmond; m. by John Burdick, Justice, July 16, 1764.
1-48   "   Sarah, and Samuel Larkin, July 16, 1764.
1-78   "   Edward, of Richmond, and Hannah Parker, of Hopkinton; m. by
              Edward Perry, Justice, Sept. 14, 1764.
1-92   "   Lucy, and Benjamin Wilbur, March 23, 1777.
1-175 "   Jesse, of Capt. David, and Mary Enos, of Benjamin, dec.; m. by
              Elder Henry Joslin, Feb. 18, 1790.
1-160 "   William, of Samuel, and Bathsheba Webster; m. by Elder Henry
              Joslin, Jan. 21, 1798.
2-45   "   Daniel, of Samuel, and Ruth Crandall, of Joseph, of Westerly; m.
              by Nathaniel T. Wilbur, Justice, Sept. 5, 1842.
2-59   "   Emily, and Ephraim A. Blanchard, July 1, 1850.
1-11   LAWTON Joseph, Jr., of Westerly, son of Joseph, and Abigail Foster, of
              Jonathan, of Richmond; m. by John Webster, Justice, March
              17, 1749.
1 —   LEWIS Izreal, and Jane Babcock, both of Westerly; m. by Tobias Saun-
              ders, Justice, about 1696.
1-10   "   Thomas, of Exeter, and Mary Bailey, of Richard, of Richmond;
              m. by John Webster, Justice, Sept. 1, 1748.
1-285 "   Nathan, of Charlestown, and Mary Adams, of Richmond; m. by
              Thomas Kenyon, Justice, Dec. 16, 1753.
1-147 "   Elnathan, of Richmond, and Margaret Tourgee; m. by Elder Joseph
              Torrey, March 22, 1767.
1-147 "   Mary, and Joseph Woodmansee, Jan. 19, 1760.
1-92   "   Martha, and Jonathan Potter, Jr., Feb. 22, 1776.
1-58   "   Isreal, of Richmond, son of Enock, and Amie Gardner, of Thomas;
              m. by Elder John Pendleton, Feb. 24, 1780.
1-72   "   Elizabeth, and Joseph Card, Oct. 8, 1789.
1-256 LILLIBRIDGE Thomas, Jr., and Mary Hoxsie; m. by Stephen Richmond,
              Justice, Dec. 12, 1754.
1-285 "   Edward, and Patience Tefft; m. by Stephen Richmond, Justice,
              Dec. 4, 1755.
1-43   "   David, of Exeter, and Marian Moore, of Richmond; m. by
              Thomas Lillibridge, Justice, Oct. 28, 1762.
1-78   "   Edward, and Thankful Wells; m. by Edward Perry, Justice, Jan.
              6, 1765.
1-135 "   Mary, and William Reynolds, April 7, 1771.
1-96   "   Sarah, and Hezekiah Tefft, March 23, 1775.
1-92   "   Deborah, and Jerah Mumford, March 14, 1776.
1-175 "   Thomas, Jr., of Thomas, and Alice Sweet, of Joshua, dec.; m.
              by Robert Stanton, Justice, June 10, 1781.
1-370 "   John, of Richmond, and Mary Kenyon, of Charlestown; m. by
              Elder Henry Joslin, Nov. 2, 1789.
2-31   "   Willett R., of Exeter, and Chloe Barber, of Richmond; m. by
              Elder Levi Meech, May 13, 1832.

2-42 LILLIBRIDGE Edward, and Mrs. Mary Clarke; m. by Elder Thomas Tillinghast, Aug. 30, 1840.

2-35 LOCKE Ezekiel J., and Mrs. Chloe Woodmansee; m. by Elder Henry C. Hubbard, Oct. 27, 1833.

2-43   "   Mrs. Elizabeth S., and Simeon C. James, Oct. 3, 1841.

M

1-550 MAXSON Sarah, and Joseph Tefft, Jr., July 17, 1757.

1-43   "   Jonathan, and Mary Woodmansee; m. by Edward Perry, Justice, Dec. 29, 1763.

1-53, 128 " Sarah, and William E. Phillips, Nov. 12, 1789.

1-175   "   Jonathan, Jr., of Col. Jonathan, of Richmond, and Elizabeth Brown, of Hopkinton, dau. of John; m. by Elder Henry Joslin, Jan. 6, 1791.

1-256 MILLEMAN Abigail, and William Bentley, April 21, 1754.

1-433 MINTURN Penelope, and Joshua Griffeth, Dec. 19, 1773.

1-433   "   Mary, and Philip Griffeth, Feb. 23, 1783.

1-123 MITCHELL Lydia, and John Bitgood, Jr., Dec. 23, 1779.

1-552 MOON Desire, and Benjamin Barber, May 28, 1761.

2-54   "   Phebe Ann, and William O. Taber, Aug. 12, 1860.

1-550 MOORE Mary, and Michael Dawley, Dec. 29, 1758.

1-43   "   Marian, and David Lillibridge, Oct. 28, 1762.

1-1   "   Lucy, and Smith Potter, Nov. 7, 1765.

1-161   "   Phebe, and George Niles, Oct. 5, 1767.

1-428   "   Silas, and Chloe Phillips; m. by Edward Perry, Justice, March 7, 1780.

2-33   "   Silas, Jr., of Richmond, and Sarah Tripp, of Exeter, dau. of Peregrine; m. by Elder Gershom Palmer, Feb. 20, 1820.

2-40   "   Mary Ann, and James Vallett, March 31, 1839.

2-49   "   Silas, and Amie A. Kenyon; m. by Elder Benedict Johnson, Jan. 1, 1843.

2-47   "   Robert E., of David, and Mary T. Hoxsie, of David; m. at East Greenwich by Elder Thomas Tillinghast, Nov. 28, 1844.

1-128   "   Mary, and Moshier Webster, Oct. 18, 1846.

2-76 MOREY Mary A., and Benjamin Worden, March 25, 1843.

1-255 MOSHIER Elizabeth, and John Webster, Jr., Dec. 6, 1751.

1-96   "   Sarah, and Charles Kelley, Dec. 28, 1775.

1-550 MUMFORD Judeth, and Gideon Foster, Oct. 12, 1758.

1-92   "   Jerah, of Jerah, late of South Kingstown, and Deborah Lillibridge, of Richmond, dau. of Thomas; m. by Robert Stanton, Justice, March 14, 1773.

N

1-161 NEY George, of Charlestown, son of Isaac, and Mercy Kenyon, of Richmond, dau. of Samuel, dec.; m. by Edward Perry, Justice, Sept. 6, 1767.

2-42 NEWTON Matthew, of Exeter, and Eliza Palmer, of Hopkinton; m. by Elder Thomas Tillinghast, April 12, 1840.

1-552 NICHOLS Elizabeth, and Amos Burdick, Feb. 4, 1761.

1-78   "   Andrew, and Anna Adams; m. by Edward Perry, Justice, June 14, 1764.

1-80   "   David, Jr., and Desire Barber; m. by Edward Perry, Justice, Jan. 23, 1766.

1-135   "   Joseph, of David, and Penelope Woodmansee, of Joseph; m. by Edward Perry, Justice, Sept. 24, 1769.

1-121   "   David, Jr., and Elizabeth Potter, of Jonathan; m. by George Webb, Justice, April 7, 1774.

1-284 NILES Elizabeth, and Caleb Barber, Jan. 26, 1755.

1-284   "   Hannah, and William Kenyon, March 9, 1755.

1-551   "   Abigail, and Moses Barber, Dec. 27, 1759.

1-48   "   Sarah, and Jeremiah Hoxsie, June 11, 1764.

1-161 NILES George, and Phebe Moore; m. by Job Tripp, Justice, Oct. 5, 1767.
2-53   NOYES Asa T., and Frances A. Babcock, of Charlestown; m. at South
          Kingstown by Elder David Culver, Dec. 1, 1850.
2-36   NEY Isabella W., and Reynolds H. Clarke, Jan. 20, 1845.

O

2-45   OLNEY John, and Caroline Sheldon; m. by Elder Pardon Tillinghast, May
          22, 1842.
3-50   "   Harriet B., and Nathan Fenner, Sept. 21, 1846.

P

2-42   PALMER Eliza, and Matthew Newton, April 12, 1840.
1-78   PARKER Hannah, and Edward Larkin, Sept. 14, 1764.
1-285 PATTERSON Amos, of Westerly, and Eunice Hall, of Richmond; m. by Syl-
          vester Kenyon, Justice, Dec. 28, 1756.
2-51   PEARCE Nelson M., and Lydia P. Burdick; m. by Elder C. C. Lewis, Sept.
          13, 1847.
2-52   "   Martha M., and James Woodmansee, Oct. 27, 1849.
2-42   PECKHAM George S., of Charlestown, and Hannah E. C. Kenyon, of Rich-
          mond; m. by Matthew B. Potter, Justice, Jan. 13, 1840.
1-428 PENDLETON Zebulon, of Westerly, son of Amos, and Thankful Wells, of
          Richmond, dau. of Joseph, of Hopkinton; m. by John Pendleton,
          Justice, Oct. 15, 1780.
2-81   PERRIN William, and Frances E. Clarke; m. by Elder C. C. Lewis, Dec. 4,
          1847.
1-13   PERRY Hannah, and Joseph Clarke, Jr., Dec. 26, 1746.
1-13   "   Samuel, Jr., and Anne Clarke, of Joseph, both of Charlestown;
          m. by Joseph Clarke, Justice, Dec. 26, 1746.
1-10   "   Simeon, of Charlestown, and Penelope Kenyon, of Richmond, dau.
          of John, Jr.; m. by John Webster, Justice, April 13, 1749.
1-159   "   Benjamin, and Alice Soul; m. by Joseph Woodmansee, Justice, Dec.
          19, 1779.
1-165   "   Alice, and Presbury Hoxsie, Feb. 27, 1791.
1-110   "   Dorcas, and Thomas James, Jr., May 30, 1805.
1-550 PETERSON Content, and Joseph Ross, Oct. 27, 1757.
1-11   PETTIS Charles, and Martha Rogers; m. by Stephen Richmond, Justice,
          Jan. 15, 1749.
1-96   "   Robert R., of Richmond, and Mary Gardiner, of South Kingstown;
          m. at South Kingstown, by Nathaniel Gardiner, Justice, Feb.
          7, 1771.
1-552 PETTY Mary, and William Douglass, May 1, 1760.
1-255 PHILLIPS Dorcas, and George Webb, Jr., Nov. 19, 1752.
1-147   "   Jerusha, and Benjamin Enos, Jan. 14, 1768.
1-147   "   John, of Joseph, of Exeter, and Elizabeth Clarke, of Thomas, of
          Richmond; m. by Samuel Tripp, Justice, Jan. 18, 1768.
1-96   "   Abigail, and Philip Potter, April 10, 1777.
1-428   "   Chloe, and Silas Moore, March 7, 1780.
1-53, 128 " William E., and Sarah Maxson; m. by Elder Henry Joslin, Nov.
          12, 1789.
2-42   "   Mary, and James Pollard, Feb. 1, 1841.
2-49   "   Martha, and Sylvester Woodmansee, April 21, 1845.
2-255 PIERCE Daniel, of Richmond, and Damaies Cahoone, of West Greenwich,
          m. by Samuel Tefft, Justice, Feb. 3, 1752.
2-42   POLLARD James, of East Greenwich, and Mary Phillips, of Richmond;
          m. by Elder Thomas Tillinghast, Feb. 1, 1841.
1-11   POTTER David, and Susannah Barber; m. by Stephen Richmond, Jus-
          tice, Jan. 5, 1748-9.
1-1   "   Smith, and Lucy Moore; m. by Thomas Lillibridge, Justice, Nov.
          7, 1765.
1-11   "   Martha, and Robert Wilcox, Dec. 24, 1749.
1-11   "   Patience, and Ezekiel Tefft, Oct. 21, 1750.

1-26 POTTER Mary, and David Kenyon, Jr., April 21, 1751.
1-284   "   Alice, and John Webb, Feb. 20, 1755.
1-550   "   Thankful, and John Dye, March 22, 1758.
1-551   "   Alice, and John Watson, May 17, 1759.
1-80   "   Daniel, and Lois Clarke; m. by Edward Perry, Justice, Dec. 1, 1765.
1-161   "   Alice, and Nathaniel Pullman, Nov. 20, 1766.
1-161   "   Desire, and James Griffith, Dec. 29, 1766.
1-135   "   Ruth, and John Rice, Oct. 13, 1768.
1-84   "   Rebecca, and William Potter, Nov. 7, 1770.
1-84   "   William, of Richmond, son of Nathaniel, of Dartmouth, Mass., (late deceased) and Rebecca Potter, of Ichabod, late of Dartmouth, Mass., deceased; m. by Aaron Wilbour, Justice, Nov. 7, 1770.
1-121   "   Elizabeth, and David Nichols, April 7, 1774.
1-96   "   Susannah, and Stephen Clarke, Nov. 24, 1774.
1-92   "   Jonathan, Jr., and Martha Lewis, of George, both of Exeter; m. by Edward Perry, Justice, Feb. 22, 1776.
1-96   "   Philip, of David, and Abigail Phillips, of Bartholomew; m. by Edward Perry, Justice, April 10, 1777.
1-165   "   Matthew, of Richmond, and Mary Braman, of Hopkinton; m. by Elder Asa Coon, Sept. 8, 1796.
2-8   "   Lucy, and Peter Barber, Feb. 13, 1814.
1-285 POWELL Threciah, and Jonathan Sherman, Aug. 31, 1755.
1-161 PULLMAN Nathaniel, Jr., now residing in Hopkinton, and Alice Potter, of Richmond; m. by Edward Perry, Justice, Nov. 20, 1766.

Q R

1-13 RATHBUN Anne, and Job Hoxsie, March 25, 1749.
1-256   "   Charity, and Nathaniel Barber, March 8, 1753.
1-286   "   Thomas, Jr., of Exeter, and Ruth Clarke, of Richmond; m. by Samuel Tefft, Justice, June 20, 1757.
1-135   "   Simeon, of Exeter, and Anne Russell, of Richmond; m. by Edward Perry, Justice, Oct. 26, 1769.
1-340 RECORD Elizabeth, and Benjamin Wilcox, Nov. 14, 1799.
1-14 REYNOLDS Mary, and John Tefft, Dec. 11, 1721.
1-12   "   Sarah, and Joseph Clarke, Nov. 15, 1727.
1-10   "   Dinah, and William Witter, Nov. 30, 1749.
1-135   "   William, Jr., and Mary Lillibridge, of Benjamin; m. by Elder James Rogers, April 7, 1771.
1-175   "   Robert, of Richmond, and Jemima Ross, of Charlestown; m. by Elder Charles Boss, Feb. 14, 1782.
1-110   "   John, of Stephen, of Exeter, and Mary Tefft, of Benjamin, of Richmond; m. by Elder Henry Joslin, June 24, 1804.
2-6   "   William, of Richmond, son of Robert, and Abigail Congdon, of West Greenwich, daughter of James; m. by Elder Gershom Palmer, Nov. 25, 1810.
2-1   "   Job, of Exeter, son of Stephen, and Joanna Barber, of Richmond, daughter of Caleb; m. by Elder Gershom Palmer, Feb. 17, 1811.
2-31   "   Wells, of Robert, and Elizabeth Barber, of Caleb; m. by Elder Gershom Palmer, May 26, 1811.
2-35   "   Robert, Jr., and Hannah Hoxsie, of Reynolds; m. by Elder Gershom Palmer, Sept. 17, 1820.
2-25   "   Lucy, and Caleb B. James, May 4, 1823.
2-25   "   Honor, and Barber Kenyon, June 8, 1823.
2-36   "   Thomas, of Robert and Jemima, and Joanna Browning, of Isaac, and Margaret; m. by Elder William Northrup, Oct. 5, 1825.
2-55   "   Robert, of Richmond, and Sarah Torrey, of Exeter; m. by Elder Nathaniel Sheffield, March 30, 1828.
2-47   "   Clarke H., of Richmond, and Alzada W. Card, of Charlestown; m. at Norwich, Conn., by Rev. D. N. Beezley, Dec. 25, 1842.
1-135 RICE John, of Captain Richard, of Coventry, R. I., and Ruth Potter, of Thomas, of Richmond; m. by Edward Perry, Justice, Oct. 13, 1768.

2-46   RICHMOND Mrs. Angeline P., and Thomas T. Barber, July 10, 1843.
2-49   "   Benjamin L., of Exeter, son of Benjamin, and Mrs. Elizabeth R.
        Smith, of Norris; m. by Elder Ezekiel J. Locke, Feb. 21, 1846.
2-50   "   Nathan L., of Exeter, and Levina Kenyon, of Richmond; m. by
        Elder C. C. Lewis, Sept. 21, 1846.
2-54   ROBBINS Sophia, and Ebenezer K. Church, Nov. 27, 1817.
1-25   ROGERS Thomas, and Zerniah Woodmansee; m. at Westerly, by Samuel
        Wilbour, Justice, Oct. 3, 1734.
1-11   "   Martha, and Charles Pettis, Jan. 15, 1749.
1-10   "   Hannah, and John Hall, Dec. 28, 1749.
1-11   "   Abigail, and Joseph Austin, Aug. 26, 1750.
1-255   "   Stephen, and Sarah Wilcox; m. by Stephen Richmond, Justice,
        Jan. 26, 1752.
1-255   "   Mary, and John Tanner, Jr., March 15, 1752.
1-285   "   Thomas, and Dinah Austin; m. by Stephen Richmond, Justice,
        Sept. 7, 1755.
1-285   "   Hannah, and Samuel Church, July 18, 1756.
1-286   "   Thomas, Jr., and Elizabeth Hoxsie; m. by Thomas Lillibridge, Jus-
        tice, March 20, 1763.
1-123   "   Mary, and Joseph Austin, Dec. 8, 1777.
1-390   "   Avis, and Thomas Rogers, Dec. 10, 1797.
1-390   "   Thomas, of Brookfield, N. Y., and Avis Rogers, of Richmond; m. by
        James Potter, Justice, Dec. 10, 1797.
1-175   ROSS Jemima, and Robert Reynolds, Feb. 14, 1782.
1-135   RUSSELL Anne, and Simeon Rathbun, Oct. 26, 1769.
2-49   "   Albert H., of Lonsdale, and Harriet N. Babcock; m. by Elder
        Daniel Avery, Aug. 25, 1845.

S

1-1   SABIN Alice, and Ezekiel Bentley, Sept. 16, 1765.
1-48   "   Elizabeth, and William James, May 14, 1767.
2-50   SANFORD George C., of North Kingstown, and Clarissa Kenyon, of Rich-
        mond; m. at Wickford by Rev. John C. Rouse, Oct. 29, 1847.
1-53   SAUNDERS Sylvia, and Thomas Kenyon, Nov. 30, 1780.
1-159   SEREL Alice, and Benjamin Perry, Dec. 19, 1779.
1-48   SHELDON William, Jr., of Richmond, and Eleanor Foster, of Hopkinton;
        m. by William Pettey, Justice, Jan. 21, 1765.
1-161   "   William, and Anne Bailey, of Samuel; m. by Edward Perry,
        Justice, June 7, 1767.
1-202   "   Elizabeth, and Samuel Clarke, June 4, 1801.
2-53   "   John T., of William J., of Coventry, and Ruth T. Hoxsie, of Rey-
        nolds, of Richmond; m. by Elder Matthew Stillman, May 10,
        1829.
2-45   "   Caroline, and John Olney, May 22, 1842.
1-285   SHERMAN Jonathan, of Benjamin, of South Kingstown, and Terceiah
        Powell, late of Plainfield, Conn.; m. by Elisha Babcock, Jus-
        tice, Aug. 31, 1755.
1-92   "   Mary, and Richard Corey, Oct. 25, 1773.
1-159   SMITH Abigail, and John Corey, Nov. 7, 1773.
2-33   "   Mrs. Mary, and Ray G Tefft, Sept. 24, 1826.
2-49   "   Mrs. Elizabeth R., and Benjamin L. Richmond, Feb. 2, 1846.
1-553   STANTON Susannah, and Samuel Clarke, Sept. 16, 1761.
1-554   "   Thomas, of Charlestown, and Susannah Baker, of Exeter; m. by
        Elder Samuel Albro, Dec. 10, 1761.
1-48   "   Elizabeth, and John Fordice, Dec. 6, 1764.
1-48   "   John, of David, of Exeter, and Sarah Fordice, of Richmond; m.
        by William Pettey, Justice, Dec. 24, 1764.
1-61   "   Elizabeth, and Peleg Kenyon, Oct. 1, 1766.
2-52   STAR Sarah, and Stephen B. Watson, March 5, 1850.
1-84   STEADMAN Sarah, and Thomas Kenyon, Nov. 15, 1764.
1-26   STEWART Hannah, and John Hide, June 9, 1751.
1-11   SUNDERLAND John, of Exeter, son of William, and Abigail Bailey, of
        Richard, of Richmond; m. by John Webster, Justice, March 2,
        1749.

1-358 SUNDERLAND Mary, and Potter Hoxsie, March 15, 1807.
1-551 SWAN Nancy, and Amos James, Oct. 1, 1758.
1-175 SWEET Alice, and Thomas Lillibridge, June 10, 1781.

T

2-46 TABER Waity M., and James W. Clarke, Dec. 29, 1839.
2-54 " William O., and Phebe Ann Moon, both of Exeter; m. at Hopkinton, by Rev. Stanton Austin, Aug. 12, 1860.
2-225 TANNER John, Jr., and Mary Rogers; m. by Stephen Richmond, Justice, March 15, 1752.
1-256 " George, and Marcy Wilcox; m. by Samuel Tefft, Justice, July 23, 1754.
1-256 " David, of Westerly, and Hopestill Worden, of Richmond; m. by Stephen Richmond, Justice, Nov. 24, 1754.
1-551 " John, of Richmond, and Susannah Hall, of Hopkinton; m. by Thomas Kenyon, Justice, Aug. 14, 1759.
1-43, 553 " Tacy, and George Crandall, Sept. 20, 1761.
1-1 " Isaac, and Hannah Boss; m. by Richard Bailey, Justice, April 28, 1765.
1-14 TEFFT John, of Richmond, and Mary Reynolds, of Westerly; m. at Westerly, by John Babcock, Justice, Dec. 11, 1721.
1-11 " Jonathan, and Mary Webb; m. by Samuel Tefft, Justice, Jan. 26, 1749.
1-11 " Ezekiel, of Richmond, and Patience Potter, of Exeter; m. by Stephen Richmond, Justice, Oct. 21, 1750.
1-284 " John, Jr., and Hannah Clarke; m. by Thomas Kenyon, Justice, March 14, 1750-1.
1-256 " John, and Elizabeth James; m. by Samuel Tefft, Justice, Dec. 26, 1752.
1-256 " William, and Mary Kenyon; m. by Stephen Richmond, Justice, March 21, 1754.
1-256 " Abigail, and Robert Tefft, March 27, 1754.
1-256 " Robert, and Abigail Tefft; m. by Stephen Richmond, Justice, March 27, 1754.
1-285 " Patience, and Edward Lillibridge, Dec. 4, 1755.
1-285 " Ruth, and Thomas Kenyon, April 15, 1756.
1-286 " Mary, and William Clarke, 3d, March 20, 1757.
1-550 " Joseph, Jr., and Sarah Maxson; m. by Edward Perry, Justice, July 17, 1757.
1-78 " Esther, and Oliver Colegrove, April 28, 1765.
1-1 " Elizabeth, and Stephen Hoxsie, Oct. 12, 1766.
1-84 " Samuel, Jr., son of Joseph, and Amie Gardiner, of George; m. by Robert Stanton, Justice, Dec. 9, 1770.
1-84 " Joseph, Jr., of Richmond, son of Joseph, and Alice Albro, of Exeter, dau. of Samuel; m. at Exeter, by Elder Solomon Sprague, May 22, 1771.
1-92 " Thomas, of Joseph, and Lydia Barber, of Benjamin; m. by Robert Stanton, Justice, Dec. 10, 1772.
1-96 " Hezekiah, of Ezekiel, and Sarah Lillibridge, of Edward, both of Exeter; m. by Edward Perry, Justice, March 23, 1775.
1-126 " Taber, of Joseph, and Sarah Barber, of Caleb; m. by Elder Charles Boss, July 25, 1782.
1-128 " Ezekiel, of Ezekiel, and Amie Wilcox, of Stephen; m. by Thomas Tefft, Justice, Oct. 13, 1785.
1-128 " Sarah, and Benjamin Barber, Oct. 16, 1785.
1-524 " Susannah, and Lawton Foster, Nov. 4, 1792.
1-110 " Mary, and John Reynolds, June 24, 1804.
1-205 " Edward, of Richmond, and Nancy Turner, of Groton, Conn.; m. by Elder John G. Weighman, Dec. 16, 1804.
1-205 " Lucy, and Thomas Tefft, Jr., Jan. 31, 1805.
1-205 " Thomas, Jr., of Richmond, son of Thomas, and Lucy Tefft, of George, of Borton, Conn.; m. by Elder Henry Joslin, Jan. 31, 1805.

2-17   TEFFT Sarah, and Luke Clarke, Feb. 28, 1806.
1-—   "   Joanna, and Joseph Clarke, Dec. 20, 1810.
2-30   "   Sarah, and John Barber, Feb. 2, 1826.
2-33   "   Ray G., of Richmond, and Mrs. Mary Smith, of South Kingstown;
             m. by Elder Henry C. Hubbard, Sept. 24, 1826.
2-49   "   Deborah, and John A. Barber, Nov. 5, 1346.
2-51   "   Sarah, and Jesse C. Barber, Dec. 27, 1847.
2-51   "   Silas W., of Silas, of Richmond, and Sarah Crandall, of Stephen,
             of Charlestown; m. by Elder E. J. Locke, Dec. 27, 1847.
1-58   TENNANT Freelove, and Job Wilcox, Nov. 30, 1779.
1-48   THOMAS Freelove, and Samuel Hull, Sept. 29, 1763.
1-202 TILLINGHAST Hannah, and Joseph Hoxsie, Nov. 16, 1797.
2-55   TORREY Sarah, and Robert Reynolds, March 30, 1828.
1-147 TOURGEE Margaret, and Elnathan Lewis, March 22, 1767.
1-43,553 TRIPP Peregrine Fry, of Exeter, and Martha Boss, of Jeremiah, of Rich-
             mond; m. at Richmond by John Webster, Justice, Sept. 14,
             1760.
1-96   "   Ruth, and Charles Boss, Feb. 9, 1775.
1-159   "   Bridget, and John Hoxsie, Feb. 14, 1779.
2-33   "   Sarah, and Silas Moore, Jr., Feb. 20, 1820.
1-256 TUCKER Jabez, of Westerly, and Elizabeth Foster, of Richmond; m. by
             John Webster, Justice, Jan. 16, 1754.
2-53   "   Brightman, and Hannah L. Braman; m. by Rev. Elbridge Cran-
             dall, Feb. 15, 1845.
2-52   TUCK Martha A., and Gilbert Fenner, Oct. 30, 1847.
1-205 TURNER Nancy, and Edward Tefft, Dec. 16, 1804.

U V

2-44   VALLETT James, and Mary Ann Moore; m. by Elder Henry B. Locke,
             March 31, 1839.

W

1-10   WATSON Simeon, and Hannah Kenyon; m. by Samuel Tefft, Justice, Oct.
             24, 1748.
1-255   "   Abigail, and Caleb Foster, Feb. 9, 1752.
1-285   "   John, and Hannah Harrington; m. by Thomas Kenyon, Justice,
             Oct. 31, 1756.
1-551   "   John, and Alice Potter; m. by Edward Perry, Justice, May 17,
             1759.
1-—   "   Joseph W., and Susannah Clarke; m. by Rev. Matthew Stillman,
             Oct. 16, 1806.
2-52   "   Stephen B., aged 45 years, and Sarah Star, widow, aged 41 years;
             m. by Elder A. D. Williams, March 5, 1850.
1-10   WEAVER John, of East Greenwich, and Abigail Kenyon, of Richmond;
             m. by Stephen Richmond, Justice, Dec. 20, 1747.
1-11   WEBB Mary, and Jonathan Tefft, Jan. 26, 1749.
1-255   "   George, Jr., and Dorcas Phillips; m. by Stephen Richmond, Justice,
             Nov. 19, 1752.
1-284   "   John, and Alice Potter; m. by Stephen Richmond, Justice, Feb. 20,
             1755.
1-43   "   Joshua, of George, and Esther Kenyon, of Thomas, son of David;
             m. by Edward Perry, Justice, Feb. 16, 1777.
1-31,255 WEBSTER Elizabeth, and John Kenyon, Jan. 18, 1748.
1-255   "   John, Jr., and Elizabeth Mosbier; m. by Stephen Richmond, Justice,
             Dec. 6, 1751.
1-552   "   Thankful, and Paul Harrington, Oct. 12, 1764.
1-80   "   Thomas, and Patience Adams; m. by Edward Perry, Justice, Nov.
             17, 1765.
1-134   "   Margaret, and Philip Griffeth, May 21, 1769.
1-159   "   Mary, and Charles Boss, April 16, 1778.
1-128   "   Moshier, and Mary Barber; m. by Elder Henry Joslin, Feb. 12,
             1789.

1-72 WEBSTER Joseph, of Richmond, and Annie Kenyon, of Charlestown; m. by Elder Henry Joslin, Nov. 29, 1789.

1-160 " Bathsheba, and William Larkin, Jan. 21, 1798.

1-255 " Elizabeth, and John Kenyon, Jan. 18, 1748.

2-38 " James T., of Jonathan, and Sally Clarke, of Luke; m. by Elder Thomas Tillinghast, Sept. 9, 1832.

1-128 " Moshier, and Mary Moore (also 2-50); m. at East Greenwich, by Elder Thomas Tillinghast, Oct. 18, 1846.

1-43 WEEKS Alice, and Joseph Hoxsie (also 5-53), April 23, 1761.

1-552 WELLS Thomas, of Hopkinton, and Sarah Clarke, of Richmond; m. by John Tefft, Justice, Sept. 17, 1761.

1-78 " Thankful, and Edward Lillibridge, Jan. 6, 1765.

1-428 " Thankful, and Zebulon Pendleton, Oct. 15, 1780.

1-26 WEST Jane, and John Hill, ——, —, 1751.

1-284 WILBOUR Samuel, and Hannah Enos; m. by Sylvester Kenyon, Justice, Mar. 16, 1755.

1-550 " William, of Richmond, and Mary Young, of Exeter; m. by Edward Perry, Justice, Dec. 28, 1758.

1-553 " Peter, of Richmond, and Hannah Jones, of Charlestown; m. by Thomas Lillibridge, Justice, Sept. 25, 1761.

1-553 " Hannah, and Daniel Wilcox, Dec. 31, 1761.

1-92 " Benjamin, and Lucy Larkin; m. by Joseph Woodmansee, Justice, March 23, 1777.

2-54 " Thomas, of Richmond, now residing in Coventry, R. I., and Sarah Briggs, of Warwick; m. at East Greenwich by Elder Thomas Tillinghast, Jan. 21, 1847.

1-11 WILCOX Robert, of Robert, dec., of South Kingstown, and Martha Potter, of William, of Richmond; m. by John Webster, Justice, Dec. 24, 1749.

1-255 " Sarah, and Stephen Rogers, Jan. 26, 1752.

1-256 " Mercy, and George Tanner, July 23, 1754.

1-286 " Amie, and Stephen Wilcox, Oct. 4, 1756.

1-286 " Stephen, and Amie Wilcox; m. by Samuel Tefft, Justice, Oct. 4, 1754.

1-285 " Job, of Exeter, and Patience James; m. by Jeremiah Crandall, Justice, Dec. 9, 1756.

1-553 " Hopson, of Exeter, and Elizabeth Holway, of Richmond; m. by Thomas Lillibridge, Justice, Dec. 10, 1761.

1-553 " Daniel, Jr., of Stonington, Conn., and Hannah Wilbour, of Richmond; m. by Thomas Lillibridge, Justice, Dec. 31, 1761.

1-43 " Stephen, of Edward, of Richmond, and Sarah Bates, of Exeter; m. by Thomas Lillibridge, Justice, April 24, 1763.

1-58 " Job, of Richmond, and Freelove Tennant, of South Kingstown; m. by Elder Thomas West, Nov. 30, 1779.

1-128 " Amie, of Ezekiel Tefft, Oct. 13, 1785.

1-128 " Noah, of Richmond, and Martha Albro, of North Kingstown; m. by Elder Henry Joslin, Nov. 15, 1789.

1-340 " Peleg, Jr., of Peleg, and Thankful Wilcox, of Stephen; m. by Elder Henry Joslin, Dec. 8, 1796.

1-340 " Thankful, and Peleg Wilcox, Dec. 8, 1796.

1-340 " Benjamin, of Peleg, and Elizabeth Record, of Thomas, dec.; m. by Elder Henry Joslin, Nov. 14, 1799.

2-8 " Champlain, of Peleg, and Elizabeth Clarke, of Simeon; m. by Elder Gershom Palmer, Oct. 14, 1815.

2-18 " Dianna, and Edward Barber, April 24, 1817.

1-10 WITTER William, and Dinah Reynolds; m. by Samuel Tefft, Justice, Nov. 30, 1749.

1-281 WOODMANSEE Abigail, and Richard Bailey, April 25, 1729.

1-25 " Zerniah, and Thomas Rogers, Oct. 3, 1734.

1-12 " Joseph, of Richmond, and Alice Closson, of Westerly; m. by Stephen Richmond, Justice, Sept. 27, 1750.

1-43 " Mary, and Jonathan Maxson, Dec. 29, 1763.

1-147 " Joseph, Jr., and Mary Lewis; m. by Edward Perry, Justice, Jan. 19, 1769.

1-135 " Penelope, and Joseph Nichols, Sept. 24, 1769.

1-92   WOODMANSEE James, of Joseph and Abigail Kenyon, of Sylvester; m. by
     Edward Perry, Justice, Jan. 7, 1773.
2-35   "   Mrs. Chloe, and Ezekiel J. Locke, Oct. 27, 1833.
2-40   "   Abner N., of Hopkinton, and Eliza Boss, of Richmond; m. at East
     Greenwich by Elder Thomas Tillinghast, Feb. 14, 1839.
2-47   "   Patience, and Anthony Hazard, Jan. 6, 1842.
2-45   "   Joseph James, of Richmond, son of Joseph, and Hannah Champlain.
     of Stephen of Exeter; m. by Elder Ezekiel J. Locke, Feb. 19,
     1843.
2-49   "   Sylvester, of Samuel, and Martha Phillips, of Nicholas; m. at Lons-
     dale, by Rev. J. P. Burbank, April 21, 1845.
2-52   "   James, and Martha M. Pearce; m. by Elder Steadman Kenyon,
     Oct. 27, 1849.
1-256 WORDEN Hopestill, and David Tanner, Nov. 24, 1754.
1-147 "   John, and Susannah Babcock; m. by Edward Perry, Justice, Jan.
     1, 1769.
2-76   "   Benjamin, of Charlestown, and Mary Ann Morey, of Richmond;
     m. by Elder Soloman Carpenter, March 25, 1843.

X Y Z

1-550 YOEMAN Hannah, and Thomas Clarke, Jr., Dec. 8, 1758.
1-550 YOUNG Mary, and William Wilbour, Dec. 28, 1758.

RICHMOND.

BIRTHS AND DEATHS.

A

1-14	ADAMS	Ezekiel, of Thomas and Mary,	Aug. 24, 1734.
1-14	"	Martha,	May 29, 1737.
1-14	"	Mary,	Sept. 13, 1739.
1-14	"	Thomas,	Sept. 24, 1742.
1-14	"	Sarah,	Feb. 11, 1745.
1-14	"	Stephen,	July 16, 1747.
1-14	"	Hannah.	April 15, 1750.

B

1-273	BABCOCK	Elisha,	May 18, 1718.
1-273	"	Elizabeth, his wife.	Nov. 3, 1719.
2-273	"	Simeon, of Elisha and Elizabeth,	May 31, 1745.
2-273	"	Eunice,	July 28, 1746.
2-273	"	Elizabeth,	Sept. 23, 1747.
2-273	"	Elisha,	Dec. 17, 1748.
2-273	"	Alice,	May 29, 1750.
2-273	"	Sarah,	April 25, 1752.
2-273	"	Susan,	Feb. 1, 1754.
2-273	"	Deliverance, (also 2-275),	May 9, 1755.
1-224	"	Phebe, of Jesse,	Dec. 3, 1785.
1-224	"	Jesse,	April 7, 1787.
1-224	"	Anne,	Feb. 13, 1789.
1-224	"	Elizabeth,	March 23, 1791.
1-224	"	George,	May 30, 1793.
1-224	"	Joseph,	June 7, 1795.
1-224	"	Mary,	May 14, 1797.
1-224	"	David,	Sept. 26, 1799.
1-281	BAILEY	Mary, of Richard and Abigail,	Dec. 18, 1729.
1-281	"	Abigail,	Jan. 16, 1731-2.
1-281	"	Elizabeth,	April 29, 1734.
1-281	"	Sarah,	Dec. 13, 1736.
1-281	"	Samuel,	May 26, 1739.
1-281	"	Richard,	May 29, 1741.
1-281	"	William,	May 12, 1743.
1-281	"	William,	d. May 26, 1757.
1-281	"	Smith,	Oct. 18, 1745.
1-281	"	Hannah,	Jan. 13, 1747-8.
1-281	"	Clarke,	Jan. 19, 1750-1.
1-72	"	William, of Richard, Jr., and Judeth,	July 11, 1762.
1-72	"	Abigail,	Aug. 26, 1765.
1-72	"	Bridget,	June 24, 1768.
1-275	BARBER	Susannah, of Samuel and Ann,	Dec. 19, 1727.
1-275	"	Edward,	Nov. 17, 1731.
1-275	"	Moses,	April, 10, 1734.
1-275	"	Samuel,	Jan. 7, 1737.
1-275	"	Hannah,	July 24, 1739.
1-275	"	Amie,	Nov. 28, 1742.

1-275	BARBER Merabah, of Samuel and Ann,	Nov. 24, 1747.
2-227	" Benjamin, of Caleb and Elizabeth,	May 25, 1756.
2-227	" Sarah,	April 17, 1762.
2-227	" Caleb,	Nov. 25, 1764.
2-227	" Mary,	Dec. 3, 1772.
1-9	" Joshua, of Ezekiel and Hannah,	Dec. 6, 1739.
1-9	" Ezekiel,	Oct. 22, 1742.
1-9	" Hannah,	Sept. 9, 1747.
1-9	" Desire,	March 20, 1745-6.
1-31	" Elizabeth,	Oct. 13, 1751.
1-31	" Benjamin,	Feb. 7, 1755.
1-31	" Susannah,	Aug. 15, 1758.
1-31	" Mary,	June 28, 1761.
1-8	" Mary, of Benjamin and Sarah,	May 11, 1747.
1-279	" Anne,	Sept. 15, 1749.
1-60	" Lydia,	Feb. 17, 1751.
1-60	" Peace, of Samuel, Jr., and Elizabeth,	Aug. 18, 1760.
1-104	" Patience,	Oct. 27, 1764.
1-104	" Samuel of Benjamin and Desire,	May 1, 1762.
1-104	" Benjamin,	June 10, 1764.
1-104	" Albro,	March 9, 1767.
1-104	" Sarah,	June 10, 1770.
1-104	" Desire,	Aug. 2, 1772.
1-194	" Jared, of Caleb, Jr., and Joanna,	July 16, 1788.
1-194	" Deborah,	March 6, 1790.
1-194	" Elizabeth,	Sept. 22, 1791.
1-194	" Joanna,	July 8, 1793.
1-419	" Caleb, of Benjamin (of Caleb) and Sarah,	May 21, 1796.
1-419	" Thankful,	March 16, 1799.
1-419	" Benjamin,	May 31, 1801.
2-278	BENTLEY James, of William and Bathsheba,	June 6, 1739.
2-278	" Greene,	March 23, 1741.
2-278	" Benjamin,	June 20, 1758.
2-278	" Benedict, of John and Elizabeth,	Jan. 1, 1741.
2-278	" Gardiner,	Oct. 1, 1744.
2-278	" Susanna,	Jan. 1, 1750.
2-278	" Lucy, of John and Elizabeth,	Nov. 15, 1752.
2-278	" Niles,	Dec. 6, 1754.
2-278	" William,	Feb. 16, 1757.
1-41	" Sarah, of William and Abigail,	Feb. 5, 1755.
1-41	" Thomas,	May 5, 1757.
1-41	" Elisha,	Oct. 21, 1759.
1-41	" Anna,	July 26, 1762.

C

1-305, 362	CARD Judeth, of Benjamin and Tacy,	Nov. 9, 1762.
1-305, 362	" Mary,	Dec. 25, 1763.
1-305, 362	" Sarah,	Aug. 27, 1765.
1-305, 362	" Joseph,	July 2, 1767.
1-305, 362	" Benjamin,	April 2, 1770.
1-305, 362	" Judeth,	Dec. 11, 1772.
1-305, 362	" Enock,	Aug. 8, 1776.
1-305, 362	" Newbury,	March 10, 1778.
2-25	" Nancy, of Enock and Mary,	Oct. 25, 1801.
2-25	" Matthew,	Sept. 22, 1803.
2-25	" Tacy, of Enock,	Feb. 17, 1807.
2-25	" Rodman S.,	Sept. 8, 1814.
1-275	CHACE Mercy, of Joshua and Mercy,	June 15, 1754.
1-3	CHAMPLAIN Mary, of Samuel and Mary,	Aug. 18, 1751
1-276	CHURCH Caleb, of Caleb and Lydia (Westerly),	March 1, 1754.
2-283	" Samuel, of Samuel and Hannah,	May 18, 1759.
2-283	" Zerniah,	Oct. 15, 1761.
2-283	" Silas,	Oct. 25, 1763.

2-283	CHURCH Sarah, of Samuel and Hannah,	Feb. 18, 1766.
2-283	" Hannah,	May 27, 1768.
2-283	" Thomas,	Nov. 7, 1770.
2-283	" Waite,	March 7, 1773.
2-283	" Rebecca,	June 10, 1775.
1-12	CLARKE Joseph, of Samuel,	Aug. 29, 1705.
1-12	" Sarah, wife of Joseph,	Oct. 21, 1709.
1-12	" Joseph, of Joseph and Sarah,	March 5, 1728.
1-12	" Anne,	Oct. 23, 1730.
1-12	" Joshua,	May 13, 1733.
1-12	" Samuel,	Dec. 1, 1737.
1-12	" John,	July 8, 1740.
1-12	" Oliver,	Nov. 21, 1743.
1-12	" Sarah,	June 15, 1745.
1-12	" James,	July 9, 1748.
1-12	" Christopher,	April 7, 1751.
2-278	" Ruth, of Thomas and Bridget,	May 20, 1733.
2-278	" William,	March 5, 1734.
2-278	" Thomas,	Dec. 27, 1736.
2-278	" Elizabeth,	Feb. 22, 1738.
2-278	" Judeth,	Feb. 8, 1742-3.
2-278	" Lois,	Dec. 3, 1744.
2-278	" Arnold,	Oct. 30, 1748.
2-278	" Moses,	Dec. 29, 1751.
1-50	" Amie, of Simeon and Elizabeth,	Aug. 23, 1737.
1-50	" Thankful,	Feb. 23, 1739.
1-50	" Sanford,	Oct. 7, 1740.
1-50	" Sanford,	died Oct. 6, 1752.
1-50	" Simeon, of Simeon and Elizabeth,	Aug. 21, 1742.
1-50	" Gideon,	Nov. 21, 1744.
1-50	" Gideon,	died Aug. 27, 1752.
1-50	" Bethiah,	Oct. 19, 1746.
1-50	" Bethiah,	d. Aug. 18, 1752.
1-50	" Esbon,	Aug. 20, 1748.
1-50	" Esbon,	Aug. 28, 1752.
1-50	" Peleg,	July 20, 1750.
1-50	" Peleg,	Aug. 22, 1752.
1-50	" Ann,	July 30, 1752.
1-13	" Rebecca, of William and Rebecca,	June 13, 1748.
1-276	" Weeden, of William, Jun., and Rebecca,	Jan. 16, 1756.
1-276	" Remington, of James and Elizabeth,	Jan. 26, 1756.
1-276	" Hannah,	Dec. 4, 1757.
1-277	" William, of William and Mary,	Oct. 11, 1757.
2-280	" Elias, of James and Elizabeth,	Aug. 2, 1760.
2-280	" Catherine,	Sept. 27, 1764.
2-280	" Rebecca,	July 20, 1767.
2-280	" William,	Feb. 20, 1770.
2-280	" James,	Oct. 12, 1772.
2-280	" Elizabeth,	Sept. 2, 1780.
1-50	" Samuel, of Simeon, Jr., and Hannah,	Nov. 20, 1767.
1-50	" Samuel,	died Dec. 10, 1767.
1-50	" Mary,	Jan. 11, 1769.
1-50	" Stennett,	Nov. 24, 1772.
1-50	" Stennett,	died Sept. 6, 1778.
1-50	" Hannah,	July 17, 1775.
1-50	" Hannah,	died Sept. 5, 1776.
1-50	" Champlain,	July 26, 1777.
1-50	" Champlain,	died Sept. 10, 1778.
1-52	" Samuel,	Feb. 7, 1780.
1-52	" Hannah,	July 6, 1782.
1-52	" Simeon,	Aug. 21, 1786.
1-68	" Rouse, of Joshua and Elizabeth,	Dec. 7, 1769.
1-68	" Elizabeth,	Oct. 17, 1771.
1-68	" William,	April 8, 1773.
1-68	" Joseph, of Joshua and Elizabeth,	April 8, 1773.

1-68	CLARKE	Joshua, of Joshua and Elizabeth,		Jan. 22, 1775.
1-68	"	Joshua,	d.	Sept. 19, 1787.
1-68	"	Wells,		Feb. 15, 1777.
1-68	"	Susannah,		Jan. 10, 1779.
1-68	"	Perry,		Nov. 21, 1780.
1-68	"	Hazard,		May 20, 1783.
1-68	"	Luke,		Aug. 15, 1785.
1-68	"	Mary,		July 10, 1787.
1-68	"	Joshua,		June 28, 1790.
1-293	"	Newman, of Moses and Alice,		Jan. 31, 1779.
2-26	"	Samuel, of Samuel and Renewed,		Nov. 21, 1796.
2-26	"	Susan S.,		May 15, 1798.
2-26	"	Benjamin S.,		Sept. 30, 1800.
2-26	"	Renewed,		Nov. 14, 1802.
2-26	"	Joshua R.,		Feb. 23, 1805.
2-26	"	Dorcas,		Feb. 1, 1808.
2-26	"	Mary,		Oct. 20, 1810.
2-17	"	Sarah, of Luke and Sarah,		Jan. 18, 1808.
2-17	"	Luke,		Aug. 23, 1809.
2-17	"	John Tefft,		Sept. 5, 1811.
2-17	"	Mary,		March 17, 1813.
2-17	"	Elizabeth,		Nov. 8, 1814.
2-17	"	Lucinda,		June 2, 1816.
2-17	"	Ruth,		Oct. 2, 1818.
2-17	"	Joshua Perry, of Luke and Sarah,		March 14, 1821.
2-17	"	Reynolds Hoxsie,		Feb. 2, 1823.
2-17	"	Harriet Wells,		Aug. 24, 1825.
2-44	"	Halsey Perry, of David and Susannah,		Aug. 9, 1818.
2-44	"	Mary Ann,		Nov. 2, 1830.
2-30	"	Susan Mursela, of Abbie,		Feb. 5, 1826.
1-165	COLDGROVE	Desire, of Oliver and Esther,		Nov. 21, 1765.
1-165	"	Ruth,		March 11, 1767.
1-165	"	Eli,		April 4, 1768.
1-165	"	William,		July 3, 1769.
1-165	"	Amos,		Nov. 18, 1770.
1-163	"	Joseph, of Oliver and Esther,		March 8, 1772.
1-163	"	Esther,		April 3, 1773.
1-163	"	William,		Sept. 14, 1774.
1-163	"	Mary,		Nov. 24, 1775.
1-163	"	Brownell,		June 12, 1777.
1-163	"	Jonathan,		Sept. 21, 1778.
1-163	"	Nathan,		Jan. 12, 1780.
1-163	"	Elizabeth,		March 31, 1781.
1-163	"	Christopher,		Feb. 13, 1783.
1-163	"	Thomas,		Feb. 22, 1785.
2-30	CONGDON	Sally Marah, of John R.,		Feb. 8, 1826.

D

1-106	DYE	Samuel, of John and Thankful.	Feb. 26, 1759.
1-106	"	Richard,	Oct. 18, 1761.
1-106	"	Elizabeth,	Feb. 8, 1765.
1-106	"	Mary,	May 21, 1768.
1-106	"	Jonah.	July 15, 1771.

E

1-273	ENOS	Marcy, of Joseph, Jr., and Kezia.	Sept. 1, 1739.
1-273	"	Catherine,	Sept. 12, 1741.

F

1-9	FOSTER	Elizabeth, of Caleb and Elizabeth.	Jan. 7, 1747.
1-9	"	John Avery, of Sanford W. and Sarah,	April 25, 1841.

G

1-163	GRIFFETH John, of James and Desire,	Nov. 12, 1767.
1-134	" Ladd, of Phillip (of Charlestown), now of Richmond,	Dec. 31, 1769.
1-134	" Desire,	Feb. 22, 1771.
2-20	GRIFFIN Stephen C., of Joseph and Mary,	May 27, 1799.
2-20	" Susan,	June 4, 1801.
2-20	" Peleg,	Dec. 8, 1802.
2-20	" Emeline,	April 11, 1806.
2-20	" George W.,	Sept. 28, 1808.
2-20	" Sarah,	May 9, 1812.
2-33	" Prillip,	died May 9, 1832.

H

1-272	HALL Isaac, of Elizabeth,	Aug. 22, 1746.
1-272	" Abner,	Dec. 10, 1747.
1-272	" Elizabeth,	June 13, 1749.
1-272	" Mary,	Jan. 30, 1750.
1-272	" Josiah,	Aug. 22, 1752.
1-153	HARRINGTON William, of William and Sarah,	March 15, 1772.
1-153	" Benjamin,	Oct. 4, 1773.
1-153	" John,	Aug. 19, 1775.
1-153	" Ezekiel,	July 23, 1777.
1-153	" Stephen,	May 18, 1779.
1-153	" Mary,	March 12, 1781.
1-153	" Anna,	Feb. 27, 1783.
1-282	HATHAWAY William, of Zepraniah and Desire,	July 24, 1759.
1-70	HOXSIE Joseph, of Joseph and Deborah,	May 15, 1729.
1-70	" Job,	May 21, 1731.
1-70	" Mary,	Sept. 19, 1733.
1-70	" Jeremiah,	Nov. 8, 1735.
1-70	" John,	Jan. 22, 1737.
1-70	" Thomas,	May 25, 1740.
1-70	" Samuel,	Dec. 25, 1742.
1-70	" Simeon,	July 31, 1745
1-70	" Elijah,	Oct. 4, 1748.
1-70	" Joseph,	died April 5, 1815.
1-108	" Frederick, of Job and Anna,	Nov. 30, 1760.
1-108	" Edith, of Barnabas and Elizabeth,	July 31, 1764.
1-108	" Stephen,	Jan. 16, 1768.
1-108	" Enock,	July 27, 1769.
1-108	" Elizabeth,	April 1, 1772.
1-108	" Esther,	May 21, 1774.
1-64	" Joseph, of Jeremiah and Sarah,	Nov. 28, 1764.
1-64	" Simeon,	March 12, 1767.
2-1	" Amie, of Gideon and Jonah,	Sept. 3, 1773.
2-1	" Susannah,	April 30, 1781.
2-1	" Potter,	Jan. 12, 1783.
2-1	" Hannah,	Feb. 26, 1785.
2-1	" Mary,	March 27, 1787.
2-1	" Gideon,	March 29, 1789.
2-1	" Rouse,	April 1, 1791.
2-1	" Almira,	May 19, 1793.
2-1	" Abigail,	Aug. 4, 1795.
2-1	" Elizabeth,	Nov. 4, 1797.
2-1	" David,	April 2, 1805.
2-47	" Reynolds,	Oct. 8, 1774.
2-47	" Mary (Tillinghast) his wife,	Jan. 21, 1776.
2-47	" Hannah Tillinghast, of Reynolds and Mary,	May 1, 1797.
2-47	" Hannah Tillinghast,	d. Jan. 23, 1849.
2-47	" Sarah Tillinghast,	March 10, 1790.
2-47	" Clarke,	Sept. 15, 1800.
2-47	" Clarke,	d. Dec. 7, 1838.

2-47	HOXSIE Reynolds, of Reynolds and Mary,		June 30, 1803.
2-47	" Samuel Albro,		April 2, 1806.
2-47	" Mary,		Jan. 14, 1808.
2-47	" Mary,		d. May 8, 1808.
2-47	" Joseph Tillinghast,		April 28, 1810.
2-47	" Joseph Tillinghast,		d. May 6, 1840.
2-47	" Ruth,		April 23, 1812.
2-47	" Anstis,		March 26, 1814.
2-47	" Mary,		March 25, 1817.
2-47	" Thomas,		Aug. 13, 1818.
1-376	" Elizabeth, of Presbury and Alice,		Sept. 9, 1792.
1-376	" Stephen,		June 24, 1795.
1-376	" Susannah,		Jan. 2, 1798.
1-376	" Alice,		Jan. 2, 1800.
1-376	HOXSIE Mary, of Presbury and Alice,		Aug. 10, 1803.
2-23	" Martha, of Joseph and Hannah (1st wife), Sept. 27, 1798.		
2-23	" Stillman L., of Joseph and Susannah (2d wife), Feb. 12, 1802.		
2-23	" Simon G.,		Sept. 3, 1805.
2-23	" Jonah,		Feb. 6, 1808.
2-23	" Sylvester P.,		Feb. 10, 1810.
2-23	" Nathaniel F.,		April 21, 1812.
2-23	" Abigail,		Oct. 30, 1814.
2-23	" Stukely T.,		Sept. 6, 1817.
2-23	" Sophie Ann,		Oct. 11, 1819.

I

1-74	IRISH Thankful, of Jonathan and Sarah (also 149, 280),		April 27, 1757.
1-74	" Sarah (also 149, 280),		Oct. 25, 1761.
1-74	" Jonathan (also 149, 280),		June 2, 1764.
1-74	" Hannah (also 149, 280),		May 13, 1767.

J

2-282	JAMES Mariam, of John and Margaret,		Jan. 13, 1750.
2-282	" Joseph,		May 13, 1753.
2-282	" Paul,		Sept. 20, 1755.
2-282	" Silas,		March 20, 1758.
2-282	" Samuel,		July 18, 1760.
1-110	" Sarah, of Thomas and Hannah,		March 15, 1770.
1-110	" Thomas,		July 8, 1772.
1-157	" Jonathan, of Robert and Anna,		June 30, 1788.
2-5	" Russell, of John and Elizabeth,		Sept. 12, 1797.
2-44	" Malinda, of Gardiner and Hannah,		Nov. 8, 1808.
2-44	" Hannah,		Aug. 12, 1810.
2-44	" William,		May 27, 1812.
2-44	" Simeon Clarke,		Sept. 18, 1814.
2-44	" Elizabeth,		March 12, 1817.
2-44	" Elizabeth,		d. March 28, 1817.
2-44	" Roxanna,		Aug. 26, 1822.
2-44	" Roxanna,		d. March 31, 1840.
2-44	" / Mary C.,		Jan. 24, 1925.
2-44	" Betsey Ann,		Aug. 7, 1820.
2-44	" Betsey Ann,		d. Nov. 25, 1838.

K

1-14	KENYON Pheneas, of David and Mary,		Oct. 8, 1744.
1-14	" John,		Oct. 22, 1747.
1-273	" Mercy, of Samuel and Hannah,		June 24, 1746.
1-118	" Martha, of David, Jr., and Lydia,		Oct. 11, 1746.
1-118	" Lydia, of David and Mary, (2d wife,)		Aug. 17, 1752.

1-118	KENYON Mary, of David and Mary,	July 26, 1755.
1-118	" William,	April 1, 1758.
1-118	" Deborah,	March 27, 1763.
1-118	" Potter,	March 25, 1768.
1-64	" Thurston, of William and Hannah,	June 8, 1755.
1-64	" David,	June 24, 1758.
1-64	" Thankful,	Sept. 30, 1763.
1-62	" Jarius, of John and Elizabeth,	Feb. 1, 1756.
1-62	" Thomas Webster,	March 9, 1758.
1-62	" Mercy,	Oct. 29, 1763.
1-70	KENYON Philip, of Thomas and Ruth,	May 17, 1758.
1-70	" Esther,	March 26, 1760.
1-70	" Patience,	Jan. 12, 1763.
1-70	" Sprague,	May 19, 1766.
1-70	" Mary,	April 8, 1768.
1-70	" Pardon,	March 19, 1770.
1-102	" Edie, of Benedict and Amie,	Aug. 11, 1760.
1-102	" Samuel,	April 17, 1762.
1-102	" Remington,	June 17, 1764.
1-102	" Silas,	Aug. 28, 1766.
1-102	" Benedict,	Dec. 26, 1768.
1-102	" John,	March 9, 1771.
1-102	" Corey,	April 13, 1773.
1-102	" Amie,	Sept. 26, 1774.
1-102	" Betsey,	Jan. 3, 1778.
1-102	" Mary,	June 30, 1780.
1-102	" George,	Feb. 9, 1783.
1-90	" Thomas, (3d son) of Thomas, Jr., and Sarah,	Feb. 3, 1765.
1-90	" Steadman, of Thomas, Jr., and Sarah,	Sept. 20, 1767.
1-90	" Hannah,	May 3, 1771.
1-90	" Simeon,	May 16, 1773.
1-90	" Sarah,	July 17, 1778.
1-188	" Jonathan, of Jonathan and Sarah,	July 13, 1782.
1-188	" Asa,	May 7, 1784.
1-188	" Beriah,	May 20, 1786.
1-188	" Beriah,	died Nov. 30, 1792.
1-188	" Elizabeth,	Feb. 28, 1789.
1-188	" Samuel J.,	Nov. 18, 1791.
1-188	" Samuel J.,	died Dec. 17, 1793.
1-188	" Samuel B.,	Dec. 16, 1793.
1-188	" Martha,	May 27, 1794.
1-188	" Mary,	July 2, 1796.
1-188	" Dorcas,	July 23, 1801.
1-188	" Solomon J,,	Aug. 8, 1804.
1-220	" Joseph, of John and Anstis,	Nov. 6, 1793.
1-220	" George,	April 23, 1795.
1-220	" Alice,	March 25. 1797.
1-220	" Amie,	Feb. 7, 1799.
1-220	" Charity,	May 7, 1801.
1-230	" Gardiner, of Silas and Mary,	May 4, 1796.
1-230	" Hannah Champlain.	June 8, 1801.
1-126	" Elizabeth, of Benedict and Orpah,	Feb. 9, 1798.
1-126	" Barber,	Oct. 4, 1799.
2-44	" Leander A., of Jarvas and Julia,	Feb. 22, 1847.
2-58	KNOWLES Kate B., of Charles A. and Abbie S.,	Dec. 20. 1852.
2-58	" James Leroy,	May 16, 1855.

L

1-274	LARKIN Sarah, of Nicholas and Sarah,	Sept. 13, 1741.
1-274	" Edward,	Nov. 18, 1742.
1-274	" Abigail,	Nov. 16, 1743.
1-274	" Kenyon,	May 14, 1750.
1-274	" Lydia,	Feb. 3, 1753.

1-74	LARKIN	Nicholas, of Nicholas and Sarah,	April 4, 1756.
1-74	"	John, of Lottansett and Prudence,	March 18, 1767.
1-74	"	Thomas,	March 15, 1768.
1-74	"	Sarah,	May 13, 1769.
1-74	"	Joseph,	Sept. 19, 1770.
1-74	"	Prudence,	Aug. 24, 1772.
1-74	"	Lot,	March 14, 1774.
1-108	"	Susannah, of Edward and Hannah,	Sept. 13, 1767.
1-108	"	Tabitha,	Feb. 4, 1770.
1-108	"	Nicholas,	April 19, 1772.
1-108	"	Sarah,	July 6, 1774.
1-108	"	Edward,	Aug. 23, 1776.
1-108	"	James,	March 16, 1779.
1-108	"	John Martin,	March 16, 1781.
1-108	"	Kenyon,	June 21, 1783.
1-272	LEWIS	Abigail, of James and Abigail,	March 28, 1717.
1-272	"	Hannah,	Aug. 5, 1720.
1-272	"	Ruth,	Feb. 2, 1724.
1-9	"	George B., of George and Sarah,	March 30, 1735.
1-9	"	Eleazer,	Jan. 11, 1737.
1-9	"	Ezekiel,	June 17, 1739.
1-9	"	Elnathan,	Jan. 4, 1742.
1-9	"	Samuel,	May 20, 1744.
1-9	"	Sarah,	March 17, 1746.
1-9	"	Benjamin,	April 10, 1748.
1-9	"	Martha,	July 16, 1750.
1-9	"	Benjamin,	died April 22, 1752.
1-271	"	Tacy, of Enock and Mary,	Sept. 29, 1743.
1-271	"	Mary,	March 26, 1745.
1-271	"	John,	May 15, 1747.
1-271	"	Isreal,	March 28, 1750.
1-271	"	Bathsheba,	Jan. 24, 1752.
1-271	"	Enock,	Feb. 19, 1754.
1-271	"	Elizabeth,	March 31, 1757.
1-271	"	Benedict,	July 11, 1759.
1-271	"	Joshua,	Sept. 24, 1762.
1-272	"	William, of James and Susannah,	May 26, 1748.
1-272	"	Gideon,	Dec. 15, 1749.
1-272	"	Patience,	Dec. 15, 1752.
1-10	"	Thomas, of Thomas and Mary,	Jan. 14, 1748-9.
1-10	"	Benoni,	Sept. 28, 1752.
2-280	"	Mary,	n. s. April 14, 1755.
2-280	"	William,	Sept. 18, 1757.
2-280	"	William 2d,	April 9, 1763.
2-280	"	Abigail,	March 26, 1765.
1-277	"	Benjamin, of George and Sarah,	Oct. 11, 1757.
1-178	"	Elizabeth, of Nathan and Mary,	July 5, 1764.
1-179	"	Nathan,	March 18, 1767.
1-179	"	Benjamin,	July 4, 1770.
1-179	"	Thomas,	Oct. 17, 1772.
1-179	"	Sarah,	Jan. 3, 1774.
1-179	"	Hannah,	March 23, 1776.
1-179	"	Anna,	June 17, 1779.

Note—Three first born Charlestown, the others Richmond.

1-149	LILLIBRIDGE	Thomas, died, in his 63d year,	Aug. 29, 1723.
1-149	"	Sarah, his wife,	d. Jan. —, 1761.
1-149	"	Thomas, Jr., died in his 55th year,	Feb. 8, 1757.
1-149	"	Mary, d. of Thomas, d. aged 14 d.,	Jan. 23, 1729.
1-149	"	Sarah (Barber), dau. of Thomas, Jr., died in her 32d year, Sept. 3, 1758.	
1-149	"	A son of Thomas, 3d,	Aug. 29, 1755.
1-149	"	A son of Thomas, 3d,	d. Sept. 8, 1755.
1-149	"	Sarah,	Aug. 27, 1758.
1-149	"	Sarah,	d. July 3, 1760.
1-149	"	A son,	March 31, 1760.

1-149	LILLIBRIDGE, a son, of Thomas 3d,	d. April 3, 1760.
2-282	" Deborah, of Thomas and Mary,	July 8, 1756.
2-282	" Thomas,	March 6, 1761.
2-282	" Joseph,	March 16, 1763.
2-282	" Edward,	April 3, 1765.
2-282	" Champlain,	March 9, 1767.
1-157	" John,	April 22, 1769.
1-157	" Mary,	March 20, 1771.
1-157	" Thankful,	April 25, 1773.
1-280	" Sarah, of Edward and Patience,	July 16, 1757.
1-280	" Lester,	Sept. 25, 1759.
1-370	" Sally, of John and Mary,	July 2, 1790.
1-370	" Thankful,	April 22, 1792.
1-370	" Thomas,	March 24, 1794.
1-370	" Deborah,	Oct. 27, 1796.
1-370	" Polly,	April 28, 1800.
1-417	" Nabby, of Amos and Phebe,	Sept. 17, 1798.
1-417	" Darcus,	Nov. 13, 1799.
1-417	" Clarissa,	June 27, 1801.
1-417	" Amos,	March 24, 1803.
2-2	" John H., of John and Hannah,	March 20, 1818.
2-2	" Nancy,	Dec. 1, 1820.

M

1-56	MAXSON Mary, of Jonathan and Mary,	June 28, 1764.
1-56	" Jemima,	Jan. 25, 1766.
1-56	" Jonathan,	June 9, 1768.
1-56	" Sarah,	Dec. 24, 1770.
1-8	MIUS Elizabeth, of Oliver,	Sept. 12, 1736.
1-8	" Mary,	April 6, 1740.
1-8	" Ann,	Jan. 20, 1742.
1-8	" Alice,	March 19, 1746.
1-8	" Oliver,	March 18, 1748.
1-76	MOON Sarah, of Robert, Jr., and Eleanor,	May 14, 1754.
1-76	" Alice,	Nov. 24, 1756.
1-76	" Augustus,	Nov. 2, 1759.
1-76	" Waite,	Jan. 21, 1762.

N

1-187	NEY Hannah, of George and Mercy,	Dec. 7, 1767.
1-187	" Samuel,	Dec. 24, 1769.
1-187	" Thurston,	May 23, 1775.
1-187	" George,	Sept. 2, 1774.
1-187	" Mercy,	March 27, 1777.
1-190	NICHOLS George, of David and Sarah,	Nov. 8, 1748.
1-190	" George,	d. Feb. 4, 1785.
1-121	" Jonathan, of David, Jr., and Desire,	July 20, 1767.
1-121	" David,	Feb. 20, 1771.
1-121	" Elizabeth, of David, Jr., and Elizabeth, 2d wife,	Jan. 7, 1775.
1-276	NILES Sarah, of Ebenezer and Sarah, born Charlestown,	May 13, 1743.
1-275	" Sarah, widow of Ebenezer,	d. Nov. 8, 1803.

O

| 2-51 | OLNEY John, born North Providence, R. I., | Nov. 14, 1804. |
| 2-51 | "   John, died Richmond, | Dec. 7, 1847. |

P

1-13	PERRY	Mary, of Samuel and Anne,	Dec. 28, 1747.
1-271	"	Samuel, of Simeon and Penelope,	June 6, 1749.
1-271	"	Mary,	Sept. 18, 1750.
1-271	"	Samuel,	May 1, 1754.
1-274	"	Benjamin, of Edward and Dorcas,	Dec. 11, 1754.
1-274	"	Susannah,	Sept. 25, 1759.
1-274	"	George,	Feb. 9, 1762.
1-138	PETTIS	Mary, of Robert and Mary,	May 11, 1771.
1-138	"	Elizabeth,	May 23, 1773.
1-138	"	Robert,	May 13, 1775.
1-271	PETTYS	Robert, of Nathaniel,	Feb. 24, 1739.
1-271	"	Elizabeth,	Dec. 17, 1741.
1-127	"	Nathaniel,	Jan. 5, 1743.
1-271	"	Ephraim,	April 13, 1745.
1-52	"	Sarah, of William and Mary,	Jan. 10, 1746.
1-52	"	Alce,	Dec. 5, 1749.
1-52	"	Stephen,	Nov. 1, 1751.
1-52	"	Mercy,	Dec. 9, 1753.
1-52	"	Joseph,	Jan. 4, 1759.
1-52	"	Hannah,	Feb. 27, 1761.
1-52	"	Mary,	Aug. 6, 1763.
1-3	PETTY	Peleg, of Benjamin and Sarah,	April 14, 1751.
1-276	"	Lydia,	June 17, 1753.
1-276	"	James,	Aug. 30, 1755.
1-276	"	Elizabeth,	Sept. 23, 1757.
1-279	"	Benjamin,	March 12, 1759.
2-54	PHILLIPS	John Edwin, of John and Rebecca,	July 31, 1851.
2-279	POTTER	Thankful, of William, Jr., and Elizabeth,	March 15, 1741.
2-279	"	Daniel,	Feb. 2, 1743.
2-279	"	Alice, of William, Jr., and Elizabeth,	Sept. 16, 1745.
2-279	"	Robert,	May 9, 1748.
2-279	"	Mary,	May 18, 1751.
2-279	"	Isabel,	Nov. 9, 1758.
2-279	"	Jonathan,	July 8, 1761.

Note—The two first of the above born in Dartmouth, Mass.

1-13	"	Ruth, of Thomas and Martha,	Sept. 13, 1746.
1-13	"	George,	Oct. 31, 1747.
1-13	"	Peleg,	May 14, 1749.
1-13	"	Mary,	Nov. 13, 1750.
1-13	"	Thomas,	Nov. 23, 1752.
1-13	"	James,	Nov. 6, 1754.
1-13	"	Paine,	Sept. 10, 175—.
1-13	"	Gideon,	Nov. 11, 175—.
1-274	"	Elizabeth, of Jonathan and Mary,	Oct. 27, 1749.
1-274	"	Mary,	June 20, 1751.
1-274	"	Sarah,	March 11, 1753.
1-274	"	Jonathan,	Aug. 26, 1754.
1-274	"	Elisha,	June 1, 1756.
1-274	"	Susannah,	March 31, 1758.
1-274	"	Lyman,	May 1, 1760.
1-274	"	Judeth,	May 1, 1762.
1-274	"	Martha,	Nov. 18, 1764.
1-274	"	Matthew,	Nov. 11, 1768.
1-11	"	Income, of David and Susannah,	July 7, 1749.
1-277	"	Silas,	April 17, 1751
1-277	"	Philip,	Sept. 13, 1753.
1-277	"	Rhoda,	June 20, 1756.
1-277	"	Ione,	Dec. 20, 1758.
1-277	"	Mary,	Jan. 17, 1762.
1-277	"	David,	(sic.) June 23, 1723.
2-277	POTTER	Stephen, of Stephen and Sarah (also 2-281),	Feb. 8, 1759.
1-62	"	Mary. of Smiteon and Lucy.	Jan. 15, 1766.
1-62	"	Joshua,	Aug. 18, 1768.

1-62	POTTER Hannah, of Smiteon and Lucy,	April 18, 1771.
1-62	" Rachel,	April 10, 1774.
1-62	" Benjamin,	May 16, 1776.
1-62	" Smiteon,	Oct. 9, 1778.
2-260	" Elisha, of Elisha and Susannah,	Jan. 8, 1788.
2-260	" Perry,	March 5, 1789.
2-260	" Dorcas,	Jan. 20, 1791.
2-8	" Mary, of Mathew and Mary,	July 12, 1797.
2-8	" Matthew Robinson,	Oct. 23, 1799.
2-8	" John Brayman,	May 10, 1803.
2-8	" Judeth,	Nov. 8, 1907.
2-8	" Jonathan,	Dec. 26, 1809.
1-196	PULLMAN George, of Jonathan and Sarah,	May 17, 1776.
1-196	" Edward,	May 17, 1776.

Q R

1-187	RECORD Jonathan, of Thomas (dec.), and Abia,	Aug. 18, 1775.
1-419	REYNOLDS Thomas, of Thomas and Jemima,	Dec. 2, 1791.
2-35	" Clarke H., of Robert and Hannah,	Dec. 1, 1821.
2-35	" Gideon,	Aug. 29, 1823.
2-35	" Mary,	Oct. 23, 1825.
2-35	" Hannah,	March 19, 1828.
2-36	" Robert Thomas, of Thomas and Joanna,	Sept. 26, 1826.
2-36	" William Henry,	Aug. 27, 1828.
2-36	" Harriet Newell,	April 14, 1830.
2-36	" Lillian J.,	Dec. 17, 1831.
2-36	" Mary Elizabeth,	Aug. 9, 1833.
2-36	" Frances W.,	Oct. 23, 1835.
1-9	RICHMOND Edward, of Stephen and Mary,	Dec. 15, 1746.
1-9	" Anne,	June 8, 1750.
1-272	ROGERS Hannah, of Thomas and Zerniah,	Sept. 21, 1735.
1-272	" Thomas,	March 10, 1741.
1-272	" Sarah,	April 1, 1744.
1-272	" Waite,	Oct. 29, 1747.
1-272	" Elizabeth,	July 7, 1750.
1-272	" Benjamin, of Jeremiah, Jr., and Patience,	April 3, 1752.
1-53	" Anne, of Thomas, Jr., and Elizabeth,	Jan. 28, 1764.
1-53	" Zuriah,	April 29, 1765.
1-53	" Elizabeth,	May 31, 1767.
1-53	" Thomas,	May 31, 1767.
1-53	" James,	May 13, 1769.
1-53	" Stephen,	April 12, 1771.
1-53	" Amie,	May 31, 1773.

S

1-56	SHELDON Susannah, of William, Jr., and Eleanor,	June 11, 1765.
1-56	" Potter,	Jan. 4, 1767.
1-272	SISSON Deborah, of Barnett and Catherine,	April 1, 1741.
1-272	" Rodman,	June 3, 1744.
1-272	" Sarah,	Nov. 20, 1751.
1-106	STAFFORD Catherine, of Andrew and Rachel,	July 21, 1775.
1-106	" James,	Oct. 6, 1777.
2-275	STANTON John, of David and Martha,	Nov. 25, 1742.
2-275	" Latham,	Jan. 13, 1745.
2-275	" Elizabeth,	April 1, 1747.
2-275	" Catherine,	March 5, 1749.
2-275	" Mary,	Dec. 28, 1751.
2-275	" Hannah,	Feb. 19, 1755.

Note—Two first born North Kingstown, third South Kingstown, fourth Exeter, the two last Richmond.

2-44	SLOCUM John H., of John and Sarah,	March 17, 1846.

T

1-14	TEFFT	John, of John,	Dec. 4, 1699.
1-14	"	Mary, wife of John, Feb.	Feb. 5, 1704.
1-14	"	Deliverance, of John and Mary,	Aug. 19, 1722.
1-14	"	Sarah,	April 27, 1725.
1-14	"	Sarah,	d. Feb. —, 1726.
1-14	"	Jonathan,	April 29, 1727.
1-14	"	John,	March 9, 1729.
1-14	"	Robert,	May 25, 1732.
1-14	'	Mary,	Sept. 20, 1734.
1-14	"	Patience,	April 21, 1737.
1-14	"	Deborah,	May 18, 1739.
1-14	"	Mehitable,	Aug. 3, 1742.
1-14	"	Elizabeth,	Feb. 10, 1744,
1-14	"	Jeremiah,	May 29, 1747.
1-14	"	William,	Jan. 16, 1749.
1-3	"	Elizabeth, of Joseph and Esther,	Dec. 20, 1730.
1-3	"	William,	Feb. 29, 1732.
1-3	"	Joseph,	March 19, 1737.
1-3	"	Ruth,	March 27, 1739.
1-3	"	Benjamin,	June 3, 1741,
1-3	"	Esther,	Aug. 6, 1743.
1-3	"	Thomas,	Nov. 10, 1745.
1-3	"	Sarah,	Aug. 24, 1747.
1-3	"	Samuel,	Aug. 29, 1749.
1-276	"	Reynolds, of John, Jr., and Hannah,	Oct. 6, 1752.
1-276	"	Reynolds,	d. July 5, 1754.
1-283	"	Clarke,	Jan. 7, 1761.
1-283	'	Hezekiah, of William and Mary,	Dec. 16, 1753.
1-282	"	Pardon,	Jan. 27, 1755.
1-282	"	Thankful,	March 21, 1757.
1-282	"	David,	April 19, 1760.
1-282	"	William,	May 21, 1763.
2-282	"	Mary,	March 13, 1766.
2-282	"	John,	May 18, 1767.
2-282	"	Mary,	April 22, 1769.
1-41	"	Caleb, of Joseph, Jr., ard Sarah,	Oct. 17, 1757.
1-41	"	Mary,	Nov. 24, 1758.
1-41	"	Taber,	March 3, 1761.
1-41	"	Jemima.	July 10, 1763.
1-41	"	Joseph,	April 6, 1766
1-41	"	Sarah,	June 12, 1768.
1-41	"	Anstice,	April 1, 1773.
1-41	"	Alice,	June 16, 1775.
1-41	"	Albro,	Sept. 27, 1778.
1-15	"	Phebe Woodmansee, of Penelope,	Jan. 3, 1765.
1-60	"	Joanna, of Benjamin and Deborah,	Feb. 7, 1766.
1-60	"	Edward,	March 12, 1768.
1-60	"	Elizabeth,	Sept. 10, 1770.
1-60	"	Asa,	June 2, 1772.
1-60	"	Jesse,	April 2, 1776.
1-179	"	Mary, of Jeremiah and Rhoda,	April 24, 1771.
1-179	"	Jeremiah,	Dec. 29, 1772.
1-179	"	John,	Dec. 18, 1778.
1-179	"	Abigail,	March 29, 1781.
1-179	"	Rhoda,	April 11, 1783.
1-102	"	George, of Samuel, Jr., and Amie,	May 7, 1772.
1-102	"	George,	d. Dec. 10, 1773.
1-102	"	Susannah,	June 30, 1775.
1-102	"	Amie,	Dec. 20, 1777.
1-102	"	George,	Oct. 18, 1780.
1-102	"	Josiah,	Sept. 12, 1782.
1-102	"	Esther,	Feb. 6, 1785.
1-102	"	Sarah,	Jan. 25, 1787.

1-102	TEFFT	Elizabeth, of Samuel, Jr., and Amie,	Nov. 16, 1788.
1-102	"	William,	Oct. 3, 1791.
1-102	"	Gardiner,	Jan. 26, 1794.
1-206	"	Benjamin, of Thomas and Lydia,	Sept. 11, 1773.
1-206	"	Sarah,	April 10, 1775.
1-206	"	Esther,	Feb. 18, 1777.
1-206	"	Esther,	d. Dec. 5, 1824.
1-206	"	Joseph,	April 6, 1779.
1-206	"	Thomas,	Feb. 23, 1781.
1-206	"	Welcome,	Oct. 4, 1782.
1-206	"	Abram,	Jan. 24, 1785.
1-206	"	Abram,	d. Oct. 9, 1785.
1-206	"	Lydia,	Aug. 4, 1786.
1-206	"	Lydia,	d. Dec. 27, 1786.
1-206	"	Mary,	Jan. 25, 1788.
1-206	"	Mary,	d. April 5, 1827.
1-206	"	Lydia,	June 29, 1790.
1-206	"	Lydia, wife of Thomas,	d. May 22, 1797.
1-206	"	Ruth, of Thomas and Lydia,	July 12, 1794.
1-206	"	Ruth,	d. Oct. 22, 1826.
2-283	"	James, of William and Mary,	Feb. 18, 1776.
2-283	"	Joseph,	March 8, 1779.
1-126	"	Caleb, of Taber and Sarah,	Oct. 14, 1782.
1-126	"	Elizabeth.	June 16, 1784.
1-181	"	Joanna, of Joseph, Jr., and Abigail,	Dec. 28, 1789.
1-181	"	Joseph Maxson,	Sept. 13, 1791.
1-181	"	William,	Jan. 20, 1794.
1-181	"	Nathan,	Oct. 4, 1798.
1-181	"	Sarah,	Feb. 21, 1800.
1-240	"	Benjamin, of Samuel Albro and Sarah,	Nov. 22, 1798.
1-240	"	Alice Albro, 1st,	Aug. 1, 1800.
2-2	"	Alice Albro, 2d,	July 29, 1802.
2-2	"	Joseph,	July 21, 1804.
2-2	"	Samuel Albro,	Aug. 7, 1807.
2-2	"	Taber,	July 23, 1809.
2-2	"	Sarah Ann,	Nov. 15, 1812.
2-2	"	Jeremiah Gardiner,	Nov. 20, 1817.
2-59	TUCKER	Ella, of Brightman and Harriet L.,	May 10, 1849.
2-59	"	Herbert,	Nov. 11, 1851.
2-59	"	Earle,	Jan. 16, 1853.
2-59	"	Wayne,	Oct. 24, 1859.

U V W

2-273	WATSON	William, of Simeon and Hannah,	July 3, 1749.
2-273	"	Hannah,	May 24, 1751.
2-273	"	Perry,	Feb. 12, 1754.
1-26	WEBB	Margeret, of John and Joanna,	Aug. 21, 1721.
1-26	"	Elizabeth,	March 27, 1724.
1-26	"	Mehitable,	Aug. 11, 1726.
1-26	"	Mary,	March 19, 1730.
1-26	"	George,	May 10, 1733.
1-26	"	John,	Oct. 10, 1735.
1-76	"	George, of George,	Aug. 15, 1753.
1-76	"	Joshua,	Jan. 23, 1755.
1-76	"	John,	May 20, 1758.
1-76	"	Joseph,	May 1, 1762.
1-76	"	Joanna,	May 1, 1762.
1-76	"	Jerusha,	May 1, 1762.
1-15	WEBSTER	Thankful, of James and Hannah,	Feb. 15, 1743.
1-15	"	Margeret,	Dec. 10, 1744.
1-15	"	Hannah,	June 8, 1747.
1-15	"	Stephen,	March 17, 1750.
1-15	"	Zerniah,	Dec. 4, 1752.

1-15	WEBSTER James, of James and Hannah,		Sept. 4, 1755.
1-15	"	John,		April 2, 1758.
1-15	"	Daniel,		Nov. 7, 1761.
1-15	"	Sarah,		May 21, 1763.
1-15	"	Elizabeth,		Sept. 25, 1767.
1-58	"	William, of John, Jr., and Elizabeth,		Jan. 27, 1753.
1-58	"	Mary,		Aug. 14, 1755.
1-58	"	Thomas,		Oct. 29, 1757.
1-58	"	Hannah,		Dec. 19, 1759.
1-58	"	Elizabeth,		April 14, 1762.
1-58	"	John,		July 24, 1765.
1-118	WILBOUR Benjamin, of Benjamin and Lucy,		June 8, 1777.
1-118	"	Anne,		Sept. 13, 1779.
1-118	"	Vincent,		April 17, 1781.
1-118	"	John,		June 6, 1783.
1-118	"	Lucy,		May 15, 1787.
1-118	"	Elizabeth,		July 11, 1789.
1-118	"	Elizabeth,	d.	Dec. 16, 1790.
1-118	"	Elizabeth, 2d,		Dec. 28, 1791.
1-118	"	Robert Morey,		May 5, 1794.
1-121	WILCOX Lyman, of Benjamin and Elizabeth,		July 17, 1800.
1-15	WOODMANSEE Joseph, of Joseph and Mary,		June 14, 1742.
1-15	"	Mary,		Feb. 7, 1744.
1-15	"	John,		Feb. 13, 1746.
1-14	"	Penelope,		Feb. 15, 1749.
1-15	"	James,		June 12, 1752.
1-15	"	Sarah,		Sept. 5, 1755.
1-15	"	David,		June 16, 1759.
1-15	"	Abigail,		June 27, 1764.
1-90	"	Hazard,		Feb. 4, 1769.
1-15	"	Mary Webster, of Margeret,		Feb. 13, 1766.

X Y Z

Vital Record of Rhode Island.

1636=1850.

FIRST SERIES.

BIRTHS, MARRIAGES AND DEATHS.

A Family Register for the People.

BY JAMES N. ARNOLD,

EDITOR OF THE NARRAGANSETT HISTORICAL REGISTER.

"Is My Name Written in the Book of Life?"

Vol. 5.   **HOPKINTON.**   **Part VII.**

Published under the Auspices of the General Assembly.

PROVIDENCE, R. I:
NARRAGANSETT HISTORICAL PUBLISHING COMPANY.
1894.

ACT INCORPORATING THE TOWN OF HOPKINTON.

AN ACT for dividing the Town of Westerly, and thereof making two distinct Townships; one to retain the name of Westerly, and the other to be designated and known by the name of Hopkinton.

Whereas, a great number of the inhabitants of the northern part of the Town of Westerly, preferred a petition, and represented into this Assembly, that the said Town being upwards of twenty miles in length, they are much aggrieved by reason many of them are obliged to travel some fifteen or sixteen miles, to get an instrument recorded, others eighteen or twenty miles, when business calls them before the Town Council, or to attend at a Court of Justices, the greater part of the public business being at this day transacted and done in the southern parts of said Town; and thereupon prayed that the same may be divided, nature having cut it into two parts, by the large river, called and known by the name of Pawcatuck; and that they may be entitled to equal privileges with the other Towns in this Colony, on consideration whereof.

Be it enacted by this General Assembly, and by the authority thereof it is enacted, that the said Town of Westerly, be, and the same is hereby, made and divided into two distinct and separate Towns; and that such part thereof as lieth to the southward of the aforesaid Pawcatuck river, shall still be and remain a Town, holding its ancient name of WESTERLY; and all the lands lying to the northward of said river, shall also be, and hereby is erected into and made a Town, to be distinguished, called and known by the name of HOPKINTON; and the inhabitants thereof shall have, hold and enjoy, all and singular, the liberties, privileges and immunities, that the other towns in this Colony are entitled to, New Shoreham and Jamestown excepted.

And be it further enacted by the authority aforesaid, that the money due unto the Town of Westerly, aforesaid, for the Cedar Swamp, shall be legally secured, both principal and intrest, unto those that live on the south side of the aforesaid Pawcatuck river; and they, in return shall be wholly and solely at the expense of defending said swamp; and the Town of Hopkinton shall not be subject to any costs, and charges on that account; that all the Town debts (except such as may have lately accrued on account of the swamp), shall be equally paid by the Towns of Westerly and Hopkinton; and all such monies as were due to what, before this act, was the Town of Westerly, shall be applied towards paying off said Town's debts, except such as are due on account of the swamp.

And be it further enacted by the authority aforesaid, that all and every of the Justices of the Peace, that were chosen and appointed such for the Town of Westerly, and who live in that part thereof, that is now made Hopkinton, be, and they hereby are. continued in their offices, with full power and ample authority, in every respect, as they had in consequence of their being chosen into and commissionated for said office and that the eldest of them issue his warrant to call the freemen of the said Town of Hopkinton to meet together at some convenient place within the same, in order to choose and appoint officers neccessary for managing and conducting the prudetial affairs of said Town.

Colonial Records of Rhode Island, Vol. VI., pages 31, 32.

HOPKINTON.

MARRIAGES.

A

1-1   ADAMS Martha, and William Douglas, Nov. 13, 1781.
1-41   ALLEN Sarah, and Gideon Foster, March 3, 1765.
1-51   "   John, Jr., and Elizabeth Matteson, both of Stonington; m. by Thomas Wells, Justice, Feb. 11, 1769.
1-1   "   Prudence, and Jonathan West, July 27, 1780.
3-10   ARNOLD Gorton W., son of Joseph, of Hopkinton, and Nancy Brown, of Francis, of Richmond; m. by Elder Matthew Stillman, Aug. 13, 1826.
3-17   "   Ruth, and Albert Bicknell, ——. —, 1843.
1-57   AUSTIN Mary, and Amos Palmer, Jr., Feb. 15, 1770.
1-47   AVERY Richardson, of Richardson, of Stonington, and Eunice Maxson, of John, Esq., of Hopkinton; m. by Thomas Wells, Justice, Jan. 1, 1766.
5-3   ATWOOD Betsey, and Albert Keeney, March 6, 1853.

B

1-116   BABCOCK Simeon, and Sarah Gardiner, Oct. 3, 1743.
1-58   "   Sarah, and Amos Langworthy, Feb. 15, 1758.
1-22   "   George's negress Mary, and Joshua Babcock's negro Port, March 9, 1758.
1-22   "   Joshua's negro Port, and George Babcock's Mary, March 9, 1758.
1-27   "   Sarah, and James Eldredge, Jan. 24, 1760.
1-32   "   Oliver, and Deborah Knowles; m. by Joshua Clarke, Justice, Dec. 2, 1761. |
1-32   "   John, and Deliverance Knowles; m. by Joshua Clarke, Justice, July 18, 1762.
2-58   "   Thankful, and George Rutter Gardiner, Sept. 12, 1767.
1-54   "   Hezekiah's Indian servant James, and Sarah ——, a mulatto; m. by Joshua Clarke, Justice, Oct. 10, 1768.
1-54   "   Martha, and Simon Rhodes, Aug. 22, 1769.
1-55   "   Rouse, of George, late of Hopkinton, dec., and Ruth Maxson, of Capt. John; m. by Elder Joshua Clarke, Oct. 12, 1769.
1-55   "   Peleg, of Oliver, Jr., and Lucy Maxson, of Samuel; m. by Joseph Crandall, Justice, Dec. 14, 1769.
1-56   "   Simeon, of Elisha, of Richmond, and Mary Perry, of Simeon, of Hopkinton, at Hopkinton; m. by Edward Perry, Justice, Jan. 7, 1770.
2-16   "   Desire, and Zaccheus Reynolds, Dec. 11, 1771.
1-69   "   Elizabeth, and Beriah Brown, Dec. 11, 1771.
1-77   "   Lois, and Benjamin Baker, Nov. 25, 1773.
1-108   "   Peleg, and Ruth Maxson; m. by Elder John Maxson, Jan. 18, 1776.
2-16   "   Phebe, and Zaccheus Reynolds, Sept. 16, 1781.
2-57   "   Daniel, of Hopkinton, and Content Potter, of Westerly, at Westerly; m. by Elder Joshua Clarke, April 8, 1784.
2-58   "   Peleg, of Stonington, and Elizabeth Wells, of Jonathan, of Hopkinton; m by Elder Joshua Clarke, June 18, 1789.

2-7 BABCOCK Barrodel, and John Tanner, March 24, 1791.
2-48 " Alice, and Rowland Lanphere, Dec. 18, 1791.
2-43 " Lois, and Stephen Tanner, March 13, 1794.
2-45 " Jonathan, of Hopkinton, and Presilla Wheeler, of Stonington,. at Stonington; m. by Elder Christopher Avery, Feb. 20, 1795.
2-54 " Rowland, of Hezekiah, and Mrs. Nabby White, of Walter; m. by Elder John Burdick, Jau. 12, 1797.
2-42 " Mary, and Joseph Clarke, Jan. 9, 1800.
2-60 " Anne, and Henry Potter, Nov. 17, 1812.
2-59 " Anna B., and Peleg Babcock, March 22, 1818.
2-59   Peleg, of Chester, New York, and Anna B. Babcock, of Westerly,. at Hopkinton; m. by Elder Matthew Stillman, March 22, 1818.
2-96 " Abbie, and John J. Maxson, Feb. 6, 1820.
2-88 " Eliza, and Samuel Gardiner, Feb. 4, 1821.
3-18 " Eliza, and Paul Babcock, Jan. 15, 1843.
3-18 " Paul, and Eliza Babcock; m. by Elder Weeden Barber, Jan. 15, 1843.
4-9 " Mary Ann, and George C. Crandall, Oct. 4, 1846.
1-77 BAGGS Margaret, and Elisha Larkin, Dec. 17, 1773.
1-112 " Elizabeth, and John Hide, March 27, 1774.
3-13 " Martha, and David Collins, May 13, 1838.
4-7 BAID Leander, of Newport, and Louisa M. Pearce, of Richmond; m. by Elder Charles C. Lewis, March 29, 1846.
1-51 BAILEY Timothy, of Richmond, and Dorcas Enos, of Hopkinton; m. by John Larkin, Justice, Feb. 16, 1769.
1-22 BAKER Ruth, and Elias Reynolds, April 17, 1758.
1-77 " Benjamin, of Richmond, and Lois Babcock, of Hopkinton, dau. of Oliver; m. by Elder John Gardiner, Nov. 25, 1773.
1-111 BARBER Mary, and Lodowick Kenyon, Jan. 16, 1777.
1-1 " Peace, and Ephraim Codner, Nov. 15, 1778.
1-1 " Benjamin, and Mary Perry, both of Hopkinton; m. by Edward Perry, Justice, Aug. 20, 1783.
2-12 " Cate, and Amos Burdick, May 11, 1790.
2-59 " Sarah, and Thomas Potter, Nov. 1, 1798.
2-59 " Dorcas, and Caleb Coon, Dec. 14, 1800.
2-46 " Samuel, of Thomas, dec., and Thankful Lewis, of James, of Exeter; m. by Elder Henry Joslin, Sept. 2, 1802.
2-65 " Susannah, and George J. Bowler, Nov. 22, 1802.
3-9 " Mary, and Amos N. Palmer, April 3, 1832.
3-10 " Abiel, of Hopkinton, and Nancy Brown, of North Stonington; m. by Elder Thomas Tillinghast, Sept. 29, 1833.
3-11   " Franklin, and Lydia Maxson; m. at Westerly by Elder Daniel Coon, Aug. 11, 1836.
3-15, 17 " John M., of Hopkinton, and Mary Hiscox, of Westerly; m. by Elder Daniel Coon, (also 4-20), March 24, 1841.
3-17 " Waitey, and George W. Richmond, —— —, 1842.
1-54 BATES Caleb, of Coventry, and Huldah Bowen of Hopkinton, daughter of Charles; m. by Elder Joshua Clarke, May 4, 1769.
1-102 BENJAMIN John, of Preston, Conn., and Grace Waite, of Hopkinton; m. by Elder Thomas West, June 29, 1775.
1-63,12 BENTLEY Susannah, and Billings Burch, Nov. 13, 1771.
2-45 " Elizabeth, and Benjamin Langworthy, Jr., Jan. 8, 1804.
2-43 " Benjamin P., and Hannah Wilbur; m. by Elder Abram Coon, Dec. 2, 1806.
2-43 " John, and Lydia Wilbur; m. by Elder Abram Coon, Dec. 3, 1806.
2-73 " Deborah, and John Tanner, Jan. 25, 1807.
1-103 BENT Catherine, and Thomas Potter Gardiner, April 15, 1773.
3-17 BICKNELL Albert, and Ruth Arnold; m. by Elder David Avery, —— —, 1843.
4-8 " Emeline Amanda, and George H. Olney, Aug. 11, 1846.
4-15 BICKNELL Mumford, and Jane Harris; m. by Elder Charles C. Lewis,. July 26, 1847.
4-15 BITGOOD Samuel C., and Eliza N. Crandall; m. by Elder C. C. Lewis, Nov. 28, 1847.

1-98 BLISS Elder William, of Newport, and Elizabeth Wand, late of Newport, but now of Hopkinton; m. by Elder Joshua Clarke, Jan. 9, 1780.

2-65 BOWLER George J., of Hopkinton, and Susannah Barber, of Westerly, at Westerly; m. by Elder Abram Coon, Nov. 22, 1802.

1-19 BOWEN Huldah, and Nathan Greene, Sept. 24, 1756.

1-54 " Huldah, and Caleb Bates, May 4, 1769.

1-108 BRAMAN James, of Hopkinton, and Isabel Millard, of Westerly; m. by Elder John Gardiner, Dec. 27, 1775.

1-111 " Mary, and Caleb Church, Nov. 27, 1777.

1-121 " James, Jr., and Hannah Lewis; m. by Elder Joseph Davis, Feb. 24, 1779.

2-43 " Mrs. Anna, and Christopher Brown, Jan. 22, 1789.

2-98 " William, and Thankful Davis; m. by Samuel Helme, Justice, Oct. 19, 1791.

4-9 " Jeremiah W., of Christopher, and Sophronia A. Foster; m. by Elder Henry Clarke, Oct. 11, 1846.

1-34 BRAND Judeth, and Isaiah Williams, Nov. 16, 1762.

2-4 " Rayzel, and Dorcas Morey; m. by David Nichols, Justice, June 8, 1788.

2-6 " Lucy, and Francis Brown, March 8, 1792.

2-57 " Nathan, and Eunice Crandall; m. by Amos Collins, Justice, April 16, 1809.

2-16 BRIGGS Nathaniel, of New Shoreham, son of Joseph and Margery, and Mary Collins, of John, of Hopkinton; m. by Elder William Northup, Aug. 27, 1793.

2-9 BRIGHTMAN Joseph, and Sarah Thomas, May 14, 1747.

2-6 " Thomas, son of Joseph, of Hopkinton, and Thankful Ney, of Caleb, of Hopkinton; m. by Elder John Pendleton, May 23, 1782.

2-6 " Martin, and Amie Larkin, of Amie, widow; m. by Elder Henry Joslin, Sept. 25, 1791.

2-76 " Joseph, and Patience Kenyon; m. by Rowland Babcock, Justice, April 3, 1814.

1-47 BROWNING Ephraim, of South Kingstown, and Susannah Davis, of Hopkinton; m. by Nathan Burdick, Justice, Feb. 23, 1768.

2-7 " Elizabeth, and Elias Lewis, Jr., Nov. 19, 1789.

2-6 " Hazard, and Hannah Lewis; m. by Daniel Babcock, Justice, Nov. 24, 1791.

2-49 " Susannah, and Stephen Cole, Nov. 21, 1794.

3-19 " Henry K., and Ann Elizabeth Card, both of Charlestown; m. by Elder Weeden Barber, Aug. 1, 1844.

4-7 " Patience B., and Silas H. Lanphere, Dec. 21, 1845.

4-7 " Thomas, of Hopkinton, and Anna Maria Powers, of Lebanon, Conn.; m. by Elder C. C. Lewis, Jan. 7, 1846.

1-25 BROWN Anna, and Joseph Mott, Feb. 18, 1761.

1-46 " Penelope, and Palmer Sheldon, Jan. 10, 1768.

2-15 " Ruth, and William Tanner, Feb. 16, 1771.

1-69 " Beriah, of North Kingstown, and Elizabeth Babcock, of George, of Hopkinton; m. by Elder Joshua Clarke, Dec. 11, 1771.

1-67 " Ruth, and William Tanner, Feb. 16, 1771, also Feb. 16, 1772.

2-19 " Fannie, and Thomas Clarke, Dec. 14, 1780.

2-43 " Christopher, and Mrs. Anna Braman; m. by Elder John Burdick, Jan. 22, 1789.

2-6 " Francis, of John, of Hopkinton, and Lucy Brand, of Samuel, of Richmond; m. by Elder Henry Joslin, March 8, 1792.

2-56 " Alphens, of Stonington, now of Hopkinton, and Hannah Burdick, of Robert; m. by Elder John Burdick, Jan. 29, 1795.

2-95 " James W., of Hopkinton, and Nabby Wilcox, of Thomas, of West Greenwich; m. by John Hazard, Justice, Sept. 12, 1819.

3-10 " Nancy, and Gorton W. Arnold, Aug. 13, 1826.

3-10 " Nancy, and Abiel Barber, Sept. 29, 1833.

5-4 " Mary Ann, and Robert Sutcliff, May 18, 1853.

1-63, 121 BURCH Billings, of Thomas, late of Stonington, dec., and Susannah Bentley, of John, of Richmond; m. by Elder Joshua Clarke, Nov. 13, 1771.

1-51	BURDICK	Sarah, and John Maxson, Oct. 30. 1740.
1-20	"	Samuel, of Stonington, and Amie Maccoon, of Hopkinton; m. by Simeon Perry, Justice, Oct. 31, 1757.
1-22	"	Bridget, and Matthew Wells, Jan. 5, 1758.
1-116	"	Eunice, and Peleg Coon, Jan. 26, 1763.
1-34	"	Hannah, and Nathan Sissel, Feb. 9. 1763.
1-42	"	Jean, and Amos Worden, March 25, 1763.
1-36	"	Margaret, and Joshua Coon, April 7, 1763.
1-35	"	William, Jr., and Mary Lamb; m. by Joshua Clarke, Justice, Sept. 23. 1763.
1-38	"	Rachel, and Rufus Burdick, Nov. 15, 1763.
1-38	"	Rufus, and Rachel Burdick; m. by Lawton Palmer, Justice, Nov. 15, 1763.
1-38	"	Lucretia, and Samuel Gardiner, March 1, 1764.
1-38	"	Elias, and Elizabeth Cottrell; m. by Job Burdick, Justice, April 23, 1764.
1-38	"	Mary, and Newman Herring, Aug. 14, 1764.
1-39	"	Deborah, and Benjamin Tefft, Sept. 20, 1764.
1-41	"	Daniel, Jr., of Stonington, and Elizabeth Robinson, of Hopkinton, at Hopkinton; m. by John Burdick, Justice, Feb. 7, 1765.
1-44	"	Phineas, of Westerly, and Penelope Hall, of Hopkinton; m. by Joseph Crandall, Justice, Feb. 5, 1767.
1-54	"	Keturah, and John Sisson, March 20, 1769.
1-55	"	Hannah, and Abraham Utter, Oct. 14, 1739.
1-57	"	Robert, of Stonington, son of Daniel, and Sarah Remington; m. by Thomas Wells, Justice, Dec. 24, 1769.
1-57	"	Daniel, of William, and Temperance Hall, of Benjamin; m. by John Larkin, Justice, March 19, 1770.
1-62	"	Tillemus, of Nathan, and Lydia Lewis, of Elisha; m. by Elder Joshua Clarke, May 15, 1771.
1-103	"	Margaret, and Leir Crandall, Jr., July 21, 1771.
1-67	"	Amie, and Benjamin Lewis, Feb. 5, 1772.
1-76	"	Anna, and Azariah Crandall, March 24, 1772.
1-71	"	Elizabeth, and Phineas Maxson, Dec. 4, 1773.
1-101	"	Elnathan, and Anne Sissons, Jan. 9, 1774.
1-78, 112	"	Dyer, and Martha Burdick; m. by Elder Thomas West, Jan. 8, 1775.
1-78, 112	"	Martha, and Dyer Burdick, Jan. 8, 1775.
1-112	"	Paul, and Mary Stanton; m. by Elder Thomas West, Feb. 18, 1775.
1-112	"	John, of Richmond, and Hannah Carpenter, of Hopkinton; m. by Elder Thomas West, Nov. 12, 1775.
1-113	"	Abel, of Hopkinton, and Comfort Palmer, of Exeter; m. by Elder Thomas West, Dec. 21, 1775.
1-113	"	Joseph, and Mary Tanner; m. by Elder Thomas West, Nov. 28, 1776.
1-114	"	Stephen Rose, and Sarah West; m. by Elder Thomas West, Aug. 14, 1777.
2-13	"	Robert, son of Robert, and Sarah Williams; m. by John Maxson, Justice, Sept. 21, 1781.
2-78	"	Prudence, and Elisha Stillman, Jr., April 24, 1782.
1-1	"	Elijah, and Rhoda Dyer, both of Hopkinton; m. by Elder Thomas West, Oct. 5, 1782.
2-11	"	Perry, and Tacy Wells, of Capt. Edward; m. by Elder John Burdick, Dec. 19, 1782.
1-102	"	Joab, and Sarah Crandall, of Benjamin; m. by Elder John Burdick, March 27, 1784.
2-16	"	Elder John, of Hopkinton, and Thankful Clarke, of Capt. Simeon, of Richmond; m. by Elder Joshua Clarke, March 9, 1788.
2-8	"	Ebenezer, and Jemima Crandall; m. by David Nichols, Justice, Jan. 31, 1789.
2-5	"	Esther, and David Crandall, Jr., Jan. 23, 1790.
2-13	"	Charles, of Hopkinton, and Phebe Davis, of Westerly; m. by Robert Burdick, Justice, March 15, 1790.
2-12	"	Amos, and Cate Barber; m. at Voluntown, Conn., by Allen Campbell, Justice, May 11, 1790.

2-17 BURDICK Joshua, and Polly Clarke; m. by Daniel Burdick, Justice, Dec. 1, 1791.

2-6 " Mark Stils, alias, son of Mary Stiles, and Martha Wilcox, of Robert, of Richmond; m. by Thomas Tefft, Justice, Rec. March 17, 1793.

2-16 " Amos, of Robert, of Hopkinton, and Catherine Clarke, of Capt. Samuel, of Westerly, at Westerly; m. by Elder John Burdick, Jan. 16, 1794.

2-56 " Hannah, and Alpheus Brown, Jan. 29, 1795.

2-60 " Ichabod, Jr., and Hannah Maxson, of Tory, dec.; m. by Elder John Burdick, Oct. 1, 1795.

2-55 " Lucy B., and Luke Burdick, Aug. 30, 1798.

2-55 " Luke, of Luke, and Lucy B. Burdick, of Samuel; m. by Elder John Burdick, Aug. 30, 1798.

2-62 " Clarissa, and Peleg Maxson, Jr., June 15, 1809.

2-68 " Abram Lewis, of James, and Catherine Burdick, of Theodoty; m. by Nathan Pendleton, Justice, April 14, 1816.

2-68 " Catherine, and Abram Lewis Burdick, April 14, 1816.

2-93 " Ichabod, Jr., of Hopkinton, and Fannie Greene, of William R., of Westerly; m. at S. K. by Elder Matthew Stillman, Nov. 22, 1818.

3-16 " Phebe A., and Allen Jordan, Oct. 4, 1840.

5-1 " Horatio N., and Thankful L. Kenyon; m. by Rev. Christopher Chester, May 27, 1838.

2-96 " Joel, Jr., and Sally Kenyon, of Benjamin; m. by Elder Matthew Stillman, Feb. 22, 1821.

2-95 " Jonathan, of Newport, and Martha Coon of Hopkinton; m. by Elder Matthew Stillman, July 22, 1826.

4-9 " William C., of Westerly, and Lucy Orella Gates, of Preston, Conn.; m. at Norwich, Conn., by Elder William Palmer, Oct. 6, 1831.

3-17 " John P., of Hopkinton, and Catherine Irving of Coventry; m. by Elder David Avery, —— —, 1842.

4-12 " Reuben, and Elizabeth Burdick; m. by Elder Weeden Barber, Jr., March 29, 1846.

4-12 " Elizabeth, and Reuben Burdick, March 29, 1846.

4-19 " Lodowick, of North Stonington, and Mary S. Kenyon, of Richmond, at Hopkinton; m. by Elder Henry Clarke, Feb. 13, 1850.

1-32 BUTTON Thankful, and David Maccoon, Nov. 26, 1761.

1-34 " Rufus, and Elizabeth Hotten; m. by John Witter, Justice, Feb. 21, 1762.

1-54 " John, Jr., and Anna Macooon; m. by John Larkin, Justice, April 23, 1769.

1-78,112 ' Mary, and Samuel Wilkinson, Aug. 14, 1774.

1-113 " Mary, and Joseph Deak, Dec. 12, 1775.

1-1 " Anne, and Joshua Palmitter, Aug. 11, 1782.

1-1 " Penelope, and Jonathan Dyer, Jan. 8, 1785.

2-4 " Lawanto Sarah, and Thomas Wright, Dec. 28, 1787.

2-8 " Amos, Jr., of Hopkinton, and Jemima Wood, of Coventry; m. by Joseph Manchester, Justice, Feb. 8, 1789.

2-46 " Ruhamah, and Lyman Potter, April 28, 1799.

2-42 " David, and Elizabeth Lanphere; m. by Josiah Witter, Justice, Oct. 29, 1803.

2-88 " Joseph, and Anne Eagleston; m. by Jedediah Randall, Justice, Jan. 26, 1807.

2-97 " Joseph, of Amos, and Elizabeth Lanphere, of Amasa; m. by Elder Matthew Stillman, March 21, 1822.

3-16 " Ann, and Joseph Jordan, Sept. 20, 1840.

1-67 BYRNES Mary, and William Worden, Oct. 4, 1764.

C

3-19 CARD Ann Elizabeth, and Henry K. Browning, Aug. 1, 1844.

1-112 CARPENTER Hannah, and John Burdick, Nov. 12, 1775.

1-1   CARPENTER Hezekiah, and Prudence Johnson, both of Hopkinton; m. by Elder Thomas West, May 20, 1778.
2-7   "   Esther, and Pardon Crandall, Dec. 19, 1799.
2-56   "   John, and Esther Crandall; m. by Elder John Burdick, Feb. 4, 1802.
4-2   CARR Ann E., and Nathan H. Langworthy, Feb. 27, 1837.
1-47   CARTRIGHT Bryant, Jr., of Hopkinton, and Elizabeth Hall, of Westerly; m. by Nathan Burdick, Justice, Sept. 17, 1767.
3-16   CASE James R., and Amelia Crumb; m. by Elder Weeden Barber, Feb. 23, 1840.
3-15   "   Gardiner, of West Greenwich, and Lucinda Vars, of Charlestown, at Hopkinton; m. by Elder Daniel Coon, March 28, 1841.
1-23   CHAMPLAIN Amia, and Nathan Lanphere, Dec. 7, 1758.
1-57   "   Nathan, and Sarah Foster; m. by Thomas Wells, Justice, Jan. 29, 1770.
2-4   "   Huldah, and Hazard Morey, Feb. 11, 1788.
2-8   "   Amie, and Daniel Wilcox, Dec. 20, 1789.
2-64   "   Ethan, and Hannah Cottrell; m. by Elder Abram Coon, July 4, 1809.
2-75   "   Sarah, and Joseph Witter, Jr., June 22, 1811.
2-67   "   Hannah, and James K. Crandall, Sept. 5, 1816.
2-88   "   Greene, of Hopkinton, and Polly Greenman, of Westerly; m. by Thomas V. Wells, Justice, Nov. 15, 1821.
1-65   CHASE Mary, and George Griffith, Dec. 8, 1771.
2-69   CHEESEBROUGH Nabby, and Nathan Langworthy, Dec. 21, 1800.
1-69   CHEVER Edward, son of Edward, of Eastham, Mass., and Susannah Maxson, of William, of Hopkinton; m. by Elder Joshua Clarke, June 28, 1772.
1-64   "   Susannah, and Fones Palmer, May —, 1783.
1-111   CHURCH Caleb, and Mary Braman; m. by Elder Joseph Davis, Nov. 27, 1777.
3-8   "   Sophia, and Nathan Wilcox, Oct. 23, 1831.
1-50   CLARKE Anna, and Job White, Jan. 6, 1759.
1-31   "   Oliver, and Mary Wells; m. by Joshua Clarke, Justice, Dec. 16, 1761.
1-38   "   Amie, and Daniel Lewis, March 16, 1763.
1-43   "   Thankful, and Amos Collins, Aug. 10, 1767.
1-55   "   Benjamin, of Stonington, son of Benjamin, and Susannah Wheeler, of Hopkinton, at Hopkinton; m. by Elder Joshua Clarke, Dec. 15, 1769.
1-57   "   Benjamin, and Susannah West; m. by Nathan Burdick, Justice, March 27, 1770.
2-9   "   Henry, and Catherine Pendleton, Dec. 5, 1776.
2-45   "   Sarah, and Peleg Maxson, Nov. 13, 1777.
1-117   "   Willett, of Hopkinton, son of Elder Joshua, and Sarah Pendleton of Sylvester, of Westerly; m. by John Maxson, Justice, April 24, 1779.
1-119   "   Hannah, and John Dodge, Nov. 14, 1779.
2-19   "   Thomas, and Phanney Brown, Dec. 14, 1780.
2-18   "   Job B., and Mrs. Mary Wells, of Jonathan; m. by Elder John Burdick, Jan. 1, 1788.
2-16   "   Thankful, and Elder John Burdick, March 9, 1788.
2-17   "   Polly, and Joshua Burdick, Dec. 1, 1791.
2-16   "   Catherine, and Amos Burdick, Jan. 16, 1794.
2-42   "   Joseph, of Leyden, Conn., and Mary Babcock, of Westerly; m. by Elder Asa Coon, Jan. 9, 1800.
2-52   "   Ruhamah, and Robert Kenyon, Jan. 1, 1801.
2-53   "   Ephraim, and Sarah Clarke; m. by Elder Asa Coon, March 15, 1801.
2-53   "   Sarah, and Ephraim Clarke, March 15, 1801.
2-45   "   Eunice, and Joseph Clarke, July 26, 1804.
2-45   "   Joseph, and Eunice Clarke; m. by Amos Collins, Justice, July 26, 1804.
2-72   "   Jesse, and Thankful Coon; m. by Allen Campbell, Justice, Nov. 7, 1805.

2-91 CLARKE Russell, of Newport, and Elizabeth Taylor, of Hopkinton; m. by Elder Abram Coon, Oct. 16, 1808.

2-91 " Russell, son of Thomas and Sarah Thurston, of George of Hopkinton; m. by Elder Matthew Stillman. Aug. 29, 1813.

2-91 " Russell, and Betsey Langworthy: m. at North Stonington by Elder Asher Miner, May 21, 1815.

2-76 " Joanna, and Rowland T. Greene, Oct. 10, 1812.

2-92 " Charles, of Job B., and Amanda Reynolds, of Zaccheus; m. by Elder Matthew Stillman, Dec. 13, 1818.

2-97 " Clarissa A., and Lester Crandall, Nov. 9, 1826.

4-5 " Henry, of Job B., Esq., and Jerusha Clarke, of Thomas; m. by Elder Matthew Stillman, Dec. 1, 1833.

4-5 " Jerusha, and Henry Clarke, Dec. 1, 1833.

3-14 " Harriet, and Leonidus Nichols, April 27, 1840.

3-16 " Nancy, and John P. Knowles, Oct. 12, 1841.

3-18 " Corydon, and Julia A. Langworthy; m. by Elder Henry Clarke, Sept. 21, 1844.

5-2 " Stephen A., of Henry B., aged 19 years, and Hannah A. Wright, aged 18 years, dau. of Samuel; m. by Elder John Greene, Nov. 5, 1853.

1-40 CLOSSON Mrs. Lydia, and John Corey, Nov. 10, 1764.

1-115 " Nathan, and Mrs. Martha Patterson; m. by Abel Tanner, Justice, Feb. 14, 1784.

1-22 CODNER Ishmeal, and Margaret Stewart; m. by Joshua Clarke, Justice, Feb. 11, 1758.

1-1 " Ephraim, of Exeter, and Peace Barber, of Richmond; m. by Elder Thomas West, Nov. 15, 1778.

1-113 COLEGROVE Jeremiah, of Hopkinton, and Hannah Webster, of Richmond; m. by Elder Thomas West, Nov. 13, 1776.

1-113 " Thankful, and William Pettey, June 2, 1776.

1-26 COLE Joseph, of Hopkinton, and Phebe Niles of Stonington; m. by Elder Waite Palmer, at Stonington, Aug. 30, 1759.

1-40,120 " Martha, and William Witter, Nov. 1, 1764.

1-99 " Joseph, and Hannah Collins; m. by Elder John Gardiner, Nov. 17, 1780.

2-49 " Stephen, of Rhode Island, and Susannah Browning, of Connecticut; m. at New London by George Williams, Justice, Nov. 21, 1794.

1-43 COLLINS Amos, and Thankful Clarke, both of Stonington; m. at Hopkinton, by Elder John Burdick, Aug. 10, 1767.

1-57 " Catherine, and Lebbeus Sweet, March 11, 1770.

1-62 " Joshua, and Mary White; m. by Elder Joshua Clarke, Feb. 7, 1771.

1-117 " Susannah, and Fones Gardiner, March 28, 1779.

1-99 " Ruth, and William White, April 5, 1780.

1-99 " Hannah, and Joseph Cole, Nov. 17, 1780.

2-16 " Mary, and Nathaniel Briggs, Aug. 27, 1793.

2-51 " John, and Elizabeth Morey; m. by Elder Samuel Northup, Oct. 19, 1795.

2-67 " Amos, M. D., and Mary Peckham, of Robert; m. by Henry Joslin, Elder, Feb. 16, 1804.

2-47 " Nathan, and Tabitha Popple, of George, of Richmond; m. by John Maxson, Justice, April 12, 1804.

2-74 " Joshua, and Mary Cross; m. at Charlestown, by Rowland Babcock, Justice, March 24, 1814.

3-13 " David, of Hopkinton, and Martha Baggs, of Richmond; m. by Elder Weeden Barber, Jr., May 13, 1838.

1-20 COON Joseph, and Elizabeth Larkin; m. by Joseph Crandall, Justice, April 14, 1757.

1-116 " Peleg, and Eunice Burdick, Jan. 26, 1763.

1-42 " Sarah, and William Ross, March 13, 1763.

1-36 " Joshua, of Hopkinton, and Margaret Burdick, of Stonington, at Stonington; m. by Elder Waite Palmer, April 7, 1763.

1-22 " Abigail, and Ichabod Prosser, —— —, 1763.

1-104 " Jemima, and David Crandall. June 16, 1764.

1-39 " Martha, and Thomas Partelow, Aug. 2, 1764.

1-45   COON Amos, and Sarah Gardiner; m. by Lawton Palmer, Justice, April 5, 1767.

1-49   "   Elias, and Phebe Ney; m. by John Larkin, Jr., Justice, May 1, 1768.

1-69   "   Samuel, of Capt. John, and Thankful Maxson, of John; m. by Elder Joshua Clarke, Jan. 7, 1773.

1-70   "   Bethany, and Sylvester Satterlee, Aug. 8, 1773.

1-112   "   Abel and Bathsheba Crandall; m. by Elder Thomas West, March 30, 1775.

1-113   "   Ann, and Asa Crandall, Jan. 7, 1776.

1-114   "   Elizabeth, and Ezra Crandall, March 5, 1778.

1-119   "   Thankful, and Joseph Enos, Jan. 5, 1780.

1-95   "   Sarah, and Stephen Potter, Jr., Nov. 29, 1780.

2-1   "   Lebbeus, and Mary Worden; m. by Elder Joseph Davis, April 13, 1785.

2-1   "   Peleg, and Anne Dye; m. by Elder Eleazer Brown, April 23, 1786.

2-4   "   Margeret, and John Whitford, Feb. 6, 1788.

2-4   "   Elizabeth, and Matthew Wells, Jr., Dec. 18, 1788.

2-18   "   Stephen, of Hopkinton, and Sarah Stillman, of Major George; m. at Westerly by Elder John Burdick, Feb. 23, 1789.

2-18   "   Lydia, and Thomas Lewis, Dec. 25, 1792.

2-61   "   Tacy, and Lewis Maxson, Jan. 27, 1797.

2-74   "   Isaac, and Martha Hull; m. by Elder Abram Coon, June 5, 1800.

2-62   "   Esther, and Samuel Larkin, Oct. 5, 1800.

2-59   "   Caleb, of Elias, and Dorcas Barber, of Levi; m. by Elder Henry Joslin, Dec. 14, 1800.

2-72   "   Thankful, and Jesse Clarke, Nov. 7, 1805.

2-95   "   Martha, and Jonathan Burdick, July 22, 1926.

4-12   "   Elias, of Hopkinton, and Mary Palmer, of Westerly; m. at Exeter by Simon Lillibridge, Justice, Sept. 29, 1840.

4-16   "   Martha, and Pardon Lewis, Feb. 13, 1848.

4-4   "   Archibald B., of Brookfield, New York, and Phebe A. Crandall, of Hopkinton; m. by Elder Henry Clarke, March 22, 1849.

4-21   "   Asa S., of North Stonington, and Lydia C. Thorp, of Hopkinton, at Hopkinton; m. by Elder C. C. Lewis, March 22, 1852.

1-40   COREY John, and Mrs. Lydia Cossen; m. by Elder John Burdick, Nov. 10, 1764.

1-34   COTTRELL Abigail, and Stephen Larkin, March 31, 1762.

1-38   "   Elizabeth, and Elias Burdick, April 23, 1764.

1-43   "   Abigail, and Thaddeus Sweet, Feb. 18, 1766.

1-113   "   Mary, and John Waite, Sept. 5, 1776.

2-51   "   Mary, and Joseph Spicer, March 6, 1796.

2-64   "   Hannah, and Ethan Champlain, July 4, 1809.

1-27   CRANDALL David, and Sarah Sherman; m. by Joshua Crandall, Justice, Feb. 19, 1761.

1-104   "   David, and Jemima Coon, June 16, 1764.

1-103   '   Levi, Jun., and Margaret Burdick; m. by John Larkin, Justice, July 21, 1771.

1-63   "   Kezia, and Paine Waite, Oct. 29, 1771.

1-76   "   Azariah, of Peter, and Anna Burdick, of Edward, March 24, 1772.

1-72   "   Amie, and Peleg Lewis, April 2, 1772.

1-78,112   "   Susannah, and Benjamin Tanner, April 21, 1774.

1-112   "   Bathsheba, and Abel Coon, March 30, 1775.

1-113   "   Asa, and Ann Coon; m. by Elder Thomas West, Jan. 7, 1776.

1-110   "   Peleg, and Eleanor Lewis; m. by Elder Joseph Davis, Nov. 9, 1777.

1-114   "   Ezra, and Elizabeth Coon; m. by Elder Thomas West, March 5, 1778.

1-102   "   Sarah, and Joab Burdick, March 27, 1784.

1-103   "   Luke, and Martha Maxson, of Capt. Matthew; m. by Elder John Burdick, Jan. 6, 1785.

2-3   "   Amherst, of Westerly, and Polly Maxson, of Samuel; m. by Elder Isaiah Wilbur, Nov. 1, 1787.

2-3   "   Archibald, and Susanna Maxson, Feb. 2, 1788.

2-8   "   Jemima, and Ebenezer Burdick, Jan. 31, 1798.

2-11 CRANDALL Rowland, of Hopkinton, and Susannah Kenyon, of Peleg, of South Kingstown, at South Kingstown; m. by Elder John Burdick, Nov. 5, 1789.

2-5 " David, Jr., and Esther Burdick; m. by Elder John Burdick, Jan. 23, 1790.

2-13 " Prudence, and Daniel Maxson, March 20, 1790.

2-71 " Pardon, of Christopher and Esther Carpenter, of Hezekiah; m. by Elder Ellet Locke, Dec. 19, 1799.

2-47 " Lucy, and William Witter, Jr., Jan. 2, 1800.

2-62 " Ruth and Nathan Maxson, April 28, 1800.

2-63 " Samuel, Jr., and Elizabeth Vinson, of Nicholas; m. by Elder John Burdick, Jan. 14, 1802.

2-56 " Esther, and John Carpenter, Feb. 4, 1802.

2-56 " Lydia, and Russell Wells, Aug. 5, 1802.

2-57 " Eunice, and Nathan Brand, April 16, 1809.

2-67 " James K., and Hannah Champlain; m. by Elder Matthew Stillman, Sept. 5, 1816.

2-98 " Lydia, and Thomas Edwards, Oct. 13, 1821.

2-97 " Nicholas, of Burney, and Abbie M. Reynolds, of Zaccheus; m. by Elder Matthew Stillman, Jan. 12, 1822.

2-94 " Susan H., and Lester T. Rogers, April 30, 1825.

2-97 " Lester, of Pheneus, and Clarissa A. Clark, of Thomas, Jr.; m. by Elder Matthew Stillman, Nov. 9, 1826.

3-16 " Judith, and Joshua Crandall, Feb. 21, 1841.

3-16 " Joshua, and Judith Crandall; m. by Elder Weeden Barber, Jr., Feb. 21, 1841.

3-16 " Hannah, and Henry Tabor, Oct. 4, 1840.

3-18 " Mary E., and Henry B. Manchester, Aug. 5, 1844.

4-9 " George C., of Their G., and Mary Ann Babcock, of Charles, both of Westerly; m. by Elder Henry Clarke, Oct. 4, 1846.

4-10 " Peleg W., and Clarissa Kenyon; m. by Elder Lucius Crandall, Oct. 18, 1846.

4-12 " Luke, of Hopkinton, son of Amherst and Mary, and Mary Ann B. White, of Walter E. and Dorcas B., of Newport, at Newport; m. by Elder Joseph Smith, March 29, 1847.

4-15 " Eliza N., and Samuel C. Bitgood, Nov. 28, 1847.

4-4 " Phebe A., and Archibald B. Coon, March 22, 1849.

4-19 " Mahala, and John S. Potter, April 21, 1850.

5-3 " Nathan M., aged 25 years, of Lester, and Almira J. Wilcox, aged 17 years, of Jeremiah W.; m. by Rev. Daniel Coon, Jan. 29, 1853.

5-2 CROCKER Nancy C., and Jerah J. Gray, Jan. 9, 1855.

2-74 CROSS Mary, and Joshua Collins, March 24, 1814.

3-16 CRUMB Amelia, and James R. Case, Feb. 23, 1840.

1-28 CULVER Thankful, and Ebenezer Hill, Sept. 10, 1744.

D

4-18 DANIELS Washington, of East Lynne, Conn., and Elizabeth Greene, of Hoxsie, of Hopkinton, at Hopkinton; m. by Elder C. C. Lewis, Nov. 30, 1848.

1-42 DARTTS Elizabeth, and Joshua Wells, Feb. 15, 1759.

1-44 DAVIS Hannah, and Samuel Maxson, Dec. 15, 1765.

1-45 " William, of Westerly, and Anna Wilbur, of Hopkinton; m. by Joseph Crandall, Justice, Feb. 26, 1767.

1-47 " Susannah, and Ephraim Browning, Feb. 23, 1768.

1-104 " Marvel, and William Scriven, Feb. 2, 1775.

1-1 " Tacy, and Nathaniel Kenyon, Jun., April 12, 1784.

1-1 " Oliver, of Jedediah, dec., and Penelope White, dau. of Oliver; m. by Robert Burdick, Justice, July 16, 1784.

2-18 " Phebe, and Charles Burdick, March 15, 1790.

2-98 " Thankful and William Braman, Oct. 19, 1791.

2-66 " Ethel, and Samuel Langworthy, July 31, 1796.

4-6 " Harriet, and George H. Spicer, Nov. 9, 1845.

4-47   DAWLEY Hannah, and Alexander Webster, March I, 1812.
4-15   "   William H., and Triphenia H. Tanner; m. by Elder C. C. Lewis, Dec. 19, 1847.
1-26   DEATS John, and Hannah Foster, both of Westerly; m. by Elder Joseph Maxson, Feb. 26, 1746-7.
1-75   "   Sarah, and Jonathan Lewis, Nov. 10, 1758.
1-39   "   Anna, and Amos Rogers, Dec. 29, 1764.
1-113   "   Joseph, of Richmond, and Mary Button, of Hopkinton; m. by Elder Thomas West, Dec. 12, 1775.
1-46   DEWEY David, of Stonington, and Sarah Witter, of Hopkinton; m. by Nathan Burdick, Justice, Jan. 12, 1768.
1-19   DODGE Daniel, of Colchester, and Mary Worden, of Westerly; m. at Westerly by Benjamin Randall, Justice, April 11, 1756.
1-119   "   John, of Westerly, and Hannah Clarke, of Hopkinton; m. by Elder Joshua Clarke, Nov. 14, 1779.
2-75   "   Lucretia, and Joseph Witter, 2d, Nov. 26, 1812.
1-1   DOUGLASS William, and Martha Adams, both of Voluntown, Conn.; m. by Elder Thomas West, Nov. 13, 1781.
5-1   "   Joel W., and Mehitable Salisbury; m. by Elder John Greene, Dec. 14, 1851.
1-35   DOWNING Mary, and Samuel Maxson, March 5, 1763.
1-1   DYER Rhoda, and Elijah Burdick, Oct. 5, 1782.
1-1   "   Jonathan, of Hopkinton, and Penelope Button, of do.; m. at Stonington by Joshua Babcock, Justice, Jan. 8, 1785.
2-1   DYE Anna, and Peleg Coon, April 23, 1786.

E

1-41   EAGLESTONE Patience, and Peter Maine, March 3, 1765.
1-113   "   Asa, and Sarah Lake; m. by Elder Thomas West, Dec. 31, 1775.
1-107   "   Jason, of Stonington, and Avis Lanphere, of Hopkinon; m. by William Tanner, Justice, April 18, 1784.
2-88   "   Anne, and Joseph Button, Jan. 26, 1809.
1-28   EDWARDS Phebe, and Henry Hall, Dec. 11, 1760.
1-108   "   Daniel, of Charlestown, and Sarah Johnson of do.; m. by Elder John Gardiner, Dec. 13, 1775.
2-73   "   Mary, and Asa Sheldon, April 26, 1800.
2-56   "   Patty, and Larkin Wilcox, Sept. 3, 1801.
2-98   "   Thomas, of Nathan, and Lydia Crandall, of James; m. by Elder Matthew Stillman, Oct. 13, 1821.
1-27   ELDREDGE James, and Sarah Babcock; m. by Lawton Palmer, Justice, Jan. 24, 1760.
1-51   ENOS Dorcas, and Timothy Bailey, Feb. 16, 1769.
1-119   "   Joseph, of Richmond, and Thankful Coon, of Hopkinton; m. at Hopkinton by Joseph Woodmansee, Justice, Jan. 5, 1780.

F

2-43   FENNER Reuben, of John, and Anstis Tanner, of William; m. by Elder John Burdick, Jan. 17, 1793.
2-43   "   Abel, of Hopkinton, and Maria Sampson, of Richmond; m. by Elder David Avery, —— —, 1842.
4-15   "   Stacy E., of Warwick, and Mary M. Greene of Hopkinton; m. by Elder C. C. Lewis, Sept. 28, 1846.
1-41   FOSTER Hannah, and John Deak, Feb. 26, 1746-7.
1-41   "   Gideon, and Sarah Allen; m. by John Burdick, Justice, March 3, 1765.
2-10   "   Lucy, and Samuel Witter, Jan. 5, 1769.
1-57   "   Sarah, and Nathan Champlain, Jan. 29, 1770.
1-98   "   Mary, and Nathaniel Palmer, Oct. 31, 1782.
4-9   "   Sophronia A., and Jeremiah W. Bramen, Oct 11, 1846.
1-57   FRINK Anna, and Timothy Maccoon, April 23, 1769.

G

2-17,45 GALLUP Wealthy, and Gardiner Wells, Dec. 23, 1792.

1-116 GARDINER Sarah, and Simeon Babcock, Oct. 3, 1743.

1-38   "   Samuel, and Lucretia Burdick; m. at Hopkinton, by Joseph Cran-
          dall, Justice, March 1, 1764.

1-45   "   Sarah, and Amos Coon, April 5, 1767.

1-46   "   Lois, and William Greene, Aug. 20, 1767.

2-58   "   George Rutter, of North Kingstown, and Thankful Babcock, of Hop-
          kinton; m. by Elder John Gardiner, Sept. 12, 1767.

1-103   "   Thomas Potter, of Samuel, and Catherine Bent, of John; m. by
          Elder John Gardiner, April 15, 1773.

1-106   "   John, Jr., of John, of Exeter, and Mary Gardiner, of Samuel,
          of Hopkinton; m. by Nathan Burdick, Justice, Dec. 14, 1775.

1-106   "   Mary, and John Gardiner, Dec. 14, 1775.

1-117   "   Fones, and Susannah Collins; m. by Elder Thomas West, March
          28, 1779.

2-62   "   Samuel, Jr., and Ruth Wells; by Elder Abram Coon, May 22,
          1803,

3-6   "   Thankful, and Phineas Stillman, Dec. 26, 1810.

2-88   "   Samuel, Esq., of Hopkinton, and Eliza Babcock, of Christopher, of
          Westerly; m. at Westerly by Elder Matthew Stillman, Feb. 4,
          1821.

3-14   "   Mary A., and Charles R. Perry, Oct. 4, 1840.

4-9 GATES Lucy Orilla, and William C. Burdick, Oct. 6, 1831.

1-111 GRANT John, of Stonington, and Thankful Lewis, of Hopkinton; m. by El-
          der John Gardiner, Oct. 6, 1776.

5-2 GRAY J., aged 38 years, of John, of New Shoreham, and Mrs. Nancy C.
          Croker, aged 26 years, of Hopkinton, dau. of Sands Palmer;
          m. by Elder Daniel Coon, Jan. 9, 1855.

2-88 GREENMAN Polly, and Greene Champlain, Nov. 15, 1821.

1-19 GREENE Nathan. of West Greenwich, and Huldah Bowen, of Westerly; m.
          at Hopkinton by Benjamin Randall, Justice, Sept. 24, 1756.

1-46   "   William, of Charlestown, and Lois Gardiner of Hopkinton; m. by
          Nathan Burdick, Justice, Aug. 20, 1767.

2-42   "   Benjamin, of Hopkinton, and Grace Rogers, of David, of New
          London; m. by Elder Zadoc Darron, Dec. 13, 1781.

2-18   "   William G., and Susannah White; m. by Daniel Babcock, Justice,
          March 9, 1793.

4-11   "   Betsey, and Benjamin Potter, March 6, 1808.

2-76   "   Rowland T., and Joanna Clarke, of Richmond; m. by Elder Abram
          Conn, Oct. 10, 1812.

2-76   "   Alpheus M., and Abbie Wells, dau. of Thompson; m. by Elder
          Matthew Stillman, Dec. 18, 1812.

2-76   "   John, Jr., and Betsey Wells, of Edward S., dec.; m. by Elder
          Matthew Stillman, April 3, 1813.

2-77   "   Caleb, of North Stonington, and Sophia Peckham, of Groton; m.
          at Groton by Christopher Morgan, Justice, March 3, 1816.

2-93   "   Fannie, and Ichabod Burdick, Nov. 22, 1818.

4-8   "   William R., and Nancy C. Kenyon; m. by Elder C. C. Lewis, July
          14, 1846.

4-15   "   Mary M., and Stacy B. Fenner, Sept. 28, 1846.

4-18   "   Elizabeth, and Washington Daniels, Nov. 30, 1848.

1-65 GRIFFETH George, of Phillip, late of Charlestown, dec., and Mary Chase, of
          Joshua, late of Westerly, dec.; m. by Nathan Burdick, Jus-
          tice, Dec. 8, 1771.

2-42 GRIFFIN Rahamah, and Peter Kenyon, April 28, 1794.

3-19 GRINNELL Lucinda, and Jonathan P. Larkin, July 26, 1843.

1-27 GOODWILL Elizabeth, and John Harris, June 15, 1760.

H

2-17 HALEY Belcher, of Stonington, and Phebe Turner, of Abel, of Hopkinton;
          m. by Elder John Burdick, Jan. 20, 1793.

1-42   HALL Mary, and Thomas Stutson, Jan. —, 1758.
1-42   "   Sarah, and Joseph Wilbur, March 25, 1758.
1-28   "   Henry, and Phebe Edwards; m. by John Larkin, Justice, Dec. 11 1760.
1-41   "   Eunice, and Edward Pierce, April 30, 1765.
1-44   "   Penelope, and Phineus Burdick, Feb. 5, 1767.
1-47   "   Elizabeth, and Bryant Cartright, Jr., Sept. 17, 1767.
1-46   "   Dorcas, and Stephen Stutson, Jan. 9, 1768.
1-57   "   Temperance, and Daniel Burdick, March 19, 1770.
1-65   "   Margaret, and Isaac Johnson, Jan. 30, 1772.
1-77   "   Esther, and William Fulman, alias Thompson, Jan. 26, 1774.
1-27   HARRIS John, of Plainfield, and Elizabeth Goodwill, of Stonington; m. by Joshua Clarke, Justice, June 15, 1760.
4-15   "   Jane, and Mumford Bicknall, July 26, 1847.
4-15   HEALEY Phebe N., and Elias H. Rathbun, Dec. 12, 1847.
1-38   HERRING, Newman, of Westerly, and Mary Burdick, of Edward, of Hopkinton; m. by John Maxson, Justice, Aug. 14, 1764.
1-112 HIDE John, of Hopkinton, and Elizabeth Baggs, of Richmond; m. by Elder Thomas West, March 27, 1774.
1-28   HILL Ebenezer, and Thankful Culiver; m. by Elder James Whitman, Sept. 10, 1744.
1-35   HISCOX Simeon, and Thankful Wells; m. by Joshua Clarke, Justice, Dec. 26, 1762.
3-15   "   Mary, and John M. Barber, (also 3-7 and 4-20), March 24, 1841.
4-15   HOOD John, of North Stonington, and Sarah L. Larkin, of Richmond; m. at Hopkinton by Elder C. C. Lewis, July 21, 1847.
1-34   HOTTEN Elizabeth, and Rufus Button, Feb. 21, 1762.
1-47   "   Joseph, of Great Brittain, and Soaeil King, of Westerly; m. by Nathan Burdick, Justice, Aug. 29, 1768.
4-18   HOXSIE Alice A., and Samuel C. Kingsley, Oct. 9, 1844.
4-1   "   William B., and Susan Wilbur; m. by Elder Weeden Barber, Jr., May 21, 1845.
4-18   "   George S., of Hopkinton, and Rachel S. Kenyon, of Richmond; m. by Elder C. C. Lewis, Sept. 9, 1848.
2-42   HULL Mary Saunders, alias, and Randall Maxson, April 18, 1793.
2-74   "   Martha, and Isaac Coon, June 5, 1800.

I

2-68   IRISH Hannah, and James Tefft Joslin, Dec. 29, 1802.
3-17   IRVING Catherine, and John P. Burdick, —— —, 1842.
3-17   "   Eliza Ann, and Horace F. Sheldon, —— —, 1843.

J

1-23   JACQUES Elizabeth, and Thomas Wilcox, Jan. 22, 1759.
1-44   "   Amie, and Ebenezer Lanphere, June 7, 1768.
1-65   JOHNSON Isaac, of Daniel, of Charlestown, and Margaret Hall, of Theodoty, of Westerly; m. by Nathan Burdick, Justice, Jan. 30, 1772.
1-108   "   Sarah, and Daniel Edwards, Dec. 13, 1775.
1-1   "   Prudence, and Hezekiah Carpenter, May 20, 1778.
1-67   "   Nabby, and Jesse Wilbur, March 4, 1784.
2-65   "   Mary, and Nathaniel Lewis, Jan. 4, 1800.
3-7   "   Mary A., and Christopher C. Stillman, Dec. 7, 1829.
3-16   JORDAN Joseph, of Coventry, and Ann Button of Hopkinton; m. by Elder Weeden Barber, Sept. 20, 1840.
3-16   "   Allen, of Coventry, and Phebe A. Burdick of Hopkinton; m. by Elder Weeden Barber, Oct. 4, 1840.
4-15   "   Edmund, and Eunice A. Tefft; m. by Elder C. C. Lewis, June 28, 1847.
2-68   JOSLIN James Tefft, of Elder Henry, and Hannah Irish, of Benjamin, formerly of Middletown, now of Hopkinton; m. by Elder Thomas Manchester, Dec. 29, 1802.

K

5-3   KEENEY Albert, and Betsey Atwood; m. by Rev. J. G. Post, March 6, 1853.

1-50   KENYON Benjamin, of Jonathan, of Charlestown, and Elizabeth Langworthy, of Samuel, late of Hopkinton, dec.; m. by Joseph Crandall, Justice, Oct. 22, 1768.

1-111   "   Lodowick, of Charlestown, and Mary Barber, of Hopkinton; m. by Elder John Gardiner, Jan. 16, 1777.

1-97   "   Eleanor, and Benjamin Langworthy, March 16, 1779.

1-1   "   Nathaniel, Jr., and Tacy Davis, both of Hopkinton; m. by Elder Thomas West, April 12, 1784.

2-1   "   Benjamin, of Hopkinton, and Mary Lanphere, of Nathan, of Westerly; m. at Westerly by Elder John Burdick, Feb. 16, 1785.

2-8   "   Benjamin, of Benjamin, and Sally Worden, of William; m. by Elder Isaiah Wilcox, Aug. 9, 1787.

2-11   "   Susanna, and Rowland Crandall, Nov. 5, 1789.

2-13   "   Rogers, and Esther Maxson; m. by Elder Isaiah Wilcox at Westerly, April 6, 1791.

2-16   "   Gideon, and Sarah Larkin, of Timothy; m. by Joseph Witter, Justice, Oct. 8, 1793.

2-42   "   Peter, of Peter, and Rahamah Griffin, of Phillip; m. by Elder Asa Coon, April 28, 1794.

2-60   "   Augustus, of Hopkinton, and Joanna Pendleton, of Westerly; m. by Joseph Potter, Justice, Oct. 11, 1798.

2-52   "   Robert, of Hopkinton, and Rahamah Clarke, of Richmond; m. by Zaccheus Maxson, Justice, Jan. 1, 1801.

2-63   "   Burdick, of Stephen, and Ruth Worden, of Arnold; m. by Elder John Burdick, Feb. 14, 1802.

2-79   "   Wealthy, and Christopher C. Lewis, April 6, 1812.

2-76   "   Patience, and Joseph Brightman, April 3, 1814.

4-17   "   Ruth, and Benjn. B. Woodmansee, Feb. 7, 1819.

2-94   "   Hannah, and Benjn. Langworthy, Aug. 1, 1819.

2-95   "   George W., of Benjamin, and Sarah Maxson, of Benjamin; m. by Elder Matthew Stillman, Dec. 30, 1819.

2-96   "   Sally, and Joel Burdick, Jun., Feb. 22, 1821.

3-12   "   Ransom, and Eliza Maynard; m. by Elder Amos R. Wells, March 27, 1838.

3-16   "   Thankful, and Horatio N. Burdick, May 27, 1838.

3-16   "   Maria, and William Kenyon, Nov. 29, 1840.

3-16   "   William, and Maria Kenyon, both of Richmond; m. by Elder Weeden Barber, Nov. 29, 1840.

3-17   "   Minerva C., and Godfrey A. Kenyon, —— —, 1842.

3-17   "   Godfrey A., of Hopkinton, and Minerva C. Kenyon, of Richmond; m. by Elder David Avery, —— —, 1842.

3-17   "   Eliza, and Charles P. White, —— —, 1843.

4-16   "   Ann Frances, and Daniel Lewis, M. D., May 24, 1846.

4-8   "   Nancy C., and William R. Greene, July 14, 1846.

4-10   "   Benjamin F., and Mary C. Langworthy; m. by Elder Lucius Crandall, Oct. 17, 1846.

4-10   "   Clarissa, and Peleg W. Crandall, Oct. 18, 1846.

4-10   "   Charles, and Sarah Langworthy; m. by Elder Lucius Crandall, Oct. 19, 1846.

4-18   "   Rachel S., and George S. Hoxsie, Sept. 9, 1848.

4-19   "   Mary S., and Lodowick Burdick, Feb. 13, 1850.

5-4   "   Merebah, and William J. Spencer, March 14, 1853.

1-40   KEZIER Mrs. Lydia, and Jonas Partelow, Sept. 27, 1764.

4-18   KINGSLEY Samuel C., and Alice A. Hoxsie; m. by Elder C. C. Lewis, Oct. 9, 1848.

1-47   KING Soueil, and Joseph Hotton, Aug. 29, 1768.

1-32   KNOWLES Deborah, and Oliver Babcock, Dec. 2, 1761.

1-32   "   Deliverance, and John Babcock, July 18, 1762.

3-16   "   John P., and Nancy Clarke; m. by Elder Daniel Coon, Oct. 12, 1841.

4-7   "   Mrs. Sarah Ann, and Samuel Waite, Nov. 27, 1845.

L

1-113   LAKE Sarah, and Asa Eaglestone, Dec. 31, 1775.

1-32   LAMB Nathan, and Lydia Plumber; m. by Joshua Clarke, Justice, July 13, 1762.

1-35   " Mary, and William Burdick, Jr., Sept. 23, 1763.

1-58   LANGWORTHY Amos, of Thomas, of New London, and Sarah Babcock, of John, of South Kingstown; m. by John Sheldon, Justice, Feb. 15, 1758.

1-50   " Elizabeth, and Benjamin Kenyon, Oct. 22, 1768.

1-59   " Samuel, of Hopkinton, and Mary Saunders, of Tobias, of Charlestown; m. by Nathan Burdick, Justice, Jan. 24, 1771.

1-62   " Rachel, and Timothy Larkin, Oct. 5, 1771.

1-108   " Joseph, and Lois Lewis; m. by Elder John Gardiner, Jan. 4, 1776.

1-97   " Benjamin, and Eleanor Kenyon, of Nathaniel; m. by Elder John Burdick, March 18, 1779.

2-66   " Samuel, Jr., of Hopkinton, of Samuel and Mary, and Ethel Davis, of Joseph and Mary, of Westerly; m. by Elder William Northup, July 31, 1796.

2-85   " Thomas, of Amos, of Hopkinton, and Waitey Peckham, of Timothy, of South Kingstown, May 6, 1797.

2-69   " Nathan, and Nabby Cheesebrough; m. at Stonington by Elder Hezekiah N. Woodruff, Dec. 21, 1800.

2-66   " Amos, Jr., and Susannah Langworthy, widow; m. by Elder Abram Coon, Jan. 21, 1802.

2-66   " Susannah, and Amos Langworthy, Jr., Jan. 21, 1802.

2-45   " Benjamin, Jr., and Elizabeth Bentley; m. by Elder Abram Coon, Jan. 8, 1804.

2-91   " Betsey, and Russell Clarke, May 21, 1815.

2-94   " Benjamin, and Hannah Kenyon; m. by Elder Matthew Stillman, Aug. 1, 1819.

4-14   " Content, and Daniel Lewis, June 26, 1823.

4-2   " Nathan H., and Ann E. Carr, Feb. 27, 1837.

3-18   " Julia A., and Corydon Clarke, Sept. 21, 1844.

3-18   " Oliver, and Phebe C. Langworthy; m. by Elder Henry Clarke, Oct. 16, 1844.

3-18   " Phebe C., and Oliver Langworthy, Oct. 16, 1844.

4-10   " Mary C., and Benjamin F. Kenyon, Oct. 17, 1846.

4-10   " Sarah, and Charles Kenyon, Oct. 19, 1846.

1-44   LANPHERE Ebenezer, of Ebenezer, of Hopkinton, and Annie Jacques, of Hannah, widow; m. by John Maxson, Justice, June 7, 1768.

1-23   " Nathan, and Amia Champlain; m. by Joshua Clarke, Justice, Dec. 7, 1758.

1-51   " Joshua, Jr., of Joshua, and Amie Satterlee, of John, both of Hopkinton; m. by John Larkin, Justice, Nov. 13, 1769.

1-67   " Latham, of Joshua, of Hopkinton, and Anna Wilbur, of Samuel, of Richmond; m. by Elder John Davis, Jan. --, 1772.

2-1   " Rowland, of Hopkinton, and Elizabeth Palmitter, of Stonington; m. by Elder John Burdick, March 25, 1777.

1-107   " Avis, and Jason Eaglestone, April 18, 1784.

2-1   " Mary, and Benjamin Kenyon, Feb. 16, 1785.

2-12   " Susey, and Ethan Maxson, Feb. 19, 1791.

2-48   " Rowland, and Alice Babcock; m. by Elder John Burdick, Dec. 18, 1791.

2-42   " Elizabeth, and David Button, Oct. 29, 1803.

2-97   " Elizabeth, and Joseph Button, March 21, 1822.

3-15   " Belinda, and Clarke A. Potter, Dec. 25, 1838.

4-7   " Silas H., and Patience B. Browning; m. by Elder C. C. Lewis, Dec. 21, 1845.

1-20   LARKIN Elizabeth, and Joseph Coon, April 14, 1757.

1-23   " Content, and John Stewart, April 8, 1758.

1-28   " Thankful, and Richmond Reynolds, Nov. 1, 1760.

1-34   " Stephen, of Hopkinton, and Abigail Cottrell, of South Kingstown; m. by John Witter, Justice, March 21, 1762.

1-36 LARKIN Timothy, of Westerly, and Sarah Ney, of Hopkington; m. by Lawton Palmer, Justice, June 9, 1763.

1-62 " Timothy, of Hopkinton, son of John, of Westerly, and Rachel Langworthy, of Samuel, late of Hopkinton; m. by Nathan Burdick, Justice, Oct. 5, 1771.

1-77 " Elisha, of Samuel, and Margaret Baggs, of John, of Richmond; m. by Elder John Gardiner, Dec. 17, 1773.

1-1 " David, Jr., of Richmond, and Sarah Utter, of Hopkinton; m. by Elder Thomas West, June 10, 1778.

2-6 " Amie, and Martin Brightman, Sept. 25, 1791.

2-16 " Sarah, and Gideon Kenyon, Oct. 8, 1793.

2-62 " Samuel, of Richmond, and Esther Coon, of Hopkinton; m. by Elder Asa Coon, Oct. 5, 1800.

3-19 " Jonathan P., of Richmond, and Lucinda Grinnell, of South Kingstown; m. by Elder Weeden Barber, July 26, 1843.

4-10 " Hannah, and Nathan B. Palmer, Oct. 17, 1846.

4-15 " Sarah L., and John Hood, July 21, 1847.

1-19 LAWTON Mary, and Francis West, Feb. 17, 1757.

1-118 " Joseph, Jr., of Hopkinton, and Anne Rathbun, of Joshua; m. by Elder John Gardiner, Dec. 17, 1778.

1-118 " Elizabeth, and Jedediah Robinson, Feb. 25, 1779.

1-1 " Ruth, and Amos Morgan, Oct. 13, 1783.

1-114 LEONARD Eunice, and Thomas Tanner, April 15, 1777.

1-75 LEWIS Jonathan, of Daniel, late of Hopkinton, and Sarah Deak, of George, late of Hopkinton; m. by Benjamin Randall, Justice, Nov. 10, 1758.

1-38 " Daniel, and Amie Clarke; m. by Lawton Palmer, Justice, March 16, 1763.

1-107 " Eleazer, and Thankful Lewis, Nov. 17, 1765.

1-107 " Thankful, and Eleazer Lewis, Nov. 17, 1765.

1-45 " William Marsh, of Stonington, and Mrs. Hannah Maxson, of Hopkinton; m. by John Burdick, Justice, Nov. 5, 1767.

1-55 " Mrs. Lydia and Sylvanus Maxson, Dec. 21, 1769.

1-100 " Isreal, and Sarah Wells; m. by Elder John Gardiner, April 28, 1771.

1-62 " Lydia, and Tillemns Burdick, May 15, 1771.

1-65 " Beriah, of Nathaniel, of Hopkinton, and Lois Wells, of Thomas, of Hopkinton; m. by John Maxson, Justice, Jan. 16, 1772.

1-67 " Benjamin, of John, and Amie Burdick, of Ezekiel; m. by Elder Joseph Davis, Feb. 5, 1772.

1-77 " Peleg, of Hopkinton, and Amie Crandall, of Charlestown, dau. of Eber; m. by Elder John Gardiner, April 2, 1772.

1-108 " Lois, and Joseph Langworthy, Jan. 4, 1776.

1-111 " Thankful, and John Grant, Oct. 6, 1776.

1-114 " Josiah, and Deborah Palmitter; m. by Elder Thomas West, Jan. 25, 1777.

1-110 " Eleanor, and Peleg Crandall, Nov. 9, 1777.

1-121 " Hannah, and James Braman, Jr., Feb. 24, 1779.

1-108 " Eunice, and Thomas Smith (Tanner), Nov. 29, 1782.

2-7 " Elias, Jr., and Elizabeth Browning; m. by Elder Joshua Clarke, Nov. 19, 1789.

2-2 " Hazard (col.), and Martha Will; m. by Peleg Cross, Justice, Nov. 6, 1791.

2-6 " Hannah, and Hazard Browning, Nov. 24, 1791.

2-18 " Thomas, and Lydia Coon, of Samuel; m. by Daniel Babcock, Justice, Dec. 25, 1792.

2-50 " Henry, and Edy Wilbur; m. by Elder Abram Coon, Feb. 5, 1794.

2-65 " Nathaniel, and Mary Johnson; m. by Elder Abram Coon, Jan. 4, 1800.

2-46 " Thankful, and Samuel Barber, Sept. 2, 1802.

2-71 " Daniel, of Daniel and Amie, and Sarah Ann Northup, dau. of Nicholas Carr and Anna, of North Kingstown; at North Kingstown by Elder William Northup (also 4-14), Sept. 5, 1805.

2-79 LEWIS Christopher C., and Wealthy Kenyon; m. by Elder Matthew Stillman, April 6, 1812.
2-93 "   Deborah H., and Edward S. Wells, April 30, 1817.
4-14 "   Daniel, and Content Langworthy; m. at North Stonington by Elder Matthew Stillman, June 26, 1823.
3-14 "   Clarinda, and William A. Marrian, Oct. 19, 1839.
4-16 "   Daniel M. D., of Stonington, and Ann Frances Kenyon, of Hopkinton; m. by Elder Daniel Coon, May 24, 1846.
4-16 "   Pardon, of Elias, dec., and Martha Coon, of Isaac, dec.; m, by Elder Henry Clarke, Feb. 13, 1848.

M

1-20 MACCOON Amia, and Samuel Burdick, Oct. 31, 1757.
1-23 "   Jonathan, and Elizabeth Stewart; m. by Joshua Clarke, Justice, Dec. 4, 1758.
1-32 "   David, and Thankful Button; m. by Elder Joseph Fish, Nov. 26, 1761.
1-54 "   Anna, and John Button, Jr., April 23, 1769.
1-54 "   Timothy, and Anna Frink; m. by John Larkin, Justice, April 23, 1769.
1-41 MAINE Peter, Jr., and Patience Eaglestone, both of Stonington, at Hopkington; m. by John Burdick, Justice, March 3, 1765.
3-18 MANCHESTER Henry B., and Mary E. Crandall; m. by Elder John Greene, Aug. 5, 1844.
3-14 MARRIAN William A., of Preston, Conn., and Clarinda Lewis, of Hopkington; m. by Elder Daniel Coon, Oct. 19, 1839.
2-12 MARRIOTT Anne, and George Maxson, Jan. 8, 1778.
2-6   "   Samuel, and Judeth Maxson; m. by Elder Joshua Clarke, May 21, 1791.
1-51 MATTESON Elizabeth, and John Allen, Jr., Feb. 11, 1769.
1-51 MAXSON John, Jr., and Sarah Burdick, of Samuel, of Westerly, Oct. 30, 1746.
1-21 "   Anna, and David Randal, Dec. 24, 1757.
1-35 "   Samuel, and Mary Downing; m. by Joshua Clarke, Justice, March 5, 1763.
1-44 "   Samuel, of Hopkinton, son of Samuel, and Hannah Davis, of John, of Westerly; m. by John Maxson, Justice, Dec. 15, 1765.
1-47 "   Eunice, and Richardson Avery, Jan. 1, 1766.
1-47 "   William, and Lucy Miner, Sept. 16, 1767.
1-45 "   Mrs. Hannah, and William Marsh, Nov. 5, 1767.
1-55 "   Ruth, and Rouse Babcock, Oct. 12, 1769.
1-55 "   Lucy, and Peleg Babcock, Dec. 14, 1769.
1-55 "   Sylvanus, and Mrs. Lydia Lewis; m. by Joshua Clarke, Justice, Dec. 21, 1769.
1-65 "   Lucy, and Ephraim Rogers, Feb. 13, 1772.
1-69 "   Susannah, and Edward Chiver, June 28, 1772.
1-69 "   Thankful, and Samuel Coon, Jan. 7, 1773.
1-71 "   Phineus, of Capt. Benjamin, and Elizabeth Burdick, of Carey; m. by Elder Joshua Clarke, Dec. 4, 1773.
1-108 "   Ruth, and Peleg Babcock, Jan. 18, 1776.
2-45 "   Peleg, and Sarah Clarke, Nov. 13, 1777.
2-12 "   George, and Anne Marriott; m. by Elder John Burdick, Jan. 8, 1778.
2-15 "   Nathan, of Hopkinton, and Nancy Vars, of Westerly; m. by Elder John Burdick, Dec. 4, 1783.
1-103 "   Martha, and Luke Crandall, Jan. 6, 1785.
2-3   "   Polly, and Amberst Crandall, Nov. 1, 1787.
2-3   "   Susanna, and Archibald Crandall, Feb. 2, 1788.
2-14 "   Elisha, of Samuel, of Hopkinton, and Rebecca Wilcox, of Voluntown; m. at Westerly, by Elder Isaiah Wilcox, March 22, 1788.
2-13 "   Daniel, of Daniel, of Westerly, and Prudence Crandall, of Benjamin, of Hopkinton; m. by Elder John Burdick, March 20, 1790.

2-12 MAXSON Ethan, of Hopkinton, and Lucy Lanphere, of Westerly; m. by Elder Joseph Clarke, Feb. 19, 1791.

2-13 " Esther, and Roger Kenyon, April 6, 1791.

2-6 " Judeth, and Samuel Marriott, May 21, 1791.

2-42 " William Miner, of Hopkinton, and Sylvia Miner, of Windham, Conn.; m. at Stonington, by Elder Eleazer Brown, March 13, 1793.

2-42 " Randall, and Mary Saunders, alias Hull; m. by Elder John Burdick, April 18, 1793.

2-60 " Hannah, and Ichabod Burdick, Jr., Oct. 1, 1795.

2-61 " Joseph, of Sylvanus, of Hopkinton, and Lydia Potter, of George, of Westerly; m. by Elder John Burdick, Dec. 17, 1795.

2-61 " Lewis, of Hopkinton, and Tacy Coon, of Hartford; m. at Montville, Conn., by Elder David Rogers, Jan. 27, 1797.

2-62 " Nathan, of Sylvanus, of Westerly, and Ruth Crandall, of Phineas, of Montville, Conn.; m. by Elder Davis Rogers, at M., April 28, 1800.

2-46 " Lydia, and Joseph Wells, May 1, 1806.

2-70 " Benjamin C., and Betsey Saunders; m. by Elder Matthew Stillman, March 26, 1807.

2-62 " Peleg, Jr., and Clarice Burdick; m. by Zeccheus Maxson, Justice, June 15, 1809.

2-96 " John J., and Abbie Babcock; m. by Elder Thomas V. Wells, Feb. 6, 1820.

2-95 " Sarah, and George W. Kenyon, Dec. 30, 1819.

3-7 " Samuel, of Elisha, dec., and Lucy Stillman, of Daniel; m. by Elder Matthew Stillman, Oct. 16, 1827.

3-11 " Lydia, and Franklin Barber, Aug. 11, 1836.

3-12 MAYNARD Eliza, and Ransom Kenyon, March 27, 1838.

1-108 MILLARD Isabel, and James Braman, Dec. 27, 1775.

1-111 MINER Hannah, and Clarke Reynolds, Dec. 20, 1767.

1-47 " Lucy, and William Maxson, Sept. 16, 1767.

2-42 " Sylvia, and Wm. Miner Maxson, March 13, 1793.

1-1 MORGAN Amos, and Ruth Lawton, both of Exeter; m. by Elder Thomas West, Oct. 13, 1783.

2-4 MOREY Hazard, of Providence, and Huldah Champlain, of Hopkinton; m. by David Nichols, Justice, Feb. 11, 1788.

2-4 " Dorcas, and Rayzel Brand, June 8, 1788.

2-51 " Elizabeth, and John Collins, Oct. 19, 1795.

1-25 MOTT Joseph, and Anna Brown (both of Voluntown); m. by John Latham, Justice, Feb. 18, 1761.

N

1-22 NEFF Arnold, and Lois Palmitter, both of Stonington; m. by Joshua Clarke, Justice, April 30, 1758.

1-36 NEY Sarah, and Timothy Larkin, June 9, 1763.

1-49 " Phebe, and Elias Coon, May 1, 1768.

1-25,62 " Catherine, and Caleb Potter, March 21, 1771.

2-6 " Thankful, and Thomas Brightman, May 23, 1782.

2-42 NICHOLS Elizabeth, and Matthew Stillman, March 13, 1794.

2-72 " John, of Hopkinton, and Elizabeth York, of William, of Charlestown; m. at Charlestown, by Elder Matthew Stillman, July 29, 1804.

3-14 " Leonidas, of Genesee, New York, and Harriet Clarke, of Charlestown; m. by Elder Daniel Coon, April 27, 1840.

1-26 NILES Phebe, and Joseph Cole, Aug. 30, 1760.

2-71 NORTHUP Sarah Ann, and Daniel Lewis (also 4-14), Sept. 5, 1805.

4-4 NOYES George W., of Stonington, son of Thomas, dec., and Martha B. Noyes, of Sanford, dec.; m. by Elder Henry Clarke, July 7, 1845.

4-4 " Martha B., and George W. Noyes, July 7, 1845.

O

4-8   OLNEY George H., of Richmond, and Emeline Amanda Bicknell, of Hopkinton; m. by Elder C. C. Lewis, Aug. 11, 1846.

P

1-46,66 PALMER Elizabeth, and Thompson Wells, Dec. 24, 1767.
1-57   "   Amos, Jr., son of Amos and Mary Austin, of Ezekiel, late of Hopkinton; m. by John Larkin, Justice, Feb. 15, 1770.
1-113 "   Comfort, and Abel Burdick, Dec. 21, 1775.
1-99   "   Hannah, and George Popple, April 13, 1780.
1-98   "   Nathaniel, of Lawton, of Hopkinton, and Mary Foster, of Gideon, of Stonington; m. by Elder Joshua Clarke, Oct. 31, 1782.
1-64   "   Fones, and Susannah Chever; m. by Joseph Clarke, Justice, May —, 1783.
2-70   "   Charlotte, and Nathen Tanner, Nov. 17, 1805.
3-9   "   Amos N., of Deacon Jabez, and Mary Barber, of Deacon Weedon; m. by Elder Thomas Tillinghast, April 3, 1832.
4-12   "   Mary, and Elias Coon, Sept. 29, 1840.
4-10   "   Nathan B., and Hannah Larkin; m. by Elder Lucius Crandall, Oct. 17, 1846.
1-114 PALMITTER Deborah, and Josiah Lewis, Jan. 25, 1777.
1-22   "   Lois, and Arnold Neff, April 30, 1758.
1-46   "   Joseph, of Joseph, dec., and Martha Tefft, of Jonathan; m. by John Burdick, Justice, Dec. 22, 1767.
1-75   "   Nathan, and Abigail Slack, Dec. 25, 1769.
2-19   "   Elizabeth, and Rowland Lanphere, March 25, 1777.
1-1   "   Joshua, and Anne Button, both of Hopkinton; m. by Elder Thomas West, Aug. 11, 1782.
1-39   PARTELOW Thomas, Jr., of Stonington, and Martha Coon, of Hopkinton; m. by Joshua Clarke, Justice, Aug. 2, 1764.
1-40   "   Jonas, and Mrs. Lydia Kezier, both of Stonington; m. by John Burdick, Justice, Sept. 27, 1764.
1-115 PATTERSON Mrs. Martha, and Nathan Closson, Feb. 14, 1784.
4-7   PEARCE Louisa M., and Leander Baid, March 29, 1846.
2-8   PECKHAM Daniel, and Avis Rogers, Feb. 16, 1775.
2-65   "   Waitey, and Thomas Langworthy, May 6, 1797.
2-67   "   Mary, and Amos Collins, Feb. 16, 1804.
2-77   "   Sophia, and Caleb Greene, March 3, 1816.
1-41   PIERCE Edward, of Charlestown, and Eunice Hall, of Hopkinton; m. by John Coon, Justice, April 30, 1765.
2-9   PENDLETON Catherine, and Henry Clarke, Dec. 5, 1776.
1-117 "   Sarah, and Willett Clarke, April 24, 1779.
2-60   "   Joanna, and Augustus Kenyon, Oct. 11, 1798.
1-35   PERKINS Ebenezer, of Newman, of Exeter, and Hannah Prosser, of Ichabod, of Hopkinton; m. by John Maxson, Justice, Dec. 25, 1762.
1-56   PERRY Mary, and Simeon Babcock, Jan. 7, 1770.
1-1   "   Mary, and Benjamin Barber, Aug. 20, 1783.
2-52   "   Lydia, and William Slocum, Nov. 28, 1802.
3-14   "   Charles R., and Mary A. Gardiner; m. by Elder Christopher Chester, Oct. 4, 1840.
1-113 PETTEY William, and Thankful Colegrove; m. by Elder Thomas West, June 2, 1776.
1-32   PLUMBER Lydia, and Nathan Lamb, July 13, 1762.
1-99   POPPLE George, and Hannah Palmer; m. by Elder John Gardiner, April 13, 1780.
2-52   "   Mary, and Samuel Witter, Nov. 12, 1796.
2-47   "   Tabitha, and Nathan Collins, April 12, 1804.
1-41   PORTER Nathan, and Hannah Witter; m. by John Burdick, Justice, Nov. 25, 1764.
1-25,62 POTTER Caleb, of Thomas, of Hopkinton, and Catherine Ney, of Caleb, and Catherine, of do.; m. by Elder Joshua Clarke, March 21, 1771.

1-72   POTTER Abigail, and Ceaser Wells, Oct. 8, 1775.
1-95   "   Stephen, Jr., and Sarah Coon, of William; m. by Elder John Bur-
                dick, Nov. 29, 1780.
1-98   "   Mrs. Susannah, and Samuel Wells, Nov. 29, 1781.
2-57   "   Content, and Daniel Babcock, April 8, 1784.
2-61   "   Lydia, and Joseph Maxson, Dec. 17, 1795.
2-59   "   Thomas, and Sarah Barber; m. by Elder Asa Coon, Nov. 1, 1798.
2-46   "   Lyman, of Jonathan, Jr., and Rabamah Button, of Isaiah; m. by
                Elder Asa Coon, April 28, 1799.
2-79   "   Sarah, and Barton Saunders, March 5, 1803.
4-11   "   Benjamin, of George, of Westerly, and Betsey Greene, of Pardon,
                of do.; m. at Newport, by Elder Henry Burdick, March 6,
                1808.
2-60   "   Henry, of Joseph, of Westerly, and Anna Babcock, of Daniel, of
                Hopkinton; m. by Elder Matthew Stillman, Nov. 17, 1812.
2-90   POTTER Content, and Joseph Spicer, Nov. 12, 1818.
3-15   "   Clarke A., of Hopkinton, and Belinda Lanphere, of Westerly; m.
                by Elder Daniel Coon, Dec. 25, 1838.
4-19   "   John S., and Mahala Crandall, dan. of Thear J., all of Westerly;
                m. at Hopkinton by Elder Henry Clarke, April 21, 1850.
4-7   POWERS Anna Maria, and Thomas Browning, Jan. 7, 1846.
1-85   PROSSER Hannah, and Ebenezer Perkins, Dec. 25, 1762.
1-22   "   Ichabod, and Abigail Coon, widow of Daniel; m. by John Maxson,
                Justice, —— —, 1763.
1-62   "   Ruth, and Jeremiah Rogers, March 22, 1771.
1-21   "   David, and Anna Maxson, both of Hopkinton; m. by Daniel Mac-
                coon, Justice, Dec. 24, 1757.

Q R

1-97   RATHBUN Martha, and Carey Rogers, Jan. 10, 1768.
1-76   "   John, Jr., of Stonington and Eunice Wells, of Thomas, of Hopkin-
                ton; m. by Elder Joshua Clarke, June 23, 1774.
1-118 "   Anne, and Joseph Lawton, Dec. 17, 1778.
4-15   "   Elias H., and Phebe N. Healey; m. by Elder C. C. Lewis, Dec. 12,
                1847.
1-57   REMINGTON Sarah, and Robert Burdick, Dec. 24, 1769.
1-22   REYNOLDS Elias, and Ruth Baker, of Stonington; m. by Joshua Clarke,
                Justice, April 17, 1758.
1-28   "   Richmond, and Thankful Larkin; m. by John Latham, Justice,
                Nov. 1, 1760.
1-87, 72 " Tacy, and Josiah Witter, Feb. 2, 1764.
1-111 "   Clarke, of Hopkinton and Hannah Miner, of Stonington, Dec.
                20, 1764.
2-16   "   Zaccheus, and Desire Babcock, Dec. 11, 1771.
2-16   "   Zaccheus, and Phebe Babcock; m. by Elder John Burdick, Sept.
                16, 1781.
2-80   "   Abbie, and Clarke Thurston, Jan. 7, 1816.
2-92   "   Amanda, and Charles Clarke, Dec. 13, 1818.
2-97   "   Abbie M., and Nicholas Crandall, Jan. 12, 1822.
4-7   "   Alcy Ann, and Simeon T. Webster, Aug. 13, 1845.
1-54   RHODES Simon, of Stonington, and Martha Babcock, of Hopkinton; m. by
                Elder Joshua Clarke, Aug. 22, 1769.
3-17   RICHMOND George W., and Waity Barber; m. by Elder David Avery, ——
                ——, 1842.
4-7   "   Samuel N., and Rachel Thayer; m. by Elder C. C. Lewis, July 5,
                1846.
2-4   RIDER Sarah, and John Wells, July 16, 1788.
1-32   ROBINSON John, Jun., and Elizabeth Wells; m. by Joshua Clarke, Jus-
                tice, Nov. 12, 1762.
1-41   "   Elizabeth, and Daniel Burdick, Jr., Feb. 7, 1765.
1-118 "   Jedediah, and Elizabeth Lawton, of Joseph; m. by Elder Thomas
                West, Feb. 25, 1779.

1-39   ROGERS Amis, of Nathan, of New London, and Anna Deak, of George, of Hopkinton; m. by John Maxson, Justice, Dec. 29, 1764.

1-41   "   Amie, and Jonathan Wells, Jr., June 6, 1767.

1-97   "   Carey, of New London, and Martha Rathbun, of Exeter; m. by Elder Joseph Davis, Jan. 10, 1768.

1-62   "   Jeremiah, of Westerly, son of Nathan, of New London, and Ruth Prosser, of Ichabod, of Hopkinton; m. by Elder Joshua Clarke, March 28, 1771.

1-65   "   Ephraim, of Jonathan, of New London, and Tacy Maxson, of John, of Hopkinton; m. by Elder Joshua Clarke, Feb. 13, 1772.

2-8   "   Avis, and Daniel Peckham, Feb. 16, 1775.

2-42   "   Grace, and Benjamin Greene, Dec. 13, 1781.

2-94   "   Lester T., of Waterford, Conn., and Susan H. Crandall; m. by Elder Matthew Stillman, April 30, 1825.

4-15   "   Charles L., of Norwich, Conn., and Lucy E. Stearns, of Griswold, Conn.; m. at Hopkinton, by Elder C. C. Lewis, Nov. 14, 1847.

1-42   ROSS William, of Charlestown, and Sarah Coon, of Hopkinton; m. by Stephen Saunders, Justice, March 13, 1763.

S

5-1   SALISBURY Mehitable, and Joel W. Douglas, Dec. 14, 1851.

2-43   SAMPSON Maria, and Abel Fenner, —— —, 1842.

1-51   SATTERLEE Amie, and Joshua Lanphere, Nov. 13, 1769.

1-70   "   Sylvester, of John, and Bethany Coon, of Elisha; m. by Elder Joshua Clarke, Aug. 8, 1773.

1-59   SAUNDERS Mary, and Samuel Langworthy, Jan. 24, 1771.

2-54   "   Esther, and John Utter, Sept. 5, 1801.

2-79   "   Barton, of Charlestown, and Sarah Potter, of Hopkinton; m. by Elder Abram Coon, March 5, 1803.

2-70   "   Betsey, and Benjamin C. Maxson, March 26, 1807.

2-69   "   Isaac, 3d, and Matilda Wells; m. by Elder Abram Coon, May 3, 1810.

1-104   SCRIVEN William, and Marvel Davis, of Elder Joseph; m. by Joseph Crandall, Justice, Feb. 2, 1775.

1-27   SHERMAN Sarah, and David Crandall, Feb. 19, 1761.

1-50   SHEFFIELD Elizabeth, and Edward Wells, Jr., Dec. 25, 1749.

1-65   "   Elizabeth, and Woodman Wilbur, Sept. 15, 1771.

1-46   SHELDON Palmer, of John, and Penelope Brown, of John, both of South Kingstown; m. by John Burdick, Justice, Jan. 10, 1768.

2-75   "   Asa, and Mary Edwards; m. by Elder Abram Coon, April 26, 1800.

3-17   SHELDON Horace F., of Hopkinton, and Eliza Ann Irving, of Coventry; m. by Elder David Avery, ——. —, 1843.

1-84   SISSEL Nathan, and Hannah Burdick; m. by Joshua Clarke, Justice, Feb. 9, 1763.

1-54   SISSON John, of Westerly, son of Thomas, and Keturah Burdick, of Peter; m. by Stephen Saunders, Justice, March 20, 1769.

1-101   "   Anne, and Elnathan Burdick, Jan. 9, 1774.

1-75   SLACK Abigail, and Nathan Palmitter, Dec. 25, 1769.

2-52   SLOCUM William, of Hopkinton, and Lydia Perry, of Stonington; m. by Elder Simeon Brown, Nov. 28, 1802.

1-108   SMITH Thomas (Tanner), and Eunice Lewis, of Elias; m. by Elder John Gardiner, Nov. 29, 1782.

4-6   SNOW Levina L., and George Watson, June 18, 1845.

5-4   SPENCER William J., of Coventry, of Pardon, aged 23 years, and Merebah Kenyon, aged 20 years, of Hopkinton, dau. of Arnold; m. by Rev. C. M. Lewis, March 14, 1853.

2-51   SPICER Joseph, and Fannie Thurston; m. by Elder Abram Coon, Nov. 10, 1793.

2-51   "   Joseph, and Mary Cottrell, of Westerly; m. by Elder Abram Coon, March 6, 1796.

2-90   "   Joseph, Jr., of Hopkinton, and Content Potter, of Westerly, dau. of George; m. at Westerly by Elder Matthew Stillman, Nov. 12, 1818.

4-6 SPICER George H., of Joseph, and Harriet Davis, of Pardon; m. by Elder
      Henry Clarke, Nov. 9, 1845.
4-6   " Mary, and Henry Whipple. Nov. 15. 1845.
4-21 " Edward D., and Eliza Wells; m. by Elder John Greene, Sept.
      4, 1851.
1-112 STANTON Mary, and Paul Burdick, Feb. 18, 1775.
4-15 STEARNS Lucy E., and Charles L. Rogers, Nov. 14, 1847.
1-22 STEWART Margaret, and Ishmeal Codner, Feb. 11, 1758.
1-23 " John, and Content Larkin; m. by Daniel Maccoon, Justice, April
      8, 1758.
1-23 " Elizabeth, and Jonathan Maccoon, Dec. 4, 1758.
2-78 STILLMAN Elisha, of Elisha, and Prudence Burdick, of Elder John, April
      24, 1782.
2-18 " Sarah, and Stephen Coon, Feb. 28, 1789.
2-42 " Matthew, and Elizabeth Nichols, of David; m. by Elder John
      Burdick, March 13, 1794.
2-67 " Fannie, and Barker Wells, Sept. 26, 1799.
3-6   " Phineas, and Thankful Gardiner, Dec. 26, 1810.
3-70 " Lucy, and Samuel Maxson, Oct. 16, 1827.
3-7   " Christopher C., of Westerly, and Mary A. Johnson, of Hopkinton;
      m. by Elder Matthew Stillman, Dec. 7, 1829.
4-6   " Aurilia E., and Thomas M. Wilcox, Oct. 12, 1845.
4-19 " Daniel G., of Westerly, and Abbie L. Wilbur, of Hopkinton; m.
      at Hopkinton, by Elder John Greene, May 13, 1849.
1-42 STUTSON Thomas, and Mary Hall; m. by Stephen Saunders, Justice, Jan.
      —, 1758.
1-46 " Stephen, of Westerly, and Dorcas Hall, of Charlestown; m. by
      Nathan Burdick, Justice, Jan. 9, 1768.
5-4   SUTCLIFF Robert, and Mary Ann Brown, both of New Shoreham; m. by
      Elder John Greene, May 18, 1853.
1-43 SWEET Theddeus, of Hopkinton, and Abigail Cottrell, of South Kings-
      town; m. by Lawton Palmer, Justice, Feb. 18, 1766.
1-51 " Lebbeus, of Thomas, of Hopkinton, dec., and Catherine Collins,
      of Hezekiah, of Hopkinton; m. by John Larkin, Justice, March
      11, 1770.

T

3-16 TABOR Henry, and Hannah Crandall; m. by Elder Weeden Barber, Oct. 4,
      1840.
1-105 TANNER Nathan, of Nathan, and Elizabeth Thurston, of Thomas, Dec. 29,
      1757.
2-15 " William, of Francis and Elizabeth, and Ruth Brown, of John; m. by
      Elder John Davis, Feb. 16, 1771.
1-67 " William, of Francis, and Ruth Brown, of John; m. by Elder John
      Davis, Feb. 16, 1772.
1-78 " Benjamin, of West Greenwich, and Susannah Crandall, of Hopkin-
      ton (also 1-112); m. by Elder Thomas West, April 21, 1774.
1-69 " Nathan, of John, and Susannah West, of Elder Thomas, Oct. 19,
      1775.
1-113 " Mary, and Joseph Burdick, Nov. 28, 1776.
1-114 " Thomas, of Richmond, and Eunice Leonard, of Preston, Conn.; m.
      by Elder Thomas West, April 15, 1777.
2-5   " William, Jr., and Hannah Utter; m. by Elder Joseph Davis, Nov.
      2, 1784.
2-7   " John, and Barrodel Babcock, of James; m. by Elder John Burdick,
      March 24, 1791.
2-43 " Anstis, and Reuben Fenner, Jan. 17, 1793.
2-17 " Phebe, and Belcher Haley, Jan. 20, 1793.
2-43 " Stephen, and Lois Babcock; m. by Elder Asa Coon, March 13,
      1794.
2-70 " Nathan, and Charlotte Palmer; m. by Elder Abram Coon, Nov.
      17, 1805.

2-73   TANNER John, and Deborah Bentley; m. by Elder Abram Coom, Jan. 25, 1807.
4-15   "   Triphenia H., and William H. Dawley, Dec. 19, 1847.
2-5   TAYLOR Benjamin, and Mrs. Mary Thurston; m. by Elder Joshua Clarke, Dec. 28, 1788.
2-72   "   Humphrey, of Thomas, and Betsey Wilbur, of Clarke; m. by Elder Matthew Stillman, Jan. 9, 1806.
2-91   "   Elizabeth, and Russell Clarke, Oct. 16, 1808.
1-39   TEFFT Benjamin, of Richmond, and Deborah Burdick, of Hopkinton; m. by John Burdick, Justice, Sept. 20, 1764.
1-46   "   Martha, and Joseph Palmitter, Dec. 22, 1767.
3-17   "   Daniel C., and Abbie A. Williams, both of Richmond; m. by Elder David Avery. —— —, 1843.
4-15   "   Eunice A., and Edmund Jordan, June 28, 1847.
4-7   THAYER Rachel, and Samuel N. Richmond, July 5, 1845.
2-9   THOMAS Sarah, and Joseph Brightman, May 14, 1747.
1-77   THOMPSON William Tolman, alias, of Hopkinton, and Esther Hall, of Charlestown; m. by Elder John Gardiner, Jan. 26, 1774.
4-21   THORP Lydia C., and Asa S. Coon, March 22, 1852.
1-105   THURSTON Elizabeth, and Nathan Tanner, Dec. 29, 1757.
1-22   "   Mary, and Nathan Wells, March 9, 1758.
2-5   "   Mrs. Mary, and Benjamin Taylor, Dec. 28, 1788.
2-51   "   Fannie, and Joseph Spicer, Nov. 10, 1793.
2-91   "   Sallie, and Russell Clarke, Aug. 29, 1813.
2-80   "   Clarke, and Abbie Reynolds; m. by Rowland Babcock, Justice, Jan. 7, 1816.

U

1-47   UTTER Abraham, of John, late of Hopkinton, dec., and Hannah White, of Roger; m. by Thomas Wells, Justice, Nov. 22, 1759.
1-55   "   Abraham, of Hopkinton, son of John, dec., and Hannah Burdick, of Hubbard; m. by Joseph Crandall, Justice, Oct. 14, 1769.
1-1   "   Sarah, and David Larkin, June 10, 1778.
2-5   "   Hannah, and William Tanner, Jr., Nov. 2, 1784.
2-54   "   John, and Esther Saunders, Sept. 5, 1801.

V

2-15   VARS Nancy, and Nathan Maxson, Dec. 4, 1783.
3-15   "   Lucinda, and Gardiner Case, March 28, 1841.
2-63   VINSON Elizabeth, and Samuel Crandall, Jr., Jan. 14, 1802

W

1-63   WAITE Paine, of Hopkinton, son of Thomas, of Tiverton, R. I., and Kezier Crandall, of Hopkinton, dau. of Jeremiah; m. by Elder John Pendleton, Oct. 29, 1771.
1-112   "   Grace, and John Benjamin, June 29, 1775.
1-113   "   John, and Mary Cottrell; m. by Elder Thomas West, Sept. 5, 1776.
4-7   "   Samuel, and Mrs. Sarah Ann Knowles; m. by Elder C. C. Lewis, Nov. 27, 1845.
4-6   WATSON George, Jr., and Levina L. Snow, both of Norwich, Conn.; m. by Elder Weeden Barber, Jr., June 18, 1845.
1-98   WAUD Elizabeth, and Elder William Bliss, Jan. 9, 1780.
1-13   WEBSTER Hannah, and Jeremiah Colegrove, Nov. 13, 1776.
2-47   "   Alexander, of Joseph, of Hopkinton, and Hannah Dawley, of Exeter, dau. of Oliver; m. by Elder Gershom Palmer, March 1, 1812.
4-7   "   Simeon T., of South Kingstown, and Alcy Ann Reynolds, of Exeter; m. by Elder C. C. Lewis, Aug. 13, 1845.

1-50	WELLS	Edward, Jr., and Elizabeth Sheffield, Dec. 25, 1749
1-22	"	Matthew, and Bridget Burdick; m. by Joshua Clarke, Justice, Jan. 5, 1758.
1-22	"	Nathan, and Mary Thurston; m. by Joshua Clarke, Justice, March 9, 1758.
1-42	"	Joshua, of Hopkinton, and Elizabeth Dartts, of Stonington; m. by Elder Walte Palmer, Feb. 15, 1759.
1-31	"	Mary, and Oliver Clarke, Dec. 16, 1761.
1-32	"	Elizabeth, and John Robinson, Jr., Nov. 12, 1762.
1-35	"	Thankful, and Simeon Hiscox, Dec. 26, 1762.
1-41	"	Jonathan, Jr., and Amie Rogers; m. by John Maxson, Justice, June 6, 1767.
1-46	"	Elizabeth, and Tanner Wells, Dec. 24, 1767.
1-46	"	Tanner, and Elizabeth Wells, Dec. 24, 1767.
1-46	"	Thompson, and Elizabeth Palmer (also 1-66); m. by John Burdick, Justice, Dec. 24, 1767.
1-100	"	Sarah, and Izreal Lewis, April 28, 1771.
1-65	"	Lois, and Beriah Lewis, Jan. 16, 1772.
1-76	"	Eunice, and John Rathbun, June 23, 1774.
1-72	"	Ceaser, servant of James, but since a soldier, and Abigail Potter; m. by Elder John Gardiner, Oct. 8, 1775.
1-98	"	Samuel, of Hopkinton, and Mrs. Susannah Potter, of Westerly; m. by Elder Joshua Clarke, Nov. 29, 1781.
2-11	"	Tacy, and Perry Burdick, Dec. 19, 1782.
2-18	"	Mrs. Mary, and Job B. Clarke, Jan. 1, 1788.
2-4	"	John, and Sarah Rider; m. by Elder John Burdick, July 10, 1788.
2-4	"	Matthew, Jr., and Elizabeth Coon, of David; m. by Elder John Burdick, Dec. 18, 1788.
2-58	"	Elizabeth, and Peleg Babcock, June 18, 1789.
2-17, 45	"	Gardiner, of Joshua, of Hopkinton, and Wealthy Gallup, of Samuel, of Voluntown; m. by Edward Burdick, Justice, Dec. 23, 1792.
2-67	"	Barker, and Fannie Stillman; m. by Elder Abram Coon, Sept. 26, 1799.
2-56	"	Russell, of Randall, and Lydia Crandall, of Phineas, of Montville, Conn.; m. by Joseph Potter, Justice, Aug. 5, 1802.
2-62	"	Ruth, and Samuel Gardiner, Jr., May 22, 1803.
2-46	"	Joseph, and Lydia Maxson; m. by Elder Abram Coon, May 1, 1806.
2-69	"	Matilda, and Isaac Saunders, 3d, May 3, 1810.
2-76	"	Abbie, and Alpheus M. Greene, Dec. 18, 1812.
2-76	"	Betsey, and John Greene, Jr., April 3, 1813.
2-93	"	Edward S., and Deborah H. Lewis; m. by Asa Church, Justice, April 30, 1817.
4-21	"	Eliza, and Edward D. Spicer, Sept. 4, 1851.
1-19	WEST	Francis, and Mary Lawton; m. by Stephen Richmond, Justice, at Westerly, Feb. 17, 1757.
1-57	"	Susannah, and Benjamin Clarke, March 27, 1770.
1-69	"	Susannah, and Nathan Tanner, Oct. 19, 1775.
1-114	"	Sarah, and Stephen Rose Burdick, Aug. 14, 1777.
1-1	"	Jonathan, of Hopkinton, and Prudence Allin, of Stonington; m. by Elder Thomas West, July 27, 1780.
2-47	"	Sabrina, and John Wright, Jr., June 29, 1788.
1-55	WHEELER	Susannah, and Benjamin Clarke, Dec. 15, 1769.
2-45	"	Presilla, and Jonathan Babcock, Feb. 20, 1795.
4-1	"	Noyes D., and Susan S. Wilbur; m. by Elder Leander E. Wakefield, Nov. 23, 1844.
4-6	WHIPPLE	Henry, of Christopher B., of Coventry, R. I., and Mary Spicer, of Joseph, of Hopkinton; m. by Elder Henry Clarke, Nov. 15, 1845.
1-50	WHITE	Job, of Roger, and Anna Clarke, widow, dau. of John Lewis; m. by Elder Joseph Davis, Jan. 6, 1759.
1-47	"	Hannah, and Abraham Utter, Nov. 22, 1759.
1-62	"	Mary, and Joshua Collins, Feb. 7, 1771.
1-62	"	Sarah, and Clarke Wilbur, Feb. 7, 1771.
1-99	"	William, and Ruth Collins; m. by Elder John Gardiner, April 5, 1780.

2-1 WHITE Godfrey, son of Oliver, of Hopkinton, and Jane Worden, of Amos, dec.; m. by Robert Burdick, Justice, Feb. 3, 1784.

1-1   "   Penelope, and Oliver Davis, July 16, 1784.

2-18   "   Susannah, and William G. Greene, March 9, 1793.

2-54   "   Mrs. Nabby, and Rowland Babcock, Jan. 12, 1797.

3-17   "   Charles P., of North Stonington, and Eliza Kenyon, of Hopkinton; m. by Elder David Avery, —— —, 1843.

4-12   "   Mary Ann B., and Luke Crandall, March 29, 1847.

2-4 WHITFORD John, of Joshua, of Little Hosick, N. Y., and Margaret Coon, of Joshua, of Hopkinton; m. by Elder John Gardiner, Feb. 6, 1788.

1-42 WILBUR Joseph, of Hopkinton, and Sarah Hall, of Stonington; m. by Stephen Saunders, Justice, March 25, 1758.

1-45   "   Anna, and William Davis, Feb. 26, 1767.

1-62   "   Clarke, and Sarah White; m. by Simeon Perry, Justice, Feb. 7, 1771.

1-65   "   Woodman, of Hopkinton, son of Thomas and Elizabeth Sheffield, of Nathan, dec.; m. by Simeon Perry, Justice, Sept. 15, 1771.

1-67   "   Anna, and Latham Lanphere, Jan. —, 1772.

1-67   "   Jesse, of Richmond, and Nabby Johnson, of Hopkinton; m. by Elder Joshua Clarke, March 4, 1784.

2-50   "   Edy, and Henry Lewis, Feb. 5, 1794.

2-72   "   Betsey, and Humphrey Taylor, Jan. 9, 1806.

2-43   "   Hannah, and Benjamin P. Bentley, Dec. 2, 1806.

2-43   "   Lydia, and John Bentley, Dec. 3, 1806.

4-1   "   Susan S., and Noyes D. Wheeler, Nov. 23, 1844.

4-1   "   Susan, and William B. Hoxsie, May 21, 1845.

4-19   "   Abbie L., and Daniel G. Stillman, May 13, 1849.

1-23 WILCOX, Thomas, of West Greenwich, and Elizabeth Jacques, of Exeter; m. by Joshua Clarke, Justice, Jan. 22, 1759.

2-14   "   Rebecca, and Elisha Maxson, March 22, 1788.

2-8   "   Daniel, of Stonington, and Amie Champlain, of Hopkinton; m. by David Nichols, Justice, Dec. 20, 1789.

2-6   "   Martha, and Mark Stiles, alias Burdick, recorded March 17, 1793.

2-56   "   Larkin, of Hopkinton, and Polly Edwards, of Westerly; m. by Elder Abram Coon, Sept. 3, 1801.

2-95   "   Nabby, and James W. Brown, Sept. 12, 1819.

3-8   "   Nathan, and Sophia Church; m. by Elder Matthew Stillman, Oct. 23, 1831.

4-6   "   Thomas M., of West Greenwich, and Aurilia E. Stillman, of Phineas, of Westerly; m. by Elder Henry Clarke, Oct. 12, 1845.

5-3   "   Almira J., and Nathan M. Crandall, Jan. 29, 1853.

1-78,112 WILKINSON Samuel, of Preston, Conn., and Mary Button, of Hopkinton; m. at Hopkinton, by Elder Thomas West, Aug. 14, 1774.

1-34 WILLIAMS Isaiah, of Plainfield, and Judeth Brand, of Hopkinton; m. by John Witter, Justice, Nov. 16, 1762.

2-13   ·   Sarah, and Robert Burdick, Sept. 21, 1781.

3-17   "   Abbie A., and Daniel C. Tefft, —— —, 1843.

2-2 WILL Martha (col.), and Hazard Lewis (col.), Nov. 6, 1791.

1-23 WITTER John, of John, and Meriam Worden, of James, of Stonington; m. by John Maxson, Jr., Justice, April 7, 1763.

1-37, 75 "   Josiah, of Joseph, and Tacy Reynolds, of Zaccheus; m. by John Burdick, Justice, Feb. 2, 1764.

1-40,120 "   William, and Martha Cole; m. by John Burdick, Justice, Nov. 1, 1764.

1-41   "   Hannah, and Nathan Porter, Nov. 25, 1764.

1-46   "   Sarah, and David Dewey, Jan. 12, 1768.

2-10   "   Samuel, and Tacy Porter, Jan. 5, 1769.

2-52   "   Samuel, Jr., son of Samuel, and Mary Popple, of William, dec.; m. by Thomas Wells, Justice, Nov. 12, 1796.

2-47   "   William, Jr., and Lucy Crandall; m. by Elder Abram Coon, Jan. 2, 1800.

2-75   "   Joseph, 2d, of Hopkinton, and Sarah Champlain, formerly of South Kingstown; m. by Elder Matthew Stillman, June 22, 1811.

2-75   "   Joseph, 2d, and Lucretia Dodge, of Joseph; m. by Elder Matthew Stillman, Nov. 26, 1812.

4-17 WOODMANSEE Benjamin B., of Asa, and Ruth Kenyon, of George; m. by
Elder Matthew Stillman, Feb. 7, 1819.
2-8 WOOD Jemima, and Ames Button, Jr., Feb. 8, 1789.
1-19 WORDEN Mary, and Daniel Dodge, April 11, 1756.
1-42 " Amos, of Stonington, and Jean Burdick, of Westerly; m. by Stephen
Saunders, Justice, March 25, 1763.
1-23 " Meriam, and John Witter, April 7, 1763.
1-67 " William, and Mary Byrnes, Oct. 4, 1764.
2-1 " Jane, and Godfrey White, Feb. 3, 1784.
2-1 " Mary, and Lebbeus Coon, April 13, 1785.
2-3 " Sally, and Benjamin Kenyon, Aug. 9, 1787.
2-63 " Ruth, and Burdick Kenyon, Feb. 14, 1802.
2-4 WRIGHT Thomas, and Lawando Sarah Button; m. by Elder Thomas West,
Justice, Dec. 28, 1787.
2-47 " John, Jr., and Sabrina West, of Francis; m. by Elder Joseph Davis,
June 29, 1788.
5-2 " Hannah A., and Stephen A. Clarke, Nov. 5, 1753.

X Y Z

2-72 YORK Elizabeth, and John Nichols, July 29, 1804.

HOPKINTON.

BIRTHS AND DEATHS.

A

1-66	ALLEN Samuel, of Stephen,	Oct. 15, 1752.
1-66	" Tamson,	Nov. 3, 1754.
1-66	" Patience,	Nov. 1, 1756.
1-66	" William,	Oct. 7, 1758.
1-66	" Stephen,	Oct. 24, 1760.
1-66	" Sarah,	Feb. 2, 1763.
1-56	" Sylvester,	Oct. 18, 1764.
1-66	" Merabah,	Oct. 26, 1766.
3-10	ARNOLD John G., of Gorton W. and Nancy,	Oct. 16, 1827.
3-10	" Francis Brown,	Dec. 15, 1828.
3-10	" Mary Elizabeth,	Sept. 13, 1830.
3-10	" Lucy Ann,	Aug. 7, 1832.
3-10	" Lucy Maria,	March 6, 1834.
3-10	" Susan Letitia T.,	March 20, 1841.

B

1-116	BABCOCK Eunice, of Simeon and Sarah,	Oct. 3, 1744.
1-116	" Jeremiah,	May 16, 1746.
1-116	" Thomas,	July 21, 1748.
1-116	" Lucy,	Jan. 11, 1750.
1-116	" Dorcas,	Dec. 1, 1753.
1-116	" Jason,	July 9, 1756.
1-116	" Lydia,	June 20, 1759.
1-116	" Hannah,	April 28, 1762.
1-116	" Lucos,	April 24, 1765.
1-116	" Jonathan,	April 18, 1768.
1-101	" Oliver, of Oliver and Patience,	June 28, 1743.
1-101	" Peleg,	Oct. 4, 1748.
1-101	" Susannah,	June 25, 1750.
1-101	" Deborah,	April 11, 1752.
1-101	" Sarah,	April 27, 1756.
1-101	" Mary,	June 11, 1758.
1-101	" Ruth,	April 20, 1760.
1-101	" Clarke,	June 10, 1762.
1-101	" Ruhamah,	May 16, 1764.
1-101	" Parah,	May 18, 1766.
1-101	" Ezra,	Sept. 17, 1769.
1-101	" Luke,	Aug. 6, 1772.
1-25	" Christopher, of Christopher,	Sept. 1, 1759.
1-34	" Martha, of Christopher and Martha,	Jan. 18, 1761.
1-34	" Mary,	Jan. 1, 1763.
1-43	" A daughter,	April 25, 1766.
1-119	" Rhoda, of Rouse and Ruth,	Dec. 17, 1769.
1-119	" Rouse,	May 12, 1773.
1-119	" Elizabeth,	March 14, 1775.
1-119	" Benjamin,	Sept. 2, 1779.

1-116	BABCOCK Eunice, dau. of Simeon and Sarah, her children.	
1-116	" Barker Wells, alias,	Dec. 19, 1769.
1-116	" Joseph Langworthy, alias,	Jan. 29, 1774.
1-116	" Lois,	June 13, 1776.
2-42	" Hezekiah, of Hezekiah and Martha,	Nov. 25, 1770.
2-42	" Rowland,	Sept. 17, 1773.
2-42	" Luke,	April 16, 1778.
2-42	" Susannah,	May 2, 1780.
2-42	" Martha,	Aug. 30, 1781.
2-42	" Dorcas,	March 13, 1785.
2-10	" Ruth, of Capt. Samuel and Ruth,	Jan. 10, 1771.
2-10	" Meriam,	Sept. 26, 1772.
2-10	" Samuel,	Oct. 19, 1775.
2-10	" George Rhodes,	May 23, 1778.
2-10	" Martha,	June 29, 1780.
2-10	" Beriah,	July 6, 1782.
2-57	" Daniel, of Daniel and Content,	Dec. 16, 1784.
2-57	" Betsey,	Feb. 21, 1787.
2-57	" Jacob Davis,	Jan. 20, 1789.
2-57	" Anna,	May 9, 1791.
2-57	" George Potter,	Nov. 4, 1795.
2-57	" Oliver,	Dec. 12, 1797.
2-57	" Lucy,	Jan. 24, 1801.
2-57	" Mary,	Nov. 2, 1806.
2-57	" Emily,	June 14, 1810.
2-58	" Elnathan, of Peleg and Elizabeth,	Sept. 30, 1790.
2-58	" Hannah,	May 30, 1792.
2-58	" Polly,	Jan. 9, 1794.
–58	" Fannie,	Nov. 5, 1795.
2-58	" Lucy,	March 11, 1790.
2-58	" Peleg,	April 7, 1801.
2-94	" Samuel Franklin, of Jared, Jr., and Lois,	March 7, 1819.
1-1	BARBER Susannah, of Nathan and Thankful,	Sept. 24, 1755.
1-1	" Moses,	July 26, 1757.
1-1	" Thankful,	May 2, 1759.
1-1	" Nathan,	Nov. 7, 1760.
1-1	" Mary,	May 27, 1762.
1-1	" Benjamin,	Nov. 20, 1763.
1-1	" John,	Dec. 21, 1765.
1-1	" Eunice,	July 22, 1769.
1-1	" Ellener,	May 15, 1775.
1-1	" Joanna,	Jan. 7, 1778.
1-1	" Lydia,	June 14, 1780.
	Note.—The two last born in Westerly, the rest in Hopkinton.	
1-64	" A son to Amie; reputed father, Peter Allen,	Aug. 29, 1769.
2-60	" Dorcas, of Levi,	July 12, 1773.
2-68	" John Ney,	March 13, 1779.
2-68	" Nicholas,	March 13, 1779.
1-1	" Benjamin Perry, of Benjamin and Mary,	Jan. 29, 1785.
2-54	" Charles Holden, of Arnold and Mary,	July 25, 1795.
2-93	" Jane G., of Paul M. and Maria,	July 3, 1830.
3-11	" Oscar Maxson, of Franklin and Lydia,	June 25, 1837.
3-15	" Mary Elizabeth, of John H. and Mary,	Sept. 24, 1844.
4-20	" Mary Elizabeth, of John H. and Mary,	died Feb. 8, 1845.
4-20	" Hannah Maria,	Nov. 5, 1846.
4-20	" John Clarke,	July 25, 1850.
1-70	BATES Charles, of Caleb,	Dec. 25, 1772.
2-80	BENTLEY Hannah, of Benjamin P. and Hannah,	Aug. 27, 1808.
2-80	" Benjamin Wilbur,	March 8, 1811.
1-108	BRAMAN James, Jr., of James and Mitheah,	July 25, 1760.
1-108	" Mitheah, wife of James,	died ——. —, 1775.
1-21	" Mason, of James and Hannah,	March 5, 1781.
1-121	" Lewis,	Oct. 14, 1783.
2-55	" Hannah,	Feb. 19, 1786.
2-55	" Benjamin, of Joseph and Cynthia,	July 1, 1786.
2-55	" Joseph,	Dec. 25, 1790.

2-55	BRAMAN Isaac, of Joseph and Cynthia,	Aug. 13, 1797,
2-55	" Washington,	March 12, 1799.
4-3	" Robert,	March 11, 1801.
4-3	" Elder William,	died Oct. 14, 1841.
4-3	" William, Jr.,	died Nov. 30, 1844.
2-98	" Nabby, of William and Thankful,	June 19, 1796.
2-98	" Dillie,	June 17, 1797.
2-98	" Sallie,	Jan. 15, 1799.
2-98	" William,	Dec. 22, 1802.
2-98	" James Woodbridge,	April 1, 1805.
2-98	" Alice,	Oct. 21, 1809.
2-98	" Zephaniah,	Sept. 28, 1811.
2-57	BRAND Nathan, of Nathan and Eunice,	Nov. 23, 1809.
2-57	" Susannah Vincent,	Nov. 22, 1811.
2-57	" Christopher Crandall,	Nov. 20, 1813.
2-57	" Samuel Babcock,	Jan. 16, 1816.
2-9	BRIGHTMAN Joseph, born	Dec. 11, 1715.
2-9	" Sarah, (Thomas), his wife, born	June 5, 1722.
2-9	" Mercy, of Joseph and Sarah,	July 22, 1748.
2-9	" Henry,	Dec. 20, 1749.
2-9	" Thomas,	Aug. 4, 1751.
2-9	" Joseph,	Nov. 17, 1753.
2-9	" Mary,	April 5, 1755.
2-9	" Martin,	May 13, 1761.
2-9	" Sarah,	Aug. 23, 1763.
2-9	" Holmes,	June 25, 1767.
1-115	" Sarah, of Henry and Hannah,	Sept. 29, 1777.
1-115	" Hannah,	March 19, 1779.
1-115	" Susannah,	May 16, 1781.
1-115	" Joseph,	March 9, 1783.
1-115	" William,	April 8, 1785.
2-6	" Esther, of Thomas and Thankful,	April 23, 1785.
2-6	" Martha,	Oct. 14, 1786.
2-6	" Sarah,	April 13, 1788.
2-6	" Mary,	April 13, 1788.
2-6	" Thomas,	Nov. 12, 1790.
2-6	" Joseph,	Nov. 13, 1792.
2-76	" Martha, of Joseph and Patience,	March 23, 1815.
2-43	BROWN James Wilson, of Christopher and Anna,	June 7, 1789.
2-43	" Nancy,	Sept. 18, 1790.
2-43	" Jeremiah,	May 28, 1792.
2-43	" Reuben,	Sept. 22, 1794.
1-54	" Clarke, of Stephen and Hannah,	Feb. 23, 1796.
2-56	" Clarke, of Alpheus and Hannah,	Feb. 23, 1796.
2-45	" Phebe, alias Irish, dau. of Ruth Brown,	Dec. 29, 1791.
1-121	BURCH Elizabeth, of Billings and Susannah,	Dec. 12, 1771.
1-121	" Thomas,	Sept. 14, 1773.
1-121	" Thomas,	died Aug. 7, 1775.
1-121	" Martha,	July 9, 1775.
1-121	" Billings,	Oct. 26, 1777.
1-121	" Samuel,	Oct. 15, 1779.
1-121	" Susannah,	Sept. 12, 1781.
1-121	" Susannah, wife of Billings,	died Sept. 24, 1781.
1-59	BURDICK William, born (N. S.) June 23, 1713.	
1-29	" Sarah, his wife, born (O. S.) Jan. 24, 1721.	
	Their children born New Style, as follows:	
1-59	" Sarah, of William and Sarah,	Feb. 14, 1742.
1-50	" William,	Aug. 17, 1744.
1-59	" Daniel,	Dec. 20, 1746.
1-59	" Luke,	April 25, 1749.
1-59	" White,	April 2, 1754.
1-59	" Perry,	Oct. 28, 1756.
1-59	" Mary,	March 11, 1764.
1-48	" Tillemus, of Nathan and Goodeth,	May 30, 1745.
1-48	" Sylvanus,	Sept. 17, 1747.

1-48	BURDICK	Goodeth, of Nathan and Goodeth,	April 17, 1751.
1-48	"	Tacy,	Oct. 12, 1754.
1-48	"	Adam,	Dec. 28, 1759.
1-48	"	Naaman,	July 18, 1762.
1-48	"	Sheppard,	Oct. 18, 1766.
1-21, 35	"	Thomas, of Edmund and Thankful,	Aug. 30, 1749.
1-21, 35	"	Margaret,	Feb. 2, 1751.
1-21, 35	"	John,	Dec. 27, 1753.
1-21, 35	"	Tacy,	Sept. 20, 1755.
1-21, 35	"	Anna,	Nov. 20, 1760.
1-21, 35	"	Sarah,	Dec. 14, 1762.
1-37	"	Samuel Hubbard, of John,	Oct. 18, 1759.
1-37	"	Prudence,	July 24, 1761.
1-37	"	Phineus,	March 13, 1764.
2-53	"	William Clarke, of William,	Dec. 10, 1762.
1-100	"	Francis, of Daniel and Elizabeth,	July 20, 1765.
1-100	"	Anne,	Dec. 28, 1767.
1-100	"	Daniel,	June 9, 1770.
1-100	"	Nathan,	July 17, 1772.
1-100	"	Robinson,	Sept. 16, 1774.
1-102	"	Abigail, of Amos and Elizabeth,	March 12, 1766.
1-102	"	Sarah,	June 2, 1768.
1-102	"	Martha.	April 11, 1770.
1-102	"	Jonathan,	Feb. 25, 1772.
1-102	"	David,	Aug. 21, 1774.
1-102	"	Patience,	March 12, 1777.
1-45	"	Abel, of John and Sybel,	Aug. 18, 1766.
1-45	"	Phebe,	Dec. 14, 1768.
1-45	"	Merabah, of Elnathan and Anne,	Sept. 25, 1774.
1-45	"	Clement,	May 1, 1776.
1-45	"	Clement,	died Sept. 21, 1778.
1-45	"	Clement Peckham,	Jan. 4, 1779.
1-45	"	Anne,	Jan. 4, 1781.
2-13	"	Phebe, of Robert and Sarah,	April 18, 1782.
2-13	"	Robert,	Jan. 12, 1784.
2-13	"	Simon,	Feb. 15, 1786.
2-13	"	Sarah,	Feb. 15, 1788.
2-13	"	Rouse,	Oct. 30, 1790.
2-13	"	Hannah, of Robert and Sarah, (born Charlestown)	Aug. 8, 1793.
2-13	"	Clarke,	March 17, 1796.
2-13	"	Gilbert,	March 19, 1799.
2-11	"	Polly, of Perry and Lucy,	Feb. 27, 1784.
2-11	"	Cynthia,	Nov. 28, 1786.
2-73	"	Billings, of Billings and Hannah,	May 21, 1788.
2-73	"	Simeon Babcock,	Sept. 29, 1789.
2-73	"	Thomas,	Aug. 16, 1791.
2-73	"	Joel,	Nov. 20, 1795.
2-73	"	Sally,	May 1, 1797.
2-73	"	Joshua,	May 17, 1800.
2-73	"	Polly,	April 11, 1803.
2-73	"	Hannah,	March 23, 1806.
2-60	"	Ichabod, of Ichabod and Hannah.	July 10, 1796.
2-60	"	Benjamin Maxson,	April 8, 1798.
2-60	"	Hannah,	May 4, 1800.
2-60	"	Martha Stillman,	Feb. 23, 1802.
2-60	"	Jonathan Trueman,	March 8, 1804.
2-60	"	Martha.	May 3, 1806.
2-60	"	Isaac Coe,	Aug. 20, 1808.
2-60	"	Welcome Clarke,	March 16, 1811.
4-9	"	William C. (born Westerly),	March 30, 1809.
4-9	"	Lucy Orilla Gates, his wife, (born Preston, Conn.,)	April 22, 1815.
4-9	"	Lucy Estelle, of Wm. C. and Lucy O.,	July 18, 1832.
4-9	"	Martha Jane,	Nov. 20, 1833.
4-9	"	William Henry,	July 31, 1835.
4-9	"	Julia Emma,	Aug. 11, 1837.

4-9	BURDICK John Perry, of Wm. C. and Lucy O.,	July 10, 1839.
4-9	" Harriet Newell,	April 20, 1841.
4-9	" Lewis,	March 16, 1844.

Note.—Two eldest born Ledyard, Conn., the rest in Hopkinton.

2-93	" Benjamin Franklin, of Ichabod and Fannie,	Nov. 3, 1819.
2-93	" George Henry,	March 23, 1821.
2-93	" Albert Stillman,	July 26, 1822.
2-93	" Frances Elizabeth,	Feb. 22, 1824.
2-93	" Martha Greene,	April 17, 1826.
2-93	" Hannah Mary,	Oct. 7, 1827.
3-12	" Mary Frances, of Henry Wilson and Abbie Moore,	Nov. 11, 1838.
1-34	BUTTON Hannah, of Nathan and Hannah,	Jan. 16, 1761.
1-34	" Sarah,	Jan. 19, 1762.
1-34	" Nathan,	Dec. 7, 1763.
1-40	" Abel, of Rufus and Elizabeth,	Jan. 5, 1763.
1-104	" Mary, of Amos and Anne,	Sept. 9, 1763.
2-88	" Sanford N., of Joseph and Anne,	April 27, 1810.
2-88	" Asher H.,	Oct. 25, 1812.
2-88	" Joseph Avery,	March 29, 1816.
2-97	" Anne, of Joseph and Elizabeth,	Jan. 20, 1823.

C

1-76	CARTRIGHT Abigail, of Bryant and Elizabeth,	Dec. 30, 1736.
1-76	" Bryant,	May 3, 1739.
1-76	" Lydia,	March 31, 1746.

Note.—These children were all born in Marthas Vineyard.

1-48	" Bryant, of Bryant, Jr., and Elizabeth,	Dec. 30, 1736.
1-48	" Elizabeth Weeks,	May 31, 1770.
1-48	" Jabez,	July 10, 1772.
1-48	" James,	July 10, 1772.
1-48	" William,	Jan. 2, 1775.
1-48	" Theodaty,	May, 29, 1777.
1-48	" Cyrus,	May 17, 1779.
1-48	" Penelope,	Oct. 7, 1782.
1-20	CHAMPLAIN Nathan, of Samuel,	(O. S.) Oct. 8, 1749.
1-20	" Mary,	(O. S.) Aug. 19, 1751.
1-20	" Jeffrey,	(N. S.) April 5, 1754.
1-20	" Hannah,	(N. S.) Nov. 5, 1757.
1-106	" Hannah, of Jeffrey and Lydia,	Nov. 5, 1774.
2-9	" Stephen,	Feb. 28, 1781.
2-9	" Barker,	Oct. 27, 1782.
2-9	" Thomas,	Oct. 3, 1784.
2-9	" George Sheffield,	Dec. 24, 1786.
2-9	" Jeffrey,	July 25, 1788.
2-9	" Lyman,	Aug. 25, 1790.
2-9	" Eunice,	Jan. 20, 1793.
2-9	" Reuben,	Feb. 2, 1795.
2-9	" Lydia,	May 31, 1797.
2-64	" Philip Cottrell, of Ethan and Hannah,	July 21, 1809.
2-64	" Sabrina, of Ethan and Hannah,	July 17, 1811.
2-64	" Pattie,	Sept. 9, 1813.
2-64	" Amey,	Jan. 23, 1816.
2-64	" Wealthy,	Aug. 8, 1817.
2-64	" Maria,	April 27, 1825.
2-55	" George C. Potter, alias, son of Betsey Potter,	March 16, 1811.
2-88	" Edward Greene, of Greene and Polly,	March 12, 1823.
2-88	" Frank,	Jan. 6, 1825.
2-88	" Lucy Maria,	Aug. 20, 1827.
2-88	" Mary Jane,	Jan. 13, 1830.
2-55	CHEESEBROUGH Pattey, of Harris and Martha,	Sept. 19, 1790.
2-55	" Harris,	July 13, 1792.
2-55	" Lydia,	July 24, 1794.
2-55	" Samuel,	April 13, 1796.

1-77	CHEVER William Maxson, of Edward and Susannah,		Feb. 21, 1774.
1-1	CHURCH Joshua, of Joshua, Jr., and Abigail,		Dec. 9, 1780.
1-1	"	Abigail,	Jan. 20, 1783.
2-42	"	Hannah, of Lodowick and Hannah,	Feb. 28, 1788.
2-42	"	Elizabeth,	Feb. 2, 1790.
2-42	"	Adam,	Feb. 17, 1792.
2-4	"	Nancy Coon, alias, of Jemima,	July 13, 1788.
2-10	"	Lodowick, Jr., born as he says	Sept. 4, 1800.
1-29	CLARKE Phineus, of Joshua and Hannah,		Feb. 23, 1740.
1-29	"	Joshua,	Aug. 17, 1741.
1-29	"	Ethan,	March 7, 1745.
1-29	"	Hannah,	May 4, 1747.
1-29	"	Thomas,	June 10, 1749.
1-29	"	Elizabeth,	Nov. 14, 1751.
1-29	"	Arnold,	March 17, 1754.
1-29	"	Henry,	Dec. 2, 1756.
1-29	"	Willett,	Oct. 20, 1759.
1-29	"	Nathan,	Feb. 7, 1762.
1-42	"	Job Bennett,	May 13, 1765.
2-9	"	Henry, of Henry and Catharine,	Dec. 16, 1777.
2-9	"	Phebe,	Sept. 28, 1779.
2-9	"	Sally,	July 25, 1781.
2-9	"	Oliver Pendleton,	March 29, 1783.
2-9	"	John Vilitt,	April 14, 1785.
2-9	"	Elizabeth,	April 30, 1787.
2-9	"	Ethan,	March 30, 1789.
2-19	"	Fannie, of Thomas and Fannie,	Sept. 11, 1781.
2-19	"	Nabby,	Aug. 21, 1783.
2-19	"	Polly, of Thomas and Fannie,	May 21, 1785.
2-19	"	Betsey,	May 4, 1787.
2-19	"	Martha,	Feb. 2, 1789.
2-19	"	Nancy,	April 6, 1791.
2-91	"	Russell, born,	April 13, 1787.
2-91	"	Elizabeth (Taylor) his 1st wife,	May 9, 1789.
2-91	"	Elizabeth (Taylor) his 1st wife,	died Dec. 17, 1812.
2-91	"	Sarah (Thurston), his 2d wife,	June 17 1793.
2-91	"	Sarah (Thurston), his 2d wife,	died Oct. 12, 1814.
2-91	"	Betsey (Langworthy), his 3d wife,	—, —, —.
2-91	"	Sarah Elizabeth, of Russell and Sarah,	June 26, 1814.
2-15	"	Amey, of Job B. and Mary,	Aug. 19, 1789.
2-15	"	Hannah,	June 10, 1791.
2-15	"	Mary,	March 30, 1793.
2-15	"	Charles, (born Newport),	April 19, 1795.
2-15	"	Cornelia,	Oct. 9, 1797.
2-15	"	Job B.,	July 28, 1800.
2-15	"	Paul,	Aug. 7, 1802.
2-15	"	Elizabeth Ann,	Jan. 12, 1805.
2-15	"	Sally H.,	March 8, 1807.
2-15	"	Henry,	May 1, 1809.
2-15	"	Caroline,	Oct. 12, 1812.
2-15	"	Corydon,	May 12, 1815.
2-57	"	Anna, of Ezra and Anna,	Nov. 9, 1797.
2-57	"	David Wright, of Thomas and Wealthy (Wright),	June 4, 1800.
4-5	"	Thomas Henry, of Henry and Jerusha,	June 15, 1836.
4-5	"	Joshua Maxson,	Feb. 15, 1838.
4-5	"	William Palmer,	Nov. 5, 1840.
4-5	"	Leander Scott,	June 2, 1843.
4-5	"	Mary Jerusha,	June 23, 1845.
2-44	COE William, of Isaac and Sarah,		May 11, 1803.
2-44	"	Mary Ann, of Isaac and Sarah,	July 14, 1806.
2-44	"	Eliza Jenckes,	May 1, 1809.
2-44	"	John Davis,	July 11, 1810.
2-44	"	Adeline,	July 26, 1812.
1-1	COLEGROVE Hannah, of Jeremiah and Susannah,		June 21, 1771.

(Vit. Rec., Vol. 5.) 32

1-1	COLEGROVE Susannah, of Jeremiah and Susannah,		June 28, 1773.
1-1	" Dinah,		Dec. 18, 1775.
1-1	" William, of Jeremiah and Hannah, born in Voluntown, Conn.		
	Feb. 9, 1781.		
1-1	" Sarah, born in Stonington, Conn.,		March 16, 1785.
1-102	COLE James, of Joseph and Phebe, 2d wife,		Aug. 21, 1760.
1-102	" Benjamin (born Stonington)		March 14, 1762.
1-102	" John,		Feb. 21, 1764.
1-102	" Stephen,		Sept. 27, 1766.
1-102	" Phebe,	Susannah, 3d, wife,	Oct. 31, 1767.
1-102	" Susannah,		Aug. 28, 1769.
1-102	" Anna,		July 5, 1772.
2-49	" Nancy, of Stephen and Susannah,		Jan. 13, 1796.
2-49	" Polly,		Dec. 9, 1797.
2-49	" Phebe,		July 25, 1801.
1-58	COLLINS Mary, of John and Mary (also 1-107),		Nov. 30, 1769.
1-107	" John,		April 19, 1771.
1-107	" Mehetable,		Nov. 19, 1773.
1-107	" Stephen,		June 18, 1776.
1-107	" Samuel,		Aug. 8, 1780.
1-107	" Daniel,		Dec. 13, 1781.
1-104	" Henry, of Joshua and Mary,		Oct. 15, 1772.
1-104	" Martha,		Aug. 13, 1774.
1-104	" Hezekiah,		April 21, 1776.
1-104	" Oliver,		Dec. 14, 1777.
1-104	" Joshua, }		Sept. 4, 1779.
2-47	" Nathan, of —— and Cynthia (Foster),		Sept. 12, 1783.
2-51	" Elizabeth, of John and Elizabeth,		Sept. 29, 1796.
2-51	" Sarah,		Feb. 22, 1798.
2-51	" Thomas,		Feb. 9, 1800.
2-51	" Benjamin,		Oct. 13, 1802.
2-51	" Anna,		March, 18, 1804.
2-51	" William,		March, 1, 1806.
2-51	" Amos,		March 5, 1808.
2-67	" Maria Almy, of Amos and Mary,		Feb. 23, 1805.
2-78	" David, of Rouse and Merehah,		May 16, 1811.
2-74	" Mary Ann, of Joshua and Mary,		Dec. 28, 1814.
1-36	COON Benjamin, of Matthew and Lydia,		Feb. 4, 1749.
1-36	" Joseph,		Jan. 18, 1751.
1-36	" Matthew,		Oct. 2, 1752.
1-36	" Jeremiah,		July 25, 1754.
1-36	" Sarah (born Richmond),		April 6, 1760.
1-36	" Anna,		Feb. 25, 1762.
1-45	" Joseph, Jr., also 2-43,		Feb. 17, 1753.
1-116	" Peleg, of Peleg and Eunice,		Oct. 12, 1763.
1-116	" Rebecca,		May 8, 1766.
1-116	" Esther,		March 14, 1769.
1-116	" Joseph,		April 7, 1771.
1-116	" Thompson,		June 26, 1773.
1-116	" Eunice,		Dec. 26, 1775.
1-116	" Arnold,		Feb. 6, 1778.
1-116	" Anna,		Oct. 7, 1780.
1-116	" Richard, of —— and Anna,		Aug. 12, 1788.
1-116	" Zerviah,		Sept. 11, 1790.
2-2	" Caleb, of Elias and Phebe,		July 25, 1769.
2-2	" Elias,		Oct. 13, 1771.
2-2	" Elias,		died Aug. 10, 1772.
2-2	" Mary,		June 10, 1773.
2-2	" Elias,		Nov. 23, 1775.
2-2	" Thankful, of Elias and Phebe,		July 21, 1778.
2-2	" Phebe,		July 6, 1782.
2-2	" Ruth,		May 5, 1784.
2-2	" George,		May 19, 1788.
2-74	" Isaac, of William,		March 26, 1774.
2-74	" Martha (Hull), his wife,		June 6, 1780.

2-74	COON Isaac, of Isaac and Martha,	Sept. 20, 1800.
2-74	" Charles,	June 6, 1803.
2-74	" Martha,	Nov. 18, 1805.
1-106	" Lebbeus, of Thomas and Anne,	Feb. 15, 1764.
1-106	" Thomas,	July 28, 1766.
1-106	" Anne,	Jan. 3, 1769.
1-106	" Lodowick,	Ang. 18, 1770.
1-106	" Elizabeth,	Oct. 31, 1772.
1-106	" Desire,	June 14, 1775.
2-1	" Eunice, wife of Peleg,	died May 24, 1783.
2-18	" Stephen, of Stephen and Sarah,	Oct. 22, 1789.
2-18	" Samuel,	June 17, 1791.
2-18	" George Stillman,	May 13, 1793.
2-48	" Mary, of Peleg and Anna,	Nov. 5, 1795.
2-59	" Moses Barber, of Caleb and Dorcas,	Feb. 9, 1801.
2-59	" Elias,	Jan. 20, 1804.
2-59	" Mary,	Feb. 21, 1807.
4-12	" Martha Ann, of Elias and Mary,	March 17, 1843.
4-12	" Ruth Mary,	June 7, 1846.
2-72	COTTRELL John, of John S. and Esther,	May 6, 1815.
2-72	" Susan,	Nov. 30, 1816.
1-33	CRANDALL Prudence, of Jeremiah and Kezier,	July 17, 1745.
1-33	" Kezier,	Feb. 17, 1749.
1-33	" Sarah,	Jan. 12, 1751.
1-33	" Jeremiah,	Dec. 17, 1752.
1-33	" Matthew,	June 30, 1755.
1-33	" Luke,	June 22, 1757.
1-33	" Ebenezer,	July 21, 1759.
1-33	" Thankful,	Feb. 9, 1762.
1-33	" Azariah, son of Peter,	Dec. 22, 1749.
1-33	" Anna (Burdick), of Edward,	Aug. 16, 1753.
1-76	" Olive, of Azariah and Anna,	Aug. 7, 1773.
1-76	" Peter,	Feb. 11, 1775.
1-76	" Sarah,	April 16, 1777.
1-32	" Sarah, of David and Sarah,	March 8, 1762.
1-32	" Sarah, wife of David, died,	March 27, 1762.
1-105	" Elias, of David and Jemima,	Feb. 17, 1765.
1-105	" David,	Dec. 12, 1766.
1-105	" Jemima,	Jan. 26, 1770.
1-105	" Zebbeus,	Nov. 22, 1774.
1-105	" Telek,	July 3, 1776.
1-105	" John,	May 16, 1778.
1-105	" Mercy,	March 19, 1780.
1-105	" Anne,	Jan. 17, 1783.
2-19	" Thankful, of Levi and Margaret,	July 22, 1772.
2-19	" Christopher,	Sept. 22, 1774.
2-19	" Samuel (born Charlestown), son of Samuel and Mary,	Aug. 11, 1780.
2-3	" Clarrissa, of Archibald and Susanna,	Dec. 2, 1788.
2-3	" Phineus Maxson, of Amherst and Polly,	June 25, 1787.
2-3	" Ethan,	Jan. 11, 1790.
2-3	" Polly,	Sept. 16, 1792.
4-13	" Luke, of Amherst and Mary,	March 22, 1795.
4-13	" Mary Ann,	July 22, 1811.
2-64	" Jairus, of Rogers and Lucy,	Jan. 17, 1799.
2-64	" Susannah,	Sept. 5, 1801.
2-64	" Rogers,	May 13, 1804.
2-53	" Anna, of Ezra and Anna,	Nov. 9, 1797.
2-71	" Hezekiah, of Pardon and Esther,	Sept. 22, 1800.
2-71	" Prudence,	Sept. 3, 1803.
2-71	" Renben,	Jan. 6, 1806.
2-63	" Mary Ann, of Samuel and Elizabeth,	Jan. 29, 1803.
2-63	" Samuel,	Jan. 27, 1805.
2-63	" William Clarke,	April 22, 1806.
2-78	" Henry Clinton, of Elijah and Susannah,	July 15, 1809.
2-78	" Samuel Wells,	March 10, 1813.
2-78	" Susannah,	May 29, 1816.

1-73	CRUMB	Sarah, of Daniel,	Jan. 20, 1765.
1-73	"	Abigail,	Oct. 22, 1766.
1-73	"	Hannah,	Dec. 25, 1768.
1-73	"	Daniel,	Oct. 22, 1770.
1-73	"	Samuel,	Aug. 2, 1772.
1-73	"	Daniel,	March 16, 1776.
1-73	"	Hunneman,	Feb. 2, 1779.
1-73	"	William,	May 2, 1781.

D

2-7	DAVIS	Martha, of Elder Joseph,	May 5, 1746.
2-7	"	Samuel,	Feb. 28, 1749.
2-7	"	Comfort,	May 18, 1753.
2-7	"	Marvel,	Sept. 6, 1755.
2-7	"	Anna,	Feb. 4, 1758.
2-7	"	Prudence,	July 7, 1760.
2-7	"	Joseph,	Oct. 11, 1764.
2-7	"	Tacy,	July 13, 1766.
2-7	"	Edward,	July 20, 1768.
2-7	"	Clarke,	Nov. 20, 1774.
2-7	"	Elizabeth,	May 8, 1776.
2-7	"	Ethan,	July 16, 1778.
2-7	"	Dorcas,	March 7, 1780.
2-7	"	Fannie,	Feb. 10, 1782.

Note.—The first two of the above children born in Shrewsbury, the next two in Westerly, the rest in Hopkinton.

1-48	"	Lydia, of David and Lydia,	May 16, 1768.
1-70	"	Lillas Hudson,	July 7, 1770.
1-70	"	David,	Oct. 31, 1772.
1-70	"	Joshua,	April 5, 1775.
2-17	"	Jedediah, of Oliver and Penelope,	May 2, 1781.
2-17	"	Pardon,	Nov. 3, 1784.
2-17	"	Peter,	June 24, 1786.
2-17	"	Oliver,	March 15, 1788.
2-17	"	Mary,	Feb. 14, 1790.
2-17	"	Hannah,	Nov. 13, 1791.
2-17	"	Sarah,	Aug. 13, 1793.
2-17	"	Lydia,	Oct. 13, 1795.
2-17	"	Susannah,	Sept. 24, 1797.
2-17	"	Walter White,	Jan. 1, 1300.
2-17	"	Elizabeth,	Jan. 14, 1802.
2-17	"	Amey,	Jan. 20, 1804.
2-84	"	David L., of Aaron and Dorcas,	June 27, 1802.
1-26	DEAK	Joshua, of John and Hannah,	June 18, 1747.
1-26	"	Christopher,	Aug. 21, 1749.
1-26	"	John,	Aug. 16, 1752.
1-26	"	Joseph,	Nov. 27, 1753.
1-26	"	Benjamin,	Nov. 27, 1753.
1-26	"	Hannah,	Dec. 16, 1755.
1-26	"	Foster,	Aug. 23, 1757.
1-26	"	Mary,	May 27, 1759.
1-33	"	William Gould, of Charles,	March 6, 1761.
1-19	DODGE	Elizabeth, (b. Charlestown) of Joseph, (O. S.)	July 19, 1744.
1-19	"	Susannah,	Nov. 12, 1747.
1-19	"	Joseph, Jr., (b. Westerly)	May 2, 1752.
1-19	"	Peter, of Daniel,	Jan. 8, 1757.
1-43	DORRANCE	Daniel, of Gershom and Margaret,	Feb. 6, 1764.
1-43	"	Margary,	Oct. 11, 1766.
1-53	"	Gershom,	March 12, 1768.

E

1-53	EDWARDS	Paine, of Peleg,	March 12, 1768.
1-105	"	Paine, 2d,	March 1, 1769.
1-105	"	Christopher,	Aug. 4, 1771.
1-105	"	Jacob,	Aug. 3, 1774,
1-105	"	Perry,	Nov. 5, 1776.
1-105	"	Sarah,	Oct. 8, 1778.
1-117	"	Mary, of Phineus and Mary,	Jan. 4, 1771.
1-117	"	Mary,	died Jan. 6, 1773.
1-117	"	Phineus,	March 18, 1773.
1-117	"	Mary,	June 18, 1775.
1-117	"	Phebe,	Aug. 9, 1777.
1-117	"	Nathan,	March 30, 1780.
1-117	"	Sarah,	Aug. 28, 1786.
1-117	"	Eunice,	March 7, 1789.
1-117	"	Putnam Lewis,	Jan. 6, 1798.
2-2	"	Rhoda, of Perry and Rhoda,	March 12, 1785.
2-2	"	Prudence,	Feb. 6, 1787.
2-2	"	Ruth,	July 6, 1789.
2-2	"	Perry,	July 12, 1791.
2-2	"	Phebe,	April 15, 1794.
2-2	"	Gardiner,	April 6, 1796.
2-2	"	Susannah,	March 3, 1800.
2-2	"	Henry,	April 21, 1805.

F

2-12	FENNER	Reuben, of John,	Sept. 8, 1769.
2-12	"	Anstis, wife of Renben,	April 19, 1776.
2-70	"	Roswell, of John,	Sept. 1, 1778.
2-70	"	Deborah (Wilcox) his wife,	Jan. 2, 1779.
2-70	"	Alice, of Roswell and Deborah,	March 27, 1796.
2-70	"	Esther,	April 23, 1798.
2-70	"	Lucinda,	Oct. 9, 1800.
2-70	"	Mary,	Feb. 23, 1804.
2-43	"	Jerah, of Renben and Anstis,	July 18, 1795.
2-43	"	Roswell Borden,	April 9, 1798.
2-43	"	Reuben,	Nov. 8, 1793.
2-43	"	Lucy Brown, (born Milton, Cayuga Co., N. Y.,) of Reuben and Anstis,	Nov. 5, 1799.
2-43	"	Anstis, wife of Renben, died at Milton, N. Y.,	Feb. 12, 1802.
1-29	FOSTER	Elizabeth, of Thomas and Mary,	July 10, 1739.
1-29	"	Jonathan,	June 24, 1741.
1-29	"	Mary,	Dec. 12, 1743.
1-29	"	Sarah,	Feb. 12, 1746.
1-29	"	William,	June 26, 1748.
1-29	"	Hannah,	Jan. 10, 1752.
1-29	"	Susannah,	Sept. 13, 1755.
1-29	"	Thomas,	July 25, 1757.
1-31	"	Elizabeth, of Jonathan and Anna,	June 2, 1755.
1-31	"	Jonathan,	July 23, 1757.
2-58	"	Christopher, of Gideon,	April 18, 1765.
2-1	"	Mary Maxson, alias, of Amey of Hopkinton,	Jan. 24, 1782.
4-8	"	Christopher,	died April 27, 1846.

G

1-103	GARDINER	Catharine, of Thomas Potter and Catharine,	Sept. 30, 1773.
1-24	GREENE	Benjamin, of Matthew and Jndeth,	March 25, 1751.
1-24	"	Hannah,	Aug. 4, 1753.
1-24	"	Sarah,	Aug. 14, 1755.
1-24	"	Humility,	April 9, 1757.

2-42	GREENE Matthew, of Benjamin and Grace,	Dec. 19, 1783.
2-42	" Benjamin,	March 15, 1786.
2-42	" David,	April 14, 1790.
2-42	" Amos,	Feb. 25, 1792.
2-42	" Esther,	May 29, 1794.
2-42	" Lucy,	April 26, 1796.
2-42	" Henry Parks,	March 28, 1798.
2-42	" Thomas Rogers,	Dec. 10, 1800.
2-42	" Paul,	Jan. 13, 1803.
2-46	" Lucy, of Wm. Gardiner and Susannah,	Dec. 8, 1793.
2-46	" Polly,	Dec. 27, 1794.
2-46	" Sophia,	April 7, 1796.
2-46	" William Gardiner,	April 1, 1798.
2-46	" Susannah,	Dec. 15, 1799.
2-77	" James Clarke Tefft, of Rowland T. and Joanna,	Dec. 29, 1812.
2-76	" Sheffield Wells, of John and Betsey,	July 15, 1814.

H

1-24	HADFALL Rachel, of William and Dorcas,	April 13, 1747.
1-24	" Dorcas,	Jan. 7, 1749.
1-24	" Joseph,	April 24, 1750.
1-24	" William,	Oct. 22, 1752.
1-24	" Sarah,	Aug. 29, 1754.
1-24	" Mary,	March 23, 1756.
1-24	" Hannah,	Feb. 17, 1758.
1-72	HALL Mary, of James and Elizabeth,	April 8, 1753.
1-72	" Rebecca,	Oct. 6, 1755.
1-72	" James,	Oct. 28, 1757.
1-72	" Elizabeth,	Sept. 15, 1759.
1-72	" Joshua,	March 25, 1762.
1-72	" Chloe,	March 13, 1764.
1-72	" Huldah,	June 29, 1766.
1-72	" Desire,	Oct. 7, 1768.
1-72	" Simeon,	Jan 27, 1772.
1-25	" Anna, of Benjamin,	Oct. 22, 1752.
1-25	" Temperance,	July 8, 1754.
1-25	" Benjamin,	July 80, 1756.
1-25	" Abigail,	Nov. 21, 1758.
1-102	" Christopher, of Henry and Phebe,	Sept. 21, 1761.
1-102	" Caleb,	April 17, 1763.
1-102	" Henry,	March 25, 1765.
1-102	" Phebe.	April 8, 1767.
1-102	" Anne,	March 3, 1772.
1-102	" Oliver,	May 18, 1773.
1-120	" John,	April 23, 1776.
1-28	HILL Mary, of Ebenezer and Thankful,	Feb. 27, 1747.
1-28	" Timothy,	June 28, 1749.
1-28	" Ebenezer,	Jan. 25, 1752.
1-28	" Josiah,	Sept. 13, 1754.
1-28	" Asa,	Jan. 11, 1758.
1-28	" Thankful,	Sept. 13, 1760.
2-5	" Martha Hall, alias Patterson, alias daughter of Mary Hill, widow. who was a Patterson,	Dec. 31, 1779.

I J

1-110	JOSLIN Elizabeth, of Elder Henry and Mary,	March 6, 1775.
1-110	" Martha,	July 7, 1777.
2-11	" James Tefft,	Oct. 31, 1782.
2-11	" Dutee,	March 8, 1786.
2-11	" Henry,	Jan. 28, 1788.
2-11	" John Fenner, of Elizabeth,	Feb. 14, 1793.

| 2-11 | JOSLIN Polly Tefft, of Pattey, | Feb. 4, 1797. |
| 2-68 | " George Sheffield, of James Tefft and Hannah, | July 4, 1803. |

K

1-24,120	KENYON Peter, of Peter and Annie (O. S.),	May 18, 1752.
1-24,120	" Arnold,	Oct. 8, 1754.
1-24,120	" Arnold,	died Dec. 3, 1776.
1-24,120	" Elizabeth,	Feb. 15, 1758.
	Note.—Another record says Arnold was born in 1755, and Elizabeth Jan. 15, 1758.	
1-120	" Naomi, of Nathaniel,	Jan. 19, 1755.
1-21	" Wells,	Jan. 16, 1758.
1-38	" Susannah, of Peleg and Joanna,	July 25, 1760.
1-38	" Joanna,	Nov. 6, 1762.
1-121	" Eleanor, of Nathaniel and Eleanor,	Dec. 23, 1761.
1-121	" Nathaniel,	Oct. 30, 1764.
2-65	" Benjamin, of Benjamin and Anne,	June 6, 1765.
2-65	" Roger, of Benjamin and Elizabeth,	Nov. 5, 1769.
2-65	" Elizabeth,	Oct. 27, 1771.
2-65	" Augustus,	Sept. 21, 1773.
2-65	" Tacy,	June 23, 1777.
1-104	" Anne, of Peter and Mary,	Feb. 18, 1772.
1-104	" Peter,	Feb. 16, 1775.
1-104	" Arnold,	Feb. 16, 1776.
1-104	" Samuel,	Sept. 7, 1782.
2-5	" James, of James and Mary,	Aug. 26, 1788.
2-89	" Mary, of Benjamin and Mary (Lanphere),	Sept. 18, 1788.
2-89	" Hannah,	Nov. 10, 1789.
2-89	" Elizabeth,	Oct. 3, 1791.
2-89	" Ethan,	Sept. 10, 1793.
2-89	" Sally,	Oct. 19, 1795.
2-89	" Jedediah,	Dec. 25, 1797.
2-89	" George W.,	Dec. 16, 1799.
2-89	" Rebecca,	Dec. 2, 1801.
2-89	" Polly,	March 7, 1804.
2-89	" Benjamin,	March 25, 1807.
4-21	" Jarvis, born in Richmond,	Jan. 2, 1784.
4-21	" Jarvis, died in Hopkinton,	Dec. 8, 1851.
2-8	" Simon, of Benjamin and Sally,	March 18, 1789.
2-8	" Pruanna,	June 21, 1791.
2-8	" Polly,	July 7, 1793.
2-8	" Benjamin Aldrich,	Dec. 4, 1795.
2-8	" Augustus,	May 17, 1798.
2-8	" Sally,	July 10, 1801.
2-8	" Aaron,	Oct. 5, 1805.
2-13	" Hannah, of Roger and Esther,	March 20, 1792.
2-13	" Esther,	July 7, 1797.
2-52	" Gardiner, of Pardon and Mary,	May 23, 1794.
2-52	" Joshua,	Dec. 14, 1795.
2-52	" Esther,	Jan. 9, 1798.
2-52	" David,	March 31, 1800.
2-42	" Arnold, of Peter and Ruhamah,	Aug. 14, 1794.
2-75	" Hannah, of Aaron and Lucretia,	Sept. 15, 1796.
2-75	" Lucretia,	Feb. 16, 1799.
2-75	" James,	March 25, 1801.
2-75	" Sands Niles,	March 26, 1803.
2-75	" Mary,	May 6, 1805.
2-75	" Aaron,	April 19, 1807.
2-60	" Polly, of Augustus and Joanna,	Oct. 31, 1799.
3-13	" Betsey, of Burdick,	June 6, 1804.
3-13	" Arnold,	Jan. 10, 1807.
3-13	" Amos,	Aug. 7, 1811.
3-13	" Ronse,	Sept. 10, 1814.
3-13	" Anne,	Oct. 7, 1817.

3-13	KENYON Lois, of Burdick,	March 10, 1821.
3-13	" Sally,	Feb. 7, 1824.
3-13	" Waitey,	July 7, 1826.
2-69	KINNEY Thankful Collins, of Jonah and Martha,	Dec. 2, 1802.

L

1-37	LAMB Joseph, of Nathan and Lydia,	May 22, 1763.
1-37	" Nathan.	Jan. 15, 1766.
1-36	LANGWORTHY Mary, of Samuel and Mary,	May 11, 1739.
1-36	" Elizabeth,	May 31, 1741.
1-36	" Rachel,	June 8, 1743.
1-36	" Samuel,	Nov. 27, 1745.
1-36	" Tacy,	Nov. 20, 1747.
1-36	" Joseph,	Feb. 6, 1749.
1-36	" Hannah,	June 21, 1752.
1-1	" Samuel, born Nov. 27, 1745.	
1-1	" Mary, his wife, born Sept. 20, 1752.	
1-1	" Samuel, of Samuel and Mary,	Sept. 11, 1771.
1-1	" Tacy,	July 1, 1773.
1-1	" Peleg,	Oct. 7, 1775.
1-1	" Nathan,	Nov. 29, 1777.
1-1	" Saundice,	Dec. 16, 1779.
1-1	" Hannah,	Feb. 19, 1782.
1-60	" Robert,	March 14, 1784.
1-60	" Benjamin, of Amos and Sarah,	Feb. 29, 1760.
1-60	" Anna,	Sept. 8, 1761.
1-60	" Sarah,	July 25, 1763.
1-60	" Amos,	March 2, 1765.
1-60	" Content,	Jan. 21, 1767.
1-60	" Thomas,	Dec. 17, 1768.
1-60	" Mary,	Aug. 26, 1770.
1-37	" Samuel (of Hopkinton),	died Aug. 1, 1763.
1-97	" Benjamin Kenyon, of Benjamin and Eleanor,	Aug. 16, 1780.
1-97	" John Davis,	July 10, 1782.
1-97	" Eleanor,	Oct. 19, 1786.
1-97	" Amos,	Feb. 12, 1789.
2-48	" Martha, of Samuel and Mercy,	Feb. 10, 1788.
2-48	" Elizabeth,	May 20, 1790.
2-48	" Daniel,	July 23, 1792.
2-48	" Mercy,	March 5, 1794.
2-48	" Aseneth,	July 28, 1797.
2-66	" Samuel, of Samuel and Ethel,	Dec. 9, 1797.
2-66	" Ethelinda,	May 30, 1800.
2-65	" Thomas, of Thomas and Waitey,	April 20, 1799.
2-65	" Waitey,	Oct. 14, 1800.
2-65	" Benjamin Peckham,	Dec. 16, 1802.
2-65	" William,	March 17, 1705.
2-65	" Sarah,	Feb. 14, 1807.
2-65	" Mary,	July 15, 1808.
2-65	" Sarah,	Oct. 22, 1810.
2-65	" Thomas,	June 17, 1812.
2-66	" Amos, of Amos and Susannah,	Jan. 6, 1803.
2-66	" Joshua Witter	June 28, 1804.
2-66	" Joseph, of Amos and Susannah,	Feb. 19, 1806.
2-66	" Lois Ann,	Dec. 6, 1807.
2-66	" Susannah,	Dec. 8, 1810.
2-66	" William Franklin, of Nathan and Nabby,	Jan. 5, 1802.
2-69	" Mary Anne,	May 18, 1803.
2-69	" Eliza,	Feb. 11, 1805.
2-65	" Thomas, Sr.,	died June 17, 1812.
2-94	" Benjamin K., of Benjamin and Hannah,	Sept. 25, 1820.
2-94	" Jeremiah T.,	April 29, 1822.
2-94	" George Edwin,	July 1, 1824.

4-2	LANGWORTHY Susan E. of Nathan H. and Ann E.,		
4-2	"	Sarah A.,	—— -, ——.
2-19	LANPHERE Nancy, of Rowland and Elizabeth,		Sept. 23, 1777.
2-19	"	Silas,	Ang. 27, 1779.
2-19	"	Elizabeth,	(sic) Feb. 10, 1780.
2-19	"	Lathana,	Nov. 22, 1782.
2-19	"	Joshua,	Aug. 23, 1784.
2-19	"	Polly,	Sept. 23, 1786.
2-19	"	Eunice,	June 25, 1788.
2-48	"	Clarke, of Roland and Alice,	Oct. 24, 1793.
2-48	"	Sylvia,	Aug 2, 1795.
1-43	LARKIN Susannah, of John and Amey,		Aug. 19, 1756.
1-43	"	Susannah,	died March 3, 1764.
1-43	"	Nathan,	March 15, 1760.
1-43	"	Anna,	April 17, 1762.
1-43	"	Joseph,	Dec. 30, 1764.
1-43	"	Mary,	March 20, 1767.
1-43	"	Amey,	Nov. 23, 1769.
1-69	"	Margaret,	Dec. 6, 1771.
1-69	"	John,	May 15, 1774.
1-69	"	Enos,	Sept 13, 1776.
1-69	"	John, Jr., died in his 47th year,	May 4, 1777.
2-19	.	John, of John and Amey, in 8y.,	died Ang. 23, 1781.
1-28	LATHAM David, of John and Lois,		May 30, 1754.
1-28	"	Joseph,	Oct. 5, 1755.
1-28	"	Sarah,	Jan. 27, 1758.
1-28	"	Sarah,	died July 18, 1759.
1-28	"	Mary,	May 10, 1760.
1-28	LEWIS Delight, of Abel and Thankful,		Nov. 4, 1760.
1-72	"	Elias, of Elias and Susannah,	July 11, 1761.
1-75	"	Sarah, of Jonathan and Sarah,	May 2, 1762.
1-75	.	Haunah,	Sept. 25, 1763.
1-75	.	Jonathan,	April 20, 1767.
1-75	"	Richard,	Sept. 4, 1771.
1-75	"	Matthew, of Eleazer and Thankful,	Feb. 18, 1767.
1-75	"	Sarah,	Sept. 10, 1769.
1-107	"	Eleazer,	Jan. 29, 1772.
1-107	"	Benjamin,	March 15, 1774.
1-107	"	Thankful,	April 12, 1776.
1-118	.	Susannah, of Ezekiel and Susannah,	March 28, 1767.
1-118	"	Ezekiel,	Jan. 27, 1769.
1-118	"	Joseph,	Nov. 13, 1771.
1-118	"	Simeon,	Aug. 29, 1773.
1-118	"	Elnathan,	Feb. 6, 1776.
1-118	"	Thomas Geer,	April 8, 1778.
1-109	"	Henry, of Moses and Hannah,	Dec. 17, 1770.
1-67	"	Nancy, of Benjamin and Amey,	May 6, 1772.
1-110	"	Ethan, of Paul and Martha,	Nov. 30, 1772.
1-110	"	Martha,	July 11, 1775.
1-110	"	Daniel,	born May 23, 1778.
4-14	"	Sarah Ann (Northnp), his wife,	July 14, 1786.
4-14	"	Content (Langworthy),	Feb. 2, 1788.
4-14	"	Sarah Ann, wife of Daniel, died at North Stonington, Conn.,	
			May 20, 1821.
2-10	"	Hannah, of Nash,	April 22, 1780.
2-9	"	Daniel, 3d, son of Jesse,	April 25, 1785.
2-48	"	Catey, of Elias and Elizabeth,	Feb. 15, 1791.
2-48	"	Lois,	March 27, 1793.
2-48	"	Elias,	Ang. 6, 1795.
2-48	"	Ephraim Browning,	May 17, 1798.
2-48	"	Betsey Browning,	May 17, 1798.
2-48	"	Pardon,	Jan. 11, 1806.
2-48	"	Fannie,	March 9, 1808.
2-48	"	Martha,	Nov. 19, 1810.
2-48	"	Eunice,	June 20, 1814.

2-61	LEWIS Simeon Paul, alias, (b. Charlestown),		Jan. 20, 1792.
2-50	"	Thomas Wilbnr, of Henry and Edy,	June 1, 1794.
2-50	"	Pardon,	June 3, 1796.
2-50	"	Matilda,	Dec. 28, 1798.
2-50	"	Moses B.,	born April 10, 1797.
2-50	"	Mary A., his wife,	Jan. 29, 1803.
4-13	"	Phebe M., of Moses B. and Mary A.,	Feb. 7, 1831.
4-13	"	Moses D.,	Jan. 28, 1833.
4-13	"	Daniel C.,	Sept. 20, 1835.
4-13	"	Hannah A.,	May 26, 1837.
4-13	"	Benjamin F.,	June 28, 1838.
4-13	"	Susan A.,	Oct. 8, 1841.
4-13	"	Francis J.,	Sept. 14, 1845.
2-65	"	George Washington, of Nathaniel and Mary,	Nov. 29, 1800.
2-71	"	Eliza, of Daniel and Sarah Ann,	Aug. 7, 1806.
2-71	"	Anna,	April 15, 1808.
2-71	"	William Bliss,	June 14, 1810.
4-14	"	Daniel C.,	Feb. 25, 1815.
4-14	"	Amey,	Nov. 16, 1813.
4-14	"	Emeline,	July 8, 1815.
4-14	"	Sarah Content, of Daniel and Content,	July 6, 1824.
4-14	"	Abbie Altoona,	Jan. 18, 1830.
4-14	"	Elizabeth, of Daniel and Ann,	Aug. 7, 1906.
4-14	"	Anne,	April 15, 1808.
4-14	"	William Bliss,	June 14, 1810.
2-79	"	Hannah B., of Christopher C. and Wealthy,	Dec. 21, 1812.
2-79	"	Christopher C.,	Feb. 22, 1815.
2-79	"	Alfred,	Jan. 31, 1817.
2-79	"	Nathan Kenyon,	Oct. 23, 1818.
2-79	"	Daniel,	Feb. 4, 1821.
2-79	"	Welcome,	July 7, 1822.
2-79	"	Edwin Ransom,	Jan. 31, 1827.
4-8	"	Edwin Augustus, of Charles C. and Frances M.,	Feb. 11, 1846.

M

1-27	MACCOON John, of John and Hannah,		Dec. 22, 1745.
1-27	"	Samuel,	Sept. 26 1747.
1-27	"	Hannah,	Aug. 3, 1749.
1-27	"	Abner,	May 25, 1752.
1-27	"	Eunice,	June 25, 1754.
1-27	"	Arnold,	May 25, 1756.
1-30	"	Marvin, of Daniel, Jr., and Abigail,	April 6, 1746.
1-30	"	Timothy,	Oct. 12, 1748.
1-30	"	Daniel,	Dec. 8, 1750.
1-30	"	Phineus,	Jan. 18, 1753.
1-30	"	James,	May 16, 1755.
1-30	"	Elizabeth,	Oct. 26, 1757.
1-30	"	Elizabeth,	died Aug. 27, 1759.
1-30	"	Abigail,	June 24, 1760.
1-45	"	Joseph, of Joseph, and Elizabeth,	Feb. 17, 1758.
1-45	"	Thankful,	April 26, 1760.
1-45	"	Mary,	Dec. 18, 1762.
1-45	"	Amey,	April 19, 1765.
3-18	MANCHESTER Henry B.,		born Jan. 11, 1818.
3-18	"	Mary E. (Crandall), his wife,	Dec. 29, 1822.
1-51	MAXSON John, Jr. (born Westerly),		Aug. 27, 1725.
1-51	"	Sarah (Burdick of Samuel), his wife,	Nov. 18, 1725.
1-51	"	Eunice, of John and Sarah,	Feb. 23, 1747.
1-51	"	Lois,	Nov. 11, 1748.
1-51	"	John,	Nov. 11, 1750.
1-51	"	Tacy,	April 3, 1753.
1-51	"	Thankful,	Aug. 2, 1755.
1-51	"	Sarah,	Feb. 11, 1758.

1-51	MAXSON Elizabeth, of John and Sarah,	July 31, 1760.
1-51	" Richard,	Oct. 11, 1763.
1-51	" Henry,	June 7, 1766.
2-11	" Samuel, of Samuel and Ruth,	Sept. 5, 1743.
2-11	" Ruth,	March 5, 1747.
2-11	" Elisha,	April 20, 1749.
2-11	" Lucy,	Aug. 27, 1751.
1-44	" Tacy,	Feb. 13, 1754.
1-44	" Judeth,	June 19, 1756.
2-11	" Phineus, of Samuel and Mary,	Jan. 11, 1765.
2-11	" Mary,	Jan. 9, 1767.
2-11	" Esther,	Dec. 31, 1768.
2-11	" Barbara,	Jan. 1, 1771.
2-11	" Nancy,	Aug. 6, 1775.
2-11	" Wealthy,	May 24, 1779.
1-44	" Stephen, of Stephen and Martha,	Aug. 25, 1757.
1-44	" Avis,	Oct. 20, 1759.
1-44	" Esther,	June 13, 1762.
1-44	" Jared,	Dec. 30, 1764.
1-44	" Joel,	March 21, 1767.
1-44	" Hannah,	Feb. 26, 1769.
1-58	" Ethan, of Samuel and Hannah,	April 28, 1768.
1-66	" Susannah, of William and Lucy,	Sept. 16, 1769.
1-66	" William Miner,	July 12, 1772.
1-66	" Lois,	Jan. 21, 1776.
1-66	" Tabor,	April 16, 1778.
1-66	" Hannah,	April 1, 1780.
1-66	" Susannah,	March 25, 1782.
1-66	" Lucy,	May 22, 1784.
1-66	" Aseneth,	June 21, 1786.
1-66	" Elon,	Nov. 8, 1788.
1-63	" Joseph, of Sylvanus and Lydia,	April 25, 1771.
1-63	" Lewis,	Dec. 17, 1772.
1-63	" Sylvanus,	Feb. 16, 1775.
1-63	" Nathan,	Oct. 5, 1777.
1-64	" Benjamin, of Stephen,	June 27, 1771.
1-64	" Thankful,	Feb. 27, 1776.
1-78	" Samuel, 3d, son of Samuel,	April 1, 1774.
1-78	" Elisha, 4th, son,	April 3, 1776.
1-78	" Davis, 5th, son,	March 13, 1784.
2-49	" Benjamin, Jr.,	born Sept. 28, 1775.
2-49	" Penelope, his wife,	Dec. 2, 1782.
2-49	" Benjamin, of Benjamin and Penelope,	Jan. 23, 1798.
2-49	" Nancy,	April 11, 1800.
2-49	" David,	Dec. 4, 1801.
2-49	" Sally,	July 8, 1804.
2-49	" Huldah,	Aug. 17, 1806.
2-12	" George, of George and Anne,	Nov. 23, 1778.
2-12	" Nancy,	Sept. 17, 1780.
2-12	" Polly,	Feb. 27, 1783.
2-12	" Freelove, of George and Anne,	Dec. 2, 1785.
2-12	" James,	March 2, 1788.
2-12	" Abel,	May 11, 1790.
2-12	" Martha,	July 7, 1792.
2-12	" Henry,	Aug. 1, 1794.
1-120	" Wealthy, of Samuel,	May 24, 1779.
2-45	" Martha, of Peleg and Sarah,	Aug. 12, 1779.
2-45	" Benjamin Clarke,	April 5, 1781.
2-45	" Peleg,	June 27, 1783.
2-15	" Nathan, of Nathan and Nancy,	Dec. 16, 1785.
2-15	" Elizabeth,	Oct. 21, 1787.
2-15	" Catharine,	Nov. 9, 1789.
2-15	" Matthew,	Nov. 27, 1791.
2-15	" Matthew,	died Dec. 30, 1791.
2-15	" Isaac Vars,	May 23, 1793.

2-15	MAXSON Edward, of Nathan and Nancy,		Aug. 20, 1797.
2-15	"	Sarah,	Sept. 16, 1799.
2-7	"	John Davis, of Samuel, Jr., and Hannah.	March 10, 1788.
2-14	"	Ezekiel, of Elisha and Rebecca.	Sept. 22, 1788.
2-14	"	Tacy,	April 6, 1790.
2 14	"	Elisha,	Jan. 26, 1792.
2-14	"	Daniel,	Nov. 6, 1793.
2-14	"	Abigail,	Nov. 6, 1795.
2-14	"	Rhoda,	March 22, 1798.
2-14	"	Rebecca,	March 21, 1800.
2-14	"	Samuel,	May 29, 1802.
2-14	"	Paul,	Dec. 20, 1807.
2-12, 14	"	Hannah, of Ethan and Susey,	April 11, 1792.
2-43	"	Charles Miner, of William M. and Sylvia,	Sept. 8, 1794.
2-50	"	Mary Clarke, of Russell and Mary,	July 16, 1795.
1-50	"	Russell, of Russell and Mary,	Aug. 25, 1797.
1-50	"	Elizabeth,	Dec. 25, 1800.
1-50	"	Paul Clarke,	Feb. 17, 1806.
2-50,90	"	George P., of Russell and Hannah,	March 26, 1824.
2-61	"	Asa, of Joseph and Lydia,	Feb. 14, 1797.
2-61	"	Joel,	Dec. 23, 1798.
2-61	"	Phebe,	May 30, 1801.
2-61	"	George Potter,	Oct. 27, 1803.
2-61	"	Lucy Crandall,	July 18, 1807.
2-61	"	Thomas,	July 19, 1811.
2-61	"	Nancy, of Lewis and Tacy,	Nov. 2, 1797.
2-61	"	Samuel Coon,	July 25, 1800.
2-62	"	Nathan, of Nathan and Ruth,	May 7, 1805.
2-62	"	Jairus Rogers Crandall,	July 11, 1807.
2-62	"	Nancy Crandall,	Dec. 22, 1809.
2-62	"	Nancy Crandall, 2d,	Dec. 22, 1810.
2-62	"	Horace,	May 17, 1812.
2-62	"	Lydia Wells,	Oct. 22, 1816.
2-62	"	Elias Irish, of Peleg and Clarrissa,	April 3, 1810.
2-90	"	Tacy Ann, of Elisha and Lydia,	Oct. 12, 1825.
2-90	"	Abbie Angeline,	July 2, 1827.
3-7	"	David Stillman, of Samuel and Lucy,	Sept. 28, 1828.
3-7	"	Nathan,	Aug. 5, 1830.
3-7	"	Samuel Ray,	Nov. 22, 1832.
3-7	"	Julia Ann,	Oct. 15, 1834.
3-7	"	Lucy Angeline,	Dec. 29, 1836.
1-27	MILLARD Sarah, of John and Catherine,		Feb. 25, 1755.
1-27	"	Elijah,	April 21, 1758.
1-27	"	Catherine,	May 24, 1761.
1-42	"	Susannah,	March 13, 1764.
1-39	MOTT Sarah, of Ebenezer and Elizabeth,		Oct. 4, 1763.

N

1-25	NEY Catherine, of Caleb and Catherine,		May 26, 1752.
2-77	"	Mary,	Oct. 22, 1761.
2-77	"	Joshua,	March 18, 1758.
2-55, 77	"	Mary, died, aged 66 years, July 5, 1788.	
2-55, 77	"	Caleb, died, aged 76 years, July 25, 1796.	
1-1	NICHOLS Andrew, of David and Elizabeth,		May 10, 1776.
1-1	"	George,	Dec. 31, 1777.
1-1	"	John,	Nov. 22, 1779.
1-1	"	Desire,	May 10, 1782.
1-1	"	Luke,	Dec. 13, 1783.
1-1	"	Martha,	Feb. 22, 1786.
1-1	"	Amey,	Dec. 4, 1787.
2-72	"	Eliza, of John and Elizabeth,	Aug. 23, 1804.
2-72	"	Maria Ann,	Feb. 16, 1806.

O P

2-3	PALMER Nathaniel, born May 13, 1757.	
2-3	" Mary, his wife, born Nov. 18, 1760.	
2-3	" Judeth, of Nathaniel and Mary,	Dec. 31, 1782.
2-3	" Mary,	Jan. 29, 1784.
2-3	" Gideon,	Feb. 23, 1785.
2-3	" Nathaniel,	Oct. 4, 1786.
2-3	" Samuel,	Aug. 15, 1788.
2-42	" Lawton, of John and Hannah,	Jan. 31, 1790.
1-75	PALMITER Phebe, of Nathan and Abigail,	Sept. 19, 1770.
1-75	" Stephen,	April 24, 1772
2-5	PATTERSON Amos (born Stonington, Conn.),	March 24, 1734.
2-5	" Eunice (Hall), his wife (born Richmond),	March 6, 1733.
2-5	" Mary, of Amos and Eunice,	June 28, 1757.
2-5	" Martha,	Oct. 18, 1761.
2-5	" Eunice,	July 8, 1763.
2-5	" Amos,	Oct. 3, 1772.
2-5	" Amos,	died Oct. 16, 1778.
	Note—First child born in Richmond, the others in Hopkinton.	
1-60	PECKHAM Hannah, of Daniel, and Avis,	April 25, 1777.
1-60	" Polly,	Nov. 27, 1778.
1-60	" Weeden,	May 2, 1782.
2-44	" Amey,	March 5, 1784.
1-19	PERRY Mary, of Simeon,	Sept. 18, 1750.
1-19	" Samuel,	May 1, 1754.
1-19	" Susannah,	June 17, 1756.
1-19	" Simeon,	Sept. 29, 1759.
1-25	" Simeon, of Simeon, and Penelope,	Sept. 29, 1769.
1-47	POPPLE Tabitha,	born March 22, 1787.
1-70	PORTER Hannah, of Nathan, and Hannah,	April 10, 1764.
1-70	" Desire,	Nov. 14, 1766.
1-70	" Nathan,	May 19, 1768.
1-70	" Fannie,	Dec. 18, 1769.
1-70	" John,	March 9, 1772.
1-70	" Mary,	April 9, 1774.
1-25	POTTER Caleb, of Thomas, and Judeth (O. S.),	Aug. 19, 1749.
1-24	" Mary, of George, and Content,	May 30, 1755.
1-24	" George,	Feb. 10, 1757.
1-24	" Joseph,	Feb. 16, 1759
1-20	" Hannah,	March 9, 1761.
1-20	" Susannah,	March 14, 1763.
1-48	" Content,	May 25, 1735.
1-48	" Lydia,	Oct. 10, 1766.
1-48	" Nathan,	May 31, 1769.
1-48	" Lucy, of George and Content,	Oct. 10, 1771.
1-48	" Elizabeth,	Sept. 19, 1775.
1-20	" Stephen, of Stephen,	Nov. 1, 1757.
1-73	" Judeth, of Caleb and Catherine,	Nov. 15, 1771.
1-73	" Judeth, of Caleb and Catherine,	died Dec. 19, 1792.
1-73	" Mary,	July 29, 1773
1-73	" Thomas,	Aug. 25, 1775.
1-73	" Caleb,	Oct. 30, 1779.
1-73	" Clarke,	Aug. 19, 1781.
1-73	" Sarah,	May 8, 1783.
1-73	" Catharine,	Feb. 17, 1788.
1-73	" Elizabeth,	Sept. 12, 1794.
1-33	" Thomas, died in his 78th year,	Jan. 8, 1773.
2-76	" Judeth, wife of Thomas, died, age 93 years,	Jan. 26, 1805.
2-76	" Judeth, of Caleb, died, age 22 years,	Dec. 19, 1779.
2-76	" Catey, of Caleb, died, age 29 years,	Dec. 4, 1816.
2-50	" Lyman, of Jonathan, Jr., and Martha,	Jan. 29, 1777.
2-50	" Lydia,	March 20, 1779.
2-50	" Lucy,	May 20, 1781.
2-50	" Luke,	June 5, 1783.

2-50	POTTER	Martha, of Jonathan, Jr., and Martha,	July 11, 1785.
2-50	"	Jonathan,	Dec. 20, 1787.
2-50	"	Sarah,	Dec. 16, 1789.
2-50	"	George,	March 30, 1793.

Note—First two born in Richmond, the others in Hopkinton.

1-95	"	William, of Stephen and Sarah,	Nov. 15, 1781.
2-3	"	Sarah,	Nov. 23, 1783.
2-3	"	Stephen,	Aug. 5, 1785.
2-3	"	Esther,	June 11, 1787.
2-3	"	Ezekiel,	July 21, 1790.
2-64	"	Rebecca, of Thomas and Sally,	Dec. 10, 1798.
2-64	"	Asa Coon, of Thomas and Sally,	May 4, 1801.
2-64	"	Asa Coon,	died Jan. 5, 1804.
2-64	"	Judith,	Nov. 4, 1803.
2-64	"	Levi Barber,	Jan. 5, 1806.
4-11	"	Benjamin, born June 16, 1785.	
4-11	"	Elizabeth (Greene), his wife, born Nov. 8, 1792.	
4-11	"	Eliza, of Benjamin and Elizabeth,	Sept. 20, 1808.
4-11	"	Maria Egerton,	Sept. 20, 1810.
4-11	"	Benjamin Franklin,	Nov. 17, 1812.
4-11	"	Elizabeth Frances,	April 7, 1815.
4-11	"	Sarah Turner,	Sept. 17, 1817.
4-11	"	Susan Greene,	July 18, 1820.
4-11	"	Luther Greene,	Nov. 8, 1823.
4-11	"	John Edwin,	Jan. 26, 1826.
2-80	"	Nancy, of Clarke and Judeth,	Jan. 2, 1809.
2-80	"	Beriah,	Feb. 23, 1811.
2-80	"	Clarke Aldrich,	Sept. 20, 1812.
2-80	"	William Wilbur,	March 8, 1814.
2-89	"	Joseph Henry, of Robert T. and Mary,	Oct. 21, 1823.
3-15	"	Harriet D., of Clarke A. and Belinda,	Dec. 28, 1839.

Q R

1-110	RANDALL	Matthew, of Lieut. Matthew and Mary,	May 17, 1775.
1-110	"	Lucy,	Dec. 16, 1776.
1-110	"	Hannah,	Feb. 5, 1779.
1-110	"	Sarah,	Feb. 10, 1781.
1-110	"	Mary,	March 4, 1783.
2-4	"	Nancy,	June 22, 1786.
2-4	"	Betsey,	Aug. 10, 1788.
1-19	REYNOLDS	Elizabeth, of Richmond,	Feb. 28, 1751.
1-19	"	Presilla,	Sept. 20, 1752.
1-19	"	Joshua, of Richmond,	March 7, 1754.
1-19	"	John,	Nov. 16, 1755.
1-19	"	Samuel, of Joseph (N. S.),	Oct. 23, 1751.
1-19	"	Thomas,	Dec. 8, 1753.
1-27	"	Simeon, of Richmond,	Jan. 15, 1758.
1-32	"	Joshua, —— and Anne, buried Jan. 28, 1760.	
1-32	"	Anne, wife of Richmond,	buried Jan. 28, 1760.
1-27	"	Thankful, of Joseph and Hannah,	June 8, 1760.
1-30	"	Rebecca, of Elias and Ruth,	Oct. 14, 1760.
1-30	"	James,	Dec. 19, 1761.
1-30	"	John,	Sept. 15, 1764.
1-30	"	Elias,	Nov. 5, 1767.
1-30	"	Silas,	March 14, 1769.
1-30	"	Amey,	April 5, 1771.
1-72	"	Susannah, of Zaccheus, Jr., and Desire,	April 2, 1773.
2-16	"	Polly,	April 23, 1775.
2-16	"	Susannah,	March 29, 1780.
1-111	"	Clarke, of Clarke and Hannah,	Aug. 10, 1777.
1-111	"	Ethan,	May 21, 1780.
1-111	"	Phineus Miner,	Dec. 24, 1787.
2-16	"	Desire, of Zaccheus and Phebe,	May 29, 1782.

2-16	REYNOLDS Phebe, of Zaccheus and Phebe,	Sept. 17, 1783.
2-16	" Sophia,	Oct. 1, 1785.
2-16	" Ira,	Dec. 5, 1787.
2-16	" Cynthia,	March 2, 1791.
2-56	" Welcome,	April 13, 1796.
2-56	" Zaccheus, father of the above children, died before his son Welcome was born.
1-39	RHODES Sarah, 4th child of James and Anna,	June 7, 1761.
1-39	" James, 5th,	Aug. 12, 1764.
1-26	ROBINSON William, of Edward and Martha,	March 29, 1736.
1-26	" Edward,	Feb. 15, 1738.
1-26	" Francis,	May 22, 1740.
1-26	" Nathan,	June 30, 1742.
1-26	" Martha,	Sept. 28, 1745.
1-26	" Elizabeth,	April 29, 1748.
1-26	" Anne,	Nov. 6, 1750.
1-26	Amey,	Feb. 6, 1853.
1-26	" Avis,	July 12, 1759.
1-58	ROGERS Amos, of Amos and Anne,	Nov. 1, 1767.
1-78	" John,	Dec. 22, 1770.
2-53	" Gleason,	June 4, 1775.
2-53	" Gleason,	d. Dec. 11, 1777.
2-53	" Elisha,	April 11, 1777.
2-53	" Anna,	Feb. 17, 1779.
2-53	" Charles Dake,	Nov. 8, 1780.
2-53	" Sally,	Nov. 17, 1785.
1-97	" Martha, of Carey and Martba,	Sept. 16, 1768.
1-97	" Clarke,	May 26, 1771.
1-97	" Benjamin,	June 6, 1773.
1-97	" Carey,	April 29, 1776.
2-74	ROSS Eliza Anna, of Lyman and Jndeth,	Feb. 5, 1810.

S

1-75	SAUNDERS William, of Henry and Aphannah,	Feb. 9, 1774.
1-75	" Mary,	March 27, 1776.
1-75	" Susannah,	Feb. 3, 1780.
1-75	" Elizabeth,	Jan. 6, 1784.
2-69	" Matilda, of Isaac and Matilda,	Feb. 7, 1811.
2-73	SHELDON Phebe, of Asa and Mary,	Sept. 27, 1801.
2-73	" Renewed,	March 26, 1803.
2-73	" Mary Ann,	Aug. 5, 1805.
2-73	" Phineus,	Sept. 13, 1807.
2-73	" Asa,	Feb. 13, 1810.
2-73	" Dennis,	April 7, 1812.
2-73	" Gilbert Gardiner,	Oct. 17, 1814.
2-51	SPICER Joseph, of Joseph and Mary,	March 9, 1797.
2-51	" Fannie,	April 26, 1799.
2-51	" George Thurston,	Aug. 4, 1802.
2-51	" John,	Aug. 26, 1804.
1-76	STILES John, of Israel and Hannah,	March 5, 1736.
1-76	" Mary,	Oct. 10, 1738.
1-76	" Israel,	April 13, 1740.
1-76	" Nathaniel,	July 28, 1742.
1-76	" Nathaniel,	d. Feb. 23, 1754.
1-76	" William,	July 29, 1744.
1-76	" Hannah,	July 13, 1746.
1-76	" Hannah,	d. July —, 1749.
1-76	" Joshua,	July 12, 1748.
1-76	" Joshua,	d. July —, 1749.
1-76	" Hannah,	July 9, 1750.
1-76	" A son born and died,	Dec. 22, 1753.
2-78	STILLMAN Elisha, of Elisha, Feb. 26, 1761.
2-78	" Prudence (Burdick, of Elder John), his wife, July 24, 1761.

2-78	STILLMAN	Prudence, of Elisha and Prudence,	Jan. 13, 1783.
2-78	"	Phineus,	May 10, 1785.
2-78	"	Polly.	Aug. 11, 1787.
2-78	"	Elisha,	Oct. 2, 1789.
2-78	"	John Burdick,	Aug. 29, 1792.
2-78	"	Clarke,	Jan. 15, 1795.
2-78	"	Susannah,	July 20, 1797.
2-78	"	Ira,	Oct. 30, 1799.
2-78	"	Thankful.	Jan. 6, 1805.
2-67	"	Phineus, born May 10, 1785.	
2-67	"	Thankful (Gardiner), his wife,	March 27, 1784.
2-67	"	Thankful, of Phineus and Thankful,	Oct. 27, 1811.
2-67	"	George P.,	March 20, 1813.
2-67	"	Boton,	July 2, 1814.
2-67	"	Prudence M.,	June 20, 1816.
2-67	"	Amelia E.,	May 5, 1818.
2-67	"	Ransome T.,	Feb. 29, 1820.
2-67	"	Charles O.,	Jan. 12, 1824.
2-67	"	Eliza C.,	Feb. 16, 1826.
2-67	"	David G.,	July 24, 1828.
2-68	"	Maria, of David and Grace,	Aug. 21, 1803.
2-68	"	Ephraim,	Jan. 8, 1806.
2-68	"	Lucy,	July 19, 1808.
2-68	"	Elizabeth,	March 7, 1811.
3-9	"	Maxson J., of Christopher C. and Mary.	Oct. 22, 1831.
2-10	STETSON	Benjamin, of Thomas,	July 9, 1772.

T

1-100	TANNER	David, of Nathan (of William) and Mary,	— —, —.
1-100	"	Nathan,	— —, —.
1-100	"	Abel,	Sept. 7, 1740.
1-35	"	Hannah, of John and Mary,	Sept. 19, 1752.
1-35	"	Nathan,	Aug. 17, 1755.
1-35	"	Mary,	Jan. 7, 1758.
1-35	"	Esther,	Dec. 17, 1760.
1-35	"	Ruth,	Nov. 8, 1763.
1-35	"	John,	Aug. 27, 1766.
1-35	"	Stephen (also 1-109),	Dec. 14, 1769.
1-47	"	Joseph, of William and Susannah,	Feb. 5, 1756.
1-47	"	Thurston,	April 15, 1758.
1-47	"	Thurston,	died May 5, 1767.
1-47	"	William,	Aug. 6, 1760.
1-47	"	Susannah,	July 23, 1763.
1-47	'	Sarah,	Dec. 15, 1765.
1-47	"	Hannah,	Jan. 29, 1768.
1-21	"	Nathan, of David,	Sept. 27, 1755.
1-21	"	Mary,	May 14, 1757.
1-105	"	Hannah, of Nathan and Elizabeth,	Sept. 6, 1760.
1-105	"	Nathan,	Feb. 22, 1763.
1-105	"	Thomas,	Sept. 14, 1767.
1-105	'	Elizabeth,	Dec. 13, 1770.
1-105	"	Sarah,	July 4, 1772.
1-105	"	Mary,	May 12, 1775.
1-31	"	Thankful, of David and Hopestill,	July 27, 1761.
1-31	"	Nathan, of John and Mary,	Aug. 17, 1755.
1-31	"	Mary,	Jan. 7, 1758.
1-31	"	Esther,	Dec. 17, 1760.
1-31	'	Hannah,	Sept. 19, 1762.
1-51	"	James, of David and Hopestill,	June 30, 1767.
1-100	"	William, of Abel and Phebe (also 2-63),	May 8, 1769.
1-100	"	Elizabeth, (also 2-63),	Feb. 6, 1771.
1-100	"	Phebe (also 2-63),	Jan. 4, 1773.
1-100	"	Mary (also 2-63),	March 26, 1775.

1-100	TANNER Hannah, of Abel and Phebe (also 2-63),	May 5, 1777.
1-100	" Nathan (also 2-63),	March 15, 1779.
1-100	" Anna (also 2-63),	May 12, 1781.
1-100	" John (also 2-63),	Oct. 4, 1783.
1-100	" Phannie (also 2-63),	Aug. 23, 1787.
1-69	" William Brown, of William and Ruth,	Oct. 13, 1772,
1-69	" Anstis,	April 19, 1776.
2-15	" Ruth,	Aug. 18, 1778.
2-15	" Susannah,	May 30, 1786.
2-15	" Francis Brown,	April 14, 1793.
1-103	" William, of William and Napple,	Oct. 13, 1772.
1-103	" Austis,	April 19, 1776.
1-103	" Mary, of William and Susannah,	Aug. 6, 1770.
1-103	" Tacy,	Dec. 16, 1772.
1-103	" Esther,	May 21, 1775.
1-103	" Susannah, wife of William, died	July 26, 1776.
1-115	" Mary, of Joshua and Thankful,	March 10, 1776.
1-115	" John,	Aug. 15, 1778.
1-d15	" Thankful,	Dec. 20, 1780.
1-115	" Susannah,	May 2, 1783.
1-115	" Elizabeth,	Dec. 25, 1785.
1-115	" Esther,	May 10, 1788.
1-115	" Pardon,	May 23, 1791.
1-119	" Nathan, of Nathan and Susannah,	Oct. 28, 1776.
1-119	" David, of David and Hopestill,	Jan. 21, 1780.
2-5	" Betsey, of William, Jr., and Hannah,	Sept. 24, 1786.
2-5	" Susey,	Jan. 5, 1788.
2-54	" Nathan, Jr., of Nathan and Charlotte,	Sept. 9, 1806.
2-2	THURSTON Taylor, of Gardiner and Lydia,	Aug. 29, 1787.
2-2	" Robert,	April 16, 1790.
2-2	" Lucy,	July 11, 1792.
2-80	" Sarah R., of Clarke and Abbie,	June 2, 1817.
2-80	" Benjamin R.,	March 31, 1819.
3-8	" Benjamin Francis, of Benjamin B.,	Nov. 7, 1829.
3-8	" George Edward,	April 11, 1831.
1-40	TEFFT Pardon, of William and Mary,	Jan. 27, 1755.
1-40	" Thankful,	March 21, 1758.
1-40	" David,	April 19, 1760.
1-40	" William,	May 21, 1763.
1-40	TRIPP Phebe Brown, alias, of Ruth,	Dec. 29, 1791.

U

2-54	UTTER James Noyes, of John and Esther,	Oct. 10, 1802.
2-54	" Esther,	June 2, 1804.
2-54	" John,	Sept. 20, 1803.

V

2-44	VINCENT Jane, of Nicholas and Anna,	March 22, 1776.
2-44	" Anna,	May 31, 1777.
2-44	" Susannah,	May 8, 1779.
2-44	" Clarke,	April 28, 1781.
2-44	" Betsey,	March 12, 1783.
2-44	" Nicholas,	Feb. 1, 1785.
2-44	" Temperance,	Oct. 20, 1787.
2-44	" Abigail,	Jan. 31, 1789.
2-44	" Lydia,	Jan. 2, 1792.

W

1-30	WAITE Paine, of Thomas and Bridget,	Dec. 12, 1745.
1-30	" Joseph,	Aug. 16, 1747.

1-30	WAITE Susannah, of Thomas and Bridget,	Dec. 12, 1745.
1-30	" Sarah,	April —, 1749.
1-30	" John,	March —, 1751.
1-30	" Job,	Aug. —, 1753.
1-30	" Grace,	June 4, 1756.
1-30	" Thankful,	Dec. 17, 1757.
1-23	WARREN Elizabeth, of Moses,	Aug. 2, 1754.
1-23	" Mary,	April 1, 1757.
1-50	WELLS Edward, Jr., born Feb. 23, 1726.	
1-50	" Elizabeth (Sheffield), his wife, born Oct. 1, 1728.	
1-50	" Sarah, of Edward and Elizabeth, Nov. 19, d. 21, 1750.	
1-50	" Catherine, of Edward and Elizabeth,	Oct. 23, 1752.
1-50	" Stephen,	April 4, 1754.
1-50	" Sheffield,	Dec. 13, 1755.
1-50	" Sheffield,	d. Nov. 11, 1759.
1-50	" Lucy,	Sept. 18, 1757.
1-50	" Cynthia,	Sept. 22, 1759.
1-50	" Phanney,	Jan. 19, 1761.
1-50	" Edward,	June 9, 1765.
1-24	" Marcy, of Joseph,	Oct. 11, 1756.
1-24	" Samuel,	Feb. 6, 1758.
1-24	" Thankful,	March 23, 1761.
1-24	" Joseph,	May 18, 1763.
1-73	" Elizabeth, of James,	Jan. 14, 1758.
1-73	" James,	Jan. 7, 1760.
1-73	" Robert,	Nov. 26, 1761.
1-73	" George,	Nov. 9, 1763.
1-73	" Polly,	April 9, 1767.
1-73	" Hannah,	April 16, 1769.
1-73	" Ruth,	Sept. 6, 1770.
1-73	" Anna,	March 5, 1774.
1-37	" Elisha, of Matthew and Bridget,	Sept. 19, 1758.
1-37	" Bathsheba,	July 6, 1760.
1-37	" Elias,	Jan. 3, 1762.
1-37	" John,	Dec. 3, 1763.
1-33	" Barbara, of Peter and Elizabeth,	Jan. 17, 1760.
1-63	" Clarke, of Thomas and Sarah,	July 8, 1762.
1-63	" Joseph,	Sept. 2, 1764.
1-63	" David,	April 2, 1766.
1-63	" Mary,	Dec. 2, 1768.
1-63	" Anne,	Jan. 1, 1770.
1-66	" Rhoda, of Thompson and Elizabeth,	May 14, 1768.
1-66	" Palmer,	March 31, 1771.
1-66	" Elizabeth,	Aug. 28, 1773.
1-66	" Thompson,	June 16, 1776.
1-66	" Mary,	Nov. 23, 1778.
1-66	" Phebe,	May 21, 1787.
1-66	" Eunice,	June 21, 1788.
1-97	" Elizabeth, of Jonathan and Amey,	Feb. 11, 1769.
1-97	" Mary,	Oct. 29, 1773.
1-59	" Gardiner, of Joshua,	March 20, 1770.
1-59	" Joshua,	July 17, 1771.
2-44	" Joseph, of Samuel and Susannah,	May 7, 1783.
2-44	" Susannah,	Nov. 14, 1788.
2-44	" Samuel,	April 27, 1791.
2-44	" George Potter,	Dec. 14, 1793.
2-44	" William Davis,	April 8, 1797.
2-44	" Thankful,	Aug. 7, 1803.
2-10	" Bathsheba, of John and Sarah,	April 19, 1789.
2-67	" Phebe, of Barker and Fannie,	Aug. 19, 1800.
2-67	" John Aldrich,	Nov. 17, 1801.
2-46	" Joseph Willard, of Joseph and Lydia,	Feb. 9, 1808.
2-46	" Daniel Babcock,	Aug. 15, 1811.
2-93	" Edward S., of Edward S. and Deborah,	Oct. 8, 1818.
1-114	WEST Jonathan, of Elder Thomas,	Nov. 28, 1754.
1-114	" Susannah,	June 3, 1756.

1-114	WEST Michael, of Elder Thomas,		Dec. 15, 1759.
1-114	"	Thomas,	Feb. 21, 1762.
1-114	"	Francis,	April 15, 1764.
1-114	"	Samuel,	Oct. 6, 1766.
1-114	"	Joseph,	Oct. 4, 1771.
1-114	"	Amie,	April 3, 1774.
1-114	"	Abigail,	July 31, 1776.
1-33	"	Sarah, of Francis and Mary,	June 5, 1758.
1-33	"	William,	Sept. 7, 1760.
2-14	WHITE Godfrey, of Oliver,		Sept. 4, 1761.
2-14	"	Susannah,	Nov. 1, 1766.
2-14	"	Amelia, of Godfrey and Jane,	Jan. 14, 1786.
2-14	"	Amos,	May 6, 1787.
2-14	"	William,	May 20, 1788.
2-14	"	Phebe,	July 28, 1789.
2-14	"	Oliver,	July 22, 1792.
2-14	"	Henry,	Dec. 31, 1793.
2-14	"	Jane,	Jan. 23, 1796.
2-14	"	Abigail Sole,	Nov. 11, 1797.
2-14	"	Gideon Sole,	April 21, 1799.
2-14	"	Susannah Greene,	July 5, 1800.
2-14	"	Walter Ellis,	Jan. 11, 1803.
2-14	"	Sophia,	Oct. 1, 1804.
1-26	"	Wealthian, of Job,	Oct. 3, 1759.
1-26	"	Sabra,	July 11, 1761.
1-26	"	Jonathan,	March 3, 1764.
1-60	"	Hannah, of Oliver, Jr., and Cynthia,	Dec. 29, 1781.
1-60	"	Clarke,	April 16, 1783.
1-29	WILBUR Dinah, of Christopher and Sarah,		Aug. 3, 1747.
1-29	"	Deborah,	July 2, 1749.
1-29	"	Mary,	May 6, 1751.
1-29	"	Elizabeth,	March 26, 1753.
1-29	"	Sarah,	Jan. 22, 1756.
1-29	"	Benjamin,	Dec. 19, 1757.
1-29	"	Lydia,	May 6, 1760.
1-35	"	John, of John and Mary,	Jan. 25, 1762.
1-35	"	Thomas,	Oct. 25, 1765.
1-35	"	Isaac, born March 26, 1774.	
1-35	"	Martha, his wife, born June 6, 1780.	
1-35	"	Isaac, of Isaac and Martha,	Sept. 20, 1800.
1-35	"	Charles,	June 6, 1803.
1-35	"	Martha,	Nov. 18, 1805.
3-8	WILCOX Nathan Asa Gates, of Nathan and Sophia,		Dec. 23, 1832.
1-115	WILKINSON Sheffield, of Samuel and Mary,		Dec. 29, 1777.
1-75	WITTER Josiah, of Joseph, born		Jan. 25, 1739.
1-75	"	Tacy (Reynolds, of Zaccheus), his wife, born	March 19, 1743.
1-75	"	Weeden, of Josiah and Tacy,	April 30, 1765.
1-75	"	Susannah,	May 7, 1767.
1-75	"	Lois,	Oct. 1, 1768.
1-75	"	Hannah,	Aug. 12, 1772.
1-75	"	Joseph,	March 28, 1773.
1-75	"	Eunice,	Oct. 31, 1775.
1-75	"	Josiah,	March 28, 1777.
1-71	"	Sarah,	Feb. 6, 1779.
1-97	"	Samuel, of John and Anne (O. S.),	June 29, 1745.
1-120	"	Sarah, of William and Martha,	Nov. 12, 1765.
1-120	"	Sarah,	died Dec. 6, 1765.
1-120	"	Sarah, 2d,	Dec. 3, 1766.
1-120	"	Martha,	April 27, 1769.
1-120	"	Elizabeth,	Aug. 4, 1771.
1-120	"	Mary,	Nov. 6, 1773.
1-120	"	Wealthy,	Feb. 17, 1776.
1-120	"	Anne,	Aug. 24, 1780.
1-120	"	Joseph,	Dec. 13, 1782.
1-120	"	William,	Aug. 26, 1778.

1-60	WITTER Mary, of Samuel and Tacy (also 2-10),		Dec. 10, 1769.
1-60	"	Huldah (also 2-10),	March 1, 1772.
1-60	"	Davis (also 2-10),	May 4, 1774.
1-60	"	Davis (also 2-10),	died Nov. 1, 1775.
1-60	"	Samuel (also 2-10),	Jan. 17, 1776.
1-60	"	Tacy (also 2-10),	Feb. 14, 1779.
1-60	"	John (also 2-10),	March 31, 1781.
1-60	"	Hannah (also 2-10),	July 27, 1784.
1-60	"	Paul (also 2-10),	Sept. 19, 1787.
2-10	"	Anne, of Samuel and Tacy,	Nov. 9, 1779.
1-51	"	Anne, of John and Meriam,	May 9, 1766.
1-51	"	John,	Dec. 19, 1768.
1-51	"	Molley,	July 14, 1772.
2-52	"	Anne, of William and Martha,	Aug. 24, 1780.
2-52	"	Joseph,	Dec. 13, 1782.
2-52	"	Dorcas, of Samuel and Mary,	April 11, 1797.
4-17	WOODMANSEE Sarah Matilda, of Benjamin B. and Ruth,		Feb. 24, 1822.
4-17	"	George K.,	March 19, 1824.
4-17	"	Thankful,	July 10, 1828.
1-31	WORDEN Lucia, of Water and Anne,		Dec. 1, 1751.
1-31	"	Dorothy,	Feb. 14, 1753.
1-31	"	Anna,	Feb. 14, 1755.
1-31	"	Sherall Waite,	Aug. 6, 1756.
1-31	"	Benjamin,	Nov. 5, 1758.
1-67	"	Mary, of William and Mary,	May 20, 1766.
1-67	"	Sarah,	Sept. 10, 1767.
1-67	"	Anne,	Aug. 19, 1769.
2-47	WRIGHT Sabrina, of John and Sabrina,		Jan. 29, 1789.
2-47	"	Francis West,	Jan. 31, 1791.
2-47	"	Nancy,	Dec. 27, 1792.
2-47	"	Esther,	July 3, 1794.
3-11	"	Daniel, of Daniel and Patience,	May 3, 1815.

X Y Z

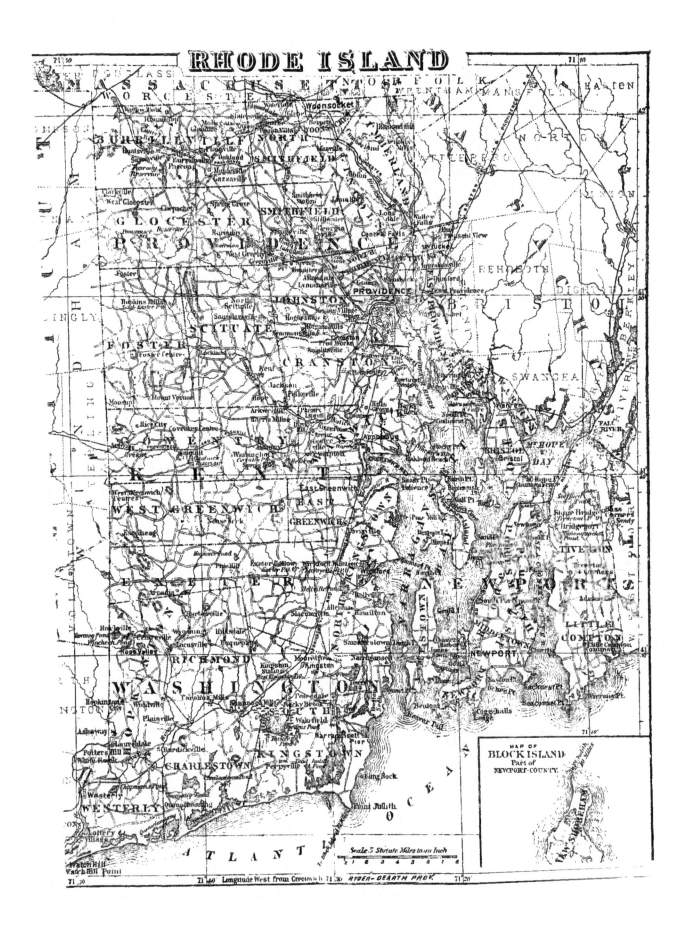

RHODE ISLAND

MAP OF
BLOCK ISLAND
Part of
NEWPORT COUNTY

Vital Record of Rhode Island.
1636=1850.

FIRST SERIES.

BIRTHS, MARRIAGES AND DEATHS.

A Family Register for the People.

BY JAMES N. ARNOLD,

EDITOR OF THE NARRAGANSETT HISTORICAL REGISTER.

"Is My Name Written in the Book of Life?"

Vol. 6.   BRISTOL COUNTY.

Published under the Auspices of the General Assembly.

—◆—

PROVIDENCE, R. I;
NARRAGANSETT HISTORICAL PUBLISHING COMPANY.
1894.

PRINTED BY THE PROVIDENCE JOURNAL CO.,
Providence, R. I.

INTRODUCTION.

BRISTOL COUNTY, formerly a part of Massachusetts, presents several sharp contrasts with Rhode Island when we examine into their mode of keeping the local records. The two original towns of the county (Bristol and Warren) bear out the same plan that appears on those of the three other towns (Cumberland, Tiverton and Little Compton), received from Massachusetts at the same time as these were, viz.: That they kept their genealogical matter in a far superior condition than our earliest colonists did theirs. Had the Rhode Island towns been as faithful, then this work would have been double its present size. While the compiler has been saved all this worry to decipher it, he regrets that it was so badly neglected, as it leaves open spaces and confusion where they apparently should not occur, and has made this work very incomplete and in many respects unsatisfactory. The compiler offers the same excuse he has given in the earlier volumes—that he realizes the great dificiency—but yet believing that half a loaf is better than none, and knowing that even this might be lost, he has in his own humble way done what he could to preserve even this much from becoming lost.

He feels a keener pride than ever that his work (rather his labor of love) has been so well received by the public at large. He appreciates the compliments paid to it by those able to judge of its merits, and thanks the authors for the interest manifested in the enterprise.

With this county we cover the entire State, and end so far as the official record goes the Vital Record of the State. There remains now to be published the "semi-official record, if it may be so termed, consisting of newspaper, church and individual items, which would make, in our opinion, as fine a volume as any that has yet appeared in this serial. While it would necessitate many repetitions, it would add many new points and strengthen materially the matter found in these pages. In our opinion this is very desirable, and should be done to add as much completeness as possible to our work.

The Honorable General Assembly has been very liberal towards us, and, if they will again look with favor upon us, we shall publish in the future a supplement to this work. containing the matter above mentioned.

It is a matter of regret with the compiler that a State so historic as ours and a city the second in New England, with a record second to none, has not historical and genealogical societies worthy of them. We trust that in the future the State will be blessed by such an institution. No more far-reaching, moralizing, better educating and enobling enterprise can be founded, and the compiler trusts that there may yet a Dexter or a Butler arise that will found for his native State a society of this nature, that will be a blessing forever to our people. May such an institution come based upon broad and liberal principles, and controlled by men of brains and ability, with a liberalty enough to reward merit, to encourage historical enterprise, wherever it may crop out, resolving to recognize genius wherever it may be found, in the palace or the hovel, or in whatever condition of life or circumstances it may be placed

—is the earnest and sincere wish of the writer, and he realizes this want fully in his own labors in these fields.

CONDITION OF THE RECORDS.

Bristol's first book is in poor condition, but has been copied into two books, which are now called No. 1 and No. 2, and which have been very carefully compared with the original. No. 3, a book of deaths, has been copied. The original in poor condition. No. 4 needs binding.

The compiler published the Bristol intentions and marriages and the births in the Bristol Phenix, in the current issue of that paper, from Jan. 31, 1885, to Sept. 10, 1887, both inclusive.

Right here we must congratulate Bristol upon being so fortunate in the selection of its Town Clerk (Hon. Herbert F. Bennett). This gentleman has done and is doing a most creditable as well as a most desirable work of putting the records into first-class condition. He has indexed the Vital Records thoroughly, and has now nearly completed an index of real estate, under one alphabet, an immense labor. The honorable gentleman has got something to work for. He has a town which is intelligent and can appreciate the importance and value of his labors. We wish, decidedly, every other town in our State had just such officers and just such enterprise behind them to encourage and push on the work so much needed and yet so universally neglected.

Warren has four books, three of which are in need of binding. No. 4 has only marriages. Warren is a small town in regard to acres, and we think the only town that has a Town Hall larger in area than the town. We admire the enterprise of the town in providing a building large enough to hold all Warren, and trust they will next be liberal enough to provide for the rebinding of their volumes of town evidence. There is nothing more neglected in our towns than the case of the Record Books. I believe the Town Clerk has a right to order his books to be rebound when, in his judgment, they need it, and I believe such a bill would be sustained by every court in the State. We do not wish the good people of Warren to think we believe their Town Records are in worse condition than other towns, but the same fact that will apply to other towns will apple here—that the books should be rebound. The wonder is, to me, a people so intelligent and enterprising as those of Warren have not looked into this affair before.

Barrington has two square books of Vital Record, in one of which several pages have been abstracted, either for a purpose or removed by the Clerk for errors committed on them. In the Ancient Town Meeting we find a few items. We were pleased to learn that means would soon be taken to rebind the Town Records. The town is to be congratulated on its very admirable hall. If a stranger will be but a little observing he can guage a township very accurately. A look at the Town Hall and its school houses is a clear index to the sterling worth of the town. Where every school house and the Town Hall floats the national flag every day the loyalty of these people can be relied on in time of dread. Barrington is such a town.

THE NAMES OF THE TOWNS.

Bristol, one of the Massachusetts towns acquired Jan. 27, 1746-7. Named from Bristol, England. A part annexed to Warren May 30, 1873. Indian name Montaup.

Warren, another Massachusetts town, acquired the same date as Bristol. Named from Sir Peter Warren, Admiral in the British navy. Indian name Sowoms.

Barrington, incorporated June 16, 1770. Taken from Warren. First incorporated in 1718 by Massachusetts, but afterwards merged into Warren.

Named, it is supposed, from an English town of that name. Indian name Popanomscnt.

ACKNOWLEDGEMENTS.

The General Assembly of the State has again been liberal and has bestowed on the work a liberal subscription, for which we thank them; and also the Honorable Committee, who favorable reported upon so desirable a matter to us, and so vital to the success of this enterprise.

We also thank the public for the favor in which they received our previous volumes, and for their good wishes towards us in the future.

PLEASE OBSERVE.

I. That the marriages are given in duplicate, but that nothing beyond the book and page of the original town record, the names and date are given where the bride is placed first. That under the groom the notes are so extended as to include all the items of the record from whence it was taken. The reader will consider the bride being placed first, therefore, as merely an index for him to consult the other entry in its proper place. Should they disagree, give the groom the preference, if possible. That the births and deaths are grouped so as to better enable the reader to see at a glance the names and dates in their natural order of the members of the family.

II. That the figures at the left of the name is the book and page of the original town record, the hyphen separating the two apart.

III. That the indexes for all the towns treated in this work are placed in the fore part of the book. No one need look farther than the index to discover whether the matter he is in search of is to be found within the covers. These indexes are so constructed as to show:

(a) The names occurring in their natural order.

(b) The names occurring promiscuously, and

(c) The places mentioned in the text.

IV. That each town is separate and distinct in itself, and the indexes are confined strictly to each town, but all are placed in the fore part of the work for the more handy reference of the reader. Should the reader want his copy rebound, he can do so, and the indexes can be differently placed with no injury to the others.

V. The spelling of the given names are as they stand on the Record in many instances, and when they are not far wrong. This accounts for the variety of spelling in this work.

VI. The acts incorporating the several towns of the county are placed before the matter itself in that particular town.

VII. Every convenience that would aid the reader, and everything that would naturally perplex him, has been carefully studied. While not claiming perfection for our work, we would say that we have spared no pains in order to make it as simple as possible, and yet be comprehensive. How well we have succeeded in this must be left, however, to the reader himself to say.

VIII. We have not changed dates here given, but we give it just as it stands on the Record itself. We have observed, however, that the Scotch year is more general in this county than in any other that has come to our notice

A REQUEST.

It would be a great favor to the compiler of this work if every reader who consults these pages would copy out and send to him at Providence, R. I., copies from his family record in the Bible, or where else the same may be recorded, or any other information he may be possessed of, in order to make these records in the future as complete as possible. It makes no difference whether the party resides in the State of Rhode Island or not. If they can connect with Rhode Island ancestry it is sufficient. While these matters may seem trifling, yet they may become of incalculable value in the future, and therefore we urgently desire that the Vital Records of Rhode Island may be made complete and that errors, wherever found, may be pointed out and corrected as soon as possible.

OUR NEW SERIAL.

The compiler of this work begs leave to announce that he has in preparation a new serial, which he flatters himself will prove of great value and interest to the historian of the State. He has entitled the serial, "RHODE ISLAND COLONIAL GLEANINGS."

Vol. I. of this serial will be "The Records of the Proprietors of the Narragansett, otherwise called the Fones Record." This volume is beyond all doubt the most historic volume of land evidence in New England. The early history of Washington county cannot be intelligently written until the historian has consulted this volume, and no scholar of that county to-day, who has any love for local history, will be without it. It will be published at a price that all can afford one, which will be most probably $1.50. Other volumes will follow this if patronage will merit publishment. None of the volumes are intended to be printed at a fancy price, but at a price that no intelligent person can take exception to as unreasonable or unjust. The compiler wishes a liberal patronage and as he intends to be liberal on his part, he therefore can expect to receive it from his friends and patrons.

The compiler's long experience in reading old manuscript, and his long and close study of our State history, places him in a position to do an able work. When it is taken into account the many perplexities and difficulties that have on every side beset his path, and of such nature that no other man in the State would have had the courage to face it, and then to see the noble work he has already done. The Vital Record alone is a monument to his industry. The grand work the city of Providence is now doing was put into successful operation by him, seconded by several thoughtful and intelligent gentlemen.

If the good people of our State will stand by us and our lamp of life holds out, we pledge ourself Rhode Island will have no need to blush for one of her sons.

The compiler of these Vital Records means business, and he proposes to be as persistent and as untiring in the future as he has been in the past, and he does not propose and will not be put down, but means to be heard. "Hew to the line" is the motto on his banner, and the preservation in print of our historical treasures shall be his object, and he asks the endorsement and good feelings of every intelligent citizen of Rhode Island in his behalf, and he asks them to see to it that he has a fair and square show.

All he asks for himself he is willing to concede to others, and stands ready to record every courtesy to others that he expects others to grant him. The field is broad enough for all, and he only demands that those who enter it shall enter as scholars should enter and conduct themselves as gentlemen should towards each other, and be willing to learn of each other and assist when occasion demands. All that enter the field with these sentiments will find every day in the week and Sundays in the compiler a friend, adviser, sympathizer and man.

INDEX.

TOWN OF BRISTOL.

I.

Names Occurring in Their Natural Order.

Marriages commence page 5; births page 61: deaths page 114.

II.

Names Occurring Promiscuously.

A

Abel, 93.
Allen, 9 132.
Almy, 28.
Avery, 7 10 34 41 48 53.

B

Bailey, 5 61 123.
Baker, 15 46 58
Ball, 98.
Bates, 11 15 39 49.
Blaine, 45.
Blake, 60.
Bonney, 7 13 21 22 27
   32 33 34 35 39 42 45
   48 56 57.
Bontecue, 11 12 13 19
   24 27 34 35 37 39 57
   59.
Bourne, 8 66 137.
Bowler, 33.
Bradford, 7 12 14 15 24
   26 30 36 38 51 54 55
   57 131 136.
Brag, 157.
Bristed. 5 10 24 25 27
   34 41 44.
Brower, 5 6 15 16 27
   28 32 36 39 43 48 57
   59.
Brown, 11 55 81.
Bullock, 16 36 114.
Burnham, 5 13 15 20 21
   27 39 50 51.
Burt, 5 6 8 9 11 12
   13 14 15 16 17 18 19
   20. 21 22 23 24 25 27
   28 29 31 32 33 34 35
   36 38 39 40 41 42 43
   44 46 47 48 50 51 52
   53 54 55 56 57 58 59
   60 122.
Byfield, 33.

C

Cady, 11 15 19 20 21
   24 25 26 34 39 40 44
   46 49 57.
Carey, 146 148 174.
Carr, 12 169.
Church, 7 16 34 41 47
   154.
Clarke, 25 124.
Coggeshall, 120 171.
Coit, 136.
Collins, 142.
Colton, 29.
Cooke, 39.
Cooper, 57.

Cotton, 17 19 22 26 27
   28 30 43 46 48 52 53
   54 58.
Cousins, 133.
Cummings, 113 175.

D

Davis, 7 11 34 37 79.
De Wolf, 66 74 164 168.
Dexter, 128.
Diman, 122.
Douglass, 51.
Durfee, 31 140 157.

E

Eames, 16.
Easterbrooks, 107.
Eddy, 26.

F

Fales, 10 12 13 14 166.
Finney, 132 134.
Fish, 94.
Foster, 9 172.
Freeman, 5 15 17 53 59.

G

Gardiner, 16.
Gifford, 105 119.
Gladding, 93 158.
Gorham, 115.
Graves, 48.
Greene, 114 115 137.
Griffin, 30 59.
Griswold, 15 25 30 31 38
   45 51 125 127.

H

Haskell, 37 56 158.
Harding, 135 147.
Hathaway, 17.
Hazard, 122.
Hitchcock, 15.
Holmes, 152.
Howe, 9 25.
Howland, 10 20 82 120
   167.
Hubbard, 8 44.
Hyde, 58.

I

Ingraham, 84 114.

J K

Kent, 18 19 36 42.
Kinnecut, 38.
Kirtland, 33.

L

Le Baron, 7.
Leigh, 58.
Liscomb, 115.
Little, 22.
Livesey, 6 7 11 19 20
   21 28 32 36 39 41 42
   48 49 51 57 58.
Lovell, 10.
Low, 171.
Luther, 53 128.

M

Manchester, 146.
Mann, 8 16 34 46.
Martindale, 61 .
Maxfield, 147 157.
May, 8.
McIntosh, 90.
McReady, 55.
McSparran, 22.
Merrett, 16 32 44.
Milton, 60.
Mingo, 116.
Mumford, 142.
Munro, 93 116 132 160
   174.

N

Noble, 37 42 46 48 49.
Norris, 121 164.
Norton, 62.

O

Oren, 42.
Osborne, 5 14 15 25 26
   31 33 36 42 46 48 51
   54 58.
Othman, 42.

P

Paine, 42 157.
Pearce, 40 114 115 168.
Peck, 100 119 167.
Pepperburgh, 138.
Pitman, 11.
Potter, 140.
Preston, 59.

III.

Names of Places.

INDEX.

TOWN OF WARREN.

I.

Names Occurring in Their Natural Order.

Marriages commence with page 5; births page 43; deaths page 97.

A

Abbott, 5 43.
Abel, 5
Adams, 5 43 97.
Albro, 5.
Alger, 5 43 97.
Allen, 5 43 97.
Ames, 44.
Anderson, 44.
Andrews, 5 44.
Angell, 5 44.
Anthony, 6.
Arnold, 6 44.
Ashworth, 44.
Asten, 6.

B

Babbitt, 45.
Bacon, 6.
Baker, 6 45 97
Ballot, 6.
Barden, 45.
Barker, 45.
Barnaby, 6 45.
Barnes, 45.
Barney, 6 45.
Barrett, 45.
Barrows, 6 46.
Bartlett, 7.
Barton, 7 46 97.
Battiat, 7.
Bean, 7 47.
Bebee, 8 49.
Bennett, 8 48.
Bennington, 48.
Beris, 8.
Besayude, 8 48.
Beverley, 8.
Bicknell, 48 97.
Biglow, 8.
Bishop, 8.
Blake, 8 48.
Blanchard, 8.
Blanding, 8.

Bliss, 8 48.
Booth, 48.
Borden, 48.
Bosworth, 8 48 97.
Bowen, 9 49 97.
Bowers, 10.
Bowington, 10.
Boynton, 10.
Bradford, 51.
Bragley, 51 97.
Braman, 51 97.
Brayton, 10 51.
Briggs, 10.
Brightman, 10.
Brown, 10 51 97.
Bucklin, 11.
Buffington, 11.
Bugbee, 11 52.
Bullock, 11 52 98.
Borden, 11.
Burgess, 11.
Burge, 11.
Burr, 11 52 98.
Burtch, 11 53.
Burt, 11 53 98.
Bushee, 11 53.
Butterfield, 12.
Butterworth, 12 53 98.
Butts, 54.

C

Camp, 12.
Capen, 12.
Carey, 54.
Carpenter, 12 54.
Carr, 12 54.
Cartee, 13 55.
Cary, 13.
Caussones, 13 55.
Champlain, 13 55.
Chapman, 56 98.
Chase, 13 56.
Chessman, 56.
Child, 13 56 98.
Churchill, 15 58.
Church, 15.

Clarke, 15 58.
Cobb, 15.
Cockrane, 15.
Coggeshall, 58.
Coghing, 15.
Coleman, 15.
Cole, 15 58 98.
Collimore, 17 62.
Collins, 17 62.
Comer, 17.
Comstock, 18 62.
Converse, 18.
Cooke, 18 62.
Cooley, 18.
Corey, 18.
Cornell, 62.
Cornwell, 18.
Corvin, 18.
Cottrell, 18.
Cowen, 18 63.
Cranston, 18 63 98.
Croade, 18 63 98.
Crowell, 63.
Cuffee, 18.
Cutler, 63.

D

Daggett, 18.
Daval, 18 63.
Davis, 18 64.
Dennis, 19.
Dexter, 19.
Diamond, 19.
Door, 64.
Dorrance, 19.
Drew, 19.
Dring, 19 64.
Driscoll, 19 64.
Drowne, 19 64.
Dunbar, 19.

E

Easterbrooks, 19 64 98.
Eaton, 20.

S

Salisbury, 35 86 100.
Sanders, 36 88 100.
Sargen, 87.
Sawtelle, 88.
Scott, 36.
Seymour, 36.
Sharkey, 88.
Sheldon, 36 89.
Sherman, 36 89.
Short, 36 89 100.
Shurtleff, 37.
Simonds, 37.
Simons, 37 89.
Simmons, 37 89.
Simms, 89.
Sisson, 37 89 100.
Slade, 37.
Smith, 37 90 100.
Snell, 38 91 100.
Sparks, 38 91.
Spellman, 91.
Spencer, 38.
Stanley, 38 91.
Steavens, 38.
Stephens, 38 91.
Stillwell, 91.
Stockbridge, 38.
Stockford, 38 91.
Stone, 91.
Surgens, 38.
Swazey, 91.
Sweet, 91.

T

Tabor, 38 100.

Talbot, 38 91.
Tallman, 38.
Tanner, 38 91.
Taylor, 38.
Thomas, 38 91 100.
Thompkins, 38.
Thompson, 38 92.
Thornton, 38 92.
Threadkill, 38.
Thurber, 38 92 100.
Thurston, 39.
Threadway, 39.
Tibbetts, 39.
Tiffany, 92 100.
Tilley, 39.
Tillinghast, 39.
Tillson, 39.
Toogood, 39 92.
Townsend, 93.
Tripp, 39 93 100.
Trott, 39 93.
Troys, 93.
Tucker, 93.
Turner, 39 93 100.
Tustin, 39.
Tyler, 39 93

U V

Vance, 39 93.
Van Doorn, 40.
Varnum, 40.
Viall, 40 93.
Vibberd, 40.
Vickery, 40.
Vinnicum, 40 94.
Vinniman, 40 100.
Vorce, 40.

W

Walden, 40.
Walker, 40.
Wardwell, 40 94.
Ware, 94.
Warner, 40 94.
Warren, 40 94.
Waterman, 40.
Watson, 40 94.
Weight, 40.
Welch, 40 94.
Westcott, 40.
West, 41 94.
Whitaker, 41.
Wheaton, 41 94 101.
Wheeler, 41 95.
Whitaker, 95.
Whitehorn, 41.
Whitely, 41.
White, 41.
Whiting, 41 95 101.
Whitman, 41.
Whitmarsh, 42 95.
Wilbour, 42.
Willard, 42 95.
Williams, 42 95 101.
Wilmarth, 42.
Wing, 42.
Winslow, 42 95.
Winston, 42.
Woodmancy, 42 96.
Wood, 42 96.
Wright, 42 96.

X Y Z

Young, 96.

II.

Names Occurring Promiscuously.

A

Adams, 7 32 39.
Alger, 23.
Allen, 5 10 11 12 15 18
  19 22 23 26 28 31 33
  40 41 42 98.
Almy, 31.
Austin, 15.

B

Baker, 5 6 7 8 9 10 11
  12 13 14 16 17 18 19
  20 21 22 23 24 25 26
  27 28 29 30 31 32 33
  34 35 36 37 38 39 40
  41 42.
Barney, 22.
Barton, 6 8 14 16 20 21
  22 24 25 27 28 30 32
  33 34 35 36 38 39 40.

Benedict, 37.
Benton, 22.
Bicknell, 18.
Bliss, 30 38.
Blodgett, 5.
Bonney, 8 17 19 24 38.
Bradford, 12 34.
Brett, 7.
Briggs, 30.
Burden, 34.
Bullock, 30.
Burlingame, 7.
Burr, 42.
Burt, 13 37.
Bushee, 40.
Butler, 21.

C

Chapman, 14 15 17.
Chase, 23.
Child, 14.

Clift, 6.
Cole, 9 14 15 20 21 23
  24 28 30 32 35 43.
Crocker, 6.
Crowell, 9 12.

D

Daval, 88.
Dayman, 37.
Dowling, 15 23 39.

E

Eddy, 10 42.

F

Ellis, 22.
Fuller, 6.
Fyfe, 10 15 19 31 34 40
  42.

III.

Names of Places.

INDEX.

TOWN OF BARRINGTON.

I.

Names Occurring in Their Natural Order.

Marriages commence with page 5; births and deaths page 20.

K

Kelley, 12 29.
Kenney, 12.
Kennicutt. 12 30.
Kent, 12 30.
Kingsley, 13.
King, 13.
Knight, 13 31.

L

Ladieu, 13.
Ladue, 13 31.
Lawton, 13.
Lilley, 13 31.
Low, 13.
Luther, 13 31.
Lyon, 13.

M

Macomber, 13.
Manchester, 13.
Marshall, 13 31.
Martin, 13 31.
Mason, 14 32.
Mathews, 14 32.
Mathewson, 14 32.
Mauran, 14 32.
Maxcy, 14.
Maxfield, 14 33.
Maxwell, 14.
May, 14 33.
Medbury, 14 33.
Medcuff, 14.
Meigs, 14.
Meone, 33.
Miller, 15 33.
Milleman, 15.
Moll, 15.
Moore, 15.
Moran, 33.
Munroe, 15 33.

N O

Olney, 33.
Ormsbee, 33.
Otis, 15.

P

Pearce, 15.
Padelford, 15.
Paine, 15.
Peck, 15 33.
Peney, 16.
Pettis, 16.
Pierce, 16.
Phillips, 34.
Phippen, 16.
Potter, 16 34.
Pomham, 16.

Q

Quam, 35.
Quash, 16.

R

Rawson, 16 35.
Read, 16 35.
Rea, 16.
Redding, 16.
Remmington, 16 35.
Rhodes, 16.
Richmond, 16 35.
Rich, 16.
Robinson, 16.
Ross, 16 35.
Rounds, 16.

S

Sabin, 17.
Salisbury, 17 35.
Sawtelle, 17 35.
Scott, 17.
Seymour, 17.
Sharp, 17.
Shears, 17.
Sheldon. 17.
Short, 17 35.
Simmons. 17.
Sisson, 17.
Smith, 17 36.
Snell, 17.
Soper, 17.
Stanley, 17 37.
Sweetland, 18.
Swift, 18.

T

Taber, 18.
Talman, 18.
Tanner, 18.
Taylor, 18.
Tew, 18 37.
Thayer, 18.
Thomas, 18 37.
Throope, 37.
Thurber, 18 37.
Tibbins, 18.
Tiffany, 18 37.
Tilley, 37.
Toogood, 18.
Torrey, 18.
Townsend, 18 37.
Tripp, 18 37.
Tyler, 18 37.

U

Utter, 18.

V

Viall, 19 38.

W

Wardwell, 19.
Waterman, 19 38.
Watson, 19 38.
Webber, 19.
Welley, 38.
West, 19.
Whaley, 19.
Wheeler, 19.
Whelen, 19.
Wheton. 19.
White, 19.
Wightman, 19.
Witherell, 19.
Worseley, 19.
Wood, 19.

X Y Z

Young, 19.

II.

Names Occurring Promiscuously.

A

Allen, 6 7 8 9 10 14 15
   16 17 19.
Andrews, 36.

B

Baker, 7 10 11 13 18.
Ball, 37.
Bonney, 17.
Bowen, 5 15

Bradford, 15.
Brown, 33.

C

Carpenter, 17.

III.

Names of Places.

Vital Record of Rhode Island.

1636=1850.

FIRST SERIES.

BIRTHS, MARRIAGES AND DEATHS.

A Family Register for the People.

BY JAMES N. ARNOLD,

EDITOR OF THE NARRAGANSETT HISTORICAL REGISTER.

"Is My Name Written in the Book of Life?"

Vol. 6.   **BRISTOL.**   **Part I.**

Published under the Auspices of the General Assembly.

PROVIDENCE, R. I:
NARRAGANSETT HISTORICAL PUBLISHING COMPANY.
1894.

AN ACT INCORPORATING THE FIVE TOWNS SECURED FROM MASSACHUSETTS.

In General Assembly at Providence, January 27, 1746-7.

AN ACT for Incorporating the Inhabitants of the Lands lately Taken Into This Colony by the Settlement of the Eastern Boundary Into Five Townships.

Whereas, His Majesty has been graciously pleased by his royal determination to settle the eastern boundaries of this Colony, whereby several large tracts of land and a great number of inhahitants are taken under Jurisdiction of this Government, and it being absolutely necessary for tbe well governing of tbe said people that the said tracts of land, with the inhabitants thereon, be set off and incorporated into Townsbips, and the same being conveniently situated for the making of five Townships;

Be it, therefore, enacted by the General Assemhly, and by the authority of tbe same it is enacted, that the aforesaid tracts of land, with tbe inhabitants thereon, be set off and incorporated into five Towns in tbe following manner, viz.:

All tbat part which heretofore has been called Bristol, with tbe inhabitants thereon, be set off and incorporated into a Township by the name of Bristol; and that part wbich was beretofore (known) as part of Tiverton, with a part of Dartmouth and Freetown, adjoining thereto, be incorporated into a Township by the name of Tiverton; and that part which bas beretofore heen a part of Little Compton and a part of Dartmouth thereto adjoining be incorporated into a Townsbip by the name of Little Compton; and that the line which formerly divided Tiverton from Little Compton he extended eastly to the Colony line, and tbe whole to be the dividing lines hetween said Towns; and tbat part wbich bas hitherto been a part of Swansey and Barrington, with a small part of Rehohoth thereto adjoining, with the inhabitants thereon, be incorporated into a Township by the name of Warren; and that part which has been commonly called and known by the name of the Gore of Land, witb the inhahitants tbereon, be incorporated into a Township by the name of Cumberland; and tbat the inhabitants of eacn respective Town, for tbe time being, shall have and enjoy equal liberties and privileges with the other Towns of this Colony, agreeably to our Charter.

And be it further enacted by tbe autbority aforesaid that a special Justice of the Peace be chosen and appointed in eacb of the above-mentioned Towns to keep His Majesty's peace and to call the inhabitants of the respective Towns together by a warrant, to meet on tbe second Tuesday in February next, to cboose such Town Officers as are directed by the laws of this Colony and also deputies to represent said Towns at the adjournment of this Assembly.

And that the said Justices be commissionated by His Honor the Governor, and to continue until the next session of this Assembly; and tbat the General Treasurer furnish eacb of tne above-mentioned Towns with a Colony law book; and that the Secretary send to each of the said Towns a copy of the late act of Assemhly, directing the manner of making freemen and regulating tbe method of voting; and that said law hooks and copies of said act be delivered to the above-mentioned Justices as soon as conveniently may be.

And be it further enacted by the authority aforesaid that every man inhabiting within the above-mentioned Towns of Bristol, Tiverton, Little-Compton, Warren and Cumberland, who is possessed of land or real estate sufficient by the laws of this Colony to qualify him for a freeman, and the eldest sons of all such freeholders, be and they are hereby declared freemen of the respective Towns, and also of this Colony; and to govern themselves in voting agreeably to the laws of this Colony.

And be it further enacted by the authority aforesaid that the following persons be and they are hereby chosen and appointed special Justices of the Peace for the above-mentioned Towns, viz.:

Jonathan Peck, Esq., for the Town of Bristol; John Manchester, Esq., for the Town of Tiverton; William Richmond, Esq., for the Town of Little Compton; Matthew Allen, Esq., for the Town of Warren; and John Bartlett, Esq., for the Town of Cumberland.

God Save the King.

R. I. Colonial Records, Vol. V., pages 204-6.

BRISTOL.

INTENTIONS AND MARRIAGES.

A

4-4   ABEL Lucy, and Bennett Munro, (also 4-12), July 6, 1818.

1-87   ABIGAIL ——, and Osque ——, (Int.) Nov. 12, 17—.

1-1   ADAMS Elisha, and Mehitable Carey, Dec. 18, 1689.

1-1   "   James, and Mary ——, Jan. 3, 1689.

1-1   "   Edward, and Elizabeth Walley, May 19, 1692.

1-62, 63   "   Elizabeth, and George Kezzer, (Int.), Dec. 23, 1718.

1-2   "   William, of Samuel and Rebecca, and Hannah Swan, dau. of Capt. John Wardwell and Hannah, his wife; m. by Rev. Henry Wight, Oct. 23, 1791.

1-2   ADY William, and Hannah Smith, July 19, 1697.

1-105   "   Mrs. Abigail, and Hezekiah Salisbury, May 17, 1753.

1-2   "   John, of Providence, and Mrs. Dorothy West, of Bristol; m. by Rev. John Burt, May 25, 1755.

1-106   "   Ruth, and Barnard Salisbury, Feb. 22, 1770.

4-52   ALDRIDGE Alvin C., and Nancy T. Sweet; m. by Rev. V. R. Osborn, Sept. 5, 1842.

4-50   ALGER Martha, and Henry Sanford, April 27, 1842.

4-53   "   Joseph, and Mary C. Penno; m. by Rev. Edward Freeman, May 14, 1842.

4-54   "   Almeda, and Albert Lake, Oct. 5, 1843.

1-15   ALLEN Mary (widow), and William Corbett, July 10, 1710.

1-5   "   Jemima, and Benjamin Bosworth, (Int.), April 15, 1727.

1-41   "   Rebecca, and John Gladding, (Int.), (also 1-42), June 19, 1730; m. July 6, 1730.

1-1   "   William, of Bristol, and Patience Luther, of Swansey, (Int.), March 22, 1735.

1-52   "   Madame Rachel, and Samuel Howland, (Int.), Feb. 18, 1741-2.

1-28   "   Mrs. Louis, and William Durs, (Int.), April 23, 1746.

1-1   "   James, and Mrs. Sarah Smith; m. by Rev. John Burt, June 9, 1751.

1-2   "   Mrs. Hannah, and Nathan Munro, Nov. 21, 1751.

1-2   "   Ebenezer, of Rehoboth, Mass., son of Ebenezer, deceased, of Barrington, R. I., and Mrs. Mary Paine, of Bristol, daughter of Thomas Bailey, of Little Compton, deceased; m. by Rev. Charles Thompson, Dec. 7, 1775.

1-2   "   William, grandson of Joseph and Joanna, and Eleanor Bailey, of Archibald and Sarah; m. by Rev. Henry Wight, March 31, 1801.

1-128   "   Mary, and Seth Whitemarsh, Nov. 7, 1911.

4-10   "   George W., of Barrington, and Harriet Jones, of Bristol; m. by Rev. John Bristed, Dec. 8, 1830.

4-10   "   Mercy Ann, and Thomas Dennis, Jan. 3, 1836.

4-83   "   Nancy A., and James G. Mason, Sept. 16, 1838.

4-48   "   John H., of Bristol, and Sarah D. Havens, of North Kingstown; m. by Rev. William L. Brower, Sept. 14, 1841.

4-53   "   Thomas N., and Hannah M. Manchester; m. by Rev. Edward Freeman, March 20, 1843.

4-59   "   Jabez L., and Abby P. Welch; m. by Rev. Hezekiah Burnham, Aug. 12, 1845.

1-2   ANDERSON James, and Philo Munro, (col.); m. by Rev. Henry Wight, March 18, 1806.

1-1   ANDROS Ephraim, and Sarah Mowry, Sept. 24, 1713.

1-18   ANTHONY Alice, and Jeremiah Church, (Indians), (Int.) June 9, 1722.

1-1   "   ——, (col.), and Sarah Howard, (col.) (Int.) Nov. 13, 1749.

1-1   "   John, and Mrs. Sarah Church; m. by Rev. John Burt, Aug. 21, 1754.

1-40   ANTILL Mary, and William Gallup, (also 1-41), (Int.) Nov. 25, 1721; m. Dec. 19, 1721.

1-1   ARCHER John, and Mehitable Shears, Jan. 5, 1692.

1-15   ARNOLD Damarius, and John Carey, March 13, 1700.

1-2   "   William, of Caleb and Leria, and Elizabeth Bosworth, of William and Elizabeth; m. by Rev. Henry Wight, March 25, 1802.

4-48   "   Rufus, and Sarah Lincoln; m. by Rev. William L. Brower, May 16, 1842.

4-69   ASHWORTH George C., and Fanny Moore, both of Warren; m. by Rev. Richard Livesey, Oct. 26, 1848.

1-74   AUDINITH Keneth, and Peter Marshall, June 2, 1808.

1-94   AUDINET Maria, and William Paul, (col.), Dec. 11, 1811.

4-34   AUSTIN Harriet N., and George T. B. Chaffee, March 18, 1839.

4-44   "   Margaret A., and George H. Munro, (also 4-48), Feb. 17, 1841.

B

4-55   BAARS J. Frederick, and Lucretia N. Luce; m. by Rev. Thomas Shepard, Aug. 22, 1842.

1-5   BAKER Amos, and Elizabeth Munro, (Int.) Jan. 1, 1724.

4-13   "   John, of Hamburg, Europe, and Ann Bainbridge, of Virginia; m. by Rev. Henry Wight, Nov. 13, 1833.

4-50   "   Martin N., and Betsey S. Brown; m. by Rev. G. F. Sanborn, June 19, 1842.

1-92   BAILEY Mrs. Mary, and Stephen Paine, Aug. 18, 1751.

1-13   "   David, of David and Elizabeth, and Rebecca Waldron of Nathaniel and Hannah; m. by Rev. Henry Wight, Jan. 18, 1801.

1-2   "   Eleanor, and William Allen, March 31, 1801.

4-7   "   Betsey, and Job Briggs, Jr., Nov. 24, 1826.

4-13   BAINBRIDGE Ann, and John Baker, Nov. 13, 1833.

4-61   BALLOU Henry G., of Cumberland, and Sarah L. Fales, of Bristol; m. by Rev. Thomas Shepard, June 8, 1846.

1-6   BALL Benjamin, and Hannah Simmons, of Swansey, (also 1-7), (Int.) Oct. 25, 1734; m. by Rev. John Usher, —gber 14, 1734.

1-44   "   Elizabeth, and John Glover, March 17, 1751.

4-50   "   Phebe R., and Samuel Mott, April 17, 1842.

4-81   BARCLAY Walter, widower, aged 40 years, born New York city, resident Newport, R. I., and Sarah B. Smith, widow, aged 29 years, born and resident of Cuba, W. I.; m. by Rev. U. T. Tracy, Feb. 26, 1876.

1-7   BARKER Samuel, Jr., of Scituate, and —— ——, of Bristol, (Int.) Oct. 15, 1839.

1-7   "   Ignatius, of Lebanon, Conn., and Jemima Gladding, of Bristol, (Int.) Feb. 27, 1740.

4-38   "   Walter C. F., and Abbie Luther; m. by Rev. Henry Sullings, Nov. 10, 1839.

4-61   BARLOW Lewis, A., and Abbie H. Dennis, both of Newport; m. by Rev. Thomas Shepard, Sept. 30, 1845.

4-65   BARNARD Albert W., of Nantucket, Mass., and Mary A. Meigs, of James, of Bristol; m. by Rev. James N. Sykes, Dec. 5, 1847.

4-48   BARNES Eliza F., and Freeborn Coggeshall, Sept. 26, 1841.

1-4   BARNEY John, and Mary Throop, Nov. 4, 1686.

1-111   "   Dorcas, and Daniel Throop, Aug. 23, 1689.

1-119   "   Sarah, and Anthony Van Santvoored, Jr., —— —, 1814.

4-13   BARNS John, son of William and Lois, of Bristol, Maine, and Nancy Waldron, of Thomas and Ruth; m. by Rev. Henry Wight, Jan. 17, 1832.

4-13 BARROWS Joseph, and Althea Clark; m. by Rev. E. K. Avery, July 14, 1833.
4-50 " Rosabella, and Francis L. D. Diman, May 16, 1842.
1-5 BARRUS Stephen, and Lydia Eddy, both of Swansey; m. by Simon Davis, Justice of the Peace, Sept. 27, 1725.
4-70 " Benjamin, and Zylphia Ann Field; m. by Rev. Richard Livesey, June 26, 1849.
1-20 BARTON Patience, and Hezekiah Child, Jan. 13, 1757.
1-16 BATES Rachel, and David Carey, (Int.) Jan. 20, 1721-2.
1-15 BATRAP, Eleanor, and William Corbet, Sept. 19, 1683.
1-12 BATT James, son of James and Mary, of Dorsetshire, England, and Hannah Waldron, dau. of Thomas and Lucretia; m. by Rev. Henry Wight, Jan. 6, 1807.
4-73 " Abby Howland, and John Bennett Munro, Dec. 25, 1846.
1-4 BAYLEY Joshua, and Mrs. Mary Gallup; m. by Col. Benjamin Church, Justice of the Peace, Jan. 9, or 10, 1711-12.
1-26 BEARCRAFT Sarah, and William Dadey, Jan. 28, 1694.
4-6 BEARS Enock, son of Timothy and Anne, and Charlotte Hathaway, of Lewis and Deborah; m. by Rev. Henry Wight, Oct. 27, 1825.
1-13 BEBEE Daniel, and Hannah Smith (Int.), July 11, 1739.
1-7 " Daniel, of Newport, and Hannah Smith, of Bristol; m. by Rev. Barnabus Taylor, Sept. 1, 1739.
1-4 BEDFORD Stephen, and Naomi Gage, Feb. 15, 1693.
1-32 BELCHER Ruth, and Joseph Eddy, (Int.) Sept. 7, 1728.
4-69 BENARD Senature, and Phebe A. Williston; m. by Rev. Richard Livesey, June 12, 1848.
1-4 BENNETT James, and Ruth Rogers, July 12, 1694.
4-28 " Messadore T., of Dighton, Mass., and Martha F. Maxwell, of Bristol; m. by Rev. Otis Thompson, April 8, 1838.
4-77 " Adams J., and Martha Abby Spooner; m. by Rev. Isaac Bonney, Nov. 1, 1853.
1-9 BICKNELL Joshua, Esq., of Warren, and Mrs. Hannah Norton, of Bristol, Sept. 10, 1763.
1-112 BILLINGS Mary, and Thomas Throop, Jr., (Int.) Feb. 17, 1732-3.
1-6,7 BIRGE Samuel, and Hannah Bragg, (Int.) Oct. 14, 1727; m. by Rev. John Usher, —gber 9, 1727.
1-71,73 BISHOP Rachel, and Charles McCartee, (Int.) May 4, 1732; m. May 18, 1732.
1-4 BLAGROVE Nathaniel, (Merchant,) and Mrs. Elizabeth Hayman, (widow.) June 18, 1690.
1-11 BLAKE Ebenezer, of Middletown, Conn., son of Jonathan, and Elizabeth Norris, of Bristol, dau. of John; m. by Daniel Bradford, Justice of the Peace, May 13, 1779.
1-57 " Elizabeth, and Philip Wheeler Ingalls, Jan. 4, 1801.
1-11 " Elizabeth, and Nathaniel Bliss, —. 5, 1809.
4-12 " Samuel, of Ebenezer and Keziah, and Martha Van Doorn, of Mark Anthony and Phebe; m. by Rev. Henry Wight, Sept. 3, 1833.
4-4 " Richard G., and Mrs. Sarah Everett; m. by Rev. Ephraim Scott, Aug. 2, 1840.
4-57 " Abby, and John Rawson, April 14, 1845.
1-42 BLANDING Mehitable, and William Gladding, (Int.) May 25, 1739 (also 1-43); m. June 30, 1739.
1-103 BLEWAT Sarah, and William Steadman, (Int.) April 20, 1720.
1-11 BLISS Nathaniel, of Oliver and Keziah, and Elizabeth Blake, of Ebenezer and Abigail; m. by Rev. Henry Wight, — 5, 1809.
4-69 " Peddy, and William Franklin, Sept. 12, 1848.
4-73 BLOSSOM Barney, and Nancy M. Davis, of Somerset; m. by Rev. Richard Livesey, Dec. 25, 1849.
4-26 BLYE William M., of William, and Emeline Hadley, of Andrew; m. by Rev. Isaac Bonney, Oct. 27, 1829.
4-50 BLY William, of New Bedford, Mass., and Martha O. Townsend, of Bristol; m. by G. F. Sanborn, May 23, 1842.
4-79 BOGERT Theodore P., and Eliza T. Howe; m. by Rev. C. F. LeBaron, Nov. 3, 1851.
4-32 BOOTH Susan J., and Henry A. Manchester, July 9, 1839.

1-58	BORDEN Elizabeth, and Benjamin Jones, Sept. 18, 1696.
1-12	"	Parker, of Capt. Joseph and Peace, and Dolly Church, of Samuel and Ann; m. by Rev. Henry Wright, March 31, 1796.
4-48	"	Hannah, and Richard D. Smith, Aug. 4, 1834.
1-5	BORLAND Francis, of Boston, and Mrs. Elizabeth McIntosh, of Bristol, (Int.) Aug. 3, 1724.
4-61	BOSS Abby, and William Guild, Aug. 4, 1845.
1-4	BOSWORTH Bellamy, and Mary Smith, Nov. 11, 1685.
1-4	"	John, and Mrs. Hannah LeFavour, both of Boston, (Int.) Sept. 13, 1718.
1-5	"	Benjamin, and Ruth Lowder, (Int.) Dec. 20, 1718.
1-5	"	Jeremiah, and Susannah Field, of Brantry, (Int.) Jan. 7, 1726.
1-5	"	Benjamin, of Bristol, and Jemima Allen, of Barrington, (Int.) April 15, 1727.
1-5	"	Nathaniel, (cooper), of Bristol, and Elizabeth Lindsey, (widow), of Newport, Aug. 18, 1727.
1-122	"	Mary, and Jeremiah Wheelwright, (Int.) Aug. 21, 1727.
1-6	"	Jacob, of Bristol, and Lydia Jones, of Taunton, (Int.) Dec. 9. 1727.
1-61	"	Sarah, and Thomas Kinnecut, (Int.) May 18, 1728.
1-17, 18	"	Hannah, and Joshua Chase, (Int.) Feb. 20, 1730; m. March 18, 1730-1.
1-71, 72	"	Sarah, and Bennett Munro, Oct. 13, 1733; m. —gber 11, 1733.
1-98, 99	"	Sarah, and Joseph Rice, (Int.) Sept. 28, 1734; m. Nov. 7, 1734.
1-90	"	Bridget, and Michael Phillips, Oct. 30, 1736.
1-90	"	Mary, and Edward Paine, (Int.) Feb. 2, 1739.
1-15, 18	"	Ruth, and Nathaniel Church, (Int.) March 14, 1740; m. May 21, 1741.
1-7	"	John, and Mary Howard, (Int.) Aug. 8, 1740.
1-90	"	Rebecca, and John Papillion, (Int.) Sept. 22, 1740.
1-8	"	John, and Mary Hayward; m. by Nathaniel Hubbard, Justice of Peace, Oct. 2, 1740.
1-91, 92	"	Rebecca, and Samuel Papillion, (Int.) June 18, 1743; m. July 3, 1743.
1-8	"	Bellamy, of Bristol, and Elizabeth Mayhew, of Chilmark, Mass., (Int.) Feb. 23, 1744.
1-8	"	William, and Mary Fales, (Int.) Feb. 27, 1744.
1-8	"	Henry, and Mrs. Phebe Eddy, (Int.) Feb. 15, 1745; m. by Rev. John Burt, March 3, 1745.
1-18, 19	"	Mrs. Elizabeth, and Thomas Church, (Int.) May 12, 1746; m. July 1, 1746.
1-19	"	Casco, servant of John, and Hagar Munro, servant of Mrs. May; m. by Shearjashub Bourne, Justice of the Peace, Jan. 11, 1749.
1-9	"	Bellamy, and Mrs. Esther Maxfield; m. by Rev. John Burt, May 17, 1750.
1-9	"	Samuel, and Mrs. Elizabeth Peck; m. by Rev. John Burt, Oct. 8, 1752.
1-9	"	Obadiah, and Mrs. Mary Lawton; m. by Rev. John Burt, Feb. 8, 1753.
1-9	BOSWORTH Benjamin, of Westport, and Mrs. Mary Church, of Bristol; m. by Rev. John Burt, July 19, 1764.
1-66	"	Mrs. Mary, and Thomas Lawton, Jan. 2, 1766.
1-10	"	William, Jr., son of William, and Elizabeth Roffney, of Solomon, dec.; m. by Rev. John Burt, Dec. 19, 1771.
1-127	"	Althea, and William Wilson, Jan. 16, 1774.
1-106	"	Elizabeth, and Thomas Swan, April 17, 1774.
1-127	"	Mary, and Thomas Wilson, May 2, 1774.
1-114	"	Elizabeth, and Amos Thurber, April 12, 1795.
1-2	"	Elizabeth, and William Arnold, March 25, 1802.
1-117	"	Mary Bradford, and Capt. Aaron Usher, May 24, 1812.
1-22	"	Ann, and Peter Church, Dec. 12, 1813.
4-2	"	Ebenezer, and Ruth B. Townsend; m. by Rev. Joel Mann, March 28, 1820.
4-2	"	Samuel, Jr., and Ann Bourne, of John W. and Noney; m. by Rev. Joel Mann, March 27, 1821.

4-16	BOSWOTH	Ann Potter, and Thomas Richmond, Aug. 10, 1829.
4-10	"	Sarah, and Scott Greene, Dec. 17, 1830.
4-40	"	Mary, and Hiram B. Munro, Sept. 2, 1840.
4-61	"	Anne Elizabeth, and Henry Waring, Sept. 3, 1844.
1-9	BOURNE	Shearjashub, and Mrs. Ruth Church, April 19, 1747.
1-20	"	Mrs. Sarah, and Job Coggeshall, Oct. 7, 1753.
1-10	"	Shearjashub, Jr., and Ruth Waldron; m. by Rev. John Burt, March 4, 1773.
1-11	"	Aaron, of Bristol, and Ruth Carr, of Warren; m. by J. Townsend, Justice of the Peace, March 10, 1781.
1-14	"	Shearjashub, of Bristol, and Rachel Kent, of Barrington; m. by Samuel Allen, Justice of the Peace, Nov. 20, 1793.
1-12	"	Allen, of Shearjashub and Ruth, and Elizabeth Smith, of Josiah and Elizabeth; m. by Rev. Henry Wight, June 7, 1805.
1-38	"	Mary, and Thomas Fales, Jan. 27, 1808.
4-1	"	Elizabeth, and John Chadwick, Jan. 27, 1821.
4-2	"	Ann, and Samuel Bosworth, Jr., March 27, 1821.
4-2	"	Mary Ann, and Penuel Corbett, March 27, 1821.
4-36	"	Ruth, and John DeWolf, Aug. 19, 1839.
4-40	"	Phillip B., and Adeline D. Tallman; m. by Rev. Chester W. Turner, Dec. 30, 1840.
1-69	BOWEN	Ruth, and John Munro, (Int.) Oct. 17, 1718.
4-6	"	Champlain, and Betsey Meigs; m. by Rev. Thomas W. Tucker, April 10, 1825.
4-6	"	Francis G., of Paul, and Mary C. Peirce, of Mason W.; m. by John Howe, Justice, April 10, 1836.
4-22	"	Abby, and Edward M. Luther, Aug. 28, 1836.
4-38	"	James M., and Charlotte M. Jones; m. by Rev. Henry Sullings, Nov. 8, 1839.
4-56	"	Mrs. Julia Ann, and Jonathan Peckham, Oct. 7, 1844.
4-59	"	Betsey M., and Charles H. Jones, Dec. 21, 1845.
4-63	"	Maria R., and Edward Goff, Sept. 8, 1846.
1-4	BOWERMAN	Tristum, and Ann Hooper, July 28, 1685.
1-61	"	Hannah, and Thomas Kinnecut, May 2, 1706.
1-4	"	Samuel, and Elizabeth Gallup, April 20, 1710.
1-26	"	Sarah, and John Dyer, (Int.) Dec. —, 1718.
1-112	"	Ann, and Samuel Toogood, (Int.) Oct. 21, 1726.
4-32	BOWERS	Wanton, and Sarah Pierce; m. by Rev. Thomas Shepard, Feb. 18, 1839.
4-42	BOWLER	Alice, and Rufus B. Drown, June 25, 1840.
4-73	"	Maria E., and Thomas F. Lindsey, Jan. 10, 1850.
1-8	BOYCE	Benjamin, and Sarah Dyer, (Int.) April 21, 1744; m. May 17, 1744.
4-73	BOYLE	Michael, of Ireland, and Catherine McDonald, of Pictou, N. S.; m. by Rev. Thomas Shepard, March 28, 1850.
1-9	BRADFORD	Daniel, and Mrs. Mary Church; m. by Rev. John Burt, Oct. 1, 1749.
1-84	"	Mrs. Hopestill, and Joseph Nash, Jan. 9, 1756.
1-9	"	Elijah, and Mrs. Mary Lindsey; m. by Rev. John Burt, Feb. 6, 1763.
1-10	"	Daniel, of Capt. Gershom, deceased, of Bristol, and Susannah Jarvis, of Leonard, of Boston; m. by Rev. John Burt, Sept. 25, 1771.
1-38	"	Elizabeth, and Nathaniel Fales, (also 4-41), Sept. 26 or 23, 1773.
1-21	"	Priscilla, and Sylvester Child, Jan. 15, 1775.
1-11	"	Major William, Esq., son of Hon. William, of Bristol, and Betsey Bloom James, of Newport; m. by Theodore Foster, Justice, July 11, 1777.
1-46	"	Polly, and Henry Goodwin, May 20, 1782.
1-30	"	Anna, and James DeWolf, Jan. 7, 1790.
1-21	"	Lydia, and Charles Collins, Oct. 8, 1797.
1-129	"	Mary, and Elijah Willard, March 28, 1799.
1-13	"	Daniel, Jr., son of Daniel and Susannah, and Sarah Reynolds, daughter of Joseph and Sarah; m. by Rev. Henry Wight, Nov. 29, 1799.

1-12 BRADFORD William, son of Major William and Elizabeth, and Mary Smith, of Nathaniel and Parnel; m. by Rev. Henry Wight, Feb. 1, 1804.

4-1 " Nancy, and Nicholas Peck, Oct. 22, 1815.

4-16 " Harriet DeWolf, and William R. Taylor, Sept. 1, 1833.

4-28 " Charles J., of Columbia, Pa., and Elizabeth Swan, of Bristol; m. by Rev. Thomas Shepard, Feb. 28, 1838.

4-36 " William, 2nd, and Ann W. Nooning; m. by Rev. Thomas Shepard, March 28, 1839.

4-32 " Peter J., and Miss Lucretia Coit; m. by Rev. John Bristed, June 16, 1839.

4-57 " Walter, of John, and Sarah W. Macumber, of Otis; m. by Rev. James N. Sykes, June 19, 1845.

4-73 " Hannah, and George H. Reynolds, June 9, 1850.

1-50 BRADLEY Susannah, and Edward Hammon, Jan. 5, 1684.

1-6, 7 " John, of New Haven, and Mrs. Elizabeth Peck, of Bristol, (Int.) Sept. 8, 1729; m. by Timothy Fales, Justice of the Peace, Dec. 5, 1729.

1-40 BRAGG Abigail, and Abraham Guy, (Int.) Jan. 20, 1721-2; m. Feb. 6, 1721.

1-6 " Nicholas, and Bethia Howland; m. by Rev. John Usher, May 19, 1725.

1-41 " Experience, and Ebenezer Gladding, (Int.) Oct. 30, 1725; m. Nov. 16, 1725.

1-5 " Henry, and Mrs. Elizabeth Davis, (Int.) July 21, 1727.

1-6, 7 " Hannah, and Samuel Birge, (Int.) Oct. 14, 1727; m. —gbr 9, 1727.

1-70, 71 " Mrs. Abagail and Samuel Morris, (Int.) Sept. 16, 1728; m. Oct. 31, 1728.

1-27 " Susannah, and Capt. John Day, (Int.) July 24, 1731.

1-27 " Mrs. Bethia, and Simeon Davis, (Int.) Aug. 8, 1733; m. Aug. 29, 1733.

1-51 " Susannah, and William Hoar, (Int.) Oct. 26, 1734; m. —gbr 14, 1734.

1-6 " John, and Mary Gallup, (Int.) June 12, 1736.

1-90, 91 " Ann, and Simeon Potter, (Int.) Feb. 7, 1740-1; m. March 5, 1740.

1-125 " Mrs. Elizabeth, and David Wilson, Sept. 12, 1751.

1-74 " Mrs. Catherine, and Nathan Munro, July 11, 1756.

4-46 BRAYLEY Martha, and Jonathan Brown, Oct. 10, 1841.

1-6 BRETLAND Thomas, of city of Erin, in Great Britain, and Mary Dowling, of do., (Int.) no date.

1-13 BREWER Philip, mariner, and Jerusha Fairbanks, (Int.) Oct. 1, 1726.

1-90, 91 " Jerusha, and Stephen Penfield, (Int.) Feb. 20, 1737-8; m. June 13, 1738.

1-11 BREWSTER Subury, and Nancy Hathaway, of Asa and Mary; m. by Rev. Henry Wight, Nov. 10, 1803.

1-7 BRIGGS Thomas, of Dighton, Mass., and Esther Drown, of Bristol, (Int.) July 12, 1740; m. by Samuel Howland, Justice of the Peace, Aug. 18, 1740.

1-11 " Lemuel Williams, son of Lemuel and Abigail, and Mary Peak, of Nicholas and Elizabeth; m. by Rev. Henry Wight, Aug. 2, 1807.

4-7 " Job, Jr., and Betsey Bailey, of Little Compton; m. by Rev. Henry Wight, Nov. 24, 1826.

4-18 " Lemuel W., and Sarah Page; m. by Rev. Shubael Lovell, Sept. 20, 1835.

4-11 BRIGHAM Erastus F., of Troy, N. Y., and Sophia DeWolf Howes, of Bristol; m. by Rev. E. K. Avery, Oct. 17, 1832.

1-24 BRISTOL Mary, and William Cox, (Int.) Dec. 12, 1739.

1-37 BRISTOW Elizabeth, and Jeremiah Finney, (Int.) May 17, 1727.

4-55 BROWER Freelove, and John Robbins (col.), June 30, 1840.

4-61 BROWNELL Beriah A., of Portsmouth, and Harriet P. Munro, of Bristol; m. by Rev. Thomas Shepard, Feb. 16, 1846.

4-11	BROWNING Jonathan T., of Little Compton, son of Christopher and Sally, and Adella W. Nooning, of Jonathan and Hannah, of Bristol; m. by Rev. Levi Bates, July 4, 1831.
1-12	BROWNSON Francisco, and Nancy Slocum, of Ebenezer and Mary; m. by Rev. Henry Wight, July 2, 1811.
1-4	BROWN Nathaniel, and Maria Searl, both of Barrington; m. by Simeon Davis, Justice of the Peace, May 29, 1718.
1-5	" Joseph, and Elizabeth Darling, (Int.) Jan. 2, 1718.
1-92	" Lydia, and William Pearse, (Int.) Jan. 8, 1741-2; m. April 22, 1742.
1-9	" James, of Warren, and Mrs. Abigail May, of Bristol; m. by Rev. John Burt, March 5, 1767.
1-13	" Benjamin, son of Benjamin and Martha, and Rebecca Westcote, of Cornelius and Rebecca; m. by Rev. Henry Wight, Aug. 16, 1795.
4-26	" James P., and Eliza Ann Easterbrooks; m. by Rev. Thomas Shepard, April 28, 1836.
4-36	" Abby M., and Allen J. Gladding, Jan. 6, 1840.
4-46	" Jonathan, and Martha Brayley; m. by Rev. Henry Sullings, Oct. 10, 1841.
4-50	" Betsey S., and Martin N. Baker, June 19, 1842.
1-108	BRYANT Charlotte, and Richard Sturch, March 9, 1829.
1-5	BUCKLIN John, of Rehoboth, Mass., and Mary Lindsey, of Bristol, (Int.) Nov. 2, 1723.
1-80	" Mary Ann, and Dr. Caleb Miller, Aug. 14, 1816.
1-9	BULLOCK, Lennox, and Submit Burton; m. by Rev. John Burt, Dec. 29, 1754.
1-10	" Lennox, son of Daniel, deceased, of Rehoboth, Mass., and Elizabeth Fuller, of Timothy, of Rehoboth; m. by Rev. John Burt, Feb. 14, 1768.
4-40	" Roby, and Zebedee Paull, Dec. 30, 1839.
4-44	" Robert H., of Bristol, and Ellen J. Mills, of Hartford, Conn.; m. by Rev. William L. Brown, Feb. 19, 1840.
4-223	" Jonathan Russell, of Nathaniel, and Susan Amelia DeWolf, of John and Lydia, Sept. 6, 1840.
4-55	" William H., and Martha B. Simmons; m. by Rev. Thomas Shepard, Nov. 27, 1842.
4-53	" Jane W., and James Wilson, March 26, 1843.
4-223	" J. Russell, of Nathaniel and Emma Westcoat, of Stephen, of West Roxbury, Mass., Dec. 23, 1868.
1-13	BUNN Lemuel, of Nathaniel and Lydia, and Abby Munro, of Joseph and Mary; m. by Rev. Henry Wight, Aug. 13, 1807.
4-30	" Nathan M., and Mrs. Lucy Ann Simmons; m. by Rev. James C. Bontecou, Aug. 7, 1838.
1-8	BURDEN John, of Portsmouth, and Mrs. Susannah Pierce, of Bristol, (Int.) Sept. 4, 1746.
1-13	BURGESS James Peckham, of Joseph and Sarah, and Hannah Reynolds, of Joseph and Sarah; m. by Rev. Henry Wight, May 6, 1810.
4-50	" Phebe J., and Charles A. Greene, Dec. 13, 1841.
4-65	" George H., and Almira W. Warren; m. by Rev. Jonathan Cady, March 27, 1847.
4-73	" John N., and Hannah Sparks; m. by Rev. Richard Livesey, Feb. 3, 1850.
1-65	BURNHAM, Miss Mary, and Edward Little (also 1-66), (Int.) April 2, 1741; m. June 18, 1741.
1-9	BURR Elisha, of Rehoboth, and Mrs. Lydia Child, of Bristol; m. by Rev. John Burt, Nov. 12, 1794.
1-11	" Samuel, and Nancy Champlain; m. by Rev. John Pitman, April 29, 1787.
1-4	BURTON Stephen, and Mrs. Elizabeth Winslow, Sept. 4, 1684.
1-6	" William (mariner), and Mary Lawson, (Int.) March 8, 1734.
1-7	" William, and Mary Jolls; M. by Rev. John Usher, March 31, 1735.
1-9	" Submit, and Lennox Bullock, Dec. 29, 1754.
1-8	BURT Rev. John, and Mrs. Abigail Viall, of Newport, (Int.) July 24, 1741.
1-10	" Rev. John, son of John, of Boston, deceased, and Ann Ellery, of Newport, only daughter of Hon. William; m. by Rev. Ezra Styles, Nov. 17, 1768.

1-12   BURT Scipeo, servant of Rev. John, deceased, and Sukey DeWolf, servant of Capt. Mark Antony DeWolf; m. by Daniel Bradford, Justice of the Peace, March 21, 1782.
1-47   "   Phillis, and Isaac Gardner (col.), May 11, 1806.
4-36   "   Ruth W., and Marcus A. DeWolf, Sept. 3, 1839.
1-6   BUSHEE John, and Rebecca Salisbury, of Swansey, (Int.) July 19, 1731; m. by Timothy Fales Justice of the Peace, Aug. 30, 1731.
1-5   BUSH Richard, and Mary Fairbanks, (Int.) Jan. 25, 1726.
1-125   "   Mrs. Abigail, and David Wilson, May 6, 1756.
4-61   "   Ann Francis, and Benjamin F. Manchester, Aug. 3, 1845.
4-61   "   Eliza, and Hezekiah Tiffany, Nov. 24, 1845.
4-34   BUTTERWORTH Gardner M., and Susan W. Richie, both of Warren; m. by Rev. James C. Bontecue, March 3, 1839.
1-44   BUTT Mrs. Abigail and John Gilot, Dec. 26, 1756.
1-88   B—— Dorothy, and James Pinnio, May 9, 1706.

C

1-100   CALDWELL Mary, and Greenwood Reynolds, Dec. 8, 1799.
1-16   CANADA Mary, and David Carey, (Int.) Oct. 2, 1725.
1-15   CAREY David, and Elizabeth ——, Dec. 9, 1687.
1-1   "   Mehitable, and Elisha Adams, Dec. 18, 1689.
1-15   "   Matthew, and Mrs. Mary Sylvester, Aug. 1, 1693.
1-15   "   John, and Damarius Arnold; m. by —— Carr, Justice of the Peace, March 13, 1700.
1-50   "   Abigail, and Samuel Howland, May 6, 1708.
1-15   "   Josiah, and Ruth Reynolds, Nov. 9, 1710.
1-16   "   David, of Bristol, and Rachel Bates, of Dorchester, Mass., (Int.) Jan. 20, 1721-2.
1-61   "   Elizabeth, and Ephraim Kidder, (Int.) April 3, 1724; m. June 1, 1724.
1-26   "   Mary, and Terrence Donnell, (Int.) June 25, 1725.
1-16   "   David, and Mary Canada, (Int.) Oct. 2, 1725.
1-41   "   Priscilla, and Joseph Gladding, (Int.) July 2, 1726.
1-41   "   Sarah, and Jonathan Gladding, (Int.) July 2, 1726.
1-17   "   Allen, of Bristol, and Hannah Church, of Little Compton, (Int.) Oct. 9, 1731.
1-42, 43 "   Jemima, and Nathaniel Gladding, (Int.) March 10, 1732-3; m. April 2, 1733.
1-17, 18 "   Benjamin, and Thankful Taylor (Int.) Dec. 8, 1733; m. by Rev. Barnabus Taylor, Dec. 26, 1733.
1-17, 18 "   Nathaniel, of Newport, and Tabitha Howland, of Bristol, (Int.) Dec. 8, 1733; m. by Rev. Barnabus Taylor, May 12, 1734.
1-113   "   Susannah, and Dann Throop, Jr., (Int.) March 12, 1736-7.
1-17   "   Nathaniel, of Bristol, and Elizabeth Wanton, of Newport, (Int.) Aug. 4, 1739.
1-17   "   Eliza, and Gamaliel Clark, (Int.) Nov. 17, 1740.
1-88, 89 "   Tabitha, and John Peckham, (Int.) April 6, 1742; m. April 22, 1742.
1-19   "   Mrs. Hannah, and Samuel Clark, April 12, 1749.
1-37   "   Mrs. Molly, and Josiah Finney, May 19, 1751.
1-37   "   Mrs. Abigail, and John Field, March 12, 1761.
1-45   "   Mrs. Susannah, and Jonathan Gladding, Feb. 8, 1764.
1-53   "   Mrs. Phebe, and William Hoar, May 31, 1764.
1-33   "   Mrs. Abigail, and William Ellery, June 28, 1767.
1-75   "   Mrs. Hannah, and William Munro, June 9, 1768.
1-20   "   Col. Nathaniel, son of Deacon Benjamin, deceased, and Ann Pearce, of Richard, deceased; m. by Rev. John Burt, Sept. 16, 1770.
1-22   "   Lieut. Ephraim, of Benjamin, of Scotland, Ct., and Abigail Waldron, of Nathaniel, of Bristol; m. by Daniel Bradford, Justice of the Peace, July 18, 1779.
1-128   "   Hannah, and Samuel Wardwell, Oct. 31, 1810.

1-16   CARPENTER Joseph, and Abigail Newton; m. by Rev. John Usher, Feb. 16, 1723.

1-89   "   Abigail, and Obadiah Papillion, (Int.) Feb. 16, 1735.

1-122   "   Mrs. Deliverance, and John Wight, (Int.) Oct. 22, 1737.

1-73   "   Mary, and Robert Marks, (Int.) Sept. 24, 1739.

4-65   CARROLL Mary M., and Samuel B. Otterson, Aug. 14, 1847.

1-64   CARR Hannah, and Samuel Little, (Int.) Dec. 8, 1739.

1-17   "   Robert, and Priscilla Waldron, (Int.) May 3, 1740.

1-11   "   Ruth, and Aaron Bourne, March 10, 1781.

1-21   "   William, of Caleb and Ruth, and Rebecca Phillips, of Nathaniel and Sarah; m. by Rev. Henry Wight, Aug. 3, 1794.

1-15   CARTER Robert, and Hannah Lucas, April 19, 1694.

1-22   "   Alfred, son of Henry and Mary, and Fidelia West, of Thomas and Catherine; m. by Rev. Henry Wight, July 31, 1812.

1-23   "   Mrs. Rhoda, and Captain Walter Cornell, Oct. 10, 1817.

4-5   "   Elizabeth, and Elias Lake, Feb. 27, 1825.

4-38   CARTEE, Alice F., and James Lawless, June 24, 1840.

4-8   CASE, Nancy, and Isaac Lake, Sept. 17, 1812.

1-16   CASTLE, Richard, and Elizabeth ——, (Int.) May 20, 1721.

4-1   CHADWICK, of John and Mary, of Charlestown, Mass., and Elizabeth S. Bourne, of Shearjashub and Rachel, of Bristol; m. by Rev. Isaac Bonney, Jan. 27, 1821.

4-14   CHAFFEE, Aaron, of Seekonk, Mass., and Mrs. Hannah Peck, of Warren, R. I.; m. by Rev. Henry Wight, Oct. 5, 1784.

4-34   "   George T. B., of Bristol, and Harriet N. Austin, of North Kingstown; m. by Rev. James C. Bontecue, March 18, 1839.

1-32   CHAMBERLAIN, Jane, and John Eldredge, (Int.) Nov. —, 1719.

1-11   CHAMPLAIN, Nancy, and Samuel Burr, April 29, 1787.

1-20   "   Thomas, of Warren, and Mrs. Phebe Throop, of Bristol; m. by Rev. John Burt, Feb. 5, 1759.

1-17   CHANDLER John, Esq., and Madam Pearce, (Int.) Jan. 12, 1739.

1-18   "   Samuel, of Woodstock, Conn., and Dorothy Church, (Int) Sept. 11, 1741.

1-18, 19   "   John, Jr., of Worcester, Mass., and Mrs. Mary Church, of Bristol, (Int.) May 10, 1746; m. June 12, 1746, by Rev. John Burt.

1-20   "   Gardner, Esq., of Worcester, Mass., and Mrs. Hannah Greene, of Bristol; m. by Rev. John Burt, Sept. 25, 1755.

4-28   CHAPPELL George, and Prudence Peters; m. by William Throop, Justice of the Peace, Nov. 19, 1837.

1-17, 18   CHASE Joshua, of Swansey, and Hannah Bosworth, of Bristol, (Int.) Feb. 20, 1730; m. by Rev. Barnabus Taylor, March 18, 1730-1.

4-30   "   Pamelia, and Samuel Lindsey, Dec. 31, 1793.

1-108   "   Elizabeth, and Rev. Benjamin Sabin, April 1, 1818.

4-54   "   Hannah, and John B. Gorton, March 19, 1844.

4-59   "   Robinson, of Prudence Island, and Catherine Liscomb, of Bristol; m. by Rev. Hezekiah Burnham, Sept. 10, 1845.

1-19   CHILD Sylvester, of Bristol, and Abigail Miller, of Warren, Jan. 19, 1748.

1-20   "   Hezekiah, of Bristol, and Patience Barton, of Warren; m. by Rev. John Burt, Jan. 13, 1757.

1 9   "   Mrs. Lydia, and Elisha Burr, Nov. 12, 1764.

1-21   "   Sylvester, of Warren, and Rebecca Miller, Aug. 1, 1773.

1-21   "   Sylvester, of Warren, son of James, late of Swansey, dec., and Priscilla Bradford, of Daniel, of Bristol; m. by Rev. John Burt, Jan. 15, 1775.

1-15   CHURCH Thomas, and Sarah Hayman, Feb. 21, 1698.

1-15   "   Charles, and Mrs. Hannah Paine; m. by Mr. Sparhawk, May 20, 1703.

1-18   "   Jeremy, and Alice Anthony, Indians, (Int.) June 9, 1722.

1-16, 17   "   Israel, and Abigail Howland, (Int.) Sept. 9, 1729; m. by Timothy Fales, Justice of the Peace, Oct. 23, 1729.

1-16   "   Benjamin, of Newport, and Elizabeth Viall, of Bristol, (Int.) Oct. 26, 1727.

1-17   "   Hannah, and Allen Carey, (Int.) Oct. 9, 1731.

1-27, 28   "   Mrs. Hannah, and Simeon Davis, Jr., (Int.) April 15, 1732; m. April 30, 1732.

1-17, 18 CHURCH Constant, and Mary Reynolds, (Int.) Jan. 6, 1732-3; m. by Rev. Barnabus Taylor, Jan. 25, 1732.

1-64 " Elizabeth, and Benjamin Lindsey, (Int.) Feb. 7, 1732-3.

1-42, 43 " Mrs. Elizabeth, and Thomas Greene, (Int.) Feb. 19, 1731-2; m. April 9, 1732.

1-104 " Abigail, and Benjamin Smith, (Int.) April 16, 1739; m. May 31, 1739.

1-15, 18 " Nathaniel, and Ruth Bosworth, (Int.) March 14, 1740; m. May 21, 1740.

1-59 " Mrs. Sarah, and Leonard Jarvis, (Int.) Aug. 1, 1741; m. Aug. 27, 1741.

1-18 " Dorothy, and Samuel Chandler, (Int.) Sept. 11, 1741.

1-18, 19 " Mrs. Mary, and John Chandler, Jr., (Int.) May 10, 1746; m. June 12, 1746.

1-18, 19 " Thomas, and Mrs. Elizabeth Bosworth, (Int.) May 12, 1746; m. by Rev. John Burt, July 1, 1746.

7-9 " Mrs. Ruth, and Shearjashub Bourne, April 19, 1747.

1-9 " Mrs. Mary, and Daniel Bradford, Oct. 1, 1749.

1-1 " Mrs. Sarah, and John Anthony, Aug. 21, 1754.

1-19 " Samuel, and Mrs. Ann Davis; m. by Rev. John Burt, Jan. 5, 1755.

1-20 " Charles, and Mrs. Eunice Peckcom; m. by Rev. John Burt, Aug. 18, 1756.

1-20 " Peter, and Mrs. Sarah Fales; m. by Rev. John Burt, March 22, 1764.

1-9 " Mrs. Mary, and Benjamin Bosworth, July 19, 1764.

1-66 " Deborah, and Joseph Lindsey, Aug. 9, 1772.

1-1 " Abraham, (negro.) servant of Peter, and —— Coggeshall, (negro.) servant of Mrs. Mowry; m. by Daniel Bradford, Justice of the Peace, Oct. 13, 1775.

1-23 " Thomas, of Samuel, and Molly Tripp, of Stephen; m. by Rev. Henry Wight, Oct. 26, 1794.

1-12 " Dolly, and Parker Borden, March 31, 1796.

1-21 " William, of Benjamin and Mehitable, and Sarah Phillips, of Captain Nathaniel and Sarah; m. by Rev. Henry Wight, Sept. 30, 1804.

1-22 " Peter, of Peter and Hannah, and Ann Bosworth, of Major Benjamin and Abigail; m. by Rev. Henry Wight, Dec. 12, 1813.

4-55 " Elizabeth W., and John H. Wardwell, Nov. 29, 1840.

4-56 " Hannah B., and Rev. Jeremiah Walcott, May 22, 1844.

4 67 " Benjamin B., son of Peter, and Betsey B. Fales, of Charles; m. by Rev. Thomas Shepard, Oct. 10, 1847.

1-17 CLARK Gamaliel, of Milford, Mass., and Eliza Carey, of Bristol, (Int.) Nov. 17, 1740.

1-19 " Samuel, of Portsmouth, and Mrs. Hannah Carey, April 12, 1749.

1-19 " Samuel, of Portsmouth, and Mrs. Mary Sampson (who deceased before April 26, 1749); m. by Rev. John Usher, Jan. 18, 1747.

1-76 " Sarah, and Bennett Munro, Jr., Nov. 12, 1772.

1-78 " Mehitable, and Jeremiah Munro, Oct. 26, 1811.

4-13 " Althea, and Joseph Barrows, July 14, 1833.

4-38 " Benjamin, and Ruth Ann Slade; m. by Rev. Henry Sullings, Aug. 25, 1839.

4-52 " Namony, and Dianna Freeman; m. by Rev. V. R. Osborn, Dec. 22, 1842.

4-69 " Louisa, and John Howland, Oct. 27, 1848.

4-55 CLEAVELAND Robert M., of Lawrenceville, Georgia, and Fanny L. Wight, of Bristol; m. by Rev. Thomas Shepard, Aug. 13, 1840.

1-17 CLIFTON Benjamin, and Mary Smith, (Int.) March 12, 1738-9: m. by Timothy Fales, Justice of the Peace, Nov. 18, 1730.

4-54 CLINTON Mrs. Sarah, and Joseph Ralph, Oct. 22, 1843.

1-15 COCKRAM John, and Lydia Potter, (Int.) Aug. 8, 1741; m. Aug. 27, 1741.

4-61 CODDINGTON Caroline L., and William Lincoln, May 24, 1846.

1-121 COFFIN Abigail, and Nathaniel Woodbury, (Int.) April 13, 1729.

1-23 " Solomon, of Providence, son of Solomon, of Nantucket, Mass., and Ann Davis Mason, of Swansey; m. by Daniel Bradford, Justice of C. C. Pleas, June 2, 1815.

1-124 COGGESHALL Mrs. Patience, and John Walker, (Int.) Aug. 18, 1746.
1-74   "   Mrs. Mary, and James Mason, Dec. 17, 1752.
1-20   "   Job, and Mrs. Sarah Bourne; m. by Rev. John Burt, Oct. 7, 1753.
1-29   "   Sarah, and Richard Drown, July 23, 1772.
1-24   "   George, and Sarah Throop; m. by Rev. Charles Thompson, Dec. 17, 1772.
1-30   "   Mrs. Martha, and Stephen Dexter, Jan. 18, 1773.
1-126   "   Hannah, and William White, Feb. 6, 1773.
1-1   "   ——, and Abraham Church, (col.) Oct. 13, 1775.
1-24   "   Job, of Bristol, and Betsey Pease, of Newport; m. by Rev. Mr. Townsend, (about) May 20, 1779.
1-38   "   Mary, and Chillingworth Foster, Aug. 9, 1807.
1-46   "   Nancy, and John Gladding, 3d, May 1, 1808.
4-75   "   George, of George and Sally, and Sally Manchester, of Captain Isaac and Priscilla; m. by Rev. Henry Wight, Oct. 28, 1812.
1-22   "   Josiah, of Captain William, and Mary P. Finney, of Captain Loring; m. by Rev. Luther Baker, Dec. 31, 1813.
4-14   "   Captain Samuel, and Elizabeth B. Munro; m. by Rev. Barnard Bates, May 15, 1821.
4-42   "   Hannah H., and Samuel M. Gladding, Oct. 12, 1840.
4-55   "   Eliza, and George Cragg (col.), Oct. 30, 1841.
4-48   "   Henry, and Sarah Ann Smith; m. by Rev. William L. Brower, May 31, 1841.
4-48   "   Freeborn, and Eliza F. Barnes; m. by Rev. William L. Brower, Sept. 26, 1841.
4-55   "   Joanna M., and Charles W. Rogers, Oct. 21, 1842.
4-53   "   George, and Abbie L. Miller; m. by Rev. Edward Freeman, Nov. 17, 1842.
4-59   "   Hannah S., and David A. Coit, Aug. 7, 1845.
4-65   "   Eliza, and Ezra E. Dyer, June 27, 1847.
1-23 COIT George M., and Mary Short; m. by Rev. Calvin Hitchcock, May 19, 1816.
4-18   "   Martha P., and Alfred L. Lewis, Nov. 10, 1835.
4-32   "   Lucretia, and Peter J. Bradford, June 16, 1839.
4-52   "   George M., and Waitey Sandford; m. by Rev. G. R. Osborn, Aug. 15, 1842.
4-55   "   Hannah L., and George T. Easterbrooks, Aug. 29, 1842.
4-59   "   David A., and Hannah S. Coggeshall; m. by Rev. Hezekiah Burnham, Aug. 7, 1845.
4-63   "   Elizabeth G., and James M. Grant, April 12, 1847.
1-45 COLE Joanna, and Benjamin Green, May 26, 1805.
1-21   "   George, and Eliza Cranston; m. by Rev. Alexander V. Griswold, Oct. 13, 1808.
1-22   "   Thomas, son of Thomas and Anna, of Warren, and Anna Trott, of Swansey; m. by Daniel Bradford, Justice Court Common Pleas, Sept. 5, 1815.
4-1   "   Thomas, and Nancy Sanders; m. by Rev. Barnard Bates, Nov. 27, 1818.
4-218   "   Lucretia G., and James N. Gladding, Feb. 26, 1838.
4-73   "   Eliza Troop, and Horace Peck, May 16, 1838.
4-46, 53   "   Martha F., and John H. Waldron, June 13, 1841.
4-53   "   Nehemiah, Jr., and Sarah A. Goff; m. by Rev. G. F. Sanborn, Jan. 19, 1843.
4-65   "   Judith, and Calvin Simmons, June 21, 1847.
4-65   "   John G., and Sarah Lawless; m. by Rev. Jonathan Cady, Dec. 29, 1847.
1-21 COLLINS Charles, of Captain Charles and Hannah, and Lydia Bradford, of Hon. William and Mary; m. by Rev. Henry Wight, Oct. 8, 1797.
1-23   "   Thomas, of Bristol, son of Peter and Mary Ann, and Mary Shaw, daughter of Mark Anthony and Mary Murray; m. by Rev. Alexander V. Griswold, Dec. 10, 1815.
4-65   "   James, and Nancy Tilling ast; m. by Rev. Jonathan Cady, Jan. 23, 1847.
4-70   "   Celia Ann, and Benjamin W. Palmer, July 3, 1848.

1-111   COLLYE Martha, and William Throop, March 20, 1698.
1-24   COLWELL Richard, and Sarah Riley, (Int.) July 8, 1725.
4-36   CONGDON Franklin E., of Warwick, and Dorcas Reynolds, of Warwick;
            m. by Elder John Gardiner, at Warwick, June 12, 1831.
1-118   COOKE Penelope, and John Verin, Aug. 30, 1683.
4-57   "   N. Bowen, and Ann R. Munro; m. by Rev. James H. Eames,
            April 22, 1846.
4-79   "   Elizabeth, and George W. Stufson, Aug. 23, 1846.
1-15   COOK Samuel, and Infield Greene, (Int.) March 6, 1718-19.
1-19   COOMER John, of Newport, and Mrs Elizabeth Kinnecut, of Bristol; m.
            by Rev. John Burt, Aug. 20, 1752.
1-15   CORBETT William, and Eleanor Batrap; m. by Captain Benjamin
            Church, Sept. 19, 1683. (First wedding in Town.)
1-15   "   William, and Mary Allen (widow), July 10, 1710.
4-2   "   Penuel, of Virginia, and Mary Ann Bourne, of Bristol; m. by Rev.
            Joel Mann, March 27, 1821.
1-23   CORNELL Captain Walter, of Bristol, and Mrs. Rhoda Carter, of Middle-
            town; m. by Rev. Daniel Webb, Oct. 10, 1817.
4-10   CORNETT William, of John and Isabella, of Morpeth, Northumberland,
            England, and Mary Tew, of Henry and Mary, of Newport;
            m. at Portsmouth, R. I., April 29, 1811.
1-20   COSINS John, and Mrs. Hannah Jones; m. by Rev. John Burt, April 22,
            1764.
1-15   COTTON Miles, and Elizabeth Joils, (Int.) July 6, 1720.
1-16   "   Rev. Nathaniel, of Bristol, and Grissell Sandford, of Newport,
            (Int.) Jan. 20, 1721-2.
4-75   COTTRELL Adeline R., and James Diman, Dec. 20, 1855.
1-23   COVINGTON, Jacob, and Patty Holbrook, both of Plymouth, Mass.; m. by
            N. Bullock, Justice of the Peace, at Bristol, Oct. 2, 1816.
1-58   COWELL Rebecca, and Morgan Jones, (Int.) Oct. 27, 1731; m. Nov. 2,
            1731.
1-24   COX William, and Mary Bristol, (Int.) Dec. 12, 1739.
1-18   "   William, and Sarah Pearce, (Int.) Feb. 1, 1741; m. by Rev. John
            Usher, March 19, 1741.
1-95   "   Hannah, and Samuel Phillips, July 4, 1802.
1-18, 19 COY John, and Sarah Woodbury, (Int.) Aug. 31, 1745; m. by Rev. John
            Burt, Oct. 27, 1745.
1-22   "   John, of Lemuel and Mary, and Rebecca Salisbury, of Barnard
            and Ruth; m. by Rev. Henry Wight, June 21, 1794.
4-55, 77 " Sarah W., and George Mutton, Sept. 17, 1840.
4-55   CRAIGG George, and Eliza Coggeshall (col.); m. by Rev. Thomas Shep-
            ard, Oct. 20, 1840.
4-48   CRANDALL Thomas F., and Rebecca S. Miller; m. by Rev. William L.
            Brower, Nov. 22, 1841.
1-15   CRANE Abraham, and Hannah Martin, (Int.) March 27, 1719.
1-78   CRANSTON Abigail, and David Munro, March 23, 1806.
1-21   "   Eliza, and George Oole, Oct. 13, 1806.
1-128   "   Phebe, and Asa West, Aug. 24, ——.
1-24   CROCKER Isaac, of Bristol, and Alice Harney, of Little Compton, (Int.)
            Oct. 31, 1741.
1-109   CROOKER Mary, and Indian Simon, (Int.) March —, 1732.
4-5   CROWELL Rev. Joshua, of Ware, Mass., and Sarah Negas, of Tiverton,
            R. I.; m. by Rev. Timothy Merrett, Nov. 12, 1824.
1-16   CUMMINGS, David, of Swansey, and Catherine Marks, widow, (Int.) Dec.
            10, 1726; m. by Rev. John Usher, Feb. 24, 1726-7.
1-43, 44 " Elizabeth, and George Gladding, (Int.) July 6, 1745; m. July
            28, 1745.
4-75   "   Lydia, and Robert Wyatt, Nov. 21, 1824.
4-32   "   Rachel S., and Thomas W. Greene, Sept. 30, 1839.
4-54, 65 " Benjamin, and Sally C. Peck; m. by Rev. G. F. Sanborn, July 19,
            1843.
4-54   "   Harriet, and Charles Simmons, Oct. 22, 1843.
4-55   CUNLIFF Cornelius S., of Providence, and Sarah W. Wardwell, of Bristol;
            m. by Rev. Thomas Shepard, Oct. 22, 1843.
1-20   CUSHING Benjamin, Esq., of Providence, and Mrs. Abigail Richmond, of
            Bristol; m. by Rev. John Burt, Sept. 11, 1765.

D

1-26 DADEY William, and Sarah Bearcroft; m. by John Saffin, Justice, Jan. 28, 1694.

1-26 DAGGETT Thomas, and Elizabeth Hawes, Jan. 22, 1683.

4-29 " Henry, son of Jethro and Hannah, and Martha Richmond, of William; m. by Rev. George Hathaway, Dec. —, 1833.

4-48 " Almira, and Nathaniel Lewis, April 24, 1843.

4-53 " John L., and Harriet M. Lawton; m. by Rev. Edward Freeman, July 20, 1842.

1-5 DARLING Elizabeth, and Joseph Brown, (Int.) Jan. 2, 1718.

1-45 DAVISON Sarah, and Richard Grant, Sept. 29, 1783.

1-26 DAVIS Simeon, and Ann Low, Sept. 24, 1685.

1-69 " Sarah, and John Miles, March 14, 1689.

1-26 " Samuel, and Bethia Howland, (Int.) June 26, 1724.

1-111, 112 " Mrs. Frances, and Ames Throop, (Int.) Nov. 28, 1724; m. Jan. 7, 1724-5.

1-5 " Mrs. Elizabeth, and Henry Bragg, (Int.) July 21, 1727.

1-27 " Simeon, and Madam Elizabeth McIntosh, (Int.) May 11, 1728; m. of Rev. John Usher, June 2, 1728.

1-71,72 " Mehitable, and Joseph Mason, (Int.) April 30, 1731; m. May 27, 1731.

1-27,28 " Simeon, Jr., and Mrs. Hannah Church, (Int.) April 15, 1732; m. by Rev. Barnabus Taylor, April 30, 1732.

1-27 " Simeon, and Mrs. Bethia Bragg, (Int.) Aug. 8, 1733; m. by Rev. John Usher, Aug. 29, 1733.

1-43 " Bethia, and Daniel Greene, (Int.) Nov. 21, 1741.

1-19 " Mrs. Ann, and Samuel Church, Jan. 5, 1755.

1-100 " Mrs. Hannah, and Ebenezer Richardson, Nov. 10, 1763.

4-73 " Nancy M., and Barney Blossom, Dec. 25, 1849.

4-48 DAWLEY Sarah, and William B. Tanner, May 24, 1841.

1-27 DAY Capt. John, and Susannah Bragg, (Int.) July 24, 1731.

4-54 " Elizabeth A., and Samuel Liscomb, July 12, 1843.

4-55 DEANE Melvin G., of Cherryfield, Me., and Sarah Shepard, of Bristol; m. by Rev. Thomas Shepard, Aug. 9, 1843.

1-26 DEAUR David, of Newport, and Elizabeth Eddy, of Bristol, (Int.) March 30, 1723; m. by Rev. Nathaniel Cotton, April 30, 1723.

1-40 DENMARK Elizabeth, and Christopher Greene, (Int.) Aug. 20, 1721.

4-10 DENNIS, Thomas, and Mercy Ann Allen; m. by Rev. Henry Wight, Jan. 3, 1836.

4-61 " Abbie H., and Lewis A. Barlow, Sept. 30, 1845.

4-10 DeWITT William Thomas, son of John and Ann, of Society Hill, Chesterfield District, N. C., and Elizabeth Mosher, of Capt. Abner and Ruth; m. by Rev. Henry Wight, Sept. 15, 1830.

1-28 DeWOLF Mark Antony, of Gaudeloupe, and Abigail Potter, of Bristol, (Int.) Aug. 11, 1744; m. Aug. 26, 1744.

1-29 " Mrs. Margaret, and Joseph Diman, Nov. 26, 1767.

1-29 " Capt. Mark Antony, of Mark A., and Elizabeth Martin, of Capt. William; m. by Rev. John Burt, Aug. 11, 1768.

1-29 " Capt. Charles, of Capt. Mark A., and Mary Taylor, of Rev. Barnabus; m. by Rev. John Burt, April 28, 1771.

1-12 " Sukey, and Scipio Burt (col.), March 21, 1782.

1-30 " James, of Capt. Mark A. and Elizabeth, and Anna Bradford, of Hon. William and Mary Gooding, of Henry and Mary; m. by Rev. Henry Wight, Jan. 7, 1790.

4-22 " Charles, of Capt. Charles and Mary, and Mary Gooding, of Henry and Mary, m. by Rev. Henry Wight, Dec. 11, 1803.

4-26 " Maria, and Robert Rogers, Dec. 27, 1814.

4-36 " John, and Ruth Bourn; m. by Rev. Thomas Shepard, Aug. 19, 1839.

4-36 " Marcus A., and Ruth W. Burt; m. by Rev. Ephraim Scott, Sept. 3, 1839.

4-223 " Susan Amelia, and Jonathan Russell Bullock, Sept. 6, 1840.

4-67 " Algernon Sidney, of John, and Clara Anna Diman, of Byron; m. by Rev. Thomas Shepard, June 30, 1847.

1-30   DEXTER Stephen, and Mrs. Martha Coggeshall, Jan. 18, 1847.

1-27,28 DIMAN Jeremiah, and Sarah Giddens, (Int.) April 14, 1733; m. by Rev.
     Barnabus Taylor, May 13, 1733.

1-103,104 "   Lucretia, and Richard Smith, (Int.) Nov. 28, 1741; m. Dec. 24,
     1741.

1-28   " Nathaniel, and Mrs. Anna Gallup; m. by Rev. John Burt, Oct.
     18, 1756.

1-29   " James, and Mrs. Ann LeFavour; m. by Rev. John Burt, March
     30, 1758.

1-86   " Mrs. Hannah, and George Oxx, Oct. 29, 1761.

1-29   " Joseph, of Deacon Jeremiah, and Mrs. Margaret DeWolf, daugh-
     ter of Capt. Mark A.; m. by Rev. John Burt, Nov. 26, 1767.

1-29   " Jonathan, of Deacon Jeremiah, and Dorothy Fales, of Nathan-
     iel; m. by Rev. John Burt, Oct. 17, 1771.

1-30   " William, of Nathaniel and Anna, and Anna Munro, of Charles and
     Anna; m. by Rev. Henry Wight, Nov. 11, 1791.

1-59   " Elizabeth Fales, and Hezekiah Jackson, May 20, 1798.

1-30   " Jeremiah, of Jonathan and Dorothy, and Rhoda Sandford, of Royal
     and Rhoda; m. by Rev. Henry Wight, Oct. 4, 1810.

4-14   " Hannah, and Billings Waldron, Feb. 16, 1812.

4-4   " Fanny Martin, and Peleg Gardiner Jones, June 26, 1821.

4-50   " Francis L. D., and Rosabella Barrows; m. by Rev. G. F. San-
     born, May 16, 1842.

4-53   " Marian, and James P. Pierce, June 13, 1843.

4-63   " Elizabeth W., and Jeremiah W. Munro, Aug. 6, 1846.

4-67   " Clara Anna, and Algernon Sidney DeWolf, June 30, 1847.

4-69   " Joanna, and Benjamin H. Whitford, Nov. 29, 1848.

4-75   " Mrs. Martha, and John Henry Schomacker, May 26, 1851.

4-75   " James, and Adeline R. Cottrell, of Athens, Vt.; m. by Rev. Asa
     Kent, Dec. 20, 1855.

1-26 DONNELS Terrence, and Mary Carey, (Int.) June 25, 1725.

4-26 DOTY Simeon, and Hannah Ingraham; m. by Rev. J. B. Wight, Sept. 3,
     1822.

4-67   " Charlotte M., and John W. Munro, Aug. 4, 1847.

4-67   " Sarah, and Benjamin T. Easterbrooks, Sept. 29, 1847.

4-9 DOUGLASS Annis, and Joseph Northup, Nov. 29, 1829.

4-8, 22 " John S., of Paris, and Beeby B. Lawton, of Peter; m. by Rev.
     Henry Sullings, June 26, 1836.

1-6 DOWLING Mary, and Thomas Bretland, (Int.) ———.

1-27 DOWSET Joseph, and Elizabeth Woodcock, (Int.) Nov. 16, 1729.

1-98 DREW Jemima, and Peter Reed, (Int.) ——— —, ———.

1-41 DROWN Esther, and William Gladding, (Int.) Sept. —, 1726.

1-103, 104 " Elizabeth, and Samuel Smith, Jr., (Int.) April 24, 1731; m. May
     10, 1731.

1-28 · " Thomas, and Sarah Paine; m. by Rev. Barnabus Taylor, March
     24, 1736.

1-42, 58 " Bathsheba, and Nathan Jones, (Int.) Sept. 18, 1736; m. Nov. 10,
     1736.

1-27   " Thomas, of Boston, and Sarah Paine, of Bristol, (Int.) Nov. 30,
     1736.

1-28   " Benjamin, and Hannah Kent, July 24, 1738.

1-42   " Mary, and John Gladding, (Int.) Aug. 14, 1738; m. Sept. 25, 1738.

1-90   " Sarah, and John Pratt, (Int.) Jan. 18, 1739-40.

1-7   " Esther, and Thomas Briggs, (Int.) July 12, 1740; m. Aug. 18,
     1740.

1-28   " Jonathan, and Mrs. Ann Durfee, June 9, 1748.

1-27   " Jonathan, and Sarah Kent, of Barrington, (Int.) ——— —, ———.

1-29   " Richard, of Jonathan, and Sarah Coggeshall, of Job, deceased; m.
     by Rev. John Burt, July 23, 1772.

1-76   " Ann, and Rufus Martin, Dec. 29, 1774.

1-77, 118 " Hannah, and William Manchester, Dec. 29, 1790.

1-107   " Mary, and Comfort Simmons, Aug. 25, 1805.

4-42   " Rufus B., and Alice Bowler; m. by Rev. Henry Sullings, June 25,
     1840.

4-54 DUBARS Waity L., and Horace Lawton, July 14, 1844.

1-92   DUFAIL Mrs. Elizabeth, and Michael Phillips, Sept. 11, 1750.
1-28   DUNBAR George, of Warwick, and Sarah Troop, of Bristol, (Int.) Sept. 6,
           1742; m. Sept. 20, 1742.
1-33   "   Mrs. Ann, and John Edgell, (Int.) July 11, 1746.
4-65   "   William, and Hannah H. Gladding; m. by Rev. Richard Livesey,
           May 1, 1848.
1-46   DUNHAM Rhoda, and George Goonerson, Sept. 13, 1812.
1-26   DURFEE Thomas, and Martha, Toman, (Int.) July 1, 1727; m. by Rev.
           John Usher, July 16, 1727.
1-28   "   Mrs. Ann, and Jonathan Drown, June 9, 1748.
1-54   "   Sarah, and Ceaser Hubbard (col.), August ——.
1-28   DURS, William, of Newport, and Mrs. Louis Allen, of Bristol, (Int.) April
           23, 1746.
1-26   DYER John, and Sarah Bowerman, (Int.) Dec. —, 1718.
1-27   "   John, and Rebecca Jones, of Taunton, (Int.) Aug. 15, 1734.
1-27, 28 "   James, of Newport, and Hannah Fairbanks, of Bristol, (Int.)
           Oct. 29, 1734; m. by Rev. Barnabus Taylor, Dec. 4, 1734.
1-28   "   John, of Bristol, and Mary Reed, of Abington, Mass., (Int.)
           March 31, 1739.
1-99   "   Mary, and Joseph Reed, (Int.) Dec. 29, 1744.
1-8   "   Sarah, and Benjamin Boyce, (Int.) April 21, 1744; m. May 17,
           1744.
1-84   "   Mrs. Martha, and Simeon Nash, March 5, 1846-47.
1-65   "   Mrs. Rebecca, and William Lawless, June 21, 1761.
4-65   "   Ezra E., and Eliza Coggeshall; m. by Rev. Jonathan Cady, June
           27, 1847.

E

1-33   EASTERBROOKS Robert, Jr., of Warren, and Mrs. Mary West; m. by
           Rev. John Burt, March 17, 1757.
1-93   "   Mariah, and Nathaniel Phillips, Dec. 23, 1770.
1-33   "   Aaron, and Leah Liscomb, May 28, 1775.
1-127   "   Mrs. Nellie, and Nathaniel H. West, March 4, 1798.
1-129   "   Amey, and Thomas Wilson, Nov. 17, 1805.
1-46   "   Sophronia, and Daniel Greer, April 27, 1806.
4-4   "   Susan Throop, and Thomas Swift, Aug. 27, 1811.
1-33   "   Crawford, of Aaron, and Hannah Hall, of Bristol, daughter of
           Robert, of Windham, N. Y.; m. by Rev. Asa Kent, Nov. 11,
           1813.
1-108   "   Mrs. Susan, and Rouse Potter Sayer, April 1, 1818.
4-6   "   John, of Bristol, and Caroline Kaull, of Newport; m. by Rev.
           Thomas W. Tucker, Feb. 6, 1825.
4-77, 222 "   Susan Wardwell, and Benjamin Tilley, Nov. 17, 1832.
4-18   "   Abby T., and John R. Howe, July 20, 1834.
4-26   "   Eliza Ann, and James P. Brown, April 28, 1836.
4-34   "   William, and Rebecca Smith Munro; m. by Rev. James C.
           Bonteone, April 21, 1839.
4-55   "   George T., and Hannah L. Coit; m. by Rev. Thomas Shepard,
           Aug. 29, 1842.
4-67   "   Benjamin T., son of Benjamin T., and Sarah Doty; m. by Rev.
           Thomas Shepard, Sept. 29, 1847.
4-69   "   John, Jr., and Harriet J. Whitford; m. by Rev. Richard Livesey,
           Nov. 23, 1848.
4-73   "   Alexander, of Jonathan, and Miriam W. Manchester; m. by Rev.
           Thomas Shepard, June 20, 1850.
1-85   EASTON Mary, and Solomon Ned, Indian, (Int.) March 18, 1731.
1-123 EDDY Sarah and David Wilson, (Int.) Oct. 4, 1720.
1-26   "   Elizabeth, and David Deaur, (Int.) March 30, 1723; m. April 30,
           1723.
1-32   "   Oliver, and Sarah Munro; m. by Rev. John Usher, Feb. 16, 1723.
1-32   "   Joseph, and Mahaliah Torrey, (Int.) Oct. 31, 1724; m. by Rev.
           Nathaniel Cotton, Dec. 2, 1724-5.

1-5	EDDY Lydia, and Stephen Barrus, Sept. 27, 1725.
1-89	"	Elizabeth, and Nathan Penny, April 8, 1726.
1-32	"	Joseph, of Bristol, and Ruth Belcher of Braintree, Mass., (Int.) Sept. 7, 1728.
1-32	"	Joseph of Newport, and Mary Smith of Bristol, (Int.) Oct. 5, 1728.
1-91,92	"	Sarah, and Jeremiah Pierce, (Int.) Nov. 19, 1744; m. Dec. 24, 1744.
1-8	"	Phebe, and Henry Bosworth, (Int.) Feb. 15, 1745; m. March 3, 1745.
1-80	"	Mrs. Mary, and Joseph Munro, Aug. 29, 1784.
4-63	"	Cyrus B., and Phebe G. Thurston; m. by Rev. Jonathan Cady, Oct. 28, 1846.
4-79	"	John D., of Bristol, and Mary W. Leach, of Providence; m. by Rev. Hezekiah Burnham, Dec. 21, 1846.
1-33	EDGELL John, of Newport, and Mrs. Ann Dunbar, of Bristol, (Int.) July 11, 1746.
4-70	EDSON, Cyrus H., of New Bedford, son of Abner and Caroline, and Rachel J. Sparks, of Samuel and Rachael; m. by Rev. Richard Livesey, —— —, 1848.
4-55	EDWARDS Pardon, of Mattapoisett, Mass., and Ann Elizabeth Newman, of Bristol; m. by Rev. Thomas Shepard, Sept. 29, 1842.
1-32	ELDREDGE John, and Jane Chamberlain, of Hull, Mass., (Int.) Nov. —, 1719.
1-32	"	John, and Martha Nibs, (Int.) Oct. 16, 1744.
1-32	"	William, and Mrs. Katherine Munro, (Int.) March 29, 1746.
1-33	ELLERY William, of Newport, and Mrs. Abigail Carey, of Bristol; m. by Rev. John Burt, June 28, 1767.
1-10	"	Ann, and Rev. John Burt, Nov. 17, 1768.
4-70	ELLIS Henry W., of Providence, and Abby M. Leonard, of Bristol; m. by Rev. Richard Livesey, Aug. 23, 1849.
1-32	ESLECK Isaac, and Mary Lawless, (Int.) April 25, 1740; m. by Samuel Howland, Justice of the Peace, May 18, 1740.
1-33	"	Isaac, and Martha Salisbury, Nov. 1, 1772.
1-33	"	Captain Isaac, 2d, and Ruth Reed, of Joseph and Mary; m. by Rev. Henry Wight, Aug. 13, 1786.
1-33	EVERETT Jesse, of Joseph, and Elizabeth Salisbury, of Benjamin; m. by Rev. John Burt, Oct. 20, 1771.
4-40	"	Mrs. Sarah, and Richard G. Blake, Aug. 2, 1840.

F

1-36	FAIRBANKS Jeremiah, and Mary Penfield, April 19, 1698.
1-36	"	David, of Bristol, and Susannah Stacy, of Newport, (Int.) Jan. 6, 1723.
1-98	"	Mary, and Benjamin Richardson, (Int.) June 13, 1724.
1-13	"	Jerusha, and Philip Brewer, Oct. 1, 1726.
1-5	"	Mary, and Richard Bush, (Int.) Jan. 25, 1726.
1-63	"	Elizabeth, and Thomas Lawrence, (Int.) May 6, 1728.
1-27, 28	"	Hannah, and James Dyer, (Int.) Oct. 29, 1734; m. Dec. 4, 1734.
1-42, 43	"	Sarah, and James Gladding, (Int.) Oct. 22, 1737; m. Dec. 1, 1737.
1-37	FALES Nathaniel, and Sarah Little, (Int.) Aug. 16, 1740.
1-8	"	Mary, and William Bosworth, (Int.) Feb. 27, 1744.
1-37	"	Jonathan, and Mrs. Hannah Peck; m. by Rev. John Burt, Dec. 20, 1750.
1-20	"	Mrs. Sarah, and Peter Church, March 22, 1764.
1-114	"	Mrs. Althea, and William Throop, March 20, 1765.
1-29	"	Dorothy, and Jonathan Diman, Oct. 17, 1771.
1-38	"	Nathaniel, Jr., and Elizabeth Bradford, Sept. 26, or 23, 1773. (Also 4-41).
1-37	"	Jonathan, Jr., of Jonathan, and Elizabeth Wardwell, of John, dec.; m. by Rev. John Burt, June 29, 1775.
1-79	"	Eliza Bradford, and Hezekiah Munro, Feb. 28, 1799.
1-80	"	Mary, and Charles Mason, Dec. 7, 1806.
1-38	"	Thomas, of Thomas and Sarah, and Mary Bourne, of Shearjashub and Ruth; m. by Rev. Henry Wight, Jan. 27, 1808.

1-38   FALES Lemuel, of Thomas and Sarah, and Hannah Vaughn, of Gideon and Patience; m. by Rev. Henry Wight, April 11, 1816.

1-119   "   Julia Ann, and Clark Vaughn, Jan. 17, 1819.

4-57   "   William C., and Elizabeth C. Mason, both of Fall River; m. by Rev. Isaac Bonney, April 10, 1845.

4-61   "   Sarah L., and Henry G. Ballon, June 8, 1946.

4-67   "   Betsey B., and Benjamin B. Church, Oct. 10, 1847.

1-36   FAUNCE Jane, and Ebenezer Finney, (Int.) May 28, 1726.

4-73   FENNER Richard, of Bristol, and Mary N. Northup, of North Kingstown; m. by Rev. Thomas Shepard, June 6, 1850.

4-55   FERRIS Alexander, and Agnes Rouse; m. by Rev. Thomas Shepard, March 11, 1844.

1-5   FIELD Susannah, and Jeremiah Bosworth, (Int.) Jan. 7, 1726.

1-37   "   John, of Providence, and Mrs. Abigail Carey, of Bristol; m. by Rev. John Burt, March 12, 1761.

4-70   "   Zylphia Ann, and Benjamin Barrus, June 26, 1849.

4-70   FINDLEY William, and Elizabeth McCormach, of Canada; m. by Rev. Thomas Shepard, May 14, 1849.

1-36   FINNEY Jonathan, and Joanna Kinnecut, Oct. 18, 1682.

1-36   "   Jeremiah, and Esther Lewis, Jan. 7, 1684.

1-36   "   Joshua, and Mercy Watts, May 31, 1688.

1-58   "   Esther, and Joseph Joy, (Int.) Oct. 31, 1719.

1-36   "   Ebenezer, and Jane Faunce, of Plymouth, (Int.) May 28, 1726.

1-37   "   Jeremiah, Jr., and Elizabeth Briston, (Int.) May 17, 1727.

1-37   "   Josiah, and Mrs. Molly Carey; m. by Rev. John Burt, May 19, 1751.

1-37   "   Daniel, of Easton, Mass., and Mrs. Mary Maxfield, of Bristol; m. by Rev. John Burt, Jan. 19, 1758.

1-37   "   Josiah, and Mrs. Martha Gibbs; m. by Rev. John Burt, Sept. 16, 1761.

1-52   "   Mrs. Abigail, and John Holmes, Dec. 13, 1761.

1-22   "   Mary P., and Josiah Coggeshall, Dec. 31, 1813.

4-65   FISHER, Beriah P., of Edgartown, Mass., and Alice G. Munro, of Bristol; m. by Rev. Jonathan Cady, June 17, 1847.

1-38   FISH David, of Preserved and Sarah, and Mary Pearce, of Thomas and Abigail; m. by Rev. Henry Wight, June 10, 1805.

4-14, 239   "   Sarah L., and Bennett J. Munro, Sept. 23, 1828.

1-115   FITCH Elizabeth, and David Taber, Oct. 26, 1811.

1-36   FORD Joseph, and Deborah Waldo, Dec. 6, 1803.

1-50   "   Eleanor, and George Harris, (Int.) March 7, 1725-6; m. March 28, 1725-6.

1-38   FOSTER Chillingworth, of Chillingworth and Margaret, and Mary Coggeshall, of William and Margaret; m. by Rev. Henry Wight, Aug. 9, 1807.

1-36   FOWLER James, of Newport, and Jane Gibbs, of Bristol, (Int.) April 1, 1727.

4-79   FRANKLIN Elisha Barney, of Elisha and Esther, and Martha Springer, of Joseph and Mary; m. by Rev. Henry Wight, Oct. 10, 1833.

4-80   "   William, and Mary Simmons; m. by Rev. Thomas Shepard, Feb. 28, 1836.

4-46   "   Hannah H., and John Mulchahy, Jan. 27, 1841.

4-50   "   Lydia D., and George W. Peckham, April 3, 1842.

4-59   "   Benjamin, and Abby Peckham; m. by Rev. Hezekiah Burnham, Dec. 14, 1845.

4-69   "   William, of Swansey, Mass., and Peddy Bliss, of Rehoboth, Mass.; m. by Rev. Richard Livesey, Sept. 12, 1848.

1-40   FRAZIER Rebecca, and Samuel Gridley, (Int.) Nov. 20, 1720.

1-36, 37   "   Alexander, and Mercy Lumber, (Int.) Dec. 17, 1728; m. by Rev. John Usher, Jan. 19, 1728.

1-95   FREDERIC Abby, and James Powell, July 7, 1812.

4-70   "   Matthias, and Mary E. Lindsey; m. by Rev. Richard Livesey, Sept. 5, 1849.

1-38   FREEBORN Thomas, of Jonathan and Martha, and Martha Hall, daughter of Captain Nehemiah Cole and Judith, his wife; m. by Rev. Henry Wight, Sept. 15, 1805.

4-40   FREEBORN James T., and Harriet T. Lane; m. by Rev. Ephraim Scott,.
          Aug. 25, 1840.
4-52   FREEMAN Dianna, and Namony Clarke, Dec. 22, 1842.
4-71   FRENCH James E., and Jemima W. Hatch; m. by Rev. Thomas Shepard,
          Nov. 13, 1849.
4-7, 63   FRIEND Mary, and Peter Gladding, Dec. 26, 1826.
4-24   "   Catherine E., and Edwin Peabody, Oct. 25, 1832.
1-36   FRY John, and Elizabeth Hummery, June 18, 1695.
1-56   "   Mary, and John Ingraham, (Int.) Nov. 27, 1723; m. Dec. 12, 1723.
1-36   "   John, and Abigail Spink, (Int.) Dec. 28, 1723; m. by Rev. Nathan-
              iel Cotton, March 26 1724.
1-36   "   Anthony, and Mercy Taylor, of Freetown, (Int.) Feb. 28, 1723; m.
              by Rev. Nathaniel Cotton, June 24, 1724.
1-98   "   Hannah, and Thomas Richmond, (Int.) March —, 1724-5; m.
              April 21, 1725.
1-10   FULLER Elizabeth, and Lennox Bullock, Feb. 14, 1768.
1-128   "   Sarah, and William West, Nov. 16, 1783.
4-6   "   Susan G., and Thomas F. Pitman, Feb. 17, 1825.
4-56   "   Susan Elizabeth, and John Sayer, Oct. 20, 1844.

G

1-4   GAGE Naomi, and Stephen Bedford, Feb. 15, 1693.
1-44   GAINDET Daniel, and Mrs. Mary Von H——; m. by Rev. John Burt, Nov.
          5, 1750.
1-98   GAINS Tabitha, and Elisha Rydor, (Int.) July 5, 1738.
1-90   "   Mary, and Joseph Prichard, (Int.) Aug. 5, 1740.
1-40   GALLUP Samuel, and Elizabeth Southworth, May 12, 1685.
1-4   "   Elizabeth, and Samuel Bowerman, April 20, 1710.
1-4   "   Mrs. Mary, and Joshua Bayley, Jan. 9 or 10, 1711-12.
1-40, 41 "   William, and Mary Antill, (Int.) Nov. 25, 1721; m. by Rev. James
              McSparran, Dec. 19, 1721.
1-47   "   Joseph, servant of William, and Peggy Little, servant of Captain
              Little (col.), Sept. 14, 1732.
1-80   "   Jennie, and Ceaser McIntosh (col.), (Int.) July 24, 1736.
1-6   "   Mary, and John Bragg, (Int.) June 12, 1736.
1-91,92   "   Mrs. Elizabeth, and Nathaniel Paine, (Int.) May 6, 1742; m.
              June 13, 1742.
1-28   "   Mrs. Anna, and Nathaniel Diman, Oct. 18, 1756.
1-75   "   Mrs. Abigail, and Nathaniel Munro, Nov. 13, 1766.
1-47   GARDINER Isaac, and Phillis Burt (col.); m. by Rev. Henry Wight, May
          11, 1806.
1-46   "   Job W., of Providence, and Harriet Richmond, of Dighton, Mass.;
              m. by Rev. Henry Wight, Jan. 22, 1810.
4-7   "   George, and Annie Titus (col.); m. by Rev. Henry Wight,
              Nov. 16, 1825.
4-56   "   George, of Warren, and Mary L. Munro, of Bristol; m. by Rev.
              Isaac Bonney, March 8, 1845.
1-40, 43 GARRETT Thomas, of Newport, and Mary Potter, of Bristol, (Int.)
              June 11, 1742; m. Oct. 19, 1742.
4-57   GAYTON George, and Levinia P. West; m. by Rev. Isaac Bonney, Oct.
          13, 1844.
1-115 GEORGE Abigail, and Isaac Truck (col.), (Int.) July 27, 1741.
1-40   GIBBS Ann, and Simon Giles, (Int.) Feb. 9, 1720-1.
1-36   "   Jane, and James Fowler, (Int.) April 1, 1727.
1-41, 42 "   John, and Sarah Jones, (Int.) Sept. 13, 1729; m. by Rev. John.
              Usher, Oct. 19, 1729.
1-42   "   James, and Martha Giddens, (Int.) April 4, 1734; m. by Rev.
              John Usher, Jan. 25, 1735.
1-43   "   James, and Mrs. Mary Ingraham, (Int.) April 29, 1742; m. by.
              Rev. John Usher, May 13, 1742.
1-44   "   John, and Sarah Gladding; m. by Rev. John Burt, April 29, 1750.
1-125   "   Mrs. Frances, and Samuel West, March 21, 1751.
1-44   "   Mrs. Mary, and Samuel Gladding, Sept. 9, 1751.
1-37   "   Mrs. Martha, and Josiah Finney, Sept. 16, 1761.

1-130 GIDDENS Martha, and Joseph Wardwell, (Int.) Dec. 22, 1709.

1-112   "   Susannah, and William Torrey, (Int.) Dec. 12, 1724; m. Dec. 29, 1724.

1-27, 28   "   Sarah, and Jeremiah Diman, (Int.) April 14, 1733; m. May 13, 1733.

1-103, 104 "   Mary, and Benjamin Salisbury, (Int.) April 13, 1734; m. May 5, 1734.

1-42   "   Martha, and James Gibbs, (Int.) April 4, 1735; m. June 25, 1735.

4-2 GIFFORD Sally, and Hezekiah C. Wardwell, Dec. 24, 1820.

4-242   "   Hannah, and Samuel Swan, Feb. 9, 1823.

1-40 GILES Simon, of Bristol, and Ann Gibbs, of Newport, (Int.) Feb. 9, 1720-1.

1-99   "   Susannah, and John Reynolds, (Int.) Jan. 11, 1743-4.

4-70   "   Martha F., and Benjamin S. Seatle, Aug. 2, 1849.

1-41 GILL Richard, of Newport, and Elizabeth Greene, of Bristol, (Int.) Oct. 27, 1725.

1-44 GILOT John, and Mrs. Abigail Batt; m. by Rev. John Burt, Dec. 26, 1756.

1-40 GINS Thomas, and Tabitha Woodcock, (Int.) Nov. 29, 1718.

1-40 GLADDING John, and Alice Wardell, Oct. 31, 1693.

1-40   "   Mary, and Robert Goof, (Int.) Feb. 14, 1718.

1-63   "   Mary, and John Lawless, (Int.) Feb. 25, 1720-1.

1-103   "   Elizabeth, and Solomon Searle, (Int.) March 23, 1723; m. April 18, 1723.

1-41   "   Ebenezer, and Experience Bragg, (Int.) Oct. 30, 1725; m. Nov. 16, 1725.

1-41   "   Jonathan, and Sarah Carey, (Int.) July 2, 1726.

1-41   "   Joseph, and Priscilla Carey, (Int.) July 2, 1726.

1-41   "   William, and Esther Drown, (Int.) Sept. —, 1726.

1-41   "   Alice, and James Gladding, (Int.) Jan. 25, 1728.

1-41   "   James, and Alice Gladding, (Int.) Jan. 25, 1728.

1-41, 42   "   John, and Rebecca Allen, of Providence, (Int.) June 19, 1730; m. by Rev. Barnabus Taylor, July 6, 1730.

1-42, 43   "   Nathaniel, and Jemima Carey, (Int.) March 10, 1732-3; m. by Rev. Barnabus Taylor, April 2, 1733.

1-86   "   Mrs. Priscilla, and Samuel Oxx, April 25, 1754.

1-42, 43   "   James, and Sarah Fairbanks, (Int.) Oct. 22, 1737; m. by Rev. Barnabus Taylor, Dec. 1, 1737.

1-42   "   John, of Newport, and Mary Drown, of Bristol, (Int.) Aug. 14, 1738; m. Sept. 25, 1738.

1-42, 43   "   William, and Mehitable Blanding, (Int.) May 25, 1739; m. by Rev. Barnabus Taylor, June 30, 1739.

1-7   "   Jemima, and Ignatius Barker, (Int.) Feb. 27, 1740.

1-91   "   Martha, and Zephaniah Pease, (Int.) Feb. 27, 1740.

1-104   "   Martha, and Samuel Smith, (Int.) July 28, 1744; m. Aug. 21, 1744.

1-43, 44   "   George, and Elizabeth Cummings, (Int.) July 6, 1745; m. by Rev. John Burt, July 28, 1745.

1-74   "   Mrs. Sarah, Jr., and John May, (Int.) Aug. 13, 1746; m. Sept. 11, 1746.

1-44   "   Mrs. Sarah, and John Gibbs, April 29, 1750.

1-56   "   Mrs. Mary, and John Ingraham, Jr., June 24, 1750.

1-44   "   Samuel, and Mrs. Mary Gibbs; m. by Rev. John Burt, Sept. 9, 1751.

1-44   "   William, and Mrs. Susannah Wardwell: m. by Rev. John Burt, Oct. 19, 1752.

1-125   "   Mrs. Alice, and William White, Sept. 15, 1760.

1-44   "   John, Jr., and Mrs. Lucretia Smith: m. by Rev. John Burt, Sept. 17, 1761.

1-114   "   Mrs. Ann, and Alexander Thomson, Aug. 12, 1762.

1-45   "   Jonathan, of Newport, and Mrs. Susannah Carey, of Bristol; m. by Rev. John Burt, Feb. 8, 1764.

1-45   "   Daniel, of John, and Susannah Wardwell, of John; m. by Rev. John Burt, Aug. 2, 1769.

1-45   GLADDING William, Jr., of William, and Rebecca Tomlin, of William, dec.;
                m. by Daniel Bradford, Justice of the Peace, Feb. 4, 1781.
1-53   "   Phebe, and LeFavour Howland, Nov. 24, 1799.
1-46   "   Nathaniel, of Capt. Daniel and Susannah, and Nancy Peck, of
                Capt. Jonathan and Mary; m. by Rev. Henry Wight, July 27,
                1800.
1-129   "   Sally, and Russell Warren, March 10, 1805.
1-47   "   Solomon, of Capt. Joshua and Sarah, and Ann Waldron, of Am-
                brose and Hannah; m. by Rev. Henry Wight, Nov. 6, 1806.
1-47   "   Stephen, of William and Susannah, and Phebe Slocum, of Peleg
                and Elizabeth; m. by Rev. Henry Wight, Feb. 28, 1807.
1-46   "   John, 3d, son of John, dec., and Nancy Coggeshall, of James;
                m. by Rev. Joseph Snelling, May 1, 1808.
1-78   "   Sally, and Bennett Munro, 2d, (also 2-12), May 16, 1808.
4-7, 63 "   Peter, of Bristol, of Daniel and Sarah, and Mary Friend, of New-
                port, dau. of John; m. by Rev. Edward T. Taylor, Dec. 26,
                1826.
4-13   "   Stephen T., and Hannah V. Harding; m. by Rev. Arthur A. Ross,
                April 13, 1830.
4-26   "   Josiah, and Susan T. Swift; m. by Rev. John Starkweather, Oct.
                20, 1833.
4-218   "   James N., and Lucretia G. Cole, Feb. 26, 1838.
4-36   "   Allen J., and Abby M. Brown; m. by Rev. John Bristed, Jan. 6,
                1840.
4-42   "   Samuel M., and Hannah H. Coggeshall; m. by Rev. Ephraim Scott,
                Oct. 12, 1840.
4 44   "   Henry W., and Abby B. Munro; m. by Rev. Ephraim Scott, Jan. 5,
                1841.
4-46   "   John, and Julia Greene; m. by Rev. Henry Sullings, March 28,
                1841.
4-46, 53 "   Mary E., and John H. Waldron, April 12, 1843.
4-53   "   Edward S., and Mary A. Greene; m. by Rev. G. F. Sanborn, June
                11, 1843.
4-56   "   Abby Ann, and Capt. Gilbert Richmond, Sept. 2, 1844.
4-57   "   Dolly C., and William E. Manchester, June 11, 1845.
4-65   "   Hannah H., and William Dunbar, May 1, 1848.
1-44   GLOVER John, and Elizabeth Ball; m. by Rev. John Burt, March 17, 1751.
1-84   "   Rebecca, and James Nooning, Oct. 20, 1771.
1-114   "   Mary, and Caleb Turner, Aug. 8, 1773.
1-44   GOFF James, of Rehoboth, and Mrs. Esther Smith, of Bristol; m. by Rev.
                John Burt, Dec. 15, 1757.
1-86   "   Mrs. Esther, and Capt. Ezra Ormsby, Oct. 12, 1764.
4-5   "   Sulvanus, of Asa and Julia, and Ann Davis Gray, of Pardon and
                Reliance; m. by Rev. Henry Wight, Aug. 31, 1817.
4-46   "   Thomas P., of Providence, and M—— Pierce, of Bristol; m. by
                Rev. Henry Sullings, May 24, 1841.
4-53   "   Sarah A., and Nehemiah Cole, Jr., Jan. 19, 1843.
4-63   "   Edward, and Maria R. Bowen; m. by Rev. Jonathan Cady, Sept.
                8, 1846.
4-63   "   Esther, and Joseph Peck, May 30, 1847.
4-22   GOODING Mary, and Charles De Wolf, Dec. 11, 1803.
4-30   "   Ann, and Lot H. Poole, March 20, 1839.
4-34   "   Josephus, and Mary Ellen Howland; m. by Rev. James C. Bon-
                tacue, April 7, 1839.
1-46   GOODWIN Henry, of Boston, son of Benjamin, and Polly Bradford, of
                Hon. William, of Bristol; m. by Daniel Bradford, Justice of
                Peace, May 20, 1782.
1-40   GOOF Robert, and Mary Gladding, (Int.) Feb. 14, 1718.
1-46   GOONERSON George, of Copenhagen, Denmark, and Rhoda Dunham, of
                Tiverton, R. I.; m. by Rev. Moses Shepard, Sept. 13, 1812.
1-86   GORHAM Mary, and Samuel Osborne, (Int.) Nov. 27, 1736.
1-61   "   Hannah, and John Kinnecut, (Int.) May 13, 1737.
1-40, 43 "   Isaac, and Jemima Potter, (Int.) Sept. 27, 1742; m. Oct. 19,
                1742.
1-43   "   Jabez, and Mary Maxfield, (Int.) March 30, 1744.

1-105 GORHAM Mrs. Mary, and Stephen Smith, Oct. 13, 1763.
1-54   "   Ruth, and Jabez Holmes, Feb. 8, 1813.
4-65   "   William T., and Mary T. Spencer; m. by Rev. Jonathan Cady, Oct. 13, 1847.
4-42 GORTON Julia A., and Stephen D. Gray, Dec. 3, 1840.
4-54   "   John B., of Warwick, and Hannah Chase, of Portsmouth; m. by Rev. V. R. Osborne, March 19, 1844.
4-56   "   William W., of Smithfield, and Susan A. Sherman, of Bristol; m. by Rev. James N. Sykes, May 5, 1844.
1-45 GRANT Richard, and Sarah Davison; m. at Albany, N. Y., by Thomas Clark, V. D. M., Sept. 29, 1783.
4-63   "   James M., and Elizabeth G. Coit; m. by Rev. Thomas Shepard, April 12, 1847.
1-40 GRAY Samuel, of Bristol, and Hannah Kent, of Barrington, (Int.) Dec. 17, 1720.
1-111   "   Dorothy, and Samuel Throop, (Int.) March 31, 1722.
1-44   "   Samuel, of Little Compton, and Deborah Peck, of Bristol; m. by Rev. John Burt, Oct. 25, 1750.
4-30   "   Ruth, and Thomas Waldron, Feb. 1, 1778.
4-5   "   Ann Davis, and Sylvanus Goff, Aug. 31, 1817.
4-42   "   Stephen D., of Bristol, and Julia A. Gorton, of Warwick; m. by Rev. Henry Sullings, Dec. 3, 1840.
1-15 GREENE Infield, and Samuel Cook, (Int.) March 6, 1718-19.
1-40   "   Christopher, and Elizabeth Denmark, (Int.) Aug. 20, 1721.
1-58   "   Sarah, and John Jones, (Int.) June 27, 1724.
1-41   "   Elizabeth, and Richard Gill, (Int.) Oct. 27, 1725.
1-51   "   Mary, and Jabez Howland, (Int.) March 11, 1727.
1-42   "   Thomas, of Newport, and Mrs. Elizabeth Church, of Bristol, (also 1-43), (Int.) Feb. 19, 1731-2; m. by Rev. Barnabus Taylor, April 9, 1732.
1-42   "   Mary, and Richard Greene (also 1-43), (Int.) April 24, 1735; m. May 10, 1735.
1-42   "   Richard, of New York, and Mary Greene, of Bristol (also 1-43), (Int.) April 24, 1735; m. by Rev. Barnabus Taylor, May 10, 1735.
1-43   "   Daniel, of Warwick, and Bethia Davis, of Bristol, (Int.) Nov. 21, 1741.
1-20   "   Mrs. Hannah, and Gardiner Chandler, Sept. 25, 1755.
1-66   "   Mary, and Rev. Abial Leonard, May 8, 1766.
1-45   "   Benjamin, of Joseph W. and Rebecca, and Joanna Cole, of Thomas and Nancy; m. by Rev. Henry Wight, May 26, 1805.
4-75   "   Richard, and Hannah Holdridge; m. by Rev. Alexander V. Griswold, Aug. 18, 1806.
4-10   "   Scott, of Portland, Me., and Sarah Bosworth; m. by Rev. John Bristed, Dec. 17, 1830.
4-22   "   Mrs. Hannah and Nathaniel Ingraham, May 2, 1834.
4-28   "   Maria Patience, and Silas Holmes, Oct. 2, 1837.
4-32   "   Thomas W., of Benjamin, of Bristol, and Richard S. Cummings, of N. Dartmouth; m. at New Bedford by Rev. Moses Howe, Sept. 30, 1839.
4-46   "   Julia, and John Gladding, March 28, 1841.
4-50   "   Charles A., of Providence, and Phebe J. Burgess, of Bristol; m. by Rev. G. F. Sanborn, Dec. 13, 1841.
4-53   "   Mary A., and Edward S. Gladding, June 11, 1843.
4-73   "   Mary A., and William H. Simmons, Dec. 9, 1849.
1-99 GREENWOOD Lydia, and Joseph Reynolds, Jr., (Int.) —— 14, 1744.
1-46 GREER Daniel, of Liverpool, Eng., and Sophronia Easterbrooks, of Daniel and Abigail, of Bristol; m. by Rev. Henry Wight, April 27, 1806.
1-40 GRIDLEY Samuel, and Rebecca Frazier, (Int.) Nov. 20, 1720.
1-45 GRIMES John, of Bow-cliff, Eng., and Olive Walker, of Abraham and Jemima, of Bristol; m. by Rev. Henry Wight, Dec. 2, 1798.
4-54 GRINNELL James, and Ruth G. Osgood; m. by Rev. V. R. Osborn, July 3, 1843.
4-54   "   Clara, and John Springer, July 12, 1843.

4-61   GUILD William, and Abby Boss, both of Newport; m. by Rev. Thomas Shepard, Aug. 4, 1845.
1-40   GUY Abraham, and Abigail Bragg, (Int.) Jan. 20, 1721-2; m. by Rev. Nathaniel Cotton, Feb. 6, 1721.
1-41   "   Timothy, and Abagail Knight, late of Woburn, Mass., (Int.) Feb. 5, 1725-6.

H

4-26   HADLEY Emeline, and William M. Blye, Oct. 27, 1829.
1-70   HAILE Ann, and Benjamin Munro, (Int.) Jan. 25, 1727-8.
2-71   "   Mary, and Hezekiel Munro, (also 2-72) (Int.) March 16, 1737.
1-113   "   Phebe, and John Throop, Jr., (Int.) Oct. 6, 1739.
1-79   "   Ruth, and Hezekiah Munro, Nov. 19, 1794.
1-53   HALL Noah, of Josiah and Abigail, and Rebecca White, of William and Alice; m. by Rev. Henry Wight, Aug. 25, 1805.
1-38   "   Martha, and Thomas Freeborn, Sept. 15, 1805.
1-33   "   Hannah, and Crawford Easterbrooks, Nov. 11, 1813.
4-227   "   Benjamin, of Bristol, son of George, of Portsmouth, and Ruth M. Rogers, of Joseph, of Middletown; m. by Rev. Michael Eddy, May 21, 1820.
4-38   "   Elizabeth, and Charles Spooner, Oct. 9, 1839.
4-52   "   Phebe A., and George W. S. Vaughn, Sept. 18, 1842.
1-50   HAMMON Edward, and Susannah Bradley, Jan. 5, 1684.
1-76   HANDY Phebe, and James Mitchell, July 8, 1779.
4-46   "   William, and Josephine B. Reed; m. by Rev. Ephraim Scott, May 23, 1841.
1-52   HARDING Joseph, and Elizabeth Moore, (Int.) Sept. 25, 1742; m. by Rev. John Usher, Oct. 24, 1742.
1-77   "   Sally, and Elisha Mason, Oct. 22, 1805.
4-13   "   Hannah V., and Stephen T. Gladding, April 18, 1830.
4-13   "   Thomas Allen, of Benjamin and Mary, and Sarah Rawson, of Samuel and Martha; m. by Rev. Henry Wight, May 3, 1833.
1-24   HARNEY Alice, and Isaac Crocker, (Int) Oct. 31, 1741.
1-50   HARRIS George, and Eleanor Ford, (Int.) March 7, 1725-6; m. March 28, 1725-6.
1-51   "   Eleanor, and William Harris, (Int.) Jan. 21, 1737-8.
1-51   "   William, and Eleanor Harris, (Int.) Jan. 21, 1737-8.
1-84   "   Mrs. Elizabeth, and John Norris, April 17, 1756.
1-53   "   William, of Benjamin and Hannah, and Hannah West, of Nathaniel and Rebecca; m. by Rev. Henry Wight, Jan. 12, 1806.
1-54   "   Capt. Benjamin, and Mrs. Elizabeth Scott, both of Boston, Mass.; m. by Rev. Henry Wight, May 10, 1816.
4-13   HARTSHORN Nancy, and Charles Willett, Nov. 10, 1833.
1-52   HART Mark, of Bristol, and Jane Markcleaner, of Scituate, (Int.) Oct. 20, 1744.
4-52   "   Frederick B., and Sarah C. Mott; m. by Rev. V. R. Osborn, Nov. 20, 1842.
1-51   HASKILL John, of the Parish of Thompson, Killingly, Conn., and Mary Smith, of Bristol, (Int.) March 11, 1731-2; m. by Rev. John Usher, April 7, 1732.
4-71   HATCH Jemima W., and James E. French, Nov. 13, 1849.
1-53   HATHAWAY John, of Asa, of Bristol, and Fanny Jackson, daughter of Anthony Dennis, of Somerset; m. by Daniel Bradford, Justice of the Peace, Oct. 23, 1803.
1-11   "   Nancy, and Seabury Brewster, Nov. 10, 1803.
4-6   "   Charlotte, and Enoch Bears, Oct. 27, 1825.
4-48   HAVENS Sarah D., and John H. Allen, Sept. 14, 1841.
4-63   HAVIER Anthony, of New Bedford, Mass., and Phebe S. Miller, of Bristol; m. by Rev. Jonathan Cady, Jan. 14, 1846.
1-26   HAWES Elizabeth, and Thomas Daggett, Jan. 22, 1683.
4-9   HAWLEY Sarah G., and Henry S. Strong, Nov. 4, 1827.
1-4   HAYMAN Mrs. Elizabeth, and Nathaniel Blagrove, June 18, 1690.
1-15   "   Sarah, and Thomas Church, Feb. 21, 1698.

1-8   HAYWARD Mary, and John Bosworth, Oct. 2, 1740.
4-220   HAZARD James Morgan Catskill, and Maria M. Howland, May 13, 1832.
1-89   HEARSON Elizabeth, and William Preston, (also 1-90) (Int.) June 25, 1734;
            m. July 9, 1734.
1-53   HEATH Jonathan, and Mrs. Ann Martindale, both of Newport; m. by
            Rev. John Burt, March 13, 1763.
4-34   "   Nathan B., and Elizabeth L. Pitman; m. by Rev. James C. Bon-
            tecue, May 6, 1839.
1-125   HICKS Mrs. Jane, and William West, April 3, 1748.
1-53   "   John, of Swansey, and Dorothy West, of Bristol, Oct. 4, 1770.
4-77   "   Sarah F., and Francis LeBaron, May 20, 1850.
1-71   HILL Sarah, and Timothy Miles, (Int.) Aug. 12, 1736.
1-108   "   Sally, and Jonathan Stead, June 13, 1802.
1-50   HINTON John, and Jane Nyles, Nov. 20, 1683.
4-55   HIXON Alfred, of Cumberland, and Julia A. Vaughn, of Bristol; m. by
            Rev. Thomas Shepard, Jan. 1. 1844.
1-50   HOAR Benjamin, and Rebecca Smith, April 10, 1699.
1-63   "   Hannah, and John Lindsey, Nov. 3, 1725.
1-51   "   William, and Susannah Bragg, (Int.) Oct. 26, 1734; m. by Rev.
            John Hsher, —gber 14, 1734.
1-74   "   Phebe, and Benjamin Marshall, (Int.) Jan. 28, 1746-7.
1-53   "   William, and Mrs. Phebe Carey; m. by Rev. John Burt, May 31,
            1764.
4-85   "   James, and Mary G. West; m. by Rev. Henry Wight, Oct. 24, 1831.
1-51   HOGINS Thomas, and Ann Pearse, (Int.) April 26, 1728; m. by Rev. John
            Usher, May 15, 1728.
1-52   "   John, and Mrs. Abigail Salisbury; m. by Rev. John Burt, Oct. 11,
            1759.
1-23   HOLBROOK Pattey, and Jacob Covington, Oct. 2, 1816.
4-75   HOLDRIDGE Hannah, and Richard Greene, Aug. 18, 1806.
1-50   HOLMES Ebenezer, of Plymouth, and Patience Phinney, of Bristol, (Int.)
            July 25, 1719.
1-122   "   —, and Benjamin Wardwell, (Int.) —— 18, 1734.
1-52   "   John, of Plymouth, and Mrs. Abigail Finney, of Bristol; m. by Rev.
            John Burt, Dec. 13, 1761.
1-54   "   Jabez, of Dr. Silas and Louisa, and Ruth Gorham, of Captain Isaac
            and Sarah; m. by Rev. Henry Wright, Feb. 8, 1815.
4-28   "   Silas, and Maria Patience Greene; m. by Rev. John Bristed, Oct.
            2, 1837.
4-44   "   Orin H., of Wrentham, Mass., and Almira Sweet, of Warwick, R.
            I.; m. by Rev. William L. Brower, May 24, 1840.
4-63   "   Thomas G., and Elizabeth C. Wardwell; m. by Rev. Thomas Shep-
            ard, Feb. 23, 1847.
1-50   HOMAN John, of London, England, and Mrs. Hannah Osborn, of Bris-
            tol, (Int.) May 8, 1725; m. by Rev. Nathaniel Cotton, May
            24, 1725.
1-4   HOOPER Ann, and Tristam Bowerman, July 28, 1685.
4-46   HORTON Almira, and Alfred Pierce, May 24, 1841.
4-56   "   Levi N., and Ann E. Wardwell; m. by Rev. Isaac Bonney, Oct.
            24, 1844.
1-7   HOWARD Mary, and John Bosworth, (Int.) Aug. 8, 1740.
1-1   "   Sarah, and —— Anthony (col.), (Int.) Nov. 13, 1749.
4-4   HOWE Captain John, of Bristol, and Abby Turner, of Warren; m. by Rev.
            John O. Welch, Sept. 11, 1823.
4-11   "   Sophia DeWolf, and Erastus F. Brigham, Oct. 17, 1832.
4-18   "   John R., of Warren, and Abby T. Easterbrooks, of Bristol; m. by
            Rev. John Starkweather, July 20, 1834.
4-59   "   William J., and Susan H. Waldron; m. by Rev. Hezekiah Burn-
            ham, Oct. 5, 1845.
4-79   "   Eliza T., and Theodore P. Bogert, Nov. 3, 1851.
1-50   HOWLAND Samuel, and Abigail Carey; m. by Rev. Mr. Sparhawk, May
            6, 1708.
1-111   "   Mercy, and Joseph Tillinghast, Jr., Aug. 6, 1722.
1,88, 89   "   Mrs. Mercy, and Captain George Pearce, (Int.) Aug. 25, 1722; m.
            Nov. 22, 1722.

1-26   HOWLAND Bethiah, and Samuel Davis, (Int.) June 26, 1724.
1-6   "   Bethiah, and Nicholas Bragg, May 19, 1725.
1-51   "   Jabez, of Bristol, and Mary Greene, of Warren, (Int.) March 11,
               1727.
1-16, 17 "   Abigail, and Israel Church, (Int.) Sept. 9, 1729; m. Oct. 23,
               1729.
1-89   "   Yetmarcy, and Captain Isaac Palmer, (Int.) Sept. 18, 1731; m.
               Oct. 17, 1731.
1-64 . "   Sarah, and Isaac Lawton, (also 1-64), (Int.) Aug. 5, 1732; m. Aug.
               27, 1732.
1-64   "   Mrs. Elizabeth, and Otis Little, (Int.) Sept. 2, 1733; m. Oct. 3,
               1733.
1-52   "   Captain Nathaniel, and Mrs. —— Palmer; m. by Rev. Barnabus Tay-
               lor, Dec. 6, 1733.
1-17   "   Tabitha, and Nathaniel Carey, (Int.) Dec. 8, 1733.
1-51   "   John, and Martha Wardwell, (also 1-52), (Int.) Sept. 13, 1735; m.
               by Rev. Barnabus Taylor, Oct. 24, 1736.
1-18   "   Tabitha, and Nathaniel Carey, May 12, 1738.
1-51   "   Samuel, Jr., of Bristol, and L—— Smith, of New Haven, Conn.,
               (Int.) July 29, 1738.
1-121   "   Phebe, and John Wardwell, (also 1-123), (Int.) Sept. —, 1741; m.
               Oct. 11, 1741.
1-52   "   Samuel, of Bristol, and Madam Rachel Allen, of Barrington, (Int.)
               Feb. 18, 1741-2.
1-123   "   Mary, and William Wardwell, (Int.) Sept. 7, 1742; m. Sept. 26,
               1742.
1-124   "   Mrs. Mehitable, and Stephen Wardwell, (Int.) Nov. 29, 1746; m.
               Dec. 18, 1746.
1-52   "   John, Jr., and Mrs. Elizabeth Lefavour; m. by Rev. John Burt,
               Oct. 25, 1759.
1-94   "   Sarah, and Samuel Pitman, Sept. 13, 1798.
1-53   "   Lefavour, of John and Elizabeth, and Phebe Gladding, of Captain
               Daniel and Susannah; m. by Rev. Henry Wight, Nov. 24, 1799.
4-220   "   Maria M., and James M. C. Hazard, May 13, 1832.
4-34   "   Mary Ellen, and Josephus Gooding, April 7, 1839.
4-42   "   Daniel L., and Eliza White; m. by Rev. Ephraim Scott, Nov. 22,
               1840.
4-69   "   John, and Louisa Clarke; m. by Rev. Richard Livesey, Oct. 27,
               1848.
1-71,72 HUBBARD Mrs. Elizabeth, and Richard Munday, (Int.) Jan. 8, 1731-2; m.
               Jan. 27, 1731-2.
1-54   "   Caezer, and Sarah Durfee, (col.) Aug. —, ——.
1-53   HULL John, and Mrs. Sarah Lindsey, both of Newport; m. by Rev. John
               Burt, Aug. 12, 1762.
1-36   HUMMERY Elizabeth, and John Fry, June 18, 1695.
1-51,52 HUMPHREY Jonas, of Barrington, and Mary Sharp, of Bristol, (Int.) May
               18, 1734; m. by Rev. Barnabus Taylor, June 13, 1734.
4-48   "   Amasa, and Clarissa P. Lake; m. by Rev. William L. Brower, March
               28, 1841.
1-50   HUNTINGTON Nathaniel, of Windham, Conn., and Mahitable Thurston, of
               Bristol, (Int.) Feb. 2, 1722; m. by Rev. Nathaniel Cotton, Feb.
               28, 1722-3.
1-52   "   Hon. Hezekiah, of Norwich, Conn., and Mrs. Dorothy Williams, of
               Bristol, March 23, 1748-9.
1-71,72 HUSBAND Sarah, and Edward Matteson, (Int.) Sept. 13, 1729; m. Oct. 26,
               1729.
4-11   HYDE Nancy, and John G. Munro, March 18, 1832.

I

1-57   INGALLS Philip Wheeler, of Elkanah and Rebecca, and Elizabeth Blake, of
               Ebenezer and Elizabeth; m. by Rev. Henry Wight, Jan. 4, 1801.
1-56   INGRAHAM Jeremiah, and Mercy Munro; m. by Job Almy, Justice of the
               Peace, July 10, 1718.

1-56 INGRAHAM Edward, and Silence Mason, (Int.) — —, 1721.
1-56 " John, and Mary Fry, (Int.) Nov. 27, 1723; m. by Rev. Nathaniel
    Colton, Dec. 12, 1723.
1-56 " Isaac, and Elizabeth Lindsey, (Int.) Oct. 2, 1725; m. by Rev. John
    Usher, Nov. 9, 1725.
1-56 " Joshua, and Martha Lawton, (Int.) Sept. 11, 1729; m. Oct. 23,
    1729.
1-56 " John, of Newport, and Mary Munro, of Bristol, (Int.) July 19,
    1736.
1-43 " Mrs. Mary, and James Gibbs, April 29, 1742; m. May 13, 1742.
1-124 " Sarah, and John Warren, (Int.) Sept. 16, 1744.
1-56 " John, Jr., and Mrs. Mary Gladding; m. by Rev. John Burt, June
    24, 1750.
1-94 " Polly, and Samuel Pitman, Nov. 29, 1792.
1-57 " Daniel, son of John and Mary, and Abigail Munro, of Nathaniel,
    1st, and Abigail; m. by Rev. Henry Wight, Feb. 3, 1793.
1-79 " Althea, and Bennett Munro, Nov. 17, 1796.
4-26 " Hannah, and Simeon Doty, Sept. 3, 1822.
4-9 " Hannah C., and Oliver S. Jones, May 10, 1829.
4-22 " Nathaniel, and Mrs. Hannah Greene; m. by Rev. Henry Sullings,
    May 2, 1834.
4-83 " Mary E., and James Winslow, Oct. 6, 1850.

J

1-59 JACKSON Hezekiah, of Nathaniel and Martha, and Elizabeth Fales Diman,
    of Jonathan and Dorothy; m. by Rev. Henry Wight, May 20,
    1798.
1-53 " Fanny, and John Hathaway, Oct. 23, 1803.
1-75 JACOB Clarissa, and William MacKarty, Nov. 7, 1770.
1-58 JAMES Benjamin, and Elizabeth Smith, (Int.) June 17, 1738.
1-58 " Benjamin, and Elizabeth Smith; m. by Rev. Barnabus Taylor,
    July 6, 1738.
1-59 " William, of Newport, and Hannah Munro, of Bristol, (Int.) Jan.
    4, 1741-2.
1-59 " Benjamin, of Newport, and Mrs. Ruth May, of Bristol; m. by
    Rev. John Burt, Oct. 27, 1765.
1-11 " Betsey Bloom, and Major William Bradford, July 11, 1777.
1-106 " Ruth, and Richard Smith, Jan. 25, 1792.
1-59 JARVIS Leonard, and Mrs. Sarah Church, (Int.) Aug. 1, 1741.
1-10 " Susannah, and Daniel Bradford, Sept. 25, 1771.
1-58 JENKINS Richard, and Mrs. Mary Peper; m. by Rev. Mr. Sparhawk, Feb.
    2, 1701.
1-59 " Joseph, and Mrs. Phebe Sharp, (Int.) Oct. 12, 1744; m. by Rev.
    John Burt, Dec. 24, 1744.
1-59 " John, and Mrs. Sarah Sharp, Oct. 8, 1747.
1-60 JENNISON William, and Violet Luther (col.); m. by Rev. Henry Wight,
    Nov. 26, 1801.
1-58 JERIUS Leonard, and Sarah Church, Aug. 27, 1741.
1-80 JETHRO Sarah, and John Mingo (col.), (Int.) Dec. 7, 1741.
1-15 JOLLS Elizabeth, and Miles Cotton, (Int.) July 6, 1720.
1-58 " Thomas, and Mehitable Ormsby, (Int.) March 15, 1732-3.
1-7 " Mary, and William Burton, March 31, 1735.
1-71, 72 " Mary, and Nathaniel Munro, (Int.) Nov. 29, 1735; m. —br 24,
    1735.
1-65 " Mary, and Hezekiah Luther, Jr., March 17, 1751.
1-63 JONES Ann, and John Lyscum, Aug. 2, 1692.
1-58 " Benjamin, and Elizabeth Borden, Sept. 18, 1696.
1-58 " John, and Sarah Greene, (Int.) June 27, 1724.
1-80 " Submit, and John Patridge, Feb. 17, 1725-6.
1-6 " Lydia, and Jacob Bosworth, (Int.) Dec. 9, 1727.
1-41, 42 " Sarah, and John Gibbs, (Int.) Sept. 13, 1729; m. Oct. 9, 1729.
1-27 " Rebecca, and John Dyer, (Int.) Aug. 15, 1730.

1-58   JONES Morgan, and Rebecca Cowell, (Int.) Oct. 27, 1731; m. by Rev.
            John Usher, Nov. 2, 1731.
1-42, 58   "   Nathan, and Bathsheba Drown, (Int.) Sept. 18, 1736; p. by Rev.
            Barnabus Taylor, Nov. 10, 1736.
1-19   "   Sarah, and William Kipp, (Int.) June 1, 1744.
1-20   "   Mrs. Hannah, and John Cosins, April 22, 1764.
4-77   "   Edward, and Lucretia Waldron; m. by Rev. Alexander V. Gris-
            wold, July 28, 1806.
1-59   "   Captain Thomas, and Harriet Waldron, daughter of Benjamin and
            Sarah; m. by Rev. Henry Wight, Aug. 30, 1813.
4-4   "   Peleg Gardiner, of Simeon and Lydia, and Fanny Martin Diman,
            of Royal and Elizabeth; m. by Rev. Henry Wight, June 26,
            1821.
4-9   "   Oliver S., of Nathaniel, and Hannah C. Ingraham, of Daniel; m.
            by Rev. Leonard B. Griffing, May 10, 1809.
4-10   "   Harriet, and George W. Allen, Dec. 8, 1830.
4-38   "   Charlotte M., and James M. Bowen, Nov. 8, 1839.
4-46   "   Delana H., and Abraham Simmons, Sept. 29, 1841.
4-59   "   Charles H., son of widow Fanny M., and Betsey M. Bowen, of
            Mrs. Philena; m. by Rev. James N. Sykes, Dec. 21, 1845.
1-63   JOSLIN Keziah, and Samuel Lindsey, (Int.) Oct. 14, 1718.
1-58   JOY Joseph, of Rehoboth, and Esther Finney, of Bristol, (Int.) Oct. 31,
            1719.
1-90, 91   "   Esther, and John Phillips, (Int.) Aug. 25, 1739; m. Sept. 20, 1739.
1-59   "   Joseph, and Mary Pearce, (Int.) Sept. 5, 1745.

K

4-6   KAULL Caroline, and John Easterbrooks, Feb. 6, 1825.
1-83   KEEN Mrs. Sarah, and Captain Shubael Norton, (Int.) July 1, 1723; m.
            July 4, 1723.
1-61   KELLEY John, and Elizabeth Rosbotham, (Int.) May 9, 1729.
1-61   "   Joseph, and Mrs. Bridget Phillips, (Int.) Jan. 20, 1736-0.
1-61   "   Joseph, and Sarah Salisbury, (Int.) Dec. 14, 1745.
1-61   KEMPTON Samuel, and Esther Throop; m. by Rev. Barnabus Taylor, Oct.
            15, 1730.
1-61   KENTON Thomas, of Plymouth, and Esther Throop, of Bristol, (Int.)
            June 19, 1730.
1-10   KENT Hannah, and Samuel Gray, (Int.) Dec. 17, 1720.
1-28   "   Hannah, and Benjamin Drown, July 24, 1738.
1-27   "   Sarah, and Jonathan Drown, ——, —, ——.
1-14   "   Rachel, and Shearjashub Bourne, Nov. 20, 1793.
1-62   "   Asa, of Bristol, son of Jacob and Abigail, of Brookfield, Mass.,
            and Susan Munro, daughter of Edward and Sarah, of Bristol;
            m. by Rev. Joel Winch, April 29, 1814.
1-62, 63   KEZZER George, of Boston, and Elizabeth Adams, of Bristol, (Int.) Dec.
            23, 1718.
1-61   KIDDER Ephraim, of Billerica, Mass., and Elizabeth Carey, of Bristol, (Int.)
            April 3, 1724; m. by Rev. Nathaniel Cotton, June 1, 1724.
4-24   KIMBALL Julia Ann, and William H. Manchester, June 15, 1828.
1-61   KIM Richard, and Abigail Thompson (col.); m. by Daniel Bradford, Jus-
            tice of the Peace, Dec. 25, 1802.
1-89   KINGSLEY Mary, and Thomas Peck, May 26, 1733.
1-36   KINNECUT Joanna, and Jonathan Finney, Oct. 15, 1682.
1-61   "   Thomas, and Hannah Bowerman; m. by Rev. Mr. Sparhawk, May
            2, 1706.
1-61   "   Thomas, and Sarah Bosworth, (Int.) May 18, 1728.
1-61   "   John, of Swansey, and Hannah Gorham, of Bristol, (Int.) May 13,
            1737.
1-19   "   Elizabeth, and John Coomer, Aug. 20, 1752.
1-74   "   Mrs. Elizabeth, and Nathan Munro, May 25, 1755.
4-3, 4   "   Abby, and Joseph Munro, Aug. 15, 1811.
1-19   KIPP William, and Sarah Jones, (Int.) June 1, 1744.
1-41   KNIGHT Abigail, and Timothy Guy. (Int.) Feb. 5, 1725-6.

4-54 KNOX Robert A., of Warwick, and Harriet G. Wheeler, of Bristol; m. by Rev. V. R. Osborne, Sept. 4, 1843.

L

1-112 LADD Elizabeth, and George Thurrell, (Int.) Jan. 16, 1724-5.

4-8 LAKE Isaac, of Portsmouth, son of Daniel, and Nancy Case, of Rehoboth; m. by Thomas Durfee, Justice of the Peace, Sept. 17, 1812.

4-5 " Elias, of Freetown, son of Pardon, and Elizabeth Cartee, of Bristol, daughter of Benjamin; m. by Rev. Thomas W. Tucker, Feb. 27, 1825

4-38 " Ann, and William C. Liscomb, March 17, 1836.

4-48 " Clarissa P., and Amasa Humphrey, March 28, 1841.

4-54 " Albert, and Almeda Alger; m. by Rev. V. R. Osborne, Oct. 5, 1843.

4-70 " Jonathan, of Bristol, and Mary Reynolds, of Fall River; m. by Rev. Thomas Shepard, Sept. 10, 1848.

4-40 LANE Harriet G., and James T. Freeborn, Aug. 25, 1840.

4-10 LANSING John Usher, of Myndert and Mary, and Elizabeth Ellery Sanford; m. by Rev. Alexander V. Griswold, Feb. 26, 1827.

1-68 LAWLESS John, and Mary Gladding, (Int.) Feb. 25, 1720-1.

1-32 " Mary, and Isaac Esleck, (Int.) April 25, 1740; m. May 13, 1740.

1-65 " William, and Mrs. Rebecca Dyer; m. by Rev. John Burt, June 21, 1761.

4-36 " Sarah, and Nathaniel Liscomb, March 27, 1819.

4-38 " James, and Alice F. Cartee; m. by Rev. Ephraim Scott, June 24, 1840.

4-40 " Martha, and James D. Wardwell, Aug. 17, 1840.

4-65 " Sarah, and John G. Cole, Dec. 29, 1847.

1-63 LAWRENCE Thomas, and Elizabeth Fairbanks, (Int.) May 6, 1728.

4-36 " Eliza, and James M. Munro, Sept. 1, 1839.

1-6 LAWSON Mary, and William Burton, (Int.) March 8, 1734.

1-88 LAWTON Susannah, and Richard Pearce, (Int.) May 4, 1723.

1-70 " Mary, and John Moore, (Int.) Aug. 17, 1724.

1-56 " Martha, and Joshua Ingraham, (Int.) Sept. 11, 1729; m. Oct. 23, 1729.

1-63, 64 " Isaac, and Sarah Howland, (Int.) Aug. 5, 1732; m. by Rev. John Usher. Aug. 27, 1732.

1-64 " Thomas, and Susannah Martin, (Int.) Jan. 29, 1736-7.

1-64 " Margaret, and Thomas Little, (Int.) Jan. 29, 1736-7.

1-66 " Reading, and Julina Russell, (col.) (Int.) ——, 1737.

1-9 " Mrs. Mary, and Obadiah Bosworth, Feb. 8, 1753.

1-105 " Mrs. Elizabeth, and Benjamin Salisbury, March 31, 1756.

1-66 " Thomas, and Mrs. Mary Bosworth; m. by Rev. John Burt, Jan. 2, 1766.

4-8, 22 " Beeby B., and John S. Douglass, June 26, 1836.

4-36 " Peter, and Nancy F. Simmons; m. by Rev. Ephraim Scott, Aug. 12, 1839.

4-53 " Harriet M., and John L. Daggett, July 20, 1842.

4-54 " Horace, and Waitey S. Dubars; m. by Rev. G. F. Sanborn, July 14, 1844.

4-79 LEACH Mary W., and John D. Eddy, Dec. 21, 1846.

4-77 LEBARON Francis, and Sarah F. Hickes; m. at Brooklyn, N. Y., by Rev. John M. Windsor, May 20, 1857.

1-64 LEE George, of Boston, and Susannah Viall, of Bristol, (Int.) Sept. 30, 1734.

1-65 " Capt. George, and Mrs. Susannah Viall; m. by Rev. Barnabus Taylor, Oct. 24, 1734.

1-64 " Susannah, and Rogers Richmond, (Int.) April 21, 1739; m. May 17, 1739.

1-4 LEFAVOUR Mrs. Hannah, and John Bosworth, Sept. 13, 1718.

1-75 " Eunice, and Bonne Norton (col.), Jan. 29, 1740.

1-65 " Daniel, and Mrs. Jemima Wardwell; m. by Rev. John Burt, Jan. 2, 1758.

1-29 " Mrs. Ann, and James Diman, March 30, 1758.

1-52 " Mrs. Elizabeth, and John Howland, Jr., Oct. 25, 1759.

1-66	LEFFINWELL	Samuel, of Norwich. Conn., and Mrs. Sarah, Russell, of Bristol; m. by Rev. John Burt, Dec. 10, 1761.
1-101	LEONARD	Mrs. Phebe, and Joseph Reynolds, (Int.) Aug. 11, 1718,
1-66	"	Rev. Abial, of Woodstock, Conn., and Mary Greene, of Bristol; m. by Rev. John Burt, May 8, 1766.
4-38	"	Phebe, and George P. Pearce, July 19, 1840.
4-69	"	John H., of Providence, and Ann C. Peabody, of Bristol; m. by Rev. Richard Livesey, Dec. 5, 1848.
4-70	"	Abby M., and Henry W. Ellis, Aug. 23, 1849.
1-69	LEWIS	Hannah, and George Mowry, Jan. 22, 1683.
1-36	"	Esther, and Jeremiah Finney, Jan. 7, 1684.
1-111	"	Hephzabeth, and James Thurber, Dec. 25, 1706.
1-66	"	John, of Aaron and Polly, and Ann Jenckes Vose, of John and Judith; m. by Rev. Henry Wight, Dec. 25, 1803.
1-96	"	Mary, and Edward Pearce (col.), Sept. 19, 1811.
4-5	"	Mrs. Ann Jenckes, and Martin Pearce, Oct. 19, 1824.
4-7	"	Sarah Ann, and George Washington Ling, Sept. 24, 1826.
4-18	"	Alfred L., of John, and Martha P. Coit, of David A.; m. by Harvey Sullings, Nov. 10, 1835.
4-24	"	Mary M., and James N. Palmer, May 29, 1837.
4-32	"	John V., and Betsey Oxx; m. by Rev. Thomas Shepard, Jan. 20, 1839.
4-48	"	Nathaniel, and Almira Daggett, both of Rehoboth, Mass.; m. by Rev. William L. Brower, April 24, 1842.
4-3	LINCOLN	Joanna, and Allen Munro, March 2, 1820.
4-7	"	Mayberry L., and Mary Lindsey; m. by Rev. Timothy Merrett, Jan. 11, 1824.
4-48	"	Sarah, and Rufus Arnold, May 16, 1842.
4-56	"	Mary L., and Seth Lincoln, Aug. 1, 1844.
4-56	"	Seth, and Mary L. Lincoln; m. by Rev. Isaac Bonney, Aug. 1, 1844.
4-61	"	William, and Caroline L. Coddington; m. by Rev. Thomas Shepard, May 24, 1846.
4-70	"	Ruth, and Elisha Partrage, June 24, 1849.
4-70	"	Eliza S., and George N. White, Sept. 3, 1849.
1-63	LINDSEY	John, and Elizabeth Munro, Aug. 29, 1694.
1-63	"	Samuel, and Keziah Joslin, of Scituate, (Int.) Oct. 14, 1718.
1-5	"	Mary, and John Bucklin, (Int.) Nov. 2, 1723.
1-86	"	Mary, and Samuel Oxx, Nov. 29, 1723.
1-56	"	Elizabeth, and Isaac Ingraham, (Int.) Oct. 2, 1725; m. Nov. 9, 1725.
1-63	"	John, and Hannah Hoar; m. by Rev. John Usher, Nov. 3, 1725.
1-5	"	Elizabeth, and Nathaniel Bosworth, Aug. 18, 1727.
1-89, 90	"	Mary, and Nathaniel Pearse, (Int.) May 4, 1731-2; m. April 6, 1732.
1-64	"	Benjamin, and Elizabeth Church, of Little Compton, (Int.) Feb. 7, 1732-3.
1-64, 65	"	John, and Elizabeth Smith, (Int.) Jan. 12, 1733; m. by Rev. Barnabus Taylor, Jan. 29, 1733-4.
1-64, 65	"	William, and Mary Wardwell, (Int.) Oct. 15, 1737; m. by Rev. Barnabus Taylor, Nov. 23, 1737.
1-122	"	Jemima, and Joseph Wardwell, Jr., (Int.) Jan. 21, 1737-8; m. Feb. 23, 1737-8.
1-122	"	Sarah, and Usal Wardwell, (Int.) Sept. 26, 1739.
1-73	"	Elizabeth, and William Martin, Jr., (Int.) Sept. 3, 1745.
1-74	"	Mrs. Hannah, and Jeremiah Munro, (Int.) May 5, 1746.
1-53	"	Mrs. Sarah, and John Hull, Aug. 12, 1762.
1-9	"	Mrs. Mary, and Elijah Bradford, Feb. 6, 1763.
1-76	"	Abigail, and George Munro, May 21, 1769.
1-86	"	Rebecca, and Samuel Oxx, April 7, 1771.
1-66	"	William, Jr., son of William, and Catherine Woodbury, of Jonathan, deceased; m. by Rev. John Burt, April 26, 1772.
1-66	"	Joseph, and Deborah Church, Aug. 9, 1772.
4-30	"	Samuel, and Pamelia Chase; m. by Rev. Henry Wight, Dec. 31, 1793.
1-94	"	Catharine, and John Peckham, Dec. 12, 1799.

1-77   LINDSEY Martha, and George Munro, Jan. 9, 1804.
1-127   "   Anstis, and Benjamin West, Aug. 25, 1805.
1-95·   "   Nancy, and Perry M. Peckham, recorded May 7, 1814.
4-3   "   Sally, and Josiah S. Wardwell, April 22, 1821.
4-7   "   Mary, and Mayberry L. Lincoln, Jan. 11, 1824.
4-5   "   Hannah, and Josiah H. Pitman, Nov. 15, 1824.
4-16   "   Sarah Luther, and Henry Wardwell, May 11, 1835.
4-18   "   Lydia Woodbury, and William Spencer, June 21, 1835.
4-52   "   Abby, and Hiram Luther, Feb. 13, 1838.
4-44   "   Nancy W., and Barney Presbury, Jan. 7, 1841.
4-70   "   Mary E., and Matthias Frederic, Sept. 5, 1849.
4-73   "   Thomas F., and Maria E. Bowler; m. by Rev. Richard Bowler, Jan. 10, 1850.
4-7   LING George Washington, of Sylvanus and Jane, and Sarah Ann Lewis, of John and Anna Jenckes; m. by Rev. Henry Wight, Sept. 24, 1826.
1-63   LISCOMB John, Jr., and Rebecca Thurston; m. by N. Byfield, Justice of the Peace, May 13, 1718.
1-123   "   Ann, and James Wardwell, Jr., (Int.) June 20, 1741; m. March 3, 1742.
1-65   "   John, Jr., and Mrs. Margaret Wilson, (Int.) Dec. 5, 1746.
1-87   "   Priscilla, and John Oldridge, March 3, 1774.
1-33   "   Leah, and Aaron Easterbrooks, May 28, 1775.
4-36   "   John, and Abigail Sanford; m. by Rev. Henry Wight, March 19, 1786.
1-107   "   Lydia, and Daniel Sanford, July 22, 1811.
4-36   "   Nathaniel, of Nathaniel and Nancy, and Sarah Lawless, of John and Sarah; m. by Rev. Henry Wight, March 27, 1819.
4-4   "   Elizabeth, and Gilbert Richmond, April 9, 1822.
4-38   "   William C., and Anne Lake; m. by Rev. Hebron Vincent, March 17, 1836.
4-38   "   Jeremiah D., and Elizabeth Wood; m. by Rev. Thomas Shepard, Nov. 20, 1839.
4-40   "   Simon DeW., and Phebe Munro; m. by Rev. Ephraim Scott, Aug. 16, 1840.
4-54   "   Samuel, and Elizabeth A. Day; m. by Rev. V. R. Osborn, July 12, 1843.
4-59   "   Catherine, and Robinson Chase, Sept. 10, 1845.
1-66   LITTLE Edward, and Mary Walker, of Thomas; m. by Rev. Mr. Sparhawk, Nov. 7, 1717.
1-63   "   Captain Samuel, of Bristol, and Mrs. Hannah Wilson, of Rehoboth, (also 1-65) (Int.) Oct. 2, 1730; m. Oct. 29, 1730.
1-47   "   Peggy, and Joseph Gallup, (col.) Sept. 14, 1732.
1-64   "   Otis, of Pembroke, and Mrs. Elizabeth Howland, of Bristol, (Int.) Sept. 2, 1733; m. by Rev. John Usher, Oct. 3, 1733.
1-64   "   Thomas, and Margaret Lawton, (Int.) Feb. 5, 1735-6.
1-64   "   Samuel, and Hannah Carr, (Int.) Dec. 8, 1739.
1-37   "   Sarah, and Nathaniel Fales, (Int.) Aug. 16, 1740.
1-65, 66   "   Edward, and Mrs. Mary Burnham, of Norwich, (Int.) April 2, 1741; m. by Rev. Mr. Kirtland, June 18, 1741.
1-99   "   Mary, and Nathaniel Reynolds, (Int.) June 13, 1741.
4-57   LIVSEY John, of Nantucket, Mass, and Elizabeth W. Reed, of Somerset, Mass.; m. by Rev. Isaac Bonney, July 22, 1845.
1-64, 65   LONGROUND Nicholas, and Judith Price, (Int.) May 9, 1746; m. by Rev. John Burt, June 3, 1746.
1-89   LORING Hannah, and Jonathan Peck, (Int.) Nov. 3, 1731.
1-5   LOWDER Ruth, and Benjamin Bosworth, (Int.) Dec. 20, 1718.
1-26   LOW Ann, and Simeon Davis, Sept. 24, 1685.
1-103   LUCAS Bethia, and Joseph Sundye, Oct. 18, 1682.
1-15   "   Hannah, and Robert Carter, April 19, 1694.
4-55   LUCE Lucretia N., and J. Frederick Baars, Aug. 22, 1842.
1-36   LUMBER Mercy, and Alexander Frazier (also 1-37), (Int.) Dec. 17, 1725; m. Jan. 19, 1726.

1-1   LUTHER Patience, and William Allen, (Int.) March 22, 1735.
1-65   "   Hezekiah, Jr., of Swansey, and Mary Jolls, of Bristol; m. by Rev.
                    John Burt, March 17, 1751.
4-61   "   Elizabeth, and Giles Luther, Oct. 10, 1796.
4-61   "   Giles, and Elizabeth Luther, Oct. 10, 1796.
1-60   "   Violet, and William Jennison, (col.), Nov. 26, 1801.
4-1   "   Sylvester, of Benjamin and Lydia, of Swansey, and Lydia P. Rey-
                    nolds, of William and Elizabeth, of Bristol; m. by Rev. Joel
                    Mann, March 16, 1820.
4-8   "   Lemira, and Caleb Munro, Sept. 6, 1821; another record reads
                    Sept. 6, 1824.
4-11   "   Samuel P., of Warren, and Eliza Vaughn; m. by Rev. E. K. Avery,
                    Aug. 13, 1832.
4-22   "   Edward M., of Obadiah, and Abby Bowen, of Silas, dec.; m. by
                    Rev. Hervey Sullings, Aug. 28, 183 .
4-52   "   Hiram, and Abby Lindsey; m. by Rev. James C. Bontecue, Feb. 13,
                    1838.
4-38   "   Abby, and Walter C. F. Barker, Nov. 10, 1839.
1-63   LYON Ebenezer, of Woodstock, and Rebecca Throop, of Bristol (also 1-65),
                    (Int.) Jan. 28, 1731-2; m. by Rev. Barnabus Taylor, March 8,
                    1731-2.
1-63   LYSEUM John, and Ann Jones, Aug. 2, 1692.

M

1-111   MACEY Deborah, and Daniel Throop, Jan. 5, 1697.
1-75   MACKARTY William, of Dennis, deceased, and Clarissa Jacob; m. by Rev.
                    John Burt, Nov. 7, 1770.
4-57   MACOMBER Sarah W., and Walter Bradford, June 19, 1845.
1-69   MANCHESTER Edward, and Mary Manchester, both of Tiverton; m. by
                    Thomas Church, Justice of the Peace, April 10, 1718.
1-69   "   Mary, and Edward Manchester, April 10, 1718.
1-69   "   Benjamin, and Martha Seabury, (Int.) July 12, 1723.
1-104   "   Mrs. Phebe, and Nathaniel Smith, Jr., (Int.) April 26, 1746; m.
                    May 21, 1746.
1-75   "   Seabury, and Mrs. Miriam Wyatt; m. by Rev. John Burt, Feb. 1,
                    1763.
1-77,118   "   William, of Seabury and Miriam, and Hannah Drown, of R—— and
                    Sarah; m. by Rev. Henry Wight, Dec. 29, 1790.
1-118   "   Phebe, and Anthony Van Doorn, May 29, 1796.
4-75,78   "   Robert, of Isaac and Alice, and Hope Miller, of Nelson and Sarah;
                    m. by Rev. Henry Wight, March 5, 1812.
4-75   "   Sally, and George Coggeshall, Oct. 28, 1812.
4-4   "   Miriam Wyatt, and William Boss Spooner, Nov. 4, 1821.
4-24   "   William H., of Bristol, and Julia Ann Kimball, of Johnston, R.
                    I.; m. by Rev. Henry Tatem, June 15, 1828.
4-83   "   Samuel S., of Providence, and Sarah Spooner; m. by Rev. Isaac
                    Bonney, May 1, 1833.
4-32   "   Henry A., and Susan J. Booth; m. by Rev. John Bristed, July 9,
                    1839.
4-53   "   Hannah, and Thomas N. Allen, March 20, 1843.
4-54   "   Mary M., and Benjamin G. West, June 4, 1843.
4-57   "   William E., of Fall River, and Dolly C. Gladding, of Bristol; m.
                    by Rev. Isaac Bonney, June 11, 1845.
4-61   "   Benjamin F., and Ann Francis Bush; m. by Rev. Thomas Shepard,
                    Aug. 3, 1845.
4-65   "   Edward, and Nancy B. Williston; m. by Rev. Jonathan Cady,
                    June 20, 1847.
4-73   "   Miriam W., and Alexander Easterbrooks, June 20, 1850.
1-113   MAN Zipomh, and Thomas Throop, (Int.) April 7, 1742.
1-113   "   Elizabeth, and Thomas Throop, Jr., (Int.) April 10, 1744.
1-113   "   Mrs. Esther, and James Tisdale, (Int.) Sept. 1, 1744; m. Sept. 25,
                    1744.
1-70   MARCY Joseph, of Woonstock, and Mary Throop, of Bristol, (Int.) April 6,
                    1728; m. by Simeon Davis, Justice of the Peace, May 31, 1728.

1-52 MAKELEANER Jane, and Mark Hart, (Int.) Oct. 24, 1744.

1-16 MARKS Catherine, widow, and David Cummings, (Int.) Dec. 10, 1726; m. Feb. 24, 1726.

2-72 " Mercy, and Thomas Munro, (Int.) April 30, 1739.

1-73 " Robert, and Mary Carpenter, (Int.) Sept. 24, 1739.

1-74 MARSHALL Benjamin, of Bristol, and Phebe Hoar, of Dighton, (Int.) Jan. 28, 1746-7.

1-74 " Peter, and Kenith Audinith; m. by Rev. Henry Wight, June 2, 1808.

4-6 MARSH Joseph, and Rosanna Eldridge Martin, (col.) both of Newport; m. by Rev. Henry Wight, Nov. 13, 1825.

1-70 MARTINDALE Isaac, and Mercy Pearce; m. by Rev. John Usher, July 9, 1724.

1-75 " Sion, of Newport, and Mrs. Sarah Peck, of Bristol; m. by Rev. John Burt, April 13, 1758.

1-53 ' Mrs. Ann, and Jonathan Heath, March 13, 1763.

1-69 MARTIN William, and Christian Pelton; m. by Rev. Mr. Sparhawk, May 7, 1706.

1-15 " Hannah, and Abraham Crane, (Int.) March 27, 1719.

1-70 " John, and Experience Rue, (widow) of Norton, Mass., Dec. 10, 1726.

1-70,72 " Thomas, and Ann Munro, (Int.) Nov. 18, 1727; m. by Rev. John Usher, —br 8, 1727.

1-72 " Thomas, and Hannah Smith, (Int.) Nov. 6, 1736.

1-64 " Susannah, and Thomas Lawton, (Int.) Jan. 29, 1736-7.

1-122 " Ann, and Philip Walker, (Int.) Feb. 17, 1737-8.

1-69,73 " John, of Barrington, and Mary Reed, of Bristol, (Int.) June 12, 1741; m. Nov. 12, 1741.

1-73 " William, Jr., and Martha Newton, (Int.) June 29, 1741.

1-73 " William, Jr., and Elizabeth Lindsey, (Int.) Sept. 3, 1745.

1-74 " Thomas, and Mrs. Hannah Potter; m. by Rev. John Burt, Jan. 25, 1753.

1-99 " Mrs. Martha, and John Russell, Oct. 15, 1761.

1-29 " Elizabeth, and Captain Mark Antony DeWolf, Aug. 11, 1768.

1-76 " Rufus, of Barrington, and Ann Drown, of Bristol, Dec. 29, 1794.

1-77 " John, of Ebenezer and Ruth, and Deborah Wilson, of William and Althea; m. by Rev. Henry Wight, Nov. 8, 1801.

4-6 " Rosanna Eldridge, and Joseph Marsh, (col.), Nov. 13, 1825.

4-56 " Ezra M., and Cynthia M. Wright; m. by Rev. Isaac Bonney, Dec. 26, 1844.

1-80 MASON Charles, of Joseph and Hannah, and Mary Fales, of Thomas and Sarah; m. by Rev. Henry Wight, Dec. 7, 1806.

1-23 " Ann Davis, and Solomon Coffin, June 2, 1815.

4-57 " Elizabeth C., and William C. Fales, April 10, 1845.

1-56 " Silence, and Edward Ingraham, (Int.) —— —, 1721.

1-71, 72 " Joseph, and Mehitable Davis, (Int.) April 30, 1731; m. by Rev. John Usher, May 27, 1731.

1-74 " James, Jr., of Warren, and Mrs. Mary Coggeshall, of Bristol; m. by Rev. John Burt, Dec. 17, 1752.

1-74 " Hezekiah, and Mrs. Parnel West; m. by Rev. John Burt, Nov. 28, 1756.

1-76, 77 " Gardiner, of Warren, son of John and Mary Munro, of Bristol, daughter of William; m. by Rev. John Burt, Feb. 27, 1772.

1-77 " Elisha, of Elisha and Sarah, and Sally Harding, of Jonathan and Mary; m. by Rev. Henry Wight, Oct. 22, 1805.

4-83 " James G., of Warren, and Nancy A. Allen of Bristol; m. by Rev. James Bontecon, Sept. 16, 1838.

1-71, 72 MATTESON Edward, of Great Britain, and Sarah Husband, of Bristol, (Int.) Sept. 13, 1729; m. by Rev. John Usher, —br 26, 1729.

1-113 MAXFIELD Mary, and John Zolode, May 19, 1708.

1-121 " Mary, and Robert Whitwell, (Int.) Aug. —, 1722; m. Sept. 13, 1722.

1-71 " Peter, and Mary Mills, (Int.) Jan. 3, 1728-9.

1-71, 72 " Daniel, and Mary Wardwell, (Int.) May 27, 1732; m. by Rev. John Usher, June 11, 1732.

1-43   MAXFIELD Mary, and Jabez Gorham, March 30, 1744.
1-9   "   Mrs. Esther, and Bellamy Bosworth, May 17, 1750.
1-74   "   Daniel, and Mrs. Mary Wilson; m. by Rev. John Burt, Dec. 14, 1755.
1-37   "   Mrs. Mary, and Daniel Finney, Jan. 19, 1758.
4-44   "   Nathaniel D., of Barrington, R. I., and Susan B. Sherman, of North Kingstown; m. by Rev. William L. Brower, Dec. 13, 1840.
4-28   MAXWELL Martha F., and Massadore T. Bennett, April 8, 1838.
1-8   MAYHEW Elizabeth, and Bellamy Bosworth, Feb 23, 1744.
1-123   MAY Elizabeth, and William West, (Int.) Aug. 14, 1740.
1-74   "   John, and Mrs. Sarah Gladding, Jr., (Int.) Aug. 13, 1746; m. by Rev. John Burt, Sept. 11, 1746.
1-105   "   Mrs. Sarah, and Benjamin Smith, Oct. 29, 1752.
1-59   "   Mrs. Ruth, and Benjamin James, Oct. 27, 1765.
1-75   "   Elijah, of Warren, and Mrs. Mary Wilson, of Bristol; m. by Rev. John Burt, Jan 1, 1767.
1-9   "   Mrs. Abigail, and James Brown, March 5, 1767.
1-126   "   Elizabeth, and Joseph Wardwell, June 22, 1769.
1-71,73   McCARTEE Charles, and Rachel Bishop, (Int.) May 4, 1732; m. by Rev. Barnabus Taylor, May 18, 1732.
1-73   McCARTE Dennis, and Margaret Woods, (Int.) Dec. 28, 1743.
4-70   McCORMICK Elizabeth, and William Findley, May 14, 1849.
4-73   McDONALD Catherine, and Michael Boyle, March 28, 1850.
4-67   McGERPHY Sarah, and William McMillan, June 18, 1848.
1-69   McINTOSH Mrs. Elizabets, and Lacklin McIntosh, (Int.) Aug. 15, 1721.
1-69   "   Lacklin, of N. Brittain, and Mrs. Elizabeth McIntosh, of Bristol, (Int.) Aug. 15, 1721.
1-5   "   Mrs. Elizabeth, and Francis Burland, (Int.) Aug. 3, 1724.
1-27   "   Madam Elizabeth, and Simeon Davis, (Int.) May 11, 1728; m. June 2, 1728.
1-80   "   Ceaser, and Jennie Gallup (col.), (Int.) July 24, 1736.
4-67   McMILLAN William, and Sarah McGerphy; m. by Rev. Thomas Shepard, Jan. 18, 1848.
4-6   MEIGS Betsey, and Champlain Bowen, April 10, 1825.
4-34   "   Sally B., and Phillip G. Wilson, March 30, 1839.
4-42   "   Elizabeth Ann, and Benjamin R. Wilson, Dec. 24, 1840.
4-65   "   Mary A., and Albert W. Barnard, Dec. 5, 1847.
4-67   "   James L., and Mary A. West; m. by Rev. Richard Livsey, May 14, 1848.
1-71   MI—— Oliver, and Mary Munro, dau. of Joseph, (Int.) April 24, 1736.
1-95   MICO Hannah, and Cato Peck (col), Jan. 3, 1805.
4-54   MIDGET Abner, and Deborah L. Vickery; m. by Rev. V. R. Osborn, Jan. 19, 1844.
1-69   MILES John, and Sarah Davis, March 14, 1689.
1-71   "   Timothy, and Sarah Hill, of Portsmouth, (Int.) Aug. 12, 1736.
1-19   MILLER Abigail, and Sylvester Child, Jan. 19, 1748.
1-106   "   Molly, and Joseph Smith, May 19, 1769.
1-21   "   Rebecca, and Sylvester Child, Aug. 1, 1773.
1-78   "   Hope, and Robert Manchester, March 5, 1812.
1-80   "   Dr. Caleb, of Bristol, and Mary Ann Bucklin, of Seekonk; m. by N. Bullock, Justice of the Peace, Aug. 14, 1816.
1-75, 78   "   Hope, and Robert Manchester, March 5, 1812.
1-79   "   James, of Nelson, and Rebecca Smith Munro, of Sylvester; m. by Rev. Asa Kent, April 7, 1814.
4-43   "   Rebecca S., and Thomas F. Crandall, Nov. 22, 1841.
4-53   "   Abbie L., and George Coggeshall, Nov. 17, 1842.
4-63   "   Phebe S., and Anthony Havier, Jan. 14, 1846.
1-71   MILLS Mary, and Peter Maxfield, (Int.) Jan. 3, 1728-9.
4-44   "   Ellen J., and Robert H. Bullock, Feb. 19, 1840.
1-80   MINGO John, and Sarah Jethro (Col.) (Int.) Dec. 7, 1739.
1-76   MITCHELL James, of Bristol, Somerset Co., England, and of Nicholas and Phebe Handy, of Swansey, dau. of Robert; m. by Daniel Bradford, Justice of the Peace, July 8, 1779.
4-24   "   Mary Ann, and William L. Peckham, April 27, 1830.

4-16 MITCHELL Priscilla B., and William Mitchell, Feb. 8, 1835.

4-16   "   William, of East Greenwich, and Priscilla B. Mitchell, of Bristol; m. by Rev. Jefferson Haskill, Feb. 8, 1835.

4-28   "   Peter T. W., of Portsmouth, and Maria Swan, of Bristol; m. by Rev. Thomas Shepard, March 11, 1838.

1-70 MOOREY Martha, and Thomas Taber, (Int.) June 24, 1723.

1-70 MOORE John, (mariner,) and Mary Lawton, (Int.) Aug. 17, 1724.

1-52   "   Elizabeth, and Joseph Harding, (Int.) Sept. 25, 1742; m. Oct. 24, 1742.

4-69   "   Fanny, and George C. Ashworth, Oct. 26, 1848.

1-70, 71 MORRIS Samuel, of Woodstock, and Mrs. Abigail Bragg, of Bristol, (Int.) Sept. 26, 1728; m. by Simeon Davis, Justice of the Peace, Oct. 31. 1728.

1-79   "   Joseph, of Emanuel and Joanna, and Mary Slocum, of Peleg and Elizabeth; m. by Rev. Henry Wight, July 8, 1810.

4-34   "   Benjamin, and Mary E. Paine; m. by Rev. James C. Bonteone, May 13, 1839.

1-72,73 MORSE, Samuel, of Mendon, and Mary Reynolds, of Bristol, (Int.) Aug. 19, 1738; m. by Rev. Barnabus Taylor, Oct. 19, 1738.

4-10 MOSHER Elizabeth, and William Thomas, DeWitt, Sept. 15, 1830.

4-50 MOTT Samuel, and Phebe R. Ball; m. by Rev. Charles Noble, April 17, 1842.

4-52   "   Sarah C., and Frederic B. Hart, Nov. 20, 1842.

1-69 MOWRY George, and Hannah Lewis, Jan. 22, 1683.

1-1   "   Sarah, and Ephraim Andros, Sept. 24, 1713.

4-46 MULCHAHY John, and Hannah H. Franklin; m. by Rev. Harvey Sullings, Jan. 27, 1841.

1-69 MUMFORD Capt. Stephen, of Newport, and Mrs. Mary Rogers, of Bristol; m. by Rev. Mr. Sparhawk, July 26, 1716.

1-71, 72 MUNDAY Richard, and Mrs. Elizabeth Hubbard, (Int.) Jan. 8, 1731-2; m. by Rev. John Usher, Jan. 27, 1731.

1-73   "   Jonathan, of Great Britain, and Mary Oxx, of Bristol, (Int.) July 13, 1745.

1-63 MUNRO Elizabeth, and John Lindsey, Aug. 29, 1694.

1-56   "   Mercy, and Jeremiah Ingraham, July 10, 1718.

1-69   "   John, of Bristol, and Ruth Bowen, of Swansey, (Int.) Oct. 17, 1718.

1-32   "   Sarah, and Oliver Eddy, Feb. 16, 1723.

1-5   "   Elizabeth, and Amos Baker, (Int.) Jan. 1, 1724.

1-70, 72   "   Ann, and Thomas Martin, (Int.) Nov. 18, 1727; m. ——br 8, 1727.

1-70   "   Benjamin, of Bristol, and Ann Haile, of Swansey, (Int.) Jan. 25, 1727-8.

1-70, 72   "   John, of Thomas, and Hannah Rosbatham, (Int.) April 9, 1728; m. by Rev. John Usher, April 29, 1728.

1-71, 72   "   Simeon, and Rebecca Wardwell, (Int.) Dec. 2, 1732; m. by Rev. John Usher, Dec. 19, 1732.

1-71, 72   "   Bennett, and Sarah Bosworth, of Nathaniel, (Int.) Oct. 13, 1733; m. by Rev. John Usher, ——ber 11, 1733.

1-71, 72   "   Nathaniel, and Mary Jolls, (Int.) Nov. 29, 1735; m. by Rev. John Usher, ——ber 24, 1735.

1-71   "   Mary, and Owen Mi——, (Int.) April 24, 1736.

1-56   "   Mary, and John Ingraham, (Int.) July 19, 1736.

1-71, 72   "   Hezekiah, and Mary Haile, of Swansey, (Int.) March 6, 1737.

1-72, 73   '   Charles, and Priscilla Smith, (Int.) April 7, 1738; m. by Rev. Barnabus Taylor, May 29, 1738.

2-72   "   Thomas, and Mercy Marks, (Int.) April 30, 1739.

1-73   "   Joseph, and Catherine Wilson, (Int.) Feb. 1, 1741; m. by Rev. John Usher, Feb. 22, 1741.

1-54   "   Hannah, and William James, (Int.) Jan. 4, 1741-2.

1-124   "   Susannah, and Jeremiah Wilson, (Int.) Aug. 17, 1744.

1-32   "   Mrs. Catharine, and William Eldredge, (Int.) March 29, 1746.

1-74   "   Jeremiah, and Mrs. Hannah Lindsey, (Int.) May 5, 1746.

1-124   "   Mrs. Mercy, and Lemuel West, (Int.) Oct. 25, 1746.

1-19   "   Hagar, and Caseo Bosworth (colored), Jan. 11, 1749.

1-88   "   Mary, and Richard Patrieke, (Int.) ——, —, ——.

1-2   MUNRO Nathan, of Bristol, and Mrs. Hannah Allen, of Rehoboth; m. by. Rev. John Burt, Nov. 21, 1751.

1-74   "   Nathan, of Warren, and Mrs. Elizabeth Kinnecutt, of Bristol; m. by Rev. John Burt, May 25, 1755.

1-74   "   Nathan, and Mrs. Catharine Bragg; m. by Rev. John Burt, July 11, 1756.

1-75   "   Mrs. Jane, and Stephen Munro, Jan. 10, 1760.

1-75   "   Stephen, and Mrs. Jane Munro; m. by Rev. John Burt, Jan. 10, 1760.

1-75   "   Simeon, and Mrs. Rachel Walker; m. by Rev. John Burt, Jan. 31, 1762.

1-75   "   Nathaniel, and Mrs. Abigail Gallup; m. by Rev. John Burt, Nov. 13, 1766.

1-75   "   William, and Mrs. Hannah Carey, June 9, 1768.

1-76   "   George, of Bennett, and Abigail Lindsey; m. by Rev. John Burt, May 21, 1769.

1-75   "   Archibald, of Simeon, and Rebecca Smith, daughter of Richard; m. by Rev. John Burt, Nov. 28, 1769.

1-76   "   Mary, and Gardiner Mason, (also 1-77), Feb. 27, 1772.

1-76   "   Hezekiah, of William and Hopestill Potter, daughter of Mr. Hopestill; m. by Rev. John Burt, May 17, 1772.

1-76   "   Bennett, Jr., and Abiah Clark, Nov. 12, 1772.

1-76   "   Stephen, and Merebah Shaw, March 28, 1773.

1-76   "   Nathaniel, (alias Maxfield), and Martha Taylor, Nov. 1, 1774.

1-76   "   Sanford, and Mrs. Mary Wardwell, Nov. 6, 1774.

1-76   "   James, and Patience Munro, Feb. 2, 1775.

1-76   "   Patience, and James Munro, Feb. 2, 1775.

1-118   "   Lydia, and Moses Van Doorn, May 27, 1779.

1-80   "   Joseph, of Bristol, and Mrs. Mary Eddy, of Warren; m. by Rev. Solomon Townsend, Aug. 29, 1784.

1-30   "   Anna, and William Diman, Nov. 11, 1791.

1-57   "   Abigail, and Daniel Ingraham, Feb. 3, 1793.

1-79   "   Hezekiah, of Capt. Nathan and Sarah, and Ruth Haile, of Amos and Ruth; m. by Rev. Henry Wight, Nov. 19, 1794.

1-79   "   Bennett, of James and Patience, and Alethea Ingraham, of William and Mary; m. by Rev. Henry Wight, Nov. 17, 1796.

1-77   "   Ephraim, of Dr. Thomas and Sarah, and Sarah Peck, of Thomas and Betsey; m. by Rev. Henry Wight, Sept. 1, 1797.

1-79   "   Hezekiah, of Hezekiah and Hopestill, and Eliza Bradford Fales, of Nathaniel, Jr., and Elizabeth; m. by Rev. Henry Wight, Feb. 28, 1799.

1-78   "   Charles, and Maria Rodman; m. by Rev. Henry Wight, Nov. 26, 1801.

1-77   "   George, of Dr. Archibald and Rebecca, and Martha Lindsey, of William and Catherine; m. by Rev. Henry Wight, Jan. 9, 1804.

1-2   "   Philo, and James Anderson (col.), March 18, 1806.

1-78   "   David, of Joseph and Mary, and Abigail Cranston, of Stephen and Sarah; m. by Daniel Bradford, Justice of the Peace, March 23, 1806.

1-13   "   Abby, and Lemuel Bunn, Aug. 13, 1807.

1-78   "   Bennett, 2d, son of Edward and Sarah, and Sally Gladding, of Daniel and Susannah; m. by Rev. Alexander V. Griswold, May 16, 1808.

4-3, 8   "   Abby, and Joseph Munro, Aug. 15, 1811.

4-3, 8   "   Joseph, son of Joseph and Mary, and Abby (Kinnecut) Munro, of Thomas Kinnecut and Rebecca; m. by Rev. Henry Wight, Aug. 15, 1811.

1-78   "   Jeremiah, of Archibald and Rebecca, and Mehitable Clarke, of Walter and Lydia; m. by Rev. Henry Wight, Oct. 26, 1811.

1-79   "   Edward, Jr., of Edward and Sarah, and Elizabeth Oxx, of Samuel and Rebecca; m. by Rev. Alexander V. Griswold, Sept. 26, 1812.

  "   Rebecca Smith, and James Miller, April 7, 1814.

1-62   "   Susan, and Asa Kent, April 29, 1814.

4-4, 12   "   Bennett, of Edward, and Lucy Abell, of Seekonk, dau. of Preserved, of Warren; m. by Rev. Jordan Rexford, July 6, 1818.

4-3   MUNRO Allen, of Maj. Hezekiah and Elizabeth, and Joanna Lincoln, of
      Capt. Seth and Phebe; m. by Rev. Henry Wight, March 2, 1820.
4-14   "   Elizabeth B., and Samuel Coggeshall, May 15, 1821.
4-3   "   Caleb, of Joseph, and Lemira Luther, of Obadiah; m. by Rev. Jor-
      dan Rexford, Sept. 6, 1821.
4-7   "   William P., of Ephraim, and Phebe Wright, of Amos; m. by Rev.
      Isaac Bonney, June 16, 1822.
4-8   "   Caleb, of Joseph, and Lemira Luther, of Obadiah, of Swansey; m.
      by Rev. Pardon Rexford, Sept. 6, 1824.
4-5   "   Angeline, and William Wheaton, Nov. 10, 1824.
4-14   "   Bennett James, of Bennett and Sarah, and Sarah L. Fish, of David
      and Mary (also 4-239); m. by Rev. Henry Wight, Sept. 23,
      1828.
4-11   "   Lydia H., and Ira P. Slade, March 4, 1832.
4-11   "   John G., of Charles and Margaret, and Nancy Hyde, of James and
      Flora; m. by Rev. Levi Bates, March 18, 1832.
4-34   "   Samuel S., and Ann Pitman; m. by Rev. James C. Bontecue, Feb.
      28, 1839.
4-34   "   Rebecca Smith, and William Easterbrooks, April 21, 1839.
4-36   "   James M., and Eliza Lawrence; m. by Rev. Ephraim Scott, Sept.
      1, 1839.
4-38   "   Ann D., and Thomas M. Paine, March 22, 1840.
4-40   "   Phebe, and Simon D. Liscomb, Aug. 16, 1840.
4-40   "   Hiram B., and Mary Bosworth; m. by Rev. Ephraim Scott, Sept.
      2, 1840.
4-42   "   Martha F., and Ira P. Slade, Dec. 15, 1840.
4-44   "   Abby B., and Henry W. Gladding, Jan. 5, 1841.
4-44, 48   "   George H., of Bristol, and Margaret A. Austin, of N. Kingstown;
      m. by Rev. William L. Brower, Feb. 17, 1841.
4-53   "   Clarrissa, and Thomas J. Thurston, April 30, 1843.
4-54   "   Mary S., and John W. Pearse, May 21, 1843.
4-54   "   Lucy R., and Jeremiah Pease, May 23, 1844.
4-56   "   Mary L., and George Gardner, March 8, 1845.
4-59   "   Abby P., and Allen M. Newman, June 25, 1845.
4-61   "   Harriet P., and Beriah H. Brownell, Feb. 16, 1846.
4-57   "   Ann R., and N. Bowen Cook, April 22, 1846.
4-73   "   John Bennett, and Abby Howland Batt; m. by Rev. James W.
      Cooke, Dec. 25, 1846.
4-63   "   Jeremiah W., and Elizabeth W. Diman; m. by Rev. Jonathan
      Cady, Aug. 6, 1846.
4-65   "   Alice G., and Beriah P. Fisher, June 17, 1847.
4-67   "   John W., and Charlotte M. Doty; m. by Rev. Thomas Shepard,
      Aug. 4, 1847.
4-70   "   Jonathan B., and Elizabeth F. Wilson; m. by Rev. Richard
      Livesey, April 13, 1849.
4-70   "   Adam J., and Martha Abby Spooner; m. by Rev. Isaac Bonney,
      Nov. 1, 1853.
1-101   MURRAY Dorcas, and Charles Stead Rawlings, Dec. 24, 1813.
1-23   "   Mary Shaw, and Thomas Collins, Dec. 10, 1815.
4-55, 57   MUTTON George, and Sarah W. Coy; m. by Rev. Thomas Shepard, Sept.
      17, 1840.

N

1-84   NASH Simeon, and Mrs. Martha Dyer, March 5, 1746-7.
1-84   "   Joseph, of Providence, and Mrs. Hopestill Bradford, of Bristol;
      m. by Rev. John Burt, Jan. 9, 1756.
1-84   "   Simeon, of Montpelier, Vt., and Abagail Throop, of Bristol; m.
      by Rev. Henry Wight, March 22, 1803.
1-85   NED Solomon, and Mary Easton, (Int.) March 18, 1731-2.
4-5   NEGUS Sarah, and Rev. Joshua Crowell, Nov. 12, 1824.
1-114   NELSON Dulcinea, and Charles Henry Tillinghast, Sept. 29, 1807.
4-55   NEWMAN Ann Elizabeth, and Pardon Edwards, Sept. 29, 1842.
4-59   "   Allen M., and Abby P. Munro; m. by Rev. Hezekiah Burnham,
      June 25, 1845.

1-16   NEWTON Abigail, and Joseph Carpenter, Feb. 16, 1723.
1-73   "   Martha, and William Martin, Jr., (Int.) June 29, 1741.
1-83   "   Mrs. Hannah, and Peter Norton, (Int.) Sept. 20, 1746; m. Oct.
                    7, 1746.
1-32,86 NIBS Martha, and John A. Oldridge, (Int.) Oct. 16, 1744.
1-83   NICHOLSON John, of Wrentham, and Mary Throop, of Bristol, (Int.) Oct.
                    14, 1736; m. Nov. 10, 1736.
4-67   NICHOLS Julia Maria, and John Fletcher Warren, May 3, 1844.
1-84   NIGARS Isaac, of Newport (mariner), son of Nathaniel (carpenter), and
                    Priscilla Oxx, of Samuel (coaster), of Bristol; m. by Rev. John
                    Usher, Jan. 3, 1784.
1-83   NOONING Timothy, and Rebecca Wilson, (Int.) May 14, 1742; m. by Rev.
                    John Burt, June 20. 1742.
1-114   "   Mrs. Mary, and Peleg Tripp, March 12, 1761.
1-84   "   James, of Timothy, deceased, and Rebecca Glover, of John; n.
                    by Rev. John Burt, Oct. 20, 1771.
4-11   "   Adelia W., and Jonathan T. Browning, July 4, 1831.
4-36   "   Ann W., and William Bradford, 2d, March 28, 1839.
1-90, 91 NORRIS Rebecca, and Joseph Phillips, Jr., (Int.) May 6, 1738; m. June
                    1, 1738.
1-84   "   John, and Mrs. Elizabeth Harris; m. by Rev. John Burt, April
                    17, 1757.
1-11   "   Elizabeth, and Ebenezer Blake, May 13, 1779.
1-107   "   Sally, and Thomas Swan, Dec. 2, 1805.
4-61   "   Mary Jane, and George W. Stetson, Feb. 6, 1845.
4-9   NORTHUP Joseph, of Christopher and Martha of Exeter, and Annis
                    Douglass, of Paris and Martha; m. by Rev. Henry Wight, Nov.
                    29, 1829.
4-73   "   Mary N., and Richard Fenner, June 6, 1850.
1-83   NORTON Captain Shubal, and Mrs. Sarah Keen, (Int.) July 1, 1723; m.
                    by Daniel Pearse, Justice of the Peace, July 4, 1723.
1-85   "   Bonney, and Eunice Lefavour (col.), (Int.) Jan. 29, 1760.
1-83   "   Peter, and Mrs. Hannah Newton, (Int.) Sept. 20, 1746; m. by
                    Rev. John Burt, Oct. 7, 1746.
1-9   "   Mrs. Hannah, and Joshua Bicknell, Sept. 10, 1763.
1-50   NYLES Jane, and John Hinton, March 20, 1683.

O

1-86   OLDRIDGE John, and Jane Chamberline, of Hull, (Int.) Nov. —, 1719.
1-86   "   John, and Martha Nibs, (Int.) Oct. 16, 1744.
1-86   "   William, and Mrs. Katherine Munro, (Int.) March 29, 1746.
1-105   "   Mrs. Susannah, and Barnard Salisbury, Aug. 5, 1748.
1-86   "   Thomas, and Mrs. Alathea Potter; m. by Rev. John Burt, Nov.
                    19, 1761.
1-86   "   Joseph, and Mrs. Elizabeth Merrill, Nov. 4, 1770.
1-87   "   John, and Priscilla Liscomb, March 3, 1774.
1-88   OLSTRA Elizabeth, and Christopher Penny, Jan. 8, 1694.
1-58   ORMSBY Mehitable, and Thomas Jolls, (Int.) March 15, 1732-3.
1-86   "   Captain Ezra, of Warren, and Mrs. Esther Goff, of Bristol; m. by
                    Rev. John Burt, Oct. 12, 1764.
1-121 OSBORN Mrs. Katherine, and Jonathan Woodbury, May 24, 1708.
1-130   "   Mrs. Margaret, and Samuel Woodbury, (Int.) July 7, 1721.
1-50   "   Mrs. Hannah, and John Homans, (Int.) May 8, 1725.
1-50   "   Mrs. Hannah, and John Homans; m. May 24, 1725.
1-86   "   Samuel, of Newport, and Mary Gorham, (Int.) Nov. 27, 1736.
4-5   "   Sally, and George Reed, Nov. 10, 1817.
4-54   OSGOOD Ruth G., and James Grinnell, July 3, 1843.
1-87   OSQUE ——, and Abigail ——, (Int.) Nov. 12, 17—.
4-65   OTTERSON Samuel B., of Bristol, and Mary M. Carroll, of Providence; m.
                    by Rev. Jonathan Cady, Aug. 14, 1847.
1-86   OXX Samuel, and Mary Lindsey; m. by Rev. John Usher, Nov. 29, 1723
1-73   "   Mary, and Jonathan Munday, (Int.) July 13, 1745.
1-113   "   Mrs. Elizabeth, and John Thurston, (Int.) April 23, 1746.

1-86 OXX Samuel, and Mrs. Priscilla Gladding; m. by Rev. John Burt, April 25, 1754.

1-86 " George, and Mrs. Hannah Diman; m. by Rev. John Burt, Oct. 29, 1761.

1-86 " Samuel, and Rebecca Lindsey, April 7, 1771.

1-84 " Priscilla, and Isaac Nigars, Jan. 3, 1784.

1-79 " Elizabeth, and Edward Munro, Jr., Sept. 26, 1812.

4-32 " Betsey, and John V. Lewis, Jan. 20, 1839.

P

1-90 PADDOCK John, and Hannah Sprague, Aug. 2, 1738.

4-18 PAGE Sarah, and Lemuel W. Briggs, Sept. 20, 1835.

1-15 PAINE Mrs. Hannah, and Charles Church, May 20, 1708.

1-121 " Dorothy, and John Williams, (Int.) Oct. 12, 1726.

1-98, 99 " Mrs. Sarah, and Joseph Russell, (Int.) May 12, 1733; m. June 10, 1733.

1-27 " Sarah and Thomas Drown, (Int.) Nov. 30, 1736; m. March 24, 1736-7.

1-90 " Edward, and Mary Bosworth, (Int.) Feb. 2, 1739.

1-91, 92 " Nathaniel, and Mrs. Elizabeth Gallup, (Int.) May 6, 1742; m. by Rev. John Usher, June 13, 1742.

1-92 " Stephen, and Mrs. Mary Bailey; m. by Rev. John Burt, Aug. 18, 1751.

1-92 " Mrs. Hannah, and Capt. Simeon Potter, March 7, 1754.

1-2 " Mrs. Mary, and Ebenezer Allen, Dec. 7, 1775.

1-119 " Mary, and William Van Doorn, Oct. 3, 1804.

4-34 " Mary E., and Benjamin Morris, May 13, 1839.

4-38 " Thomas M., and Ann D. Munro; m. by Rev. Ephraim Scott, March 22, 1840.

4-44 " Prudence W., and William Wyatt, (Int.) Dec. 31, 1840.

4-50 " Harriet A., and John R. Slade, Sept. 20, 1841.

1-88 PALMER Cotton, and Susannah Fearse; m. by Thomas Church, Justice of the Peace, Jan. 10, 1711.

1-89 " Isaac, and Yetmarcy Howland, (Int.) Sept. 18, 1731.

1-91 " Capt. Isaac, and Yetmarcy Howland; m. by Rev. Barnabus Taylor, Oct. 17, 1731.

1-52 " Mrs. ——, and Capt. Nathaniel Howland, Dec. 6, 1733.

4-24 " James N., of Cambridge, Mass., and Mary M. Lewis, of Bristol; m. by Rev. Allan Bristed, May 29, 1837.

4-65 " Mary Ann, and Samuel J. C. Wells, Aug. 30, 1847.

4-70 " Benjamin W., and Celia Ann Collins; m. by Rev. Thomas Sheperd, July 3, 1848.

1-92 PALMENTER Benjamin, of Boston, and Hannah Tripp, of Bristol, (Int.) July 27, 1745.

1-88 PAPILLION Mrs. Bridget, and James Pecker, (Int.) ——. 1722; m. Nov. 29, 1722.

1-89 " Obadiah, and Abigail Carpenter, (Int.) Feb. 16, 1735.

1-90 " John, and Rebecca Bosworth, (Int.) Sept. 22, 1740.

1-91, 92 " Samuel, and Rebecca Bosworth, (Int.) June 18, 1743; m. by Rev. John Usher, July 3, 1743.

4-44 PARKER Emma, and Rev. John C. Welch, Aug. 17, 1840.

4-70 PATRAGE Elisha, and Ruth Lincoln; m. by Rev. Richard Livesey, June 24, 1849.

1-88 PATRICHE Richard, and Mary Munro, (Int.) ——. —, ——.

1-89 PATRIDGE John, and Submit Jones, of Dighton, Mass., Feb. 17, 1725-6.

1-94 PAULL Zebedee, of William and Hannah, and Alethea Wilson, of William and Alathea; m. by Rev. Henry Wight, Jan. 4, 1801.

1-94 " William, and Maria Audinet, (col.); m. by Rev. Henry Wight, Dec. 11, 1811.

4-40 " Zebedee, and Robey Bullock; m. by Rev. Henry Sullings, Dec. 30, 1839.

4-24 PEABODY Edwin, of Newport, and Catherine E. Friend, of Bristol; m. by Rev. E. K. Avery, Oct. 25, 1832.

4-67   PEABODY Fitz Herbert, and Phebe M. Pearse; m. by Richard Livesey, May 18, 1848.

4-69   "   Ann C., and John H. Leonard, Dec. 5, 1848.

1-88   PEARSE Susannah, and Cotton Palmer, Jan. 11, 1711.

1-88, 89   "   Capt. George, and Mrs. Mercy Howland, (Int.) Aug. 25, 1722; m. by Rev. James Orem, Nov. 22, 1722.

1-88   "   Richard, Jr., of Bristol, and Susannah Lawton, of Portsmouth, (Int.) May 4, 1723.

1-70   "   Mercy, and Isaac Martindale, July 9, 1724.

1-121   "   Ann, and William Williams, (Int.) April 17, 1725.

1-51   "   Ann, and Thomas Hogins, (Int.) April 26, 1728; m. May 15, 1728.

1-89, 90   "   Nathaniel, and Mary Lindsey, (Int.) May 4, 1731-2; m. by Rev. John Usher, April 6, 1732.

1-103   "   Experience, and Ichabod Simmons, (Int.) Aug. 31, 1737.

1-17   "   Madam, and John Chandler, (Int.) Jan. 12, 1739.

1-92   "   William, of Bristol, and Lydia Brown, of Barrington, (Int.) Jan. 8, 1741-2.

1-18   "   Sarah, and William Cox, (Int.) Feb. 1, 1741; m. March 18, 1741.

1-92   "   William, of Bristol, and Lydia Brown, of Barrington, April 22, 1742.

1-59   "   Mary, and Joseph Joy, (Int.) Sept. 5, 1745.

1-93   "   Nathaniel, Jr., and Mrs. Lydia Peckham, Nov. 15, 1767.

1-20   "   Ann, and Col. Nathaniel Carey, Sept. 16, 1770.

1-93   "   Thomas, of Jeremiah, dec., and Abigail Wardwell, of Stephen; m. by Rev. John Burt, Dec. 5, 1771.

1-95   "   Josiah, of Thomas and Abigail, and Sarah Wilson, of James and Jemima: m. by Rev. Henry Wight, Jan. 1, 1804.

1-38   "   Mary, and David Fish, Jan. 10, 1805.

1-96   "   Edward, and Mary Lewis (col.); m. by Rev. Henry Wight, Sept. 19, 1811.

4-5   "   Martin, of Martin and Sarah, and Mrs. Ann Jenckes Lewis, daughter of John Vose and Judith, his wife; m. by Rev. Henry Wight, Oct. 19, 1824.

————   "   George P., and Phebe Leonard; m. by Rev. Ephraim Scott, July 19, 1840.

4-38   "   John W., and Mary S. Munro; m. by Rev. V. R. Osborn, May 21, 1843.

4-54

4-67   "   Phebe M., and Fitz Herbert Peabody, May 18, 1848.

1-91   PEASE Zephaniah, of Newport, and Martha Gladding, Jr., Bristol, (Int.) Feb. 27, 1740.

1-24   "   Betsey, and Job Coggeshall, (about) May 20, 1779.

4-52   "   Sylvanus L., of Edgartown, and Nancy Sayer, of Bristol; m. by Rev. Bartholomew Othman, June 19, 1842.

4-54   "   Jeremiah, Jr., of Edgartown, Mass., and Lucy R. Munro, of Bristol; m. by Rev. V. R. Osborn, May 23, 1844.

1-88   PECKER James, of Boston, and Mrs. Bridget Papillion, —— ——. (Int.) 1722; m. by Rev. Nathaniel Cotton, Nov. 29, 1722.

1-88, 91   PECKHAM John, of Newport, and Tabitha Carey, of Bristol, (Int.) April 6, 1742; m. April 22, 1742.

1-20   "   Mrs. Eunice, and Charles Church, Aug. 13, 1756.

1-93   "   Nathaniel, of Newport, and Mrs. Lydia Peck; m. by Rev. John Burt, Jan. 10, 1760.

1-93   "   Mrs. Lydia, and Nathaniel Pearse, Jr., Nov. 15, 1767.

1-94   "   John, of Joshua and Deborah, and Catherine Lindsey, of William and Catherine; m. by Rev. Henry Wight, Dec. 12, 1799.

1-95   "   Perry M., son of Levi, of Middletown, and Nancy Lindsey, of Joseph, of Bristol; m. by Rev. Asa Kent, recorded May 7, 1814.

4-24   "   William L., and Mary Ann Mitchell, both of Woonsocket; m. by Rev. Jacob Sanborn, April 27, 1830.

4-16   "   Ann, and Joseph Simmons, Jan. 1, 1835.

4-50   "   George W., and Lydia D. Franklin; m. by Rev. Charles Noble, April 3, 1842.

4-56   "   Jonathan, of Fall River, and Mrs. Julia Ann Bowen, of Bristol; m. by Rev. Isaac Bonney, Oct. 7, 1844.

4-59   "   Abby, and Benjamin Franklin, Dec. 14, 1845.

1-88 PECK Jonathan, and Elizabeth Throop, March 31, 1695.

1-88 " Jonathan, of Bristol, and Hannah Wood, of Little Compton, (Int.) Dec. 16, 1720.

1-89, 96 " William, and Elizabeth Throop, (Int.) July 23, 1723-4; m. by Rev. Nathaniel Cotton, May 13, 1725.

1-6 " Mrs. Eliza, and John Bradley, (Int.) Sept. 8, 1729.

1-7 " Elizabeth, and John Bradley, Dec. 5, 1729.

1-89 " Jonathan, and Hannah Loring, of Little Compton, (Int.) Nov. 3, 1731.

1-89 " Thomas, of Bristol, and Mary Kingsley, of Swansey, (Int.) May 26, 1733.

1-121, 123 " Rebecca, and Joseph Waldron, Jr., (Int.) May 3, 1741; m. July 16, 1741.

1-91 " William, and Rebecca Talbot, Jr., of Dighton, Mass., (Int.) Oct. 24, 1741.

1-44 " Deborah, and Samuel Gray, Oct. 25, 1750.

1-37 " Mrs. Hannah, and Jonathan Fales, Dec. 20, 1750.

1-9 " Mrs. Elizabeth, and Samuel Bosworth, Oct. 8, 1752.

1-93 " Jonathan, and Mrs. Mary Throop; m. by Rev. John Burt, Oct. 29, 1757.

1-75 " Mrs. Sarah, and Sion Martindale, April 13, 1758.

1-93 " Mrs. Lydia, and Nathaniel Peckham, Jan. 10, 1760.

1-93 " Thomas, and Mrs. Mary Richmond; m. by Rev. John Burt, Dec. 2, 1762.

1-93 " Thomas, Jr., of Swansey, and Mrs. Elizabeth Sanford, of Bristol; m. by Rev. John Burt, Dec. 11, 1766.

1-93 " Loring, and Mrs. Sarah Richmond; m. by Rev. John Burt, June 4, 1767.

1-95 " Nathaniel, of Thomas and Mary, and Mary Wilson, of John and Mary; m. by Rev. Henry Wight, Dec. 14, 1791.

4-243 " Elizabeth, and William Reynolds, Feb. 2, 1797.

1-77 " Sarah, and Ephraim Munro, Sept. 1, 1797.

1-46 " Nancy, and Nathaniel Gladding, July 27, 1800.

1-100 " Lydia, and Thomas Richmond, Feb. 7, 1802.

1-94 " John, of Capt. Jonathan and Mary, and Ann Reynolds, of Joseph and Sarah; m. by Rev. Henry Wight, May 16, 1802.

1-95 " Cato, and Hannah Mico (col.); m. by Rev. Henry Wight, Jan. 3, 1805.

1-11 " Mary, and Lemuel William Briggs, Aug. 2, 1807.

4-1 " Nicholas, of Nicholas and Elizabeth, and Nancy Bradford, of John; m. by Rev. Henry Wight, Oct. 22, 1815.

4-14 " Mrs. Hannah, and Aaron Chaffee, Oct. 5, 1834.

4-73 " Horace, of John, and Eliza Troop Cole, of Luther; m. by Rev. John C. Welch, May 16, 1838.

4-48 " John H., of Barrington, and Charlotte Tanner, of Bristol; m. by Rev. William L. Brower, April 26, 1841.

4-54 " Sally C., and Benjamin Cummings, (also 4-65), July 19, 1843.

4-63 " Joseph, of Nicholas, dec., and Esther Goff, of James, dec.; m. by Rev. Paul Townsend, May 30, 1847.

1-91 PIERCE Jeremiah, and Sarah Eddy, (also 1-92), (Int.) Nov. 19, 1744; m. by Rev. John Burt, Dec. 24, 1744.

1-8 " Mrs. Susannah, and John Burden, (Int.) Sept. 4, 1746.

4-6 " Mary C., and Francis G. Bowen, April 10, 1836.

4-32 " Sarah, and Wanton Bowers, Feb. 18, 1839.

4-46 " M——, and Thomas P. Goff, May 24, 1841.

4-46 " Alfred, and Alvira Horton; m. by Rev. Henry Snilings, May 24, 1841.

4-50 " Mason W., Jr., and Lydia M. Townsend; m. by Rev. G. F. Sanborn, June 19, 1842.

4-53 " James P., and Miriam Diman; m. by Rev. G. F. Sanborn, June 13, 1843.

1-69 PELTON Christian, and William Martin, May 7, 1706.

1-36 PENFIELD Mary, and Jeremiah Fairbanks, April 19, 1698.

1-90, 91 " Stephen, of Middletown, Conn., and Jerusha Brewer, of Bristol, (Int.) Feb. 20, 1737-8; m. by Rev. Barnabus Taylor, June 13, 1738.

4-53 PENNO Mary C., and Joseph Alger, May 14, 1842.

1-88 PENNY Christopher, and Elizabeth Olsra, Jan. 8, 1694.

1-89 " Nathan, and Elizabeth Eddy, of Norton, Mass., April 8, 1726.

1-58 PEPER Mrs. Mary, and Richard Jenkins, Feb. 3, 1701.

4-28 PETERS Prudence, and George Chappell, Nov. 19, 1837.

4-65 PHELPS William M., of Bristol, and Susan F. Pike, of Newport; m. by Rev. Jonathan Cady, April 18, 1848.

1-90 PHILLIPS Michael, and Bridget Bosworth, Oct. 30, 1736.

1-90, 91 " Joseph, Jr., and Rebecca Norris, (Int.) May 6, 1738; m. by Rev. Barnabus Taylor, June 1, 1738.

1-61 " Bridget, and Joseph Kelley, (Int.) Jan. 20, 1738-9.

1-90, 91 " John, and Esther Joy, (pub.) Aug. 25, 1739; m. by Rev. Barnabus Taylor, Sept. 20, 1739.

1-92 " Joseph, and Sarah Vanis, July 13, 1749.

1-92 " John, and Mrs. Elizabeth Tomkins; m. by Rev. John Burt, Aug. 23, 1750.

1-92 " Michael, and Mrs. Elizabeth Dufail; m. by Rev. John Burt, Sept. 11, 1750.

1-125 " Mrs. Sarah, and Captain Thomas Wickes, June 2, 1757.

1-03 " Nathaniel, and Sarah Easterbrooks, Dec. 23, 1770.

1-21 " Rebecca, and William Carr, Aug. 3, 1794.

1-95 " Samuel, of Captain Nathaniel and Sarah, and Hannah Cox, of William and Mary; m. by Rev. Henry Wight, July 4, 1802.

1-21 " Sarah, and William Church, Sept. 30, 1804.

1-50 PHINNEY Patience, and Ebenezer Holmes, (Int.) July 25, 1719.

1 93 PIKE William, of Newport, and Mrs. Martha Sandford, of Bristol; m. by Rev. John Burt, June 16, 1763.

4-65 " Susan F., and William M. Phelps, April 18, 1848.

1-88 PINNIO James, and Dorothy B——; m. by Rev. Mr. Sparhawk, May 9, 1706.

4-2 PITCHER Susannah, and Solomon Sherman, Jan. 15, 1820.

1-93 PITMAN Peleg, of Newport, and Mary Wardwell, of Bristol, July 7, 1770.

1-94 " Samuel, of Peleg and Mary, and Polly Ingraham, of John and Mary; m. by Rev. Henry Wight, Nov. 29, 1792.

1-94 " Samuel, of Peleg and Mary, and Sarah Howland, of John and Elizabeth; m. by Rev. Henry Wight, Sept 13, 1798.

4-5 " Josiah H., and Hannah Lindsey; m. by Rev. Timothy Merrett, Nov. 15, 1824.

4-6 " Thomas F., of Newport, and Susan G. Fuller, of Bristol; m. by Rev. Thomas W. Tucker, Feb. 17, 1825.

4-34 " Ann, and Samuel S. Munro, Feb. 28, 1839.

4-34 " Elizabeth L., and Nathan B. Heath, May 6, 1839.

" John Howland, and Eliza F. Slade; m. by Rev. John Bristed, Jan. 16, 1840.

1-98 PITTS Mercy, and Nathaniel Reynolds, (Int.) Dec. 12, 1739.

1-122 POND Mrs. Mary, and John Wight, (Int.) May 25, 1728.

4-30 POOLE Lot H., of Boston, Mass., and Ann Gooding, of Bristol; m. by Rev. John Bristed, March 20, 1839.

1-90, 91 POTTER Simeon, and Ann Bragg, (Int.) Feb. 7, 1740-1; m. by Nathaniel Hubbard, Justice of the Peace, March 5, 1740.

1-15 " Lydia, and John Cockrum, (Int.) Aug. 8, 1741; m. Aug. 27, 1741.

1-40, 43 " Mary, and Thomas Garrett, (Int.) June 11, 1742; m. Oct. 19, 1742.

1-40, 43 " Jemima, and Isaac Gorham, (Int.) Sept. 27, 1742; m. Oct. 19, 1742.

1-28 " Abigail, and Mark Antony De Wolf, (Int.) Aug. 11, 1744; m. Aug. 26, 1744.

1-74 " Mrs. Hannah, and Thomas Martin, Jan. 25, 1753.

1-92 " Capt. Simeon, and Mrs. Hannah Paine; m. by Rev. John Burt, March 7, 1754.

1-86 " Mrs. Alathea, and Thomas Oldridge, Nov. 19, 1761.

1-76 " Hopestill, and Hezekiah Munro, May 17, 1772.

1-129 " Content, and Joseph Whiting, Feb. 23, 1800.

1-108 " Nancy, and Jonathan Slade, May 14, 1807.

1-95 POWELL James, and Abby Frederic; m. by Rev. Henry Wight, July 7, 1812.

1-90 PRATT John, and Sarah Drown, (Int.) Jan. 18, 1739-40.

4-14 " Spencer, and Sarah Ann White, of Pawtucket; m. by Rev. John Blaine, May 18, 1834.

1-64,65 PRICE Judith, and Nicholas Longround, (Int.) May 9, 1746; m. June 3, 1746.

1-90 PRICHARD Joseph, and Mary Gains, (Int.) Aug. 5, 1740.

1-118 PRINCE Elizabeth, and Samuel Vernon, (Int.) Nov. 23, 1724; m. Jan. 12, 1724-5.

4-44 PRESBURY Barney, of Taunton, Mass., and Nancy W. Lindsey, of Bristol; m. by Rev. Ephraim Scott, Jan. 7, 1841.

1-89,90 PRESTON William, and Elizabeth Hearson, (Int.) June 25, 1734; m. by Rev. John Usher, July 9, 1734.

Q R

4-54 RALPH Joseph, and Mrs. Sarah Clinton; m. by Rev. G. F. Sanborn, Oct. 22, 1843.

4-229,36 RAMIERES Thomas, of Minorca Islands, and Rachel T. Waldron, of Bristol, R. I.; m. by Rev. Ephraim Scott, Oct. 14, 1839.

4-44,48 RANDALL Elizabeth R., and Job Williston, Jr., Jan. 31, 1841.

1-101 RAWLINS Charles Stead, of William and Mary, and Dorcas Murray, of Anthony and Mary; m. by Rev. Alexander V. Griswold, Dec. 24, 1813.

1-98,99 RAWSON Thomas, and Anne Waldron, (Int.) March 30, 1737; m. by Rev. Barnabus Taylor, April 14, 1737.

1-99 " Grindall, of Mendon, Mass., and Ann Raynolds, of Bristol, (Int.) May 17, 1743.

1-99 " Stephen, and Elizabeth Walker, (Int.) March 29, 1745.

4-13 " Sarah, and Thomas Allen Harding, May 3, 1833.

4-34 " Mary Ann, and Nathan Warren, Jr., May 13, 1839.

4-57 " John, and Abby Blake; m. by Rev. Isaac Bonney, April 14, 1845.

1-121 REYNOLDS Mary, and John Woodbury, May 18, 1694.

1-15 " Ruth, and Josiah Carey, Nov. 9, 1710.

1-101 " Joseph, of Bristol, and Mrs. Phebe Leonard, of Norton, Mass., (Int.) Aug. 11, 1718.

1-17 " Mary, and Constant Church, (also 1-18) (Int.) Jan. 6, 1732-3: m. Jan. 25, 1732.

1-98 " Eleazer, and Mercy Throop, (also 1-99) (Int.) April 7, 1733; m. by Rev. Barnabus Taylor. May 6, 1733.

1-72 " Mary, and Samuel Morse, (also 1-73) (Int.) Aug. 19, 1738; m. Oct. 19, 1738.

1-98 " Nathaniel, of Bristol, and Mercy Pitts, of Dighton, Mass., (Int.) Dec. 12, 1739.

1-99 " Nathaniel, and Mary Little, (Int.) June 13, 1741.

1-99 " John, of Bristol, and Susannah Giles, of Salem, Mass., (Int.) Jan. 11, 1743-4.

1-124 " Elizabeth, and John Watson, (Int.) March 17, 1743-4; m. Sept. 6, 1744.

1-99 " Ann, and Grindall Rawson, (Int.) May 17, 1743.

1-99 " Joseph, Jr., of Bristol, and Lydia Greenwood, of Rehoboth, Mass., (Int.) —— 14, 1744.

1-124 " Mrs. Phebe, and Daniel Waldron, (Int.) Sept. —, 1746; m. Sept. 28, 1746.

1-125 " Mrs. Sarah, and Edmund Weld, April 15, 1752.

1-106 " Mrs. Elizabeth, and Josiah Smith, Aug. 22, 1776.

4-243 " William, and Elizabeth Peck, daughter of Captain Jonathan; m. by Rev. Henry Wight, Feb. 2, 1797.

1-13 " Sarah, and Daniel Bradford, Jr., Nov. 29, 1799.

1-100 " Greenwood, of Joseph and Sarah, and Mary Caldwell, of Robert and Elizabeth; m. by Rev. Henry Wight, Dec. 8, 1799.

1-94 " Mary Ann, and John Peck, May 16, 1802.

1-13 " Hannah, and James Peckham Burgess, May 6, 1810.

4-1 " Lydia P., and Sylvester Luther, March 16, 1820.

4-36 " Dorcas, and Franklin E. Congdon, June 12, 1831.

4-70 " Mary, and Jonathan Lake, Sept. 10, 1848.

4-73 REYNOLDS George H., and Hannah Bradford; m. by Rev. Thomas Sheperd, June 9, 1850.

1-28 REED Mary, and John Dyer, (Int.) March 31, 1739.

1-99 " Joseph, of Bridgewater, Mass., and Mary Dyer, of Bristol, (Int.)
Dec. 29, 1740.

1,69, 75 " Mary, and John Martin, (Int.) June 12, 1741; m. Nov. 12, 1741.

1-98 " Peter, and Jemima Drew, of Middleboro, Mass., (Int.) ——. —,
—.

1-100 " Mrs. Mary, and David Richardson, Sept. 8, 1765.

1-33 " Ruth, and Captain Isaac Esheck, 2d, Aug. 13, 1786.

4-5 " George, of Bristol, and Sally Osborn, of Providence; m. by Rev.
V. R. Osborn, Nov. 10, 1817.

1-130 " Betsey, and George Wilson, Oct. 5, 1818.

4-46 " Josephine B., and William Handy, May 23, 1841.

4-50 " Daniel D., and Charlotte White; m. by Rev. Charles Noble, Nov.
18, 1841.

4-57 " Elizabeth W., and John Livesey, July 22, 1845.

4-65 " Julia A., and Samuel Reed, Jan. 26, 1847.

4-65 " Samuel, and Julia A. Reed; m. by Rev. Jonathan Cady, Jan. 26,
1847.

1-98,99 RICE Joseph, and Sarah Bosworth, (Int.) Sept. 28, 1734; m. by Rev.
Barnabus Taylor, Nov. 7, 1734.

1-98 RICHARDSON Benjamin, of Newport, and Mary Fairhanks, of Bristol, (Int.)
June 13, 1724.

1-100 " Ebenezer, of Newport, and Mrs. Hannah Davis, of Bristol; m. by
Rev. John Burt, Nov. 10, 1763.

1-100 " David, and Mrs. Mary Reed; m. by Rev. John Burt, Sept. 8, 1765.

4-34 RICHIE Susan W., and Gardiner M. Butterworth, March 3, 1839.

1-98 RICHMOND Thomas, of Taunton, and Hannah Fry, of Bristol, (Int.) March
—, 1724-5; m. by Rev. Nathaniel Cotton, April 21, 1725.

1-98 " Rogers, of Little Compton, and Susannah Lee, of Bristol, (Int.)
April 21, 1739; m. by Rev. Barnabus Taylor (also 1-99, 101),
May 17, 1739.

1-99 " Ichabod, of Little Compton, and Mrs. Mary ——, of Bristol; m. by
Rev. John Burt, Nov. 15, 1753.

1-93 " Mrs. Mary, and Thomas Peck, Dec. 2, 1762.

1-20 " Mrs. Abigail, and Benjamin Cushing, Sept. 11, 1765.

1-93 " Mrs. Sarah, and Loring Peck, June 4, 1767.

1-100 " Edward, son of Captain Perez, late of Dartmouth, Mass., and Eliza
Throop, of Thomas, of Bristol; m. by Rev. John Burt, Oct.
25, 1770.

1-100 " Gilbert, of Gamaliel, and Judith, and Prudence West, of John and
Lydia; m. by Rev. Henry Wight, Oct. 16, 1797.

1-100 " Thomas, of Edward and Reliance, and Lydia Peck, of Captain Jonathan and Mary; m. by Rev. Henry Wight, Feb. 7, 1802.

1-46 " Harriet, and Job W., Gardiner, Jan. 20, 1810.

4-4 " Gilbert, and Elizabeth Liscomb; m. by Rev. Joel Mann, April 9,
1822.

4-16 " Thomas, of Edward and Reliance, and Ann Potter Bosworth, of
Benjamin and Hanoah; m. by Rev. Henry Wight, Aug. 10,
1829.

4-29 " Martha, and Henry Daggett, Dec. —, 1833.

4-56 " Captain Gilbert, and Abby Ann Gladding, daughter of Captain
John; m. by Rev. James W. Sykes, Sept. 2, 1844.

4-55 RICH John C., of Troy, N. H., and Mary Ann Simmons, of Bristol; m. by
Rev. Thomas Sheperd, Feb. 14, 1841.

1-24 RILEY Sarah, and Richard Colwell, (Int.) July 8, 1725.

1-129 ROBBINS Rebecca, and Benjamin Wing (col.), Nov. 22, 1801.

4-55 " John, and Freelove Brower (col.); m. by Rev. Thomas Sheperd,
June 30, 1840.

1-78 RODMAN Maria, and Charles Munro (col.), Nov. 26, 1801.

1-10 ROFFEY Elizabeth, and William Bosworth, Jr., Dec. 19, 1771.

1-4 ROGERS Ruth, and James Bennett, July 12, 1694.

1-69 " Mrs. Mary, and Captain Stephen Mumford, July 26, 1716.

1-100 " David, of Bristol, and Mrs. Lydia Sheffield, of Barrington; m.
by Rev. Luther Baker, Nov. 12, 1803.

4-26 ROGERS Robert, son of Daniel and Ann, and Maria DeWolf, of Col. William and Charlotte; m. by Rev. Henry Wight, Dec. 27, 1814.

4-227 " Ruth M., and Benjamin Hall, May 21, 1820.

4-55 " Charles W., of Utica, N. Y., and Joanna M. Coggeshall, of Bristol; m. by Rev. Thomas Sheperd, Oct. 21, 1842.

1-103 ROSBOTHAM Mrs. Elizabeth, and John Sampson, Sept. 11, 1717.

1-70 " Hannah, and John Munro, (Int.) April 9, 1728, (also 1-72); m. April 29, 1728.

1-61 " Elizabeth, and John Kelley, (Int.) May 9, 1729.

4-55 ROUSE Agnes, and Alexander Ferris, March 11, 1844.

4-9 ROWLAND William Maltby, son of Samuel and Sarah, of Fairfield, Conn., and Clarrissa Leonard Wight, of Providence, daughter of Henry and Clarrissa; m. by Rev. Henry Wight, Aug. 22, 1830.

1-70 RUE Experience, and John Martin, (Int.) Dec. 10, 1726.

1-98 RUSSELL Joseph, of Barnstable, Mass., and Mrs. Sarah Paine, of Bristol (also 1-99), (Int.) May 12, 1733; m. by Rev. Barnabus Taylor, June 10, 1733.

1-66 " Julianna, and Reding Lawton (col.), (Int.) ——, 1737.

1-99 " John, of Providence, and Mrs. Martha Martin, of Bristol; m. by Rev. John Burt, Oct. 15, 1761.

1-66 " Mrs. Sarah, and Samuel Leffinwell, Dec. 10, 1761.

1-101 " John Willard, son of Nathaniel and Elizabeth, and Nancy Smith, of Nathaniel and Parnell; m. by Rev. Henry Wight, June 1, 1802.

1-98 RYDOR Elisba, and Tabitha Gains, (Int.) July 5, 1738.

S

4-32 SABIN Sarah Smith, and Oliver Wilson, June 1, 1814.

1-108 " Rev. Benjamin, of Bristol, son of Peter, deceased, of Thompson, Conn., and Elizabeth Chace, dau. of James, of Swansey, Mass.; m. by Rev. Jordan Rexford, April 1, 1818.

1-6 SALISBURY Rebecca, and John Busbee, (Int.) July 19, 1731; m. Aug. 30, 1731.

1-103 " Benjamin, and Mary Giddens (also 1-104), (Int.) April 13, 1734; m. by Rev. Barnabus Taylor, May 5, 1734.

1-123 " Prudence, and Samuel Wheaton, Jr., (Int.) March 8, 1741-2.

1-104 " Archibald, and Sarah Wardwell, (Int.) Nov. 28, 1741.

1-61 " Sarah, and Joseph Kelley, (Int.) Dec. 14, 1745-6.

1-105 " Barnard, and Mrs. Susannah Oldridge, Aug. 5, 1748.

1-105 " Hezekiah, and Mrs. Abigail Ady; m. by Rev. John Burt, May 17, 1753.

1-105 " Benjamin, and Mrs. Elizabeth Lawton; m. by Rev. John Burt, March 31, 1756.

1-114 " Mrs. Mary, and Capt. Nathan Tyler, June 2, 1757.

1-52 " Mrs. Abigail, and John Hogins, Oct. 11, 1759.

1-106 " Barnard, and Ruth Ady, Feb. 22, 1770.

1-33 " Elizabeth, and Jesse Everett, Oct. 20, 1771.

1-33 " Martha, and Isaac Esleck, Nov. 1, 1772.

1-127 " Lydia, and Nathaniel Waldron, Jr., Nov. 20, 1781.

1-22 " Rebecca, and John Coy, June 21, 1794.

1-103 SANDYE Joseph, and Berhia Lucas, Oct. 18, 1682.

1-103 SAMPSON John, and Mrs. Elizabeth Rosbotham; m. by Benjamin Church, Justice of the Peace, Sept. 11, 1717.

1-122 SAMSON Mrs. Elizabeth, and Capt. Samuel Woodbury, (Int.) —— —. 1739; m. June 18, 1739.

1-19 " Mrs. Mary, and Samuel Clarke, Jan. 18, 1747.

1-16 SANDFORD Grissel, and Rev. Nathaniel Cotton, Jan. 20, 1721-2.

1-104 " Samuel, of Newport, and Hannah Wardwell, of Bristol, (Int.) July 6, 1740.

1-105 " Eben, of Newport, and Mrs. Martha Smith, May 28, 1749.

1-93 " Mrs. Martha, and William Pike, June 16, 1763.

1-105 " Restcome, and Mrs. Abigail Wardwell; m. by Rev. John Burt, Jan. 14, 1764.

1-93 " Mrs. Elizabeth, and Thomas Peck, Jr., Dec. 11, 1766.

4-36	SANDFORD Abigail, and John Liscomb, March 19, 1786.
1-30	"	Rhoda, and Jeremiah Diman, Oct. 4, 1810.
1-107	"	Daniel, of Royal and Rhoda, and Lydia Liscomb, of Richard and Lydia; m. by Rev. Henry Wight, July 22, 1811.
4-10	"	Elizabeth Ellery, and John Usher Lansing, Feb. 26, 1827.
4-50	"	Allen B., and Julia A. D. Wood; m. by Rev. Charles Noble, April 17, 1842.
4-50	"	Henry, and Martha Alger; m. by Rev. Charles Noble, April 27, 1842.
4-52	"	Waitey, and George M. Coit, Aug. 15, 1842.
4-52	"	Leonard, and Harriet B. Slade, daughter of Jonathan; m. by Rev. V. R. Osborn, Sept. 27, 1842.
4-71	"	Mary L., and Isaiah D. Simmons, Oct. 3, 1849.
4-1	SAUNDERS Nancy, and Thomas Cole, Nov. 27, 1818.
1-108	SAYER Rouse Potter, son of Lewis, deceased, of Newport, and Mrs. Susan Easterbrooks, of Bristol, daughter of the late Joseph Wardwell, of Bristol; m. by Rev. Jordan Rexford, April 1, 1818.
4-52	"	Nancy, and Sylvanus L. Pease, June 19, 1842.
4-56	"	John, of Bristol, and Susan Elizabeth Fuller, of Cumberland; m. by Rev. Isaac Bonney, Oct. 20, 1844.
4-75	SCHOMACKER John Henry, of Germany, and Mrs. Martha Diman, of Bristol; m. by Rev. Joseph M. Graves, May 26, 1851.
4-61	SCOLLEY Clara, and Samuel B. Wight, Oct. 9, 1845.
1-54	SCOTT Elizabeth, and Captain Benjamin Harris, May 10, 1816.
1-69	SEABURY Martha, and Benjamin Manchester, (Int.) July 12, 1723.
1-4	SEARL Marian, and Nathaniel Brown, May 29, 1718.
1-103	"	Solomon, and Elizabeth Gladding, (Int.) March 23, 1723; m. by Nathaniel Cotton, April 18, 1723.
4-70	SEATLE Benjamin S., and Martha F. Giles; m. by Rev. Richard Livesey, Aug. 2, 1849.
1-115	SHANTOM Bridget, and Jacob Truck, Feb. 23, 1732-3.
1-109	"	Jacob, and Delle Siman, (Int.) Aug. —, 1741.
1-51, 52	SHARP Mary, and Jonas Humphrey, (Int.) May 18, 1734; m. June 13, 1734.
1-59	"	Mrs. Phebe, and Joseph Jenkins, (Int.) Oct. 12, 1744; m. Dec. 24, 1744.
1-59	"	Mrs. Sarah, and John Jenkins, Oct. 8, 1747.
4-48	"	Thomas, of Newport, and Sybil Vaughn, of Bristol; m. by Rev. William L. Brower, May 2, 1841.
1-76	SHAW Merebah, and Stephen Munro, March 23, 1773.
1-1	SHEARS Mehitable, and John Archer, Jan. 5, 1692.
1-100	SHEFFIELD Mrs. Lydia, and David Rogers, Nov. 12, 1803.
	SHELDON Rebecca, and Nathaniel Hicks, Feb. 2, 1786.
4-55	SHEPERL Sarah, and Melvin G. Deane, Aug. 9, 1843.
4-2	SHERMAN Solomon, and Susanna Pitcher; m. by Rev. Isaac Bonney, Jan. 15, 1820.
4-13	"	Gideon, and Seraphina Thurber; m. by Rev. E. K. Avery, Dec. 25, 1832.
4-44	"	Susan B., and Nathaniel D. Maxfield, Dec. 13, 1840.
4-53	"	Maria B., and Daniel Wilcox, April 27, 1843.
4-56	"	Susan A., and William W. Gorton, May 5, 1844.
1-23	SHORT Mary, and George M. Coit, May 19, 1816.
4-38	"	Judith Eliza, and Henry Van Doorn, Dec. 17, 1839.
1-109	SIMAN Delle, and Jacob Shantom, (Int.) Aug. —, 1741.
1-106	"	Joseph, of Thomas and Merian, and Mary Wilson, of Thomas and Mary; m. by Rev. Henry Wight, Feb. 2, 1801.
1-6, 7	SIMMONS Hannah, and Benjamin Ball, (Int.) Oct. 25, 1734; m. —gbr, 14, 1734.
1-103	"	Ichabod, of Newport, and Experience Pearce, of Bristol, (Int.) Aug. 31, 1737.
1-125	"	Mrs. Experience, and Samuel Whitaker, Aug. 15, 1753.
1-107	"	Ephraim, son of Constant and Lydia, and Prescilla West, of Nathaniel and Rebecca; m. by Rev. Henry Wight, July 12, 1801.
1-107	"	Comfort, of Comfort and Abigail, and Mary Drown, daughter of Jonathan Jenckes and Hannah Drown; m. by Rev. Henry Wight, Aug. 25, 1805.

4-16	SIMMONS	Joseph, of Fairhaven, Mass., and Ann Peckham, of Bristol; m. by Rev. Henry Wight, Jan. 1, 1835.
4-80	"	Mary, and William Franklin, Feb. 28, 1836.
4-30	"	Mrs. Lucy Ann, and Nathan M. Bunn, Aug. 7, 1838.
4-36	"	Nancy F., and Peter Lawton, Aug. 12, 1839.
4-55	"	Mary Ann, and John C. Rich, Feb. 14, 1841.
4-46	"	Abraham, of Cranston, R. I., and Delana H. Jones, of Bristol; m. by Rev. Henry Sullings, Sept. 29, 1841.
4-55	"	Martha B., and William H. Bullock, Nov. 27, 1842.
4-54	"	Charles, of Dighton, Mass., and Harriet Cummings, of Bristol; m. by Rev. G. F. Sanborn, Oct. 22, 1843.
4-65	"	Calvin, and Judith Cole; m. by Rev. Jonathan Cady, June 21, 1847.
4-67	"	Isaac, and Mary E. Warren, of Nathan; m. by Rev. Thomas Sheperd, Jan. 24, 1848.
4-71	"	Isaiah D., and Mary L. Sandford; m. by Rev. Richard Livesey, Oct. 3, 1849.
4-71	"	Robert M., of S. Rochester, Mass., and Patience W. Wilcox, of Bristol; m. by Rev. Thomas Sheperd, Nov. 13, 1849.
4-73	"	William H., and Mary A. Greene; m. by Rev. Richard Livesey, Dec. 9, 1849.
1-109	SIMON	Indian, and Mary Crooker, (Int.) March —, 1732.
1-115	"	—, son of Tom, and Hannah ——, (Int.) June 9, 1722.
1-108	SLADE	Jonathan, son of Job and Prudence, and Nancy Potter, of Thomas and Ruth; m. by Rev. Henry Wight, May 14, 1807.
4-8	"	Charlotte, and William Christopher Van Doorn, Oct. 29, 1827.
4-11	"	Ira P., of Jonathan and Nancy, and Lydia H. Munro, of Benjamin and Rebecca; m. by Rev. Lewis Bates, March 4, 1832.
4-38	"	Ruth Ann, and Benjamin Clark, Aug. 25, 1839.
4-42	"	Ira P., and Martha F. Munro; m. by Rev. Ephraim Scott, Dec. 15, 1840.
	SLADE	Eliza F., and John Howland Pitman, June 16, 1840.
4-50	"	John R., and Harriet Paine; m. by Rev. Charles Noble, Sept. 20, 1841.
4-52	"	Harriet B., and Leonard Sandford, Sept. 27, 1842.
1-47	SLOCUM	Phebe, and Stephen Gladding, Feb. 28, 1807.
1-79	"	Mary, and Joseph Morris, July 8, 1810.
1-12	"	Nancy, and Francisco Brownson, July 2, 1811.
4-69	"	William L., of Newport, and Hannah A. Vaughn, of Bristol; m. by Rev. Richard Livesey, Sept. 26, 1848.
1-4	SMITH	Mary, and Bellamy Bosworth, Nov. 11, 1685.
1-2	"	Hannah, and William Ady, July 19, 1697.
1-111	"	Rebecca, and John Throop, Nov. 26, 1697.
1-50	"	Rebecca, and Benjamin Hoar, April 10, 1699.
1-111	"	Sarah, and Joseph Throop, (Int.) July 6, 1724; m. Feb. 24, 1724-5.
1-32	"	Mary, and Joseph Eddy, (Int.) Oct. 5, 1728.
1-103, 104	"	Samuel, Jr., and Elizabeth Drown, (Int.) April 24, 1731; m. by Rev. Barnabus Taylor, May 10, 1731.
1-51	"	Mary, and John Haskill, (Int.) March 11, 1731-2; m. April 7, 1732.
1-64, 65	"	Elizabeth, and John Lindsey, (Int.) Jan. 12, 1733; m. Jan. 29, 1733-4.
1-103, 104	"	Abigail, and Ralph Stanhope, (Int.) Jan. 3, 1735-6; m. March 28, 1735-6.
1-72	"	Hannah, and Thomas Martin, (Int.) Nov. 6, 1736.
1-17	"	Mary, and Benjamin Clifton, (Int.) March 12, 1738-9; m. Nov. 18, 1739.
1-72, 73	"	Priscilla, and Charles Munro, (Int.) April 7, 1738; m. May 29, 1735-6.
1-103, 104	"	John, and Hannah Thompson, (Int.) April 12, 1738; m. by Rev. Barnabus Taylor, May 25, 1738.
1-58	"	Elizabeth, and Benjamin James, (Int.) June 17, 1738; m. July 6, 1738.

1-51   SMITH L——, and Samuel Howland, Jr., (Int.) July 29, 1738.
1-104   "   Benjamin, and Abigail Church, (Int.) April 16, 1739; m. by Rev.
              Barnabus Taylor, May 31, 1739.
1-7, 13   "   Hannah, and Daniel Beebe, (Int.) July 11, 1739; m. Sept. 1, 1739.
1-103, 104 "   Richard, and Lucretia Diman, (Int.) Nov. 28, 1741; m. Dec. 24,
              1741.
1-104   "   Samuel, and Martha Gladding, (Int.) July 28, 1744; m. Aug. 21,
              1744.
1-104   "   Nathaniel, Jr., and Mrs. Phebe Manchester, (Int.) April 26, 1746;
              m. by Rev. John Burt, May 21, 1746.
1-105   "   Mrs. Martha, and Eben Sandford, May 28, 1749.
1-1   "   Mrs. Sarah, and James Allen, June 9, 1751.
1-105   "   Benjamin, and Mrs. Sarah May; m. by Rev. John Burt, Oct. 29,
              1752.
1-125   "   Mrs. Elizabeth, and Benjamin West, June 7, 1753.
1-133   "   Mrs. Joyce, and Isaac Young, Dec. 22, 1753.
1-44   "   Mrs. Esther, and James Goff, Dec. 15, 1757.
1-44   "   Mrs. Lucretia, and John Gladding, Jr., Sept. 17, 1761.
1-105   "   Stephen, and Mrs. Mary Gorham; m. by Rev. John Burt, Oct. 13,
              1763.
1-105   "   Josiah, and Mrs. Eleanor Taylor; m. by Rev. John Burt, July 5,
              1764.
1-105   "   Benjamin, and Mrs. Jemima Wardwell; m. by Rev. John Burt,
              Sept. 18, 1764.
1-106   "   James, of Samuel, deceased, and Phebe Wardwell, of John; m. by
              Rev. John Burt, Dec. 2, 1767.
1-105   "   Nathaniel, of Benjamin, and Parnel Taylor, of Rev. Barnabus, de-
              ceased; m. by Rev. John Burt, Oct. 27, 1768.
1-106   "   Joseph, and Molly Miller, both of Warren, May 18, 1769.
1-75   "   Rebecca, and Archibald Munro, Nov. 28, 1769.
1-126   "   Sarah, and Benjamin Wardwell, June 8, 1773.
1-106   "   Josiah, and Mrs. Elizabeth Raynolds; m. by Joseph Raynolds, Aug.
              22, 1776.
1-106   "   Richard, of Bristol, and Ruth James, of Providence; m. by Rev.
              Joseph Snow, Jan. 25, 1792.
1-101   "   Nancy, and John Willard Russell, June 1, 1802.
1-12   "   Mary, and William Bradford, Feb. 1, 1804.
1-12   "   Elizabeth, and Allen Bourne, June 7, 1805.
1-130   "   Lucy, and George Walkine (col.), Nov. 16, 1815.
4-3   "   James, of James and Sarah, and Martha Van Doorn, of Anthony
              and Phebe; m. by Rev. Henry Wight, Feb. 8, 1818.
4-48   "   Richard D., of Comanico, Cuba, and Hannah Borden, of Bristol;
              m. by Rev. John Starkweather, Aug. 4, 1834.
4-48   "   Sarah Ann, and Henry Coggeshall, May 31, 1841.
4-57   "   Sarah U., and Nathaniel J. Wardwell, July 3, 1845.
4-59   "   Solen H., and Sarah M. Waldron; m. by Rev. Hezekiah Burnham,
              Nov. 22, 1845.
4-81   "   Sarah B., and Walter Barclay, Feb. 26, 1876.
1-40   SOUTHWORTH Elizabeth, and Samuel Gallup, May 12, 1685.
1-111   "   Priscilla, and Samuel Talbot, March 1, 1689.
1-122   SPARHAWK Madam Priscilla, and Jonathan Waldo, (Int.) Feb. 11, 1726-7.
4-70   SPARKS Rachel J., and Cyrus H. Edson, —— —, 1848.
4-73   "   Lydia W., and James Francis Stoughton, Jan. 13, 1850.
4-73   "   Hannah, and John N. Burgess, Feb. 3, 1850.
4-18   SPENCER William, of New York, and Lydia Woodbury Lindsey, of Jonathan
              W. and Hannah; m. by Rev. Henry Wight, June 21, 1835.
4-65   "   Mary T., and William T. Gorham, Oct. 13, 1847.
1-36   SPINK Abigail, and John Fry, (Int.) Dec. 28, 1723; m. March 26, 1724.
4-4   SPOONER William Boss, of John Wing, and Marian Wyatt Manchester, of
              William; m. by Rev. Henry Wight, Nov. 4, 1821.
4-38   "   Charles, and Elizabeth Hall; m. by Rev. Thomas Sheperd, Oct. 9,
              1839.
4-83   "   Sarah, and Samuel S. Manchester, May 1, 1833.
4-70   "   Elizabeth W., and Joseph M. Wardwell, May 31, 1849.
4-70, 77   "   Martha Abby, and Adams J. Bennett, Nov. 1, 1853.

1-90 SPRAGUE Hannah, and John Paddock, Aug. 2, 1738.

3-107 SPRINGER Joseph, son of John, and Martha, of Bristol, and Mary Vickery, dau. of Joseph and Susannah, of Newport; m. by Rev. Alexander V. Griswold, July 10, 1808.

4-79 " Martha, and Elisha Barney Franklin, Oct. 10, 1833.

4-54 " John, and Clara Grinnell: m. by Rev. V. R. Osborn, July 12, 1843.

1-36 STACY Susannah, and David Fairbanks, (Int.) Jan. 6, 1723.

1-111 STANBURY Elizabeth, and William Throop, Jr., (Int.) September 19, 1719.

1-109 STANDISH Miles, and Mehitable ——, (and then removed to Preston, Conn.), Dec. 5, 1700.

1-103 STANHOPE Ralph, of Newport, and Abigail Smith, of Bristol, (Int.) Jan. 3, 1735-6 (also 1-104); m. by Rev. Barnabus Taylor, March 28, 1735-6.

• 1-103 STEADMAN William (mariner) and Sarah Blewat, late of Maryland, (Int.) April 20, 1720.

1-108 STEAD Jonathan, of Providence, son of Job, and Sally Hill, of Ebenezer, of Providence; m. by Rev. James Wilson, June 13, 1802.

4-61 STETSON George W., and Mary Jane Norris; m. by Rev. Thomas Sheperd, Feb. 6, 1845.

4-6 STODDARD Rev. Isaac, of Groton, Conn., and Eleanor Wardwell, of Bristol; m. by Rev. Thomas W. Tucker, June 22, 1825.

1-103 STONE William, and Hannah Walley, June 2, 1686.

4-73 STOUGHTON James Francis, and Lydia W. Sparks; m. by Rev. Richard Livesey, Jan. 13, 1850.

4-9 STRONG Henry S., of New Hampton, Mass., son of Levi and Mary, and Sarah G. Hawly, of Andrew and Mary; m. by Rev. Henry Wight, Nov. 4, 1827.

1-108 STURCH Richard, and Charlotte Bryant; m. by Daniel Bradford, Justice of the Peace, March 9, 1820.

4-79 STUTSON George W., and Elizabeth Cooke; m. by Rev. Hezekiah Burnham, Aug. 23, 1846.

1-126 SWAN Mrs. Hannah, and John Wardwell, Jr., Jan. 5, 1766.

1-106 " Thomas, of Ebenezer, of Boston, Mass., and Elizabeth Bosworth, daughter of Samuel, of Bristol; m. by Rev. John Burt, April 17, 1774.

1-2 " Hannah, and William Adams, Oct. 23, 1791.

1-107 " Thomas, son of Thomas and Elizabeth, and Sally Norris, daughter of Capt. John and Hannah; m. by Rev. Henry Wight, Dec. 2, 1805.

4-242 " Samuel, and Hannah Gifford, daughter of Ephraim and Ruth; m. by Rev. Alexander G. Griswold, Feb. 9, 1823.

4-28 " Elizabeth, and Charles J Bradford, Feb. 28, 1838.

4-28 " Maria, and Peter T. W. Mitchell, March 11, 1838.

1-108 SWEETING Henry, and Bethia Wood, (Int.) ——.

4-44 SWEET Almira, and Orin H. Holmes, May 24, 1840.

4-52 " Nancy T., and Alvin C. Aldridge, Sept. 4, 1842.

4-4 SWIFT Thomas, of Capt. Charles and Sarah, and Susan Troop Easterbrooks, of Daniel and Abigail; m. by Rev. Henry Wight, Aug. 27, 1811.

4-26 " Susan T., and Josiah Gladding, Oct. 20, 1833.

1-15 SYLVESTER Mrs. Mary, and Matthew Carey, Aug. 1, 1693.

T

1-111 TABER Thomas, of Tiverton, and Martha Moorey, (Int.) June 24, 1723.

1-115 " David, of Edmond and Patience, and Elizabeth Fitch, of Amos and Lydia; m. by Rev. Henry Wight, Oct. 26, 1811.

1-113 TALBY Edward, and Mrs. Austis Waldron; m. by Rev. John Burt, Oct. 17, 1751.

1-111 TALBOT Samuel, and Priscilla Southworth, March 1, 1689.

1-91 " Rebecca, Jr., and William Peck, (Int.) Oct. 24, 1741.

1-91 " Josiah R., and Dorothea B. Wilson; m. by Rev. Latherlord Douglass, July 6, 1826.

1-115 TALLMAN Abel, of John and Mary, and Lucy Vose, of William and Lucy.;
            m. by Rev. Henry Wight, May 13, 1813.
4-40   "   Adeline D., and Phillip B. Bourne, Dec. 30, 1840.
4-48   TANNER Charlotte, and John H. Peck, April 26, 1841.
4-46   "   William B., of Providence, and Sarah Dawley, of Bristol; m. by
            Rev. Henry Sullings, May 24, 1841.
1-36   TAYLOR Mercy, and Anthony Fry (Int.) Feb. 28, 1723; m. June 24, 1724.
1-112 "   Mrs. Susannah, and John Throop, (Int.) Oct. 9, 1732.
1-17,18 "   Thankful, and Benjamin Carey, (Int.) Dec. 8, 1733; m. Dec. 26,
            1733.
1-105 "   Mrs. Eleanor, and Josiah Smith, July 5, 1764.
1-105 "   Parnel, and Nathaniel Smith, Oct. 27, 1768.
1-29   "   Mary, and Capt. Charles DeWolf, April 28, 1771.
1-76   "   Martha, and Nathaniel Munro, Nov. 1, 1774.
1-128 "   Freelove, and Nathaniel Wilson, Nov. 4, 1799.
4-16   "   William R., and Harriet DeWolf Bradford; m. by Rev. John.
            Starkweather, Sept. 1, 1833.
4-63   TEEL William H., and Ruth H. Wardwell; m. by Rev. Thomas Sheperd,
            April 13, 1847.
4-10   TEW Mary, and William Carnett, April 29, 1811.
1-115 THAYER Rufus, of Elijah, and Lydia, and Parmelia Throop, daughter
            of Samuel and Elizabeth; m. by Rev. Henry Wight, Feb. 8,
            1795.
1-103 THOMPSON Hannah, and John Smith, (Int.) April 12, 1738 (also 1-104);
            m. May 25, 1738.
1-114 "   Alexander, of Newport, and Mrs. Ann Gladding, of Bristol; m.
            by Rev. John Burt, Aug. 12, 1762.
1-61   "   Abigail, and Richard Kim, (col.) Dec. 25, 1802.
1-4   THROOP Mary, and John Barney, Nov. 4, 1686.
1-111 "   Daniel, and Dorcas Barney, Aug. 23, 1689.
1-88   "   Elizabeth, and Jonathan Peck, March 31, 1695.
1-111 "   John, and Rebecca Smith, Nov. 25, 1697.
1-111 "   Daniel, and Deborah Macey, Jan. 5, 1697.
1-111 "   William, and Martha Collye, March 20, 1698.
1-121 "   Anna, and Cornelius Waldron, (Int.) Nov. —, 1718.
1-111 "   William, Jr., and Elizabeth Stanbury, of Pembroke, (Int.) Sept.
            19, 1719.
1-111 "   Samuel, of Bristol, and Dorothy Gray, of Newport, (Int.) March
            31, 1722.
1-89   "   Elizabeth, and William Peck, (Int.) July 23, 1723.
1-111 "   Joseph, and Sarah Smith, (Int.) July 6, 1724.
1-111 "   Amos, and Mrs. Francis Davis (also 1-112), (Int.) Nov. 28, 1724;
            m. by Rev. Nathaniel Cotton, Jan. 7, 1724-5.
1-112 "   Joseph, and Sarah Smith; m. by Rev. Nathaniel Cotton, Feb. 24,
            1724-5.
1-96   "   Elizabeth, and William Peck, May 13, 1725.
1-118 "   Martha, and Daniel Vangn, (Int.) Nov. 6, 1725; m. Nov. 23, 1725.
1-70   "   Mary, and Joseph Marcy, (Int.) April 6, 1728; m. May 31, 1728.
1-61   "   Esther, and Thomas Kenton, (Int.) June 19, 1730.
1-61   "   ——, and Thomas Kempton, Oct. 15, 1730.
1-63,65 "   Rebecca, and Ebenezer Lyon, (Int.) Jan. 28, 1731-2; m. March
            8, 1731-2.
1-112 "   Dea. John, of Bristol, and Mrs. Susannah Taylor, of Barnworth,
            (Int.) Oct. 9, 1732.
1-112 "   Thomas, Jr., of Bristol, and Mary Billings, of Little Compton,
            (Int.) Feb. 17, 1732-3.
1-98,99 "   Mercy, and Eleazor Reynolds, (Int.) April 7, 1733; m. May 6,
            1733.
1-83   "   Mary, and John Nicholson, (Int.) Oct. 14, 1736; m. Nov. 10, 1736.
1-113 "   Dann, Jr., of Lebanon, and Susannah Carey, Jr., of Bristol, (Int.)
            March, 12, 1736-7.
1-113 "   John, Jr., of Bristol, and Phebe Hall, of Swansey, (Int.) Oct. 6,
            1739.
1-28   "   Sarah, and George Dunbar, Sept. 6, 1742; m. Sept. 20, 1742.
1-113 "   Thomas, of Bristol, and Zporah Man, of Wrentham, (Int.) April 7,
            1742.

1-113   THROOP Thomas, Jr., of Bristol, and Elizabeth Man, of Wrentham, (Int.) April 10, 1744.

1-125   "   Mrs. Hannah, and Nathaniel Waldron, Oct. 19, 1755.

1-93   "   Mrs. Mary, and Jonathan Peck, Oct. 29, 1757.

1-20   "   Mrs. Phebe, and Thomas Champlain, Feb. 5, 1759.

1-114   "   William, and Mrs. Alathea Fales; m. by Rev. John Burt, March 20, 1765.

1-100   "   Eliza, and Edward Richmond, Oct. 25, 1770.

1-24   "   Sarah, and George Coggeshall, Dec. 17, 1772.

1-115   "   Parmelia, and Rufus Thayer, Feb. 8, 1795.

1-114   "   William, of Bristol, son of William and Alathea, dec., and Hannah Walker, of Tiverton, dau. of David, dec., and Sarah; m. by Rev. Mase Sheperd, at Tiverton, Oct. 22, 1795.

1-84   "   Abigail, and Simeon Nash, March 22, 1803.

1-111   THURBER James, of Swansey, and Hephzebah Lewis, of Bristol; m. by Rev. Mr. Luther, Dec. 25, 1706.

1-114   "   Amos, of John, and Elizabeth Bosworth, of William and Mary; m. by Rev. Henry Wight, April 12, 1795.

4-13   "   Serephina, and Gideon Sherman, Dec. 25, 1832.

1-112   THURRILL George, of Bristol, and Elizabeth Ladd, of William, of Little Compton, (Int.) Jan. 16, 1724-5.

1-126   "   Mary, and John West, Jr., Dec. 8, 1765.

1-127   "   Elizabeth, Jr., and Edward Winslow, Aug. 12, 1770.

1-86   "   Elizabeth, and Joseph Oldridge, Nov. 4, 1770.

1-63   THURSTON Rebecca, and John Liscomb, Jr., May 13, 1718.

1-50   "   Mahitable, and Nathaniel Huntington, (Int.) Feb. 2, 1722; m. Feb. 28, 1722-3.

1-113   "   John, of Newport, and Mrs. Elizabeth Oxx, (Int.) April 23, 1746.

4-53   "   Thomas J., and Clarrissa Munro; m. by Rev. Edward Freeman, April 30, 1843.

4-63   "   Phebe G., and Cyrus B. Eddy, Oct. 28, 1846.

4-61   TIFFANY Hezekiah, and Eliza Bash, both of Barrington; m. by Rev. Thomas Sheperd, Nov. 24, 1846.

4-77, 222   TILLEY Benjamin, (21 years) and Susan Wardwell Easterbrooks, (21 years) m. by Rev. E. K. Avery, Nov. 17, 1832.

1-111   TILLINGHAST Joseph, Jr., of Tiverton, and Mercy Howland, of Bristol, Aug. 6, 1722.

1-114   "   Charles Henry, son of Joseph and Ann, and Dulcina Nelson, of Major Paul and Grace; m. by Rev. Henry Wight, Sept. 29, 1807.

4-65   "   Nancy, and James Collins, Jan. 23, 1847.

1-113   TISDALE James, and Esther Man, (Int.) Sept. 1, 1744; m. Sept. 25, 1744.

4-7   TITUS Anne, and George Gardner, (col.) Nov. 16, 1825.

1-26   TOMAN Martha, and Thomas Durfee, (Int.) July —, 1727; m. July 16, 1727.

1-45   TOMLIN Rebecca, and William Gladding, Feb. 4, 1781.

1-113   **TOMKINS** Nathaniel, of Little Compton, and Elizabeth Wardwell, of Bristol, (Int.) June 14, 1744; m. Aug. 2, 1744.

1-92   "   Mrs. Elizabeth, and John Phillips, Aug. 28, 1750.

1-112   TOOGOOD Samuel, late resident of Swansey, and Ann Bowerman, of Bristol, (Int.) Oct. 21, 1726.

1-129   TOPHAM Betsey, and Amos Wright, April 26, 1812.

1-32   TORREY Maluliah, and Joseph Eddy, (Int.) Oct. 31, 1724; m. Dec. 2, 1724-5.

1-112   "   William, and Susannah Giddens, (Int.) Dec. 12, 1724; m. by Rev. Nathaniel Cotton, Dec. 29, 1724.

1-112   "   Samuel, of Boston, and Silener Torrey, of Bristol, (Int.) Dec. —, 1725; m. by Rev. Nathaniel Cotton, Feb. 3, 1725-6.

1-112   "   Silener, and Samuel Torrey, (Int.) Dec. —, 1725; m. Feb. 3, 1725-6.

4-2   TOWNSEND Ruth B., and Ebenezer Bosworth, March 28, 1820.

4-50   "   Martha O., and William Bly, May 23, 1842.

4-50   "   Lydia M., and Mason W. Peirce, Jr., June 19, 1842.

1-92   TRIPP Hannah, and Benjamin Palmenter, (Int.) July 27, 1745.

1-113   "   James, of Bristol, and Martha White, of Barrington, (Int.) Sept. 2, 1745.

1-114 TRIPP Peleg, of Dartmonth, and Mrs. Mary Nooning, of Bristol; m. by Rev. John Burt, March 12, 1761.
1-23   " Molly, and Thomas Church, Oct. 26, 1794.
1-22 TROTT Anna, and Thomas Cole, Sept. 5, 1815.
1-115 TRUCK Jacob, and Bridget Shantom, Feb. 23, 1732-3.
1-115   " Isaac, and Abigail George, (col.), (Int.) July 27, 1741.
4-70 TRUSSELL Richard, of New York, and Sarah Augusta Wardwell, of Bristol; m. by Rev. Thomas Sheperd, Nov. 15, 1848.
1-112 TURNER Nathaniel, and Mary Wardwell, of Benjamin, (Int.) May 27, 1731.
1-114   " Caleb, of Warren, and Mary Glover, of Bristol, Aug. 8, 1773.
4-4   " Abbie, and Capt. George Howe, Sept. 11, 1823.
1-114 TYLER Captain Nathan, of Mendon, Mass., and Mrs. Mary Salisbury, of Bristol; m. by Rev. John Burt, June 2, 1757.

U

1-117 USHER Capt. Aaron, of Allen, dec., of Bristol, and Mary Bradford Bosworth, of Benjamin, dec., of Warren; m. by Daniel Bradford, J. C. C. P., May 24, 1812.
4-34   " Benjamin B., son of Aaron, and Abby W. Peck, of Joseph; m. at Warren, by Rev. Shipley W. Willson, Sept. 16, 1838.

V

1-118 VAN DOORN Moses, and Lydia Munro; m. by Rev. Solomon Townsend, May 27, 1779.
1-118   " Anthony, and Phebe Manchester: m. by Rev. Solomon Townsend, May 29, 1796.
1-119   " William, son of Moses and Lydia, and Mary Paine, daughter of Capt. William C. and Sarah, Oct. 3, 1804.
4-3   " Martha, and James Smith, Feb. 8, 1818.
4-8   " William Christopher, of William and Mary, and Charlotte Slade, of Col. Jonathan and Sarah; m. by Rev. Henry Wight, Oct. 29, 1827.
4-12   " Martha, and Samuel Blake, Sept. 3, 1833.
4-38   " Henry, and Judith Eliza Short: m. by Rev. John C. Welch, Dec. 17, 1839.
1-119 VAN SANTVOORED Anthony, Jr. (merchant), of Albany, N. Y., and Sarah Barney, dau. of Peleg, of Swansey; m. by Daniel Bradford, J. C. C. P., ——, 1814.
1-92 VANIS Sarah, and Joseph Phillips, July 13, 1749.
1-118 VAUGHN Daniel, and Martha Throop, (Int.) Nov. 6, 1725; m. by Rev. Nathaniel Cotton, Nov. 23, 1725.
1-38   " Hannah, and Lemuel Fales, April 11, 1816.
1-119   " Clark, of Gideon and Patience, and Julia Ann Fales, of Thomas and Sarah; m. by Rev. Henry Wight, Jan. 17, 1819.
4-11   " Eliza, and Samuel P. Luther, Aug. 13, 1832.
4-48   " Sybel, and Thomas Sharpe, May 2, 1841.
4-52   " George W. G., and Phebe A. Hall; m. by Rev. V. R. Osborn, Sept. 18, 1842.
4-55   " Julia A., and Alfred Hixon, Jan. 1, 1844.
4-63   " Mary B., and Nathan T. Verry, Sept. 6, 1847.
4-69   " Hannah A., and William L. Slocum, Sept. 26, 1848.
1-118 VERIN John, and Penelope Cooke; m. at Seaconnet, Aug. 30, 1683.
1-118 VERNON Samuel, of Newport, and Elizabeth Prince, of Bristol, (Int.) Nov. 23, 1724; m. by Nathaniel Cotton, Jan. 12, 1724-5.
4-63 VERRY Nathan T., of Cumberland, and Mary B. Vaughn, of Clarke, of Bristol; m. by Rev. James N. Sykes, Sept. 6, 1847.
1-16 VIALL Elizabeth, and Benjamin Church, (Int.) Oct. 26, 1727.
1-64, 65   " Mrs. Susannah, and Capt. George Lee, (Int.) Sept. 30, 1734; m. Oct. 24, 1734.
1-118   " Hezekiah, of Boston, and Abigail Wanton, of Newport, (Int.) Sept. 2, 1736.

1-64 VIALL Susannah, and Rogers Richmond, (Int.) April 21, 1739.
1-8   "   Mrs. Abigail, and Rev. John Burt, (Int.) July 24, 1741.
1-107 VICKERY Mary, and Joseph Springer, July 10, 1808.
4-48 "   Thomas, and Mary Wilson, both of Fall River; m. by Rev. William L. Brown, Dec. 27, 1841.
4-54 VICKERY Deborah L., and Abner Midget, June 19, 1844.
1-130 VIRGIN Mrs. Priscilla, and Capt. Ezra Weston, July 4, 1817.
1-44 VON H—— Mrs. Mary, and Daniel Saindet, Nov. 5, 1750.
1-66 VOSE, Ann Jenckes, and John Lewis, Dec. 25, 1803.
1-115 "   Lucy, and Abel Tallman, May 13, 1813.

W

4-56 WALCOTT Rev. Jeremiah, of Auburn, N. Y., and Hannah B. Church, daughter of Edward, of Bristol; m. by Rev. James N. Sykes, May 22, 1844.
1-36 WALDO Deborah, and Joseph Ford, Dec. 6, 1683.
1-122 "   Jonathan, of Boston, and Madam Priscilla Sparhawk, of Bristol, (Int.) Feb. 11, 1726-7.
1-121 WALDRON Cornelius, and Anne Throop, (Int.) Nov. —, 1718.
1-98, 99 " Ann, and Thomas Rawson, (Int.) March 30, 1737; m. April 14, 1737.
1-17 "   Priscilla, and Robert Carr, (Int.) May 3, 1740.
1-121, 123 " Joseph, Jr., and Rebecca Peck, (Int.) May 3, 1741; m. July 16, 1741.
1-124 "   Daniel, and Mrs. Phebe Reynolds, (Int.) Sept. —, 1746; m. by Rev. John Burt, Sept. 28, 1746.
1-113 "   Mrs. Austis, and Edward Talby, Oct. 17, 1751.
1-125 "   Nathaniel, and Mrs. Hannah Throop; m. by Rev. John Burt, Oct. 19, 1755.
1-125 "   Mrs. Sarah, and Isaac Wardwell, Sept. 9, 1756.
1-126 "   Isaac, and Mrs. Abigail West; m. by Rev. John Burt, Feb. 14, 1765.
1-10 "   Ruth, and Shearjashub Bourne, Jr., March 4, 1773.
4-30 "   Thomas, of Nathaniel, and Ruth Gray, of Col. Thomas; m. by Daniel Bradford, Justice, Feb. 1, 1778.
1-22 "   Abigail, and Lieut. Ephraim Carey, July 18, 1779.
1-127 "   Nathaniel, Jr., son of Nathaniel, and Lydia Salisbury, of Caleb; m. by Daniel Bradford, Justice Court Common Pleas, Nov. 20, 1781.
1-13 "   Rebecca, and David Bailey, Jan. 18, 1801.
4-77 "   Lucretia, and Edward Jones, July 28, 1806.
1-47 "   Ann, and Solomon Gladding, Nov. 6, 1806.
1-12 "   Hannah, and James Batt, Jan. 6, 1807.
1-127 "   Abigail Coggeshall, and George Wilson, Feb. 3, 1811.
4-14 "   Billings, son of Ambrose and Hannah, and Hannah Diman, daughter of Jonathan and Dolly; m. by Rev. Jordan Rexford, Feb. 16, 1812.
1-59 "   Harriet, and Capt. Thomas Jones, Aug. 30, 1813.
4-13 "   Nancy, and John Burns, Jan. 17, 1832.
4-229, 35 " Rachel T., and Thomas, Remieres, Oct. 14, 1839.
4-46, 53 " John H., of Leonard, and Martha F. Cole, of Nehemiah; m. by Rev. C. S. McCready, June 13, 1841.
4-46, 53 " John M., and Mary E. Gladding; m. by Rev. G. F. Sanborn, April 12, 1843.
4-59 "   Susan H., and William J. Howe, Oct. 5, 1845.
4-59 "   Sarah M., and Solon H. Smith, Nov. 22, 1845.
1-66 WALKER Mary, and Edward Little, Nov. 7, 1717.
1-122 "   Phillip, of Rehoboth, and Ann Martin, of Bristol, (Int.) Feb. 17, 1737-8.
1-123 "   Mary, and Elisha Weaver, (Int.) Sept. 9, 1743; m. Oct 2, 1743.
1-99 "   Elizabeth, and Stephen Rawson, (Int.) March 29, 1745.
1-124 "   John, and Mrs. Patience Coggeshall, (Int.) Aug. 18, 1746.
1-75 "   Mrs. Rachel, and Simeon Munro, Jan. 31, 1762.

1-114 WALKER Hannah, and William Throop, Oct. 22, 1795.
1-45   "   Olive, and John Grimes, Dec. 2, 1798.
1-130 WALKINE George, and Lucy Smith (col.); m. by Rev. Henry Wight, Nov. 16, 1815.
1-103 WALLEY Hannah, and William Stone, June 2, 1686.
1-1   "   Elizabeth, and Edward Adams, May 19, 1692.
1-118 WANTON Abigail, and Hezekiah Viall, (Int.) Sept. 2, 1736.
1-17   "   Elizabeth, and Nathaniel Carey, (Int.) Aug. 4, 1739.
1-40 WARDELL Alice, and John Gladding, Oct. 31, 1693.
1-130   "   Joseph, and Martha Giddens, (Int.) Dec. 22, 1709.
1-122   "   Benjamin, of Bristol, and —— Holmes, of Norton, Mass., (Int.) —— 18, 1734.
1-122   "   Joseph, Jr., and Joanna Lindsey, (Int.) Jan 21, 1737-8.
1-123   "   James, Jr., and Ann Liscomb, (Int.) June 20, 1741.
1-121, 123   "   John, and Phebe Howland, (Int.) Sept. —, 1741; m. Oct. 11, 1741.
1-121, 123   "   William, and Mary Howland, Sept. 26, 1742.
1-112   "   Mary, and Nathaniel Turner, (Int.) May 27, 1731.
1-71, 72   "   Mary, and Daniel Maxfield, (Int.) May 27, 1732; m. June 11, 1732.
1-71, 72   "   Rebecca, and Simeon Munro, (Int.) Dec. 2, 1732; m. Dec. 19, 1732.
1-51, 52   "   Martha, and John Howland, (Int.) Sept. 13, 1735; m. Oct. 24, 1736.
1-64, 65   "   Mary, and William Lindsey, (Int.) Oct. 15, 1737; m. Nov. 23, 1737.
1-122   "   Joseph, and Jemima Lindsey; m. by Rev. Barnabus Taylor, Feb. 23, 1737-8.
1-122   "   Usal, and Sarah Lindsey, (Int.) Sept. 26, 1739.
1-104   "   Hannah, and Samuel Sandford, (Int.) July 6, 1740.
1-104   "   Sarah, and Archibald Salisbury, (Int.) Nov. 28, 1741.
1-123   "   James, and Ann Liscomb; m. by Rev. John Usher, March 3, 1742.
1-123   "   William, and Mary Howland, (Int.) Sept. 7, 1742.
1-113   "   Elizabeth, and Nathaniel Tompkins, (Int.) June 14, 1744; m. Aug. 2, 1744.
1-124   "   Stephen, and Mrs. Mehitable Howland, (Int.) Nov. 29, 1746; m. by Rev. John Burt, Dec. 18, 1746.
1-44   "   Mrs. Susannah, and William Gladding, Oct. 19, 1752.
1-125   "   Isaac, of Providence, and Mrs. Sarah Waldron; m. by Rev. John Burt, Sept. 9, 1756.
1-65   "   Mrs. Jemima, and Daniel Lefavour, Jan. 2, 1758.
1-105   "   Mrs. Abigail, and Restcome Sanford, Jan. 4, 1764.
1-105   "   Mrs. Jemima, and Benjamin Smith, Sept. 18, 1764.
1-126   "   John, Jr., and Mrs. Hannah Swan; m. by Rev. John Burt, Jan. 5, 1766.
1-106   "   Phebe, and James Smith, Dec. 2, 1767.
1-126   '   Joseph, son of John, and Elizabeth May, of John; m. by Rev. John Burt, June 22, 1769.
1-45   "   Susannah, and Daniel Gladding, Aug. 2, 1769.
1-93   "   Mary, and Peleg Pitman, July 7, 1770.
1-93   "   Abigail, and Thomas Pearse, Dec. 5, 1771.
1-126   "   Benjamin, son of William, deceased, and Sarah Smith, of Richard; m. by Rev. John Burt, June 8, 1773.
1-76   "   Mrs. Mary, and Sanford Munro, Nov. 6, 1774.
1-37   "   Elizabeth, and Jonathan Fales, Jr., June 29, 1775.
1-128   "   Samuel, son of Samuel and Lydia, and Hannah Carey, daughter of Captain Simeon Munro and Abigail; m. by Rev. Henry Wight, Oct. 31, 1810.
4-2   "   Hezekiah C., son of Samuel, deceased, and Sally Gifford, of Ephraim; m. by Rev. Isaac Bonney, Dec. 24, 1820.
4-3   "   Josiah S., of Captain Allen, and Sally Lindsey, daughter of Captain Jonathan W.; m. by Rev. Isaac Bonney, April 22, 1821.
4-6   "   Eleanor, and Rev. Isaac Stoddard, June 22, 1825.
4-16   "   Henry, and Sarah Luther Lindsey; m. by Rev. Jefferson Haskill, May 11, 1835.
4-40   "   James D., and Martha Lawless; m. by Rev. Ephraim Scott, Aug. 17, 1840.

4-55 WARDELL John H., of Albany. N. Y., and Elizabeth W. Church, of Bristol; m. by Rev. Thomas Sheperd, Nov. 29, 1840.

4-55 " Sarah W., and Cornelius S. Cunliff, Oct. 22, 1843.

4-56 " Ann E., and Levi N. Horton, Oct. 24, 1844.

4-57 " Nathaniel J., and Sarah U. Smith; m. by Rev. Isaac Bonney, July 3, 1845.

4-63 " Elizabeth C., and Thomas G. Holmes, Feb. 23, 1847.

4-67 " Joseph, son of John, and Elizabeth G. Wyatt, of William; m. by Rev. Thomas Sheperd, Aug. 10, 1847.

4-63 " Ruth H., and William H. Teel, April 13, 1847.

4-70 " Sarah Augusta, and Richard Trussell, Nov. 15, 1848.

4-70 " Joseph M., and Elizabeth W. Spooner; m. by Rev. Thomas Sheperd, May 31, 1849.

4-61 WARING Henry, and Ann Elizabeth Bosworth; m. by Rev. Thomas Sheperd, Sept. 3, 1844.

1-124 WARREN John, of Newport, and Sarah Ingraham, of Bristol, (Int.) Sept. 16, 1744.

1-129 " Russell, of Gamaliel and Ruth, and Sally Gladding, of Capt. Joshua and Sarah; m. by Rev. Henry Wight, March 10, 1805.

4-34 " Nathan, Jr., and Mary Ann Rawson; m. by Rev. James C. Bontecuc, May 13, 1839.

4-65 " Almira W., and George H. Burgess, March 27, 1847.

4-67 ' Mary E., and Isaac Simmons, Jan. 24, 1848.

4-67 " John Fletcher, and Julia Maria Nichols; m. by Rev. Richard Livesey, May 3, 1848.

1-131 WATERMAN Hannah, and Jeremiah Williams (col.), (Int.) June 7, 1729.

1-124 WATSON John, of Plymouth, and Elizabeth Raynolds, of Bristol, (Int.) March 17, 1743-4; m. Sept. 6, 1744.

1-36 WATTS Mercy, and Joshua Finney, May 31, 1688.

1-123 WEAVER Elisha, of Newport, and Mary Walker, of Bristol, (Int) Sept. 9, 1743; m. by Rev. John Usher, Oct. 2, 1743.

1-121 WELCH Henry, late of Dighton, and Judith Whitmore, of Bristol, (Int.) Aug. —. 1721.

4-44 " Rev. John C., and Emma Parker; m. by Rev. William L. Brower, at Warren, R. I., Aug. 17, 1844.

4-59 " Abby P., and Jabez L. Allen, Aug. 12, 1845.

1-125 WELD Edmund, of Roxbury, and Mrs. Sarah Raynolds, of Bristol; m. by Rev. John Burt, April, 15, 1752.

4-65 WELLS Samuel J. C., and Mary Ann Palmer; m. by Rev. Jonathan Cady, Aug. 30, 1847.

1-13 WESTCOTE Rebecca, and Benjamin Brown, Aug. 16, 1795.

4-223 " Emma, and J. Russell Bullock, Dec. 23, 1868.

1-130 WESTON Capt. Ezra, of Duxborough, Mass., and Mrs. Priscilla Virgin, daughter of Richard Cooper, of Bristol; m. by Daniel Bradford, J. C. C. P., July, 4, 1817.

1-123 WEST William, and Elizabeth May, (Int.) Aug. 14, 1740.

1-123 " Ebenezer and Hannah Wilson, (Int) Sept. 25, 1742.

1-124 " Samuel, and Mrs. Mercy Munro, (Int.) Oct. 25, 1746.

1-125 " William, and Mrs. Jane Hicks; m. by Rev. John Burt, April 3, 1748.

1-125 " Samuel, and Mrs. Frances Gibbs; m. by Rev. John Burt, March 21, 1751.

1-125 " Benjamin, and Mrs. Elizabeth Smith; m. by Rev. John Burt, June 7, 1753.

1-2 " Mrs. Dorothy, and John Ady, May 25, 1755.

1-74 " Mrs. Parnel, and Hezekiah Mason, Nov. 28, 1756.

1-33 " Mrs. Mary, and Robert Easterbrooks, Jr., March 17, 1757.

1-126 " Mrs. Abigail, and Isaac Waldron, Feb. 14, 1765.

1-126 " John, Jr., and Mary Thurrell; m. by Rev. John Burt, Dec. 8, 1765.

1-53 " Dorothy, and John Hicks, Oct. 4, 1770.

1-126 " James, of Ebenezer, deceased, and Lydia West, of John; m. by Rev. John Burt, Nov. 4, 1771.

1-126 " Lydia, and James West, Nov. 4, 1771.

1-128 " William, of Bristol, and Sarah Fuller, of Swanzey; m. by Rev. Charles Thomson, Nov. 16, 1783.

1-127 WEST Nathaniel Hicks, son of John and Lydia, and Rebecca Sheldon, of William and Lydia; m. by Rev. Henry Wight, Feb. 2, 1786.

1-100 " Prudence, and Gilbert Richmond, Oct. 16, 1797.

1-127 " Nathaniel H., of Bristol, and Mrs. Nellie Easterbrooks, of Warren; m. by Rev. Luther Baker, March 4, 1798.

1-107 " Priscilla, and Ephraim Simmons, July 12, 1801.

1-127 " Benjamin, of Asa and Phebe, and Austis Lindsey, daughter of Samuel and Priscilla; m. by Rev. Henry Wight, Aug. 25, 1805.

1-53 " Hannah, and William Harris, Jan. 12, 1806.

1-128 " Jemima, and William Wilson, Nov. 3, 1811.

1-22 " Fidelia, and Alfred Carter, July 31, 1812.

1-130 " Fidelia, and Luther Wheeler, Aug. 15, 1814.

4-9 " Maria, and Hezekiah Willard, Sept. 27, 1828.

4-85 " Mary G., and James Hoar, Oct. 24, 1831.

4-54 " Benjamin G., and Mary M. Manchester; m. by Rev. V. R. Osborn, June 4, 1843.

4-57 " Levina P., and George Gayton, Oct. 13, 1844.

4-67 " Mary A., and James L. Meigs, May 14, 1848.

1-129 " Asa, of Bristol, and Phebe Cranston, of Warren; m. by Rev. Charles Thompson, Aug. 24, ——.

4-5 WHEATON William, of Newport, son of Ephraim, and Angeline Munro, of Bristol, daughter of Ichabod; m. by Rev. Thomas W. Tucker, Nov. 10, 1824.

1-130 WHEELER Luther, son of William and Hannah, of Rehoboth, and Fidelia West, of Thomas and Catherine; m. by Rev. Edward Hyde, Aug. 15, 1814.

4-54 " Harriet G., and Robert A. Knox, Sept. 4, 1843.

1-122 WHEELWRIGHT Jeremiah, of Boston, and Mary Bosworth, of Bristol, (Int.) Aug. 21, 1727.

1-123 WHETON Samuel, Jr., of Swansey, and Prudence Salisbury, of Bristol, (Int.) March 8, 1741-2.

1-125 WHITAKER Samuel, of Rehoboth, and Mrs. Experience Simmons, of Bristol; m. by Rev. John Burt, Aug. 15, 1753.

1-128 WHITEMARSH Seth, son of Joseph and Susannah, and Mary Allen, of Dr. Samuel and Hannah; m. by Rev. Henry Wight, Nov. 7, 1811.

1-113 WHITE Martha, and James Tripp, (Int.) Sept. 2, 1745.

1-125 " William, and Mrs. Alice Gladding; m. by Rev. John Burt, Sept. 15, 1760.

1-126 " William, of Providence, son of Philip, late of Boston, deceased, and Hannah Coggeshall, of George, deceased, of Bristol; m. by Rev. John Burt, Feb. 6, 1773.

1-53 " Rebecca, and Noah Hall, Aug. 25, 1805.

4-14 " Sarah Ann, and Spencer Pratt, May 18, 1834.

4-42 " Eliza, and Daniel L. Howland, Nov. 22, 1840.

4-50 " Charlotte, and Daniel D. Reed, November 18, 1841.

4-70 " George N., and Eliza S. Lincoln. m. by Rev. Richard Livesey, Sept. 3, 1849.

4-69 WHITFORD Harriet J., and John Easterbrooks, Nov. 23, 1848.

4-69 " Benjamin H., and Joanna Diman; m. by Rev. Richard Livesey, Nov. 29, 1848.

1-129 WHITING Joseph, and Content Potter; m. by Henry Wight, Feb. 23, 1800.

1-121 WHITMORE Judith, and Henry Welch, (Int.) Aug. —, 1721.

1-121 WHITWELL Robert, and Mary Maxfield, (Int.) Aug. —. 1722; m. by Rev. Nathaniel Cotton, Sept. 13, 1722.

1-125 WICKES Capt. Thomas, of Warwick, and Mrs. Sarah Phillips, of Bristol. m. by Rev. John Burt, June 2, 1757.

1-122 WIGHT John, of Bristol, and Mrs. Mary Pond, of Dedham, Mass., (Int.) May 25, 1728.

1-122 " John, of Bristol, and Mrs. Deliverance Carpenter, of Rehoboth, (Int.) Oct. 22, 1737.

4-9 " Clarissa Leonard, and William Mottby Rowland, Aug. 22, 1830.

4-55 " Fanny L., and Robert M. Cleveland, Aug. 13, 1840.

4-61 " Samuel B., of Wightville, Ga., grandson of late Henry, of Bristol, and Clara Scolley, of Capt. Glover, of Ashburnbam, Mass.; m. by Rev. Edward Leigh, Oct. 9, 1845.

4-53 WILCOX Daniel, and Maria B. Sherman; m. by Rev. Edward Freeman, April 27, 1843.
4-71 " Patience W., and Robert M. Simmons, Nov. 13, 1849.
1-129 WILLARD Elijah, of Hezekiah and Mary, and Mary Bradford, of Major William and Elizabeth; m. by Rev. Henry Wight, March 28, 1799.
4-9 " Hezekiah, and Maria West; m. by Rev. Leonard B. Griffing, Sept. 27, 1828.
4-13 WILLETT Charles, and Nancy Hartshorn; m. by Rev. Faranda Preston, Nov. 10, 1833.
1-121 WILLIAMS William, late of Swansey, and Ann Pearce, of Bristol, (Int.) April 17, 1725.
1-121 " John, late of Boston, and Dorothy Paine, of Bristol, (Int.) Oct. 12, 1726.
1-131 " Jeremiah, of Swansey, and Hannah Waterman, of Bristol, (col.) (Int.) June 7, 1729.
1-52 " Mrs. Dorothy, and Hon. Hezekiah Huntington, March 23, 1748-9.
4-44, 48 WILLISTON Job, Jr., and Elizabeth R. Randall; m. by Rev. William L. Brower, Jan. 31, 1841.
4-65 " Nancy B., and Edward Manchester, June 20, 1847.
4-69 " Phebe A., and Senatore Benard, June 12, 1848.
1-123 WILLSON David, and Sarah Eddy, of Swansey, (Int.) Oct. 4, 1724.
1-63, 65 " Mrs. Hannah, and Capt. Samuel Little, (Int.) Oct. 2, 1734; m. Oct. 29, 1730.
1-73 WILSON Catherine, and Joseph Munro, (Int.) Feb. 1, 1741; m. Feb. 22, 1741.
1-83 " Rebecca, and Timothy Nooning, June 20, 1742.
1-123 " Hannah, and Ebenezer West, (Int.) Sept. 25, 1742.
1-124 " Jeremiah, and Susannah Munro, (Int.) Aug. 17, 1744.
1-65 " Mrs. Margaret, and John Liscomb, Jr., (Int.) Dec. 5, 1746.
1-125 " David, and Mrs. Elizabeth Bragg; m. by Rev. John Burt, Sept. 12, 1751.
1-74 " Mrs. Mary, and Daniel Maxfield, Dec. 14, 1755.
1-125 " David, and Mrs. Abigail Bush; m. by Rev. John Burt, May 6, 1756.
1-75 " Mis. Mary, and Elijah May, Jan. 1, 1767.
1-127 " William, and Alathea Bosworth, Jan. 16, 1774.
1-127 " Thomas, and Mary Bosworth, May 2, 1774.
1-95 " Mary, and Nathaniel Peck, Dec. 14, 1791.
1-128 " Nathaniel, of Jeremiah and Susannah, and Freelove Taylor, of Samuel and Phebe; m. by Rev. Henry Wight, Nov. 4, 1799.
1-94 " Alathea, and Zebedee Paull, Jan. 4, 1801.
1-106 " Mary, and Joseph Simons, Feb. 2, 1801.
1-77 " Deborah, and John Martin, Nov. 8, 1801.
1-95 " Sarah, and Josiah Pearse, Jan. 1, 1804.
1-129 " Thomas, son of Thomas and Mary, and Amey Easterbrooks, of Eleanor; m. by Rev. Henry Wight, Nov. 17, 1805.
1-127 " George, of James and Mary, and Abigail Coggeshall Waldron, daughter of Isaac and Martha; m. by Rev. Henry Wight, Feb. 3, 1811.
1-128 " William, of John and Mary, and Jemima West, of Thomas and Catherine; m. by Rev. Henry Wight, Nov. 3, 1811.
4-32 " Oliver, of Calvin, and Submit, and Sarah Smith Sabin, of Capt. John and Lucretia; m. by Rev. Henry Wight, June 1, 1814.
1-130 " George, of Nathaniel, and Betsey Reed, of Benjamin; m. by Rev. Thomas W. Tucker, Oct. 5, 1818.
1-91 " Dorothea B., and Josiah R. Talbot, July 6, 1826.
4-34 " Phillip G., and Sally B. Meigs; m. by Rev. James C. Bontecue, March 30, 1839.
4-42 " Benjamin R., and Elizabeth Ann Meigs; m. by Rev. Ephraim Scott, Dec. 24, 1840.
4-48 " Mary, and Thomas Vickery, Dec. 27, 1841.
4-53 " James, of Bristol, and Jane W. Bullock, of S. Kingstown; m. by Rev. Edward Freeman, March 26, 1843.
4-70 " Elizabeth F., and Jonathan B. Munro, April 19, 1849.
1-129 WING Benjamin, and Rebecca Robbin, (col.); m. by Rev. Henry Wight, Nov. 22, 1801.

1-4	WINSLOW Mrs. Elizabeth, and Stephen Burton, Sept. 4, 1684.
1-127	" Edward, of Providence, and Elizabeth Thurrell, Jr., of Bristol, Aug. 12, 1770.
4-83	" Joseph, and Mary E. Ingraham; m. by Rev. George W. Milton, Oct. 6, 1850.
1-121	WOODBURY John, and Mary Reynolds, May 18, 1694.
1-121	" Jonathan, and Mrs. Katherine Osborn; m. by Rev. Mr. Sparhawk, May. 24, 1708.
1-121	" Nathaniel, and Abigail Coffin, of Mendon, Mass., (Int.) April 13, 1720.
1-130	" Samuel, and Mrs. Margaret Osborn, (Int.) July 7, 1721.
1-122	" Capt. Samuel, and Mrs. Elizabeth Sampson, (Int.) — —, 1739; m. by Rev. Barnabus Taylor, June 18, 1739.
1-18, 19	" Sarah, and John Coy, (Int.) Aug. 31, 1745; m. Oct. 27, 1745.
1-66	" Catherine, and William Lindsey, Jr., April 26, 1772.
1-40	WOODCOCK Tabitha, and Thomas Gins, (Int.) Nov. 29, 1718.
1-27	" Elizabeth, and Joseph Dowset, (Int.) Nov. 16, 1729.
1-88	WOOD Hannah, and Jonathan Peck, (Int.) Dec. 16, 1720.
1-73	" Margaret, and Dennis McCarte, (Int.) Dec. 28, 1743.
1-108	" Bethia, and Henry Sweeting, (Int.) — —, ——.
4-38	" Elizabeth, and Jeremiah D. Liscomb, Nov. 20, 1839.
4-50	" Julia A. D., and Allen B. Sanford, April 17, 1842.
1-129	WRIGHT Amos, son of Amos and Sarah, and Betsey Topham, of Theophilus and Margaret; m. by Rev. Henry Wight, April 26, 1812.
4-7	" Phebe, and William P. Munro, June 16, 1822.
4-56	" Cynthia M., and Ezra M. Martin, Dec. 26, 1844.
1-75	WYATT Mrs. Marian, and Seabury Manchester, Feb. 1, 1763.
4-75	" Robert, and Lydia Cummings; m. by Rev. Ebenezer Blake, Nov. 21, 1824.
4-44	" William, 2d, of Bristol, and Prudence W. Paine, of Freetown, Mass.; m. at Freetown, (Int.) Dec. 31, 1840.
4-67	" Elizabeth G., and Joseph Wardwell, Aug. 10, 1847.

X Y

1-133	YOUNG Isaac, of Newport, and Mrs. Joyce Smith, of Bristol; m. by Rev. John Burt, Dec. 22, 1753.

Z

1-133	ZOLODE John, and Mary Maxfield; m. by Rev. Mr. Sparhawk, May 19, 1708.

BRISTOL.

BIRTHS.

A

1-134	ADAMS	Lydia, of Elisha and Mehitable,	Jan. 17, 1690.
1-134	"	William,	June 3, 1693.
1-134	"	Mehitable,	Aug. 3, 1695.
1-135	"	Elisha,	Sept. 11, 1697.
1-134	"	Elizabeth, of Edward and Elizabeth,	April 7, 1693.
1-134	"	Edward,	Aug. 28, 1694.
1-135	"	Hannah,	May 26, 1696.
1-135	"	Thomas,	March 28, 1698.
1-135	"	Elisha,	May 9, 1699.
1-135	"	Lydia,	July 22, 1701.
1-136	"	Nathaniel,	April 22, 1704.
1-136	"	Bethia,	Aug. 15, 1706.
1-134	"	James, of James and Mary.	Oct. —, 1691.
1-134	"	James,	June 28, 1693.
1-134	"	Sarah,	April 27, 1695.
1-135	"	Mary,	April 26, 1697.
1-135	"	Sarah,	Jan. 21, 1699-1700.
1-135	"	Ebenezer,	Dec. 20, 1702.
1-136	"	John.	Dec. 18, 1704.
1-136	"	Christian,	Nov. 26, 1706.
1-136	"	Elizabeth,	Feb. 19, 1707.
1-136	"	Elizabeth,	July 26, 1711.
1-137	"	Nancy Martindale, of James Hervey and Sally Martindale,	March 6, 1809.
1-137	"	George James,	Feb. 17, 1811.
1-137	ADEE	Dorcas, of John and Dorothy,	— 27, 1758.
1-137	"	John. of Belcher and Susannah,	Jan. 10, 1761.
1-136	ADEWITTE	Margaret, of Bryan and Rachel,	Feb. 11, 1702.
1-136	"	Bryan, of Bryan and Rachel (Salem, Mass.),	July 3, 1692.
1-137	ADY	Abigail, of Joseph and Ruth,	Feb. 10, 1731.
1-137	"	Elizabeth,	Feb. 6, 1737.
1-137	AJUBA	——, son of Ayun and Abigail,	Oct. 27, 1750.
4-222	ALGER	Julia Ann, of Joseph and Mary C.,	Feb. 9, 1851.
4-222	"	Lizzie A.,	May 7, 1854.
1-137	ALLEN	Augustine, of William and Lydia,	Feb. 25, 1731.
4-249	"	William, of William and Eleanor (Bailey),	April 23, 1802.
4-249	"	Lydia,	June 25, 1804.
4-249	"	John B.,	March 7, 1807.
4-249	"	Hezekiah,	Aug. 5, 1809.
4-249	"	Archibald St. Clair,	Oct. 16, 1811.
4-249	"	Thomas N.,	Feb. 5, 1814.
4-225	"	Susan Elizabeth, of Jabez L. and Abby P.,	July 26, 1846.
1-137	ANDERSON	Nancy, of James and Phila,	Sept. 22, 1807.
1-134	ANDROS	Edmund, of John and Alice,	June 7, 1693.
1-134	"	Samuel,	Oct. 15, 1695.
1-135	"	Abigail,	March 1, 1698.
1-135	"	James,	June 30, 1697.
1-136	"	Sarah, of Ephraim and Sarah,	July 10, 1714.
1-136	"	Mary,	April 1, 1716.

1-136	ANDROS Abigail, of Ephraim and Sarah.	July 13, 1717.
1-137	" Ephraim,	Jan. 10, 1718.
1-137	" Hannah,	Sept. 2, 1720.
4-235	ANTHONY Chandler, of Moses and Elizabeth B.,	March 14, 1844.
4-235	" Charles Waterman,	May 17, 1850.
1-134	ARCHER Edward, of John and Mehitable.	Oct. 1, 1693.
1-134	" John,	Oct. 15, 1695.
1-1	" Elizabeth,	Jan. 31, 1698.
1-1	" Abigail,	Sept. 5, 1702.
1-136	" Mary,	Oct. 18, 1707.
1-136	" Benjamin,	Nov. 25, 1708.
1-134	ATHERTON Samuel, of Watking and Elizabeth,	June 25, 1686.

B

4-225	BAARS John Frederick, and Lucretia (Norton), his wife, and children.	
4-225	" Annie Frederica,	Sept. 21, 1845.
4-225	" Wilhelmina Dobbertien,	April 5, 1847.
4-225	" John Frederic,	April 21, 1849.
4-225	" William Henry,	Feb. 20, 1851.
4-225	" George Schultz,	March 24, 1853.
1-140	BAKER Hannah, of Joseph and Hannah,	last of February, 1692.
1-142	" Ebenezer,	June 29, 1697.
1-148	BALL Sarah, of Benjamin and Hannah,	Aug. 12, 1735.
1-148	" Serviah,	March 19, 1737-8.
1-140	BARNEY Mary, of John and Mary,	Nov. 14, 1688.
1-140	" John.	May 13, 1689.
1-140	" Elizabeth.	Oct. 4, 1691.
1-140	" Anna,	Nov. 23, 1693.
1-141	" Jacob,	Jan. 16, 1695.
1-142	" John,	Sept. 27, 1698.
1-143	" William,	May 26, 1701.
1-52	BURROWS Sarah, of John and Sarah.	March 25, 1774.
1-152	" George,	June 18, 1776.
1-155	BUTT Richard Waldron, of James and Hannah,	Nov. 24, 1809.
1-155	" James Ellsbree,	Oct. 26, 1807.
1-156	" William,	Feb. 8, 1812.
4-244	" Mary Harvey, of James,	July 13, 1820.
4-244	" Abby Howland,	Jan. 10, 1824.
1-139	BAYLEY Joshua, of John and Rachel,	Sept. 10, 1685.
1-139	" John,	Feb. 17, 1687.
1-139	" Mary,	Feb. 3, 1699.
1-141	BEARS Mary, of Ephraim and Mary,	Dec. 27, 1692.
1-142	" John,	April 27, 1695.
1-143	" Elnathan,	Aug. 26, 1697.
1-141	BEDFORD Rebecca, of Stephen and Naomi,	Nov. 19, 1694.
1-142	" Stephen,	Aug. 24, 1696.
1-140	BIRGE Samuel, of John and Sarah,	Aug. 1, 1691.
1-140	BIRCH Jonathan, of Thomas and Batshua,	Jan. 25, 1691.
1-141	" Hannah,	Sept. 7, 1894.
1-142	" Hannah,	March 17, 1697.
1-143	BISHA John, of Phillip and Mary,	Feb. 20, 1708-9.
1-145	" Mary,	Oct. 22, 1710.
1-145	" James,	Sept. 26, 1712.
1-146	" Phillip,	Jan. 25, 1714-5.
1-146	" Sarah,	March 12, 1716-7.
1-146	" Elizabeth,	March 27, 1719.
1-146	" James,	July 11, 1721.
1-146	" Abigail,	July 12, 1723.
1-146	" Benjamin,	May 20, 1726.
1-148	" Patience,	April 13, 1729.
1-156	BLAKE Samuel, of Ebenezer, Jr., and Keziah,	Jan. 14, 1795.
1-157	" Allen,	June 14, 1802.
4-235	" Mary Elizabeth, of Samuel and Mary Ann,	Sept. 27, 1836.

4-235	BLAKE	Sarah Pearse, of Samuel and Mary Ann,	July 23, 1840.
4-228	"	Charles, of Joseph M, and Hope E. T.,	— —, —.
4-228	"	Hunt,	— —, —.
4-246	BLIVEN	Sarah, of Isaac R. and Nancy,	Dec. 24, 1812.
4-233	BLYE	William Thomas, of William M. and Emeline,	Sept. 16, 1830.
4-233	"	Andrew Mason,	Oct. 5, 1832.
4-233	"	Andrew Mason,	d. April 12, 1837.
4-233	"	Mary Emeline,	Dec. 15, 1835.
1-139	BOSWORTH	Bridget, of Bellamy and Mary,	Oct. 29, 1686.
1-139	"	Benjamin,	June 26, 1689.
1-139	"	Esther,	Jan. 7, 1692.
1-139	"	Nathaniel,	March 3, 1693.
1-143	"	Mary,	July 29, 1701.
1-143	"	Bellamy,	Jan. 16, 1703.
1-143	"	Hannah, of Edward and Merry,	March 16, 1696.
1-143	"	John, of John, Jr., and Elizabeth (H——),	May 9, 1708.
1-143	"	Elizabeth,	May 6, 1711.
1-144	"	Henry,	Oct. 12, 1713.
1-143	"	Sarah, of Edward and Elizabeth,	Dec. 4, 1710.
1-144	"	Sarah, of —— and Mary,	Oct. 17, 1712.
1-144	"	Mehitable, of Edward, Jr., and Mehitable,	May 24, 1715.
1-144	"	Edward,	Aug. 28, 1717.
1-144	"	Bridget, of Nathaniel and Lydia,	July 6, 1715.
1-144	"	Bellamy,	Nov. 26, 1716.
1-144	"	Nathaniel,	Nov. 26, 1716.
1-146	"	Ann,	March 1, 1720-1.
1-146	"	Ebenezer,	Feb. 9, 1723-4.
1-146	"	Lydia,	Feb. 9, 1723-4.
1-145	"	Sarah, of Nathaniel (of John) and Sarah,	Feb. 2, 1715-6.
1-145	"	Rebecca,	Nov. 20, 1717.
1-147	"	Mary,	Oct. 6, 1719.
1-147	"	Priscilla,	Oct. 6, 1722.
1-147	"	James,	Oct. 17, 1725.
1-145	"	Judeth, of Benjamin and Judeth,	Nov. 25, 1718.
1-145	"	Jonathan,	Aug. 16, 1720.
1-145	"	Hannah,	Aug. 16, 1720.
1-145	"	Abigail,	April 14, 1722.
1-146	"	Benjamin,	Oct. 8, 1724.
1-145	"	Ruth, of Benjamin and Ruth,	Sept. 7, 1721.
1-145	"	Samuel,	Jan. 6, 1722-3.
1-146	"	William,	Sept. 5, 1724.
1-147	"	Hannah, of Benjamin and Jemima,	March 26, 1728.
1-147	"	Hopestill,	Sept. 7, 1729.
1-147	"	Elizabeth, of Nathaniel and Elizabeth,	Oct. 10, 1728.
1-147	"	Lydia,	May 26, 1730.
1-148	"	Daniel,	Sept. 26, 1731.
1-148	"	Obadiah,	Sept. 26, 1731.
1-147	"	Benjamin,	Jan. 9, 1732-3.
1-148	"	Peleg,	Sept. 27, 1734.
1-149	"	John, of John, Jr., and Mary,	July 7, 1741.
1-149	"	Mary,	Feb. 28, 1742-3.
1-149	"	Aaron,	Jan. 15, 1744-5.
1-149	"	Mary, of William and Mary,	April 22, 1746.
1-149	"	Benjamin,	Jan. 24, 1747-8.
1-150	"	William,	June 26, 1751.
1-150	"	Allethia,	Oct. 2, 1754.
1-150	"	Ruth,	Feb. 14, 1756.
1-151	"	Timothy,	Feb. 22, 1758.
1-151	"	Deborah,	Sept. 11, 1760.
1-151	"	Elizabeth,	April 4, 1763.
1-149	"	Molly, of Henry and Phebe,	May 8, 1746.
1-150	"	Sarah, of John and Mary,	May 2, 1747.
1-150	"	Hannah,	March 10, 1749.
1-150	"	Caleb,	Feb. 2, 1751.
1-150	"	Samuel,	Dec. 15, 1755.

1-150	BOSWORTH	Elizabeth, of Henry and Phebe,	July 2, 1748.
1-150	"	Nathaniel,	Sept. 2, 1750.
1-150	"	William,	Dec. 5, 1752.
1-150	"	Benjamin,	April 22, 1755.
1-151	"	Martha,	March —, 1757.
1-152	"	Daniel,	July 14, 1760.
1-152	"	Phebe,	April 27, 1763.
1-152	"	Sarah,	Dec. 9, 1766.
1-152	"	George,	July 23, 1769.
1-151	"	Elizabeth, of Samuel and Elizabeth,	May 25, 1753.
1-151	"	Samuel,	Sept. 9, 1755.
1-152	"	Jonathan,	Sept. 3, 1757.
1-152	"	Ruth,	July 28, 1760.
1-152	"	Ebenezer, of Bellamy and Esther,	Oct. 5, 1754.
1-156	"	Jonathan, of Benjamin and Sarah,	Feb. 18, 1783.
1-154	"	Allen,	April 13, 1785.
1-154	"	William,	March 12, 1787.
1-154	"	George,	Sept. 14, 1789.
1-154	"	Gardiner,	Feb. 21, 1792.
1-154	"	Polly,	Sept. 18, 1794.
1-154	"	Timothy,	Oct. 20, 1797.
1-154	"	Elizabeth,	Nov. 6, 1799.
1-154	"	Ruth,	Dec. 3, 1801.
1-154	"	William,	Sept. 8, 1804.
1-155	"	Samuel, of Samuel and Tabitha,	Oct. 18, 1785.
1-155	"	Jonathan,	Aug. 22, 1788.
1-155	"	Nathaniel,	Aug. 14, 1791.
1-155	"	Elizabeth,	Dec. 29, 1795.
1-155	"	Samuel,	July 5, 1798.
1-155	"	William, of William, Jr., and Elizabeth,	May 10, 1790.
1-154	"	Samuel, of Samuel, Jr., and Ruth,	July 5, 1799.
1-154	"	Eliza,	March 8, 1797.
1-154	"	Timothy,	Oct. 29, 1801.
1-154	"	William,	Feb. 24, 1803.
1-154	"	Henry,	Dec. 11, 1808.
1-154	"	Mark Antony,	Dec. 2, 1811.
1-146	BOURNE	Hannah, of Dr. Aaron and Hannah,	Dec. 26, 1728.
1-147	"	Aaron,	Jan. 17, 1730-1.
1-147	"	Sarah,	Aug. 5, 1734.
1-148	"	Michael,	April 27, 1736.
1-149	"	Martha, of Shearjashub and Ruth,	Aug. 15, 1748.
1-149	"	Shearjashub,	Dec. 4, 1751.
1-149	"	Benjamin,	Dec. 9, 1755.
1-151	"	Michael, of Michael and Hannah,	June 13, 1755.
1-151	"	Aaron,	July 24, 1757.
1-152	"	Elizabeth, of Shearjashub and Ruth,	July 14, 1774.
1-152	"	Ruth,	Jan. 24, 1776.
1-152	"	Hannah,	Jan. 24, 1776.
1-152	"	Shearjashub,	Oct. 1, 1777.
1-152	"	John Waldron,	Oct. 1, 1777.
1-152	"	Allen,	June 25, 1779.
1-152	"	Hannah,	Aug. 10, 1781.
1-152	"	Martha,	Aug. 10, 1781.
1-152	"	Benjamin,	Aug. 10, 1781.
1-153	"	Charlotte, of Shearjashub and Rachel,	Aug. 21, 1794.
1-153	"	Mary Ann,	March 21, 1796.
1-155	"	Shearjashub,	April 23, 1798.
1-155	"	Ezra,	Aug. 20, 1800.
4-225	"	Elizabeth S.,	March 28, 1802.
1-156	"	Ann, of John W. and Nancy,	Feb. 6, 1800.
1-156	"	Benjamin Smith,	Nov. 2, 1801.
1-156	"	George Smith, of Allen and Betsey,	Feb. 26, 1806.
1-156	"	Ruth Waldron,	Nov. 19 or 20, 1807.
1-156	"	Rebecca Smith,	Dec. 23 or 28, 1809.
1-156	"	Betsey Allen,	March 1, 1812.

Note—Also recorded (4-245).

4-225	BOURNE Frances G., of Philip B. and Adeline D.,		Oct. 5, 1841.
4-225	" Almira,		Jan. 13, 1844.
1-142	BOWEN Mary, of Samuel and Elizabeth,		Feb. 9, 1698.
1-142	" Clesson,		Feb. 12, 1700-1.
1-149	" Elizabeth, of Amos and Elizabeth,		Oct. 11, 1750.
1-139	BOWERMAN Samuel, of Tristam and Anna,		Oct. 22, 1685.
1-139	" Hannah,		Nov. 22, 1688.
1-139	" Mary,		Jan. 2, 1689.
1-140	" Mehitable,		Oct. 11, 1692.
1-141	" John,		Sept. 13, 1694.
1-142	" Jonathan,		Oct. 6, 1696.
1-158	" Anna,		Nov. 20, 1698.
1-143	" Sarah,		April 22, 1701.
1-143	" Bellamy,		Jan. 16, 1703.
1-143	" Bellamy,		d. Jan. 20, 1703.
1-143	" Edward, of Samuel and Elizabeth,		Nov. 22, 1711.
1-144	" Elizabeth,		Feb. 25, 1713-4.
1-149	BRADFORD Elizabeth, of Daniel and Mary, (also 4-41),		June 5, 1750.
1-151	" Priscilla,		March 1, 1752.
1-150	" William, of Dr. William and Mary, (b. Warren),		Sept. 15, 1752.
1-150	" Lebarron,	(b. Bristol),	March 31, 1754.
1-151	" John,		Oct. 9, 1758.
1-151	" Mary,		Sept. 3, 1760.
1-151	" Hannah,		June 14, 1767.
1-152	" John,		—. —, 1768.
1-153	" Daniel, of Daniel and Susannah, (b. Attleboro),		June 27, 1778.
1-153	" Leonard J.,	(b. Bristol),	May 22, 1780.
1-153	" Samuel,	(b. Bristol),	May 6, 1783.
1-153	" Mary, of William, Jr., and Elizabeth (b. Taunton),		Dec. 30, 1778.
1-153	" William (Rehoboth),		Feb. 2, 1781.
1-153	" Elizabeth Bloom (Rehoboth),		Feb. 18, 1785.
1-153	" Henry (Rehoboth),		Feb. 18, 1787.
1-153	" Peter James (Rehoboth),		Feb. 6, 1790.
1-154	" John Willis (Rehoboth),		Dec. 26, 1793.
1-154	" Sarah (Bristol),		Jan. 29, 1799.
1-154	" Mary Le Barron, of John, and Jemima,		June 18, 1801.
1-154	" Eleanor,		Dec. 18, 1804.
1-154	" Lydia,		Feb. 9, 1806.
1-156	" Walter,		Aug. 13, 1809.
1-156	" Nancy,		Aug. 16, 1795.
1-155	" Benjamin Wardwell,		June 24, 1797.
1-155	" Le Barron,		April 18, 1799.
1-157	" Charles Jarvis, of Daniel, Jr., and Sarah (Reynolds, of Joseph), Aug. 17, 1800.		
1-157	" Joseph Reynolds,		Nov. 15, 1802.
1-157	" Sally Russell,		March 10, 1805.
1-157	" Mary Sparhawk,		Nov. 23, 1806.
1-157	" Jane Angusta,		Aug. 22, 1809.
1-157	" Daniel, Jr.,		March 9, 1811.
1-157	" Leonard Jarvis,		Feb. 4, 1813.
1-157	" Susannah Jarvis,		June 4, 1815.
1-158	" Susannah Jarvis, of Leonard Jarvis, and Sally (Turner of Capt. Moses, of Warren, R. I.), March 18, 1802.		
1-158	" Sally Leonard,		Nov. 18, 1803.
1-158	" Harriet Turner,		Feb. 11, 1806.
1-158	" Leonard Jarvis,		March 29, 1808.
1-158	" Durfee Turner,		March 14, 1810.
1-156	" William Parnell, of William, 3d, and Mary,		May 29, 1805.
1-156	" Edward James,		Sept. 29, 1806.
1-156	" Allen Taylor Smith,		Sept. 2, 1808.
1-156	" Nancy Smith,		April 7, 1811.
1-158	" Samuel, Jr., of Samuel, and Elizabeth (Reynolds of Joseph), May 10, 1807.		
1-158	" William Greenwood,		March 4, 1809.

1-158	BRADFORD Elizabeth, of Samuel and Elizabeth,		Feb. 2, 1811.
1-158	" Ann Peck,		Dec. 1, 1814.
1-140	BRAGG John, of Henry and Elizabeth,		Aug. 15, 1693.
1-141	" Sarah,		Nov. 3, —.
1-142	" Nicholas,		May 23, 1696.
1-142	" Hannah,		Sept. 27, 1698.
1-142	" Abigail,		Jan. 23, 1700-1.
1-142	" Mary, of John and Elizabeth,		July 17, 1697.
1-142	" Experience,		April 2, 1700.
1-143	" Benjamin,		Nov. 22, 1702.
1-144	' Abigail, of Henry and Susannah (also 1-143),		May 1, 1709.
1-145	" Susannah,		July 28, 1712.
1-145	" John,		Feb. 14, 1714-5.
1-145	" Anne,		May 25, 1717.
1-146	" Henry,		June 8, 1719.
1-147	" Elizabeth, of Henry and Elizabeth.		July 10, 1728.
1-148	" William, of Nicholas and Bithiah,		Feb. 25, 1729-30.
1-148	" John, of John and Mary,		Jan. 28, 1737-8.
1-149	" Susannah,		Feb. 18, 1740-1.
1-149	" Ann,		Dec. 6, 1742.
1-149	" Henry,		Sept. 1, 1745.
1-139	BRENTON Benjamin, of William and Hannah,		Dec. 23, 1686.
1-140	" Jahleel,		Aug. 15, 1691.
1-140	" Ebenezer, of Ebenezer and Priscilla (Swansey),		Dec. 7, 1687.
1-141	" Martha (Swanzey),		Jan. 4, 1689.
1-141	" William,	(Bristol), Nov. 28, 1694.	
1-142	" Sarah (Bristol),		May 6, 1697.
1-146	BREWER William, of Philip and Jerusha,		May 26, 1727.
4-247	BRIGGS Abby Paul, of Lemuel W. and Mary,		Aug. 10, 1808.
4-247	" Lemuel Williams,	(also 1-155), May 21, 1811.	
4-247	" Walter Dean,	(also 1-155), July 5, 1818.	
1-144	BRISTOW Elizabeth, of Thomas and Elizabeth,		Dec. 14, 1706.
1-144	" Mary,		Oct. 23, 1711.
1-144	" Thomas,		March 10, 1714-5.
4-242	BROWNING Elizabeth, of Beriah G. and Lydia,		Feb. 28, 1822.
4-242	" Ann Emily, of Beriah G. and Marian,		April 1, 1826.
1-158	BROWN Sarah, of William and Sarah,		Aug. 14, 1697.
1-154	" James, of James and Mary,		May 17, 1789.
1-155	" Jonathan W.,		March 7, 1791.
1-154	" Polly,		Nov. 5, 794.
4-240	" Henry, and Nancy (Bourne) his wife, children,	—, —.	
4-240	" Henry Horace,		Aug. 13, 1828.
4-240	" Catherine Metcalf,		May 12, 1831.
4-240	" Sarah Anne,		Sept. 11, 1833.
4-240	" William Osborn,		Aug. 24, 1835.
4-235	" Ann Elizabeth, of George, and Ruth M.,		Sept. 17, 1836.
4-246	BULLOCK, Stephen Smith, of Nathaniel and Ruth (also 1-156),		
			July 25, 1813.
4-246	" Jonathan Russell (also 1-57),		Sept. 6, 1815.
4-246	" Benjamin Smith (also 1-157),		March 25, 1818.
4-246	" Benjamin Smith,	died Nov. 10, 1819.	
4-246	" Harriet Smith,		Jan. 25, 1820.
4-246	" Ann Russell,		March 10, 1822.
4-246	" Henry Smith,		Feb. 18, 1825.
4-246	" Nathaniel Bullock,		April 17, 1827.
4-225	" Sylvia Russell, of Jonath		July 16, 1841.
	Alton, Ill.), an Russell and Susan Amelia (DeWolf) (b.		
4-225	" Anna Amelia,		June 30, 1843.
4-225	" Charles Russell, Feb. 9, 1848,	died Sept. 1, 1849.	
4-225	" Elizabeth Mickelson,		July 28, 1858.
4-225	" Susan Amelia, wife of J. R.,	died Oct. 7, 1866.	
4-225	' Emma Russell, of Jonathan R., and Emma (Westcott), his 2d		
	wife, Sept. 25, 1869.		
1-141	BUMPUS Samuel, of Phillip and Sarah,		Feb. 20, 1687.
1-141	" Phillip,		Feb. 13, 1689.

1-141	BUMPUS Lydia, of Philip and Sarah,	April 2, 1692.
1-141	" Matthew,	June 8, 1695.
1-158	" Josiah,	April 9, 1698.
1-156	BUNN Nathan Munro, of Lemuel and Abigail,	July 3, 1808.
1-156	" Lydia,	Sept. 16, 1809.
1-156	" Lemuel,	June 19, 1811.
4-231	" Abby S., of Nathan M., and Lucy Ann,	June 2, 1839.
4-231	" Elizabeth,	May 22, 1841.
4-231	" Mary A.,	Nov. 16, 1844.
4-231	" Cornelia C.,	July 28, 1847.
4-231	" Martha' S.,	Jan. 20, 1852.
1-156	BURGESS Sally, of James P. and Hannah,	March 9, 1811.
1-139	BURRELL Elizabeth, of James and Dinah,	Sept. 26, 1685.
1-157	" Samuel,	died Feb. 13, 1686-7.
1-139	" James,	Feb. 14, 1687.
1-141	" James,	Oct. 2, 1689.
1-139	BURROUGHS Thomas, of James and Sarah,	July 12, 1685.
1-141	" Ezekiel, of James and Ann,	May 5, 1694.
4-225	BURRY Ellen, of John and Sarah,	Sept. 9, 1846.
1-153	BURR Shubael, of Samuel and Nancy,	May 13, 1791.
1-153	" Nancy,	Feb. 6, 1794.
1-153	" Samuel Champlain,	Aug. 17, 1795.
1-153	" Peter Turner,	Aug. 29, 1798.
1-139	BURTON Penelope, of Stephen and Elizabeth,	Aug. 8, 1686.
1-158	" Thomas,	March 19, 1692-3.
1-148	BUSHEE Rebecca, of John and Rebecca,	Oct. 14, 1733.
1-148	" Zubath,	Feb. 20, 1736-7.
1-148	" Martha,	May 18, 1739.
1-148	" Susannah,	July 9, 1741.
1-147	BUSH Abigail, of Richard and Mary,	Feb. 6, 1731-2.
1-143	B—— Sarah, of Obadiah and Mary,	April 19, 1708.

C

1-162	CAHOON John, of Joseph and Hannah,	July 24, 1692.
1-162	" Joseph,	Aug. 3, 1690.
1-163	" Hannah,	March 22, 1696.
1-166	CALDWELL Margeret, of Robert and Amey,	July 17, 1699.
1-166	" Mary,	Nov. 4, 1700.
1-166	" Robert,	June 26, 1702.
1-166	" Amey,	June 23, 1703.
1-166	" Richard,	March 23, 1705.
1-166	" Elizabeth,	Sept. 4, 1706.
1-166	" John,	July 12, 1708.
1-166	" William,	Dec. 23, 1709.
1-166	" Sarah,	June 11, 1711.
1-166	" Ruth,	June 30, 1713.
1-167	CARPENTER Sarah, of Joseph and Abigail,	Feb. 3, 1724-25.
1-167	" Joseph,	Oct. —, 1726.
4-240	CARD Martha E., of Henry and Sally,	Aug. 4, 1813.
4-240	" Henry B.,	Sept. 13, 1815.
4-240	" Mary A.,	June 18, 1817.
4-240	" Sarah T.,	June 18, 1819.
4-240	" Elizabeth B.,	Jan. 17, 1821.
4-240	" Julia Sophia,	Nov. 5, 1822.
4-240	" George M.,	April 26, 1824.
4-240	" Caroline M.,	Aug. 31, 1828.
1-163	CARTER Samuel, of Robert and Hannah,	May 12, 1695.
1-163	" John,	March 3, 1697.
1-163	" Sarah,	(b. Phila., Pa.) Aug. 4, 1699.
1-163	" Hannah,	April 18, 1701.
1-165	" William,	June 23, 1707.
1-161	CARY John, of John and Abigail,	(b. Bridgewater) Nov. 6, 1671.
1-161	" John,	buried Dec. 29, 1671.

1-161	CARY	Seth, of John and Abigail,	(b. Bridgewater) Jan. 28, 1672-3.
1-161	"	John,	(b. Bridgewater) Dec. 9, 1674.
1-161	"	Nathaniel,	(b. Bridgewater) Nov. 24, 1676.
1-161	"	Eleazer.	(b. Bridgewater) Sept. 27, 1678.
1-161	"	James,	(b. Bridgewater) June 10, 1680.
1-161	"	Benjamin,	(b. Bridgewater) Oct. 29, 1681.
1-161	"	Elizabeth,	(Bristol) May 23, 1683.
1-162	"	Abigail.	(Bristol) Aug. 31, 1684.
1-162	"	Josiah,	(Bristol) May 6, 1686.
1-162	"	Timothy,	(Bristol) Feb. 15, 1687-8.
1-162	"	Elizabeth. of David and Elizabeth,	March 7, 1691-2.
1-162	"	Mehitable,	Aug. 14, 1693.
1-162	"	Beersheba,	Aug. 14, 1693.
1-163	"	daughter,	June 11, 1695.
1-163	"	Bethia,	Dec. 9, 1696.
1-163	"	David.	June 22, 1698.
1-163	"	daughter,	Nov. 24, died 29, 1700.
1-164	"	Peter,	Nov. 9, 1701.
1-164	"	Mary.	Nov. 6, 1703.
1-164	"	Sarah.	Jan. 21, 1706-7.
1-165	"	Priscilla,	May 9, 1709.
1-165	"	Henry,	June 24, 1711.
1-165	"	Phebe, of John and Damarias, (also 1-164)	March 5, 1701-2.
1-165	"	John,	(Newport) Nov. 21, 1704.
1-165	"	Abigail,	(Newport) Nov. 4, 1707.
1-164	"	Abigail, of Eleazer and Lydia,	Jan. 30, 1703-4.
1-164	"	Lydia,	Feb. 12, 1705-6.
1-165	"	Ann,	Sept. 21, 1708.
1-165	"	Elizabeth.	March 25, 1711.
1-166	"	Eleazer,	Sept. 19, 1713.
1-167	"	Mary,	March 23, 1715-6.
1-167	"	Martha,	March 1, 1717-8.
1-165	"	Alice. of Benjamin and Susannah.	(b. Swansey) July 9, 1708.
1-166	"	Nathaniel,	Nov. 5, 1711.
1-167	"	Bethiah,	Feb. 8, 1716-7.
1-167	"	Abigail,	Feb. 11, 1719-0.
1-167	"	Elizabeth.	Feb. 4, 1720-1.
1-167	"	Mehitable.	Sept. 23, 1722.
1-167	"	John,	Sept. 23, 1728.
1-168	"	Joseph,	Nov. 22, 1733.
1-168	"	Seth.	Nov. 22, 1733.
1-165	"	Seth, of James and Bridget,	(Newport) Sept. 5, 1708.
1-165	"	Deborah,	(Newport) May 17, 1707.
1-165	"	Jemima, of Josiah and Ruth,	July 25, 1711.
1-167	"	Nathaniel,	Feb. 6, 1713-4.
1-168	"	David, of David and Mary,	Nov. 23, 1729.
1-168	"	Edward,	May 1, 1732.
1-168	"	Thomas,	March 23, 1733-4.
1-169	"	Mary,	Aug. 9, 1735.
1-169	"	Nathaniel,	Feb. 5, 1737-8.
1-169	"	Michael,	Jan. 29, 1739-40.
1-168	"	Molly, of Allen and Hannah,	Dec. 3, 1732.
1-168	"	Benjamin,	Jan. 10, 1734-5.
1-169	"	Abigail,	Dec. 23, 1736.
1-169	"	Susannah,	Aug. 7, 1740.
1-169	"	Hannah,	Sept. 26, 1742.
1-169	"	Josiah, of Nathaniel and Tabitha,	(b. Newport) Feb. 24, 1738-9.
1-169	"	Abigail, of Nathaniel and Elizabeth,	Nov. 12, 1742.
1-176	CASEY	Mary, of Richard and Betsey,	Nov. 10, 1813.
1-175	CATALOGNE,	children of Joseph Dominick Catalogne, of France, an inhabitant of Havana, Cuba, and Emilia Michaella Digneron.	
1-175	"	John Baptist Adolphus.	June 12, 1810.
1-175	"	John Baptist Gustavus,	Feb. 8, 1812.
1-175	"	Emelia Aimie Felicite,	Aug. 16, 1814.

4-249	CHAFFEE Lucinda Thomas, of Stephen and Deborah (Usher),	Oct. 4, 1813.
4-249	" George Tew Barker,	May 27, 1816.
4-249	" Eunice Foster,	April 26, 1818.
4-249	" Stephen James,	June 6, 1820.
1-172	CHAMPLAIN Thomas, of Thomas and Phebe,	Sept. 1, 1759.
1-172	" Phebe Hail,	July 3, 1762.
1-172	" Martha,	Dec. 23, 1763.
1-174	" Nancy,	Aug. 4, 1765.
1-174	" Bridget,	June 7, 1767.
1-174	" John,	March 1, 1769.
1-174	" Joshua,	Dec. 9, 1771.
1-174	" James,	June 21, 1773.
1-174	" William,	May 5, 1776.
1-175	" Charlotte, of William and Rebecca,	Jan. 11, 1805.
1-171	CHASE Persis, of John and Ruth,	Sept. 22, 1758.
1-172	" John,	July 1, 1760.
1-177	CHEAUVETEAUX Serafine Sophia, of J. J. and Serafine,	June 6, 1810.
1-177	" Francis Evarist,	Oct. 24, 1811.
1-161	CHURCH Charles, of Benjamin and Alice,	May 9, 1682.
1-161	" Elizabeth,	March 26, 1684.
1-162	" Nathaniel,	July 1, 1686.
1-162	" Nathaniel	died Feb. 20, 1687.
1-163	" Sarah, of Thomas and Sarah,	Jan. 15, 1700-1.
1-163	" Sarah, of Thomas and Sarah,	died Aug. 29, 1701.
1-164	" Elizabeth,	Sept. 9, d. 27, 1702.
1-164	" Thomas,	Aug. 20, 1704.
1-164	" Alice,	July 11, 1696.
1-164	" Abigail, of Edward and Martha,	March 4, 1702-3.
1-164	" Benjamin,	Oct. 8, 1704.
1-165	" Constant, of Charles and Hannah,	Dec. 12, 1708.
1-166	" Elizabeth,	Dec. 24, 1710,
1-166	" Hannah,	Feb. 20, 1712-3.
1-167	" Martha, of Benjamin and Elizabeth,	Oct. 25, 1728.
1-168	" Nathaniel, of Israel and Abigail,	March 10, 1730-1.
1-177	" Abigail,	Jan. 13, 1732-3.
1-177	" Sarah,	Feb. 19, 1734-5.
1-169	" Constant, of Constant and Mary,	Nov. 5, 1733.
1-169	" Charles,	Nov. 5, 1733.
1-169	" Peter,	Dec. 1, 1737.
1-169	" Mary,	April 2, 1740.
1-169	" Hannah, of Nathaniel and Ruth,	July 31, 1743.
1-170	' Nathaniel,	Feb. 3, 1744-5.
1-170	" Nathaniel, of Thomas and Elizabeth,	June 11, 1750.
1-170	" Deborah,	March 6, 1753.
1-171	" Elizabeth,	Nov. 29, 1756.
1-171	" Hannah, of Samuel and Anna,	Dec. 14, 1755.
1-172	" Samuel,	June 4, 1757.
1-172	" Benjamin,	March 28, 1759.
1-172	" Thomas,	Feb. 15, 1761.
1-173	" Hezekiah,	Oct. 14, 1764.
1-173	" Elizabeth,	Aug. 16, 1766.
1-173	" Dorothy,	May 4, 1770.
1-174	" Edward,	July 6, 1776.
1-171	" Charles, of Charles and Eunice,	March 16, 1757.
1-171	" Constant,	Dec. 30, 1758.
1-172	" Mary,	Feb. 24, 1761.
1-172	" Hannah,	Feb. 17, 1763.
1-172	" Sarah,	March 2, 1765.
1-173	" Abigail,	April 27, 1767.
1-173	" Nathaniel, of Peter and Sarah,	Aug. 30, 1766.
1-173	" Charlotte,	Dec. 12, 1768.
1-174	" George,	April 1, 1771.
1-174	" Thomas, of Nathaniel and Sarah,	June 2, 1776.
1-174	" Nathaniel,	Sept. 10, 1779.
1-174	" William, of Col. Peter and Sarah,	April 4, 1776.

1-174	CHURCH Peter, of Col. Peter and Hannah,		Feb. 26, 1791.
1-174	"	Hannah,	Sept. 13, 1792.
4-232	"	Benjamin, of Thomas and Mary,	Aug. 7, 1795.
4-232	"	Polly,	Oct. 31, 1796.
4-232	"	Benjamin, (also 1-176)	Nov. 13, 1798.
4-232	"	Thomas, (also 1-176) Nov. 9, or 11, 1801.	
4-232	"	Samuel Wardwell,	Feb. 13, 1803.
4-232	"	Sarah Ann,	May 6, 1805.
4-232	"	Stephen Tripp,	Jan. 14, 1808.
4-232	"	William Howe,	Jan. 23, 1810.
4-232	"	Mary Tripp,	April 23, 1813.
4-232	"	Hezekiah Ward,	Aug. 27, 1815.
4-232	"	Betsey Wardwell,	April 26, 1818.
4-236	"	Le Baron B., of Thomas, Jr., and Mary Eleanor,	June 28, 1824.
4-236	"	Benjamin T.,	Jan. 8, 1827.
4-236	"	William B.,	April 24, 1829.
4-236	"	Eleanor B.,	June 6, 1831.
4-236	"	Elizabeth G.,	Feb. 27, 1835.
4-236	"	Mary T.,	June 20, 1839.
1-162	CLARKE Samuel, of Timothy and Sarah,		April 19, 1688.
1-171	"	Gamaliel, of Gamaliel and Elizabeth,	July 9, 1744.
1-171	"	Oliver Allen,	Dec. 16, 1747.
1-171	"	Nanthaniel, Cary,	April 1, 1752.
1-171	"	Mehitable,	March 15, 1754.

Note.—Above children born Milford, Conn., except last born Bristol.

1-170	"	Hannah, of Samuel and Hannah,	Jan. 10, 1750-1.
1-170	"	Sarah,	April 11, 1753.
1-176	"	Joseph, of John and Nancy,	March 29, 1800.
1-162	CORBETT Sarah, of Samuel and Sarah,		Jan. 3, 1689.
1-162	"	Samuel,	Aug. 16, 1693.
1-162	"	Thomas,	Oct. 18, 1695.
1-163	"	John,	Oct. 9, 1696.
1-177	COCKRAM Deborah, of John and Lydia,		May 26, 1742.
1-170	"	John,	Feb. 1, 1743-4.
1-170	"	Lydia,	Jan. 16, 1745-6.
1-177	"	Simeon Potter,	May 20, 1747.
1-170	COGGESHALL John, of George and Hannah,		June 22, 1750.
1-170	"	George,	Feb. 8, 1752.
1-172	"	Hannah,	Feb. 8, 1754.
1-170	"	Elizabeth, of Newby and Mary,	April 19, 1752.
1-173	"	William,	Jan. 28, 1754.
1-173	"	Mary,	Nov. 9, 1755.
1-173	"	Haile,	Oct. 28, 1757.
1-173	"	James,	Nov. 1, 1759.
1-173	"	Nancy,	Jan. 8, 1762.
1-173	"	Henry,	March 5, 1764.
1-173	"	John,	Feb. 14, 1767.
1-170	"	Abigail, of Job and Sarah,	Aug. 15, 1754.
1-175	"	Patience, of George and Sally,	Sept. 4, 1773.
1-175	"	William,	Nov. 4, 1778.
1-174	"	Margaret, of William and Margaret,	July 8, 1773.
1-175	"	Thomas, of George and Lucy,	Sept. 26, 1789.
1-175	"	George,	Feb. 27, 1790.
1-176	"	William, of William and Hannah,	June 4, 1797.
1-176	"	Ruth Easton, of John M. and Betsey,	Feb. 5, 1798.
4-239	"	Johannah Munro, of Samuel and Elizabeth,	April 14, 1822.
4-239	"	Isabella Lafayette,	July 20, 1824.
4-239	"	Isabella Lafayette,	d. Aug. 3, 1825.
4-239	"	Allen Munro,	March 15, 1827.
4-239	"	Elizabeth Bradford,	Sept. 14, 1832.
4-239	"	Samuel Bradford,	June 15, 1835.
4-228	"	Lucy Melvora, of George and Abby L.,	Sept. 24, 1843.
1-176	COIT Mary Mumford, of Joseph and Eunice,		Aug. —. 1809.
1-176	"	Charlotte Allen,	July —, 1811.

1-176	COIT Eunice Gladding, of Joseph and Eunice,		March 31, 1813.
1-176	"	Hannah Martin,	Jan. 31, 1815.
1-176	"	William Henry Bowen, of Thomas B. and Rachel,	March 25, 1815.
4-246	"	Lucy Ann, of George M. and Mary, (also 1-177)	Feb. 12, 1817.
4-246	"	Joseph Martin,	Feb. 9, 1818.
4-246	"	Elizabeth G.,	May 21, 1819.
4-246	"	John,	Oct. 21, 1820.
4-246	"	John,	d. Oct. 6, 1821.
4-246	"	Benjamin W.,	Dec. 30, 1823.
4-246	"	Infant,	b. and d. ——, 1824.
1-175	COLE Luther, of Luther and Betsey,		April 12, 1807.
1-177	"	Samuel Nichols,	May 19, 1800.
1-175	"	Eliza Ann, of George and Eliza,	May 13, 1809.
4-249	"	Martha Davis, of Thomas and Nancy,	Feb. 7, 1820.
4-247	"	John Throop,	Feb. 25, 1822.
4-243	"	Thomas, of Thomas and Anna,	Oct. 16, 1824.
4-231	"	Mary Emily, of Luther and Elizabeth,	June 31, 1832.
4-231	"	Mary Emily,	died July 29, 1844.
4-231	"	Samuel Bradford,	Oct. 11, 1833.
4-231	"	William Bradford,	Sept. 14, 1836.
4-231	"	Luther,	March 13, 1839.
4-231	"	Henry Jarvis,	June 21, 1841.
4-231	"	George Gilbert,	April 5, 1843.
4-231	"	Charles Russell,	July 8, 1845.
1-175	COLLINS Charles, of Charles, Jr., and Lydia,		Aug. 35, 1803.
1-175	"	Charlotte,	Aug. 30, 1803.
1-172	COOMER John, of John and Elizabeth,		May 8, 1755.
1-172	"	Thos. Pinnecut,	July 11, 1757.
1-174	"	Thomas K., of Thomas K. and Mary,	Aug. 19, 1781.
1-176	"	Sally K.,	Dec. 17, 1782.
1-176	"	Nicholas, of John, Jr., and Halley,	Feb. 11, 1793.
1-176	"	John, 3d.	May 8, 1787.
4-241	"	Nicholas, of Henry and Prudence,	Oct. 15, 1821.
4-241	"	George Henry,	Dec. 13, 1825.
4-241	"	Prudence L.,	Feb. 13, 1829.
4-241	CORNETT William, of William and Mary,		Sept. 13, 1812.
4-241	"	Henry,	Aug. 30, 1816.
1-161	CORPS Hope, son of John and Deliverance (First English child born in this town),		Nov. 8, 1681.
1-161	"	Anna, of John and Deliverance,	Feb. 23, 1683-4.
1-161	"	Mary,	Nov. 2, 1685.
1-162	"	Elizabeth,	March 14, 1687-8.
1-162	"	Sarah,	Nov. 30, 1690.
1-162	CORTIS Nathaniel, of Solomon and Prudence.		April 24, 1687.
1-163	"	Mary,	Aug. 1, 1695.
1-163	"	Mary,	died Aug. 22, 1695.
1-167	COTTON Roland, of Rev. Nath'l and Grizzell,		Jan. 21, 1722-3.
1-168	"	Elizabeth,	Feb. 28, 1723-4.
1-168	"	Nathaniel,	Feb. 15, 1724-5.
1-168	"	Elizabeth,	Feb. 25, 1725-6.
1-168	"	Ann,	Feb. 20, 1726-7.
1-168	"	John,	March 25, 1728.
4-58	COX Susannah,		May 20, 1755.
1-171	COY John, of John and Sarah (also 1-170),		Sept. 25, 1746.
1-171	"	Samuel, (also 1-170)	Oct. 25, 1748.
1-171	"	William,	Oct. 16, 1750.
1-171	"	Sarah,	Aug. 28, 1752.
1-171	"	Jonathan Woodbury,	March 7, 1757.
1-175	CRANSTON Abigail, of Stephen and Sarah,		July 29, 1791.
1-175	CUMMINGS Oliver Simmons, of Lovet and Lydia,		July 22, 1795.
1-177	CURTIS Samuel, of Solomon and Prudence,		Dec. 4, 1683.
1-164	"	Solomon, of Solomon, Jr., and Abigail,	March 23, 1703-4.
1-164	"	Abigail,	July 26, 1705.
1-165	"	Eleazer,	Nov. 13, 1709.

D

1-179	DADEE William, of William and Sarah,	Nov. 15, 1695.
1-180	" Sarah,	Dec. 6, 1700.
1-179	DAGGETT Samuel, of Thomas and Elizabeth,	June 10, 1685.
1-179	" Hannah,	May 27, 1687.
4-240	" Richmond, of Henry and Martha,	April 13, 1835.
4-240	" Hope,	Sept. 21, 1839.
4-240	" Frances,	Sept. 21, 1839.
1-188	DALTON Walter W., of Walter and Eliza,	March 21, 1806.
1-186	DARLING William Munro, of John and Lydia,	May 12, 1794.
1-188	" John,	Feb. 17, 1782.
1-188	" James Brown,	May 20, 1787.
1-187	" Elizabeth Pearce, of John and Sarah,	Feb. 19, 1809.
1-187	" Sarah,	Sept. 27, 1810.
1-187	" Patience Fortnough,	Dec. 10, 1813.
1-179	DAVENPORT Thomas, of Jonathan and Hannah (born Dorchester, Mass.),	Dec. 10, 1681.
1-179	" Jonathan,	Nov. 3, 1684.
1-179	DAVIS Nicholas, of Simon and Ann,	Oct. 9, 1686.
1-179	" Sarah,	June 15, 1689.
1-179	" Ann,	Sept. 23, 1694.
1-179	" Hannah,	Jan. 12, 1696.
1-179	" Samuel,	June 30, 1698.
1-180	" Elizabeth,	Aug. 8, 1699.
1-180	" Simon,	Oct. 11, 1701.
1-180	" Frances,	Sept. 23, 1703.
1-181	" Hannah, of Galus and Mehitable,	June 9, 1719.
1-185	" Ichabod, of Hezekiah and Rebecca,	March 30, 1789.
1-179	DAWERTZ William, of Briant and Rachel,	Nov. 24, 1694.
1-180	" Rachel,	Feb. 12, 1700-1.
1-186	DEARTH Henry Bradford, of Golden and Eliza,	Jan. 2, 1809.
1-188	DEVOL William Henry, of George and Mary,	June 15, 1808.
1-188	" George W.,	Sept. 16, 1809.
1-188	" Eliza,	Oct. 2, 1815.
1-188	" Obadiah Bosworth,	March 28, 1813.
1-188	" Thomas Russell,	Nov. 25, 1814.
1-183	DEWOLF Charles, of Mark Antony and Abigail,	Feb. 25, 1744-5.
1-184	" Mary, of Charles and Mary,	May 3, 1772.
1-184	" Martha,	May 13, 1774.
1-184	" Abigail,	March 6, 1776.
1-185	" George,	Dec. 8, 1778.
1-189	" Charles,	July 3, 1780.
1-187	" William, of William and Elizabeth, (also 1-186),	Dec. 8, 1788.
1-187	" Henry,	March 21, 1785.
1-187	" Charlotte,	June 17, 1793.
1-187	" Maria,	Oct. 26, 1795.
1-187	" Abigail,	April 18, 1798.
1-186	" James, of James and Ann,	Oct. 10, 1790.
1-186	" Mary Ann,	April 14, 1795.
1-186	" Frances L. B.,	Dec. 2, 1797.
1-186	" Mark Antony,	Sept. 28, 1799.
1-186	" William Henry,	May 15, 1802.
1-186	" Harriet,	May 28, 1804.
1-186	" Catherine H.,	July 16, 1806.
1-186	" Nancy Bradford,	July 3, 1808.
1-186	" William Bradford,	Oct. 30, 1810.
4-222	" Mary Taylor, of Charles, Jr., and Mary,	Jan. 10, 1805.
4-222	" Charles Henry,	March 8, 1806.
4-222	" Allen Munro,	Dec. 11, 1808.
4-222	" Abby B.,	April 4, 1810.
4-222	" Martha G.,	Dec. 12, 1811.
	Note—Also recorded 4-232.	
1-189	" John, of John and Betsey,	Sept. 11, 1807.
1-187	" Wm. Frederic, of Henry and Anna Eliza,	April 21, 1811.

1-188	DEWOLF	Josephine Maria, of James and Nancy,	Sept. 4, 1812.
4-225	"	James F., of Francis L. B., and Ellen,	April 15, 1823.
4-233	'	Winthrop, of John J. and Annette H.,	March 14, 1830.
4-233	"	Elizabeth,	Dec. 15, 1833.
4-233	"	Halsey,	Nov. 21, 1836.
4-233	"	James Andrews,	Oct. 11, 1839.
1-183	DIMAN	Nathaniel, of Jeremiah and Sarah,	Jan. 29, 1734.
1-183	"	James,	Oct. 19, 1735.
1-183	"	Sarah,	Feb. 11, 1738.
1-183	"	Jeremiah,	July 13, 1740.
1-183	"	Jonathan,	Oct. 19, 1742.
1-183	"	Hannah,	Oct. 19, 1742.
1-183	"	William,	Dec. 10, 1744.
1-185	"	William, of Nathaniel and Anna (also 4-81),	Nov. 1, 1759.
1-187	"	Jeremiah,	Jan. 4, 1767.
1-185	"	Royal, of Joseph and Margaret,	May 26, 1768.
1-185	"	Jeremiah,	March 26, 1770.
1-185	"	Margaret,	Dec. 27, 1773.
1-185	"	Joseph,	Aug. 16, 1785.
1-185	"	Sarah, of Jonathan and Dorothy,	May 2, 1772.
1-185	"	Betsey Fales,	Feb. 20, 1774.
1-185	"	Jonathan,	Sept. 16, 1775.
1-186	•	Willard, of Timothy and Ruth,	Nov. 23, 1781.
1-186	"	John, of Timothy and Elizabeth,	June 24, 1791.
1-188	"	John, of William and Nancy,	Jan. 2, 1794.
1-187	"	James, of Jeremiah, 2d, and Abigail,	March 15, 1795.
1-187	"	Byron, of Jeremiah and Hannah,	Aug. 5, 1795.
1-188	"	George Howe,	Aug. —, 1797.
1-186	"	Francis Moore, of Royal and Elizabeth,	June 8, 1796.
1-188	"	Royal,	April 4, 1798.
4-237	"	Jonathan, of Billings and Hannah (Butts),	Dec. 8, 1810.
4-237	"	Elizabeth Jackson,	Oct. 17, 1814.
1-188	"	George Byron, of Byron and Abby Alden (Wight),	May 16, 1824.
1-188	"	Clara Anna,	April 1, 1828.
1-188	"	Jeremiah Lewis,	May 1, 1831.
1-188	"	Henry Wight,	April 2, 1835.
1-188	."	Abby Byron,	May 7, 1838.
1-181	DONELLY	Catherine, of Tarence and Mary,	Oct. 6, 1722.
4-232	DOTY	Charlotte, of Simeon and Hannah,	Aug. 17, 1826.
4-232	"	Henry,	Oct. 11, 1829.
4-232	"	Mary,	Aug. 12, 1833.
4-232	"	John,	July 22, 1836.
1-180	DOWNS	Edward, of William and Elizabeth,	June 22, 1701.
1-180	"	William,	Sept. 17, 1703.
1-180	"	Samuel,	Oct. 2, 1705.
1-180	DROWNE	Solomon, of Solomon and Hester,	Oct. 4, 1700.
1-181	"	Solomon,	Oct. 4, 1706.
1-181	"	Esther,	Oct. 26, 1708.
1-181	"	Elizabeth,	(Boston) Sept. 8, 1710.
1-181	"	Joseph,	(Boston) Feb. 8, 1712-3.
1-181	"	Bathsheba,	June 10, 1715.
1-182	"	Benjamin,	June 9, 1717.
1-182	"	Mary,	June 7, 1719.
1-182	"	Samuel,	July 31, 1721.
1-182	"	Sarah,	July 23, 1723.
1-182	'	Jonathan,	July 29, 1725.
1-182	"	Shem,	June 13, 1728.
1-182	"	Joshua, of Jonathan and Sarah,	Nov. 20, 1733.
1-182	"	Alithea,	Sept. 18, 1735.
1-183	"	Mary,	Aug. 24, 1737.
1-183	"	Nathaniel,	Sept. 21, 1740.
1-183	"	Solomon, of Jonathan and Anne,	Dec. 21, 1748.
1-184	"	Richard,	Aug. 5, 1750.
1-184	"	Jonathan,	March 23, 1751-2.
1-184	"	Jonathan,	Feb. 4, 1756.
1-184	"	Anne,	Oct. 7, 1753.

1-184	DROWNE Thomas, of Jonathan and Anne,	Nov. 23, 1757.
1-184	" Philip,	March 16, 1759.
1-184	" John,	March 28, 1761.
1-184	" Sarah,	March 3, 1763.
1-184	" Simeon, of Jonathan and Sarah,	July 10, 1765.
1-184	" Levi,	July 10, 1765.
1-185	" Samuel,	June 6, 1767.
1-185	" Molly, of Jonathan and Rhoda,	June 2, 1773.
1-185	" James, of Solomon and Sarah,	Nov. 7, 1774.
1-185	" Jonathan,	Sept. 4, 1779.
1-185	" Sarah,	Jan. 20, 1784.
4-244	DRURY William Cowper, of Luke and Lydia Potter (DeWolf), his wife,	Oct. 20, 1821.
1-180	DRYER Anna, of William and Hester,	June 23, 1710.
1-181	DURFEE Ann, of Thomas and Martha,	June 7, 1728.
1-182	" Richard,	Aug. 1, 1730.
1-182	" Martha,	May 10, 1731-2.
1-183	" James, of Thomas and Mary,	Jan. 11, 1741-2.
1-183	" Benjamin,	Jan. 6, 1743-4.
1-183	" Oliver,	March 19, 1745-6.
1-179	DUTCH Thomas, of Robert and Hannah,	Sept. 13, 1685.
1-179	" Elizabeth,	Sept. 8, 1695.
1-188	" Hannah,	Aug. 31, 1683.
1-181	DYER Ebenezer, of John and Sarah,	April 19, 1720.
1-181	" Mary,	May 21, 1722.
1-181	" John,	Sept. 10, 1724.
1-181	" Sarah,	Aug. 28, 1726.
1-181	" Jonathan,	June 28, 1729.
1-181	" Martha,	June 28, 1729.
1-180	" Ann, of Samuel and Mary,	May 30, 1701.
1-180	" Ann,	d. June 11, 1701.
1-180	" Anne,	Oct. 1, 1702.
1-182	" Edward,	April 20, 1705.
1-182	" Lydia, of John and Rebecca,	May 16, 1733.
1-182	" Abigail,	Feb. 25, 1734-5.
1-182	" Jones,	March 13, 1736-7.
1-189	" Rebecca,	Oct. 31, 1731.

E

1-193	EASTERBROOK Samuel, of Aaron and Leah,	Aug. 21, 1789.
1-193	EDDY Joseph, of William and Hannah,	Aug. 26, 1699.
1-191	" William,	March 22, 1702.
1-191	" Elizabeth,	April 17, 1704.
1-191	" John,	June 17, 1707.
1-191	" Phebe, of Oliver and Sarah,	Nov. 10, 1725.
1-191	" Mary,	July 7, 1727.
1-191	" Martha,	May 23, 1732.
1-191	" Hannah, of Joseph and Malatiah,	Dec. 22, 1725.
1-191	" Belcher, of Joseph and Ruth,	Oct. 19, 1729.
1-191	" Rebecca,	Jan. 31, 1733-4.
1-192	" Joseph,	Feb. 3, 1735-6.
1-192	" Ruth,	May 19, 1740.
1-192	" Sarah,	Aug. 26, 1742.
1-192	" Joyce,	Oct. 3, 1745.
1-191	" Mary, of Joseph and Mary,	March 23, 1733-4.
4-238	" Alfred Lewis, of Cyrus B. and Eunice,	April 22, 1834.
4-238	" Mary Anna,	Oct. 2, 1841
4-238	" Rensselaer Osborn, of Cyrus B. and Phebe,	March 7, 1843
4-238	" Susan Amelia,	Aug. 18, 1848
1-192	EDGILL Elizabeth, of John and Ann,	Dec. 7, 1747.
1-191	ELLERY Anstis, of Benjamin and Abigail,	Feb. 19, 1697-8.
1-191	" Abigail,	Feb. 24, 1698-9
1-191	" William,	Oct. 31, 1701

1-191	ELLERY Benjamin, of Benjamin and Abigail,		March 23, 1705-6.
1-192	" Christopher, of Christopher and Mary,		Nov. 5, 1768.
1-192	" Samuel,		Sept. 29, 1770.
1-193	ELLIOTT John Reed, of Nathaniel and Elizabeth,		Nov. 14, 1784.
1-193	" Sarah Martin,		Aug. 8, 1780.
1-193	" Mary Reed,		Aug. 6, 1782.
1-193	" Abigail,		March 6, 1787.
1-193	ELLSBREE Hannah James, of James and Hannah,		June 7, 1805.
4-247	EPPINGER James, of James, of Savannah, Ga., and	Juliana, his wife,	
			Aug. 30, 1821.
1-192	ESLICK Samuel, of Isaac and Mary,		Jan. 8, 1740-1.
1-192	" John,		Sept. 17, 1743.
1-192	" Isaac,		Feb. 8, 1744-5.
1-192	" Mary,		Nov. 12, 1746.
1-192	" Allen, of Isaac, 2d., and Ruth,		Sept. 29 1787.
1-192	" John,		March 30, 1790.
1-193	" Lydia,		Aug. 28, 1792.
1-193	" Sally,		March 4, 1795.
1-193	EVERETT James, of John and Susan,		May 30, 1801.
1-193	" James,		May 30, 1800.

F

1-196	FAIRBANKS Mary, of Jeremiah and Mary,		Aug. 22, 1692.
1-197	" David,		Feb. 7, 1700-1.
1-197	" Abigail,		April 17, 1703.
1-197	" Sarah,		April 4, 1705.
1-197	" Hannah,		April 28, 1710.
1-197	" Elizabeth,		April 4, 1707.
1-197	" Jerusha,		Sept. 5, 1708.
1-197	" Deborah,		Feb. 8, 1712-3.
1-197	" Jonathan,		March 29, 1714.
1-198	" Nathaniel,		March 2, 1716.
1-198	" Jeremiah,		Jan. 8, 1717-8.
1-198	" Rebecca,		Jan. 25, 1719-20.
1-201	" Benjamin,		May 23, 1722.
1-196	FALES Timothy, of Capt. Timothy and Allthea,		Sept. 14. 1718.
1-198	" Nathaniel,		July 4, 1720.
1-198	" Altthea,		Aug. 25, 1722.
1-198	" Mary,		Sept. 12, 1724.
1-198	" Jonathan,		May 25, 1727.
1-198	" Deborah,		April 1, 1731.
1-199	" Samuel,		Sept. 28, 1733.
1-199	" Sarah, of Nathaniel and Sarah,		Feb. 12, 1740-1.
1-199	" Alethea,		March 5, 1742-3.
1-199	" Dorothy,		June 10, 1744.
1-199	" Timothy,		Feb. 7, 1745-6.
1-199	" Mary,		Oct. 12, 1747.
1-199	" Nathaniel,		May 11, 1749.
1-199	" Samuel,		Sept. 15, 1750.
1-200	" Thomas,		Oct. 22, 1752.
1-200	" Elizabeth,		Nov. 11, 1754.
1-200	" Stephen,		April 15, 1756.
1-200	" William,		March 6, 1758.
1-200	" John,		June 13, 1760.
1-200	" Hannah,		Oct. 12, 1763.
4-70	" Jonathan,		Oct. 5, 1751.
1-199	" Jonathan, of Jonathan and Hannah,		May —, 1752.
1-199	" Ammarentia,		March 18, 1754.
1-199	" William, of Jonathan, Jr., and Elizabeth,		Jan. 14, 1776.
1-199	" Jonathan,		Jan. 6, 1778.
1-200	" Bradford,		Oct. 22, 1778.
1-200	" William, of Thomas and Sarah,		March 13, 1782.
1-201	" Thomas,		May 29, 1786.

1-200	FALES	Stephen Smith, of William and Mary,	Nov. 24, 1783.
1-201	"	William,	March 5. 1788.
4-232	FALES	Charlotte, of John and Martha,	Jan. 5, 1784.
4-232	"	Fidelia,	Dec. 27, 1785.
4-232	"	Timothy,	July 23, 1788.
4-232	"	James Gibbs,	Oct. 10, 1789.
4-232	"	James,	Jan. 20, 1791.
4-232	"	Betsey P.,	March 29, 1792.
4-232	"	Abby F.,	March 23, 1794.
4-232	"	Nancy C.,	March 23, 1796.
4-232	"	Joseph Jackson,	April 10, 1798.
4-232	"	Henry DeWolf,	Feb. 8, 1800,
4-232	"	Martha G.,	March 10, 1802.
1-201	"	Joseph Jackson, of John and Martha,	May 9, 1799.
1-201	"	Henry DeWolf,	March 30, 1801.
1-202	"	Avis Bicknell, of James (b. Newport),	July 6, 1806.
1-202	"	Elizabeth Smith, (b. Newport),	Feb. 15, 1808.
1-202	"	James, (b. Bristol),	Nov. 10, 1810.
1-202	"	Harriet,	April 17, 1812.
1-202	"	Peter,	Nov. 2, 1813.
1-202	"	Giles Sanford,	Feb. 26, 1816.
1-202	"	William Henry,	Nov. 23, 1817.
1-201	"	William, of William and Harriet,	May 4, 1815.
4-226	"	George Augustus, of Charles and Lydia.	Feb. 18, 1818.
4-226	"	Charles,	June 14, 1819.
4-226	"	Mary Ann Frances,	Dec. 23, 1820.
4-226	"	Mary Ann Frances,	d. Sept. 21, 1822.
4-226	"	Sarah Little,	Dec. 9, 1822.
4-226	"	Nathaniel,	Aug. 22, 1824.
4-226	"	Nathaniel,	d. Dec. 4, 1839.
4-226	"	Mary Ann,	Oct. 21, 1826.
4-226	"	Mary Ann,	d. Jan. 1, 1844.
4-226	"	Elizabeth Bradford, of Charles and Lydia,	Jan. 12, 1828.
4-226	"	Abby Bosworth,	Jan. 29, 1830.
4-226	"	Abby Bosworth,	d. Feb. 13, 1841.
4-226	"	Frances,	June 20, 1831.
4-226	"	Frances,	d. Feb. 26, 1833.
4-226	"	Alexander,	Dec. 23, 1833.
4-226	"	Lydia Bosworth,	May 22, 1834.
1-196	FANNING	William, of John and Rebecca,	Feb. 28, 1698.
1-201	FENNER	Leonard Bardin, of Edward and Hannah,	Aug. 9, 1804.
1-201	"	Edward,	March 3, 1806.
1-201	"	Benjamin Smith,	Feb. 9, 1808.
1-201	"	Albert,	Sept. 10, 1810.
1-201	"	George,	Jan. 24, 1813.
1-197	FENTON	Hannah, of Thomas and Hannah,	Dec. 29, 1713.
1-197	"	Mary,	June 23, 1715.
1-195	FINNEY	Joanna, of Jonathan and Joanna,	Nov. 30, 1683.
1-195	"	Jonathan,	Nov. 3, ——.
1-196	"	Mary, of Jeremiah and Esther,	March 26, 1686.
1-196	"	Hannah,	Jan. 14, 1687-8.
1-196	"	Mehitable,	May 8, 1687.
1-196	"	John,	Aug. 3, 1690.
1-196	"	Rebecca,	Feb. 24, 1691.
1-196	"	Esther, of Jeremiah and Esther,	May 5, 1693.
1-196	"	John,	April 13, 1696.
1-196	"	Abigail,	April 17, 1697.
1-196	"	Joshua, of Joshua and Mercy, (also 1-195),	May 7, 1689.
1-196	"	Elizabeth,	Sept. 25, 1693.
1-196	"	Mary,	April 12, 1694.
1-196	"	John,	Aug. 15, 1696.
1-196	"	Samuel,	May 20, 1699.
1-196	"	Josiah,	July 26, 1701.
1-198	"	Josiah, of Jeremiah and Elizabeth (also 1-197),	July 1, 1728.
1-198	"	Jeremiah,	March 19, 1732-3.

1-202	FINNEY Thomas, of Jeremiah and Elizabeth,	Nov. 16, 1737.
1-199	" Mary,	Nov. 7, 1742.
1-199	" Esther,	Nov. 14, 1744.
1-198	" Nelson, of Ebenezer and Jane,	July 8, 1728.
1-200	" Elizabeth, of Thomas and Elizabeth,	Aug. 22, 1761.
1-200	" Clark,	Nov. 6, 1762.
1-200	" Molly,	Dec. 5, 1763.
1-200	" Josiah Morton,	Nov. 10, 1765.
1-200	" Ruth,	April 7, 1768.
1-201	" Levi Loring, of Loring and Experience,	Dec. 28, 1791.
4-229	FISH Betsey Wardwell, of David and Mary,	Dec. 8, 1805.
4-229	" Betsey,	d. Jan. 11, 1828.
4-229	" Sarah Lawton,	Dec. 31, 1807.
4-229	" George Pearse,	Nov. 15, 1810.
4-229	" Rowland Greene,	Aug. 17, 1812.
4-229	" Abby Wardwell,	March 4, 1816.
4-229	" Abby Wardwell,	d. Aug. 4, 1838.
4-229	" Henry Doty,	Oct. 25, 1818.
4-229	" Mary Pearse,	Jan. 25, 1821.
4-229	" Hannah Bushee,	July 1, 1824.
1-195	FORD Deborah, of Joseph and Deborah,	Sept. 27, 1784.
1-195	" Joseph,	July 26, 1686.
4-225	FRANCIS Ann Elizabeth, of Antonio and Eliza (Waldron, of Joseph), his wife,	Oct. 16, 1848.
4-229	FRANKLIN Josephus, of Elisha B. and Martha,	Nov. 21, 1840.
1-201	FREEBORN Martha Brownell, of Thomas and Martha H.,	Aug. 29, 1810.
1-200	FRENCH Nancy, of Asa and Betsey,	Feb. 20, 1801.
1-195	FRY James, of Anthony and Hannah,	March 7, 1684-5.
1-195	" Mercy,	April 15, 1687.
1-195	" Stephen, of John and Deliverance,	June 19, 1695.
1-196	" John,	Dec. 18, 1696.
1-196	" Antony,	Sept. 4, 1698.
1-196	" Mary,	July 24, 1700.
1-197	" Hannah,	June 4, 1702.
1-197	" Martha,	April 29, 1704.
1-197	" Nathaniel,	Dec. 26, 1705.
1-198	" John, of Anthony and Mercy,	May 9, 1725.
1-198	' Anthony,	Nov. 19, 1726.

G

1-208	GAINS Thomas, of Thomas and Tabitha,	July 29, 1722.
1-208	" Nathan,	July 29, 1722.
1-208	" Mary,	Jan. 1, 1723-4.
1-204	GALLUP Elizabeth, of Samuel and Elizabeth,	April 26, 1688.
1-204	" Samuel,	Oct. 9, 1690.
1-204	" Mary,	Oct. 22, 1692.
1-204	" William,	Aug. 18, 1695.
1-205	" Nathaniel,	June 5, 1698.
1-207	" Mary, of Samuel and Mary (Groton, Conn.,)	Dec. 16, 1716.
1-207	" Samuel,	Oct. 26, 1718.
1-205	GEREARDY John, of John and Deliverance,	Dec. 22, 1696.
1-205	" Sweet,	(b. Warwick), May 15, 1699.
1-209	GIBBS Elizabeth, of John and Sarah,	Oct. 12, 1731.
1-209	" Mary,	Oct. 21, 1732.
1-211	" James, of James and Mary,	Feb. 23, 1742-3.
1-211	" John, of John and Sarah,	Oct. 20, 1751.
1-213	' Elizabeth, of Jabez and Hannah,	Feb. 21, 1806.
1-207	GIDDINGS Sarah, of Joseph and Grace,	June 28, 1710.
1-207	" Martha,	Nov. 16, 1712.
1-214	GILMAN Eliza Ann Fox Goodhue, of Caleb and Lydia	(b. Newport, April 9, 1809.
1-214	" Jesse Porter, of Caleb and Lydia (b. Bristol),	Feb. 2, 1812.

4-133	GIFFORD	John N., of Hugh N. and Ruth S.,	Aug. 8, 1826.
4-133	"	A. H.,	Aug. 30, 1828.
4-133	"	Elizabeth W.,	Jan. 18, 1830.
4-133	"	W. M.,	Jan. 1, 1832.
4-133	"	H. C.,	Jan. 25, 1834.
4-133	"	Ruth Ann,	April —, 1836.
4-133	"	Robert N.,	May 25, 1839.
1-204	GLADDING	Joshua, of John and Elizabeth,	May 6, 1685.
1-204	"	Sarah,	Nov. 20, 1691.
1-216	"	Daniel,	Nov. 8, 1687.
1-204	"	John, of John, Jr., and Alice,	Sept. 18, 1694.
1-205	"	Mary,	Nov. 30, 1696.
1-205	"	William,	Oct. 13, 1698.
1-205	"	Jonathan,	Jan. 5, 1700-1.
1-205	"	Ebenezer,	Dec. 8, 1702.
1-206	"	Joseph,	Oct. 2, 1704.
1-206	"	Alice,	March 24, 1705-6.
1-206	"	Elizabeth,	Sept. 13, 1708.
1-206	"	Nathaniel,	Dec. 16, 1709.
1-207	"	Sarah, died, age 8 days,	May 27, 1712.
1-207	"	Sarah, of John, Jr.,	May 21, 1715.
1-206	"	Mary, of William, Jr., and Mary,	Dec. 7, 1700.
1-206	"	Samuel,	May 19, 1703.
1-206	"	Elizabeth,	Aug. 6, 1705.
1-206	"	James,	Sept. 21, 1707.
1-207	"	John, of John and Martha,	June 30, 1717.
1-207	"	Charles,	June 10, 1719.
1-208	"	Daniel,	May 20, 1721.
1-208	"	Martha,	April 10, 1723.
1-208	"	George,	March 26, 1724-5.
1-208	"	Samuel,	March 25, 1728.
1-209	"	Phebe,	Aug. 21, 1730.
1-209	"	Mary,	Aug. 23, 1732.
1-208	"	John, of Ebenezer and Experience,	Oct. 28, 1726.
1-209	"	Rebecca,	June 8, 1728.
1-209	"	Elizabeth,	July 22, 1730.
1-208	"	Esther, of William and Esther,	July 30, 1727.
1-209	"	William,	June 1, 1730.
1-209	"	Bathsheba,	Jan. 15, 1731-2.
1-209	"	Esther,	April 19, 1733.
1-210	"	Solomon,	March 20, 1734-5.
1-208	"	Sarah, of Jonathan and Sarah,	Sept. 1, 1727.
1-209	"	Elizabeth,	Sept. 22, 1729.
1-209	"	Priscilla,	April 9, 1733.
1-210	"	Nathaniel,	Oct. 6, 1735.
1-210	"	Jonathan,	Oct. 12, 1737.
1-210	"	Timothy,	Nov. 18, 1740.
1-210	"	Benjamin,	June 22, 1743.
1-209	"	James, of James and Alice,	April 19, 1731.
1-210	"	Rebecca, of Nathaniel, and Jemima,	Aug. 14, 1734.
1-210	"	Sarah, of James and Sarah,	Dec. 20, 1738.
1-210	"	Alice,	Aug. 20, 1740.
1-211	"	William,	Jan. 24, 1744-5.
1-210	"	John, of John and Mary,	Jan. 3, 1739-40.
1-210	"	Josiah, of Jonathan and Mary,	Aug. 12, 1741.
1-216	"	Samuel, of James and Sarah,	March 16, 1749-50.
1-211	"	Samuel, of Samuel and Mary,	Oct. 19, 1751.
1-211	"	Nathaniel,	April 28, 1754.
1-211	"	George,	April 9, 1756.
1-211	"	Mary,	Sept. 2, 1758.
1-212	"	John,	June 23, 1761.
1-212	"	Solomon, of Solomon and Ann,	Feb. 23, 1762.
1-212	"	John, of John, Jr. and Lucretia,	Nov. 19, 1762.
1-212	"	Hannah,	Aug. 27, 1764.
1-212	"	Lucretia,	July 25, 1766.

1-212	GLADDING Samuel, of John, Jr., and Lucretia,		April 4, 1768.
1-212	"	Richard,	May 8, 1770.
4-116	"	Mrs. Rachel ——, widow of John, born	Nov. 31, 1764.
1-212	"	Nancy, of Daniel and Susannah,	Dec. 24, 1770.
1-212	"	Nathaniel,	Aug. 14, 1777.
1-214	"	Joseph, of William, Jr., and Rebecca,	(Bristol) Jan. —, 1783.
1-214	"	William,	(Rehoboth) ——. —, 1785.
1-214	"	Ebenezer,	(Bristol) Jan. 3, 1787.
1-214	"	Josiah,	April 12, 1789.
1-214	"	Dorcas,	Dec. 14, 1791.
1-214	"	Jeremiah,	Sept. 10, 1794.
1-214	"	Simeon,	July 12, 1797.
1-212	"	John, of John, Jr., and Rachel,	Oct. 23, 1785.
1-213	"	Edward Talbee, of John and Rachel,	Dec. 21, 1787.
1-213	"	Lydia,	Jan. 17, 1790.
1-213	"	Benjamin,	Feb. 9, 1792.
1-213	"	Hannah T.,	Aug. 6, 1794.
1-213	"	Samuel,	April 16, 1797.
1-213	"	Rachel,	Oct. 21, 1800.
1-213	"	Stephen T.,	Feb. 21, 1803.
1-215	"	Eunice, of Samuel, 2d, and Charlotte,	Oct. 12, 1789.
1-215	"	Allen Ingraham,	Aug. 16, 1791.
1-215	"	Samuel,	Feb. 22, 1794.
1-215	"	Richard Smith,	Feb. 25, 1796.
1-215	"	John,	May 8, 1798.
1-215	"	Edmund,	Oct. 8, 1800.
1-213	"	Gilbert Richmond,	March 4, 1802.
1-215	"	Samuel,	Feb. 28, 1804
1-215	"	Martha James,	Sept. 7, 1806.
1-215	"	Mary Ingraham,	Sept. 14, 1808.
		Note—Also recorded 1-213.	
1-214	"	Nathaniel, of Capt Nathaniel and Nancy,	July 14, 1801.
1-214	"	Jonathan Peck,	Feb. 16, 1804.
1-214	"	John	Aug. 26, 1805.
1-214	"	Nancy,	March 24, 1808.
1-214	"	Susannah W.,	Nov. 26, 1809.
1-216	"	Peter, of Daniel and Saly,	July 27, 1805.
1-215	GLADING Elizabeth, of Samuel, 3d, and Nancy,		Jan. 14, 1847.
1-215	"	Martha Townsend,	Aug. 13, 1810.
1-215	"	Nathaniel,	Aug. 2, 1812.
1-213	"	Martha Turner, of John, 3d, and Nancy,	Aug. 4, 1810.
1-215	"	Anstis,	Nov. 25, 1811.
1-215	"	James Coggshall,	Nov. 14, 1813.
1-240	"	John Greene, of Stephen and Hannah,	Dec. 24, 1830.
1-240	"	Samuel,	Oct. 29, 1832.
1-216	"	William Osborn, of Peter and Mary,	July 14, ——.
1-216	"	Daniel Henry,	—— —, ——.
1-216	"	Charles Joseph,	—— —, ——.
1-216	"	Peter Russell,	—— —, ——.
4-218	GLADDING Lucretia James, of James N. and Lucretia G.,		Jan. 21, 1839.
4-218	"	Julia Ann T.,	Feb. 10, 1840.
4-218	"	Rachael Talbee,	Sept. 8, 1841.
4-218	"	Alzada,	Feb. 14, 1843.
4-218	"	James Nickerson,	June 3, 1844.
4-218	"	John.	Jan. 25, 1846.
4-218	"	Sarah Cole,	Dec. 13, 1846.
4-218	"	Anne,	May 4, 1849.
4-218	"	Ella Frances,	June 22, 1851.
4-218	"	Ellen Fales,	March 15, 1853.
4-218	"	Daniel,	Jan. 23, 1855.
4-218	"	Benjamin S.,	April 3, 1857.
1-205	GLOVER Henry, of Henry and Mary,		July 17, 1706.
1-206	"	Hannah,	June 4, 1712.
4-246	GOFF Sylvanus, of Sylvanus and Ann (Davis), his wife,		Aug. 27, 1818.
4-246	"	Lydia Waldron,	Jan. 27, 1823.

4-246	GOFF Ann Davis, of Sylvanus and Ann,		Jan. 27, 1823.
4-243	" Pardon Gray,		March 8, 1825.
	Note—Also recorded 4-248.		
4-223	" Mary, of Nathan and Nancy,		June 1, 1834.
4-223	" Elizabeth L.,		Aug. 26, 1840.
4-223	" Nancy,		Feb. 10, 1843.
4-223	" Susan I.,		Oct. 5, 1845.
1-213	GOODING Josiah, of Josiah and Ann,		July 15, 1806.
1-213	" James Madison,		March 4, 1809.
1-214	" Horatio,		July 6, 1811.
1-214	" Iranaeus,		Feb. 14, 1815.
1-216	" Joseph,		March 17, 1817.
1-207	GOOF Mary, of Robert and Mary,		Sept. 9, 1720.
1-209	" Bathania, of Anthony and Elizabeth,		Nov. 20, 1730.
1-204	GORHAM Samuel, of Jabez and Hannah,		April 15, 1682.
1-204	" Jabez,		Jan. 31, 1683-4.
1-204	" Sheebal,		April 12, 1686.
1-204	" Isaac,		Feb. 1, 1689.
1-204	" John,		Nov. 8, 1690.
1-204	" Joseph,		Aug. 22, 1692.
1-204	" Hannah,		Feb. 21, 1693-4.
1-205	" Benjamin,		Dec. 11, 1695.
1-205	" Thomas,		Oct. 30, 1701.
1-207	" Samuel, of Jabez and Leah,	(b. Newport)	Nov. 27, 1707.
1-207	" Elizabeth,	(b. Newport)	April 9, 1710.
1-207	" Sheball,	(b. Bristol)	March 29, 1713.
1-208	" Nathan,	(b. Bristol)	Jan. 8, 1725-6.
1-206	" Isaac, of Isaac and Mary,		May 28, 1712-13.
1-207	" Hezekiah,		Feb. —, 1714-15.
1-207	" Benjamin, of Benjamin and Bethia,		Aug. 22, 1718.
1-208	" Bethiah,		Oct. 10, ——.
1-208	" Sarah,		Sept. 15, 1723.
1-210	" Mary, of Isaac and Jemima,		July 28, 1743.
1-211	" Hannah,		Sept. 25, 1745.
1-213	" William, of Isaac and Sally,		July 10, 1788.
1-212	GRANT William Jadine, of Richard and Sarah,		Sept. 3, 1784.
1-212	" Elizabeth Jannet,		Sept. 30, 1786.
1-212	" Frances Morris,		June 14, 1789.
1-213	" James Lamb,		Oct. 12, 1791.
1-213	" Richard Tillinghast,		Sept. 22, 1795.
4-134	" Henry Thomas, of Thomas C. and Elizabeh,		Feb. 28, 1853.
1-215	GRAY Susan, of Elijah and Lydia,		March 8, 1813.
4-235	" Martha Ann, of John and Alethea,		May 27, 1827.
4-235	" Alethea,		May 3, 1830.
4-235	" Julia Catherine Hascall,		May 15, 1835.
4-242	" William Bramun, of Gideon and Hannah,		Dec. 12, 1827.
1-205	GREENE Sarah, of John and Elizabeth,		Aug. 1, 1704.
1-205	" Elizabeth,		Dec. 25, 1705.
1-206	" Mary,		April 8, 1709.
1-206	" Daniel,		Nov. 5, 1710.
1-206	" Martha,		May 19, 1714.
1-210	" Thomas, of Thomas (of Thomas) and Elizabeth (b. Newport),		March 21, 1732-3.
1-210	" Hannah (b. Newport),		Nov. 25, 1734.
1-210	" Elizabeth,		Nov. 14, 1736.
1-211	" Nathaniel,		May 23, 1738.
1-211	" Mary,		June 18, 1743.
1-213	" Thomas Ingraham, of Joseph Whipple Greene and Rebecca,		Sept. 20, 1784.
4-248	" Thomas Whipple, of Benjn. and Joanna		Aug. 7, 1819.
4-225	" Rebecca Ingraham, of Thomas W. and Rachel S.,		Nov. 10, 1844.
4-225	" Mary Frances,		March 6, 1847.
1-211	" Benjamin, of Thomas and Elizabeth,		March —, 1755.
3-6	GRIMES Sally, of John and Leah,		April 20, 1786.
3-6	" Polly,		June 10, 1788.

3-6	GRIMES Elizabeth, of John and Leah,	Jan. —, 1787.
3-6	" Charlotte,	July 8, 1789.
3-6	" Nabby,	June 8, 1792.
8-6	" Polly, 2d,	June —, 1794.
3-6	" Leah,	Nov. 1, 1800.
1-215	GREER Betsy Mann, of Daniel and Sophronia,	April 30, 1807.
4-229	GRIFFIN Sarah Thomas, of Charles and Sarah,	March 20, 1834.
4-229	" Ann Frances,	Dec. 15, 1836.
1-216	GROSS Dixie, of Edward and Mary,	March 6, 1701-2.
1-205	" Benjamin,	Sept. 17, 1703.
1-205	" Priscilla,	June 23, 1705.

H

1-226	HAIL Gardner, of Bernard and Mary,	Aug. 30, 1795.
1-226	" Mary Ann,	Jan. 15, 1798.
4-227	HALL George Rogers, of Benjamin and Ruth (Miller),	March 25, 1821.
4-227	" Frances Maria,	Dec. 10, 1822.
4-227	" Ruth Ann,	Jan. 14, 1824.
4-227	" Sarah,	March 23, 1828.
4-227	" Mary Jane,	April 19, 1834.
1-218	HAMMON William, of Edward and Susannah,	Dec. 31, 1685.
1-219	" Edward,	Dec. 1, 1687.
1-219	" Margeret,	June 24, 1690.
1-219	" Martha,	March 10, 1694-5.
1-218	HAMTON Katheren, of Henry and Sarah,	June 25, 1683.
1-218	" Henry,	Feb. 25, 1684-5.
1-219	" Abigail,	March 2, 1687.
4-243	HANDY Albert, of Pardon and Ardeliza, (also 1-225),	Sept. 16, 1811.
4-243	" William Arnold,	Aug. 1, 1813.
4-243	" Christopher Greene,	Dec. 23, 1815.
4-243	" Charlotte,	May 22, 1818.
4-243	" Caroline,	Aug. 5, 1820.
4-243	" Lydia Greene,	Sept. 18, 1822.
4-243	" Alice Holmes,	Oct. 29, 1824.
4-243	" Mary Ann,	Sept. 29, 1826.
1-225	HARDING Richard, of William and Hannah,	April 28, 1764.
1-225	" Ruth, of James and Hannah,	Jan. 31, 1793.
4-225	HARGRAVES Joseph Thomas, of Joseph and Maria,	April 28, 1844.
1-222	HARRIS Benjamin, of George and Eleanor,	Nov. 13, 1726.
1-222	" George,	Feb. 14, 1728-9.
1-222	" Elizabeth,	April 21, 1731.
1-222	" Frances,	May 10, 1733.
1-225	" William, of William and Hannah,	Oct. 2, 1806.
1-225	" Hannah,	Jan. 1, 1811.
1-221	HARTSHORN Hannah, of Jacob and Martha,	Nov. 7, 1725.
1-222	" Elizabeth,	July 24, 1727.
1-222	" John,	Sept. 6, 1729.
1-222	HART Catherine, of Mark and Mary,	Nov. 3, 1729.
1-222	" Mary,	Nov. 20, 1726.
1-222	" Mark,	Oct. 24, 1728.
1-222	" Cornelius,	Jan. 26, 1730-1.
4-249	" Restcome Sanford, of Restcome and Amey,	April 20, 1803.
4-249	" John Brown, of Restcome and Sally (Brown), his 2d wife, July 25, 1805.	
4-249	" Samuel Hopkins, of Restcome and Sarah (Sanford), his 3d wife, May 16, 1814.	
4-249	" William Tennant, of his third wife, May 24, 1818.	
4-249	" Henry Wight, of his third wife, March 5, 1820.	
1-223	HASKELL Sarah, of John and Mary,	May 25, 1738.
4-230	HATCH Jemima W., of William and Lydia,	Feb. 22, 1830.
4-230	" William,	June 14, 1833.
1-218	HAYMAN Grace, of Capt. Nathan and Elizabeth,	Jan. 31, 1684-5.
1-219	" John,	Dec. 22, 1687.

1-219	HAYNES Frances, of Charles and Frances,		Sept. 21, 1699.
4-220	HAZARD James Morgan Catskill, Sept. 18, 1801; d. Feb. 12, 1864.		
4-220	" Maria M. (Howland), his wife, April 23, 1812.		
4-219	" Anne E. P., of James and Maria M.,	.	Jan. 20, 1833.
4-219	" Maria James, July 22, 1834,	died May 29, 1855.
4-219	" James Fowler,		July 14, 1836.
4-219	• " Mary Eliza,		Jan. 9, 1839.
4-219	" Victoria, April 6, 1841;	died May 20, 1855.
4-219	" Daniel,		May 1, 1842.
4-219	". William James, Feb. 13, 1845;	died June 5, 1845.
4-219	" Julia Anne, April 2, 1846;	died May 24, 1855.
4-219	" Jabez Holmes,		March 12, 1849.
4-219	" John Thomas,		Nov. 2, 1852.
4-219	" Cornelius Williams,		Jan. 10, 1855.
1-218	HEDG Elizabeth, of William and Elizabeth,	Feb. 15, d. 16, 1682-3.
1-219	" John,		April 4, 1685.
1-219	" Elizabeth,		May 5, 1687.
1-222	HEIFERLAND Mercy, of Samuel and Mary,	July 10, 1729.
1-222	" William,		March 23, 1730-1.
1-223	" Elizabeth, (	Feb. 29, 1732-3.
1-223	" Samuel,		March 7, 1734-5.
1-225	HEIRLEHY Thomas, of William and Sarah,	Oct. 3, 1772.
1-225	HILL Patty, of Jonathan and Sally,	Feb. 24, 1793.
1-218	HINTON Mary, of John and Jane,	Oct. 17, 1684.
1-218	" Mercy,		Oct. 17, 1684.
1-219	HOAR Hannah, of William and Hannah,	Aug. 26, 1689.
1-219	" Mary,		March 10, 1692.
1-219	" Hannah, of Benjamin and Rebecca,	Aug. 15, 1700.
1-219	" Rebecca,		Aug. 17, d. 21, 1702.
1-219	" Benjamin,	(Newport), Oct. 11, 1711.
1-226	" William, of William and Sarah,	May 21, 1710.
1-223	" Hannah, of William and Susannah,	Oct. 27, 1735.
1-223	" William,		July 28, 1743.
1-223	" Benjamin,	(sic) Oct. 19, 1743.
1-223	" Sarah,		Feb. 4, 1744-5.
1-223	" Ann,		Jan. 30, 1745-6.
1-222	HOGINS John, of Thomas and Ann,	March 11, 1728-9.
1-224	HOLMES William, of Capt. William and Ruth,	July 24, 1755.
1-224	" Thomas,		July 23, 1757.
1-224	" William,		Sept. 1, 1760.
1-224	" Ebenezer, /	Jan. 6, 1763.
4-230	" Silas, of Dr. Jabez, and Ruth (also 1-225),	Oct. 20, 1815.
4-230	" Thomas G.,		Feb. 13, 1818.
4-230	" Thomas G.,	d. Jan. 10, 1819.
4-230	" Thomas G., 2d,	Oct. 10, 1819.
4-230	" Louisa,		Dec. 19, 1821.
4-230	" Catherine,		Jan. 13, 1824.
4-230	" Julia G.,		May 21, 1826.
4-230	" Gertrude R.,		Dec. 11, 1829.
4-230	" Jabez,		Dec. 20, 1832.
4-230	" Jabez,		d. July 25, 1836.
4-230	" Richmond,		Oct. 18, 1835.
4-230	" Mary Ellen, of Thomas and Eleanor,	Feb. 5, 1830.
4-230	" Thomas Otis,		May 10, 1832.
1-221	HOMANS John, of John and Hannah,	March 3, 1725-6.
1-226	HOWE Mark Antony DeWolf, of John and Louisa,	April 5, 1809.
4-235	" Abby Turner, of George and Abby,	Aug. 10, 1824.
4-235	" Eliza Turner,		March 4, 1826.
4-235	" Harriet, (	Jan. 27, 1828.
4-235	" Lavinia Cady,		Jan. 3, 1831.
4-235	" Julia,		March 6, 1834.
4-245	" Abby Turner, of John R. and Abby T. (also 4-239), July 28, 1836.
1-218	HOWLAND Judah, of Jabez and Bethiah,	May 7, 1683.
1-218	" Seth,		Jan. 5, 1684.
1-218	" Samuel,		May 16, 1686.

1-218	HOWLAND Experience (L. B.), of Jabez and Bethiah,		May 19, 1687.
1-219	" Joseph,		Oct. 14, 1692.
1-219	" Bethiah, of Jabez, Jr., and Patience,		Dec. 5, 1702.
1-220	" Mary,		Jan. 27, 1704.
1-220	" Elizabeth,		May 15, 1707.
1-220	" Elizabeth,		July 17, 1709.
1-220	" Sarah,		April 30, 1711.
1-220	" Jabez,		July 20, 1713.
1-220	" Patience,		March 23, 1716-7.
1-221	" Thomas,		Feb. 5, 1719-20.
1-220	" Samuel, of Samuel and Abigail,		April 3, 1709.
1-220	" Abigail,		Oct. 18, 1710.
1-220	" John,		Sept. 27, 1713.
1-220	" Tabitha,		Jan. 13, 1715.
1-221	" Seth,	July 9;	died Aug. 6, 1719.
1-221	" Phebe,		March 9, 1720-1.
1-221	" Mary,		March 18, 1722-3.
1-221	" Mehitable,		Feb. 1, 1724-5.
1-226	" Yetmercy, of Josiah and Yetmercy,		March 11, 1712-3.
1-221	" Josiah,		April 9, 1717.
1-220	" Lydia, of Joseph and Bathsheba,		Nov. 6, 1715.
1-220	" Joseph,		Dec. 6, 1717.
1-221	" Elizabeth,		Feb. 14, 1719-20.
1-223	" Nathaniel, of Nathaniel and Yetmercy,		April 3, 1735.
1-223	" John, of John and Martha,		Jan. 29, 1736-7.
1-223	" John,		March 9, 1738-9.
1-223	" John,		Jan. 29, 1736.
1-223	" Abigail, of Samuel, Jr., and Abigail (b. Portsmouth),	Aug. 4, 1744.
1-223	" Elizabeth,		March 16, 1745.
1-224	" Samuel, of John, Jr., and Elizabeth,		June 13, 1760.
1-224	" John,		Sept. 20, 1761.
1-224	" Elizabeth,		Sept. 8, 1763.
1-224	" Daniel,		Feb. 11, 1765.
1-224	" Martha,		Nov. 7, 1766.
1-224	" Abigail,		Feb. 5, 1768.
1-224	" Peleg,		Aug. 26, 1769.
1-224	" Nathaniel,		Sept. 9, 1772.
1-224	" Sarah,		Aug. 1, 1774.
1-224	" Sarah,		Dec. 17, 1775.
1-225	" LeFavor,		June 6, 1778.
1-225	" Josiah,		March 6, 1780.
1-225	" Wm. Martin,		June 26, 1788.
1-225	" Sophia, of Cato and Susannah,		— 16, 1797.
1-225	" John, 2d, of Nathaniel and Hannah,		July 12, 1798.
1-225	" Daniel LeFavour, of LeFavour and Phebe,		June 16, 1803.
1-221	HUMPHREY Josiah, of Josiah and Hannah (b. Swansey),	Oct. 13, 1717.
1-221	" Samuel,		Dec. 24, 1719.
1-221	" Hannah,		Jan. 2, 1721-2.
4-225	HYDE Caroline K., of Isaac B. and Eunice S.,		July 30, 1825.
4-225	" Isaac L.,		Feb. 19, 1838.
4-225	" Geneverie Eveline (also recorded 4-233),		March 14, 1842.

I

1-228	INGRAHAM William, of William, Jr., and Elizabeth.		Feb. 17, 1690.
1-228	" Mary,		Dec. 8, 1692.
1-228	" Jeremiah,		Feb. 11, 1694-5.
1-228	" Samuel,		April 11, 1697.
1-228	" Samuel,		died May 25, 1697.
1-228	" Hezekiah,		Oct. 3, 1698.
1-228	" Timothy, of Timothy and Sarah,		Jan. 7, 1691.
1-228	" Sarah,		Sept. 23, 1695.
1-228	" Jeremiah,		Jan. 18, 1697.
1-228	" Edward,		Nov. 2, 1699.

1-228	INGRAHAM John, of Timothy and Sarah,	Dec. 8, 1701.
1-228	" Joshua,	Feb. 12, 1704-5.
1-228	" Isaac,	May 17, 1706.
1-228	" Timothy, son of Margaret Maxfield and Timothy Ingraham,	
		Feb. 1, 1712.
1-229	" Timothy, of John and Mary,	Dec. 20, 1724.
1-229	" Mary,	May 12, 1726.
1-229	" John,	Jan. 25, 1727-8.
1-230	" Abigail,	Jan. 12, 1729-30.
1-230	" Jeremiah,	Dec. 8, 1731.
1-230	" Rachel,	Dec. 24, 1733.
1-230	" Thomas,	Jan. 17, 1736-7.
1-230	" Joseph,	May 11, 1738.
1-230	" Samuel,	March 17, 1740.
1-230	" Martha,	Sept. 14, 1742.
1-229	" Elizabeth, of Isaac and Elizabeth,	June 23, 1729.
1-229	" Joshua, of Joshua and Martha,	Sept. 13, 1730.
1-229	" Lawton,	Dec. 23, 1732.
1-229	" Margaret,	March 4, 1735.
1-229	" Ruth,	April 16, 1737.
1-229	" William,	Dec. 16, 1738.
1-229	" Martha,	Aug. 31, 1740.
1-229	" Allen,	July 9, 1742.
1-229	" Sarah,	July 7, 1744.
1-230	" Timothy,	March 2, 1745.
1-231	" Simeon,	April 24, 1749.
1-231	" Anna,	Feb. 14, 1753.
1-231	" Hannah, of Joshua and Mary,	June 11, 1765.
1-231	" Charlotte,	July 2, 1767.
1-231	" Phebe,	Nov. 27, 1768.
1-231	" Molly,	Sept. 5, 1771.
1-231	" Martha,	June 26, 1774.
1-229	" John, of John and Mary,	June 19, 1738.
1-230	" Jeremiah,	June 4, 1751.
1-230	" William,	Sept. 25, 1754.
1-230	" Simeon, of Jeremiah and Rebecca,	Jan. 12, 1755.
1-230	" Jeremiah,	Jan. 27, 1758.
1-230	" Rebecca,	Nov. 14, 1760.
1-231	" George,	July 8, 1764.
1-231	" Mary,	Aug. 20, 1768.
1-231	" James, of Joshua and Elizabeth,	Feb. 13, 1758.
1-230	" Martha, of Timothy and Sarah,	Feb. 10, 1770.
1-231	" Sarah,	Feb. 20, 1772.
1-231	" William, of William and Mary,	Nov. 30, 1778.
1-231	" Allethea,	Jan. 5, 1777.
1-231	" Lydia, of Jeremiah, 2d, and Priscilla,	Dec. —, 1778.
1-231	" Benjamin,	March 20, 1782.
1-232	" Priscilla,	Jan. 14, 1784.
1-232	" Betsey,	Oct. 10, 1790.
1-232	" Samuel, of Nath'l and Mary,	Nov. 13, 1792.
1-232	" Allen, of Daniel and Abigail,	Oct. 27, 1793.
1-232	" Daniel, Jr.,	March 10, 1797.
1-232	" Henry,	June 19, 1795.

J

1-238	JACOBS Joseph (b. Hingham), (also 2-64), May 1, 1646.
1-238	" Hannah, his wife (b. Hull), April 30, 1650.
1-238	" Joseph, of Joseph and Hannah, (b. Hingham), April 10, 1675.
1-238	" Benjamin, (b. Hingham), April 10, ——.
1-238	" Nathaniel, (b. Hingham), June 26, 1683.
1-238	" Mary, (b. Hingham), Sept 16, 1683 (sic).
1-234	" Mary, of Nathaniel and Mercy, Aug. 28, 1715.
1-234	" Joseph, July 12, 1717.
1-234	" Benjamin, April 26, 1719.

1-234	JENKINS Anstis, of Richard and Mary,		Oct. 28, 1702.
1-235	" Sarah, of Joseph and Phebe,		Feb. 20, 1745-6.
1-236	" Phebe,		July 7, 1747.
1-236	" William,		March 1, 1748-9.
1-236	" George,		Nov. 7, 1750.
1-236	" Joseph,		Feb. 3, 1753.
1-236	" Abiah,		Feb. 5, 1755.
1-236	JENNINGS William, of Stephen and Mary,		March 31, 1747.
1-236	" Molly,		Sept. 7, 1749.
1-234	JOLLS Thomas, of Robert and Experience,		
		(b. Bridgewater),	Nov. 9, 1703.
1-234	" John,	(b. Scituate),	Oct. 2, 1705.
1-234	" Mary,	(b. Bristol),	Sept. 3, 1715.
1-234	" Susannah, of Thomas and Mehitable,		March 22, 1733-4.
1-235	" Mary,		May 7, 1735.
1-235	" Robert,		Oct. 10, 1736.
1-235	" Lydia,		March 1, 1738-9.
1-235	" Hannah,		Oct. 20, 1740.
1-235	" Thomas,		Jan. 16, 1741-2.
1-235	" John,		Nov. 18, 1743.
1-235	" Sarah,		Aug. 7, 1745.
1-235	" Ebenezer,		Jan. 28, 1746-7.
1-236	" Mehitable,		April 24, 1749.
1-236	" Jeremiah,		Oct. 10, 1750.
1-236	" Betty,		Jan. 15, 1755.
1-236	" Thomas, of Robert and Sarah,		June 7, 1762.
1-236	" Anna,		July 18, 1764.
1-236	" James,		Feb. 24, 1767.
1-237	" Sarah,		Nov. 18, 1772.
1-237	" Robert,		Aug. 16, 1775.
1-237	" Lydia, of John and Mary,		Oct. 5, 1767.
1-237	" Polly,		Dec. 22, 1768.
1-237	" Mercy,		Sept. 11, 1770.
1-237	" Benjamin,		Oct. 16, 1772.
1-237	" John,		March 16, 1774.
1-237	" Haile,		Dec. 2, 1782.
1-236	" Simeon, of Thomas and Phebe,		May 29, 1768.
1-237	" Elizabeth,		Dec. 28, 1769.
1-237	" Gardner, of Ebenezer and Molly,		May 23, 1770.
1-237	" Sylvester,		July 9, 1771.
1-237	" Abigail,		June 3, 1774.
1-237	" Samuel Wheaton,		Sept. 27, 1777.
1-234	JONES Cornelius, of Cornelius and Mercy,		Nov. 1, 1693.
1-234	" Ichabod,		Nov. 1, 1693.
1-234	" Elizabeth, of Benjamin and Elizabeth,		July 12, 1697.
1-234	" Sarah, of John and Sarah,		Oct. 2, 1725.
1-234	" John,		Jan. 18, 1726-7.
	Note.—John, Sr., had deceased about this latter date.		
1-235	" Nathan, of Nathan and Bathsheba,		July 6, 1738.
1-235	" Benjamin,		Feb. 15, 1739-40.
1-235	" Solomon,		March 22, 1740-1.
4-242	" Francis LeRoy, of Capt. Peleg G. and Fanny,		March 28, 1822.
4-242	" Charles Henry,		June 30, 1823.
4-242	" William Augustus,		Oct. 21, 1824.
1-235	JOY Elizabeth, of Joseph (late of Rehoboth) and Esther, his wife,		June 27, 1725.
1-234	" Elizabeth, of Joseph and Mary,		Aug. 24, 1746.

K

1-239	KEEN William, of Shadrack and Elizabeth,		Feb. 22, 1741-2.
1-239	KENNECUTT Thomas, of Thomas and Hannah,		May 1, 1707.
1-239	" Elizabeth, of Thomas and Sarah,		March 27, 1731.
1-239	" Sarah,		Feb. 27, 1732-3.

1-239	KENT Abigail, of Rev. Asa and Abigail,	June 17, 1813.
1-239	KILLEY Mary, of Joseph and Bridget,	Dec. 5, 1739.
1-239	" Daniel,	Jan. 29, 1742-3.
4-221	KINDER Sarah E., of Samuel and Sarah,	May 3, 1866.
1-239	KIPP Cornelia, of William and Sarah,	May 26, 1746.

L

1-240	LADAR John, of Briant and Rachel,	Feb. 9, 1696.
1-240	" Daniel,	May 5, 1699.
4-242	LAKE Ann, of Isaac and Nancy,	May 20, 1815.
4-242	" Albert,	May 1, 1818.
4-242	" Mavina F.,	Sept. 4, 1821.
4-242	" Clarrissa P.,	March 19, 1824.
4-238	" Daniel Gardner,	Aug. 9, 1828.
4-238	" Sarah Abby,	Aug. 9, 1828.
4-238	" Elizabeth West,	Dec. 30, 1833.
4-238	" Ellen Pitman,	April 7, 1837.
1-240	LANDON Mercy, of Daniel and Anna,	June 2, 1682.
1-240	" Martha,	Feb. 4, 1683-4.
1-240	" James,	March 29, 1685.
1-242	LAWLESS Mary, of John and Mary,	Sept. 27, 1720.
1-242	" John,	March 3, 1722-3.
1-243	" Margaret,	Aug. —, —.
1-243	" Sarah,	—. —, —.
1-244	" Powers,	April 7, 1732.
1-243	LAWRENCE Margaret, of Thomas and Elizabeth,	March 30, 1728-9.
1-243	" William,	Nov. 16, 1730.
1-245	" Anna,	March 23, 1733.
1-245	" Thomas,	Sept. 27, 1735.
1-245	" Jonathan,	Dec. 31, 1737.
1-245	" Mary,	May 16, 1741.
1-245	" Henry,	Sept. 26, 1743.
1-250	LAWSON Alice, of Richard and Mary,	March 12, 1708-9.
1-250	" Elizabeth, of Mary,	Oct. 6, 1724.
1-241	LAWTON Ruth, of Thomas and Margaret (Prudence Isle),	Feb. 26, 1708.
1-241	" Isaac,	Oct. 6, 1709.
1-241	" Martha,	Sept. 12, 1712.
1-241	" Thomas,	Oct. 14, 1714.
1-243	" Job,	April 12, 1725.
1-243	" Margaret,	March 28, 1719.
1-244	" Ruth,	March 26, 1721.
1-244	" Elizabeth,	Jan. 16, 1727.
1-244	" Mary,	June 26, 1730.
1-244	" John, of Isaac and Sarah,	Nov. 22, 1734.
1-244	" William,	Oct. 3, 1737.
1-245	" Ruth, of Thomas, Jr., and Susannah,	Oct. 10, 1739.
1-245	" Thomas,	March 14, 1741.
1-246	" Isaac, of Joseph and Sarah,	Sept. 4, 1740.
1-246	" Patience,	Feb. 26, 1743.
1-247	" Thomas, of Job and Phebe,	July 20, 1745.
1-247	" William,	Sept. 11, 1746.
1-247	" Joshua, of Isaac and Sarah,	March 8, 1746-7.
1-248	" Thomas, of Thomas and Molly,	Nov. 14, 1766.
1-248	" John,	Nov. 14, 1766.
1-249	" Charles Westcott, of Peter and Hannah,	Dec. 23, 1814.
1-243	LEFAVOUR Timothy, of Timothy and Elizabeth,	Feb. 11, 1731-2.
1-244	" Daniel,	Aug. 30, 1733.
1-244	" Annah,	Feb. 1, 1735-6.
1-245	" Sarah,	June 27, 1738.
1-245	" Elizabeth,	May 28, 1741.
1-247	LENTHORN Elizabeth, of Thomas and Elizabeth,	March 8, 1756.
1-247	" Benjamin,	Feb. 16, 1758.
1-247	" Martha,	Jan. 27, 1760.

2-240	LEWIS Abigail, of Thomas, Jr., and Elizabeth,	Jan. 8, 1691.
2-240	" Nathaniel,	Dec. 14, 1689.
1-249	LINCOLN Mayberry Luther, of Seth and Phebe,	Feb. 25, 1800.
1-249	" Seth,	March 8, 1805.
1-240	LINSEY Samuel, of John and Elizabeth,	Aug. 8, 1697.
1-240	" Mary,	Jan. 15, 1699.
1-240	" John,	May 17, 1703.
1-240	" Elizabeth,	Dec. 19, 1705.
1-241	" Benjamin,	March 11, 1709-10.
1-241	" William,	July 2, 1713.
1-241	" Lydia,	Dec. 2, 1715.
1-242	" Jemima,	May 20, 1719.
1-242	" Sarah, of Samuel and Keziah,	Sept. 17, 1719.
1-242	" John,	Nov. 10, 1721.
1-242	" Mary,	Dec. 20, 1723.
1-242	" Samuel,	Feb. 29, 1727-8.
1-242	" Jemima,	March 21, 1730-1.
1-243	" Hannah, of John and Hannah,	Aug. 20, 1724.
1-243	" Elizabeth,	Aug. 20, 1726.
1-243	" Lydia,	June 9, 1732.
1-244	" John,	May 15, 1733.
1-244	" Benjamin	June 12, 1735.
1-245	" William,	June 11, 1738.
1-245	" Mary,	Aug. 26, 1741.
1-246	" Mary, of William and Mary,	Nov. 12, 1738.
1-246	" Rebecca,	March 23, 1739.
1-246	" Martha,	Oct. 16, 1741.
1-246	" Lydia,	Aug. 23, 1743.
1-246	" William,	March 1, 1744-5.
1-246	" Benjamin,	May 2, 1753.
1-248	" Mary, of William and Katherine,	Feb. 22, 1774.
1-249	" Katherine,	Dec. 3, 1776.
1-249	" Jonathan Woodbury,	June 18, 1778.
1-249	" William, (also 1-248),	Aug. 23, 1780.
1-249	LINDSEY Joseph, of Joseph and Deborah,	Dec. 20, 1779.
1-249	" Thomas,	Feb. 14, 1785.
1-249	" Daniel,	April 4, 1797.
1-249	" Martha, of William and Katherine,	Oct. 30, 1782.
1-249	" Woodbury,	Jan. 15, 1785.
1-249	" Sarah,	Oct. 24, 1787.
1-249	" Nathaniel,	April 14, 1790.
1-249	" Allen,	June 20, 1793.
1-249	" Nathaniel,	July 9, 1796.
1-249	" William, of William and Mary (also 1-247)	March 24, ——.
1-250	" Jonathan Woodbury, and Hannah's children.	
1-250	" Sarah,	July 12, 1798.
1-250	" Hannah,	Aug. 5, 1800.
1-250	" Martha,	June 24, 1802.
1-250	" Mary,	Aug. 18, 1804.
1-250	" Lydia,	April 2, 1807.
1-250	" Jonathan Woodbury,	March 10, 1809.
1-250	" Catherine Woodbury,	Aug. 4, 1811.
1-240	LISCOMB John, of John and Anne,	July 31, 1693.
1-240	" Isaac,	Sept. 20, 1695.
1-240	" Thomas,	Nov. 30, 1697.
1-241	" Nathaniel,	April 23, 1701.
1-241	" Elizabeth,	April 14, 1703.
1-241	" Anne, of John and Rebecca,	Feb. 8, 1718-9.
1-242	" John,	March 5, 1720-1.
1-242	" Hannah,	March 28, 1723.
1-242	" Samuel,	March 13, 1726-7.
1-242	" Elizabeth,	Nov. 30, 1730.
1-244	" Sarah,	July 14, 1733.
1-244	" Phebe,	July 20, 1736.
1-245	" Nathaniel,	March 14, 1739-40.

1-247	LISCOMB John, of John, Jr., and Margaret,		Aug. 27, 1747.
1-247	"	Wilson,	April 9, 1750.
1-247	"	William,	April 13, 1752.
1-248	"	Priscilla, of Samuel and Leah,	Jan. 2, 1753.
1-248	"	Leah,	Oct. 27, 1757.
1-248	"	Samuel,	Jan. 3, 1760.
1-248	"	Rebecca,	April 13, 1762.
1-248	"	John,	June 2, 1764.
1-248	"	Isaac,	July 15, 1765.
1-248	"	Isaac, 2d,	July 2, 1766.
1-248	"	Nathaniel,	Feb. 19, 1768.
1-248	"	Benjamin,	June 28, 1771.
1-250	"	Samuel, of Isaac and Margaret,	— —, —.
1-250	"	Amanda,	— —, —.
1-250	"	Harriet,	— —, —.
1-250	"	Simon De Wolf,	Aug. 17, 1798.
1-250	"	Abigail Howe,	— —, —.
1-250	"	Isaac,	— —, —.
1-250	"	Joseph Diman,	— —, —.
1-250	"	Jeremiah Diman,	— —, —.
1-249	LITTLEFIELD Enock, of Caleb and Hannah,		April 23, 1801.
1-241	LITTLE Thomas, of Samuel and Mary,		Dec. 17, 1714.
1-241	"	Samuel,	March 18, 1715-6.
1-241	"	Mary,	March 30, 1718.
1-242	"	Sarah, of Edward and Mary (also 1-244),	Oct. 15, 1718.
1-242	"	Sarah,	died Oct. 22, 1718.
1-242	"	Edward,	July 1, 1720.
1-242	"	Mary,	May 15, 1721.
1-242	"	Thomas,	Oct. 18, 1722.
1-246	"	Lemuel,	Aug. 26, 1726.
1-246	"	Elizabeth,	March 8, 1724-5.
1-246	"	Nathaniel,	April 10, 1729.
1-246	"	Edward,	May 16, 1733.
1-246	"	Rebecca,	Feb. 22, 1736-7.
1-247	"	William,	June 15, 1742.
1-247	"	Benjamin,	March 25, 1744.
1-247	"	Lucy,	Oct. 17, 1746.
1-244	"	Mary, of Thomas and Margaret,	May 4, 1738.
1-250	"	Samuel, of Samuel and Hannah,	Feb. 27, 1740.
1-245	LUTHER Sylvester, of Benjamin and Lydia,		Nov. 19, 1789.
1-245	"	William R., of Sylvester and Lydia G.,	Sept. 18, 1820.
1-245	"	William R.,	died Oct. 11, 1820.
1-245	"	Elizabeth R.,	Nov. 21, 1821.
1-245	"	George,	May 3, 1823.
1-245	"	William,	Dec. 10, 1824.
1-245	"	William,	died Feb. 13, 1827.
1-245	"	Benjamin,	Feb. 25, 1827.
1-245	"	John Adams,	Feb. 13, 1829.
1-245	'	Mary Beverly,	Dec. 4, 1830.
4-238	"	Arthur Boss,	April 22, 1834.
4-238	"	Arthur Boss,	died Aug. 5, 1840.
4-238	"	Sylvester,	May 13, 1836.
1-249	"	Loesa Simmons, of William and Deborah,	Nov. 18, 1811.
4-227	"	Abby Frances, of Hiram and Abby,	March 8, 1839.
4-227	"	Caroline,	Jan. 15, 1845.
4-227	"	Hiram,	May 30, 1847.
4-227	"	Celistina,	March 2, 1849.

M

1-262	MACKARTY William, of Dennis and Margaret,		Jan. 7, 1745-6.
1-262	"	Anne,	June 17, 1752.
1-262	"	Elizabeth,	June 17, 1752.
1-268	"	Margaret, of William and Clarissa,	Jan. 29, 1772.

1-269	MAKIM Joseph, of Mary,		Sept. 25, 1778.
1-258	MANCHESTER Ruth, of Benj. and Martha,		Jan. 15, 1726-7.
1-258	" Rachel,		Oct. 14, 1729.
1-259	" Seabury,		March 30, 1732.
1-259	" Mary,		April 2, 1733.
1-259	" William,		Feb. 12, 1735-6.
1-260	" Seabury,		Aug. 27, 1740.
1-262	" Nathaniel,		(sic.) April 2, 1740.
1-268	" Martha, of Seabury and Meriam,		Aug. 2, 1764.
1-268	" William,		April 16, 1767.
1-268	" Benjamin,		April 9, 1769.
1-268	" William,		April 27, 1772.
1-269	" Phebe,		Nov. 27, 1775.
1-267	" Nathaniel, of Nathaniel and Elizabeth,		March 4, 1777.
1-271	" Simeon, of Isaac and Priscilla,		May 7, 1798.
1-272	" William Cox, of John and Rebecca,		Feb. 18, 1799.
1-272	" Robert, of Robert and Hope,		Oct. 7, 1812.
4-234	" George Henry, of William H. and Julia Ann (b. Coventry), also 4-24),		Oct. 7, 1829.
4-234	" Eliza Antonette,		Jan. 3, 1832.
4-234	" Julia A.,		Jan. 16, 1834.
4-234	" Almy Luther,		March 26, 1836.
4-249	MANN Samuel Vernon, of Rev. Joel and Catherine,		Feb. 10, 1817.
4-249	" Joel Edward,		May 20, 1818.
4-249	" Mary Elizabeth,		Feb. 20, 1821.
1-257	MARKS Ann, of William and Catherine,		July 31, 1716.
1-257	" Robert,		April 11, 1718.
1-257	" Mary,		June 22, 1719.
1-258	" William,		July 14, 1721.
1-260	" Molly, of Robert and Molly,		Aug. 31, 1740.
1-261	" William,		Sept. 2, 1742.
1-253	MARSHALL Mehitable, of Peter and Abigail,		Dec. 12, 1696.
1-264	MARTINDALE Hannah, of William and Lydia, (b. Little Compton), May 15, 1755.		
1-264	" Susannah,	(b. Bristol), Aug. 20, 1756.	
1-264	" Lydia,	(b. Bristol), April 15, 1758.	
1-264	" Desire,	(b. Bristol), March 20, 1760.	
1-268	" Sarah, of Sihon and Sarah,		Jan. 18, 1759.
1-268	" Nancy,		Feb. 22, 1762.
1-268	" Patty,		Nov. 29, 1767.
1-252	MARTIN Joseph, of John and Mary,		Jan. 15, 1684-5.
1-252	" Mary,	(b. Malden), April 19, 1674.	
1-252	" Thomas,	(b. Malden), June 8, 1675.	
1-252	" John,	(b. Malden), Sept. 14, 1679.	
1-252	" Abigail,	(b. Swansey) July 19, 1681.	
1-252	" Benjamin,	(b. Swansey), May 24, 1686.	
1-252	" Ebenezer,	(b. Swansey), Sept. 28, 1689.	
1-252	" Martha,	(b. Swansey), Feb. 11, 1691.	
1-254	MARTIN John, of John, Jr., and Hannah,		May 14, 1703.
1-254	" Mary,		Jan. 7, 1704-5.
1-254	" Thomas,		Aug. 18, 1706.
1-254	" William, of William and Christian,		Dec. 20, 1707.
1-254	" John,		March 19, 1708-9.
1-255	" William,		Feb. 17, 1712-3.
1-255	" Thomas,		April 7, 1715.
1-256	" Susannah,		Sept. 9, 1717.
1-254	" Jonathan, of Joseph and Mary,	Jan. 17 or 19, 1707-8.	
1-261	" William, of Thomas and Hannah,		May 19, 1740.
1-261	" Christian,		Dec. 2, 1742.
1-262	" Elizabeth, of William, Jr., and Elizabeth (also 1-263),		Oct. 10, 1747.
1-262	" Mary,		Jan. 16, 1748-9.
1-262	" Patience,		Dec. 1, 1750.
1-262	" Abigail,		Dec. 7, 1752.
1-262	" Allen,		Jan. 1, 1755.

1-262	MARTIN Sarah, of William, Jr., and Elizabeth,	May 4, 1757.
1-262	" Lydia,	July 10, 1759,
1-262	" Nancy,	Nov. 12, 1761.
1-272	MASON Charles, of Charles and Mary,	April 19, 1811.
1-253	MAXFIELD Margeret, of Samuel and Christian,	April 2, 1695.
1-253	" Mary, of Ebenezer and Anne,	Nov. 21, 1703.
1-254	" Peter,	March 31, 1706.
1-254	" Samuel,	July 27, 1708.
1-256	" Daniel,	Sept. 8, 1712.
1-255	" Sarah, of Joseph and Mary,	June 24, 1715.
1-256	" Nathaniel,	Oct. 2, 1718.
1-257	" Jeremiah,	March 20, 1721-2.
1-259	" Daniel, of Daniel and Mary,	March 6, 1732-3.
1-259	" Ann,	April 17, 1736.
1-260	" Cathcrine,	Dec. 25, 1738.
1-270	MAY Mehitable, of Elisha and Hannah,	Aug. 5, 1788.
1-270	" John,	Nov. 14, 1791.
4-245	McINTIRE Abby Mayberry, of Joseph and Nancy,	Oct. 4, 1826.
1-258	McINTOSH Elizabeth, of Laughlan and Elizabeth, (grand-daughter of Col. Henry McIntosh),	Sept. 13, 1722.
1-258	" Mary, of Laughlan and Elizabeth,	Aug. 22, 1723.
1-252	MEAD Ebenezer, of Nicholas and Elizabeth,	March 22, 1685-6.
1-256	MILLER Nathan, of Samuel and Ruth,	Aug. 21, 1717.
1-256	" Samuel,	Feb. 7, 1718-9.
1-272	" Richard Carmichael, of Dr. Caleb and Mary Ann,	May 20, 1817.
4-217	" Sarah M., of James and Rebecca,	Oct. 7, 1814.
4-217	" Augustus N.,	Feb. 9, 1816.
4-217	" William Jones,	Jan. 19, 1818.
4-217	" Abby Lindsey,	April 3, 1820.
4-217	" Rebecca Smith,	March 19, 1822.
4-217	" Phebe Sylvester,	July 28, 1824.
4-217	" James, Jr.,	March 26, 1826.
4-217	" James Allen,	June 1, 1827.
4-217	" Isabella Alice,	June 30, 1829.
4-217	" Hope Nelson,	Sept. 8, 1831.
4-217	" Mary Louisa,	Jan. 16, 1834.
4-217	" Helen Marion,	Dec. 6, 1835.
4-217	" Nelson,	May 26, 1838.
4-241	MITCHELL William Henry, of Daniel and Susan,	July 5, 1827.
4-241	" Samuel Hix,	June 18, 1829.
4-241	" Julia Ann,	April 30, 1832.
4-241	" Mary Ellen,	March 5, 1834.
4-241	" Daniel Augustus,	July 10, 1836.
1-267	MOOR Thomas Martin, of Francis and Elizabeth,	Jan. 8, 1782.
1-252	MORY John, of George and Hannah,	Oct. 3, 1684.
1-252	" Mary,	March 24, 1687-8.
1-252	" Sarah,	March 4, 1690-1.
1-252	" Hannah,	March 18, 1693-4.
1-253	" George,	Aug. 31, 1696.
1-253	" Martha,	March 12, 1698-9.
1-253	" Abigail,	Feb. 27, 1701-2.
1-254	" Benjamin,	April 18, 1705.
1-254	" Thomas,	Jan. 1, 1708-9.
1-252	" Hannah, of John and Hannah,	Feb. 1, 1687.
1-256	" Linsford, of John and Margeret,	June 21, 1708.
1-256	" Ephraim, of John and Margeret, (b. Long Island),	July 31, 1710.
1-256	" John,	May 13, 1712.
1-272	MOSHIER John, of Abner and Ruth, (b. Dighton),	Aug. 11, 1791.
1-272	" William Henry, of Abner and Ruth, (b. Bristol),	Feb. 8, 1798.
1-272	" Ruth Ann,	April 7, 1802.
1-272	" Elizabeth,	April 20, 1804.
1-272	" Emily,	March 24, 1811.
1-253	MUNRO Joseph, of John and Mehitable,	Dec. 18, 1696.
1-253	" Elizabeth, of Thomas and Mary,	Sept. 11, 1699.
1-253	" John,	May 14, 1701.

1-253	MUNRO	Samuel, of Thomas and Mary,	May 15, 1703.
1-253	"	William, of George and Mary,	Dec. 24, 1701.
1-254	"	Sarah,	Feb. 23, 1705 6.
1-255	"	Benjamin,	April 26, 1711.
1-255	"	Simeon (also 1-272),	July 30, 1713.
1-255	"	Thomas,	Oct. 21, 1715.
1-253	"	Hezekiah, of William and Mary,	July 27, 1702.
1-253	"	Hezekiah,	d. Aug. 15, 1702.
1-253	"	William,	Nov. 20, 1703.
1-254	"	Nathan,	June 11, 1706.
1-254	"	Bennet,	Oct. 1, 1708.
1-255	"	George,	Aug. 31, 1710.
1-255	'	Nathaniel,	Oct. 27, 1712.
1-255	"	Benjamin,	Nov. 16, 1714.
1-256	"	Mary,	Dec. 15, 1716.
1-257	"	Susannah,	Dec. 20, 1720.
1-255	"	Ann, of Joseph and Mary,	Feb. 8, 1711-2.
1-255	"	Joseph,	Oct. 25, 1713.
1-256	"	Mary,	Oct. 23, 1715.
1-256	"	Simeon, of George and Mary,	July 30, 1713.
1-256	"	Tabitha,	May 24, 1718.
1-257	"	Hannah,	Jan. 28, 1721-2.
1-255	"	Henry, of Benjamin and Mary,	April 23, 1715.
1-257	"	Charles,	Jan. 9, 1716-7.
1-257	"	Shubael,	Jan. 2, 1719-20.
1-257	"	Mercy,	Nov. 2, 1721.
1-257	"	Mary,	Feb. 14, 1723-4.
1-255	"	Andrew, of Thomas and Margeret,	May 17, 1715.
1-256	"	Ebenezer, of John and Elizabeth,	Jan. 16, 1717-8.
1-256	"	Joseph,	March 20, 1719-20.
1-257	"	Thomas,	April 16, 1722.
1-257	"	Jeremiah,	June 24, 1724.
1-258	"	William,	May 16, 1726.
1-258	"	John,	July 21, 1728.
1-258	"	George,	Sept. 22, 1730.
1-259	"	Elizabeth,	Feb. 7, 1732-3.
1-260	"	Thankful,	Oct. 11, 1738.
1-260	"	Ebenezer,	May 9, 1736.
1-260	"	——, dau. of Joseph, (also 1-257),	March 16, 1722-3.
1-258	"	Lydia, of John and Ruth,	April —, 1724.
1-258	"	Priscilla,	Dec. 25, 1726.
1-258	"	Susannah,	Oct. —, 1720.
1-258	"	Martha,	Oct. —, 1721.
1-258	"	Comfort, of John and Hannah,	March 22, 1728-9.
1-259	"	Nathan,	Sept. 29, 1730.
1-259	"	Stephen,	April 22, ——.
1-259	"	Rothbotham,	Feb. 9, 1733-4.
1-262	"	Benjamin,	Feb. 5, 1735-6.
1-262	"	Elizabeth,	Aug. 6, 1738.
1-262	"	Samuel,	Sept. 25, 1740.
1-262	"	John,	Dec. 23, 1742.
1-262	"	Mary,	Jan. 5, 1744-5.
1-262	"	Alice,	Jan. 1, 1746-7.
1-262	"	Thomas,	Dec. 3, 1748.
1-259	"	Dorcas, of Simeon and Rebecca,	April 2, 1733.
1-259	"	Rebecca,	April 30, 1736.
1-260	"	Mary,	Nov. 20, 1738.
1-260	"	William,	March 30, 1741.
1-261	"	Simeon,	March 11, 1743-4.
1-263	"	Archibald, (also 1-272),	Nov. 11, 1746.
1-263	"	Sarah,	Oct. 16, 1749.
1-259	"	Nathan, of Bennett and Sarah,	Oct. 3, 1734.
1-259	"	Nathaniel,	Oct. 20, 1736.
1-260	"	William,	April 7, 1738.
1-260	"	George,	Aug. 26, 1740.

1-261	MUNRO	Sarah, of Bennett and Sarah,	Nov. 25, 1742
1-261	"	James, of Bennett and Sarah, 2d w.,	March 10, 1744-5.
1-263	"	Edward,	April 14, 1747.
1-263	"	Bennett,	July 28, 1749.
1-264	"	Henry,	July 30, 1752.
1-272	"	Benoni,	Aug. 11, 1754.
1-265	"	Jemima,	March 30, 1757.
1-265	"	Samuel,	Nov. 27, 1758.
1-266	"	Royal,	Oct. 8, 1762.
1-260	"	Mary, of Nathaniel and Mary,	Oct. 10, 1736.
1-260	"	Rebecca,	July 12, 1738.
1-261	"	Nathaniel,	Aug. 1, 1741.
1-261	"	Phebe,	June 16, 1743.
1-261	"	Margaret,	Jan. 23, 1744-5.
1-263	"	Timothy,	Feb. 6, 1746-7.
1-263	"	Robert,	Aug. 15, 1748.
1-263	"	Rebecca,	May 19, 1750.
1-263	"	Deborah,	Dec. 11, 1751.
1-264	"	Benjamin,	March 23, 1754.
1-264	"	Stephen,	Jan. 4, 1758.
1-264	"	Benjamin, of Charles and Priscilla,	May 20, 1739.
1-260	"	Lydia,	Oct. 7, 1740.
1-260	"	Nathaniel,	Nov. 8, 1742.
1-261	"	William, son of Elizabeth Corey,	Sept. 1, 1741.
1-261	"	Thomas, of Joseph and Katherine,	Feb. 12, 1742-3
1-262	"	Elizabeth,	April 8, 1745.
1-263	"	Mary, of William and Elizabeth,	Jan. 16, 1748-9.
1-263	"	Patience,	Dec. 1, 1750.
1-264	"	Mary,	Dec. 7, 1752.
1-264	"	Allen,	Jan. 1, 1755.
1-264	"	Sarah,	May 4, 1757.
1-265	"	Lydia,	July 10, 1759.
1-265	"	Nancy,	Nov. 12, 1761.
1-261	"	Jane,	May 14, 1743.
1-261	"	Elizabeth,	Nov. 26, 1744.
1-261	"	Elizabeth,	Oct. 10, 1747.
1-263	"	Hezekiah,	Nov. 11, 1746.
1-262	"	Benjamin, of Jeremiah and Hannah (also 1-263),	May 4, 1748.
1-264	"	Jeremiah,	July 18, 1751.
1-264	"	William,	July 15, 1753.
1-264	"	John Linsey,	March 4, 1756.
1-265	"	Hannah,	Sept. 22, 1758.
1-265	"	Benjamin,	March 25, 1760.
1-269	"	Abner, of Charles and Anne,	Dec. 19, 1754.
1-269	"	Bernice,	May 3, 1756.
1-269	"	Anne,	May 13, 1759.
1-269	"	Matthias,	June 17, 1762.
1-266	"	Samuel, of Nathan and Catherine,	Jan. 31, 1757.
1-267	"	Elizabeth,	June 1, 1761.
1-267	"	Allen,	Oct. 2, 1763.
1-267	"	Mary,	July 13, 1766.
1-268	"	Anne,	July 26, 1768.
1-265	"	Sarah, of Nathan and Sarah,	April 15, 1757.
1-265	"	Nathan,	Sept. 3, 1759.
1-265	"	Joseph,	March 12, 1762.
1-265	"	Elizabeth,	Sept. 26, 1765.
1-268	"	Thomas Kinnecut,	Oct. 23, 1767.
1-268	"	Hezekiah,	May 15, 1770.
1-266	"	Elizabeth, of Stephen and Jane,	Feb. 17, 1762.
1-266	"	William,	July 26, 1765.
1-265	"	Mary, of Nathaniel, Jr., and Sarah,	July 1, 1764.
1-265	"	Sarah,	April 11, 1765.
1-265	"	Elizabeth,	Sept. 1, 1766.
1-266	"	Samuel, of Nathaniel and Abigail,	Oct. 23, 1767.
1-266	"	Lydia,	Aug. 20, 1769.
1-266	"	Abigail,	July 30, 1771.

1-266	MUNRO	Nathaniel, of Nathaniel and Abigail,	Oct. 11, 1773.
1-267	"	William Wardwell, of Nathaniel and Abigail, 2d w.,	Oct. 9, 1781.
1-267	"	Matthais,	April 24, 1785.
1-269	"	Rebecca, of Daniel and Rebecca,	April 17, 1768.
1-269	"	Priscilla,	Jan. 4, 1770.
1-269	"	Daniel,	—— —, 1773.
1-265	"	Gideon, of Elizabeth, single woman, and of Nathan Munro, son of Bennett,	Dec. 13, 1768.
1-266	"	George, of Dr. Thomas and Sarah,	July 7, 1770.
1-267	"	Henry, of Edward and Sarah,	May 28, 1771.
1-268	"	Sylvester, of George and Abigail,	June 4, 1770.
1-268	"	Abigail,	Feb. 17, 1772.
1-269	"	Phebe,	Sept. 22, 1773.
1-269	"	Sarah,	Aug. 12, 1776.
1-266	"	Stephen, of Stephen and Merehah,	Nov. 26, 1773.
1-266	"	Palmer,	Nov. 9, 1775.
1-266	"	Ellery, (Swansey),	April 27, 1778.
1-266	"	Bennett, of James and Patience,	Dec. 30, 1775.
1-267	"	Hannah, of Henry and Amarentine,	Jan. 17, 1778.
1-272	"	Mary, of Archibald and Rebecca,	Sept. 24, 1779.
1-272	"	George,	Jan. 7, 1782.
1-272	"	Rebecca,	Feb. 2, 1784.
1-272	"	Jeremiah,	March 31, 1791.
1-268	"	Josiah,	April 5, 1771.
1-269	"	David, of Joseph and Mary,	Dec. 18, 1784.
1-269	"	Joseph,	April 23, 1786.
1-244	"	George, of Nathan, Jr., and Elizabeth,	Oct. 21, 1785.
1-244	"	Thomas,	Jan. 9, 1788.
1-244	"	Hezekiah,	March 16, 1790.
1-244	"	Edward B.,	Aug. 6, 1792.
1-271	"	Sarah, of Edward and Sarah,	April 3, 1777.
1-270	"	Bennett, (also 2-12),	Dec. 19, 1785.
4-247	"	Bennett, of Edward and Sarah,	Dec. 19, 1785.
4-247	"	Sally, (Glading, of Daniel and Susannah), his wife, June 23, 1790; d. Oct. 12, 1817.	
4-247	"	Lucy, (Abel, of Preserved, of Seekonk, Mass.), his wife, July 14, 1797.	
4-247	"	Edward, of Bennett and Sally,	April 28, 1810.
4-247	"	Phebe Howland,	Aug. 19, 1812.
4-247	"	Phebe Howland,	d. Oct. 8, 1815.
4-247	"	Eleanor,	Oct. 6, 1814.
4-247	"	Sally Glading, of Bennett and Lucy,	Jan. 22, 1810.
4-247	"	John Bennett,	Sept. 20, 1820.
4-247	"	Permelia Abel,	Oct. 11, 1822.
4-247	"	George,	Jan. 2, 1825.
4-247	"	Otis,	Nov. 10, 1827.
4-247	"	Lucy Bennett,	Jan. 15, 1830.
4-247	"	Frances Sidney,	Aug. 3, 1831.
4-247	"	Crawford,	Feb. 16, 1834.
4-247	"	Anne Durfee,	July 30, 1837.
4-247	"	Charles Bennett; (also recorded 4-12),	Nov. 17, 1839.
1-267	"	Allen, of Nathaniel and Martha (also 1-270),	April 6, 1787.
1-271	"	Abigail, of Joseph and Mary,	Sept. 30, 1787.
1-270	"	John, of Daniel and Betsey,	Nov. 13, 1789.
1-270	"	Edward, of Joseph and Elizabeth,	Aug. 6, 1792.
1-270	"	Thomas, of Thomas and Sibel,	Oct. 5, 1793.
1-271	"	Sarah,	Jan. 19, 1792.
1-271	"	Thomas,	Oct. 5, 1794.
1-271	"	Mary Turner,	May 5, 1798.
1-271	"	George,	July 17, 1800.
1-271	"	Abraham,	Oct. 23, 1802.
1-271	"	Peter,	Sept. 15, 1808.
1-271	"	Sybil,	Dec. 26, 1810.
1-272	"	Bateman,	June 25, 1813.
1-271	"	George, 4th son of James and Patience,	Dec. 4, 1794.

1-266	MUNRO Hezekiah, of Hezekiah, 2d, and Ruth,	Aug. 24, 1795.
1-270	" George, of Ichabod and Margeret,	Jan. 5, 1798.
1-270	" Charles,	Feb. 17, 1800.
1-270	" Angeline,	May 17, 1802.
1-270	" Eunice,	Jan. 28, 1804.
1-270	" Sukey,	May 17, 1807.
1-270	" Nathan P.,	Jan. 11, 1810.
1-269	" Martin Easterbrook, of Jonathan Bliss and Sally,	Aug. 3, 1799.
1-270	" Henry, of Thomas and Phila (col.),	April 12, 1800.
4-244	" William G., of Ephraim,	March 9, 1801.
4-244	" Ruth Ann, of William P.,	July 1, 1823.
1-269	" Sarah, of George and Martha,	July 26, 1804.
1-271	" George,	Nov. 4, 1813.
1-267	" Lucretia Smith, of George, 2d, and Martha,	March 4, 1807.
1-267	" Martha,	July 5, 1811.
1-271	" Abigail West, of David and Abigail,	April 13, 1808.
1-271	" Stephen Cranston,	May 9, 1810.
1-270	" Susannah, of Bennett, 2d, and Sarah,	Jan. 14, d. 28, 1809.
1-271	" Edward,	April 28, 1810.
1-271	" Phebe Howland,	Aug. 19, 1812.
1-272	" Eleanor,	Oct. 6, 1814.
4-239	" Bennett James, of Bennett and Sarah,	April 3, 1809.
4-239	" Sarah L. (Fish) of David and Mary, his wife,	Dec. 31, 1807.
4-239	" Bennett James, of Bennett J. and Sarah L.,	April 23, 1829.
4-239	" Bennett James,	d. Aug. 28, 1830.
4-239	" Sarah Bennett,	Dec. 11, 1830.
4-239	" James Tucker,	Dec. 24, 1832.
4-239	" Betsey Wardwell,	Feb. 26, 1835.
4-239	" Abby Davis,	Nov. 17, 1837.
4-239	" Isidore Williams,	Dec. 4, 1840.
4-239	" Lewis Sheperd,	May 18, 1844.
4-239	" Silas Holmes,	April 2, 1849.
4-239	" Mary Leeman,	April 2, 1849.
4-239	" Sally Glading, of Bennett and Lucy,	June 22, 1819.
4-239	" John B.,	Sept. 20, 1820.
4-239	" Pamelia Abel,	Oct. 10, 1822.
4-225	" Benjamin Fuller, of Henry, Jr., and Martha T.,	Dec. 28, 1845.
4-224	" Myra Williams, of John B. and Abby H.,	Oct. 31, 1847.
4-224	" Myra Williams,	d. Nov. 15, 1848.
4-224	" Wilford Harold,	Aug. 20, 1849.
4-221	MUTTON Rebecca J.,	June 25, 1941.
4-221	" George T.,	May 22, 1843.
4-221	" Annie E.,	Sept. 1, 1845.
4-221	" Mary Elizabeth,	Aug. 25, 1852.
4-221	" John W.,	May 7, 1855.
4-221	" Lewis E.,	——. —, ——.
4-133	" James Madison, of James M. and Eliza V.,	Dec. 5, 1842.

N

1-277	NELSON Abby, of Dr. Thomas and Nancy,	Oct. 3, 1803.
1-277	" Angeline,	April 13, 1806.
1-277	" Catherine,	Dec. 11, 1809.
1-275	NEWDEGATE Sarah, of Nathaniel and Sarah,	July 14, 1704.
1-275	" Hannah,	Jan. 9, 1712-13.
4-224	NEWMAN Mary Augustus, of Simeon A. and Mary A.,	March 29, 1853.
1-225	NEWTON Thomas, of John and Anne,	March 21, 1714-15.
1-276	" John,	Jan. 29, 1716-17.
1-276	" Martha,	March 10, 1718-19.
1-276	" Simeon,	June 25, 1720.
1-276	" Daniel,	Aug. 1, 1722.
1-276	" Anne,	Feb. 27, 1724-5.
1-276	" Hannah,	May 4, 1727.
1-276	" Sarah,	May 11, 1730.

1-275	NIBS Thomas, of Thomas and Martha,		July 11, 1'
1-275	" Ebenezer,		July 11, 1'
1-276	NOONING Mary, of Timothy and Rebecca,		Aug. 6, 1'
1-276	" James,		June 18, 1
1-276	" Rebecca,		April 14, 1
1-276	" Timothy, of James and Rebecca,		April 25, 1'
1-276	" Sarah,		Aug. 30, 1'
1-275	NORRIS Rebecca, of Samuel and Rebecca,		Aug. 24, 1
1-275	" Samuel,		Jan. 19, 172
1-275	" Samuel,		Aug. 17, 1'
1-275	" Thomas,		May 14, 1'
1-275	" Abigail,		May 14, 1'
1-275	" John,		Feb. 24, 173
1-276	" John, of John and Elizabeth,		Jan. 31, 1'
1-277	" Elizabeth,		Oct. 4, 1'
1-277	" Mary,		Feb. 17, 1'
1-277	" Paul Uniee,		Feb. 17, 1'
1-277	" Benjamin,		Nov. 17, 1'
1-277	" Rebecca,		May 9, 1'
1-277	" Gilbert,		April 11, 1'
1-277	" Thomas,		April 2, 1'
1-277	" Hannah,		Feb. 17, 1'
4-248	" Hezekiah, of Benjamin,		March 11, 1'
4-248	" John,		Sept. 28, 1'
4-248	" William,		Oct. 12, 1'
4-248	" Benjamin,		Oct. 13, 1'
4-248	" Mary,		Feb. 28, 1'
4-248	" Ann,		July 19, 1'
4-248	" Hannah,		March 23, 1'
4-248	" Rebecca,		June 1, 1'
1-275	NORTON Peter, of Shubael and Sarah,		Jan. 12, 172
1-275	" Shubael,		Feb. 2, 172
1-275	" Sarah,		Aug. 24, 1'

O

1-275	OCQUA Ann, dau. of Ocqua and Abigail (also 1-281),		Dec. 10, 1'
1-275	" Abigail (also 1-281),		July 27, 1'
1-279	OLDRIDGE John, of John and Jane,		Aug. 5, 17
1-279	" William,		April 24, 1'
1-279	" Susannah,		Sept. 23, 17
1-279	" Joseph,		March 27, 1'
1-279	" John,		Sept. 17, 1'
1-280	" Visciler,		June 8, 1'
1-280	" John, of William and Catherine,		Feb. 6, 174
1-280	" William,		March 17, 1749
1-280	" Joseph,		May 12, 1'
1-280	" Yetmercy,		July 20, 1'
1-280	" Thomas,		April 2, 1'
1-280	" Alethea, of Thomas and Alethea,		March 16, 1'
1-280	" William, of John,		Nov. 5, 1'
1-282	" Hannah Talbee,		Sept. 21, 1
1-280	" John,		July 4, 1'
1-280	" Samuel,		Aug. 27, 1'
1-280	ORMSBY Thomas, of Joseph and Hannah,		March 10, 1
1-280	" Sarah, of John and Sarah.		Nov. 26, 1'
1-279	OSBAND Robert, of Jeremiah and Mercy,		Aug. 11, 1'
1-279	" Katherine,		Nov. 12, 1
1-279	" John,		Oct. 31, 1
1-279	" Jeremiah,		July 25, 1
1-279	" Margaret,		May 27, 1
1-279	" Sarah,		May 11, 1
1-279	" Jeremiah,		June 21, 1

1-279	OX Elizabeth, of Samuel and Mary,	June 14, 1725.
1-280	" Benjamin, of William and Hannah,	Sept. 12, 1788.
1-281	" Peleg,	Dec. 26, 1783.
1-281	" Lewis,	April 11, 1792.
1-281	" William,	Jan. 27, 1805.

P

1-282	PAINE Hannah, of Nathaniel and Dorothy,	April 20, 1685.
1-282	" Nathaniel,	March 9, 1688.
1-282	" Edward,	Oct. 7, 1690.
1-283	" Jonathan,	April 18, 1695.
1-283	" Alethea,	Aug. 28, 1697.
1-284	" Sarah,	May 5, d. 8, 1699.
1-285	" Dorothy,	March 19, 1706-7.
1-285	" Sarah,	March 19, 1706-7.
1-286	" Sarah, of Nathaniel, Jr., and Sarah,	Aug. 17, 1716.
1-286	" Nathaniel,	June 17, 1719.
1-286	" Edward,	(b. Boston), April 18, 1714.
1-288	" Dorothy,	Jan. 20, 1723-4.
1-288	" Samuel,	Sept. 3, 1725.
1-288	" Sam'l Clarke,	Feb. 11, 1727-8.
1-288	" Timothy,	July 8, 1730.
	Note.—Nathaniel died about this time.	
1-290	" Stephen, of Stephen and Priscilla,	Sept. 14, 1725.
1-290	" Royal,	March 12, 1730-1.
1-290	" Hannah,	Jan. 5, 1732 3.
1-290	" Elizabeth,	Feb. 5, 1735-6.
1-290	" Mary,	Feb. 16, 1738-9.
1-290	" Sarah, of Nathaniel, Jr., and Elizabeth,	Jan. 5, 1742-3.
1-291	" Sarah, of Edward and Mary,	June 22, 1743.
1-294	" Stephen, of Stephen and Mary,	Dec. 22, 1754.
1-294	" Samuel Royal,	April 23, 1757.
1-294	" Thomas,	Oct. 16, 1758.
1-294	" Betsey, of Stephen and Elizabeth,	Dec. 29, 1776.
1-295	" Mary, of Royal and Olive,	May 5, 1778.
1-295	" Priscilla,	June 17, 1780.
1-296	" Samuel Royal, of Sam'l Royal and Elizabeth,	Aug. 2, 1788.
1-296	" Nathaniel Terry,	May 8, 1790.
1-296	" Stephen,	Dec. 15, 1792.
1-296	" Betsey Torrey, of Samuel Royal and Abigail,	Jan. 4, 1812.
4-233	" Royal Luther, of Samuel Royal and Bethia,	Oct. 19, 1823.
1-282	PAPILLEON Ebenezer, of Peter and Joan,	March 13, 1687-8.
1-282	" Samuel,	(b. Boston) Nov. 16, 1690.
1-282	" Mary,	Jan. 28, 1679-80.
1-282	" Peter,	(b. Boston) March 6, 1682.
1-282	" John,	(b. Boston) July 20, 1685.
1-283	" Obadiah,	May 19, 1692.
1-285	" Peter, of Peter and Katberine,	Sept. 20, 1710.
1-285	" Ebenezer, of John and Bridget,	April 9, 1712.
1-287	" Hester, of Obadiah and Hester,	Oct. 17, 1717.
1-287	" John,	April 8, 1718.
1-287	" Samuel,	Nov. 25, 1721.
1-288	" Mary,	Nov. 3, 1724.
1-288	" Peter,	March 27, 1727.
1-290	" Esther, of Obadiah and Abigail,	Sept. 18, 1738.
1-295	PARKER Charles, of William and Susannah,	Feb. 25, 1781.
1-297	PAULL Zebedee, of Zebedee and Alethea,	Feb. 3, 1802.
1-297	" William,	Feb. 14, 1804.
1-283	PEARSE Abigail, of Richard and Experience,	Oct. 3, 1690.
1-283	" Mary,	Aug. 17, 1693.
1-283	" Jeremiah,	Aug. 29, 1695.
1-284	" Anne,	Feb. 11, 1698-9.
1-284	" Benjamin,	Jan. 11, 1703-4.

1-284	PEARSE Nicholas, of Jonathan and Elizabeth,	Nov. 11, 1700.
1-284	" William,	March 17, 1702-3.
1-284	" Isaac, 2d,	May 21, 1706.
1-285	" Elizabeth,	Nov. 13, 1707.
1-285	" Mercy,	Dec. 11, 1709.
1-285	" Thomas,	Aug. 7, 1711.
1-286	" Abijah,	Sept. 23, 1713.
1-286	" Jonathan died about this time.	
1-285	" Samuel, of Richard and Sarah,	March 2, 1706-7.
1-285	" Nathaniel,	Nov. 23, 1708.
1-286	" Sarah,	Feb. 8, 1710.
1-286	" Richard,	Oct. 6, 1713.
1-286	" William,	Sept. 18, 1715.
1-287	" Experience,	July 5, 1718.
1-287	" Mary,	June 29, 1720.
1-287	" Jonathan, of Jeremiah and Submit,	May 13, 1718.
1-291	" Jeremiah,	June 2, 1738.
1-288	" Susannah, of Richard and Susannah,	Feb. 12, 1723-4.
1-288	" Ann,	Sept. 21, 1725.
1-288	" Elizabeth,	May 9, 1728.
1-289	" Samuel, of Nathaniel and Mary,	Oct. 25, 1733.
1-289	" John,	March 28, 1735.
1-290	" Nathaniel,	Aug. 5, 1739.
1-290	" Christopher,	July 5, 1741.
1-290	" Elizabeth,	Feb. 17, 1742-3.
1-291	" Richard,	June 15, 1737.
1-291	" Thomas,	March 6, 1744-5.
1-291	" George, of Jeremiah and Sarah,	March 20, 1745-6.
1-291	" Thomas,	July 27, 1749.
1-292	" Sarah, of William and Lydia,	Dec. 21, 1742.
1-292	" George,	Sept. 15, 1744.
1-292	" Susannah,	Aug. 31, 1746.
1-292	" Elizabeth,	June 20, 1748.
1-292	" Mary, of Nathaniel and Mary,	April 3, 1747.
1-292	" Thomas,	Nov. 24, 1749.
1-292	" William,	April 2, 1753.
1-293	" Sarah,	Aug. 26, 1754.
1-293	" Mary, of Samuel and Mary,	June 27, 1755.
1-293	" John,	Feb. 4, 1760.
1-293	" Phebe, of Richard and Phebe,	Oct. 5, 1760.
1-293	" Richard,	Oct. 27, 1762.
1-293	" Nathaniel,	Oct. 4, 1764.
1-294	" Lydia,	Feb. 13, 1767.
1-294	" Mary,	July 2, 1771.
1-295	" Timothy,	Feb. 14, 1775.
1-294	" William, of George and Hannah, (also 4-82),	March 2, 1766.
1-294	" George,	April 24, 1763.
1-294	" Mary,	June 4, 1770.
1-295	" Hannah,	Dec. 22, 1772.
1-295	" William, of Thomas and Abigail,	Nov. 3, 1772.
1-295	" Stephen,	Dec. 29, 1775.
1-295	" Jeremiah,	Jan. 21, 1778.
1-295	" Mary, of Richard, Jr., and Candace, (b. Rehoboth),	Feb. 4, 1782.
1-295	" Jonathan, of Richard, Jr., and Candace, (b. Bristol),	April 7, 1784.
1-296	" George, of William and Elizabeth,	Nov. 14, 1787.
1-296	" Mary, of George R. and Lucy,	Aug. 1, 1803.
1-247	" Ann, of Jarvis B. and Nancy,	Sept. 14, 1828.
1-248	" Jarvis G.,	May 15, 1820.
4-227	" Harriet Smith, of Richard S. and Hope C.,	Sept. 20, 1832.
4-227	" Elizabeth Buck,	July 6, 1834.
4-227	" George Thomas,	Feb. 7, 1837.
4-227	" Richard Smith,	April 2, 1839.
4-227	" William Fales,	April 20, 1841.
4-227	" Mary A.,	May 13, 1844.

4-227	PEARSE	Thomas E., of Richard S. and Hope C.,	May 13, 1844.
4-228	"	Oliver Chase,	April 10, 1848.
4-228	"	Susan Thomas, of George P. and Phebe,	Feb. 9, 1842.
1-292	PECKCOME	Robert, of John and Tabitha, (b. Newport),	Jan. 16, 1742-3.
1-292	"	Abigail,	Nov. 4, 1744.
1-292	"	Samuel,	March 19, 1746.
1-293	"	Tabitha, of John and Tabitha, (b. Bristol),	Jan. 22, 1748.
1-293	"	William,	Feb. 1, 1750-1.
1-293	"	Sarah	Jan. 15, 1753.
1-293	"	Josia	Feb. 10, 1756.
1-296	"	John, of John and Catherine,	July 1, 1801.
1-296	"	William Linsey,	July 12, 1803.
4-234	PECKHAM	Mary Catherine, of William L. and Mary Anne,	Aug. 23, 1833.
4-234	"	William Byron,	June 11, 1843.
1-283	PECK	Mary, of Jonathan and Elizabeth,	Jan. 23, 1697.
1-283	"	Jonathan,	Sept. 12, 1698.
1-287	"	Rebecca, of Jonathan and Hannah,	Sept. 26, 1721.
1-288	"	Nicholas,	March 14, 1726-7.
1-288	"	Hannah,	Feb. 20, 1728-9.
1-288	"	John,	April 24, 1723.
1-289	"	Jonathan,	Jan. 4, 1724-5.
1-289	"	Hannah,	March 14, 1729-30.
1-289	"	Deborah,	Feb. 23, 1732-3.
1-289	"	Thomas,	June 24, 1736.
1-289	"	Sarah,	Feb. 11, 1737-8.
1-290	"	Lydia,	March 16, 1739-40.
1-291	"	Mary,	Dec. 31, 1741.
1-291	"	Abigail,	May 11, 1743.
1-291	"	Loring,	Jan. 19, 1744-5.
1-291	"	Nathaniel,	Dec. 3, 1746.
1-288	"	William, of William and Elizabeth,	Aug. 23, 1729.
1-289	"	Martha,	Feb. 1, 1730-1.
1-289	"	Nicholas,	March 23, 1731-2.
1-289	"	Elizabeth, (b. New Haven),	Sept. 15, 1726.
1-289	"	Mary,	Dec. 3, 1727.
1-289	"	Martha,	Sept. 13 or 14, 1728.
1-290	"	Benjamin,	Sept. 13, 1741.
1-289	"	John (so-called), son of Elizabeth Ball,	July 10, 172—.
1-289	"	George, of Jeremiah and Sarah,	March 20, 1745-6.
1-289	"	Thomas,	July 27, 1749.
1-293	"	Abigail, of Jonathan and Mary,	Aug. 14, 1758.
1-293	"	Jonathan,	June 5, 1760.
1-293	"	Nicholas,	May 6, 1762.
1-294	"	John,	March 2, 1764.
1-294	"	Sarah,	Feb. 19, 1766.
1-294	"	Mary,	Sept. 28, 1767.
1-294	"	Samuel Vial, of Thomas and Mary,	Oct. 22, 1763.
1-294	"	Hannah,	May 29, 1765.
1-295	"	Nathaniel,	March 20, 1767.
1-295	"	Rogers Richmond,	Sept. 19, 1771.
1-295	"	Sarah, of Loring and Sarah,	March 8, 1772.
1-295	"	Lydia, of Capt. Jonathan and Mary,	— —, 177-.
1-296	"	Nancy,	Aug. 29, 1779.
1-296	"	—, of Belinda (col.),	Dec. 10, 1788.
1-296	"	John, 2d, of Nicholas and Elizabeth,	Sept. 26, 1791.
1-296	"	Emma, of John and Patience,	May 21, 1796.
1-296	"	Jonathan,	Feb. 24, 1798.
1-296	"	Susan,	Aug. 25, 1799.
1-296	"	John Turner,	July 12, 1801.
1-296	"	William, of John and Ann, 2d w.,	June 16, 1803.
1-296	"	Henry,	Dec. 4, 1804.
1-296	"	Horace,	July 1, 1806.
1-296	"	George Reynolds,	April 20, 1808.
1-296	"	Ann, (also recorded 1-297),	Jan. 25, 1810.
3-6	"	Daniel, of Nicholas 2d,	Oct. 30, 1785.

3-6	PECK	William, of Nicholas, 2d,	Nov. 19, 1787.
3-6	"	Jerusha,	April 21, 1789.
3-6	"	Lydia,	July 18, 1791.
3-6	"	Nicholas,	Feb. 6, 1793.
3-6	"	Polly,	July 1, 1795.
3-6	"	Thereza,	May 9, 1800.
1-296	"	John Bradford, of Nicholas, Jr., and Nancy,	July 21, 1816.
1-249	"	Benjamin Bradford,	May 9, 1818.
1-249	"	John N.,	March 15, 1821.
1-282	PELTON	Henry, of Samuel and Mary,	Dec. 10, 1690.
1-283	"	Sarah,	March 23, 1692-3.
1-284	"	Benjamin,	Sept. 3, 1698.
1-282	PENFIELD	Isaac, of Samuel and Mary,	July 27, 1685.
1-282	"	Hannah,	Oct. 29, 1687.
1-282	"	Jonathan,	Nov. 21, 1689.
1-283	"	Rebecca, of Samuel and Anne, 2d w.,	Oct. 23, 1692.
1-283	"	Abigail,	Oct. 23, 1692.
1-283	"	Benjamin, of Samuel and Mary, 3d w.,	April 26, 1696.
1-284	"	Samuel, of Samuel, Jr., and Hannah,	July 19, 1700.
1-284	"	Peter,	July 14, 1702.
1-284	"	Abigail,	Dec. 22, 1704.
1-285	"	Nathaniel,	Feb. 10, 1706-7.
1-283	PENNY	Christopher, of Christopher and Elizabeth,	April 2, 1695.
1-283	"	Oliver,	April 2, 1695.
1-284	"	Katherine,	June 7, 1697.
1-285	"	Mary,	April 4, 1699.
1-285	"	Isaac,	June 7, 1701.
1-285	"	Nathan,	June 14, 1704.
1-233	PERRY	James De Wolf, of Raymond H. and Mary Ann,	Sept. 2, 1815.
1-233	"	Nancy B.,	Jan. 13, 1819.
1-233	"	Alexander,	May 4, 1822.
1-286	PHILLIPS	Joseph, of Joseph and Susannah,	Oct. 7, 1711.
1-286	"	Michael,	Feb. 8, 1712-3.
1-286	"	Susannah,	April 27, 1714.
1-287	"	John,	June 5, 1719.
1-287	"	Bridget,	March 31, 1719-20.
1-287	"	Susannah,	Jan. 26, 1720-1.
1-298	"	Esther, of John and Esther,	March 15, 1742-3.
1-291	"	Bridget, of Michael and Bridget,	May 25, 1745.
1-291	"	Michael,	Oct. 16, 1746.
1-292	"	Thomas, of Joseph, Jr., and Sarah,	May 31, 1750.
1-296	"	Thomas, of Nathaniel and Sarah,	Oct. 3, 1790.
1-297	"	Samuel Wardwell, of Nathaniel, Jr., and Martha,	March 18, 1799.
1-286	PHINNEY	Joshua, of Joshua and Martha,	May 11, 1716.
1-285	PINIO	James, of James and Dorothy,	April 19, 1707.
1-285	"	Elizabeth,	Feb. 22, 1709.
1-286	"	Sarah,	Dec. 19, 1712.
1-286	"	Daniel,	July 28, 1715.
1-286	PITMAN	James Davis, of Samuel and Mary,	Aug. 27, 1793.
1-297	"	John Howland, of Samuel and Sarah,	April 30, 1814.
1-297	"	Elizabeth Lefavour,	April 30, 1814.
1-298	"	Josiah Howland,	May 14, 1799.
1-298	"	Samuel,	May 17, 1801.
1-298	"	Sarah,	March 19, 1804.
1-298	"	George,	Dec. 5, 1805.
1-298	"	Abigail,	Sept. 9, 1808.
1-298	"	Ann,	Feb. 8, 1811.
4-247	"	Allen W., of Benjamin,	Aug. 29, 1800.
4-247	"	Allen W.,	d. Sept. 8, 1800.
4-247	"	Ruth S.,	March 3, 1802.
4-247	"	Benjamin,	Sept. 13, 1804.
4-247	"	Mary W.,	Aug. 20, 1806.
4-247	"	William H.,	March 6, 1809.
4-247	"	Joseph H.,	Jan. 19, 1811.
4-247	"	Francis,	April 10, 1813.
4-247	"	Francis,	d. Oct. 23, 1813.

1-284	PRATT	Elizabeth, of Joseph and Elizabeth,	March 30, 1706.
1-285	"	Elizabeth,	Sept. 30, 1708.
1-286	"	Mary, of Micah and Mercy,	Oct. 7, 1716.
1-291	"	John, of John and Sarah,	Nov. 17, 1741.
1-291	"	Hannah,	Nov. 7, 1743.
1-291	"	Sarah,	Aug. 11, 1746.
1-291	"	Mary,	Aug. 11, 1746.
1-292	PRITCHARD	Joseph, of Joseph and Mary,	July 29, 1741.
1-292	"	Gaius, (b. Milford, Conn.),	March 17, 1843-4.
1-282	PUMP	Jemina, of Phillip and Sarah,	Jan. 7, 1687.

Q R

4-229	RAMIERES	Mary Thomas, of Thomas and Rachel,	Nov. 11, 1840.
4-229	"	Frances T.,	April 16, 1842.
4-229	"	Eliza G.,	Jan. 31, 1844.
1-300	RANGER	Stephen, of Edmund and Mary,	March 24, 1681-2.
1-300	"	Mary,	Sept. 9, 1685.
1-300	"	Amos,	Feb. 17, 1687.
1-301	RAWSON	William, of Thomas and Ann,	Nov. 11, 1738.
4-239	"	Ethan Allen, of Joseph and Rebecca,	Oct. 22, 1798.
1-300	RAYNOLDS	Benjamin, of Nathaniel and Priscilla,	May 10, 1686.
1-300	"	Ruth,	Dec. 9, 1688.
1-300	"	Peter, of Peter and Mary,	Nov. 26, 1700.
1-300	"	Eleazer,	March 12, 1703-4.
1-301	"	Priscilla, of Benjamin and Susannah,	April 13, 1711.
1-301	"	Ann,	July 12, 1715.
1-301	"	Mary,	July 12, 1715.
1-301	"	Mary,	Nov. 20, 1716.
1-301	"	John,	April 1, 1718.
1-301	"	Benjamin,	Nov. 15, 1722.
1-301	"	Grindall,	July 11, 1726.
1-302	"	Joseph, of Joseph and Phebe,	Nov. 15, 1719.
1-302	"	George,	April 30, 1721.
1-302	"	Elizabeth,	Jan. 15, 1722.
1-302	"	Phebe,	Aug. 3, 1725.
1-302	"	Samuel,	July 14, d. 30, 1727.
1-302	"	Samuel,	Jan. 9, 1728.
1-302	"	Jonathan,	Sept. 28, 1732.
1-302	"	John, of Eleazer and Mercy,	June 26, 1744.
1-303	"	Priscilla, of John, Jr., and Susannah,	June 3, 1745.
1-303	"	Samuel, of John, Jr., and Dorothy,	April 3, 1754.
1-303	"	Grindall,	Oct. 12, 1755.
1-304	"	Benjamin,	March 17, 1757.
1-302	"	Lydia, of Joseph, Jr., and Lydia,	Nov. 14, 1749.
1-303	"	Joseph,	Sept. 20, 1748.
1-303	"	Elizabeth,	Sept. 21, 1750.
1-304	"	Mary,	Nov. 11, 1752.
1-304	"	Mercy,	Nov. 11, 1752.
1-304	"	Phebe,	Oct. 15, 1754.
1-304	"	George,	Nov. 7, 1756.
1-304	"	Hannah,	Dec. 24, 1758.
1-304	"	Samuel,	Dec. 26, 1760.
1-304	"	Jonathan,	Jan. 29, 1768.
4-234	"	William, Feb. 29, 1772.	
4-243	"	Elizabeth (Peck), his wife, Dec. 26, 1774.	
4-243	"	Lydia Peck, of William and Elizabeth,	Nov. 10, 1797.
4-243	"	William,	Oct. 20, 1799.
4-243	"	Mary Peck,	June 1, 1804.
4-243	"	George,	Aug. 11, 1809.
4-243	"	George,	d. Sept. 14, 1809.
4-243	"	George H.,	Aug. 11, 1809.
4-243	"	Elizabeth,	Sept. 29, 1913.
1-306	"	Sarah, of Joseph and Sarah,	Oct. 25, 1773.

1-306	REYNOLDS Ann, of Joseph and Sarah,		April 15, 1778.
1-304	"	Lydia, of George and Abigail,	May 4, 1785.
1-305	"	Jonathan Peck,	Nov. 9, 1786.
1-305	"	George,	Nov. 15, 1788.
1-305	"	Abigail,	July 11, 1791.
1-305	"	Joseph,	June 21, 1794.
4-244	"	William, Jr., Oct. 20, 1799.	
1-303	REED Joseph, of Joseph and Mary,		Sept. 2, 1749.
1-303	"	Hannah,	April 8, 1752.
1-303	"	Samuel,	Nov. 30, 1753.
1-303	"	Elizabeth,	July 16, 1755.
1-305	"	Joseph, of Benjamin and Deborah,	April 1, 1783.
1-305	"	Samuel,	Feb. 7, 1785
1-305	"	Shearjashub,	April 3, 1789.
1-305	"	George,	May 19, 1794.
1-305	"	Josiah,	Aug. 17, 1798.
1-305	"	John, of John (dec.) and Elizabeth,	Feb. 12, 1792.
1-305	"	Hannah, of Joseph and Joanna,	April 27, 1808.
1-305	"	Mary,	Jan. 28, 1810.
1-305	"	Eliza Ann,	Nov. 28, 1811.
4-248	"	Joseph,	Jan. 16, 1814.
4-248	"	Levinia,	Jan. 6, 1816.
4-248	"	Daniel,	April 21, 1818.
4-248	"	Patience,	Jan. 4, 1820.
4-246	"	Josiah, of George,	Sept. 12, 1817.
4-246	"	James Osborn,	June 30, 1821.
1-302	RICHMOND Viall, of Rogers and Susannah,		March 8, 1740-1.
1-301	"	Samuel Viall,	Nov. 25, 1742.
1-302	"	Susannah,	Feb. 15, 1740.
1-302	"	Elizabeth,	Jan. 26, 1743-4.
1-303	"	Sarah,	Jan. 17, 1746.
1-303	"	Mary,	April 15, 1745.
1-304	"	Nathaniel, of Dr. Ichabod and Abigail (died soon after), Aug. 16, 1761.	
1-304	"	——, (a son),	Jan. 5, 1760.
1-306	"	Thomas Paddock, of Thomas and Lydia,	Feb. 4, 1811.
4-236	"	Lydia Ann, of Thomas and Ann P.,	April 24, 1832.
1-304	ROFFEY Elizabeth, of Solomon and Sarah,		April 2, 1753.
1-304	"	Christopher,	March 6, 1756.
1-304	"	Solomon,	Sept. 25, 1758.
1-304	ROGERS Abby Nelson, of David and Lydia,		Sept. 15, 1803.
1-304	"	Wm. Hinman,	Aug. 17, 1806.
1-300	ROSBOTHAM Benjamin, of Joseph and Elizabeth,		Dec. 21, 1701.
1-300	"	Alice,	Aug. 26, 1704.
1-300	"	Benjamin,	Dec. 21, 1701.
1-300	"	Elizabeth,	Sept. 7, 1708.
1-300	"	Hannah,	June 20, 1711.
1-303	ROSS Elizabeth, of Elizabeth,		March 25, 1753.
1-305	ROUNDS Mary, of Seth and Mary,		March 29, 1811.
1-300	ROYAL Mary of Samuel and Hannah,		Dec. 1, 1707.
1-301	RUSSELL Anna, of Joseph and Sarah,		May 10, 1734.
1-301	"	Sarah,	Aug. 30, 1735.
1-301	"	Jonathan,	March 22, 1736-7.
1-301	"	Nathaniel,	Nov. 16, 1738.
1-301	"	Anna,	Dec. 11, 1747.
1-306	"	Betsey Bourne, of John Willard and Nancy,	Sept. 11, 1803.
1-306	"	Parnell Taylor,	Oct. 1, 1805.
1-306	"	Nancy Smith,	Oct. 15, 1807.
1 306	"	John,	May 25, 1810.

S

1-314	SABIN William, of Elijah and Susannah,		July 9, 1757.
1-314	"	Samuel,	July 9, 1757.

1-312	SALISBURY Mary, of Benjamin and Mary,		May 5, 1735.
1-312	"	Elizabeth,	April 7, 1739.
1-313	"	Sarah, of Archibald and Sarah,	Jan. 30, 1742-3.
1-314	"	Sarah, of Bernard and Elizabeth,	Nov. 25, 1754.
1-314	"	Benjamin,	Jan. 2, 1758.
1-315	"	Benjamin, of Benjamin and Elizabeth,	Jan. 30, 1757.
1-317	"	Levi, of Levi and Phebe,	March 5, 1768.
1-317	"	William,	July 5, 1770.
1-318	"	Royal,	March 10, 1773.
1-317	"	Simeon,	July 11, 1775.
1-317	"	Rebecca, of Bernard and Ruth,	April 20, 1770.
1-318	"	James, of Jemima,	Oct. 14, 1732.
1-310	SAMPSON John, of John and Elizabeth,		Jan. 20, 1718-9.
1-310	"	Mary,	Jan. 20, 1718-9.
1-312	"	John, (b. New Haven),	May 31, 1722.
1-308	SANDERS Elizabeth, of Christian and Elizabeth,		Oct. 13, 1684.
1-308	"	Lovett,	March 7, 1683-4.
1-314	SANDFORD George, of Joshua and Waite,		April 6, 1754.
1-315	"	Abigail,	Sept. 16, 1756.
1-315	"	Royal,	May 15, 1760.
1-314	"	Mary, of Esbon and Martha,	May 27, 1757.
1-308	SANDY Joseph, of Joseph and Bethiah,		March 6, 1682-3.
1-308	"	Mary,	Jan. 23, 1684-5.
1-308	"	Sarah.	Oct. 7, 1687.
1-309	"	Benjamin,	July 30, 1689.
1-309	"	Bethia,	May 11, 1693.
1-309	"	Elizabeth,	May 7, 1691.
1-309	"	John,	Jan. 21, 1694-5.
1-313	SANFORD Honorah, of Samuel and Hannah,		June 25, 1745.
1-318	"	Stephen, of Joshua and Waite,	Aug. 12, 1762.
1-318	"	Ellery,	—— ——, ——.
1-318	"	Thomas,	—— ——, ——.
1-318	"	Content,	Aug. 25, 1771.
1-319	"	Royal, of Royal and Rhodia,	Oct. 8, 1793.
1-319	"	Daniel,	May 18, 1787.
1-311	SHARP Mary, of William and Phebe,		March 19, 1713-14.
1-311	"	Phebe,	Oct. 3, 1716.
1-312	"	Abigail,	Dec. 25, 1718.
1-312	"	Susannah,	April 24, 1721.
1-312	"	Sarah,	Oct. 17, 1723.
1-309	SHEPERD John, of Thomas and Hannah,		Aug. 9, 1696.
1-309	"	Elizabeth,	July 27, 1698.
4-232	"	Charlotte Maria, of Thomas and Sarah W.,	Feb. 4, 1838.
4-237	SIMMONS Davenport S., (b. New Bedford),		July 16, 1809.
4-237	"	Jonathan R.,	Oct. 21, 1811.
4-237	"	William S.,	Sept. 24, 1813.
4-237	"	Nancy F.,	Sept. 4, 1815.
4-237	"	Robert M.,	April 12, 1817.
4-237	"	Allen S.,	June 17, 1919.
4-237	"	Charles F.,	July 20, 1821.
4-237	"	Isaac B.,	July 10, 1824.
4-237	"	James F.,	May 24, 1826.
4-237	"	Theodore E.,	July 23, 1828.
4-237	"	Theodore E.,	d. Aug. 13, 1829.
4-237	"	Leonard G.,	Aug. 14, 1830.
4-237	"	Eunice C.,	Aug. 24, 1832.
4-237	"	Rebecca A.,	Nov. 25, 1835.
4-237	"	John Calvin, of Calvin and Bernice,	July 14, 1829.
4-237	"	John Calvin,	d. Oct. 23, 1934.
4-237	"	Charles Carroll,	July 4, 1831.
4-137	"	Nancy Diman,	Feb. 21, 1834.
4-247	SLADE Charlotte, of Jonathan and Sally,		Feb. 6, 1803.
4-247	"	Benjamin Powers,	Dec. 18, 1804.
4-247	"	Sally,	Dec. 29, 1806.
4-247	"	Ira Potter, of Jonathan and Nancy.	June 5, 1808.

4-247	SLADE	Sally Hill, of Jonathan and Nancy,	May 11, 1810.
4-247	"	Nancy Russell,	Feb. 8, 1812.
4-247	"	Ruth Ann,	April 24, 1814.
4-247	"	Mary Ahby,	March 20, 1821.
4-247	"	Harriet Bradford,	Sept. 14, 1823.
4-244	"	George,	July 3, 1826.
4-241	"	Leonard Potter,	Feb. 16, 1829.
4-241	"	Caroline,	Dec. 31, 1831.
1-308	SMITH	Nathaniel, of Richard and Joyce,	May 17, 1681.
1-308	"	Samuel,	June 24, 1683.
1-308	"	Daniel,	March 2, 1687-8.
1-309	"	Mary, of John and Susannah,	Aug. 14, 1686.
1-308	"	John,	Oct. 28, 1689.
1-309	"	Thomas,	Oct. 19, 1692.
1-309	"	Joseph, of Joseph and Mercy,	Oct. 25, 1707.
1-311	"	Mary, of Nathaniel and Abigail,	April 12, 1709.
1-311	"	Abigail,	Feb. 19, 1711.
1-311	"	Nathaniel,	June 29, 1712-3.
1-310	"	Hannah,	April 4, 1715.
1-310	"	Priscilla,	May 16, 1717.
1-311	"	Mercy,	Jan. 29, 1719-20.
1-311	"	Lydia,	June 8, 1722.
1-312	"	Martha,	March 11, 1724-5.
1-312	"	William,	Jan. 14, 1727-8.
1-309	"	Sarah, of Samuel and Sarah,	April 24, 1710.
1-310	"	Elizabeth,	May 22, 1713.
1-310	"	Benjamin,	July 2, 1716.
1-311	"	Richard,	May 25, 1720.
1-310	"	Daniel, of Daniel and Elizabeth,	July 7, 1713.
1-310	"	John,	Jan. 20, 1714-5.
1-311	"	Elizabeth,	March 15, 1717-8.
1-312	"	William,	March 3, 1724-5.
1-312	"	Nathan,	July 1, 1730.
1-312	"	Joyce,	July 1, 1730.
1-312	"	Sarah, of Samuel, Jr., and Elizabeth,	Feb. 16, 1731-2.
1-312	"	Elizabeth,	Dec. 14, 1733.
1-313	"	Mary,	Jan. 25, 1736-7.
1-313	"	Samuel,	April 11, 1739.
1-313	"	Stephen,	April 22, 1741.
1-313	"	Hannah,	April 30, 1743.
1-313	"	James,	May 3, 1745.
1-313	"	Benjamin, of Benjamin and Abigail,	March 1, 1739-40.
1-313	"	Josiah,	June 7, 1742.
1-313	"	Nathaniel,	Jan. 30, 1744-5.
1-313	"	Joseph,	Aug. 25, 1747.
1-314	"	Samuel,	June 28, 1749.
1-313	"	Lucretia, of Richard and Lucretia,	May 7, 1743.
1-313	"	Thomas,	March 11, 1744-5.
1-314	"	Richard,	March 10, 1747-8.
1-314	"	Rebecca,	July 1, 1750.
1-314	"	Richard,	April 16, 1753.
1-314	"	Sarah,	June 28, 1755.
1-314	"	Hannah,	Jan. 3, 1758.
1-315	"	Nathaniel, of Nathaniel, Jr., and Phebe,	Jan. 5, 1747-8.
1-315	"	Samuel, of Benjamin and Sarah,	Oct. 27, 1760.
1-315	"	Mary, of Stephen and Mary,	July 18, 1764.
1-315	"	Elizabeth,	June 5, 1766.
1-315	"	Hannah,	March 23, 1768.
1-315	"	Lydia Potter,	March 11, 1770.
1-316	"	Susannah,	May 26, 1773.
1-316	"	Stephen,	Dec. 24, 1774.
1-315	"	Abigail, of Josiah and Eleanor,	Oct. 3, 1765.
1-315	"	Rebecca,	Dec. 13, 1767.
1-316	"	Benjamin,	Nov. 8, 1769.
1-316	"	Susannah,	Dec. 5, 1771.

1-316	SMITH Barnabus Taylor, of Josiah and Eleanor,		Jan. 22, 1774.
1-316	" Mary, of John and Sarah,		Oct. 13, 1765.
1-316	" John,		Sept. 14, 1768.
1-316	" William,		Dec. 9, 1770.
1-316	" Sarah,		May 8, 1773.
1-317	" Daniel,		May 20, 1776.
1-315	" Martha, of James and Phebe,		Sept. 8, 1768.
1-316	" Phebe,		July 15, 1770.
1-316	" Elizabeth,		March 21, 1772.
1-315	" Nancy, of Nathaniel and Parnel,		Jan. 16, 1770.
1-316	" Martha,		Dec. 1, 1771.
1-316	" Allen Taylor,		April 25, 1773.
1-316	" Nancy,		May 7, 1775.
1-318	" Eleanor,	(b. Rehoboth),	Feb. 11, 1777.
1-318	" Nathaniel,		Jan. 14, 1772.
1-318	" Polly,		—, —.
1-318	" Allen Taylor,		Jan. 10, 1781.
1-317	" Josiah, of Josiah and Elizabeth,		Aug. 24, 1779.
1-317	" George Reynolds,		Sept. 5, 1781.
1-319	" Jonathan,		May 15, 1784.
1-319	" Elizabeth,		Feb. 27, 1786.
1-319	" Mary,		Feb. 4, 1788.
1-317	" Henry, of Stephen and Ruth,		Dec. 10, 1787.
1-317	" Louisa,		April 25, 1789.
1-317	" Ruth,		Jan. 8, 1792.
1-317	" Benjamin Bosworth,		June 13, 1794.
1-317	" Allen Taylor, of Nathaniel and Amarentia,		July 27, 1797.
1-319	" Mark Antony De Wolf, of Bernard and Elizabeth,		Feb. 5, 1798.
1-319	" Sukey,		April 5, 1800.
1-319	" Samuel D. W.,		Jan. 30, 1802.
1-320	" John Munro, of Nathaniel, Jr., and Rebecca,		June 3, 1802
1-320	" Margaret, of Bernard and Margaret,		July 19, 1815.
1-320	" Samuel, of Henry and Amelia,		July 20, 1816.
4-248	" William, of James and Martha,		May 3, 1820.
4-248	" Sarah Ann,		Jan. 25, 1822.
4-241	" Samuel D. W., of Mark Antony DeWolf Smith,		Feb. 18, 1824.
4-241	" George,		Jan. 18, 1826.
1-308	SOLARO John, of Dennis, and Elizabeth,		Aug. 8, 1688.
1-309	" Priscilla,		Feb. 23, 1689-90.
1-310	SOUTHWORTH Nathaniel, of Nathaniel and Mary,		Feb. 13, 1714-15.
1-310	" William,		Jan. 9, 1716-17.
1-311	" Josiah,		Sept. 4, 1719.
1-311	" Elizabeth, of Samuel and Abigail,		Sept. 11, 1717.
1-311	" Eleazer,		Sept. 11, 1717.
1-311	" —, dau.,		July —, 1716.
1-311	" William,		Jan. 8, 1719.
1-311	" Rebecca,		Oct. 14, 1721.
1-310	SPARHAWK John, of John and Priscilla,		Sept. 1, 1713.
1-310	" Nathaniel,		March 4, 1714-5.
4-220	SPOONER William Boss, of William H. and Sarah E.,		March 7, 1862.
4-220	" Anne Church,		Aug. 18, 1863.
4-220	" Catherine Frances,		March 7, 1867.
1-317	SPRINGER Joseph, of John and Martha (Newport),		Oct. 24, 1779.
1-317	" Martha, of Joseph and Mary,		Nov. 12, 1808.
1-317	" Susan,		Sept. 17, 1811.
4-240	STARKWEATHER John Henry, of Rev. John and Mercy H.,		June 17, 1832.
1-309	STARLIN William, of Richard and Grace,		Sept. 5, 1695.
1-319	STEAD Charlotte, of Jonathan and Sally, (Providence),		Feb. 6, 1803.
1-319	" Benjamin Bowers,		Dec. 16, 1804.
1-319	" Sally,		Dec. 29, 1806.
1-318	" Ira Potter, of Jonathan and Nancy,		June 5, 1808.
1-318	" Sally Hill,	May 11, d. 18, 1810.
1-318	" Nancy Russell,		Feb. 8, 1812.
1-318	" Ruth Ann,		April 24, 1814.
1-318	" Mary Abby, of Jonathan and Nancy,		March 20, 1821.

1-318	STEAD Harriet Bradford, of Jonathan and Nancy,		Sept. 14, 1823.
1-318	" George,		July 3, 1826.
1-318	" Leonard Potter,		Feb. 16, 1829.
1-318	" Caroline,		Dec. 31, 1831.
1-308	STONE Hannah, of William and Hannah,		March 26, 1687.
1-318	" Abigail,		July 9, 1689.
1-309	" William,		June 27, 1693.
4-241	STRONG Henry Goodwin, of Henry S. and Sarah,		Sept. 12, 1828.
1-310	SWAN Jeremiah Osborn, of Thomas and Elizabeth,		Aug. 31, 1774.
4-242	" Samuel,		Oct. 18, 1801.
4-242	" Annah (Gifford), of Portsmouth, his wife,		July 15, 1806.
4-242	" Samuel Osborn, of Samuel and Hannah,		March 15, 1823.
4-242	" Mary Hall,		March 7, 1825.
4-242	" William Pearse,		Sept. 4, 1826.
4-242	" Hannah Church,		April 12, 1828.
1-312	SWEETING Bethiah, of Henry and Bethiah,		Nov. 1, 1723.
4-247	SWIFT Thomas, of Thomas and Susan,		Oct. 1, 1812.
4-247	" Saravah,		Dec. 16, 1813.
4-247	" Susan Thomas,		April 2, 1815.
1-317	SYLVESTER Betsey Topham, of Josiah B. and Abigail,		Feb. 18, 1808.
1-319	" Mary Almy, of Joseph and Phebe,		Feb. 15, 1808.
1-319	" Elizabeth Denham,		June 11, 1810.
1-319	" Phebe Taber,		April 6, 1812.
1-319	" Almira,		Jan. 17, 1815.

T

1-325	TABER Timothy, of Thomas and Martha,		May 13, 1724.
1-325	" Benjamin,	(Swansey),	Jan. 26, 1725-6.
1-326	" Thomas,		Aug. 16, 1728.
1-322	TAFT Benjamin, of Robert and Sarah,		March 31, 1684.
1-322	TALBEE Stephen, of Samuel and Priscilla,		Aug. 26, 1693.
1-322	" Hannah,		Sept. 21, 1698.
1-325	" Priscilla, of Stephen and Alice,		Aug. 18, 1725.
1-325	" Samuel,		Feb. 28, 1727-8.
1-326	" Edward,		July 19, 1730.
1-327	" Hannah, of Edward and Anstis,		Sept. 15, 1754.
1-329	" Edward,		Nov. 20, 1759.
1-328	" Priscilla,		Oct. 15, 1762.
1-329	" Rachel,		Nov. 3, 1764.
1-329	" Stephen,		Oct. 3, 1766.
4-224	TALBOT Virginia R., of Capt. Josiah R.,		July 20, 1835.
4-224	" Sarah H.,		Nov. 20, 1848.
4-224	" Josiah R.,		July 17, 1850.
1-329	TANNER James, of Ceaser and Bridget,		Sept. 8, 1795.
1-329	" Almira Rodman,		April 20, 1798.
1-329	" Patience,		July 3, 1804.
1-329	" Sippio,		July 11, 1807.
4-248	" Timothy Ingraham, of William and Margaret,		March 21, 1803.
4-248	" William,		Aug. 11, 1804.
4-248	" Sarah Ingraham,		June 21, 1806.
4-248	" Bennett Munro,		June 19, 1808.
4-248	" Bennett Munroe	d. ——, 1818.	
4-248	" Margeret,		May 21, 1810.
4-248	" A son,	b. and d. Nov. 25, 1812.	
4-248	" Henry,		June 9, 1813.
4-248	" Mariah,		Nov. 14, 1815.
1-326	TAYLOR Martha, of Rev. Barnabus and Martha,		March 2, 1734-5.
4-236	" John Bradford, of Wm. R. and Harriet,		Oct. 14, 1834.
4-236	" Harriet Frances,		Oct. 1, 1836.
4-236	' Sarah LeBaron,		Aug. 21, 1838.
4-240	THOMPSON Louisa, of Samuel and Sybel,		—— ——, ——.
4-240	" Samuel,		—— ——, ——.
4-240	" Lothrop,		—— ——, ——.

4-240	THOMPSON Hannah, of Samuel and Sybel,	— —, —.	
4-240	" William,	July 31, 1809.	
4-240	" Gilbert,	— —, —.	
4-240	" Charles,	— —, —.	
4-240	" Lucinda,	— —, —.	
4-240	" Nathaniel,	— —, —.	
4-240	" Almira,	— —, —.	
1-322	THROOP (see also TROOP), Lydia, of William and Mary,	July 15, 1686.	
1-322	" Mary, of Dan and Dorcas,	Oct. 31, 1691.	
1-322	" Dorcas,	Dec. 3, 1693.	
1-322	" William,	Sept. 30, 1695.	
1-322	" Mercy, of Dan and Deborah,	Oct. 14, 1698.	
1-323	" Deborah,	March 17, 1702.	
1-323	" Samuel, (Taunton),	April 25, 1700.	
1-323	" Submit,	Dec. 25, 1706.	
1-323	" Dan,	July 31, 1715.	
1-323	" Joseph,	Feb. 26, 1716-7.	
1-323	" John, of John and Rebecca,	Jan. 24, 1698.	
1-323	" Ann,	Dec. 27, 1699.	
1-323	" Amos,	March 28, 1702.	
1-323	" Mary,	Sept. 9, 1704.	
1-323	" Hester,	Dec. 31, 1706.	
1-322	" William, of William and Martha,	Jan. 8, 1699-00.	
1-323	" Joseph,	July 23, 1701.	
1-323	" Abigail, of Thomas and Abigail,	Nov. 17, 1703.	
1-323	" William,	Nov. 29, 1706.	
1-324	" Lydia,	May 10, 1708.	
1-324	" Thomas,	May 26, 1710.	
1-324	" William,	Jan. 25, 1712-3.	
1-324	" Mercy,	Jan. 25, 1712-3.	
1-234	" Mary,	Oct. 29, 1717,	
1-325	" Sarah, of Joseph and Sarah, (also 1-330),	Sept. 26, 1726.	
1-325	" Hannah, of Thomas, Jr., and Mary,	Oct. 20, 1733.	
1-326	" Billings,	May 31, 1735.	
1-326	" Mary,	May 30, 1737.	
1-326	" William,	June 13, 1739.	
1-326	" Abigail,	July 9, 1741.	
1-326	" Sarah,	Oct. 1, 1743.	
1-326	" Phebe, of John, Jr., and Phebe,	Nov. 18, 1740.	
1-327	" Samuel, of Thomas, Jr., and Elizabeth,	March 18, 1744-5.	
1-327	" Esther,	March 16, 1745-6.	
1-327	" Elizabeth,	Sept. 15, 1747.	
1-327	" Lydia,	March 1, 1748-9.	
1-327	" a daughter,	May 21, 1750.	
1-327	" Jerusha,	June 12, 1751.	
1-327	" Jerusha,	d. July 3, 1751.	
1-327	" Thomas,	June 4, 1752.	
1-327	" George,	March 15, 1754.	
1-328	" Susannah,	May 20, 1755.	
1-328	" George,	Nov. 21, 1756.	
1-328	" Benjamin,	June 25, 1758.	
1-328	" Abigail,	March 20, 1760.	
1-327	" Sarah, of John, Jr., and Sarah,	Oct. 29, 1753.	
1-328	" Abigail, of Billings and Hannah,	Sept. 24, 1759.	
1-328	" Molly,	Dec. 25, 1760.	
1-329	" Hannah,	Jan. 24, 1763.	
1-329	" Sarah,	March 15, 1765.	
1-329	" Betsey,	March 11, 1767.	
1-329	" Peggy,	Sept. 20, 1770.	
1-329	" Thomas,	— —, 1772.	
1-328	" Pamella, of Samuel and Elizabeth,	March 12, 1770.	
1-329	" Mary,	Jan. 18, 1772.	
1-329	" William, of William and Alethea,	Aug. 15, 1771.	
1-329	" John, of John and Elizabeth,	July 7, 1786.	
1-330	" Thomas, of William, Jr., and Hannah,	Jan. 26, 1797.	

1-330	THROOP Juliana, of William, Jr., and Hannah,	Sept. 9, 1798.
1-330	" Juliana,	(died soon) April 6, 1803.
1-330	" Jane Augusta,	Dec. 31, 1811.
1-327	THURREL Elizabeth, of George and Elizabeth,	March 3, 1749-50.
1-330	" Ruth,	June 13, 1753.
1-328	" Mary,	Aug. —, 1755.
1-330	THURSTON David, of John and Sarah,	Jan. 30, 1684-5.
1-324	THWING John, of John and Mercy,	April 5, 1717.
1-322	TIFFANY James, of James and Bethia,	Nov. 28, 1697.
1-322	" Isaiah, of Thomas and Hannah,	Feb. 22, 1697.
4-222	TILLEY Benjamin, and Sarah W. (Easterbrooks), his wife, children.	
4-222	" A son, April 19,	died April 20, 1833.
4-222	" Henry Henry,	July 26, 1834.
4-222	" Samuel Easterbrooks,	March 28, 1837.
4-222	" Susan Elizabeth,	Jan. 14, 1841.
4-222	" William James,	Sept. 16, 1845.
4-222	" Benjamin Franklin,	March 29, 1848.
4-222	" Catherine Metcalf,	Sept. 20, 1850.
4-222	" George Annable,	Aug. 20, 1853.
4-222	" Anne Pease,	May 5, 1856.
1-327	TOBEY Deborah, of Elisha and Desill,	July 6, 1747.
1-328	TOMLIN William, of William and Dorcas,	Nov. 14, 1761.
1-328	" Rebecca,	Nov. 3, 1763.
1-325	TOOGOOD Samuel, of Samuel and Anne,	Oct. 27, 1727.
1-326	" Nathaniel,	Aug. 26, 1729.
1-326	" Simeon,	April 18, 1731.
1-322	TORREY Siliner, of Angell and Hannah,	May 3, 1699.
1-322	" William,	Dec. 17, 1700.
1-325	" William, of William and Susannah,	Oct. 24, 1725.
1-330	TOWNSEND Nathaniel Church, of Samuel and Martha,	Nov. 8, 1790.
1-330	" Ruth Bourne,	Feb. 28, 1793.
1-330	" Martha,	Jan. 24, 1795.
1-130	" Benjamin Bourne,	Sept. 8, 1799.
1-130	" Sally,	March 21, 1802.
1-324	TRIPP Joseph, of Abiel and Eleanor,	May 25, 1717.
1-323	TROOP Elizabeth, of William, Jr., and Martha,	May 27, 1703.
1-323	" Martha,	June 30, 1705.
1-324	" Mary,	Jan. 11, 1707-8.
1-324	" Bathsheba,	Jan. 11, 1707-8.
1-324	" John,	March 11, 1710-1.
1-324	" Benjamin,	June 9, 1712.
1-324	" Lydia, of Dea. John and Rebecca,	March 15, 1713-4.
1-325	" John,	May 27, 1716.
1-325	" Ebenezer,	Nov. 25, 1718.
1-324	" William, of William and Elizabeth,	July 11, 1720.
1-325	" George,	March 10, 1723-4.
1-325	" Elizabeth,	March 9, 1725-6.
1-325	" Josiah,	July 13, 1727.
1-325	" Nathaniel, of Amos and Frances,	March 11, 1725-6.
	See also Throop.	
1-330	TRUCK Benjamin, of Jack and Abigail,	Nov. 8, 1739.
4-234	TUCKER Thomas Winthrop, of Rev. Thomas W. and Mary,	March 17, 1820.

U

1-332	USHER John, of Rev. John and Elizabeth,	Sept. 27, 1723.
1-332	" Samuel,	Jan. 20, 1724-5.
1-332	" Hezekiah,	Nov. 13, 1726.
1-332	" Allen,	Aug. 14, 1728.
1-332	" Edward,	March 19, 1729.
1-332	" Thomas,	April 25, 1731.
1-332	" James,	Sept. 20, 1733.
1-332	" Elizabeth,	April 7, 1736.
1-332	" Edward, of Allen and Rebecca,	Nov. 17, 1762.

1-332	USHER Hezekiah, of Allen, Jr., and Susannah,		Oct. 8, 1793.
1-332	" Susan,		June 8, 1796.
1-332	" Allen, of Edward and Phebe,		Aug. 15, 1796.
4-241	" William Henry, of William and Phebe,		Aug. 29, 1829.
4-231	" Mary Abby, of Benjamin B. and Abby W.,		May 7, 1839.
4-231	" Elizabeth,		May 7, 1841.

V

1-324	VAN DOORN Moses, of Anthony and Ruth,		May 19, 1758.
1-324	" Anthony,		May 4, 1775.
1-324	" Hannah,		—— —, ——.
1-324	" William, of Moses and Lydia,		Aug. 23, 1781.
1-324	" David,		Dec. 8, 1785.
1-324	" Elizabeth,		Jan. 3, 1788.
1-325	" Sally, of Joshua and Nancy,		Jan. 6, 1788.
1-325	" Ruth,		Dec. 31, 1790.
1-325	" Sophia,		July 2, 1793.
1-324	" Hannah Swan, of Moses and Sally,		July 6, 1791.
1-324	" Anthony,		Oct. 14, 1792.
1-324	" John,		Dec. 25, 1793.
1-324	" Lydia,		May 8, 1795.
1-324	" Philip Zimmerman,		Nov. 29, 1796.
1-325	" Sarah,		April 30, 1798.
1-325	" Frederic,		Oct. 6, 1799.
1-325	" Abraham Peppersburg,		Dec. 11, 1801.
1-325	" Martha, of Anthony and Phebe,		Aug. 21, 1797.
1-325	" Joshua,		Feb. 2, 1800.
1-325	" Moses,		Dec 20, 1801.
1-325	" William C., of William and Mary P.,		Jan. 31, 1806.
1-325	" Henry,		Oct. 26, 1810.
1-325	" Joseph Russell,		Dec. 25, 1813.
4-224	" Joseph Russell, of William Christ'r and Charlotte,	Aug. 30, 1830.
4-224	" William Henry,		Jan. 28, 1832.
4-224	" Sarah H.,		Aug. 29, 1834.
4-224	" Sarah H.,		died Aug. 10, 1836.
4-224	" Lydia Leonard,		Aug. 29, 1837.
4-224	" John Frederic,		Dec. 8, 1839.
4-224	" John Frederic,		died Sept. 26, 1840.
4-224	" Charlotte E.,		Sept. 7, 1842.
4-224	" Charlotte E.,		died Sept. 1, 1843.
4-224	" Mary Christopher,		May 20, 1845.
4-229	" Anna Russell, of Henry and Judeth Eliza,	Nov. 26, 1840.
4-229	" Edward Paine,		June 25, 1844.
4-229	" Clara Haile,		Aug. 26, 1846.
1-334	VAUGHN Mary, of Daniel and Martha,		Sept. 3, 1726.
4-248	" Julia Ann, of Clark L. and Julia Ann,		Dec. 21, 1819.
4-248	" Julia Ann,		Aug. 5, 1821.
1-334	VEREN Mercy, of John and Penelope,		Aug. 21, 1684.
1-334	VIAL Josiah, of Samuel and Susannah,		July 23, 1714.
1-334	" Hezekiah,		Nov. 2, 1715.
1-334	VON HUINEN Mary, of Solomon and Mary,		July 22, 1742.

W

1-337	WALDRON Isaac, of George and Rachel,		March 7, 1683-4.
1-337	" Thomas,		April 29, 1686.
1-337	" Jacob,		April 23, 1689.
1-338	" Samuel,		July 26, 1691.
1-338	" Hannah,		Sept. 2, 1692.
1-339	" Cornelius,		Sept. 4, 1697.
1-339	" Martha,		Dec. 30, 1701.

1-340	WALDRON Anne, of Cornelius and Anne (also 1-343),	Sept. 25, 1720.
1-340	" (son),	Aug. 6, 1720.
1-340	" Joseph, of Joseph and Martha,	Oct. 6, 1718.
1-344	" Priscilla,	—. —. 1724.
1-334	" Priscilla,	d. Sept. 15, 1741.
1-344	" Rachel,	Dec. 27, 1726.
1-344	" Anstis,	Jan. 5, 1728.
1-344	" Leah,	May 17, 1729.
1-344	" Nathaniel,	March 25, 1731.
1-344	" Sarah,	Feb. 10, 1734.
1-344	" Willoby,	Nov. 13, 1736.
1-344	" John,	Dec. 20, 1738.
1-334	" Isaac,	June 1, 1742.
1-341	" Nathaniel, of Joseph and Martha,	Aug. 9, 1721.
1-341	" Daniel,	Dec. 14, 1724.
1-342	" John,	March 26, 1727,
1-342	" Nathaniel, of Joseph, Jr., and Rebecca,	March 16. 1741-2.
1-344	" Joseph,	Dec. 22, 1747.
1-344	" Jonathan,	Jan. 15, 1749-50.
1-345	" Rebecca,	May —, 1752.
1-346	" Hannah,	March 14, 1756.
1-346	" Elizabeth,	April 14, 1759.
1-347	" Joseph,	March 27, 1762.
1-347	" Daniel, of Daniel and Phebe,	Dec. 22, 1749.
1-340	" George,	April 7, 1754.
1-346	" Samuel,	Oct. 11, 1755.
1-346	" Phebe,	May 22, 1758.
1-348	" Leonard,	May 26, 1760.
1-349	" Elizabeth,	Jan. 29, 1762.
1-349	" Molly,	Jan. 5, 1764.
1-350	" Nancy,	Dec. —, 1767.
1-345	" Ruth, of John and Elizabeth,	Nov. 21, 1751.
1-346	" Allen,	Dec. 20, 1755.
1-348	" Priscilla,	Jan. 4, 1758.
1-346	" Nathaniel, of Nathaniel and Hannah,	June 10, 1756.
1-346	" Billings,	Feb. 4, 1758.
1-347	" John,	Feb. 13, 1760.
1-347	" Abigail,	Feb. 13, 1760.
1-347	" Thomas,	Jan. 16, 1762.
1-349	" Ambrose,	June 1, 1764.
1-349	" Rebecca.	June 16, 1766.
1-350	" Joseph,	Feb. 8, 1768.
1-350	" Benjamin,	Feb. 8, 1768.
1-350	" William Throop,	Aug. 29, 1770.
1-350	" Samuel	May 11, 1772.
1-350	" William, of Isaac and A	Feb. 1, 1766.
1-350	" George,	March 22, 1767.
1-350	" Isaac,	April 16, 1770.
1-350	" Daniel,	Feb. 6, 1773.
1-350	" Elizabeth,	April 23, 1776.
1-351	" Anne,	Feb. 9, 1779.
1-353	" Leonard, of Ambrose and Hannah,	Feb. 2, 1787.
1-353	" Nancy,	Dec. 22, 1788 or 9.
1-351	" Billings,	(also 1-354), Aug. 27, 1790.
1-351	" Polly,	April 6, 1792.
1-351	" John,	March 9, 1794.
1-354	" Nathaniel,	Oct. 8, 1795.
1-354	" Marshall,	Aug. 24, 1797.
1-354	" Hannah,	March 7, 1799.
1-354	" Rebecca,	May 20, 1803.
1-354	" Abby Cary,	May 4, 1805.
1-354	" Richard S.,	Nov. 20, 1807.
2-2	" Thomas, of Thomas and Ruth,	Aug. 22, 1790.
1-353	" John,	April 12, 1797.
1-352	" Leonard, of Newton and Frances,	Jan. 13, 1795.

1-352	WALDRON Benjamin Bosworth, of Newton and Frances,	Sept. 1, 1797.
1-352	" Frances,	April 12, 1800.
1-352	" Ann,	Oct. 9, 1805.
4-245	" Joseph, of George and Sarah,	Dec. 6, 1800.
2-1	" Lydia, of Leonard and Elizabeth,	July 27, 1809.
2-1	" Ambrose,	Feb. 1, 1813.
2-1	" Jonathan Diman, of Billings and Hannah,	Dec. 8, 1812.
2-1	" Elizabeth Jackson,	Oct. 17, 1814.
1-337	WALKER John, of Thomas and Elizabeth,	Oct. 1, 1685.
1-337	" William,	Aug. 5, 1687.
1-338	" Mary,	July 28, 1693
1-339	" John, of William and Hannah,	March 17, 1714-5.
1-339	" Rachel,	Oct. 24, 1716.
1-341	" Elizabeth,	Jan. 15, 1720-1.
1-341	" Mary,	Oct. 23, 1722.
1-343	" William, of John and Patience,	July 25, 1748.
1-344	" Elizabeth,	Dec. 25, 1750.
1-346	" John,	Oct. 28, 1753.
1-346	" Abigail,	March 16, 1758.
1-347	" Rebecca,	Nov. 6, 1759.
1-338	WALLEY Elizabeth, of John and Sarah,	Nov. 1, 1685.
1-338	" Lydian,	Sept. 2, 1688.
1-338	" John,	Sept. 11, 1691.
1-338	WALTER Thomas, of Thomas and Elizabeth,	Feb. 8, 1688-9.
1-338	WATTS ——, dau. of John and Mary,	Dec. 6, 1694. d. soon.
1-338	" Mary,	Dec. 4, 1695.
1-338	" Elizabeth,	March 17, 1697.
1-337	WARDALL James, of Uzal and Grace,	June 30, 1684.
1-337	" Joseph,	July 30, 1686
1-337	" Benjamin,	April 9, 1688.
1-338	" William,	May 13, 1693.
1-338	" Rebecca,	May 13, 1693.
1-339	" Mary, of Joseph and Martha,	Sept. 22, 1710.
1-339	" Mary,	Aug. 2, 1713.
1-340	" Joseph,	June 3, 1715.
1-340	" Martha,	Nov. 29, 1716.
1-340	" Joseph,	Oct. 6, 1718.
1-340	" a son,	Aug. 6, d. 18, 1720.
1-340	" Rebecca, of James and Sarah,	March 22, 1714-5.
1-340	" James,	May 4, 1717.
1-340	" Hannah,	April 5, 1720.
1-341	" John, of Joseph and Martha,	Oct. 12, 1720.
1-342	" Jemima, of Joseph, Jr., and Jemima,	Dec. 18, 1738.
1-342	" Elizabeth,	Aug. 20, 1741.
1-342	" Martha,	Dec. 14, 1743.
1-343	" Lydia,	Dec. 13, 1745.
1-342	" John, of John and Phebe,	June 19, 1742.
1-342	" Nathaniel,	March 29, 1744.
1-344	" Phebe,	Jan. 23, 1748-9.
1-343	WARDWELL Mary, of Uzal and Sarah,	Sept. 3, 1740.
1-343	" Sarah,	March 10, 1743-4.
1-343	" Rebecca, of James, Jr., and Anne,	Jan. 21, 1743-4.
1-343	" Abigail, of William and Mary,	June 3, 1745.
1-343	" William.	(sic.) Dec. 3, 1744.
1-343	" Joseph, of John and Phebe,	March 1, 1746-7.
1-345	" Susannah,	Jan. 15, 1750-1.
1-345	" Mary,	Jan. 6, 1753.
1-345	" Elizabeth,	Jan. 6, 1753.
1-346	" Samuel,	April 25, 1755.
1-345	" Elizabeth, of Stephen and Mehitable (also 4-70),	July 7, 1749.
1-345	" Abigail,	Dec. 24, 1751.
1-349	" Stephen,	Nov. 5, 1754.
1-349	" Josiah,	July 20, 1757.
1-349	" James,	Jan. 9, 1760.
1-349	" Hannah,	Nov. 6, 1762.

1-348	WARDWELL Lydia, of Isaac and Sarah,		June 15, 1757.
1-348	"	Sarah,	Dec. 4, 1758.
1-348	'	Jonathan,	May 25, 1760.
1-348	"	Anna,	Aug. 13, 1762.
1-348	"	Willoby,	June 4, 1764.
1-253	"	Allen, of John and Phebe,	March 1, 1765.
1-348	"	Samuel Woodbury, of John, Jr., and Hannah,	Sept. 17, 1776.
1-351	"	Lucretia, of Benjamin and Sarah,	May 30, 1777.
1-351	"	Sarah,	Nov. 11, 1779.
4-246	"	Ellen, of Allen and Abigail,	July 3, 1789.
4-246	"	Ellen,	d. Sept. 2, 1791.
4-246	"	Allen,	July 29, 1791.
		Died July 27, 1821, in a foreign land.	
4-246	"	Eleanor, of Allen and Abigail,	May 7, 1793.
4-246	"	George Smith,	Jan. 21, 1795.
4-246	"	Josiah Smith,	Jan. 18, 1797.
4-246	"	William Taylor,	Jan. 16, 1799.
4-246	"	Nancy Russell,	Sept. 7, 1803.
4-246	"	Mary Smith,	Oct. 11, 1806.
1-353	"	Henry, of Samuel and Lydia,	July 9, 1792.
1-353	"	William Munro, of Samuel, Jr., and Hannah,	Aug. 13, 1811.
4-237	"	Elizabeth, of Benjamin and Elizabeth,	Nov. 6, 1827.
4-230	WARREN Mary Abbey, of Thomas and Martha,		May 29, 1813.
4-230	"	George E.,	Aug. 20, 1818.
4-230	"	Charles D. W.,	Aug. 6, 1823.
1-342	WEAVER Mary, of Thomas and Sary (b. on R. Island),		Feb. 11, 1736-7.
1-342	"	Ruth,	Oct. 9, 1742.
1-343	"	Thomas,	May 3, 1746.
1-343	"	John, of Elisha and Mary,	March 10, 1743-4.
1-343	"	William,	March 15, 1744-5.
1-339	WELCH Samuel, of James and Mercy,		Oct. 15, 1693.
1-339	"	Thomas,	March 1, 1695.
1-339	"	Ebenezer,	Feb. 13, 1697.
1-339	"	John,	April 17, 1699.
4-241	WELSH George, of Stillman and Betsey,		Jan. 8, 1826.
4-241	"	James,	Sept. 24, ——.
4-241	"	Charles,	Sept. 24, ——.
1-345	WEST Oliver, of John and Lydia,		Oct. 28, 1741.
1-345	"	John,	April 16, 1743.
1-345	"	Dorothy,	Sept. 10, 1746.
1-345	"	Lydia,	March 7, 1748-9.
1-345	"	Nathaniel Hix,	Nov. 23, 1751.
1-347	"	Asa,	Oct. 7, 1757.
1-347	"	William,	Aug. 30, 1760.
1-349	"	Prudence,	April 26, 1763.
1-346	"	Nathaniel, of Wm. and Jane,	Jan. 1, 1750-1.
1-346	"	Mary,	Aug. 5, 1755.
1-346	"	Alethea,	Feb. 23, 1758.
1-347	"	William,	July —, 1761.
1-347	"	Thomas,	July —, 1761.
1-349	"	Sarah,	July 28, 1764.
1-348	"	Jonathan,	March 28, 1767.
1-350	"	Ebenezer, of James and Lydia,	Nov. 16, 1771.
1-350	"	Rebecca,	Sept. 3, 1773.
1-352	"	James,	Nov. 15, 1774.
1-351	"	Nancy, of William and Sarah,	Feb. 1, 1785.
1-351	"	Sarah,	April 15, 1787.
1-351	"	Olive,	July 6, 1789.
1-351	"	Ansel,	July 8, 1796.
1-352	"	Jonathan, of Nathaniel and Rebecca,	Aug. 23, 1786.
1-351	"	Royal,	Sept. 27, 1789.
1-351	"	Nathan, of Asa and Phebe,	Sept. 9, 1787.
1-352	"	Gardner,	June 22, 1791.
1-352	"	Nancy,	Aug. 31, 1793.
1-352	"	Stephen,	March 2, 1797.

1-353	WEST	George, of Asa and Phebe,	Sept. 16, 1800.
1-352	"	William, of Thomas and Catherine,	May 8, 1788.
1-352	"	William, of Nathaniel Hix and Nellie,	Feb. 9, 1799.
1-352	"	Rebecca,	April 8, 1801.
1-352	"	Susannah Easterbrooks,	May 11, 1805.
2-1	"	William, Henry, of Benjamin and Anstis,	July 9, 1906.
2-1	"	Maria,	June 20, 1808.
2-1	"	Ann,	Aug. 28, 1811.
2-2	"	William Coomer, of Jonathan and Sally,	Dec. 12, 1808.
2-2	"	Sarah Ann,	Dec. 20, 1810.
2-2	"	Jonathan,	Feb. 2, 1813.
1-353	"	James Gardner, of Joseph and Patience,	Sept. 6, 1809.
2-1	"	Joseph,	Sept. 3, 1812.
4-247	"	Betsey, of Nathan and Hannah,	May 17, 1810.
1-353	"	William Henry, of John and Prudence,	June 14, 1810.
2-1	"	Mary Gardiner,	Oct. 15, 1812.
1-353	"	James, of Royal and Rohy,	June 8, 1811.
2-1	"	Henry Clarke,	Oct. 8, 1813.
1-348	WHEEDEN	Martha, of Amos and Martha,	Oct. 17, 1761.
1-339	WHIPPLE	Job, of John and Lydia of Providence (b. Taunton),	Dec. 25, 1690.
1-349	WHITE	Sarah, of William and Alice,	May 19, 1761.
1-349	"	Mary,	Sept. 1, 1763.
1-349	"	Elizabeth,	July 22, 1766.
1-349	"	Rebecca,	Jan. 9, 1768.
1-349	"	Samuel,	Dec. —, 1771.
1-353	WHITING	Joseph, of Joseph and Tent,	June 19, 1801.
1-353	"	Eliza,	Oct. 16, 1803.
1-353	"	Sophia,	Dec. 25, 1806.
1-353	"	Frederic,	April 6, 1808.
1-353	"	Caroline,	June 29, 1810.
1-353	"	Mary Ann,	June 11, 1813.
1-353	"	Phillip, of Joseph and Mary,	Dec. 13, 1821.
1-342	WIGHT	Anne, of John and Mary,	March 5, 1732-3.
1-342	"	Daniel,	May 3, 1735.
2-2	"	John,	July 15, 1729.
4-43	"	Rev. Henry (b. Medfield, Mass.),	May 26, 1752.
1-351	"	John Burt, of Rev. Henry and Alice,	May 7, 1790.
1-353	"	Henry,	Nov. 5, 1791.
1-351	"	Adeliza,	April 8, 1794.
1-353	"	Alice Burrington, of Rev. Henry and Clarrissa,	Feb. 10, 1800.
1-352	"	Abigail Alden,	Oct. 21, 1802.
1-353	"	Charlotte DeWolf,	Feb. 1, 1805.
1-353	"	Martha Gibbs,	July 25, 1807.
1-337	WILKINS	Samuel, of John and Anstis,	May 31, 1683.
1-337	"	Mehitable,	May 2, 1685.
4-230	WILLISTONE	Ann M., of Masa B. and Ann,	Dec. 2, 1836.
1-337	WILSON	Benjamin, of John and Esther,	June 1, 1689.
1-338	"	Esther,	Aug. 20, 1691.
1-338	"	Mary,	Aug. 17, 1693.
1-340	"	David, of David and Martha,	June 7, 1718.
1-340	"	Margaret,	May 2, 1721.
1-341	"	Catherine,	June 9, 1723.
1-340	"	Rebecca, of James and Mary,	Sept. 15, 1718.
1-343	"	Mary, of Jeremiah and Susannah,	Feb. 13, 1744-5.
1-347	"	Thomas,	Aug. 18, 1747.
1-347	"	William,	Feb. 25, 1750.
1-347	"	James,	June 5, 1752.
1-347	"	Nathaniel,	Jan. 2, 1755.
1-347	"	Sarah,	March 28, 1757.
1-348	"	Samuel,	Oct. 4, 1759.
1-348	"	Elizabeth,	Feb. 11, 1763.
1-348	"	David, of David and Elizabeth,	Sept. 7, 1753.
1-348	"	Ammiel, of David and Bethiah,	June 4, 1763.
1-350	"	Mary,	July 3, 1764.
1-352	"	James, of Samuel and Patience,	May 10, 1790.

2-1	WILSON Samuel, of Samuel and Patience,	July 10, 1797.
2-1	" George, of Nathaniel and Freelove,	Nov. 15, 1800.
4-247	" Dorothea, of James B., and Anne,	Jan. 17, 1810.
4-228	" John S., of Oliver and Sarah S.,	June 4, 1817.
4-236	" George Henry, of George and Mary T.,	Jan. 5, 1835.
4-236	" Joseph A.,	April 18, 1837.
1-337	WOODBURY Samuel, of Benjamin and Mary,	Aug. 30, 1683.
1-337	" Jonathan, of Samuel and Mary,	May 5, 1685.
2-2	" Samuel,	Nov. 5, 1688.
1-338	" Sarah,	Sept. 18, 1690.
1-339	" Nathaniel, of John and Mary,	June 23, 1697.
1-341	" Mary, of Nathaniel and Abigail.	Aug. 1, 1721.
1-341	" Abigail,	June 2, 1723.
1-341	" Priscilla,	May 2, 1725.
1-341	" Jonathan, of Samuel and Margaret,	April 11, 1722.
1-341	" Sarah,	Sept. 16, 1723.
1-341	" Margaret,	Nov. 30, 1724.
1-342	" Samuel,	Nov. 1, 1726.
1-345	" Katherine, of Jonathan, Jr., and Lydia,	Dec. 11, 1752.
1-342	WOODS Christopher, of Paul and Margaret,	Nov. 30, 1734.
2-2	" Ann,	March 12, 1736-7.
1-340	WOOD John, of John and Charity.	Feb. 27, 1716-7.
2-1	WYATT Robert, Nov. 5, 1789, died Oct. 5, 1844.	
2-1	" Lydia (Cummings), his wife, Aug. 12, 1789, died March 7, 1841.	
2-1	" Nancy Perry, of Robert and Lydia,	Aug. 5, 1831.
2-1	" Sarah Jane, (also recorded 4-75),	Jan. 30, 1833.
2-1	" Susan Mendall, of Benjamin and Elizabeth W.,	Oct. 6, 1805.
2-1	" Eliza Bailey,	Nov. 3, 1808.
2-1	" Lemuel,	April 7, 1811.

X Y

2-4	YOUNG Elizabeth, of Isaac and Joyce,	Feb. 23, 1756.
2-4	" George,	May 12, 1759.
2-4	" William,	Sept. 12, 1761.
2-4	" Sarah,	April 8, 1764.
2-4	" Daniel,	April 8, 1764.

Z

2-5	ZOLODE Joseph, of John and Mary,	Nov. 5, 1711.
2-5	" Mary,	April 29, 1715.

(Vit. Rec., Vol. 6.) 8

BRISTOL.

DEATHS.

A

4-56	ABEL Lucy, widow of Preserved, of Seekonk, 82 years, (buried there) March 26, 1840.
3-1	" Abigail, 63 years, Jan. 3, 1786.
2-6	" Absalom, an Indian (at Isaac Anthony at the camp), Dec. —, 1834.
4-21	ADAMS Sarah M., widow of James H., 49 years.
4-31	" Ann Elizabeth, of John, 2 years, 8 months, March 24, 1836.
4-56	" John Henry, 2 years, 7 months, March 18, 1840.
4-56	" Charles Edwin, 14 months, March 30, 1840.
2-6	ADEE Rebecca, of Joseph, aged 27 years, Nov. 21, 1759.
2-7	" Belcher, May 27, 1769.
2-7	" Joseph, 42 years, Aug. —, 1778.
2-7	" Ruth, widow, Oct. —, 1778.
2-7	ADEY Joseph, 65y., Nov. 9, 1763.
2-8	" Mrs. Hannah, 83y, Jan. 16, 1755.
2-6	ADONIS Sarah, of James, Aug. 9, 1696.
2-6	" Elizabeth, March 9, 1709-10.
2-8	AJUBA, mulatto, (at Samuel Purs's), March 24, 1761.
4-160	ALDEN Abner, A. M., 62y., (also 3-25), Aug. 23, 1820.
2-8	ALFREY Godfrey, (in prison), Dec. 13, 1744.
2-6	ALGER John, Jan. —, 1717.
2-6	ALLEN ——, wife of William, Sept. 27, 1734.
2-6	" Elizabeth, of Newport, (at Major Greene's) July 23, 1752.
2-8	" Nathan, apprentice to John Waldron, 21y., May 11, 1764.
2-7	" ——, child of James, b. March 22; d. 23, 1765.
2-7	" James (at sea), Dec. 7, 1769.
2-7	" Sarah, widow, 41 years, Dec. 14, 1772.
2-7	" ——, a young woman of Barrington, R. I. (at Capt. Ingraham's), Nov. 18, 1774..
2-7	" ——, child of Sarah, Feb. 8, 1775.
2 7	" Lydia, of James, April 17, 1776.
3-1	" Sarah, wife of James, July 20, 1785.
3-7	" ——, of James, 3 days, Oct. 5, 1791.
3-12	" Ethan, of Gen. Thomas (lost at sea), Dec. 26, 1796.
3-12	" Joseph, 25 years, Sept. 3, 1797.
2-7	" James, a member of the Town Council, 57 years (in heaving down his vessel for the purpose of graving, the rigging parted, and the mast fell and gave him a mortal wound, after which accident he survived about five days), (also 3-21), Oct. 16, 1811.
2-7	" Charlotte, 26 years, (at John Bullock's, and interred the 7th inst., at Tiverton), May 6, 1812.
2-7	" Mary, widow, 81 years, (also 3-22), Nov. 13, 1814.
3-30	" Samuel, 2d, July 16, 1830.
4-33	" Sarah, widow of James, 73 years, March 31, 1836.
4-40	" Francisco, (born Fayal, W. I.), 23 years, July 25, 1838.
4-68	" George, 66 years, Nov. 22, 1841.
4-80	" Samuel S., 48 years, Nov. 25, 1843.
4-82	" George A., 41 years, July 22, 1844.
4-110	" John Nelson, of Thomas N., 3 years, 8 months, April 7, 1849.
4-112	" Abby Ann, 13 months, April 29, 1849.

4-130	ALLEN Eleanor, widow of William, 76 years, May 7, 1851.
4-132	" Harriet, 56 years, June 14, 1851.
2-6	ALMY ——, child of Indian, Jan. 12, 1743.
2-6	" ——, wife of Jack, March 25, 1744.
4-56	" Amey ——, child of (col.), 3 years, March 26, 1840.
3-4	" Anna, 73 years, Nov. 4, 1788.
3-5	" Anna, 39 years, Oct. 6, 1790.
2-6	ANTHONY ——, child of John, July 8, 1758.
2-6	" ——, wife of John, Aug. 26, 1759.
2-7	" Mrs. Susannah (dau. of William Pearse), 31 years, Aug. 4, 1777.
3-10	" Nancy, of John, 18 years, Sept. 26, 1795.
3-14	" Polly, wife of William, Dec. 19, 1800.
3-26	" Peleg, 87 years, June —, 1822.
4-128	" Charles Waterman, of Moses, 8 months, 11 days, Jan. 28, 1851.
2-8	ANTONIO, an old negro (at the Mount), Jan. 22, 1759.
2-6	AQUAS ——, child of Nab, 1 year, Oct. 24, 1756.
2-6	" Abigail, Feb. 7, 1757.
2-6	ARCHER Sarah, of John and Mehitable, Nov. 30, 1707.
2-6	" John, Feb. 8, 1717.
4-47	ARMSTRONG Whiting (born Cape Elizabeth, Me.), mariner, 22 years, May 11, 1838.
2-8	ARNOLD Nancy, wife of ——, of Cumberland, formerly widow of Nathaniel Liscomb, late of Bristol, died at said Cumberland, but brought to Bristol and interred, April 13, 1815.
4-94	" ——, child of Lyman, Nov. 27, 1846.
4-94	ATTWOOD Betsey (at the Asylum), about 60 years, Nov. 27, 1846.

B

4-82	B——, E——, of J. B., 20 months, Nov. 9, 1844.
2-19	BABBITT Jacob, Sept. 30, 1811.
2-19	" ——, child of Jacob, 5 days, Sept. 16, 1812.
4-88	" Jacob William, of Jacob, Jr., 4 years, Dec. 2, 1845.
4-120	" Jacob, 81 years, March 8, 1850.
4-94	BABCOCK ——, child of Adelaide, 1 year, Aug. 3, 1846.
2-13	BAILEY ——, adopted child of Mr., 9 years, Aug. 10, 1742.
2-20	" Joshua, 82 years, June 5, 1767.
2-17	" Mrs. Mary, 78y., Aug. 6, 1767.
2-17	" Mary, widow of Joshua, 79y., Sept. 23, 1771.
2-12	BAKER ——, child of Amos, June 20, 1736.
2-15	" Capt. Thomas, (born London, Eng.), at Isaac Gorham's, July 18, 1751.
3-31	" Sarah Ann, widow of Nathaniel Greene, 21y., June 5, 1832.
4-80	" Mary, wife of James, 52y., Dec. 24, 1843.
4-124	" Mary C., wife of Benjamin, of Providence, dau. of Jonathan West, 34y., Aug. 22, 1850.
4-49	BALLITT Rosanna (col.), 65y., Sept. 7, 1838.
2-12	BALL Jonathan, at Surinam, June 6, 1737.
2-13	" ——, child of Benjamin, Dec. 20, 1741.
2-13	" ——, wife of Francis, Aug. 17, 1743.
2-14	" ——, child of John, Dec. 13, 1743.
2-14	" Francis, Aug. 26, 1745.
2-17	" ——, child of Benjamin, June 29, 1766.
2-17	" Benjamin, April 23, 1769.
3-18	" Sarah, widow, 86y., Feb. 9, 1807.
4-21	" Phebe, 70y., Dec. 10, 1834.
4-58	" Susannah, 85y., (at the Asylum), May 9, 1840.
4-53	BARKER Mary, widow of Richard, of Newport, 73y., May 18, 1839.
4-74	" George, 64y., Dec. 21, 1842.
4-82	BARNARD Lydia, widow, 52y., June 20, 1844.
4-47	BARNES John, (born Bristol, Me.), 35y., Jan. —, 1835.
2-13	" Stephen, (at Jamaica), Dec. 20, 1743.
2-19	BARNEY ——, child of John, Sept. —, 1814.
3-26	BARRETT William S., 46y., Aug. 9, 1823.

4-118	BARRETT J. Wadsworth, 40y., Dec. 10, 1849.
4-25	BARROWS ——, child of Joseph, 1y., April 9, 1835.
3-9	BARRUS Dr. Isaac, 34y., Nov. 5, 1794.
3-13	BARTON Andrew, drowned April 20, 1798.
4-80	" Samuel, (col.) 82y. (at the Asylum), March 25, 1844.
4-90	" Katy, widow of Samuel, (col.), formerly Katy Mingo, 92y., March 22, 1846.
3-28	BATT Lydia, 64y., Oct. 11, 1826.
4-29	" Capt. Jones, (on passage to West Indies), ——, —, 1835.
2-10	BAYLEY, about 38y., March 4, 1690.
2-13	" an Indian child, at Mr., July 13, 1741.
4-110	" Samuel Z., formerly of Portsmouth, N. H., son of Capt. Samuel S., (at Rio Grande), Dec. 5, 1848.
3-20	BAYLIES Hannah, wife of Dr. Gustavus, July 6, 1811.
2-12	BEARD Nathaniel, Jan. 19, 1734-5.
2-10	BENNETT Richard, July —, 1716.
2-11	" Mrs. ——, July 19, 1730.
4-20	" Capt. Martin (on passage to Europe), Sept. 7, 1835.
4-82	" George Sheldon, of East Greenwich, 29y. (buried there), July 6, 1844.
4-92	" Ferdinand Reginold, of Massadore T., 2m., Aug. 1, 1846.
4-53	BENSON Samuel (at Guadaloupe) 55y., May —, 1839.
2-15	BETTEY, old Indian, Dec. 28, 1755.
2-15	" Old negro woman (at the Mount), May 12, 1758.
4-33	BELLINGTON Abigail, late of Newport, widow of Capt. Elisha, 75y., April 24, 1836.
2-17	BIRDGE Hannah, widow, 71y., Jan. 13, 1769.
2-12	" John, Sept. 5, 1733.
2-10	BISHA James, of Phillip and Mary, Jan. 31, 1720.
2-12	BISHERS ——, child of John, Nov. 24, 1733.
3-35	BISHOP William James of Nathan A., 7m., Oct. 3, 1836.
4-110	" Mary, wife of Nathan A. (dau. of Edward Munro, Jr.,), 38y., Jan. 13, 1849.
4-130	" Sarah Ann, of Nathan A., 18y., March 28, 1851.
2-19	BLACK James, of Tiverton, belonging to Gunboat No. 1, drowned in Bristol Harbor, July 15, 1813
2-11	BLAGROVE ——, negro child of Mr., June 21, 1731.
2-11	" ——, Jan. —, 1733.
2-13	" ——, July, 5, 1742.
2-13	" ——, June 26, 1744.
2-18	" Boson, an old negro of Mr. (100y. by his own account, by others said to be 103y.), Jan. 19, 1772.
2-17	BLAKE ——, child of Ebenezer, 5y., Dec. 8, 1771.
3-7	" Abigail, wife of Ebenezer, 44y., Oct. 25, 1791.
2-19	" Ebenezer, Jr., March 19, 1812.
4-169	" ——, child of Samuel, Jr., March 26, 1820.
4-169	" Allen, of Ebenezer, dec., 18y., July 23, 1820.
3-28	" Ebenezer (born Dorchester, Mass.), 89y., Feb. 28, 1827.
3-29	" Samuel, 52y., July 2, 1828.
3-31	" Esther, widow, 87y., Sept. 2, 1832.
4-25	" Samuel N., formerly of this place, now a resident of Hudson, N. Y., 55y., May 23, 1835.
4-51	" George Henry, of Samuel, 18m., Nov. 1, 1838.
4-53	" Samuel, 44y., June 3, 1839.
4-74	" Susan, wife of William M., 42y., Oct. 5, 1842.
4-78	" Samuel, 48y., Sept. 26, 1843.
2-19	BLIVEN Isaac R., from on board the privateer schooner Hiram, which blew up at sea Aug. 10, 1812, caused by magazine taking fire. On board the schooner were 33 men, all lost but five, who were four and one-half days at sea.
4-41	BLY Andrew Mason, of William M., 5y., April 12, 1837.
4-78	" Bradford Durfee, 2y. 11m., Nov. 5, 1843.
4-80	" Eliza Covel, 7m., Dec. 31, 1843.
4-118	" William, of Capt. Isaac, of New Bedford (at San Francisco, Cal.), Nov. 2, 1849.

4-51	BONNEY William, of Martin D., 1y. 10m., Sept. 27, 1838.
2-19	BOOTH ——, child of Joseph, July 31, 1814.
4-62	" Joseph, 62y., Nov. 9, 1840.
2-15	BORDEN ——, child of Benjamin, Aug. 12, 1754.
2-19	" Sybel, widow, 74y., (carried to Portsmouth and there interred), July 29, 1815.
3-32	" Elizabeth, Dec. 29, 1833.
4-15	" Henry, formerly of Portsmouth, 67y., Jan. 6, 1834.
4-25	" Dorothy, of Parker, 65y., May 12, 1835.
4-51	" Sarah, widow of Henry, 71y., Nov. 9, 1838.
4-52	" Julianna, of Isaac, 18y., Dec. 25, 1838.
4-70	" Elizabeth, 14y., April 20, 1842.
4-72	" Parker, 78y., Sept. 19, 1842.
2-13	BOSTON ——, a negro (drowned), Dec. 20, 1739.
2-10	BOSWORTH Dea. Nathaniel, Aug. 31, 1690.
2-11	" Elizabeth, wife of John, Jr., Nov. 27, 1716.
2-11	" Bellamy, March 16, 1717.
2-11	" Jerome, March 19, 1717.
2-11	" Judeth, wife of Benjamin, Feb 2, 1725-6.
2-11	" Lydia, wife of Nathaniel, (suddenly), May 11, ——.
2-11	" Hannah, of Benjamin and Jemima, Dec. 21, 1729.
2-10	" Jonathan, of Benjamin and Judeth, Oct. 4, 1720.
2-12	" Sarah, widow, (at Barrington, but buried in this town), 79y., April 6, 1735.
2-12	" Mary, (school dame), 78y., April 21, 1735.
2-12	" ——, negro man of Nathaniel, Aug. 1, 1735.
2-12	" ——, negro child of John, May 14, 1736.
2-12	" ——, son of Capt. ——, July 23, 1736.
2-12	" ——, child of Capt. ——, Oct. 10, 1738.
2-12	" ——, Indian woman of John, Jan. 5, 1738.
2-13	" Lydia, 9y., Dec. 9, 1738.
2-13	" a stranger at Mr. ——, May 13, 1739.
2-13	" Mrs. Mary, 73y., April 20, 1740.
2-13	" Benjamin, Oct. 13, 1740.
2-13	" Ebenezer, (at Surinam), Dec. 26, 1741.
2-13	" Edward, Feb. 22, 1743.
2-13	" ——, negro man of John, April 11, 1743.
2-13	" ——, child of Mrs., June 16, 1743.
2-14	" Capt. Nathaniel (at Attleboro), Aug. 17, 1745.
2-14	" Ann, of Capt. Nathaniel, Aug. 21, 1745.
2-14	" Indian child, of John, March 4, 1746.
2-14	" Ceaser servant of John (at sea), Dec. 31, 1746.
2-14	" Mulatto girl, of John, Feb. 19, 1747.
2-14	" ——, wife of John, Aug. 20, 1747.
2-14	" Maria, servant of Mr. ——, Dec. —, 1748.
2-14	" Negro girl, of John, Jan. 10, 1748.
2-14	" Indian child, Jan. 30, 1749.
1-14	" Child, of James, Sept. 26, 1749.
2-14	" Child, of William, Dec. 29, 1749.
2-14	" ——, widow of Edward, Jan. 15, 1750.
2-14	" Dr. Nathaniel (at Hispaniola), April 10, 1750.
2-15	" Negro child, of John, June 14, 1750.
2-15	" Grandchild, May 19, 1751.
2-15	" Benjamin, of Ashford, Aug. 8, 1753.
2-15	" John, Oct. 24, 1754.
2-15	" A stranger, at John, June 22, 1755.
2-15	" Child of John, Jan. 16, 1755.
2-15	" Indian boy, of John, May 14, 1755.
2-20	" Mrs. Elizabeth, Dec. 7, 1751.
2-16	" Ruth, widow, June 19, 1758.
2-16	" Esther, wife of Bellamy, 42y., July 7, 1758.
2-16	" ——, child of Henry, July 24, 1758.
2-16	" Samuel, 39y., Oct. 8, 1761.
2-16	" Nathaniel, of Bellamy, 12y., Dec. 15, 1763.
2-17	" Susannah, wife of Jeremiah, 70y., Jan. 26, 1768.

2-17	BOSWORTH	Nathaniel, 78y., Jan. 17, 1771.
2-17	"	Sarah, widow of Nathaniel, 89y., Oct. 11, 1771.
2-18	"	Child of Benjamin, Oct. 17, 1773.
2-18	"	Prince, servant of Benjamin, May 13, 1774.
2-18	"	Jonathan, 18y., Nov. 10, 1774.
2-18	"	Jeremiah, about 80y., Sept. 26, 1777.
2-18	"	—, child of Benjamin, Feb. 10, 1775.
3-2	"	Bellamy, 70y., Dec. 12, 1786.
3-4	"	Sarah, of Benjamin, 5y., June 26, 1789.
3-5	"	Daniel, Sept. 25, 1790.
3-5	"	—, child of Benjamin 1st, 4w., Oct. 13, 1790.
3-8	"	Simeon Potter, of Benjamin 2d, Sept. 11, 1792.
3-8	"	Mary, wife of William 1st, 68y., July 30, 1793.
3-9	"	Charles, of Benjamin 2d, 20y., (at Havana, W. I.), Oct. —. 1794.
3-10	"	Timothy, of William, Jr., Nov. 30, 1794.
2-10	"	Samuel, of Samuel and Tabitha, Oct. 8, 1795.
3-10	"	Samuel, of Samuel, 10y., Sept. 20, 1795.
3-11	"	James, 72y., Dec. 31, 1795.
3-14	"	Hannah, wife of Major Benjamin, 46y., Nov. 9, 1800.
3-17	"	Mary, widow, 77y., Sept. 6, 1804.
3-17	"	William, of Timothy, 17y., (at Havana, W. I.), Nov. 24, 1804.
3-17	"	Elizabeth, 72y., March 31, 1806.
3-18	"	William, (lost at sea), Nov. —, 1806.
3-18	"	Mary, widow, 76y., Feb. 24, 1807.
3-19	"	William, 86y., Nov. 15, 1808.
2-116	"	Mrs. Betsey, (dau. of Capt. Thomas Swan), — —, 1811.
3-22	"	Capt. Peleg, 27y., (also 2-18), Dec. 21, 1814.
2-18	"	Samuel, died in the Army, — —, 1814.
3-23	"	Henry, (drowned in mill pond in a gale), Sept. 23, 1815.
3-24	"	Elizabeth, wife of William, 58y., May 6, 1817.
3-24	"	Jonathan, 30y., Sept. 8, 1818.
3-27	"	Benjamin, Esq., 72y., July 1, 1825.
3-27	"	Benjamin. "of 60 acres," 79y., Nov. 3, 1825.
3-28	"	Samuel, Esq., 71y., Sept. 6, 1826.
3-30	"	William, 80y., Jan. 9, 1830.
4-37	"	Sarah, widow of Benjamin, 80y., Nov. 14, 1836.
4-51	"	Sarah E., of Jeremiah, 1y. 3m., Sept. 19, 1838.
4-60	"	George A., 1y. 8m., Oct. 9, 1840.
4-68	"	Tabitha, widow of Samuel, 84y., Jan. 8, 1842.
4-118	"	Sarah, widow of Benjamin, 78y., (at Buffalo, N. Y.), Dec. 25, 1849.
2-14	BOURNE	—, negro child, Dr., July 26, 1744.
2-14	"	—, May 13, 1745.
2-14	"	—, Nov. 11, 1747.
2-15	"	Wife of Dr., Feb. 20, 1751.
2-15	"	Dr. Aaron, May 2, 1752.
2-16	"	—, child of Aaron, 1 1-2y., June 26, 1758.
2-16	"	Aaron (at Berbeccia), March 15, 1762.
2-28	"	Ceaser, servant of Mr. (at the Lakes), — —, 1758.
2-18	"	—, child of Shearjashub, Oct. 2, 1773.
2-18	"	—, child of Shearjashub, Jr., June 13, 1776.
2-18	"	Dinah, servant of Mr., Dec. —, 1779.
2-43	"	Frank, servant of Mr., Feb. 16, 1780.
3-1	"	Samuel Irving, of Aaron, 6w., March 26, 1786.
3-2	"	Aaron, of Aaron, 13y., Oct. 13, 1786.
3-2	"	Zarid, natural son of widow Ruth, Dec. 13, 1786.
3-5	"	child of Aaron, 1w., Oct. —, 1790.
3-8	"	Ruth, wife of Shearjashub, 42y., Jan. 28, 1793.
3-8	"	Shearjashub, of Shearjashub, 17y., (at Guadaloupe, W. I.), Oct. 21, 1793.
3-11	"	Ruth, widow, 76y., Oct. 31, 1796.
3-12	"	Ruth, wife of Aaron, 36y., Jan. 23, 1797.
3-19	"	Hon. Benjamin, Esq., 53y., Sept. 17, 1808.
2-18	"	Hope, widow of Benjamin, — —, 1811.
3-22	"	Allen, Esq., 35y., (also 2-19), Dec. 8, 1814.
3-24	"	Mary, widow (at Providence), Oct. 12, 1818.

3-26	BOURNE Shearjashub, 70y., Nov. 24, 1821.	
3-26	"	John Waldron, 46y., Aug. 8, 1823.
3-29	"	Ruth, of Allen, 22y., Aug. 3, 1829.
4-15	"	Almira, wife of Francis (dau. of Ephraim Gifford), 27y., Feb. 11, 1834.
4-47	"	Almira, of Francis, 47y., March 15, 1838.
4-84	"	Rachel, widow of Shearjashub, 76y., Nov. 21, 1844.
4-116	"	Rachel, widow of Shearjashub, Sept. 21, 1849.
2-15	BRADFORD ——, child of Daniel, June 14, 1750.	
2-16	"	Levi, 19y., Nov. 7, 1756.
2-16	"	Capt. Gersham, 66y., April 4, 1757.
2-16	"	——, negro child of do., Dec. 30, 1761.
2-16	"	——, child of do., 10m., Sept. 5, 1763.
2-16	"	——, child of Elijah, Dec. —, 1763.
2-16	"	——, child of do., —— —, 1764.
2-16	"	——, son of do., 8y., Oct. 30, 1765.
2-17	"	——, negro child of do., Aug. 16, 1766.
2-10	"	John, of Dr. William and Mary, Oct. 30, 1765.
2-17	"	Mrs. Mary, April 16, 1772.
2-18	"	——, negro child of do., ——. 13, 1773.
2-18	"	Mrs. Mary, 44y., Oct. 3, 1775.
2-18	"	——, son of Capt. Job, 12y., March 12, 1775.
2-18	"	Mrs. Priscilla, 85y., Sept. 12, 1778.
3-8	BRADFORD Le Baron, 40y., Sept. 25, 1793.	
3-19	"	Hon. William, Esq., 79y., July 6, 1808.
3-20	"	Daniel, Esq., 89y., July 22, 1810.
3-21	"	Major William, 59y. (also 2-19), Oct. 29, 1811.
3-21	"	Capt. Leonard, Jr., 32y., (also 2-19), July 27, 1812.
3-22	"	Francis (at sea with schooner O. H. Perry), Dec. —, 1814.
3-23	"	Susanna, widow, 75y., Dec. 31, 1815.
3-25	"	Daniel, Esq. 42y., (also 4-168), Feb. 27, 1821.
3-32	"	John, 67y., July 7, 1833.
4-70	"	Henry, Jr., 22y., July 6, 1842.
4-72	"	Jemima, widow of John, Sept. 5, 1842.
4-98	"	Seraphina, of Hasey, 28y., July 12, 1847.
4-100	"	Robert Nimme, of Durfee T., Dec. 24, 1847.
4-114	"	Hersey, 79y. (at Middletown), Sept. 1, 1849.
4-124	"	Ann P., of Capt. Samuel, 35y., July 6, 1850.
4-130	"	Capt. William, 70y., April 23, 1851.
2-11	BRAGG ——, child of Henry, April 9, 1730.	
2-11	"	——, child of Nicholas, Feb. 6, 1731.
2-11	"	Capt. Nicholas (at Surinam), Feb. 8, 1732.
2-12	"	——, negro woman, of ——, Nov. —, 1734.
2-12	"	——, child of Mr. ——, May 19, 1735.
2-13	"	Mary, June 26, 1739.
2-13	"	Mrs. Elizabeth, Sept. 9, 1741.
2-14	"	——, Indian boy, of John, April 11, 1744.
2-14	"	——, child, of Mrs. Henry, Nov. 23, 1743.
2-14	"	——, negro child, of Mr. ——, June —, 1750.
2-12	"	Capt. John (at St. Estatious), April 18, 1746.
2-15	"	Samuel (at Surinam), Oct. 15, 1755.
2-16	"	William, 77y., Feb. 21, 1758.
2-16	"	Sarah, April 22, 1764.
2-17	"	Henry, about 90y., Jan. 23, 1768.
2-10	BRENTON Hannah, wife of William, 36 or 37y., July 17, 1695.	
2-10	"	Priscilla, wife of Major Ebenezer, May 14, buried 16th, 1705.
4-168	"	Robert (sailor of New York), 48y., March 2, 1821.
3-17	BREWSTER Seabury, Nov. 24, 1804.	
2-19	BRIGGS ——, widow (at Benjamin Wardwell's), —— —, 1815.	
3-23	"	Ruth, widow, 90y., Feb. 5, 1815.
4-1	"	Mary, wife of Dr. Samuel W. (dau. of Nicholas Peck), 47y., July 9, 1834.
4-56	"	Dr. Lemuel W., 54y., March 8, 1840.
4-62	"	Isadore, of Dr. Lemuel W., 2y. 10m., Dec. 10, 1840.
2-13	BRISTOL, a negro (drowned), Dec. 20, 1739.	

2-13 BRISTOW, Mrs. ——, April 3, 1740.
3-6   BROWNELL Capt. Thomas (at Cape Francis), 31y., Jan. 26, 1791.
3-7   "   Martha, of late Capt. Thomas, 19m., Sept. 13, 1791.
3-24 "   Philadelphia, widow, 57y., Sept. 1, 1817.
4-80 "   Adelaide, wife of Jonathan, 34y., Jan. 15, 1844.
4-104 "   Rachel Frances, of Beriah, 1y. 11m., Aug. 8, 1848.
4-114 "   Geraldine Gardner, 18y., Aug. 27, 1849.
2-19 BROWNINGSON, Francisco, a child of, Sept. 18, 1813.
2-19 BROWNSON, child of Francis, Aug. 19, 1875.
2-10 BROWN William, of William, buried, Oct. 26, 1683.
2-10 "   William (burial from Mr. Jabez Howland's), Dec. 3, 1683.
2-10 "   Bethia, Feb. ——, 1689.
3-9   "   ——, child of James, 18m., Sept. ——, 1794.
3-16 "   John, 56y., March 24, 1804.
3-19 "   Elizabeth, wife of William, 19y., Jan. 6, 1809.
2-19 "   Betsey, wife of Obadiah D., April 17, 1815.
3-20 "   Hope, widow, 54y., Aug. 7, 1811.
4-169 "   Charles (col.), 55y., Oct. 12, 1820.
4-15 "   Sylvester, of Reuben, 20y., Jan. 24, 1834.
3-35 "   Rev. Palmer (at Woonsocket), 50y., Sept. 19, 1836.
4-45 "   Charles (col.), 13y., Aug. 11, 1837.
4-58 "   Abby, wife of Thomas, dau. of Stephen Talby (at New Bedford),
             June 29, 1840.
4-70 "   Sarah Ann., of James P., 8m., March 27, 1842.
4-80 "   Georgiana, of George, 10m., April 10, 1844.
4-82 "   Mary, widow of James, 90y., Sept. 13, 1844.
4-96 "   Nancy Titus, wife of Reuben, 70y., Jan. 15, 1847.
4-112 "   Joseph, 72y., May 23, 1849.
2-11 BOWERMAN Samuel, Dec. 29, 1729.
2-15 BOWEN ——, wife of Amos, Dec. 6, 1750.
2-15 "   —— (a child), at Newby Coggeshall, Aug. 12, 1754.
4-45 "   Mrs. Hannah, widow of Ephraim, of Rehoboth, 78y., Aug. 25,
             1837.
4-54 "   Aaron, 84y. (Revolutionary pensioner), June 27, 1839.
4-62 "   child of James, 6w., Oct. 11, 1840.
4-62 "   Hannah, 38y., Oct. 28, 1840.
4-94 "   Mary, widow of Martin, both of Rehoboth, 76y., Nov. 14, 1846.
4-104 "   Paul, 64y., Aug. 7, 1848.
4-23 BOWLER Joseph J. (at sea), 28y., Sept. ——, 1834.
4-39 "   Elizabeth, of John, 1y. 10m., Jan. 17, 1837.
4-60 "   Mary Ann, of Joseph J., deceased, 12y., Sept. 2, 1840.
4-66 "   James J., 27y., Sept. 9, 1841.
2-16 BULLOCK, ——, wife of Lennox, 28y., April 25, 1774.
2-18 "   ——, child of Lennox, 2y., Sept. 3, 1773.
2-18 "   ——,   June 20, 1774.
2-18 "   ——,   Aug. 12, 1775.
2-18 "   Lennox (at Rehoboth),   Dec 21, 1779.
2-20 "   Benjamin Smith, of Nathaniel and Ruth (also 4-246), Nov. 10, 18—.
3-27 "   Coomer, 63y., Oct. 4, 1823.
3-27 "   Mary, wife of Simeon, 72y., Feb. 20, 1824.
3-30 "   Ruth, wife of Nathaniel, 35y., Nov. 11, 1829.
4-17 "   child of Simeon, 1 day, March 24, 1834.
4-23 "   Lenox, 40y., March 1, 1835.
4-51 "   Simeon (a Revolutionary pensioner), 84y., Nov. 9, 1838.
4-84 "   Eliza, of Ebenezer W., 17y., Nov. 27, 1844.
4-88 "   Joseph, 79y., Aug. 30. 1845.
4-104 "   Rebecca, widow of Coomer, 77y. (also 4-110), May 23, 1848.
4-110 "   Sarah, of David, 18y., Jan. 9, 1849.
4-114 "   Charles Russell, of J. Russell, and Susan Amelia (also 4-223), 1-6-23,
             Sept. 1, 1849.
4-223 "   Susan Amelia, wife of J. Russell, Oct. 7, 1866.
4-122 "   David, 59y., April 23, 1850.
4-74 BUNN Maria, of Nathan M., 6w., March 23, 1843.
2-130 BURDICK Mrs. Ann, formerly of South Kingstown, 93y., March 9, 1851.
4-23 BURGESS Joseph M. Blake, of John (strangled), 1y 8m., Feb. 26, 1835.

4-49	BURGESS James C. H., of John, 18m., Aug. 21, 1838.	
4-53	" Stephen (a Revolutionary pensioner), 86y. (Interred at Middleboro, Mass.), April 14, 1839.	
4-74	" John, 49y., Oct. 24, 1842.	
4-106	" William Frederick, of Frederick A., 1y. 4m., Oct. 5, 1848.	
4-106	" Ruth, wife of James W., 54y., Sept. 28, 1848.	
4-116	" James W., 50y., Nov. 2, 1849.	
4-23	BURR Nancy, 41y., Jan. 27, 1835.	
4-66	" Mary E., wife of Gersham, eldest dau. of Benjamin Norris (at Ottawa, La Salle Co., Ill.), Aug. 20, 1841.	
2-10	BURTON Abigail, wife of Stephen, buried March 30, 1684.	
2-10	" Stephen, July 22, 1693.	
2-13	" Mary, Oct. 31, 1740.	
2-15	BURT, ——, negro child of Mr ——, May 19, 1751.	
2-15	" ——,	Sept. 30, 1753.
2-15	" ——,	May 26, 1754.
2-17	" ——,	July 14, 1766.
2-17	" Mrs. Abigail, 50y., March 13, 1768.	
2-17	" Dide, servant of Mr. ——, 11y., Dec. 29, 1768.	
2-17	" Hannah,	Feb. 6, 1769.
2-17	" Phillis,	April 28, 1769.
2-17	" Judith,	April 28, 1769.
2-17	" ——, negro child of ——,	June 11, 1769.
2-17	" Judee, servant of ——,	April 22, 1770.
2-17	" Prince,	May 9, 1770.
2-18	" Rev. John, 59y., Oct. 7, 1775.	
2-18	" Prince, servant of Mrs. ——, at Dighton,	April —, 1776.
3-2	" Philip, negro servant of John Waldron, Jr., 18y., Nov. 11, 1786.	
3-7	" Cato Russell, of Scipio (col.) 12y.,	Aug. 31, 1791.
3-7	" Abram, 2w.,	Sept. 21, 1792.
3-8	" Sarah, 9w.,	May 4, 1793.
3-17	" Ann, widow, 74y., May 27, 1806.	
2-11	BUSHEE ——, child of Richard, Jan. —, 1730.	
2-12	" ——, child of Mary, Jan. 18, 1734-5.	
2-15	" ——, dau. of John, 18y., May 18, 1754.	
2-15	" Phillip, 16y.,	Oct. 30, 1756.
2-11	BUSH Richard, Sept. 27, 1732.	
2-13	" Mary, May 7, 1743.	
3-12	" Jane, widow, 80y., Jan. 12, 1797.	
4-104	" Col. Arnold H., 52y., May 25, 1848.	
4-25	BUTHFORD George, 47y., April 12, 1835.	
4-25	BUTTS John, of Samuel, 43y., (a man but little known to fame, being a cripple from his birth), Jan. 6, 1834.	
4-33	" Coggeshall, a Revolutionary prisoner, formerly of Newport, 86y., March 27, 1836.	
4-45	" Deborah, wife of Samuel, 76y., Oct. 22, 1837.	

C

4-70	CARD ——, child of William H., 2y., April 1, 1842.	
4-126	" Matilda, wife of James, 37y., Sept. 16, 1850.	
2-24	CARPENTER Joseph, 19y., (at Surinam), Feb. 4, 1745.	
2-25	" Sarah, Feb. 22, 1748.	
3-17	" Mrs. Hannah, 29y., June 30, 1805.	
2-24	CARR ——, wife of Robert, Sept. 15, 1741.	
4-88	CASHMAN Sylvia, wife of Jacob, 68y., Oct. 14, 1845.	
4-112	" Jacob, formerly of Middleboro, Mass., 78y., May 16, 1849.	
4-25	CASS John (col.), 92y., July 30, 1835.	
2-28	CARTER Alfred, of Henry, Sept. 5, 1812.	
2-28	" ——, child of Benjamin, April 14, 1814.	
1-161	CARY John, of John and Abigail, buried, Dec. 29, 1671.	
2-22	" John, Jr., of Newport, (at his father's house in Bristol), 37y., April 25, 1711.	
2-22	" Nathaniel, of Benjamin and Susannah, 1m.,	Dec. 2, 1711.

2-22	CARY David, of Benjamin and Susannah,	—— —, 1718.	
2-22	" Dea. John, July 14, 1721.		
2-22	" Joseph, of Josiah, Nov. 9, 1729.		
2-23	" ——, child of David, Aug. 6, 1733.		
2-23	" Benjamin,	Jan. 20, 1734-5.	
2-23	" Seth, of Benjamin and Susannah, March 10, 1734-5.		
2-23	" Joseph,	May 10, 1736.	
2-23	" Abigail,	May 22, 1736.	
2-23	" Lydia,	May 27, 1736.	
2-23	" John,	May 29, 1736.	
2-23	" Mehitable,	June 4, 1736.	
2-23	" Bethiah,	June 7, 1736.	
2-23	" Thomas, of David and Mary, June —, 1735.		
2-24	" Allen (died at sea on board schooner Ann on her passage home from Antiguia), —— —, ——.		
2-24	" Mrs. Ruth, July 3, 1737.		
2-24	" ——, child of Susannah, March 9, 1735.		
2-24	" ——, child of Benjamin, Jan. 5, 1738.		
2-24	" Josiah, of Nathaniel, June 26, 1739.		
2-24	" ——, child of Allen, June 26, 1739.		
2-24	" Nathaniel, Dec. 11, 1739.		
2-30	" David, Nov. —, 1746.		
2-26	" Indian woman, servant of Mrs. ——, 29y., Aug. 12, 1753.		
2-26	" Benjamin, Oct. 7, 1753.		
2-20	" Ben, formerly servant of Dea. Cary, April 7, 1762.		
2-29	" Mrs. Susannah, 77y., Aug. 29, 1764.		
2-26	" Elizabeth, widow of Col. Nathaniel, Sept. 18, 1769.		
2 80	" Jethro, formerly servant of Dea. Cary, about 80y., April 10, 1774.		
2-28	" Cudjo, servant of Col. Cary, April —, 1779.		
3-6	" ——, negro servant of late Nathaniel, 73y., July 7, 1791.		
2-29	" Henry, of David and Elizabeth (in Vermont), 90y., ——, 1801.		
4-15	" Ann, wife of Stephen, dau. of Scipio Burt, dec. (col.), 27y., Jan. 3, 1834.		
2-27	CATO ——, child of ——, 5m., July 24, 1770.		
2-24	CEAZER (Mrs. Waldron's servant), Nov. 2, 1744.		
2-22	CHADWELL Moses, buried April 27, 1684.		
3-15	CHAFFEE Barney (on ship Hope at Batavia), Dec. —, 1801.		
2-28	" Mrs. ——, Oct. 22, 1811.		
4-15	" Lucinda, of Stephen, 20y., Jan. 26, 1834.		
4-106	" Harriet M., of George T. B., 1y. 3m., Oct. 3, 1848.		
4-114	" Montemon Le Baron, of Thomas, 1m., July 24, 1849.		
4-132	" Cyrel B., of Stephen, 21y., July 18, 1851.		
2-30	CHAMBERLAIN Mrs. ——, Feb. 22, 1737.		
2-25	" Ebenezer (at Cape Breton), Dec. 31, 1746.		
2-26	CHAMPLAIN ——, child of Thomas, —— —, 1761.		
2-26	" wife of Thomas, Sept. 14, 1778.		
4-17	CHADWICK Mary Elizabeth, of Nathaniel, 19 days, June 11, 1834.		
4-29	" ——, child of Nathaniel (at Providence, 4w., June 1, 1835.		
3-10	CHAMPLAIN Delight, wife of Jeffry Hazard, 18y., Oct. 11, 1795.		
3-17	" Capt. John, 72, Feb. 16, 1805.		
2-24	CHANDLER Devonshire, servant, of Mrs. ——, May 22, 1740.		
2-24	" Madame Mary, March 9, 1745.		
2-28	CHASE Isaac (an apprentice to James Dimon, at the Camp), —— —, 1760.		
3-10	" Perry, 22y. (at Gombia river), Sept. —, 1795.		
3-21	" Nancy, wife of Barney, 24y., (also 2-28), July 14, 1812.		
2-28	" ——, child of Barney, Sept. 6, 1812.		
4-45	" Rebecca, wife of Thorndike, 28y., Aug. 17, 1837.		
4-84	" Lydia, widow of Levi, Jr., 28y., Jan. 27, 1845.		
4-92	" Mary Louise, of Robinson, Aug. 1, 1846.		
4-98	" Ellen M., of Joseph E., 9y. 9m., July 3, 1847.		
4-98	" Frank Judson, of Joseph E., 2y., Sept. 2, 1847.		
4-128	" Thorndike, 40y., Nov. 26, 1850.		
4-29	CHILD ——, child of Nathan, 20m., Dec. 11, 1835.		
4-31	" Sarah, wife of Nathan, of Warren, 37y., Jan. 8, 1836.		

2-26	CHRISTOPHER ——, child of William, June 13, 1766.		
2-27	" Eliza,	Sept. 15, 1773.	
2-27	" ——,	—— 23, 1775.	
2-27	" Billy,	Dec. 9, 1775.	
3-26	CHURCHILL Ann, widow, 77y., July 14, 1822.		
2-22	CHURCH ——, negro child of Col. ——, Aug. 23, 1730.		
2-23	" Izrael, 28y., Aug. 29, 1735..		
2-23	" Nathaniel, of Izrael and Abigail,	July 28, 1738.	
2-23	" Abigail,	Aug. 8, 1737.	
2-24	" Constant, 32y., May 8, 1740.		
2-25	" Col. Charles, 64y., Dec. 31, 1746.		
3-25	" ——, child of Thomas, April 26, 1747.		
2-24	" ——, son of widow, Nov. 20, 1740.		
2-24	" ——, child of Nathaniel, April 7, 1742.		
2-24	" Nathaniel, 27y., Aug. 26, 1744.		
2-25	" ——, child of widow Ruth, Feb. 27, 1745.		
2-25	" Constant (Mr. Bailey's apprentice), killed on privateer, Aug. 21, 1745.		
2-25	" Rina, servant of Mrs., Aug. 1, 1747.		
2-25	" ——, child of Thomas, May 16, 1748.		
2-25	" ——, child of Thomas, March 7, 1749.		
2-25	" ——, servant of Mrs., Jan. 11, 1750.		
2-26	" Mrs. Hannah, Oct. 16, 1755.		
2-26	" ——, child of Thomas, —— —, 1762.		
2-27	" Charles, 33y., Nov. 14, 1766.		
2-27	" ——, negro child of Thomas, April —. 1769.		
2-27	" Elizabeth, wife of Thomas, 42y., Jan. 27, 1770.		
2-27	" Samuel, of Samuel (at sea), 20y., ——. —, 1776.		
2-27	" Benjamin, of Samuel (at New London), 18y., ——. —, 1776.		
2-29	" Jack, servant of Charles, Mar. 6, 1763.		
2-29	" Alice, of Capt. Thomas and Sarah, 69y., July 10, 1775.		
3-1	" Nathaniel, of Nathaniel, 6y., Oct. 25, 1785.		
3-2	" Hezekiah, of Samuel, 20y., Sept. 24, 1786.		
3-9	" Samuel, Esq., 64y., Feb. 5, 1794.		
3-9	" Col. Thomas, 72y., April 22, 1794.		
3-12	" Ann, widow, 66y., July 13, 1797.		
3-13	" William, 22y., Nov. —, 1798.		
3-16	" Hannah, 60y., Jan. 25, 1803.		
2-28	" ——, child of Nathaniel, Sept. 12, 1812.		
3-22	" Capt. William (drowned in Providence river), Oct. 12, 1812.		
2-28	" He came ashore at Warwick Neck Oct. 14; buried at Bristol Nov. 22, 1812.		
2-28	" Martha, wife of Edward, April 8, 1813.		
3-26	" Col. Peter, 84y., Oct. 21, 1821.		
3-26	" Nathaniel (at the asylum), 72y., Jan. 23, 1823.		
3-29	" Hannah, widow, 80y., Jan, 6, 1828.		
3-31	" Albert, of Peter, dec., 22y., May 19, 1831.		
3-32	" Capt, Edward, 66y., July —, 1833.		
4-35	" Thomas, of Samuel, M. (at Taunton, Mass.), 1y. 8m., Aug. 21, 1836.		
4-37	" Sarah Ann, of Nathaniel, Jr., 1y. 2m., Oct. 18, 1836.		
4-37	" Charles Collins,	20y., Nov. 17, 1836.	
4-41	" Charlotte, of Col. Peter, dec., 69y., June 29, 1837.		
4-51	" Thomas, Jr., 39y., Oct. 20, 1838.		
4-55	" Charlotte, of George, 11y., Dec. 8, 1839.		
4-56	" Emma, of Stephen T., 1y., Feb. 25, 1840.		
4-68	" Matilda, widow, of Benjamin, 41y., Nov. 9, 1841.		
4-68	" Peter, of Nathaniel, 28y., Dec. 20, 1841.		
4-68	" Ann, wife of Col. Peter, 51y., Jan. 20, 1842.		
4-72	" Edward Payson, of William H., 2y., Aug. 17, 1842.		
4-76	" Nathaniel, 76y., April 16, 1843.		
4-76	" Thomas, 83y., May 16, 1843.		
4-92	" Ann Frances, of Col. Peter, 16y., May 8, 1846.		
4-98	" Mary, widow of George, 75y. (at Port Henry, Essex Co., N. Y.), Aug. 4, 1847.		

4-112	CHURCH Eveline, of Samuel, Esq., 2y. 2m., June 22, 1849.	
4-132	" Eleanor B., 20y., June 27, 1851.	
2-15	CLARKE John, 28y., May 9, 1801.	
3-24	" Lemuel, 80y., May 1, 1817.	
3-26	" Elizabeth, widow, 77y., April 29, 1823.	
4-112	" Amey, of Paine (col.), 72y., June 25, 1849.	
2-25	" ——, wife of Samuel, Aug. 23, 1748.	
2-28	" Samuel, 60y., Jan. 30, 1759.	
2-28	" Abigail, wife of Weston, June 13, 1813.	
2-28	" ——, child of Prince (col), May —, 1814.	
2-28	" James (col.), at Samuel Clarke's, 13y., June 1, 1814.	
2-29	" Charles (drowned on passage from New York from off schooner O. H. Perry, which foundered off Fishers Island Race, Sept. 25, 1814, on board of which were 7 persons, two of which come ashore at Montauk Point).	
2-29	" Dorcas, child of, Oct. 1, 1814.	
4-128	CLINTON John A., formerly of Newport, 21y., at Honolulu, S. I., Oct. 14, 1850.	
2-22	COBBOTT Thomas, of Samuel and Sarah, Dec. 2, 1695.	
2-25	COCKRAN ——, wife of John (in the West Indies), Sept. 26, 1749.	
2-25	" John, of John, Sept. 4, 1750.	
2-26	" John (at Martinique), 18y., Oct. 9, 1759.	
4-104	CODDINGTON Eliza Jane, of William, 1y., Aug. 1, 1848.	
2-25	COGGESHALL ——, dau. of William, 18y., Feb. 6, 1749.	
2-28	" William (found dead), 77y., Nov. 2, 1752.	
2-28	" ——, child of George, Dec. 17, 1758.	
2-28	" Job, 28y., May 13, 1759.	
2-26	" March, servant of George, —— —, 1762.	
2-26	" George, Feb. 16, 1766.	
2-27	" John, 19y., Oct. 25, 1768.	
2-29	" Elizabeth, of Newby and Mary, Aug. 19, 1769.	
2-27	" ——, child,	Nov. 16, 1773.
2-27	" ——, negro child of do., —— —, ——.	
2-27	" ——, wife of William, Nov. 12, 1772.	
2-8	" Adam, (negro servant) of Newby, (drowned) Aug. 30, ——.	
3-1	" Sarah D., of George, Feb. 10, 1785.	
2-29	" ——, wife of George, 32y., June 9, 1785.	
3-2	" Elizabeth,	Aug. 30, 1786.
3-1	" Sarah, wife of George, June 9, 1785.	
3-3	" Elizabeth, of William, 2d, 5y., Feb. 9, 1787.	
3-3	" Margaret,	12y., March 14, 1787.
3-4	" Nicholas, 20y., Aug. 13, 1788.	
3-4	" Martha, of James, 5y., Dec. 22, 1788.	
3-5	" Mary, wife of William, 2d. May 19, 1790.	
3-11	" William, Esq., 74y., May 13, 1796.	
3-12	" Martha, dau. of widow Margaret, 17y., Feb. 17, 1797.	
3-17	" Hannah, wife of William, May 18, 1805.	
3-17	" Mary, wife of Newby, July 29, 1806.	
3-18	" Newby, 81y., Jan. 1, 1807.	
3-18	" Henry, 42y., Jan. 10, 1807.	
3-20	" Margaret, widow, 64y., March 18, 1809.	
3-20	" Hannah, widow, 82y., Jan. 31, 1811.	
2-28	" George, 62y., July 18, 1812.	
3-21	" George, 60y., July 19, 1812.	
2-29	" Peggy (col.), March 14, 1815.	
3-24	" Sarah, widow, 84y., Nov. 6, 1818.	
3-26	" Capt. William, 69y., May 10, 1823.	
3-28	" Dr. John, 62y., Feb. 28, 1826.	
3-30	" Evelyn, wife of Nathaniel, 25y., April 19, 1830.	
3-31	" Pearce, 47y., April 24, 1831.	
3-31	" Sarah Ann, wife of Thomas (at Taunton), Sept. 2, 1832.	
2-29	" William Henry Bowen, of Thomas B. and Rachel, 11m., Feb. 23, 1815.	
3-31	" Rebecca, 24y., Dec. 17, 1832.	
4-21	" Samuel, 43y., Dec. 27, 1834.	

4-25	COGGESHALL	Sally L., of William, 40y., May 21, 1835.
4-27	"	Sarah, wife of Henry G., 34y., Aug. 9, 1835.
4-33	"	William, of Pearce, dec., 17y., June 12, 1836.
4-37	"	Ruth E., of Dr. John M., dec., 39y., Nov. 7, 1836.
4-62	"	Eveline, of Nathaniel, 11y., Dec. 20, 1840.
4-64	"	Charlotte M., wife of George, 23y., Aug. 22, 1841.
4-74	"	Free-born, 33y., (at Cuba, W. I.,) Oct. 5, 1842.
4-104	"	——, child of Henry, 11m., April 27, 1848.
4-106	"	Sarah Ann, wife of Henry, 27y., Oct. 10, 1848.
4-169	COIT	Elizabeth, of David, 15m., Nov. 1, 1820.
4-246	"	John, of George M., Oct. 6, 1821.
4-246	"	son, b. and d. —— —, 1824.
3-29	"	Mary, wife of George M., 31y., June 6, 1828.
4-33	"	William, of David A., 23y., April 11, 1836.
3-13	COLE	Lucy, 35y., July 31, 1798.
3-17	"	Judeth, wife of Nicholas, 52y., July 17, 1806.
3-21	"	Nehemiah, 62y.; (also 2-28). May 21 or 22, 1812.
4-39	"	Perry Munro, of Jonathan F., 14m., Feb. 19, 1837.
4-45	"	Jonathan F., 32y., (killed from fall from roof of the M. E. Church), Sept. 13, 1837.
4-58	"	Anna, widow of Thomas, (b. Warren, R. I.), 83y., June 13, 1840.
4-64	"	Clement, of David, 28y., April 13, 1841.
4-82	"	Mary Emily, of Luther, 12y. 6m., July 29, 1844.
4-88	"	——, child of Nathaniel, Jr., Aug. 30, 1845.
3-9	COLLIMORE	Sarah, of Peleg, 16 m., Jan. 27, 1794.
3-10	"	Susanna, Nov. 26, 1794.
3-12	"	Peleg, of Peleg, 19y., Jan. 7, 1797.
3-12	"	Davis, 21y., Aug. 29, 1797.
3-17	"	Bethiah, wife of Peleg, 47y., July 25, 1806.
3-18	COLLINS	Augustus (at Charlestown, S. C.), 25y., July 4, 1807.
2-28	"	Elizabeth, widow of Augustus (dau. of Rev. A. V. Griswold), at Sudbury, Conn., Dec. 31, 1810, interred at Bristol, Jan. 5, 1811.
2-29	"	——, child of Charles, Jr., April 5, 1813.
2-29	"	Charles, June 21, 1813.
2-29	"	——, Jan. 2, 1815.
2-29	"	——, Feb. —, 1815.
3-21	COLEMAN	Sanford (drowned in Mount Hope Harbor), May 13, 1812.
2-22	COLWELL	Ruth, of Robert and Amey, Oct. 2, 1713.
3-14	COOKE	Mrs. Elizabeth, 64y., Oct. 19, 1799.
4-169	"	William, of Portsmouth, 55y., drowned Jan. 15, 1820.
4-23	"	Emily C., of Stephen W., of Portsmouth, 8m. 21d., March —, 1835.
3-8	COOMER	——, child of John, 2w., (sic.) Feb. 30, 1788.
3-16	"	Thomas, Jr., Oct. —, 1802.
3-22	"	Mary, wife of Thomas H. (also 2-28), July 11, 1813.
3-23	"	John, 90y., Dec. 30, 1816.
3-30	"	Mason, 33y., March 26, 1830.
4-15	"	John, 79y., Feb. 27, 1834.
4-39	"	Dyer, of Stephen D., 2y., Nov. 23, 1836.
4-45	"	Thomas K., 81y., Oct. 22, 1837.
4-52	"	Polly, of Thomas K., 50y., Nov. 22, 1838.
4-64	"	Stephen D., 43y., May 11, 1841.
4-64	"	William Rogers, of Stephen D., 3y., May 27, 1841.
3-16	"	Elizabeth, wife of John, 72y., Dec. 17, 1842.
4-19	CORBETT	Mary Ann, wife of Panuel, 37y., July 16, 1834.
2-26	COREY	Caleb, (at Berbeccia), July 17, 1762.
3-21	CORNELL	Ruth, wife of Walter (also 2-28), 41y., March 26, 1812.
4-126	"	Mary, 54y., (at the Asylum), Sept. 14, 1850.
2-130	"	David, 55y., (at the Asylum), March 16, 1851.
2-22	CORPS	John, Nov. 1, 1691.
1-163	CORTIS	Mary, of Solomon and Prudence, Aug. 22, 1695.
2-22	COTTON	Rev. N., July 3, 1729.
2-22	"	——, child of do., July 6, 1729.
2-22	"	——, child of Madame, May 31, 1730.
2-24	COX	——, wife of Mr. —— —, —— —, 1741.

2-27 COX ——, wife of William, 62y., July 25, 1771.
2-27 " Dr. William, 72y., May 14, 1776.
3-11 " Mary, wife of William, 50y., Dec. 26, 1796.
3-28 " William, 82y., Aug. 18, 1826,
4-58 " Susannah, widow of William, dau. of Thomas Throop, 85y. 1m. 23d., July 13, 1840.
3-27 COY John, 62y., Oct. 11, 1825.
2 29 " Tite, negro servant of Mr. —— (at Fort William Henry), —— —, ——.
2-26 COZZINS ——, child of John, Nov. 9, 1765.
2-27 " ——, b. and d., —— —, 1768.
2-27 " John, (drowned on passage from West Indies), May 5, 1769.
2-28 CRANE Abraham, at Newport, (on return from the camp), —— —, 1758.
2-29 " widow ——, 80y., Nov. 29 or 30, 1769.
3-7 CRANSTON Stephen, 25y., (drowned at the Narrows), Sept. 28, 1792.
3-29 " Capt. Fred, 31y., April 30, 1829.
4-60 " Sarah, widow of Stephen, 86y., Sept. 16, 1840.
3-16 CROSSMAN Dr. Luther Andrew (at sea), June 10, 1804.
3-10 CUDWORTH Lucy, 14y., Sept. 14, 1795.
4-114 CULLEN Brian (born Ireland), 71y., Aug. 7, 1849.
2-22 CUMMINS Philip, of Dartmouth, a resident here sometime, confined for debt to the province Treasurer, Nov. 21, 1707.
2-23 " ——, dau. of David, Aug. 29, 1735.
2-24 " ——, child, Oct. 31, 1742.
2-25 " David (at Cape Breton), Oct. 19, 1745.
2-25 " Benjamin (lost on back of the Cape coming from Surinam, vessel and cargo lost), Dec. 29, 1747.
2-28 " widow ——, (at New York), —— —, 1757.
3-16 " Lydia, widow, Feb. 12, 1803.
4-58 " ——, child of Lemuel, 5y., April 23, 1840.

D

3-20 DAILEY John (Irishman), 36y., Feb. 14, 1810.
3-19 DALTON Capt. Walter, 54y., Dec. 20, 1808.
3-4 DARLING child of William, 1w., Aug. 7, 1789.
2-36 " William M., (lost from sloop Manhattan on voyage to West Indies), Feb. 16, 1814.
3-22 " William (at sea with sch. O. H. Perry), Dec. —, 1814.
4-49 " James F., of James, 16m., Sept. 8, 1838.
4-58 " James F., 2d, 11 m., May 13, 1840.
4-126 DAWSON Benjamin S., of Bridgewater, Conn., 29y., Sept. 27, 1850.
2-32 DAVIS Mr. ——, 63y., May 29, 1730.
2-32 " Gains. Aug. 8, 1730.
2-32 " Samuel, March 23, 1732.
2-32 " Simeon, 76y., Sept. 11, 1736.
2-32 " ——, child of Capt. ——, Aug. 22, 1743.
2-32 " ——, negro child of Capt. ——, May 30, 1744.
2-34 " Simeon, (at Cape Frau), Jan, —, 1750.
2-34 " Nathaniel O., 6y., Sept. 14, 1751.
2-34 " Mrs. Hannah, Oct. 23, 1751.
2-34 " ——, negro child of Capt. ——. May 26, 1754.
2-34 " ——, Sept. 12, 1760.
2-34 " Simeon, 66y., Jan. 16, 1767.
2-36 " ——, negro woman of Capt. ——, May 14, 1761.
3-21 " ——, wife of Capt. Simeon, (also 2-35), 46y., Oct. 3, 1811.
3-24 " Cornelius, 52y., Dec. 1, 1818.
3-30 " David, 30y., Jan. 27, 1830.
3-32 " Capt. Simeon, 83y., Jan. 8, 1832.
4-21 " Abby, of William, 16y., Oct. 25, 1834.
4-42 " Abby W., wife of Benjamin G., 22y., (at Tioga, Penn.), Aug. 2, 1838.
4-53 " Mary Abby, of William, Jr., 6m., April 20, 1839.
4-54 " Benjamin G., 25y., (at Brookfield, Pa.), June 18, 1839.

4-66	DAVIS John J., 33y., (at Providence), Sept. 16, 1841.	
4-74	" William, 72y., March 22, 1843,	
4-76	" Rebecca, widow of Jesse, 75y., June 2, 1843.	
4-92	" Abby Betsey, of Elbridge G., 7y., May 1, 1846.	
4-120	" Mary Maria, of Solomon T., 7y., Jan. 22, 1850.	
4-120	" William Solomon,	5y., Jan. 29, 1850.
2-130	" Charles H.,	13m., March 16, 1851.

4-122   DAVOL William, of Capt. George, 40y. (at Bernice, Cal., was 2d mate of
             ship Hopewell), Feb. 23, 1850.

4-90   DAWLEY Cynthia, wife of Joseph, Dec. 8, 1845.

4-9, 69   DAYTON Catharine, widow of Capt. Benedick, of Newport (buried there),
             May 7, 1846.

4-96   DEAN Sarah A., wife of Malvin G., dau. of Rev. Thomas Shepherd, 23y.,
             May 12, 1847.

4-74   DEARTH Mary G., wife of John W., 27y., Nov. 30, 1842.

4-122   "   Eliza E., widow of Golden, 66y., (at Providence), April 30, 1850.

4-47   DE COSTA Joseph, (b. Portugal), 67y., April 14, 1838.

2-36   DE LIZENA Bartholomew, of St. Domingo, (at Shearjashub Bourne's
             house, being thrown from his chaise, his horse taking fright),
             Nov. 9, ——.

2-34   DENISON ——, wife of Mr. ——, Feb. 25, 1770.

2-34   "   ——, child of Mr. ——, Feb. 25, 1770.

2-34   DENMARK A negro, —— —, 1778.

2-36   DENNIS ——, child of Arthur, Sept. 30, 1811.

4-55   "   Mary, of James W., 13m., Sept. 30, 1839.

4-74   "   Mary Ann, wife of Thomas, 27y., Feb. 8, 1843.

	DEWEY Nancy, widow, 81y., April 10, 1830.	
2-30	DE WOLF Quash, servant of Mark Antony (at sea),	Dec. 6, 1748.
2-34	" ——, child of M., July 22, 1752.	
2-34	" ——, negro child of Capt. ——, (drowned), 7y., May 28, 1767.	
2-34	" ——, the twins of Capt. ——. ——. —, 1768.	
2-36	" ——, negro man, of Capt. ——, Oct. 25, 1760.	
2-34	" ——, child of Capt. ——, 4y., May 16, 1778.	
2-35	" Martha, of Capt. Charles and Mary, (at Dighton), May 17, 1778.	
3-2	" Mary, wife of Capt. Charles, June 19, 1786.	
3-4	" James, of John, 2y., Jan. 20, 1789.	
3-4	" Amelia, of Capt. John, 9m., April 16, 1790.	
43-8	" ——, child of Capt. Charles, 1m., March 22, 1793.	
3-8	" Capt. Mark Antony, 69y., Nov. 9, 1793.	
3-9	" Francis, of Capt. James, 17m., Sept. 19, 1794.	
3-10	" Mark Antony, (in Africa), Aug. 24, 1795.	
3-11	" Simeon, (in Africa), 19y., May 20, 1796.	
3-12	" Simeon, (lost at sea), —— —, 1796.	
3-13	" Mary, of Charles. 26y., Oct. —, 1798.	
3-13	" Mark Antony, of Levi, 2y., Nov. 1, 1798.	
3-14	" Capt. Samuel, 21y., Sept. 1, 1799.	
3-14	" Elizabeth, wife of Capt. Charles, 42y., Feb. 5, 1801.	
3-19	" Abigail, widow, 83y., Feb. 7, 1809.	
2-35	" ——, child of George, Aug. 5, 1813.	
2-35	" ——, child of Henry, Oct. 15, 1813.	
2-35	" William, of Charles, (at New York), —— —, 1814.	
3-24	" Elizabeth, wife of John, 32y., Jan. 5, 1818.	
3-26	" Capt. Charles, 77y., Aug. 20, 1822.	
3-27	" Levi, Jr., 21y., April —, 1824.	
3-29	" Major William, 66y., April 19, 1829.	
3-29	" Charlotte, widow of William, 65y., May 15, 1829.	

4-17   "   Sylvia, wife of John, Jr., (dau. of Rev. Alexander V. Griswold),
             34y., April 20, 1834.

4-41   "   Abigail, widow of Charles, (at Cambridgeport, Mass.,) 80y., April
             18, 1837.

4-45   "   James, (in New York), 74y., Dec. 21, 1837.

4-47   "   Ann B., widow of James, 68y., Jan. 2, 1838.

4-47   "   Allen M., of Charles, Jr., dec., 30y., (at Cuba, W. I.), March 22,
             1838.

4 52   "   Sukey, wife of John, Esq., 80y., Dec. 29, 1838.

4-56	DE WOLF	Mary, of William B., 2y. 3m., March 13, 1840.
4-66	"	John, Esq., 82y., Oct. 10, 1841.
4-68	"	Amey, (col.), 27y., Dec. 26, 1841.
4-80	"	Charles Russell, of William B., 14m., March 14, 1844.
4-82	"	Mark A., of Mark A., 22y., Aug. 27, 1844.
4-90	"	George B., of George, dec., about 38y., (at Cuba, W. I.,) Nov. 14, 1845.
4-104	"	Capt. Levi, 82y., July 18, 1848.
4-108	"	Caroline, wife of Francis L. B., dau. of Samuel Dexter, of Providence, 25y., Dec. 27, 1848.
4-110	"	Levi, 82y., ——. —, 1848.
4-114	"	Marcus A., (col.), 29y., June 26, 1849.
2-130	"	Mark Antony, of Hon. James, 51y., March 21, 1851.
2-32	DIMAN	——, wife of Thomas, Dec. 22, 1744.
2-32	"	Thomas, May —. 1745.
2-32	"	Thomas, May —. 1754.
2-32	"	Jeremiah, Jr., (at Albany on return from the Camp), 21y., ——. —, 1760.
2-36	"	——. child of Jeremiah, May 13, 1745.
2-33	"	——, child of Nathaniel, May 10, 1762.
2-33	"	——, May 2, 1763.
2-33	"	——. child of James, 18m., Feb. 15, 1773.
2-33	"	——, child of Nathaniel 2y., March 5, 1773.
2-33	"	——, son of James, (drowned), 7y., Aug. 24, 1775.
2-34	"	Capt. Benjamin, Dec. 31, 1777.
2-34	"	——, child of James, June —, 1778.
3-4	"	Deborah, of Thomas, Jan. 21, 1789.
3-4	"	Phebe, 72y., Sept. 14, 1789.
3-5	"	Sarah, wife of Deacon Jeremiah, 81y., Oct. 13, 1790.
3-5	"	York, negro servant of James, (at sea), Dec. —, 1790.
3-6	"	Anna, wife of Nathaniel, March 7, 1791.
3 9	"	Mary, of Timothy, Sept. 11, 1794.
3-9	"	Jonathan, Jr., 20y., (at Havana, W. I.), Nov. 18, 1794.
3-10	"	Melvin, 19y., (in Africa), July 25, 1795.
3-13	"	Anna, wife of James, 61y., Jan. 4, 1798.
3-13	"	Deacon Jeremiah, 88y., Nov. 10, 1798.
3-14	"	Elizabeth, wife of Timothy, 42y., April 8, 1801.
3-15	"	Benjamin, 25y. (at sea), June 19, 1802.
3-17	"	Joseph, of Joseph, 11y., Nov. 24, 1804.
3-18	"	Henry, 33y., Sept. 5, 1806.
3-19	"	James, 2d., (at sea), Dec. 28, 1807.
3-19	"	John (lost at sea with sloop Minerva), Dec. 29, 1807.
3-19	"	Anna, wife of William, Nov. 4, 1808.
3-19	"	Willard, 28y., Feb. 23, 1809.
3-20	"	James, 73y., May 30, 1809.
3-20	"	Margaret, wife of Joseph, 62y., Jan. 7, 1811.
3-20	"	Mary, widow, 30y., Feb. 15, 1811.
3-21	"	Nathaniel (also 2-35), May 24, 1812.
2-35	"	——, child of Lefavour, Oct. 11, 1812.
2-35	"	——, Oct. 12, 1812.
2-35	"	William, of Timothy, (died in England in prison, taken in the war), —— —, 1814.
2-35	"	George Howe, of Jeremiah and Hannah (Luther), Dec. 2, 1815.
3-24	"	Salome, wife of Thomas, 90y., Dec. 26, 1818.
3 24	"	Jonathan, 77y., April 30, 1819.
3-25	"	Royal, of Royal, 20y., Sept. 22, 1819.
3 25	"	Royal, 53y., (also 4-169), Aug. 17, 1820.
3-26	"	Joseph, 73y., Oct. 19, 1821.
3-29	"	Dorothy, widow, 84y., May 3, 1828.
3-29	"	Rebecca, 86y., Dec. 16, 1828.
4-19	"	Elizabeth, wife of Thomas, 72y., July 20, 1834.
4-36	"	Thomas, 90y., Jan. 14, 1836.
4-39	"	Virginia, of Francis M., 7y., Feb. 10, 1837.
4-39	"	Frances Maria, 3y., Feb. 15, 1837.
4-45	"	Anna, 75y., Oct. 30, 1837.

4-47	DIMAN	Royal, of Henry W., 9y., May 21, 1838.
4-49	"	Henry W., June 23, 1838.
4-49	"	Abby Byron, of Byron and Abby Alden (Wight), (also 2-35), 3m., Aug. 10, 1838.
4-51	"	Elizabeth, widow of Willard, 51y., Sept. 19, 1838.
4-54	"	Hannah, wife of John, 40y., Aug. 23, 1839.
4-58	"	Hannah, wife of Dea. Jeremiah, 70y., June 7, 1840.
4-74	"	William H., of Henry W., dec., 19y., Dec. 12, 1842.
4-78	"	Abby A., wife of Byron, 41y., Aug. 4, 1843,
4-84	"	William, 85-1-18, Dec. 18, 1844.
4-84	"	James, of Lefavour, 30y., Feb. 2, 1845.
4-102	"	Jeremiah, 80y., —— —, 1847.
4-126	"	Martha V., of Major Benjamin, dec., 76y., Nov. 7, 1850.
2-32	DORMAN, a negro, —— —, 1732.	
4-106	DORRANCE	Amey Richmond, wife of William T., of Providence, 30y., Aug. 13, 1848.
3-27	DOTY	Rebecca, wife of Benjamin W., 55y., March 17, 1825.
4-82	"	Benjamin W., 72y., Aug. 3, 1844.
4-86	"	Sarah, widow of Benjamin W., 60y., July 24, 1845.
4-98	"	——, child of Benjamin, 11m., Sept. 14, 1847.
4-25	DOUGLASS	——, child of George, 18 days, May 12, 1837.
4-88	"	Amey C., wife of Purvis, 43y., Oct. 9, 1845.
2-32	"	Solomon, 49y., Oct. 10, 1730.
2-32	"	——, Indian woman, of Jonathan, Oct. 12, 1788.
2-32	"	——, child, Oct. 20, 1738.
2-36	"	——, child, of Mr., —— —, 1739.
2-35	"	Jonathan, of Jonathan and Anne, 5m 15d., Sept. 13, 1751.
2-35	"	Thomas, Jan. 30, 1758.
2-35	"	Sarah, Jan. 20, 1764.
2-35	"	Simeon, March 17, 1766.
2-33	DROWNE	——, child of Irene, Oct. 2, 1753.
2-33	"	Anne, wife of Jonathan, Jan. 30, 1758.
2-33	"	Irene, Jan. 27, 1760.
2-34	"	——, child of Jonathan, 11m., Jan. 20, 1764.
2-34	"	——, child of James, April —, 1766.
2-34	"	Joseph, 56y., Aug. 18, 1769.
2-34	"	——, wife of Jonathan, Feb. 13, 1771.
2-34	"	——, child of Solomon, Dec. 16, 1775.
2-34	"	Jonathan, Jr., 22y., July —, 1777.
3-7	"	Nathaniel Bosworth, of Solomon, 2y., Sept. 28, 1791.
3-9	"	Jonathan, May 7, 1794.
3-11	"	Richard, 47y., Aug. 17, 1796.
3-15	"	Solomon, 53y., Sept. 3, 1801.
4-31	"	Sarah, widow of Richard, 80y., Jan. 11, 1836.
4-31	"	Sarah, widow of Solomon, 88y., Jan. 26, 1836.
4-37	"	James, Oct. 28, 1836.
4-74	"	William H., 33y., Oct. 1, 1842.
3-27	DRUBY	Lydia Potter, wife of Luke, May 16, 1825.
2-33	DUEN	Thomas, Nov. —, 1751.
2-32	DUNBAR	——, negro man, of Mr. (drowned), Feb. 19, 1747.
2-33	"	George (at Providence), Feb. 10, 1754.
3-14	"	Robert (at Havana), May 14, 1798.
3-14	"	William, May 22, 1799.
3-14	"	William, 19y., (lost at sea), —— —, 1800.
4-168	"	Robert, of Newport, about 68y., May 1, 1821.
4-76	"	Mary Frances, of Robert, 7m 10d., July 4, 1843.
4-78	"	Reynolds, 51y., (buried at Newport), July 24, 1843.
4-60	DUNHAM	Lydia C., wife of Serenas, of Fall River, Mass., 20y., Sept. 25, 1840.
2-32	DURFEE	——, negro child of Thomas, July —, 1733.
2-32	"	Thomas (at Jamaica), Nov. —, 1734.
2-32	"	——, child of Thomas, —— —, 1748.
4-88	DWYER	Margaret P., wife of Thomas, dau. of Capt. Thomas Swan, 24y., Sept. 5, 1845.

2-32 DYER Sarah, wife of John, July 13, 1729.
2-32   "   Rebecca, wife of John, Aug. 20, 1738.
2-32   "   John, Sept. 6, 1748.
2-32   "   Ebenezer, April 3, 1751.
2-34   "   Mrs. Mary, 83y., Dec. —, 1777.
3-18   "   John, 83y., Jan. 28, 1807.

E

3-19 EARL Capt. John B. (at sea), Dec. 28, 1807.
2-38 EASTERBROOKS ——, child of John, ——. —, 1764.
        "   ——, wife of John, May 24, 1769.
        "   ——, child of John, Sept. 26, 1769.
        "   Samuel, 23y., Nov. 2, 1812.
3-11   "   Sally, of Aaron, 16y., Nov. 19, 1796.
3-11   "   Sarah, wife of Aaron, 38y., Dec. 23, 1796.
3-22   "   Samuel, 23y., Nov. 3, 1812.
3-22   "   George, (at sea with Sch. O. H. Perry), Dec. —, 1814.
4-169   "   Benjamin, about 50y., (also 3-25), April 29, 1820.
4-168   "   ——, child of Jonathan, March 11, 1821.
3-27   "   Hannah, wife of Crawford, 29y., June 10, 1825.
3-28   "   Patience, wife of Jonathan, 35y., April 14, 1827.
3-28   "   Aaron, of Abel, 25y., Oct. 1, 1827.
3-30   "   Mary, widow, 60y., Feb. 27, 1831.
4-33   "   Abigail, widow of Daniel, 75y., April 10, 1836.
4-39   "   Crawford, 49y., March 3, 1837.
4-47   "   William J., of Benjamin, 18y. 4m., May 1, 1838.
4-49   "   Lydia, wife of Abel, 62y., Aug. 18, 1838.
4-56   "   Benjamin Franklin, of Crawford, 3y., March 7, 1840.
4-62   "   William H., of William, 11w., Oct. 11, 1840.
4-68   "   Aaron, 91y., 5m., 11d., Dec. 26, 1841.
4-78   "   Hannah H., of Crawford, 10m., Aug. 13, 1843.
4-92   "   Benjamin, of Benjamin, 3m., June 2, 1846.
4-116   "   Julia Ann, of William and Rebecca, 8m. 12d., Oct. 6, 1849.
4-132   "   Abel, 76y., June 23, 1851.
4-126   "   Thomas T., of Providence, son of Jonathan, of this town (at Sacramenta, Cal.), 32y., July 27, 1850.
2-38 EDDY Malatiah, wife of Joseph, Jan. 29, 1725-6.
2-38   "   ——, child of Oliver, Dec. 22, 1729.
2-38   "   ——, April —, 1731.
2-38   "   Oliver, Feb. 4, 1734.
3 26   "   Sarah, widow, 71y., March 20, 1822.
4 90   "   Catherine, wife of Comfort (buried at Providence), Feb. 9, 1846.
4-90   "   Eunice G., wife of Cyrus B., formerly of Providence, 43y., May 8, 1846.
2-38 EDGILL John (lost at sea on back of the Cape on passage from Surinam, vessel and cargo lost), Dec. 29, 1747.
3-20 EDWARD Thomas, of Baltimore, 35y., June 13, 1811.
3-23 ELLIOTT ——, widow, 75y., Aug. 31, 1816.
3-30   "   Mary, 54y., May 4, 1830.
2 38 EMMERSON Mrs. Mary, March 11, 1748.
2-38 ESLICK Isaac (at West Indies), Feb. —, 1752.
2-38   "   ——, child of Isaac, Feb. 24, 1774.
2-38   "   Mary, widow, 35y., April 15, 1776.
3-12 ESTES Ruth, wife of Capt. Isaac, 39y., May 17, 1797.
4-25 EVERETT Hannah, widow of John, 60y., June 15, 1835.

F

2 40 FAIRBANKS Abigail, 20y., Nov. 6, 1730.
2-40   "   Jonathan, 19y., Jan. 18, 1733.
2-40   "   Jeremiah, 60y., March 28, 1735.
2 40   "   Jeremiah, 17y., Aug. 28, 1735.

2-41	FAIRBANKS —, negro child of widow, June —, 1748.		
2-41	"	Benjamin, — —, 1756.	
2-42	"	Rebecca, 50y., April 12, 1760.	
2-40	FALES —, dau. of Capt., July 20, 1733.		
2-41	"	—, son of Capt., Aug. 8, 1737.	
2-41	"	Timothy, Jr., June —, 1739.	
2-41	"	—, child of Capt., 14m., July 1, 1740.	
2-41	"	negro woman of Capt. —, Sept. 24, 1742.	
2-47	"	Mrs. Althea, 52y., Sept. 19, 1747.	
2-42	"	Sambo, servant of Mrs. (drowned or lost in a snow storm), Feb. 1, 1769.	
2-42	"	Timothy (at Taunton), 86y., April 30, 1777.	
2-42	"	Jonathan, 50y., May 8, 1777.	
2-42	"	—, child of, Dec. —. 1777.	
2-42	"	Hannah, widow, Oct. 1, 1811.	
2-43	"	—, dau. of James, 7y., Oct. 13, 1812.	
2-43	"	John, Oct. 4, 1813.	
2-43	"	Mary, of William, Oct. 5, 1814.	
3-1	"	—, child of Nathaniel Jr., 1d., Nov. 11, 1785.	
3-1	"	Robert, 50y., — —, 1785.	
3-2	"	Reuben, negro servant of Nathaniel, 25y., April 30, 1786.	
3-2	"	Isaac, of William, 6m., Sept. 17, 1786.	
3-3	"	Sarah, wife of Nathaniel, 60y., May 16, 1787.	
3-5	"	James Gibbs, of John, 9w., Oct. 20, 1790.	
3-7	"	—, child of Nathaniel, Jr., 2m., Sept. 22, 1791.	
3-7	"	child of John, 5w., — 22, 1792.	
3-8	"	Thomas, Dec. —, 1793.	
3-10	"	Nathaniel, of Thomas, 2y., Aug. 6, 1795.	
3-12	"	William, 39y., Jan. 22, 1797.	
3-12	"	Mehitable, widow, 89y., March 1, 1797.	
3-13	"	Amey, wife of Nathaniel, Esq., 72y., Sept. 21, 1798.	
3-14	"	Bradford, 21y., at Havanna, Jan. —, 1799.	
3-14	"	Deborah, 68y., Aug. 22, 1799.	
2-15	"	Jonathan, Jr., (at St. Croix), June 26, 1801.	
3-15	"	Nathaniel, Esq. (at Taunton), 82y., Dec. 13, 1801.	
3-19	"	Robert (lost at sea with sloop Minerva), Dec. 29, 1807.	
3-21	"	—, widow, 53y., Oct. 1, 1811.	
3-21	"	Capt. Timothy, (in sloop lost at sea), Dec. —, 1811.	
3-22	"	John, 53y., Oct. 4, 1813.	
3-22	"	Mary, widow, 50y., Oct. 5, 1814.	
3-24	"	Hannah, widow, 90y., March 23, 1817.	
3-24	"	Capt. Thomas, (lost at sea), 31y., Aug. 2, 1817.	
3-25	"	Sarah, wife of Thomas, 60y., Aug. 1, 1819.	
4-226	"	Mary Ann Frances, of Charles and Lydia M., Sept. 21, 1822.	
4-226	"	Nathaniel,	Dec. 4, 1839.
4-226	"	Mary Ann,	Jan. 1, 1844.
4-226	"	Abby Bosworth,	Feb. 13, 1841.
4-226	"	Frances,	Feb. 26, 1833.
3-30	"	Thomas, 78y., Nov. 14, 1830	
3-31	"	Elizabeth, wife of Jonathan, 79y., Oct. 23, 1831.	
3-31	"	Nathaniel, 85y., Feb. 12, 1834.	

Note—Mr. Fales was born May 11, 1749, and was youngest of 13 children of Nathaniel and Sarah, all of whom lived to marry and leave heirs, and many lived to advanced age, 7 sons, 6 daughters.

4-17	"	Rebecca, widow of Jonathan, Jr., 55y., April 29, 1834.	
4-29	"	Edmund, 20y. (drowned), Sept. 8, 1835.	
4-41	"	Elizabeth, widow of Nathaniel, 86y. 10m. (dau. of Daniel Bradford), April 29, 1837.	
4-41	"	Nathaniel,	Feb. 12, 1832.
4-51	"	Sarah, of Timothy, 56y., Nov. 3, 1838.	
4-54	"	Capt. Stephen S., 55y. (for many years a resident of Cuba, W. I.), June 22, 1839.	
4-55	"	Phebe, wife of Capt. Stephen S., dec., 55y., Sept. 26, 1839.	
4-55	"	Nathaniel, of Charles, 16y., Dec. 4, 1839.	

4-55   FALES Dolera, (col.), 11y., Feb. 19, 1840.
4-62   "   Abby M.,, of Charles, 12y., Feb. 13, 1841.
4-70   "   Jonathan, 91y., June 22, 1842.
4-76   "   Martha, widow of John, at Providence, April 13, 1843.
4-80   "   Mary Ann, of Charles, 17y., Jan. 1, 1844.
3-18   FAULKNER Samuel (Englishman , 45y., Feb. 22, 1807.
4-37   FELIX Ann Elizabeth Parnell, of Henry, 1y., Nov. 16, 1836.
4-39   "   Louisa Antoine, 3y., 10m., Nov. 29, 1836.
4-106   "   Henry Adolph Ferris, 10w. 2d., Aug. 29, 1848.
4-116   "   Clarence Ferris, 11w., Sept. 17, 1849.
4-120   "   Nancy S., wife of Henry, 43y., Feb. 21, 1850.
4-31   FENNER Edward, Jr. (at sea), 30y., March —, 1836.
4-37   "   Leander, of Richard, 2y., 6m., Nov. 14, 1836.
4-102   "   Lydia, wife of Richard, dau. of James Allen, dec., 41y., Jan. 27,
                 1848.
4-120   "   Sarah, of Richard (18y., Feb. 21, 1850), March 20, 1850.
4-120   "   Sarah, of Richard, 20y., March 20, 1850.
4-124 FERRIS Agnes Roan, wife of Alexander (born New Solway, Scotland),
                 28y., June 29, 1850.
2-43   FERRY, negro child at the, July 10, 1758.
3-19   FINLEY Susanna, widow, 89y., April 6, 1808.
2-40   FINNEY Elizabeth, wife of John, buried Feb. 9, 1683-4.
2-40   "   Elizabeth, of Joshua and Mercy, Sept. 19, 1701.
2-40   "   John, of Jeremiah and Esther, Oct. 23, 1690.
2-40   "   —, child of Jeremiah, Feb. 27, 1730.
2-40   "   —, child of Ebenezer, Aug. 23, 1730.
2-41   "   —, child of Capt. —, March 26, 1744.
2-41   "   Esther, of Jeremiah and Elizabeth, March 26, 1745.
2-41   "   Elizabeth, of Joseph, 2y., Sept. 21, 1756.
2-41   "   —, child of Josiah, July 31, 1758.
2-41   "   Mary, wife of Daniel, 34y., April 30, 1759.
2-41   "   Elizabeth, 28y., May 14, 1759.
2-41   "   —, negro girl of Jeremiah, Jr., July 30, 1759.
2-42   "   Capt. Jeremiah, 59y., Oct. 21, 1759.
2-42   "   —, child of Jeremiah, 2y., March 8, 1760.
2-42   "   Molly, wife of Josiah, 28y., Sept. 18, 1760.
2-42   "   Mrs. Elizabeth, 54y., Nov. 8, 1760.
2-42   "   —, child of Thomas, Dec. 16, 1761.
2-42   "   Elizabeth, of Thomas and Elizabeth, Dec. 16, 1761.
2-42   "   —, child of Thomas, 7 weeks, Jan. 15, 1763.
2-42   "   Clarke, of Thomas and Elizabeth, Jan. 17, 1763.
2-42   "   Jeremiah, 21y., July 25, 1773.
2-43   "   Sabina, servant of Capt. —, May 7, 1757.
3-7   "   George, 22y. (at sea), May 9, 1792.
3-11   "   Abigail, 20y., Oct. 16, 1796.
3-14   "   Jeremiah, Jr., 25y., Jan. 15, 1799.
3-16   "   Josiah, Esq., 76y., July 23, 1804.
3-18   "   Jeremiah, 74y., July 17, 1807.
3-26   "   Mary, widow, 74y., Sept. 20, 1821.
3-26   "   Martha, 84y., May 29, 1823.
3-28   "   Capt. Loring, 66y., March 8, 1827.
4-29   "   Experience, widow of Loring, 74y., Dec. 11, 1835.
4-55   "   Ann, of Josiah, dec., 66y., Dec. 17, 1839.
4-126 FISHER Mary, wife of Thomas, dau. of Archibald Munro, 18y., Nov. 14,
                 1850.
3-5   FISH Peter (at Cape Francis), 95y., Dec. —. 1790.
2-43   "   —, child of Sally, Nov. 20, 1812.
4-229   "   Betsey Wardwell, of David and Mary, Jan. 11, 1828.
4-229   "   Abby Wardwell,   Aug. 4, 1838.
3-34   "   David, 50y., July 2, 1830.
4-56   "   William F., of George P., 4y., April 16, 1840.
4-90   "   Harriet Williams,   2y. 7m., Feb. 2, 1846.
4-118   "   Cyrus, formerly of Swansey, 51y., Dec. 30, 1849.
3-20   FITCH Merebah, 88y., Feb. 27, 1811.
4-102   "   Susan, widow of Capt. Oliver, of Norwich, Conn., dau. of Josiah
                 Finney, 73y. (also 4-110), Jan. 8, 1848.

2-130 FLETCHER Capt. John, 64y., Feb. 4, 1851.
3-29 FORBES Dr. George, 26y., Aug. 22, 1828.
2-41 FORTUNE, a negro (at the Mount), July 2, 1756.
2-42 FOSTER ——, child of Chillingworth, Jan. 18, 1812.
2-185 " Chillingworth (killed on privateer Hiram), (see Nathan West), (also 2-42), Aug. 19, 1812.
2-41 FOWLER ——, child of James, Sept. 24, 1759.
2-41 " Perscilla, wife of James, Jan. 25, 1760.
4-41 FRANKLIN Ann Maria, of Marcus, 1y. 3m., April 2, 1837.
4-98 " Elisha Barney, 38y., Sept. 10, 1847.
4-104 " Elisha, 76y. (also 4-110), June 22, 1848.
2-4 FRAZIER Alexander, Jan. —, 1717.
2-43 FREEBORN, child of Isaac, —— —, 1813.
2-43 " ——, April 12, 1814.
4-17 " Polly, of Dinah (col.), 11y., March 26, 1834.
4-25 " Amanda, widow of Theophilus, 42y., April 4, 1835.
4-25 " Thomas, 52y., May 29, 1835.
4-84 " Harriet, of Isaac (at Fall River), 35y., Nov. 24, 1844.
1-120 FREEMAN Rosanna (col.), 67y., April 7, 1850.
3-8 FRENCH Cudjo, negro servant of Capt. J. Cousines, 80y., Dec. 2, 1793.
4-49 " Timothy, 74y., July 7, 1838.
4-53 " Lydia, widow of Timothy, 73y., June 10, 1839.
4-56 FRISBEE Catharine Adelbert, of Hiram, 5y., March 24, 1840.
2-40 FRY John, Jan. 12, 1705.
2-43 " Norton, a West India gentleman, July 28, 1736.
3-18 FULLER Edward, 76y., March 19, 1807.
2-40 FULTON Dr. William, 79y., Aug. 27, 1729.
2-40 " Madame, June 5, 1732.

G

4-128 GALLAGHER Andrew (seaman), 34y., Dec. 2, 1850.
2-45 GALLUP Elizabeth, wife of Capt. Samuel (fell from a horse Aug. 12), died —— 15, 1709.
2-45 " Capt. Samuel, March 24, 1717.
2-45 " ——, of William, April 27, 1730.
2-46 " ——, child of ——. July 4, 1737.
2-46 " Capt. ——, —— —, ——.
2-46 " ——, an apprentice of ——, —— —, 1739.
2-46 " ——, negro child of Capt. ——, —— —, ——.
2-46 " ——, negro woman of William, June 12, 1743.
2-46 " ——, negro child of Capt. ——, Oct. 18, 1743.
2-47 " Nathaniel, Oct. 4, 1746.
2-47 " Capt. Samuel, child of ——, Feb. 12, 1747.
2-47 " Mrs. Mary, March 12, 1750.
2-48 " Mrs. Eliza, Feb. 4, 1752.
2-48 " William, Feb. 12, 1752.
2-49 " Mary, wife of William, Feb. 20, 1762.
2-50 " William (at Cambridge), 80y., Nov. —. 1774.
2-48 GAINDETS Mrs. ——, her negro child, Nov. —. 1752.
2-48 " ——, Aug. 12, 1755.
2-48 " ——, March 17, 1758.
2-48 " ——, Sept. 25, 1759.
2-45 GAINS Thomas, died at sea, Nov. —, 1729.
2-51 GARDINER Isaac, child of —— (col.), May 2, 1815.
4-169 " Mille (col.), 21y., Nov. 3, 1820.
4-33 " Joseph, of Stephen, 10m., April 24, 1836.
4-62 " Ann, wife of John (at Savannah), Nov. 28, 1840.
4-70 " ——, child of Joseph L., 20 days, March 6, 1842.
4-78 " George Henry, of Dr. C., of Dixon, Ill., 1y., Oct. 3, 1843.
4-86 " Martha, (born Stockport, Eng.), 56y., July 3, 1845.
4-168 GAVIN Mary, 84y., Jan. 1, 1821.
3-2 " George (at sea), Jan. 9, 1789.
4-51 " George M., of Nathaniel S., 2y., Nov. 14, 1838.

2-51	GEERS John, of Richard, died in England, in prison, a prisoner of war, —— —, 1814.
2-45	GIBBS John, June 1, 1731.
2-46	" ——, of John, July 5, 1734.
2-46	" Martha, wife of James, May 6, 1740.
2-46	" Sarah, wife of John, April 20, 1746.
2-47	" ——, wife of John, April 24, 1746.
2-47	" Capt., a negro child of, April 2, 1748.
2-48	" Nathaniel, of Capt. James, drowned, 7y., May 31, 1756.
2-48	" Mrs. Sarah, 82y., Oct. 8, 1756.
2-51	" James, of Capt. James (drowned at sea), —— —, 1760.
3-11	" Capt. James, 89y., Nov. 17, 1795.
3-17	" Capt. John, 83y., Jan. 7, 1806.
3-29	" Elizabeth, 23y., March 17, 1829.
2-45	GIDDENS ——, of Mary, Aug. 14, 1729.
2-49	" Mrs. Grace, 90y., May 1, 1768.
4-33	GIFFORD Gideon, 4w., April 26, 1836.
4-60	" Almira, of Gideon, 2y., Sept. 16, 1840.
4-84	" John Nelson, of Hugh N., 19y., Dec. 22, 1844.
4-86	" Elizabeth, of Gideon, 10y., June 11, 1845.
4-92	" Susan Thomas. 16y., July 1, 1846.
4-108	" Susan, wife of Gideon, dau. of Joseph Simmons, 44y., Dec. 10, 1848.
3-3	GILES Thomas, of —— Finney, Esq. (at sea), 19y., Oct. 4, 1787.
4-124	GLACKING John (born Ireland), about 66y., July 19, 1850.
2-45	GLADDING Mr. ——, 50y., March 23, 1730.
2-45	" Sarah, Aug. 5, 1730.
2-45	" ——, of William, Feb. 8, 1732.
2-46	" John, May 3, 1732.
2-51	" William, child of, Dec. —, 1733.
2-46	" Alice, 30y., Aug. 25, 1734.
2-46	" Nathaniel, 27y., Sept. 13, 1735.
2-46	" William, 38y., Oct. 22, 1735.
2-46	" Ebenezer, Feb. 26, 1737.
2-46	" William, July 10, 1737.
2-47	" ——, child of James, June 17, 1743.
2-47	" Jonathan, Oct. 27, 1743.
2-47	" John, child of, Jan. 10, 1747.
2-47	" George (lost on back of the cape, on passage from Surinam, with vessel and cargo). Dec. 29, 1747.
2-47	" William, wife of (at Palmer's river), July 10, 1751.
2-47	" John, child of, Oct. 28, 1751.
2-48	" John (died at Newport), Sept. —, 1754.
2-48	" Alice (child of, by William White), Jan. 9, 1759.
2-49	" William, 84y., March 17, 1759.
2-49	" Mary, wife of John, 40y., April 15, 1759.
2-48	" James (on return from camp at Lake George), —— —, 1760.
2-48	" John, of Samuel and Mary, March 11, 1762.
2-49	" Samuel, child of, 9m., March 11, 1762.
2-49	" Samuel, 34y., April 16, 1762.
2-49	" Solomon, 27y., April 29, 1762.
2-49	" Daniel, child of, b. and d. Oct. 27, 1769.
2-48, 50	" Richard, of John, Jr., and Lucretia, 5y., June 14, 1775.
2-50	" Solomon, summer of 1776.
2-50	" John, Jr., child of, Sept. —. 1777.
2-50	" Peter, Dec. 6, 1777.
3-1	" Capt. John, 69y., Nov. 16, 1785.
3-2	" Sarah, widow, 83y., Dec. 26, 1786.
3-3	" Esther, widow, 79y., Nov. 18, 1787.
3-3	" Hannah, widow, 69y., Feb. 29, 1788.
3-7	" George, of Capt. Joshua, 18m., Sept. 14, 1791.
3-8	" Jeremiah (at sea), Dec. —. 1793.
2-50	" Samuel, of Samuel and Charlotte, Dec. 22, 1796.
3-14	" William, 71y., Jan. 7, 1801.
2-50	" Edmund, Aug. 17, 1801.

3-18	GLADDING Susannah, widow, 78y., Dec. 14, 1806.	
3-19	" Susanna, widow, 58y., Aug. 15. 1808.	
2-50	" Solomon, 27y., May 7, 1811.	
2-50	" Nathaniel, child of, 22m., Sept. 26, 1811.	
2-50	" Susannah W., of Capt. Nathaniel and Nancy, Sept. 26, 1811.	
2-50	" Edward, child of, Oct. 5. 1811.	
3-21	" Allen, of Samuel, in sloop Sally, from Havana), Dec. —, 1811.	
3-22	" Lucretia, wife of John, 70y. (also 2-51), May 5, 1813.	
251	" Samuel, 2d., Dec. 8, 1813.	
2-51	" Molly, of William, Dec. 31, 1813.	
2-51	" —, child of Daniel, 9d, Jan. 31, 1814.	
2-51	" ——, child of Stephen, 1y., Oct. 5, 1814.	
2-51	" Joseph, of William (died in prison in England, a prisoner of war), —— —, 1814.	
2-51	" ——, child of Stephen, June 5, 1815.	
3-24	" Sarah, wife of Joshua, 60y., Jan. 27, 1819.	
3-25	" John, 81y. (also 4-169), Sept. 25, 1820.	
3-25	" Rebecca, wife of William, 56y. (also 4-169), Oct. 2, 1820.	
3-26	" Joseph, 59y., Oct. 20. 1821.	
3-29	" Capt. Joshua, 71y., Feb. 3, 1828.	
3-32	" Sarah Ann, wife of Samuel, 26y., Feb. 3, 1832.	
3-31	" Thomas, 59y., July 11, 1832.	
4-17	' son of Jonathan, 10d., May 11, 1834.	
4-31	" Nancy, wife of Nathaniel, 57y., Jan. 5, 1836.	
4-37	" Charlotte, widow of Capt. Samuel, 69y., Nov. 6, 1836.	
4-45	" Miss Mary, 87y., Aug. 29, 1837.	
4-47	" Capt. Nathaniel, 60y. (on passage home from New Orleans on sch. Le Bruce), March 28, 1838.	
4-52	" John, 53y. (at Pharsalia, Chenango Co., N. Y.), Jan. 1, 1839.	
4-56	" Abigail Howe, of Josiah, 3y., March 11, 1940.	
4-56	" Josiah, 7m., March 12, 1840.	
4-58	" Daniel W., of Peter, 5y., April 30, 1840.	
4-64	" William James, of James H., 2-8-13 April 13, 1841.	
4-68	" ——, child of Nathaniel, 1y., Dec. 8, 1841.	
4-70	" Stephen, 78y., May 24, 1842.	
4-72	" Peter, of Peter, 4y., Aug. 17, 1842.	
4-72	" —, child of John, 3d., Sept. 2, 1842.	
4-72	" Henrietta, of Daniel, 15y., Sept. 3, 1842.	
4-72	" Charles J., of Peter, 5y., 7m., Sept. 12, 1842.	
4-78	" Philip, of Samuel, 20y., July 24, 1843.	
4-86	" Capt. John, mate of brig Neptune (at Matanzas), 45y., June 27, 1845.	
4-98	" Benjamin, of John, dec., 56y, (at Waterville, Oneida Co., N. Y., left a wife and 10 children), Sept. 12, 1847.	
4-104	" Abby Ann, of John H., 1y., 5m., March 26, 1848.	
4-106	" Susan Thomas, of Capt. Josiah, 10m., Aug. 24, 1848.	
4-114	" Hannah V., wife of Stephen T., youngest dau. of James Harding, dec. (at Smithfield, Bradford Co., Pa.), 40y., July 29, 1849.	
4-116	" Rachel, widow of John. 85y., Sept. 14, 1849.	
4-124	" Adaliza, 53y., June 17, 1850.	
4-126	" Samuel, 66y., Sept. 18, 1850.	
4-132	" Frank Henry, of John H. and Fanny L., 1y., 7m., 15d. (at Newport), July 2, 1851.	
4-218	" Alzada, of James N. and Lucretia G., March 5, 1856.	
4-218	" James Nickerson,	July 3. 1864.
4-218	" John,	Jan. 25, 1846.
4-33	GLASHING Betsey, wife of John, May 9, 1836.	
3-3	GLOVER Elizabeth, 72y., April 24, 1787.	
4-19	GOFF Thomas, of Thomas, dec., 24y., Aug. 12, 1834.	
4-35	" James, 76y., Aug, 6, 1836.	
4-112	" Mary N., 19y., May 13, 1849.	
2-51	GOODING Josiah, child of ——, Sept. 28, 1812.	
2-51	" ——, 6y., March 27, 1813.	
2-50	" Henry (died at the Havanna), —— —, ——.	

3-4   GOODWIN Henry, Esq., 28y., May 31, 1789.
4-15   "   Mary, widow of Henry, dau. of William Bradford, dec. (at Newport), 73y., Jan. 14, 1834.
4-169 GOONERSON ——, child of George, June 6, 1820.
2-45   GORHAM Hannah, of Jabez (smothered in a tub of slus and water), March 28, 1682.
2-48   "   Hezekiah, of Isaac and Mary, Dec. —, 1715.
2-45   "   Mary, wife of Isaac, Sept. 11, 1716.
2-45   "   John, of Jabez and Hannah, Jan. —, 1717.
2-45   "   ——, Indian child of Benjamin, Aug. —, 1730.
2-46   "   Shubael, —— —, 1734.
2-46   "   Samuel, 53y., Nov. 24, 1735.
2-48   "   ——, wife of Jabez, May 13, 1739.
2-47   "   Jabez, Nov. 21, 1745.
2-49   "   Isaac, dau. of ——, 3y., May 10, 1759.
2-49   "   Isaac, 50y., Dec. 1, 1760.
2-50   "   William, of Isaac (perished with cold; vessel driven on shore at the Vineyard), Dec. 26, 1778.
3-6   "   Flora, negro servant of widow Joanna, 16y., April 8, 1791.
3-10   "   Capt. Isaac (at sea), 48y., Sept. —, 1795.
3-13   "   Isaac (at sea), 21y., Aug. 21, 1798.
3-18   "   Jemima, widow, 88y., Oct. 10, 1806.
3-20   "   William, 21y. (at sea), June 6, 1809.
4-23   "   Sarah, widow of Capt. Isaac, 85y., Feb. 25, 1835.
4-51   "   Lafayette, of Amos T., 3y. 2m., Oct. 7, 1838.
4-130   "   Ann Janette, of Daniel, dec., 22y., March 24, 1851.
2-49   GOULD John (died in the army), —— —, 1759.
2-51   "   Grace, an Indian, Jan. —, 1730.
3-18   GRANT Rebecca, wife of Benjamin, 32y., Sept. 17, 1806.
4-169   "   Mary Ann, of Benjamin, 12y., June 10, 1820.
4-169   "   ——, child, 5y., Sept. 1, 1820.
3-29   "   Allen, 24y., Jan. 15, 1828.
4-15   "   Sarah, widow of Richard, 85y., Jan. —, 1834.
4-52   "   Barbara, widow of John, of Warren, 78y., April 1, 1833.
4-122   "   Mrs. Elizabeth Gardiner, wife of J. M., dau. of Dea. George M. Coit, 31y., April 26, 1850.
4-126 GRAVES Rev. H. A., 37y., Nov. 3, 1850.
3-7   GRAY Sukey, negro servant of Col. Thomas, June —, 1792.
3-16   "   Col. Thomas (at Tiverton), 74y., Nov. 8, 1803.
3-18   "   Mary, wife of Gideon, 29y., Dec. 12, 1806.
3-19   "   Capt. Gideon (at sea), Dec. 28, 1807.
3-22   "   Sarah, widow of Thomas, Esq. (also 2-51), buried at Tiverton, 88y., Sept. 14, 1813.
2-51   "   Richard,   Sept. 25, 1814.
3-23   "   Thomas, of Tiverton, 33y., Nov. 26, 1815.
2-51   "   Nancy (col.), March 6, 1815.
4-169   "   ——, wife of Thomas, July 3, 1820.
3-26   "   Thomas, 33y., Sept. 1, 1822.
4-51   "   Reliance, widow of Pardon, 74y., Nov. 9, 1838.
4-55   "   Morilla Fiske, of Gideon, 10m., Nov. 27, 1839.
4-72   "   Eliza Jane, of Gideon, 15y., Aug. 22, 1842.
4-114   "   Nimine (col.), 44y., July 3, 1849.
2-130   "   Lydia, wife of Elijah, 59y., Feb. 4, 1851.
2-46   GREENE ——, child of Capt. ——, —— —, 1742.
2-46   "   ——, June —, 1742.
2-47   "   John, dau of ——, Feb. 1, 1746.
2-46   "   Martha, of John and Elizabeth, Feb. 1, 1745-6.
2-47   "   ——, child of Major, April 24, 1747.
2-47   "   John,   May 24, 1749.
2-48   "   Elizabeth, dau. of Major, Sept. 26, 1752.
2-48   "   ——, negro child, of Major, Jan. —, 1754.
2-48   "   ——,   June 16, 1758.
2-49   "   Col. ——, negro child, —— —, 1760.
2-49   "   Elizabeth, widow of John, 87y., Feb. 14, 1763.
2-48   "   Hannah, of Thomas and Elizabeth (at Worcester), Dec. 1, 1765.

2-49 GREENE Thomas, Esq., 57y., Nov. 4, 1769.
2-113   "   Sipeo, late servant of T. Greene (at Providence), —— —, 1769.
2-49   "   Mrs. ——, negro child, Feb. 3, 1770.
2-49   "   Mrs. Elizabeth (at Woodstock), 64y., April 22, 1774.
2-51   "   Henry, of Samuel, March, 27, 1814.
3-19   "   Jacob, Esq., 68y., Nov. 7, 1808.
3-26   "   Rebecca, of Joseph W., 61y., Sept. 23, 1821.
3-29   "   Capt. Joseph Whipple, 68y., April 27, 1829.
4-68   "   Julia B., wife of Albert G., dau. of Benjamin · Bourne, dec., 52y., Jan. 4, 1842.
4-74   "   Nathaniel S., of Nathaniel S., 1y., March 23, 1843.
4-80   "   Child of Jeremiah J., 7w., Dec. 24, 1843.
4-102   "   Child of Nathaniel S., 6m., Jan. 19, 1848.
4-106   "   Susan W., of Henry N., 3y., 8m., Aug. 10, 1848.
2-47 GREENHILL, Tower Hill, negro servant, of Mr. ——, Nov. 29, 1748.
2-48   "   Joseph, Dec. 6, 1754.
2-47   "   Mr. ——, negro child of ——; —— —, ——.
2-45 GRIDLEY, Elizabeth, wife of Samuel, Oct. 20, 1720.
2-46   "   Rebecca, 80y., March 16, 1738.
2-47   "   Samuel, Jan. 22, 1748.
4-52 GRIFFIN, Sarah, wife of Charles (col.), Jan. 31, 1839.
4-62   "   Child of Charles (col.), 4m., May 2, 1839.
4-53   "   Child of Charles (col.), 5m., May 23, 1839.
4-62   "   Child of Charles (col.), 4y., Oct. 30, 1840.
3-2 GRIMES, child of John, 5m., Sept. 23, 1786.
3-2   "   Sally, of John, 11w., Dec., 28, 1786.
3-3   "   Child of John, 11m., July, 10, 1788.
3-13   "   Leah, wife of John, 37y., June 9, 1798.
2-50 GRISWOLD Viets, of Rev. Alexander V., 24y., May 1, 1812.
3-24   "   Elizabeth, wife of Rev. Alexander V., 49y., Sept. 20, 1817.
3-28   "   Miss Julia, 27y., April 16, 1826.
3-30   "   Rev. George, 27y., Sept. 27, 1829.
2-50 GWIN Andrew, 71 or 72y., April 10, 1776.
2-49   "   ——, wife of Andrew, Oct. 5, 1763.
3-25   "   Miss Mary, 84y., Jan. 1, 1821.

H

2-58 HADLEY Andrew, child of ——, Aug. 14, 1812.
4-169   "   Andrew (died in a fit), about 50y., Aug. 16, 1820.
3-26 HAILEY Samuel, 84y., Aug. 18, 1823.
3-15 HAILE Mary, wife of Barnard, March 7, 1802.
3-20   "   ——, widow of Dea. ——, 69y., July 24, 1809.
3-21   "   Capt. —— (in sloop Sally, in last passage from Havana), Dec. —, 1811.
2-58   "   Nathan B., of Barnard (buried at Warren), Nov. 11, 1813.
3-24   "   Dea. ——, 82y., Sept. 4, 1818.
4-96   "   Barnard, 88y., (also 4-102), May 8, 1847.
4-112   "   Coomer, a Revolutionary pensioner, 84y., April 22, 1849.
4-132 HALL Ruth M., wife of Benjamin, 56y., (at Steubenville, O.) June 16, 1851.
2-54 HAMMON Edward, Jan. —, 1717.
2-55   "   Susannah, Jan. 17, 1731.
4-169 HANDY William, Dec. 10, 1820.
3-30   "   Sophia, widow of Russell N., 71y., Oct. 4, 1830.
4-21   "   William A., 9m., Oct. 6, 1834.
4-73   "   Joanna, of Luther, 20y., July 24, 1843.
4-112   "   William, 49y., March, 21, 1849.
2-54 HANNAH, an Indian, May 14, 1730.
2-56 HANNOH (at Narragansett), Sept. --, 1746.
2-57 HARDING Joseph, child of ——, Nov. 5, 1759.
2-57   "   ——, wife of Joseph, June 14, 1766.
2-57   "   Mary, child of ——, —— --, 1774.
3-2   "   Joseph, 73y., Feb. 1, 1787.

3-7	HARDING Elizabeth, of Richard, 16m., Sept. 12, 1791.	
3-9	" Johannah (Pepperburgh), wife of James, 26y., Sept. 25, 1794.	
3-9	" Nancy, of James, 11m., Oct. 6, 1794.	
3-10	" Joseph, 20y. (at Havanna), Nov. 30, 1794.	
3-12	" Martha, wife of Richard, 30y., Feb. 8, 1797.	
3-14	" Charles (at sea), Jan. —, 1799.	
3-16	" William, July 20, 1804.	
3-19	" Deborah, wife of Richard, Dec. 6, 1807.	
2-58	" James, child of —, Feb. 17, 1814.	
3-23	" William, (drowned in mill pond in a gale), Sept. 23, 1815.	
3-24	" James, 50y., Oct. 20, 1817.	
3-28	" Hannah, widow, 84y., July 28, 1826.	
4-15	" Sarah, wife of John G., 64y., Jan. 19, 1834.	
4-47	" Lorenzo Dow, of Benjamin, 21y., May 12, 1838.	
4-47	" William P., of John G., 2d, 1y., 8m., May 22, 1838.	
4-56	" John S., 33y., March 4, 1840.	
4-58	" Theodore O., 27y., April 25, 1840.	
4-58	" Martha, of Thomas A., 2y., June 20, 1840.	
4-84	" Sarah, wife of Thomas A., 29y., Nov. 12, 1844.	
4-112	" Hannah, 75y., June 20, 1849.	
4-114	" William, 84y., Aug. 24, 1849.	
4-118	" Mary Elizabeth, widow of James, 82y., Feb. 4, 1850.	
4-122	" Sarah, widow of Richard, 82y., May 7, 1850.	
4-124	" John Glover, 81y., June 25, 1850.	
4-126	" Sylvester, 79y., Oct. 30, 1850.	
2-55	HARRIS George, child of —, Feb. 14, 1736.	
2-55	" George (at Newport), April —, 1736.	
2-56	" Frank (at Surinam), —, 1753.	
2-57	" Eleanor, widow, Sept. 19, 1768.	
4-169	" William (at Georgetown, S. C.), 39y., Nov. 3, 1820.	
3-31	" Harris, 47y., June 10, 1831.	
4-27	" Hannah, wife of — (col), 24y., Nov. 7, 1835.	
2-56	HART Mark, wife of —, Oct. 4, 1743.	
2-58	" Asa, child of —, — —, 1811.	
2-58	" —, of Asa, June —, 1812.	
2-55	HASKELL John, son of —, July 4, 1736.	
2-55	" —, child of —, July 24 1737.	
2-55	" John (at Woodstock), Nov. —, 1737.	
2-57	" Mary, widow, Nov. 6, 1775.	
2-58	" Song, child of —, 7y., Nov. 24, 1812.	
3-4	" Lucy, negro servant of Sarah —, 54y., July 7, 1789.	
3-24	" Sarah, 81y., Oct. 12, 1818.	
4-45	" Susannah T., of John (col.), 8y., Aug. 18, 1837.	
4-58	" Maria, wife of Song (col.), 66y., April 30, 1840.	
4-90	" Song (col.), 75y., April 24, 1846.	
4-120	" Mary, wife of John (col.), 42y., April 11, 1850.	
2-55	HATCH Nathaniel, of Newport, June —, 1739.	
4-29	" Capt. William (on the African coast), April 22, 1835.	
2-57	HAUGH Richard, Jr. (mortally wounded by a pump falling on him), Sept. 10, 1773.	
2-54	HAYMAN Capt. Nathan, July 27, 1689.	
4-94	HAY John, 60y., (born Great Britain) Sept. 11, 1846.	
4-219	HAZARD James Morgan Catskill, and Maria M., his wife, their children's deaths.	
4-219	" William James,	June 5, 1845.
4-219	" Victoria,	May 20, 1855.
4-219	" Julia Ann,	May 24, 1855.
4-219	" Maria Jane,	May 29, 1855.
4-219	" Barbara Howland,	Feb. 28, 1861.
4-219	" James M. C., father of above, 62y., Feb. 12, 1864.	
3-27	HEATH Winchester, 42y., July 10, 1825.	
2-54	HEDGE John, of William and Elizabeth, July 17, 1687.	
2-55	HEIFERLAND —, child of —,	April 11, 1736.
2-55	HERLE Richard, March 3, 1742.	
2-57	" Mrs. Mary, 85y., April 23, 1757.	

2-57	HERLIHEY William, child of, Oct. 18, 1772.	
3-25	HERRESHOFF Charles F., 50y., (in N. Y. State), Dec. 19, 1819.	
4-92	" Sarah, widow of Charles F., 74y., Aug. 2, 1846.	
2-57	HICKS Benjamin, child of, Sept. 9, 1758.	
2-57	" Mary, widow, 69y., Sept. 11, 1763.	
3-17	HILL Betsey, 26y., Jan. 11, 1806.	
2-56	HILTON Dudley, child of, June 25, 1743.	
2-56	" Dudley, child of, Sept. —, 1745.	
2-56	" Dudley (lost on the back of the Cape on passage from Surinam, vessel and cargo lost), Dec. 29, 1747.	
2-54	HINTON Mary, of John and Jane, buried Oct. 14, 1684.	
2-54	HOAR William, Nov. 27, 1698.	
1-219	" Rebecca, of Benjamin and Rebecca, Aug. 21, 1702.	
2-55	" —, child of William, May 18, 1737.	
2-56	" William, child of —, Feb. 23, 1744.	
2-54	" Mrs. Hannah, Sept. 28, 1746.	
2-57	" —, child of William, April —, 1754.	
2-57	" —,	Nov. 17, 1754.
2-54	" Benjamin, of Benjamin and Deborah, July 3, —.	
1-219	" Rebecca, of Benjamin and Rebecca, Aug. 21, 1702.	
3-2	" William, 77y., Oct. 22, 1786.	
3-29	" Benjamin, March 21, 1829.	
4-25	" Priscilla, widow of Benjamin, 77y., April 16, 1835.	
4-47	" Betsey, 56y., March 1, 1838.	
4-55	" John Henry, of James, Oct. 17, 1839.	
4-106	" Mary, wife of William, 54y., Aug. 27, 1848.	
2-57	HOGEN Anne, widow, 67y., Feb. 25, 1765.	
2-57	" John, child of, (scalded by drinking hot tea), 3y., Feb. 2, 1768.	
2-58	" John, 46y., Dec. 17, 1775.	
2-55	HOLMES Mary, Sept. 20, 1734.	
2-57	" Capt. William, a son of, 4y., July 16, 1759.	
2-57	" Joanna, Oct. 7, 1775.	
2-58	" William, of Capt., (at sea), — —, 1775.	
3-15	" Ruth, widow, (at Swansey), Nov. 4, 1801.	
4-35	" Jabez, of Dr. Jabez, 3y., 7m., July 25, 1836.	
4-54	HONFLEUR Susan Frances, dau. of Dr. William Rogers, dec., of Philadelphia, Pa., (at Jeffersonville, Ind.), Sept. 6, 1839.	
3-30	HORSWELL Betsey, widow, 66y., Dec. 3, 1829.	
4-94	HORTON Mary, wife of Eliphalet, formerly of Rehoboth, (buried there), 77y., Oct. 25, 1846.	
4-124	" Delight, wife of Levi, 50y., July 3, 1850.	
2-54	HOWELL John, Nov. 18, 1729.	
3-16	HOWE James, 21y. (at sea), March —, 1802.	
3-16	" William, 24y. (at sea), March —, 1802.	
3-16	" Mark Antony (at sea), March —, 1802.	
4-17	" Louisa, wife of John, dau. of Stephen Smith, 45y., April 21, 1834.	
4-35	" Abby T., wife of John R., 24y., Aug. 7, 1836.	
4-35	" Abby, of John R., 12w., Sept. 22, 1836.	
4-45	" George, 46y., Oct. 24, 1837.	
2-57	HOWLAND Seth, of Jabez and Bethiah, (buried) April 12, 1685.	
2-54	" —, of Jabez and Patience, Oct. 5, 1707.	
2-54	" Elizabeth,	—. —, 1707.
2-54	" Josiah, Feb. 8, 1717.	
2-55, 54	" Jabez, 64y., Oct. 17, 1732.	
2-55	" —, son of Capt. Nathaniel, July 18, 1736.	
2-55	" Abigail, wife of Samuel, 53y., Aug. 6, 1737.	
2-55	" Yet Mercy, wife of Nathaniel, Aug. 8, 1737.	
2-55	" Joseph, Aug. 16, 1737.	
2-55	" —, son of John, Dec. 20, 1737.	
2-55	" Jabez, (at sea), May —, 1739.	
2-56	" Mary, of John and Joanna, of Barnstable, Mass., Sept. 28, 1745.	
2-56	" Shem, servant of Mrs. Yet Mercy, May 6, 1747.	
2-56	" —, negro child,	Jan. —, 1748.
2-56	" —, negro girl,	May —, 1748.
2-56	" Josiah, Feb. 6, 1748.	

2-56	HOWLAND Samuel, May 15, 1748.	
2-57	" John, child of (still born), —— —, 1771.	
2-58	" Sarah, of John, Jr., and Elizabeth, Dec. 31, 1775.	
2-58	" Judah, of Jabez and Bethiah, (buried), Nov. 12, 1783.	
1-221	" Seth, of Samuel and Abigail, —— —, ——.	
3-3	" Pompey, negro servant of John, 22y., April 10, 1787.	
3-5	" Child of John, Jr., 5 days, Oct. 1, 1790.	
3-5	" Peleg, Oct —, 1790.	
3-7	" Child of John, Jr., Sept. 24, 1792.	
3-7	" John, Esq., 54y., Dec. 6, 1792.	
3-9	" Martha, widow, 78y., July 9, 1794.	
3-9	" Daniel, 31y (at Gambia river), Sept. —, 1795.	
3-12	" Joseph, 20y. (lost from brig "Little Joseph" at sea), Dec. 26, 1796.	
3-14	" Elizabeth, 54y., Jan. 27, 1801.	
3-16	" William Martin (in Africa), May —, 1804.	
3-17	" Capt. Nathaniel, 32y., March 18, 1805.	
3-25	" Hannah, widow, 45y., July 7, 1819.	
4-169	" Charity (col.), 20y., Jan. 1, 1820.	
3-27	" Charles, of Judge, 21y., June 28, 1825.	
3-28	" Thankful, 61y., Sept. 22, 1827.	
3-31	" John, Esq., 60y., April 25, 1831.	
4-17	" Sukey, wife of John (col.), 28y., May 3, 1834.	
4-19	" John, of Capt. Nathaniel (at Buffalo, N. Y.), 35y., Aug. 18, 1834.	
4-21	" Dau. of James (col.), 5y., Oct. 3, 1834.	
4-21	" Dau. of James (col.), 5y March 10, 1836.	
4-88	" Hannah (col.), about 57y., Oct. 4, 1845.	
4-88	" Barbara, Feb. 28, 1861.	
2-55	HUBBARD Mrs. Sarah, 68y., Jan. —, 1743.	
2-56	" William (at Cape Breton), May —, 1744-5.	
2-56	" ——, negro child of Mrs., Dec. —, 1746.	
2-56	" Hon. N. (at Rehoboth), Jan. 10, 1748.	
2-56	" John, child of, May —, 1748.	
2-57	" John, wife of, 53y., Sept. 12, 1775.	
2-57	" John, 65y., Oct. 1, 1775.	
3-19	HUMPHREY Selena, 59y., Feb. 23, 1809.	
4-169	HYMES Arnold, child of, Aug. 16, 1820.	

I

4-31	IDE Mary Ann Chickering, of Isaac, 5y., March 26, 1836.	
2-60	INDIAN woman found dead at Papoose Squaw, Jan. —, 1740.	
2-60	" man, at do., Oct. 17, 1742.	
2-60	" man, on board ship, with Capt. Potter, April 25, 1745.	
——	" man, at Thomas Durfee's, Jan. 18, 1747.	
2-60	INGRAHAM Jer., child of, Sept. —, 1732.	
2-60	" Isaac, child of, March 3, 1733.	
2-60	" Mary, of Edward, Jan. 11, 1734-5.	
2-60	" ——, son of, 12y., July 19, 1736.	
2-60	" Capt. Joshua, negro man of, July 10, 1737.	
2-60	" Mercy, May 30, 1743.	
2-60	" Joshua, son of, (drawned) 5y., June 10, 1743.	
2-60	" Timothy, Nov. 22, 1743.	
2-60	" Mrs. ——, 75y., —— —, 1743.	
2-60	" Edward, (at Cape Breton), Sept. —, 1745.	
2-60	" Timothy, June 29, 1748.	
2-60	" Joshua, twin child of,	Oct. 28, 1751.
2-60	" ——,	Nov. 5, 1751.
2-60	" ——, child of,	Jan. 10, 1752.
2-60	" ——, negro child of Joshua, Sept. 18, 1761.	
2-61	" John, Jr., child, died Sept. 18, 1761.	
2-61	" Capt., negro child of ——, April —, 1762.	
2-61	" Martha, of Capt. Joshua, 22y., July 19, 1762.	
2-61	" Martha, his wife,	Oct. 24, 1762.
2-61	" ——, infant child of ——,	Oct. 25, 1763.

2-61	INGRAHAM ——, his negro child, —— —, 1764.		
2-61	" ——,		Sept. 13, 1765.
2-61	" ——,		Dec. 20, 1787.
2-61	" ——,		—— —, 1770.
2-61	" ——, his negro woman, June 17, 1774.		
2-61	" Elizabeth, wife of Joshua, Jr., 38y., Oct. 7, 1769.		
	" ——, infant child of ——,		Sept. or Oct. —, 1769.
2-61	" Timothy, child of ——, 2y., Nov. 17, 1771.		
2-61	" ——, child of do., —— 8, 1775.		
2-61	" Benjamin, of John, Jr., (perished with cold on ship board wrecked at the Vineyard), Dec. 26, 1778.		
3-1	" Capt. John, 85y., Feb. 17, 1786.		
3-2	" Richard, negro servant of S., April 30, 1786.		
3-2	" ——, infant child of George, 12d., Jan. 29, 1787.		
3-4	" Mary, of Jeremiah, 16m., Sept. 30, 1789.		
3-7	" Lydia Pearce, of Nathaniel, 20m., Sept. 29, 1791.		
3-7	" Fanny Usher,		3y., Sept. 30, 1791.
3-7	" Henry, of George, 3y., Nov. 4, 1791.		
3-8	" Capt. Joshua, 89y., March 1, 1793.		
3-8	" Mary, of Jeremiah, 25y., May 8, 1793.		
3-9	" Agnes, wife of Capt. Jeremiah, Feb. 28, 1794.		
3-11	" James Davis, 26y., Sept. 18, 1796.		
3-14	" John, 72y., Aug. 3, 1799.		
3-14	" William (at sea), Sept. —, 1799.		
3-18	" Capt. Jeremiah, 75y., Sept. 30, 1807.		
3-19	" Mary, widow, Nov. 6, 1807.		
3-20	" Mary, widow, 78y., March 19, 1810.		
3-20	" Benjamin (in Africa), Oct. 18, 1810.		
3-21	" Jeremiah, 60y., Aug. 28, 1811.		
2-62	" Daniel, child of ——, 1d., July 29, 1812.		
2-62	" ——,		8d., Aug. 5, 1812.
2-62	" ——,		12d., Aug. 9, 1812.
3-22	" Joseph, of Boston, Mass., (at Mrs. Slocum's), (also 2-61), 44y., June 28, 1813.		
4-169	" ——, child of Allen, 13m., Aug. 31, 1820.		
4-17	" Priscilla, widow of Jeremiah, 85y., April 20, 1834.		
3-30	" Mary, wife of Capt. Nathaniel, 66y., April 12, 1830.		
4-37	" Nathaniel, 72y., Oct. 18, 1836.		
4-56	" Patience, wife of James D., 24y., April 16, 1840.		
4-64	" Thomas (at Amenia, Datchess Co., N. Y.), 70y., May 12, 1841.		
4-68	" Daniel, 73y., Nov. 5, 1841.		
4-116	" Abby, of Capt. Daniel, 79y., Oct. 16, 1849.		
4-86	INMAN Phila., 17y., Feb. 19, 1845.		
3-6	" Isaac, of Capt. Isaac, 2y., Aug. —, 1791.		
2-61	IRENS Peter, child of ——, July 24, 1812.		
2-60	" Isaac, old Bowson, (at Guadaloupe), —— —, 1742.		

J

2-64	JACOBS Joseph, Feb. 9, 1708.		
2-64	" Benjamin, of Joseph and Hannah, Aug. 17, 1703.		
2-64	" Joseph, Jr.,		Nov. 1. 1703.
2-64	" Mary (at Hingham), March 22, 1696.		
2-64	" Indian, a child of ——, Oct. 31, 1744.		
2-64	JENKINS Deborah, widow, Feb. 4. 1707-8.		
2-65	" Joseph, child of ——, Sept. 30, 1746.		
2-65	" ——, May —, 1750.		
2-65	" Sarah, widow, child of ——, —— —, 1749.		
2-65	JENNINGS Stephen, Nov. 13, 1750.		
2-65	JETHRO Tom (mulatto), Dec. —, 1776.		
2-64	JOLLS Mrs. ——, negro child of ——, —— —, 1736.		
2-64	" Thomas, child of ——, Feb. —, 1738.		
2-64	" Robert, his Indian woman, —— —, 1738.		
2-64	" ——, negro child of ——, Feb. 3, 1738.		

2-64	JOLLS Robert, 63y., Jan. 17, 1739-40.	
2-64	" Mr——, his negro child, Dec. 19, 1741.	
2-65	" ——,	May 27, 1745.
2-65	" ——,	July 2, 1758.
2-65	" Old Mrs. (from a burn received the day before), 84y., Dec. 15, 1757.	
2-65	" Thomas, 58y., Oct. 16, 1760.	
4-52	" Phillis (col.), 90y., Jan. 34, 1839.	
2-64	" Cornelius, of Cornelius and Mercy (buried), July 16, 1694.	
2-64	" Ichabod, of do., (buried) July 16, 1694.	
2-64	" Benjamin (after a long illness), Jan. 12, 1717.	
2-65	" Mrs. Bathsheba, Sept. 17, 1740.	
2-65	" John (at Surinam), Oct. 3, 1748.	
2-65	" Abel, child of ——, April 6, 1812.	
3-23	JONES Abel, 35y., Oct. 1, 1815.	
4-15	" Oliver S., formerly of Hartford, Conn., 39y., Feb. 17, 1834.	
4-31	" John (col.), 25y., March 25, 1836.	
4-66	" Caroline, widow of Le Roy, 34, Oct. 10, 1841.	
2-64	JOY Mrs., child of ——, 8y., July —, 1734.	
2-65	" Esther, widow, May 26, 1754.	
3-19	JUDSON Joseph (lost at sea with sloop Minerva), Dec. 29, 1807.	
3-7	JULY Charles (free black at sea as servant of Charles Collins), Aug. 22, 1792.	

K

4-52	KAWL John A., 89y., (a native of Germany, a soldier and Revolutionary pensioner), March 31, 1839.	
2-67	KELLEY, Daniel, Nov. —, 1730.	
2-67	" widow, child of, March 2, 1731.	
2-67	" George (drowned at Surinam), April —, 1740.	
2-67	" Joseph, wife of, Nov. 20, 1743.	
2-67	" —— child of, Feb. 15, 1746.	
2-67	" Joseph (lost on back of the Cape coming from Surinam; vessel and cargo lost), Dec. 29, 1747.	
2-68	" Edward (drowned from privateer Yankee while at anchor), Feb. —, 1814. Taken up and interred April 30, 1814.	
4-62	KEMPTON Eunice, widow of Daniel, of Mendon, Mass., Dec. 28, 1840.	
4-128	KENDRICK Edward, 10y., Jan. 5, 1851.	
3-30	KENNEDY Ann, widow, 85y., Feb. 20, 1831.	
4-41	KENNEY Pardon Tillinghast, of Lorenzo D., 4y. 1m., March 23, 1837.	
4-41	" William Henry,	1y. 8m., March 29, 1837.
2-68	KENT Abigail, of Rev. Asa, 34y., Aug. 11, 1813.	
4-66	KENYON Mrs. Sarah, 22y., (buried at Providence), Sept. 26, 1841.	
4-122	KERSHAW John, 53y., (born England), May 2, 1850.	
3-14	KINGSLEY Elizabeth, wife of Mason, April 14, 1801.	
4-169	" Hezekiah, of Mason, 2y., Jan. 12, 1820.	
4-169	" Hannah,	Nov. 1, 1820.
4-56	KING Pamela F., of George W., 8m., March 9, 1840.	
2-67	KINNECUTT Thomas (blacksmith), Feb. 2, 1707-8.	
2-67	" ——, child of Thomas, 2y., Dec. 12, 1736.	
2-67	" ——,	March 26, 1739.
2-67	" ——,	Aug. 16, 1740.
2-67	" ——,	Aug. 22, 1744.
2-67	" Bosworth, Aug. 9, 1755.	
2-68	" Thomas, 57y., —— —, 1763.	
3-14	" Sarah, widow, 91y., March 22, 1801.	
4-64	KINS Hannah, 38y., (col.), April 23, 1841.	
2-67	KIPP Cornelia, of William and Sarah, 2m., 4d., July 30, 1746.	
2-67	" ——,	July 31, 1746.
2-67	" William, wife of, (drowned coming from Newport), Oct. 15, 1747.	
2-67	" William, (on return from camp at Lake George), —— —, 1756.	
2-68	KNIGHT John, (apprentice to Thomas Mumford, drowned at Surinam), Aug. —, 1747.	

3-20   KNOWLES Joseph, of Providence, (drowned in Bristol harbor), May 18, 1810.

L

4-110   LADUCE Samuel, 60y., April 1, 1849.
4-21   LAKE Betsey, wife of Elias, 25y., Dec. 10, 1834.
4-29   "   Ann Elizabeth, of Elias, 10m., (at Taunton), Oct. 4, 1835.
4-31   "   Hannah, of Joseph, of Tiverton, 24y., March 24, 1836.
4-76   "   Isaac, 56y., April 3, 1843.
4-118   "   Malvina, of Albert and Almeda, 3y., Oct. 23, 1849.
4-118   "   Albert Bliven,   7m. 5d., Nov. 12, 1849.
2-71   LAKEMAN John, (at Cape Breton), Nov. —, 1745.
2-70   LAMBERT Caleb, wife of, March 25, 1682.
2-73   LAMB Mrs. Sarah, 74y., Aug. 29, 1774.
4-98   LANSING Elizabeth Allen, widow of Garrett, granddau. of Rev. John Usher, (at New York), June 28, 1847.
2-72   LAWLESS John, (at Cape Breton), March 3, 1746.
2-74   "   Joseph (on return from camp), — —, 1756.
2-73   "   William, child of —, Jan. 1, 1762.
2-73   "   Mary, widow, 67y., March 30, 1763.
2-73   "   William, child of, 2y., June 28, 1771.
3-6   "   Capt. James, 55y., March 15, 1791.
4-21   "   Margaret, 42y., Oct. 24, 1834.
4-27   "   Sarah, widow of John, 71y., Nov. 22, 1835.
4-56   "   —, child of John Y., 7m., March 18, 1840.
3-18   LAWRENCE Henry, 25y., Aug. 27, 1807.
2-70   "   Thomas, child of —, Oct. —, 1730.
2-72   "   Elizabeth, Sept. 30, 1748.
2-72   "   Thomas, 17y., Jan. 18, 1753.
2-72   "   Jonathan, 20y., Jan. 11, 1758.
3-18   "   Henry, 25y., Aug. 27, 1807.
4-52   LAWS Nancy, wife of Dennis (col.), 29y., Dec. 12, 1838.
2-74   LAWSON Alice, Oct. 15, 1775.
2-70   LAWTON Capt., his negro woman, Aug. —. 1730.
2-70   "   child,   Aug. —, 1730.
2-70   "   —,   July —, 1731.
2-70   "   —,   — —, 1732.
2-70   "   —,   April —, 1734.
2-70   "   Capt., child of, March —, 1733.
2-74   "   Isaac, child of, June —. 1733.
2-71   "   Capt., his negro woman, July —, 1736.
2-71   "   ——, his daughter, 16y., July 24, 1736.
2-71   "   Thomas, Jr. (at Surinam), June —, 1744.
2-71   "   ——, his wife, Jan. 29, 1745.
2-72   "   Job, wife of, Oct. 2, 1746.
2-72   "   Isaac, March 7, 1749.
2-72   "   Capt. Thomas, April 24, 1752.
2-72   "   Thomas, (at the West Indies), — —, 1753.
2-73   "   Gardiner, 21y., Feb. 13, 1760.
2-73   "   Joseph, (at Crown Point), — —, 1760.
4-33   LE BARON William Henry, of James, 2y. 8m., April 18, 1836.
4-100   LEEMAN Mary P., wife of Henry W., dau. of David Fish, dec., 28y., (at Charlestown, Mass.), Nov. —, 1847.
3-16   LEE Charles, (at sea), 16y., March —, 1802.
3-16   "   Samuel, (at sea), 18y., March —, 1802.
2-70   LEFAVOUR Timothy, child of, June 27, 1732.
2-71   "   Timothy, Sept. —, 1741.
2-72   "   Mrs., infant child of, April —, 1746.
2-72   "   her negro child, Jan. 24, 1747.
2-72   "   Mrs., March 3, 1748.
2-72   "   Daniel, child of, Dec. 19, 1759.
2-72   "   Jemima, wife of Daniel, 21y., Dec. 25, 1759.
3-11   "   Martha, wife of Daniel, 53y., May 6, 1796.
3-12   "   Daniel, 64y., (drowned at East Greenwich), July 1, 1797.

2-72	LENTHARNS Thomas, child of, Jan. —. 1755.	
2-72	" Mrs., child of, March —, 1735.	
2-73	" Margaret, of Thomas, 2y., Feb. 22, 1762.	
2-73	" Benjamin,	6y., Oct. 15, 1763.
4-29	LESAVAN Howland, 57y., Dec. 15, 1835.	
2-70	LEWIS Mary, of Thomas and Hannah, March 26, 1686.	
2-70	" Thomas, about 76y., April 26, 1709.	
2-70	" Hannah, widow, Jan. —, 1717.	
3-16	" Bathsheba, widow, 38y., March 25, 1804.	
4-82	" Elizabeth, of Joseph, late of St. George, Delaware, 16m., Oct. 5, 1844.	
3-8	LINCOLN Rose, negro servant of Freeman, 18y., July 2, 1793.	
3-21	" Elizabeth, widow, 85y., (also 2-74), Sept. 12, 1811.	
4-76	" Phebe, widow of Capt. Seth, 70y., March 26, 1843.	
4-104	" Capt. Seth, 54y., Aug. 6, 1848.	
2-72	LINDSEY Samuel, (at Surinam), —— —, 1756.	
2-72	" William, of Capt. John, (at Dartmouth, Eng.,) 20y., —— —. 1758.	
2-72	" John, Jr., child of, Jan. 7, 1759.	
2-73	" Capt. John, 58y., April 1, 1761.	
2-73	" John, child of, May 6, 1763.	
2-73	" Mary, of William, 25y., May 22, 1763.	
2-73	" Eliza,	1y., Dec. 8, 1769.
2-73	" Jemima,	14y., Aug. 31, 1770.
2-73	" Mrs. Hannah, widow of Capt. John, 66y., Nov. 11, 1765.	
2-73	" John (at Surinam), Aug. —, 1766.	
2-74	" William, (at Rehoboth), 64y., May 17, 1777.	
2-74	" Mrs. Mary, (at Rehoboth), 65y., June 3, 1777.	
3-6	" Anna, of Joseph, 3y., Aug. 24, 1791.	
3-7	" Mary, of Samuel, 16y., Aug. 29, 1791.	
3-7	" Jemima, 62y., Oct. 14, 1792.	
3-8	" Prescilla, wife of Samuel. 30y., Jan. 4, 1793.	
3-5	" ——, child of Joseph, 1w., Oct. —. 1790.	
3-5	" ——, child, 9 days, Oct. —, 1790.	
3-11	" Rebecca, widow, 39y., Dec. 19, 1796.	
3-12	" Lydia, 20y., Sept. 1, 1797.	
3-12	" Joseph, 49y., Sept. 4, 1797.	
3-15	" Joseph (at New York), June —, 1802.	
2-74	" Samuel, child of ——, 5 weeks, April 14, 1813.	
2-74	" Woodbury, child of ——, Aug. 18, 1813.	
2-74	" Sophia, of Thomas, May 24, 1815.	
2-74	" ——, Aug. 20. 1815.	
3-23	" Deborah, widow, 63y., Nov. 3, 1815.	
3-25	" Rhodie, wife of Thomas, 35y., Oct. 29, 1819.	
4-169	" Sophia, of Thomas, 8m., June 6, 1820.	
3-28	" William, 80y., March 22, 1826.	
3-30	" Miss Lydia, 86y., July 4. 1830.	
4-31	" William James, of Joseph, 6y., March 3. 1836.	
4-39	" ——, son of Jonathan, W., Jr., 10d., March 7, 1837.	
4-45	" Abby Ann, of Daniel, 20m., Oct. 13, 1837.	
4-62	" Benjamin,	18y., Feb. 3, 1841.
4-64	" Catherine, widow of William, 88y., March 7, 1841.	
4-74	" Daniel, 46y., Dec. 15, 1842.	
4-114	" Jemima, 63y., Sept. 7, 1849.	
4-124	" Pamela, widow of Samuel, 77y., Aug. 4, 1850.	
2-130	" Hannah V., wife of Capt. Jonathan W., 72y., March 21, 1851.	
2-71	LINSEY Capt. John,, his Indian woman, April —, 1734.	
2-71	" Capt. John, (at Surinam), July —, 1734.	
2-71	" ——, his negro woman, July 12, 1737.	
2-71	" Benjamin, child of ——, Nov. 3, 1734.	
2-71	" Samuel, his mulatto girl, —— —, 1735.	
2-71	" Samuel, child,	June 6, 1737.
2-71	" Keziah, Oct. 29, 1740.	
2-71	" Capt. John, son of about 9y., Nov. 18, 1743.	
2-71	" William, child of ——, May —, 1745.	
2-72	" Benjamin, (at Jamaica), Aug. —. 1747.	
2-72	" Mrs. Eliza, March —, 1755.	

2-71	LISCOMB Ann, June 6, 1738.	
2-73	"	John, Jr., at Berbacia, July 11, 1762.
2-74	"	John, 68 or 69y., Nov. 21, 1761.
2-73	"	Sarah, 33y., Sept. 2, 1765.
2-74	"	Samuel, 79y., Dec. 18, 1775.
2-74	"	Elizabeth, 73y., March 25, 1776.
2-74	"	Nathaniel, of William and Katherine, Sept. 6, 1795.
2-74	"	Nathaniel, Jr., of ditto, Sept. 21, 1796.
3-7	"	——, child of Nathaniel, 2 days, —— —, 1792.
3-15	"	Nathaniel, Aug. 30, 1802.
3-16	"	Samuel, 77y., May 17, 1804.
2-74	"	Nancy, of John, dec., April 28, 1813.
2-74	"	Isaac, child of ——, July 1, 1818.
2-74	"	Sarah, widow of John, June 6, 1815.
3-23	"	Leah, widow, 86y., June 7, 1815.
4-169	"	Sarah, wife of Simon, 26y., Dec. 10, 1820.
3-29	"	Mary, 40y. (at Providence), March 31, 1828.
3-29	"	Samuel, 37y., Nov. 24, 1828.
4-33	"	Benjamin, 66y., June 23, 1836.
4-37	"	Raymond, of Jeremiah D., 5y., 7m., Oct. 20, 1836.
4-37	"	Eleanor, wife of Jeremiah D., 28y., Nov. 3, 1836.
4-39	"	Isaac, 72y., Jan. 21, 1837.
4-80	"	Simon DeW., 45y., March 10, 1844.
4-102	"	Abigail, 83y., —— —, 1847.
4-116	"	Rosalie, of William C., 4m., Sept. 29, 1849.
4-128	"	Jeremiah D., 43y., Jan. 1, 1851.
3-20	LITTLEFIELD Capt. Caleb (at sea), 35y., Oct. 18, 1810.	
4-118	"	Capt. George (master of ship Hopewell of Warren), at Benecia, Cal., 44y., Oct. 6, 1849.
4-116	"	Hannah M., widow of Capt. Caleb, 69y. (at Warren), (also 4-118), Nov. 30, 1849.
2-70	LITTLE Lieut. Samuel, Jan. 16, 1707.	
2-70	"	Captain, wife of ——, July —, 1729.
2-70	"	——, negro man, March 23, 1732.
2-75	"	Mrs. Sarah, Feb. 14, 1736-7.
2-71	"	Mrs. Mary, Feb. 11, 1737.
2-71	"	Thomas, May 14, 1739.
2-71	"	Capt. Samuel, 49 or 50y., Jan. 8, 1739-40.
2-71	"	Mary, wife of Edward, Jan. 25, 1739-40.
4-120	LIVESEY Jane M., of Rev. Richard, 32y. (buried at Lowell, Mass.), Feb. 16, 1850.	
4-41	LUCE Harriet B., of Abijah, 18y., June 18, 1837.	
4-64	"	Sarah T., wife of Abijah, 39y., June 27, 1841.
4-74	"	Nancy M., of Abijah, 18y., Feb. 5, 1843.
2-74	LUTHER Alfred, Nov. 21, 1812.	
4-169	"	——, child of Sylvanus, Oct. 10, 1820.
4-37	"	Nathaniel, of Ebenezer, 22y. (at Mattapoisett), Nov. 7, 1836.
4-54	"	Allen, 70y., Sept. 6, 1839.
4-60	"	Arthur Boss, of Sylvester and Lydia P., 6y. 4m., (also 4-238), Aug. 5, 1840.
4-62	"	Col. Giles, 66y., Jan. 4, 1841.
4-76	"	Obadiah (formerly of Swansey), 72y., April 15, 1843.
4-86	"	Mary, of Josiah, 27y., July 2, 1845.
4-100	"	Elizabeth, widow of Barney, 88y. (Revolutionary pensioner), Dec. 30, 1847.
4-102	"	Elizabeth, 87y., —— —, 1847.

M

2-81	MACKARTY Dennis (on board man-of-war), —— —, 1760.	
2-82	"	Eliza, of widow Eliza, 10y., April —, 1762.
4-116	MACKINSON John, 45y., Nov. 22, 1849.	

2-85	MACLINTOCK Sally, of Joseph, May 2, 1813.
2-85	MACMAN Margaret, widow, Nov. 20, 1814.
4-85	MACUMBER ——, son of Otis, 5m., Aug. 13, 1836.
4-68	" Abby, wife of Otis, 48y., Dec. 17, 1841.
4-72	" Emily, of Otis, 9m., Aug. 12, 1842.
2-85	MAKIM Abigail, of Richard, Nov. 7, 1812.
2-80	MANCHESTER Seabury, of Benjamin and Martha, May 13, 1732.
2-78	" Job (drowned), Dec. 26, 1739.
2-79	" Benjamin, dau. of ——, Feb. 19, 1744.
2-80	" William (on coast of Africa), 22y., Aug. —, 1757.
2-81	" Benjamin, May 15, 1760.
2-82	" Seabury, child of, April 17, 1768.
2-82	" Nathaniel, child of, Dec. 1, 1770.
2-83	" Seabury, child of, Aug. 3, 1774.
2-84	" Martha, widow, Jan. 25, 1780.
3-9	" Marian, of Benjamin, 15m., March 26, 1794.
3-10	" Benjamin, 27y., Sept. —, 1795.
3-12	" Marian, wife of Seabury, 53y., Feb. 13, 1797.
3-14	" Sabra, wife of Seabury, 52y., March 19, 1801.
3-22	" Wyatt, 26y., Dec. 10, 1812.
2-85	" Wyatt, of Seabury, Dec. 13, 1812.
4-169	" Hannah, wife of Benjamin, 20y., Sept. 17, 1820.
3-26	" Elizabeth, wife of Nathaniel, 73y., Jan. 11, 1823.
3-26	" Almy, wife of Seabury, 38y., Sept. 6, 1823.
3-30	" Seabury, 89y., Aug 10, 1829.
4-19	" William, 63y., Aug. 21, 1834.
4-52	" John, Jr., 18m., Jan. 30, 1839.
4-56	" George Henry, of William H., 10y., March 26, 1840.
4-110	" Julia, 16y., March 20, 1840
4-62	" Susan, of Joseph, 4y., Dec. 30, 1840.
4-68	" child, 20m., Nov. 16, 1841.
4-88	" Hannah, widow of William, 73y., Dec. 3, 1841.
4-68	" child of Henry R., 3m., Feb. 1, 1842.
4-70	" M., 27y., May 12, 1842.
4-92	" Benjamin F., of Henry H., 3m., May 16, 1846.
4-94	" Sarah, wife of Philip A., 36y., Nov. 2, 1846.
4-94	" Susan J., wife of Henry A., 31y. 11m., Dec. 24, 1846.
4-102	" John, 73y., —— —, 1847.
4-114	" Philip A., 39y., Aug. 28, 1849.
4-116	" Emily Frances, of William, 1y. 4m., Oct. 7, 1849.
4-120	" William Henry, of Seabury, 42y., March 27, 1850.
4-122	" Ann Frances, wife of Capt. Benjamin F., and dau. of Arnold H. Manchester, 25y., May 7, 1850.
4-124	" George, of John, dec., 32y., June 30, 1850.
4-124	" John, of John, dec., 45y., Sept. 9, 1850.
4-126	' Seth Lincoln, of Henry R., 5m., Sept. 29, 1850.
3-14	MANSFIELD Daniel, 68y., March 30, 1801.
4-104	MANN Hannah, widow of Noah, 66y., April 23, 1848.
4-120	MARCHANT John Herbert, of Henry C. and Lucy A., 11y. 1m., Feb. 23, 1850.
3-4	" Margaret, widow, 73y., Oct. 3, 1788.
4-124	MARSTON Helen F., of John, dec., of Boston, 47y., Aug. 22, 1850.
3-1	MARTHA, wife of Col. Isaac, 45y., Jan. 20, 1786.
2-86	MARSHALL John, Jr., 19y., Oct. 17, 1748.
2-81	" Dinah, an Indian woman (at Major Carey's), June 4, 1761.
2-81	MARTINDALE Sion, child of, Nov. 30, 1761.
2-82	" William, child of, 4y., Feb. 15, 1768.
2-83	" Nancy, 14y., Sept. 28, 1775.
3-1	" Capt. Sion, 52y., May 21, 1785.
3-9	" Sarah, widow, 57y., Nov. 22, 1794.
2-78	MARTIN Thomas, child of, (also 2-77), Feb. —, 1735.
2-78	" ——, Oct. 16, 1736.
2-78	" ——, 2y., April —, 1740.
2-79	" William, wife of, June 18, 1741.
2-79	" William, Jr., wife of, 27y., Feb. 4, 1745.

2-78   MARTIN Hannah, wife of Thomas, (also 2-79), July 13, 1746.
2-79   "   Capt. William (at Jamaica), Jan. —, 1748.
2-80   "   Thomas (at sea), Sept. 19, 1750.
2-80   "   Thomas, his negro man, July 27, 1752.
2-81   "   Thomas (at Antigua), —— —, 1758.
2-81   "   Rachel, widow, child of, 9y., Sept. 26, 1759.
2-82   "   William, 91y., April 30, 1767.
2-82   "   Rachel, widow, 43y., March 13, 1769.
2-83   "   Charity, 65y., April 5, 1776.
4-94   "   Harry, of Samuel, 25y., Nov. 10, 1846.
4-106   "   Mrs. Betsey, dau. of William Harding, 77y. (at Rehoboth), Aug. 30, 1848.
2-77   MASON Joseph, child of, May 3, 1732.
2-83   "   Content, of James, 13y., Oct. 11, 1775.
3-12   "   Mary, widow, 74y., June 3, 1797.
4-27   "   Sarah, wife of Joseph, 54y., Dec. 2, 1835.
4-72   "   child of Asa, 6y., Sept. 20, 1842.
4-90   "   Hannah, wife of Asa, 65y., Dec. 14, 1845.
4-86   MATHEWSON James Edwin, of John and Amey, 10m., June 7, 1845.
2-85   MATTHEWS William, child of, Aug. 9, 1814.
2-77   MAXFIELD Joseph, wife of, March 10, 1732.
2-86   "   Joseph, Jr., Oct. 22, 1747.
2-86   "   Ebenezer, July 11, 1737.
2-7b   "   Daniel, Feb. 27, 1740.
2-78   "   Ann (at Killingly), May —, 1740.
2-79   "   Nathaniel (at Boston), Nov. 17, 1745.
2-79   "   Jeremy (at sea), —— —, 1745.
2-85   "   Abigail, Sept. 13, 1747.
2-85   "   Joseph, 78y., March 6, 1768.
2-83   "   Sarah, 61y., June 30, 1776.
3-15   "   Almira, of Daniel, 18m., Oct. 4, 1801.
3-19   "   Mary, widow, 75y., Feb. 7, 1809.
3-31   "   Deborah, wife of Daniel, 66y., Oct. 25, 1831.
4-17   "   Merebah, wife of David, 72y., April 26, 1834.
4-17   "   Daniel, 67y., June 5, 1834.
4-37   "   David, a Revolutionary pensioner, 80y., Nov. 23, 1836.
4-78   "   William, 50y., Oct. 16, 1843.
4-122   "   Eunice, of Abel, 19y., May 13, 1850.
2-78   MAY Elisha, 19y., Feb. 28, 1737.
2-79   "   Abigail, May 20, 1746.
2-80   "   Hannah, wife of Elisha, 68y., Nov. 14, 1756.
2-82   "   Hannah, of Elisha, Nov. —, 1763.
2-83   "   Elisha, 79y., Nov. 27, 1773.
3-5   "   John, July 14, 1790.
3-8   "   John, July 8, 1793.
3-9   "   Elisha, 30y., Feb. 17, 1794.
3-22   "   Sarah, widow of John, 87y., (also 2-85) Oct. 11, 1812.
3-35   "   John, of John, of Charleston, S. C. (drowned), Sept. 26, 1836.
4-116   McCANN James, 2d, officer of brig Rio (born Scotland) (at sea) 24y., Sept. 25, 1849.
4-102   McCARTNEY William, of Adam, 1y., 4m., Jan. 29, 1848.
3-23   McCARTY Clarissa, widow, 74y., Jan. 7, 1817.
4-86   MEIGS Elizabeth, widow of Ansel, 70y., Aug. 4, 1845.
2-79   MELLIS Nehemiah, wife of, Nov. 22, 1741.
2-84   MIKE Dick, of John, 12y., April 23, 1812.
2-77   MILLER Josiah, May 28, 1694.
2-81   "   Jonathan (apprentice to Joseph Maxfield at the Camp), —— —, 1760.
4-168   "   child of Allen, March 19, 1821.
4-217   "   James, of James and Rebecca, March 26, 1826.
4-217   "   Isabella A., Dec. 6, 1830.
4-217   "   Mary L., Nov. 10, 1835.
3-28   "   Allen, 45y., June 1, 1826.
4-27   "   Mary Louisa, of James, 1y. 10m., Nov. 12, 1835.
4-49   "   Sarah, wife of Nelson, 86y., June 13, 1838.
4-56   "   Nelson, a Revolutionary pensioner, 86y., March 2, 1840.

4-62	MILLER	Allen, 24y., (at Havana), Nov. 8, 1840.
4-64	"	Harriet Augusta, of Augustus N. and Harriet J., 4y., April 17, 1841.
4-84	"	William, 5y., Feb. 3, 1845.
4-86	"	Nelson, of James, 7y., March 11, 1845.
4-88	"	Susan Chickering, of John N., 5y. 8m., Oct. 28, 1845.
4-94	"	James, of Nelson and Sarah, 52y., April 20, 1846.
2-79	MINGO	John, child of ——, Jan. ——, 1747.
2-79	"	——, May 22, 1748.
2-80	"	Cudd, child of ——, 28y., Dec. 28, 1751.
2-86	"	Cudd (at sea), Nov. 2, 1752.
2-80	"	——, a negro (at the Mount), Dec. 9, 1756.
2-81	"	Charles (mulatto), an apprentice to Major Carey, 13y., July 3, 1761.
2-82	"	Sarah, wife of John, Jan. 11, 1772.
2-83	"	Joseph, mulatto (at the West Indies), —— ——, 1773.
2-83	"	John, child, died June 30, 1775.
3-1	"	John, 40y., Feb. 6, 1786.
2-85	"	Abigail (col.), child of ——, April 27, 1815.
4-55	"	Lucy (col.), Dec. 19, 1839.
3-13	MINPELIEUR	Monsieur (Frenchman), 55y., Oct. 16, 1797.
3-18	MOORE	Capt. Benjamin, 39y., Nov. 2, 1806.
3-23	"	Capt. Thomas Martin, Jan. 28, 1816.
3-30	"	Samuel M., 29y., Aug. 8, 1829.
4-76	"	Susan, widow of Thomas M., 61y., May 24, 1843.
4-128	"	Capt. Francis, master of barque Winthrop (at Panama), 43y., Nov. 14, 1850.
2-80	MOREY	Hannah, of John and Hannah, April 26, 1687.
2-77	"	Hannah, of George Dec. ——, 1717.
4-96	MORRICE	Daniel N., 83y (also 4-102), Jan. 13, 1847.
4-118	MORRISON	Richard (born Ireland), about 50y., Jan. 18, 1850.
4-78	MORRIS	Nicholas D., of Daniel N., 4y., Nov. 18, 1843.
2-85	MOSHIER	Capt. Abner (news received of his death at New Orleans), Aug. 25, 1815.
4-21	MOSHER	Susan J. B., wife of William H., 33y., Dec. 22, 1834.
4-41	MOTT	Gustavus, Taylor, of James, 13m., March 30, 1837.
2-77	MUNDAY	Mrs. ——, June 21, 1731.
2-80	"	Mrs. ——, a stranger at ——. Jan. 28, 1753.
2-83	"	Jonathan, wife of ——, 76y., March 18, 1775.
3-2	"	Java, 86y., May 18, 1786.
2-77	MUNRO	Mary, wife of Thomas, Feb. 13, 1705.
2-77	"	Thomas, of Thomas, Feb. 24, 1717.
2-77	"	William, son of, Feb. 22, 1730.
2-77	"	——, negro child of, Feb. ——, 1732.
2-77	"	John, son of, Feb. ——, 1730.
2-77	"	——, Dec. ——, 1734.
2-78	"	William, his negro woman, Dec. ——, 1735.
2-78	"	——, his negro child, Aug. ——, 1736.
2-78	"	George, wife of, Oct. 13, 1736.
2-78	"	John —— ——, 1739.
2-78	"	William, his negro child, April ——, 1740.
2-78	"	Nathaniel, child of, 2y., May 27, 1740.
2-79	"	Mr., his negro child, Aug. 20, 1741.
2-79	"	Benjamin, child of, April 28, 1742.
2-79	"	——, Feb. 27, 1743.
2-79	"	—— (still born), May ——, 1744.
2-79	"	John, wife of, Dec. 9, 1743.
2-79	"	Thomas, Jan. 11, 1744.
2-79	"	George, Sept. 9, 1744.
2-79	"	Joseph, child of ——, Oct. 6, 1744.
2-79	"	——, —— ——, 1744.
2-78	"	William, April 28, 1746.
2-79	"	Mr. ——, his negro man, Peleg, Aug 30, 1748.
2-80	"	Jere, child of ——, June 14, 1750.
2-80	"	Thomas, his Indian boy, Sept. 22, 1751.

2-80	MUNRO	Charles, wife of, Feb. 19, 1753.
2-80	"	Capt. Bennett, wife of, 40y., Aug. 12, 1754.
2-80	"	Thomas, ——, —— —, 1755.
2-80	"	Allen, of William, 21m., Oct. 31, 1756.
2-80	"	Elizabeth, 12y., Oct. 12, 1756.
2-80	"	Mrs. ——, her negro woman, Oct. 27, 1756.
2-80	"	Mary, alias Salisbury, 17y., Feb. 15, 1757.
2-81	"	Nathaniel, his negro child, Aug. 24, 1758.
2-81	"	Charles, child of, May 28, 1759.
2-81	"	William, dau. of, 2 1-2y., Nov. 1, 1759.
2-81	"	William, Jr., of William (in army and supposed dead), ——, 1759.
2-81	"	Stephen, child of, b. and d. Sept. 5, 1760.
2-81	"	Mrs. Mary, 86y., Nov. 8, 1760.
2-81	"	Rebecca, wife of Simeon, Sept. 28, 1761.
2-81	"	Nathan, of Bennett, Dec. 20, 1761.
2-82	"	Capt. Bennett, child of (scalded), July 11, 1763.
2-82	"	Nathan, her negro girl, Jan. 13, 1764.
2-82	"	Capt. Bennett, child of, May 5, 1765.
2-82	"	Thankful, child of, May —, 1765.
2-82	"	Jeremiah, child of, April —, 1766.
2-82	"	Nathaniel, his negro child, ——, 1766.
2-82	"	Mrs. Mary, widow of Joseph, 82y., Jan. 10, 1770.
2-82	"	Stephen, child of, Jan. 27, 1771.
2-82	"	——, Feb. 13, 1771.
2-82	"	Stephen, wife of, 29y., Jan. 11, 1772.
2-83	"	Bennett, his negro woman, Sept. 18, 1775.
2-83	"	——, his negro girl, Sept. 27, 1775.
2-83	"	Capt. Bennett, 67y., Sept. 25, 1775.
2-83	"	William, Jr., dau. of, 9y., Oct. 4, 1775.
2-83	"	Daniel, wife of, Oct. 23, 1775.
2-83	"	——, child of, Oct. —, 1775.
2-83	"	George, child of, Aug. 22, 1776.
2-83	"	Thankful, child of, Sept. ——, 1776.
2-38	"	William, Esq., 74y., Oct. 7, 1777.
2-84	"	Nathaniel, wife of, 38y., Jan. 1, 1779.
2-84	"	Andrew (at Rehoboth), 64y., April 30, 1779.
2-84	"	Samuel of Bennett, 21y. (at sea), —— —, 1779.
2-84	"	Royal, (at New York), —— —, 1779.
2-84	"	Charles, grandchild of, —— —, 1779.
3-1	"	Charles, negro servant of Hezekiah, April 30, 1786.
3-2	"	——, child of Nathaniel, 6w., May 3, 1786.
3-3	"	Capt. William, 26y., July —, 1787.
3-4	"	Simeon, 76y., May 23, 1789.
3-5	"	Daniel, (at Norfolk, Va.), 21y., Dec. —, 1790.
3-6	"	Gideon, of Betsey, 23y., Jan. 1, 1791.
3-6	"	Mary, widow, 71y., March 23, 1791.
3-7	"	James, of James, 6y., Oct. 30, 1791.
3-8	"	Isaiah, Sept. 24, 1792.
3-8	"	Capt. Nathan, Jr., Sept. 7, 1793.
3-9	"	Allen, of Hezekiah and Hovannah, 20y., May 27, 1794.
3-10	"	Lydia, of Hezekiah, 23y., April 17, 1795.
3-10	"	Mary, 20y., Sept. 20, 1795.
3-11	"	Nathaniel, of Nathaniel 2d (a sea), 18y., Dec. 7, 1795.
3-11	"	Anna, wife of Charles, 77y., Feb. 7, 1796.
3-11	"	Sarah, 46y., Aug. 12, 1796.
3-12	"	Capt. Simon (lost from brig Little Joseph at sea), 28y., Dec. 26, 1796.
3-12	"	William, 59y., Jan. 28, 1797.
3-12	"	Sarah, wife of Sylvester, June 30, 1797.
3-13	"	Charles, 82y., Jan. 11, 1798.
3-13	"	Alathea, of Bennett, 21y., Nov. 23, 1798.
2-15	"	Capt. Nathan, June 12, 1801.
3-15	"	William, 2d, (lost at sea), Dec. —, 1801.
3-15	"	Susanna, wife of Bateman, 27y., Nov. 29, 1802.
3-17	"	Nathaniel, 62y., Dec. 9, 1804.

3-17	MUNRO	Elizabeth, widow, 86y., Nov. 2, 1805.
3-18	"	Mary, widow, 66y., Nov. 10, 1806.
3-18	"	William Wardwell (at Gambia river, Africa), 25y., Jan. 30, 1807.
3-18	"	Allen, 34y. (at sea), June 10, 1807.
3-18	"	Capt. John, 31y., Sept. 12, 1807.
3-18	"	Prescilla, 43y., Sept. 22, 1807.
3-19	"	Elizabeth, wife of Sylvester, Feb. 9, 1809.
3-19	"	Bennett, 1st, 33y., Feb. 22, 1809.
2-85	"	Lucretia Smith, of George, 2d, and Martha, Dec. 18, 1809.
3-20	"	Miss Sarah, 32y., July 31, 1810.
2-84	"	William, child of ——, 5m., May 10, 1811.
2-84	"	Molly, wife of Thomas, 63y., Sept. 24, 1811.
3-21	"	Mary, wife of Thomas, 64y., Sept. 24, 1811.
3-21	"	Sarah, widow of Capt. Bennett (clothes caught fire, died a few days after), (also 2-84), 92y., Sept. 25, 1811.
2-84	"	Edward, Jr., child of ——, Oct. 31, 1811.
2-84	"	Mary, wife of Edward, Nov. 7, 1811.
2-84	"	Deacon Archibald, 65y., (also 3-21), Jan. 15, 1812.
2-84	"	Patience, wife of James, 61y., Feb. 2, 1812.
3-21	"	Mary, widow, 54y., May 12, 1812.
2-84	"	Henry, child of ——, 15m., May 29, 1812.
2-85	"	Ephraim, child of ——, July —, 1813.
2-85	"	——, 6 weeks, July 3, 1814.
2-85	"	Nathaniel, 2d, child of ——, Aug. —, 1813.
2-85	"	Elizabeth, wife of William, 2d, Dec. 2, 1813.
2-85	"	Hezekiah, Jr., child of, ——. March —. 1814.
2-85	"	Mehitable, wife of Jeremiah, 23y., May —, 1414.
2-85	"	Josiah, 2d, child of ——, Sept. —, 1814.
1-271	"	Phebe Howland, of Bennett and Sally, Oct. 8, 1815.
3-23	"	Thomas, 69y., Feb. 29, 1816.
3-23	"	Martha, wife of Nathaniel, 1st, 59y., July 12, 1816.
3-24	"	Phebe, wife of Henry, 44y., Jan. 17, 1819.
3-25	"	Hopestill, wife of Hugh, 81y., Nov. 1, 1819.
4-169	"	Thankful, 83y., March 26, 1820.
3-25	"	Miss Thankful, 83y., March 26, 1820.
4-169	"	Joanna, wife of Allen, 2d, 21y., Oct. 23, 1820.
4-169	"	Bernice, 64y., Nov. 8, 1820.
4-168	"	Sylvester, of Sylvester, 16y., Feb. 8, 1821.
4-168	"	Jeremiah, 30y., March 23, 1821.
3-26	"	Sarah, of Nathaniel, 32y., Sept. 18, 1821.
3-26	"	Abigail, widow, 90y., Feb. 11, 1823.
3-27	"	Sarah, wife of Sylvester, 50y., Nov. 6, 1825.
3-28	"	James, 81y., April 28, 1826.
3-28	"	Benjamin, 45y., Jan. 8, 1826.
3-28	"	Abigail, widow, 81y., July 30, 1826.
3-28	"	Edward, 48y., Dec. 6, 1826.
3-28	"	Hezekiah, 80y., Dec. 7, 1826.
3-28	"	Dea. William, 86y., July 11, 1827.
3-28	"	Rebecca, widow, 78y., (dau. of Richard Smith), Nov 3, 1827.
3-30	"	James, of Nathaniel, 23y., Aug. 31, 1830.
3-31	"	Capt. George, 63y., Dec. 5, 1831.
3-31	"	Mary, wife of Jeseph, 68y., Dec. 28, 1831.
3-31	"	Rebecca, widow, 48y., July 3, 1832.
4-23	"	Sarah, 78y., Jan. 18, 1835.
4-23	"	George Edward, of Henry, 11m. 5d., Feb. 10, 1835.
4-23	"	Edward, 87-10-25, March 10, 1835.
4-25	"	Sally, 47y., April 14, 1835.
4-25	"	James N., of James N., 1-1-24, May 7, 1835.
4-27	"	Sarah, wife of Nathaniel, 63y., Oct. 26, 1835.
4-31	"	Perry P. Greene, of Joseph, 21y., Nov. 25, 1835.
4-33	"	Rev. Matthias, formerly of Bridgewater, Mass., 51y., April 8, 1836.
4-41	"	Elizabeth B., wife of Hezekiah, 56y., (at Charlestown, Mass.,) April 13, 1837.
4-47	"	Huile, 35y., May 10, 1838.
4-52	"	Nathaniel, 87y., a Revolutionary Pensioner, Dec. 4, 1838.

4-54	MUNRO ——, child of Caleb, 17y. Sept. 25, 1839.
4-60	" ——, child of John P., 4w., Aug. 10, 1840.
4-60	" Amey, 52y. (col.), Sept. 7, 1840.
4-60	" Ephraim, 66y., Sept. 16, 1840.
4-60	" Henry, of Henry, Jr., 5w., Sept. 21. 1840.
4-64	" Ann Maria, of Nathaniel, Jr., of Somerset, 20y., March 28, 1841.
4-64	" Ichabod (col.), 77y., March 31, 1841.
4-66	" Rebecca, wife of Thomas K., 73y., Oct. 17, 1841.
4-88	" Elizabeth, wife of Jeremiah, 29y., Dec. 5, 1841.
4-70	" Josiah, 52y., Feb. 11, 1842.
4-47	" Rhoda M., of David, 18y., Dec. 10, 1842.
4-76	" Martha, widow of George, 60y., April 20, 1843.
4-78	" Nathaniel, 67y., (drowned), July 24, 1843.
4-80	" Mary, widow of William, 80y., Dec. 7, 1843.
4-80	" Eliza Jane, of Nathaniel, Jr., of Somerset, 22y., April 10, 1844.
4-82	" Betsey, wife of Henry, 54y., June 15, 1844.
4-82	" George, of George, 15y. (col.), July 29, 1844.
4-86	" George, of George, 2d, 10m., April 22, 1845.
4-86	" Eliza F., widow of Nathaniel, Jr., of Somerset, 45y., July 8, 1845.
4-88	" William H., of Henry, Jr., 1y. 8m., Oct. 10, 1845.
4-88	" Mary, wife of Joseph, 61y., Dec. 1, 1845.
4-96	" Sarah, widow of Nathaniel, 2d., 70y (at Providence), July 14, 1846.
4-96	" Isabella, of William W., 16m., Feb. 9, 1847.
4-96	" Charles (col.) 74y., March 27, 1847.
4-96	" Louisa Anna M., of Mary Ann (col.), 3y., May 20, 1847.
4-98	" Capt. Henry, 76y., Sept. 23, 1847.
	. (Also 4-100 and 102).
4-99	" Betty, widow of Daniel (col.), 96y., Nov. 9, 1847.
4-102	" Charles (col.), 74y., —— ——, 1847.
4-102	" Henry, 76y., —— ——, 1847.
4-110	" Thomas K., 83y., —— —— ——. 1848.
4-106	" Myra Williams, of John B., 12m. 15d., Nov. 15, 1848.
4-108	" Thomas K., 82y., Nov. 30, 1848.
4-110	" Martha, widow of Ephraim, 77y., Jan. 6, 1849.
4-114	" James Augustus, of George, 2d., 3y., July 21, 1849.
4-112	" Joseph, a Revolutionary pensioner, 89y., April 26, 1849.
4-112	" Miss Abigail, 78y., May 8, 1849.
4-116	" child of Henry, 3w., Oct. 13, 1849.
4-116	" Catherine (col.), 52y., Nov. 20, 1849.
4-120	" Anna, (col.), 14y., Feb. 12, 1850.
4-122	" William James Diman, of Jeremiah, 6m., April 30, 1850.
4-124	" Martha, of John (col.), of Warren, 18y., Sept. 8, 1850.
4-132	" Caleb, 53y., June 25, 1951.
3-13	MURRAY Anthony, 60y., Sept. 10, 1797.
2-84	" Mary, of Anthony, May 12, 1812.
4-92	MUTTON Mary Elizabeth, of George, 10m., July 9, 1846.

N

4-23	NASH Betsey, wife of Rev. Sylvester, dau. of Stephen Smith (at East Greenwich), Jan. 3, 1835.
4-114	NAVY Martha (col.), (at the asylum), about 60y., Aug. 5, 1849.

2-88	NEGRAS Benjamin, child of,	June 18, 1757.
2-77	" negro child, at the Mount,	April —, 1731.
2-77	"	June —, 1733.
2-77	"	Feb. —, 1735.
2-78	"	Oct. —, 1736.
2-78	"	June —, 1737.
2-78	"	July —, 1737.
2-78	" girl,	March 19, 1738.
2-78	" child,	—— ——, 1739.
2-78	" woman,	July 4, 1740.
2-89	" negro man (at Mr. Reed's, he came from Maryland), Dec. 11, 1772.

2-88   NEGRAS woman, March 1, 1733.
3-15   NELSON Susannah, wife of Dr. Thomas, 29y., April 23, 1802.
3-22   "   Paul, 21y. (at sea), Oct. 15, 1813.
3-22   "   Dr. Thomas, 44y. (also 2-89), March 2, 1814.
2-88   NEWBY, alias Bonsignore (at Antigua), —— —, 1757.
4-39   NEWMAN Albert, of James T., 1y. 2m., Dec. 1, 1836.
4-45   "   Mary Abby,   15y., Dec. 14, 1837.
4-55   "   James T., 43y., Nov. 21, 1839.
4-72   "   Abby H., widow of James T., 46y., Sept. 10, 1842.
2-88   NEWTON Capt., his mulatto woman, July 26, 1737.
2-88   "   his negro woman, Dec. 26, 1741.
2-88   "   Capt. John, 57y., Jan. 2, 1747.
2-88   "   Mrs., her negro girl, 8y., Aug. 12, 1759.
2-89   "   Daniel (at sea), 43y., —— —, 1765.
2-89   "   Mrs. Anna, 76y., May 7, 1770.
3-14   "   Capt. Peter, April 3, 1801.
3-15   "   •   Ann, 78y., Oct. 24, 1802.
4-72   NICKERSON Elsey, of James, 20m., Aug. 24, 1842.
2-88   NIBBS Ebenezer (at Surinam), Nov. —, 1744.
2-89   NICHOLS Herbert, child of, June 21, 1739.
2-88   NOONING Timothy, Feb. 14, 1752.
3-3   "   James, 42y., May 15, 1788.
3-9   "   Rebecca, widow, 70y., June 2, 1788.
3-9   "   Rebecca, of widow Rebecca, 13y., April 27, 1794.
3-24   "   Rebecca, widow, 74y., Jan. 19, 1819.
3-29   "   Hannah, wife of Jonathan, 42y., Nov. 27, 1827.
4-102   "   Isabella, of Jonathan, 23y., Jan. 27, 1848.
2-88   NORRIS Samuel, child of, Dec. 29, 1729.
2-88   "   Abigail, of Thomas and Rebecca, Dec. 25, 1729.
2-88   "   Mrs. Rebecca, March 3, 1745.
2-89   "   John, child of, 17m., Sept. 25, 1769.
2-89   "   Samuel, of John (perished of cold at the Vineyard), Dec. 26, 1778.
3-8   "   Martha, wife of Paul W., Nov. 28, 1793.
3-9   "   child of John, 1 day, July 18, 1794.
3-13   "   Capt. John, 40y. (lost at sea), Feb. 5, 1798.
3-13   "   Capt. Samuel M., 38y. (at sea), Nov. —, 1798.
3-19   "   John, 77y., July 5, 1808.
3-26   "   Elizabeth, widow, 81y., Oct. 30, 1822.
3-31   "   Elizabeth, wife of William E., 25y., Nov. 10, 1832.
4-31   "   Charles Carr, of Hezekiah, 1y. 8m., March 15, 1836.
4-88   "   Samuel, 58y., Sept. 3, 1845.
4-104   "   Julia Griswold, wife of Samuel, 3d dau. of Dr. Jabez Holmes, 22y., May 11, 1848.
4-106   "   Julia Holmes, of Samuel, 5m. 22d., Sept. 2, 1848.
4-112   "   Hezekiah, of Benjamin (at Providence), May 23, 1849.
4-49   NORTHUP Lydia, 23y., Aug. 26, 1838.
4-51   "   Christopher, formerly of North Kingstown, 68y., Oct. 9, 1838.
2-88   NORTON Capt. ——, his negro woman, Nov. 28, 1729.
2-88   "   ——, his Indian girl, Nov. 26, 1733.
2-89   "   Capt. Shubael (at sea), ——, 1737.
2-88   "   Mrs. Sarah, Aug. 23, 1744.
2-88   "   Sarah, Aug. —, 1747.
2-88   "   Peter, an Indian man, June —, 1750.
4-60   NYE Mary Ann. of widow Mary L., 19y., Sept. 25, 1840.

O

4-60   OATLEY Henry Martin, of Reuben, 1y. 6m., Dec. 24, 1843.
2-02   OLDRIDGE Mrs., Oct. 15, 1742.
2-91   "   John, Jr. (at Surinam), ——, 1746.
2-91   "   William, child of ——, Sept. 15, 1751.
2-91   "   John, his negro child, Dec. —, 1751.
2-91   "   William, daughter of, 3y., Dec. 27, 1757.
2-91   "   William, Aug. 4, 1760.

2-91	OLDRIDGE —, son of widow, —, Aug. 5, 1761.	
2-91	" —, daughter of widow, —, 1766.	
2-91	" Catherine, widow, May 30, 1762.	
2-91	" Thomas (at Philadelphia), Dec. 16, 1765.	
2-92	" Joseph (at sea), 22y., Feb. 1, 1774.	
2-92	" John, wife of —. 74y., April 4, 1775.	
2-92	" John, about 83y., Jan. 29, 1776.	
3-9	" Joseph, 67y., Sept. 10, 1794.	
3-12	" Elizabeth, widow, 70y., July 5, 1797.	
3-15	" Joseph, 40y., Nov. 25, 1802.	
3-20	" Alatbea, widow, 78y., Nov. 17, 1810.	
3-25	" Priscilla, wife of John, 68y., Oct. 15, 1819.	
3-26	" John, 75y. (at the asylum), Jan. 16, 1823.	
3-29	" Mary, widow, 52y., April 17, 1828.	
2-92	OLNEY Stephen, of Providence, 40y. (on board privateer McDonough in Bristol harbor), (also 3-23), March 20, 1815.	
2-91	OSBORN Robert, of Jeremiah and Mercy, 1y., 3w., buried Sept. 2, 1685.	
2-91	" Jeremiah, of do., Jan. 24, 1683-4.	
2-91	" Mercy, wife of Jeremiah, Feb. 16, 1732-3.	
3-19	OTTERSON Samuel (from Ireland) (at sea), Dec. 28, 1807.	
2-92	OXX Capt., a child of, — —, 1739.	
2-91	" Samuel (at Berlisha), — —, 1743.	
2-91	" —, child of —. Sept. 11, 1762.	
2-91	" —, wife of —, 38y., June 22, 1770.	
2-91	" —, child of —, Jan. 30, 1771.	
2-91	" George, child of —, 5m., July 22, 1768.	
2-92	" —, Sept. —, 1777.	
3-1	" Benjamin, 23y., May 29, 1785.	
3-15	" George (in ship Hope at, Batavia), Dec. —, 1801.	
3-15	" Peleg (at sea) 21y., Feb. 7, 1805.	
3-18	" Capt. Samuel, 76y., Nov. 16, 1806.	
3-21	" Rebecca, widow of Samuel, 71y (also 2-92), June 25, 1812.	
2-92	" William, 3d, child of ——, 2y., Sept. 11, 1812.	
2-92	" William, of William, 2d, (drowned from on board Water Witch from Bristol to Newport,) June —, 1815.	
3-23	" William, 3d, (in army at the Lakes), (also 2-92), Feb. 27, 1815.	
3-23	" Hannah, wife of Capt. George, 73y., Jan. 5, 1816.	
3-25	" Capt. George, 80y., Aug. 28, 1819.	
3-27	" Lydia, wife of William, 55y., July 3, 1825.	
4-39	" William, 96y., Jan. 5, 1837.	
4-68	" . William, 72y., Dec. 28, 1841.	

P

2-94	PAINE Dorothy, of Nathaniel and Dorothy, Feb. 17, 1699-1700.	
2-94	" Jonathan,	Dec. 26, 1707.
2-95	" Hon. Col., 63y., Dec. 9, 1729.	
2-97	" Nathaniel, child of —, Dec. 9, 1746.	
2-97	" Nathaniel, (at Annapolis), Jan. 15, 1747.	
2-97	" Col. Stephen, 48y., Sept. 21, 1749.	
2-98	" Eliza, of widow —, 17y., Nov. 4, 1752.	
2-98	" Stephen, child of —, Dec. —, 1752.	
2-98	" —, — —, 1754.	
2-98	" Madame Dorothy, 93y., Jan. 2, 1755.	
2-103	" Ben, servant of Madame —, near 90y., June 18, 1756.	
2-99	" Mary, of Stephen, 20y., July 9, 1758.	
2-99	" Mary, wife of Edward, 40y., May 23, 1759.	
2-99	" Capt. Stephen, child of, —, b. and d. June 23, 1760.	
2-99	" —. b. and d. July 8, 1761.	
2-99	" —, b. and d. July 3, 1762.	
2-99	" Capt. Stephen (at Berbeccia), March 16, 1762.	
2-100	" Sarah, of Nathaniel and Dorothy, Jan. 10, 1764.	
2-100	" Royal (at Boston), 34y., June 17, 1764.	
2-100	" Elizabeth, widow, May 11, 1768.	

2-100   PAINE Mrs. ——, her negro child, Oct. 23, 1769.
2-100   "   Mrs. Prescilla, 66y., Feb. 24, 1772.
2-101   "   Dorothy, of Nathaniel and Dorothy (at Norwich), Feb. 27, 1774.
2-101   "   Edward (at Worcester), 65y., Nov. —, 1777.
2-101   "   Elizabeth, wife of Stephen, 23y., —— —, 1777.
2-102   "   Edward, of Nathaniel and Sarah (at Worcester), Nov. —, 1778.
2-102   "   Mary, of Royal and Olive, Oct. 10, 1779.
3-3   "   Samuel R., of Samuel R., 4y., July 6, 1787.
3-15   "   Elizabeth, wife of Samuel R., Feb. 12, 1802.
2-102   "   Nathaniel T., child of ——, 17m., Feb. 16, 1813.
2-102   "   Timothy F., of John, 10m., Sept. 17, 1814.
3-23   "   Abigail, wife of Samuel R., 40y., Jan. 14, 1817.
4-19   "   William Henry Richmond, of Nathaniel T., 8m., Aug. 28, 1834.
4-47   "   Nathaniel T., 48y., March 22, 1838.
4-52   "   Samuel Royal, a Revolutionary pensioner, 82y., Dec. 26, 1838.
4-54   "   Ann Franklin, of John, 27y., (at Providence), Sept. 17, 1839.
4-45   PALMER Louisa, widow of Elijah, of Stonington, Conn., 8—y., Dec. 26, 1837.
4-94   "   Josephine, of Benjamin W., 13y., Oct. 13, 1846.
4-94   "   ——, wife of Benjamin, 36y., Nov. 25, 1846.
2-95   PAPILLION Obadiah, his negro child, Oct. —, 1729.
2-95   "   Esther, of Obadiah, Jan. 20, 1731-2.
2-96   "   John (at Newport), Oct. 29, 1740.
2-97   "   Samuel (at Jamaica) Feb. 24, 1745.
2-97   "   Peter (at sea) —— —, 1746.
2-99   "   Obadiah (news of his death at South Carolina), Jan. 13, 1760.
2-101   "   Rebecca, widow of Samuel, 58y., Feb. 21, 1775.
3-5   PARKER Wanton, of William, 4y., Nov. 27, 1790.
3-13   "   John, of William, 20y., Sept. 21, 1797.
4-104   PARTRIDGE Betsey, wife of Elisha, 59y., May 18, 1848.
2-99   PATTERSON Andrew, child of about 4m., Sept. 10, 1759.
3-17   PAUL Alathea, wife of Zebedee, 26y., Aug. 29, 1805.
4-51   "   ——, son of William, 1m, Oct. 22, 1838.
4-51   "   George H., 11m, 8d., Sept. 27, 1840.
4-51   "   ——, child of ——, 7w., Sept. 19, 1842.
4-98   "   Sarah B., wife of William, and dau. of Capt. Edward Church, Sept. 13, 1847.
3-21   PEABODY John, of Providence, 77y., (also 2-102), May 8, 1812.
4-169   "   ——, child of Thomas, 9m., Sept. 5, 1820.
4-168   "   Deborah, widow, 77y., (also 3-25), Feb. 3, or 8, 1821.
4-98   "   William Thomas, of Alfred, 11m., July 27, 1847.
2-94   PEARSE Isaac, of Jonathan and Elizabeth, May 21, 1706.
2-94   "   Mercy, June 25, 1710.
2-94   "   Jonathan (at Rehoboth), July 2, 1713.
2-94   "   Abijah, of Elisha, widow of Jonathan, dec., April 15, 1714.
2-94   "   Sarah, wife of Richard, Jr., July 4, 1720.
2-94   "   Experience, wife of Richard, July 17, 1720.
2-95   "   Renew, of Jeremiah, Jan. 16, 1734-5.
2-95   "   Jeremiah, dau. of, 11y., Jan. 17, 1735.
2-95   "   Nathaniel, child of, —— —, 1736.
2-96   "   Richard, son of (at sea), June —, 1737.
2-96   "   Simon (at Surinam), —— —, 1737.
2-97   "   Capt. Nathaniel, child of, 3y., Nov. 27, 1743.
2-103   "   Mr. Richard, Oct. 25, 1744.
2-96   "   Elizabeth, of Richard and Susannah, 18y., 2m., 26d., Aug. 5, 1746.
2-97   "   Eliza, Aug. 6, 1746.
2-97   "   Capt., child of (scalded), Dec. 23, 1748.
2-97   "   negro child of, —— —, 1749.
2-98   "   Jeremiah, child of, Nov. 2, 1750.
2-98   "   Capt., child of, Jan. 16, 1755.
2-99   "   William, negro child of, Aug. 7, 1758.
2-99   "   Samuel, child of, Dec. 26, 1760.
2-99   "   his wife, 25y., Dec. 30, 1760.
2-99   "   child of, —— —, 1761.

2-99	PEARSE —, Dec. 24, 1762.	
2-99	"	Jeremiah, 65y., Jan. 22, 1761.
2-100	"	Col., negro, Quash, April 10, 1771.
2-100	"	William (his mulatto girl), 7y., Feb. 29, 1772.
2-101	"	George, 31y., Jan. 13, 1775.
2-101	"	Col., his negro man, Jan., 22, 1775.
2-101	"	William, negro child, March 13, 1775.
2-101	"	Widow, child of, Aug. 19, 1775.
2-101	"	Thomas, child of, Sept. or Oct. —, 1777.
2-101	"	Capt. Benjamin (perished with cold at the Vineyard), Dec. 26, 1778.
3-1	"	Sarah, widow, 83y., April 16, 1785.
3-2	"	Olive, wife of Samuel R., July 14, 1786.
3-2	"	child of Samuel R., 7d., July 18, 1786.
3-4	"	William, 74y., Sept. 13, 1788.
3-4	"	Lydia, wife of Nathaniel, Jr., 48y., Oct. 23, 1788.
3-4	"	Dick, negro servant of William, 70y., Oct. —, 1789.
3-5	"	Jude, negro servant of Capt. Nathaniel, 62y., Dec. 3, 1790.
3-6	"	Stephen, of Thomas (drowned at shore), Aug. 3, 1791.
3-8	"	Nathaniel, Esq., 85y., March 7, 1793.
3-11	"	Miss Abigail, 41y., Dec. 20, 1796.
2-15	"	Lydia, widow, 77y., June 22, 1801.
3-17	"	Noah, 27y., April 5, 1805.
3-18	"	Lydia, wife of Christopher, Aug. 28, 1807.
3-19	"	Capt. Jeremiah, 30y. (lost at sea with sloop Minerva), Dec. 29, 1807.
3-20	"	George, 24y. (at Havanna), May 7, 1810.
2-102	"	Mary, of Jeremiah (dec.), 5y., Aug. 6, 1812.
2-102	"	Josiah, 33y. (also 3-22), Aug. 11, 1814.
2-103	"	Josiah, child of, Oct. 11, 1814.
2-103	"	Peleg (col.), Dec. —. 1814.
3-22	"	Josiah, 33y., Aug. 11, 1814.
3-27	"	Thomas, 74y., Nov. 20, 1823.
3-28	"	Ebenezer, 57y. (fell from Job Williston's store, broke his neck), Feb. 26, 1826.
3-30	"	Deacon William, 22y., March 18, 1830.
4-23	"	Jeremiah, of William, 2d, 23y., Jan. 5, 1835.
4-29	"	Marian, of Albert J., 13m., Dec. 8, 1835.
4-31	"	James, of William, 3d, 13y., March 1, 1836.
3-35	"	Fanny, wife of Benjamin of Swansey, 80y. (died here, buried at Swansey), Oct. 5, 1836.
4-47	"	Bradford, of John S., 11m., April 12, 1838.
4-47	"	Isabella L., of John L., 3y. 4m., April 27, 1838.
4-49	"	Thomas H., 42y., July 26, 1838.
4-55	"	William, late of Rehoboth, 66y., Oct. 24, 1839.
4-58	"	Lurame, of Mason W., 5 1-2y., April 29, 1840.
4-64	"	Jarvis G., of Jarvis B., 21y., April 24, 1841.
4-76	"	Le Baron, of John S., 2y. 3m., June 11, 1843.
4-78	"	Sarah, wife of William, 2d, Aug. —, 1843.
4-78	"	Martha Esther, of Walter, 8y. 1m., Nov. 12, 1843.
4-80	"	George P., master of brig Emeline, lost at sea, Nov. 19, 1843.
4-82	"	William, Esq., 79y., June 19, 1844.
4-84	"	Marian, wife of James, 20y., Nov. 13, 1844.
4-110	"	William, 2d, Feb. 19, 1849.
4-112	"	child of David, April 26, 1849.
4-120	"	Thomas, of Josiah, dec., 46y., April 12, 1850.
4-106	PEARK Thomas Eccles, of Capt. Richard S., 4-5-19, Nov. 2, 1848.	
2-97	PECKHAM John, child of, Sept. 4, 1750.	
2-99	"	Abigail, of John, 18y., Dec. 9, 1762.
2-102	"	Peleg, child of (buried at Rehoboth), —— —, 1811.
2-102	"	Mr., child of, —— —, 1813.
3-35	"	Mary, of Perry M., 14y. (at Fall River), Sept. 7, 1836.
4-54	"	Sarah, wife of James (buried at Middletown), 38y., June 30, 1839.
4-60	"	George, of Nathaniel, 11m., Aug. 24, 1840.
4-92	"	John, 73y., May 15, 1846.

2-94	PECK	Mary, of Jonathan and Elizabeth, Dec. 4, 1697.
2-95	"	Jonathan, wife of, June 14, 1729.
2-95	"	Hannah, wife of Jonathan, June 14, 1730.
2-95	"	Nichols, of Jonathan (at Little Compton), Sept. 20, 1731.
2-95	"	Martha, of William and Elizabeth, April 16, 1731.
2-95	"	William, child of, April 16, 1731.
2-95	"	——, Aug. 1, 1735.
2-95	"	Joseph, of William and Elizabeth, Aug. —, 1735.
2-96	"	William, child of, July —, 1736.
2-96	"	Elizabeth, wife of William, Nov. 12, 1740.
2-96	"	Mr. ——, child of, —— —, 1741.
2-96	"	Mr. ——, a mulatto woman, (at ——), Jan. —, 1743.
2-97	"	Capt. ——, his negro boy, July —, 1747.
2-98	"	his negro woman, May 21, 1752.
2-98	"	John, 32y., Aug. 2, 1754.
2-98	"	Hannah, wife of Jonathan, 50y., Aug. 11, 1756.
2-98	"	Nathaniel, of Jonathan, 10y., Oct. 22, 1756.
2-98	"	Jonathan, Esq., 59y., Feb. 25, 1757.
2-100	"	Loring, child of, b. and d., July 10, 1768.
2-100	"	——, / July 14, 1771.
2-100	"	Thomas, 27y., Nov. 21, 1771.
2-100	"	Thomas, child of, 13m., Oct. 20, 1772.
2-100	"	Loring, child of, 1y., 5m., Aug. 8, 1773.
2-101	"	Capt., his negro child, Dec. 30, 1773.
2-101	"	Loring, wife of, 28y., April 20, 1774.
2-101	"	Capt. Jonathan, his negro child, Nov. 3, 1775.
2-101	"	——, his child, Sept. 14, 1777.
3-1	"	Nero, negro servant of Capt. James, 45y., July 31, 1785.
3-4	"	Henry, of Loring, 6m., June 6, 1789.
3-5	"	Richard, of Capt. Loring, 11y., March 7, 1790.
3-10	"	Thomas, 60y., Aug. 10, 1795.
3-10	"	Hannah, 30y., Sept. 28, 1795.
3-11	"	Elizabeth, wife of Nicholas, 30y., May 20, 1796.
3-11	"	Eliza Smith, of Nathaniel, 4m., Sept. 30, 1796.
3-11	"	Hannah, wife of Samuel W., 36y., Nov. 16, 1796.
3-13	"	Capt. Jonathan, 73y., Oct. 7, 1797.
3-13	"	Betsey, wife of Thomas, 1st., July 11, 1798.
3-13	"	Jemima, of Nicholas, 23y., Nov. 7, 1798.
3-15	"	Patience, wife of John, July 12, 1801.
3-16	"	Mary, widow, 68y., Nov. 7, 1803.
3-16	"	Nathaniel Viall, 40y., (drowned at Bristol Harbor), Feb. 21, 1804.
3-18	"	Nancy, wife of Joshua, May 17, 1807.
3-21	"	Thomas, 71y., buried at Swansey, (also 2-102), Feb. 29, 1812.
2-102	"	Cato (cast away at the Ponobscot), March 5, 1812.
2-102	"	Reuben, of Belinda (col.), 23y., Sept. 28, 1812.
2-102	"	Titus, April 4, 1813.
2-102	"	Jonathan, child of, Aug. 31, 1814.
2-102	"	Charlotte, of Cato (col.), Sept. —, 1814.
4-168	"	George M., of George B., 8 months, Feb. 2, 1821.
3-28	"	Miss Abigail, 82y., Jan. 22, 1826.
3-29	"	John, Esq., 65y., March 1, 1829.
3-32	"	Jonathan, 43y., Dec. 14, 1833.
4-17	"	John, of Nicholas, 42y., (formerly of this town, for many years resident of Fredericksburg, Va., died at Baltimore, Md., while on his way here), May 25, 1834.
4-27	"	Susan, widow of Jonathan, 40y., Aug. 14, 1835.
4-49	"	Elizabeth Smith, of Nicholas, Jr., 15m., Sept. 12, 1838.
4-55	"	Jenny (col.), about 60y., Jan. 9, 1840.
4-74	"	Albert, 27y., Feb. 13, 1843.
4-76	"	Waitey, 75y., April 20, 1843.
4-90	"	Abigail, wife of Joseph, 64y., Feb. 20, 1846.
4-110	"	Martha, widow of Samuel Viall, dec., 82y., Jan. 14, 1849.
4-96	"	Nicholas, Esq., 86y., June 11, 1847.
4-100	"	Horace North, of John Y., (at Leroy, Penn.), 10-11-26, Oct. 19, 1847.

4-102	PECK Nicholas, 85y., —— —, 1847.	
4-104	" Theresa, wife of Winchester, and dau. of David Maxfield, 62y., April 6, 1848.	
4-120	" Esther, wife of Joseph, 61y., April 11, 1850.	
2-95	PEGG, a mulatto woman, July 30, 1734.	
2-96	PENNIMAN John, Oct. 30, 1740.	
4-19	PERRY Meltiah Z., late of New Bedford, Mass., 39y., Sept. 21, 1834.	
4-23	" Daniel, Jan. 25, 1835.	
4-74	" Phebe, wife of Dea. Daniel, 87y., Sept. 27, 1842.	
4-112	PETERSON Mary, wife of Capt. John B., May 15, 1849.	
2-96	PETER, a French boy of Surinam (at Mr. John Bragg's), May 13, 1741.	
2-96	" Peter (Thomas Durfee's ferryman, drowned), Sept. 16, 1742.	
3-15	PETIT John (Frenchman), drowned from ship Jefferson, Sept. 8, 1801.	
4-33	PHELPS Laura, of William S., May 21, 1836.	
2-96	PHILLIPS Michael, child of, Sept. 13, 1741.	
2-96	" John, child of, March 16, 1742.	
2-96	" Susannah, June 16, 1743.	
2-97	" Michel, child of, July 2, 1743.	
2-97	" John, wife of, Aug. 2, 1747.	
2-97	" Joseph, Jr., wife of, Sept. 24, 1747.	
2-97	" Michael, wife of, July 2, 1750.	
2-98	" ——, child of, July —, 1751.	
2-98	" John, child of, Sept. 8, 1751.	
2-98	" Joseph, 68y., July 9, 1758.	
2-99	" John, Jr. (at Martinico), Aug. 14, 1762.	
2-100	" Susannah, 86y., June 2, 1770.	
2-101	" Thomas, of Joseph, Jr., and Sarah, —— —, 1771.	
3-4	" Thomas, of Capt. Nathaniel (at sea), 18y., Nov. 1, 1789.	
3-5	" Thomas, of Capt. Nathaniel (at sea), Nov. 3, 1790.	
3-10	" James (at Gambria River), Sept. —, 1795.	
3-24	" Capt. Samuel, 38y., Nov. 19, 1817.	
3-34	" Samuel, of Martha, 19y., (at sea), March —, 1818.	
3-21	" Capt. Nathaniel, news of death received March 5, 1812, 65y., (at sea), (cast away at the Penobscot) (also 2-102), Feb. 1, 1812.	
4-27	" Nathaniel Brenton, of Capt. Samuel, dec., 23y., (in the hospital at Staten Island, N. Y.), Aug. 17, 1835.	
4-49	" Sarah, widow of Capt. Nathaniel, 86y., Sept. 2, 1838.	
4-55	" Laura, of William S., 2y. 6m., Nov. 30, 1839.	
2-101	PHILLIS Old, formerly servant of Madame Paine, 72y., Dec. 3, 1775.	
2-94	PHINNEY Joshua, of Joshua and Martha, Nov. 29, 1716.	
2-96	" Mr. Jer., 85y., Feb. 18, 1743.	
2-96	" Mrs. Esther, April 11, 1743.	
2-94	PINUS James, of James and Dorothy, June 6, 1707.	
3-12	PITMAN Mary, of Capt. Samuel, 25y., May 2, 1797.	
4-247	" Allen W., of Benjamin, Sept. 8, 1800.	
4-247	" Francis,	Oct. 23, 1813.
3-19	" William, 34y., Dec. 5, 1807.	
3-24	" Peleg, 65y., (also 2-102), Feb. 25, 1812.	
2-103	" Nathaniel, (drowned at Fisher's Island Race from on board schooner O. O. Perry), Sept. 25, 1814.	
3-25	" Mary, widow, 79y., Dec. 1, 1819.	
4-39	" Elisha Adams, of Josiah K., 9m., Feb. 28, 1837.	
4-45	" Nancy, wife of William H., Nov. 1, 1837.	
4-53	" Samuel (at Brooklyn, N. Y.), 30y., April —, 1839.	
4-56	" Helen, of Benjamin, Jr., 2y. 6m., March 30, 1840.	
4-56	" Benjamin,	6y. 5m., April 3, 1840.
4-70	" William A., of William, dec., 2 1-2y., March 20, 1842.	
4-72	" Mary Anna, of James D., 19y., Sept. 22, 1842.	
4-88	" Sarah Russell, of Josiah K., 2y. 2m., Oct. 27, 1845.	
4-88	" Benjamin, of Benjamin, Jr., 4y. 8m., Nov. 9, 1845.	
4-90	" Mary,	15y., April 16, 1846
4-104	" Capt. Benjamin, 75y., Aug. 7, 1848.	
4-110	" Benjamin, 74y., —— —, 1848.	
2-94	POPE John, (found dead near the ferry), buried April 2, 1686.	

4-17   PORTER Emily, of James (col.), 13y., April 13, 1834.
4-45   "   Susan J., (col.), 13y., Dec. 14, 1837.
4-96   "   Violet, (col.), Jan. 4, 1847.
2-97   POTTER Mr., his negro boy, Feb. 28, 1745.
2-97   "   Capt., his negro man, (lost on the back of the cape on passage
                   from Surinam, vessel and cargo lost), Dec. 29, 1747.
2-97   "   Capt., his negro man Ceazer, April 16, 1748.
2-97   "   Capt. Sim, wife of, July 30, 1750.
2-98   "   Mr., his mulatto girl, April 7, 1751.
2-98   "   Levi, Jan. 5, 1754.
2-98   "   Sim, his negro Bristow, March 11, 1754.
2-98   "   Capt., his Indian Tom. March —, 1755.
2-98   "   his negro Prince, (at sea), March —, 1755.
2-98   "   his mulatto child, Jan. 31, 1757.
2-100   "   his negro York (drowned), Dec. 12, 1764.
2-100   "   Mrs. Hopestill, 74y., Jan. 6, 1770.
2-103   "   Capt., his negro child, Sept. 22, 1773.
2-100   "   —,   June 29, 1773.
3-3   "   Hannah, of Simeon, 56y., March 14, 1788.
3-17   "   Simeon, 86y., Feb. 21, 1806.
4-39   "   Mary, wife of Peleg, of Prudence Island, 25y., Jan. 11, 1837.
4-132   "   Mary Ann, 17y., July 15, 1851.
2-94   PRATT Elizabeth, of Joseph and Elizabeth, Nov. 14, 1707.
2-96   "   John, child of, Oct. 3, 1740.
2-101   "   John, wife of, 53y., Aug. 17, 1775.
4-126   "   Lavina, widow of Spencer, 77y., Nov. 15, 1850.
3-7   PRINCE, negro servant, of Benjamin Haskell, 6y., —. —, —.
4-60   PUTNAM Samuel Viall, of James N., 11m., Sept. 24, 1840.

Q

4-114   QUINN Lydia R., wife of Thomas, dau. of Capt. Nathaniel Gladding, dec.,
                32y., June 23, 1849.

R

4-60   RALPH Ann, of Joseph, 58y., Aug. 17, 1840.
4-82   RAMNAS Thomas (born Isle of Minerva, a resident of Matanzas, Cuba),
                52y., July 16, 1844.
3-22   RANDALL James, 35y. (drowned from gunboat), July 15, 1813.
4-66   "   William H., of Thomas, dec., 18y. (at sea), Oct. 19, 1841.
4-21   RANDOLPH Anthony (col.), 64y., Dec. 16, 1834.
2-108 RANS, widow, child of, Sept. 2, 1814.
4-31   RAWSON Martha, wife of Samuel, 51y., Jan. 22, 1836.
3-4   REBECCA —, wife of Capt. James, 55y., Sept. 20, 1789.
4-116 REDFORD Mary, wife of Joseph, 34y. (born England), Sept. 23, 1849.
2-108 REED Samuel, 22y., Sept. 7, 1758.
2-108   "   Samuel (at New York), —— —, 1778.
2-108   "   Joseph, child of Joseph, Oct. 7, 1813.
3-4   "   —, son of Benjamin, 27y., Sept. 10, 1788.
3-6   "   John, 27y., (drowned in Bristol harbor), June 4, 1791.
3-13   "   Mary, wife of Joseph, Esq., 77y., Jan. 10, 1798.
3-13   "   Joseph, Esq., 82y., July 2, 1812.
3-23   "   John (drowned in Mill Pond in a gale), Sept. 23, 1815.
3-23   "   Josiah (drowned in Mill Pond in a gale), Sept. 23, 1815.
4-169   "   Benjamin, 59y. (also 3-25), Oct. 23 or 24, 1820.
3-30   "   Hannah, wife of Capt. Samuel, Sept. 9, 1830.
4-39   "   Virginia, of Samuel, 3y. 8m., March 7, 1837.
4-39   "   Thomas Jefferson, 2y., March 19, 1837.
4-49   "   Abby, 67y., Sept. —, 1838.
4-54   "   John Francis, of John, (col.), 3y., 3m., Sept. 15, 1839.
4-76   "   Samuel (at sea), 60y., July 9, 1843.
4-110   "   John (col.), 42y., March 12, 1849.

2-105	REYNOLDS Capt. Nathaniel (suddenly), July 10, 1703.	
2-105	" Joseph,, his negro child, June —, 1734.	
2-105	" ——,	May 19, 1735.
2-105	" ——,	March 13, 1740.
2-105	" Mrs. Mary, 70y., Jan. 8, 1740.	
2-105	" Joseph, his negro child, Sept. 16, 1742.	
2-105	" ——,	Dec. 18, 1743.
2-105	" ——,	Feb. 10, 1744.
2-105	" Priscilla, Jan. 24, 1744.	
2-106	" Joseph, wife of, 49y., Dec. 18, 1744.	
2-106	" George, Oct. 18, 1745.	
2-106	" Eleazer (at Capt. Breton), ——. —, 1745.	
2-106	" Nathaniel (at Jamaica), Sept. —, 1746.	
2-106	" Benjamin, his negro man London, Jan. 3, 1749.	
2-106	" Jonathan, 20y., Jan. 21, 1753.	
2-106	" Samuel, April 27, 1753.	
2-106	" John, 90y., Jan. 30, 1757.	
2-106	" Joseph, 82y. 0m. 7d., Jan. 16, 1759.	
2-107	" Sarah, wife of Benjamin, March 11, 1762.	
2-107	" Capt. Joseph, child of, 2y., July 2, 1767.	
2-107	" Capt., his negro child, Nov. 16, 1767.	
2-107	" ——,	Sept. 3, 1768.
2-107	" Benjamin, 85y., Aug. 4, 1770.	
2-107	" Capt., his old negro woman, Aug. 29, 1770.	
2-107	" ——, his negro child,	Nov. 5, 1770.
2-107	" ——,	Nov. 4, 1773.
2-108	" Phebe, of Capt., 25y., Oct. 16, 1779.	
3-3	REYNOLDS Joseph, of Joseph, 11y., Feb. 17, 1788.	
3-4	" Joseph, Esq., 70, Sept. 11, 1789.	
3-10	" Marcy, widow, 83y., Sept. 23, 1795.	
3-16	" Lydia, widow, 80y., May 1, 1804.	
3-23	" Sarah, 80y., July 28, 1816.	
3-24	" Joseph, 70y., Oct. 10, 1818.	
3-25	" Lydia, 75y., (also 4-169), Nov. 30, 1820.	
4-19	" Eliza, wife of Samuel G., 29y., (at Pawtucket), July 12, 1834.	
4-25	" Robert C., 30y., May 21, 1835.	
4-29	" Samuel, 75y., Dec. 28, 1835.	
4-39	" Mary, 84y. 21d., Dec. 2, 1836.	
4-49	" Sarah, widow of Joseph, 93y., Sept. 6, 1838.	
4-58	" Elizabeth, wife of William, 65y., May 15, 1840.	
4-62	" Greenwood, 64y., Nov. 21, 1840.	
4-74	" William, 71y., Oct. 14, 1842.	
4-76	" Jane, of Samuel G., 13y., May 12, 1843.	
4-76	" Jane G., 32y., July 3, 1843.	
4-86	" Jonathan, 83y., June 29, 1845.	
4-118	" Mary, wife of George H. and dau. of Capt. James Usher, dec., 40y., Dec. 25, 1849.	
4-124	" Susan, of George H., 17y., June 12, 1850.	
3-1	RHODES ——, child of, 3y., April 12, 1786.	
2-107	RICHARDSON David, child of, 3y., Dec. 2, 1768.	
3-30	" Hannah, widow, 71y., July 17, 1810.	
4-169	" Nancy, widow, 48y., (also 3-25), Sept. 30, 1820.	
2-105	RICHMOND ——, child of Mr. ——, July 23, 1740.	
2-105	" ——, Feb. 13, 1742.	
2-105	" ——, his negro child, May 26, 1743.	
2-106	" ——, Jan. —, 1746.	
2-106	" Rogers ——, his negro child, March 7, 1748.	
2-106	" Dr. Ichabod, Jr., child of ——. —— —, 1756.	
2-106	" ——,	b. and d. Jan. 5, 1760.
2-108	" Samuel (at Albany on return from the camp), 19y., —— —, 1760.	
2-106	" Mrs. Rogers, 45y., Feb. 6, 1762.	
2-107	" Dr., 59y., Sept. 29, 1762.	
2-107	" ——, wife of William, Esq., of Little Compton (at Bristol), 61y., Oct. 9, 1762.	
2-107	" Eliza, of Rogers, 23y., July 31, 1766.	

2-108	RICHMOND Mary, of Rogers and Susannah, Nov. 21, 1771.
2-107	" Mrs. Susannah, 64y., July 6, 1776.
3-201	" Gamaliel, 83y., May 16, 1809.
4-168	" Gilbert, of Newport, 56y., (also 3-25), May 1, 1821.
3-26	" Capt. William, 45y., Aug. 19, 1823.
4-29	" ——, child of William H., April 14, 1835.
3-29	" Lydia, wife of Thomas, 56y., Dec. 18, 1827.
4-49	" Grace W., wife of Gilbert, dau. of Matthias Munro, dec., of South Bridgewater, Mass., June 11, 1838.
4-52	" John Henshaw, of Lemuel C., 21y., Jan. 3, 1839.
4-62	" Thomas P., 30y., Nov. 3, 1840.
4-68	" Ruth Pearce, of William A., 2y., Feb. 2, 1842.
4-80	" Isaac Gorham, of Lemuel C., 24y., Jan. 30, 1844.
4-86	" Abby Ann, of Gilbert, 23y., June 19, 1845.
4-92	" Hannah, wife of Lemuel C., 63y., Aug. 1, 1846.
4-106	" Simeon, 50y., Aug. 18, 1848.
4-112	" ——, child of William H., 19m., April 22, 1849.
2-106	RIDING (a free negro), Nov. 11, 1758.
2-105	RISDON Elisha (at Newport), July —, 1741.
2-106	" Tabitha, widow, Dec. 9, 1755.
2-106	RIX John (at Cape Breton), ——, —, 1745.
4-80	ROAN Matthew (born Scotland), 24y., Dec. 11, 1843.
4-80	" Isabella (born Scotland), 20y., June 25, 1844.
2-108	ROBBINS Elizabeth, child of ——, Feb. 18, 1813.
4-66	ROBERTSON Walter W., 56y. (a foreigner, but had resided here a number of years), Sept. 14, 1841.
2-106	ROBINSON Sion, child of, Nov. 5, 1760.
4-128	ROCKE William, child of, Feb. 2, 1851.
2-107	ROFFEY Solomon (at New Providence), —— —, 1762.
2-107	" Mrs. Sarah, March 8, 1764.
3-23	ROGERS William De Wolf, of Robert, 4m., March 18, 1816.
4-116	" Susan Maria, of Rev. William, 89y., Nov. 8, 1849.
2-107	ROSBOTHAM Peleg, servant of Benjamin, Feb. 5, 1776.
2-107	" Prince, July 18, 1776.
2-107	" Mrs. Sarah, Feb. 16, 1776.
2-108	" Benjamin (at Rehoboth) 77y., July 20, 1777.
2-108	" Benjamin, his negro woman (at Rehoboth), —— —, 1777.
4-168	ROSY Sarah, widow, 91y., Feb. 12, 1821.
4-110	ROWEBOTHAM ——, child of Joseph, 2y. 6m., April 5, 1849.
2-130	" George W., of Joseph, 1y., Feb. 5, 1851.
2-105	ROYALL Mary, in 32y., April 2, 1739.
2-105	" Samuel, 64y., June 13, 1743.
2-106	" Mrs. Hannah, 68y., Jan. 25, 1749.
2-105	RUSSELL Anna, of Joseph and Sarah, Sept. 7, 1735.
2-108	" Sarah, of Anna, (at Norwich), Oct. 22, 1763.
2-107	" Mrs. Sarah, 57y., Jan. 10, 1764.
2-108	" Hon. Joseph, 78y., July 31, 1780.
2-108	" Jonathan, Esq., 78y., July 17, 1814.
3-18	" Ann, widow, 43y., Sept. 8, 1807.
3-20	" Nancy, wife of Capt. John W., 36y., Sept. 5, 1810.
3-22	" Capt. John Willard, 44y., (also 2-108), Aug. 20, 1814.
3-23	" Jonathan, 78y., July 17, 1815.
3-25	" Capt. Thomas, 28y., July 21, 1819.
3-26	" Miss Ann, 76y., May 22, 1823.
4-128	RUTHERFORD George H., of Providence, 24y., (on board steamer Panama), Nov. 14, 1850.
3-3	" Ruth, wife of Samuel, 27y., Dec. 30, 1787.

S

2-112	SABIN Elijah (at the Camp), —— —, 1758.
3-19	" Capt. John, 28y., (at sea), Dec. 28, 1807.
3-20	" Susanna, widow, 89y., Aug. 14, 1811.
3-21	" Lucretia, widow of Capt. John (also 2-115), 34y., Sept. 11, 1811.

3-2	SAMUEL ——, wife of, 25y., Jan. 4, 1787.	
2-110	SALISBURY John, child of, July 26, 1734.	
2-111	" Archibald (at Newport), May 22, 1743.	
2-110	" Sarah, of Archibald and Sarah, March —. 1745-6.	
2-113	" William, widow of, formerly of this town, 82y., May 14, 1767.	
2-112	" Barnard, wife of, Nov. —, 1751.	
2-116	" Mrs. Mary, Feb. 12, 1752.	
2-113	" Nathaniel (killed at Crown Point), —— —. 1759.	
2-113	" Barnard, wife of, June 1, 1769.	
2-114	" ——, child of, Jan. 31, 1772.	
2-115	" Levi, March 26, 1776.	
2-115	" Joseph (at New York), Aug. —. 1776.	
2-115	" Benjamin, 77y., Dec. 24, 1779.	
2-115	" Elizabeth widow, Feb. 25, 1780.	
2-112	" Hezekiah (in captivity in old France), ——. —. ——.	
2-115	" Thomas June 6, 1813.	
2-116	" Thomas (dec.), child of, Nov. 13, 1813.	
2-110	SAMPSON Capt. John, Jan. 12, 1734-5.	
2-111	SAMSON John, killed by the French at Cayenne), —— —, 1744.	
2-110	SANDY Elizabeth, of Joseph and Bethia (by a blow from a horse), Aug. 27, 1694.	
2-112	SANFORD Esbon (at Newport), Jan. 22, 1759.	
2-113	" Hannah, widow, June 5, 1759.	
2-113	" Joshua, wife of, July 9, 1759.	
2-113	" Martha, widow, child of, 1y., March 5, 1760.	
2-113	" Restcome, child of, Oct. 11, 1767.	
2-114	" Restcome, child of (burnt), about 2y., Oct. 17, 1771.	
2-116	" Joshua, about 81 y., May 16, 1774.	
2-114	" Restcome, child of, Sept. 28, 1775.	
2-112	" Samuel (in captivity in old France)) —— —, ——.	
3-4	" Joshua, 67y., Aug. 10, 1789.	
3-13	" Joshua, widow of, 73y., Sept. 14, 1797.	
3-17	" Thomas, 37y., Feb. 23, 1806.	
3-20	" Stephen (lost at sea), Oct. 18, 1810.	
3-21	" Stephen, 22y. (in sloop Sally from Havana), Dec. —, 1811.	
3-24	" Ellery, 53y., Jan. 6, 1819.	
4-168	" Waitstill, of Royal, 31y., Feb. 14, 1821.	
3-29	" Hezekiah, 82y., April 19, 1828.	
3-29	" Rhoda, wife of Royal, 66y., Aug. 2, 1829.	
3-31	" George, 80y., Dec. 1, 1832.	
4-21	" Royal, 74y., Dec. 30, 1834.	
4-45	" James R., 38y., Dec. 16, 1837.	
4-88	" George, of Henry, 5m., Aug. 30, 1845.	
4-126	" Emma, of Leonard, 17m., Oct. 12, 1850.	
4-128	" John, 35y. (at Ithica, N. Y.,), Dec. 26, 1850.	
2-15	" Salisbury Barnard, 73y., June 8, 1801.	
3-17	" Ruth, widow, 65y., March 15, 1805.	
3-22	" Thomas, 47y., June 6, 1813.	
4-80	" James (at the Asylum), 67y., Dec. 7, 1843.	
3-1	SARAH ——, widow, 85y., Jan. 29, 1786.	
3-1	SCIPIO child of, 1y., March 19, 1786.	
4-60	SCOTT Sophronia E., of Rev. Ephraim, 13m., Sept. 15, 1840.	
3-22	SEAMANS Joseph, 37y., Feb. 24, 1813.	
2-111	SHARP William, dau. of, 16y., June 5, 1740.	
2-112	" wife of, April 30, 1751.	
2-112	" William, July 8, 1752.	
2-111	SHANTON Jacob, Indian (at Newport), Oct. 29, 1746.	
4-51	SHAW Joanna S., of Elnathan T., 9y., Oct. 14, 1838.	
3-8	SHENE Madame —— (friend lady), 38y., Oct. 10, 1793.	
4-102	SHEPHERD Eliza Barrett, eldest dau. of Rev. Thomas (at Portland, Me.), 25y., Jan. 16, 1848.	
2-116	SHERMAN Isaac, wife of, Sept. 8, 1813.	
2-114	SHORT Theophilus (at Dartmouth), ——. —, 1769.	
2-110	SHOVE Edward, formerly of Dighton, (also 2-111), Oct. 12, 1746.	

2-111	SIMMONS Ichabod (at Cape ——), Jan. 1, 1750.	
2-115	" Joseph, Feb. 20, 1813.	
3-24	" Mary, widow, 63y., May 2, 1819.	
3-25	" Elizabeth, widow, 72y., Dec. 4, 1819.	
4-237	" Theodore S., Aug. 13, 1829.	
4-21	" John Colvin, of Colvin, 5y. 3m. (also 4-237), Oct. 29, 1834.	
4-237	" Nancy Diman,	1-9-8, Nov. 23, 1835.
4-41	" Comfort, 54y., April 30, 1837.	
4-51	" George Gooding, of Isaac, 11m., Sept. 27, 1838.	
4-54	" Maria, of Comfort, dec. July 3, 1839.	
4-54	" ——, child of Edward, 1y., Sept. 24, 1839.	
4-58	" ——, child of John P., 3w., June 23, 1840.	
4-74	" Albert Newton, of Isaiah; 11y., Oct. 8, 1842.	
4-76	" Abby Julia,	14y., March 30, 1843.
4-86	" Mary, widow of Joseph, 67y., July 15, 1845.	
4-92	" Georgiana, of Colvin, 9y., June 29, 1846.	
4-106	" Sarah Jenckes, of Jason D., 2y., Aug. 23, 1848.	
4-114	" Smith B., 43y., July 4, 1849.	
4-106	SKINNER Carroll J., of Parmenas, 1y., Sept. 4, 1848.	
4-70	SLADE Ira Potter, of Ira P., 5 1-2m., March 6, 1842.	
4-76	" ——, child of Daniel, 6m., April 25, 1843.	
4-94	" Betsey, (col.), 17y., Oct. 31, 1846.	
4-96	" William, of John (col.), 13m., Jan. 28, 1847.	
4-124	" Henry, of Daniel, 1y., Aug. 17, 1850.	
3-9	SLOCUM Samuel, of Capt. Samuel, 7m., Sept. 21, 1794.	
3-10	" Martha, wife of Capt. Samuel, 26y., Jan. 8, 1795.	
3-23	" James, 23y. (lost from sloop Henry at sea), Feb. 19, 1817.	
3-27	" Sarah, widow, 58y., April 16, 1825.	
4-25	" Mary (col.), 40y., May 29, 1835.	
4-64	" Christopher, formerly of New Bedford, recently of Newport, 51y., May 21, 1841.	
4-70	" Mary, of Samuel, 20y. (at Providence), Feb. 27, 1842.	
4-108	" Elizabeth, widow of Peleg, 95y., a Revolutionary pensioner, Jan. 1, 1849.	
2-110	SMITH Joseph, Dec. 30, 1707.	
2-110	" Daniel, child of, Aug. 10, 1729.	
2-116	" Mrs., about 95y., Aug. —, 1734.	
2-110	" Nathaniel, son of, 8y., Aug. 13, 1736.	
2-110	" Sarah, Dec. 17, 1738.	
2-111	" Joseph, his negro child, Aug. 20, 1740.	
2-111	" Daniel, 54y., Aug. 21, 1741.	
2-111	" Samuel, wife of, April —, 1744.	
2-111	" Gideon, 69y., June 30, 1744.	
2-111	" John (drowned at sea), April —, 1746.	
2-111	" Samuel, Jr., Sept. 6, 1746.	
2-111	" Richard, child of, Oct. 29, 1746.	
2-112	" Nathaniel, Jr., (died as was supposed), Dec. 26, 1747.	
2-111	" Nathaniel (lost on back of the Cape coming from Surinam. Vessel and cargo lost), —— —, 1747.	
2-111	" David (at Newport), Oct. —, 1749.	
2-111	" Richard, child of, Sept. 26, 1749.	
2-111	" Daniel, child of, Dec. —, 1750.	
2-111	" Nathaniel, 70y., March 22, 1751.	
2-112	" Samuel, of Benjamin and Abigail, Aug. 2, 1751.	
2-112	" Abigail, wife of Benjamin, 40y., Aug. 9, 1751.	
2-112	" Elizabeth, widow, dau. of, 10y., June 10, 1752.	
2-112	" Nathan (at sea), Sept. —, 1752.	
2-112	" Will, servant of, widow, March 18, 1754.	
2-112	" three children (triplets), of Benjamin, b. and d. —— —, 1756.	
2-112	" Richard, negro girl of 13y., May 7, 1758.	
2-112	" Hannah, of Richard, 9m., Oct. 10, 1758.	
2-112	" Benjamin, child of, b. and d. Jan. 14, 1759.	
2-113	" Abigail, widow, Dec. 9, 1759.	
2-113	" Elizabeth, widow of Gideon, Aug. 25, 1759.	
2-113	" Joseph (at Newport), 54y., Aug. 21, 1760.	

2-113	SMITH Benjamin, child of, b. and d. —— —, 1763.	
2-113	" Sarah, wife of Benjamin, March 17, 1764.	
2-113	" Elizabeth, widow of Samuel, Jr., 56y., May 6, 1765.	
2-113	" Samuel, 85y., Nov. 18, 1766.	
2-113	" . Mrs. Martha, 73y., June 6, 1767.	
2-114	" Stephen, his negro child, May 19, 1772.	
2-114	" Nathaniel, child of, 6m., July 16, 1772.	
2-114	" Elizabeth, widow of Daniel, 81y., Sept. 1, 1772.	
2-114	" Stephen, his negro woman, Aug. 2, 1773.	
2-114	" Josiah, child of, 1y., Jan. 19, 1775.	
2-114	" Stephen, child of, about 9m., Sept. 16, 1775.	
2-114	" James, child of, 11m., Sept. 17, 1775.	
2-114	" Allen, of Nathaniel, 2y. 2m., Sept. 18, 1775.	
2-114	" Nathaniel, child of, 6y., named Nancy,	Sept. 24, 1775.
2-114	" Josiah, child of, b. and d. —— —, 1775.	
2-114	" ——, wife of,	Oct. 16, 1775.
2-115	" Benjamin (dumb man), 36y., Oct. 31, 1775.	
2-115	" Phebe, widow, 59y., Jan. 19, 1776.	
2-115	" Josiah, child of, Oct. 22, 1777.	
2-115	" James, child of, June —, 1777.	
2-115	" ——,	—— —, 1777
2-116	" Sarah, of Richard and Lucretia, Nov. 20, 1779.	
3-1	" Mary, wife of Stephen, Jan. 12, 1785	
3-1	" Richard, of Richard, Jr., 3w., Aug. 23, 1785.	
3-2	" Mary, wife of Nathaniel June 12, 1786.	
3-3	" Francis, 34y. (drowned) March 29, 1787.	
3-3	" Louisa, of Stephen, 1y., Sept. 22, 1787.	
3-5	" Lucretia, of Richard, Esq., 71y., Jan. 31, 1790.	
3-5	" child of Richard, Jr., 12 hours, Sept. 18, 1790.	
3-7	" child, •	12 days, April 22, 1792.
3-9	" Elizabeth, of Barnard, Sept. 10, 1794.	
3-10	" Allen Taylor, of Nathaniel and Parnel (also 2-116), 15y., July 28, 1795.	
3-10	" Nathaniel, of Nathaniel, 2d., 20y., Sept. 16, 1795.	
3-11	" Jemima, widow, 78y., Sept. 9, 1796.	
3-11	" Josiah, Jr., 21y. (at Charleston, S. C.), Sept. 18, 1796.	
3-11	" Elizabeth, wife of Benjamin, 23y., Oct. 11, 1796.	
3-12	" Mary, dau. of James, 14y., Sept. 7, 1797.	
3-13	" Elizabeth, wife of Josiah, 47y., Oct. 2, 1797.	
3-13	" Stephen, of Stephen, Esq., 15y., Oct. 6, 1797.	
3-13	" Jonathan, of Josiah, Oct. 13, 1797.	
3-13	" Susannah, 25y., Oct. 15, 1797.	
3-13	" Eleanor, 8y., Oct. 21, 1797.	
3-14	" Stephen, Esq., 59y., Nov. 3, 1799.	
2-15	" Capt. Benjamin, May 6, 1801.	
2-15	" Samuel, of Richard, 14y., June 23, 1801.	
3-16	" Elizabeth, wife of Barnard, July 15, 1804.	
3-17	" George, 25y., April 27, 1805.	
3-17	" Miss Mary, 18y., April 19, 1806.	
3-17	" James, Jr., July 25, 1806.	
2-115	" Nathaniel (also 2-115), June —, 1811.	
3-22	" Richard, 92 or 93y., Feb. 6, 1813.	
3-22	" Mary, wife of Cornelius, 44y., April 25, 1814.	
2-116	" John, wife of, April 25, 1814.	
3-23	" Sarah, 42y., widow, July 22, 1816.	
4-168	" William C., 40y., (also 3-25), March 11, 1821.	
3-26	" Nathaniel, 74y., March 21, 1822.	
3-26	" Ruth, widow, 63y., March 25, 1823.	
2-116	" William C., child of, Aug. 28, 1815.	
3-26	" Samuel, 63y., Sept. 14, 1823.	
3-29	" Capt. James, 32y., March 20, 1828.	
3-29	" Nathaniel, 84y., Oct. 9, 1828.	
3-30	" Capt. Allen Taylor, Oct. 1, 1830.	
3-31	" Richard, Esq., 80y., Oct. 17, 1832.	
4-27	" Ruth Ann, of Benjamin, 5m., Nov. 8, 1835.	

3-35   SMITH Mary, wife of Isaiah, 83y., Sept. 21, 1836.
4-37   "   ——, child of Benjamin, 5m., Oct. 15, 1836.
4-39   "   John W., of John W., 1y., 7m., Feb. 25, 1837.
4-41   "   Josiah, 95y., June 22, 1837.
4-53   "   John (at Cuba), Feb. 27, 1839.
4-60   "   Phebe, widow of James, 92y., Sept. 23, 1840.
4-64   "   Ammanntia, widow of Nathaniel, 87y., May 1, 1841.
4-66   "   Susan, widow of Richard, Aug. 31, 1841.
4-68   "   Bristol, 73y. (col.), Jan. 15, 1842.
4-70   "   Allen T., 44y., May 11, 1842.
4-72   "   William Henry, of William, 1y., Aug. 19, 1842.
4-90   "   John, of John (col.), 8y., Dec. 5, 1845.
4-90   "   Samuel DeWolf, of Mark A. DeWolf Smith, 22y., Dec. 7, 1845.
4-90   "   Delia (col.), 38y., Dec. 10, 1845.
4-92   "   Rebecca, of Josiah, dec., 79y., June 4, 1846.
4-102   "   Phebe, 87y., —— —. 1847.
4-106   "   Betsey, widow of Nathaniel, 99y. 7m., Oct. 29, 1848.
4-110   "   Betsey, 97y., —— —. 1848.
4-110   "   Capt. John M., 49y., mate of schooner Hard Times (at Mobile, Ala.), March 30, 1849.
4-118   "   Barnard, 81y. (formerly Judge Court of Common Pleas), Feb. 11, 1850.
4-102   SNELL Miss Ruth, of Seth, dec., 77y., Jan. 27, 1848.
4-110   "   Ruth, 78y., —— —, 1848.
4-130   SOLEY John, Esq., of Charlestown, Mass., 86y., April 6, 1851.
2-110   SOUTHWORTH Elizabeth, widow, June 24, 1682.
4-72   "   Mary L., of Sylvester S., 38y., Aug. 17, 1842.
4-72   "   Rebecca, 15y., Aug. 23, 1842.
2-110   SPARHAWK Rev. John (minister of this town for 23y.), April 22, 1718.
4-47   SPARKS Charity, widow of Joseph, 75y., March 27, 1838.
3-16   SPAULDING Edward, 36y., Feb. 9, 1804.
3-20   "   Susan, widow, 36y., April 21, 1809.
2-116   SPINK Samuel, child of, Dec. 10, 1814.
2-116   "   ——, Dec. 13, 1814.
3-22   "   Samuel, 29y., Dec. 15, 1814.
4-19   SPOONER Mary Anna, of Charles, 16m., Sept. 9, 1834.
4-23   "   ——, child of John, 5w., Feb. 22, 1835.
4-27   "   Walter, of John W., 10m., Nov. 12, 1835.
4-52   "   Eleanor, wife of Charles, 33y., Jan. 14, 1839.
4-104   "   Emily Frances, of William B., 4y. 5m., Aug. 2, 1848.
2-116   SPRAGUE Ephraim, child of, Sept. 27, 1814.
3-22   SPRINGER John, 85 or 86y. (also 2-115), May 27, 1813.
3-27   "   Martha, widow, 83y., March 28, 1824.
4-60   "   ——, child of Joseph, Jr., Sept. 15, 1840.
4-27   STANDISH Ann Amanda, of David, 3y., Oct. 9, 1835.
3-24   STANHOPE Hannah, 93y., Aug. 28, 1818.
2-116   STARLIN Samuel, of Richard and Grace, Jan. 11, 1694-5.
4-23   STARRS Otis, 32y., formerly of Mansfield, Conn., March 18, 1835.
2-115   STEAD Sally, of Jonathan, 6w. 1d., Feb. 14, 1807.
2-115   "   Sally, his wife, 29y., March 11, 1807.
2-115   "   Sally Hill, his daughter, 7 days, May 18, 1810.
4-128   STEPHENS Alexander G., 22y., Jan. 18, 1851.
4-98   STRONG Esther, 19y. (buried at Freetown, Mass.), Sept. 29, 1847.
4-78   STUDLEY child of John, 3y., Aug. 4, 1843.
3-20   STUTSON Luther, 61y., March 22, 1810.
4-86   "   Mary Jane, wife of George W., and dau. of John Norris, 2d, 18y., March 5, 1845.
2-113   SUCA (at the Mount), Dec. 19, 1763.
4-19   SUMNER Mary Ann, wife of William H., eldest dau. of James DeWolf, Esq., 39y., July 14, 1834.
2-100   SUSANNAH Mrs., 80y., July 27, 1768.
2-113   SWAN Sarah, 21y., April 17, 1767.
2-114   "   Thomas, child of, 13m., Sept. 22, 1775.
2-114   "   ——,   Dec. 24, 1775.
2-116   "   William, child of, Feb. —, 1815.

3-8 SWAN Margaret, widow, 69y., April 27, 1793.
3-17 " Capt. Samuel (at Havana), 21y., Nov. 24, 1804.
3-17 " Thomas, Esq., 56y., July 30, 1805.
3-27 " William, 36y., Oct. 16, 1825.
4-19 " Abby, of Nathaniel P., 17y., Aug. 16, 1834.
4-96 " Caroline, wife of Samuel B., 21y., April 24, 1847.
4-104 " Charlotte DeWolf, of Samuel, 13y., Aug. 3, 1848.
3-22 SWIFT Capt. Thomas (at sea with schooner O. H. Perry), Dec. —, 1814.
3-30 SYLVESTER Phebe, widow, 49y., Feb. 28, 1831.
2-116 " Joseph, child of, April 4, 1815.

T

2-118 TABOR widow, child of, Feb. 10, 1730.
4-68 " Sophronia, widow of Capt. William, 57y., Nov. 11, 1841.
2-121 TALBEE Edward, child of, Aug. —, 1754.
2-120 " William, child of, 3y., May 9, 1769.
2-120 " ——, b. and d. Aug. 26, 1770.
2-120 " Hannah, of Edward, 21y., Dec. 8, 1774.
3-11 " Anstis, wife of Edward, 70y., Sept. 26, 1796.
3-31 " Mary, wife of Stephen, 98y., Dec. 28, 1832.
4-92 " Stephen, 90y., June 22, 1846.
4-104 " Ann, widow of Edward, 95y., July 23, 1848.
4-110 " Anne, 95y., —— —, 1848.
3-31 TALBOT Dolly, wife of Capt. ——. 22y., June 6, 1832.
4-51 " Hannah, wife of Josiah, R., 23y., Oct. 27, 1838.
4-94 " Josephine Howes, of Josiah R., 16m., Aug. 19, 1846.
4-116 " Harriet R., 13y., Oct. 24, 1849.
4-126 " Bridget (col.), 87y. (at the asylum), Nov. 8, 1850.
4-104 TAYER Capt. Edward, of Newport, July 1, 1848.
3-30 TANNER Abigall, widow, late of Warren, 74y., Jan. 17, 1830.
4-53 " Elizabeth, of James, dec., 12y. (col.), June 8, 1839.
4-74 " Edward Payson, of Timothy J., 3m., Nov. 3, 1842.
4-84 " Deborah, wife of Daniel, 59y., Jan. 15, 1845.
4-98 " Louisa, of James, dec. (col.), 23y., Sept. 29, 1847.
4-108 " Scipeo, 44y. (col.), (at the asylum), Nov. 13, 1848.
4-108 " Mary Elizabeth, wife of Daniel (col.), 20y., Nov. 18, 1848.
4-118 " Maria, of William, dec., 33y. (at Philadelphia, Pa.), Dec. 3, 1849.
4-122 " Charlotte (col.), 54y., April 24, 1850.
2-121 TAYLOR Mr., his Indian girl, Aug. 24, 1740.
2-121 " Abigall, 18y., Oct. 3, 1755.
2-119 " Allen (news comes of his death at sea), 26y., May 2, 1758.
2-120 " Bille, alias William, 17y., Nov. 3, 1773.
2-121 " Susannah (at Newport), 49y., —— —, 1779.
3-4 " Martha, widow, 66y., Jan. 22, 1789.
4-37 " George B., of Samuel, 18y., Oct. 25, 1836.
4-49 " Hannah C., wife of Albert, and dau. of Samuel Wardwell, 25y. (at Ellisburgh, N. Y.), May 7, 1838.
4-72 " Jemima, of William R., 1y., 6m., Aug. 18, 1842.
4-72 " Sarah LeBaron, 4y., Aug. 20, 1842.
4-53 TENNANT James, formerly of Newport, 80y. (a resident of this town for many years, died at Exeter at the burning of the Exeter Poor House, where he and several others perished. Was a revolutionary pensioner), April 10, 1839.
4-92 " Louisa B., of John, of Newport, 21y. (buried at Newport), July 23, 1846.
4-21 THATCHER Rebecca, 73y., Dec. 22, 1834.
4-110 THAYER Edward, 75y., —— —, 1848.
4-106 THOMAS Zenas, 66y., Aug. 31, 1848.
2-121 THOMPKINS Nathaniel, child of, Oct. 15, 1747.
3-121 " Nathaniel, (at Jamaica), Feb. —, 1748.
3-32 THOMPSON Samuel, 60y., Dec. 29, 1833.
4-31 " Lucinda, of Samuel, dec., 23y., March 18, 1836.
4-33 " Isabella, of Samuel, 2y. 2m., April 5, 1836.

4-33	THOMPSON Eliza Ann, 4y., April 7, 1836.	
4-33	" George Gilbert, 10y., June 5, 1836.	
4-92	" John (col.), June 30, 1846.	
4-108	" Charlotte, of Rev. Otis, of Utica, N. Y., formerly of Rehoboth, Mass., dau. of John Fales, dec., 60y., Dec. 12, 1848.	
4-114	" Sybel, widow of Samuel, 68y. (at Hudson, N. Y.), July 13, 1849.	
4-130	" Charles E., of Capt. Peleg, 38y. (at Philadelphia, Pa.), Feb. 27, 1851.	
4-74	THORNTON John Tyler, of William, 1y., 10m., March 1, 1843.	
2-121	THOM (Indian), at Papoose Squaw Neck, Nov. 26, 1746.	
2-121	THRESHER widow, Aug. 14, 1813.	
4-51	" Julia A., only child of Deacon Royal, 22y., Nov. 22, 1858.	
2-118	THROOPE William, of Dan and Dorcas, buried March 28, 1696.	
2-118	" Mary,	April 11, 1696.
2-118	" John, of William and Martha, about 3m., May 7, 1711.	
2-118	" William, of Thomas and Abigail, —— —, 1712-3.	
2-118	" Abigail,	Jan. —, 1717.
2-118	" Nathaniel, of Amos and Frances, Sept. 17, 1726.	
2-118	" Elizabeth, of William, Jr., and Elizabeth, about 17m., Aug. 29, 1727.	
2-118	" Rebecca, of Deacon John, Dec. 19, 1731.	
2-118	" Mrs. Mary, June —, 1732.	
2-119	" Ebenezer, 17y., Aug. 10, 1736.	
2-122	" Mrs. Lydia, 22y., May 21, 1737.	
2-122	" Thomas, wife of, July —, 1740.	
2-121	" John, wife of, Dec. 18, 1740.	
2-121	" Dea., his negro woman, Nov. 12, 1741.	
2-121	" his negro man, May —, 1742.	
2-121	" Thomas, wife of. Dec. 20, 1743.	
2-121	" his Indian boy (at Cape Breton), Nov. —, 1746.	
2-122	" John, child of, July 23, 1747.	
2-121	" Thomas, Jr., his Indian child, May —, 1750.	
2-121	" Thomas, child of, May —, 1751.	
2-119	" George, of Thomas, Jr., and Elizabeth, in 3d y., Sept. 14, 1756.	
2-119	" Thomas, 75y. 0m. 14d., Sept. 18, 1756.	
2-119	" Abigail, of Thomas and Mary, in 16th y., Oct. 12, 1756.	
2-120	" Thomas, widow of, 84y., Jan. 25, 1767.	
2-120	" William, infant child of, —— —, 1767.	
2-120	"	July 23, 1763.
2-120	" Susannah, wife of Dea., 85y., Oct. 13, 1768.	
2-120	" William, child of, about 5y., Jan. 2, 1770.	
2-120	" Billings, child of, Sept. 11, 1770.	
2-120	" Thomas, 61y., June 2, 1771.	
2-120	" Dea. John, 96y., Jan. 25, 1772.	
2-120	" Capt. Billings, child of, Sept. 23, 1775.	
2-120	" Capt. Billings, 44y., Jan. 24, 1776.	
2-120	" Samuel, 31y., Jan. 28, 1776.	
3-4	" Alathea, of Capt. William, 46y., June 19, 1789.	
3-16	" John, Esq., 86y., Dec. 2, 1802.	
4-169	" John, of John, 84y., (also 3-25), Sept. 15, 1820.	
4-19	" Mary, widow of Capt. William, 90y., June 17, 1834.	
4-112	" Hannah, wife of William, Esq., 79y., June 2, 1849.	
4-122	" Hon. William, Esq., 79y., May 30, 1850.	
2-121	THURBER James, June 10, 1747.	
2-122	" Hephzibah, widow, Nov. 11, 1753.	
4-17	" Betsey, widow of Amos, 72y., June 12, 1834.	
4-29	" Mary Michie, alias, (col.), 71y., Dec. 7, 1835.	
2-119	THURREL George, child of, Aug. 19, 1736.	
2-119	" dau. of, Jan. 9, 1739-40.	
2-121	" child of, Jan. 13, 1752.	
2-121	" George, (at Cape Breton), Oct. —, 1745.	
2-121	" child of George, ab. 5y., May 14, 1759.	
2-119	" George, May 1, 1760.	
2-119	" child of widow, about 2y., July 5, 1761.	
2-120	" William, at the Havanna, —— —, 1762.	

4-37 THURSTON Ruth, widow of Capt. Peleg, of Portsmouth, 77y., Oct. 28, 1836.
2-100 TIFFANY Peter, formerly servant of Mrs., Jan. 16, 1764.
4-132 TILLEY Samuel Easterbrooks, of Benjamin and Susan W., (at North Dighton, Mass.,) Aug. 10, 1839.
4-90   " Francis G.. of William B., 10m., March 26, 1846.
4-132   " Anna Pearse, of Benjamin and Snsan W., 2m., 17d., July 22, 1856.
4-88 TILLINGHAST child of George, 8m., Aug. 23, 1845.
4-102 TITUS Nancy, 70y., —— —, 1847.
2-120 TOMPKINS dau. of Capt., an only child, (at Hez Usher's), (born in New Providence Island), July 24, 1770.
2-121 TOMLIN John, (at sea), Feb. —, 1749.
2-120   " William, March 10, 1769.
2-118 TORREY Ebenezer, (drowned at sea), Feb. — 1730.
2-119   " Josiah, of John, Sept. 26, 1746.
2-121   " Josiah, (apprentice of Dea. Howland), Sept. 26, 1746.
3-28 TOWNSEND Nathaniel Church, 35y., Jan. 6, 1826.
3-28   " Capt. Samuel, 38y., Jan. 17, 1826.
4-27   " Lydia. widow of Nathaniel C., 42y., Aug. 2, 1835.
4-168 TREN Mary, wife of Peter, 50y., Feb. 4, 1821.
3-27 TRIPP Sarah, widow, 76y., Oct. 12, 1823.
2-119 TRUCK Ben, mulatto, at Mr. Peck's, Feb. 10, 1762.
4-58 TINE Lydia, of Peter, 5y., June 2, 1840.
4-58   " Joseph T., 3y., June 5, 1840.
4-68   " Peter, 65y., (at North Smithfield, Bradford county, Pa.,) Dec. 31, 1841.
2-119 TUNGUEr Daniel. Indian (killed at Ticonderoga), —— —, 1758.
2-118 TWING Benjamin (drowned in the bay and not found), —— —, 1680.

U

2-124 UNIS Paul, child of, Aug. 17, 1773.
2-124   " ——, April 18, 1736.
2-124   " Capt. Paul (at sea), Jan. 20, 1737.
2-124   " Mrs. Alice, 69y., July 10, 1775.
3-3 UNKNOWN (drowned at Bristol Ferry), Dec. 23, 1787.
2-124 USHER Edward, of Rev. John and Elizabeth, April 1, 1730.
2-124   " Elizabeth, wife of Rev. John, Dec. 5, 1769.
2-124   " Thomas (at sea), April 16, 1752.
2-124   " Samuel (drowned at Essequebo), May 15, 1755.
2-124   " John, child of, May 22, 1769.
2-124   " John, of John, Jr. (at Newport), Jan. 9, 1770.
2-124   " Allen, wife of, July 29, 1773.
2-124   " Rev. John, 75y., April 30, 1775.
2-124   " James (at Bayonne, France), —— —, ——.
3-1   " Clarrissa (at Newport), 30y., July 4, 1785.
3-3   " son of Edward, 2m., April 19. 1787.
3-4   " Elizabeth, wife of George D., 23y., Jan. 13, 1790.
3-8   " Anna, wife of Hezekiah, Esq., 71y., Dec. 11, 1793.
3-9   " Allen, 67y., Oct. 16, 1794.
3-10   " Capt. Hezekiah, 33y., (at Gambia river), Sept. 15, 1795.
3-11   " Allen, 32y., Sept. 24, 1796.
3-13   " Capt. George Dunbar, 32y., May —, 1798.
3-14   " John, Jr. (at Havana) Nov. 4, 1799.
2-15   " Rebecca, widow, 63y., June 15, 1801.
3-15   " Hezekiah, Esq., 75y., Feb. 26, 1802.
3-16   " Hannah, wife of Aaron, 35y., April 20, 1804.
3-16   " Rev. John, rector of St. Michael's Church, 81y., July 5, 1804.
3-19   " Elizabeth, wife of Edward, Sept. 18, 1808.
3-21   " Elizabeth, wife of Aaron, 33y.. (also 2 124) Sept. 17, 1811.
3-24   " Allen (at sea), April —, 1818.
3-25   " Capt. Aaron, 53y., Nov. —, 1819.
3-25   " Sarah, wife of Edward, 58y., (also 4-169), Jan. 11, 1820.

4-169	USHER Sarah, widow, 52y., (also 3-25), May 4, 1820.	
3-27	" Martha, wife of Capt. George F., 28y., July 29, 1825.	
3-29	" Ebenezer, 65y., Sept. 28, 1828.	
3-30	" Susanna, wife of Capt. James, Sr., 60y., Aug. 16, 1829.	
3-30	" Sylvia, wife of ——, 72y., Aug. 25, 1829.	
3-31	" Capt. James, 72y., Dec. 11, 1832.	
4-37	" child of William, Oct. 18, 1836.	
4-39	" William Henry, of William, 8y., March 11, 1837.	
4-41	" Ann Elizabeth, of Allen, 7y., March 25, 1837.	
4-41	" Charles Henry, 1y., 11m., March 29, 1837.	
4-60	" James, 5y., July 28, 1840.	
4-62	" Susan, widow of James, 52y., Dec. 10, 1840.	
4-66	" Allen, of Allen T., 10m., Sept. 14, 1841.	
4-88	" Miss Sarah, 40y., Nov. 18, 1845.	

V

3-1	VAN DOORN child of Moses, 2 days, Dec. 10, 1785.	
3-3	" child of Joshua, 1m., Sept. 13, 1787.	
3-4	" Lydia, wife of Moses, 30y., Sept. 10, 1788.	
3-5	" Sarah, 18y., May 13, 1790.	
3-5	" Mary, of Joshua, 16m., Oct. 26, 1790.	
3-7	" Ruth, widow, Oct. 15, 1791.	
3-7	" Martha, 22y., June 22, 1792.	
3-12	" Joshua, 36y., April 25, 1797.	
3-16	" Anthony, 29y, Sept. 29, 1803.	
3-17	" Phebe, widow, 29y., Jan. 15, 1804.	
3-27	" Philadelphia, wife of Joshua, 25y., July 5, 1825.	
4-60	" John F., of William C., 9m. 14d., Sept. 26, 1840.	
4-84	" Mary P., of William, 66y., Feb. 6, 1845.	
2-126	VANDORIN Mr., child of, 1y. 8m., Aug. —, 1767.	
2-126	" Elizabeth, 16y., Sept. 5, 1775.	
2-126	" Anthony, child of, Sept. 19, 1775.	
2-126	VARNUM Eliza, wife of ——, dau. of Charles DeWolf, (at New York), buried at Bristol, d. April 10, bur. 16, 1815.	
4-45	" Martha, widow of Gen. James Mitchell Varnum, 87y., Oct. 10, 1837.	
4-55	VAUGHN Susan, of George, 8y., (buried at East Greenwich), Dec. 14, 1839.	
4-104	" Patience, of Gideon, 78y., May 2, 1848.	
4-108	" Deriah, wife of Bowen, 56y., Nov. 23, 1848.	
4-110	" Patience, 78y., —— —, 1848.	
2-126	VICKERY Reuben C., Sept. 5, 1812.	
4-33	" John, of Capt. Samuel, dec., (at New Orleans), 25y., April —, 1836.	
4-112	" Charlotte, wife of Isaiah, 52y., June 25, 1849.	
2-126	VERNON Mrs. Elizabeth, 79y., March 15, 1759.	
2-126	VIALL Susannah, of Samuel, Nov. 16, 1715.	
2-126	" Samuel,	April 25, 1729.
2-126	" Benjamin,	Aug. 11, 1729.
2-126	" Hez, May 4, 1739.	
2-126	" Samuel, 82y., June 10, 1749.	
2-23	" Cuffee, servant of Mrs., Jan. 13, 1752.	
2-126	VON HENEN Mr., boy Daniel (at sea, —— —, 1743.	
2-126	" Solomon, Nov. —, 1745.	

W

4-96	WADSWORTH John, of Dr. John A., of Providence, 77y., May 22, 1847.	
4-102	" John, 76y., —— —, 1847.	
2-132	WALCH Gregory (at William Pearse), about 26y., May 31, 1759.	
2-128	WALDRON Samuel, of George and Rachel, Oct. 25, 1691.	
2-128	" Rachel, of George, Nov. 25, 1706.	
2-129	" George, Dec. 12, 1739.	
2-129	" Isaac, June 23, 1740.	

2-130	WALDRON	widow, her negro man, April 9, 1741.
2-130	"	Prescilla, of Cornelius and Ann, wife of Robert Carr, Sept. 15, 1741.
2-130	"	Daniel, child of, July —, 1747. .
2-131	"	Joseph, Jr., child of, b. and d. —— —, 1754.
2-131	"	Samuel, of Capt. Daniel, Aug. 4, 1756.
2-132	"	Joseph, of Joseph, 9y., Oct. 10, 1756.
2-132	"	John, Dec. 17, 1756.
2-132	"	Mrs. Martha, 77y., Dec. 10, 1759.
2-132	"	Joseph, 67y., Aug. 14, 1760.
2-133	"	Capt. Daniel (on coast of Africa), 44y., Dec. 27, 1767.
2-133	"	Hannah, widow, 79y., Jan. 30, 1768.
2-133	"	Nathaniel, of Joseph, Jr., and Rebecca (at Newport), Jan. 27, 1769.
2-134	"	Prince, negro servant of John, Sept. 27, 1770.
2-134	"	Daniel, 26y., March 9, 1775.
2-134	"	John (negro), June —, 1778.
2-135	"	Cornelius (at Rehoboth), 81y., Sept. 22, 1778.
2-135	"	Rose, of John (aged negro), —— —, 1780.
3-1	"	Lucretia, wife of Thomas, 22y., Feb. 22, 1786.
3-2	"	Anna, 18y., July 5, 1786.
3-2	"	Capt. George (at sea), 33y., Oct. 9, 1786.
3-4	"	Phebe, widow, 64y., March 3, 1789.
3-4	"	Sarah, 50y., April 13, 1789.
3-5	"	Anna, widow, 91y., Aug. 7, 1790.
3-5	"	Isaac, servant of John, 54y., Aug. 18, 1790.
3-6	"	Elizabeth, widow, May 25, 1793.
3-9	"	Joseph, 3w., Aug. 25, 1794.
3-9	"	John, of John, 1m., Sept. 16, 1794.
3-13	"	John, Esq., 72y., Nov. 28, 1798.
3-14	"	Daniel, of Capt. Daniel, 20y., April —, 1800.
3-15	"	Elizabeth, widow, July 19, 1801.
3-17	"	George (at sea), 22y., Feb. 1, 1806.
3-18	"	Daniel, Sept. 24, 1767.
3-19	"	Richard Smith, 1st (at sea), Dec. 28, 1807.
3-20	"	Hannah, wife of Nathaniel, 78y., June 22, 1811.
3-21	"	Sarah, wife of George (also 2-135), July 26, 1812.
2-136	"	——, dau. of George, 11y., Sept. 18, 1813.
2-136	"	——, child of Samuel, Oct. 13, 1813.
3-23	"	Nathaniel, 87y., Jan. 22, 1817.
3-24	"	Miss Willoughby, 82y., Nov. 6, 1818.
4-109	"	Daniel, 24y., Dec. 29, 1820.
3-26	"	Thomas, 59y., Sept. 11, 1821.
3-27	"	Billings, 66y., Nov. 1, 1823.
3-27	"	Isaac, 82y., June 21, 1824.
3-27	"	Abigail, 81y., June 25, 1824.
3-27	"	Charlotte, wife of Joseph, 57y., Sept. 16, 1824.
3-28	"	Hannah, wife of William, 67y., Feb. 8, 1826.
3-28	"	Miss Phebe, 68y., Aug. 13, 1926.
3-28	"	Sarah, widow, 55y., Oct. 1, 1826.
3-28	"	Newton, 75y., March 17, 1827.
3-29	"	Mary, wife of Samuel, 57y., Sept. 11, 1828.
3-31	"	Elizabeth, widow, 75y., Jan. 9, 1832.
4-17	"	——, child of Henry, 9m., April 4, 1834.
4-19	"	Sarah Martindale, widow of Capt. George, 75y., Aug. 4, 1834.
4-27	"	——, child of William T., Jr., Aug. 21, 1835.
4-33	"	Isaac Liscomb, of John, 4y., June 30, 1836.
4-33	"	Mary Freeborn, 1y. 4m., July 9, 1836.
4-37	"	Hannah Maxfield, of Richard S., 3y. 11m., Nov. 14, 1836.
4-49	"	Isaac P., of Edmund, 14m., Sept. 11, 1838.
4-54	"	Hannah, wife of Billings, 52y., July 26, 1839.
4-55	"	Joseph, 72y., Feb. 1, 1840.
4-56	"	——, child of Edmund, 1y., Feb. 23, 1840.
4-58	"	Samuel, 68y., June 4, 1840.
4-64	"	William Henry, of Joseph, 2y. 7m., April 8, 1841.
4-66	"	Allen, Jr., of Allen, 21y. Aug. 31, 1841.

4-66	WALDRON William T., of W. T., Jr., 15y., Sept. 17, 1841.	
4-66	" Mary, wife of Thomas, 53y., Nov. 2, 1841.	
4-70	" Emma S., of Nathaniel, April 24, 1842.	
4-78	" William Throop, of Nathaniel and Hannah, 73y., July 10, 1843.	
4-88	" ——, child, of Edmund, 15m., Aug. 29, 1845.	
4-94	" Ambrose, 82y. 3m., Sept. 7, 1846.	
4-94	" William, 81y., Nov. 26, 1846.	
4-96	" John Howland, of Leonard, 28y., June 29, 1847.	
4-102	" Allen, of William T., 54y., March 13, 1848.	
4-112	" Ruth, widow, 85y., a Revolutionary pensioner, June 19, 1849.	
4-124	" Hannah, widow of Ambrose, 85y. 10m., June 25, 1850.	
4-128	" Frances, widow of Newton, 82y., Jan. 27, 1851.	
2-129	WALKER Capt. William, July 17, 1735.	
2-130	" Mrs. Elizabeth, 94y., Nov. 6, 1742.	
2-131	" John, child of, Nov. —, 1748.	
2-131	" ——,	Feb. —, 1755.
2-133	" ——, dau. of, 6y., Oct. 29, 1765.	
2-134	" John, 59y., April 3, 1773.	
2-134	" Mrs. Hannah, 82y., May 2, 1774.	
3-6	" Patience. widow, 66y., Feb. 28, 1791.	
2-128	WALLEY Mrs. Sarah, March 2, 1692.	
3-21	WALLACE James (with sloop lost at sea), Dec. —, 1811.	
4-120	WALTON John N., 38y. (at the mines 40 miles from San Francisco, Cal., one of the company which sailed on the barque Winthrop from this port), Jan. 22, 1850.	
2-129	WORDALL Mary, of Joseph W., and Martha, Aug. 7, 1712.	
2-129	" James. his negro child, Dec. —. 1731.	
2-129	" Uzal, 93y., Oct. 25, 1732.	
2-129	" Benjamin, wife of, May 2, 1733.	
2-129	" ——, wife of, June 6, 1737.	
2-129	" Benjamin, June —, 1739.	
2-129	" Benjamin, Jr. (at sea). June —, 1739.	
2-130	" Old Mrs. Grace, May 9, 1741.	
2-130	WARDWELL William, of William and Mary, Feb. 15, 1744-5.	
2-130	" James, Jr., April 9, 1745.	
2-130	" Jonathan (killed at Cape Breton), May —, 1745.	
2-130	" Uzal (at Cape Breton), Sept. —, 1745.	
2-130	" David, his brother (at Cape Breton), Sept. —, 1745.	
2-130	" Joseph, Jr., Sept. 10, 1746.	
2-131	" Stephen, Nov. 13, 1747.	
2-131	" Jemima, widow, child of, 10y., April 12, 1752.	
2-131	" William, child of, April 18, 1754.	
2-131	" Joseph, 69y., March 10, 1755.	
2-132	" James, 74y., March 14, 1757.	
2-132	" William, infant child of, June 19, 1757.	
2-132	" ——, son of, 10m., May 14, 1759.	
2-132	" William (drowned at sea), —— —, 1760.	
2-133	" Sarah, widow, April 2, 1761.	
2-133	" John, child of, Nov. 10, 1762.	
2-133	" Mehitable, wife of Stephen, Feb. 13, 1764.	
2-133	" Isaac, child of, 2y., June 23, 1766.	
2-134	" Nathaniel, (on Coast of Africa), June 2, 1770.	
2-134	" Mrs. Hannah, wife of John, 28y., May 21, 1772.	
2-134	" Stephen, child of, Dec. 15, 1772.	
2-134	"	—— —, 1773.
2-134	" John, 31y., Feb. 9, 1773.	
2-134	" child of Joseph, Jan. 31, 1775.	
2-134	"	5y., Feb. 7, 1775.
2-134	" Mrs. Martha, 88y., Aug. 11, 1775.	
2-134	" infant child of Benjamin, April 21, 1776.	
2-135	" child of Joseph, Sept. —, 1778.	
2-135	" wife of Benjamin, 25y., Nov. 20, 1779.	
3-3	" William, of Benjamin, 1y., Sept. 22, 1787.	
3-5	" Susanna, wife of Dea. Joseph, 13m., July 14, 1790.	
3-6	" Maria, of Samuel, 2d, 5m., Aug. 17, 1791.	

4-246	WARDWELL	Ellen, of Allen and Abigail, Sept. 2, 1791.
4-246	"	Allen, Jr., (in a foreign land), July 27, 1821.
3-7	"	Eleanor, of Capt. Allen, 3y., Sept. 2, 1791.
3-7	"	child of Benjamin, 8w., Oct. 15, 1791.
3-8	"	Samuel Woodbury, (at Guadaloupe), Oct. 24, 1793.
3 9	"	Abigail, of Col. Samuel, 1w., Sept. 3, 1794.
3-10	"	Phebe, widow, 74y., Nov. 30, 1794.
3-11	"	Benjamin, of Stephen and Hannah, 20y., July 28, 1796.
3-11	"	John, 22y., (on the Dolphin at Nassau, N. P.), Aug. —, 1796.
3-12	"	Capt. Samuel, 38y., Aug. 12, 1797.
3-14	"	Stephen, 77y., Aug. 6, 1799.
3-15	"	William, 22y., (drowned at sea), March —, 1802.
3-16	"	Catherine, wife of Benjamin, Jan. 14, 1803.
3-17	"	Jonathan (lost in brig —— in the West Indies). 21y., Dec. 9, 1804.
3-20	"	Lydia, 64y., March 8, 1809.
3-20	"	Isaac, 80y., May 7, 1810.
3-135	"	child of Benjamin, Jr., Oct. 2, 1811.
2-135	"	Sarah, widow of Isaac, 79y. (also 3-21), July 5, 1812.
2-136	"	Jemima, widow of Stephen, 83y. (also 3-23), Aug. 19, 1813.
3-23	"	James, 56y., Oct. 2, 1815.
3-23	"	Capt. Henry, 24y., Aug. 4, 1816.
3-24	"	Deacon Joseph, 70y., July 25, 1817.
3-24	"	Lydia, wife of Col. Samuel, 60y., Aug. 18, 1817.
3-25	"	Col. Samuel, 65y., Nov. 22, 1819.
4-169	"	Elizabeth, widow, Sept. 27, 1820.
3-28	"	Martha, widow, 77y., Jan. 19, 1827.
3-20	"	Major Benjamin, 78y., Feb. 28, 1830.
3-31	"	Elizabeth, widow, 79y., April 17, 1831.
4-56	"	Allen, 76y., March 31, 1840.
4-64	"	Lucy, widow of Col. Samuel, and formerly widow of George Coggeshall, 36y., March 14, 1841.
4-70	"	Elizabeth, 93y., July 18, 1842.
4-82	"	Abigail, widow of Allen, 79y., Oct. 6, 1844.
4-84	"	Sally, widow of Josiah, 46y. (at Providence), Nov. 13, 1844.
4-86	"	Mary Ann, of Capt. Allen, Jr., 24y., April 11, 1845.
4-96	"	Nathaniel P., of Nathaniel, of Ellisburgh, N. Y., 33y. (at Watertown, Jefferson Co., N. Y.), Feb. 15, 1847.
4-102	"	Hannah, wife of Capt. John and dau. of Henry and Amarenthia Munro 70y., (also 4-110), Jan. 8, 1848.
4-120	"	Anna Russell, of Nathaniel J., 8m. 12d., Feb. 21, 1850.
4-128	"	Nathaniel J., 28y. (went to California in ship Audley Clarke, went to Panama on business), Oct. 27, 1850.
4-126	"	Elizabeth W., wife of Joseph M., dau. of Dea. William B. and Marian W. Spooner, 22y. (at Warren), Nov. 24, 1850.
2-128	WARD	Hugh (drowned from Mr. Antbony Low's sloop), buried July 24, 1684.
3-18	WARREN	Perice, wife of Abraham, 34y., Aug. 14, 1807.
3-24	"	Sarah, wife of Russell, 30y., March 17, 1817.
4-29	"	child of Henry R , 4 days, Aug. 8, 1835.
4-35	"	Harriet Nelson, of Nathan, 4y. 5m., Aug. 11, 1836.
4-60	"	Russell, of Henry R., 16m., Aug. 27, 1840.
4-72	"	Emogene, 19m. 7d., Aug. 23, 1842.
4-76	"	Cerelia, 2m., May 6, 1843.
4-112	"	child of William H., 13m., April 28, 1849.
4-128	"	William H., 1st officer of ship Thomas Church (at New Orleans), 32y., Nov. 29, 1850.
2-130	WATERMAN	John (an Indian), April 18, 1745.
2-129	"	Hannah (an Indian), Nov. 4, 1732.
3-17	WATSON	Cearer, 65y., Sept. 6, 1804.
2-128	WATTS	Jeremiah, buried, Dec. 31, 1694.
2-128	"	Mary, of John and Mary, Feb. 19, 1695-6.
2-128	"	Elizabeth, Feb. 23, 1695-6.
2-129	"	Rev. Robert, March 15, 1740.
2-128	WEBB	Margaret, wife of George, of Little Compton, Nov. 3, 1707.
4-130	WEEDEN	Elmira, of Warren G., 20m., May 10, 1851.

2-130	WEST	Samuel, wife of, Aug. 24, 1747.
2-130	"	William, Sept. 30, 1747.
2-131	"	Joseph (at Surinam), Aug. 3, 1748.
2-131	"	Henry, wife of, Nov. 24, 1748.
2-131	"	William, child of, Jan. 15, 1749.
2-131	"	William, Aug. 23, 1751.
2-131	"	Samuel, child of, Dec. 3, 1752.
2-131	"	William, child of, Feb. —, 1754.
2-132	"	Samuel, infant child of, Dec. 30, 1757.
2-132	"	William, child of, Nov. 23, 1758.
2-133	"	William, of William and Jane, June 6, 1762.
2-133	"	widow, Nov. 20, 1768.
2-134	"	William, wife of, Dec. 4, 1773.
2-134	"	Samuel, his wife's grandchild, 6y., Oct. 22, 1775.
3-1	"	Elizabeth, of William, 42y., Aug. 3, 1785.
3-1	"	Hannah, of James, 3y., March 26, 1786.
3-2	"	child of William, 2d., July 1, 1786.
3-3	"	James, 44y., May 22, 1787.
3-3	"	John, 72y., Aug. 28, 1787.
3-5	"	child of Thomas, 6w., Dec. 18, 1790.
3-8	"	Ruth, of Jonathan, 18m., Sept. 10, 1793.
3-9	"	James, of Nathaniel, 2y. 6m., Sept. 20, 1794.
3-10	"	Hannah, 80y., Oct. 12, 1795.
3-12	"	Rebecca, wife of Nathaniel H., 47y., Jan. 10, 1797.
3-13	"	William, 37y., Sept. 8, 1797.
3-14	"	Jonathan, (lost at sea), Nov. —, 1798.
3-14	"	Samuel, 78y., Jan. 29, 1799.
3-14	"	Catherine, wife of Thomas, 39y., Feb. 18, 1801.
3-15	"	James, (at sea), 24y., June 18, 1802.
3-20	"	Thomas, 46y., Sept. 12, 1810.
3-21	"	Asa, 57y., (also 2-135), July 11 or 12, 1812.
2-135	"	Nathan, (killed on privateer Hiram), Aug. 19, 1812,

> Intelligence came Oct. 9, 1812, of the death of James Willson, Chillingworth Foster, Nathan West, Gardiner West, William West and Henry Wing, who were all lost on board the privateer schooner Hiram, which blew up at sea in lat. — the 19th of August last, occasioned by the magazine taking fire. On board of the schooner were 33 men, who were all lost but five, who were at sea 4 1-2 days and providentially arrived at the Island of ——.

3-135	"	Gardiner, (see above), Aug. 19, 1812.
2-135	"	William, (see above), Aug. 19, 1812.
2-135	"	child of Nathan, dec., March 3, 1813.
2-136	"	child of Benjamin, Dec. 10, 1813.
2-136	"	William C., of Jonathan, 6 1-2y., June 8, 1815.
3-23	"	Lydia, widow, 101y., 5m. June 19, 1816,
4-169	"	Elizabeth, widow of Gardner, 30y., Nov. 4, 1820.
3-27	"	Oliver, 83y., Feb. 22, 1824.
3-27	"	Abigail, 90y., widow, May 6, 1824.
3-27	"	Benjamin, 26y., (at the Asylum), July 23, 1825.
3-29	"	Nathaniel, 80y., Oct. 21, 1828.
3-30	"	Rebecca, 71y., Nov. 12, 1829.
3-32	"	Patience, wife of John, 52y., Jan. 6, 1832.
4-30	"	Nathaniel Hix, 85y., Jan. 31, 1836.
4-45	"	Miss Sarah G., 29y., Nov. 13, 1837.
4-53	"	Richard, 55y., Feb. 22, 1840.
4-56	"	Sarah, widow of William, dec., 82y., April 1, 1840.
4-94	"	child of William H., 6y., Oct. 13, 1846.
4-96	"	Benjamin, 62y., Feb. 25, 1847.
4-106	"	Henry Russell, of Benjamin G., 6m., Oct. 2, 1848.
4-110	"	John, 70y., April 1, 1849.
4-114	"	Harriet Williams, of Capt. William H., 7m., Aug. 13, 1849.
4-120	"	Benjamin C. (at Benecia, Cal., on board ship Hopewell), Dec. 14, 1849.
4-130	"	Hannah, widow of Richard, 76y., April 4, 1851.

2-132	WHEATON Abigail, wife of Ephraim (midwife), 62y., Oct. 12, 1762.	
2-133	WHEEDON Amos, child of, Oct. 5, 1761.	
2-133	" Amos (at sea), March —, 1762.	
2-133	WHILEY Thomas (apprentice to Allen Usher) (at the Camp), —— —, 1760.	
2-133	WHITAKER Samuel, child of, 6m., May 30, 1765.	
3-6	" Samuel, 36y., Aug. 5, 1791.	
3-18	" Samuel, 80y., Sept. 15. 1807.	
4-126	" Orion, of Asa., dec., of Rehoboth, formerly of Bristol (at New-York), 36y., Aug. 17, 1850.	
3-3	WHITE William, 70y., April 1, 1787.	
2-135	" Adeliza, of Rev. Henry and Alice, Sept. 13, 1794.	
2-135	" child of James, —— —, 1811.	
2-136	" child of,	Oct. 13, 1814.
3-31	" Olive, widow, 92y., May 22, 1832.	
3-35	" Samuel Pearce, of Samuel, 4y., Sept. 7, 1836.	
4-55	" Elizabeth, wife of Samuel G., 68y., Dec. 5, 1839.	
4-55	" Sally, widow of James, 62y., Dec. 26, 1839.	
4-62	" Henry, 38y., Oct. 10, 1840.	
4-66	" Jacob Frances, of James B., 2y. 6m., Aug. 30, 1841.	
4-70	" Betsey, 75y., April 14, 1842.	
4 70	" Susan J., of James B., 18y., July 15, 1842.	
4-74	" child of Thomas N., 6m., March 20, 1843.	
4-78	" Betsey, widow of Henry, 45y., July 25, 1843.	
4-86	" Mary, 81y., Feb. 22, 1845.	
4-90	" Sarah, 85y. (at Swansey), April 26, 1846.	
4 106	" child of Thomas N., 4m., Sept. 5, 1848.	
4-124	" Anna B., wife of Samuel, 40y., July 4, 1850.	
2-130	" Samuel G., 80y., March 12, 1851.	
4-169	WHITING Content, wife of Joseph (col.), April 25, 1820.	
4-116	WHITEMARSH Anna, of Ephraim, 10m., Nov. 6, 1849.	
2-129	WIGHT Mary, wife of John, June 19, 1735.	
2-129	" John, child of, July 20, 1740.	
2-129	"	July 26, 1740.
3-9	" Adeliza, of Rev. Henry and Alice, 5m., 5d., Sept. 13, 1794.	
3-12	" Alice, wife of Rev. Henry, 35y., April 19, 1797.	
3-20	" Charlotte DeWolf, wife of Rev. Henry, 44y., July 24, 1809.	
2-136	" child of Rev. Henry, April 4, 1815.	
4-169	" Abigail Wardwell, of Henry, Jr., 13m., Oct. 9, 1820.	
4-31	" Amos. 63y., March 8, 1836.	
4-43	" Rev. Henry, 86y., Aug. 12, 1837.	
4-54	" Almira, of Allen, 77y., Aug. 7, 1839.	
4-84	" William Henry (at New York), 27y., Jan. 5, 1845.	
2-132	WILBUR Benjamin, child of, Nov. 28, 1759.	
4-169	WILCOX Martha Munro, of John, 1y., Nov. 4, 1820.	
4-33	WILKINSON Sarah DeWolf, of George, of Pawtucket, 6y., July 24, 1836.	
4-90	" Ann Maria, of John, 4y., 5m., Dec. 7, 1845.	
2-134	WILKINS Mehitable, of Jonh and Anstess, 92y., July or Aug. 1776.	
3-10	WILLARD Patty, wife of Hezekiah, Jr., Nov. 29, 1794.	
3-10	" Hezekiah, Jr. (at Trent bridge), Oct. 23, 1795.	
3-12	" Hezekiah, 56y., May 29, 1797.	
2-136	" ——, child of Elijah, 1 1-2y., Oct. 30, 1814.	
4-29	" Philip, of Gardiner, 25y., (at New Orleans), Sept. 5, 1835.	
4-120	" Capt. Hezekiah, (at Benecia, Cal., on ship Hopewell), Dec. 6, 1849.	
4-124	" Mary, widow of Capt. Elijah, 72y., July 5, 1850.	
4-51	" William A., of Alfred L., 10m., Sept. 18, 1838.	
2-130	WILLIAMS Mr., his negro child, Nov. 13, 1743.	
2-136	WILLISTON Child of Job, Oct. 17, 1813.	
3-29	" Phebe, wife of Isaac, 27y., July 31, 1828.	
4-39	" Mase B., 28y., Dec. 8, 1836.	
4-76	" Child of Job, Jr., 9w., May 12, 1843.	
4-96	" Catherine, 19y., March 24, 1847.	
3-10	WILLIS John (at Havanna), Nov. 30, 1794.	
2-130	WILLSON James Jr. (at Jamacia), Jan. —, 1744.	
2-130	" James, Feb. 6. 1744.	
2-111	" Reuben (apprentice to Samuel Smith), March 4, 1746.	

2-131	WILLSON Samuel, Feb. 7, 1755.	
2-131	"	David, wife of, Oct. 26, 1755.
2-132	"	—— infant child of, Jan. 20, 1757.
2-132	"	Mary, widow, March 23, 1757.
2-132	"	Abigail, wife of David, May 3, 1759.
2-133	"	David (at Philadelphia, Pa.), Dec. 19, 1765.
2-133	"	Ammiel, of David and Bethiah, Nov. 29, 1767.
2-134	"	Jeremiah, dau. of, 11y., Oct. 14, 1773.
2-134	"	David (killed at New York), 22y., Sept. —. 1776.
2-135	"	Thomas, Sept. —, 1778.
3-3	"	Alethea, wife of William, May 15, 1788.
3-4	"	John, 53y., Dec. 5, 1788.
3-7	"	Jeremiah, 76y., Nov. 9, 1791.
3-9	"	James, of William, 20y., May 27, 1794.
2-15	"	William, 51y., June 25, 1801.
2-135	"	Molly, wife of Thomas, May 24, 1812.
3-21	"	Mary, wife of Thomas Wilson, May 24, 1812.
3-22	"	Patience, wife of Samuel, 47y., Nov. 8, 1814.
2-135	"	James (see Nathan West), Aug. 19, 1812.
2-136	"	wife of Samuel, Nov. 9, 1814.
4-168	"	Jemima, widow of William, Aug. 27, 1819.
4-166	"	Catherine, of George and Elizabeth, Sept. 25, 1825.
4-166	"	Nathaniel, 71-4-29 (also 3-28), May 21, or 31, 1826.
3-30	"	Benjamin, 78y., Oct. 29, 1830.
3-31	"	Samuel, 72y., March 21, 1831.
4-27	"	Thomas, 88y., Oct. 27, 1835.
4-39	"	Freelove, widow of Nathaniel, 65y., March 6, 1837.
4-47	"	William, 61y., April 23, 1838.
4-53	"	Oliver (at Cuba, W. I.), Feb. 28, 1839.
4-55	"	Jemima, widow of James, 83y., Jan. 24, 1840.
4-64	"	Betsey, wife of George, 38y., June 26, 1841.
4-66	"	——, child of Philip, 20m., Oct. 19, 1841.
4-80	"	Nancy, of Thomas, 22y., Dec. 3, 1843.
4-88	"	James, 5m., Sept. 13, 1845.
4-108	"	Philip G., 28y., Dec. 16, 1848.
3-2	WING Ichabod, negro servant of N. Carey, 50y., Oct. 29, 1786.	
3-8	"	John (mulatto), (at sea), Dec. —, 1793.
2-135	"	Henry (see Nathan West), Aug. 19, 1812.
3-11	WINSLOW Job, 46y. (drowned at India bridge), Dec. 7, 1795.	
4-98	"	Charles Henry, of Capt. James, 1-6-23, Sept. 18, 1847.
3-2	WOODARD Dea. John, 73y., Aug. 24, 1786.	
2-128	WOODBURY Mary, wife of Benjamin, Oct. 11, buried 13, 1685.	
2-128	"	John, of Hugh and Mary, March 3, 1698-9.
2-128	"	Hugh, April 17, 1702.
2-128	"	Mary, widow of Hugh, —— —, 1705.
2-128	"	Mrs. Mary, Sept. 27, 1718.
2-129	"	Jonathan, infant child of, June —, 1730.
2-128	"	Margaret, wife of Samuel, Oct. —, 1730.
2-129	"	Capt., his negro child, —— —, 1739.
2-130	"	——, a boy of, April 12, 1741.
2-131	"	——, Aug. —, 1751.
2-131	"	——, a woman of, May 15, 1752.
2-131	"	Jonathan (at Surinam), —— —, 1752.
2-132	"	Capt. Samuel, 69y., March 24, 1757.
2-132	"	Mrs., alias Sampson, 74y., July 17, 1757.
2-133	"	Jonathan, Esq., 81y., Jan. 21, 1766.
2-34	"	Dido, servant of Capt., Oct. 30, 1768.
2-135	"	Lydia, widow of Jonathan (also 3-21), 83y., July 28, 1812.
2-129	WOODCOCK Mr., a negro boy of, 9y., Feb. 16, 1740.	
2-130	"	Mrs. Mary, Aug. 10, 1747.
2-129	WOOD Paul, child of, 3y., June 18, 1740.	
2-130	"	Paul, (never heard of) since Sept., 1740.
2-131	"	——, (apprentice to Simeon Munro, drowned at sea), Dec. —. 1749.
3-1	"	Elizabeth, wife of James, Aug. 22, 1785.
3-3	"	Anna, of Joseph, 11y., Aug. 19, 1787.

3-3	WOOD	Mary, of Benjamin, 3y., Oct. 7, 1787.
3-4	"	Henry, of Benjamin, 8m., Oct. 12, 1789.
3-8	"	Hannah, wife of Joseph. Sept. 8, 1793.
3-9	"	Hannah, widow, 84y., Aug. 28, 1794.
4-41	"	Miss Mary, of Thomas, 32y., Aug. 10, 1837.
4-110	"	Thomas, 72y., Feb. 11, 1849.
4-35	WRIGHT	Edward Allen, of Leonard, 5y., Aug. 31, 1836.
4-35	"	Charles Leonard, 11m., Sept. 7, 1836.
4-90	"	child of William, 4m., Dec. 15, 1845.
2-136	WYATT	Elizabeth, of Benjamin, 34y. (also 3-22), Nov. 1, 1813.
2-136	"	child of Benjamin, Jan. 29, 1814.
3-28	"	Susanna, wife of Stutely, 79y., March 26, 1827.
3-19	"	Stutely, Nov. 6, 1828.
4-51	"	Tillinghast, of William, 1y., 5m., Sept. 18, 1838.
4-62	"	Lydia, wife of Robert, 50y., March 7, 1841.
4-82	"	Robert (at Fall River), 55y. (also 4-75), Oct. 5, 1844.
4-75	"	Lydia (Cummings), wife of Robert, March 7, 1841.
4-88	"	Rebecca, wife of Benjamin, 72y., Oct. 26, 1845.

X Y Z

4-98	YONA	John (born Scotland), of Philadelphia, 18y., Nov. 9, 1847.
2-138	YOUNG,	——, infant child of Isaac, June.15. 1758.
2-138	"	——, dau. of, about 5y., May 24, 1759.
2-138	"	——, child of, about 2y., Feb. 23, 1773.
2-138	"	Isaac, Oct. 15, 1773.
3-17	"	Joice, widow, 74y., Jan. 16, 1804.
5-58	"	Mary, widow of William, 92y., April 25, 1840.

Vital Record of Rhode Island.

1636=1850.

FIRST SERIES.

BIRTHS, MARRIAGES AND DEATHS.

A Family Register for the People.

By James N. Arnold,

EDITOR OF THE NARRAGANSETT HISTORICAL REGISTER.

"Is My Name Written in the Book of Life?"

Vol. 6. WARREN. Part II.

Published under the Auspices of the General Assembly.

PROVIDENCE, R. I:
NARRAGANSETT HISTORICAL PUBLISHING COMPANY.
1894.

AN ACT INCORPORATING THE FIVE TOWNS SECURED FROM MASSACHUSETTS.

In General Assembly at Providence, January 27, 1746-7.

AN ACT for Incorporating the Inhabitants of the Lands lately Taken Into This Colony by the Settlement of the Eastern Boundary Into Five Townships.

Whereas, His Majesty has been graciously pleased by his royal determination to settle the eastern boundaries of this Colony, whereby several large tracts of land and a great number of inhabitants are taken under Jurisdiction of this Government, and it being absolutely necessary for the well governing of the said people that the said tracts of land, with the, inhabitants thereon, be set off and incorporated into Townships, and the same being conveniently situated for the making of five Townships;

Be it, therefore, enacted by the General Assembly, and by the authority of the same it is enacted, that the aforesaid tracts of land, with the inhabitants thereon, be set off and incorporated into five Towns in the following manner, viz.:

All that part which heretofore has been called Bristol, with the inhabitants thereon, be set off and incorporated into a Township by the name of Bristol; and that part which was heretofore (known) as part of Tiverton, with a part of Dartmouth and Freetown, adjoining thereto, be incorporated into a Township by the name of Tiverton; and that part which has heretofore been a part of Little Compton and a part of Dartmouth thereto adjoining be incorporated into a Township by the name of Little Compton; and that the line which formerly divided Tiverton from Little Compton be extended eastly to the Colony line, and the whole to be the dividing lines between said Towns; and that part which has hitherto been a part of Swansey and Barrington, with a small part of Rehoboth thereto adjoining, with the inhabitants thereon, be incorporated into a Township by the name of Warren; and that part which has been commonly called and known by the name of the Gore of Land, with the inhabitants thereon, be incorporated into a Township by the name of Cumberland; and that the inhabitants of each respective Town, for the time being, shall have and enjoy equal liberties and privileges with the other Towns of this Colony, agreeably to our Charter.

And be it further enacted by the authority aforesaid that a special Justice of the Peace be chosen and appointed in each of the above-mentioned Towns to keep His Majesty's peace and to call the inhabitants of the respective Towns together by a warrant, to meet on the second Tuesday in February next, to choose such Town Officers as are directed by the laws of this Colony and also deputies to represent said Towns at the adjournment of this Assembly.

And that the said Justices be commissionated by His Honor the Governor, and to continue until the next session of this Assembly; and that the General Treasurer furnish each of the above-mentioned Towns with a Colony law book; and that the Secretary send to each of the said Towns a copy of the late act of Assembly, directing the manner of making freemen and regulating the method of voting; and that said law books and copies of said act be delivered to the above-mentioned Justices as soon as conveniently may be.

And be it further enacted by the authority aforesaid that every man inhabiting within the above-mentioned Towns of Bristol, Tiverton, Little Compton, Warren and Cumberland, who is possessed of land or real estate sufficient by the laws of this Colony to qualify him for a freeman, and the eldest sons of all such freeholders, be and they are hereby declared freemen of the respective Towns, and also of this Colony; and to govern themselves in voting agreeably to the laws of this Colony.

And be it further enacted by the authority aforesaid that the following persons be and they are hereby chosen and appointed special Justices of the Peace for the above-mentioned Towns, viz.:

Jonathan Peck, Esq., for the Town of Bristol; John Manchester, Esq., for the Town of Tiverton; William Richmond, Esq., for the Town of Little Compton; Matthew Allen, Esq., for the Town of Warren; and John Bartlett, Esq., for the Town of Cumberland.

God Save the King.

R. I. Colonial Records, Vol. V., pages 204-6.

WARREN.

INTENTIONS AND MARRIAGES.

A

4-1   ABBOTT Lieut. Joel, U. S. N., son of Charles, dec., and Susan Wheaton;
         m. by Rev. John C. Welch, Nov. 29, 1825.

1-63   ABEL Abigail, and John Easterbrooks, Nov. 5, 1747.

1-68   ADAMS James, and Mrs. Lydia Kennicutt; m. by Rev. John Usher, April
         29, 1762.

1-82   "   Joseph, and Lydia Child; m. by Rev. John Pitman, Sept. 23,
         1787.

1-83   "   Lydia, and Dr. Nathan Miller Burr, Nov. 30, 1788.

4-10   "   Betsey S., and George S. Browne, July 1, 1838.

4-23   "   Mary, and Nathan Kent. Oct. 6, 1839.

4-23   "   Hannah Kennicutt, and Thomas B. Hall, Wickford (also 4-13),
         Oct. 11, or 13, 1840.

4-14   "   Louisa, and Josiah T. Horton, April 17, 1842.

4-27   "   John Q., and Mary J. Phinney; m. by Rev. R. W. Allen, June 7,
         1849.

4-10   ALBRO Benjamin, of James, of Newport, and Elizabeth Barton, of Samuel,
         of Warren; m. by Rev. George W. Hathaway, May 15, 1836.

1-98   ALGER Abbey B., and William Maxwell, Oct. 21, 1806.

1-100 "   Abigail, and Phillip Randall, June 29, 1809.

1-113 "   Lucinda, and Samuel Bowington, Nov. 3, 1813.

1-62   ALLEN Elizabeth, and David Joy, Dec. 1, 1747.

1-64   "   Rachel, and Lamech Blanding, Dec. 14, 1749.

1-65   "   Sarah, and Daniel Bliss, Nov. 16, 1752.

1-65   "   Ruth, and Samuel Viall, July 25, 1754.

1-69   "   Joseph, and Mary Humphrey; m. by Rev. Solomon Townsend,
         Dec. 23, 1759.

1-69   "   Joseph, Jr., and Joanna Whitehorn; m. by Rev. Solomon Town-
         send, June 2, 1765.

1-70   "   William, and Rachel Blanchard; m. by Rev. James Manning, Oct.
         30, 1766.

1-77   "   Mary, and John Linzey Munroe, April 21, 1777.

1-96   "   Paschal, of William, of Providence (Limner), and Mary H. Croude,
         of John, of Warren; m. by Eld. Luther Baker, June 24, 1804.

1-117 "   Paschal, of William, dec., late of Providence, and Elouisa Bow-
         ers, of Capt. David, dec., of Somerset; m. by Eld. Luther Baker,
         Sept. 25, 1806.

4-11   "   Paschal, of Warren, and Mary Tillinghast, of Pawtucket, Mass.;
         m. at Pawtucket, by Rev. Constantine Blodgett, Nov. 27, 1838.

4-14   "   John J., and Mary T. Bowen, March 9, 1842.

4-16   "   Mary A., and James P. Bowen, Nov. 13, 1842.

4-17   "   Capt. Samuel, and Mary Ann Luther; m. by Rev. Josiah P. Tus-
         tin, Jan. 15, 1843.

4-9   ANDREWS Hiram, of Warren, of John, of Dighton, Mass., and Eliza
         Ladien, of Curtis, of Barrington; m. by Rev. Jordan Rexford,
         May 14, 1826.

1-121 ANGELL Samuel, of Warren, son of Hope, of North Providence, and
         Aseneth Lewis, of Warren, dau. of Isaac, of Wilbraham, Mass.;
         m. by Rev. Silas Hall, Jan. 1, 1817.

4-24   ANTHONY Henry, of Fall River, and Betsey Mason, of Swansey; m. by
            Rev. John C. Welch, Nov. 12, 1839.
4-23   "   Caroline M., and Nathan A. Chase, March 1, 1841.
1-62   ARNOLD William, and Charity Miller; m. by Benjamin Miller, Justice,
            Dec. 18, 1747.
1-77   "   Ruth, and James Bowen, May 3, 1778.
1-81   "   Patience, and John Pearce, Nov. 27, 1785.
1-89   "   Benedick, and Polly Phillips; m. by Elder John Mason, Nov. 17,
            1793.
1-89   "   Parmelia, and Frederick Luther, Feb. 12, 1795.
1-117   "   Mrs. Polly, and James Wood, June 30, 1805.
1-65   ASTEN Benjamin, and Mrs. Susannah Chase, both of Swansey; m. by John
            Kennicutt, Justice, Feb. 14, 1757.

B

4-30   BACON Henry A., and Annie R. Eddy; m. by Rev. N. B. Crocker, June
            6, 1855.
1-69   BAKER Jesse, and Louis Cole; m. by Rev. James Manning, March 17,
            1768.
1-79   "   Jesse, and Lillis Cole; m. by William Burton, Justice, April 11,
            1782.
1-85   "   Jesse, of Warren, and Hannah Smith, of Barrington; m. by Rev.
            Solomon Townsend, July 17, 1791.
1-118   "   Eld. Luther, of Jesse, and Peggy Thompson, of Eld. Charles, Oct.
            11, 1795.
1-101   "   Sarah S., and Daniel W. Barnaby, March 2, 1820.
2-110   "   Capt. Thomas, of Capt. Thomas, dec., of Warren, and Elizabeth
            Bowers of Capt. David, of Somerset; m. by Rev. Flavel Shurt-
            leff, Aug. 25, 1820.
3-171   "   Jesse, of Warren, and Mary Mason, of Benjamin, of Swansey; m.
            by Rev. Flavel Shurtleff, Oct. 27, 1821.
4-6   "   Ruel Holden, of Luther, of Warren, and Jerusha Ellis Horton, of
            Seth, of Dighton; m. by Rev. Luther Baker, Dec. 5, 1830.
4-8   "   Nancy, and Benjamin Ingle, July 26, 1835.
4-30   "   William, of Warren, son of Rev. R. H. and Jerusha E., and Mar-
            tha G. Peck, of George and Mary, of Swansey; m. by Rev.
            William Clift, May 26, 1853.
1-121   BALLOT Robert, of Warren, and Rosanna Fales, of Bristol; m. by Rev.
            Henry Wight, Dec. 8, 1816.
1-113   BARNABY Daniel W., of Warren, and Sarah M. Winston, of Swansey;
            m. at Swansey, by John Mason, Justice, Oct. 24, 1816.
1-109   "   Daniel W., of Warren, and Sarah S. Baker, of Swansey; m. by
            Rev. Benjamin Taylor, March 2, 1820.
4-23   "   Ambrose, of Daniel, dec., and Hannah G. Vinnicum, of John, dec.;
            m. by Rev. George W. Hathaway, June 27, 1839.
1-71   BARNEY Abigail, and Solomon Peck, Jr., Dec. 8, 1763.
1-79   "   Jonathan, of Swansey, and Elizabeth Mason, of Warren; m. by
            William Barton, Justice, March 24, 1782.
1-82   "   Comfort, and Polly Kelley; m. by William Barton, Justice,
            March 15, 1787.
4-5   "   John K., of Comfort, and Mary Cole, of Ephraim; m. by Rev.
            Luther Baker, Aug. 27, 1807.
4-20   "   John K., of Warren, and Mary J. Spencer, of North Providence;
            m. by Rev. Edward K. Fuller, Sept. 29, 1839.
4-18, 21 "   Julia A., and Edmund G. Johnson, Nov. 27, 1843.
1-87   BARROWS Isaac, and Elizabeth Miller; m. by Rev. John Usher, May 17,
            1787.
3-167   "   Capt. Daniel B., of Dr. Daniel, and Sylvania A. Winslow, of
            Ebenezer; m. by Rev. John C. Welch, July 31, 1823.
4-12   "   Nathan L., of Dr. Daniel, and Abby M. Haile, of John; m. by
            Rev. John C. Welch, Sept. 23, 1839.
4-22   "   Prudence C., and Leonard B. Biglow, Nov. 4, 1846.

1-92   BARTLETT David, of Cumberland, and Hannah Joslin, of said town; m. by William T. Miller, Justice, Aug. 21, 1798.
1-66   BARTON Mrs. Patience, and Hezekiah Child, Jan. 13, 1757.
1-65   "   Mrs. Anne, and Peleg Thurston, Feb. 3, 1757.
1-66   "   Benjamin, Jr., and Mrs. Lois Butterworth; m. by John Kennicutt, Justice, March 23, 1758.
1-68   "   Mrs. Rebecca, and Nathan Miller, Jan. 8, 1764.
1-71   "   William, and Ruth Thomas; m. by Rev. James Manning, Jan. 10, 1768.
1-70   "   Lillis, and Caleb Carr, Sept. 20, 1768.
1-72   "   Rufus, and Prudence Cole; m. by Rev. Solomon Townsend, April 7, 1771.
1-74   "   Haile, and Elizabeth Phinney; m. by Rev. Charles Thompson, Dec. 19, 1773.
1-75   "   David, of Warren, and Rebecca Brightman, of Freetown; m. by Rev. Silas Brett, Oct. 30, 1774.
1-80   "   Susannah, and Joseph Whitmarsh, May 15, 1777.
1-80   "   William, and Elizabeth Miller; m. by William T. Miller, Justice, April 25, 1779.
1-85   "   Lillis, and Ansel Churchill, March 18, 1792.
1-86   "   William, and Sally Bowen; m. by Elder Luther Baker, Nov. 24, 1793.
1-87   "   Benjamin, and Lydia Child; m. by Elder Luther Baker, May 31, 1795.
1-90   "   Rebecca, and James Reed, Oct. 27, 1796.
1-93   "   Polly, and Daniel Sanders, Sept. 20, 1801.
1-94   "   Rebecca, and William Barton, Jan. 3, 1802.
1-94   "   William, of Rufus, and Rebecca Barton, of David; m. by Elder Luther Baker, Jan. 3, 1802.
1-98   "   Samuel, of William, and Sally Viall, of Josiah; m. by Rev. Samuel Watson, July 4, 1805.
1-99   "   Lydia, and Elisha G. Phinney, Dec. 14, 1806.
1-101 "   Rebecca, and Seth Snell, June 27, 1809.
1-112 "   Polly, and Seth Barton, May 9, 1813.
1-112 "   Seth, of Col. David and Polly Barton, of Benjamin, Jr.; m. by Joseph Adams, Justice, May 9, 1813.
3-172 "   Capt. Alfred, of William, dec., and Margaret C. Turner, of Capt. William; m. by Rev. Jordan Rexford, Oct. 15, 1820.
4-2   "   William J., of Benjamin, and Eliza Luther, of Frederick; m. by Rev. Jordan Rexford, Nov. 20, 1826.
4-8   "   Charles, of Samuel, of Warren, and Mary Bowen, of Barrington; m. by Rev. Elias Vernon, May 22, 1833.
4-9   "   George, of Samuel, and Rebecca M. Phillips, of William; m. by Rev. George W. Hathaway, Aug. 14, 1834.
4-9   "   Laura, and John Duval, Aug. 31, 1834.
4-9   "   Samuel, of William, and Hannah Smith, dau. of Josiah Viall, of Barrington; m. by Rev. George W. Hathaway, Nov. 2, 1834.
4-8   "   Capt. David Brightman, of Jonathan, and Eliza Burr, of Capt. Shubael; m. by Rev. John C. Welch, Aug. 2, 1835.
4-10   "   Elizabeth, and Benjamin Albro, May 15, 1836.
4-10   "   James M., of Samuel, and Mary Randall, of Philip and Abigail; m. by Rev. William R. Stone, March 31, 1836.
4-24   "   Catherine, and Joseph H. Luther, Nov. 3, 1839.
4-14   "   Hannah, and Henry Walter Eddy, March 27, 1842.
4-14   "   Rebecca S., and George Clinton Carr, June 19, 1842.
4-21   "   Alfred, Jr., of Warren, and Ann Elizabeth Bowen of Nathan, of Coventry; m. at Coventry by Rev. James Burlingame, April 20, 1846.
3-170 BATTIOT John, and Susan Parker; m. by Rev. Flavel Shurtleff, Aug. 7, 1820 (?).
4-20   BEAN Sarah, and Stephen Smith, Sept. 20, 1844.
4-22   "   William H., of New York, and Eliza Davol, of Stephen, of Warren; m. by Rev. Josiah P. Tustin, June 16, 1846.
1-90   BEBEE Clement Stanton, and Ruth Carr; m. by Eld. Luther Baker, May 27, 1798.

1-95 BEBEE Allen, and Patty Warren; m. by Eld. Luther Baker, April 10, 1803.

3-168   "   Patty, and John Butts, Aug. 21, 1817.

4-3   "   Henry, of Allen, and Eliza Ann Wood, of Jonathan; m. by Rev. Jordan Rexford, Jan. 17, 1828.

4-3   "   Allen, and Hannah Hubbard; m. at New York by Rev. John Truan, July 21, 1826.

3-167 BENNETT Mary Ann, and Haile Child, June 29, 1823.

4-13, 14   "   Charles Edwin, of Warren, son of Cornelius and Abby Lewis Cole, of Jonathan; m. by Rev. George W. Hathaway, Feb. 13, 1842.

4-17   "   Caroline A., and George R. Marble, May 16, 1843.

1-99 BERIS Angell, and Abigail S. Goodwin, of Middletown, Conn.; m. at Middletown by Rev. Benjamin Graves, Feb. 10, 1807.

1-79 BESAYUDE Lewis, and Elizabeth Cranston; m. by Rev. Charles Thompson, Jan. 24, 1779.

1-119   "   Betsey, and Noah Pearce, April 4, 1801.

1-62 BEVERLY Tabitha, and Valentine Easterbrooks, Dec. 13, 1747.

4-22 BIGLOW Leonard B., of Providence, and Prudence C. Barrows, of Warren; m. by Rev. Josiah P. Tustin, Nov. 4, 1846.

1-73 BISHOP Zadock, of Rehoboth, and Elizabeth Haile, of Swansey; m. by John Kennicutt, Justice, May 11, 1772.

4-3   "   Hannah, and William Bowen, Aug. 19, 1827.

4-4 BLAKE Samuel, of Samuel, and Mary Ann Ladieu, of Curtis; m. by Rev. Luther Baker, Nov. 25, 1827.

1-70 BLANCHARD Rachel, and William Allen, Oct. 30, 1766.

1-64 BLANDING Lameck, and Rachel Allen; m. by Edward Luther, Justice, Dec. 14, 1749.

1-65 BLISS Daniel, of Rehoboth, and Sarah Allen, of Warren; m. by James Smith, Justice, Nov. 16, 1752.

1-77   "   Jonathan, and Mary Bowen; m. by Rev. Charles Thompson, April —. 1777.

1-80   "   Sarah, and William Warren, Aug. 19, 1784.

1-81   "   Mary, and John Child, —— —, 1784(?)

1-116   "   Sally T., and Job Smith, Oct. 4, 1813.

1-62 BOSWORTH Mrs. Lydia, and John Kelley, Oct. 18, 1747.

1-63   "   Ichabod, of Rehoboth, and Bethiah Wood, of Swansey; m. by Benjamin Miller, Justice, Nov. 19, 1748.

1-63   "   Jonathan, and Mrs. Mary Humphrey; m. by Rev. Solomon Townsend, March 19, 1748-9.

1-78   "   Ebenezer, and Patience Easterbrooks; m. by Rev. Charles Thompson, April 22, 1781.

1-88   "   Samuel, of Bristol, and Ruth Cole, of Warren; m. by Eld. Luther Baker, Sept. 25, 1794.

1-92   "   Benjamin, of Benjamin, and Anna Haile, of Nathan; m. by Eld. Luther Baker, Jan. 19, 1800.

1-116   "   Burrell, of Benjamin, and Roby Cole, of Ichabod, Nov. 10, 1811.

3-168   "   Hopestill, and John Thurber, Jr., June 22, 1823.

4-2   "   Jonathan, of Swansey, son of Joseph, of Warren, and Mary Salisbury, of Caleb, of Warren; m. by Rev. Jordan Rexford, March 22, 1827.

4-7   "   Ann H., and Sylvester Child, March 10, 1833.

4-8   "   Benjamin M., and Eliza Miller; m. by Rev. John C. Welch, March 6, 1835.

4-17   "   Alfred, and Lydia L. Vinnicum; m. by Rev. William R. Stone, Aug. 17, 1835.

4-10   "   Peleg, of Peleg, dec., and Betsey, and Hannah Driscoll Burt, of Joseph and Content; m. by Rev. John C. Welch, Nov. 13, 1835.

4-3   "   Alfred, of Daniel, and Harriet N. Child, of Shubael P.; m. by Rev. John C. Welch, Dec. 13, 1835.

4-10   "   Alfred, of Daniel, and Ann Collins, of William; m. by Rev. George W. Hathaway, Oct. 11, 1838.

4-18   "   Benjamin M., and Elizabeth Luther; m. by Rev. Isaac Bonney, Dec. 28, 1843.

4-21   "   Susan C., and Amasa S. Westcott, April 7, 1845.

4-28   "   Almira S., and Shearjashub T. Viall, April 18, 1850.

1-63	BOWEN	Mrs. Mary, and Ebenezer Martin, May 22, 1748.
1-63	"	Sarah, and Benjamin Cranston, Feb. 19, 1748-9.
1-66	"	Amos, of Warren, and Elizabeth Lewis, of Bristol; m. by Benjamin Miller, Justice, May 3, 1750.
1-65	"	Amos, and Mrs. Elizabeth Simons; m. by John Kennicutt, Justice, March 7, 1754.
1-66	"	James, of Warwick, and Mrs. Patience Miller, of Warren; m. by Benjamin Miller, Justice, March 3, 1755.
1-68	"	Mrs. Olive, and Barnard Miller, Aug. 10, 1755.
1-66	"	Jonathan, and Mrs. Elizabeth Munroe; m. by John Kennicutt, Justice, Nov. 7, 1759.
1-67	"	Peleg, and Mrs. Elizabeth Easterbrooks; m. by Ebenezer Cole, Justice, April 24, 1760.
1-67	"	Mrs. Lydia, and Oliver Salisbury, Feb. 7, 1762.
1-68	"	Stephen, of Warren, and Mrs. Mary Lee, of Rehoboth; m. by John Wheaton, Justice, April 7, 1762.
1-68	"	Nathan, and Mrs. Herren Easterbrooks; m. by John Kennicutt, Justice, Oct. 7, 1762.
1-68	"	Mrs. Elizabeth, and Samuel Warren, March 7, 1764.
1-70	"	Jeremiah, and Lillice Haile; m. by Rev. James Manning, July 16, 1767.
1-73	"	Mrs. Hannah, and Jeremiah Comstock, Dec. 13, 1772.
1-73	"	Josiah, and Ann Haile; m. by Rev. Charles Thompson, Jan. 9, 1772.
1-77	"	John, and Dorcas Wheaton; m. by Rev. Charles Thompson, June 22, 1774.
1-77	"	Mrs. Mary, and Benjamin Cranston, Feb. 6, 1777.
1-89	"	James Easterbrooks and Lydia Jolls; m. by Rev. Solomon Townsend, Oct. 21, 1792.
1-77	"	Sarah, and Thomas Fales, April 10, 1777.
1-77	"	Mary, and Jonathan Bliss, April —, 1777.
1-77	"	James and Ruth Arnold; m. by Rev. Charles Thompson, May 3, 1778.
1-78	"	Elizabeth, and Thomas Champlain, April 8, 1781.
1-80	"	Mary, and Spencer Cole, Oct. 16, 1783.
1-87	"	Jonathan, and Betsey Taylor, Oct. 7, 1787.
1-85	"	Molly, and William Hoar, Nov. 30, 1788.
1-88	"	Nancy, and Spencer Wheaton, April 13, 1790.
1-84	"	James, and Joanna Easterbrooks; m. by William Barton, Justice, March 27, 1791.
1-91	"	Haile, and Polly Tyler; m. by Rev. Solomon Townsend, Oct. 16, 1791.
1-84	"	Sally, and Caleb Child, Jr., Oct. 30, 1791.
1-86	"	Sally, and William Barton, Nov. 24, 1793.
1-86	"	Sally, and Nathaniel Sanders, June 8, 1794.
1-88	"	Martin, and Nancy Corwin; m. by Elder Luther Baker, Aug. 3, 1794.
1-88	"	James, 2d, of Barrington, and Sarah Kelley, of Warren; m. by William T. Miller, Justice, Sept. 28, 1794.
1-88	"	Betsey, and George Sanders, Nov. 2, 1794.
1-89	"	Olive, and Samuel Haile, Nov. 13, 1796.
1-90	"	Olive, and James Thurber, Dec. 15, 1796.
1-91	"	Avis, and John Phinney, July 8, 1798.
1-93	"	Peleg, of James, and Ruth Martin, of Ebenezer; m. by Elder Luther Baker, Sept. 13, 1801.
1-95	"	Polly, and Stephen Davoll, Oct. 20, 1803.
1-100	"	Isaac, of Stephen, and Polly Luther, of Barnabee; m. by Rev. Joshua Crowell, Nov. 16, 1808.
1-119	"	Henry, of Warren, and Bathsheba Marvel, of Somerset; m. by William Barton, Justice, June 11, 1815.
1-117	"	Reuben, and Mrs. Betsey Cranston; m. by Rev. Silas Hall, July 16, 1815.
2-110	"	John, of James E., dec., and Mary Haile, of Comer; m. by Rev. Jordan Rexford, April 11, 1819.
3-164	"	Alvira, and Royal Packard, Nov. 27, 1825.

4-3	BOWEN	William, of Jonathan, and Hannah Bishop, of Ebenezer; m. by Rev. Isaac Stoddard, Aug. 19, 1827.
4-3	"	Harriet, and John T. Martin, Nov. 8, 1827.
4-4	"	John G., and Prescilla Child Salisbury, of Simeon; m. by Rev. John C. Welch, Nov. 22, 1827.
4-8	"	Mary, and Charles Barton, May 22, 1833.
4-12	"	Lydia, and Lucius Warner, April 18, 1838.
4-14	"	Mary T., and John J. Allen, March 9, 1842.
4-14	"	Mrs. ——, and Joseph S. Jayne, July 3, 1842.
4-14	"	Laura Maria, and John Champlain Hoar, Sept. 11, 1842.
4-16	"	James P., of Niles, N. Y., and Mary A. Allen, dau. of James Goff, dec.; m. by Rev. Josiah P. Tustin, Nov. 13, 1842.
4-19	"	Jndith R., and William Parker, Sept. 25, 1843.
4-21	"	Henry A., and Deborah L. Bushee, of Sylvanus H.; m. by Rev. Josiah P. Tustin, June 15, 1845.
4-21	"	Hannah B., and Viall Stanley, Nov. 2, 1845.
4-26	"	Edwin S., and Margaret A. Child; m. by Rev. Thorndike C. Jameson, Nov. 25, 1845.
4-25, 21	"	Charles Perry, and Sarah Ann Drowne; m. by Rev. Josiah P. Tustin, March 22, 1846.
4-21	"	Ann Elizabeth, and Alfred Barton, Jr., April 20, 1846.
4-21	"	John H., and Mary L. Cooley; m. by Lowell Greene, Justice, June 21, 1846.
4-25	"	Joseph, of Barrington, son of James, and Martha Fales, of Lemuel, of Warren; m. by Rev. Paul Townsend, Jan. 1, 1848.
4-28	"	Daniel K., of Barrington, and Ruth B. Sanders, of Warren; m. by Rev. R. W. Allen, Jan. 28, 1850.
3-173	"	Anne E., and Henry F. Drowne, Feb. 5, 1850.
4-28	"	Jonathan M., and Abby P. Luther; m. by Rev. R. A. Fyfe, May 22, 1850.
1-117	BOWERS	Elarvisa, and Paschal Allen, Sept. 25, 1806.
2-110	"	Elizabeth, and Capt. Thomas Baker, Aug. 25, 1820.
1-113	BOWINGTON	Samuel, of Samuel, and Lucinda Alger, of Preserved; m. by Eld. Artemus Stebbens, Nov. 3, 1813.
2-111	BOYNTON	Mrs. Lucinda, and Elijah Hall, June 4, 1820.
1-87	BRAYTON	Content, and James Maxwell, March 28, 1793.
1-88	"	Patience, and Samuel Whitman, Sept. 25, 1794.
1-92	"	Benjamin, and Rebecca Read; m. by Elder Luther Baker, June 20, 1799.
1-93	"	Hannah, and William More Hubbard, March 7, 1801.
1-96	"	Susan, and Wilson Kent, Feb. 26, 1804.
3-171	"	William, of James, of Warren, and Mary Tallman, of Edward, of Providence; m. by Rev. Flavel Shurtliff, June 6, 1821.
4-18	"	Seranus A., and Mrs. Eliza A. Luther; m. by Rev. Josiah P. Tustin, Sept. 18, 1843.
4-29	"	Clara Sophia, and John Haile, Jr., Sept. 10, 1847.
1-79	BRIGGS	Mary, and Curtis Cole, Sept. 2, 1781.
4-17	"	Alfred C., of Little Compton, and Elvina M. Cole, of Warren; m. by Rev. Josiah P. Tustin, April 12, 1843.
4-26	"	Richard, of Thomas, dec., and Ann Dunbar, of Robert; m. by Rev. Paul Townsend, Jan. 4, 1849.
1-75	BRIGHTMAN	Rebecca, and David Barton, Oct. 30, 1774.
1-64	BROWN	Elizabeth, and John Daggett, Jr., June 13, 1751.
1-65	"	Jarvis, and Anne Kennicutt; m. by Rev. John Usher, Dec. 5, 1754.
1-65	"	Keziah, and Benjamin Viall, Jan. 23, 1755.
1-75	"	James, of Swansey, and Mrs. Hannah Glover, of Warren; m. by Rev. Charles Thompson, Aug. 8, 1776.
1-90	"	Sarah, and James Smith, Nov. 8, 1795.
1-91	"	John, and Sally Steavens; m. by Rev. Michael Eddy, at Newport, Oct. 28, 1798.
1-115	"	Lydia G. and Shubael Kennicutt, June 7, 1807.
1-113	"	Joseph, of Warren, son of William, of Dighton, Mass., and Mary Bushee, of Swansey, dau. of James; m. by Eld. Luther Baker, Jan. 12, 1812.
3-168	"	Mrs. Mary, and Moses W. Wardwell, March 13, 1823.

4-18   BROWN Charles Frederick, of John, and Sarah Gardiner Wilbur, of David;. m. by Rev. George W. Humphrey, May 3, 1835.

4-10   "   George S., and Betsey S. Adams; m. by Rev. John C. Welch, July 1, 1838.

4-19   "   Noah M., and Sarah Parker, of Benjamin; m. by Rev. Josiah P. Tustin, March 21, 1844.

4-22   "   Jabez, of Jabez, and Susan S. Kelley, of Lawton; m. by Rev. Josiah P. Tustin, Aug. 6, 1846.

4-19   BUCKLIN Minerva Oliver, and Charles Whitefield Sanders, Dec. 15, 1844.

4-7   BUFFINTON Esther, and Samuel Mason, Jr., May 25, 1834.

1-116   BUGBEE ——, of Hezekiah, of Connecticut, and Elizabeth Dorrance, of Samuel, of Foster, R. I.; m. by Eld. Luther Baker, Dec. 26, 1811.

1-63   BULLOCK John, of Rehoboth, and Mrs. Jerusha Smith, of Warren; m. by Rev. Solomon Townsend, March 16, 1748-9.

1-64   "   Richard, and Abigail Kennicutt; m. by Rev. John Usher, June 6, 1751.

1-100   "   Joseph, of Calvin and Abigail Davis, of John; m. by Rev. Henry Wight, Nov. 24, 1808.

4-8   "   Dr. Otis, of Dr. Samuel, of Rehoboth, and Martha M. Randall, of Samuel; m. by Rev. John C. Welch, Aug. 17, 1836.

4-16   "   Otis, of Samuel, and Elizabeth Hicks Sanders, of George; m. by Rev. George W. Hathaway, Oct. 5, 1842.

1-73   BURDEN Elizabeth, and William Owen, March 3, 1771.

1-114   "   Hattie, and John Thurber, May 5, 1818.

4-3   "   Luther Mason, and Eliza Pehrce; m. by Rev. Flavel Shutleff, June 4, 1820.

4-23   BURGESS Sarah, and James Smith, Jr., Aug. 24, 1845.

4-18   BURGE Esther T., and Simeon Rounds, Feb. 18, 1844.

1-67   BURR Shubael, of Rehoboth, and Mrs. Betsey Miller, of Warren; m. by Rev. Solomon Townsend, Nov. 8, 1759.

1-82   "   Samuel, and Anne Champlain; m. by Rev. John Pitman, April 29, 1787.

1-83   "   Dr. Nathan Miller, and Lydia Adams; m. by Rev. John Pitman, Nov. 30, 1788.

1-88   "   Shubael, and Anne Cole; m. by Rev. Luther Baker, Nov. 9, 1794.

1-89   "   Polly, and Joshua Ormsbee, June 4, 1795.

1-100   "   Nathan M., of Shubael and Lucy Willard, of Ephraim; m. by Eld. Luther Baker, Dec. 13, 1807.

1-115   "   Shubael, of Samuel, and Betsey Cole, of Allen, dec.; m. by Eld. Luther Baker, July 7, 1811.

1-116   "   Betsey, and John Thorp Child, Sept. 19, 1811.

1-119   "   Sarah Marsh, and Robert Miller Cole, July 17, 1817.

4-8   "   Lucy Ann, and Jeremiah Goff, Dec. 11, 1817.

4-2   "   Nancy, and Capt. John Watson (also 4-1 and 3-164), Oct. 8, 1826.

4-8   "   Eliza, and Capt. David Brightman Barton, Aug. 2, 1835.

4-29   "   Mary Newell, and Nathaniel Drowne, Nov. 25, 1838.

4-7   "   Ephraim W., of Nathan M., and Abby Miller Child, of John T.; m. by Rev. George W. Hathaway, Sept. 20, 1831.

4-11   BURTCH Henry, of Stanton and Abby F. Salisbury, of John; m. by Rev. S. W. Willson, Aug. 12, 1838.

1-97   BURT Alvin, of Alvin, of New York, and Mary Cole, of Benjamin, of Warren; m. by Eld. Luther Baker, May 15, 1805.

4-10   "   Hannah Driscoll, and Peleg Bosworth, Nov. 13, 1835.

4-14   "   Samuel L., and Mary J., Bushee, of Swansey; m. by Rev. Benjamin R. Allen, Jan. 20, 1842.

4-16, 18   "   George L., of Alvan and Mary Ann Hood; m. by Rev. Josiah P. Tustin, Jan. 1, 1843.

4-18   "   Delina C., and Robert McMillion, Nov. 30, 1843.

4-21   "   Mary C., and Lewis Leonard, July 21, 1845.

1-66   BUSHEE James, and Mrs. Bathshela Tripp; m. by James Miller, Justice, July 19, 1751.

1-68   "   Susannah, and William Child, Oct. 10, 1761.

1-75   "   James, and Lydia Sheldon; m. by Rev. James Manning, Feb. 1, 1768.

1-113   BUSHEE Mary, and Joseph Brown, Jan. 12, 1812.
4-14   "   Mary J., and Samuel L. Burt, Jan. 20, 1842.
4-21   "   Deborah L., and Henry A. Bowen, June 15, 1845.
3-162   BUTTERFIELD Porter Putnam, aged 30 years, born Hudson, N. Y., son
                of Jonathan, and Emily Mansfield Luther, aged 19 years, born
                Warren. R. I., dau. of Gardiner; m. by Rev. George W. Hath-
                away, July 7, 1844.
1-62   BUTTERWORTH Sarah, and Nathan Cole, Dec. 13, 1747.
1-64   "   John, and Mrs. Isabel Pollard; m. by John Kennicutt, Justice,
                April 15, 1750.
1-64   "   Alice, and Joseph Pettey, Dec. 14, 1752.
1-66   "   Mrs. Lois, and Benjamin Barton, Jr., March 23, 1758.
1-75   "   Lillis, and Andrew Cole, April 8, 1770.
1-89   "   Betsey, and Rufus Frink, Dec. 14, 1794.
1-97   "   Samuel, of Hezekiah, and Mary Mason, of Gardiner; m. by James
                Sisson, Justice, Nov. 25, 1804.
1-111   "   Sally, and Samuel Place, Oct. 11, 1812.
3-168   "   Butts John, of Peleg and Patty Bebee, dau. of widow Alice; m.
                by Rev. John Lindsey, Aug. 21, 1817.
1-119   "   Mary, and George Munroe, Jan. 22, 1818.
4-20   "   Betsey, and William Martin, Oct. 22, 1835.
4-16   "   Benjamin Ellis, of Seekonk, Mass., son of Benjamin, and Abby
                Nelson White, of Warren, dau. of William H.: m. by Rev.
                George W. Hathaway, Aug. 18, 1842.

C

1-65   CAMP William, and Bethiah Medbury, both of Rehoboth; m. by Matthew
                Allen, Justice, Jan. 21, 1755.
4-26   CAPEN Annie, and John Q. Thurber, Oct. 5, 1848.
1-81   CARPENTER Nathan, of Cranston, R. I., and Hannah Thomas, of War-
                ren; m. by Rev. Charles Thompson, March 10, 1780.
1-88   "   Peter, and Patience Rogers; m. by Elder Luther Baker, Oct.
                11, 1794.
1-69   CARR Robert, and Lydia Turner; m. by Rev. James Manning, Aug. 30,
                1767.
1-70   "   Caleb, and Lillis Barton; m. by Rev. James Manning, Sept. 20,
                1768.
1-84   "   Mary, and Benajah Cole, Nov. 30, 1777.
1-90   "   William, and Elizabeth Hoar; m. by Elder John Pitman, March
                16, 1788.
1-90   "   Lydia, and James Vance, Aug. 8, 1797.
1-87   "   Samuel, and Sally Jolls, Sept. 13, 1792.
1-86   "   Elizabeth, and John Champlain, Jan. 12, 1794.
1-86   "   John, and Patty Davis; m. by Elder Luther Baker, June 15,
                1794.
1-86   "   Caleb, and Olive Miller; m. by Elder Luther Baker, June 26,
                1794.
1-88   "   Lillis, and Alfred Carter, Oct. 11, 1794.
1-90   "   Ruth, and Clement Stanton Bebee, May 27, 1798.
1-92   "   Hailey, and William Cole, Oct. 5, 1800.
1-96   "   Patience, and Cassander Kingman, May 27, 1804.
1-99   "   Caleb, of Caleb, dec., and Sally Warren, dau. of William Bliss,
                dec.; m. by Daniel Bradford, Jr., Justice, Nov. 1, 1807.
1-100   "   Jonathan, of Jonathan, of Warren, and Ann Tredway, of James,
                of Connecticut; m. by Rev. Joshua Crowell, Feb. 25, 1809.
3-172   "   Capt. William, Jr., of Capt. William, and Temperance Smith, of
                Joseph, Jr.; m. by Rev. Jordan Rexford, Sept. 3, 1820.
4-1, 9   "   Turner, of Caleb, and Sally J. Sanders, of Joseph; m. by Rev.
                Jordan Rexford, May 31, 1822.
4-4   "   Maria, and William Haile, Jr., Oct. 19, 1828.
4-4   "   Clarissa, and Alvan Cole, Nov. 22, 1829.
4-14   "   George Clinton, and Rebecca S. Barton; m. by Rev. William
                Livesey, June 19, 1842.

4-18   CARR Caleb, Jr., and Hannah Sherman; m. by Rev. A. M. Swinton, Sept. 29, 1844.

4-25   "   Caleb A., of Capt. George W., of Newport, and Martha S. Gladding, of Capt. Richard E., of Bristol; m. by Rev. Paul Townsend, June 11, 1848.

1-88   CARTEE Alfred, and Lillis Carr; m. by Elder Luther Baker, Oct. 11, 1794.

1-98   "   Mrs. Lillis, and John Brinsmond Gibson, —— —, 1805.

1-111   "   Mrs. Susannah, and John Lawrence, Nov. 2, 1812.

4-25   CARY Elizabeth, and Horace Luther, May 25, 1848.

1-88   CAUSSONES John, and Nancy Wheaton; m. by Rev. John Pitman, July 6, 1788.

1-78   CHAMPLAIN Thomas, and Elizabeth Bowen; m. by Rev. Charles Thompson, April 8, 1781.

1-82   "   Anne, and Samuel Burr, April 29, 1787.

1-86   "   John, and Elizabeth Carr; m. by Elder Luther Baker, Jan. 12, 1794.

1-89   "   James, and Hannah Snell; m. by Elder Luther Baker, May 24, 1795.

1-97   "   Abigail, and Benjamin Parker, July 10, 1805.

1-120   "   Mary, and Allen C. Hoar, March 20. 1817.

2-112   "   Eliza, and Benjamin Drowne, June 2, 1817.

3-171   "   Capt. Joshua, and Hannah Martin; m. by Rev. Flavel Shurtleff, June 28, 1821.

3-166   "   Capt. William and Eliza Kennicutt Phinney, of Daniel; m. by Rev. Jordan Rexford, Sept. 15, 1823.

4-4   "   Henry, of James and Elizabeth Haile, of Capt. John; m. by Rev. John C. Welch, Sept. 24, 1829.

4-12   "   Jonathan C., and Lydia Jolls; m. by Rev. John C. Welch, May 12, 1836.

1-65   CHASE Mrs. Susannah, and Benjamin Asten, Feb. 14, 1757.

1-68   "   Elisha, of Swansey, and Mrs. Sarah Sisson of Warren; m. by John Kennicutt, Justice, March 20, 1760.

1-67   "   Mrs. Rachel, and Jonathan Ormsbee, Nov. 13, 1760.

1-70   "   Naomi, and Joseph Garzia, Aug. 10, 1765.

1-83   "   Patience, and Isaac Ormsbee, Feb. 8, 1789.

1-90   "   Edward, and Betsey Grant; m. by Eld. Luther Baker, Oct. 18, 1795.

3-168   "   Mrs. Sally, and Col. Seth Peck, Dec. 29, 1822.

4-8   "   Elizabeth H., and Samuel Pearce, Oct. 27, 1833.

4-23   "   Nathan A., and Caroline M. Anthony, both of Somerset, Mass.; m. by Rev. William Livesey, March 1, 1841.

4-13   "   Angustus, and Rhody Lake, both of Tiverton; m. by Rev. William Livesey, Sept. 1, 1841.

4-16   "   Benjamin Hathaway, of Richard, and Sarah Slade, of William, both of Swansey, Mass.; m. by Rev. George W. Hathaway, June 2, 1842.

4-26   "   Mervin B., of Fall River, son of Henry, and Caroline Fales, of Warren, dau. of Lemuel; m. by Rev. Paul Townsend, Sept. 27, 1848.

1-66   CHILD Cromwell, and Roby Eddy; m. by Benjamin Miller, Justice, Oct. 21, 1749.

1-66   "   Mrs. Patience, and Thomas Easterbrooks, Aug. 18, 1753.

1-66   "   Hezekiah, and Mrs. Patience Barton; m. by Rev. John Burt, Jan. 13, 1757.

1-68   "   Mrs. Mary, and Jonathan Salisbury, May 11, 1758.

1-66   "   John, 2d, and Mrs. Rosabella Cole; m. by John Kennicutt, Justice, Nov. 23, 1758.

1-67   "   Mrs. Abigail, and Edward Eddy, Jr., Jan. 20, 1760.

1-68   "   William, of Warren, and Susanna Bushee; m. by Timothy Wilmarth, Justice, Oct. 10, 1761.

1-70   "   James, and Mary Jenkins; m. by Rev. James Manning, March 2, 1766.

1-70   "   Cromwell, and Patience Miller; m. by Rev. James Manning, Nov. 9, 1766.

1-70	CHILD	Jeremiah, and Patience Cole; m. by Rev. James Manning, Jan. 31, 1768.
1-72	"	Martha, and James Mitchell Varnum, Feb. 8, 1770.
1-72	"	Prudence, and Barnard Salisbury, Oct. 21, 1770.
1-73	"	Mrs. Sarah, and Charles Thompson, Nov. 26, 1770.
1-74	"	Mrs. Abigail Miller, and William M. Lewis, Dec. 13, 1772.
1-74	"	Caleb, and Mary Cole; m. by Rev. Charles Thompson, Feb. 16, 1774.
1-75	"	Hope, and Benjamin Dimond, Sept. 8, 1774.
1-77	"	Mrs. Elizabeth, and Peter Turner; int. March 17, m. 21, 1776.
1-87	"	Haile, and Amey Kennicutt; m. by Rev. Solomon Townsend, Feb. 22, 1781.
1-81	"	William, 2d, and Betsey Ormsbee; m. by Rev. Charles Thompson, Oct. 7, 1784.
1-81	"	John, and Mary Bliss; m. by William Barton, Justice, —— —, 1784(?).
1-81	"	Elizabeth, and John Croade, April 3, 1785.
1-81	"	Bethiah, and John Luther, —— —, 1786.
1-82	"	Lydia, and Joseph Adams, Sept. 23, 1787.
1-82	"	John T., and Molly Miller; m. by Rev. John Pitman, Dec. 9, 1787.
1-82	"	William, and Abigail Payne; m. at Johnston, by Rev. Samuel Winsor, Jan. 20, 1788.
1-83	"	Samuel, and Nancy Luther; m. by Rev. John Pitman, July 23, 1789.
1-84	"	Caleb, Jr., and Sally Bowen; m. by Elder Nathaniel Cole, Oct. 30, 1791.
1-84	"	Patience, and Jonathan Hix, Feb. 21, 1791.
1-87	"	Mary, and Edward Eddy, June 3, 1792.
1-85	"	Nathan, and Dorcas Tibbetts; m. by Elder Luther Baker, Nov. 17, 1793.
1-86	"	Sylvester, and Patience Luther; m. by Elder Solomon Townsend, June 23, 1794.
1-89	"	Lydia, and Benjamin Barton, May 31, 1795.
1-90	"	Elizabeth, and Thomas Cranston, Oct. 11, 1795.
1-89	"	Oliver, and Hannah Hoar; m. by Elder Luther Baker, Dec. 4, 1796.
1-91	"	Priscilla, and Simeon Salisbury, Aug. 26, 1798.
1-92	"	Jeremiah, and Sally Macomber; m. by Elder Luther Baker, Jan. 31, 1799.
1-94	"	Abby, and John Fessenden, March 25, 1802.
1-95	"	Patience, and George Rex, Oct. 29, 1802.
1-94	"	Lydia, and Lewin Cranston, Oct. 31, 1802.
1-96	"	Rosahellar, and Edward Gardiner, Feb. 20, 1803.
1-96	"	Varnum, of Jeremiah and Nancy Thurber; m. by Elder Luther Baker, May 24, 1804.
1-100	"	William, of Haile and Lucinda Thurber; m. by William Barton, Justice, March 7, 1806.
1-99	"	Benjamin, of William and Ann Comer, of John; m. by Rev. John B. Gibson, March 6, 1807.
1-100	"	Prescilla, and Shubael Child, May 7, 1807.
1-100	"	Shubael, of Caleb and Prescilla Child, of Sylvester; m. by Josiah Humphrey, Jr., Justice, May 7, 1807.
1-101	"	John T., of John and Mrs. Elizabeth Croade, dau. of Col. Sylvester Child, Dec. 2, 1809.
1-101	"	James, of Capt. Haile, of Warren, and Betsey Pettis, of Somerset; m. by Elder Luther Baker, Nov. 4, 1810.
1-112	"	Mary T., and John T. Croade, Nov. 4, 1810.
1-116	"	John Throop, of John Throop, and Betsey Burr, of Nathan Miller Burr; m. by Elder Luther Baker, Sept. 19, 1811.
1-116	"	Thomas C., of Jeremiah, and Nancy B. Thurber, of Caleb; m. by Elder Luther Baker, Jan. 12, 1812.
1-120	"	Daniel, and Mary Anna Cole; m. by Rev. Daniel Chapman, July 11, 1819.
2-110	"	John K., and Mary Ann Newhall; m. by Rev. Daniel Chapman, Aug. 18, 1819.
1-120	"	Margaret B., and William B. Child, Nov. 16, 1819.

1-120   CHILD William B., and Margaret B. Child; m. by Rev. Daniel Chapman, Nov. 18, 1819.

3-167   "   Halle, and Mary Ann Bennett; m. by James Sisson, Justice, June 22, 1823.

4-7   "   Abby Miller, and Ephraim W. Burr, Sept. 20, 1831.

4-7   "   Sylvester, of Warren, son of Joseph, of Portsmouth, and Ann H. Bosworth, of Benjamin; m. by Rev. George W. Hathaway, March 10, 1833.

4-8   "   Harriet N., and Alfred Bosworth, Dec. 13, 1835.

4-12   "   Henry, and Ann Eliza Hale; m. by Rev. John C. Welch, Oct. 15, 1837.

4-12   "   Joseph B., and Elizabeth C. Drowne; m. by Rev. John Dowling, July 16, 1840.

4-17   "   Shubael P., and Adeline Croude; m. by Rev. Josiah P. Austin, May 21, 1843.

4-26   "   Margaret A., and Edwin S. Bowen,, Nov. 25, 1845.

4-28   "   Samuel Smith, of Ezra and Betsey, and Ellen Maria Easterbrooks, of George and Rebecca; m. by Rev. R. A. Fyfe, Nov. 18, 1849.

4-30   "   Ezra O., and Sarah Martin; m. by Rev. John C. Welch, May 14, 1850.

1-85   CHURCHILL Ansel, and Lillis Barton; m. by Rev. Charles Thompson, March 18, 1792.

4-26   CHURCH Samuel T., of Bristol, son of George, and Sally M. Drowne, of Warren, of Solomon, dec.; m. by Rev. Paul Townsend, Jan. 1, 1849.

1-110   CLARKE Ezekiel, of Fairhaven, and Mary Eddy, of Warren; m. by Rev. Jordan Rexford, April 22, 1818.

4-23   COBB Allen, and Polly Simmons; m. by Rev. William Livesey, Feb. 14, 1841.

1-70   COCKRAM Lydia, and William Turner Miller, Nov. 2, 1766.

1-113   "   Lydia, and William T. Miller, May 18, 1817.

3-163   COGHING Timothy, and Susan Price; m. by Rev. R. W. Allen, Dec. 10, 1850.

4-20   COLEMAN Ann Maria, and William E. Perkins, Nov. 11, 1844.

1-62   COLE Nathan, and Sarah Butterworth; m. by Benjamin Miller, Justice, Dec. 13, 1747.

1-64   "   Benjamin, of Warren, and Hannah Luther, of Swansey; m. by Edward Luther, Justice, Sept. 26, 1749.

1-63   "   Joseph, of Warren, and Mrs. Susannah Jolls, of Bristol; m. by John Kennicutt, Justice, Nov. 30, 1749.

1-66   "   Mrs. Hope, and Benjamin Miller, Jr., Jan. 10, 1751.

1-66   "   Mrs. Patience, and Elkanah Eddy, May 22, 1751.

1-64   "   Hannah, and Benjamin Harding, Nov. 15, 1753.

1-64   "   Abigail, and Samuel Toogood, Feb. 28, 1754.

1-66   "   Mrs. Elizabeth, and Ezra Ormsbee, Jan. 30, 1755.

1-65   "   Jonathan, and Mrs. Abigail Easterbrooks; m. by Ebenezer Cole, Justice, March 2, 1756.

1-66   "   John, and Elizabeth Halle; m. by John Kinnecutt, Justice, March 16, 1758.

1-66   "   Mrs. Rosabellar, and John Child, 2d, Nov. 23, 1758.

1-67   "   Mrs. Esther, and Theophilus Luther, March 13, 1760.

1-68   "   Mrs. Elizabeth, and Nehemiah Hopkins, March 11, 1762.

1-68   "   Mrs. Mehitable, and Barnabus Luther, Oct. 14, 1762.

1-78   "   Anna, and Martin Luther, Nov. 4, 1762.

1-69   "   Ruth, and John Thurber, Jr., March 2, 1763.

1-68   "   Curtis, of Warren, and Mrs. Sarah Eddy, of Bristol; m. by Rev. Solomon Townsend, April 8, 1764.

1-69   "   Patience, and Peter Reynolds, Jan. 3, 1765.

1-69   "   Sarah, and Caleb Eddy, March 14, 1765.

1-69   "   Sarah, and John Martin, April 18, 1765.

1-70   "   Mary, and Oliver Easterbrooks, —— —, 1765.

1-70   "   Mary, and John Jolls, Feb. 5, 1767.

1-70   "   Lydia, and Thomas Easterbrooks, March 12, 1767.

1-70	COLE	Richard, and Lydia Kelley; m. by Rev. James Manning, Dec. 10, 1767.
1-70	"	Patience, and Jeremiah Child, Jan. 31, 1768.
1-69	"	Lois, and Jesse Baker, March 17, 1768.
1-72	"	Elizabeth, and John Kelley, April 9, 1769.
1-75	"	Andrew, and Lillis Butterworth; m. by Rev. James Manning, April 8, 1770.
1-73	"	Edward, and Sarah Perce; m. by William T. Miller, Justice, Aug. 20, 1771.
1-72	"	Prudence, and Rufus Barton, April 7, 1771.
1-74	"	Seabury, and Peres Wheaton, May 18, 1773.
1-74	"	Ichabod, and Robie Cole; m. by Rev Charles Thompson, Dec. 19, 1773.
1-74	"	Robie, and Ichabod Cole, Dec. 19, 1773.
1-74	"	Mary, and Caleb Child, Feb. 16, 1774.
1-77	"	Lindall, and Elizabeth Varce; m. by Rev. Solomon Townsend, Aug. 24, 1777.
1-84	"	Benajah, and Mary Carr; m. by Rev. Charles Thompson, Nov. 30, 1777.
1-78	"	Amey, and Martin Easterbrooks, March 5, 1780.
1-78	"	Mary, and Peleg Kingsley, June —, 1780.
1-83	"	Isaac, and Phebe Perce; m. by Rev. Charles Thompson, Nov. 12, 1780.
1-83	"	Ebenezer, and Patty Ingraham; m. by Rev. Solomon Townsend, Dec. 7, 1780.
1-82	"	Abigail, and Luther Salisbury, Feb. 11, 1781.
1-79	"	Thomas, and Anne Vosce; m. by Rev. Charles Thompson, April 2, 1781.
1-79	"	Curtis, and Mary Briggs; m. at Attleboro, Mass., by Rev. Mr. Thatcher, Sept. 2, 1781.
1-79	"	Lillis, and Jesse Baker, April 11, 1782.
1-80	"	Spencer, and Mary Bowen; m. by Rev. Solomon Townsend, Oct. 16, 1783.
1-80	"	Abigail, and Seth Cole, April 9, 1784.
1-80	"	Seth, and Abigail Cole; m. by William Barton, Justice, April 9, 1784.
1 81	"	Benjamin, 2d, of Warren, and Sarah Luther, of Swansey; m. by Rev. Charles Thompson, Oct. 24, 1784.
1-80	"	Mary, and Daniel Trogood, Nov. 25, 1784.
1-82	"	Rachel, and Martin Luther, July 9, 1786.
1-92	"	Isaac, and Abigail Pearce; m. by William Barton, Justice, Feb. 24, 1792.
1 88	"	Ruth, and Samuel Bosworth, Sept. 25, 1794.
1-88	"	Anne, and Shubael Burr, Nov. 9, 1794.
1-92	"	William, of Allen, and Halley Carr, of Robert; m. by Elder Luther Baker, Oct. 5, 1800.
1-93	"	Ebenezer, of Curtis, and Polly Salisbury, of William; m. by Elder Luther Baker, Dec. 21, 1800.
1-96	"	Benjamin, of Ebenezer, and Patience Cole of Allen; m. by Elder Luther Baker, Feb. 19, 1804.
1-96	"	Patience, and Benjamin Cole, Feb. 19, 1804.
1-97	"	Mary, and Alvin Burt, May 15, 1805.
1-97	"	Allen, of Allen, and Betsy Wheaton, of Perez; m. by Elder Luther Baker, July 10, 1805.
1-99	"	Elizabeth, and Martin Salisbury, Aug. 24, 1806.
1-98	"	Joseph, of Ichobod, and Mary Mason, of Samuel; m. by Elder Luther Baker, Dec. 14, 1806.
4-5	"	Mary, and John K. Barney, April 27, 1807.
1-115	"	Simmons, of Isaac and Sarah Mason, of Samuel; m. by Elder Luther Baker, Feb. 10, 1811.
1-115	"	Martha, and John Folson Phillips, May 26, 1811.
1-115	"	Betsey, and Shubuel Burr, July 7, 1811.
1-116	"	Roby, and Burrell Bosworth, Nov. 10, 1811.
1-115	"	James, of Ebenezer, and Sally Smith, of Joseph; m. by Elder Luther Baker, Nov. 11, 1811.

1-111 COLE Elijah, of Seth, and Mary Easterbrooks, of Nathaniel; m. by Elder Luther Baker, Dec. 20, 1812.

1-112 " Capt. Jonathan, of Warren, son of Capt. Curtis, of Cambridge, N. Y., and Abigail Lewis, of William, dec., of Warren; m. by Elder Luther Baker, Sept. 19, 1813.

1-110 " Thomas E., and Emma Phinney; m. by Rev. Daniel Chapman, Aug. 23, 1818.

1-118 " Luther, of Col. Benjamin, and Sally Salisbury, of Luther; m. by Rev. Silas Hall, Sept. 8, 1816.

1-119 " Robert Miller, of Warren, son of Capt. Jonathan and Mrs. Betsey, and Sarah Marsh Burr, of Capt. Rufus and Nancy; m. by Rev. Jordan Rexford, July 17, 1817.

1-120 " Mary Anna, and Daniel Child, July 11, 1819.

3-171 " Christiana, and Cornelius S. Thompson, June 17, 1821.

3-170 " Eliza, and Rev. Flavel Shurtleff, Aug. 1, 1821.

3-171 " Samuel, of Allen, dec., and Patience Greene Maxwell, of James; m. by Elder Luther Baker, Aug. 30, 1821.

3-166 " Betsey, and Abraham Parsons, Feb. 8, 1824.

3-165 " Jeremiah, of Warren, son of Lundall, and Rebecca Vinniman, of Rev. John, dec., of New Jersey; m. by Rev. Jordan Rexford, Oct. 3, 1824.

4-4 " Alvon, of Benjamin, and Clarissa Carr, of Samuel; m. by Rev. John C. Welch, Nov. 22, 1829.

4-6 " Betsey Smith, and Stephen Duval, Sept. 12, 1830.

4-7 " Alvan, of Benjamin, and Lydia Burr Hoar, of Samuel; m. by Rev. George W. Hathaway, Feb. 3, 1833.

4-9 " Andrew, and Mrs. Phebe Short; m. by Rev. John C. Welch, Nov. 10, 1836.

4-10 " George, and Rachel Weight; m. by Rev. Isaac Bonney, Jan. 18, 1838.

4-10 " Abby, and Edward T. Martin, Sept. 5, 1838.

4-18 " Edmund, of Capt. Luther, of Warren, and Olive M. Wheeler, of David, of Seekonk; m. at Seekonk, by Rev. John C. Welch, April 22, 1841.

4-13, 14 " Abby Lewis, and Charles Edwin Bennett, Feb. 13, 1842.

4-17 " Elvina M., and Alfred C. Briggs, April 12, 1843.

4-17 " Capt. Samuel, and Mary B. Martin; m. by Rev. William Phillips, July 9, 1843.

4-20 " Robert, and Mary V. Sisson; m. by Rev. Robert M. Hatfield, Aug. 8, 1845.

4-22 " William, of Benjamin, and Maria Munroe, of Philip, dec.; m. by Rev. Paul Townsend, May 23, 1847.

4-24 " Content M., and Charles Collins, Nov. 29, 1847.

4-27 " Elizabeth H., and James Miller, May 27, 1849.

4-29 " Margaret Smith, and Samuel Angustus Driscoll, Oct. 2, 1850.

4-4 COLLIMORE Luther, and Hannah Kelley; m. by Rev. N. S. Spaulding, May 7, 1830.

1-73 COLLINS Charles, and Hannah Turner; m. by Rev. Charles Thompson, Oct. 20, 1771.

1-91 " William, and Polly Haile; m. by Elder Luther Baker, May 20, 1798.

1-95 " Hannah, and Henry Sisson, Aug. 31, 1803.

4-2 " Haile, of William and Mary Maxwell, of James; m. by Rev. Luther Baker, Oct. 28, 1824.

4-17 " Haile, of William and Emeline Sanders, dau. of James Maxwell; m. by Rev. Nathan Paine, Sept. 8, 1830.

4-6 " William, of William, and Mary French, of Ephraim; m. by Rev. Luther Baker, Nov. 23, 1830.

4-10 " Ann, and Alfred Bosworth, Oct. 11, 1838.

4-22 " Margaret Rhodes, and Joseph Mason Smith, Dec. 24, 1845.

4-24 " Charles, and Content M. Cole, of Samuel; m. by Rev. Josiah P. Tustin, Nov. 29, 1847.

1-91 COMER Betsey, and Daniel Phinney, June 14, 1798.

1-99 " Ann, and Benjamin Child, March 6, 1807.

1-74   COMSTOCK Jeremiah, and Mrs. Hannah Bowen; m. by Rev. Charles Thompson, Dec. 13, 1772.

4-24   CONVERSE Horace, of Gloucester, Mass., and Adeline Lawton, of Swansey; m. by Rev. John C. Welch, Aug. 25, 1839.

4-16   COOKE George Lewis, of New York, son of Joseph S., and Laura Francis Wheaton, of Nathan M.; m. by Rev. George W. Hathaway, Dec. 14, 1842.

4-21   COOLEY Mary L., and John H. Bowen, June 21, 1846.

4-28   COREY Mrs. Adeline H., and Charles W. Carey, March 15, 1850.

4-28   "   Charles W., and Mrs. Adeline H. Carey, both of Dartmouth; m. by Rev. R. W. Allen, March 15, 1850.

3-106 CORNWELL Clarissa S., and Dea. Stephen Davol, Jan. 4, 1824.

1-88   CORVIN Nancy, and Martin Bowen, Aug. 3, 1794.

4-7   COTTRELL Susan A., and Martin L. Salisbury, Oct. 9, 1831.

1-71   COWEN John, and Mary Miller; m. by John Kennicutt, Justice, Aug. 6, 1769.

1-80   "   Mary, and James Hayes, Feb. 10, 1784.

1-91   "   John, and Elizabeth Kelley; m. by Elder Luther Baker, July 22, 1798.

1-63   CRANSTON Benjamin, and Sarah Bowen; m. by Benjamin Miller, Justice, Feb. 19, 1748-9.

1-72   "   Caleb, of Benjamin, and Rachel Lewin, of William, dec.; m. by William Turner Miller, Justice, Aug. 5, 1770.

1-77   "   Benjamin, and Mrs. Mary Bowen; m. by Rev. Charles Thompson, Feb. 6, 1777.

1-79   "   Elizabeth, and Lewis Besaynde, Jan. 24, 1779.

1-79   "   Keziah, and Joshua Ormsbee, April 10, 1783.

1-90   "   Thomas, and Elizabeth Child; m. by Eld. Luther Baker, Oct. 11, 1795.

1-94   "   Lewin, of Caleb and Lydia Child, of Haile; m. by Eld. Luther Baker, Oct. 31, 1802.

1-117 "   Mrs. Betsey, and Reuben Bowen, July 16, 1815.

1-81   CROADE John, and Elizabeth Child; m. by Rev. Solomon Townsend, April 3, 1785.

1-96   "   Mary H., and Paschal Allen, June 24, 1804.

1-101 "   Mrs. Elizabeth, and John T. Child. Dec. 2, 1809.

1-112 "   John T., of John, and Mary T. Child, of John T.; m. by Eld. Luther Baker, Nov. 4, 1810.

4-17   "   Adeline, and Shubael P. Child, May 21, 1843.

1-63   CUFFEE ——, servant of Lient. John Adams, and Phebe, servant of widow Tiffany; m. by Rev. Solomon Townsend, Dec. 17, 1747.

1-67   "   Curtis Simeon, and Mrs. Rebecca Manchester; m. by Joshua Bicknell, Justice, Jan. 18, 1761

D

1-64   DAGGETT John, Jr., and Elizabeth Brown, both of Rehoboth; m. by Matthew Allen, Justice, June 13, 1751.

1-95   DAVAL Nathan and Prudence Kelley; m. by Elder Luther Baker, Sept. 19, 1803.

1-95   "   Stephen, of Pardon, and Polly Bowen, of Jeremiah; m. by Eld. Luther Baker, Oct. 20, 1803.

3-166 "   Dea. Stephen and Clarissa S. Cornwell; m. by Rev. John C. Welch, Jan. 4, 1824.

4-6   "   Stephen, of Dea. Stephen and Betsey Smith Cole, of widow Mahala; m. by Rev. John C. Welch, Sept. 12, 1830.

4-9   "   John, of Stephen, and Laura Barton, of Samuel; m. by Rev. George W. Hathaway, Aug. 31, 1834.

4-11   "   Maria, and Edward Sanders, Oct. 1, 1837.

4-22   "   Eliza, and William H. Benn, June 16, 1846.

1-87   DAVIS Nancy, and David Sanders, June 8, 1788.

1-86   "   Patty, and John Carr, June 15, 1794.

1-100 "   Abigail, and Joseph Bullock, Nov. 24, 1808.

4-28   "   Ann M., and Ransom Randall, Feb. 3, 1850.

4-28 DAVIS Lysander W., of Somerset, Mass., son of Leonard B. and Tryphenia A. Marble, of Samuel; m. by Rev. R. A. Fyfe, Feb. 3, 1850.

1-67 DENNIS James, and Sarah Medbury, both of Rehoboth; m. by Matthew Allen, Justice, April 12, 1761.

4-19 DEXTER George T., of Providence, and Mntha Salisbury; m. by Rev. C. S. Macreading, Oct. 31, 1844.

1-75 DIMOND Benjamin, of Bristol, and Hope Child, of Warren; m. by Rev. Charles Thompson, Sept. 8, 1774.

1-116 DORRANCE Elizabeth, and James Bugbee, Dec. 26, 1811.

1-97 DREW Ezra, of Carver, Mass., and Sally Woodmancy, of Warren; m. by Rev. John B. Gibson, Oct. 13, 1805.

1-69 DRING Richard, and Mrs. Priscilla Munroe; m. by Barnard Miller, Justice, Aug. 2, 1764.

1-98 DRISCOLL James, of New Brunswick, son of Jeremiah and Hannah Maxwell, of James, of Warren; m. by Eld. Luther Baker, June 11, 1804.

4-6 " William H., of Capt. James and Eliza Tyler Martin, of Capt. Samuel; m. by Rev. John C. Welch, Nov. 4, 1830.

4-5 " Jeremiah, of Warren, and Elizabeth B. Kingsley, of Providence; m. by Rev. Charles G. Summers, May 23, 1843.

4-29 " Samuel Augustus, and Margaret Smith Cole; m. by Rev. Isaac Bonney, Oct. 2, 1850.

1-64 DROWNE Benjamin, and Hannah Jenckes; m. by Edward Luther, Justice, Oct. 13, 1751.

1-75 " Daniel, of Barrington, and Mrs. Freelove Luther, of Warren; m. by Rev. Charles Thompson, Feb. 8, 1776.

1-89 " Chloe, and Lawton Kelley, March 1, 1795.

1-95 " Samuel, of Benjamin, and Hannah Kelley of Daniel; m. by Rev. John Hill, May 26, 1799.

1-96 " Jerusha, and Oliver Round, Dec. 23, 1804.

2-112 " Benjamin, of Barrington, son of Jonathan J., and Eliza Champlain, of Warren, dau. of John; m. by Rev. Silas Hall, June 2, 1817.

3-172 " Samuel, of Capt. Samuel, dec., and Ann Luther, of Hezekiah, dec.; m. by Rev. Jordan Rexford, April 30, 1820.

3-168 " Philip, of Warren, son of Philip, of Barrington, and Mary Stanley, of Barrington, dau. of Comfort, dec.; m. by Rev. Jordan Rexford, Jan. 24, 1822.

4-29 " Nathaniel, of Jeremiah S., of Barrington, and Mary Newell Burr, of Dr. Nathan M., dec.; m. by Rev. John C. Welch, Nov. 25, 1838.

4-12 " Elizabeth C., and Joseph B. Child, July 16, 1840.

4-17 " Joshua C., of Benjamin, of Warren, and Malvina F. Lake, of Bristol; m. by Rev. Josiah P. Tustin, March 4, 1843.

4-25, 21 " Sarah Ann, and Charles Perry Bowen, March 22, 1846.

4-22 " Rebecca S., and John Trott, June 21, 1846.

4-26 " Sally M., and Samuel T. Church, Jan. 1, 1849.

3-173 " Henry F., and Ann E. Bowen; m. by Rev. Junius Marshall Wiley, at Stonington, Conn., Feb. 5, 1850.

4-26 DUNBAR Ann, and Richard Briggs, Jan. 4, 1849.

E

1-62 EASTERBROOKS William, and Abigail Martin; m. by Samuel Miller, Justice, Nov. 1, 1747.

1-63 " John, of Warren, and Abigail Abel, of Rehoboth; m. by Rev. John Greenwood, Nov. 5, 1747.

1-62 " Valentine, and Tabitha Beverly; m. by Benjamin Miller, Justice, Dec. 13, 1747.

1-62 " Elizabeth, and William Hill, Dec. 20, 1747.

1-64 " William, Jr., and Susannah Luther; m. by John Kennicutt, Justice, Feb. 18, 1753.

1-66	EASTERBROOKS Thomas, Jr., and Mrs. Patience Child; m. by Benjamin Justice, Aug. 18, 1753.
1-65	" Benjamin, and Mrs. Sarah Hill; m. by John Kennicutt, Justice, Jan. 1, 1756.
1-65	" Mrs. Anne, and David Luther, Jan. 29, 1756.
1-65	" Mrs. Abigail, and Jonathan Cole, March 2, 1756.
1-65	" Mrs. Abiah, and Barnard Mason, July 22, 1756.
1-67	" Mrs. Ruth, and Amos Haile, May 18, 1758.
1-66	" Mrs. Jemima, and Trusterham Toogood, Dec. 14, 1758.
1-67	" Levi, and Mrs. Mary Esterbrooks; m. by Ebenezer Cole, Justice, June 19, 1759.
1-67	" Mrs. Mary, and Levi Easterbrooks, June 19, 1759.
1-67	" Mrs. Elizabeth, and Peleg Bowen, April 24, 1760.
1-67	" Mrs. Mary, and Barnard Hix, Jan. 20, 1762.
1-68	" Mrs. Herren, and Nathan Bowen, Oct. 7, 1762.
1-70	" Oliver, and Mary Cole; m. by Rev. James Manning, —— —, 1765.
1-69	" Rebecca, and Barnabee Luther, Jan. 1, 1767.
1-70	" Thomas, and Lydia Cole; m. by Rev. James Manning, March 12, 1767.
1-75	" Anne, and Amos Fisk, Aug. 7, 1768.
1-70	" Elizabeth, and Edward Thurber, Aug. 18, 1768.
1-71	" Warren, and Rosannah Haile; m. by Rev. James Manning, Jan. 18, 1770.
1-72	" Peleg, and Rebecca Salisbury; m. by Rev. James Manning, March 6, 1770.
1-73	" Mrs. Frances, and Samuel Nash, Jr., Dec. 13, 1770.
1-83	" Abial, and Ruth Miller, Nov. 3, 1774.
1-75	" Mrs. Lydia, and Nathaniel Easterbrooks, July 17, 1776.
1-75	" Nathaniel, of Pomfret, Conn., and Mrs. Lydia Easterbrooks, of Warren; m. by Rev. Charles Thompson, July 17, 1776.
1-77	" Sarah, and James Vance, June 1, 1777.
1-78	" Martin, and Amey Cole; m. by Rev. Charles Thompson, March 5, 1780.
1-78	" Patience, and Ebenezer Bosworth, April 22, 1781.
1-78	" Edward, and Mrs. Deborah Hill; m. by William Barton, Justice, Nov. 11, 1781.
1-83	" Royal, and Hannah Salisbury; m. by Elder Russell Mason, Feb. 10, 1789.
1-87	" William, and Polly Kelley; m. by Rev. John Pitman, Oct. 4, 1789.
1-84	" Joanna, and James Bowen, March 27, 1791.
1-85	" David, and Dinah Rogers; m. by Rev. Solomon Townsend, Sept. 1, 1791.
1-85	" David, and Massy Jolls; m. by William Barton, Justice, Sept. 2, 1792.
1-86	" Elizabeth, and Caleb Harding, Feb. 23, 1794.
2-111	" Nelly, and Nathaniel Hicks West, March —, 1798.
1-91	" William, and Lois Kelley; m. by Elder Luther Baker, Oct. 14, 1798.
1-94	" Sally, and Jonathan Munroe, Nov. 6, 1798.
1-97	" Nancy, and Clarke Parker, Oct. 20, 1805.
1-111	" Mercy, and Elijah Cole, Dec. 20, 1812.
1-118	" John, and Mary Wheaton; m. by Rev. Silas Hall, Jan. 22, 1816.
1-121	" Sarah, and Seth Lincoln, Oct. 13, 1816.
3-171	" Nathaniel, Jr., and Harriet Harding; m. by Rev. Flavel Shurtleff, Nov. 19, 1820.
3-167	" Joseph, of Swansey, and Almy Cole Luther, of Martin, of Warren, about 1820 (?)
4-26	" Abby, and David E. Luther, March 14, 1848.
4-28	" Ellen Maria, and Samuel Smith Child, Nov. 18, 1849.
4-22	EATON Elizabeth A., and Robert Goddard, Aug. 6, 1840.
1-64	EDDY Anne, and John Kennicutt, Feb. 3, 1725.
1-66	" Roby, and Cromwell Child, Oct. 21, 1749.
1-66	" Elkanah, of Warren, and Mrs. Patience Cole, of Swansey; m. by Benjamin Miller, Justice, May 22, 1751.

1-65 EDDY Joseph, of Warren, and Mrs. Lydia Jolls, of Bristol; m. by Ebenezer Cole, Justice, June 13, 1756.

1-67 " Edward, Jr., and Mrs. Abigail Child; m. by John Kennicutt, Justice, Jan. 20, 1760.

1-68 " Mrs. Sarah, and Curtis Cole, April 8, 1764.

1-69 " Caleb, and Sarah Cole; m. by Rev. James Manning, March 14, 1765.

1-74 " Joice, and William Salisbury, March 20, 1774.

1-87 " Oliver, and Sarah Wheaton; m. by Rev. Charles Thompson, Dec. 15, 1774.

1-84 " Elizabeth, and Joseph Kelley, May 9, 1785.

1-87 " Edward, and Mary Child; m. by Rev. Solomon Townsend, June 3, 1792.

1-85 " Caleb and Nabby Maxwell; m. by Elder Luther Baker, Dec. 12, 1793.

1-88 " Benjamin, and Abigail Kelley; m. by Elder Luther Baker, Nov. 9, 1794.

1-91 " Enos, and Elizabeth Will'ams; m. by William T. Miller, Justice, April 14, 1796.

1-92 " Nancy, and Benajah Jobls, Dec. 16, 179—.

1-110 " Mary, and Ezekiel Clarke, April 22, 1818.

4-3. " William, of Enos, and Hannah G. Wilbur, of Benjamin; m. by Rev. Jordan Rexford, Nov. 14, 1822.

4-7 " Rebecca Maxwell, and John Robert Wheaton, Nov. 9, 1825.

4-6 " Abby Child, and George Tibbitts Gardiner, Nov. 21, 1830.

4-14 " Henry Walter, of Caleb, and Hannah Barton, of Samuel; m. by Rev. George W. Hathaway, March 27, 1842.

4-30 " Anne R., and Henry A. Bacon, June 6, 1855.

4-10 ELBRIDGE Abby Cole, and Gerry Wheaton, Nov. 4, 1838.

3-170 ELLIOTT John R., of Nathaniel, and Mrs. Lois Luther, dau. of Joseph Barton; m. by Rev. Luther Baker, Aug. 24, 1814.

F

1-77 FALES Thomas, and Sarah Bowen; m. by Rev. Charles Thompson, April 10, 1777.

1-121 " Rosanna, and Robert Ballot, Dec. 8, 1816.

4-25 " Martha, and Joseph Bowen, Jan. 1, 1848.

4-26 " Caroline, and Mervin B. Chase, Sept. 27, 1848.

1-94 FESSENDEN John, of John, and Abby Child, of Sylvester; m. by Elder Luther Baker, March 25, 1802.

4-25 FISHER Sarah M., and Egbert J. Richards, May 16, 1848.

1-69 FISK Samuel, and Judeth Rowell, both of Nottingham, N. H.; m. at Nottingham by Rev. Benjamin Butler, March 6, 1764.

1-75 " Amos, and Anne Easterbrooks; m. by Rev. James Manning, Aug. 7, 1768.

4-30 " Sarah E., and Rufus B. Goff, Dec. 23, 1849.

4-19 FOLLENSBEE James, and Maria Sherman, both of Swansey; m. by Rev. C. S. Macreading, Aug. 12, 1844.

4-13 FOSTER Abby W., and John Salisbury, Oct. 17, 1841.

1-79 FOWLER Olive, and Gideon Luther, March 24, 1782.

1-62 FRANKLIN Elizabeth, and William Haile, July 9, 1747.

4-6 FREENCH Mary, and William Collins, Nov. 23, 1830.

4-24 FRIEZE John, and Jane Young Smith; m. by Robert M. Hatfield, July 28, 1846.

1-89 FRINK Rufus, of Stonington, and Betsey Butterworth, of Warren; m. by William Barton, Justice, Dec. 14, 1794.

3-164 " Eliza, and James Haile, May 22, 1825.

4-16 " Sarah H., and Henry A. Parrington, Oct. 4, 1842.

1-73 FULLER Caleb, and Mrs. Rebecca Peck, both of Rehoboth; m. by John Kennicutt, Justice, Sept. 10, 1772.

4-22 " Nathaniel L., of New Bedford, Mass., and Elizabeth E. Harding, of Warren; m. by Rev. John C. Welch, June 18, 1837.

G

1-96	GARDINER	Edward, of Edward, and Rosabella Child, of John; m. by Elder Luther Baker, Feb. 20, 1803.
1-99	"	Izrael, of William, and Rebecca Kelley, of Daniel; m. by Rev. John B. Gibson, April 19, 1807.
1-118	"	Elizabeth, and Haile Mason, March 10, 1816.
1-114	"	Hezekiah, of Swansey, son of Samuel and Almira Mason, of Samuel, of Warren; m. by Rev. Silas Hall, Jan. 25, 1817.
4-2	"	Zerviah, and Capt. John Mason, March 18, 1827.
4-6	"	George Tibbitts, of Capt. Edward, and Abby Child Eddy, of Capt. Enos; m. by Rev. John C. Welch, Nov. 21, 1830.
4-8	"	George Tibbitts, of Edward, of Warren, and Harriet Byron Viall, of Benjamin, of Seekonk; m. by Rev. James O. Barney, Feb. 15, 1835.
4-26	"	Maria N., and William F. Mason, Oct. 11, 1848.
1-70	GARZIA	Joseph, and Naomi Chase; m. by Rev. James Manning, Aug. 10, 1765.
1-98	GIBSON	John Brinsmead, and Mrs. Lillis Carter, dau. of Caleb Carr; m. by William Barton, Justice, —— —, 1805.
1-66	GLADDING	Mrs. Sarah, and Thomas Lorain, April 5, 1759.
1-68	"	Mrs. Judah, and John Wilson Low, Sept. 28, 1762.
4-25	"	Martha S., and Caleb A. Carr, June 11, 1848.
1-75	GLOVER	Mrs. Hannah, and James Brown, Aug. 8, 1770.
4-22	GODDARD	Robert, of Brunswick, Me., and Elizabeth A. Eaton, of Warren; m. by Rev. William Livesey, Aug. 6, 1840.
1-62	GOFF	Rebecca, and John Salisbury, Nov. 8, 1747.
1-92	"	James, and Prescilla Pearce; m. by Elder Charles Thompson, June 4, 1780.
1-78	"	James, and Priscilla Pears; m. by Rev. Charles Thompson, June 22, 1780.
1-88	"	James, and Jemima Salisbury; m. by Elder Luther Baker, Aug. 17, 1794.
1-95	"	James, of James and Prescilla, and Judith Peck; m. by James Ellis, Justice, Oct. 25, 1801.
1-94	"	Rebecca, and George Woodmancy, Dec. 5, 1802.
1-115	"	James, of James, of Warren, and Deborah Simmons, of Joseph, of Little Compton, May 4, 1806.
4-8	"	Jeremiah, of James and Lucy Ann Burr, of Capt. Rufus; m. by Rev. Jordan Rexford, Dec. 11, 1817.
4-2	"	Nathan, of Warren, son of James, of Bristol, and Nancy Ingraham, of Thomas; m. by Rev. Jordan Rexford, March 29, 1827.
4-4	"	Martha, and George Woodmancy, July 28, 1829.
4-9	"	Mrs. Lucy Ann, and Joseph Hoar, Aug. 28, 1836.
4-27	"	Nathan, Jr., of Bristol, and Sally S. Surgens, of Warren; m. by Rev. R. W. Allen, Nov. 20, 1849.
4-30	"	Rufus B., of Warren, and Sarah E. Fish, of Portsmouth; m. by Rev. Nathan Paine, Dec. 23, 1849.
4-29	"	Henry P., and Judeth G. Ingraham; m. by Rev. Sanford Benton, July 4, 1852.
1-99	GOODWIN	Abigail S., and Angell Berls, Feb. 10, 1807.
1-04	GORHAM	Hannah, and John Kennicutt, May 30, 1737.
1-75	"	Isaac, of Bristol, and Sarah Thomas, of Warren; m. by Rev. Charles Thompson, Sept. 4, 1774.
4-26	GOULD	Mary E., and Henry W. Mason, May 5, 1848.
1-86	GRANT	Ransey, and Jonathan Luther, July 13, 1794.
1-89	"	Lois, and Daniel Kelley, April 26, 1795.
1-90	"	Betsey, and Edward Chase, Oct. 18, 1795.
1-95	"	Marian, and Samuel Kelley, Jan. 16, 1803.
1-100	"	Izrael, of Shubael, and Patty Viall, of Joshua, both of Barrington; m. by Elder Luther Baker, July 6, 1809.
4-3	"	Mrs. Polly, and Peter Tabor, July 29, 1827.
3-165	GREENE	Capt. Abraham, of Warren, and Susan De Wolf Smith, of Bristol, dau. of Barnard; m. by Rev. Jordan Rexford, Feb. 12, 1821.

4-28   GRIFFETH Ellis, of Providence, and Olive B. Wheaton, of Warren; m. by
              Rev. R. W. Allen, May 12, 1850.

H

1-62   HAILE Richard, and Hannah Phinney; m. by James Mason, Justice, June
              21, 1747.
1-62   "   William, and Elizabeth Franklin; m. by Benjamin Miller, Justice,
              July 9, 1747.
1-66   "   Elizabeth, and John Cole, March 16, 1758.
1-67   "   Amos, and Mrs. Ruth Easterbrooks; m. by Ebenezer, Cole, Justice,
              May 18, 1758.
1-67   "   Mrs. Anne, and James Miller, Dec. 3, 1761
1-70   "   Lillice, and Jeremiah Bowen, July 16, 1767.
1-71   "   James, and Hannah Hix; m. by John Kennicutt, Justice, Nov. 2,
              1768.
1-71   "   Lydia, and Constant Martin, Sept. 10, 1769.
1-71   "   Rosannah, and Warren Easterbrooks, Jan. 18, 1770.
1-73   "   Ann, and Josiah Bowen, Jan. 9, 1772.
1-73   "   Elizabeth, and Zaddock Bishop, May 11, 1772.
1-82   "   Sarah, and James Vance, Nov. 7, 1787.
1-84   "   Elizabeth, and John Harris, June 29, 1790.
1-85   "   Mary, and Robertson Hill, Nov. 6, 1791.
1-89   "   Samuel, and Olive Bowen; m. by Elder Luther Baker, Nov. 13,
              1796.
1-91   "   Polly, and William Collins, May 20, 1798.
1-92   "   Anna, and Benjamin Bosworth, Jun. 19, 1800.
1-95   "   John, of John, and Mary Ann Lewis, of William; m. by Elder
              Samuel Watson, Dec. 26, 1802.
1-114   "   Margaret, and Zephaniah Talbot (also 3-166), April 26, 1818.
2-110   "   Mary, and John Bowen, April 11, 1819.
3-165   "   Ann, and Levi Haile, April 5, 1824.
3-165   "   Levi, of Aaron, of Warren, and Ann Haile, of Joseph, dec., of
              Providence; m. by Rev. Stephen Gano, April 5, 1824.
3-165   "   Betsey, and Stillman Welch, Jan. 16, 1825.
3-164   "   James, of Amos, dec , and Eliza Frink; m. by Rev. John C.
              Welch, May 22, 1825.
4-9   "   Mary Theresa, and John Pearce, Oct. 2, 1825.
4-4   "   William, Jr., and Maria Carr, of Caleb; m. by Rev. John C. Welch,
              Oct. 19, 1828.
4-4   "   Elizabeth, and Henry Champlain, Sept 24, 1829.
4-12   "   Ann Elizabeth, and Henry Child, Oct. 15, 1837.
4-23   "   Hon. Levi, and Phebe Alm'ra Tanner; m. by Rev. John C. Welch,
              Feb. 4, 1839.
4-12   "   Abby M., and Nathan L. Barrus, Sept. 23, 1839.
4-29   "   John, Jr., and Clara Sophia Brayton; m. by Rev. John Dowling,
              Sept. 10, 1847.
1-62   HALLETT Elizabeth, and Benjamin Thurber, Nov. 1, 1747.
2-111   HALL Elijah, of Elisha, of Taunton, and Mrs. Lucinda Boynton, dau. of
              Preserved Alger, dec., of Warren; m. by Rev. Jordan Rexford,
              June 4, 1820.
4-23   "   Thomas Bickford, of Lee, N. H., son of Andrew and Hannah Ken-
              nicutt. of Joseph, dec., of Warren; m. by Rev. George W.
              Hathaway (also 4-13), Oct. 11 or 13, 1840.
1-63   HAMMOND Nathan, and Bethiah Luther; m. by Benjamin Miller, Justice,
              Jan. 15, 1748-9.
1-71   "   Martha, and Noah Wheaton, Dec. 25, 1768.
1-86   HANDY Job, and Patty Mason; m. by Edward Chase, Justice, March 6,
              1794.
1-64   HARDING Benjamin, and Hannah Cole, both of Providence; m. by John
              Kennicutt, Justice, Nov. 15, 1753.
1-70   "   John, and Phebe Salisbury; m. by Rev. James Manning, Sept. 1,
              1765.

1-86   HARDING Caleb, and Elizabeth Easterbrooks; m. by Elder Luther Baker, Feb. 23, 1794.
3-171   "   Harriet, and Nathaniel Easterbrooks, Jr., Nov. 19, 1820.
4-22   "   Elizabeth E., and Nathaniel L. Fuller, June 18, 1837.
1-84   HARRIS John, and Elizabeth Haile; m. by Rev. John Pitman, June 29, 1790.
1-118   "   Mary, and John Kelley, Dec. 3, 1815.
4-2   "   Elizabeth, and Jeremiah Woodmancy, Aug. 29, 1824.
4-27   HATHAWAY Susan T., and William E. Williams, June 10, 1849.
1-80   HAYES James, and Mary Cowen; m. by Rev. Charles Thompson, at Swansey, Feb. 10, 1784.
4-2   HAZARD Hannah, Mary and Cyrel C. Wheeler, May 9, 1827.
4-29   "   George G., and Mary J. Tilley; m. at Newport, by Rev. John West, Sept. 8, 1835.
1-63   HEATH Mrs. Mary, and Nathaniel Paine, Feb. 9, 1748-9.
1-66   "   Mrs. Esther, and John Woodmancy, April 10, 1751.
1-68   HICKS Mrs. Elizabeth, and Barnard Miller, March 18, 1746.
1-67   "   Samuel, and Mrs. Bethiah Salisbury; m. by Ebenezer Cole, Justice, Feb. 3, 1757.
1-67   "   Barnard, of Rehoboth, and Mrs. Mary Easterbrooks, of Warren; m. by John Kennicutt, Justice, Jan. 20, 1762.
1-71   "   Hannah, and James Haile, Nov. 2, 1768.
1-84   "   Jonathan, and Patience Child; m. by William Barton, Justice, Feb. 21, 1791.
1-93   "   Henry, of Samuel, and Elizabeth Sanders, of Jacob; m. by Elder Luther Baker, Dec. 21, 1800.
1-94   "   Sarah, and Church Kelley, April 18, 1802.
3-170   "   Sarah, and Philip Short, Oct. 8, 1821.
4-6   "   Ambrose, of Roxbury, N. Y., and Mary Carr Snell, of Warren; m. by Rev. John C. Welch, June 14, 1832.
4-30   HILLING Charles, of Warwick, and Ann Maria Sparks, of Edward, of Warren; m. by Rev. Josiah P. Tustin, July 29, 1849.
1-62   HILL William, and Elizabeth Easterbrooks; m. by Benjamin Miller, Justice, Dec. 20, 1747.
1-65   "   Mrs. Sarah, and Benjamin Easterbrooks, Jan. 1, 1756.
1-69   "   Elizabeth, and William Miller (also 1-70), June 27, 1765.
1-85   "   Barnard, and Hannah Wheaton; m. by Rev. Solomon Townsend, Dec. 9, 1770.
1-78   "   Sarah, and David Vibbard, Feb. 7, 1779.
1-78   "   Mrs. Abigail, and Level Maxwell, May 6, 1781.
1-78   "   Mrs. Deborah, and Edward Easterbrooks, Nov. 11, 1781.
1-85   "   Robertson, of Stonington, Conn., and Mary Haile, of Warren; m. by Elder Nathaniel Cole, Nov. 6, 1791.
2-111   "   Jonathan, of Tiverton, and Cynthia Vickery, of said town; m. by Elisha Hicks, Justice, Jan. 23, 1821.
4-26   HISCOX Edwin, of Warren, son of Pardon, and Nancy Munroe, of Bristol, dau. of Bosworth; m. by Rev. Paul Townsend, Oct. 2, 1848.
1-90   HOAR Elizabeth, and William Carr, March 16, 1788.
1-85   "   William, and Molly Bowen; m. by Rev. John Pitman, Nov. 30, 1788.
1-86   "   Allen, and Hannah Sanders; m. by Rev. John Pitman, March 14, 1790.
1-89   "   Hannah, and Oliver Child, Dec. 4, 1796.
1-120   "   Allen C., of Major Allen and Mary Champlain, of Capt. John, dec.; m. by Rev. Silas Hall, March 20, 1817.
1-114   "   Hope S., and Levi Sherman, Sept. 7, 1817.
4-7   "   Lydia Burr, and Alvin Cole, Feb. 3, 1833.
4-9   "   Joseph, of Allen, and Mrs. Lucy Ann Goff, widow of Jeremiah; m. by Rev. Isaac Bonney, Aug. 28, 1836.
4-11   "   Elizabeth, and George Maxwell Randall, May 28, 1839.
4-14   "   John Champlain, and Laura Maria Bowen, of Haile; m. by Rev. Josiah P. Tustin, Sept. 11, 1842.
1-100   HOLDEN Sally, and Joshua Viall, June 7, 1809.
4-16   HOOD Mary Ann, and George L. Burt (also 4-18), Jan. 1, 1843.

4-27 HOOKER Edward, of Farmington, Conn., and Elizabeth M. Wardwell, of
          Warren; m. by Rev. Robert M. Hatfield, March 28, 1847.
1-68 HOPKINS Nehemiah, and Mrs. Elizabeth Cole, both of Scituate; m. by
          John Kennicutt, Justice, March 11, 1762.
1-99   "   Nathan, of South Kingstown, and Sally Luther, of James. of War-
          ren; m. by Rev. John B. Gibson, March 22, 1807.
1-65 HORTON Jonathan, Jr., and Mrs. Phebe Ormsbee; m. by John Kennicutt,
          Justice, Dec. 5, 1754.
4-6   "   Jerusha Ellis, and Ruel Holden Baker, Dec. 5, 1830.
4-23   "   Josephus W., of Rehoboth, and Ann A. Watson, of Warren; m. by
          Rev. John C. Welch, Jan. 27, 1839.
4-14   "   Josiah T., and Louisa Adams; m. by Rev. William Livesey, April
          17, 1842.
1-84 HOW Thomas, and Sarah Luther; m. by William Barton, Justice, Jan. 30,
          1791.
1-93 HUBBARD William More, of John, and Hannah Brayton, of James W.;
          m. by Rev. John Hill, March 7, 1801.
4-3   "   Hannah, and Allen Bebee, July 21, 1826.
4-12   "   Roby E., and Jeremiah Martin, July 6, 1835.
1-70 HUDSON Reuben, of Swansey, and Abigail Sisson, of Warren; m. by John
          Kennicutt, Justice, Nov 1, 1767.
1-98   "   Eliza, and Jabez Rounds, April 20, 1806.
1-63 HUMPHREY Mrs. Mary and Jonathan Bosworth, March 19, 1748-9.
1-69   "   Mary, and Joseph Allen, Dec. 23, 1759.
1-69   "   Elkanah, and Sarah Smith; m. by Rev. James Manning, March
          28, 1765.
1-92 HUNTER Rufus, of Eldad, and Patience Round, of Oliver; m. by Elder
          Luther Baker, Oct. 19, 1800.
4-13 HUSE Peter Henry, of Warren, and Isabella Hystops, of Pictou, N. S.; m.
          by Rev. William Livesey, April 18, 1841.
4-13 HYSTOPS Isabella, and Peter Henry Huse, April 18, 1841.

I

1-64 IDE Mary, and Ebenezer Medbury, May 12, 1751.
4-8   INGLE Benjamin, of Jonathan, of Taunton, Mass., and Nancy Baker, of
          Thomas, dec., of Warren; m. by Rev. George W. Hatha-
          way, July 26, 1835.
1-83 INGRAHAM Patty, and Ebenezer Cole, Dec. 7, 1780.
1-90   "   Lydia, and Barnard Miller, Dec. 22, 1796.
1-92   "   Daniel, and Temperance Turner; m. by Elder Luther Baker, Oct.
          21, 1798.
4-2   "   Nancy, and Nathan Goff March 29, 1827.
4-16   "   James Davis, of Daniel, and Elizabeth Smith, of Samuel C., both
          of Bristol; m. by Rev. George W. Hathaway, Sept. 25, 1842.
4-25   "   Olive, and Philip Randall, Jan. 2, 1848.
4-29   "   Judeth G., and Henry P. Goff, July 4, 1852.

J

4-14 JAYNE Joseph S., and Mrs. —— Bowen; m. by Rev. Josiah P. Tustin, July
          3, 1842.
1-64 JENCKES Hannah, and Benjamin Drowne, Oct. 13, 1751.
1-70 JENKINS Mary, and James Child, March 2, 1766.
4-18,21 JOHNSON Edmund Y., of Suffield, Conn., and Julia A. Barney, of War-
          ren; m. by Rev. Josiah P. Tustin, Nov. 27, 1843.
4-19   "   Sarah L., and Elisha W. Peckham, July 1, 1844.
1-97 JOHANNET Oliver, of Daniel, and Lydia Kennicutt, of Hezekiah; m. by
          Elder Luther Baker, March 3, 1805.
4-11   "   Caroline, and Joseph Rawson, April 19, 1839.
1-63 JOLLS Susannah, and Joseph Cole, Nov. 30, 1749.
1-65   "   Mrs. Lydia, and Joseph Eddy, June 13, 1756.
·1-67   "   Mrs. Hannah, and John Ormsbee, July 27, 1760.

1-68	JOLLS Mrs. Sarah, and John Ormsbee, March 14, 1762.	
1-70	"	John, and Mary Cole; m. by Rev. James Manning, Feb. 5, 1767.
1-71	"	Ebenezer, and Mary Wheaton; m. by Rev. James Manning, April 7, 1769.
1-74	"	Jeremiah, and Mrs. Robe Salisbury, both of Bristol; m. by Rev. Charles Thompson, Dec. 30, 1772.
1-82	"	Polly, and Gideon Luther, —— —, 1786 (?)
1-85	"	Massy, and David Easterbrooks, 2d, Sept. 2, 1792.
1-87	"	Sally, and Samuel Carr, Sept. 13, 1792.
1-89	"	Lydia, and James Easterbrooks Bowen, Oct. 21, 1792.
1-91	"	John, and Sally Whitaker; m. by Elder Luther Baker, July 22, 1798.
1-92	"	Benajah, and Nancy Eddy; m. by Elder Luther Baker, Dec. 16, 179—.
4-7	"	Jeremiah, of Benajah and Hannah F. Wheeler, of Cyrus; m. by Rev. John C. Welch, Feb. 3, 1833.
4-12	"	Lydia, and Jonathan C. Champlain, May 12, 1836.
1-92	JOSLIN Hannah, and David Bartlett, Aug. 21, 1798.	
1-62	JOY David, and Elizabeth Allen, both of Rehoboth; m. by Joseph Allen, Justice, Dec. 1, 1747.	
4-16	JUSTIN Henry, and Henrietta Martin, of Metcalf; m. by Rev. Josiah P. Tustin, Oct. 29, 1842.	

K

1-62	KELLEY John, and Mrs. Lydia Bosworth; m. by Benjamin Miller, Justice, Oct. 18, 1747.	
1-70	"	Lydia, and Richard Cole, Dec. 10, 1767.
1-72	"	John, and Elizabeth Cole; m. by Rev. James Manning, April 9, 1769.
1-71	"	Edward, and Mary Thomas; m. by John Kennicutt, Justice, Dec. 2, 1769.
1-84	"	Joseph, and Elizabeth Eddy; m. by Rev. Solomon Townsend, May 9, 1785.
1-82	"	Polly, and Comfort Barney, May 15, 1787.
1-87	"	Polly, and William Easterbrooks, Oct. 4, 1789.
1-87	"	John, and Prudence Thurber; m. by Rev. John Pitman, Oct. 11, 1789.
1-88	"	Sarah, and James Bowen, 2d, Sept. 28, 1794.
1-88	"	Abigail, and Benjamin Eddy, Nov. 9, 1794.
1-89	"	Lawton, and Chloe Drowne; m. by Elder Luther Baker, March 1, 1795.
1-89	"	Daniel, and Lois Grant; m. by Elder Luther Baker, April 26, 1795.
1-91	"	Elizabeth, and John Cowen, July 22, 1798.
1-91	"	Lois, and William Easterbrooks, Oct. 14, 1798.
1-95	"	Hannah, and Samuel Drowne, May 26, 1799.
1-93	"	Polly, and Ebenezer Winslow, Aug. 21, 1800.
1-94	"	Joseph, of Joseph, and Phebe Cornwell Treadway, of Phebe; m. by Rev. John Hill, Oct. 24, 1800.
1-94	"	Church, of Joseph, and Sarah Hicks, of James; m. by Elder Luther Baker, April 18, 1802.
1-93	"	Samuel, of Joseph, and Marian Grant, of Shubael; m. by Elder Luther Baker, Jan. 16, 1803.
1-95	"	Prudence, and Nathan Davol, Sept. 19, 1803.
1-98	"	James, of Edward, and Betsey Newman; m. by Rev. John B. Gibson, Feb. 16, 1806.
1-99	"	Rebecca, and Izrael Gardiner, April 19, 1807.
1-99	"	Church, of Joseph, and Patience Mason, of Marmaduke; m. by Elder Luther Baker, July 9, 1807.
1-118	"	John, and Mary Harris; m. by Rev. Silas Hall, Dec. 3, 1815.
1-121	"	William, of Warren, son of Daniel, and Ruth Luther, of Warren, dau. of Hezekiah, of Swansey; m. by Rev. Silas Hall, Jan. 5, 1817.

3-164 KELLEY Sally, and Samuel J. Mathewson, May 23, 1821.
4-2   "   Mary, and Joshua Orne Lewis, Nov. 1, 1826.
4-4   "   Hannah, and Luther Collimore, May 7, 1830.
4-22   "   Susan T., and Jabez Brown, Aug. 6, 1846.
4-29   "   Maria, and Charles S. Sisson, June 29, 1851.
1-64 KENNICUTT John, and Anne Eddy; m. by Rev. Ephraim Wheaton, Feb. 3, 1725.
1-64   "   John, and Hannah Gorham; m. by Rev. John Usher, May 30, 1737.
1-64   "   Elizabeth, and Hooker Low, May 31, 1750.
1-64   "   John, Jr., and Roby Sherman; m. by Rev. Job Mason, May 16, 1751.
1-64   "   Abigail, and Richard Bullock, June 6, 1751.
1-65   "   Anne, and Jarvis Brown, Dec. 5, 1754.
1-67   "   Daniel, and Mrs. Hannah Kent; m. by Rev. Solomon Townsend, July 23, 1758.
1-67   "   Mrs. Hannah, and John Roger Richmond, Dec. 10, 1761.
1-68   "   Mrs. Lydia, and James Adams, April 29, 1762.
1-74   "   Hezekiah, and Lydia Luther; m. by Rev. Charles Thompson, Dec. 23, 1773.
1-87   "   Amey, and Haile Child, Feb. 22, 1781.
1-94   "   Shubael, and Elizabeth Mason; m. by Elder Luther Baker, Nov. 4, 1802.
1-97   "   Bethiah, and John Vinnecum, Jan. 11, 1805.
1-97   "   Lydia, and Oliver Johannot, March 3, 1805.
1-115   "   Shubael, of Shubael, of Warren, and Lydia G. Brown, of Seth, of Swansey; m. by ——, June 7, 1807.
1-100   "   Sally, and Luther Richards, April 20, 1809.
1-67 KENT Mrs. Hannah, and Daniel Kinnecutt, July 23, 1758.
1-96   "   Wilson, of Joshua, and Susan Brayton, of James W.; m. by Elder Luther Baker, Feb. 26, 1804.
4-23   "   Nathan, and Mary Adams; m. by Rev. John C. Welch, Oct. 6, 1839.
1-96 KINGMAN Cassander, and Patience Carr; m. by Elder Luther Baker, May 27, 1804.
1-78 KINGSLEY Peleg, and Mary Cole; m. by William Barton, Justice, June ——, 1780.
4-5   "   Elizabeth B., and Jeremiah Driscoll, May 23, 1843.

L

4-9 LADIEU Eliza, and Hiram Andrews, May 14, 1826.
4-4   "   Mary Ann, and Samuel Blake, Nov. 25, 1827.
1-98 LAKE Mary, and John L. Winslow, —— ——, 1806 (?).
4-13   "   Rhoda, and Augustus Chase, Sept. 1, 1841.
4-17   "   Malvina F., and Joshua C. Drowne, March 4, 1843.
1-111 LAWRENCE John, of Warren, and Mrs. Susanna Cartee, of Newport; m. by Rev. Artemus Stebbins, Nov. 2, 1812.
4-6 LAWTON William B., and Sarah Smith; m. by Rev. John C. Welch, March 23, 1830.
4-24   "   Adeline, and Horace Converse, Aug. 25, 1839.
4-27 LEERING Ellen, and Henry Whitaker, Sept. 12, 1840.
1-68 LEE Mrs. Mary, and Stephen Bowen, April 7, 1762.
4-21 LEONARD Lewis, of New Bedford, and Mary C. Burt, of Joseph; m. by Rev. Josiah P. Tustin, July 21, 1845.
1-72 LEWIN Rachel, and Caleb Cranston, Aug. 5, 1770.
1-66 LEWIS Elizabeth, and Amos Bowen, May 3, 1750.
1-74   "   William M., of Boston, and Mrs. Abigail Miller Child, of Warren; m. by Rev. Charles Thompson, Dec. 13, 1772.
1-95   "   Mary Ann, and John Haile, Dec. 26, 1802.
1-112   "   Abigail, and Capt. Jonathan Cole, Sept. 19, 1813.
1-121   "   Aseneth, and Samuel Angell, Jan. 1, 1817.
4-2   "   Joshua Orne, of Cumberland, and Mary Kelley, of Warren; m. by Rev. John C. Welch, Nov. 1, 1826.

4-27   LEWIS Andrew A., and Eliza A. Newhall, of Bristol; m. by Rev. R. W. Allen, June 4, 1849.
1-121 LINCOLN Seth, and Sarah Easterbrooks; m. by Rev. Silas Hall, Oct. 13, 1816.
2-112 LONGHEAD Charles Thompson, and Sarah Miller Thompson; m. by Rev. Samuel Watson, April 9, 1809.
1-66   LORAIN Thomas, of Warren, and Mrs. Sarah Gladding, of Bristol; m. by John Kennicutt, Justice, April 5, 1759.
1-64   LOW Hooker, and Elizabeth Kennicutt; m. by Rev. John Usher, May 31, 1750.
1-68   "   John Wilson, of Warren, and Mrs. Judah Gladding, of Rehoboth; m. by John Wheaton, Justice, Sept. 28, 1762.
1-63   LUTHER Daniel, and Hannah Martin, April 27, 1737.
1-63   "   Bethiah, and Nathan Hammond, Jan. 15, 1748-9.
1-64   "   Hannah, and Benjamin Cole, Sept. 26, 1749.
1-66   "   Calvin, of Swansey, and Mrs. Sarah Salisbury, of Warren; m. by Benjamin Miller, Justice, Jan. 11, 1753.
1-64   "   Susannah, and William Easterbrooks, Jr., Feb. 18, 1753.
1-64   "   Elizabeth, and Caleb Salisbury, Feb. 10, 1754.
1-65   "   David, and Mrs. Anne Easterbrooks; m. by John Kennicutt, Justice, Jan. 29, 1756.
1-67   "   Theophilus, and Mrs. Esther Cole; m. by Ebenezer Cole, Justice, March 13, 1760.
1-68   "   Barnabus, of Swansey, and Mrs. Mehitable Cole, of Warren; m. by John Wheaton, Justice, Oct. 14, 1762.
1-78   "   Martin, and Anna Cole; m. by Rev. Solomon Townsend, Nov. 4, 1762.
1-69   "   Barnabee, and Rebecca Easterbrooks; m. by Rev. James Manning, Jan. 1, 1767.
1-73   "   Robe, and Nathaniel Whiting, Sept. 12, 1771.
1-73   "   Ebenezer, and Mrs. Jemima Toogood; m. by Rev. Charles Thompson, Oct. 23, 1772.
1-74   "   Lydia, and Hezekiah Kennicutt, Dec. 23, 1773.
1-75   "   Mrs. Freelove, and Daniel Drowne, Feb. 8, 1776.
1-89   "   Susannah, and Peter Richards, July 12, 1779.
1-79   "   Gideon, and Olive Fowler; m. by William Barton, Justice, March 24, 1782.
1-81   "   Sarah, and Benjamin Cole, 2d, Oct. 24, 1784.
1-82   "   Martin, and Rachel Cole; m. by Rev. Solomon Townsend, July 9, 1786.
1-81   "   John, and Bethiah Chill; m. by William Barton, Justice, —— —, 1786.
1-82   "   Gideon, and Polly Jolls; m. by William Barton, Justice, —— —, 1786 (?).
1-82   "   Anne, and Simeon Whitaker, June 8, 1787.
1-83   "   Nancy, and Samuel Child, July 23, 1789.
1-84   "   Sarah, and Thomas Howe, Jan. 30, 1791.
1-84   "   Patience, and Caleb Salisbury, April 10, 1791.
1-86   "   Patience, and Sylvester Child, June 23, 1794.
1-86   "   Jonathan, and Ramsey Grant; m. by Elder Luther Baker, July 13, 1794.
1-92   "   Mary, and John Pearce, Dec. 17, 1794.
1-89   "   Frederick, and Parmelia Arnold; m. by Elder Russell Mason, Feb. 12, 1795.
1-90   "   James, and Sebra Wheaton; m. by Elder Luther Baker, May 27, 1798.
1-91   "   Barnabee, and Elizabeth Monroe; m. by Elder Luther Baker, July 19, 1798.
1-99   "   Asa, of William, and Betsey Eddy Woodmancy, of Reuben; m. by Elder Luther Baker, March 17, 1805.
1-101 "   Deborah Cooke, and Haile Mason Sisson, Jan. 25, 1807.
1-99   "   Sally, and Nathan Hopkins, March 22, 1807.
1-100 "   Polly, and Isaac Bowen, Nov. 16, 1803.
1-111 "   Rebecca, and Dr. Jeremiah Williams, Oct. 5, 1812.
3-170 "   Mrs. Lois, and John R. Elliott, Aug. 24, 1814.

1-118 LUTHER Job, of Warren, son of Hezekiah, of Swansey, and Polly Pearce, of
John, of Warren; m. by Rev. Silas Hall, Oct. 21, 1816.
1-121 " Ruth, and William Kelley, Jan. 5, 1817.
3-172 " Ann, and Samuel Drowne, April 30, 1820.
3-167 " Almy Cole, and Joseph Easterbrooks, —— —, 1820 (?)
3-170 " Jeremiah C., of Martin, and Mary T. Wheeler, of Cyrel, dec.; m.
by Rev. Jordan Rexford, April 7, 1822.
4-2, 1 " Eliza, and William J. Barton, Nov. 20 or 26, 1826.
4-7 " Mary Pearce, and Thomas Goodwin Turner, April 4, 1833.
4-12 " Sophronia, and James A. Thornton, Nov. 19, 1837.
4-24 " Joseph H., and Catherine Barton; m. by Rev. John C. Welch, Nov.
3, 1839.
4-13 " Elizabeth, and James M. Peck, Nov. —, 1841.
4-17 " Mary Ann, and Capt. Samuel Allen, Jan. 15, 1843.
4-18 " Mrs. Eliza A., and Seranns A. Brayton, Sept. 18, 1843.
4-18 " Elizabeth, and Benjamin M. Bosworth, Dec. 28, 1843.
3-162 " Emily Mansfield, and Peter Putoam Butterfield, Joly 7, 1844.
4-20 " Jonathan, of Warren, and Sarah C. Muloy, of Bristol; m. by Rev.
Josiah P. Tustin, Nov. 21, 1844.
4-25 " Phebe P., and Esek B. Simmons, Jan. 25, 1857.
4-21 " Sarah L., and Job Miller, Oct. 1, 1846.
4-25 " Ann Jane, and Peter C. Smith, Jan. 1, 1848.
4-26 " David E., and Abby Easterbrooks; m. by Rev. Josiah P. Tustin.
March 14, 1848.
4-25 " Horace, of Daniel B., of Warren, and Elizabeth Cary, of Robert, of
Bristol; m. by Rev. Paul Townsend, May 25, 1848.
4-28 " Abby P., and Jonathan M. Bowen, May 22, 1850.
4-29 " Sylvia C., and John T. Place, Feb. 5, 1853.

M

1-92 MACUMBER Sally, and Jeremiah Child, Jan. 31, 1799.
4-20 MALOY Sarah W., and Jonathan Luther, Nov. 21, 1844.
1-67 MANCHESTER Mrs. Rebecca, and Simeon Curtis, Jan. 18, 1761.
1-90 " Jane, and John Stackford, June 12, 1791.
4-13 MANLEY Louisa, and Jeremiah Woodmancy, April 8, 1841.
3-168 MARBLE Rebecca, and Samuel Wheaton, Nov. 24, 1822.
4-17 " George R., of Warren, son of George R., of Bristol, and Caroline
A. Bennett; m. by Rev. Josiah P. Tustin, May 16, 1843.
4-28 " Tryphenia A., and Lysander W. Davis, Feb. 3, 1850.
1-63 MARTIN Hannah, and Daniel Luther, April 27, 1737.
1-62 " Abigail, and William Easterbrooks, Nov. 1, 1747.
1-63 " Ebenezer, and Mrs. Mary Bowen; m. by Rev. Solomon Townsend,
May 22, 1748.
1-69 " John, and Sarah Cole; m. by Rev. James Manning, April 18, 1765.
1-71 " Constant, of Rehoboth, and Lydia Haile, of Warren; m. by John
Kennicutt, Justice, Sept. 10, 1769.
1-82 " Ruth, and Samuel Perce, Feb. 26, 1788.
1-93 " Ruth, and Peleg Bowen, Sept. 13, 1801.
3-171 " Hannah, and Capt. Joshua Champlain, June 28, 1821.
3-165 " Charlotte D., and John Vinnicnm, Aug. 26, 1824.
4-3 " John T., of Samuel and Harriet Bowen, of Jonathan; m. by Rev.
Luther Baker, Nov. 8, 1827.
4-6 " Eliza Tyler, and William H. Driscoll, Nov. 4, 1830.
4-12 " Jeremiah, of Warren, son of John, of Barrington, and Roby E.
Hubbard, of William M.; m. by Rev. John C. Welch, July 6,
1835.
4-20 " William, and Betsey Butts; m. by Rev. John C. Welch, Oct. 22,
1835.
4-10 " Edward T., of Cincinoati, Ohio, son of Samuel, dec., and Abby
Cole, of Benjamin, dec.; m. by Rev. John C. Welch, Sept. 5,
1838.
4-13 " Samuel, of Samuel and Ruth, and Patience Salisbury; m. by Rev.
William Livesey, Feb. 13, 1842.

4-16   MARTIN Henrietta, and Henry Justin, Oct. 29, 1842.
4-17   "   Mary B., and Capt. Samuel Cole, July 9, 1843.
4-22   "   George, and Ellen E. Surgens; m. by Rev. Josiah P. Tustin, Jan.
              10, 1847.
4-30   "   Sarah, and Ezra O. Child, May 14, 1856.
1-119   MARVEL Bathsheba, and Henry Bowen, June 11, 1815.
1-65   MASON Barnard, and Mrs. Abiah Easterbrooks; m. by Ebenezer Cole, Jus-
              tice, July 22, 1756.
1-83   "   Sarah, and James Sisson, Nov. 12, 1780.
1-79   "   Elizabeth, and Jonathan Barney, March 24, 1782.
1-79   "   Marmaduke, and Elizabeth O'Kelley; m. by William Barton, Jus-
              tice, Dec. 12, 1782.
1-86   "   Patty, and Job Handy, March 6, 1794.
1-94   "   Elizabeth, and Shubael Kennicutt, Nov. 4, 1802.
1-96   "   Sally, and James Smith, Dec. 18, 1803.
1-97   "   Mary, and Samuel Butterworth, Nov. 25, 1804.
1-98   "   Mary, and Joseph Cole, Dec. 14, 1806.
1-99   "   Patience, and Church Kelley, July 9, 1807.
1-115   "   Sarah, and Simmons Cole, Feb. 10, 1811.
1-118   "   Haile, of Warren, and Elizabeth Gardiner, of Swansey; m. by Rev.
              Philip Slade, March 10, 1816.
1-114   "   Almira, and Hezekiah Gardiner, Jan. 25, 1817.
1-113   "   Content, and James Short, Jr., March 5, 1817.
3-171   "   Mary, and Jesse Baker, Oct. 27, 1821.
4-2   "   Capt. John, of Capt. Samuel, of Warren, and Zerviah Gardiner, of
              Swansey, dau. of William; m. by Rev. Benjamin Taylor, March
              18, 1827.
4-4   "   Zephaniah S., and Susan Vinnicum; m. by Rev. Isaac Stoddard,
              Dec. 18, 1828.
4-6   "   Benjamin, and Sally Vinnicum; m. by Rev. N. S. Spaulding,
              March 25, 1830.
4-9   "   Eliza Ann, and George Sisson, Jan. 13, 1833.
4-7   "   Samuel, Jr., of Samuel, of Warren, and Esther Buffington, of John,
              of Swansey; m. by Rev. Jesse Briggs, May 25, 1834.
4-24   "   Betsey and Henry Anthony, Nov. 12, 1839.
4-20   "   Ann Maria and Samuel Fisher Randall, Nov. 13, 1845.
4-30   "   Sarah Ann and Daniel Sanders, April 2, 1846.
4-26   "   Henry W. and Mary E. Gould, both of Providence; m. by Rev.
              Josiah P. Tustin, May 5, 1848.
4-26   "   William F., of Fall River, son of Edward, dec., and Maria N.
              Gardiner, of Warren, dau. of Joseph; m. by Rev. Paul Town-
              send, Oct. 11, 1848.
3-164   MATHEWSON Samuel J., of Warren, son of Daniel and Sally Kelley, of
              Barrington, dau. of Duncan; m. by Rev. Flavel Shurtleff, May
              23, 1821.
4-19   MAURAN Mary Tyler, and John Calvin Stockbridge, Nov. 14, 1844.
1-79   MAXWELL James, and Rebecca Nooning; m. by Rev. Charles Thompson,
              Oct. 16, 1774.
1-78   "   Level, and Mrs. Abigail Hill; m. by Rev. Charles Thompson, May
              6, 1781.
1-87   "   James, and Content Brayton; m. by Stephen Bullock, Justice, March
              28, 1793.
1-85   "   Nabby, and Caleb Eddy, Dec. 12, 1793.
1-98   "   Hannah, and James Driscoll, June 11, 1804.
1-98   "   William, of Level, and Abby B. Alger, of Preserved; m. by Elder
              Luther Baker, Oct. 21, 1806.
1-101   "   Patty, and Samuel Randall, Aug. 13, 1809.
1-101   "   Rebecca, and William Phillips, April 11, 1810.
1-101   "   Level, of Squire, of Warren, and Henrietta Smith, of Greenwich, R.
              I.; m. by Elder Luther Baker, Nov. 1, 1810.
1-112   "   Content B., and Nathan M. Wheaton, Nov. 25, 1813.
1-119   "   Emeline M., and George Sanders, Aug. 24, 1820.
3-171   "   Patience Greene, and Samuel Cole, Aug. 30, 1821.
4-1, 2 "   Mary, and Haile Collins, Oct. 28, 1824.
4-3   "   Joanna, and Lieut. Lewis E. Simonds, Nov. 4, 1827.

4-18   McMILLION Robert, of Smithfield, and Delina C. Burt, of Alvan, of Warren; m. by Rev. Josiah P. Tustin, Nov. 30, 1848.

1-64   MEDBURY Ebenezer, and Mary Ide; m. by Matthew Allen, Justice, May 12, 1751.

1-65   "   Bethiah, and William Camp, Jan. 21, 1755.

1-67   "   Sarah, and James Dennis, April 12, 1761.

1-68   MILLER Barnard, and Mrs. Elizabeth Hicks, both of Swansey; m. by Benjamin Herrendon, Justice, March 18, 1746.

1-62   "   Charity, and William Arnold, Dec. 18, 1747.

1-63   "   Samuel, of Warren, and Mrs. Mary Reynolds, of Bristol; m. by Rev. Solomon Townsend, March 31, 1749.

1-66   "   Benjamin, Jr., and Mrs. Hope Cole; m. by Benjamin Miller, Justice, Jan. 10, 1751.

1-66   "   Mrs. Patience, and James Bowen, March 3, 1755.

1-68   "   Barnard, and Mrs. Olive Bowen; m. by Benjamin Miller, Justice, Aug. 10, 1755.

1-67   "   Mrs. Betsey, and Shubael Burr, Nov. 8, 1759.

1-70   "   Ruth, and Peleg Rogers, Sept. 22, 1760.

1-67   "   James, and Mrs. Anne Haile; m. by John Kennicutt, Justice, Dec. 3, 1761.

1-74   "   Samuel, of Warren, and Elizabeth Peirce, of Portsmouth; m. by John Almy, Assistant, Oct. 13, 1763.

1-68   "   Nathan, and Mrs. Rebecca Barton; m. by Rev. Solomon Townsend, Jan. 8, 1764.

1-69, 70   "   William, and Elizabeth Hill; m. by Rev. James Manning, June 27, 1765.

1-70   "   William Turner, and Lydia Cockrane; m. by Rev. James Manning, Nov. 2, 1766.

1-70   "   Patience, and Cromwell Child, Nov. 9, 1766.

1-71   "   Molly, and Joseph Smith, May 18, 1769.

1-71   "   Mary, and John Cowen, Aug. 6, 1769.

1-72   "   Patience, and William Williams, Feb. 25, 1770.

1-75   "   Elizabeth, and Edward Wing, Aug. 7, 1774.

1-83   "   Ruth, and Abial Easterbrooks, Nov. 3, 1774.

1-80   "   Elizabeth, and William Barton, April 25, 1779.

1-81   "   Abigail, and Charles Wheaton, Sept. 26, 1784.

1-87   "   Elizabeth, and Isaac Barrows, May 17, 1787.

1-82   "   Molly, and John T. Child, Dec. 9, 1787.

1-86   "   Olive, and Caleb Carr, June 26, 1794.

1-90   "   Barnard, and Lydia Ingraham; m. by Elder Luther Baker, Dec. 22, 1796.

1-113   "   William T., of Nathan, and Lydia Cockran, of Simeon S.; m. by Rev. Silas Hall, May 18, 1817.

4-8   "   Eliza, and Benjamin M. Bosworth, March 6, 1835.

4-21   "   Job, and Sarah L. Luther; m. at New York, by Rev. Thomas Lyell, Oct. 1, 1846.

4-27   "   James, and Elizabeth H. Cole; m. by Rev. R. W. Allen, May 27, 1849.

1-100   MOREY Ralph, of Attleboro, and Lydia Whitaker, of Warren; m. by Elder Luther Baker, April 30, 1808.

4-11   MOORE Thomas Paine, of Warren, son of Thomas, of Chester, Mass., and Abby Wheaton, of Nathan M., of Warren; m. by Rev. George W. Hathaway, Nov. 7, 1831.

4-27   MORSE Chancey Almore, of Newark, N. J., and Ann Eliza Wright, of Warren; m. by Rev. R. W. Allen, May 6, 1849.

4-28   MULCHAHEY Charles M., and Patience R. Smith; m. by Rev. R. A. Fyfe, May 19, 1850.

1-66   MUNROE Lydia, and William Sheldon, Nov. 23, 1750.

1-66   "   Mrs. Elizabeth, and Jonathan Bowen, Nov. 7, 1759.

1-68   "   Mrs. Prescilla, and Richard Dring, Aug. 2, 1764.

1-77   "   John Linzey Munroe, and Mary Allen, both of Bristol; m. by Rev. Charles Thompson, April 21, 1777.

1-91   "   Elizabeth, and Barnabee Luther, July 19, 1798.

1-94   MUNROE Jonathan, of Hector, and Sally Easterbrooks, of Martin; m. by Rev. John Hill, Nov. 6, 1798.

1-93   "   Palmer, of Warren, son of Stephen, and Anna Whitaker, dau. of Barnabee Luther, of Warren; m. by Rev. John Hill, May 18, 1800.

1-117   "   Stephen, of Swansey, and Sybel Peirce, of Warren; m. by Joseph Adams, Justice, July —, 1813.

1-119   "   George, of Warren, son of James, of Bristol, and Mary Butts, of Peleg, of Warren; m. by Rev. Jordan Rexford, Jan. 22, 1818.

3-172   "   Sarah Haile, and James B. Trott, Aug. 2, 1820.

4-10   "   Maria B., and George Williams, Sept. 2, 1838.

4-22   "   Maria, and William Cole, May 23, 1847.

4-26   "   Nancy, and Edwin Hiscox, Oct. 2, 1848.

N

1-73   NASH Samuel, Jr., of Abington, Mass., and Mrs. Frances Easterbrooks, of Warren; m. by Rev. Solomon Townsend, Dec. 13, 1770.

1-88   NEMO Henry, of Virginia, and Roby Turner, of Warren; m. by Elder Luther Baker, Oct. 12, 1794.

2-110   NEWHALL Mary Ann, and John K. Child, Aug. 18, 1819.

3-167   "   Hetty, and John Watson, Sept. 25, 1822.

4-27   "   Eliza A., and Andrew A. Lewis, June 4, 1849.

1-98   NEWMAN Betsey, and James Kelley, Feb. 16, 1806.

1-79   NOONING Rebecca, and James Maxwell, Oct. 16, 1774.

O

1-79   O'KELLEY Elizabeth, and Marmaduke Mason, Dec. 12, 1782.

1-65   ORMSBEE Mrs. Phebe, and Jonathan Horton, Jr., Dec. 5, 1754.

1-66   "   Ezra, and Mrs. Elizabeth Cole; m. by Benjamin Miller, Justice, Jan. 30, 1755.

1-67   "   Joseph, of Warren, and Mrs. Hannah Jolls, of Bristol; m. by John Kennicutt, Justice, July 27, 1760.

1-67   "   Joshua, and Mrs. Rachel Chase; m. by Ebenezer Cole, Justice, Nov. 13, 1760.

1-68   "   John, of Warren, and Mrs. Sarah Jolls, of Bristol; m. by John Kennicutt, Justice, March 14, 1762.

1-79   "   Joshua, and Keziah Cranston; m. by William Barton, Justice, April 10, 1783.

1-81   "   Betsey, and William Child, 2d, Oct. 7, 1784.

1-83   "   Isaac, and Patience Chase; m. by Rev. John Pitman, Feb. 8, 1789.

1-89   "   Joshua, and Polly Burr; m. by Elder Luther Baker, June 4, 1795.

1-73   OWEN William, and Elizabeth Burden; m. by William T. Miller, Justice, March 3, 1771.

P

3-164   PACKARD Royal, of Providence, and Alvira Bowen, of Johnston; m. by Rev. Jordan Rexford, Nov. 27, 1825.

1-63   PAINE Nathaniel, of Rehoboth, and Mrs. Mary Heath, of Warren; m. by Rev. Solomon Townsend, Feb. 9, 1748-9.

1-82   "   Abigail, and William Child, Jan. 20, 1788.

1-97   PARKER Benjamin, of William, and Abigail Champlain, of Thomas; m. by Elder Luther Baker, July 10, 1805.

1-97   "   Clarke, of William, and Nancy Easterbrooks, of William; m. by Elder Luther Baker, Oct. 20, 1805.

3-170   "   Susan, and John Battlot, Aug. 7, 1820 (?).

4-19   "   William, of Benjamin, of Warren, and Judith R. Bowen, of James, of Barrington; m. by Rev. John C. Welch, Sept. 25, 1843.

4-19   "   Sarah, and Noah M. Brown, March 21, 1844.

4-16 PARRINGTON Henry A., of New Bedford, and Sarah H. Frink, of Capt. Rufus, of Warren; m. by Rev. Josiah P. Tustin, Oct. 4, 1842.
3-166 PARSONS Abraham, of Jackson, N. Y., and Betsey Cole, of Warren; m. by Rev. John C. Welch, Feb. 8, 1824.
1-92 PEARCE Prescilla, and James Goff, June 4, 1780.
1-79 " Susannah, and Caleb Turner, Nov. 12, 1783.
1-81 " John, and Patience Arnold; m. by William Barton, Justice, Nov. 27, 1785.
1-82 " Samuel, and Ruth Martin; m. by James Miller, Justice, Feb. 26, 1788.
1-92 " Abigail, and Isaac Cole, Feb. 24, 1792.
1-92 " John, and Mary Luther; m. by Elder Luther Baker, Dec. 17, 1734.
1-119 " Noah, of Noah, of Rehoboth, and Betsey Bessayude, of Lewis, of Warren; m. by Elder Luther Baker, April 4, 1801.
1-118 " Polly, and Job Luther, Oct. 21, 1816.
2-110 " Phebe, and Benjamin C. Short, April 16, 1820.
4-3 " Eliza, and Luther Mason Burden, June 4, 1820.
4-9 " John, of John and Mary Theresa Haile, of James; m. by Rev. Jordan Rexford, Oct. 2, 1825.
4-8 " Samuel, of John and Elizabeth H. Chase, of Allen, dec.; m. by Rev. George W. Hathaway, Oct. 27, 1833.
1-78 PEARS Priscilla, and James Goff, June 22, 1780.
4-19 PECKHAM Elisha N., of Newport, and Sarah L. Johnson, of Somerset, Mass.; m. by Rev. Josiah P. Tustin, July 1, 1844.
1-63 PECK Mrs. Margaret, and James Short, April 18, 1748.
1-63 " Simeon, and Prescilla West; m. by Rev. Solomon Townsend, Nov. 24, 1748.
1-71 " Solomon, Jr., and Abigail Barney; m. by Rev. Solomon Townsend, Dec. 8, 1763.
1-73 " Mrs. Rebecca, and Caleb Fuller, Sept. 10, 1772.
1-95 " Judeth, and James Goff, Oct. 25, 1801.
1-110 " Temperance, and William Thompson, May 15, 1819.
3-168 " Col. Seth, and Mrs. Mary Chase; m. at Bristol, by Rev. Henry Wight, Dec. 29, 1822.
4-13 " James M., of Rehoboth, and Elizabeth Luther, of Warren; m. by Rev. William Livesey, Nov. —, 1841.
4-30 " Martha G., and William Baker, May 26, 1853.
1-74 PEIRCE Elizabeth, and Samuel Miller, Oct. 13, 1763.
1-117 " Sybel, and Stephen Munroe, July —, 1813.
1-73 PERCE Sarah, and Edward Cole, Aug. 20, 1771.
1-83 " Phebe, and Isaac Cole, Nov. 12, 1780.
4-20 PERKINS William E., of Providence, and Ann Maria Coleman, of Warren; m. by Rev. Josiah P. Tustin, Nov. 11, 1844.
4-27 PETTERSON John B., and Mrs. Sarah T. Simmons, of Bristol; m. by Rev. R. W. Allen, Oct. 18, 1849.
1-64 PETTY Joseph, of Dartmouth, and Alice Butterworth, of Warren; m. by John Kennicutt, Justice, Dec. 14, 1752.
1-101 PETTIS Betsey, and James Child, Nov. 4, 1810.
1-63 " Phebe, and Cuffee, Dec. 17, 1747.
1-87 PHILLIPS Nathaniel, and Robe Waterman; m. at Warwick, by Elder Charles Holden, Feb. 7, 1779.
1-89 " Polly, and Benedick Arnold, Nov. 17, 1793.
1-101 " William, of Nathaniel and Rebecca Maxwell, of James; m. by Elder Luther Baker, April 11, 1810.
1-115 " John Folson, of Nathaniel, and Martha Cole, of Capt. Ebenezer; m. by Elder Luther Baker, May 26, 1811.
4-6 " Hannah P., and John B. Thompson, July 4, 1830.
4-9 " Rebecca M., and George Barton, Aug. 14, 1834.
1-62 PHINNEY, Hannah, and Richard Haile, June 21, 1747.
1-69 " Elisha, and Jemima Threodkill; m. by Rev. Solomon Townsend, May 5, 1763.
1-74 " Elizabeth, and Haile Barton, Dec. 19, 1773.
1-88 " Benjamin, and Betsey Varce; m. by William T. Miller, Justice, Aug. 31, 1794.

1-91   PHINNEY Daniel, and Betsey Comer; m. by Eld. Luther Baker, June 14, 1798.

1-91   "   John, and Avis Bowen; m. by Eld. Luther Baker, July 8, 1798.

1-99   "   Elisha G., of Elisha and Lydia Barton, of David; m. by Rev. John B. Gibson, Dec. 14, 1806.

1-110   "   Emma, and Thomas E. Cole, Aug. 23, 1818.

3-166   "   Eliza Kennicutt, and Capt. William Champlain, Sept. 15, 1823.

4-27   "   Mary J., and John Q. Adams, June 7, 1849.

1-111   PLACE Samuel, and Sally Butterworth; m. by Daniel Bradford, Jr., Justice, Oct. 11, 1812.

4-19   "   Capt. Samuel, and Mary Sherman; m. by Rev. C. S. Macreading, Aug. 14, 1844.

4-29   "   John T., and Sylvia C. Luther; m. by Rev. Moses Howe, Feb. 5, 1853.

1-64   POLLARD Mrs. Isabel, and John Butterworth, April 15, 1750.

4-24, 12 PRICE Eliza A., and George W. Scott, Dec. 12, or 21, 1839.

3-163   "   Susan and Timothy Coghing, Dec. 10, 1850.

Q R

1-100   RANDALL Philip, of Samuel and Abigail Alger, dau. of Joseph Kelley; m. by Daniel Bradford, Jr., Justice, June 29, 1809.

1-101   "   Samuel, of Joseph, of Sharon, Mass., and Patty Maxwell, of James, of Warren; m. by Eld. Luther Baker, Aug. 13, 1809.

4-7   "   Charles, of Warren, son of John, of Sharon, Mass., and Lydia Brown Reed of Capt. Leonard; m. by Rev. John C. Welch, May 8, 1831.

4-10   "   Mary, and James M. Barton, March 31, 1836.

4-8   "   Martha M., and Dr. Otis Bullock, Aug. 17, 1836.

4-11   "   George Maxwell of Fall River, son of Samuel, of Warren, and Elizabeth Hoard, of Lewis, of Warren; m. by Rev. George W. Hathaway, May 28, 1839.

4-20   "   Samuel Fisher, of Samuel and Ann Maria Mason, of Rhodick, dec.; m. by Rev. George W. Hathaway, Nov. 13, 1845.

4-25   "   Philip, of Providence; son of Philip, dec., and Olive Ingraham, of Warren, dau. of John; m. by Rev. Paul Townsend, Jan. 2, 1848.

4-28   "   Ranson, of Spencer, Mass., son of Ranson and Priscilla, and Ann M. Davis, of Philip, of Somerset; m. by Rev. R. A. Fyfe, Feb. 3, 1850.

1-71   RAWSON Ann, and Dennis Smith, Feb. 15, 1770.

4-11   "   Joseph, of Barzillai, and Caroline Johannot, of Oliver; m. by Rev. Shirley W. Wilson, April 19, 1839.

1-65   REED Stephen, and Abigail Sallsbury; m. by John Kennicutt, Justice, June 14, 1756.

1-90   "   James, and Rebecca Burton; m. by Eld. Job Burden, Oct. 27, 1796.

1-92   "   Rebecca, and Benjamin Brayton, June 20, 1799.

3-166   "   Barton, and Betsey Sinders; m. by William Barton, Justice, Aug. 26, 1820.

4-7   "   Lydia Brown, and Charles Randall, May 8, 1831.

4-19   "   Bradford, of Warren, and Julia A. Rounds; m. by Rev. C. S. Macreading, Oct. 7, 1844.

4-20   REMINGTON Henrietta Eliza, and Simeon Talbot, Jr., Dec. 18, 1844.

1-63   REYNOLDS Mrs. Mary, and Samuel Miller, March 31, 1748.

1-69   "   Peter, and Patience Cole; m. by Rev. James Manning, Jan. 3, 1765.

1-95   REX George, of George and Patience Child, of Jeremiah; m. by Eld. Luther Baker, Oct. 29, 1802.

1-89   RICHARDS Peter, and Susannah Luther; m. by William T. Miller, Justice, July 12, 1779.

1-100   "   Luther, of Peter, and Sally Kennicutt, of Hezekiah; m. by James Sisson, Justice, April 20, 1809.

4-25   "   Egbert J., of Spencer, dec., and Sarah M. Fisher, of Ellis, dec., both of Attleboro; m. by Rev. Paul Townsend, May 16, 1848.

1-67   RICHMOND John Roger, of Rehoboth, and Mrs. Hannah Kennicutt, of Warren; m. by Rev. John Usher, Dec. 10, 1761.

4-11   "   Charles, Jr., of New York city, and Ruth Miller Williams, of Warren; m. by Rev. John C. Welch, Dec. 18, 1837.

4-24   RIEGEWAY James, and Sarah Welch, both of Boston; m. by Rev. John C. Welch, Nov. 19, 1839.

1-70   ROGERS Peleg, and Ruth Miller, Sept. 22, 1760.

1-85   "   Dinah, and David Easterbrooks, Sept. 1, 1791.

1-88   "   Patience, and Peter Carpenter, Oct. 11, 1794.

1-72   ROUNDS Oliver, and Anna Salisbury; m. by Rev. James Manning, April 12, 1770.

1-92   "   Patience, and Rufus Hunter, Oct. 19, 1800.

1-96   "   Oliver, of Oliver, of Warren, and Jerusha Drowne, of Jonathan, of Barrington; m. by Elder Luther Baker, Dec. 23, 1804.

1-98   "   Jabez, of Oliver and Eliza Hudson, of Rueben; m. by Rev. John B. Gibson, April 20, 1806.

4-18   "   Simeon, of Taunton, and Esther T. Burke, of Warren; m. by Rev. Josiah P. Tustin, Feb. 18, 1844.

4-19   "   Julia A., and Bradford Reed, Oct. 7, 1844.

1-69   ROWELL Judith, and Samuel Fisk, March 6, 1764.

S

1-62   SALISBURY John and Rebecca Goff; m. by Benjamin Miller, Justice, Nov. 8, 1747.

1-66   "   Mrs. Sarah, and Calvin Luther, Jan. 11, 1753.

1-64   "   Caleb and Elizabeth Luther; m. by John Kennicutt, Justice, Feb. 10, 1754.

1-65   "   Abigail and Stephen Reed, June 14, 1756.

1-67   "   Mrs. Bethiah, and Samuel Hicks, Feb. 3, 1757.

1-68   "   Jonathan, and Mrs. Mary Child; m. by Rev. Solomon Townsend, May 11, 1758.

1-67   "   Mrs. Abigail, and George Salisbury, March 12, 1761.

1-67   "   George, and Mrs. Abigail Salisbury; m. by John Kennicutt, Justice, March 12, 1761.

1-67   "   Oliver, and Mrs. Lydia Bowen; m. by John Wheaton, Justice, Feb. 7, 1762.

1-70   "   Phebe, and John Harding, Sept. 1, 1765.

1-72   "   Rebecca, and Peleg Easterbrooks, March 6, 1770.

1-72   "   Anne, and Oliver Rounds, April 12, 1770.

1-72   "   Barnard, and Prudence Child; m. by Rev. James Manning, Oct. 21, 1770.

1-74   "   Mrs. Robe, and Jeremiah Jolls, Dec. 30, 1772.

1-74   "   William, and Joice Eddy; m. by Rev. Charles Thompson, March 20, 1774.

1-75   "   James, and Susannah Thomas; m. by Rev. Charles Thompson, Sept. 18, 1774.

1-78   "   Mrs. Anne, and James Shot, Nov. 1, 1778.

1-82   "   Luther, and Abigail Cole; m. by Rev. Solomon Townsend, Feb. 11, 1781.

1-83   "   Hannah, and Royal Easterbrooks, Feb. 10, 1789.

1-84   "   Jonathan, and Elizabeth Thurber; m. by William Barton, Justice, Dec. 29, 1790.

1-84   "   Caleb, and Patience Luther; m. by Elder Nathaniel Cole, April 10, 1791.

1-88   "   Jemima, and James Goff, Aug. 17, 1794.

1-91   "   Simeon, and Priscilla Child; m. by Elder Luther Baker, Aug. 26, 1798.

1-93   "   Polly, and Ebenezer Cole, Dec. 21, 1800.

1-99   "   Martin, of Luther and Elizabeth Cole, of Benjamin; m. by Elder Luther Baker, Aug. 24, 1806.

1-118   "   Sally, and Luther Cole, Sept. 8, 1816.

4-2   "   Mary, and Jonathan Bosworth, March 22, 1827.

4-4   SALISBURY Charles H., of Daniel, and Rebecca Sisson, of Essex; m. by Rev. Jordan Rexford, Sept. 27, 1827.
4-4   "   Priscilla Child, and John G. Bowen, Nov. 22, 1827.
4-7   "   Martin L., of Martin and Elizabeth, of Warren, and Susan A. Cottrell of Jesse and Mary, of North Kingstown; m. at South Kingstown, by Elder William Northup, Oct. 9, 1831.
4-11 "   Abby F., and Henry Burtch, Aug. 12, 1838.
4-13 "   John, of John and Betsey, and Abby W. Foster, of Benjamin and Hannah; m. by Rev. William Livesey, Oct. 17, 1841.
4-13 "   Patience, and Samuel Martin, Feb. 13, 1842.
4-19 "   Martha, and George T. Dexter, Oct. 31, 1844.
1-72 SANDERS Jacob, and Elizabeth Whiting; m. by John Kennicutt, Justice, Nov. 15, 1770.
1-87 "   David, and Nancy Davis, June 8, 1788.
1-86 "   Hannah, and Allen Hoar, March 14, 1790.
1-86 "   Nathaniel, and Sally Bowen; m. by Elder Luther Baker, June 8, 1794.
1-88 "   George, and Betsey, Bowen; m. by Elder Luther Baker, Nov. 2, 1794.
1-93 "   Elizabeth, and Henry Hicks, Dec. 21, 1800.
1-93 "   Daniel, of Jacob, and Polly Barton, of William; m. by Elder Luther Baker, Sept. 20, 1801.
1-119 "   George, of Philadelphia, Pa., son of Capt. George, dec., of Warren, and Emeline M. Maxwell, of James, of Warren; m. by Rev. Luther Baker, Aug. 24, 1820.
3-166 "   Betsey, and Barton Reed, Aug. 26, 1820.
4-1, 9 " Sally J., and Turner Carr, May 31, 1822.
4-17 "   Emeline, and Haile Collins, Sept. 8, 1830.
4-11 "   Edward, and Maria Davol; m. by Rev. John C. Welch, Oct. 1, 1837.
4-16 "   Elizabeth Hicks. and Otis Bullock, Oct. 5, 1842.
4-24 "   Henry, of Warren, and Martha V. Viall, of Seekonk; m. by Rev. John C. Welch, Feb. 7, 1843.
4-19 "   Charles Whitefield, and Minerva Olivia Bucklin; m. by Rev. Josiah P. Tustin, Dec. 15, 1844.
4-20 "   Daniel, of Daniel, and Sarah Ann Mason, of Roderick; m. by Rev. George W. Hathaway, April 2, 1846.
4-28 "   Ruth B., and Daniel K. Bowen, Jan. 28, 1850.
4-12, 24 SCOTT George W., of Scarborough, Eng., and Eliza A. Price, of Warren; m. by Rev. John C. Welch, Dec. 12, or 21, 1839.
4-29 SEYMOUR Anna G., and Marcus Wilmarth, July 14, 1850.
1-66 SHELDON William, and Lydia Munroe; m. by Benjamin Miller, Justice, Nov. 23, 1750.
1-75 "   Lydia, and James Bushee, Feb. 1, 1768.
1-64 SHERMAN Roby, and John Kennicutt, Jr., May 16, 1751.
1-78 "   Christopher, and Mrs. Grizzell Sherman; m. by William Barton, Justice, Feb. 18, 1779.
1-78 "   Mrs. Grizzell, and Christopher Sherman, Feb. 18, 1779.
1-80 "   Caleb, and Mary Sherman, both of Swansey; m. by William Burton, Justice, Oct. 7, 1784.
1-80 "   Mary, and Caleb Sherman, Oct. 7, 1784.
1-114 "   Levi, of Levi and Hope S. Hoar, of Allen; m. by Rev. Jordan Rexford, Sept. 7, 1817.
4-19 "   Maria, and James Follensbee, Aug. 12, 1844.
4-19 "   Mary, and Capt. Samuel Place, Aug. 14, 1844.
4-18 "   Hannah, and Caleb Carr, Jr., Sept. 29, 1844.
1-62 SHORT Mrs. Joanna, and Jabez Wood, April 7, 1748.
1-63 "   James, of Warren, and Mrs. Margaret Peck, of Rehoboth; m. by Rev. Solomon Townsend, April 18, 1748.
1-78 "   James, and Mrs. Anne Salisbury; m. by Rev. Charles Thompson, Nov. 1, 1778.
1-113 "   James, Jr., of James, of Warren, and Content Mason, of Caleb, of Swansey; m. by Rev. Silas Hall, March 5, 1817.
2-110 "   Benjamin C., of James, of Warren, and Phebe Pearce, of Somerset, dau. of David, of Rehoboth; m. by Rev. Jordan Rexford, April 16, 1820.

3-170 SHORT Philip, of James, and Sarah Hicks, of Jonathan; m. by **Rev.**
        Jordan Rexford, Oct. 8, 1821.
4-9   "   Mrs. Phebe, and Andrew Cole, Nov. 10, 1836.
4-24   "   Jndith Eliza, and Henry Van Doorn, Dec. 17, 1839.
3-17 SHURTLEFF Rev. Fluvel, and Eliza Cole; m. by Rev. **David** Benedick,
        Ang. 1. 1821.
4-3 SIMONDS Lient. Lewis E., U. S. N., and Joanna Maxwell. of James; m.
        by Eld. Luther Baker, Nov. 4, 1827.
1-65 SIMONS Mrs. Elizabeth, and Amos Bowen, March 7, 1754.
1-115 SIMMONS Deborah, and James Goff, May 4, 1806.
4-23   "   Polly, and Allen Cobb, Feb. 14, 1841.
4-25   "   Esek B., and Phebe P. Luther, of William; m. by **Rev.** Josiah
        P. Tustin, Jan. 24, 1847.
4-27   "   Mrs. Sarah T. and John B. Petterson, Oct. 18, 1849.
1-68 SISSON, Mrs. Sarah, and Elisha Chase, March 20, 1760.
1-70   "   Abigail, and Reuben Hudson, Nov. 1, 1767.
1-83   "   James, and Sarah Mason; m. by Rev. Solomon Townsend, Nov. 12,
        1780.
1-95   "   Henry, of Gideon and Hannah Collins, of Charles; m. by Elder Ln-
        ther Baker, Aug. 31, 1803.
1-101   "   Halle Mason, of Warren and Deborah Cooke Luther, of Somerset;
        m. by Elder Philip Slade, Jan. 25, 1807.
3-165   "   Susan, and George Wheaton, Jan. 10, 1825.
4-4   "   Rebecca, and Charles H. Salisbury, Sept. 27, 1827.
4-9   "   George, of James and Eliza Ann Mason, of Benajah; m. by Rev.
        George W. Hathaway, Jan. 13, 1833.
4-25   "   Elizabeth B. and Samuel Wheaton, Sept. 12, 1836.
4-20   "   Almira R., and George Stanley, June 27, 1845.
4-20   "   Mary V., and Robert Cole. Aug. 8, 1845.
4-29   "   Charles S., and Maria Kelley; m. at Providence by Rev. Robert
        M. Hatfield, June 29, 1851.
4-16 SLADE Sarah, and Benjamin Hathaway Chase, June 2, 1842.
1-63 SMITH Mrs. Jerusha, and John Bullock, March 16, 1748-9.
1-69   "   Sarah, and Elkanah Humphrey, March 28, 1765.
1-71   "   Joseph, of Warren, son of Benjamin, of Bristol, and Molly Miller,
        of Barnard, of Warren; m. by Rev. John Bnrt, May 18, 1769.
1-71   "   Dennis, of Freetown, and Ann Rawson, of Warren; m. by Rev.
        James Manning, Feb. 15, 1770.
1-85   "   Hannah, and Jesse Baker, July 17, 1791.
1-90   "   James, and Sarah Brown; m. by Rev. Solomon Townsend, at Bar-
        rington, Nov. 8, 1795.
1-91   "   Joseph, and Hannah Wheaton; m. by Eld. Luther Baker, Aug. 26,
        1798.
1-96   "   James, of Joseph, and Sally Mason, of Joseph; m. by Eld. Lnther
        Baker, Dec. 18, 1803.
1-101   "   Mary, and Nathaniel M. Wheaton, Dec. 24, 1809.
1-101   "   Henrietta, and Level Maxwell, Nov. 1, 1810.
1-115   "   Sally, and James Cole, Nov. 11, 1811.
1-116   "   Job, of Joseph, of Warren and Sally T. Bliss, of Jesse, of Reho-
        both; m. by Eld. Luther Baker, Oct. 4, 1813.
1-117   "   Eliza, and Thomas Williams, May 15, 1814.
3-172   "   Temperance, and Capt. William Carr, Jr., Sept. 3, 1820.
3-165   "   Susan DeWolf, and Capt. Abraham Greene, Feb. 12, 1821.
4-6   "   Sarah, and William B. Lawton, March 23, 1830.
4-9   "   Hannah, and Samuel Barton, Nov. 2, 1834.
4-23   "   Charlotte Townsend, and James Smith, Nov. 16, 1834.
4-23   "   James, of James, and Charlotte Townsend Smith, Nov. 16, 1834.
4-16   "   Elizabeth, and James Davis Ingrabam, Sept. 25, 1842.
4-20   "   Stephen, of Providence, and Sarah Bean, of Warren; m. by **Rev.**
        Josiah P. Tustin, Sept. 22, 1844.
4-23   "   James, Jr., of Warren, and Sarah Burgess, of Providence; m. by
        Rev. Joseph B. Dayman, Aug. 24, 1845.
4-22   "   Joseph Mason, of James and Margaret Rhodes Collins, of William; m.
        by Rev. George W. Hathaway, Dec. 24, 1845.
4-24   "   Jane Young, and John Frieze, July 28, 1846.

4-25   SMITH Peter C., and Ann Jane Luther, of Joseph; m. by Rev. Josiah T.
           Tustin, Jan. 1, 1848.
4-29   "   S. T., and Edward Williams, June 25, 1848.
4-28   "   Patience R., and Charles M. Mulchahey, May 19, 1850.
1-89   SNELL Hannah, and James Champlain, May 24, 1795.
1-90   "   William and Anstis Stackford; m. by Eld. Luther Baker, Oct. 25,
           1797.
1-93   "   Abigail, and Gardiner Willard, Oct. 26, 1800.
1-101   "   Seth, of Seth and Rebecca Barton, of William, June 27, 1809.
4-6   "   Mary Carr, and Ambrose Hicks, June 14, 1832.
4-30   SPARKS Ann Maria, and Charles Hilling, July 29, 1849.
4-20   SPENCER Mary J., and John K. Barney, Sept. 29, 1839.
3-168 STANLEY Mary, and Philip Drowne, Jan. 24, 1822.
4-20   "   George, of Viall, dec., of Barrington, and Almira R. Sisson, of
           Thomas, of Warren; m. by Rev. John C. Welch, June 27, 1845.
4-21   "   Viall, and Hannah B. Bowen; m. by Rev. Josiah P. Tustin, Nov.
           2, 1845.
1-91   STEAVENS Sally, and John Brown, Oct. 28, 1798.
1-79   STEPHENS John, and Tabitha Vosce; m. by William Barton, Justice,
           Dec. 14, 1783.
4-19   STOCKBRIDGE John Calvin, of Waterville, Me., and Mary Tyler Mauran
           of Suchet, of Warren; m. by Rev. George W. Hathaway, Nov.
           14, 1844.
1-90   STOCKFORD John, and Jane Manchester; m. at Middletown, by Elder
           William Bliss, June 12, 1791.
1-90   "   Anstis, and William Snell, Oct. 25, 1797.
4-22   SURGENS Ellen E., and George Martin, Jan. 10, 1847.
4-27   "   Sally S., and Nathan Goff, Jr., Nov. 20, 1849.

T

4-3   TABER Peter, of Barrington, son of Peter, and Mrs. Polly Grant, dau.
           of Jonah Viall; m. by Rev. Isaac Stoddard, July 29, 1827.
1-114 TALBOT Zephaniah, of Warren, son of Zephaniah, dec., of Dighton, and
           Margaret Haile, of Comer, of Warren; m. by Rev. Jordan Rex-
           ford, (also 3-166), April 26, 1818.
4-20   "   Simeon, Jr., and Henrietta Eliza Remington, of Samuel; m. by
           Rev. Josiah P. Tustin, Dec. 18, 1844.
3-171 TALLMAN Mary, and William Brayton, June 6, 1821.
4-23   TANNER Phebe Almira, and Hon. Levi Haile, Feb. 4, 1839.
1-87   TAYLOR Betsey, and Jonathan Bowen, Oct. 7, 1787.
1-71   THOMAS Ruth, and William Barton, Jan. 10, 1768.
1-71   "   Mary, and Edward Kelley, Dec. 2, 1769.
1-75   "   Sarah, and Isaac Gorham, Sept. 4, 1774.
1-75   "   Susannah, and James Salisbury, Sept. 18, 1774.
1-81   "   Hannah, and Nathan Carpenter, March 10, 1780.
3-171 THOMPKINS Cornelius S., of Pawtucket, son of John, of Little Compton,
           and Christiana Cole of Warren, dau. of James, of Barnard, Vt.;
           m. by Rev. Jordan Rexford, June 17, 1821.
1-73   THOMPSON Charles, and Mrs. Sarah Child; m. by Rev. Solomon Townsend,
           Nov. 26, 1770.
1-118   "   Peggy, and Elder Luther Baker, Oct. 11, 1795.
2-112   "   Sarah Miller, and Charles Thompson Longhead, April 9, 1809.
1-110   "   William, of Warren, son of Rev. Charles, of Charlton, Mass., and
           Temperance Peck, of Josiah, of Seekonk; m. at Providence by
           Elder Luther Baker, May 15, 1819.
4-6   "   John B., of Dr. William, dec., and Hannah P. Phillips, of Wil-
           liam, dec.; m. by Eld. Luther Baker, July 4, 1830.
4-12   THORNTON James A., and Sophronia Luther; m. by Rev. Isaac Bonney,
           Nov. 19, 1837.
1-69   THREADKILL Jemima, and Elisha Phinney, May 5, 1763.
1-62   THURBER Benjamin, and Elizabeth Hallett; m. by Samuel Miller, Jus-
           tice, Nov. 1, 1747.

1-69	THURBER John, Jr., and Ruth Cole; m. by Rev. Solomon Townsend, March 2, 1763.
1-70	" Edward, of Swansey, and Elizabeth Easterbrooks, of Warren; m. by Rev. James Manning, Aug. 18, 1768.
1-87	" Prudence, and John Kelley, Oct. 11, 1789.
1-84	" Elizabeth, and Jonathan Salisbury, Dec. 29, 1790.
1-90	" James, and Olive Bowen; m. by Elder Luther Baker, Dec. 15, 1796.
1-96	" Nancy, and Varnum Child, May 24, 1804.
1-100	" Lucinda, and William Child, May 7, 1806.
1-116	" Nancy B., and Thomas C. Child, Jan. 12, 1812.
1-114	" John, of Bristol, and Hattie Burden, of Warren; m. by Joseph Adams, Justice, May 5, 1818.
3-168	" John, Jr., of Warren, son of John, and Hopestill Bosworth, of Warren, dau. of Joseph, of Rehoboth; m. by Rev. Jordan Rexford, June 22, 1823.
4-14	" Abby, and Moses L. Tillson, June 5, 1842.
4-30	" Collins, and Maria Vickery; m. by Rev. Robert M. Hatfield, Oct. 27, 1846.
4-26	" John Q., of George T., dec., and Amina Capen, of James; m. by Rev. Paul Townsend, Oct. 5, 1848.
1-65	THURSTON Peleg, of Freetown, and Mrs. Amey Barton, of Warren; m. by John Kennicutt, Justice, Feb. 3, 1757.
1-85	TIBBETTS Dorcas, and Nathan Child, Nov. 17, 1793.
4-29	TILLEY Mary J., and George G. Hazard, Sept. 8, 1835.
4-11	TILLINGHAST Mary, and Paschal Allen, Nov. 27, 1838.
4-14	TILLSON Moses L., of Bridgewater. Mass., and Abby Thurber. of Warren; m. by Rev. William Livesey. June 5, 1842.
1-64	TOOGOOD Samuel, of Swansey, and Abigail Cole, of Warren; m. by John Kennicutt, Justice, Feb. 28, 1754.
1-66	" Trusterham, of Swansey, and Mrs. Jemima Easterbrooks, of Warren; m. by John Kennicutt, Justice, Dec. 14, 1758.
1-73	" Mrs. Jemima, and Ebenezer Luther, Oct. 23, 1772.
1-80	" Daniel and Mary Cole; m. by William Barton, Justice, Nov. 25, 1784.
1-94	TREADWAY Phebe Cornwell, and Joseph Kelley, Oct. 24, 1800.
1-100	" Ann, and Jonathan Carr, Feb. 25, 1809.
1-66	TRIPP Mrs. Bathsheba, and James Bushee, July 19, 1751.
3-172	TROTT James B., of Warren, and Sarah Haile Munroe, of Hezekiah, of Bristol; m. by Rev. Jordan Rexford, Aug. 2, 1820.
4-22	" John, and Rebecca S. Drowne; m. by Rev. Josiah P. Tustin, June 21, 1846.
1-69	TURNER Lydia, and Robert Carr, Aug. 30, 1767.
1-73	" Hannah, and Charles Collins, Oct. 20, 1771.
1-77	" Peter, and Mrs. Elizabeth Child; m. by Rev. Solomon Townsend, (Int. March 17); m. —— 21, 1776.
1-83	" Temperance, and John Wheaton, Feb. 28, 1779.
1-79	" Caleb, and Susannah Pearce: m. by Rev. Charles Thompson, Nov. 12, 1783.
1-88	" Roby, and Henry Nemo, Oct. 12, 1794.
1-92	" Temperance, and Daniel Ingraham, Oct. 21, 1798.
3-172	" Margaret C., and Capt. Alfred Barton, Oct. 15, 1820.
4-7	" Thomas Goodwin, of William, and Mary Pearce Luther, of Jonathan: m. by Rev. John C. Welch, April 4, 1833.
4-13	TUSTIN Rev. Josiah P., and Rebecca H. Williams, of Jeremiah; m. by Rev. John Dowling, Sept. 7, 1841.
1-91	TYLER Polly, and Haile Bowen, Oct. 16, 1791.

U V

1-77	VANCE James, and Sarah Easterbrooks; m. by Rev. Charles Thompson, June 1, 1777.
1-82	" James, and Sarah Haile; m. by Rev. John Pitman, Nov. 7, 1787.
1-90	" James, and Lydia Carr; m. by Elder Luther Baker, Aug. 8, 1797.

4-24   VAN DOORN Henry, of Bristol, and Judith Eliza Short, of Samuel, dec., of Warren; m. by Rev. John C. Welch, Dec. 17, 1839.

1-72   VARNUM James Mitchell, and Martha Child; m. by Rev. James Manning, Feb. 8, 1770.

1-65   VIALL Samuel, and Ruth Allen; m. by Matthew Allen, Justice, July 25, 1754.

1-65   "   Benjamin, and Keziah Brown, both of Rehoboth; m. by Matthew Allen, Justice, Jan. 23, 1755.

1-98   "   Sally, and Samuel Barton, July 4, 1805.

1-100   "   Joshua, of Joshua, and Sally Holden, of James; m. by Elder Luther Baker, June 7, 1809.

1-100   "   Patty, and Izrael Grant, July 6, 1809.

4-8   "   Harriet Byron, and George Tibbetts Gardner, Feb. 15, 1835.

4-24   "   Martha B., and Henry Sanders, Feb. 7, 1843.

4-28   "   Shearjashub T., and Almira S. Bosworth; m. by Rev. R. A. Fyfe, April 18, 1850.

1-78   VIBBARD David, of Hartford, Conn., and Sarah Hill, of Warren; m. by Rev. Charles Thompson, Feb. 7, 1779.

2-111   VICKERY Cynthia, and Jonathan Hill, Jan. 23, 1821.

4-30   "   Maria, and Collins Thurber, Oct. 27, 1846.

1-97   VINNICUM John, of John, and Bethiah Kennicutt, of Hezekiah; m. by James Sisson, Justice, Jan. 11, 1805.

3-165   "   John, Jr., of Warren, and Charlotte D. Martin, of Swansey; m. by Rev. Benjamin Taylor, Aug. 26, 1824.

4-4   "   Susan, and Zepbaniah S. Mason, Dec. 18, 1828.

4-6   "   Sally, and Benjamin Mason, March 25, 1830.

4-17   "   Lydia L., and Alfred Bosworth, Aug. 17, 1835.

4-23   "   Hannah G., and Ambrose Barnabee, June 27, 1839.

3-165   VINNIMAN Rebecca, and Jeremiah Cole, Oct. 3, 1824.

1-77   VORCE Elizabeth, and Lindall Cole, Aug. 24, 1777.

1-79   "   Anne, and Thomas Cole, April 2, 1781.

1-79   "   Tabitha, and John Stephens, Dec. 14, 1783.

1-88   "   Betsey, and Benjamin Phinney, Aug. 31, 1794.

W

3-167   WALDEN Sarah, and John Thomas Walker, Oct. 19, 1823.

3-167   WALKER John Thomas, of North Providence, son of John, of Pembroke, N. S., and Sarah Walden, of Warren; dau. of widow Lydia, of Westport, Mass.; m. by Rev. Jordan Rexford, Oct. 19, 1823.

3-168   WARDWELL Moses W., of Warren, son of Joseph, of Rumford, Me., and Mrs. Mary Brown, dau. of James Bushee, of Warren; m. by Rev. Jordan Rexford, March 13, 1823.

4-27   "   Elizabeth M., and Edward Hooker, March 28, 1847.

4-12   WARNER Lucius, of Barrington, of Ebenezer, and Lydia Bowen, of James, dec.; m. by Rev. John C. Welch, April 18, 1838.

1-68   WARREN Samuel, of Uptown, and Mrs. Elizabeth Bowen, of Warren; m. by Barnard Miller, Justice, March 7, 1764.

1-80   "   William, and Sarah Bliss; m. by William Barton, Justice, Aug. 19, 1784.

1-95   "   Patty, and Allen Beebe, April 10, 1803.

1-99   "   Sally, and Caleb Carr, Nov. 1, 1807.

1-87   WATERMAN Robe, and Nathaniel Phillips, Feb. 7, 1779.

3-167   WATSON John, and Hetty Newhall; m. by Rev. Jordan Rexford, Sept. 25, 1822.

3-164   "   Capt. John, and Nancy Burr; m. by Rev. John C. Welch (also 4-2), Oct. 8, 1826.

4-23   "   Ann A., and Josephus W. Horton, Jan. 27, 1839.

4-10   WEIGHT Rachel, and George Cole, Jan. 15, 1838.

3-165   WELCH Stillman, of Warren, and Betsey Haile, of Bristol; m. by Rev. John C. Welch, Jan. 16, 1825.

4-24   "   Sarah, and James Ridgway, Nov. 19, 1839.

1-70   WESTCOTT Abigail, and Oliver West, Jan. 2, 1766.

4-21   "   Amasa S., and Susan C. Bosworth; m. wy Rev. Josiah P. Tustin, April 7, 1845.

1-63 WEST Prescilla, and Simeon Peck, Nov. 24, 1748.
1-70 " Oliver, and Abigail Westcott; m. by Rev. James Manning, Jan. 2, 1766.
2-111 " Natahniel Hicks, of Bristol, and Nelly Easterbrooks, of Warren; m. by Rev. Luther Baker, March —, 1798.
1-82 WHITAKER Simeon, and Anne Luther; m. by Rev. John Pitman, June 8, 1787.
1-91 " Sally, and John Jolls, July 22, 1798.
1-93 " Anna, and Palmer Munroe, May 18, 1800.
1-100 " Lydia, and Ralph Morey, April 30, 1808.
4-27 " Henry, and Ellen Leering, of Fall River; m. by Rev. R. W. Allen, Sept. 12, 1849.
1-71 WHEATON Noah, and Martha Hammond; m. by Rev. James Manning, Dec. 25, 1768.
1-71 " Mary, and Ebenezer Jolls, April 7, 1769.
1-85 " Hannah and Barnard Hill, Dec. 9, 1770.
1-74 " Peres, and Seabury Cole; m. by Rev. Charles Thompson, May 18, 1773.
1-77 " Dorcas, and John Bowen, June 22, 1774.
1-87 " Sarah, and Oliver Eddy, Dec. 15, 1774.
1-83 " John, and Temperance Turner; m. by Rev. Solomon Townsend, Feb. 28, 1779.
1-81 " Charles, and Abigail Miller; m. by Rev. Solomon Townsend, Sept. 26, 1784.
1-88 " Nancy and John Caussones, July 6, 1788.
1-88 " Spencer, and Nancy Bowen; m. by Rev. John Pitman, April 13, 1790.
1-90 " Sebra, and James Luther, May 27, 1798.
1-91 " Hannah, and Joseph Smith, Aug. 26, 1798.
1-97 " Betsey, and Allen Cole, July 10, 1805.
1-101 ' Nathaniel M., of Charles, and Mary Smith, of Joseph, Dec. 24, 1809.
1-112 " Nathan M., of Charles and Content B. Maxwell, of James; m. by Elder Luther Baker, Nov. 25, 1813.
1-118 " Mary, and John Easterbrooks, Jan. 22, 1816.
3-168 " Samuel, of Perez, dec., of Warren and Rebecca Marble, of Robert, of Freetown; m. by Rev. Jordan Rexford, Nov. 24, 1822.
3-165 " George, of Warren, son of Charles, Esq., and Susan Sisson, of Edward, of Charlestown, Mass.; m. by Rev. John C. Welch, Jan. 10, 1825.
4-7 " John Robert, of Charles, and Rebecca Maxwell Eddy, of Caleb; m. by Rev. Jordan Rexford, Nov. 9, 1825.
4-1 " Susan, and Lieut. Joel Abbott, Nov. 29, 1825.
4-11 " Abby, and Thomas Paine Moore, Nov. 7, 1831.
4-25 " Samuel, of Charles, dec., and Elizabeth B. Sisson, of Freetown; m. by Rev. George W. Hathaway, Sept. 12, 1836.
4-10 " Elbridge Gerry, of Nathan M., of Warren, and Abby Cole, of Luther, dec., of Bristol; m. by Rev. George W. Hathaway, Nov. 4, 1838.
4-16 " Laura Frances, and George Lewis Cooke, Dec. 14, 1842.
4-28 " Olive B., and Ellis Griffith, May 12, 1850.
3-170 WHEELER Mary T., and Jeremiah C. Luther, April 7, 1822.
4-2 " Cyrel C., of Warren, and Hannah Mary Hazard, of Newport; m. by Rev. William Gammell. May 9, 1827.
4-7 " Hannah F., and Jeremiah Jolls, Feb. 3, 1833.
4-18 " Olive M., and Edmund Cole, April 22, 1841.
1-69 WHITEHORN Joanna, and Joseph Allen, Jr., June 2, 1765.
4-12 WHITELY Elkanah, of Fall River, of John, and Mary V. Woodmancy, of George, of Warren; m. by Rev. S. W. Willson, Oct. 29, 1839.
4-16 WHITE Abby Nelson, and Benjamin Ellis Butts, Aug. 18, 1842.
1-72 WHITING Elizabeth, and Jacob Sanders, Nov. 15, 1770.
1-71 " Nathaniel, and Roby Luther; m. by Rev. Charles Thompson, Sept. 12, 1771.
1-88 WHITMAN Samuel, and Patience Brayton, both of Rehoboth; m. by Elder Luther Baker, Sept. 25, 1794.

1-80   WUITMARSH Joseph, and Susannah Barton; m. by Rev. Charles Thompson, May 15, 1777.

4-3   WILBOUR Hannah G., and William Eddy, Nov. 14, 1822.

4-18   "   Sarah Gardiner, and Charles Frederick Brown, May 3, 1835.

1-93   WILLARD Gardiner, of Hezekiah, and Abigail Snell, of Seth; m. by Elder Luther Baker, Oct. 26, 1800.

1-100   "   Lucy, and Nathan M. Burr, Dec. 13, 1807.

1-72   WILLIAMS William, and Patience Miller; m. by Rev. James Manning, Feb. 25, 1770.

1-91   "   Elizabeth, and Enos Eddy, April 14, 1796.

1-111   "   Dr. Jeremiah, of Warren, son of George, of Dighton, and Rebecca Luther, dau. of Samuel Hicks; m. by Elder Luther Baker, Oct. 5, 1812.

1-117   "   Thomas C., of Warren, son of John, of Newport, and Eliza Smith. of Joseph, of Warren; m. by Elder Luther Baker, May 15, 1814.

4-11   "   Ruth Miller, and Charles Richmond, Jr., Dec. 18, 1837.

4-10   "   George, of Randolph, Mass., son of Thomas C., and Maria B. Munroe, of Warren, dau. af George; m. by Rev. Shipley W. Willson, Sept. 2, 1838.

4-13   "   Rebecca H., and Rev. Josiah P. Tustin, Sept. 7, 1841.

4-29   "   Edward, and S. T. Smith; m. at New York City by Elder Oliver Barr, June 25, 1848.

4-27   "   William E., of Warren, and Susan T. Hathaway, of Dighton; m. by Rev. R. W. Allen, June 10, 1849.

4-29   WILMARTH Marcus, of Smithfield, and Anna G. Seymore, of Warren; m. by Rev. R. A. Fyfe, July 14, 1850.

1-75   WING Edward, and Elizabeth Miller; m. by Rev. Charles Thompson, Aug. 7, 1774.

1-93   WINSLOW Ebenezer, of Ebenezer, and Polly Kelley, of Duncan; m. by Rev. John Hill, Aug. 21, 1800.

1-98   "   John L., of Warren, and Mary Lake, of David, of Portsmouth; m. by Rev. Michael Eddy, at Newport —— —, 1806 (?).

3-167   "   Silvania A., and Capt. Daniel B. Barrus, July 31, 1823.

1-113   WINSTON Sarah M., and Daniel W. Barnabee, Oct. 24, 1816.

1-66   WOODMANCY John, and Mrs. Esther Heath, both of Swansey; m. by Benjamin Miller, Justice, April 10, 1751.

1-94   "   George, of Rhubin, and Rebecca Goff, of James; m. by Elder Luther Baker, Dec. 5, 1802.

1-99   "   Betsey Eddy, and Asa Luther, March 17, 1805.

1-97   "   Sally, and Ezra Drew, Oct. 13, 1805.

4-2   "   Jeremiah, of George. and Elizabeth Harris (orphan); m. by Rev. Jordan Rexford, Aug. 29, 1824.

4-4   "   George, and Martha Goff; m. by Rev. N. S. Spaulding, July 28, 1829.

4-12   "   Mary V., and Elkanah Whiteley, Oct. 29, 1839.

4-13   "   Jeremiah, of Warren, and Louisa Manley, of Mendon, Mass.; m. by Rev. William Livesey, April 8, 1841.

1-62   WOOD Jabez, of Middleboro, Mass., and Mrs. Joanna Short, of Warren; m. by Matthew Allen, Justice, April 7, 1748.

1-63   "   Bethiah, and Ichabod Bosworth, Nov. 19, 1748.

1-117   "   James, of Warren, son of James, of Swansey, and Mrs. Polly Arnold, of Warren; m. by Elder Luther Baker, June 30, 1805.

4-3   "   Eliza Ann, and Henry Beebee, Jan. 17, 1828.

4-27   WRIGHT Ann Eliza, and Chauncey Almore Moore, May 6, 1849.

X Y Z

WARREN.

BIRTHS AND DEATHS.

A

3-75	ABBOTT Lydia Lord, of Joel and Laura W.,	Sept. 14, 1826.
3-62	" John Pickens,	June 26, 1828.
3-22	" Charles Wheaton,	Nov. 18, 1829.
3-143	" Trevett,	July 2, 1831.
3-96	" Mary,	Dec. 29, 1832.
3-75	" Laura Wheaton,	March 10, 1835.
3-98	" Nathan M.,	Dec. 25, 1836.
3-100	" Mary,	May 1, 1839.
3-162	" Walter (born U. S. Navy Yard, Charlestown, Mass.),	Oct. 14, 1841.
1-50	ADAMS Stephen, of John and Elizabeth,	May 6, 1743.
1-37	" Newdigate,	June 13, 1753.
1-51	" Sarah, 2d wife,	July 13, 1755.
1-8	" Chloe,	Sept. 4, 1758.
1-16	" Ebenezer, of James and Lydia,	Oct. 13, 1762.
1-26	" Joseph,	Nov. 22, 1764.
1-51	" Samuel, of Samuel and Rebecca,	Jan. 11, 1768.
1-56	" William,	Dec. 6, 1769.
1-30	" Lydia, of James and Ruth,	Sept. 10, 1769.
2-1	" Ardelia, of Joseph and Lydia,	Aug. 29, 1788.
2-52	" James,	June 18, 1790.
2-55	" Joseph,	July 21, 1792.
2-36	" Eben Wheaton,	Dec. 13, 1794.
2-47	" Hannah Kinnecutt,	Dec. 13, 1794.
3-64	" Joseph, of Nathaniel and Mary (b. Barrington),	Sept. 9, 1819.
3-94	" Mary,	Nov. 11, 1822.
3-51	" Hannah Hubbard,	March 14, 1825.
3-62	" John Quincy,	May 26, 1828.
3-31	" Elizabeth Annah,	Jan. 12, 1831.
3-137	" Samuel Martin,	Aug. 14, 1834.
1-41	ALGER Preserved, son of Preserved Alger and Comfort Cole,	
		March 10, 1762.
2-52	" James, of Preserved and Charlotte (b. Pomfret, Conn.),	
		Feb. 22, 1784.
2-2	" Abigail,	June 13, 1787.
2-73	" Lucinda,	July 25, 1790.
1-43	" Preserved,	March 23, 1792.
1-58	" William,	June 20, 1794.
2-45	" Hannah,	Feb. 29, 1796.
2-74	" Lucinda,	May 10, 1798.
2-101	" Sarah Ann,	May 10, 1801.
2-109	" William M.,	April 7, 1806.
3-58	" James Benjamin,	Feb. 2, 1813.
2-10	" Betsey Eddy, of James and Abigail,	Nov. 12, 1803.
1-50	ALLEN Samuel, of Samuel and Mercy,	Feb. 14, 1743.
1-55	" Viall,	Dec. 9, 1744.
1-25	" Jerusha,	Feb. 18, 1748.
1-25	" James, of Samuel, (of Samuel), and Mary,	Oct. 13, 1750.
1-55	" William, of Ebenezer, Jr., and Elizabeth,	July 27, 1746.
1-18	" George,	April 6, 1748.

1-14	ALLEN	Elizabeth, of Ebenezer, Jr., and Elizabeth,		Nov. 14, 1749.
1-46	"	Rebecca, of Timothy, and Mollie,		April 3, 1755.
1-46	"	Rachel,		March 30, 1757.
1-41	"	Polly,		Jan. 27, 1760.
1-27	"	Jabez Brown,		Dec. 6, 1761.
1-51	"	Sarah Norton,		May 14, 1764.
1-39	"	Oliver,		Aug. 14, 1766.
1-4	"	Asa, of Samuel, 2d, and Ruth,		Oct. 15, 1760.
1-26	"	Joseph Viall,		Sept. 23, 1762.
1-45	"	Rachel,		Sept. 18, 1765.
2-95	"	Samuel, (in middle of remarkable eclipse),		Jan. 19, 1768.
2-95	"	Sylvester,		Feb. 20, 1770.
1-51	"	Squire, of Joseph. Jr., and Joanna,		July 30, 1765.
1-26	"	James,		Jan. 29, 1768.
2-47	"	Hannah Bowen, of Paschall and Elouisa,		Oct. 2, 1807.
2-87	"	Paschall,	(also 2-129),	June 27, 1809.
2-73	"	Mary Elouisa,	(also 3-90)	June 30, 1813.
2-6	"	Ann Mary,		July 23, 1816.
2-61	"	Jonathan Bowers,		Aug. 1, 1821.
2-6	"	Ann Elizabeth,	(b. Marah)	March 12, 1823.
2-61	"	John Jay, of Ira and Abigail,		Dec. 26, 1818.
3-139	"	Shearjashub B.,		Dec. 3, 1818.
3-162	"	James Wheaton, of Wheaton and Maria (page 66 says Jan. 26, 1848), Jan. 26, 1846.		
3-37	AMES	Charles Robert, of Robert N. and Rosamond,		Feb. —, 1851.
3-96	ANDERSON	Martha, of John C. and Martha,		Nov. 14, 1836.
1-26	ANDREWS	Jonathan, of William and Bethiah,		June 29, 1761.
1-51	"	Susannah,		June 6, 1764.
1-46	"	Rachel,		April 2, 1766.
3-22	"	Charles Augustus, of John and Hannah,		Feb. 11, 1816.
3-94	"	Mary Ann, of Hiram and Eliza,		Nov. 7, 1826.
3-160	"	William Hathaway,		Dec. 24, 1828.
3-52	"	Hiram Francis,		Jan. 7, 1832.
3-96	"	Mary Anna,		April 10, 1834.
3-41	"	George Augustus,		July 7, 1836.
3-35	ANGELL	Francis Hendrick, of Samuel and Aseneth,		March 22, 1818.
3-92	"	Maria,		Sept. —, 1821.
3-61	"	James Manning (also 3-93),		May 18, 1824.
1-32	ARNOLD	Mary, of William and Charity,		Aug. 10, 1750.
1-55	"	William,		Sept. 26, 1752.
1-5	"	Benjamin,		Dec. 12, 1754.
1-45	"	Ruth,		March 20, 1757.
1-40	"	Peleg,		Feb. 12, 1759.
2-51	"	James,		March 20, 1761.
1-43	"	Iramillice,		April 4, 1763.
1-9	"	Charity,		March 4, 1765.
1-7	"	Benedick,		June 4, 1770.
2-44	"	Hannah,		June 20, 1772.
1-42	"	Phebe, of William and Elizabeth,		Aug. 6, 1779.
1-42	"	Patience,		May 26, 1782.
1-57	"	William,		May 27, 1784.
2-51	"	James,		April 19, 1786.
1-43	"	Peleg,		April 25, 1788.
2-81	"	Nelly, of Benedick and Polly,		Aug. 25, 1782.(?)
2-99	"	Seth Lincoln, of Hannah,		May 27, 1794.
2-38	"	George Miller,		May 26, 1801.
3-125	"	Reuben M., of George W. and Sophia, (b. Glocester, R. I.,)		Nov. 3, 1779.
3-7	ASHWORTH	Ann E., of George O. and Fanny,		March 7, 1849.
3-99	"	Mary Jane,		June 22, 1850.
3-98	"	Nancy,		Dec. 29, 1857.

B

1-60	BABBITT Zebe, of Elkanah and Hannah,	Feb. 22, 1808.
2-116	" Luther R.,	Feb. 22, 1808.
1-28	BAKER Jesse, of Jesse and Lois,	Oct. 3, 1769.
1-30	" Luther,	June 11, 1770.
1-57	" William (also 1-56),	Nov. 17 or 18, 1772.
2-53	" John Smith, of Jesse and Hannah,	Feb. 29, 1792.
2-81	" Nancy,	April 29, 1795.
2-80	" Nancy, of Thomas and Freeborn,	June 9, 1793.
2-38	" George Tew,	July 1, 1802.
1-10	" Charles Thompson, of Elder Luther and Peggy,	Sept. 27, 1797.
2-18	" Caleb Hill,	Nov. 20, 1799.
2-94	" Ruel Holden,	Oct. 6, 1808.
3-160	" William Longhead (b. Providence),	Oct. 7, 1818.
3-137	" Samuel Young (b. Providence),	March 15, 1821.
3-128	" Robert Simington (b. Providence),	Sept. 3, 1823.
2-77	" Margaret Spencer, of Luther and Margaret,	June 29, 1802.
2-77	" Mary Child,	April 3, 1806.
3-89	" Mary Child,	April 17, 1811.
3-73	" Luther,	Nov. 22, 1813.
3-159	" William B., of Ruel H. and Jerusha E.,	Aug. 30, 1832.
3-25	" David,	Sept. 7, 1834.
3-101	" William Hillman, of William L. and Emeline M.,	Jan. 3, 1847.
3-155	" Virginia,	Dec. 24, 1859.
3-67	" Isabel Wheaton,	Jan. 4, 1861.
1-33	BARDEN Molly of Nathan and Mary,	April 11, 1767.
1-37	" Nancy,	Dec. 1, 1769.
1-6	" Betsey,	June 27, 1772.
2-96	" Sarah,	July 5, 1775.
1-38	" Nathan,	Aug. 28, 1778.
2-44	" Hannah,	May 18, 1782.
3-75	" Luther Mason, of Luther Mason and Eliza V.,	Aug. 28, 1823.
3-19	BARKER Charles, of Benjamin and Abigail,	Sept. 13, 1813.
1-12	BARNABY Daniel Wilbour, of Daniel and Hope,	Sept. 29, 1793.
3-28	" Enock, of Daniel W. and Sarah,	Aug. 16, 1817.
3 29	" Elizabeth Wilbour,	Jan. 15, 1821.
3-29	" Edwin,	March 29, 1822.
1-40	BARNES Peleg, of Thomas and Ruth,	June 7, 1746.
1-45	" Ruth,	March 25, 1751.
1 49	" Samuel,	Sept. 9, 1756.
1-26	" John, of Levi and Ruth,	Oct. 20, 1760.
1 26	" Jerusha,	Dec. 7, 1763.
1-33	" Mary,	July 28, 1765.
2 56	" James, of James and Rebecca,	Aug. 3, 1795.
2 93	" Rosabella Child, of Daniel and Nancy,	July 21, 1802.
2-60	" John Child,	Oct. 4, 1805.
2-5	" Abigail Miller,	March 31, 1807.
3-67	" Josephine, of Nathan L. and Abby M.,	Jan. 4, 1844.
2-60	BARNEY John Kelley, of Comfort and Mary,	May 9, 1788.
2-10	" Betsey,	Nov. 14, 1790.
2-60	" Josiah,	Oct. 20, 1793.
2 90	" Polly Kelley,	July 23, 1799.
2-35	" Eliza,	(sic.) Nov. 15, 1799.
2-129	" Patience Miller,	Oct. 15, 1802.
3-135	" Sarah Ann,	Feb. 3, 1809.
3-2	" Abby,	May 27, 1913.
3-74	" Laura,	April 23, 1815.
2-109	" William, of John Kelley and Mary,	April 8, 1808.
3-61	" John Kelley,	Dec. 19, 1811.
3-101	" Mary B.,	Dec. 15, 1814.
3-66	" Julia A.,	May 8, 1817.
3-101	" Maria Antonette, of John K. and Mary J.,	March 19, 1840.
3-67	BARRETT John Joseph, of Patrick A. and Catherine C.,	Feb. 12, 1845.
3-162	" William Francis,	Jan. 2, 1847.

3-67	BARRETT James Thomas, of Patrick A. and Catherine C.,	Jan. 16, 1849.
2-99	BARROWS Sally, of Isaac and Elizabeth,	April 21, 1788.
2-8	" Betsey,	Jan. 11, 1790.
2-54	" Isaac Briggs,	April 30, 1792.
2-54	" Job Miller,	March 28, 1794.
2-108	" William Lewis, of Dr. Daniel and Nancy Esther (Usher), Jan. 13, 1797.	
2-100	" Sukey Lewis,	July 1, 1798.
1-13	" Daniel Briggs,	May 25, 1800.
2-108	" William Lewis,	Dec. 25, 1803.
2-61	- " John Throop Child,	Feb. 25, 1809.
3-97	" Nathan Child Lewis,	Dec. 13, 1810.
3-1	" Abigail Miller Child,	April 22, 1813.
3-119	" Prudence Briggs Cole,	Sept. 23, 1814.
3-59	" Joseph Cornell,	Aug. 18, 1818.
3-61	" James Barnet,	April 2, 1822.
3-93	" Mary Ann Winslow, of Daniel B. and Sylvania,	July 20, 1824.
3-95	" Mary Kelley,	May 14, 1828.
3-21	" Charles Leonard, of William Lewis and Harriet,	Sept. 7, 1827.
3-159	" William Lewis,	July 24, 1829.
3-52	" Horace Granville,	April 24, 1831.
3-76	" Lewis Haile, of Nathan L. and Abby M.,	July 12, 1851.
3-55	" Ida L., of James B. and Hannah L.,	May 3, 1854.
1-11	BARTON David, of Benjamin and Lydia,	Dec. 9, 1746.
1-55	" William,	May 26, 1748.
1-4	" Anne,	Sept. 1, 1749.
1-50	" Susannah,	Aug. 18, 1751.
1-50	" Seth,	July 29, 1759.
1-25	" Joseph, of Benjamin, Jr., and Lois,	Dec. 12, 1758.
1-6	" Benjamin,	March 29, 1762.
1-46	" Rebecca,	Sept. 22, 1766.
1-1	" Andrew,	April 7, 1769.
1-18	" Gardner, of Richard and Anne,	Nov. 28, 1762.
1-33	" Mary,	Dec. 9, 1764.
1-46	" Richard,	Jan. 4, 1770.
1-1	" Amos Thomas, of William and Ruth,	Oct. 5, 1768.
1-30	" Lillis,	Sept. 17, 1770.
1-56	" William,	Aug. 20, 1772.
1-42	" Patience,	Aug. 13, 1774.
1-7	" Benjamin, of Rufus and Prudence,	Sept. 21, 1771.
1-9	" Caleb,	March 11, 1774.
1-57	" William,	Aug. 1, 1777.
1-9	" Caleb, •	July 3, 1780.
1-36	" Mary,	Nov. 20, 1782.
1-36	" Martha,	July 9, 1785.
2-92	" Rufus,	June 27, 1788.
2-80	" Nathan Sisson,	May 8, 1791.
2-73	" Lillis Turner,	Aug. 30, 1793.
1-53	" Turner,	May 24, 1796.
2-86	" Ebenezer Cole, (b. Cambridge, N. Y.,)	April 14, 1790.
1-34	" Molly, of Haile and Elizabeth,	Aug. 21, 1774.
1-47	" Rose,	Sept. 30, 1775.
2-32	" Elizabeth,	June 23, 1777.
2-95	" Susannah, of David and Rebeckah,	Jan. 4, 1775.
1-7	" Betsey,	May 10, 1776.
1-60	" Anne,	(also 2-4), April 19, 1778.
1-47	" Rebeckah,	Feb. 21, 1779.
2-92	" Rebeckah,	Feb. 21, 1780.
2-72	. " Lydia,	(also 2-74), Jan. 29, 1782.
2-97	" Seth,	(also 2-100), Jan. 27, 1784.
2 56	" James,	(sic) Feb. 12, 1784.
1-13	" Dianna,	Jan. 1, 1788.
1-10	" Charlotte,	Jan. 20, 1790.
1-13	" David Brightman,	March 19, 1791.
2 56	" Jonathan Brown,	March 19, 1791.

1-35	BARTON Molly, of William and Elizabeth,	March 28, 1780.
2-96	" Samuel,	June 26, 1782.
1-52	" Thomas,	Sept. 23, 1784.
2 91	" Rebeckah,	Nov. 11, 1787.
2 2	" Alfred,	Dec. 12, 1790.
2-8	" Betsey,	Jan. 31, 1793.
2 91	" Ruth, of Joseph and Ruth,	Feb. 18, 1781.
2-73	" Lois,	July 15, 1786.
2-33	" Elizabeth,	Aug. 19, 1788.
2 51	" John Hathaway, of Richard and Hannah,	Jan. 28, 1782.
2-72	" Luther,	Sept. 15, 1783.
1-38	" Nathan Sims,	Aug. 10, 1785.
2-91	" Rufus,	April 14, 1787.
2-8	" Betsey Barnaby, of Benjamin and Hannah,	April 2, 1790.
2-89	" Polly,	Feb. 6, 1792.
_ 9	" Benjamin,	April 30, 1793.
2-99	" Sally,	Jan. 2, 1794.
2-3	" Andrew,	April 10, 1796.
2-101	" Samuel,	April 20, 1800.
2-46	", Haile,	March 15, 1802.
2-108	" William Ira,	March 11, 1804.
2-98	" Sally, of William, Jr., and Sally,	March 4, 1794.
2-4	" Amos Thomas,	Feb. 11, 1797.
2-35	" Eliza,	—— —, 1800 (?).
2-3	" Anthony, of Benjamin, 3d, and Lydia,	May 29, 1796.
2-100	" Seth,	Aug. 3, 1797.
2-4	" Albert,	June 10, 1799.
2-35	" Emma,	April 11, 1801.
2-75	" Lydia,	July 26, 1803.
2-75	" Lois,	Nov. 7, 1805.
2-94	" Rufus,	May 15, 1808.
2-102	" Seth, of William and Rebeckah,	Nov. 16, 1802.
2-94	" Rebeckah Brightman,	Sept. 13, 1804.
2-5	" Alemea,	Aug. 1, 1806.
2-38	" George, of Samuel and Sally,	Feb. 4, 1807.
2-61	" James Winchester,	Oct. 27, 1808.
3-19	" Charles,	July 31, 1810.
3-73	" Laura,	May 22, 1812.
3-132	" Hannah,	Aug. 20, 1814.
3-28	" Elizabeth,	Feb. 17, 1817.
3-134	" Sarah,	Oct. 22, 1821.
3-92	" Maria,	Aug. 21, 1823.
3-51	" Henry,	May 23, 1825.
2-78	" Mary Mason, of James and Charlotte,	Oct. 3, 1808.
3-25	" David Brightman, of Jonathan B., and Deborah,	Aug. 3, 1810.
3-49	" Harriet, of Seth and Polly,	Feb. 3, 1814.
3-90	" Mary Ann,	May 4, 1816.
3-115	" Ophelia,	June 30, 1817.
3-71	" Lydia Matilda,	Sept. 28, 1819.
3-115	" Ophelia, 2d,	May 17, 1822.
3-3	" Alfred, of Alfred and Margaret C.,	July 12, 1921.
3-158	" William Turner,	Dec. 24, 1823.
3-126	" Robert,	April 4, 1827.
3-143	" Thomas Haile,	Jan. 14, 1830.
3-51	" Haile Barnaby, of William and Eliza,	Nov. 4, 1826.
3-21	" Caroline, of James C. and Sally,	June 4, 1827.
3-31	" Emily, of Charles and Mary, (b. Barrington),	Feb. 4, 1834.
3-31	" Eliza, of David B. and Eliza,	July 13, 1836.
3-42	" Georgiana, of George and Rebecca M.,	Sept. 25, 1847.
3-107	" Nora Clara, of James W. and Mary R.,	Jan. 15, 1848.
3-50	BEAN Horace, of Benson and Sally,	——. 10, 1819.
3-159	" William Henry,	Sept. 25, 1820.
3-136	" Sally,	April 8, 1824.

2-9	BEBEE Betsey, of Clement Stanton and Ruth,	Sept. 24, 1798.
2-5	" Allen, of Allen and Patty,	Feb. 22, 1804.
2-47	" Henry,	Feb. 4, 1806.
3-92	" Martha,	May 27, 1815.
3-32	BENNETT Edwin Francis, of Charles E. and Abby L.,	Nov. 17, 1842.
3-23	" Charles Herbert,	April 29, 1846.
3-119	BENNINGTON Preserved Alger, of Samuel and Lucinda,	July 30, 1814.
1-7	BESAYADE Betsey, of Lewis and Elizabeth,	Feb. 29, 1780.
1-2	BICKNELL Abigail, of Joshua, Jr., and Ruth,	Feb. 9, 1746-7.
1-22	" James,	Feb. 2, 1748-9.
1-20	" Hannah,	Sept. 4, 1750.
1-44	" Ruth,	Oct. 29, 1752.
1-39	" Olive,	Nov. 11, 1754.
1-24	" Joshua, of Joshua and Jerusha,	Jan. 14, 1759.
1-55	" Winchester,	March 31, 1761.
1-25	" Jerusha,	Jan. 20, 1763.
1-25	" Joseph,	Jan. 20, 1763.
1-17	" Freeborn (dau.),	Jan. 9, 1768.
1-2	" Amey, of Peter and Rachel,	Aug. 24, 1751.
3 61	" John J., of Charles and Betsey, (b. Boston, Mass.),	Feb. 12, 1800.
3-169	" Pomp, of Pomp and Jane (col.),	Sept. 4, 1804.
3-41	" George Henry, of John and Jane M.,	June 7, 1831.
3-135	BLAKE Samuel, of Samuel and Polly (at Bristol),	Aug. 24, 1800.
3-21	" James Curtis, of Samuel C., and Mary Ann (also 3-62),	
		Dec. 15, 1828.
3-41	" George Edwin,	Feb. 16, 1833.
1-21	BLISS Henry, of William and Hartey,	Nov. 30, 1770.
1-17	" Fanny,	Feb. 1, 1772.
1-39	" Oliver, of Patience,	Dec. 16, 1776.
2-44	" Harte (dau.), of Jonathan and Mary,	Nov. 12, 1777.
1-42	" Polly,	March 22, 1780.
2-89	" Patty,	March 22, 1780.
2-8	" Barbara,	June 15, 1782.
1-7	" Barbace,	June 15, 1783.
2-55	" James,	Oct. 20, 1785.
2-8	" Betsey,	Sept. 11, 1788.
2-55	" Jonathan,	Sept. 15, 1791.
2-93	" Rebeckah Miller,	Sept. 22, 1795.
2-93	" Robey Bowen,	July 9, 1798.
2-81	" Nancy, of William and Betsey,	May 1, 1794.
3-51	" Henry Hiram,	May 4, 1808.
3-139	BOOTH Sarah Elizabeth, of William and Lucinda,	July 3, 1853.
2-74	BARDEN Luther Mason, of Thomas and Sarah,	April 14, 1797.
2-76	" Martin Easterbrooks,	Feb. 2, 1800.
2-104	" Thomas Sisson,	March 13, 1806.
1-31	BOSWORTH Molly, of Jonathan and Mary,	Jan. 18, 1751.
1-37	" Nathaniel,	April 12, 1753.
1-5	" Betsey,	May 27, 1755.
1-24	" Jonathan.	May 20, 1757.
1-1	" Anne, of Samuel and Elizabeth,	Oct. 26, 1769.
1-38	" Nancy, of Ebenezer and Patience,	Feb. 12, 1782.
2-89	" Peleg, of Benjamin and Abigail,	Dec. 20, 1787.
2-3	" Ann,	April 5, 1790.
2-9	" Burrell,	Dec. 20, 1791.
2-34	" Ebenezer,	Sept. 25, 1793.
2-74	" Lydia,	Oct. 17, 1795.
2-6	" Abigail Munro, of Peleg and Betsey,	Feb. 21, 1809.
3-1	" Alfred, of Daniel and Susan.	Jan. 28, 1812.
3-10	" Cyrus,	June 4, 1817.
3-136	" Susan Carpenter, (also 3-135),	May 11 or 16, 1823.
3-52	" Hannah Mason,	Aug. 20, 1826.
3-110	" Olive Mason,	April 26, 1829.
3-143	" Timothy Sabins, of Timothy and Deborah,	March 8, 1826.
3-32	" Emily, of Benjamin M. and Elizabeth M.,	March 2, 1837.
3-5	" Abby Elizabeth,	March 20, 1840.

3-32	BOSWORTH	Edmund Burke, of Benj. M. and Elizabeth M.,	Dec. 9, 1844.
3-138	"	Sarah,	March 14, 1846.
3-11	"	Benjamin Miller,	Jan. 17, 1848.
3-110	"	Orrin Luther,	April 19, 1849.
3-161	"	Walter Spencer,	Jan. 10, 1851.
3-101	"	Martin Luther,	Oct. 16, 1852.
3-23	"	Charles Demetries, of Peleg and Hannah,	Jan. 10, 1838.
3-120	"	Peleg,	July 26, 1840.
3-53	"	Hannah Frances,	Dec. 4, 1842.
3-26	"	Emily Miller,	Aug. 20, 1845.
3 37	"	Clara Ellis,	Aug. 15, 1848.
1-22	BOWEN	Jeremiah, of James and Ann,	Nov. 30, 1744.
1-23	"	Josiah,	July 25, 1752.
1-38	"	Mary,	Aug. 15, 1755.
1-45	"	Robe,	Feb. 19, 1757.
1-21	"	Huldah,	June 9, 1759.
1 4	"	Anne.	June 23, 1761.
1-26	"	James, (also 1-27),	July 14 or 15, 1765.
1-34	"	Margaret,	Aug. 1, 1768..
1-2	"	Anne, of Nathaniel and Esther,	April 11, 1749.
1-23	"	John,	May 14, 1751.
1-44	"	Reuben,	Nov. 24, 1753.
1-25	"	James,	May 11, 1755.
1-32	"	Mary,	Nov. 12, 1757.
1-4	"	Avis,	Dec. 12, 1758.
1-55	"	William,	Sept. 25, 1760.
1-4	"	Anne,	June 2, 1766.
1-20	"	Hannah, of Amos and Elizabeth,	Nov. 10, 1754.
1-24	"	John, of Josiah and Huldah,	Jan. 12, 1759.
1-41	"	Patience,	Jan. 17, 1761.
1-33	"	Margaret,	Nov. 29, 1762.
1-26	"	James Easterbrooks,	Feb. 14, 1765.
1-51	"	Sarah,	April 14, 1767.
1-34	"	Martin,	Aug. 15, 1770.
1-27	"	Jonathan, of Jonathan and Elizabeth,	Nov. 14, 1760.
1-21	"	Haile,	Dec. 30, 1762.
1-41	"	Pardon,	June 7, 1764.
1-33	"	Mary,	Sept. 20, 1768.
1-51	"	Samuel, of Smith and Mary,	Oct. 18, 1760.
1-51	"	Sarah,	Jan. 11, 1759.
1-16	"	Elizabeth,	Oct. 21, 1762.
1-33	"	Mary,	Jan. 21, 1765.
1-27	"	James,	Feb. 2, 1767.
1-1	"	Anne,	Aug. 19, 1769.
1-1	"	Aaron,	Aug. 12, 1771.
2-3	"	Amey,	Feb. 12, 1774.
1-39	"	Olive,	March 5, 1778.
1-41	"	Peleg, of Peleg and Elizabeth,	Sept. 17, 1761.
1-6	"	Benjamin, of Nathan and Herren,	Oct. 4, 1763.
1-37	"	Nathan,	Dec. 9, 1765.
1-41	"	Patience,	July 16, 1768
1-28	"	Joanna,	May 15, 1771.
2-95	"	Sarah (also 2-96),	May 4, 1774.
1-47	"	Ruth,	Sept. 29, 1777.
1-42	"	Polly,	Aug. 22, 1790
1-7	"	Betsey,	Oct. 10, 1782.
1-37	"	Nathan, of Thomas and Penelope,	Sept. 11, 1765.
1-37	"	Nathaniel Aldrich,	Jan. 29, 1767.
1-6	"	Betsey, of Jeremiah and Lillis,	Nov. 25, 1767.
2-1	"	Anne,	Oct. 23, 1769.
2-99	"	Sally T., of Jonathan and Betsey,	May 28, 1769.
1-39	"	Olive, of John and Dorcas,	July 13, 1773.
1-18	"	George,	May 9, 1775.
1-47	"	Rebekah,	March 11, 1777.
1-12	"	Dorcas,	Feb. 17, 1779.

2-51	BOWEN	John, of John and Dorcas,	Feb. 27, 1781.
1-57	"	Wheaton,	March 24, 1783.
1-58	"	William, of Stephen and Deborah,	Jan. 1, 1774.
2-88	"	Peleg, of James and Ruth,	Sept. 19, 1778.
2-2	"	Avis,	Feb. 24, 1780.
2-54	"	James,	March 6, 1782.
1-58	"	William,	Feb. 28, 1784.
2-88	"	Polly,	Dec. 2, 1785.
2-91	"	Reuben,	Feb. 24, 1788.
1-10	"	Cranston,	March 16, 1792.
2-91	"	Ruth,	March 16, 1792.
2-80	"	Nancy,	April 21, 1794.
2-5	"	Arnold,	Jan. 28, 1798.
2-10	"	Betsey,	Jan. 9, 1801.
2-82	"	Nathaniel,	Dec. 15, 1802
2-33	"	Elizabeth, of William and Lydia (b. Little Compton), Nov. —, 1779.
1-57	'	William, of Benjamin and Rebeckah,	June 1, 1788.
2-45	"	Henry,	March 12, 1791.
2-33	"	Elizabeth, of Nathan and Betsey,	March 11, 1791.
2-57	"	Jonathan, of Haile and Pattey,	Aug. 7, 1792.
2-90	"	Polly T.,	Oct 25, 1795.
2-90	"	Pardon,	Oct. 10, 1797.
2-56	"	John, of James Easterbrooks and Lydia,	March 4, 1793.
2-59	"	James E.,	May 1, 1796.
2-108	"	William,	April 1, 1798.
2-38	"	George,	July 29, 1800.
2-75	"	Lydia,	Aug. 30, 1802.
3-94	"	Mary T., of James E., Jr., and Betsey,	Dec. 31, 1828.
3-31	"	Elizabeth F.,	May 30, 1831.
2-8	"	Betsey, of Jonathan and Betsey,	April 25, 1793.
2-54	"	Jonathan,	July 4, 1794.
2-47	"	Harriet,	May 26, 1796.
1-36	"	Edward Tyler,	Feb. 19, 1798.
2-45	"	Haile, of Haile and Phebe,	April 7, 1794.
2-76	"	Martin, of Martin and Nancy,	Aug. 6, 1795.
1-10	"	Caleb,	June 9, 1797.
2-57	"	John Greene,	Feb. 13, 1799.
2-58	"	Josiah,	March 18, 1801.
2-56	"	Jarvis Brown, of Aaron and Lydia,	Dec. 25, 1796.
3-132	"	Samuel,	April 7, 1799.
2-128	"	Patty, of Peleg and Ruth,	March 11, 1802.
2-47	"	Hannah,	July 4, 1804.
2-103	"	Sally Ann,	Jan. 1, 1807.
2-109	"	William B.,	April 1, 1809.
3-31	"	Ebenezer Martin.	March 21, 1814.
2-36	"	Elvira, of Wheaton and Sarah,	Nov. 22, 1805.
2-109	"	William Cranston,	May 14, 1807.
3-143	"	Thomas Owens, of Nancy,	Dec. 4, 1809.
2-109	"	William Henry, of Samuel Turner and Betsey,	Dec. 25, 1809.
2-73	"	Levi Salisbury, of Isaac and Mary,	Feb. 18, 1813.
3-91	"	Maria,	Sept. 22, 1815.
3-96	"	Mary Carr,	Oct. 18, 1819.
3-52	"	Henry,	Jan. 25, 1825.
3-55	"	Ira Beers, of James, Jr., and Rebecca,	Sept. 20, 1813.
3-2	"	Almira,	May 13, 1818.
3-157	"	William Henry, of Henry and Bathsheba P.,	March 21, 1817.
3-20	"	Charles Perry,	April 16, 1819.
3-125	"	Rebecca Cole,	Oct. 19, 1824.
3 93	"	Mary Elizabeth,	May 9, 1926.
3-74	"	Laura Maria, of Haile and Betsey,	Sept. 14, 1818.
3-50	"	Henry Augustus,	Oct. 14, 1820.
3 92	"	Mary T.,	July 7, 1823.
3-62	"	John Haile,	April 6, 1826.
3-42	"	George Saunders,	Jan. 17, 1831.
3-10	"	Betsey Johonnett.	March 26, 1833.

3-23	BOWEN Charles William, of Haile and Betsey,	June 18, 1836.
3-61	" James Easterbrooks, of John and Mary,	March 29, 1822.
3-51	" Hannah Burr,	Oct. 16, 1826.
3-159	" William, of George and Betsey,	Aug. 18, 1828.
3-95	" Mary,	Nov. 14, 1829.
3-4	" Ann Elizabeth, of Allen and Betsey.	June 20, 1829.
3-96	" Mary Stanley,	July 23, 1832.
3-94	" Mary Frances, of John Greene and Priscilla C.,	Jan. 15, 1830.
3-95	" Martin,	Jan. 24, 1832.
3-77	" Nancy,	Dec. 19, 1833.
3-96	" Mary Miller,	Sept. 16, 1836.
3-65	" John Miller,	Dec. 27, 1845.
3-63	" Jonathan, of Cyrel and Sally,	July 26, 1831.
3-160	" William Henry, of Arnold and Matilda,	Feb. 28, 1833.
3-76	" Laura Frances,	Nov. 22, 1834.
3-76	" Lewis Henry, of William H. and Maria B.,	March 27, 1839.
3-35	" Fanny Rogers,	July 3, 1841.
3-107	" Nora Melville,	Aug. 3, 1844.
3-37	" Clara Watson,	Oct. 3, 1850.
3-66	" James Bradford, of Ira and Nancy,	Oct. 7, 1839.
3-139	" Samuel Luther,	Dec. 22, 1843.
3-6	" Almira Simmons,	Sept. 16, 1846.
3-8	" Amanda Bailey,	Jan. 23, 1849.
3-33	" Emma Rebecca,	May 3, 1851.
3-25	" Deborah Josephine, of James P. and Mary S.,	April 23, 1844.
3-101	" Mary Adelaide,	May 10, 1846.
3-23	" Charles Andrew, of Henry A. and Deborah L.,	Feb. 7, 1847.
3-126	" Rebecca Cole, of Charles P. and Sarah Ann,	July 29, 1847.
3-161	" William Child, of Edwin S. and Margaret A.,	Nov. 5, 1847.
3-6	" Amelia Milton, of Ira B. and Nancy,	July 18, 1853.
2-72	BRADFORD Le Baron, of Le Baron and Sarah,	Dec. 21, 1780.
1-22	BRAGLEY Johannah, of John and Johannah,	March 26, 1747.
3-26	BRAMAN Elizabeth A., of Elijah and Mary A.,	Oct. 19, 1836.
3-139	" Sylvanus H.,	July 8, 1838.
3-26	" Elijah F.,	Sept. 12, 1839.
3-6	" Ann Augusta,	Sept. 29, 1842.
3-6	" Alice,	Jan. 25, 1846.
3-101	" Mary Frances,	June 8, 1846.
1-7	BRAYTON Benjamin, of James Wheaton and Robe,	March 2, 1778.
2-44	" Hannah,	July 4, 1781.
2-97	" Susannah,	Sept. 23, 1783.
2-91	" Roby (at Freetown).	July 30, 1786.
2-88	" Patience,	Feb. 23, 1789.
2-7	" Betsey,	Jan. 2, 1791.
2-53	" James,	March 17, 1793.
1-58	" William,	March 17, 1796.
2-74	" Luther,	Aug. 2, 1798.
2-90	" Parthenia, of Benjamin and Rebecca,	Jan. 28, 1800.
2-77	" Maria,	Sept. 15, 1801.
2-93	" Rebeckah,	Nov. 19, 1803.
3-10	" Benjamin,	May —, 1806.
3-40	" George Wheaton, of William and Mary,	March 25, 1825.
3-159	" William,	Nov. 9, 1827.
3-62	" Jeremiah Williams,	July 8, 1829.
3-22	" Clara Sophia,	Aug. 16, 1831.
3-64	" James Wheaton,	Sept. 1, 1833.
3-64	" John Thurber,	Nov. 21, 1837.
1-5	BROWN Becca, of James and Rebecca,	April 17, 1738.
1-22	" James, 1st,	June 11, 1739.
1-31	" Molly,	June 22, 1740.
1-22	" James, 2d,	Aug. 19, 1742.
1-22	" James, 3d,	July 3, 1744.
1-8	" Cyrel,	June 11, 1746.
1-44	" Rebeckah,	Feb. 7, 1747.
1-31	" Micha (dau.),	Feb. 21, 1749.

1-11	BROWN David, of James and Rebecca,	Jan. 21, 1752.
1-11	" Deborah, of Jeremiah and Rebeckah,	May 18, 1747.
1-23	" John, of John, Jr., and Phebe,	May 7, 1752.
1-27	" John, 2d,	Jan. 6, 1755.
1-49	" Sarah, of James and Sarah,	Jan. 11, 1754.
1-4	" Asa, of Asa and Chloe,	Jan. 13, 1761.
1-4	" Amey, of William and Allthiah,	Aug. 1. 1762.
1-33	" Martin,	Feb. 4. 1764.
1-30	" Kent,	Dec. 27, 1765.
1-17	" Frances (dau.),	Nov. 20, 1769.
2-19	" Cynthia, of John and Betsey (also 3-22),	Jan. 26, 1779.
2-51	" John Stafford,	Aug. 25, 1782.
2-18	" Charles Frederick,	Oct. 13, 1796.
2-46	" Henry.	Jan. 7, 1800.
2-2	" Asa, of Samuel M. and Abigail (at Pomfret, Conn.),	Aug. 3, 1782.
1-12	" Debe (at Pomfret, Conn.),	Dec. 16, 1783.
2-2	" Abigail	Sept. 19, 1785.
2-33	" Esek.	Sept. 17, 1787.
2-91	" Rebeckah,	Sept. 4, 1790.
2-91	" Rebeckah, 2d,	Dec. 11, 1791.
2-45	" Hannah,	March 3, 1794.
2-58	" Jere. of John and Sally,	March 7, 1800.
2-108	" William S.,	Feb. 4, 1804.
2-94	" Rebeckah Miller,	April 28, 1606.
3-93	" Mark Anthony, of John and Lucinda,	April 11, 1809.
2-61	" Joseph Rogers, of David and Patience,	Jan. 26, 1810.
3-131	" Sarah Ann,	March 16, 1811.
3-25	" David Easterbrooks,	June 20, 1812.
3-59	" Jane,	Jan. 7, 1814.
3-119	" Peleg Rogers,	Dec. 1, 1815.
3-92	" Mary,	May 14, 1822.
3-125	" Roland Greene, of John and Mary,	March —, 1811.
3-41	" George S., of John and Malinday,	Jan. 28, 1813.
3-73	" Mary Ann Bowen, of Joseph and Maria,	Jan. 30, 1813.
3-92	" Mary Ann,	Jan. 30, 1814.
3-161	" William Mathewson, of William L. and Sally,	Jan. 16, 1827.
3-23	" Charles Palmer,	June 29, 1831.
3-100	" Marietta,	April 28, 1833.
3-5	" Ann Frances,	July 21, 1835.
3-138	" Sarah Elizabeth,	Aug. 9, 1837.
3-53	" Harrison Tyler,	Feb. 20, 1840.
3-32	" Elizabeth Folger, of Charles F. and Sarah G.,	Jan. 26, 1836.
3-115	" Octavia Frederick,	Oct. 10, 1842.
3-55	" Isabella Fredonia,	April 2, 1845.
3-37	" Charles Frederick,	Sept. 25. 1846.
3-35	" Frederick Montrose,	May 18, 1848.
3-32	" Elizabeth Frances. of George and Betsey,	May 1, 1839.
3 58	BUGBEE James Henry, of James and Elizabeth,	Dec. 5. 1812.
3-90	" Mary Ann,	Aug. 29, 1814.
1-55	BULLOCK William, of Richard and Abigail,	March 27, 1752.
1-3	" Ann,	Jan. 31, 1754.
1-24	" Joseph,	April 8, 1755.
1-3	" Abigail,	March 23, 1757.
1-45	" Richard,	Nov. 19, 1759.
3-96	" Martha Otis, of Dr. Otis and Martha,	May 8, 1637.
3-53	" Herbert Dorrance, of Otis and Elizabeth H.,	May 28, 1844.
3-43	" George Sanders,	Jan. 10, 1849.
1-50	BURR Samuel, of Shubael and Betsey,	May 5, 1761.
1-6	" Betsey,	June 17. 1763.
1-51	" Sarah,	Sept. 14, 1764.
1-37	" Nathan Miller,	Jan. 27. 1766.
1-41	" Patience,	April 9, 1767.
1-51	" Sarah,	June 30, 1768.
1-27	" Josiah,	April 25, 1770.
1-46	" Rebecca,	Aug. 4, 1772.

1-57	BURR	William Turner Miller. of Shubael and Betsey,	March 27, 1777.
2-108	"	William, of Rufus and Anna,	Nov. 8, 1788.
2-101	"	Sally,	March 28, 1793.
2-92	"	Rufus,	Oct. 27, 1795.
2-74	"	Lucy Ann,	Aug. 17, 1798.
2-7	"	Betsey, of Nathan Miller and Lydia (born at Pittstown, N. Y., in a log house),	Dec. 17, 1791.
2-58	"	James Adams,	Dec. 24, 1793.
2-81	"	Nathan Miller,	Dec. 4, 1795.
2-57	"	John Fessenden,	Aug. —, 1799.
2-37	"	Ephraim Willard, of Nathan Miller and Lucy,	March 7, 1809.
3-119	"	Polly Newell,	Jan. 12, 1811.
3-98	"	Norman Goodman, of Nathan Miller, Jr., and Martha G.,	Dec. 26, 1836.
3-98	"	Norman Goodman, 2d,	Aug. 3, 1838.
3-76	"	Lydia Adams,	Nov. 4, 1840.
2-45	"	Henry Willard, of Isaiah and Polly,	Nov. 20, 1794.
2-77	"	Martha Martindale,	May 20, 1796.
2-77	"	Mary,	July 31 1801.
1-58	"	William, of Shubael and Anna,	June 18, 1795.
2-82	"	Nancy,	March 8, 1799.
2-101	"	Shubael,	Nov. 22, 1801.
3-27	"	Eliza, of Shubael and Betsey,	April 11, 1812.
3-132	"	Shubael,	Oct. 22, 1814.
3-50	"	Henry,	Jan. 25, 1818.
3-40	"	Gerard,	Feb. 16, 1820.
3-160	"	Willard, child of Ephraim W. and Abby M. (also 3-162),	Aug. 12, 1836.
3-37	"	Clarence,	Dec. 18, 1838.
3-76	"	Lucy Elizabeth,	June 15, 1841.
3-101	"	Mary Smith,	May 11, 1844.
3-33	"	Edmund Coffin,	April 14, 1846.
3-32	"	Eveline Estella, of Henry and Eunice H.,	Sept. 15, 1840.
3-52	BURTCH	Henry, of Stanton and Phebe (b. New Bedford),	June 21, 1817.
3-32	"	Emily, of Henry and Abby F.,	May 11, 1839.
2-6	BURT	Alvan Cole, of Alvan and Mary,	Oct. 4, 1908.
2-103	"	Sally Luther,	Oct. 31, 1810.
3-89	"	Mary,	April 12, 1813.
3-24	"	Delana Caroline,	Oct. 28, 1814.
3-157	"	Wealtby Austin,	July 12, 1817.
3-134	"	Samuel Zelotes,	Sept. 3, 1920.
3-40	"	George,	Dec. 7, 1822.
3-75	"	Lillis Cole,	Feb. 5, 1825.
3-62	"	John,	Feb. 17, 1829.
3-49	"	Hannah Driscoll, of Joseph and Content,	July 13, 1814.
3-90	"	Mary,	Jan. 3, 1816.
3-20	"	Abigail Wheaton,	Jan. 14, 1819.
3-60	"	Joseph,	Feb. 21, 1921.
3-30	"	Enos, Jr., of Enos and Winefred,	May 9, 1825.
3-3	"	Angeline Winefred,	April 10, 1826.
3-158	"	William Henry,	Oct. 11, 1827.
3-136	"	Seth Enos,	Oct. 25, 1829.
1-14	BUSHEE	Elizabeth, of James and Bathsheba,	Jan. 20, 1753.
1-24	"	James,	Sept. 16, 1754.
1-49	"	Sarah,	Oct. 29, 1756.
1-4	"	Anna,	July 21, 1758.
1-25	"	Jonathan,	Feb. 5, 1761.
1-8	"	Consider,	May 10, 1763.
1-28	"	Jesse. of James and Lydia,	June 4, 1768.
2-60	"	Jane, of Jonathan and Anstis,	Oct. 31, 1907.
3-120	"	Prescilla Luther, of John W. and Prescilla (Talby),	April 11, 1834.
1-22	BUTTERWORTH	Joseph, of Benjamin and Mellicent,	July 28, 1747.
1-7	"	Betty, of Hezekiah and Elizabeth,	July 22, 1768.
1-7	"	Benjamin,	May 29, 1771.
2-96	"	Samuel,	March 20, 1781.

BUTTERWORTH Gardner M., of Samuel and Mary,   July 24, 1805.
"   Eliza,   Aug. 7, 1808.
"   Daniel Gould of Benjamin and Polly,   Dec. 30, 1809.
"   Hezekiah, of Gardner M. and Susan W.,   Dec. 22, 1839.
"   John,   Aug. 11, 1842.
"   Addison G.,   April 3, 1844.
"   Joseph,   June 11, 1846.
"   Benjamin,   Aug. 30, 1848.
"   Mary Ann,   Jan. 6, 1855.
BUTTS Job, of Samuel and Deborah,   Oct. 14, 1797.
"   Nancy, of George and Avis,   Oct. 30, 1798.
"   George,   Sept. 20, 1800.
"   Enock,   Nov. 9, 1803.
"   Philena,   July 26, 1805.
"   Almira,   Dec. 27, 1807.
"   William Cole (also 3-159),   June 5, 1810.
"   James,   June 30, 1813.
"   Betsey,   Oct. 9, 1813.

C

CAREY Mariah, of Nathan and Rosalinda,   June 8, 1831.
"   James Ford,   Aug. 9, 1832.
CARPENTER Asaph, of Benjamin and Anne,   July 2, 1746.
"   Joseph,   Feb. 24, 1749.
"   Lucinda,   March 6, 1751.
"   Lois,   Sept. 8, 1753.
"   Morris Thomas, of Nathan and Hannah,   June 25, 1781.
"   Nabby, of Peter and Patience,   July 23, 1795.
"   Eliza Miller,   Aug. 5, 1802.
"   Moriah,   Feb. 28, 1804.
"   Rebeckah Hicks,   Nov. 18, 1807.
"   Mary, of Elisha and Hannah,   March 24, 1798.
"   Loiza,   Nov. 28, 1799.
CARR Caleb, of Caleb and Ruth,   Sept. 4, 1743.
"   John,   Jan. 12, 1746.
"   Samuel,   Dec. 8. 1748.
"   Jonathan,   March 8. 1751.
"   Robert,   May 5. 1752.
"   Hannah,   April —. 1753.
"   Mary,   June 19. 1755.
"   Nathan,   April 3. 1757.
"   Philip,   June 4. 1759.
"   Ruth,   Aug. 15, 1761.
"   Caleb, of Robert and Lydia,   Feb. 26, 1768.
"   Turner,   Sept. 6, 1769.
"   Lydia,   Jan. 29, 1772.
"   Robert,   Dec. 6, 1773.
"   Haile (dau.),   Dec. 25, 1776.
"   Philip,   Feb. 14, 1782.
"   Patience,   Jan. 27, 1784.
"   Samuel, of Caleb and Lillis,   April 19, 1769.
"   John,   Feb. 12, 1771.
"   Lillis,   Sept. 30, 1775.
"   Caleb,   Oct. 2, 1778.
"   Stephen,   Sept. 20, 1780.
"   Elizabeth, of Jonathan and Elizabeth,   June 29, 1772.
"   Ruth,   Feb. 24, 1776.
"   Lillis,   Feb. 22, 1778.
"   Abigail,   Oct. 24, 1780.
"   Polly,   Nov. 4, 1782.
"   Jonathan,   Feb. 27, 1785.
"   William, of William and Elizabeth,   April 14, 1790.
"   James, of Samuel and Sally,   June 7, 1793.

2-100	CARR	Sophia, of Samuel and Sally,	May 31, 1795.
2-101	"	Sally,	Sept. 25, 1797.
3-40	"	George Clinton,	April 26, 1809.
2-55	"	John, of John and Patty,	April 7, 1795.
2-5,	"	James Davis,	June 6, 1797.
2-102	"	Stephen,	May 14, 1802.
2-5	"	Ann Eliza,	Jan. 22, 1806.
1-53	"	Turner, of Caleb and Olive,	Sept. 21, 1795.
2-90	"	Philip,	Aug. 15, 1798.
2 81	"	Nathan, of William and Rebecca,	March 24, 1796.
2 10	"	Betsey,	March 22, 1798.
2-46	"	Henry Philip,	Nov. 5, 1799.
2 93	"	Rebeckah,	Jan. 17, 1802.
2 75	"	Lydia Miller,	June 21, 1805.
2 39	"	George Washington,	April 18, 1808.
3-1	"	Abigail Phillips,	Dec. 20, 1810.
3-19	"	Charles,	Sept. 6, 1813.
3-90	"	Mary,	July 4, 1815.
3 50	"	Henry Phillips,	Feb. 16, 1821.
2-93	"	Rebecca, of John and Martha,	Sept. 19, 1800.
2-18	"	Caleb,	Feb. 28, 1804.
2-5	"	Alfred Coste, of Stephen and Polly,	Dec. 26, 1804.
2-36	"	Elizabeth Miller, of Caleb and Alice,	Nov. 11, 1807.
3-89	"	Mary Ann, of Jonathan, Jr., and Ann,	April 5, 1811.
3-157	"	William Hill,	July 24, 1812.
3-157	"	William, of William, Jr., and Temperance,	July 9, 1821.
3-10	"	Betsey,	April —, 1824.
3-157	"	Seraphine Smith,	Oct. 29, 1836.
3-65	"	Josephine,	Jan. 8, 1839.
3-119	"	Phillip, of Turner and Sally J.,	Feb. 23, 1823.
3-143	"	Turner,	July 18, 1824.
3-5	"	Abby Elizabeth,	Jan. 18, 1828.
3-22	"	Caleb Sanders,	Oct. 28, 1829.
3-64	"	Joseph Sanders,	March 20, 1832.
3-23	"	Clarence Lyndon, of George W. and Elizabeth,	July 18, 1842.
3-5	"	Alice Elizabeth,	Sept. 12, 1845.
3-55	"	John Tyler, of Philip and Mary Elizabeth,	Feb. 22, 1848.
3-6	"	Anne Majus,	Oct. 24, 1850.
3-120	"	Philip Angustus,	Nov. 14, 1852.
2-89	CARTEE	Polly, of Alfred and Lillis,	April 30, 1795.
2-100	"	Seth,	Nov. 3, 1797.
2-116	"	Louisa,	Aug. 24, 1799.
2-53	CAUSSANES	John, of John and Nancy,	July 5, 1785.
2-80	"	Nancy,	July 3, 1790.
2-89	"	Polly Sophia,	Jan. 20, 1792.
1-52	CHAMPLAIN	Thomas, of Thomas and Charity,	Dec. 14, 1779.
1-53	"	Thomas, 2d,	Sept. 9, 1784.
2-56	"	Joshua, of John and Elizabeth,	Sept. 25, 1794.
2-34	"	Eliza,	April 10, 1796.
2-90	"	Polly,	March 14, 1798.
2-58	"	John,	Dec. 11, 1800.
2-104	"	Thomas,	Sept. 2, 1802.
2-60	"	Jotham Carr,	Nov. 30, 1804.
2-39	"	George Thompson,	May 28, 1807.
2-90	"	Phebe, of James and Hannah,	Aug. 29, 1795.
2-47	"	Hannah,	June 28, 1797.
2 57	"	James,	(also 2-60), May 15, 1799.
2-47	"	Henry,	Sept. 11, 1803.
2-58	"	John Bowman, of William and Rebecca,	May 29, 1798.
2-108	"	William,	May 16, 1800.
3-63	"	John Martin, of Joshua and Hannah,	March 12, 1824.
3-63	"	Joshua,	Aug. 6, 1825.
3-136	"	Samuel Martin,	April 18, 1828.
3 95	"	Moses Tyler,	Jan. 20, 1830.
3-53	"	Henry, of Henry and Elizabeth,	Jan. 28, 1833.

3-33	CHAMPLAIN Edna Elizabeth. of Henry and Elizabeth,	Jan. 6, 1844.
3-42	" George Thompson, of George T. and Hannah,	Jan. 28, 1835.
3-65	" John,	Feb. 16, 1837.
3-9	CHAPMAN Benjamin Hallett, of Daniel and Christian,	Jan. 4, 1819.
1-45	CHASE Royal, of Elisha and Sarah,	Oct. 11, 1760.
1-29	" Lydia,	Sept. 2, 1762.
1-6	" Bethany,	May 23, 1768.
1-33	" Mary, of Edward and Joanna,	June 9, 1768.
1-34	" Maxwell,	July 17, 1770.
2-33	" Edward,	March 5, 1774.
1-35	" Mary, of James and Mary,	July 11, 1777.
2-82	" Nancy, of Edward and Betsey,	Sept. 4, 1796.
2-76	" Maxwell,	Jan. 7, 1798.
2-35	" Edward,	Jan. 22, 1799.
2-10	" Betty,	Dec. 1, 1800.
2-35	" Elmina, of Joshua and Anna,	March 24, 1800.
3-49	" Harriet Viall, of Allen and Sally,	March 23, 1809.
3-27	" Elizabeth Haile,	March 26, 1812.
3-59	" John Haile,	May 19, 1814.
3-75	" Laura,	April 10, 1816.
3-8	" Allen,	April 20, 1818.
3-56	" John Horn, of Peleg, and Polly,	April 19, 1811.
3-157	" William Millbery,	May 22, 1813.
3-115	" Obadiah, of Anthony and Isabel.	April 12, 1818.
3-10	" Benjamin Anthony,	March 6, 1820.
3 4	" Abigail,	March 13, 1824.
3-37	" Charles Anthony, of Obadiah and Esther, 12 m,,	—— 22, 1846.
3-34	" Emma,	May 22, 1853.
3-133	CHESSMAN Samuel Hallett, of Daniel and Christina,	Jan. 7, 1820.
1-24	CHILD John, of James and Sarah,	Jan. 20, 1733.
1-22	" James, of John and Abigail,	Jan. 27, 1745.
1-22	" Jeremiah,	April 22, 1747.
1-32	" Martha, of Cromwell and Roby,	Dec. 5, 1748.
1-15	" Elizabeth,	Sept. 17, 1752.
1-20	" Hope,	May 14, 1756
1-26	" John,	Jan. 16, 1761.
1-40	" Prudence, of Sylvester and Abigail,	Aug. 5, 1749.
1-23	" James,	March 6, 1750-1.
1-49	" Sarah,	Ang. 27, 1752.
1-3	" Abigail Miller,	Oct. 16, 1756.
1 8	" Cromwell, of Caleb and Bethiah,	Jan. 30, 1757.
1-8	" Caleb,	Nov. 24, 1761.
1-5	" Benjamin, of Hezekiah and Patience,	Dec. 13, 1757.
1-20	" Haile,	Jan. 25, 1759.
1-56	" William,	March 29, 1761.
1-29	" Lillis Turner,	Jan. 3, 1763.
1-41	" Patience,	June 23, 1765.
1-1	" Anne,	Oct. 3, 1767.
1-34	" Mary,	Oct. 2, 1769.
1-4	" Abigail, of Sylvester and Joanna,	Sept. 5, 1759.
1-18	" Gardner,	April 9, 1761.
1-51	" Sylvester,	Sept. 14, 1764.
1-16	" Elizabeth,	July 2, 1766.
1-3	" Abigail Miller, of John 2d, and Rosabella,	Sept. 26, 1759.
1-25	" John Throop,	Nov. 6, 1761.
1-51	" Samuel,	Jan. 21, 1765.
1-37	" Nathan,	July 18, 1767.
1-47	" Rosabella,	July 25, 1778.
1-33	" Margary, of James and Hannah,	June 18, 1762.
1-26	" James Kelley,	Aug. 30, 1763.
1-52	" Thomas,	April 17, 1765.
1-51	" Simeon, of William and Susannah,	March 6, 1763.
1-57	" William,	April 10, 1766.
2-91	" Roby,	Nov. 7, 1768.
1-6	" Bethiah. of James and Mary,	July 8, 1767.

2-1	CHILD	Anne, of James and Mary,	June 25, 1768.
1-28	"	James,	March 16, 1772.
2-1	"	Abigail,	Oct. 27, 1774.
1-34	"	Mary,	Nov. 19, 1770.
2-72	"	Lydia, of Sylvester and Jean,	Oct. 28, 1768.
1-27	"	Jeremiah, of Jeremiah and Patience,	Dec. 10, 1768.
1-6	"	Betsey,	March 5, 1770.
2-32	"	Elizabeth,	March 14, 1773.
1-39	"	Oliver,	Jan. 28, 1775.
2-76	"	Martin,	April 16, 1777.
1-54	"	Varnum,	May 18, 1781.
2-89	"	Patience,	March 31, 1784.
1-53	"	Thomas,	April 21, 1788.
1-9	"	Christopher, of Caleb and Mary,	Sept. 20, 1775.
2-96	"	Shubuel Peck,	Sept. 28, 1779.
1-12	"	Daniel.	Nov. 17, 1782.
2-97	"	Samuel Cole,	Aug. 22, 1787.
2-90	"	Polly Reynolds, of Sylvester and Prescilla,	May 26, 1779.
2-90	"	Prescilla Bradford,	May 27, 1781.
2-3	"	Abigail Miller,	July 1, 1783.
1-19	"	Gardner,	Dec. 27, 1788.
2-56	"	Joanna,	Dec. 16, 1790.
1-19	"	George Washington, of James and Lydia,	Feb. 20, 1780.
2-88	"	Prescilla, of Cromwell, 2d, and Sally,	Jan. 3, 1781.
2-88	"	Peggy,	Oct. 26, 1782.
2-83	"	Edward Anthony,	Oct. 23, 1784.
2-73	"	Luther,	Aug. 22, 1788.
2-45	"	Henry,	May 4, 1790.
2-73	"	Lydia, of Haile and Amey,	Nov. 26, 1781.
1-53	"	William,	April 10, 1784.
1-19	"	Gardner,	April 8, 1786.
2-54	"	James,	Oct. 7, 1788.
2-45	"	Haile (son),	April 19, 1791.
2-54	"	John Kennicutt,	June 10, 1794.
1-13	"	Daniel,	Oct. 29, 1796.
2-82	"	Nathan,	Jan. 21, 1799.
2-46	"	Henry,	March 5, 1801.
2-38	"	George.	Sept. 18, 1803.
2-7	"	Benjamin, of William and Betsey,	Jan. 1, 1785.
2-53	"	Joseph.	Jan. 1, 1785.
2-98	"	Samuel,	Feb. 5, 1787.
1-58	"	William Henry,	June 11, 1789.
2-7	"	Betsey,	Oct. 4, 1791.
2-80	"	Nancy.	April 18, 1794.
2-34	"	Ezra Ormsbee,	May 5, 1796.
2-108	"	William Barton,	May 5, 1796.
2-4	"	Amanda,	June 26, 1798.
2-101	"	Sally,	May 7, 1800.
1-36	"	——, of John Throop and Molly,	Dec. 23, 1788.
2-53	"	John Throop,	May 7, 1790.
1-36	"	Molly Turner,	Nov. 20, 1792.
2-10	"	Betsey, of Simeon and Patience,	Dec. 16, 1789.
2-46	"	Henry Arnold,	Feb. 24, 1793.
1-38	"	Nancy, of Samuel and Nancy,	April 14, 1790.
2-55	"	Julian,	June 18, 1794.
2-7	"	Bethiah Cole, of Caleb, Jr., and Peggy,	Aug. 13, 1786.
2-90	"	Peggy Bowen, of Caleb, Jr., and Sarah,	June 10, 1792.
2-9	"	Betsey, of Oliver and Hannah,	July 18, 1797.
2-93	"	Robert, of Christopher and Polly,	May 17, 1799.
2-18	"	Christopher,	July 9, 1803.
2-46	"	Hannah, of Cromwell and Sarah,	July 18, 1799.
3-74	"	Louisa, of Ruth,	Feb. 25, 1805.
3-89	"	Mary Ann, of Varnum and Nancy,	Feb. 27, 1805.
3-131	"	Sylvester,	May 12, 1810.
2-78	"	Mary Cole, of Shubael Peck and Priscilla B.,	Nov. 26, 1808.

3-49	CHILD	Harriet Newell, of Shubael Peck and Priscilla B.,	Jan. 27, 1815.
3-19	"	Charles Thompson,	Oct. 11, 1816.
2-37	"	Eliza Ann, of William and Lucinda.	Jan. 13, 1809.
3-39	"	Gardner,	Jan. 20, 1811.
3-73	"	Lydia,	June 25, 1813.
3-50	"	Haile (son),	May 18, 1816.
3-2	"	Amey Kennicutt,	April 25, 1819.
3-51	"	Henry,	July 24, 1823.
3-60	"	John Henry, of Thomas C. and Nancy B.,	Feb. 11, 1810.
3-119	"	Pardon Bowen,	April 22, 1821.
3-89	"	Maria, of Edward A. and Betsey,	July 22, 1810.
3-27	"	Eloiza,	Nov. 20, 1811.
3-132	"	Sally,	July 3, 1815.
3-91	"	Maria,	March 26, 1817.
3-28	"	Edward Anthony,	Jan. 26, 1819.
2-6	"	Arnold, of Simeon,	—— —, 1810 (?)
3-4	"	Abby Miller, of John Throop and Elizabeth,	March 6, 1811.
3-57	"	Joseph Bowen, of Henry W. and Betsey,	March 26, 1812.
3-49	"	Henry W.,	Sept. 13, 1814.
3-59	"	Jonathan Bowen,	Aug. 18, 1817.
3-24	"	Daniel Thomas, of Thomas E. and Nancy,	Dec. 11, 1812.
3-19	"	Caleb Oliver,	Oct. 17, 1815.
3-60	"	James Champlain, of Benjamin and Phebe,	Oct. 14, 1819.
3-119	"	Phebe Ann,	March 21, 1821.
3-9	"	Benjamin Smith,	Oct. 18, 1822.
3-93	"	Maria Matilda,	May 27, 1824.
3-9	"	Betsey Kennicutt, of Daniel and Mary Ann,	Jan. 16, 1820.
3-91	"	Mary,	Feb. 9, 1821.
3-3	"	Abby Cole,	Nov. 4, 1823.
3-134	"	Samuel Smith, of Ezra O. and Betsey,	Sept. 9, 1820.
3-30	"	Ezra O.,	Sept. 17, 1822.
3-75	"	Louisa,	Aug. 19, 1827.
3-134	"	Sarah, of William B. and Peggy B.,	Sept. 29, 1820.
3-29	"	Elizabeth,	Nov. 3, 1822.
3-60	"	John Newhall, of John K. and Mary Ann,	Feb. 7, 1821.
3-51	"	Hetty Newhall,	April 28, 1824.
3-51	"	Henry,	July 4, 1827.
3-53	"	Henry William, of Henry and Ann Eliza,	Sept. 13, 1838.
2-91	CHURCHILL	Ruth, of Ansel and Lillis,	Feb. 19, 1794.
2-4	"	Ansel,	Feb. 3, 1797.
3-24	CLARKE	David Eddy, of Ezekiel and Mary,	May 17, 1819.
2-83	COGGESHALL	Nicholas Easton, of John M. and Betsey,	Sept. 16, 1796.
1-15	COLE	Esther, of Benjamin and Mary,	Dec. 15, 1738.
1-32	"	Mehitable,	April 19, 1741.
1-40	"	Patience,	Sept. 12, 1744.
1-31	"	Mary,	Dec. 27, 1746.
1-45	"	Robe,	Aug. 2, 1756.
1-14	"	Elizabeth, of Ebenezer and Prudence,	Dec. 28, 1738.
1-44	'	Rosabella,	Jan. 4, 1739.
1-8	"	Curtis,	April 4, 1742.
1-44	"	Ruth,	July 24, 1744.
1-48	"	Sarah,	Dec. 3, 1746.
1-31	"	Mary,	Jan. 9, 1748.
1-15	"	Edward,	Oct. 25, 1751.
1-40	"	Prudence,	Oct. 22, 1753.
1-15	"	Ebenezer,	Feb. 22, 1756.
1-5	"	Benjamin,	Dec. 3, 1759.
2-91	"	Roby,	Dec. 12, 1761.
1-49	"	Sarah, of Thomas and Christian,	Feb. 6, 1742.
1-3	"	Anne,	Dec. 19, 1743.
1-11	"	Dorcas,	Jan. 31, 1746.
1-20	"	Haite (dau.),	March 11, 1748.
1-11	"	Deborah,	April 1, 1750.
1-3	"	Abigail,	Nov. 15, 1752.
1-24	"	James,	April 21, 1755.

1-33	COLE Mary, of Thomas and Christian,	July 10, 1757.
1-6	" Bethiah,	March 14, 1761.
1-30	" Loisanah,	Oct. 5, 1762.
1-40	" Peter, of Peter and Mary,	March 29, 1745.
1-31	" Mary,	Dec. 25, 1746.
1-2	" Joanna, of Isaac and Sarah,	Dec. 20, 1746.
1-22	" Ichabod,	Dec. 17, 1748.
1-23	" Isaac,	Oct. 1, 1735.
1-52	" Thomas,	July 1, 1758.
1-45	" Reuben Butts,	Dec. 12, 1762.
1-2	" Allen, of David and Anna,	Oct. 16, 1747.
1-2	" Anna,	March 1, 1750-1.
1-49	" Simeon,	June 26, 1752.
1-11	" David,	Nov. 19, 1754.
1-14	" Elizabeth, of Nathan and Sarah,	Feb. 22, 1747-8.
1-23	" John,	May 16, 1751.
2 95	" Sarah,	Feb. 21, 1756.
1-40	" Peace,	May 16, 1760.
1-29	" Lydia, of Benjamin, 2d, and Mary,	Aug. 4, 1749.
1-48	" Samuel, of Daniel and Amey,	Sept. 1, 1749.
1-29	" Landall,	Nov. 28, 1751.
1-14	" Elijah,	Oct. 25, 1753.
1-32	" Mary,	Aug. 31, 1755.
1-11	" Daniel,	Aug. 8, 1757.
1 50	" Seth,	May 12, 1760.
1 51	" Spencer,	Sept. 12, 1762.
1-46	" Rachel,	Nov. 16, 1766.
1-27	" Jeremiah,	Oct. 18, 1769.
1-1	" Amey,	July 24, 1772.
1-5	" Benjamin, of Benjamin and Hannah,	July 7, 1750.
1 49	" Sebra, of William and Elizabeth,	Nov. 8, 1751.
1-55	" William,	Oct. 8, 1753.
1-18	" Gideon,	Nov. 15, 1755.
1-52	" Thomas, of Isaiah and Ellinor,	Nov. 29, 1751.
1-15	" Elizabeth,	April 25, 1753.
1-3	" Andrew,	Jan. 30, 1755.
1-24	" James,	June 1, 1757.
1-37	" Nathaniel,	Nov. 20, 1759.
1-4	" Abigail,	May 26, 1763.
1-34	" Mary,	Oct. 27, 1765.
2-95	" Samuel,	March 3, 1769.
1-15	" Edward, of Jonathan and Elizabeth,	Aug. 14, 1754.
1 3	" Aubrey, of Jonathan and Abigail,	July 14, 1756.
1-41	" Patience,	Oct. 20, 1759.
1-32	" Martin,	Jan. 17, 1762.
1-30	" Levi, of Eddy and Ruth,	June 11, 1761.
1-33	" Mary,	Oct. 23, 1765.
1-42	" Patience,	Nov. 16, 1771.
1-16	" Edward, of Samuel and Keziah,	Nov. 13, 1763.
1-51	" Samuel,	July 26, 1765.
1-37	" Nathaniel Hix,	Aug. 7, 1767.
1-24	" Mary, of Richard and Lydia,	May 29, 1764.
1-21	" Hannah,	Sept. 18, 1768.
1-45	" Rebecca, of Curtis and Sarah,	Dec. 4, 1764.
1-57	" William,	March 17, 1766.
1-26	" Jonathan,	Oct. 12, 1767.
1-41	" Prudence,	July 8, 1769.
1-6	" Betsey,	May 14, 1771.
2-95	" Sarah,	Feb. 19, 1773.
2 96	" Sarah, 2d,	July 8, 1774.
2-32	" Ebenezer,	June 8, 1778.
1-35	" Mary,	Oct. 17, 1780.
1-30	" Levi, of Edward and Sarah,	Nov. 20, 1771.
2-32	" Elizabeth,	Sept. 1, 1773.
1-42	" Paul,	July 8, 1776.

1-9	COLE	Caleb Pears, of Edward and Sarah,		March 14, 1777.
1-52	"	Tillinghast,		Sept. 10, 1778.
2-96	"	Samuel,		Nov. 17, 1780.
2-97	"	Sally,		Dec. 25, 1783.
1-6	"	Burden, of Isaac and Abigail,		June 9, 1772.
1-56	"	William, of Allen and Patience.		July 2, 1773.
1-1	"	Anne,		Feb. 9, 1776.
1-42	"	Patience,		April 5, 1778.
2-41	"	Allen,		Feb. 18, 1781.
1-43	"	Pattey,		June 10, 1783.
1-12	"	David,		May 10, 1786.
2-8	"	Betsey,		Nov. 12, 1788.
2-99	"	Samuel,		Sept. 4, 1792.
2-9	"	Benjamin, of Ichabod and Robe.		Feb. 19, 1775.
2-51	"	Joseph,		Feb. 4, 1783.
2-99	"	Sarah,	(also 2-97), March 30 or 31, 1785.
2-91	"	Roby,		May 31, 1791.
1-53	"	Thomas Easterbrooks,		Dec. 17, 1797.
2-74	"	Luther. of Luther and Elizabeth,		May 1, 1776.
1-53	"	Thomas,		May 24, 1781.
1-47	"	Rachel, of John and Elizabeth,		April 25. 1779.
1-38	"	Nathan.		about 1780.
2-52	"	Jeremiah,		March 13. 1782.
2-97	"	Sarah,		May 11, 1785.
1-35	"	Mary, of Daniel and Zilpha,		Dec. 18, 1780.
1-60	"	Abigail, •		March 30, 1782.
2-97	"	Samuel,		Feb. 17, 1784.
2-51	"	Isaac, of Thomas and Anne,		Nov. 9, 1781.
2-52	"	Joanna,		July 18, 1785.
1-53	"	Thomas,		Aug. 15, 1788.
1-18	"	George, of Landall and Elizabeth,		Jan. 31, 1782.
1-12	"	Daniel,		June 23, 1788.
2-55	"	Jeremiah,		Aug. 9, 1794.
2-97	"	Sylvester, of Spencer and Mary,		Oct. 4, 1784.
1-52	"	Thomas, of James and Abigail,		Jan. 3, 1785.
2-32	"	Elizabeth, of Seth and Abigail,		April 1, 1785.
2-56	"	Elijah,		Feb. 16, 1788.
2-2	"	Andrew,		Nov. 25, 1791.
2-56	"	Isaiah,		July 9, 1797.
2-35	"	Eleanor,		Oct. 22, 1801.
2-77	"	Mary Ann,		Oct. 22, 1801.
2-72	"	Lillis, of Benjamin and Sarah,		Nov. 13, 1785.
1-36	"	Mary,		April 24, 1787.
2-33	"	Elizabeth,		April 24, 1787.
2-73	"	Luther,		Jan. 12, 1792.
2-100	"	Sarah,		Dec. 20, 1793.
2-9	"	Benjamin Miller,		Dec. 7, 1797.
2-52	"	James, of Ebenezer and Patty,		May 12, 1786.
1-43	"	Patty,		June 15, 1790.
2-33	"	Eben,		May 15, 1793.
1-19	"	Gibbs,		March 10, 1797.
1-36	"	Eliza,		April 25, 1803.
2-7	"	Bottey, of Isaac and Phebe,		July 17, 1786.
2-88	"	Patience, of Reuben and Molly,		May 10, 1787.
1-53	"	Thomas, of Benajah and Mary,		Aug. 1, 1789.
2-92	"	Roby, of Curtis and Mary,		July 11, 1790.
2-9	"	Betsey,		April 22, 1792.
2-92	"	Robert Miller, of Jonathan and Betsey,		March 24, 1793.
2-10	"	Betsey,		Dec. 23, 1795.
2-77	"	Mary Ann,		March 27, 1798.
2-102	"	Sarah Eddy,		May 9, 1802.
2-128	"	Polly Miller,		April 2, 1804.
2-47	"	Henry,		Oct. 15, 1806.
2-18	"	Catherine,		May 7, 1809.
2-38	"	George Salisbury, of Ebenezer, 2d, and Mary,		Feb. 3, 1801.

1-59	COLE	William, of William and Haile,	Nov. 11, 1801.
2-129	"	Patience,	April 19, 1805.
2-11	"	Betsey Smith,	May 15, 1808.
2-61	"	James Vance,	Jan. 11, 1810.
2-36	"	Eliza, of Allen and Betsey,	Dec. 18, 1805.
2-6	"	Allen,	March 12, 1808.
2-47	"	Henry,	Jan. 18, 1810.
3-27	"	Eliza,	March 4, 1813.
3-132	"	Samuel,	Nov. 14, 1815.
3-157	"	Wheaton,	Feb. 14, 1818.
3-133	"	Susannah Tibbetts,	Feb. 9, 1820.
2-5	"	Alvin, of Benjamin and Patience,	Aug. 3, 1806.
2-6	"	Abigail,	May 27, 1810.
3-39	"	George,	Feb. 26, 1812.
3-90	"	Maria,	March 8, 1814.
3-157	"	William,	Jan. 9, 1818.
2-103	"	Sarah, of Joseph and Mary,	May 30, 1810.
3-131	"	Sarah M., of David and Polly,	March 18, 1811.
3-19	"	Clement,	April 10, 1813.
3-90	"	Mary,	June 24, 1816.
3-50	"	Hannah,	March 28, 1820.
3-92	"	Martha Martin,	Aug. 19, 1821.
3-29	"	Elizabeth Burr,	March 25, 1823.
3-21	"	Charles,	Sept. 11, 1825.
3-119	"	Patience Hill,	Jan. 9, 1827.
3-136	"	Shubael Burr,	Oct 17, 1828.
3-125	"	Rebecca, of Jonathan and Betsey,	Oct. 12, 1811.
3-2	"	Abigail, of Jonathan and Abigail,	June 29, 1815.
3-19	"	Caroline, of Simmons and Sarah,	April 24. 1813.
3-53	"	Hanan Wilbour,	Aug. 30, 1816.
3-65	"	John Vinneman,	April 26, 1822.
3-58	"	Julian Easterbrooks, of Elijah and Marcy,	Sept. 4, 1813.
3-9	"	Betsey Easterbrooks,	Aug. 4, 1814.
3-95	"	Margaret Smith, of James and Sally,	June 15, 1815.
3-24	"	Daniel, of Thomas and Anne,	April 22, 1817.
3-50	"	Henry,	Aug. 20, 1820.
3-143	"	Thomas,	July 19, 1823.
3 28	"	Edmund, of Luther and Sally,	June 2, 1817.
3-73	"	Luther Salisbury,	Nov. 13, 1818.
3 133	"	Sophia Carr,	July 26, 1820.
3-135	"	Sarah,	July 5, 1823.
3-30	"	Elizabeth,	July 27, 1828.
3 96	"	Maria Pickens,	April 28, 1834.
3-133	"	Sarah, of George and Eliza,	Oct. 26, 1818.
3-133	"	Sally, of Thomas E. and Emma,	July 21, 1819.
3-9	"	Benjamin,	March 28, 1821.
3-10	"	Betsey Phinney,	April 19, 1825.
3-4	"	Adeline,	March 11, 1829.
3-10	"	Burrell Bosworth,	Dec. 22, 1836.
3-126	"	Robert, of Robert and Sally,	Feb. 25, 1820.
3-10	"	Betsey,	Jan. 1, 1825.
3-20	"	Content Maxwell, of Samuel and Patience G.,	June 10, 1822.
3-51	"	Hannah Driscoll,	June 12, 1824.
3-135	"	Samuel,	Sept. 7, 1826.
3-41	"	George Sanders,	Feb. 1, 1829.
3-159	"	William Allen,	June 11, 1831.
3-137	"	Samuel,	April 29, 1834
3-31	"	Emeline Mayberry,	June 5, 1836.
3-136	"	Sally Carr, of Alvin and Clarrissa,	Sept. 27, 1830.
3-31	"	Elizabeth Haile,	May 13, 1832.
3-31	"	Elizabeth Sherman, of Isaiah and Anna,	Sept. 25, 1832.
3-4	"	Aseneth Wilbour,	March 9, 1834.
3-5	"	Abby Anna,	June 28, 1838.
3-24	"	Daniel,	Feb. 10, 1845.
3-96	"	Mary Hoar, of Alvin and Lydia B.,	Jan. 17, 1834.

3-76	COLE	Lydia Burr, of Alvin and Lydia B.,	March 30, 1838.
3-7	"	Alice Hathaway (b. Cincinnati, O.),	April 5, 1840.
3-120	"	Patience,	March 10, 1844.
3-75	"	Lydia Williams, of Allen and Abby P.,	March 21, 1835.
3-71	"	Isabella, of George and Rachel,	Jan. 18, 1839.
3-102	"	Mary Elizabeth, of Samuel, 2d, and Mary Ann,	Aug. 6, 1842.
3-11	"	Abby Phillips,	Sept. 8, 1846.
3-102	"	Martha Davis,	Feb. 1, 1849.
3-11	"	Anna Bullock,	March 16, 1851.
3-139	"	Susan Wheaton,	April 7, 1954.
3-32	"	Emily Frances, of Edmund and Olive M.,	Aug. 29, 1844.
3-6	"	Adela Maria,	Feb. 7, 1849.
3-101	"	Mary Maria, of Betsey,	Dec. 8, 1845.
3-162	"	Walter Joyce, of Abram and Lydia,	April 6, 1846.
3-161	"	Walter Stanley, of Robert and Mary N.,	Dec. 6, 1846.
3-35	"	Frank Clafton,	April 11, 1949.
3-37	"	Charles H., of William and Maria,	June 17, 1847.
3-37	"	Clara W.,	Aug. 22, 1848.
3-33	"	Eliza Wheaton, of Wheaton and Eliza (Stockford),	April 26, 1849.
3-66	"	James Allen,	May 23, 1850.
3-139	"	Susan Frances, of John G. and Sarah J.,	June 7, 1849.
3-43	"	Gilbert Richmond,	Feb. 11, 1851.
2-75	COLLIMORE	Luther, of Nymphus and Sally,	March 13, 1806.
2-60	"	John Stephens,	May 13, 1807.
3-143	"	Thomas Cole,	Nov. 13, 1810.
3-24	"	Dorcas Stephens,	April 30, 1814.
3-19	"	Charles Henry,	July 28, 1817.
3-60	"	James Stillwell,	April 4, 1821.
3-106	"	Sarah Caroline, of Luther and Hannah,	Jan. 14, 1831.
3-52	"	Hannah,	March 12, 1832.
3-96	"	Mariah,	Aug. 15, 1834.
3-101	"	Mary Studson, of Thomas C. and Mary Ann,	Oct. 11, 1839.
1-9	COLLINS	Charles, of Charles and Hannah,	March 24, 1773.
1-57	"	William,	Aug. 7, 1776.
2-44	"	Hannah,	July 3, 1780.
2-45	"	Haile, of William and Sally,	May 30, 1798.
1-10	"	Charles Bradford, of Charles and Lydia,	Oct. 16, 1798.
2-18	"	Caroline,	Jan. 27, 1801.
2-77	"	Maria, of William and Polly,	March 8, 1801.
2-77	"	Mary,	June 22, 1803.
2-109	"	William,	Feb. 2, 1805.
2-47	"	Henry,	April 8, 1807.
2-83	"	Nancy,	June 2, 1810.
3-49	"	Hannah Turner,	May 23, 1812.
3-20	"	Charles,	May 30, 1818.
3-20	"	Clara,	Feb. 22, 1820.
3-93	"	Margaret Rhodes,	July 25, 1823.
3-160	"	William Henry,	Oct. 26, 1833.
3-51	"	Henry, of Hon. C. and Mary,	Oct. 20, 1826.
3-54	"	Henry, of Haile and Mary,	Nov. 28, 1825.
3-62	"	John Haile,	Dec. 8, 1823.
3-42	"	George Sanders, of Haile and Emeline,	Dec. 29, 1833.
3-160	"	William Haile,	Feb. 25, 1836.
3-100	"	Mary Frances,	Oct. 9, 1839.
3-101	"	Mary Maxwell, of Henry and Mary Ann,	July 27, 1852.
2-32	COMSTOCK	Elizabeth, of Jeremiah and Hannah,	Feb. 7, 1774.
1-1	"	Anne,	May 27, 1775.
1-28	"	Joseph Butterworth,	Jan. 7, 1778.
2-96	"	Samuel,	March 5, 1780.
3-42	COOKE	George Lewis, of George Lewis and Laura Frances,	June 29, 1849.
1-18	CORNELL	Gideon, of Gideon and Hepzebeth,	Sept. 11, 1760.
1-56	"	William,	June 16, 1762.
1-38	"	Nancy,	Jan. 27, 1768.
3-65	"	Joseph Edwin, of Alfred and Mary,	Nov. 7, 1837.

3-35	CORNELL Frances Elizabeth Driscoll, of Alfred and Mary,	Nov. 6, 1838.	
3-23	" Charles Henry,	July 14, 1842.	
3-23	" Charles Henry,	July 17, 1844.	
1-38	COWEN Nancy, of John and Mary,	Nov. 20, 1769.	
2-7	" Betsey,	June 2, 1772.	
2-52	" John,	June 13, 1774.	
2-35	" Eliza, of John and Elizabeth,	Aug. 9, 1796.	
2-59	" John K.,	March 22, 1802.	
2-102	" Sally,	Oct. 25, 1804.	
2-78	" Martin Kelley,	Aug. 7, 1807.	
2-79	" Mary Miller,	Jan. 22, 1810.	
3-97	" Nancy,	April 21, 1813.	
1-48	CRANSTON Samuel, of Benjamin and Elizabeth,	Sept. 17, 1737.	
1-8	" Caleb, of Benjamin and Sarah,	Feb. 12, 1749-50.	
1-5	" Benjamin,	Feb. 7, 1754.	
1-49	" Sarah,	Sept. 8, 1755.	
1-15	" Elizabeth,	July 2, 1757.	
1-41	" Phebe,	March 21, 1762.	
1-56	" William,	Feb. 1, 1764.	
1-42	" Peleg,	March 2, 1770.	
1-49	" Samuel, of Caleb and Mary,	May 17, 1755.	
1-50	" Samuel,	March 7, 1757.	
1-24	" John,	April 7, 1761.	
1-33	" Mary,	Feb. 2, 1764.	
1-30	" Lydia, of Caleb and Rachel,	April 18, 1771.	
1-52	" Thomas,	Feb. 28, 1773.	
2-72	" Lewin,	March 5, 1780.	
1-47	" Rachel,	June 15, 1782.	
1-9	" Caleb,	Sept. 22, 1787.	
2-96	" Sarah, of Benjamin and Mary,	Oct. 16, 1777.	
1-47	" Reuben Bowen,	July 18, 1779.	
1-57	" William,	May 11, 1783.	
2-44	" Harte, (dau.) of Benjamin and Keziah,	May 3, 1778.	
2-51	" John, of Samuel and Elizabeth,	March 2, 1785.	
1-10	" Caleb,	April 29, 1789.	
2-50	" Ira, of Peleg and Mary,	Nov. 19, 1793.	
1-53	" Thomas, of Thomas and Elizabeth,	Jan. 29, 1797.	
2-75	" Laura, of Lewin and Lydia,	March 30, 1804.	
2-116	" Lydia Child,	Dec. 24, 1808.	
3-73	" Lydia Child, 2d,	June 26, 1816.	
3-90	" Mary Newhall,	June 26, 1816.	
2-78	" Mary Davis, of William and Eliza,	July 23, 1808.	
2-109	" William Benjamin,	April 23, 1810.	
1-42	CROADE Polly, of John and Mary,	March 30, 1783.	
1-7	" Betsey, of John and Betsey,	March 9, 1786.	
2-8	" Betsey,	(sic.), March 17, 1786.	
2-54	" Johannah,	March 20, 1787.	
2-54	" John Thomas,	Nov. 5, 1788.	
2-3	" ——, (son),	Sept. 13, 1790.	
2-34	" Eliza,	Nov. 8, 1791.	
2-92	" Robert Child,	March 17, 1794.	
2-4	" Adeline,	Feb. 23, 1796.	
2-57	" Joanna,	Sept. 30, 1797.	
2-75	" Lydia Adams,	May 26, 1804.	
2-6	CROWELL Ardelia, of Joshua and Morey,	Nov. 22, 1808.	
3-38	CUTLER Charles Russell, of Charles R. and Celinda (also 3-26),	Nov. 13, 1848.	
3-26	" Mary Darling,	(also 3-102), April 17, 1851.	

D

2-60	DUVAL Joseph Bowen, of Stephen and Polly,	Sept. 15, 1804.	
2-103	" Stephen,	June 6, 1806.	
2-78	" Mary Ann,	Nov. 19, 1807.	

3-58	DUVAL John, of Stephen and Polly,		April 8, 1811.
3-131	" Sarah,		Feb. 20, 1813.
3-64	" John Francis, of John and Laura,		March 17, 1836.
3-161	" William Henry,		Feb. 4, 1840.
3-138	" Stephen Augustus, of Stephen, Jr., and Betsey S.,		March 27, 1840.
3-65	" James Cole,		March 6, 1842.
3-67	" Julia Maria, of William L. and Maria F.,		April 27, 1853.
2-128	DAVIS Polly, of Jesse and Rebeckah,		June 7, 1786.
2-75	" Lucinda,		March 23, 1790.
2-3	" Anthony,		Oct. 9, 1794.
1-13	" David,		July 9, 1798.
2-4	" Amanda,		May 6, 1802.
3-59	" John J. F.,		Dec. 4, 1808.
3-20	" Charles, of John and Celia (b. Dighton, Mass.),		Aug. 16, 1801.
3-34	" Edgar Maurice, of Sturges and Mary Kelley,		May 10, 1852.
3-101	" Mary Louisa,		April 25, 1854.
1-28	DOOR James, of James and Peace,		July 7, 1779.
1-33	DRING Mary, of Richard and Prescilla,		May 11, 1765.
2-60	DRISCOLL James Maxwell, of James and Hannah,		March 26, 1805.
2-109	" William Henry,		Feb. 26, 1807.
3-131	" Samuel Augustus,		April 2, 1810.
3-58	" Jeremiah,		March 31, 1814.
3-137	" Stephen· Gano,		April 13, 1816.
3-60	" John Flavel,		June 11, 1820.
3-91	" Mary Eliza, of William H. and Eliza T., (also 3-97),		Jan. 30, 1833.
3-64	" Josephine Frances,		Oct. 22, 1835.
3-6	" Antoinette Tyler,		Aug. 9, 1842.
3-6	" Annie,		March 14, 1845.
3-37	" Charles,		Nov. 5, 1948.
3-137	" Sarah James, of Samuel A. and Margaret (Smith),		June 26, 1837.
3-35	" Frederick Augustus,		Feb. 13, 1841.
1-30	DROWNE Lydia, of Benjamin and Hannah,		Feb. 1, 1740.
2-95	" Solomon,		March 1, 1742.
1-20	" Hannah,		Jan. 24, 1745.
1-5	" Benjamin,		Nov. 25, 1747.
1-11	" Daniel,		July 5, 1750.
1-8	" Caleb,		March 4, 1753.
1-49	" Simeon,		March 15, 1754.
1-5	" Betty,		July 16, 1755.
1-28	" Jonathan Jenckes,		Aug. 30, 1760.
2-4	" Almira, of Samuel and Hannah,		May 3, 1799.
2-102	" Samuel,		Oct. 3, 1801.
2-47	" Hannah,		April 21, 1804.
2-47	" Hannah, of Samuel and Ann,		May 16, 1808.
3-135	" Sarah Ann,		Feb. 21, 1822.
3-1	" Ann, of Samuel and Nancy,		June 17, 1809.
3-27	" Emeline,		Dec. 21, 1810.
3-39	" George, of James and Rebecca,		April 27, 1812.
3-59	" John,		April 13, 1814.
3-50	" Henry Frances, of Benjamin and Eliza (b. Barrington),,		April 21, 1818.
3-29	" Elizabeth Carr,		Sept. 9, 1819.
3-10	" Benjamin,		Dec. 19, 1826.
3-96	" Mary Jolls,	(also 3-101),	May 30, 1831.
3-66	" James Barnes,		Sept. 20, 1835.
3-6	" Albert Newell, of Nathaniel and Mary N.,		Dec. 9, 1839.
3-35	" Frank Scott,		Nov. 5, 1842.
3-161	" Willard Burr,		Feb. 15, 1845.
3-33	" Eliza Merriman,		Dec. 4, 1849.

E

1-20	EASTERBROOKS Harin, (dau.) of Benjamin and Joanna,		Nov. 6, 1741.
1-52	" Thomas,		April 6, 1744.

1-44	EASTERBROOKS Rhoda, of Benjamin and Joanna,		March 29, 1748.
1-5	"	Benjamin,	April 5, 1750.
1-48	"	Samuel,	May 4, 1752.
1-37	"	Nathaniel, of Nathaniel and Sarah,	March 15, 1744-5.
1-8	"	Calvin,	Sept. 21, 1749.
1-5	"	Benjamin. of Robert and Sarah,	Feb. 4, 1745-6.
1-55	"	Warren,	Aug. 23, 1748.
1-8	"	Caleb,	May 28, 1751.
1-14	"	Elizabeth, of William. 2d, and Abigail,	June 10, 1748.
1-18	"	Grizzell,	Aug. 31, 1751.
1-55	"	William,	Nov. 18, 1752.
1-2	"	Abel, of John and Abigail,	Aug. 31, 1748.
1-3	"	Aaron,	July 15, 1750.
1-48	"	Sarah, of John, 2d, and Abigail,	Aug. 2, 1752.
1-25	"	John,	Feb. 2, 1755.
1-8	"	Charles,	May 15, 1757.
1-25	"	Joanna,	June 9, 1760.
1-4	"	Abigail,	July 19, 1762.
1-17	"	Frances, of John and Frances,	April 9, 1753.
1-49	"	Sarah,	Aug. 10, 1754.
1-15	"	Edward,	June 1, 1756.
1-6	"	Byall, of William, Jr., and Susannah,	Aug. 14, 1753.
1-32	"	Martin,	Oct. 30, 1754.
1-40	"	Patience,	June 8, 1756.
1-50	"	Susannah,	Feb. 1, 1758.
1-45	"	Roby,	May 4, 1759.
2-95	"	Sarah,	March 9, 1765.
1-56	"	William,	Oct. 2, 1768.
2-32	"	Elizabeth.	Jan. 15, 1771.
1-40	"	Patience, of Benjamin and Sarah,	Sept. 19, 1756.
1-11	"	Daniel,	March 16, 1758.
1-26	"	Jonathan,	June 14, 1761.
1-4	"	Alexander,	Nov. 23, 1762.
1-40	"	Priscilla, of Robert, Jr., and Mary,	Dec. 16, 1757.
1-24	"	Jabez,	March 13, 1760.
1-24	"	James, of Levi, and Mary,	Sept. 12, 1759.
1-55	"	William,	Feb. 5, 1761.
1-9	"	Coomer,	May 11, 1767.
1-26	"	James, of Oliver, and Mary,	Oct. 20, 1765.
1-30	"	Lydia,	Jan. 16, 1769
2-32	"	Elizabeth,	Oct. 13, 1771.
1-46	"	Royal, of Thomas, 3d, and Lydia,	Oct. 4, 1767.
1-12	"	David,	Oct. 29, 1769.
1-28	"	Joanna,	Aug. 18, 1771.
1-46	"	Reuben. of Peleg and Rebecca,	Sept. 6, 1769.
2-1	"	Abigail,	June 23, 1771.
2-95	"	Sarah,	July 8, 1773.
1-42	"	Patience,	Oct. 23, 1775.
2-72	"	Levi,	July 17, 1778.
2-51	"	Jesse,	Jan. 22, 1787.
1-6	"	Barnard, of Moses and Abigail,	Dec. 6, 1769.
1-57	"	William, of Abial and Ruth,	July 25, 1775.
1-43	"	Patience Miller,	Oct. 3, 1777.
1-10	"	Caleb,	June 19, 1780.
1-36	"	Martin,	Oct. 16, 1782.
1-38	"	Nathan,	Oct. 25, 1784.
2-7	"	Betsey,	Feb. 10, 1787.
2-73	"	Lydia Adams,	March 26, 1789.
1-43	"	Persis, of Nathaniel and Lydia,	Sept. 15, 1777.
1-36	"	Mary,	Nov. 9, 1784.
2-72	"	Lydia,	Jan. 24, 1787.
2-102	"	Sarah,	May 16, 1789.
2-77	"	Marcy,	Sept. 14, 1791.
2-82	"	Nathaniel,	Sept. 5, 1797.
2-98	"	Sally, of Martin, and Aney,	Feb. 20, 1781.

2-55	EASTERBROOKS John, of Edward and Deborah,		Jan. 9, 1782.
1-42	"	Polly Hill,	March 4, 1783.
1-10	"	Caleb,	Sept. 5, 1784.
2-55	"	James,	Nov. 14, 1786.
2-34	"	Edward,	May 26, 1788.
2-8	"	Barnard,	March 9, 1790.
2-73	"	Lydia,	May 29, 1791.
2-81	"	Nancy,	Dec. 14, 1792.
2-97	"	Sally, of Daniel and Nabby,	April 3, 1784.
2-97	"	Sophronia,	Sept. 4, 1785.
2-55	"	Jonathan,	March 1, 1787.
2-8	"	Benjamin Throop,	July 7, 1789.
2-99	"	Sukey,	July 4, 1791.
1-17	"	George Throop,	June 7, 1794.
1-13	"	Daniel,	May 21, 1797.
2-1	"	Amy Cole, of Nellie,	Feb. 7, 1785.
1-38	"	Nancy, of William and Molly,	Dec. 13, 1789.
2-3	"	Amos,	May 21, 1792.
2-7	"	Betsey, of Royal and Hannah,	July 7, 1790.
1-53	"	Thomas,	April 13, 1792.
1-12	"	David, of David and Dianna,	April 11, 1793.
2-110	"	William, of William and Lois,	Sept. 15, 1800.
3-91	"	Martin,	Oct. 14, 1802.
3-40	"	George,	March 7, 1807.
3-133	"	Sally Wheaton, of John and Mary,	Nov. 13, 1816.
3-91	"	Mary,	Dec. 7, 1818.
3-3	"	Abby,	March 14, 1821.
3-61	"	James,	April 28, 1823.
3-158	"	William, of Joseph and Amey C.,	April 17, 1825.
3-62	"	James,	Nov. 29, 1828.
3-75	"	Levi,	April 10, 1831.
3-42	"	George Clarence, of Levi and Jane.	July 25, 1846.
3-33	"	Ezra Otis,	Nov. 24, 1847.
1-22	EDDY Joseph, of Joseph and Mary,		Feb. 24, 1729.
1-8	"	Charles,	March 1, 1731.
1-2	"	Abigail,	Dec. 7, 1736.
1-40	"	Patience,	Sept. 28, 1738.
1-31	"	Mary,	March 16, 1739.
1-39	"	Oliver,	March 15, 1741.
1-55	"	William, of Caleb and Mehitable,	April 25, 1746.
1-8	"	Caleb,	May 2, 1751.
1-8	"	Caleb, of Joseph, Jr., and Lydia,	June 27, 1757.
1-5	"	Betty,	Oct. 7, 1759.
1-25	"	John,	April 15, 1761.
2-92	"	Roby,	Nov. 16, 1770.
2-55	"	Jeremiah,	Jan. 10, 1772.
2-34	"	Ebenezer,	June 1, 1773.
2-100	"	Samuel,	Sept. 4, 1775.
1-3	"	Amey, of Elkanah and Patience,	Jan. 31, 1752.
1-8	"	Caleb, of Edward and Abigail,	May 2, 1763.
1-16	"	Edward,	June 12, 1766.
1-16	"	Enos,	Dec. 22, 1767.
2-52	"	John Cummins,	March 29, 1775.
1-16	"	Elizabeth, of Caleb and Sarah,	May 16, 1766.
1-9	"	Caleb,	June 12, 1768.
1-7	"	Benjamin, of Sarah,	Aug. 7, 1772.
2-72	"	Little Reynolds,	Jan. 11, 1780.
2-34	"	Edward, of Edward and Mary,	Aug. 29, 1792.
2-128	"	Polly, of Nancy,	Jan. 29, 1795.
2-100	"	Sarah, of Benjamin and Abigail,	April 28, 1795.
2-100	"	Sylvester,	June 19, 1797.
2-10	"	Benjamin, of Benjamin and Abigail,	March 18, 1804.
2-78	"	Mary K.,	Feb. 27, 1808.
3-55	"	John Lawton,	April 21, 1811.
2-81	"	Nabby, of Caleb and Nabby,	Sept. 3, 1795.

2-18	EDDY Caleb, of Caleb and Nabby,		May 11, 1799.
2-35	"	Elizabeth,	Dec. 11, 1800.
2-93	"	Rebeckah Maxwell,	March 8, 1804.
2-5	"	Anjanette,	Feb. 7, 1807.
2-78	"	Mongomery,	Nov. 10, 1808.
2-57	"	James Maxwell,	Feb. 8, 1811.
3-49	"	Henry Walter,	Jan. 1, 1813.
3-157	"	William Phillips,	Sept. 25, 1816.
3-133	"	Samuel Randall,	Oct. 2, 1818.
2-108	"	William Williams, of Enos and Betsey,	Sept. 2, 1796.
2-34	"	Eliza Williams,	April 23, 1798.
2-58	"	John Enos,	Jan. 1, 1802.
2 60	"	Jane Matilda,	June 29, 1804.
2-5	"	Abby Child,	Jan. 23, 1807.
2-37	"	Eliza Williams,	July 21, 1809.
3-35	"	Ferdinand Smith,	Feb. 27, 1812.
3-61	"	John Lawton, of Sylvester and Tomah,	Jan. 14, 1825.
3-62	"	John Enos, of William W. and Hannah,	Sept. 12, 1825.
3-159	"	William Sayles,	July 27, 1827.
3-30	"	Elizabeth, of Sylvester and Mahala,	Jan. 17, 1827.
3-21	"	Charles Cantero,	Jan. 27, 1829.
3-5	"	Abby K.,	March 22, 1834.
3-41	"	George Henry,	Feb. 26, 1837.
3-100	"	Mary Taylor, of Henry Walter and Hannah,	June 5, 1843.
3-5	"	Anjanette,	July 11, 1945.
3-33	"	Emily,	Dec. 15, 1850.
3-23	"	Caleb Montgomery, of William P. and Nancy G.,	Feb. 28, 1844.
3-33	"	Edward Taylor Clarke,	Jan. 14, 1846.
3-37	"	Clara Frances, of Samuel R. and Abby E.,	Nov. 29, 1848.
1-17	ELLIOTT Francis, of Nathaniel and Elizabeth,		Aug. 15, 1794.
3-61	"	John Edmund, of John and Lois,	Dec. 20, 1822.
3-94	EMERY Mary Ann, of John and Nancy Grant,		March 17, 1826.
3-63	ESTES Joseph Anthony, of Joseph and Eunice,		8m. 21, 1831.

F

2-59	FESSENDEN John Milton, of John and Abigail,		Dec. 23, 1802.
2-38	"	Guy,	March 30, 1804.
1-51	FISK Sarah, of Samuel and Judeth,		March 9, 1765.
1-26	"	Jonathan,	Nov. 20, 1766.
2-95	"	Samuel,	May 1, 1769.
1-35	"	Mary, (also 3-94)	June 26, 1774.
1-47	"	Rice Powell,	Jan. 11, 1776.
1-34	"	Mary, of Amos and Mary,	March 25, 1767.
1-9	"	Caleb,	Dec. 24, 1768.
3-89	FOSTER Mary Ann, of Peregrine P. and Rebecca,		Nov. 3, 1818.
1-49	FOWLER Sarah, of Samuel and Hannah,		Oct. 20, 1753.
1-15	"	Ezekiel,	Dec. 23, 1755.
1-32	"	Marcy,	Aug. 24, 1756.
1-24	"	Isaac,	Aug. 3, 1758.
3-100	"	Mary Haile, of Samuel M. and Mary C. (b. Pawtucket, R. I.), May 22, 1831.	
1-25	FREDWELL James, of James and Sarah,		Oct. 19, 1755.
1-50	"	Sarah,	Aug. 31, 1757.
1-32	"	Molly,	July 13, 1759.
1-15	"	Edminster,	Aug. 31, 1761.
1-33	"	Molly Martin, of Eleazer and Hannah,	Dec. 11, 1762.
2-101	FRENCH Stanton, of Rufus and Betsey,		Jan. 11, 1799.
3-90	"	Mary, of Ephraim and Mary (b. Bristol),	July 14, 1807.
2-48	"	Henry,	Aug. 13, 1809.
3-49	"	Henry, 2d,	Aug. 25, 1812.
3-63	"	James,	Oct. 23, 1815.
3-139	FRIEZE Sarah Lyman, of John and Jane Y.,		Feb. 22, 1850.
3-35	FRINK Francis Denison, of Rufus and Sally S.,		April 25, 1826.

3-98	FULLER Nathaniel C., of Nathaniel L. and Elizabeth,		April 2, 1838.
3-6	" Albert E.,		July 3, 1842.

G

2-1	GARDINER Anne, of Edward and Elizabeth,	Sept. 13, 1777.
2-51	" John,	April 6, 1780.
2-97	" Sarah Brown,	Jan. 24, 1784.
2-53	" Joseph,	Jan. 19, 1787.
2-88	" Polly,	Nov. 25, 1789.
2-82	" Nancy (b. Somerset),	Oct. 25, 1794.
2-90	" Philip Smith,	Oct. 17, 1798.
1-13	" Daniel,	Aug. 15, 1799.
2-59	" John Child, of Edward and Rosabella,	Nov. 28, 1803.
2-38	" George Tibbetts,	Feb. 16, 1805.
2-18	" Charles,	Jan. 1, 1808.
2-11	" Betsey Winslow,	Nov. 12, 1809.
3-9	" Betsey Paine,	Dec. 23, 1811.
3-125	" Robert St. Kitts,	March 19, 1814.
2-61	" Ira, of Israel and Rebecca,	Jan. 21, 1808.
3-53	" Ira Williams,	Nov. 11, 1811.
3-132	" Sarah Ann,	Aug. 23, 1814.
3-24	" Daniel Kelley,	June 26, 1816.
3-20	" Charles,	April 14, 1818.
3-55	" Ira W., of Fred and Rebecca,	Nov. 8, 1811.
3-39	" Lydia, of Joseph and Lavice, (also 3-73),	June 26, 1812.
3-28	" Elizabeth Brown,	March 14, 1816.
3-60	" Joseph,	July 27, 1821.
3-94	" Maria Nelson,	Feb. 27, 1826.
3-4	" Abby Child, of George T. and Abby C.,	Dec. 14, 1831.
3-126	" Robert, of George T. and Harriet B.,	March 6, 1836.
3-42	" George Tibbetts,	Nov. 12, 1839.
3-53	" Harriet Frances,	Jan. 10, 1844.
3-33	" Esther Alice,	May 30, 1846.
3-43	" Georgianna,	Sept. 1, 1848.
3-54	" Horace Richmond,	Aug. 12, 1851.
3-32	" Edward LeRoy, of Daniel and Sally,	March 12, 1837.
2-109	GIBSON William, of John Brinsmead and Lillis,	Aug. 23, 1806.
2-57	GOFF James, of James and Priscilla,	Oct. 25, 1780.
2-57	" Joseph Pearce,	Oct. 15, 1782.
2-92	" Rebecca,	May 30, 1784.
2-34	" Esther,	Dec. 3, 1788.
2-9	" Betsey,	Oct. 2, 1790.
2-57	" Jeremiah,	July 31, 1792.
2-74	" Luther, of James and Jemima,	April 1, 1795.
2-57	" John,	April 4, 1797.
2-103	" Samuel,	Jan. 10, 1800.
2-83	" Nathan,	March 26, 1802.
2-36	" Ezra, of James and Judeth,	June 29, 1802.
2-79	" Mary, of James, Jr., and Deborah,	Oct. 24, 1807.
3-51	" Hiram,	Sept. 7, 1816.
3-52	" Henry Payson, of Jeremiah and Lucy Ann,	Feb. 2, 1819.
3-55	" Jeremiah,	Feb. 4, 1822.
3-126	" Rufus Burr,	July 27, 1826.
3-97	" Nathan, of Nathan and Nancy,	Aug. 5, 1827.
3-143	" Thomas Ingraham,	July 7, 1829.
3-99	" Martha (also 3-100),	Nov. 29, 1831.
3-34	" Elizabeth Eugenia, of Hiram and Martha,	July 5, 1841.
3-43	" George Henry,	Nov. 14, 1855.
3-67	" Jeremiah Wallis, of Rufus B. and Sarah E.,	Feb. 12, 1852.
1-27	GRANT John, of Shubael and Elizabeth,	Jan. 10, 1766.
1-27	" James,	July 13, 1767.
1-27	" Edward,	July 13, 1767.
2-92	" Richard Tillinghast, of Richard,	Sept. 22, 1795.

2-78	GRANT	Martha Smith, of Daniel, and Rachel,	Jan. 18, 1808.
3-125	"	Sylvester (also 3-131),	Oct. 18, 1810.
3-55	"	Izrael Jackson, of Izrael and Mary,	July 24, 1810.
3-9	"	Betsey, of Daniel and Ruth,	Oct. 18, 1810.
3-1	"	Anna Elvira, of Joseph and Sally,	Dec. 5, 1810.
3-131	"	Sylvester, of Sylvester and Betsey,	Sept. 7, 1812.
3-157	"	William Nimmo, of John and Nancy L.,	March 26, 1816.
3-75	"	Laura,	Oct. 11, 1817.
3-97	"	Nancy Adeline,	Dec. 25, 1819.
3-41	"	George Dimon,	Nov. 16, 1821.
3-21	"	Charles Luther,	Jan. 13, 1824.
3-63	"	John,	March 8, 1828.
1-28	GREATREAKS	John, of John, and Hannah,	May 12, 1773.
3-169	GREENE	Abraham, of Nancy (col.),	Sept. 12, 1807.
3-158	"	William Smith, of Abraham and Susan,	April 8, 1824.
1-42	GREENMAN	Polly Hix, of George and Susannah,	Feb. 24, 1773.
1-7	"	Betsey,	Aug. 19, 1775.
3-57	GREGORY	John, of John and Sarah,	May 31, 1809.
3-39	"	George,	Nov. 8, 1811.
3-1	"	Albert,	April 27, 1815.
3-32	GUSHEE	Elizabeth Williams, of Almond and Elizabeth Richmond,	Dec. 7, 1837.
3-76	"	Lydia Leonard,	July 30, 1840.
3-98	"	Nathaniel Williams,	March 24, 1843.
3-102	"	Mary Reynolds,	March 12, 1845.
3-144	"	Thomas Cobb,	Aug. 15, 1847.
3-139	"	Sarah Annie,	Sept. 11, 1852.

H

1-40	HAILE	Phebe, of Barnard, Jr., and Mary,	June 27, 1741.
1-22	"	Jonathan,	Nov. 12, 1742.
1-31	"	Mary,	Aug. 29, 1744.
1-14	"	Elizabeth,	Aug. 9, 1746.
1-48	"	Sarah,	Jan. 17, 1747.
1-29	"	Lydia, of Walter and Mary,	Feb. 15, 1747.
1-32	"	Mary,	April 8, 1750.
1-14	"	Elizabeth,	Dec. 18, 1752.
1-20	"	Hannah, of Richard and Hannah,	May 31, 1748.
1-3	"	Anne,	Oct. 28, 1751.
1-25	"	Jonathan,	March 22, 1753.
1-5	"	Barnard,	Aug. 4, 1755.
1-45	"	Richard,	April 11, 1758.
1-24	"	John,	Aug. 11, 1760.
1-16	"	Elizabeth,	Sept. 25, 1765.
2-95	"	Samuel,	Sept. 5, 1770.
1-5	"	Barnard, of Amos and Ruth,	May 3, 1758.
1-50	"	Sarah, (also 1-51),	April 16 or 17, 1761
1-21	"	Hannah,	Aug. 16, 1763.
1-9	"	Coomer,	July 28, 1765.
1-1	"	Amos,	July 7, 1767.
1-6	"	Benjamin,	Jan. 16, 1770.
2-2	"	Amos, of Nathan and Bethiah,	April 8, 1768.
2-53	"	Joseph,	Oct. 9, 1772.
2-53	"	James,	Nov. 20, 1775.
2-2	"	Aaron,	Sept. 16, 1777.
2-2	"	Asa,	March 13, 1780.
2-2	"	Anne,	April 13, 1781.
2-80	"	Nathan,	Nov. 22, 1782.
1-46	"	Richard, of James and Hannah,	Aug. 14, 1769.
1-21	"	Hezekiah,	Aug. 17, 1770.
1-34	"	Mary,	Jan. 15, 1772.
1-35	"	Mary, of Barnard and Mary,	April 24, 1778.
2-8	"	Betsey,	Aug. 26, 1790.

1-19	HAILE George, of Barnard and Mary,		June 12, 1793.
2-55	" John, of John and Sarah,		Nov. 30, 1780.
2-99	" Sally,		Nov. 17, 1784.
2-99	" Sylvester,		May 18, 1787.
2-99	" Sylvester, of Coomer and Hannah,		June 11, 1788.
1-53	" Thomas Burr,		April 3, 1797.
3-19	" Coomer,		Nov. 6, 1799.
2-80	" Nancy, of Amos and Lydia,		June 29, 1793.
2-100	" Sarah,		Jan. 14, 1795.
2-46	" Hannah,		April 30, 1798.
2-58	" James,		March 8, 1801.
2-5	" Amos,		Dec. 16, 1803.
2-109	" William,		March 24, 1807.
2-74	" Lydia, of Benjamin and Keziah,		April 7, 1795.
2-58	" John E.,		Sept. 7, 1796.
2-76	" Mason,		Nov. 20, 1800.
2-93	" Ruth,		March 11, 1803.
2-10	" Benjamin,		Nov. 6, 1806.
2-6	" Allen,		Oct. 5, 1808.
2-100	" Sarah, of Aaron and Polly,		Sept. 16, 1795.
2-74	" Levi,		May 29, 1797.
1-13	" Delight,		Sept. 12, 1799.
2-58	" James,		Aug. 14, 1801.
2-34	" Eliza Wheaton, of Samuel and Olive,		Feb. 12, 1797.
2-101	" Samuel,		Sept. 27, 1798.
2-35	" Emeline,		Dec. 4, 1800.
2-102	" Sally, of William and Peggy,		June 26, 1797.
2-128	" Polly,		April 7, 1799.
1-59	" William,	(also 2-108),	Oct. 12, 1803.
2-5	" Ann Eliza,		May 27, 1805.
2-59	" James, of John and Mary Ann,		June 22, 1803.
2-77	" Mary Ann Lewis,		May 6, 1805.
2-37	" Elizabeth,		Jan. 30, 1808.
3-1	" Abigail Miller,		Dec. 12, 1810.
3-89	" Maria,		July 28, 1813.
3-132	" Sally Brown,		July 8, 1816.
3-61	" John,		Sept. 4, 1821.
2-78	" Mary, of Amos and Nancy,		Jan. 10, 1809.
2-6	" Anthony,		April 17, 1810.
3-75	" Lydia Kent, of James and Eliza,		March 1, 1826.
3-159	' William Rufus, of William, Jr., and Maria,		Aug. 20, 1829.
3-110	" Olive Elizabeth,		Nov. 5, 1835.
3-163	" William Bradford, of Levi Walter and Phebe Eliza,		Feb. 17, 1848.
3-66	" John, of John, Jr., and Clara S.,		Nov. 14, 1849.
3-37	" Clarence,		Aug. 2, 1852.
2-54	HARDING Jonathan, of John and Phebe,		May 2, 1766.
1-10	" Caleb,		Jan. 10, 1768.
2-54	" James,		Jan. 30, 1770.
2-34	" Elizabeth,		Sept. 13, 1774.
2-3	" Amey,		June 2, 1777.
1-58	" William,		Sept. 13, 1784.
2-54	" John,		Dec. 8, 1786.
1-27	" John, of Richard and Abigail,		May 23, 1768.
1-27	" Jonathan,		May 23, 1768.
2-56	" James, of Caleb and Elizabeth,		Feb. 24, 1795.
2-100	" Susannah,		Sept. 12, 1797.
2-46	" Harriett,		July 4, 1799.
2-93	" Ruth,		March 19, 1803.
3-21	" Caleb,		May 5, 1805.
3-27	" Elizabeth Easterbrooks,		April 30, 1812.
3-65	" James Hidden, of Caleb and Betsey,		July 5, 1840.
2-138	" Sarah Elizabeth,		Sept. 20, 1842.
2-88	HARRIS Polly, of John and Elizabeth,		June 21, 1791.
2-53	" John Haile,		June 7, 1793.
2-9	" Betsey,		Oct. 26, 1794.

2-81	HARRIS Nancy, of John and Elizabeth,	Aug. 25, 1796.
2-98	HAYES Sally, of James and Mary,	Dec. 24, 1779.
3-33	HAZARD Eliza Stockford, of George G. and Mary J.,	May 25, 1836.
3-37	" Clarissa Ellery,	May 15, 1838.
3-66	" Jane Maria,	Jan. 7, 1840.
1-30	HEALEY Lydia, of Ithamer and Molly,	Feb. 25, 1766.
1-27	" James,	Oct. 4, 1768.
1-40	HEATH Peleg, of Peleg and Jerusha.	March 23, 1747.
3-31	HENDRICK Eleanor Amelia, of Garrett and Catherine,	Sept. 17, 1836.
3-100	" Mary Ann Elizabeth,	July 6, 1839.
1-40	HILL Patience, of William and Elizabeth,	Oct.17, 1748.
1-14	" Elizabeth,	July 2, 1750.
1-55	" William,	May 11, 1752.
1-32	" Molly,	June 8, 1755.
1-3	" Abigail,	July 8, 1757.
1 45	" Ruth,	March 21, 1759.
1-50	" Sarah,	April 25, 1762.
2-95	" Samuel,	Nov. 28, 1771.
2-98	" Sarah, of Barnard and Hannah,	Aug. 12, 1771.
2-53	" John,	May 29, 1775.
2-45	" Hailey Blanchard,	Oct. 14, 1780.
2-8	" Barnard,	Dec. 27, 1784.
1-12	" Deborah, of Jonathan and Sally,	June 10, 1795.
2-101	" Sally,	June 3, 1798.
2-78	" Marcy Sabin,	Sept. 19, 1806.
2-61	" Jonathan,	April 5, 1809.
2-101	" Sally, of John and Rebecca,	April 27, 1800.
2-76	" Maria, of John and Roby,	Sept. 4, 1801.
3-19	" Caleb, of Holmes and Mary,	Dec. 31, 1810.
3-1	" Almira,	Oct. 31, 1812.
1-48	HIX Samuel, of Samuel and Thankful,	Nov. 19, 1747.
1-22	" Josiah,	April 17, 1749.
1-14	" Elizabeth,	July 20, 1751.
1-40	" Patience,	Dec. 10, 1752.
1-45	" Rebecca,	Feb. 20, 1755.
1-3	" Ambrose,	Feb. 23, 1757.
1-41	" Polly,	May 12, 1759.
1-25	" Ira,	March 30, 1761.
1-29	" Keziah, of Samuel and Bethiah,	Nov. 2, 1757.
1-25	" Jonathan,	Sept. 19, 1761.
1-34	" Molly,	July 10, 1768.
1-42	" Peleg Rogers, of Samuel and Ruth,	Oct. 8, 1773.
1-21	" Hannah,	Jan. 31, 1777.
1-47	" Rebeckah,	April 24, 1780.
2-99	" Samuel, of Jonathan and Patience,	Sept. 24, 1791.
2-99	" Sally,	Sept. 25, 1792.
3-50	HOARD Henry, of Noble and Sally,	Jan. 8, 1807.
2-7	HOAR Benjamin, of William and Phebe,	June 12, 1774.
2-44	" Hannah,	July 19, 1778.
2-98	" Samuel,	Aug. 15, 1781.
2-73	" Lewis,	Jan. 30, 1786.
2-7	" Betsey, of William and Molly,	Sept. 10, 1789.
1-58	" William,	Aug. 18, 1791.
2-90	" Pardon Bowen,	June 18, 1793.
1-19	" George,	June 30, 1796.
2-56	" John,	June 30, 1796.
2-60	" John, 2d,	Sept. 26, 1799.
2-83	" Nathan,	Sept. 15, 1801.
2-10	" Benjamin,	June 20, 1804.
2-78	" Mary Bowen,	Aug. 6, 1806.
3-73	" Lewis Thomas,	Nov. 3, 1810.
2-88	" Phebe, of Allen and Hannah,	Feb. 13, 1791.
2-2	" Allen Carey,	Oct. 8, 1793
2-56	" Joseph Sanders,	July 23, 1795.
2-46	" Hopey Sanders,	Jan. 27, 1798.

1-13	HOAR David, of Allen and Hannah,	Jnue 20, 1803.
2-82	" Nancy, of Benjamin and Elizabeth,	— —, 1796.
2-116	" Lydia Burr,	Feb. 13, 1808.
3-27	" Elizabeth, of Lewis and Frances,	June 15, 1813.
3-59	" John R.,	Sept. 5, 1816.
3-91	" Maria Rogers,	Nov. 26, 1817.
3-60	" John Champlain, of Allen C. and Mary,	March 30, 1818.
3-20	" Charles,	Sept. 1, 1820.
3-135	" Samuel, of Samuel and H nnah,	July 6, 1822.
3-5	" Allen, of Joseph S. and L cy Ann,	July 2, 1837.
3-100	" Mary Rogers, of John R. and Sarah B.,	June 11, 1841.
3-54	" Henry Irvine,	Dec. 15, 1842.
3-2	HOOD Adeline, of Noble and Sophia,	Dec. 28, 1917.
3-74	" Lewis,	Sept. 18, 1820.
3-98	HORTON Nancy Baker, of Josiah T. and Lovice,	July 28, 1845.
3-42	" George Leonard,	Dec. 31, 1846.
3-55	" Isabella,	Jan. 11, 1849.
3-76	" Lovice,	Aug. 28, 1851.
1-54	HUBBARD Eunice, of William More and Hannah,	March 8, 1801.
2-102	" Sally Borden,	June 29, 1803.
1-46	HUDSON Ruth, of Reuben and Abigail,	Feb. 22, 1768.
1-18	" George,	Feb. 16, 1770.
1-48	HUMPHREY Samuel, of Samuel and Elizabeth,	March 15, 1747-8.
1-23	" James,	April 11, 1750.
1-29	" Lydia,	May 15, 1752.
1-29	" Lydia,	Nov. 24, 1754.
1-24	" John,	April 4, 1757.
1-33	" Molly,	April 19, 1759.
1-45	" Rachel,	Feb. 8, 1762.
1-45	" Ruth,	May 31, 1764.
1-37	" Nathaniel, of Nathaniel and Eunice,	Aug. 22, 1759.
1-1	" Amos,	May 3, 1761.
1-1	" Amey,	June 17, 1764.
1-30	" Lewis,	Aug. 22, 1767.
2-128	HUNTER Polly, of Rufus and Patience,	July 21, 1801.
1-13	" Daniel,	May 11, 1803.
2-94	" Rufus,	June 18, 1805.
2-36	" Eliza,	May 1, 1807.
3-159	" William Salisbury,	June 4, 1810.

I

2-128	INGRAHAM Polly Turner, of Daniel and Temperance,	March 31, 1799.
2-59	" John Turner,	Jan. 7, 1801.
2-128	" Pattey,	July 19, 1802.
3-126	" Rebecca Carr, of Mason and Rebecca,	May 26, 1835.
3-5	" Alis Lyndon,	July 13, 1839.
3-23	" Charles Ernest,	Aug. 12, 1844.

J

3-65	JAYNE Josephine, of Joseph S. and Betsey Jane,	April 17, 1843.
3-138	" Seraphine,	April 17, 1843.
3-42	" George,	Oct. 4, 1845.
3-54	" Henry Walter,	Feb. 22, 1849.
2-9	JENCKES Brown, of Abner and Sally, (b. North Providence),	March 14, 1792.
2-101	" Sylvester,	Sept. 17, 1798.
2-108	" William Henry,	March 23, 1799.
2-102	" Sally,	Nov. 14, 1804.
1-45	JOLLS Robert, of Thomas and Phebe,	March 17, 1766.
1-34	" Mehitable, of Jeremiah and Roby,	March 12, 1774.
2-101	" Sally, of John and Sally,	March 25, 1799.

2-47	JOLLS Harriet, of John and Sally,	Oct. 5, 1801.
2-75	" Lydia,	March 19, 1804.
2-78	" Mary,	Dec. 28, 1807.
3-58	" Joseph Haile,	May 17, 1814.
1-53	" Thomas, of Benijah and Nancy,	Aug. 18, 1800.
2-59	" Jeremiah,	March 14, 1802.
2-58	" Jane Makensie,	Jan. 24, 1904.
2-58	" James,	April 4, 1806.
3-125	" Rebecca,	April 23, 1808.
2-58	" John Flavel,	June 23, 1811.
3*169	JOHNSON William, of William and Violet, (col.),	Dec. 20, 1804.
3-169	" Loiza, of William and Princess, (col.),	July 11, 1810.
3-55	" John Allen, (also 3-169), (col.),	Feb. 3, or 8, 1912.
3-138	" Susan Brown, of Rodolphus B. and Mary L.,	June 6, 1838.
3-76	" Lois Bardwell,	April 7, 1840.
3-126	" Rodolphus H.,	April 13, 1842.
3-35	" Frank Olin,	Feb. 8, 1846.
2-4	JOHONETT Andrew, of Daniel and Robe,	March 21, 1799.
2-18	" Caroline, of Oliver and Lydia,	Nov. 21, 1809.
3-39	" George Gorham,	Dec. 11, 1811.
3-96	" Mary Louisa, of George G. and Mary Ann,	Oct. 30, 1844.
1-15	JONES Eneck, of John and Constant,	Feb. 28, 1754.
1-35	" William,	Nov. 28, 1755.
1-49	" Susanna,	Sept. 16, 1757.
1-1	" Abigail,	Oct. 2, 1759.
1-25	" John,	Nov. 25, 1762.

K

1-21	KELLEY Hannah, of John, 2d, and Margary,	Nov. 24, 1739.
1-31	" Molly,	April 12, 1746.
1-55	" William,	Nov. 13, 1748.
1-24	" Jonathan,	Oct. 28, 1750.
1-40	" Patience,	March 23, 1753.
1-49	" Sarah,	Aug. 4, 1755.
1-37	" Naomi,	Aug. 29, 1757.
1-50	" Susanna,	July 3, 1759.
1-24	" John,	March 27, 1761.
1-39	" Oliver, of John and Lydia,	Sept. 20, 1748.
1-29	" Lydia,	Oct. 21, 1750.
1-11	" Duncan,	April 19, 1753.
1-40	" Patience,	July 14, 1755.
1-32	" Molly,	Jan. 15, 1757.
1-26	" John, of Joseph and Molly,	June 15, 1762.
1-26	" Joseph,	Aug. 31, 1764.
1-16	" Ebenezer,	Feb. 10, 1767.
1-34	" Molly,	April 10, 1769.
2-72	" Lawton,	March 7, 1772.
2-1	" Abigail,	Jan. 4, 1776.
1-9	" Church,	June 4, 1778.
2-97	" Samuel,	Aug. 14, 1781.
1-11	" Duncan, of Edward and Elizabeth,	Oct. 11, 1764.
1-4	" Abigail, of William and Rebecca,	Nov. 8, 1767.
1-16	" Elizabeth,	Aug. 25, 1769.
1-12	" Daniel, of Daniel and Elizabeth,	April 26, 1770.
2-32	" Elizabeth,	March 13, 1772.
2-96	" Sally,	May 2, 1774.
1-21	" Hannah,	April 29, 1776.
1-43	" Prescilla,	Nov. 20, 1781.
1-7	" Bears,	(also 2-7), May 30, 1784.
2-92	" Rebecca,	June 4, 1786.
2-80	" Nixon,	July 19, 1790.
1-58	" William,	March 18, 1792.
1-34	" Mary, of John D. and Elizabeth,	Sept. 27, 1770.

1-34	KELLEY Martin, of John D. and Elizabeth,	April 16, 1773.
2-1	"	Abigail, of Joseph and Elizabeth,	Sept. 13, 1785.
1-10	"	Caleb,	Oct. 11, 1787.
2-33	"	Ebenezer,	Oct. 23, 1789.
2-9	"	Benjamin,	Nov. 20, 1793.
2-57	"	Jeremiah,	March 30, 1796.
2-58	"	James Greene.	May 1, 1798.
2-53	"	John, of John and Prudence,	Feb. 27, 1790.
1-43	"	Polly,	Nov. 26, 1791.
2-34	"	Esek,	Oct. 5, 1793.
2-74	"	Lawton,	Feb. 9, 1796.
2-8	"	Betsey, of Duncan and Mary,	June 10, 1791.
2-18	"	Charles, of Joseph and Phebe,	March 31, 1802.
2-60	"	Joseph James,	Feb. 5, 1806.
2-18	"	Caleb,	May 18, 1807.
3-58	"	Julia Ann,	Nov. 27, 1812.
3-9	"	Benjamin Greene,	Jan. 29, 1815.
2-38	"	George Lewis, of Edward and Pattey,	Sept. 17, 1802.
2-71	"	Kezia,	Sept. 11, 1804.
2-38	"	George,	Oct. 28, 1806.
2-6	"	Amanda,	Aug. 25, 1808.
2-73	"	Lewis,	Nov. 12, 1810.
3-27	"	Eliza,	Oct. 17, 1812.
3-28	"	Eliza, 2d,	Jan. 10, 1818.
2-102	"	Sally, of Church and Sally,	May 16, 1804.
2-10	"	Betsey, of James and Betsey,	Nov. 21, 1806.
2-37	"	Edward,	July 10, 1808.
3-73	"	Lorenzo Dow,	April 8, 1811.
2-103	"	Samuel, of Samuel and Mary Ann,	March 3, 1807.
2-78	"	Mary Ann,	March 21, 1809.
3-49	"	Haman,	Feb. 14, 1814.
3-135	"	Sylvester Eddy,	July 30, 1816.
3-93	"	Mary, of Church and Patience, (also 2-129), May 15 or 18, 1808.
2-61	"	Joseph Church,	March 16, 1810.
3-1	"	Abigail,	Sept. 17, 1811.
3-27	"	Eliza,	June 13, 1813.
3-157	"	William,	March 15, 1815.
3-90	"	Martha, of Edward and Martha,	Nov. 18, 1814.
3-50	"	Henry Bears, of William and Ruth,	July 8, 1818.
3-29	"	Elizabeth,	Sept. 14, 1822.
3-126	"	Rebecca,	April 14, 1825.
3-94	"	Maria,	Feb. 1, 1828.
3-4	"	Amelia,	Jan. 29, 1831.
3-96	"	Mary,	Dec. 31, 1834.
3-20	"	Charles Lawton, of Lawton and Susan,	Nov. 4, 1820.
3-135	"	Susan Turner,	July 2, 1822.
3-30	"	Eliza Day,	Sept. 25, 1825.
3-95	"	Mary Maria,	May 5, 1829.
3 63	"	John Lawton,	April 22, 1831.
3-66	"	Joseph Augustus, of Benjamin Greene and Ann,	April 12, 1847.
3-37	"	Charles Greene,	March 25, 1849.
2-96	KINGSLEY Sarah, of Peleg and Mary,	Nov. 8, 1780.
2-59	"	Julian, of Haile and Sally,	Sept. 17, 1800.
2-4	"	Allen,	Oct. 24, 1802.
3-19	"	Charlotte Townsend,	Jan. 1, 1811.
3-169	"	George, of William and Betsey (col.),	May 1, 1818.
3-21	KING Keziah Mason Haile, of William and Lydia,	March 20, 1825.
1-14	KINNECUTT Elizabeth, of John and Anne,	Jan. 18, 1726-7.
1-23	"	John,	Oct. 17, 1728.
1-2	"	Abigail,	Sept. 20, 1730.
1-2	"	Anne,	Sept. 17, 1732.
1-11	"	Daniel,	July 14, 1735.
1-48	"	Shubael, of John and Hannah,	March 28, 1738.
1-20	"	Hannah,	Feb. 28, 1739-40.
1-29	"	Lydia,	Jan. 17, 1741-2.

1-20	KINNECUTT Hezekiah, of John and Hannah,		March 24, 1743-4.
1-44	"	Rebekah,	Jan. 20, 1745-6.
1-5	"	Bettey,	March 4, 1748.
1-48	"	Sarah,	April 15, 1751.
1-52	"	Thomas,	May 20, 1753.
1-15	"	Edward,	April 7, 1755.
1-15	"	Edward, 2d,	April 25, 1759.
1-15	"	Elizabeth, of John and Robe,	Jan. 28, 1753.
1-24	"	John,	March 20, 1754.
1-11	"	Daniel,	Dec. 3, 1755.
1-24	"	Jonathan,	Oct. 24, 1757.
1-45	"	Roby,	April 20, 1760.
1-28	"	John,	May 21, 1762.
1-34	"	Mary,	May 31, 1764.
1-30	"	Levi,	June 27, 1766.
1-46	"	Roby,	Feb. 12, 1768.
1-46	"	Robert,	April 4, 1770.
1-28	"	Jonathan, 2d,	Oct. 28, 1772.
2-72	"	Lydia,	April 27, 1775.
1-4	"	Anne, of Daniel and Hannah,	May 15, 1759.
1-4	"	Amey,	Feb. 8, 1761.
1-16	"	Edward,	Feb. 24, 1763.
1-26	"	Josiah,	April 2, 1765.
1-30	"	Lydia,	May 22, 1767.
1-12	"	Daniel,	Nov. 17, 1769.
1-28	"	John,	March 8, 1772.
1-37	"	Nathaniel, of Shubael and Elizabeth,	Jan. 11, 1767.
1-52	"	Thomas,	Aug. 13, 1768.
1-16	"	Elizabeth,	Sept. 29, 1770.
1-34	"	Mary,	March 12, 1773.
2-95	"	Shubael,	Dec. 24, 1774.
1-56	"	William,	April 8, 1777.
2-96	"	Simon,	Oct. 26, 1779.
2-52	"	Joseph Adams, of Edward and Nancy,	Jan. 20, 1783.
1-57	"	William,	Nov. 11, 1784.
2-98	"	Samuel DeWolf,	March 8, 1786.
2-4	"	Amanda, of Thomas and Amey,	Nov. 24, 1794.
2-35	"	Eliza,	Sept. 5, 1796.
2-58	"	Julian,	July 14, 1798.
2-104	"	Thomas,	Nov. 30, 1800.
3-131	"	Seth Brown, of Shubael and Lydia G.,	Aug. 15, 1809.
3-132	"	Shubael,	Dec. 22, 1811.
3-2	"	Augusta,	May 15, 1814.
3-28	"	Edward,	July 16, 1816.
1-22	KENT Joshua, of Josiah and Alethea,		Feb. 28, 1746.
1-25	"	John, of Samuel and Ruth,	Sept. 11, 1759.
1-25	"	Jerusha,	Nov. 14, 1760.
1-26	"	Joseph,	July 3, 1762.
1-51	"	Samuel,	May 26, 1765.
1-46	"	Rachel,	Feb. 26, 1767.
3-134	"	Susan Drowne, of Ira and Sukey Ann,	Aug. 24, 1821.
3-131	KNIGHT Sophia Smith, of George and Ruth,		Dec. 17, 1811.

L

3-134	LADIEU Seth Snell, of James and Betsey,		Feb. 26, 1822.
3-136	"	Sarah Elizabeth,	May 12, 1828.
3-64	"	James Thomas,	June 30, 1830.
3-160	"	William Ira,	Aug. 19, 1834.
3-32	"	Edwin Seekell,	Aug. 5, 1837.
1-26	LADU James, of Nicholas and Prudence,		Oct. 16, 1760.
1-8	"	Curtis,	Dec. 12, 1763.
3-132	LAWRENCE Samuel Wheaton, of John and Susan,		Sept. 20, 1813.

1-25	LAWTON John, of William and Molly,	Oct. 8, 1759.
1-45	" Rebecca,	April 5, 1761.
3-158	" William Bennett, of Samuel and Abigail (b. Newport),	
		Feb. 6, 1809.
3-137	" Samuel, of William B. and Sarah,	July 12, 1831.
3-54	" Leonard Henry Lewis, of Lewis, Jr., and Mary E.,	June 27, 1846.
3-66	" James Douglass,	Oct. 22, 1848.
1-55	LEWIN William, of William and Sarah,	July 19, 1747.
1-44	" Rachel,	Nov. 14, 1749.
1-52	" Thomas,	Aug. 16, 1753.
1-52	" Thomas, 2d,	June 26, 1756.
2-2	LEWIS Abigail, of William and Abigail (also 1-1),	Sept. 6 or 7, 1775.
2-80	" Nancy,	April 15, 1777.
1-36	" Mary Anna,	Jan. 11, 1780.
2-80	" Nathan Child,	Dec. 18, 1790.
3-4	" Abby Kelley, of Joshua O. and Mary,	April 8, 1832.
3-133	LINCOLN Susan, of Seth and Sarah,	Sept. 12, 1817.
3-133	" Sally,	Feb. 16, 1819.
3-134	" Seth Flavel,	Dec. 20, 1820.
3-158	" William,	March 12, 1823.
3-115	LONGHEAD Orphelia Caroline, of Charles T. and Sally,	Jan. 2 or 3, 1811.
3-134	" Susan,	Nov. 20, 1814.
1-55	LOW Wilson, of Hooper and Elizabeth,	July 13, 1751.
1-15	" Wilson, 2d,	Feb. 12, 1753.
1-50	" Sarah,	Sept. 3, 1754.
1-21	" Hooker,	March 11, 1756.
1-56	" Wilson,	Jan. 5, 1758.
1-4	" Anstress,	July 15, 1759.
1-4	" Amey,	April 11, 1761.
1-26	" John Wilson,	Jan. 6, 1764.
1-29	" Lydia, of John Wilson and Lydia,	Aug. 10, 1754.
1-14	" Rachel,	Feb. 26, 1756.
1-24	" John Wilson,	Oct. 25, 1757.
1-18	LUTHER George, of Daniel and Hannah,	Jan. 12, 173/8.
1-29	" Lydia,	Oct. 15, 1739.
1-20	" Hannah,	Nov. 22, 1741.
1-48	" Sarah,	Oct. 6, 1744.
1-11	" Daniel,	Aug. 8, 1748.
1-11	" Martin,	(also 1-31), Aug. 8, 1748.
1-11	" Deborah, of Ebenezer, Jr., and Johannah,	June 14, 1753.
1-18	" Gideon, of Ebenezer and Mercy,	May 26, 1756.
1-37	" Nehemiah,	Sept. 16, 1758.
1-4	" Amos,	April 19, 1761.
1-16	" Ebenezer,	Feb. 14, 1763.
1-6	" Benjamin Sisson,	Dec. 9, 1764.
1-34	" Marcy,	Dec. 22, 1767.
1-50	" John, of John, 2d, and Margaret,	Oct. 17, 1757.
1-11	" David,	April 12, 1759.
1-27	" Josiah,	May 25, 1761.
1-37	" Nathaniel,	Jan. 3, 1764.
1-27	" John,	March 14, 1766.
1-50	" Sarah, of Elisha and Patience,	Aug. 11. 1760.
1-50	" Samuel, of Samuel and Elizabeth,	Aug. 9, 1762.
1-41	" Preserved,	Nov. 22, 1763.
1-51	" Samuel, 2d.,	March 7, 1766.
1-56	" Welcome,	May 20, 1769.
1-60	" Zebedee,	May 21, 1772.
2-33	" Elizabeth,	Oct. 21, 1775.
1-35	" Martin,	April 21, 1780.
1-17	" Frederick, of Frederick and Joanna,	June 8, 1763.
1-45	" Rebecca,	April 17, 1765.
2-95	" Samuel,	April 11, 1768.
1-33	" Martha, of Jabez and Alice,	July 3, 1764.
1-46	" Rhubramah,	March 8, 1767.
1-1	" Alice,	June 24, 1769.

1-37	LUTHER	Nancy, of Barnaby and Rebecca,	Sept. 11, 1767.
1-21	"	Hannah,	July 16, 1769.
2-95	"	Sarah,	Dec. 21, 1772.
1-56	"	William,	May 10, 1774.
1-38	"	Nancy, of Martin and Anne,	Jan. 20, 1770.
1-43	"	Patience,	June 1, 1773.
1-28	"	James Miller, of William and Patience,	Oct. 23, 1776.
1-21	"	Hezekiah,	Nov. 26, 1778.
1-60	"	Asa,	April 24, 1781.
1-57	"	William,	April 1, 1784.
2-32	"	Edward, of Abner and Harte,	Aug. 16, 1780.
2-44	"	Henry, of Barnaby and Phebe,	Aug. 19, 1781.
1-47	"	Rebecca,	June 15, 1783.
2-1	"	Amey,	Dec. 21, 1784.
1-9	"	Coomer,	Oct. 1, 1786.
2-89	"	Polly,	April 2, 1789.
1-36	"	Mary, of Jabez and Lydia,	Aug. 26, 1782.
1-57	"	William,	Dec. 29, 1784.
1-19	"	George Perce,	June 30, 1787.
2-46	"	Hannah, of Gideon and Mary,	July 5, 1783.
2-35	"	Ebenezer,	July 12, 1785.
2-44	"	Hannah, of Gideon and Olive.	July 5, 1783.
2-33	"	Ebenezer,	July 12, 1785.
1-57	"	William, of Amos and Elizabeth.	May 15, 1786.
2-72	"	Lydia,	March 2, 1789.
1-12	"	David, of John and Bethiah.	Aug. 3, 1786.
1-10	"	Cromwell,	Dec. 14, 1791.
2-80	"	Nathaniel,	March 14, 1793.
2-82	"	Nancy,	July 3, 1795.
2-76	"	Margaret.	June 25, 1798.
2-128	"	Patty,	April 7, 1800.
2-108	"	William Jenkins.	March 12, 1802.
3-24	"	David,	June 20, 1809.
1-43	"	Polly. of Martin and Rachel,	Nov. 30, 1786.
2-98	"	Samuel,	Aug. 24, 1788.
2-81	"	Nancy,	May 25, 1791.
2-45	"	Hannah,	May 6, 1793.
1-108	"	Jeremiah Cole,	March 2, 1796.
2-4	"	Amey,	Feb. 24, 1799.
2-77	"	Martin,	April 21, 1802.
2-5	"	Alfred,	March 20, 1805.
2-37	"	Ellery Spencer,	Dec. 16, 1808.
3-27	"	Elizabeth,	June 29, 1911.
2-98	"	Sally, of James and Phelinda,	Feb. 23, 1788.
2-55	"	James,	June 30, 1794.
2-59	"	John, of Jonathan and Rosamond.	June 11, 1795.
1-13	"	Daniel Kelley,	July 9, 1797.
2-18	"	Charles,	Sept. 15, 1803.
1-19	"	Gardner, of Frederick and Parmella,	Sept. 11, 1795.
2-3	"	Allen,	March 7, 1797.
2-9	"	Betsey,	Dec. 31, 1799.
2-58	"	Joanna,	July 27, 1801.
1-36	"	Eliza,	Nov. 12, 1804.
2-97	"	Nathan, of Ebenezer and Johanna,	Oct. 12, 1795.
2-81	"	Nathan,	Oct. 12, 1796.
2-57	"	Joanna,	March 2, 1798.
2-38	"	George,	Nov. 18, 1800.
1-36	"	Edward,	Jan. 29, 1803.
2-47	"	Henry Sisson,	Sept. 25, 1805.
3-27	"	Ebenezer,	Dec. 28, 1807.
3-9	"	Betsey B.,	July 28, 1810.
3-89	"	Mary B.,	July 28, 1810.
3-132	"	Susan,	July 3, 1813.
2-9	"	Betsey, of James Miller and Sebra,	May 2, 1800.
2-128	"	Philip,	March 15, 1802.

2-116	LUTHER Leonard, of Asa and Betsey,	June 16, 1806.
3-131	"	Sarah Seward,	March 15, 1810.
3-90	"	Mary Pearce, of Jonathan and Rosabella,	Feb. 3, 1808.
2-47	"	Henry Hicks, of George and Rebecca,	Sept. 21, 1808.
2-18	"	Charles Simmons, of Joseph and Elizabeth,	April 20, 1809.
2-103	"	Samuel Brown, of William and Deborah,	Oct. 25, 1809.
1-39	"	George Perry, of Coomer and Nancy,	Nov. 29, 1811.
3-131	"	Sophronia, of Samuel and Elizabeth,	June 14, 1812.
3-73	"	Levi S., of Harvey and Ann,	March 8, 1816.
3-24	"	David Easterbrooks, of Job and Polly,	Aug. 12, 1817
3-92	"	Mary Ann,	Sept. 25, 1819.
3-64	"	John Eddy, of Cromwell and Delana,	April 11, 1820.
3-64	"	Jane Ann,	July 9, 1824.
3-41	"	George Alfred,	June 22, 1826.
3-160	"	William Henry,	Aug. 22, 1831.
3-20	"	Charles Frederick, of Allen and Nancy,	June 21, 1820.
3-92	"	Margaret Maria, of John and Mary,	Sept. 17, 1821.
3-20	"	Cyrus Carpenter, of Jeremiah C. and Mary T.,	May 2, 1823.
3-61	"	Jeremiah Jolls,	April 13, 1825.
3-51	"	Horace, of Daniel B. and Polly,	March 21, 1825.
3-24	"	Daniel B.,	April 21, 1827.
3-95	"	Mary Ann,	March 3, 1831.
3-5	"	Abby Elizabeth,	March 4, 1837.
3-53	"	Harriet,	June 18, 1842.
3-75	"	Lydia Maria, of Charles and Eliza Ann,	Aug. 24, 1826.
3-33	"	Ella Frances, of Horace and Elizabeth,	March 9, 1849.
2-59	LYON Judeth Delight, of Nathan and Polly,	April 16, 1798.
2-82	"	Nancy,	Oct. 22, 1802.

M

1-2	MARTIN Abigail, of John and Mary,	Oct. 9, 1745.
1-48	"	Samuel,	March 17, 1749-50.
1-5	"	Benjamin,	March 23, 1755.
1-14	"	Ebenezer, of Ebenezer and Mary,	July 12, 1749.
1-23	"	James,	Aug. 3, 1751.
1-15	"	Edward,	April 17, 1754.
1-45	"	Rufus,	July 1, 1755.
1-50	"	Samuel,	March 24, 1757.
1-32	"	Molly,	Aug. 2, 1759.
1-4	"	Anne,	Oct. 15, 1761.
1-27	"	John,	June 1, 1767.
1-29	"	Luther, of Nathaniel and Susannah,	Jan. 20, 1752.
1-3	"	Anna,	April 13, 1753.
1-37	"	Nathaniel,	Oct. 1, 1754.
1-3	"	Alathier,	Feb. 20, 1756.
1-29	"	Kent,	Dec. 25, 1757.
1-3	"	Anthony,	April 21, 1760.
1-51	"	Susannah,	Nov. 25, 1761.
1-30	"	Kent,	Sept. 9, 1767.
1-9	"	Calvin,	Oct. 28, 1769.
1-28	"	Judah, (dau.),	Oct. 11, 1773.
2-76	"	Moses Tyler, of Samuel and Hannah (b. Barrington),	April 11, 1792.
2-101	"	Samuel, (b. Barrington),	March 8, 1794.
2-57	"	John Tyler,	March 14, 1796.
2-46	"	Hannah,	Aug. 17, 1798.
2-35	"	Edward Tyler,	Sept. 7, 1800.
2-79	"	Mary Bowen,	Nov. 4, 1802.
3-93	"	Moses Tyler,	Feb. 22, 1808.
3-29	"	Eliza Tyler,	Jan. 12, 1810.
2-5	"	Abby Sprague, of Ephraim and Abigail,	May 17, 1806.
3-169	"	Levi Sheldon, of Metcalf and Dinah (col.),	Sept. 12, 1807.
3-169	"	Henrietta (col.),	Dec. 18, 1809.
3-169	"	David Brayton (col.),	Oct. 23, 1819.

3-20	MARTIN	Cyrel Read, of Cyrel and Sally,	Aug. 13, 1820.
3-137	"	Samuel,	June 22, 1823.
3-137	"	Sarah Tyler,	April 23, 1828.
3-63	"	James Blake, of John and Hannah,	Dec. 14, 1828.
3-23	"	Charles Henry, of Joseph E. and Sarah Ann.,	March 25, 1835.
3-11	"	Benjamin Baker,	June 25, 1839.
3-67	"	Jeremiah,	Feb. 4, 1842.
3-139	"	Sarah Ann,	July 11, 1846.
3-33	"	Eudorah,	March 15, 1849.
3-6	"	Anna Wilmarth,	Dec. 25, 1851.
3-66	"	Julia Maria, of William and Betsey,	Feb. 9, 1839.
3-5	"	Adelaide Cole,	March 18, 1843.
3-54	"	Henrietta, of Henry and Maria,	Dec. 11, 1848.
3-6	"	Abby Frances,	Jan. 5, 1847.
3-100	"	Mary Emily,	Jan. 10, 1845.
1-18	MASON	Garner, of John and Sarah,	Aug. 28, 1744.
1-14	"	Edward,	June 22, 1746.
1-20	"	Haile,	Nov. 12, 1748.
1-20	"	Holden,	Dec. 18, 1750.
1-44	"	Rose,	Oct. 2, 1752.
1-20	"	Hannah,	Feb. 9, 1755.
1-49	"	Samuel,	Oct. 2, 1757.
1-50	"	Sarah,	June 1, 1759.
1-15	"	Edward, of Marmaduke and Hannah,	June 18, 1752.
1-3	"	Anthony,	Feb. 17, 1754.
1-24	"	James,	(also 1-25), Dec. 20, 1755.
1-3	"	Alexander,	Dec. 3, 1757.
1-25	"	Joseph,	Aug. 7, 1759.
1-16	"	Elizabeth,	Feb. 21, 1766.
1-23	"	James, of James, Jr., and Mary,	March 3, 1753.
1-32	"	Mary,	July 19, 1754.
2-51	"	James N.,	Dec. 14, 1763.
1-23	"	Joseph, of Augustus and Constance,	May 24, 1753.
1-3	"	Anne,	June 9, 1755.
1-33	"	Molly, of Barnard and Abiah,	May 4, 1757.
1-45	"	Rufus,	July 3, 1759.
1-41	"	Prudence,	May 24, 1761.
1-41	"	Patience,	June 8, 1763.
1-30	"	Lilliee,	Dec. 20, 1765.
1-1	"	Anthony, of Edward and Sarah,	Oct. 17, 1770.
1-47	"	Rosezinca Matilda,	March 3, 1773.
1-18	"	Gardner,	May 26, 1775.
1-28	"	John,	May 22, 1777.
1-60	"	Anna,	Sept. 19, 1780.
2-32	"	Edward Margrave,	March 24, 1783.
1-35	"	Mary,	Aug. 7, 1785.
1-39	"	Obadiah,	Jan. 14, 1787.
1-36	"	Miller,	Sept. 26, 1789.
1-59	"	Sarah, of Gardner and Mary,	Nov. 11, 1772.
1-38	"	Nancy,	Feb. 28, 1775.
1-36	"	Mary,	March 19, 1783.
2-52	"	James,	Feb. 24, 1785.
1-21	"	Hopestill, of Holden and Margaret,	April 1, 1774.
1-35	"	Martha, of James and Lillis,	Jan. 6, 1775.
1-35	"	Marmaduke,	May 6, 1776.
1-28	"	James,	June 29, 1778.
2-108	"	Wilbor,	July 18, 1780.
2-4	"	Asa,	Feb. 25, 1782.
2-108	"	William,	Sept. 17, 1785.
1-13	"	Daniel,	Feb. 23, 1789.
2-46	"	Hannah,	Jan. 2, 1795.
2-4	"	Anthony,	April 29, 1797.
1-2	"	Alexander, of Joseph and Lavina,	Oct. 21, 1778.

2-44	MASON	Hannah, of Joseph and Lavina,	July 12, 1781.
1-7	"	Betsey,	Feb. 2, 1783.
2-52	"	Joseph,	Sept. 12, 1784.
2-52	"	John Augustus,	June 20, 1786.
2-73	"	Levina,	April 15, 1788.
1-19	"	George,	Nov. 24, 1789.
2-3	"	Alexander, of Alexander and Barbara,	June 27, 1780.
2-92	"	Roderick,	Sept. 4, 1782.
1-42	"	Patience, of Marmaduke and Elizabeth,	March 1, 1783.
2-72	"	Lydia, of Samuel and Hannah,	June 15, 1783.
1-36	"	Mary,	July 10, 1785.
2-44	"	Haile,	March 13, 1787.
2-34	"	Esther,	April 7, 1789.
2-99	"	Sarah,	Sept. 2, 1790.
2-54	"	Job Anthony,	Nov. 16, 1792.
2-3	"	Almira,	Sept. 14, 1796.
2-46	"	Hannah,	April 13, 1798.
2-58	"	John,	May 31, 1800.
2-102	"	Samuel,	Sept. 8, 1802.
1-60	"	Zephaniah,	Feb. 27, 1804.
3-131	"	Samuel,	April 22, 1809.
1-139	"	Thomas, of Bosan and Flora (col.),	March 18, 1789.
1-139	"	Jack,	(col.), April 18, 1792.
1-19	"	Gardner Smith, of Gardner and Hannah,	July 12, 1797.
2-46	"	Hannah Anthony,	April 16, 1799.
2-35	"	Edward,	May 3, 1801.
2-10	"	Betsey Smith,	Dec. 26, 1803.
2-103	"	Sarah Arnold,	Feb. 23, 1806.
2-78	"	Martha Barney,	April 30, 1808.
2-97	"	Nancy,	Sept. 26, 1810.
3-1	"	Anna,	June 4, 1814.
2-36	"	Eliza Ann, of Stephen and Lydia,	July 9, 1806.
2-103	"	Stephen,	Oct. 1, 1808.
3-131	"	Sophia,	June 22, 1811.
3-1	"	Amasa,	Sept 16, 1813.
3-40	"	George Freeborn,	Nov. 28, 1815.
3-49	"	Hannah F.,	July 3, 1817.
3-74	"	Lydia,	Nov. 22, 1820.
3-92	"	Mary Jane,	May 9, 1822.
3-61	"	John Reuben,	March 17, 1824.
3-61	"	John Reuben, 2d.,	Jan. 7, 1826.
3-62	"	James Luther,	Nov. 24, 1827.
3-27	"	Edward, of James and Hannah,	Nov. 12, 1810.
3-1	"	Anna, of Edward M. and Phebe,	Aug. 28, 1811.
3-2	"	Adeline, of James, 2d., and Hannah,	Nov. 5, 1813.
3-2	"	Allen Chase,	April 8, 1815.
3-60	"	Julia,	Dec. 3, 1816.
3-133	"	Sarah,	Sept. 10, 1818.
3-21	"	Charles, of Marmaduke and Mary,	March 12, 1815.
3-50	"	Howland, of Haile and Elizabeth, (b. Swansey),	May 19, 1817.
3-28	"	Elizabeth Gardner,	May 23, 1819.
3-92	"	Marmaduke, of Anthony and Betsey,	April 11, 1818.
3-92	"	Mark Anthony.	May 3, 1820.
3-3	"	Anthony,	July 30, 1823.
3-161	"	William, of Zephaniah S. and Susan,	June 5, 1831.
3-6	"	Ann Frances,	Nov. 14, 1834.
3-23	"	Caroline Cole,	Dec. 12, 1839.
3-52	"	Henry Newton, of Samuel and Esther,	Feb. 23, 1836.
3-97	MATHEWSON	Nathan Fuller, of Samuel J. and Rebecca, (b. Thompson, Conn.), Sept. 7, 1814.	
3-93	"	Mary Stanly, of Samuel J. and Sally,	Oct. 23, 1819.
3-61	"	James,	March 17, 1822.
3-135	"	Sarah Kelley,	Dec. 18, 1823.
1-24	MAXWELL	James, of Squire and Joanna, (b. Rehoboth),	Aug. 8, 1752.
1-29	"	Level,	Sept. 29, 1754.

1-41	MAXWELL Philip, of James and Hannah, (b. Rehoboth),	Dec. 22, 1753.
1-50	"	Squire,	April 29, 1756.
1-15	"	Elizabeth,	Oct. 7, 1759.
1-51	"	Samuel,	July 20, 1762.
1-38	"	Nabby, of James and Rebecca,	June 26, 1776.
2-44	"	Hannah,	Feb. 23, 1783.
2-91	"	Rebekah,	Aug. 7, 1787.
2-89	"	Polly,	May 25, 1790.
1-43	"	Pattey,	May 25, 1790.
2-97	"	Squire, of Level and Abigail,	Nov. 27, 1781.
2-51	"	Joanna,	May 6, 1783.
1-59	"	William,	July 27, 1785.
1-36	"	Elizabeth,	April 19, 1789.
2-5	"	Abigail,	Aug. 5, 1793.
2-89	"	Patience Greene, of James and Content,	Jan. 5, 1794.
1-53	"	Tenty Brayton,	Dec. 25, 1796.
2-35	"	Emeline Maybury,	April 23, 1798.
2-58	"	James,	May 11, 1800.
2-59	"	James, 2d,	Feb. 28, 1802.
2-77	"	Mary,	April 20, 1803.
2-75	"	Level, of Squire and Lydia,	Sept. 5, 1802.
2-5	"	Abigail Hill,	Feb. 17, 1804.
2-103	"	Samuel,	Dec. 31, 1805.
2-36	"	Emily,	Aug. 7, 1807.
2-116	"	Lydia,	April 27, 1809.
3-57	"	James,	March 26, 1811.
3-157	"	William,	Feb. 21, 1813.
2-18	"	Charlotte Maria, of William and Abigail,	May 16, 1808.
3-37	McELROY Catherine, of Owen and Mary,	Feb. 4, 1847.
3-120	"	Patrick,	Sept. 28, 1849.
1-28	McMILLION James, of Joseph and Alice.	May 4, 1776.
1-47	"	Reuben,	March 11, 1778.
2-52	"	James, of Peter and Sarah.	—— —, 1782 (?)
2-51	"	Joseph, of Joseph and Avis.	June 14, 1782.
1-18	"	Ginney,	Feb. 18, 1783.
1-6	MEDBURY Bettey, of Nathaniel and Sarah,	April 10, 1762.
1-11	"	Deliverance, of Rebecca,	Sept. 3, 1763.
1-15	MILLARD Experience, of John and Susannah,	Aug. 28, 1748.
1-11	"	Dorcas,	May 6, 1752.
1-41	"	Prudence,	Feb. 5, 1754.
1-52	"	Tabitha,	May 22, 1756.
1-8	"	Consider.	Sept. 7, 1760.
1-22	MILLER James, of Benjamin and Mehitable,	Oct. 20, 1733.
1-40	"	Patience,	April 1, 1736.
1-44	"	Rachael,	May 2, 1738.
1-31	"	Mehitable,	Sept. 2, 1740.
1-44	"	Robert,	March 1, 1742-3.
1-31	"	Mary,	March 4, 1744-5.
1-48	"	Sarah,	Jan. 19, 1746.
1-5	"	Betsey, of Nathan and Patience,	Jan. 2, 1741.
1-37	"	Nathan,	March 20, 1743.
1-55	"	William Turner,	April 15, 1745.
1-40	"	Patience,	Nov. 4, 1747.
1-44	"	Rebecca,	Jan. 25, 1749-50.
1-32	"	Mary,	Aug. 23, 1752.
1-8	"	Caleb,	Feb. 16, 1759.
1-33	"	Molly Turner,	Sept. 8, 1762.
1-56	"	William, of Samuel and Elizabeth,	Jan. 13, 1744-5.
1-26	"	Jonathan,	March 25, 1765.
1-23	"	Job, of Barnard and Elizabeth,	Dec. 16, 1746.
1-32	"	Molly,	Feb. 14, 1750.
1-52	"	Thomas, of Samuel and Mary,	June 18, 1749.
1-14	"	Elizabeth,	Nov. 25, 1750.
1-32	"	Mehitable, of Benjamin, Jr., and Hope,	June 18, 1753.
1-32	"	Elizabeth,	June 18, 1753.

1-37	MILLER Nelson, of Benjamin, Jr., and Hope,	July 26, 1755.
1-20	" Hope,	Nov. 25, 1757.
1-29	" Luraine, of James and Mary,	May 22, 1754.
1-40	" Patience,	Dec. 21, 1756.
1-5	" Barbary,	April 22, 1759.
1-37	" Nathan, of Nathan and Rebecca,	Nov. 23, 1764.
1-4	" Abigail,	Dec. 26, 1766.
1-21	" Haile, of William and Elizabeth,	May 18, 1766.
1-51	" Samuel,	Feb 24, 1768.
1-41	" Perry, (also 1-42),	Jan. 4, 1770.
2-32	" Ebenezer,	Jan. 14, 1772.
1-56	" William,	Dec. 7, 1773.
1-7	" Betsey, (b. Cumberland),	Nov. 22, 1777.
1-38	" Nathan, (b. Cumberland),	Jan. 17, 1780.
1-7	" Betsey, of Mehitabl , Jr.,	April 24, 1770.
2-32	" Elizabeth, of Job and Elizabeth,	Sept. 16, 1770.
1-7	" Barnard,	Aug. 5, 1773.
1-39	" Olive,	April 20, 1776.
2-52	" Job,	July 10, 1780.
1-58	" William Turner, of Samuel and Nancy,	July 30, 1780.
2-99	" Sally Johnson,	March 4, 1782.
1-139	" Cenzer, of Bristol and Peg (col.),	Dec. 28, 1781.
1-139	" Flora (col.),	Dec. 22, 1788.
2-9	" Benjamin, of James and Elizabeth,	Nov. 24, 1791.
1-39	" Olive, of Barnard and Lydia,	Nov. 27, 1797.
2-75	" Lydia Wilbur,	Aug. 15, 1799.
2-93	" Robert,	June 3, 1803.
3-139	" Sarah Emily, of Job and Sarah L.,	July 7, 1849.
3-97	MOORE Nathan Wheaton, of Dr. Thomas P. and Abby,	Nov. 30, 1832.
3-100	" Mary Elizabeth,	Sept. 26, 1834.
3-33	MULCHAHEY Edward Irving, of Charles M. and Patience R.,	
		March 5, 1851.
1-56	MUNRO William, of Thomas and Sarah,	May 8, 1762.
1-52	" Thomas,	Jan. 18, 1765.
1-6	" Bateman,	June 8, 1767.
2-93	" Rebeckah, of Josiah and Sarah,	Sept. 28, 1794.
2-101	" Sarah,	March 28, 1798.
2-76	" Mary Mason,	June 14, 1799.
2-60	" Josiah Smith,	Sept. 24, 1805.
2-101	" Sally Easterbrooks, of Jonathan and Sally,	Oct. 31, 1800.
2-93	" Rebeckah, of Palmer and Anna,	Jan. 16, 1801.
2-102	" Sally,	Feb. 25, 1803.
2-75	" Luther Palmer,	Sept. 2, 1805.
3-27	" Eliza, of Philip and Patience,	Jan. 11, 1812.
3-40	" George,	Oct. 28, 1816.
3-49	" Horace, of John and Nancy,	Dec. 21, 1813.
3-91	" Maria, of George and Mary,	June 22, 1819.
3-29	" Elizabeth Diman,	Jan. 8, 1822.
3-41	" George, of George and Mary B.,	Dec. 15, 1826.
3-52	" Henry Bowen,	Jan. 8, 1830.
3-95	" Mary Abby, of George and Mary Ann,	Jan. 15, 1833.
3-160	" William Henry,	April 24 or 27, 1834.
3-5	" Alexander Griswold,	July 18, 1835.
3-65	" James,	April 2, 1837.
3-5	" Ann Frances,	Sept. 16, 1839.
3-101	" Mary Emily,	April 23, 1841.
3-161	" William,	Aug. 30, 1843.
3-53	" Henry Augustus, of Gardner and Sarah B.,	June 12, 1835.
3-138	" Sarah Gardner,	March 18, 1838.
3-23	MYERS Clement Lawrence Perkins, of Allen B. L. and Huldah P.,	
		Nov. 12, 1840.

N

3-25	NEWMAN Daniel, of Joseph P. and Sarah L.,	July 13, 1827.
3-42	" George L., of Sylvester S. and Eliza,	Oct. 9, 1828.
3-137	" Sarah Ann,	Jan. 2, 1834.
3-157	NEWTON William Henry, of Martin and Deborah,	April 11, 1821.

O

1-28	O'BRIEN Jonathan, of William and Lucinda,	Sept. 15, 1771.
1-47	" Rebecca,	July 22, 1774.
1-56	" William,	Nov. 24, 1776.
2-32	O'KELLEY Elizabeth, of John and Elizabeth,	March 24, 1775.
1-60	ORMSBY Zurniah, of Ebenezer and Hannah,	Aug. 26, 1746.
1-5	" Benjamin,	Oct. 26, 1749.
1-14	" Ezra,	March 30, 1751.
1-14	" Elisha,	Feb. 28, 1753.
1-20	" Hannah,	April 21, 1756.
1-15	" Ebenezer,	Aug. 22, 1760.
1-33	" Mary,	Dec. 18, 1763.
1-24	" John, of Ezra, Jr., and Elizabeth,	Aug. 11, 1756.
1-32	" Mary, of Joshua and Rachel,	Aug. 13, 1761.
1-9	" Caleb,	July 24, 1763.
1-25	" Isaac,	June 21, 1765.
1-27	" Joshua,	Nov. 13, 1767.
1-1	" Anna,	Feb. 12, 1770.
1-56	" William, of Joseph and Hannah,	May 13, 1763.
1-39	" Oliver,	April 28, 1765.
1-33	" Mahitable,	Nov. 11, 1766.
1-27	" Joseph,	May 26, 1768.
1-46	" Robert,	March 6, 1770.
1-6	" Betty, of John and Sarah.	Sept. 5, 1763.
1-26	" John,	March 16, 1765.
1-27	" James,	Aug. 20, 1768.
1-1	" Anne,	Dec. 7, 1770.
1-46	" Roby,	Sept. 22, 1772.
1-46	" Rose,	July 15, 1774.
1-16	" Elizabeth, of Ezra and Esther,	March 29, 1766.
1-60	" Zerviah, of Isaac and Patience,	Feb. 4, 1790.
2-53	" Ira,	June 23, 1792.
2-128	" Philip, of Joshua and Polly,	July 1, 1799.
2-76	" Mary Ann,	March 20, 1801.

P

2-57	PARKER John, of Benjamin and Abigail,	March 25, 1805.
3-49	" Henry William,	Feb. 3, 1807.
3-9	" Betsey Bowen,	Nov. 12, 1809.
3-39	" George,	Oct. 23, 1811.
2-95	PEARS Samuel, of Samuel and Bettey,	March 19, 1764.
1-23	" James,	Dec. 10, 1765.
1-28	" John,	Feb. 15, 1768.
2-1	" Abigail,	Jan. 10, 1770.
1-7	" Betsey,	July 27, 1772.
1-34	" Mary,	March 2, 1775.
2-88	PEARCE Polly, of Samuel and Ruth,	Jan. 25, 1794.
3-88	" Maria, of Noah, Jr., and Betsey,	Jan. 10, 1802.
3-74	" Lewis Desabaye Besayade,	June 13, 1803.
3-26	" Ezekiel Robinson,	Oct. 23, 1804.
2-82	" Noah, (also 3-98),	Dec. 6, 1805.
2-59	" John, of John and Mary,	May 28, 1802.
3-132	" Samuel, of John and Anna,	Dec. 30, 1810.
3-30	" Elizabeth, of Lewis and Sarah Ann,	May 19, 1827.

3-159	PEARCE	William Henry, of Lewis and Sarah Ann,	May 15, 1828.
3-75	"	Lewis,	March 7, 1830.
3-31	"	Elizabeth Haile, of Samuel and Elizabeth (Haile),	Aug. 1, 1834.
3-75	"	Laura,	Aug. 6, 1836.
3-38	"	Charles Sumner, of Isaac and Elizabeth A.,	June 4, 1856.
1-49	PECK	Solomon, of Solomon and Kezia,	Oct. 29, 1738.
1-29	"	Keziah,	Aug. 3, 1740.
1-20	"	Hannah,	Feb. 4, 1743.
1-49	"	Samuel,	Dec. 30, 1744.
1-5	"	Benjamin,	June 9, 1747.
1-3	"	Amos,	May 1, 1749.
1-15	"	Esther,	May 18, 1751.
1-11	"	Daniel,	March 24, 1753.
1-20	"	Hannah,	Oct. 17, 1755.
1-37	"	Nathaniel,	Dec. 17, 1759.
1-16	"	Ebenezer,	Dec. 11, 1762.
1-23	"	James, of Izrael and Sarah,	July 5, 1747.
1-23	"	Izrael,	Feb. 20, 1748-9.
1-23	"	Izrael, 2d,	Dec. 6, 1750.
1-31	"	Mehitable,	July 21, 1752.
1-31	"	Martha, of Prescilla,	March 5, 1748-9.
1-5	"	Bethiah, of Simeon and Prescilla,	Oct. 3, 1751.
1-23	"	Joseph Kelley,	Jan. 10, 1754.
1-5	"	Bettey,	July 16, 1755.
1-49	"	Simeon,	Feb. 6, 1756.
1-32	"	Mary,	April 17, 1758.
1-37	"	Nathaniel,	Aug. 17, 1760.
1-49	"	Sarah, of Nathaniel, Jr., and Mary, (also 1-50),	Feb. 2, 1754.
1-56	"	Winchester,	Feb. 7, 1762.
1-26	"	Jerusha,	June 18, 1764.
1-4	"	Abigail, of Solomon, Jr., and Abigail,	May 12, 1764.
1-30	"	Keziah,	Sept. 10, 1766.
2-95	"	Solomon,	Feb. 13, 1769.
3-119	"	Patience, of Seth and Lillis,	Aug. 25, 1792.
3-59	"	John Greene,	Sept. 7, 1800.
1-58	"	William, of Hezekiah, and Abigail,	May 15, 1794.
2-45	"	Hezekiah,	Aug. 23, 1796.
2-90	"	Peleg,	Dec. 11, 1798.
3-139	"	Sarah Arnold, of Isaac L. and Jane D.,	Sept. 15, 1840.
3-139	"	Samuel Luther.	Dec. 17, 1845.
3-66	"	James Clarence, of James M. and Elizabeth L.,	Jan. 29, 1850.
1-36	PERCE	Mary, of Jeremiah and Nancy,	July 31, 1785.
2-7	"	Betsey,	July 31, 1785.
2-52	"	Joseph,	June 1, 1787.
2-91	"	Robe,	Jan. 25, 1790.
2-98	"	Sanford, of Samuel and Ruth,	Nov. 23, 1789.
2-2	"	Abigail,	Dec. 25, 1791.
2-90	"	Polly, of John and Mary,	March 12, 1797.
1-45	PETTIS	Rhoda, of John and Rachel,	July 20, 1757.
1-15	"	Elizabeth,	June 23, 1757.
1-11	"	Daniel,	Feb. 8, 1759.
2-45	PHILLIPS	Hannah Proctor, of Nathaniel and Robe, (b. Johnston),	
			Jan. 8, 1780.
1-58	"	William,	Nov. 30, 1785.
2-54	"	John,	Nov. 16, 1787.
2-54	"	Joseph,	Jan. 20, 1790.
2-92	"	Resolved,	Jan. 4, 1793.
2-80	"	Nathaniel,	Sept. 22, 1793.
3-89	"	Mary Jane, of John F. and Martha,	May 7, 1812.
3-58	"	John Gibbs.	Nov. 17, 1813.
3-49	"	Hannah Proctor, of William and Rebecca,	Jan. 29, 1811.
3-125	"	Rebecca Maxwell,	June 27, 1812.
1-26	PHINNEY	Jonathan, of Elisha and Jemima,	Jan. 30, 1764.
2-1	"	Aaron, of Elisha and Rebecca,	April 24, 1767.
1-12	"	Daniel,	Sept. 14, 1768.

1-6	PHINNEY Benjamin, of Elisha and Rebecca,	Oct. 8, 1771.
1-34	" Mima,	March 29, 1773.
2-32	" Elisha Peck,	Oct. 13. 1774.
2-92	" Reuben,	Sept. 22, 1777.
2-45	" Hannah,	Oct. 11. 1779.
2-81	" Nathan,	Oct. 5, 1782.
2-74	" Lydia Peck, of Benjamin and Betsey,	April 8, 1795.
2-35	" Emma, of Daniel and Eliza,	April 13, 1900.
2-36	" Eliza Kinnecutt,	May 15, 1802.
2-4	PITCHER Allen Greene, of Edward and Sarah,	March 20, 1802.
2-33	PITMAN Elizabeth, of John and Rebecca,	Sept. 29, 1787.
3-35	PLACE Frank Thornton, of John T. and Sylvia C.,	June —, 1853.
1-19	PONE George, of Samuel and Ruth,	July 1, 1788.
2-37	PRICE Eliza Ann, of Richard and Mary,	Sept. 10. 1809.
3-9	" Benjamin Arnold,	Nov. 23, 1811.
3-19	" Caroline Bowen,	Aug. 14. 1814.
3-28	· Edward Enos,	Jan. 6, 1817.
3-125	" William Henry,	July 21, 1821.
3-3	" Ardelia,	Oct. 20, 1824.
3-135	" Susan White Slocum,	July 13, 1826.
3-67	PRIOR John William, of Charles and Celia,	Sept. 11, 1848.
3-139	" Samuel Irving,	July 4, 1853.

Q R

2-19	RANDALL Charles, of John and Nancy, (b. Sharon, Mass.),	Aug. 6, 1806.
2-57	" Jane Gordon, of Philip and Abby,	Jan. 27, 1811.
3-39	" Geo. Maxwell, of Samuel and Patty,	Nov. 23, 1810.
3-89	" Martha M.,	Sept. 15, 1813.
3-132	" Samuel Fisher,	March 31, 1816.
1-134	" Seraphine,	April 20, 1819.
3-21	" Chas. Theodore,	Sept. 5, 1825.
3-1	" Abby, of Philip and Abigail,	Nov. 13, 1813.
3-90	" Mary,	May 22, 1815.
3-119	" Philip,	May 14, 1817.
3-3	" Abby Eddy,	Feb. 8, 1821.
3-135	" Sophia,	July 23, 1824.
3-66	" James,	May 7, 1829.
3-137	" Seraphine, of Charles and Lydia B.,	Nov. 10, 1838.
3-138	" Seraphine, of George Maxwell and Elizabeth, (b. Tiverton), July 3, 1843.
1-2	RAWSON Ann, of Elijah and Mary,	Nov. 9, 1747.
1-22	" James Paddock,	April 5, 1750.
1-11	" David,	Aug. 3, 1752.
1-14	" Elijah,	March 22, 1755.
1-24	" James Paddock, 2d,	Sept. 30, 1757.
1-50	" Samuel,	July 16, 1760.
1-16	" Edward,	March 20, 1763.
1-33	" Mary,	Nov. 27, 1765.
1-31	REED Mary, of Benjamin and Elizabeth,	March 27, 1747.
1-2	" Anne, of Samuel and Sybel,	Sept. 11, 1747.
1-40	" Phebe,	Nov. 20, 1748.
1-24	" Jonathan,	Jan. 14, 1751.
1-29	" Lillis,	Aug. 18, 1753.
1-50	" Squire,	Sept. 18, 1756.
2-79	" Mary Ann, of L. Leonard and Mary,	Feb. 21, 1806.
2-79	" Lydia Brown,	Aug. 9, 1808.
2-79	" Laura Greene,	Oct. 30, 1813.
3-29	" Elizabeth, of Andrew Barton and Betsey,	June 30, 1822.
3-30	" Ellen,	Jan. 3, 1825.
3-63	" James,	Feb. 16, 1827.
3-4	" Andrew,	Jan. 20, 1829.
1-20	REMINGTON Hepzebeth, of Matthew and Rachael,	July 24, 1749.
1-32	" Molly, of Enock and Molly,	Nov. 11, 1757.

1-30	REMINGTON Lydia, of Enock and Molly,		July 20, 1765.
2-59	REX John, of George and Patience,		Jan. 23, 1803.
1-36	"	Eliza,	Dec. 20, 1804.
2-104	"	Thomas White,	March 31, 1809.
3-89	"	Mary Child,	Oct. 29 1811.
3-59	"	Jeremiah Child (at Pawtucket),	March 24, 1814.
1-34	REYNOLDS Molly, of Peter and Ptience,		May 10, 1765.
1-38	"	Nathaniel,	Oct. 31, 1768.
1-1	"	Anne,	June 6, 1772.
3-33	"	Elizabeth Adelaide, of William L. and Maria,	Oct. 31, 1845.
3-33	"	Evelyn,	Sept. 13, 1847.
2-76	RICHARDS Margaret, of Peter and Susannah,		Sept. 14, 1779.
2-73	"	Luther,	Sept. 19, 1783.
2-56	"	James.	June 26, 1796.
3-132	"	Susanna, of Luther and Sarah,	Dec. 15, 1812.
3-119	"	Polly Kinnecutt,	July 10, 1818.
3-40	"	George Pearce, of James and Abby,	July 3, 1825.
3-58	RILEY James Madison, of Owen and Deborah,		Jan. 23, 1813.
1-24	ROGERS Joseph, of Peleg and Ruth,		July 3, 1762.
1-12	"	Dianna,	Aug. 14, 1764.
1-27	"	John Rogers,	Dec. 6, 1766.
1-41	"	Pati nce,	July 21, 1769.
3-125	"	Rebecca Almy, of Peleg and Lydia,	June 18, 1817.
3-133	"	Sarah Ann,	March 28, 1818.
2-89	"	Peleg, of John and Anna,	Nov. 7, 1791.
1-60	ROSS Zephaniah, of John and Sarah,		April 2, 1743.
1-31	"	Mica (son),	Dec. 31, 1744.
1-12	ROUNDS Daniel, of Oliver and Anna,		June 5, 1771.
2-96	"	Sybel,	May 1, 1773.
2-1	"	Abigail,	March 1, 1775.
1-9	"	Calvin,	Oct. 3, 1776.
1-42	"	Patience,	March 1, 1778.
2-98	"	Spencer,	Feb. 26, 1780.
1-39	"	Oliver,	Feb. 26, 1780.
2-53	"	Jabez,	Nov. 20, 1782.
2-103	"	Spencer,	Oct. 24, 1805.
3-57	"	James, of Oliver, Jr., and Jerusha,	May 20, 1812.
3-158	"	William E., of Philip and Elizabeth (b Barrington).	June 8, 1808.
3-58	"	Julia Ann, of Spencer and Cynthia,	March 17, 1814.
3-2	"	Ardelia,	Nov. 13, 1815.
3-91	"	Mason H.,	Oct. 11, 1817.
3-30	"	Eliza Ann, of Henry C. and Mary Anne	Nov. 15, 1826.

S

1-3	SALISBURY Anna, of William and Mary,		Sept. 20, 1743.
1-55	"	William,	Jan. 20, 1745-6.
1-22	"	Jonathan,	June 5, 1748.
1-44	"	Rebecca,	Jan. 3, 1751.
1-32	"	Mary,	April 4, 1753.
1-4	"	Anne,	May 17, 1756.
1-45	"	Roby, of Jonathan and Mary,	Sept. 27, 1758.
1-6	"	Bethiah,	April 25, 1761.
1-27	"	John,	Nov. 11, 1764.
1-27	"	James,	Nov. 11, 1764.
1-4	"	Archibald,	Nov. 29, 1766.
1-34	"	Molly,	April 6, 1770.
2-32	"	Elizabeth,	Dec. 9, 1772.
1-41	"	Patience, of Levi and Phebe,	May 5, 1764.
1-41	"	Phebe.	Nov. 22, 1765.
1-51	"	Samuel, of George and Abigail,	April 27, 1765.
2-95	"	Sally,	May 18, 1768.
1-21	"	Halle, of Oliver, Jr., and Hannah,	Sept. 23, 1766.
2-32	"	Elizabeth,	July 8, 1767.

2-95	SALISBURY Sarah, of Oliver, Jr., and Hannah,	Jan. 26, 1770.
1-18	" Gardner, of Barnard and Prudence,	July 12, 1771.
2-95	" Sylvester Child,	Aug. 12, 1773.
2-32	" Elizabeth,	June 14, 1774.
2 9	" Barnard,	April 1, 1778.
1-18	" George Sisson, of William and Elizabeth,	Feb. 14, 1771.
1-12	" Daniel,	Sept. 5, 1772.
2-3	" Amos,	April 14, 1774.
1-36	" Mary,	May 7, 1776.
2-45	" Hopestill,	April 28, 1779.
1-30	" Luther, of Caleb and Hannah,	Sept. 18, 1772.
1-28	" Joanna,	May 16, 1774.
1-38	" Nehemiah,	April 3, 1779.
1-60	" Abigail, of Theophilus and Abigail,	March 28, 1783.
1-52	" Theophilus, of Theophilus and Abigail,	May 27, 1781.
1-35	" Martin Luther, of Luther and Abigail,	July 11, 1783.
1-36	" Martin,	June 3, 1785.
2-7	" Betsey,	March 26, 1788.
2-73	" Luther,	Dec. 25, 1789.
2-57	" John, of John and Abigail,	Aug. 29, 1789.
2-91	" Rebecca Cranston, of Pardon and Lydia,	May 1, 1792.
2-76	" Mary, of Caleb and Patience,	July 26, 1795.
2-128	" Pasha Miller,	June 30, 1802.
2-38	" Genet, of Simeon and Prescilla,	April 11, 1801.
2-128	" Prescilla Child,	Dec. 22, 1802.
2-77	" Margaret,	Jan. 4, 1806.
2-37	" Edward Child,	July 4, 1809.
3-22	" Charles H., of Daniel and Mary,	Nov. 8, 1804.
2-83	" Nabby Throop, of Theophilus and Polly,	Oct. 17, 1807.
2-61	" Julian,	Dec. 24, 1808.
3-9	" Billings Throop,	May 29, 1811.
3-143	" Theophilus,	Aug. 16, 1813.
3-50	" Henry Bryant,	Jan. 10, 1816.
3-132	" Samuel,	Jan. 6, 1818.
3-92	" Mary,	May 18, 1820.
3-51	" Hannah,	Aug. 8, 1822.
3-93	" Maria,	June 1, 1825.
3-30	" Elizabeth,	June 18, 1828.
2-108	" Sarah Luther, of Martin and Elizabeth,	Nov. 29, 1807.
3-93	" Martin Luther,	March 4, 1810.
3-1	" Amelia,	March 4, 1812.
3-28	" Elizabeth,	July 9, 1814.
3-59	" John Goff,	Jan. 22, 1817.
3-10	" Benjamin Cole,	Dec. 26, 1821.
3-119	" Patience Cole,	March 6, 1824.
3-4	" Abby Cole,	Feb. 9, 1829.
3-9	" Abby Fisher, of John and Betsey, (also 3-2),	May 1, 1817.
3-60	" John,	Feb. 23, 1819.
3-74	" Levi,	Oct. 27, 1821.
3-93	" Maria, (also 3-40),	May 16, 1824.
3-93	" George, (also 3-40),	May 16, 1824.
3-95	" Mary Hall, of Charles H. and Rebecca,	Nov. 20, 1928.
3-160	" William H.,	Sept. 17, 1831.
3-95	" Mary Elizabeth, of Martin L. and Susan A.,	July 13, 1832.
3-128	" Ruth Stanton,	Sept. 22, 1835.
3-25	" Daniel Stanton,	Sept. 12, 1837.
3-25	" Susan Louisa, (also 3-138),	July 8, 1839.
3-65	" Josephine, of Billings and Nancy,	Jan. 27, 1839.
3-42	" George Leonard,	Sept. 18, 1840.
3-161	" William Henry, of John and Abby W.,	July 6, 1842.
3-100	" Maria Adelaide,	Jan. 21, 1844.
3-54	" Herman,	Feb. 2, 1851.
3-158	SARGEN William Henry, of Hammond and Roby,	Feb. 9, 1826.
3-135	" Sally Sanders,	Feb. 9, 1827.
3-30	" Ellen Elizabeth,	Jan. 21, 1829.

3-41	SARGEN George Hammond, of Hammond and Roby,		June 7, 1830.
3-37	" Charles R.,		April 27, 1832.
3-33	" Edward Luther,		Aug. 23, 1836.
3-101	" Mary Cole,		Nov. 18, 1937.
1-18	SANDERS George, of Jacob and Elizabeth.		Aug. 31, 1771.
2-81	" Nathaniel,		March 10, 1774.
1-12	" Daniel,		Dec. 19, 1775.
2-34	" Elizabeth,		April 12, 1778.
1-58	" William,		March 22, 1782.
2-81	" Nelly,		April 8, 1784.
1-58	" Wheaton of Benjamin and Anna,		Jan. 6, 1787.
2-8	" Betsey,		June 25, 1789.
2-8	" Benjamin,		April 8, 1791.
2-3	" Anna,		Dec. 14, 1792.
2-82	" Nancy,		Dec. 14, 1792.
1-13	" Daniel,		March 26, 1795.
2-75	" Lydia,		May 14, 1797.
2-59	" James,		Dec. 11, 1799.
2-77	" Mary,		Dec. 11, 1799.
2-4	" Amasa,		March 25, 1802.
2-32	" Elizabeth, of James and Elizabeth,		July 6, 1773.
2 53	" John, of David and Nancy,		July 29, 1789.
2-80	" Nancy,		April 20, 1791.
2-45	" Hopestill,		July 6, 1793.
2-100	" Sarah, of Nathaniel and Sarah,		Dec. 10, 1794.
2-82	" Nathaniel Whiting,		Feb. 13, 1796.
2-93	" Roby,		Feb. 23, 1798.
1-59	" William,		July 7, 1800.
2-47	" Henry,		Sept. 6, 1802.
2-83	" Nathan Bowen,		May 13, 1804.
2-60	" Jacob,		July 21, 1807.
2-19	" Charles Whitfield,	(also 3-20),	Dec. 3, 1808.
3-39	" George, 2d,		April 20, 1811.
3-26	" Edward,		April 8, 1814.
3-26	" Edwin,		April 8, 1814.
1-19	" George, of George and Betsey,		May 15, 1796.
2-10	" Betsey, of Daniel and Molly,		July 13, 1802.
2-77	" Maria,		April 17, 1804.
2-78	" Mary Little,		Oct. 2, 1807.
1-13	" Daniel,		June 24, 1809.
3-131	" Samuel,		July 29, 1811.
3-132	" Seth,		Sept. 3, 1813.
3-57	" John, of Jeremiah and Mary,		April 22, 1812.
3-29	" Elizabeth Hicks, of George and Emeline,		Sept. 20, 1821.
3-137	" Sarah Elizabeth, of Charles W. and Catherine,		Feb. 16, 1833.
3-65	" Jacob Gustavus, of Jacob and Mary H.,		Feb. 10, 1838.
3-98	" Nathaniel Thomas, of Edwin and Henrietta M.,		
	(b. Fairhaven, Mass.), April 2, 1838.		
3-53	" Henry,		Jan. 4, 1841.
3-100	" Maria Louisa, of Edward and Maria (Davol),		July 7, 1838.
3-67	" Clara Davol,		Oct. 28, 1841.
3-38	" Clara Davol, 2d,		Oct. 28, 1842.
3-34	" Edward Francis,		June 7, 1849.
3-85	" Florence Eliza,		Jan. 7, 1854.
3-161	" William, of Henry and Martha B.,		Dec. 10, 1843.
3-66	" Julia Whitfield,		March 13, 1847.
3-25	" Daniel Walter, of Daniel and Sarah A.,		Dec. 29, 1946.
3-38	" Clara Collins.		May 2, 1850.
3-57	SAWTELLE James Bugbee, of Joel and Dinah,		Sept. 11, 1811.
3-74	" Lucinda Barnes,		Sept. 12, 1813.
3-50	" Hollis,		Feb. 2, 1816.
3-60	" Joseph.		Nov. 25, 1818.
3-66	" James Bugbee, of Joseph and Betsey M.,		July 18, 1848.
3-55	SHARKEY James, of Michael and Betsey, (b. Ireland),		Aug. —, 1834.
3-120	" Patrick,	(b. Ireland),	—— —, 1836.

3-101	SHARKEY Michael, of Michael and Betsey,	(b. Ireland), — —,	1838.
3-101	" Mary,	(b. Ireland), — —,	1840.
3-23	" Edward,	(b. Ireland), — —,	1844.
3-139	" Susan,	(b. Ireland), — .—,	1845.
3-37	" Catherine, of Patrick and Betsey,	(b. Ireland), — —,	1835.
1-52	SHELDON Thomas, of Ephraim and Rebecca,	Jan. 9, 1748-9.	
1-44	" Rebecca, of William and Lydia,	Dec. 31, 1750.	
1-55	" William,	Feb. 28, 1751-2.	
1-40	" Prescilla,	Nov. 15, 1753.	
1-15	" Edward,	Nov. 5, 1755.	
1-40	" Patience,	Oct. 13, 1757.	
3-60	SHERMAN Joseph Henry, of Levi and Hopey,	Aug. 5, 1818.	
3-51	" Hannah,	Sept. 22, 1822.	
3-93	" Mary,	June 6, 1825.	
3-119	" Phebe Maria,	Sept. 27, 1827.	
1-29	SHORT Lydia, of James and Margaret,	Sept. 15, 1748.	
1-23	" James, of John and Phebe,	April 6, 1753.	
1-49	" Samuel,	March 9, 1755.	
1-25	" John,	Feb. 14, 1757.	
1-45	" Rachel,	Feb. 6, 1759.	
1-41	" Philip,	March 19, 1761.	
1-41	" Phebe,	July 11, 1764.	
1-34	" Monoseth, (son),	May 26, 1766.	
1-21	" Hannah,	Dec. 25, 1767.	
1-57	" William, of James and Anna,	Aug. 14, 1779.	
1-36	" Mary,	June 24, 1781.	
2-98	" Samuel,	March 31, 1784.	
2-88	" Philip,	May 29, 1786.	
2-53	" James,	Aug. 25, 1789.	
2-8	" Benjamin,	Oct. 24, 1793.	
2-55	" Joseph, of Upham and Rebecca,	Oct. 1, 1794.	
2-56	" John Vinnecome,	Sept. 5, 1797.	
2-75	" Luther Cole,	Aug. 17, 1803.	
3-19	" Caleb Mason, of James, Jr., and Content,	March 24, 1818.	
3-91	" Mary Ann,	Aug. 23, 1820.	
3-10	" Betsey,	Aug. 2, 1823.	
3-64	" James Gardner,	Feb. 28, 1834.	
1-22	SIMMONS Joseph, of George and Elizabeth,	Sept. 23, 1747.	
3 63	SIMONS Joseph Noble, of Lewis E. and Joanna,	June 26, 1831.	
1-50	SIMMS Sampson, of John and Mercy,	May 18, 1758.	
1-7	" Benjamin, of Sampson and Mary,	Sept. 27, 1786.	
2-52	" John,	Nov. 11, 1789.	
2-89	" Polly,	Feb. 10, 1792.	
2-74	" Lloyd Hokey,	March 4, 1795.	
2-82	" Nathan Anthony, (b. Portsmouth),	March 25, 1798.	
1-1	SISSON Sarah, of George and Drosilla,	March 28, 1739.	
1-46	" Ruth,	May 10, 1741.	
1-46	" Richard,	July 16, 1743.	
1-2	" Abigail,	Aug. 18, 1745.	
1-22	" Jonathan,	Oct. 20, 1747.	
1-27	" James,	Feb. 22, 1750.	
1-16	" Elizabeth,	Aug. 27, 1751.	
1-1	" Anna,	Aug. 23, 1753.	
1-18	" George,	Oct 22, 1754.	
1-25	" John, of John and Mary,	Feb. 17, 1758.	
1-8	" Caleb,	April 14, 1760.	
1-16	" Esek,	Aug. 11, 1762.	
1-26	" Jane,	Sept. 27, 1764.	
1-18	" Gardner,	March 7, 1767	
1-17	" Fones,	June 7, 1769.	
1-35	" Mary,	Nov. 13, 1771.	
2-72	" Lydia,	July 13, 1774.	
2-1	" Anstress, of Gideon and Abigail,	May 11, 1765.	
1-17	" Freeborn (son),	Jan. 16, 1767.	
1-16	" Edward,	Oct. 14, 1768.	

1-21	SISSON	Henry, of Gideon and Abigail,		Oct. 12, 1770.
1-18	"	Gideon,		Oct. 10, 1772.
2-72	"	Linda,		Jan. 11, 1776.
1-35	"	Marvel,		March 9, 1778.
2-44	"	Haile Mason, of James and Sarah,		Jan. 1, 1792.
1-9	"	Charlotte,		April 6, 1783.
1-10	"	Charlotte, 2d,		May 1, 1785.
2-92	"	Rodman.		Aug. 6, 1792.
2-38	"	George,		July 22, 1795.
2-37	"	Freeborn, of Freeborn,		——, ——.
2-43	"	Freeborn, of Freeborn and Jane, (also 2-79),		April 17, 1810.
3-39	"	Gideon,		Oct. 15, 1812.
3-28	"	Elizabeth Blackstick,		March 15, 1816.
3-20	"	Charles Nathan,		April 14, 1818.
3-28	"	Edward,		Feb. 14, 1820.
3-40	"	Gideon,		May 4, 1823.
2-79	"	Maria Maxwell, of Gideon and Jane,		Feb. 10, 1802.
2-129	"	Philip Allen, of Esek and Sabra,		Dec. 28, 1806.
2-47	"	Henry Collins, of Henry and Hannah,		March 10, 1809.
3-19	"	Caroline Maria,		April 25, 1814.
3-89	"	Mary Slade Mason, of James and Hannah,		April 21, 1809.
3-5	"	Anjanette Mason, of George and Eliza Ann,		Nov. 14, 1833.
3-5	"	Abby Hudson,		April 12, 1838.
1-21	SMITH	Hannah, of James, Jr., and Avis May,		May 24, 1767.
1-27	"	John,		Oct. 2, 1768.
1-6	"	Barnard, of Joseph and Molly,		May 30, 1770.
1-6	"	Benjamin,		April 3, 1773.
1-28	"	Joseph,		July 19, 1775.
1-57	"	William,		Dec. 12, 1777.
1-28	"	James,		April 2, 1780.
2-1	"	Anthony,		Dec. 28, 1783.
2-51	"	Job,		May 28, 1786.
1-35	"	Molly,		May 28, 1786.
2-98	"	Sally,		April 23, 1789.
2-33	"	Eliza,		June 23, 1793.
2-56	"	James, of James and Sarah,		Sept. 11, 1796.
2-10	"	Benjamin,		Aug. 29, 1804.
2-102	"	Sally,		Nov. 27, 1805.
2-47	"	Howland,		Oct. 22, 1807.
3 59	"	James,		Feb. 14, 1809.
3-2	"	Anthony,		Oct. 12, 1813.
3-59	"	Joseph,		Aug. 9, 1815.
3-20	"	Charles Mason,		May 31, 1818.
3-40	"	George,		July 26, 1820.
3-29	"	Eliza,	(sic,), April 31, 1822.
1-53	"	Tempe, of Joseph and Hannah.		Feb. 14, 1799.
2-59	"	Joseph,	(also 2-59), May 9 or 10, 1803.
3-00	"	Mary,	(at Bristol), Nov. 9, 1805.
3-58	"	John Wheaton,	(at Bristol), Aug. 19, 1808.
3-97	"	Nancy,		Jan. 24, 1813.
2-48	"	Hannah,		Jan. 10, 1818.
2-18	"	Charles, of Jonathan and Abigail,		Dec. 19, 1801.
2-59	"	Julian,		Feb. 15, 1804.
2-109	"	William,		July 27, 1808.
2-103	"	Sally,		Nov. 19, 1809.
3-27	"	Elisha Glowshy,		May 21, 1812.
3-90	"	Martha Glowshey,		May 12, 1815.
3-91	"	Maria,		April 27, 1817.
3-25	"	Darius,		Nov. 10, 1819.
3-134	"	Seth Wheaton,		June 12, 1821.
3-3	"	Abby Caroline,		Nov. 3, 1824.
2-37	"	Elizabeth, of Barnard and Margaret,	(also 2-11), Aug. 13, 1806.
2-10	"	Barnard,		Dec. 1, 1807.
2-109	"	William,		Oct. 11, 1809.
3-57	"	James Arnold, of Michael and Hannah,		Aug. 21, 1812.

3-90	SMITH	Mary, of Job and Sally,	Sept. 15, 1814.
3-28	"	Ellen,	Dec. 6, 1816.
3-51	"	Henry Greene,	April 16, 1819.
3-62	"	John Young,	March 11, 1825.
3-136	"	Susan Thompson,	June 24, 1827.
3-163	"	Zerah Bradford, (b. Troy, Penn.),	July 3, 1830.
3-10	"	Barnard,	Jan. 11, 1822.
3-2	"	Ann Wood, of Eleazer and Experience S.,	March 5, 1816.
3-157	"	William Barney,	Nov. 12, 1818.
3-28	"	Eliza Miller Carpenter, of Elisha G. and Abby,	June 30, 1819.
3-40	"	George Leonidas,	Nov. 24, 1823.
3-21	"	Charles Sidney,	Oct. 4, 1828.
3-119	"	Peter Carpenter,	June 14, 1826.
3-95	"	Mary Elizabeth, of Joseph, 3d, and Betsey,	Nov. 3, 1827.
3-4	"	Ann Frances,	April 16, 1829.
3-137	"	Seraphine Randall,	July 18, 1830.
3-52	"	Hannah Wheaton,	Jan. 26, 1832.
3-138	"	Samuel Watson, of James and Charlotte T.,	Dec. 6, 1835.
3-161	"	William Armington,	Sept. 4, 1838.
3-65	"	John Day, of E. G. and A.,	Feb. 12, 1840.
3-161	"	William Collins, of Joseph M. and Margaret R.,	Sept. 27, 1846.
3-42	"	George Emily (dau.) of James and Sarah,	June 26, 1847.
3-142	"	Sarah Reynolds,	Nov. 13, 1850.
3-33	"	Emma Stephens, of Peter C. and Ann J.,	Feb. 23, 1849.
3-76	"	Lyra Niles,	Dec. 29, 1851.
3-76	"	Lucy Carpenter,	Aug. 22, 1853.
3-126	"	Roswell Cunningham, of Charles S. and Levina W.,	March 27, 1851.
1-31	SNELL	Mary, of John and Freelove,	——. 27, 1748.
1-46	"	Ruth, of Seth and Hannah,	Sept. 13, 1772.
1-56	"	William,	March 11, 1774.
1-21	"	Hannah,	Feb. 20, 1776.
1-38	"	Nathan,	Feb. 6, 1778.
1-35	"	Mary Carr,	April 3, 1780.
2-97	"	Seth,	Nov. 8, 1782.
1-60	"	Abigail,	Aug. 25, 1784.
2-89	"	Philip,	Jan. 22, 1787.
1-53	"	Thomas,	March 14, 1789.
1-10	"	Caleb,	Aug. 7, 1791.
1-12	"	Deliverance,	Oct. 15, 1793.
2-10	"	Betsey,	March 21, 1797.
2-82	"	Nathan, of William and Amstress K.,	Jan. 15, 1798.
2-110	"	William Barton, of Seth, Jr., and Rebecca (also 3-158),	July 25, 1810.
2-33	SPARKS	Edward Cole, of Joseph and Charity,	June 1, 1788.
2-52	"	Joseph,	April 19, 1790.
2-100	"	Samuel Cole,	Sept. 2, 1796.
3-24	SPELLMAN	David Easterbrooks, of John and Persis,	July 16, 1810.
3-34	STANLEY	Elizabeth Martin, of Viall and Hannah B.,	Nov. 11, 1848.
3-37	"	Charles Henry, of George and Almira K.,	Feb. 11, 1848.
2-100	STEPHENS	Sally, of John and Dorcas,	May 12, 1784.
3-128	STILLWELL	Rebecca Gardner, of Stephen and Sarah Ann,	Jan. 16, 1832.
2-34	STACKFORD	Eliza, of John and Jean,	Sept. 8, 1796.
3-62	STONE	Jacob, of Jacob and Anne (b. Lancaster, Mass.),	March 6, 1803.
3-126	SWAZEY	Rebecca W., of Stephen S. and Sarah R.,	Jan. 7, 1825.
2-116	SWEET	Leonard, of Leonard and Lemira,	May 10, 1806.

T

3-158	TALBOT	William Haile, of Zephaniah and Margaret,	Jan. 26, 1819.
3-101	TANNER	Mary Maria H., of Clarke H. and Maria Louisa,	June 13, 1852.
1-44	THOMAS	Rachel, of Richard and Mary,	Jan. 26, 1727-8.
1-2	"	Asa,	Sept. 30, 1729.
1-44	"	Ruth,	Dec. 19, 1731.
1-48	"	Sanford,	April 24, 1734.

1-31	THOMAS Mary, of Richard and Mary,		Sept. 9, 1736.
1-22	"	Isaac,	May 5, 1739.
1-8	"	Caleb,	March 28, 1741.
1-14	"	Elizabeth,	Sept. 9, 1743.
1-48	"	Sarah,	Jan. 30, 1745-6.
1-2	"	Anne,	Dec. 3, 1748.
1-44	"	Ruth, of Amos and Jemima,	May 27, 1846.
1-48	"	Sarah,	Sept. 3, 1749.
1-40	"	Prudence,	April 11, 1752.
1-49	"	Susanna,	April 8, 1755.
1-56	THOMPSON William, of Charles and Sarah,		Oct. 23, 1771.
1-1	"	Abigail Miller,	Oct. 3, 1773.
1-42	"	Peggy,	July 17, 1777.
2-76	"	Maria, of William and Sally (b. Pittstown, N. Y.),	June 22, 1794.
2-103	"	William Baker (b. Pittstown, N. Y.),	Aug. 6, 1796.
2-74	"	Louisa Hill,	May 25, 1799.
3-24	"	Daniel Wales,	Aug. 4, 1801.
2-60	"	John Brown,	Nov. 1, 1805.
2-39	"	George Smith, (also 3-40),	Dec. 15, 1807.
3-90	"	Mary Child,	Aug. 28, 1811.
3-22	"	Charles Henry, of John B. and Hannah P.,	June 10, 1832.
3-160	"	William Phillips,	April 2, 1835.
3-52	"	Hannah Phillips,	June 9, 1837.
3-67	"	John Everett,	Oct. 3, 1840.
3-162	"	Walter Florence,	June 4, 1843.
3-102	"	Malcom Brennan,	Jan. 27, 1846.
3-6	"	Araline,	April 14, 1848.
3-38	"	Charles,	March 27, 1850.
3-65	THORNTON James Arnold, of James A. and Sophronia		Nov. 7, 1838.
3-100	"	Mary Elizabeth,	Dec. 3, 1840.
3-66	"	James Clarence,	May 5, 1843.
1-44	THURBER Ruth, of Lemuel and Agatha,		Feb. 24, 1746.
1-2	"	Agatha,	July 28, 1748.
1-48	"	Lemuel, of Samuel and Eliss,	Feb. 28, 1750.
1-11	"	Deliverance,	Oct. 22, 1752.
1-16	"	Esek, of John and Ruth,	March 17, 1764.
1-41	"	Prudence,	June 22, 1766.
1-16	"	Elizabeth,	Jan 13, 1769.
2-88	"	Polly, of Caleb and Lucretia,	Jan. 9, 1769.
1-10	"	Collins,	April 2, 1770.
2-53	"	James,	Feb. 28, 1773.
1-19	"	George,	April 9, 1779.
2-80	"	Nancy,	May 30, 1787.
2-129	"	Penelope, of Esek and Mary,	Oct. 30, 1784.
2-94	"	Roby,	Dec. 11, 1795.
2-61	"	James, of George and Jemima,	Nov. 11, 1800.
2-39	"	George Leonard,	Oct. 4, 1802.
3-19	"	Collins,	Dec. 26, 1804.
3-157	"	William Henry,	Feb. 17, 1807.
3-2	"	Anna,	Nov. 23, 1809.
3-73	"	Lois Leonard,	Dec. 31, 1814.
3-2	"	Abby Fuller,	Sept. 3, 1817.
3-6	"	Anna Collins, of Collins and Maria,	Feb. 10, 1848.
1-48	TIFFANY Sarah, of Hezekiah and Sarah. Feb. 9, 1727-8.		
1-14	"	Elizabeth, of Ephraim and Esther, Jan. 22, 1745.	
1-44	"	Rachel,	Sept. 22, 1748.
1-31	"	Molly,	June 1, 1751.
1-14	"	Ebenezer,	June 10, 1753.
1-3	TOOGOOD Anne, of Lemuel, Jr., and Abigail, Sept. 7, 1754.		
1-60	"	Zilpha,	Feb. 10, 1757.
1-32	"	Mary,	Feb. 28, 1762.
1-11	"	Daniel, of Trustam and Jemima,	Nov. 11, 1759.
1-25	"	Joseph,	Jan. 8, 1762.
1-16	"	Elizabeth, of Joseph, and Bete,	Jan. 28, 1765.
1-33	"	Mary, of Simeon and Mary (also 1-34),	Jan. 6, 1764.

1-16	TOOGOOD Elizabeth. of Simeon and Mary,	Jan. 2, 1766.
1-28	" James.	July 31, 1769.
2-95	" Sally,	July 10, 1775.
2-51	" Joseph, of Daniel and Mary,	April 18, 1786.
1-48	TOWNSEND Solomon, of Solomon and Rebecca,	June 24, 1748.
1-44	TRIPP Rebecca, of William and Abigail,	Sept. 26, 1745.
1-55	" William.	June 24, 1748.
1-20	" Hannah.	April 23, 1750.
1-31	" Mehitable,	March 4, 1752.
1-15	" Elizabeth.	May 17, 1755.
1-8	" Consider,	May 25, 1757.
1-4	" Anne, of John and Elizabeth,	March 3, 1758.
2-83	" Noel Allen, of William and Betsey,	Jan. 18, 1808.
3-29	TROTT Eliza Stockford, of James and Sally,	July 20, 1821.
1-139	TROYS Cloe, of Abigail (Indian),	Jan. 6, 1748-9.
1-32	TUCKER Mary, of John and Susannah,	Aug. 15, 1751.
1-25	" John,	Feb. 26, 1756.
1-20	TURNER Hannah, of Caleb and Hannah,	Dec. 18, 1750.
1-52	" Temperance,	Oct. 17, 1752.
2-51	" John, of Caleb and Mary,	Jan. 31, 1774.
1-35	" Mary,	April 16, 1775.
1-9	" Caleb,	June 28, 1776.
1-52	" Temperance,	Nov. 16, 1779.
1-9	" Cyrus,	Dec. 24, 1785.
1-43	" Polly,	Feb. 15, 1775.
2-92	" Roby, of Moses and Abigail,	July 14, 1775.
1-54	" Varnum,	Dec. 18, 1777.
1-12	" Durfee,	Nov. 20, 1778.
2-89	" Patience,	March 27, 1784.
2-89	" Pattey,	March 7, 1788.
2-34	" Eliza,	Feb. 22, 1791.
2-45	" Harriet,	Feb. 22, 1791.
1-39	" Oliver Cromwell, of Peter and Elizabeth,	Feb. 4, 1777.
1-9	" Cyrus, of Caleb and Susanna,	Dec. 24, 1785.
2-46	" Haile (son), of William and Abiah (b. Middletown, Ct.),	
		June 11, 1795.
2-76	" Margaret Clay,	April 20, 1800.
2-5	" Abiah Goodwin,	June 5. 1803.
2-109	" William Henry,	March 17. 1808.
3-143	" Thomas Goodwin,	Oct. 24, 1810.
3-22	" Caroline, of William H. and Ann Eliza,	Dec. 8, 1833.
3-53	" Haile (son),	April 15, 1836.
3-161	" William Henry,	Sept. 5, 1838.
3-128	" Robert Northam,	Nov. 9, 1840.
3-32	" Elizabeth Howard,	Dec. 29, 1842.
3-24	" Daniel Luther, of Thomas G. and Mary P.,	Feb. 11, 1834.
3-137	" Sarah Cole,	Aug. 4, 1836.
3-161	" William,	May 26, 1841.
3-42	" George Thomas,	April 19, 1843.
1-21	TYLER Hannah, of Moses and Elizabeth,	April 4, 1764.
1-16	" Elizabeth,	Feb. 24, 1766.
1-33	" Mary,	Feb. 18, 1768.
1-27	" John,	Nov. 26, 1769.
2-61	" John, of John and Mary,	March 26, 1802.

U V

2-98	VANCE Stephen Collins, of James and Robe,	Nov. 6, 1789.
2-73	" Lucia,	Oct. 13, 1791.
2-99	" Samuel James,	Oct. 15, 1793.
2-58	" Joseph Carey, of James and Lydia,	Feb. 16, 1798.
2-101	" Sally,	Sept. 4, 1799.
1-8	VIALL Caleb, of Constant and Sarah,	May 17, 1747.
1-51	" Sarah,	June 13, 1755.

1-6	VIALL Benjamin, of Constant, Jr., and Sybel,	Jan. 11, 1762.
1-56	" Winchester, of James and Lydia,	Oct. 30, 1763.
2-58	VINNECOME John, of John and Sarah,	Aug. 27, 1799.
2-74	" Lydia Luther,	March 29, 1801.
2-38	" George Gorham, of John and Bethany,	Dec. 27, 1805.
2-103	" Susanna,	March 30, 1807.
2-103	" Sally,	March 14, 1809.
3-49	" Hannah Gorham,	Jan. 26, 1811.
3-39	" George Kennicutt,	May 6, 1813.
3-91	" Mary Kinnecutt,	Nov. 5, 1818.

W

3-94	WARDWELL Moses Hemmenway, of Moses H. and Mary,	Jan. 1, 1827.
3-30	" Elizabeth Moore,	June 22, 1829.
3-132	WARE Susan, of Paul and Mahala,	Oct. 27, 1817.
3-74	" Lawton Ingraham,	March 29, 1819.
3-91	" Mahala,	Aug. 17, 1821
3-120	" Paul,	Oct. 19, 1824.
3-138	WARNER Sarah Elizabeth, of Lucius and Lydia,	Jan. 30, 1839.
2-88	WARREN Patty, of William and Sarah,	Oct. 31, 1783.
2-92	WATSON Mary, of John and Hetty,	June 20, 1823.
3-63	" John Clifford, of John and Nancy,	Sept. 25, 1830.
3-31	" Eleanora,	April 15, 1833.
3-135	WELSH Stillman, of Thomas and Louisa (b. Boston, Mass.),	
		Oct. 23, 1796.
1-29	WEST Lydia, of Judah and Prescilla,	Jan. 22, 1745.
1-20	WHEATON Hannah, of John and Hannah,	April 19, 1745.
1-49	" Sarah,	Jan. 7, 1748.
1-23	" John,	Nov. 2. 1751.
1-32	" Mary,	Feb. 22, 1755.
2-96	" Samuel,	Aug. 18, 1758.
1-4	" Anne,	Sept. 15, 1762.
1-50	" Spencer, of Samuel and Prudence,	June 2, 1762.
2-56	" Joseph, of Perez and Sebra,	Jan. 15, 1774.
1-47	" Roby, of Prudence,	Nov. 1, 1775.
1-21	" Hannah,	Sept. 19, 1777.
2-44	" Hannah, of John and Temperance,	Oct. 27, 1779.
2-90	" Perez, of Perez and Betsey,	March 9, 1783.
2-102	" Samuel,	Jan. 14, 1792.
2-104	" Thomas,	April 22, 1794.
1-38	" Nathan Miller, of Charles and Abigail,	June 28, 1785.
2-97	" Seth,	Sept. 25, 1786.
2-2	" Abigail,	May 21, 1789.
1-10	" Charles,	June 28, 1791.
2-54	" John Robert,	Nov. 1, 1793.
2-38	" George,	Nov. 24, 1795.
2-38	" — (still born),	April —, 1797.
2-102	" Samuel,	April 24, 1799.
2-75	" Laura,	March 15, 1801.
1-13	" Daniel Bowen,	Aug. 3, 1803.
1-59	" William Turner,	Jan. 26, 1806.
2-73	" Levi, of Spencer and Nancy,	June 29, 1790.
2-5	" Ardelia A., of Joseph and Polly,	June 23, 1803.
3-1	" Abby, of Nathan M. and Mary,	Feb. 24, 1811.
3-28	" Elbridge Gerry, of Nathan M. and Content B.,	Feb. 16, 1816.
3-91	" Mary Smith,	April 11, 1818.
3-29	" Emeline Maxwell,	June 9, 1820.
3-74	" Laura Frances,	March 26, 1823.
3-126	" Rebecca Miller,	Jan. 20, 1825.
3-138	" Susan,	May 11, 1827.
3-21	" Charles,	May 29, 1829.
3-41	" Elizabeth Saunders,	-(also 3-32), Jan. 7 or 8, 1832.

3-64	WHEATON Joel Abbott, of Nathan M. and Content B.,	Sept. 20, 1837.
3-3	" Anne Elizabeth, of John R. and Rebecca (Maxwell),	Sept. 26, 1826.
3-3	" Abby Eddy, .	July 26, 1828.
3-22	" Catherine,	Oct. 7, 1830.
3-4	" Alice,	Feb. 6, 1833.
3-64	" John R.,	March 21, 1835.
3-128	" Rebecca Eddy,	Aug. 11, 1837.
3-161	" William Turner,	Dec. 10, 1839.
3-35	" Florence,	Dec. 1, 1846.
3-136	" Sarah Gibbs, of Charles and Abiah G.,	Feb. 10, 1931.
3-41	" George,	Feb. 6, 1833.
3-22	" Charles,	May 30, 1835.
3-138	" Stockford,	Oct. 18, 1837.
3-110	" Olive Bowen, of Levi and Louisa,	Aug. 17, 1831.
3-75	" Levi,	Sept. 23, 1834.
3-53	" Henry, of Elbridge G. and Abby,	Nov. 25, 1839.
3-65	" James Maxwell,	March 10, 1842.
3-42	" George Lewis Cooke, (b. Bristol),	June 1, 1844.
3-23	" Clara,	Jan. 28, 1847.
3-42	" Grace,	Aug. 24, 1849.
3-59	WHEELER Jonathan M., of Jonathan M. and Barbara,	Sept. 8, 1817.
1-51	WHITAKER Simeon, of Rufus and Deborah,	Jan. 13, 1764.
1-26	" James,	Jan. 7, 1766.
1-46	" Rufus,	Sept. 18, 1767.
1-30	" Lydia,	March 11, 1771.
2-96	" Sarah,	Dec. 12, 1775.
2-44	" Hannah,	——— —, 1776(?)
2-1	" Asa,	May 25, 1778.
2-57	" Joseph,	Sept. 29, 1783.
2-81	" Nancy, of Simeon and Anna,	May 10, 1793.
1-30	WHITING Lurana, of Joshua and Mary,	Jan. 4, 1764.
1-56	" William,	April 3, 1765.
1-12	" David,	June 5, 1770.
1-12	" Daniel,	June 22, 1775.
1-21	" Haile, of Whitfield and Rachel,	Nov. 12, 1771.
2-32	" Eliza,	Nov. 2, 1775.
2-97	WHITMARSH Seth, of Joseph and Susannah,	Oct. 18, 1782.
2-72	" Lydia,	Aug. 4, 1784.
2-3	" Amey,	April 1, 1792.
2-60	" Joseph Winslow, of Seth and Hannah,	Aug. 31, 1804.
2-103	" Susanna Barton,	March 21, 1806.
2-78	" Mary Beverly Chew,	July 15, 1808.
2-57	" Joseph Allen,	Dec. 5, 1810.
2-76	WILLARD Mary Ann, of Gardner and Abigail,	Dec. 7, 1800.
2-60	" John,	May 9, 1803.
3-119	" Polly Newhall,	Oct. 15, 1806.
3-119	" Philip Snell, ·	Nov. 8, 1808.
1-56	WILLIAMS William Turner, of William and Patience,	Jan. 2, 1771.
1-46	" Rebecca,	Oct. 16, 1772.
3-125	" Ruth Miller, of Dr. Jeremiah and Rebecca,	Sept. 24, 1813.
3-125	" Rebecca Hicks,	Aug. 10, 1817.
3-59	" John, of Thomas C. and Eliza,	Feb. 6, 1815.
3-40	" George,	Feb. 12, 1817.
3-143	" Thomas,	Feb. 25, 1821.
3-3	" Albert,	July 10, 1824.
3-158	" William Earl,	March 12, 1827.
3-26	" Eugene Palmer, of Edward and S. S.,	May 11, 1849.
2-81	WINSLOW, Nancy, of Job and Sarah,	Aug. 7, 1785.
2-55	" John Perry,	May 8, 1788.
1-19	' " Gardner,	Dec. 20, 1790.
2-55	" Job,	Oct. 30, 1793.
1-13	" David L., of John L. and Mary,	April 2, 1805.
2-109	" William Brayton,	Dec. 11, 1806.
3-89	" Mary Ann,	Aug. 19, 1808.

(Vit. Rec., Vol. 6.) 18

3-49	WINSLOW Henry Augustus, of John L. and Mary,		June 9, 1811.
3-57	"	John Perry, of John Perry and Lelia,	April 7, 1811.
3-131	"	Sally Haile, of Ebenezer and Polly,	—— 22, 1813.
3-10	"	Benjamin,	Dec. 7, 1814.
3-61	"	James,	Oct. 17, 1816.
3-41	"	Gardiner, of Gardner and Martha,	Sept. 13, 1814.
3-94	"	Mary Ann,	Nov. —, 1815.
2-90	WRIGHT Phebe, of Amos and Ruth,		Jan. 20, 1799.
2-75	"	Leonard,	Nov. 21, 1802.
2-128	WOODMANSEE Prescilla, of George and Rebecca,		Oct. 9, 1805.
2-60	"	Jeremiah,	Sept. 30, 1808.
3-39	"	George Pickering,	Jan. 10, 1813.
3-94	"	Mary Vinniman,	Feb. 25, 1816.
3-136	"	Samuel Geoff,	June 22, 1823.
1-43	WOOD Polly, of Jonathan and Ruth,		Oct. 8, 1788.
2-93	"	Perry Horton, of Jonathan and Phelema,	
		(also 2-128),	March 28, 1802.
2-37	"	Eliza Ann,	June 11, 1807.
3-59	"	Jonathan Perry, of Jonathan and Hannah,	Jan. 2, 1817.
3-97	"	Nelly Reed, of James and Polly,	March 29, 1806.
2-88	"	Phebe, of Izrael and Candas,	May 7, 1794.

X Y Z

3-136	YOUNG Samuel, of Samuel Simmons and Margaret (Spencer), Feb. 10, 1827.
3-22	" Charles Baker, Feb. 26, 1832.

WARREN.

DEATHS.

A

1-105	ADAMS Lydia, wife of James, 24y. 10d.,		Feb. 7, 1766.
1-108	" James, of Joseph and Lydia, 16m.,		Nov. 21, 1792.
1-107	ALGER Lucinda, of Preserved and Charlotte,		Oct. 9, 1793.
1-105	ALLEN Samuel, of Samuel and Mercy,		Nov. 14, 1743.
1-105	" Jerusba,		Jan. 7, 1751.
1-105	" James,		Jan. 12, 1752.
1-102	" John, Dec. 13, 1747.		
1-105	" Deborah, of Joseph, June 9, 1759.		
2-47	" Hannah Bowen, of Paschal and Elouisa,		July 18, 1808.
2-79	" Mary Elouisa,		Aug. 15, 1814.
2-6	" Ann Mary,		Nov. 20, 1819.
2-6	" Ann Elizabeth	(born Marah),	Sept. 1, 1850.
3-90	" Mary Elouisa,		Nov. 10, 1820.
2-87	" Paschal,	(also 2-129),	July 18, 1845.

B

1-108	BAKER John Smith, of Jesse and Hannah,		Sept. 29, 1793.
1-107	BARTON Ruth, wife of William, in 30th y.,		Feb. 11, 1777.
1-108	" Caleb, of Rufus and Prudence,		July 9, 1779.
2-91	" Ruth, of Joseph and Ruth,		May 19, 1781.
1-108	" Rebecca, wife of Col. David,		March 23, 1791.
1-108	" Charlotte, of Col. David and Rebecca,		June 30, 1790.
1-108	" Anthony, of Benjamin and Lydia,		Sept. 10, 1796.
1-109	" Caleb, of Rufus and Prudence,		May 13, 1809.
1-109	" William, Esq., 64y., 2m., 11d.,		Aug. 15, 1809.
1-104	BICKNELL Joshua, Feb. 6, 1752.		
1-105	" Jerusha, of Joshua and Jerusha,		March 13, 1763.
1-05	" Jerusha, wife of Joshua,		April 9, 1763.
1-107	POSWORTH Ebenezer, (at New York),		July 26, 1781.
1-102	BOWEN Sarah, wife of Samuel,		June 7, 1747.
1-102	" Josiah, (drowned),		Feb. 11, 1747-8.
1-104	" Elizabeth, wife of Amos,		Sept. 8, 1756.
1-106	" Patience, of Nathan and Herren,		Aug. 7, 1770.
1-124	" William Child, of Edwin S. and Margaret, 10m., 23d., Sept. 28, 1848.		
1-42	" Polly, of Nathan and Herren,		April —, 1866.
1-124	BRAMAN Sylvanus H., of Elijah and Mary A.,		Oct. 19, 1842.
1-124	" Elijah F.,		Sept. 13, 1842.
1-124	" Alice,		May 4, 1847.
1-102	BRAYLEY Joanna, of John and Joanna,		March 26, 1747.
1-108	BROWN Becca, of James and Rebecca,		May 3, 1738.
1-103	" James,		Nov. 14, 1743.
1-102	" Micha, Jan. 5, 1747-8.		
1-104	" Rebecca, wife of James, in 36th year,		Jan. 31, 1752.
1-104	" John, of John and Phebe,		Sept. 23, 1753.
1-104	" Rebecca, of James and Rebecca,		Jan. 21, 1754.
1-106	" John, Jan. 20, 1775.		

1-105	BULLOCK William, of Richard and Abigail.	(1-6-16), Oct. 24, 1753.
1-105	" Richard, March 10, 1764.	
1-106	BURR Sarah, of Shubael and Betsey.	Nov. 7, 1767.
1-106	" Patience.	Dec. 2, 1768.
1-106	" Sarah.	Nov. 20, 1769.
1-109	" Lydia, wife of Nathan M..	—— ——, 1808 (?)
3-98	" Norman Goodman, of Nathan M. and Martha.	Oct. 3, 1837.
3-30	BURT Enos, Jr., of Enos and Winefred.	May 24, 1825.
1-103	BUTTERWORTH Hannah, of Joseph and Hopestill,	March 18, 1749-50.

C

1-109	CHAPMAN Benjamin Hattitti, of Daniel and Christiana,	Jan. 26, 1819.
1-107	CHILD ——, son of John Throop and Sally,	Dec. 24, 1788.
1-124	" Julia Ann, of Samuel and Nancy, (born, died and buried at Roxbury, Mass.),	Sept. 15, 1844.
1-104	COLE Dorcas, of Thomas and Christiana, 1y. 8m.,	Oct. 11, 1747.
1-103	" John, June 25, 1748.	
1-103	" Sarah, widow of John, Jan. 16, 1748-9.	
1-105	" Elijah, of Daniel and Amey, 1y. lacking 1 day,	Oct. 24, 1754.
1-105	" Elizabeth, wife of Jonathan,	May 8, 1755.
1-105	" ——, of Thomas and Christian,	June 14, 1759.
1-105	" Nathan, Aug. 4, 1760.	
1-107	" Sarah, wife of Curtis, in 30y., Oct. 23, 1780.	
1-109	" Caroline, of Simmons and Sarah, Nov. 14, 1836.	
1-104	CRANSTON Samuel, of Samuel,	Feb. 3, 1755.
1-106	" Caleb, 35y. in Jan. next,	July 18, 1765.
1-106	" Sarah, wife of Benjamin,	Sept. 21, 1771.
1-106	" Anne, of Benjamin and Sarah,	July 15, 1771.
1-107	CROADE Mary, wife of John, in 24y.,	June 22, 1784.
1-108	" Betsey, of John and Elizabeth,	Sept. 6, 1786.
1-108	" Johannah,	June 26, 1789.
1-108	" Infant son,	Nov. 27, 1790.
1-96	" Mary H., dau. of John, (wife of Paschal Allen),	May 31, 1805.

D E

1-104	EASTERBROOKS Joanna, wife of Thomas,	July 3, 1746.
1-103	" Aaron, of William and Patience,	Aug. 8, 1748.
1-103	" Prescilla, Dec. 24, 1749.	
1-103	" Patience, of William and Patience,	—— ——, 1749 (?).
1-105	" Joanna, wife of Benjamin,	Sept. 7, 1754.
1-104	" Lois, of Thomas,	March 23, 1757.
1-105	" Patience, of Benjamin and Sarah,	Jan. 14, 1761.
1-105	" Benoni, Dec. 22, 1762.	
1-106	" William, Aug. 12, 1772.	
1-103	EDDY Caleb, of Caleb and Mehitable,	Sept. 14, 1750.
3-164	" Capt. Benjamin, Dec. 15, 1845.	

F

| 1-106 | FISK Samuel, of Samuel and Judeth, | Sept. 26, 1769. |

G

| 1-106 | GREATUX Jeremiah, of John and Hannah, | Jan. 20, 1775. |
| 1-106 | "   Hannah, wife of John, | Oct. 31, 1775. |

H

1-108   HICKS Peleg Rogers, of Samuel and Ruth,
                                    (at Marteneco, W. I.,), March 24, 1794.

I J

1-102   JENKINS Bethiah, wife of John,   March 29, 1747.

K

1-102   KENT Josiah, —— —, 1747(?).
1-104   KENNICUTT Elizabeth, of Elizabeth, 82y. in Dec. —, 1753, Aug. 14, 1754.
1-104   "   Lydia, 38-1-9, Jan. 21, 1754.
1-105   "   Daniel, of John Jr., and Robie,   (also 1-106), Oct. 6, 1756.
1-106   "   Jonathan,   (also 1-105), May 7, 1759.
1-106   "   John,   (also 1-105), May 16, 1759.
1-106   "   Roby,   Nov. 19, 1765.
1-105   "   Edward, of John and Hannah, 40-0-22,   April 29, 1759.
1-106   "   Thomas,   8m., 20d., Feb. 18, 1766.
1-107   "   Mary, of Shubael and Elizabeth,   March 6, 1777.
1-102   KNOWLES William, March 2, 1747-8.
1-103   "   Mary, Jan. 4, 1750-1.

L

3-158   LAWTON William Burnett, of Samuel and Abigail,   Aug. 6, 1875.
1-104   LEWIN Thomas, of William,   Jan. 5, 1756.
1-104   LUTHER Mary, Jan. 8, 1741.
1-102   "   Joshua, Dec. 18, 1747.
1-103   "   Elizabeth, wife of Edward,   Dec. 29, 1749.
1-105   "   Samuel, of Samuel and Elizabeth,   June 1, 1765.
1-106   "   Daniel, March 31, 1770.
1-106   "   Hannah, wife of Daniel, in 45th y.,   July 7, 1762.
1-106   "   John, Jan. 4, 1771.
1-106   "   Zebedee, of Samuel and Elizabeth,   June 29, 1773.
1-107   "   Rebeckah, wife of Barnaby,   Jan. 12, 1777.
1-107   "   William, (at sea), May 11, 1784.
1-108   "   Rebecca, of Barnaby and Phebe,   June 21, 1794.
1-109   "   Alfred, of Martin and Rachel,   March 12, 1807.
3-27   "   Ebenezer, of Ebenezer and Joanna,   June 30, 1868.

M

1-104   MARTIN Samuel, of John and Mary,   Oct. 14, 1756.
1-102   MASON Rose, wife of James, in 56th y.,   March 7, 1747-8.
1-102   "   Elder Joseph, May 19, 1748.
1-103   "   Anne, of James, June 29 1748.
1-104   "   Anthony, of Marmaduke and Hannah,   Nov. 14, 1754.
1-104   "   James, of James, Jr., and Mary,   Dec. 17, 1754.
1-102   MILLER Samuel, 55y., April 6, 1748.
1-108   "   Anna, wife of James, Esq.,   April 30, 1786.
1-108   "   Mary, his wife, Jan. 18, 1761.
1-108   "   Barbara, his daughter, Jan. 13, 1761.
1-109   "   Lydia, wife of William T., 70y.,   March 27, 1816.

N O P

1-108   PEARCE Samuel, Esq., Dec. 2, 1793.
1-108   "   Mary, of Samuel and Bettey,   Nov. 13, 1798.

1-109	PEARCE Bettey, wife of Noah, Dec. 10, 1806.	
1-107	" George, of Samuel and Ruth,	Aug. 29, 1789.
1-104	" Izrael, of Izrael and Sarah.	April 11, 1750.
1-104	" Dea. Nathaniel, Aug. 5, 1751.	
1-105	" Hannah, of Solomon and Kezia, Aug. 17, 1752.	
1-105	PETTIS Elizabeth, of John and Rachel,	Jan. 22, 1758.
1-106	PHINNEY Jemima, of Elisha,	Feb. 19, 1764.
1-108	" Jonathan, of Elisha and Jemima.	Oct. 11, 1779.
1-103	POLLARD Thomas, Jan. 19, 1748-9.	

Q R

1-109	RANDALL Charles Leonard, of Charles and Lydia B., 3y. 1m. 27d.	
		Aug. 10, 1837.
1-104	RAWSON James Paddock, of Elijah and Mary,	Oct. 24, 1754.
1-104	REMINGTON Lydia, of Matthew and Rachel,	July 23, 1748.
1-104	" Mary,	Aug. 31, 1750.
1-104	" Prudence, Oct. 23, 1750.	
1-102	ROSS Sarah, March 18, 1747-8.	

S

1-105	SALISBURY Mary, of William and Mary,	Oct. 4, 1756.
1-105	" Jonathan,	Oct. 6, 1756.
1-105	" William,	Nov. 2, 1763.
1-107	" Martin Luther, of Luther and Abigail,	July 3, 1784.
1-107	" Mary, widow of William,	Nov. 1, 1793.
1-109	" Abigail, widow of Luther	April 20, 1809.
1-107	SANDERS John, of David and Nancy,	Sept. 27, 1790.
1-107	" Hopestill,	April 9, 1794.
1-107	" Nancy, wife of David,	May 7, 1794.
1-108	" Jacob.	April 10, 1791.
2-83	" Nathan Bowen, of Nathaniel and Sally,	Feb. 12, 1807.
1-105	SHORT Joanna, wife of Philip, in 74th year,	Aug. 22, 1756.
1-105	" Philip, of John and Phebe. 5m. 8d.,	Aug. 27, 1761.
1-105	" Philip, in 85y., Oct. 17, 1763.	
1-106	" Hannah, of John and Phebe,	Dec. 28, 1768.
1-9	SISSON Charlotte, of James and Sarah, (also 1-107), Dec. 28, 1783.	
1-104	SMITH Benjamin, of Benjamin and Mercy,	Aug. 8, 1752.
1-124	" William Armington, of James and Charlotte T.,	Aug. 20, 1844.
1-124	" Charlotte Townsend, wife of James, May 5, 1842.	
1-109	SNELL Rebecca, of Seth, Jr., Aug. 28, 1810.	

T

1-103	TABOR Benjamin, Aug. 11, 1749.	
1-107	THOMAS Jemima, widow of Amos,	—— —, 1776 (?).
1-103	THURBER Egatha, wife of Samuel,	Jan. 17, 1748-9.
1-102	TIFFANY Ebenezer, Feb. 10, 1746-7.	
1-105	TRIPP Consider, of William and Abigail, 3y. 9m., 3d.	Feb. 28, 1761.
1-105	TURNER Caleb, in 37th y.,	July 20, 1757.
1-54	" Varnum, of Moses and Abigail,	Jan. —, 1778.
2-89	" ——,	March 30, 1784.

U V

1-109	VENNIMAN Polly, of John and Bettey,	Aug. 27, 1814.

W

1-108	WHEATON Seth, of Charles and Abigail,	May 17, 1789.
3-164	" Abigail, widow of Charles,	April 7, 1847.
1-106	WHITING Eleanor, wife of David,	Jan. 10, 1771.
1-106	WILLIAMS William Turner, of William and Patience,	Feb. 9, 1771.

X Y Z

Vital Record of Rhode Island.

1636=1850.

FIRST SERIES.

BIRTHS, MARRIAGES AND DEATHS.

A Family Register for the People.

By James N. Arnold,

EDITOR OF THE NARRAGANSETT HISTORICAL REGISTER.

"Is My Name Written in the Book of Life?"

Vol. 6.   BARRINGTON.   Part III.

Published under the Auspices of the General Assembly.

PROVIDENCE, R. I:
NARRAGANSETT HISTORICAL PUBLISHING COMPANY.
1894.

ACT INCORPORATING THE TOWN OF BARRINGTON.

AN ACT for Incorporating the West Part of the Town of Warren Into a Township to be Distinguished and known by the Name of Barrington.

Be it enacted by this General Assembly and by the authority thereof: It is enacted that the Town of Warren be and the same is hereby divided into two distinct and separate towns, that the bounds between them be as the river between Bristol and Rumstick extends itself northerly to Miles Bridge, that all the lands on the westerly side of the said river be and they are hereby erected and made into a Township to be distinguished, called and known by the name of BARRINGTON, and that the inhabitants thereof shall choose two deputies to represent them in the General Assembly, and shall have, hold and enjoy all and singular the liberties, privileges and immunities which the other towns in this Colony have, enjoy and are entitled to.

And be it further enacted by the authority aforesaid that all debts due and money belonging to the Town of Warren before the division thereof by this Act made shall be divided according to the last tax, that all debts due from the said Town before the division shall be settled and made in the same manner, and that the poor of the said Town be divided between the said two Towns in proportion to their taxes and debts.

And be it further enacted by the authority aforesaid that all and every of the Justices of the Peace and Military Officers who were chosen and appointed for the Town of Warren and live in that part thereof which is now Barrington be and they are hereby continued in their respective offices with as full power and ample authority in every particular as they had in consequence of their being chosen into and commissionated for the offices by them respectively sustained, and that James Brown, Esq., be and he is hereby authorized and fully empowered to issue a warrant and call the Freemen of the Town of Barrington to meet together at such time and place within said Town as he shall think fit on or before the 8th day of July next in order to choose and appoint all officers necessary for managing and conducting the prudential affairs of said Town agreeably to the laws of this Colony.

And be it further enacted by the authority aforesaid that the said Town of Barrington shall send three grand and two petit jurors to each of the Superior and Inferior Courts which shall be holden in the County of Bristol, and that the Town of Warren shall send three grand and four petit jurors to each of the said Courts.

And be it further enacted by the authority aforesaid that Nathaniel Fales, Thomas Throop and Daniel Bradford, Esqs., all of Bristol, be and they are appointed a committee to settle and proportion the debts and poor of said Town agreeably to the last tax of said Town.

God Save the King.

Rhode Island Colonial Records, Vol. VII., pages 15, 16, 17.

BARRINGTON.

INTENTIONS AND MARRIAGES.

A

93	ADAMS	Ebenezer, and Hannah Allen; int. Jan. 8, 1736-7.
1-158	"	John, and Martha Hunt; int. Nov. 16, 1745.
1-159	"	Sarah, and Izrael Peck; int. April 29, 1746; m. (1-173), Sept. 18, 1746.
2-29	"	Nudigate, and Frances Low; m. by Rev. Solomon Townsend, ——— —, 1775.
2-11	"	Abigail, and Sylvester Viall, Oct. 23, 1790.
2-30	"	William, and Hannah Wardwell, Oct. 23, 1791.
2-36	"	Rachel, and John Short, Jr., Dec. 11, 1803.
2-49	"	John, and Joanna Reding, April 22, 1804.
2-68	"	Ebenezer, and Persiller Dunham, Jan. 24, 1813.
2-75	"	Nathaniel, of Barrington, and Mary Hunter, of Warren; m. by Rev. Daniel Chipman, May 31, 1818.
1-153	AGAR	Amity, and Abel Percey; int. July 30, 1743; m. (1-166), Nov. 18, 1743.
1-147	ALGER	Nancy, and Anderson Martin, (also 2-60), Feb. 15, 1799.
93	ALLEN	Joseph, of Barrington, and Deborah Dunn, of Taunton; int. Feb. 28, 1735-6.
94	"	John, and Mary Celley; int. Jan. 8, 1736-7.
93	"	Hannah, and Ebenezer Adams; int. Jan. 8, 1736-7.
83	"	Mrs. Abigail, and Joshua Bicknell; int. Sept. 23, 1738; m. (82), Oct. 12, 1738.
1-149	"	Elizabeth, and Aaron Lyon; int. April 5, 1740.
1-149	"	Joseph, Jr., and Sarah Bosworth; int. Oct. 2, 1740.
1-150	"	Christian, and Nathan Phippen; int. Nov. 6, 1740.
1-150	"	Ruth, and William Mathews; int. Jan. 24, 1740-1.
1-150	"	Daniel, Jr., and Hannah Humphrey; int. Feb. 28, 1740-1.
1-171	"	Joseph, Jr., of Barrington, and Mrs. Sarah Butterworth, of Rehoboth; m. by Thomas Bowen, Justice, May 21, 1741.
1-151	"	Jerusha, and Japheth Bicknell; int. Sept. 12, 1741.
1-152	"	Madame Rachel, and Samuel Howland, Esq.; int. Feb. 10, 1741-2.
1-152	"	Samuel, and Marcy Viall, int. March 6, 1741-2.
1-153	"	Mrs. Neoma, and Abiezer Peck; int. March 15, 1742-3; m. (1-166) April 28, 1743.
1-153	"	Daniel, of Barrington, and Ann Chaffee, of Rehoboth; int. July 30, 1743; m. by Rev. Solomon Townsend, Oct. 15, 1743.
1-159	"	Ebenezer, Jr., and Elizabeth Bosworth; int. Jan. 11, 1745-6.
1-159	"	Timothy, and Ann Torrey; int. May 24, 1746.
1-37	"	Viall, and Rachel Humphrey, March 22, 1766.
1-64	"	Asa, and Abigail Blunt; m. at Andover, Mass., Nov. 1, 1781.
2-9	"	Elizabeth, and John Barnes, Nov. 9, 1783.
1-81	"	Squire, and Elizabeth Hews (also 2-17), Dec. 26, 1790.
2-9	"	Cyrus, and Julanie Taylor, March 10, 1793.
1-184	"	Phillis, and Cato Enston, April 16, 1793.
2-44	"	Patience, and Samuel Bosworth, Nov. 28, 1794.
1-118	"	Samuel, Jr., and Fanny Brown, June 7, 1795.
2-12	"	Amey, and John Horn, Feb. 20, 1796.
2-12	"	Rachel, and Anthony Comstock, Sept. 17, 1797.

1-145 ALLEN Syllivan, and Susannah Kent; m. by Rev. Samuel Watson, May 13, 1798.
1-184 " Pero, and Jennie King; m. by Rev. Samuel Watson, Aug. 12, 1798.
1-145 " Thomas, Jr., and Mary Heath Paine, of Rehoboth; m. by Rev. Samuel Watson, Sept. 9, 1798.
2-32 " Eunice, and Kent Brown, Sept. 22, 1799.
2-43 " Thomas, and Sarah R. Paine, March 27, 1802 (also 2-35); m. by Rev. Samuel Watson, March 28, 1802.
2-51 " Ira, and Abigail Shears; m. by Rev. Samuel Watson, May 12, 1805.
2-50 " Sylvester, and Nancy Luther; m. by Rev. Samuel Watson, Feb. 15, 1807.
2-72 " Eliza, and John Medbury, Dec. 30, 1813.
2-97 " John, and Lemira Round; m. by Rev. Francis Wood, Aug. 7, 1823.
2-104 " Jeremiah B., of Capt. Samuel, of Seekonk, Mass., and Hannah, his wife, and Julia M. Rawson, of Barrington, of Hon. Joseph and Rebecca, his wife; m. by Rev. Joseph H. Patrick, Jan. 21, 1823.
2-126 " Ira, and Rosamond Britman, May 5, 1833.
2-146 " Sarah, and John Pierce, Aug. 19, 1846.
2-150 " Amey A., and Benjamin F. Drown, Feb. 4, 1848.
2-152 " Mercy, and Abraham Francis, April 30, 1848.
2-155 " Jemima, and Jonathan William Henry Simmons, March 26, 1849.
1-36 ANDREWS William, and Rebecca Curtis; m. by Lemuel Allen, Justice, April 29, 1769.
1-153 ANDROS Elizabeth, and Samuel Humphrey, Jr., Int. Nov. 27, 1742; m. (1-J 66) Feb. 27, 1742-3.
2-85 ANTHONY Cordelia, and James W. Young, Aug. 17, 1815.
1-149 ARMSBY Mary, and Hezekiah Bowen, Int., Sept. 20, 1740.
2-8 ARMINGTON Ruth, and Enock Remington, Aug. 5, 1790.
2-31 " Charlotte, and Solomon Townsend, Jr., April 2, 1794.
2-8 " Walker, and Mercy Remington, Aug. 31, 1794.
2-47 " Lucy, and Samuel Smith, Aug. 18, 1805.
2-70 ARNOLD Phebe, and Asa Smith, May 1, 1808.
2-125 " Jabez R., of Glocester, and Mary A. Heath, of Barrington; m. by Rev. Benjamin R. Allen, July 7, 1829.

B

1-152 BACKER Rebecca, and Solomon Townsend; int. Oct. 9, 1742.
1-68 BAKER Thomas, and Freeborn Bicknell, Aug. 16, 1787.
2-146 " Tacy, and Lewis S. Bliss, July 4, 1846.
83 BARNEY Mary, and Capt. Joseph Hodges; int. Sept. 25, 1738; (92), m. Oct. 26, 1738.
2-140 " Almira M., and Josias Tanner, Dec. 19, 1844.
2-144 " Rodman Sisson, of Mason, of Swansey, Mass., and Elizabeth Wiver Seymour, of Joseph, of Barrington; m. by Rev. Joseph P. Tustin, April 14, 1846.
93 BARNES Thomas, and Ruth Swift; int. Feb. 28, 1735.
90 " Keziah, and Solomon Peck; int. Nov. 19, 1737.
1-152 " Eunice, and James Franklin; int. May 1, 1742.
2-9 " John, and Elizabeth Allen; m. by Rev. Solomon Townsend, Nov. 9, 1783.
2-10 " Ruth, and John Potter, Oct. 21, 1797.
2-61 " Samuel, and Sarah Heath, March 3, 1811.
2-89 " Alfred, of Barrington, and Keziah Daggett, of Seekonk; m. by Rev. John Pitman, March 1, 1818.
2-89 " Alfred, and Lydia Daggett, April 9, 1826.
2-148 BEAN Catherine Amanda, and Hiram Horton, Dec. 6, 1846.
90 BEERY Elizabeth, and Jonathan Tibbins; int. May 7, 1737.
2-65 BLAKE Hannah, and Capt. John Martin, Jr., June 3, 1827.

2-146 BLISS Lewis S., of Rehoboth, and Tacy Baker, of Natick; m. by Rev. Charles Peabody, July 4, 1846.

1-64 BLUNT Abigail, and Asa Allen, Nov. 1, 1781.

83 BICKNELL Joshua, and Mrs. Abigail Allen; int. Sept. 23, 1738; m. (No. 82) by George Tibbetts, Justice, Oct. 12, 1738.

1-151   "   Japheth, and Jerusha Allen; int. Sept. 12, 1741.

1-166   "   James, of Rehoboth, and Mary Peck, of Barrington; m. by Rev. Solomon Townsend, March 20, 1743.

1-153   "   Hannah, and Jonathan Padelford; int. April 22, 1743; m. (1-166) May 26, 1743.

1-156   "   Joshua, Jr., and Ruth Bicknell; int. Feb. 16, 1744-5.

1-156   "   Ruth, and Joshua Bicknell, Jr., Feb. 16, 1744-5.

1-159   "   Japheth, and Dorothy Franklin, Int. Aug. 9, 1746.

1-159   "   Japheth, and Martha Medcaff; int. Sept. 27, 1746.

2-2   "   Asa, and Elizabeth Low; m. by Rev. Solomon Townsend, June 25, 1769; Int. (1-63) June 25, 1769.

2-3   "   Olive, and Joseph Carlo Mauran, —— —, 1773.

1-61   "   Joshua, and Amy Brown, April 18, 1782; m. by Rev. Solomon Townsend (2-16) same date.

1-77   "   Joseph, and Alethea Viall, Nov. 19, 1786.

1-68   "   Freeborn, and Thomas Baker, Aug. 16, 1787.

2-21   "   Martha, and Rev. Samuel Watson, Dec. 5, 1799.

2-52   "   John W., and Keziah Paine, April 14, 1805.

2-90   "   Col. Allen, of Joshua, and Harriet Byron, Kennicutt, of Josiah; m. by Rev. Luther Wright, Dec. 23, 1817.

1-146 BISHOP Ebenezer, and Lydia Grant; m. by Rev. Luther Baker (also 2-20), Oct. 12, 1797.

2-105   "   Hannah, and William Bowen, Aug. 19, 1827.

91 BOSWORTH Nathaniel, of Rehoboth, and Jane Brown, of Barrington; int. June 9, 1738.

1-150   "   Patience, and John Bullock; int. Sept. 6, 1740.

1-149   "   Sarah, and Joseph Allen, Jr.; int. Oct. 2, 1740.

1-153   "   Joseph, Jr., of Rehoboth, and Ann Low, of Barrington; int. Aug. 6, 1743; m. (1-166) by Rev. Solomon Townsend, Dec. 10, 1743.

1-159   "   Elizabeth, and Ebenezer Allen, Jr.; int. Jan. 11, 1745-6.

2-6   "   Nancy, and Daniel Mathewson, Oct. 27, 1789.

2-44   "   Samuel, and Patience Allen, Nov. 28, 1794.

2-6   "   Joseph, and Ruth Taylor; m. by Rev. Solomon Townsend, Sept. 11, 1796.

2-27   "   Betsey, and Thomas Champlain, Jan. 8, 1800.

2-87   "   Lydia, and Simon Smith, Jan. 2, 1807.

2-64   "   Pearce, and Celinda Ingraham, Sept. 27, 1812.

2-98   "   Polly Taylor, and Lawton Ingraham, Aug. 30, 1819.

1-81 BOURNE Shearjashub, Esq., of Bristol, and Rachel Kent, of Barrington; m. by Samuel Allen, Justice, Nov. 20, 1793.

84 BOWEN Margary, and John Healey, Aug. 9, 1739.

1-140   "   Hezekiah, and Mary Armsby; int. Sept. 20, 1740.

1-155   "   James, and Ann Thurber; int. June 2, 1744.

1-80   "   Jeremiah, and Lillis Haile, July 16, 1767.

1-71   "   Asa, of Rehoboth, and Ruth Viall, of Barrington; m. by Rev. Solomon Townsend, May 4, 1788.

1-82   "   James, Jr., and Chloe Thayer, March 22, 1789.

1-143   "   Betsey, and John Martin, Jr. (also 2-26), Dec. 31, 1789.

1-82   "   Stephen, and Betsey Hall, Sept. 11, 1791.

2-18   "   James, and Sally Kelley, Sept. 28, 1794.

1-118   "   Margaret, and Ambrose Hicks, March 1, 1795.

2-15   "   Hall, and Sally Stephens Witherell, Sept. 1, 1796.

2-62   "   Sally T., and Cyrel Martin, Aug. 23, 1812.

2-67   "   Sylvester, and Amelia Ladue, Jan. 10, 1813.

2-79   "   Sally, and Samuel R. Martin, Oct. 2, 1814.

2-49   "   Haile, of Haile, dec., and Elizabeth Johonnat, of Daniel, dec., both of Warren; m. by Rev. Luther Wright, Dec. 2, 1817.

2-91   "   Sophia, and Capt. Suchet Mauran, Sept. 10, 1818.

2-18   "   Capt. James, and Miss Elizabeth Tiffany, Nov. 15, 1821.

2-93   BOWEN Allen, of James and Betsey Stanley, of Comfort; m. by Rev. Jordan Rexford, Nov. 18, 1821.
2-106   "   Samuel, of Haile, dec., and Abigail Peck; m. by Rev. Jordan Rexford, July 4, 1826.
2-105   "   William, and Hannah Bishop; m. by Rev. Isaac Paddock, Aug. 19, 1827.
2-165   "   Capt. Albert, and Susan K. Smith; m. by Rev. Benjamin R. Allen, Sept. 2, 1841.
2-159   "   Jonathan N., of Barrington, and Abby P. Luther, of Warren; m. by Rev. A. Tyfe Warren, May 22, 1850.
2-160   "   Abigail, and Edwin F. Peck, June 6, 1850.
2-84   BRADFORD William B., of Boston, and Nancy Child, of Warren, Aug. 3, 1815.
2-53   BRAYTON Susannah, and Wilson Kent, Feb. 28, 1804.
2-83   "   Betsey, and John Salisbury, July 2, 1815.
2-19   BRIGGS William, and Nancy Read, June 26, 1796.
2-126   BRITMAN Rosamond, and Ira Allen, May 5, 1833.
91   BROWN Abijah and Josiah Humphrey; int. Nov. 4, 1737.
91   "   Jane, and Nathaniel Bosworth; int. June 9, 1739.
1-150   "   Jabez, and Abigail Whelen; int. Feb. 14, 1740-1.
1-151   "   Lydia, and William Pearce; int. Jan. 9, 1741-2.
1-33   "   Rebecca, and Caleb Luther, Dec. 16, 1773.
2-103   "   Rachel, and Josiah Humphrey, April 30, 1775.
1-61   "   Amey, and Joshua Bicknell (also 2-16), April 18, 1782.
1-76   "   Bebee, and William Jones, Oct. 31, 1782.
2-5   "   Huldah, and Ebenezer Peck, Dec. 2, 1785.
2-15   "   Martin, and Sally Mathewson; m. by Rev. Solomon Townsend, March 31, 1789.
2-32   "   Kent, and Betsey Cole, —— —, 1793.
1-118   "   Fanny, and Samuel Allen, Jr., June 7, 1795.
2-17   "   Abigail, and Duncan Kelley, Nov. 24, 1797.
2-32   "   Kent, and Eunice Allen; m. by Rev. Samuel Watson, Sept. 22, 1799.
2-66   "   Jabez, and Susanna Lawton, Jan. 7, 1813.
2-99   "   Nathaniel, of Darius Kent, and Martha Townsend Kennicutt, of Josiah; m. by Rev. Luther Wright, April 12, 1821.
2-101   "   Allen Mathewson, and Elizabeth Drowne, Aug. 2, 1824.
2-134   "   Sarah M., and Charles W. Rhodes, Aug. 7, 1843.
2-151   "   Mary Elizabeth, and Albert G. Rea, Feb. 2, 1848.
1-35   "   Rebecca, and Samuel Conant —— —, —.
1-152   BUCKLIN James, and Mary Peck; int. Oct. 11, 1742.
1-166   BUGBEE James, of Woodstock, Conn., and Mary May, of Barrington; m. by Rev. Solomon Townsend, May —, 1744; int. (1-156) March 23, 1744.
1-93   BULLOCK William, of Rehoboth, and Susannah Kent, of Barrington; int. Jan. 8, 1737-8.
1-150   "   John, and Patience Bosworth; int. Sept. 6, 1740.
1-155   "   Hezekiah, and Jemima Garnsey; int. April 7, 1744.
2-23   "   Elizabeth, and John Humphrey, Nov. 14, 1782.
1-84   "   Mary Ann, and Ebenezer Tiffany, Feb. 2, 1783; in 2-42 it reads Feb. 12, 1783.
2-94   "   Rebecca, and Joseph Rawson, Dec. 21, 1797.
2-25   BUSHEE James, and Deborah Luther, April 4, 1776.
1-85   "   Jonathan, and Anstis Sisson, —— —, 1787.
1-171   BUTTERWORTH Mrs. Sarah, and Joseph Allen, Jr., May 21, 1741.

C

1-184   CAMBRIDGE ——, and Jane, servants of Mathew Watson; int. published by Town Clerk Josiah Humphrey, Oct. 19, 1744; m. (1-167) by Rev. Solomon Townsend, Nov. 26, 1744.
1-149   CAMP Anna, and John Medbury; int. Oct. 4, 1740.
91   CARPENTER Mehitable, and William Mathews, May 22, 1735.
1-158   "   Lydia, and Andrew Wheaton; int. Oct. 19, 1745.

2-12 CARPENTER Anthony, and Rachel Allen, Sept. 17, 1797.
2-108 " Eliza, and Capt. Thomas W. Cooke, Dec. 27, 1827.
2-111 " Edmund, of Otis and Mehitable, and Lemira Tiffany, of Ebenezer and Mary Ann; m. by Rev. Henry Wight, Sept. 1, 1830.
1-28 CARY Micha. and Martha Gurnsey, Aug. 26, 1770.
2-34 " Ebenezer G., and Polly Moore, March 4, 1798.
94 CELLEY Mary, and John Allen; int. Jan. 8, 1736-7.
1-153 CHAFFEE Annas or Ann, and Daniel Allen; int. July 30, 1743; m. (1-166), Oct. 15, 1743.
2-83 " Huldah, and Capt. Benjamin Peck, Nov. 9, 1817.
2-27 CHAMPLAIN Thomas, and Betsey Bosworth; m. by Rev. Samuel Watson, Jan. 8, 1800.
2-69 " Betsey, and Jabez Heath, April 25, 1813.
2-86 CHASE Grindall, and Lucretia Watson; m. by John Howe, Justice, June 10, 1816.
1-184 CHEESE Walley, and Mary Pomham; int. published by Town Clerk Josiah Humphrey, March 3, 1743-4; m. (1-172), by Josiah Howland, Justice, April 19, 1744.
1-145 CHILD Christopher, and Polly Child, both of Warren; m. by Rev. Samuel Watson, Aug. 14, 1798.
1-145 " Polly, and Christopher Child, Aug. 14, 1798.
2-80 " Dyer, of Woodstock, Conn., and Betsey Maxfield, of Bristol, Nov. 13, 1814.
2-84 " Nancy, and William B. Bradford, Aug. 3, 1815.
2-115 " Sally, and William G. Ingraham, Oct. 16, 1825.
90 CLARKE Susannah, and Benjamin Mory; int. Jan. 15, 1736-7.
2-34 COBB Mary, and Peleg Cranston, Feb. 7, 1793.
2-73 COGGESHALL Thomas B., and Rachel Drowne, Feb. 14, 1814.
2-156 COLBY Augustus G., of Salem, Mass., of Samuel and Sally P., and Abby Jane Jefferds, of Rev. Forrest and Sarah C., of Barrington; m. by Rev. Forrest Jefferds, Nov. 21, 1849.
2-32 COLE Betsey, and Kent Brown, —— ——, 1793.
1-35 CONANT Samuel, and Rebecca Brown, —— —, ——.
2-76 COOKE Phebe E., and William Fowler, Sept. 4, 1814.
2-108 " Capt. Thomas W., of Portsmouth, son of John B., and Eliza Carpenter, of Barrington, dau. of Anthony; m. by Rev. Jordan Rexford, Dec. 27, 1827.
2-34 CRANSTON Peleg, of Warren, and Mary Cobb, of Barrington; m. by Rev. Solomon Townsend, Feb. 7, 1793.
1-36 CURTIS Rebecca, and William Andrews, April 29, 1769.

D

2-89 DAGGETT Keziah, and Alfred Barnes, March 1, 1818.
2-89 " Lydia, and Alfred Barnes, April 9, 1826.
92 DEXTER John, of Barrington, and Ruth Utter, of Warwick; int. Jan. —, 1735-6.
84 DROWNE Benjamin, and Mrs. Hannah Kent, Nov. 25, 1738.
1-67 " Benjamin, Jr., and Rachel Scott, Jan. 10, 1773.
1-71 " Daniel, and Freelove Luther (also 2-37), Feb. 8, 1776.
1-62 " Caleb, and Mehitable Tripp; m. by Samuel Allen, Justice, Dec. 24, 1783.
1-69 " Philip, and Anne Martin (also 2-24), Aug. 14, 1785.
2-10 " Jeremiah Scott, and Betsey Grant, March 17, 1797.
2-35 " Lydia, and Squire Maxwell, March 7, 1802.
2-55 " Sally, and Thomas Grant, Jr., Jan. 20, 1807.
2-71 " Ann, and John Maxfield, Jan. 12, 1814.
2-73 " Rachel, and Thomas Coggeshall, Feb. 14, 1814.
2-73 " Sukey Ann, and Ira Kent, Oct. 11, 1818.
2-48 " Alfred, of Major Jeremiah, and Frances Humphrey; m. by Rev. Luther Wright, Nov. 8, 1818.
2-101 " Elizabeth, and Allen Mathewson Brown, Aug. 2, 1824.
2-102 " Simeon, and Mary Ann Kelley, Sept. 2, 1824.
2-165 ' Hannah, and George R. Kernicutt, Jan. 25, 1826.

2-114. DROWNE Emeline, and Hiram Drew Drowne, Dec. 31, 1828.
2-114   "   Hiram Drew, and Emeline Drowne; m. by Rev. Isaac Stoddard,
                  Dec. 31, 1828.
2-132   "   Julia R., and Benjamin Martin, June 22, 1837.
2-150   "   Benjamin F., of Alfred and Frances, and Amey A. Allen, of
                  Thomas and Sarah; m. by Rev. Forrest Jefferds, Feb. 4, 1848.
1-184   DUCHESS ——, and Jack; int. Dec. 14, 1745; m. (1-167), Jan. 30, 1745-6.
2-68   DUNHAM Persiller, and Ebenezer Adams, Jan. 24, 1813.
  93   DUNN Deborah, and Joseph Allen; int. Feb. 28, 1735-6.

E

1-184   EASTON Cato, of Newport, and Phillis Allen, of Warren; m. by Rev. Sam-
                  uel Watson, April 16, 1793.

F

1-158   FIEF Abigail, and William Tripp; int. Nov. 21, 1744; m. (1-172) Jan. 21,
                  1744-5.
2-7   FISH Lucy, and Joel Peck, May 20, 1792.
2-76   FOWLER William, and Phebe E. Cooke, Sept. 4, 1814.
2-152   FRANCIS Abraham, of Fall River, son of John and Polly, and Mercy
                  Allen, of Stephen and Chloe, of Barrington; m. by Rev. Forrest
                  Jefferds, April 30, 1848.
  91   FRANKLIN James, of Providence, and Hannah Talman, of Barrington; int.
                  April 13, 1738.
1-152   "   James, and Eunice Barnes; int. May 1, 1742.
1-172   "   John, and Mary Wood, both of Rehoboth; m. by Josiah Howland,
                  Justice, Aug. 18, 1743.
1-159   "   Dorothy, and Japheth Bicknell; int. Aug. 9, 1746.
  89   FRANK Mary, and Job; int. Dec. 18, 1738.
  92   FRISSELL Benjamin, of Woodstock, Conn., and Naoma May, of Rehoboth;
                  m. by Samuel Allen, Justice, March 11, 1735-6.

G

1-149   GARNSEY Rosamond, and Joseph Grant; int. May 10, 1740.
1-155   "   Jemima, and Hezekiah Bullock; int. April 7, 1744.
1-159   "   Biah, and Joseph Munroe; int. Aug. 2, 1746.
1-28   "   Martha, and Micha Cary, Aug. 26, 1770.
1-184   GENENS Freelove, and John Hill; int. July 5, 1746; m. (1-167) Aug. 6,
                  1746.
1-62   GLADDING Joseph, and Anna Martin, July 4, 1776.
2-30   "   Judeth, and Watson Ingraham, May 10, 1801.
2-100   "   George, and Nancy Martin; m. by Rev. Samuel Watson, May 13,
                  1810.
1-149   GRANT Joseph, and Rosamond Garnsey; int. May 10, 1740.
2-10   "   Betsey, and Jeremiah Scott, March 17, 1797.
1-146   "   Lydia, and Ebenezer Bishop, (also 2-20), Oct. 12. 1797.
1-147   "   William, and Lois Laduc; m. by Rev. Luther Baker, Feb. 22, 1798.
2-54   "   Joshua, and Mary Martin, Feb. 24, 1805.
2-55   "   Thomas, Jr., and Sally Drowne, Jan. 20, 1807.
2-145   GREENWOOD George W., of Rome, N. Y., and Sally Ingraham, of Bar-
                  rington; m. by Rev. Charles Peabody, May 25, 1846.
  92   GREEN Isabel, and Samuel Low; int. Jan. 31, 1735-6.

H

1-80   HAILE Lillis, and Jeremiah Bowen, July 16, 1767.
1-82   HALL Betsey, and Stephen Bowen, Sept. 11, 1791.
2-14   HARDING John, and Ruth Humphrey, —— —. 1794.

84   HEALEY John, of Swansey, and Margary Bowen, of Barrington, Aug 9, 1739.
1-149 HEATH Rev. Peleg, and Mrs. Bethiah Peck; Int. Aug. 9, 1740; m. (1-171) by Sylvester Richmond, Justice, Aug. 26, 1740.
1-154 "   Rev. Peleg, and Jerusha Peck; Int. Nov. 12, 1743; m. (1-172) by Josiah Howland, Justice, Dec. 8, 1743.
1-147 "   Nathaniel, Jr., and Nabby Salisbury; m. by Eld. Luther Baker, Nov. 30, 1797.
2-58 "   Cynthia, and Nath'l Peck, May 29, 1808.
2-61 "   Sarah, and Samuel Barnes, March 3, 1811.
2-63 "   Capt. Benjamin, and Bebee Peck, Sept. 13, 1812.
2-69 "   Jabez, and Betsey Champlain, April 25, 1813.
2-78 "   Wilmarth, and Mary Humphrey, Sept. 18, 1814.
2-125 "   Mary A., and Jahez R. Arnold, July 7, 1829.
2-158 "   Thomas Champlain, of Jabez, and Avis Smith Martin, of Anderson; m. by Rev. George W. Hathaway, March 21, 1850.
1-81 HEWS Elizabeth, and Squire Allen (also 2-77), Dec. 26, 1790.
1-118 HICKS Ambrose, and Margaret Bowen, March 1, 1795.
1-158 HILL Sarah, and Samuel Miller; Int. July 30, 1745.
1-184 "   John, and Freelove Geneus; int. published by Town Clerk Josiah Humphrey, July 5, 1746; m. (1-167) by Rev. Solomon Townsend, Aug. 6, 1746.
2-26 "   Prescilla, and Josiah Luther, Nov. 3, 1785.
2-31 "   Sarah, and Ellis Peck, Dec. 10, 1801.
2-20 "   David, and Kezia Read; m. by Rev. Samuel Watson, July 8, 1802.
2-157 HINSMAN Francis S., of Meriden, N. H., son of Ephraim and Rebecca, and Susan K. Miller, of James and Wealtha, of Barrington; m. by Rev. Forrest Jefferds, Jan. 6, 1850.
92   HODGES Capt. Joseph, of Norton, Mass., and Mrs. Mary Barney, of Barrington; m. by George Leonard, Justice, Oct. 26, 1738; int. (83) Sept. 25, 1738.
93   HOLBROOK Mrs. Sarah, and Samuel Humphrey; int. Dec. 18, 1736.
2-12 HORN John, and Amey Allen; m. by Rev. Solomon Townsend, Feb. 20, 1796.
2-45 "   Daniel, and Alethea Kent, Feb. 14, 1801.
2-148 HORTON Hiram, of Fall River, son of Aaron, and Catherine Amanda Bean, of Barrington, dau. of Joseph; m. by Rev. Josiah P. Tustin, Dec. 6, 1846.
1-146 HOWARD Thomas, of Warwick, and Polly Humphrey, of Barrington; m. by Rev. Samuel Watson, Nov. 28, 1798.
1-152 HOWLAND Samuel, Esq., and Madame Rachel Allen; int. Feb. 19, 1741-2.
93   HUMPHREY Samuel, and Mrs. Sarah Holbrook; Int. Dec. 18, 1736.
91   "   Josiah, and Abijah Brown; int. Nov. 4, 1737.
1-150 "   Hannah, and Daniel Allen, Jr.; int. Feb. 28, 1740-1.
1-153 "   Samuel, Jr., and Elizabeth Andros; int. Nov. 27, 1742; m. (1-166) by Rev. Solomon Townsend, Feb. 27, 1742-3.
1-155 "   Sarah, and David Peck; int. June 30, 1744.
1-37 "   Rachel, and Viall Allen, March 22, 1766.
2-1   "   Lillis, and Nathaniel Smith, Dec. 6, 1770.
2-103 "   Josiah, and Rachel Brown, April 30, 1775.
1-143 "   Eliza, and Luther Martin, Nov. 16, 1775.
2-23 "   John, and Elizabeth Bullock, Nov. 14, 1782.
2-7   "   Jerusha, and Calvin Martin, Dec. 4, 1788.
1-118 "   Anna, and James Ingraham (also 2-11), Sept. 16, 1790.
2-14 "   Ruth, and John Harding, —— ——, 1794.
1-146 "   Polly, and Thomas Howard, Nov. 28, 1798.
2-35 "   Eliza, and John Martin, Dec. 26, 1802.
2-78 "   Mary, and Wilmarth Heath, Sept. 18, 1814.
2-48 "   Frances, and Alfred Drowne, Nov. 8, 1818.
2-33 "   Emerson, of John, dec., and Huldah Peck, of Major Ebenezer, dec.; m. by Rev. Luther Wright, Dec. 31, 1818.
2-75 HUNTER Mary, and Nathaniel Adams, May 31, 1818.
1-154 HUNT Nathaniel, and Elizabeth Thomas; int. Dec. 10, 1743.
1-158 "   Martha, and John Adams; int. Nov. 16, 1745.
2-129 HUTCHINS Ann Eliza, and Samuel W. Remington, March 5, 1840.

I

2-74	IDE Timothy P., and Althea Tiffany, April 7, 1814.
1-118	INGRAHAM James, and Anna Humphrey; m. by Rev. Solomon Townsend, (also 2-11), Sept. 16, 1790.
2-30	" Watson, and Judeth Gladding; m. by Rev. Samuel Watson, May 10, 1801.
2-64	" Celinda, and Pearce Bosworth, Sept. 27, 1812.
2-98	" Lawton, son of James, dec., and Polly Taylor Bosworth, of Joseph, dec.; m. by Rev. Luther Wright, Aug. 30, 1819.
2-115	" William G., and Sally Child; m. by Rev. Jordan Rexford, Oct. 16, 1825.
2-145	" Sally, and George W. Greenwood, May 25, 1846.

J

1-167	JACK servant of Hezekiah Tiffany, of Barrington, and Duchess, servant of Mr. Pearce, of Bristol; m. by Rev. Solomon Townsend, Jan. 30, 1745-6; int. (1-184), published by Town Clerk Josiah Humphrey, Dec. 14, 1845.
1-184	" Jane, and Cambridge; int. Oct. 19, 1744; m. Nov. 26, 1744.
2-156	JEFFERDS Abby Ann, and Augustus G. Colby, Nov. 21, 1849.
89	" Job, and Mary Frank; int. Dec. 18, 1738.
2-153	JOHNSON George W., of West Greenwich, son of Truman and Martha, and Esther V. Peck, of Barrington, dau. of Ebenezer and Esther; m. by Rev. Forrest Jefferds, June 26, 1848.
2-49	JAHONAT Elizabeth, and Haile Bowen, Dec. 2, 1817.
1-76	JONES William, and Bebee Brown, Oct. 31, 1782.
2-8	" Abigail, and Ebenezer Mathewson, Feb. 22, 1798.
2-142	" Louisa, and Ellis Peck, Jr., Feb. 28, 1830.

K

1-155	KELLEY Priscilla, and Judah West; int. April 14, 1744.
2-17	" Duncan, and Mary Short, Nov. 15, 1779.
2-18	" Sally, and James Bowen, Sept. 28, 1794.
2-17	" Duncan, and Abigail Brown, Nov. 24, 1797.
2-17	" John, and Louisa Martin; m. by Rev. Flavel Shurtleff, May 20, 1821.
2-102	" Mary Ann, and Simeon Drowne, Sept. 2, 1824.
1-69	KENNEY Thomas, of Worthington, Mass., and Mrs. Eunice Toogood, of Barrington (also 1-36); m. by Rev. Solomon Townsend, Feb. 23, 1775.
1-44	KENNICUTT Hezekiah, and Lydia Luther, Dec. 23, 1773.
1-77	" Josiah, and Rebecca Townsend; m. by Rev. Solomon Tounsend (also 2-28), Nov. 8, 1787.
2-59	" Hannah, and Benjamin Viall, Jan. 1, 1809.
2-90	" Harriet Byron, and Col. Allen Bicknell, Dec. 23, 1817.
2-99	" Martha Townsend, and Nathaniel Brown, April 12, 1821.
2-165	" George R., and Hannah Drowne, Jan. 25, 1826.
2-154	" Nancy D., and Horace A. Martin, Aug. 23, 1848.
2-162	" George R., Jr., and Sophia M. Smith; m. at East Killingly, Conn., by Rev. John Chaney, Aug. 20, 1854.
93	KENT Susannah, and William Bullock; int. Jan. 8, 1737-8.
84	" Mrs. Hannah, and Benjamin Drowne, Nov. 25, 1738.
1-154	" Lydia, and Joseph Whelen, Jr.; int. Oct. 7, 1743.
1-158	" Mary, and Joseph Munroe; int. Dec. 15, 1744.
2-22	" Joshua, and Anna Low, Jan. 15, 1771.
1-81	" Rachel, and Shearjashab Bourne, Nov. 20, 1793.
2-24	" Huldah, and Solomon Peck, Dec. 10, 1795.
1-145	" Susannah, and Syllivan Allen, May 13, 1798.
2-45	" Alethea, and Daniel Horn, Feb. 14, 1801.

2-53   KENT Wilson, and Susannah Brayton, Feb. 26, 1804.
2-40   "   Elizabeth, and Thomas Whaley, Oct. 16, 1807.
2-73   "   Ira, of Joseph, and Sukey Ann Drowne, of Daniel; m. by Rev.
           Luther Wright, Oct. 11, 1818.
2-116 KINGSLEY Huldah B., and Amaziah Lilley, Aug. 15, 1815.
2-184 KING Jennie, and Pero Allen, Aug. 12, 1798.
2-56   KNIGHT George, and Ruth Townsend, Jan. 1, 1806.

L

2-74   LADIEW James, of Barrington, son of Capt. Curtis, and Betsey Snell, of
           Warren, dau. of Seth; m. by Rev. Luther Wright, Oct. 20,
           1819.
1-144 LADUE Curtis, and Rachel Tew, June 15, 1787.
1-147 "   Lois, and William Grant, Feb. 22, 1798.
2-67   "   Amelia, and Sylvester Bowen, Jan. 10, 1813.
2-66   LAWTON Susanuah, and Jabez Brown, Jan. 7, 1813.
2-136 LESTER Martha, and Henry Smith, Dec. 7, 1837.
2-116 LILLEY Amaziah, of Barrington, and Huldah B. Kingsley, of Swansey,
           Aug. 15, 1815.
92   LOW Samuel, of Barrington, and Isabel Green, of Warwick; int. Jan. 31,
           1735-6.
1-153 "   Ann, and Joseph Bosworth, Jr.; int. Aug. 6, 1743; m. (1-166)
           Dec. 10, 1743.
1-63   "   Elizabeth and Asa Bicknell (also 2-2), June 25, 1769.
2-22   "   Anna, and Joshua Kent, Jan. 15, 1771.
2-29   "   Frances, and Nudigate Adams. —— —, 1775.
1-151 LUTHER Lydia, and Philip Short, Jr.; int. Oct. 31, 1741.
1-33   "   Caleb, and Rebecca Brown, Dec. 16, 1773.
1-44   "   Lydia, and Hezekiah Keunicutt, Dec. 23, 1773.
1-71   "   Freelove, and Daniel Drowne (also 2-37), Feb. 8, 1776.
2-26   "   Josiah, and Prescilla Hill, Nov. 3, 1785.
2-25   "   Deborah, and James Bushee, April 4, 1776.
2-50   "   Nancy, and Sylvester Allen, Feb. 15, 1807.
2-82   "   Mary, and Benjamin Pecke Feb. 12, 1815.
2-159 "   Abby P., and Jonathan N. Bowen, May 22, 1850.
1-149 LYON Aaron. and Elizabeth Alleu; int. April 5, 1740.

M

2-149 MACUMBER Otis. and Maria Meigs, both of Bristol; m. by Rev. Josiah P.
           Tustin, Feb. 9, 1847.
1-149 MANCHESTER Eunice, and Nathaniel Toogood; int. Aug. 16, 1740.
2-33   MARSHALL Daniel Greene, and Hannah Read, Dec. 11, 1799.
1-150 MARTIN John, and Mary Read; int. June 10, 1741.
1-143 "   Luther, and Eliza Humphrey, Nov. 16, 1775.
1-62   "   Anna, and Joseph Gladding, July 4, 1776.
1-59   "   Benjamin, and Sarah Read, March 31, 1782.
1-69   "   James, and Judeth Read, (also 2-38), Sept. 12, 1782.
1-69   "   Anna, and Philip Drowne (also 2-24), Aug. 14, 1785.
2-7   "   Calvin, and Jerusha Humphrey; m. by Rev. Solomon Townsend,
           Dec. 4, 1788.
1-143 "   John, Jr., and Betsey Bowen (also 2-26), Dec. 31, 1789.
2-4   "   Susannah, and Noel Mathewson, Aug. 20, 1796.
1-147 "   Anderson, of Nathaniel and Nancy Alger, of Jonathan; m. by Rev.
           Luther Baker (also 2-60), Feb. 15, 1799.
2-35   "   John, and Eliza Humphrey; m. by Rev. Samuel Watson, Dec.
           26, 1802.
2-54   "   Mary, and Joshua Grant, Feb. 24, 1805.
2-65   "   John, Jr., and Mary Witherell, April 2, 1809.
2-100 "   Nancy, and George Gladding, May 13, 1810.
2-62   "   Cyrel, and Sally T. Bowen, Aug. 23, 1812.
2-79   "   Samuel R., and Sally Bowen, Oct. 2, 1814.

2-17   MARTIN Louisa, and John Kelley, May 20, 1821.
2-92   "   Lillis, and Viall Stanley, Aug. 19, 1821.
2-65   "   Capt. John, Jr., of Barrington, son of Capt. John and Hannah
                Blake, of Bristol, dau. of Samuel; m. by Rev. Jordan Rexford,
                June 3, 1827.
2-109   "   Eliza, and John Tyler, Oct. 23, 1827.
2-132   "   Benjamin, and Julia R. Drowne, of Jeremiah S.; m. by Rev.
                Thomas Williams, June 22, 1837.
2-123   "   Anna D., and Lewis B. Smith Nov. 14, 1839.
2-131   "   Sarah A., and James L. Sweetland, Oct. 3, 1841.
2-134   "   Syllivan, and Esther V. Tiffany; m. by Rev. Charles Peabody,
                Oct. 2, 1843.
2-141   "   Eliza, and Philander Soper, Sept. 9, 1845.
2-154   "   Horace A., of Anderson and Nancy, and Nancy D. Kennicutt, of
                George R. and Hannah; m. by Rev. Forrest Jefferds, Aug. 23,
                1848.
2-158   "   Avis Smith, and Thomas Champlain Heath, March 21, 1850.
2-75   MASON Babara, and Jonathan M. Wheeler, May 15, 1814.
91   MATHEWS William, and Mehitable Carpenter; m. by Samuel Allen, Justice,
                May 22, 1735.
91   "   Jeremiah, of Providence, and Susannah Medbury, of Barrington;
                int. Dec. 24, 1737.
1-150   "   William, and Ruth Allen; int. Jan. 24, 1740-1.
1-151   "   Mercy, and Andrew Robinson; int. Sept. 26, 1741.
2-15   MATHEWSON Sally, and Martin Brown, March 31, 1789.
2-6   "   Daniel, and Nancy Bosworth; m. by Rev. Solomon Townsend,
                Oct. 27, 1789.
2-4   "   Noel, and Susannah Martin; m. by Rev. Solomon Townsend, Aug.
                20, 1796.
2-8   "   Ebenezer, and Abigail Jones, Feb. 22, 1798.
2-130   "   Noel, of Providence, and Hannah B. Smith, of Barrington; m. by
                Rev. Benjamin R. Allen, July 15, 1841.
2-3   MAURAN Joseph Carlo, and Olive Bicknell; m. by Rev. Solomon Townsend,
                —— —, 1773.
2-14   "   Wait, and Nathaniel Smith, Jr., Sept. 21, 1794.
2-41   "   Carlo, and Sally Smith; m. by Rev. Samuel Watson, March 28,
                1805.
2-91   "   Capt. Suchet, of Providence, son of Joseph C., dec., and Sophia.
                Bowen, of Capt. Pardon, dec.; m. by Rev. Luther Wright, Sept.
                10, 1818.
1-155 MAXCY Martha, and Benjamin May; int. July 7, 1744.
2-71   MAXFIELD John, and Ann Drowne, Jan. 12, 1814.
2-80   "   Betsey, and Dyer Child, Nov. 13, 1814.
2-107   "   James, and Ann Eliza Watson; m. by Rev. Joel Mann, Oct. 10,
                1819.
2-137   "   Ann Elvira, and Amariah L. Medbury, March 7, 1844.
1-151 MAXWELL Samuel, and Sarah Tiffany; int. Oct. 14, 1741.
2-35   "   Squire, and Lydia Drowne; m. by Rev. Samuel Watson, March 7,
                1802.
92   MAY Naomi, and Benjamin Trissell, March 11, 1735-6.
90   "   Benjamin, of Barrington, and Susannah Clarke, of Rehoboth; int.
                Jan. 15, 1736-7.
1-166   "   Mary, and James Bugbee, May —, 1745; int. (1-156) March 23,
                1744-5.
1-155   "   Benjamin, and Martha Maxey; int. July 7, 1744.
91   MEDBURY Susannah, and Jeremiah Matthews; int. Dec. 24, 1737.
1-149   "   John, and Anna Camp; int. Oct. 4, 1740.
2-72   "   John, and Eliza Allen, Dec. 30, 1813.
2-137   "   Amariah L., of Providence, and Ann Elvira Maxfield, of Barring-
                ton; m. by Rev. Charles Peabody, March 7, 1844.
2-138   "   Hannah C., and George H. Smith, June 30, 1844.
2-155   "   Lucy A., and William G. Sheldon, Feb. 4, 1849.
1-159 MEDCAFF Martha, and Japheth Bicknell; int. Sept. 27, 1746.
2-149 MEIGS Maria, and Otis Micumber, Feb. 9, 1847.

1-158   MILLER Samuel, and Sarah Hill ; int. July 30, 1745.
2-119   "   James E., of Thompson, Conn., son of John, and Elizabeth S. Raw-
            son, of Barrington, dau. of Liberty, of Mendon, Mass ; m. by
            Rev. William R. Stone, Sept. 23, 1835.
2-157   "   Susan K., and Francis S. Hinsman, Jan. 6, 1850.
1-43   MILLEMAN George, and Elizabeth Tripp ; m. by Samuel Allen, Justice,
            June 13, 1779.
1-184   MOLL ——, and Quash ; int. Dec. 22, 1744 ; m. (1-165), Jan. 9, 1743-4.
2-34   MOORE Polly, and Ebenezer G. Cary, March 4, 1798.
1-158   MUNROE Joseph, and Mary Kent ; int. Dec. 15, 1744.
1-159   "   Joseph, and Biah Garnsey ; int. Aug. 2, 1746.

N O

90   OTIS Robert, and Margaret Sabin ; int. Jan. 15, 1736-7.

P

1-151   PEARCE William, and Lydia Brown ; int. Jan. 9, 1741-2.
1-153   PADELFORD Jonathan, and Hannah Bicknell ; int. April 22, 1743 ; (1-166),
            he of Taunton, she of Barrington ; m. by Rev. Solomon Town-
            send, May 26, 1743.
92   PAINE Samuel, of Pomfret, Conn., and Lydia Smith, of Barrington ; m. by
            Paris Bradford, Justice, May 15, 1735.
1-145   "   Mary Heath, and Thomas Allen, Jr., Sept. 9, 1798.
2-57   "   Roxalana, and Ichabod Richmond, Jan. 4, 1801.
2-43   "   Sarah R., and Thomas Allen, March 27, 1802.
2-35   "   says March 28, 1802.
2-40   "   Dolly, and Hezekiah Salisbury, Sept. 16, 1804.
2-50   "   Keziah, and John W. Bicknell, April 14, 1805.
90   PECK Solomon, and Kaziah Barnes ; int. Nov. 19, 1737.
1-149   "   Mrs. Bethiah, and Rev. Peleg Heath ; int. Aug. 9, 1740 : m.
            (1-171), Aug. 26, 1740.
1-152   "   Mary, and James Bucklin ; int. Oct. 11, 1742.
1-166   "   Mary, and James Bicknell, March 20, 1743.
1-153   "   Abiezer, of Rehoboth, and Mrs. Neoma Allen, of Barrington ; int.
            March 15, 1742-3 ; m. (1-166), by Rev. Solomon Townsend, April
            28, 1743.
1-154   "   Jerusha, and Peleg Heath ; int. Nov. 12, 1743 ; m. (1-172), Dec.
            8, 1743.
1-155   "   David, and Sarah Humphrey ; int. June 30, 1744.
1-159   "   Israel, and Sarah Adams ; int. April 29, 1746 ; m. (1-173), at
            Providence, by Jabez Bowen, Justice, Sept. 18, 1746.
2-7   "   Joel, and Lucy Fish, May 20, 1792.
2-5   "   Ebenezer, and Huldah Brown ; m. by Rev. Solomon Townsend, Dec.
            2, 1785.
2-24   "   Solomon, and Huldah Kent ; m. by Rev. John Ellis, Dec. 10, 1795.
2-31   "   Ellis, and Sarah Hill ; m. by Calvin Martin, Justice, Dec. 10, 1801.
2-58   "   Nathaniel, and Cynthia Heath ; m. by Rev. Samuel Watson, May 29,
            1808.
2-63   "   Bebee, and Capt. Benjamin Heath, Sept. 13, 1812.
2-82   "   Benjamin, of Swansey, and Mary Luther, of Warren, Feb. 12, 1815.
2-88   "   Capt. Benjamin, of Barrington, and Huldah Chaffee, of Seekonk ;
            m. by Rev. John Pitman, Nov. 9, 1817.
2-110   "   Leonard, and Harriet Cook Short ; m. by Rev. Luther Wright, Nov.
            27, 1817.
2-33   "   Huldah, and Emerson Humphrey, Dec. 31, 1818.
2-106   "   Abigail, and Samuel Bowen, July 4, 1826.
2-142   "   Ellis, Jr., of Barrington, and Louisa Jones, of Seekonk ; m. by
            Rev. Mr. Grafton, Feb. 28, 1830.
2-120   "   Asa, and Lucretia S. Remington ; m. by Rev. Benjamin R. Allen,
            —— —, 1839.
2-128   "   Clarissa, and Robert T. Smith, April 7, 1841.

2-153   PECK Esther V., and George W. Johnson, June 26, 1848.
2-160   "   Edwin F., of Seekonk, and Abigail Bowen, of Barrington; m. by
                    Rev. Forrest Jefferds, June 6, 1850.
1-153   PENEY Abel, and Amity Agor; int. July 30, 1743; m. (1-166) by Rev.
                    Solomon Townsend, Nov. 18, 1743.
1-145   PETTIS Thomas, of Rehoboth, and Susannah Tew, of Barrington; m. by
                    Rev. Samuel Watson, Sept. 26, 1798.
2-146   PIERCE John, and Sarah Allen; m. by Rev. Charles Peabody, Aug. 19,
                    1846.
2-150   PHIPPEN Nathan, and Christian Allen; int. Nov. 6, 1740.
2-1C   POTTER John, and Ruth Barnes, Oct. 21, 1797.
1-184   POMHAM Mary, and Walley Cheese; int. March 3, 1743-4; m. (1-172),
                    April 19, 1744.

Q

1-166   QUASH and Molly, colored servants of widow Smith; m. by Rev. Solomon
                    Townsend, Jan. 9, 1743-4; int. (1-184), published by Town
                    Clerk Josiah Humphrey, Dec. 22, 1743.

R

2-94   RAWSON Joseph, of Bristol, son of Edward, and Sarah, of Mendon, Mass.,
                    and Rebecca Bullock, widow of Capt. William, of Providence,
                    dau. of Gen. Thomas Allen, of Barrington; m. by Rev. Henry
                    White, Dec. 21, 1797.
2-104   "   Julia M., and Jeremiah B. Allen, Jan. 21, 1828.
2-119   "   Elizabeth S., and James E. Miller, Sept. 23, 1835.
  95   READ William, and Elizabeth Wood, of Rehoboth; int. Feb. 16, 1739-40.
1-150   "   Mary, and John Martin; int. June 10, 1741.
1-59   "   Sarah, and Benjamin Martin, March 31, 1782.
1-69   "   Judeth, and James Martin, (also 2-38), Sept. 12, 1782.
2-19   "   Nancy, and William Briggs, June 26, 1796.
2-33   "   Hannah, and Daniel Greene Marshall, Dec. 11, 1799.
2-20   "   Kezia, and David Hill, July 8, 1802.
2-95   "   Joshua, and Patience West, of Joseph, of Seekonk; m. by Rev.
                    John Pitman, Dec. 26, 1819.
2-151   REA Albert G., of Providence, son of William and Frances B., and Mary
                    Elizabeth Brown, of Nathaniel and Martha T.; m. by Rev.
                    Forrest Jefferds, Feb. 2, 1848.
2-49   REDING Joanna, and John Adams, April 22, 1804.
2-8   REMINGTON Enock, and Ruth Armington, Aug. 5, 1790.
2-8   "   Mercy, and Walker Armington, Aug. 31, 1794.
2-81   "   Enock, and Phebe Short, Nov. 13, 1814.
2-120   "   Lucretia S., and Asa Peck, —— —, 1839.
2-129   "   Samuel W., of Barrington, and Ann Eliza Hutchins, of Seekonk,
                    Mass.; m. by Rev. Benjamin R. Allen, March 5, 1840.
2-134   RHODES Charles W., of Providence, and Sarah M. Brown, of Barring-
                    ton; m. by Rev. Charles Peabody, Aug. 7, 1843.
2-57   RICHMOND Ichabod, and Roxalana Paine, Jan. 4, 1801.
2-127   "   Ardelia, and George K. Viall, April 4, 1841.
2-112   RICH Mary, and Ebenezer Tiffany, Oct. 3, 1830.
2-147   "   Eliza, and Hezekiah Tiffany, Nov. 24, 1846.
1-151   ROBINSON Andrew, and Mercy Mathews; int. Sept. 26, 1741.
1-151   ROSS John, and Sarah Torrey; int. Nov. 14, 1741. (1-171) he of Edenton,
                    N. C., she of Barrington; m. by Samuel Howland, Justice,
                    June 20, 1742.
90   ROUNDS Hannah, and John Webber; int. March 8, 1736-7.
2-97   "   Lemira, and John Allen, Aug. 7, 1823.

S

90	SABIN Margary, and Robert Otis; int. Jan. 15, 1736-7.
1-147	SALISBURY Nabby, and Nathaniel Heath, Jr., Nov. 30, 1797.
2-40	" Hezekiah, and Dolly Paine; m. by Rev. Samuel Watson, Sept. 16, 1804.
2-83	" John, and Betsey Brayton, July 2, 1815.
2-139	SAWTELLE Hollis, of Warren, and Betsey B. Tanner, of said town; m. by Rev. Isaac Bonney, Nov. 30, 1843.
1-67	SCOTT Rachel, and Benjamin Drowne, Jr., Jan. 10, 1773.
1-65	" Betsey, and John Short, Jr., (also 1-145 and 2-13), Sept. 30, 1779.
2-144	SEYMOUR Elizabeth Wiver, and Robinson Sisson Barney, April 14, 1846.
1-154	SHARP Susannah, and Elijah Taber; int. Dec. 24, 1743.
2-51	SHEARS Abigail, and Ira Allen, May 12, 1805.
2-155	SHELDON William G., of Providence, and Lucy A. Medbury, of Nathaniel, of Barrington; m. by Rev. Forrest Jefferds, Feb. 4, 1849.
1-151	SHORT Philip, Jr., and Lydia Luther; int. Oct. 31, 1741.
1-65	" John, Jr., of Barrington, and Betsey Scott of Cumberland; m. by Jonathan Carpenter, Justice (also 1-145 and 2-13), Sept. 30, 1779.
2-17	" Mary, and Duncan Kelley, Nov. 15, 1779.
2-36	" John, Jr., and Rachel Adams; m. by Rev. Samuel Watson, Dec. 11, 1803.
2-81	" Phebe, and Enock Remington, Nov. 13, 1814.
2-110	" Harriet Cooke, and Leonard Peck, Nov. 27, 1817.
2-155	SIMMONS Jonathan William Henry, son of Mrs. Jennie of Swansey, Mass., and Jemima Allen, of Mrs. Margaret of Barrington; m. by Rev. Forrest Jefferds, March 26, 1849.
1-85	SISSON Austis, and Jonathan Bushee, —. —, 1797.
92	SMITH Lydia, and Samuel Paine, May 15, 1735.
2-1	" Nathaniel, and Lillis Humphrey, Dec. 6, 1770.
1-85	" Simon, and Rachel Tiffany, May 3, 1779.
2-14	" Nathaniel, Jr., and Waite Mauran; m. by Rev. Solomon Townsend, Sept. 21, 1794.
2-19	" Ebenezer, and Martha Townsend; m. by Rev. Samuel Watson, Sept. 4, 1800.
2-35	" Amey, and Peter Taylor, Dec. 2, 1802.
2-41	" Sally, and Carlo Mauran, March 28, 1805.
2-47	" Samuel, and Lucy Armington, Aug. 18, 1805.
2-87	" Simon, and Lydia Bosworth, Jan. 2, 1807.
2-70	" Asa, of Barrington, and Phebe Arnold, of Woodstock, Conn., May 1, 1808.
2-136	" Henry, and Martha Lester; m. at Pleasant Ridge, Hamilton county, Ohio, Dec. 7, 1837.
2-123	" Lewis B., and Anna D. Martin; m. by Rev. Benjamin R. Allen, Nov. 14, 1839.
2-130	" Hannah B., and Noel Mathewson, July 15, 1841.
2-128	" Robert T., and Clarissa Peck; m. by Rev. Benjamin R. Allen, April 7, 1841.
2-165	" Susan K., and Capt. Albert Bowen, Sept. 2, 1841.
2-133	" Lydia B., and George W. Wightman, May 10, 1843.
2-138	" George H., of Providence, and Hannah C. Medbury, of Benjamin, of Barrington; m. by Rev. Charles Peabody, June 30, 1844.
2-162	" Sophia M., and George R. Kennicutt, Aug. 20, 1854.
2-74	SNELL Betsey, and James Ladien, Oct. 20, 1819.
2-141	SOPER Philander, of Rome, N. Y., son of Amos, and Eliza Martin, of Anderson, of Barrington; m. by Rev. George W. Hathaway, Sept. 9, 1845.
1-146	STANLEY Comfort, and Molly Viall; m. by Rev. Solomon Townsend (also 1-71), June 2, 1785.
2-92	" Viall, of Comfort, and Lillis Martin, of John; m. by Rev Flavel Shurtleff, Aug. 19, 1821.
2-93	" Betsey, and Allen Bowen, Nov. 18, 1821.

2-131 SWEETLAND James L., of James, of Pawtucket, R. I., and Sarah A. Martin, of Capt. Samuel R., of Barrington; m. at Seekonk, by Rev. John C. Welsh, Oct. 3, 1841.

93 SWIFT Ruth, and Thomas Barnes; int. Feb. 28, 1735.

T

1-154 TABER Elijah, and Susannah Sharp; int. Dec. 24, 1743.

91 TALMAN Hannah, and James Franklin; int. April 13, 1738.

2-139 TANNER Betsey B., and Hollis Sawtelle, Nov. 30, 1843.

2-140 " Josias, and Almira M. Barney; m. by Rev. Charles Peabody, Dec. 19, 1844.

2-9 TAYLOR Julanie, and Cyrus Allen, March 10, 1793.

2-6 " Ruth, and Joseph Bosworth, Sept. 11, 1796.

2-35 " Peter, and Amey Smith; m. by Rev. Samuel Watson, Dec. 2, 1802.

1-144 TEW Rachel, and Curtis Ladieu, June 15, 1787.

1-145 " Susannah, and Thomas Pettis, Sept. 26, 1793.

1-82 THAYER Chloe, and James Bowen, Jr. March 22, 1789.

1-154 THOMAS Elizabeth, and Nathaniel Hunt; int. Dec. 10, 1743.

1-154 THURBER Sarah, and John Wood; int. Sept. 10, 1743.

1-155 " Ann, and James Bowen; int. June 2, 1744.

90 TIBBINS Jonathan, and Elizabeth Beery; int. May 7, 1737.

1-151 TIFFANY Sarah, and Samuel Maxwell; int. Oct. 14, 1741.

1-155 " Ephraim, and Esther Viall; int. Nov. 3, 1744; m. (1-167), by Rev. Solomon Townsend, Dec. 27, 1744.

1-85 " Rachel, and Simon Smith, May 3, 1779.

1-84 " Ebenezer, and Mary Ann Bullock, Feb. 2, 1783. (2-42) says Feb. 12, 1783.

2-74 " Althea, and Timothy P. Ide, April 7, 1814.

2-18 " Elizabeth, and Capt. James Bowen, Nov. 15, 1821.

2-96 " Lydia, and Rev. Francis Wood, Sept. 9, 1825.

2-111 " Lemira, and Edmund Carpenter, Sept. 1, 1830.

2-112 " Ebenezer, and Mary Rich, of Ezekiel, and Rachel; m. at Troy, N. H., by Rev. Ezekiel Rich, Oct. 3, 1830.

2-134 " Esther V., and Sullivan Martin, Oct. 2, 1843.

2-147 " Hezekiah, and Eliza Rich; m. by Rev. Thomas Shepherd, Nov. 24, 1846.

1-149 TOOGOOD Nathaniel, and Eunice Manchester; int. Aug. 16, 1740.

1-36 " Mrs. Eunice, and Thomas Kenney (also 1-69), Feb. 23, 1775.

1-151 TORREY Sarah, and John Ross; int. Nov. 14, 1741; m. (1-171), June 20, 1742.

1-159 " Ann, and Timothy Allen; int. May 24, 1746.

1-152 TOWNSEND Solomon, and Rebecca Backer; int. Oct. 9, 1742.

1-77 " Rebecca, and Josiah Kennicutt (also 2-28), Nov. 8, 1787.

2-31 " Solomon, Jr., and Charlotte Armington; m. by Rev. Solomon Townsend, April 2, 1794.

2-19 " Martha, and Ebenezer Smith, Sept. 4, 1800.

2-56 " Ruth, and George Knight, Jan. 1, 1806.

1-158 TRIPP William, and Abigail Fief; int. Nov. 21, 1744; m. (1-172) by Josiah Howland, Justice, Jan. 21, 1744-5.

1-158 " James, and Martha White; int. Sept. 7, 1745, he of Bristol, she of Barrington; m. (1-167) by Rev. Solomon Townsend, Dec. 12, 1745.

1-43 " Elizabeth, and George Milleman, June 13, 1779.

1-62 " Mehetable, and Caleb Drowne, Dec. 24, 1783.

2-109 TYLER John, and Eliza Martin; m. by Rev. Luther Baker, Oct. 23, 1827.

U

92 UTTER Ruth, and John Dexter, Feb. —, 1735-6.

V

1-152 VIALL Mercy, and Samuel Allen int. March 6, 1741-2.
1-155 " Esther, and Ephraim Tiffany; int. Nov. 3, 1744; m. (1-167), Dec. 27, 1744.
1-71 " Molly, and Comfort Stanly, (also 1-146), June 2, 1785.
1-77 " Alethea, and Joseph Bl knell, Nov. 19, 1786.
1-71 " Ruth, and Asa Bowen, May 4, 1788.
2-11 " Sylvester, and Abigail Adams; m. by Rev. Solomon Townsend, Oct. 23, 1790.
2-59 " Benjamin, and Hannah Kennicutt, Jan. 1, 1809.
2-127 " George K., of Warren, and Ardelia Richmond, of Barrington; m. by Rev. Benjamin R. Allen, April 4, 1841.

W

2-30 WARDWELL Hannah, and William Adams, Oct. 23, 1791.
2-35 WATERMAN Lucretia, and Martha Watson, (also 2-48), Nov. 28, 1802.
2-35 " Ann, and John Watson, (also 2-39), Nov. 20, 1803.
2-21 WATSON Rev. Samuel, and Martha Bicknell; m. by Rev. Mr. Wilder, Dec. 5, 1799.
2-35 " Matthew, and Lucretia Waterman; m. by Rev. Samuel Watson, (also 2-48), Nov. 28, 1802.
2-35 " John, and Ann Waterman; m. by Rev. Samuel Watson, (also 2-39), Nov. 20, 1803.
2-86 " Lucretia, and Grindall Chase, June 10, 1816.
2-107 " Ann Eliza, and James Maxfield, Oct. 10, 1819.
90 WEBBER John, of Barrington, and Hannah Rounds, of Rehoboth; int. March 8, 1736-7.
1-155 WEST Judah, and Prescilla Kelley; int. April 14, 1744.
2-95 " Patience, and Joshua Read, Dec. 26, 1819.
2-40 WHALEY Thomas, of South Kingstown, and Elizabeth Kent, of Barrington; m. by Rev. Samuel Watson, Oct. 16, 1807.
2-75 WHEELER Jonathan M., of Swansey, and Barbara Mason, of Warren, May 15, 1814.
1-150 WHELEN Abigail, and Jabez Brown; int. Feb. 14, 1740-1.
1-154 " Joseph, Jr., of Rehoboth, and Lydia Kent.; int. Oct. 7, 1743.
1-158 WHETON Andrew, and Lydia Carpenter; int. Oct. 19, 1745.
1-158 WHITE Martha, and James Tripp; int. Sept. 7, 1745; m. (1-167) Dec. 12, 1745.
2-133 WIGHTMAN George W., and Lydia B. Smith; m. by Rev. Charles Peabody, May 10, 1843.
2-15 WITHERELL Sally Stephens, and Haile Bowen, Sept. 1, 1796.
2-65 " Mary, and John Martin, Jr., April 2, 1809.
2-129 WORSELEY Pardon E. A., and Sarah Wood, both of Pawtucket, Mass.; m. by Rev. Benjamin R. Allen, Sept. 17, 1840.
95 WOOD Elizabeth, and William Read; int. Feb. 16, 1739-40.
1-172 " Mary, and John Franklin, Aug. 18, 1743.
1-154 " John, and Sarah Thurber; int. Sept. 10, 1743.
2-96 " Rev. Francis, of Mark and Rachel, and Lydia Tiffany, of Ebenezer and Mary Ann; m. by Rev. Henry Wight, Sept. 9, 1823.
2-129 " Sarah, and Pardon E. A. Warseley, Sept. 17, 1849.

X Y Z

2-85 YOUNG James W., and Cordelia Anthony, of Providence, Aug. 17, 1815.

BARRINGTON.

BIRTHS AND DEATHS.

A

96	ADAMS	Christian, of James and Mary,	d. March 9, 1713-14.
1-16	"	Joseph, of Ebenezer and Hannah,	May 25, 1739.
1-16	"	James,	Sept. 6, 1740.
1-16	"	Mary,	July 12, 1742.
1-18	"	Rachel,	June 1, 1744.
1-34	"	John, Esq., d. Nov. 28, 1772.	
1-25	"	Molly, of James and Ruth,	June 7, 1771.
1-33	"	Molly,	d. March 29, 1774.
1-34	"	Rachel,	May 9, 1774.
1-25	"	Hannah, of Samuel and Rebecca,	Oct. 10, 1771.
1-34	"	John,	July 6, 1773.
1-55	"	James, d. June 8, 1775.	
1-35	"	Ruth, widow, d. Sept. 7, 1775.	
2-29	"	Nathaniel, of Nudigate and Frances,	Aug. 6, 1776.
2-29	"	Nathaniel,	d. Sept. 13, 1777.
2-29	"	John,	Sept. 27, 1777.
2-29	"	John,	d. Oct. 25, 1780.
2-29	"	John, (	Jan. 8, 1781.
2-29	"	Nudigate,	(1-64) Oct. 30, 1783.
2-29	"	Rachel,	(1-66) Nov. 8, 1785.
2-29	"	Samuel,	(1-76) June 9, 1788.
2-29	"	Ebenezer,	(1-76) Oct. 7, 1790.
2-29	"	Joseph,	(1-82) May 14. 1793.
2-29	"	Nathaniel,	(1-118) Sept. 2, 1795.
2-29	"	Nudigate, Sr., died.	Jan. 5, 1798.
		Note—Three first also recorded 1-58.	
1-42	"	Hannah, widow, died,	Sept. 7, 1777.
1-148	"	Samuel W., of William and Hannah (also 2-30),	Sept. 29, 1793.
2-49	"	John Moses, of John and Joanna,	Oct. 13, 1805.
2-68	"	Betsey Short, of Ebenezer and Prescilla.	Dec. 2, 1813.
2-68	"	George William,	Nov. 18, 1815.
2-68	"	Luvisa,	June 10, 1818.
2-68	"	Rachel,	Nov. 4, 1823.
2-68	"	Henry Augustus,	Sept. 15, 1829.
2-68	"	Abby Ann,	March 26, 1832.
		Note—(2-29) reads George William (above), born Nov. 28, 1815.	
2-75	"	Joseph, of Nathaniel and Mary,	Sept. 9, 1819.
2-46	ALGER	Lydia, of Jonathan and Dorothy,	June 23, 1786.
2-46	"	Joseph,	July 14, 1788.
2-46	"	Henrietta,	June 16, 1790.
2-46	"	Jonathan,	June 1, 1794.
1-10	ALLEN	Hannah, of Joseph and Hannah,	March 27, 1717.
1-10	"	Joseph,	June 30, 1719.
1-10	"	Samuel,	Dec. 22, 1721.
1-10	"	Jerusha,	March 22, 1724.
1-10	"	Rachel,	March 4, 1727.
1-10	"	Rachel,	d. Oct. 18, 1740.

1-10	ALLEN Molly, of Joseph and Hannah,	Dec. 16, 1732.
	Note—Also recorded (84).	
1-7	"	Elizabeth, of Matthew and Ruth.	Oct. 31, 1726.
1-7	"	Mercy,	Sept. 24, 1728.
1-7	"	Anne,	March 4, 1731-2.
1-7	"	Ruth,	April 14, 1733.
1-7	"	Rebecca,	March 17, 1735.
1-7	"	Rachel,	July 16, 1737.
1-7	"	Abigail,	Nov. 19, 1739.
1-15	"	Ann, of Thomas and Alethea,	Dec. 22, 1729.
1-15	"	Alethea,	Oct. 19, 1731.
1-15	"	Hannah,	Nov. 5, 1733.
1-3	"	Samuel, reputed son of Samuel Allen and Eunice Manchester, March 25, 1739.
1-8	"	Mercy, of Matthew and Ruth,	d. Aug. 21, 1740.
1-8	"	Abigail,	d. Sept. 4, 1740.
1-8	"	Anna,	d. Sept. 9, 1740.
1-8	"	Rebecca,	d. Sept. 10, 1740.
1-8	"	Rachel,	d. Sept. 15, 1740.
1-16	"	Nathan, of Daniel, and Hannah,	Oct. 6, 1743.
1-21	"	Viall, of Samuel and Mercy,	Dec. 9, 1744.
1-21	"	Samuel,	April 8, 1746.
1-21	"	Hannah,	Sept. 19, 1745.
1-29	"	Asa, of Samuel, 2d, and Ruth,	Oct. 15, 1760.
1-29	"	Joseph Viall,	Sept. 23, 1762.
1-29	"	Rachel,	Sept. 28, 1765.
1-30	"	Samuel,	Jan. 19, 1768.
1-30	"	Sylvester,	Feb. 20, 1770.
	Note—Samuel above, born in the middle of a remarkable eclipse, which occurred that day ; above all taken from Warren records.
1-30	"	James, of Samuel, 2d, and Ruth,	Oct. 10, 1772.
1-37	"	Jerusha, of Viall and Rachel,	Sept. 10, 1766.
1-38	"	Rebecca,	May 13, 1769.
1-38	"	Rachel,	April 27, 1771.
1-38	"	James,	Dec. 9, 1773.
2-27	"	Elizabeth, of Matthew and Elizabeth,	March 18, 1767.
2-27	"	Ruth, of Matthew and Bathsheba,	Sept. 20, 1769.
2-27	"	Huldah,	March 6, 1771.
2-27	"	Matthew,	Oct. 16, 1774.
2-27	"	Sullivan,	Sept. 25, 1776.
2-27	"	Chloe,	Feb. 14, 1780.
2-27	"	Mercy,	May 21, 1783.
1-113	"	William, of Thomas and Amey,	Aug. 17, 1768.
1-113	"	Rebecca,	Feb. 11, 1770.
1-113	"	Rachel,	Feb. 20, 1772.
1-113	"	Amey,	Nov. 7, 1773.
1-113	"	Thomas,	Aug. 12, 1775.
1-113	"	Ethan,	Oct. 7, 1777.
1-113	"	Ira,	Oct. 18, 1780.
1-113	"	Anna,	July 10, 1783.
1-113	"	Shearjashub B.,	June 30, 1785.
1-113	"	Elizabeth,	June 9, 1787.
1-113	"	George Washington,	June 25, 1789.
1-113	"	John Jay,	Dec. 13, 1791.
1-37	"	James, of Samuel, 2d, and Ruth.	d. Nov. 16, 1774.
1-37	"	Eunice,	Oct. 6, 1775.
1-37	"	Sylvester,	d. Dec. 21, 1776.
1-42	"	Sylvester, 2d,	Sept. 16, 1778.
1-44	"	James,	Aug. 23, 1780.
1-37	"	Major Samuel, died, aged 56y. 9m., wanting 3 days	March 25, 1777.
1-64	"	Joseph Viall, of Asa and Abigail,	May 12, 1783.
1-85	"	Prince, of Prince,	Sept. 16, 1788.
2-77	"	James, of Squire and Elizabeth,	May 16, 1791.

2-77	ALLEN Mercy, of Squire and Elizabeth,	Aug. 29, 1792.
2-77	" Elizabeth,	(1-82), May 1, 1794.
2-77	" Squire,	March 2, 1797.
2-77	" Calvin,	March 18, 1799.
2-77	" Joanna,	March 4, 1803.
2-77	" Ira,	Feb. 2, 1805.
2-77	" Paschal,	April 6, 1809.
	Note—Two eldest recorded (1-81).	
2-9	" James, of Cyrus and Julanie,	June 14, 1793.
2-9	" Pamelia,	Sept. 5, 1795.
2-9	" Daniel,	Nov. 3, 1797.
1-118	" Avery, of Samuel, 2d, and Fanny,	June 19, 1796.
1-144	" Ethan,	April 3, 1798.
2-18	" Gen. Thomas, d. in his 59th y., May 30, 1800.	
2-43	" Mary Paine, of Thomas and Sarah R.,	July 27, 1902.
2-43	" Ethan,	Sept. 29, 1804.
2-43	" Thomas Richmond,	Aug. 30, 1806.
2-43	" Sarah,	Dec. 24, 1813.
2-43	" Amey Ann,	March 15, 1809.
2-51	" Ira Richard, of Ira and Abigail,	Feb. 24, 1806.
2-51	" Thomas Irvine,	April 29, 1808.
2-50	" Martha Watson, of Sylvester and Nancy,	March 11, 1809.
2-50	" Samuel,	March 2, 1811.
2-50	" Joseph Kennicutt,	Feb. 21, 1813.
2-104	" Benjamin Clifford, of Jeremiah B. and Julia Ann,	Oct. 13, 1828.
2-156	" Theodore Hughes, of Ira and Rosamond,	Aug. 31, 1834.
2-156	" Charles Crawford,	Sept. 22, 1837.
2-156	" Emily Frances,	June 29, 1839.
1-70	ARMINGTON Gardiner, of Joseph and Esther,	July 6, 1785.
1-70	" Gardiner,	d. April 14, 1786.
1-70	" Hannah Baster,	Aug. 21, 1787.
1-75	" James Gardiner,	Sept. 9, 1789.
1-77	" Daniel,	Oct. 12, 1791.
1-118	" Hervey, of Asa and Bethia,	July 26, 1793.
1-118	" Ira,	April 28, 1795.
2-8	" Joseph, of Walker and Mercy,	July 9, 1795.
2-8	" Mercy,	d. Oct. 16, 1795.
2-125	ARNOLD William Albert, of Jabez R. and Mary A., May 30, 1840.	

B

1-74	BAKER Thomas, of Thomas and Freelove,	Nov. 10, 1788.
1-77	" Jeremiah, of Joseph and Mary,	Aug. 4, 1792.
1-13	BARNES Thomas, of Samuel and Jean,	April 25, 1713.
1-13	" Keziah,	April 1, 1718.
1-13	" Lois,	Jan. 3, 1719-20.
1-14	" Lois,	d. Sept. 20, 1740.
1-13	" Eunice,	Aug. 26, 1721.
1-13	" Hannah,	April 1, 1726.
1-14	" Hannah,	d. Sept. 29, 1740.
1-13	" Huldah,	Nov. 12, 1727.
1-14	" Huldah,	d. Oct. 5, 1740.
1-13	" Zerdiah,	Feb. 27, 1730.
1-14	" Zerdiah,	d. Oct. 8, 1740.
1-13	" Samuel,	Dec. 20, 1732.
1-14	" Samuel,	d. Oct. 21, 1740.
1-13	" Benjamin,	Dec. 20, 1732.
1-17	" Benjamin,	Feb. 25, 1744-5.
1-83	" Elizabeth, of Samuel and Hannah,	May 31, 1775.
1-83	" Esther,	Dec. 22, 1777.
1-83	" Amey,	April 12, 1780.
1-83	" Hannah,	March 22, 1783.
1-83	" Thomas,	May 28, 1785.
1-83	" Samuel,	April 8, 1788.

1-83	BARNES Peleg, of Samuel and Hannah,		May 11, 1790.
1-83	" Alfred,		Dec. 14, 1793.
1-42	" Alethea Viall, of Peleg and Rachel,		Jan. 16, 1777.
2-9	" Betsey, of John and Elizabeth,		March 31, 1794.
2-9	" Levi,		April 3, 1786.
2-9	" Nancy,		Aug. 21, 1788.
2-9	" John,		Sept. 26, 1790.
2-9	" Mary,		April 3, 1793.
2-9	" Otis.		Feb. 26, 1796.
2-9	" Almira,		May 8, 1798.
2-18	" Thomas, died in his 88th year.		June 29, 1800.
2-89	" Thomas, of Alfred and Keziah.		June 13, 1819.
2-89	" Keziah, wife of Alfred,		d. July 14, 1825.
2-89	" John Woodbury, of Alfred and Lydia,		Oct. 18, 1826.
2-89	" Keziah Daggett,		Oct. 23, 1828.
2-89	" Alfred.		Dec. 15, 1830.
2-89	" Lydia Peck,		Jan. 25, 1833.
2-89	" Hannah Peck,		April 13, 1835.
1-77	BARNEY Jonathan, of Nathaniel and Sarah,		May 19, 1785.
1-77	" Enock.		April 9, 1787.
1-160	" Wheaton, of Peleg,		Sept. 7, 1791.
1-16	BICKNELL Allen, of Joshua and Abigail,		July 19, 1743.
1-16	" Allen,		d. Oct. 1, 1743.
1-19	" Thomas. of Joshua, Jr., and Ruth.		Feb. 11, 1745-6.
2-2	" Asa, of Asa and Elizabeth.		Aug. 11, 1771.
2-2	" Asa,		d. Sept. 21, 1787.
2-2	" Otis.		Aug. 29, 1773.
2-2	" Otis,		d. Sept. 21, 1795.
2-2	" Releaf,		Dec. 3, 1776.
2-2	" John Wilson,		April 16, 1781.
2-2	" William.		May 2, 1782.
2-2	" Elizabeth,		Feb. 18, 1784.
2-2	" Benjamin Ellery,		Dec. 10, 1786.
2-2	" Asa,		Dec. 8, 1788.
2-2	" Frances,		March 27, 1793.
2-2	" Asa, Esq., died June 12, 1799.		
	Note.—The six eldest recorded also (1-63), and the two eldest (1-36).		
1-28	" Wait, of Joshua and Freeborn.		Nov. 9, 1771.
1-28	" Freeborn,		Jan. 9, 1776 or 9.
1-58	" Joshua. Esq., died Nov. 30, 1781.		
2-16	" Jerusha, of Joshua and Amey,	(1-61),	March 5, 1783.
2-16	" Mary,	(1-75),	Nov. 19, 1784.
2-16	" Allen.	(1-75),	April 13, 1787.
2-16	" Amey,	(1-75),	Aug. 16, 1789.
2 16	" Freeborn,	(1-112),	Nov. 5, 1791.
2-16	" Freeborn,	(1-112),	d. Nov. 22, 1791.
2-16	" Joshua,	(1-112),	Nov. 19, 1792.
2-16	" James,	(1-112),	Nov. 4, 1795.
2-16	" Elizabeth,		Feb. 22, 1799.
2-16	" Joseph Peck,		Aug. 19, 1801.
2-52	" George Willson, of John W. and Keziah,		Nov. 7, 1807.
2-90	" Joshua, of Col. Allen and Harriet B.,		Oct. 29, 1818.
2-90	" George Augustus,		June 30, 1822.
2-90	" Daniel Kennicutt,		Sept. 25, 1829.
2-90	" Thomas Williams,		Sept. 6, 1834.
2-20	BISHOP Elizabeth, of Ebenezer and Lydia,	(1-146),	Sept. 12, 1798.
2-20	" Lydia		June 13, 1800.
2-161	" Sarah Whipple, of James and Sarah,		Jan. 26, 1848.
1-26	BOSWORTH Sarah, of Jacob and Lydia,		June 5, 1732.
1-26	" Rebecca,		Feb. 27, 1736.
1-26	" Hannah,		Sept. 9, 1740.
1-26	" Submit,		Oct. 16, 1742.
1-31	" Molly, of Jonathan and Molly,		Jan. 29, 1751.

(Vit. Rec., Vol. 6.) 20

1-31	BOSWORTH	Nathaniel, of Jonathan and Molly,	April 12, 1753.
1-31	"	Betsey,	May 27, 1755.
1-31	"	Jonathan,	May 20, 1757.
1-31	"	Mehitable,	Nov. 4, 1759.
1-32	"	Susannah,	March 10, 1762.
1-32	"	Susannah,	d. July 11, 1766.
1-82	"	Hannah,	June 12, 1764.
1-32	"	Edward,	April 4, 1767.
1-32	"	Susannah,	Feb. 28, 1770.
1-119	"	Anna, of Samuel and Elizabeth,	Oct. 26, 1769.
1-119	"	Joseph,	June 3, 1771.
1-119	"	Samuel,	Sept. 20, 1773.
1-119	"	Mary,	Oct. 30, 1779.
1-119	"	Elizabeth,	May 13, 1782.
2-6	"	Polly Taylor, of Joseph and Ruth,	Jan. 15, 1797.
2-6	"	Richard,	Feb. 26, 1799.
2-6	"	Richard,	d. Dec. 5, 1811.
2-6	"	Joseph,	Aug. 14, 1806.
2-44	"	Sally, of Samuel and Patience,	April 23, 1798.
2-44	"	Almira,	Sept. 7, 1801.
2-44	"	Sylvania,	April 9, 1803.
2-44	"	Job Allen,	July 6, 1805.
2-44	"	Elizabeth T.,	May 16, 1808.
2-44	"	Julia W.,	Dec. 8, 1810.
2-44	"	Abby C.,	Aug. 17, 1813.
2-44	"	John D.,	Nov. 17, 1815.
2-64	"	Eliza Ann, of Pearce and Celinda,	Oct. 24, 1813.
2-64	"	Richard Taylor,	Aug. 14, 1815.
2-64	"	Mary Pearce,	Sept. 5, 1823.
2-64	"	Nancy Ingraham,	July 1, 1825.
2-64	"	James Ingraham,	March 30, 1819.
2-64	"	Leonard S.,	June 20, 1821.
2-64	"	Caroline S.,	April 4, 1830.
1-12	BOWEN	Josiah, of Josiah and Margaret,	July 29, 1734.
1-12	"	Margaret,	Nov. 12, 1736.
1-12	"	Nathan,	Jan. 24, 1738-9.
1-33	"	Hannah, of Henry and Mary,	May 3, 1766.
1-33	"	Henry,	Sept. 18, 1774.

Note—Eldest born Woodstock, Conn., youngest Barrington.

1-80	"	Betsey, of Jeremiah and Lillis,	Nov. 25, 1767.
1-80	"	Anna,	Oct. 22, 1769.
1-80	"	James,	Dec. 15, 1773.
1-80	"	Haile,	Nov. 6, 1776.
1-80	"	Ruth,	Oct. 5, 1779.
1-80	"	Joseph,	March 4, 1782.
1-80	"	Mary,	April 3, 1784.
1-80	"	Sarah,	March 2, 1787.
1-80	"	Susannah,	June 23, 1790.
1-29	"	Jeremy, of Josiah and Anna,	May 27, 1772.
1-74	"	William,	May 10, 1774.
1-74	"	Haile,	Aug. 6, 1777.
1-74	"	Samuel,	Nov. 22, 1782.
1-74	"	Josiah,	Nov. 22, 1782.
1-74	"	Hannah,	Oct. 13, 1785.
1-74	"	Jonathan,	May 24, 1787.
1-74	"	Jonathan,	d. Sept. 24, 1787.
1-74	"	Sylvester,	April 10, 1789.
1-43	"	Mary, wife of Henry, died Oct. 30, 1778.	
1-58	"	Elizabeth, of Henry and Elizabeth,	Oct. 6, 1781.
1-82	"	Amasa, of James and Chloe,	Dec. 31, 1789.
1-82	"	Abner,	March 17, 1792.
1-82	"	Eseck,	Sept. 11, 1794.
1-80	"	Capt. James, died,	Sept. 28, 1793.
1-82	"	Sally, of Stephen and Betsey,	May 12, 1794.
1-113	"	Rebecca,	Sept. 6, 1796.

2-18	BOWEN Allen, of James and Sally,	March 19, 1797.
2-18	" Daniel,	Feb. 24, 1799.
2-18	" James,	July 23, 1805.
2-15	" James, of Halle and Sally S.,	April 4, 1797.
2-15	" Betsey,	March 16, 1800.
2-15	" Samuel,	June 8, 1802.
2-15	" Halle,	Aug. 5, 1805.
2-15	" Mary,	Sept. 9, 1809.
2-15	" Susanna,	Aug. 27, 1812.
2-67	" Hannah, of Sylvester and Amelia,	July 16, 1816.
2-67	" William James,	July 5, 1818.
2-67	" Sylvester,	April 23, 1820.
2-93	" Edwin, of Allen and Betsey,	July 9, 1823.
2-93	" Mary Drowne,	April 2, 1827.
2-93	" Mary Drowne,	d. Jan. 10, 1828.
2-93	" James,	Dec. 2, 1839.
2-18	" William Haile, of Capt. James and Elizabeth,	Aug. 5, 1828.
2-159	" Ella Augusta, of Jonathan N. and Abby P.,	April 2, 1851.
1-17	BRALEY James, of John and Johannah,	May 1, 1744.
2-19	BRIGGS William, of William and Nancy,	May 7, 1797.
2-19	" Nancy,	May 16, 1799.
1-12	BROWN Simon, of Daniel and Sarah,	Jan. 5, 1719-20.
1-6	" Mary, of Isaac and Esther,	Feb. 20, 1730-1.
1-6	" Thomas,	April 16, 1733.
1-6	" Daniel,	Jan. 18, 1726-7.
1-19	" Keziah, of Hezekiah and Joannah,	Sept. 22, 1735.
1-19	" William,	Sept. 10, 1737.
1-19	" Nathaniel,	May 31, 1739.
1-17	" Becca, of James and Rebecca,	April 17, 1738.
1-17	" Becca,	d. May 5, 1738.
1-17	" James,	June 11, 1739.
1-17	" James,	d. June 12, 1739.
1-18	" Mollie,	June 22, 1740.
1-18	" James, 2d,	Aug. 19, 1742.
1-18	" James, 2d,	d. Nov. 14, 1743.
1-18	" James, 3d,	July 3, 1744.
1-21	" Cerrel,	June 11, 1746.
1-160	" Pero, of Prince and Wattie (also 1-181),	April 2, 1766.
1-144	" Russell, of William and Alethea,	Oct. 23, 1772.
1-144	" Annah,	Aug. 4, 1776.
1-144	" Allen,	Jan. 6, 1780.
1-16	" Ruben, of Pero and Jennie,	June 15, 1790.
2-15	" Jabez, of Martin and Sally,	Aug. 28, 1790.
2-15	" Harvey,	Nov. 28, 1792.
2-15	" Martin,	Feb. 24, 1798.
2-15	" Allen,	July 16, 1803.
2-32	" Polly, of Kent and Betsey, (1-144),	Oct. 3, 1794.
2-32	" Nathaniel,	(1-144), Aug. 20, 1796.
2-32	" Betsey, wife of Kent, died April ——. ——.	
22-32	" Betsey, of Kent and Eunice,	Aug. 2, 1800.
2-32	" Asa,	Nov. 17, 1802.
2-32	" William,	Nov. 11, 1804.
2-32	" Allen,	Jan. 14, 1808.
2-32	" Samuel Allen,	March 3, 1810.
2-32	" Lyman,	March 12, 1815.
2-99	" Mary Elizabeth, of Nathaniel and Martha S.,	Feb. 2, 1823.
2-101	" George Harvey, of Allen M. and Elizabeth,	June 29, 1826.
1-18	BULLOCK Josiah, of Israel and Sarah,	Sept. 30, 1733.
1-18	" Sarah,	June 8, 1735.
1-18	" Prudence,	Sept. 29, 1736.
1-18	" Anna,	Jan. 15, 1739-40.
1-18	" Comfort,	April 14, 1741.
1-15	" Jabez, of John and Patience,	April 19, 1741.
2-25	BUSHEE Susannah, of James and Deborah,	(1-45), May 10, 1776.
2-25	" Rebecca,	(1-43), June 5, 1778.

2-25	BUSHEE James, of James and Deborah,		July 25, 1780.
2-25	"	Sarah,	Feb. 16, 1783.
2-25	"	Luther,	June 16, 1786.
2-25	"	Bashabee,	Jan. 6, 1789.
2-25	"	Deborah,	Jan. 22, 1791.
2-25	"	Mary,	June 2, 1793.
2-25	"	Sylvanus Hathaway,	Dec. 31, 1795.
2-25	"	John Wilbur,	Aug. 22, 1800.
1-148	"	Jonathan, reported son of Jonathan Bushee and Sarah Salisbury, March 2, 1781.
1-85	"	Nancy, of Jonathan and Anstis,	July 8, 1788.

C

2-12	CARPENTER Eliza, of Anthony and Rachel,		April 12, 1799.
2-12	"	Thomas,	Aug. 7, 1800.
2-12	",	John Horn,	Oct. 24, 1803.
2-12	"	Ann,	Dec. 14, 1811.
1-35	CARY David, of Micah and Martha,		Dec. 9, 1774.
1-28	"	Ebenezer Garnsey,	June 11, 1771.
2-34	"	Amey Brown, of Ebenezer G. and Polly,	Sept. 18, 1802.
2-34	"	Nathan,	April 1, 1804.
2-34	"	Caleb,	May 23, 1806.
2-34	"	Angeline,	Feb. 28, 1812.
2-86	"	Chase Emeline Watson, of Grindall and Lucretia,	Jan. 29, 1818.
1-94	CLEANNAN Anna, of Henry and Mary,		Dec. 2, 1735.
1-35	CONANT Benajah, of Samuel and Rebecca,		— —, —.
2-108	COOKE Mary Ann, of Capt. Thomas W. and Eliza,		Jan. 20, 1829.
2-34	CRANSTON Ira, of Peleg and Mary,		Nov. 19, 1798.
1-3	CURTIS Samuel, of Samuel and Katherine,		May 4, 1729.
1-3	"	Nathaniel,	Sept. 18, 1731.
1-3	"	Simeon,	June 30, 1734.
1-3	"	Prudence,	April 26, 1737.

D

1-70	DEHANE Jacob, merchant of Newport, died in his 58th year, Sept. 1, 1751.		
94	DEXTER Jonathan, of Thomas and Mary,		March 30, 1733-4.
1-5	DROWNE Lydia, of Benjamin and Hannah,		Feb. 1, 1739.
1-5	"	Solomon,	March —, 1741-2.
1-67	"	Chloe, of Benjamin and Rachel,	Dec. 8, 1773.
1-67	"	Jeremiah Scott,	April 21, 1775.
1-67	"	Benjamin,	Aug. 9, 1777.
1-67	"	Samuel,	June 23, 1779.
1-67	"	Lydia,	April 5, 1781.
1-68	"	Sarah,	Nov. 28, 1783.
1-68	"	Rachel,	Dec. 27, 1785.
2-37	"	Hannah, of Daniel and Freelove, (1-74), (1-37), Dec. 21, 1776.
2-37	"	Solomon, (1-74), Sept. 9, 1779.
2-37	"	Joanna, (1-74), June 16, 1782.
2-37	"	Rebecca, (1-74), Aug. 17, 1785.
2-37	"	Daniel,	Sept. 19, 1791.
2-37	"	Sukey Ann,	March 6, 1796.
1-64	"	Molly, of Jonathan Jenckes and Hannah, March 22, 1782.
1-64	"	Jerusha,	May 5, 1784.
1-112	"	Jason,	May 30, 1797.
1-75	"	Simeon, of Caleb and Mehitable, (1-68), July 8, 1784.
1-75	"	Caleb, (1-68), April 23, 1786.
1-75	"	Abigail,	Nov. 15, 1788.
2-24	"	James, of Philip and Anna,	April 12, 1786.
1-69	"	Tamer, (1-70), April 12, 1786.
1-70	"	Anna,	Dec. 8, 1787.
2-24	"	Philip,	April 4, 1789.

2-24	DROWNE Adelia, of Philip and Anna,	Jan. 22, 1792.
2-24	" Jonathan,	March 25, 1794.
2-24	" Rachel.	April 16, 1796.
2-24	" Ethan,	July 24, 1798.
1-85	" Betsey, of Jonathan T. and Hannah,	Oct. 21, 1786.
1-112	" Jonathan,	Jan. 12, 1789.
1-112	" Benjamin,	Feb. 9, 1791.
1-112	" James Barnes,	Oct. 9, 1793.
2-4	" Nathaniel, of Benjamin and Rachel,	Feb. 25, 1788.
2-4	" Nancy,	Oct. 10, 1790.
1-144	" Philip, of Philip, April 4, 1789.	
1-144	" Paschal, April 16, 1796.	
1-119	" Ethan, July 25, 1798.	
2-10	" Alfred, of Jeremiah Scott and Betsey,	Aug. 7, 1797.
2-10	" Hiram,	Dec. 13, 1798.
2-10	" Eliza,	Aug. 18, 1800.
2-10	" Sally,	Feb. 23, 1802.
2-10	" Mary Ann,	Sept. 9, 1803.
2-10	" Candace,	July 20, 1805.
2-10	" Jeremiah,	Sept. 24, 1808.
2-10	" Nathaniel,	Sept. 28, 1810.
2-10	" Julia Rawson,	Dec. 25, 1812.
1-143	" Hannah, of Jonathan J. and Hannah,	Nov. 2, 1799.
1-148	" Prudence,	March 24, 1803.
2-165	" Hannah, of Samuel and Nancy, (b. Warren),	May 16, 1808.
2-48	" Almira Scott, of Alfred and Frances,	Oct. 12, 1819.
2-48	" Benjamin Franklin,	March 20, 1822.
2-102	" Simeon, of Simeon and Mary A.,	July 13, 1925.
2-102	" Thomas,	Feb. 3, 1827.
2-114	" Samuel Marvin, of Hiram D. and Emeline,	Jan. 1, 1831.
2-114	" Ann Frances,	Dec. 12, 1832.
2-114	" Charles Ellery,	Jan. 14, 1836.
2-114	" Adeline Eliza,	June 18, 1837.

E F

94	FRANKLIN Viall, of John and Elizabeth,	Feb. 9, 1735-6.
1-13	" Lois, of James and Eunice,	Nov. 25, 1742.
1-21	" James,	May 15, 1746.

G

1-11	GARNSEY Molly, of Ebenezer and Martha,	Jan. 25, 1739-40.
1-62	GLADDING William, of Joseph and Anna,	Oct. 19, 1779
1-62	" Judeth,	Sept. 10, 1781.
1-62	" George,	Nov. 25, 1783.
1-76	" Joseph,	Nov. 2, 1790.
2-100	" George Anthony, of George and Nancy,	Aug. 6, 1822.
1-15	GRANT Shubael, of Joseph and Rosamond,	June 23, 1743.
1-119	" Shubael, of Samuel and Elizabeth,	Aug. 1, 1778.
1-119	" Pearce,	June 20, 1776.
1-119	" Lydia,	Aug. 16, 1784.
1-119	" Pearce, 2d,	Oct. 12, 1787.
2-45	" Izrael, of Shubael and Elizabeth,	June 1, 1783.
1-160	" Abel, of Abel.	Jan. 13, 1788.
1-147	" Samuel, of William and Lois,	Nov. 24, 1798.
2-54	" Julia, of Joshua and Mary,	Nov. 4, 1805.
2-54	" Cyrel Read,	April 15, 1807.
2-54	" Nancy,	April 24, 1809.
2-54	" Mary,	Aug. 4, 1811.
2-54	" James	April 4, 1814.
2-54	" Joseph,	March 27, 1816.
2-54	" Lydia Wheaton,	Sept. 17, 1818.

2-54	GRANT Albert, of Joshua and Mary,		Oct. 13, 1820.
2-55	" Jeremiah, of Thomas and Sally,		Aug. 11, 1807.

H

2-14	HARDING Eddy, of John and Ruth,		Feb. 22, 1795.
2-14	" Harriet,		April 27, 1797.
2-14	" John Jay,		Nov. 8, 1805.
1-9	HEATH Mary, of Peleg and Sarah,		Feb. 24, 1731-2.
1-9	" Peleg,		Aug. 27, 1734.
1-9	" Peleg,	(94), d.	Feb. 10, 1735-6.
1-9	" Peleg, 2d,		March 3, 1735-6.
1-9	" Peleg, 2d,	(94), d.	Oct. 24, 1740.
1-9	" Nathaniel,		Feb. 20, 1737-8.
1-9	" Nathaniel,		d. Nov. 15, 1740.
1-9	" Sarah, wife of Peleg, d. in 28th y.,		Oct. 9, 1739.
1-9	" Bethiah, wife of Peleg, d. in 23d y.,		Oct. 28, 1740.
1-9	" Nathaniel, of Peleg and Jerusha,		Jan. 29, 1744-5.
1-24	" Peleg, of Peleg and Anna,		March 31, 1771.
1-148	" Jabez,		April 16, 1781.
1-148	" Wilmarth, of Nathaniel and Rebecca,		Aug. 30, 1787.
1-147	" William Peck, of Nathaniel, Jr., and Nabby,		Aug. 8, 1798.
2-63	" Mary Anne, of Capt. Benjamin and Bebee,		March 15, 1813.
2-63	" Benjamin,		Dec. 15, 1814.
2-63	" Huldah Peck,		Oct. 10, 1816.
2-63	" William Peck,		March 21, 1819.
2-63	" Clarissa,		Dec. 9, 1821.
2-69	" Elizabeth, of Jabez and Betsey,		May 29, 1816.
2-69	" Thomas Champlain,		March 23, 1818.
2-158	" William Champlain, of Thomas C. and Avis,		April 4, 1851.
1-59	HOLMES William, of Simeon and Amey,		July 20, 1784.
2-12	HORN John, of John and Amey,		Sept. 5, 1796.
2-12	" John,		d. Dec. 26, 1800.
2-12	" John, Sr., died Dec. 18, 1796.		
2-45	" Mary Ann, of Daniel and Alethea,		March 1, 1803.
2-45	" John,		May 18, 1805.
2-52	HORTON James, of Simeon and Elizabeth,		Sept. 25, 1787.
1-112	HUGHES Joseph, of Spurr and Mary,		Oct. 11, 1790.
1-2	HUMPHREY Samuel, of Josiah and Hannah,		Dec. 24, 1719.
1-2	" Josiah,		Oct. 13, 1717.
1-2	" Hannah,		Jan. 2, 1721-2.
1-2	" Nathaniel,		Nov. 24, 1724.
1-2	" Nathaniel,		d. June 15, 1726.
1-2	" Mary,		July 7, 1729.
1-2	" Sarah,		July 11, 1731.
1-2	" Nathaniel,		Nov. 26, 1735.
1-2	" Ruth,		March 1, 1737-8.
1-5	" Elkanah, of Josiah and Abijah,		Feb. 18, 1738-9.
1-5	" Rachel,		April 16, 1742.
1-5	" Lillis,		May 7, 1745.
1-4	" William, of Jonas and Mary,		Jan. 24, 1734.
1-4	" William,		d. Oct. 28, 1740.
1-4	" Nathan,		May 7, 1737.
1-4	" Nathan,		d. Nov. 2, 1740.
1-4	" Micah,		Aug. 15, 1739.
1-4	" Micah,		d. Oct. 19, 1740.
1-4	" Sarah,		May 15, 1741.
1-14	" Molly,		Aug. 31, 1743.
1-14	" Jonah,		Sept. 7, 1745.
1-27	" Elizabeth, of Samuel and Elizabeth,		(1-16), Oct. 5, 1743.
1-27	" Hannah,		(1-21) May 1, 1746.
1-27	" Samuel,		March 15, 1748.
1-27	" James,		April 11, 1750.
1-27	" Lydia,		May 4, 1752.

1-27	HUMPHREY	Sarah, of Samuel and Elizabeth,	Nov. 24, 1754.
1-27	"	John,	April 8, 1757.
1-27	"	Molly,	April 17, 1759.
1-27	"	Rachel,	Feb. 8, 1762.
1-27	"	Ruth,	May 31, 1764.
2-103	"	Polly, of Josiah and Rachel,	July 12, 1776.
2-103	"	Elizabeth,	Oct. 30, 1777.
2-103	"	William,	Sept. 5, 1779.
2-103	"	William,	d. Feb. 28, 1815.
2-103	"	Olive,	April 5, 1781.
2-103	"	Rebecca,	Sept. 17, 1783.
2-103	"	Rebecca,	d. Feb. 14, 1807.
2-103	"	Amasa,	Nov. 13, 1791.
2-23	"	Nancy, of John and Elizabeth,	Feb. 26, 1783.
2-23	"	Eliza,	March 12, 1785.
2-23	"	John,	Oct. 4, 1787.
2-23	"	Polly,	Oct. 3, 1789.
2-23	"	Emerson,	Oct. 24, 1792.
2-23	"	James,	March 11, 1795.
2-23	"	James,	d. Oct. 7, 1795.
2-23	"	Fanny,	Aug. 25, 1797.
2-33	"	Albert Nelson, of Emerson and Huldah,	April 20, 1820.
2-33	"	Samuel Newell,	April 20, 1820.
2-33	"	John Bullock,	Feb. 24, 1824.
2-33	"	Maria Louisa,	June 23, 1826.
2-33	"	Nancy Augusta,	Nov. 2, 1828.
2-33	"	Ann Eliza,	June 1, 1831.

I

2-11	INGRAHAM	Selinda, of James and Anna,	(1-118), April 27, 1791.
2-11	"	Lawton,	(1-118), Feb. 4, 1793.
2-11	"	Anna,	(1-118), March 18, 1796.
2-11	"	Anna,	d. Oct. 15, 1798.
2-11	"	Sarah,	Jan. 20, 1799.
2-11	"	James,	May 30, 1802.
2-11	"	Nancy,	May 30, 1802.
2-11	"	George Gibbs,	April 5, 1804.
2-30	"	William Gladding, of Watson and Judeth,	Oct. 2, 1801.
2-30	"	Nancy Watson,	Nov. 4, 1803.
2-30	"	Matthew Watson,	Dec. 3, 1805.
2-30	"	Lydia Miller,	Aug. 18, 1808.
2-30	"	Mary Ann,	Feb. 28, 1811.
2-30	"	Matthew, 2d.,	Oct. 10, 1814.
2-98	"	Peter Taylor, of Lawton and Polly T.,	April 17, 1821.
2-98	"	Amey Taylor,	Feb. 10, 1826.
2-98	"	Joseph Lawton,	Aug. 5, 1830.
2-115	"	William Oliver, of William G. and Sally,	June 17, 1827.
2-115	"	Judeth Gladding,	March 24, 1829.

J

1-76	JONES	Bebee, of William and Bebee,	May 28, 1783.
1-76	"	Hannah,	June 6, 1786

K

1-19	KELLEY	John, of John and Elizabeth,	Jan. 27, 1733-4.
1-19	"	Joseph,	April 10, 1737.
1-12	"	Elizabeth,	Sept. 16, 1742.
1-19	"	Daniel,	Feb. 11, 1744-5.
1-12	"	Hannah, of John and Margary,	Nov. 24, 1739.

1-29	KELLEY Rachel, of William and Rebecca,		April 9, 1773.
1-25	"	William,	June 18, 1774.
1-59	"	James,	March 27, 1782.
1-43	"	Ebenezer, of William and Elizabeth,	Nov. 29, 1779.
2-17	"	Lydia, of Duncan and Mary,	Dec. 16, 1780.
2-17	"	Betsey,	March 24, 1782.
2-17	"	Polly,	Oct. 14, 1783.
2-17	"	Joanna,	Feb. 10, 1785.
2-17	"	Joanna,	d. Dec. 10, 1785.
2-17	"	Peggy,	May 10, 1787.
2-17	"	Peggy,	d. July 4, 1787.
2-17	"	Sally,	April 1, 1789.
2-17	"	Mary, wife of Duncan, died July 24, 1794.	
2-17	"	John, of Duncan and Abigail, Dec. 1, 1798.	
1-64	"	Joseph, of William and Bebee,	Oct. 10, 1784.
2-17	"	John Ed, of John and Loiza,	Feb. 23, 1822.
2-17	"	George Henry,	Sept. 27, 1829.
2-17	"	Esek Brown,	Oct. 10, 1832.
2-17	"	Ann Caroline,	April 10, 1838.
2-17	"	Charles Duncan,	Oct. 8, 1839.
2-17	"	William Winslow, of John and Sarah J.,	May 1, 1854.
1-44	KENNICUTT Sarah, of Hezekiah and Lydia,		March 15, 1775.
1-44	"	Sarah,	d. April 4, 1775.
1-44	"	Lydia,	May 28, 1776.
1-44	"	Bethany,	Feb. 2, 1778.
1-44	"	George Garcham,	Oct. 5, 1780.
1-45	"	Sarah,	Nov. 30, 1782.
1-63	"	Sarah,	Nov. 30, 1783.
1-58	"	Polly,	(1-77), Jan. 27, 1792.
2-28	"	Hannah Baker, of Josiah and Rebecca,	June 22, 1788.
2-28	"	Harriet Byron,	(1-77), Sept. 10, 1791.
2-28	"	Benjamin Townsend,	(1-85), Aug. 6, 1794.
2-28	"	Patty Townsend,	(1-147), April 21, 1799.
2-28	"	Nancy Brown,	Aug. 15, 1801.
2-28	"	George Robert,	March 30, 1805.
2-165	"	Nancy D., of George R. and Hannah,	Feb. 1, 1827.
2-165	"	Harriet B.,	Aug. 5, 1828.
2-165	"	George R.,	Sept. 27, 1829.
2-165	"	Julia F.,	May 12, 1832.
2-165	"	Amanda L.,	Oct. 12, 1833.
2-165	"	Horace T.,	June 18, 1836.
2-165	"	Henry W.,	Nov. 16, 1838.
2-165	"	William E.,	Dec. 24, 1843.
2-166	"	Emeline F.,	Aug. 24, 1847.
2-166	"	Harriet B.,	d. Jan. 9, 1829.
2-166	"	George R.,	d. Aug. 21, 1863.
2-166	"	Julia F.,	d. Dec. 4, 1832.
2-166	"	Horace T.,	d. Oct. 20, 1838.
1-20	KENT Susannah, of Josiah and Alethea,		May 4, 1732.
1-20	"	Samuel,	Jan. 19, 1733-4.
1-20	"	Anies,	June 26, 1743.
1-20	"	Annah,	April 16, 1745.
94	"	Hannah,	March 13, 1737.
1-15	"	Josiah,	April 8, 1741.
2-22	"	Lydia, of Joshua and Anna.	(1-45), May 16, 1772.
2-22	"	Susanna,	(1-45), Dec. 26, 1774.
2-22	"	Alethea,	(1-45), Feb. 27, 1777.
2-22	"	Willson,	(1-45), April 8, 1779.
2-22	"	Desire,	(1-45), Feb. 8, 1781.
2-22	"	Elizabeth,	(1-70), Jan. 5, 1783.
2-22	"	Joshua,	(1-65), March 2, 1785.
2-22	"	Anna,	March 25, 1787.
2-22	"	William,	Aug. 10, 1789.
2-22	"	Fanny,	April 12, 1792.
2-22	"	Ellery,	July 7, 1795.

2-22	KENT Amariah, of Joshua and Anna,	Oct. 14, 1798.
1-84	" Samuel, of John and Huldah,	Feb. 27, 1787.
1-84	" Ira,	Aug. 15, 1792.
2-53	" William, of Willson and Susannah,	Nov. 13, 1807.
2-53	" Ann Genette,	July 8, 1806.
2-53	" Ann Genette,	d. Jan. 16, 1807.
2-53	" Lydia,	Aug. 3, 1809.
2-53	" Rebecca Barton,	Sept. 3, 1810.
2-73	" Ira Bicknell, of Ira and Sukey Ann,	April 18, 1819.
2-73	" Joseph Henry,	July 8, 1831.
2-56	KNIGHT Caroline, of George and Ruth,	Dec. 16, 1806.
2-56	" Martha Bourne,	Feb. 27, 1809.

L

1-144	LADUE James, of Curtis and Rachel,	July 18, 1787.
1-144	" James,	d. Dec. 7, 1791.
1-144	" Samuel,	April 19, 1789.
1-144	" Prudence,	April 23, 1791.
1-144	" Amelia,	March 31, 1793.
1-144	" James,	July 10, 1795.
2-9	" Ira,	Dec. 3, 1798.
2-116	LILLEY Asa Kingsley, of Amaziah and Huldah B.,	March 18, 1820.
2-116	" Huldah B.,	June 22, 1827.
2-116	" Phebe Ann,	March 4, 1829.
2-116	" Hannah Cook,	Dec. 4, 1834.
2-116	" Mary Elizabeth,	Oct. 21, 1836.
2-26	LUTHER John, of Josiah and Presilla,	May 9, 1787.
2-26	" Nancy,	Nov. 9, 1789.
2-26	" Curus,	Dec. 18, 1791.
2-26	" Sally,	July 1, 1796.
2-26	" Joseph,	Sept. 30, 1798.

M

2-33	MARSHALL Mary Ann, of Daniel G. and Hannah,	Aug. 28, 1800.
2-33	" Eliza,	May 21, 1802.
1-12	MARTIN John, of John and Mary,	July 24, 1742.
1-12	" John,	died Dec. 13, 1742.
1-12	" Mary,	Oct. 7, 1743.
1-143	" Susannah, of Luther and Eliza,	Nov. 8, 1776.
1-143	" Nathaniel A.,	March 8, 1779.
1-43	" Luther,	Feb. 17, 1782.
1-143	" Ambrose,	May 11, 1784.
1-143	" Elizabeth,	Aug. 16, 1786.
1-143	" Sullivan,	Jan. 31, 1789.
1-143	" Nancy,	March 3, 1792.
1-143	" Sterry,	Aug. 20, 1794.
1-143	" Josiah,	May 1, 1798.
1-148	" Ebenezer, of Edward, Nov. 8, 1778.
1-59	" Samuel Read, of Benjamin and Sarah,	Nov. 15, 1782.
1-66	" Mary,	(1-69) April 16, 1786.
2-38	" Mary, of James and Judith,	March 19, 1783.
2-38	" Serrel,	(1-69) Feb. 15, 1785.
2-38	" James,	(1-69) July 13, 1787.
2-38	" Judeth,	(1-69) July 13, 1787.
2-38	" Nancy,	Dec. 28, 1789.
2-38	" Sally,	March 8, 1792.
2-38	" Pamelia,	March 31, 1794.
2-38	" Harry,	Jan. 10, 1797.
2-38	" Louisa,	July 29, 1799.
2-38	" Eliza,	May 1, 1802.
1-45	" Lydia, of Anthony and Susannah,	Sept. 13, 1781.

1-61	MARTIN	Kent, of Anthony and Susannah,		Dec. 4, 1783.
1-65	"	Bosworth,		March 10, 1785.
1-68	"	Susaunah,		Dec. 20, 1786.
2-7	"	Sally, of Colvin and Jerusha,		Oct. 24, 1789.
2-7	"	Jerusha,		Dec. 7, 1791.
2-7	"	Pamela,		April 17, 1794.
2-7	"	Almeda,		Oct. 1, 1796.
2-7	"	Ardelia,		Oct. 4, 1798.
2-26	"	John, of John, Jr., and Betsey,	(1-143)	Oct. 7, 1790.
2-26	"	Joseph,	(1-143)	Oct. 19, 1793.
2-26	"	Lillis,		Dec. 18, 1797.
1-147	"	Eliza, of Anderson and Nancy,	(2-60)	June 9 or 19, 1799.
2-60	"	Joseph,		Feb. 9, 1807.
2-60	"	William Smith,		Nov. 7, 1807.
2-60	"	Julian,		Aug. 12, 1809.
2-60	"	Luther,		July 21, 1811.
2-60	"	Abby Gladding,		July 9, 1813.
2-60	"	Nancy Alger,		April 29, 1816.
2-60	"	Alice Smith,		Jan. 29, 1818.
2-60	"	Horace Anderson,		Aug. 18, 1820.
2-60	"	Paschal Allen,		Aug. 18, 1822.
2-4	"	Luther, died Aug. 12, 1799.		
2-65	"	Betsey, of John, Jr., and Mary,		Sept. 22, 1809.
2-65	"	Joseph Ellbridge,		Dec. 29, 1811.
2-65	"	Jeremiah,		March 13, 1813.
2-65	"	Hannah,		Sept. 21, 1814.
2-65	"	Mary Jane,		April 10, 1817.
2-65	"	John,		April 24, 1818.
2-65	"	George,		July 6, 1819.
2-79	"	Benjamin, of Samuel R. and Sally,		Aug. 28, 1815.
2-79	"	Sarah Ann,		June 18, 1819.
2-79	"	Joseph Bowen,		April 28, 1823.
2-122	"	Luther Ambrose, of Sterry and Mary,		March 8, 1824.
2-122	"	Ann Elizabeth,		June 22, 1835.
2-65	"	James, of Capt. John, Jr., and Hannah,		Dec. 14, 1828.
2-65	"	Nancy Emily,		Jan. 10, 1839.
2-65	"	Amanda Simmons,		June 18, 1841.
2-65	"	Lillis,		July 18, 1848.
2-132	"	Charles Ellery, of Benjamin, and Julia R.,		Feb. 27, 1838.
2-132	"	Samuel Read,		July 4, 1842.
2-132	"	Sarah Elizabeth,		April 18, 1844.
2-132	"	Jeremiah Drowne,		Nov. 22, 1846.
2-132	"	Julia Maria,		Feb. 4, 1851.
2-163	"	George L., of George S. and Betsey S.,		May 7, 1847.
1-30	MASON	Joseph, of Joseph and Han,		July 10, 1774.
2-6	MATHEWSON	Lewis, of Daniel and Nancy,		Aug. 28, 1789.
2-6	"	Lewis,		d. Dec. 11, 1789.
2-6	"	Samuel Joy,		Dec. 10, 1790.
2-6	"	Ira Allen,		Nov. 8, 1792.
2-6	"	Lewis Bosworth,		Aug. 23, 1794.
2-6	"	Allen Durfee,		Aug. 12, 1796.
2-6	"	Nancy Low,		Oct. 5, 1798.
2-4	"	John, of John and Susannah,		June 3, 1797.
2-4	"	Maria,		July 8, 1799.
2-4	"	Waite,		Oct. 18, 1806.
2-4	"	Noel,		May 24, 1810.
2-8	"	Ebenezer, of Ebenezer and Abigail,		Jan. 3, 1799.
2-119	"	Permillia Allen, of Ebenezer,		May 5, 1827.
2-119	"	Augustus Watson,		Dec. 21, 1829.
2-130	"	John Bourne, of Noel and Hannah B.,		Nov. 21, 1843.
1-14	MATHEWS	Jeremiah, of Jeremiah and Susannah,		April 13, 1740.
2-3	MAURAN	Joseph, of Joseph Carlo and Olive,		July 10, 1774, d. May 4, 1795.
2-3	"	Walt, of Joseph Carlo and Olive,		Aug. 27, 1776.
2-3	"	Carlo,	(1-44)	March 12, 1779.

2-3	MAURAN Joshua, of Joseph Carlo and Olive,	(1-44), March 23, 1782.
2-3	" Abigail,	(1-65) Aug. 31, 1784.
2-3	" Ira,	June 2, 1786.
2-3	" Olive,	Feb. 9, 1789.
2-3	" Orendatis,	Nov. 28, 1791.
2-3	" Suchet,	April 3, 1794.
2-3	" Joseph,	Dec. 21, 1796.
2-41	" Nathaniel ·Smith, of Carlo and Sally,	Dec. 29, 1805.
2-91	" Mary Tyler, of Capt. Suchet and Sophia,	Jan. 12, 1820.
2-91	" Suchet,	July 29, 1821.
2-91	" Charles Joseph,	March 10, 1824.
2-91	" John Tyler,	Nov. 20, 1826.
2-91	" William Azal,	June 26, 1829.
2-91	" Sophia Bowen,	June 29, 1831.
2-71	MAXFIELD Daniel Drowne, of John and Ann,	Jan. 13, 1815.
2-107	" Dehorah S., of James and Anna Eliza,	Dec. 27, 1821.
2-107	" William,	Feb. 18, 1823.
2-107	" Ann Eliza,	Oct. 28, 1826.
2-107	" James, Jr.,	Feb. 5, 1828.
1-21	MAY Mary, of Elijah and Jean,	July 10, 1723.
1-22	" Hezekiah,	March 10, 1735-6
1-22	" Samuel,	Nov. 13, 1739.
1-22	" Elijah,	Nov. 27, 1742.
1-14	" Elizabeth, of Benjamin and Susannah,	Dec. 1, 1741.
1-16	MEDBURY Nathaniel, of John and Anna,	July 29, 1741.
1-16	" Chloe,	Oct. 6, 1743.
1-60	MEONE Mason, born Oct. 9, 1795.	
1-17	MILLER Jonathan, of Samuel and Elizabeth,	Oct. 27, 1744.
1-17	" Samuel,	Feb. 17, 1742-3.
1-17	" William,	Jan. 13, 1744-5.
1-17	" Elizabeth, wife of Samuel, died,	Jan. 21, 1744-5.
1-34	MORAN Joseph, of Joseph and Olive,	July 10, 1774.
1-35	MUNROE Mary, widow; died (sic Transit Gloria Mundi), (sic) Feb. 29, 1775.	

N O

1-75	OLNEY Isaac, of Isaac and Nancy,	Feb. 12, 1780.
95	ORMSBEE Joseph, of Ezra and Mary,	Nov. 17, 1736.
1-82	" Philanda, of Isaac and Patience,	Sept. 26, 1794.
1-85	" Nancy,	April 6, 1796.

P

1-23	PECK David, of David and Sarah,	Aug. 18, 1746.
1-23	" Sarah,	March 19, 1749-50.
1-23	" John,	March 8, 1751-2.
1-23	" Ezra,	July 3, 1748.
1-24	" Ezra,	Oct. 5, 1753.
1-24	" Ezra,	d. Jan. 5, 1754.
1-24	" Rachel,	Oct. 20, 1754.
1-24	" Lewis,	Oct. 8, 1757.
1-24	" Joel,	Aug. 28, 1759.
1-24	" Lewis,	May 30, 1761.
1-24	" John,	May 12, 1763.
1-24	" John,	d. Oct. 10, 1763.
1-24	" Noah,	March 31, 1765.
1-24	" Sarah, 2d,	March 7, 1767.
1-24	" Sarah, 1st,	d. March 31, 1752.
1-24	" Ezra, 1st,	d. April 12, 1752.
2-5	" Ebenezer, Dec. 11, 1762.	
2-5	Huldah (Brown), his wife, March 4, 1753.	
2-5	" Nathaniel, of Ebenezer and Huldah,	Jan. 16, 1786.
2-5	" Ebenezer,	Aug. 31, 1787.

2-5	PECK	Huldah, of Ebenezer and Huldah,	Aug. 3, 1789.
2-5	"	Beebe,	June 18, 1791.
2-5	"	Benjamin,	July 10, 1793.
2-5	"	Samuel,	Oct. 15, 1795.
2-5	"	William Heath,	June 5, 1798.
1-29	"	Bathsheba, died Dec. 13, 1769.	
1-29	"	Davis, of Solomon, Jr., and Abigail,	June 25, 1772.
1-35	"	Ellis,	Aug. 2, 1774.
1-42	"	Bebee,	June 1, 1777.
2-7	"	Horatio, of Joel and Lucy,	Dec. 3, 1793.
2-7	"	Elnathan,	Jan. 27, 1796.
2-7	"	Bela,	Jan. 29, 1798.
2-7	"	Wealthy,	Sept. 22, 1800.
2-7	"	Seeba,	Jan. 25, 1803.
2-7	"	Fanny,	Sept. 6, 1805.
2-7	"	Bethiah,	Aug. 4, 1808.
2-7	"	Clarissa,	Dec. 13, 1812.
2-24	"	Huldah, of Solomon and Huldah,	Oct. 3, 1796.
2-31	"	Sarah, of Ellis and Sarah,	Sept. 10, 1802.
2-31	"	Abigail,	March 29, 1804.
2-31	"	Ellis,	May 11, 1806.
2-31	"	Hannah,	June 27, 1810.
2-31	"	Asa,	April 7, 1812.
2-31	"	Hannah,	May 26, 1815.
2-31	"	William Hill,	May 8, 1817.
2-31	"	William Hill,	d. June 29, 1817.
2-58	"	Nathaniel, of Nathaniel and Cynthia,	April 24, 1809.
2-58	"	William Brown,	June 4, 1812.
2-58	"	William Brown,	d. Dec. 27, 1819.
2-58	"	Samuel Heath,	Oct. 6, 1814.
2-58	"	Samuel Heath,	d. Sept. 29, 1820.
2-58	"	Ebenezer,	May 24, 1817.
2-58	"	Joseph,	Sept. 13, 1819.
2 58	"	Joseph,	d. June 5, 1822.
2-58	"	Cynthia Heath,	Dec. 31, 1821.
2-58	"	Willmarth Heath,	Dec. 15, 1825.
2-88	"	Amanda Malvina, of Capt. Benjamin and Huldah,	Sept. 23, 1818.
2-88	"	Benjamin Brown,	July 28, 1820.
2-88	"	Benjamin Brown,	d. Dec. 18, 1820.
2-88	"	Benjamin Walker,	Sept. 28, 1825.
2-110	"	Harriet Newell, of Leonard and Harriet C.,	May 8, 1821.
2-110	"	William Heath,	Oct. 10, 1823.
2-110	"	Betsey Scott,	Sept. 14, 1825.
2-110	"	Sarah Drowne,	May 7, 1827.
2-110	"	Julia Mason,	Jan. 23, 1829.
2-110	"	Charles Collins,	Feb. 7, 1831.
2-110	"	Tristam Burgess,	Jan. 17, 1833.
2-110	"	Amanda Cook,	Jan. 15, 1834.
2-110	"	Anna Cornelia,	Dec. 5, 1835.
2-142	"	William Jones, of Ellis, Jr., and Louisa,	June 5, 1833.
2-142	"	Sarah Elizabeth,	Sept. 8, 1836.
2-142	"	Arabelle Louisa,	Sept. 4, 1845.
2-120	"	Adalaide Eliza, of Asa and Lucretia S.,	March 22. 1840.
2-120	"	Leander Remington,	Feb. 12, 1843.
2-120	"	Joliette Lucretia,	Nov. 7, 1843.
1-157	PHILLIPS	John Jay, born Dighton, Mass.,	Aug. 5, 1781.
2-10	POTTER	Ira, of John and Ruth,	March 30, 1798.
2-10	"	Sally,	May 5, 1799.
2-10	"	John,	April 20, 1801.
2-10	"	James Barnes,	April 23, 1805.
2-10	"	Eliza,	May 10, 1807.
2-10	"	William,	May 14, 1809.
2-10	"	Henry,	Sept. 18, 1814.

Q

1-160 QUAM Joshua, of Joshua and Mary,   Dec. 11, 1773.

R

2-94	RAWSON Ethan Allen, of Joseph and Rebecca,	Oct. 22, 1798.
2-94	" Julia Mauran,	Aug. 17, 1801.
2-94	" Mary Ann,	Oct. 6, 1804.
2-93	" William Bullock,	Aug. 20, 1807.
2-94	" William Bullock,	d. May 10, 1810.
2-94	" Joseph William,	June 2, 1810.
2-94	" Rebecca, wife of Joseph,	d. July 22, 1817.
1-5	READ Elizabeth, of William and Elizabeth,	Aug. 17, 1741.
1-5	" Bethiah,	Sept. 12, 1742.
1-42	" John, of David and Mary,	March 3, 1778.
1-66	" Nancy,	Nov. 15, 1779.
1-66	" Hannah,	Feb. 17, 1782.
1-66	" David,	March 26, 1784.
1-67	" James,	Sept. 14, 1786.
1-84	" Eliza,	May 12, 1791.
2-95	" Joshua, of Joshua and Patience,	Oct. 13, 1820.
2-95	" Ann Eliza,	May 18, 1823.
2-8	REMINGTON Samuel Watson, of Enoch and Ruth,	Jan. 4, 1791.
2-8	" Enoch,	May 3, 1792.
2-8	" Enoch,	d. Jan. 1, 1795.
2-8	" Ruth,	Dec. 28, 1794.
2-81	" Samuel W., of Enoch and Phebe,	Sept. 30, 1817.
2-81	" Lucretia S.,	Jan. 15, 1820.
2-81	" William H.,	March 29, 1822.
2-81	" George A.,	Sept. 26, 1824.
2-81	" Jeremiah S.,	Feb. 6, 1827.
2-81	" Daniel S.,	March 3, 1829.
2-81	" Phebe A.,	March 12, 1831.
2-81	" George A.,	March 31, 1833.
1-17	RICHMOND Peleg, of Peleg and Mary,	March 1, 1743-4.
2-57	" John R., of Ichabod and Roxalana,	March 30, 1802.
2-57	" William,	Dec. 20, 1806.
2-113	" Ardelia A., of Perez, Nov. 7, 1819.	
2-113	" Sarah C., April 20, 1822.	
2-113	" Hannah F., Oct. 26. 1827.	
2-113	" Henry P., July 20, 1832.	
1-22	ROSS Zephaniah, of John and Sarah,	April 2, 1743.
1-22	" Micah,	Dec. 31, 1744.

S

1-23	SALISBURY Freeborn, of George and Abigail,	Oct. 10, 1770.
1-28	" Hezekiah,	Nov. 20, 1772.
1-35	" Abigail,	Sept. 10, 1776.
1-43	" George,	Aug. 12, 1778.
2-139	SAWTELLE Joseph, of Hollis and Betsey B.,	Oct. 5, 1844.
1-16	SHORT Daniel, of Philip and Lydia,	Sept. 12, 1742.
1-65	" Upham, of John and Phebe,	Jan. 13, 1770.
2-13	" John, of John, Jr., and Betsey,	(1-65), July 10, 1781.
2-13	" Daniel Cooke,	(1-66), July 10, 1782.
2-13	" Jeremiah Scott,	(1-66), March 17, 1784.
2-13	" Nathaniel,	(1-66), Sept. 6, 1786.
2-13	" Betsey,	Feb. 16, 1788.
2-13	" Rebecca,	March 7, 1790.
2-13	" Lucretia,	May 27, 1792.
2-13	" Phebe,	April 9, 1797.
2-13	" Harriet Cooke,	Sept. 29, 1801.

Note—All the above except the youngest are also recorded 1-145.

2-34	SHORT	John, reputed son of John Short, Jr., and Mary Cranston, April 1, 1803.	
2-36	"	Eliza, of John, Jr., and Rachel,	Nov. 17, 1804.
2-36	"	Nathaniel Scott,	Sept. 17, 1806.
2-36	"	John,	May 8, 1810.
2-36	"	Timothy Waterman,	June 7, 1812.
2-36	"	Albert Galleton,	Oct. 9, 1815.
2-36	"	Samuel,	July 10, 1818.
2-36	"	Jeremiah Scott,	March 16, 1821.
2-124	"	Judeth Eliza, of Samuel,	Oct. 10, 1819.
2-124	"	Phebe Ann,	Feb. 28, 1822.
2-124	"	Clarrissa,	Feb. 9, 1824.
2-143	"	Susan Martin, of John, Jr.,	Dec. 20, 1842.
2-143	"	John Calvin,	Jan. 17, 1844.
2-164	"	Anne Davis, of Albert G. and Anne D.,	Dec. 5, 1852.
1-60	SMITH	Hannah, of James and Avis,	May 24, 1767.
1-60	"	John.	Oct. 2, 1768.
1-60	"	James.	Dec. 1, 1769.
1-60	"	Joshua.	Feb. 8, 1771.
1-60	"	Caleb.	Dec. 29, 1772.
1-60	"	William,	Feb. 14, 1774.
2-1	"	Josiah, of Nathaniel and Lillis.	May 21, 1772.
2-1	"	Josiah.	d. April 28, 1774.
2-1	"	Nathaniel.	Jan. 23, 1774.
2-1	"	Bicknell,	July 15, 1776.
2-1	"	Bicknell.	d. Oct. 4, 1777.
2-1	"	Ebenezer.	May 21, 1778.
2-1	"	Simeon.	Sept. 26, 1781.
2-1	"	James,	Oct. 15, 1783.
2-1	"	Sarah.	Sept. 14, 1785.
2-1	"	Asa.	Feb. 18, 1788.
1-83	"	James, Esq., died April 30, 1774.	
1-61	"	Jerusha, of James and Avis,	Feb. 8, 1776.
1-61	"	Amey,	Oct. 8, 1777.
1-85	"	Samuel, of Simon and Rachel,	Nov. 23, 1779.
1-70	"	Simon and William, reputed sons of William Smith and Rachel Andrews,	Feb. 11, 1787.
1-180	"	Gardiner (col.), born Jan. 15, 1793.	
2-14	"	Joseph Mauran, of Nathaniel, Jr., and Waite,	Jan. 6, 1795.
2-14	"	Olive Bicknell,	Sept. 11, 1800.
2-14	"	Nathaniel,	Oct. 12, 1811.
2-34	"	James, reputed son of Ebenezer Smith and Mary Cranston, April 29, 1798.	
2-4	"	Capt. James, died July 5, 1799.	
2-19	"	Lovisa, of Ebenezer and Martha,	Aug. 23, 1800.
2-19	"	Sophia,	Aug. 19, 1804.
2-19	"	George Knight,	July 13, 1805.
2-19	"	Asa,	Jan. 8, 1807.
2-47	"	Elizabeth, of Samuel and Lucy,	Nov. 23, 1805.
2-47	"	Lucy,	April 4, 1808.
2-47	"	Susannah Kent,	Jan. 15, 1811.
2-47	"	Charlotte Townsend,	Oct. 3, 1813.
2-47	"	Samuel Watson,	Jan. 23, 1816.
2-47	"	Rachel Tiffany,	Nov. 6, 1819.
2-70	"	James Arnold of Asa and Phebe,	May 31, 1810.
2-70	"	Henry,	Nov. 1, 1812.
2-70	"	Sarah Ann,	Nov. 30, 1814.
2-70	"	Elizer Chandler,	Nov. 11, 1817.
2-87	"	William Henry, of Simon and Lydia,	March 25, 1816.
2-87	"	Lewis Bosworth,	Sept. 14, 1817.
2-87	"	Lydia,	Feb. 7, 1822.
2-87	"	Elizabeth Joy,	Jan. 25, 1825.
2-87	"	Harriet,	Aug. 1, 1827.
2-136	"	Mary E., of Henry and Martha,	Oct. 20, 1838.
2-136	"	Ellen H.,	June 5, 1840.

2-136	SMITH Sarah Ann L., of Henry and Martha,		Oct. 12, 1843.
2-136	"	Hannah C.,	July 19, 1845.
2-136	"	Frank H.,	Sept. 13, 1847.
2-123	"	George Lewis, of Lewis B. and Anna D.,	Sept. 23, 1840.
1-146	STANLEY Samuel, of Comfort and Molly,	(1-71),	Sept. 16, 1787.
1-146	"	Polly,	May 1, 1789.
1-146	"	Nancy,	Oct. 22, 1791.
1-146	"	Viall,	July 27, 1793.
1-146	"	Ruth,	June 16, 1795.
1-146	"	Betsey,	Feb. 22, 1798.
2-92	·	George, of Viall and Lillis,	May 5, 1822.
2-92	"	Viall,	June 24, 1824.
2-92	"	John Martin,	Nov. 24, 1825.
2-92	"	Henry Martin,	April 1, 1829.
2-92	"	Jeremiah Bowen.	July 29, 1833.

T

1-43	TEW Susannah, reputed daughter of Benedick Tew and Lydia Ball,		
			Sept. 27, 1780.
1-11	THOMAS John, of John and Elizabeth.		Sept. 30, 1727.
1-11	"	Elizabeth,	Aug. 11, 1723.
1-11	"	Elizabeth, wife of John,	d. April 7, 1725.
1-11	"	Sarah, of John and Mercy,	Oct. 26, 1738.
1-21	"	Molly, of James and Mary.	Jan. 27, 1737-8.
1-25	THROOPE Thomas Billings, of Billings and Hannah,		Aug. 29, 1771.
1-26	THURBER Elizabeth, of Edward and Elizabeth,		Feb. 16, 1772.
1-14	TIFFANY Sarah, of Hezekiah and Sarah.		Feb. 9, 1727-8.
2-42	"	Elizabeth, of Ebenezer and Mary Ann.	Oct. 14, 1784.
2-42	"	Sarah.	Jan. 27, 1786.
2-42	"	Alethea,	Feb. 26, 1788.
2-42	"	Mary Ann,	Feb. 17, 1790.
2-42	"	Esther Viall,	Feb. 13, 1793.
2-42	"	Susanna Kent,	Feb. 13, 1793.
2-42	"	Susanna Kent,	d. April 5, 1803.
2-42	"	Ebenezer,	July 13, 1795.
2-42	"	Lydia,	(2-18), March 23, 1798.
2-42	"	Hezekiah,	(2-18), Jan. 18, 1800.
2-42	"	Lemira,	Feb. 3, 1802.
		Note—Above, except three youngest, recorded 1-84.	
1-84	"	Esther, widow, d. March 19, 1792.	
2-112	"	Susan Kent, of Ebenezer and Mary,	Oct. 11, 1832.
2-112	"	William Bullock,	June 14, 1834.
2-112	"	Ebenezer,	Feb. 16, 1836.
2-112	"	John Crane,	Jan. 7, 1838.
2-112	"	Mary Louisa,	Feb. 8, 1840.
2-112	"	Sarah Eliza,	Feb. 11, 1844.
2-112	"	Samuel Mills,	July 4, 1846.
2-112	"	Rachel Ann,	Nov. 13, 1849.
1-81	TILLEY Hannah Cooke, of Ammariah and Anna,		June 7, 1793.
1-23	TOWNSEND Samuel, of Solomon and Martha,		Oct. 11, 1767.
1-23	"	Rebecca,	Oct. 18, 1768.
1-25	"	Shearjashub Bourne, ,	Dec. 29, 1771.
1-33	"	Solomon,	May 6, 1774.
1-36	"	Benjamin Bourne,	Nov. 3, 1776.
1-58	"	Patty,	Jan. 14, 1779.
1-68	"	George Robert,	May 20, 1782.
1-68	"	Ruth,	May 8, 1785.
1-31	"	Shearjashub Bourne, of Solomon, Jr., and Charlotte,	April 14, 1795.
1-19	TRIPP Rebecca, of William and Abigail,		Sept. 26, 1745.
1-59	TYLER Sarah, of Moses, Esq., and Betsey,		Dec. 19, 1771.
2-109	"	Mary Elizabeth, of John and Eliza,	July 28, 1828.

U V

94	VIALL	John, of Nathaniel and Alethea,	May 25, 1734.
94	"	Elizabeth,	Feb. 21, 1735.
1-15	"	Constant, of Constant and Sarah,	Oct. 10, 1734.
1-15	"	Sarah,	Dec. 25, 1735.
1-15	"	James,	Aug. 31, 1741.
1-16	"	Josiah,	March 11, 1743-4.
1-3	"	Ruth, of Joseph and Ruth,	Nov. 28, 1736.
1-3	"	Jonathan,	Sept. 11, 1739.
1-3	"	Joseph,	Jan. 25, 1740-1.
1-11	"	Elizabeth,	March 4, 1742-3.
1-76	"	James, of Caleb and Elizabeth,	March 28, 1769.
1-76	"	Mary,	July 17, 1772.
1-26	"	Ruth Bicknell, of Josiah and Hannah,	Jan. 3, 1772.
1-113	"	Joshua,	May 5, 1779.
1-30	"	Winchester W., of Josiah, June 20, 1779.	
1-61	"	Elizabeth Gaylord, of Joseph and Rachel,	Dec. 5, 1781.
2-11	"	Joseph, of Sylvester and Abigail,	Aug. 23, 1791.
2-11	"	Sylvester,	Oct. 10, 1792.
2-11	"	Eliza,	Oct. 20, 1794.
2-11	"	Samuel,	May 5, 1796.
2-11	"	Stephen,	Nov. 13, 1798.
2-11	"	Ruth,	April 6, 1800.
2-11	"	James,	Nov. 17, 1801.
2-11	"	James,	d. Sept. 26, 1803.
2-11	"	James, 2d,	Sept. 21, 1805.
2-11	"	William,	Sept. 9, 1807.
2-11	"	Ethan,	May 20, 1809.
2-59	"	Benjamin Bourn, of Benjamin and Hannah,	Oct. 9, 1809.

W

1-148	WATERMAN	Nicholas Cooke,	Nov. 9, 1787.
1-10	WATSON	Abigail, of Mathew and Bethiah,	Jan. 13, 1733-4.
1-10	"	Molly,	March 5, 1734-5.
1-10	"	Rachel,	July 14, 1736.
1-10	"	Mercy,	March 30, 1738.
1-10	"	Bethiah,	Oct. 12, 1739.
1-10	"	Matthew,	April 4, 1741.
1-20	"	Lydia,	Dec. 17, 1742.
1-20	"	William,	June 25, 1744.
1-20	"	John,	Oct. 5, 1746.
1-25	"	Elizabeth, of Matthew, Jr., and Avis,	March 4, 1771.
1-30	"	Samuel,	April 1, 1773.
1-34	"	Matthew,	April 1, 1775.
1-43	"	John,	June 8, 1778.
2-21	"	Matthew, of Rev. Samuel and Martha,	Sept. 2, 1800.
2-21	"	Elizabeth,	June 3, 1802.
2-21	"	John Dexter,	Oct. 28, 1804.
2-21	"	Samuel,	July 16, 1807.
2-21	"	Sabra Bicknell,	Jan. 24, 1810.
2-21	"	George B.,	April 7, 1813.
2-21	"	George B.,	d. Feb. 16, 1814.
2-48	"	Ann Eliza, of Matthew and Lucretia,	Sept. 16, 1804.
2-39	"	Robert Sterry, of John and Ann,	Sept. 29, 1804.
2-39	"	John William,	Oct. 2, 1806.
2-39	"	Julia Ann,	July 17, 1809.
1-4	WELLEY	John, of Thomas and Charity,	Oct. 31, 1726.

X Y Z

9 789353 864804